ASP.NET: Tips, Tutorials, and Code

Scott Mitchell
Steve Walther
Doug Seven
Donny Mack
Chris Payne
Billy Anders
Adam Nathan
Dan Wahlin

201 West 103rd St., Indianapolis, Indiana, 46290 USA

ASP.NET: Tips, Tutorials, and Code

Copyright © 2002 by Sams Publishing

All rights reserved. No part of this book shall be reproduced, stored in a retrieval system, or transmitted by any means, electronic, mechanical, photocopying, recording, or otherwise, without written permission from the publisher. No patent liability is assumed with respect to the use of the information contained herein. Although every precaution has been taken in the preparation of this book, the publisher and authors assume no responsibility for errors or omissions. Nor is any liability assumed for damages resulting from the use of the information contained herein.

International Standard Book Number: 0-672-32143-2

Library of Congress Catalog Card Number: 00-111729

Printed in the United States of America

First Printing: August 2001

04 03 02 01   4 3 2 1

Trademarks

All terms mentioned in this book that are known to be trademarks or service marks have been appropriately capitalized. Sams cannot attest to the accuracy of this information. Use of a term in this book should not be regarded as affecting the validity of any trademark or service mark.

Warning and Disclaimer

Every effort has been made to make this book as complete and as accurate as possible, but no warranty or fitness is implied. The information provided is on an "as is" basis. The authors and the publisher shall have neither liability nor responsibility to any person or entity with respect to any loss or damages arising from the information contained in this book or from the use of the CD or programs accompanying it.

EXECUTIVE EDITOR
Shelley Kronzek

DEVELOPMENT EDITOR
Rob Tidrow

MANAGING EDITOR
Charlotte Clapp

PROJECT EDITOR
Leah Kirkpatrick

COPY EDITOR
Bart Reed

INDEXER
Tim Tate

PROOFREADER
Kevin Laseau
Juli Cook

TECHNICAL EDITOR
John Kolat

MEDIA DEVELOPER
Dan Scherf

INTERIOR DESIGNER
Gary Adair

COVER DESIGNER
Gary Adair

CONTENTS AT A GLANCE

FOREWORD   1

INTRODUCTION   3

CHAPTER 1	Common ASP.NET Page Techniques	7
CHAPTER 2	Common ASP.NET Code Techniques	29
CHAPTER 3	Form Field Input Validation	123
CHAPTER 4	Enabling Better Browser Support	155
CHAPTER 5	Creating and Using User controls	171
CHAPTER 6	Data Manipulation with ADO.NET	195
CHAPTER 7	Data Presentation	233
CHAPTER 8	Using XML	303
CHAPTER 9	ASP.NET Error Handling	347
CHAPTER 10	Debugging ASP.NET Applications	379
CHAPTER 11	ASP.NET Deployment and Configuration	399
CHAPTER 12	Security with ASP.NET	417
CHAPTER 13	Web Services	473
CHAPTER 14	Managing State	513
CHAPTER 15	ASP.NET Performance Tips	539
CHAPTER 16	Separating Code from Content	579
CHAPTER 17	Mobile Controls	611
CHAPTER 18	ASP.NET Http Runtime	659
CHAPTER 19	COM and Win32 in ASP.NET Web Pages	723

APPENDIXES

APPENDIX A	Upgrading to Visual Basic.NET	799
APPENDIX B	Commonly Used Regular Expressions	807
APPENDIX C	Commonly Used Stored Procedure Templates	813

INDEX   823

TABLE OF CONTENTS

FOREWORD 1
INTRODUCTION 3
CHAPTER 1: Common ASP.NET Page Techniques 7
   1. Using `Page_Load`: Executing Code When a Page Is Loaded ... 8
   2. Using Forms in ASP.NET 11
      Using the Two-Page Form Processing Technique 11
      Using the Postback Form Processing Technique 15
   3. Responding to a Form Postback 19
   4. Creating Event Handlers for Web Control Events 23
   Summary 26
   Other Resources 27
CHAPTER 2: Common ASP.NET Code Techniques 29
   1. Using Collections 30
      Working with the `ArrayList` Class 31
      Working with the `Hashtable` Class 35
      Working with the `SortedList` Class 38
      Working with the `Queue` Class 41
      Working with the `Stack` Class 44
      Similarities Among the Collection Types 49
      Conclusion 53
   2. Working with the File System 53
      Reading, Creating, and Deleting Directories 54
      Reading, Writing, and Creating Files 60
   3. Using Regular Expressions 68
   4. Generating Images Dynamically 75
      Saving Dynamically Created Images on the Web Server 75
      Sending Dynamically Created Images to the Browser 80
   5. Sending Email from an ASP.NET Page 83
   6. Network Access via an ASP.NET Page 86
   7. Uploading Files from the Browser to the Web Server
      via an ASP.NET Page 93
      Saving an Uploaded File to the Web Server's File System . 94
      Working Directly with an Uploaded File 97
   8. Using `ProcessInfo`: Retrieving Information About a Process ... 100
      Displaying Information for the Currently Executing
         aspnet_wp.exe Process 100
      Displaying Information for Past Instances of the
         aspnet_wp.exe Process 102

CONTENTS

- 9. Accessing the Windows Event Log 105
  - Reading from the Event Log 105
  - Writing to the Event Log 111
- 10. Working with Server Performance Counters 113
- Summary 121
- Other Resources 122

CHAPTER 3: Form Field Input Validation 123
- 1. Validating Form Field Input with ASP.NET's Validation Controls ... 124
- 2. Using the `RequiredFieldValidator` Control 125
- 3. Using the `CompareValidator` Control 131
- 4. Using the `RangeValidator` Control 135
- 5. Using the `RegularExpressionValidator` Control 139
- 6. Using the `CustomValidator` Control 141
  - Creating Server-Side Validation Functions for the
    `CustomValidator` Control 142
  - Creating Client-Side Validation Functions for the
    `CustomValidator` Control 145
- 7. Using the `ValidationSummary` Control 148
- Summary 152
- Other Resources 152

CHAPTER 4: Enabling Better Browser Support 155
- 1. Determining a Visitor's Browser Capabilities with the
  `HttpBrowserCapabilities` Class 156
- 2. Dynamically Redirecting a User Based on His Browser's Capabilities 164
- 3. Testing Various Types of Server Control Output Through the
  `ClientTarget` Property 165
- Summary 168
- Other Resources 169

CHAPTER 5: Creating and Using User Controls 171
- 1. Creating User Controls 172
- 2. Registering a User Control 174
- 3. Properties and Methods 175
  - Inherent Properties and Methods 175
  - Custom Properties and Methods 178
- 4. Dynamically Loading User Controls 190
- Summary 194
- Other Resources 194

CHAPTER 6: Data Manipulation with ADO.NET 195
- 1. Overview of ADO.NET 196
- 2. Using ADO.NET to Accomplish Common Database Tasks 197
  - Opening a Database Connection 198
  - Inserting Data Using ADO.NET 200

Updating Data Using ADO.NET 202
Deleting Data Using ADO.NET 204
Querying Data Using ADO.NET 207
3. Using Parameters with SQL Commands 210
4. Using Stored Procedures with ADO.NET 214
Using Output Parameters 216
5. Retrieving Data with DataSets 218
6. Understanding DataTables 221
Building a DataTable Programmatically 223
Filtering and Sorting Data in a DataTable 225
Understanding DataRelations 226
7. Understanding the DataAdapter 228
Summary 230
Other Resources 231

CHAPTER 7: Data Presentation 233
1. Saving Form Data 234
2. Displaying Database Information in ASP.NET Server Controls 241
Binding Data to the Repeater Control 242
Binding Data to the `DropDownList` Control 251
Binding Data to the `HyperLink` Control 255
3. Using the `DataList` Control 258
Controlling `DataList` Table Properties 258
Event Bubbling in a `DataList` Control 262
Editing an Item in a `DataList` Control 271
4. Using the `DataGrid` Control 276
Controlling Which Columns Are Displayed in a `DataGrid` Control 277
Showing and Hiding Columns 279
Editing Data in a `DataGrid` Control 281
Sorting Data in a `DataGrid` Control 289
Paging Through a `DataGrid` 292
Summary 302
Other Resources 302

CHAPTER 8: Using XML 303
1. XML Support in .NET 303
2. Why Use XML? 304
3. What's in the `System.Xml` Assembly 306
4. Reading XML Documents Using the `XmlTextReader` Class 307
Pull Versus Push Models 307
Using the `XmlTextReader` Class to Read an XML Document ...308
Associating `XmlTextReader` with the `XmlNameTable` Class 314
5. Validating XML Documents Against XML Schemas 314

    6. Creating XML Documents Using the `XmlTextWriter` Class 318
    7. Working with XML Documents Using the Document
       Object Model (DOM) 322
         In-Memory Versus Forward Only Cursor-Based Parsing 324
         DOM Classes 325
         Adding Nodes to an XML Document Using the DOM 327
         Recursion in the DOM 327
         Selecting Nodes in the DOM Using XPath 330
    8. Transforming XML Documents with XSLT 331
         XSLT Classes in the .NET Platform 333
    9. XML Support in ADO.NET 339
         Introducing the `DataSet` Class 339
         Reading and Writing XML Using the `DataSet` Class 343
         Mapping XSD Schemas to a DataSet 343
    Summary 345
    Other Resources 345

CHAPTER 9: ASP.NET Error Handling Techniques 347
    1. Error Handling and the .NET Runtime 347
    2. Stopping Errors Before They Occur 348
         `Option Explicit` 348
         `Option Strict` 349
         The Exception Class 352
    3. Structured Error Handling 354
         Catching General Exceptions 355
         Catching Specific Exceptions 356
         Throwing Exceptions 360
         Creating Custom Exceptions 360
    4. Page Level Error Handling 363
         Using the Page Objects Error Event 363
         Using the `@Page` Directive To Handle Page Redirection 365
    5. Application-Level Error Handling 368
         Using the `Application_Error` Event 368
         Implementing an Application-Wide Error Page Redirect 372
    Summary 377
    Other Resources 377

CHAPTER 10: Debugging ASP.NET Applications 379
    1. Tracing Code Execution 379
         Page-Level Tracing 380
         Adding to the Trace Output 381
         Application-Level Tracing 383
         Viewing an Entire Application's Trace Information in One Place 384

viii ASP.NET: TIPS, TUTORIALS, AND CODE

    2. Debugging with the CLR Debugger 385
        Enabling Debugging 385
        Attaching to Your Application 386
        Working with Breakpoints 387
        Stepping Through Your Application 389
        Examining Variables 391
        Cross-Language Debugging 392
        Debugging Exceptions 396
    Summary 398
    Other Resources 398

CHAPTER 11: ASP.NET Deployment and Configuration 399
    1. Deploying Components to the `\bin` Directory 399
    2. Configuring Applications to Use Specific Component Versions 401
        The Global Assembly Cache 401
        Building a Versioned Assembly 402
        Creating a Key File for Strong Named Assemblies 404
        Compiling a Strong Named Assembly 404
        Registering an Assembly with the Global Assembly Cache 405
        Using a Registered Assembly 406
        Adding a New Assembly Version to the Global Assembly Cache 408
        Using Multiple Assembly Versions 410
    3. Common `web.config` Configuration Settings 412
        `machine.config` Sections 413
        `web.config` Sections 416
    4. Reading Custom Configuration Settings from `web.config` 419
        Adding Application Configuration Settings .419
        Reading Application Configuration Settings 420
        Adding Custom Configuration Sections 421
        Reading Custom Configuration Sections 422
    5. Enabling Worker Process Restarts 423
    6. Using Web Gardens: Enabling Multiprocessor Functionality 428
    Summary 430
    Other Resources 431

CHAPTER 12: Security with ASP.NET 433
    An Overview of Authentication and Authorization 433
    1. Authentication 434
        Integrated Windows Authentication 435
        Forms-based Authentication 437
        Passport Authentication 467

    2. Authorization 479
        File Authorization 479
        URL Authorization 481
        Impersonation 485
    Summary 487
    Other Resources 488

CHAPTER 13: Web Services 489
    1. What Is a Web Service? 490
    2. Creating and Exposing a Simple Web Service 492
    3. Consuming a Web Service Through an ASP.NET Page 498
        Creating a Proxy Class 498
        Making Synchronous Calls to the Web Service 507
        Making Asynchronous Calls to the Web Service 510
    4. Returning Database Data from a Web Service 512
        Using Database Data in a Web Service to Make Decisions 513
        Creating Web Services That Return Datasets .514
    5. Security and Web Services 516
    6. Design Considerations When Creating and Using Web Services 521
        Security Concerns 521
        Responding to Web Service Failures 522
        Interface-Based Programming Challenges 524
    Summary 527
    Other Resources 528

CHAPTER 14: Managing State 529
    1. Managing Page-Level State with ViewState 529
    2. Managing ASP.NET Session State 535
        Controlling Session Expiration 535
        Controlling Session Initialization 536
    3. Managing Session State with SQL Server 538
    4. Managing Session State with Cookies 543
    5. Cookieless Session State Management 546
    6. Using the Session State Server 547
        Running the Session State Server InProc 548
        Running the Session State Server Out-of-Proc 548
    7. Managing Application State 550
    Summary 553
    Other Resources 554

CHAPTER 15: ASP.NET Performance Tips 555
    1. What Is Caching? 555
    2. Caching Entire ASP.NET Web Forms with Page Output Caching 556
        Using the `@OutputCache` Directive's `VaryByParam` Attribute 562
        Using the `@OutputCache` Directive's `Location` Attribute 564
        Using the `@OutputCache` Directive's `VaryByCustom` Attribute 565
        Using the `@OutputCache` Directive's `VaryByHeader` Attribute 566
    3. Caching Portions of ASP.NET Web Forms—Fragment Cachine 567
        Using the `VaryByControl` Attribute In a User Control 572
    4. Obtaining Page-Level Information with `Response.Cache` 574
    5. Enabling Output Caching with Web Services 576
    6. Programmatically Caching Using the `Cache` Class 578
        The `Insert` Method 579
        The `Remove` Method 585
        The `Get` Method 586
        The `GetEnumerator` Method 587
    7. ASP.NET Web Forms Performance Checklist 588
        Using ASP.NET Performance Counters 590
    8. Database Performance Checklist 592
    9. Web Services Performance Checklist 592
    Summary 593
    Other Resources 593

CHAPTER 16: Separating Code from Content 595
    1. Using Code Behind 596
        Code-Behind Techniques for ASP.NET Web Forms 596
        Code-Behind Techniques for User Controls 602
    2. Localization 612
        Using the `System.Globalization` Namespace 612
        Specifying Character Encodings 613
    3. Using Resource Files 618
    Summary 625
    Other Resources 626

CHAPTER 17: Mobile Controls 627
    1. Using Mobile Device Software Simulators 627
    2. Introduction to the Wireless Application Protocol 629
    3. Building WML Pages 630
        Configuring Internet Information Server 630
        WML and XML 631
        Creating a Deck of Cards 631
        Linking Files with WML 633

- 4. Using ASP.NET Mobile Controls 634
  - Creating Mobile Forms 634
  - Dynamically Activating a Mobile Form 637
  - Displaying Text 638
  - Displaying Lists 642
  - Creating Interactive Lists 646
  - Creating Object Lists 650
  - Creating Text Boxes 655
  - Validating User Input 658
  - Displaying Images 660
  - Placing Phone Calls 661
  - Displaying Advertisements with Mobile Controls 662
  - Displaying Calendars with Mobile Controls 664
- 5. Creating Cross-Device-Compatible Mobile Pages 666
  - Detecting Mobile Capabilities 667
  - Choosing Devices with `DeviceSpecific` 669
  - Using Form Template Sets 671
- Summary 672
- Other Resources 673

CHAPTER 18: ASP.NET Http Runtime 675
- 1. Http Runtime Overview 675
  - Interception Events 678
  - Using the Application-Level Events 679
- 2. `Global.asax` Event Handlers 681
  - Intercepting Events Using the `global.asax` Application File 681
  - Intercepting Events Using HTTP Modules 690
  - `IHttpHandlers` 695
  - The `HttpContext` Class 699
  - The `HttpRequest` Class 702
- 3. Using Directives 723
  - Using the `Application` Directive 724
  - Using the `Import` Directive 725
  - Assemblies and Using the `Assembly` Directive 727
  - Using `Object` Tags 729
  - Code Declarations 733
  - Server-Side Includes 735
- Summary 736
- Other Resources 737

CHAPTER 19: COM and Win32 in ASP.NET Web Pages 739
1. Using COM Components in an ASP.NET Web Page 740
Using COM Objects Created with the `<object>` Tag 741
Using COM Objects Created in the Source Code 745
Getting Type Information for COM Components 754
Taking Advantage of Type Information 759
Common Interactions with COM Objects 765
Deployment 773
2. Calling Win32 APIs in an ASP.NET Web Page 774
Calling Win32 APIs Using VB.NET 774
Calling Win32 APIs Using C# 777
Choosing the Right Parameter Types 779
Customizing Parameters 785
Calling APIs with Complex Types 788
Customizing `Declare` and `DllImport` 796
3. Using the `AspCompat` Directive 807
Executing on an STA Thread 808
ASP Intrinsics 810
4. Performance Concerns 811
Summary 812
Other Resources 813

APPENDIXES

APPENDIX A: Upgrading to Visual Basic.NET 815
1. Variables 815
The `Variant` Data Type 816
The `Currency` Data Type 816
The `Integer` and `Long` Data Types 816
Code Blocks and Local Variables 816
Array Bounds 817
2. Short-Circuiting Operators 817
3. Functions and Subroutines 818
Parentheses Required for Calling Subroutines and Functions 818
Function and Subroutine Parameters Now `ByVal` by Default 819
4. The `While` Statement 820
5. Default Properties 820

APPENDIX B: Commonly Used Regular Expression Templates 823
    1. Zip Code Validation 824
    2. Social Security Validation 825
    3. Telephone Number Validation 825
    4. E-mail Address Validation 826
    5. Censoring Offensive Language 827

APPENDIX C: Commonly Used Stored Procedure Templates 829
    1. Selecting Rows 829
    2. Inserting New Rows 830
    3. Updating Existing Rows 831
    4. Deleting Rows 832
    5. Selecting the Top 10 Rows 832
    6. Selecting Rows That Contain a Certain Substring 832
    7. Insert a Record if It Does Not Already Exist 833
    8. Update the Record if It Exists, or Else Insert the Record 834
    9. Checking for a Valid Username/Password 835
    10. Retrieving SQL Server System Objects 837

INDEX 839

ACKNOWLEDGMENTS

The entire group of authors would like to extend their deepest thanks to the Microsoft ASP.NET team, specifically Scott Guthrie, Rob Howard, and Mark Anders, all of whom have donated countless hours of time and energy to this project. Additionally, this book would not have been possible without the hard work of Shelley Kronzek, lead editor, Rob Tidrow, development editor, John Kolat, technical editor, Leah Kirkpatrick, project manager, and Dan Scherf, media development. Thanks everyone!

DEDICATION

Scott Mitchell

This book is dedicated to my loving family. Their support, love, and encouragement have made any obstacle surmountable. This book is also dedicated to Jisun, whose mere presence brightens my day and makes life overwhelmingly fun.

This book would not have been possible if it weren't for the brilliance and hard work of Scott Guthrie, Rob Howard, and Mark Anders, the two co-creators of ASP.NET. Hats off to the entire ASP.NET team as well for creating the best Web programming technology ever.

Steve Walther

I want to thank my beautiful wife, Ruth Walther, for her support and encouragement while writing this book. I'd also like to thank Rob Howard and Scott Guthrie from Microsoft for taking time from their busy schedules to discuss the chapters of this book.

Doug Seven

In fondest memory of Leo Seven.

I would like to extend my deepest appreciation to the entire Sams Publishing team. They have done an outstanding job at pulling this book together and making it happen through constant changes in the beta versions of the .NET Framework. They have put up with me, and that alone is worthy of an acknowledgement. My thanks also goes to Scott Mitchell, Rob Tidrow, Shelley Kronzek, and my co-authors for all the fun and support we provided each other throughout the writing of this book; John Cline for his years of support and camaraderie; Donny Mack, for being the Mack; Jon Serious for something; Lance Hayes for what Serious didn't cover; and my family for not killing me when they had the chance. My most heart-felt appreciation is reserved for Dawniel, who put up with me while I finished my work on this book, pushed me to get it done, and watched over my shoulder while I reviewed it for the last time.

Billy Anders

I would like to thank my beautiful mother, Lucy, the one that has kept me on-track, in-line and deeply rooted in her heart for my entire life. I cannot even begin to thank you enough. To my dad, Billy Sr., thank you for introducing me to, and subsequently funding, my early PC adventures. As he said back then, "I think these things are going to be everywhere one day." Pops, looks like you were right! Thanks to my beautiful best friend, Toni, for your inspiration, encouragement and understanding during the long nights that this industry oftentimes demands. Big thanks to Erik Olson and Lance Olson for all of their help and timely details during this writing project. You guys are da' bomb! And an extra thank you goes out to one of the co-creators of ASP.NET, Scott Guthrie, for recommending me to the Sams Publishing team. Good lookin' out, Scott! Lastly, sincere thanks go out to Scott Mitchell, Shelley Kronzek, and Rob Tidrow for their patience, professionalism and attention to detail during the writing of this book. You guys are great.

Adam Nathan

I would like to thank the great people at Sams who worked on this book, most notably Shelley Kronzek. I'd also like to thank many people at Microsoft, including Chris Waldron, Kory Srock, David Mortenson, Dennis Angeline, Sonja Keserovic, and Mahesh Prakriya. Most importantly, I want to thank my beautiful wife, Lindsay, for her never-ending patience and support. I also can't forget to thank our kitten, Shadow, for keeping Lindsay company while I was writing.

Dan Wahlin

I would like to thank my wife Heedy and my two boys Danny and Jeffery for their patience as I worked on this book. I'd also like to thank my mom and dad (Elaine and Danny) for bringing me up in such a pleasant environment and pushing me to succeed in life. I couldn't have asked for better parents or for a better wife and kids.

The authors and publisher would like to thank Christophe Wille for his contributions to Chapter 10 and Rob Gottschalk for his contributions to Chapter 13.

TELL US WHAT YOU THINK!

As the reader of this book, *you* are our most important critic and commentator. We value your opinion and want to know what we're doing right, what we could do better, what areas you'd like to see us publish in, and any other words of wisdom you're willing to pass our way.

As an Executive Editor for Sams, I welcome your comments. You can e-mail or write me directly to let me know what you did or didn't like about this book—as well as what we can do to make our books stronger.

Please note that I cannot help you with technical problems related to the topic of this book, and that due to the high volume of mail I receive, I might not be able to reply to every message.

When you write, please be sure to include this book's title and author as well as your name and phone or fax number. I will carefully review your comments and share them with the author and editors who worked on the book.

Email: `feedback@samspublishing.com`

Mail: Shelley Kronzek
        Sams Publishing
        201 West 103rd Street
        Indianapolis, IN 46290 USA

FOREWORD

In learning something new, there's no substitute for experience, although, of course, there are a number of ways to get it. When I wanted to learn how to ride a bike, for example, I did it the old-fashioned way—I just got on the bike and tried to ride. Naturally, at first, I spent most of my time falling down. After a while, though, and with practice, I was able to ride around all day with no skinned knees.

Learning to play the guitar was a little different in that I couldn't just pick it up and do it. I needed to learn from experienced guitar players. I needed teachers. I actually had a number of teachers, and I learned different things from all of them. Whether it was picking up fantastic "licks" from people such as Jimi Hendrix, Eddie Van Halen, and Eric Clapton, or sitting down with more experienced players and having them give me tips on certain techniques, taking advantage of their experience made me a better player. Although it took me much longer to learn to play the guitar than to ride a bike, I don't think I ever skinned my knees in the process.

Thankfully, learning ASP.NET is far easier than learning to play the guitar, and when you make a mistake, it's much less painful than falling off a bike! ASP.NET was designed to make developing and deploying applications and services easier than ever before. One of the key features that developers love is the new architecture for building pages using reusable controls, which provides a programming model similar to Visual Basic. There's a fantastic method for creating XML-based Web services, and "xcopy" deployment allows you to deploy your application by simply copying all the resources for your app, such as pages, compiled components, and configuration data, with no registration required. You can even deploy updates to a running app, and the app is gracefully migrated to the new version! ASP.NET also contains a number of less-obvious features that, nonetheless, provide huge benefits. For example, the tracing features have drawn spontaneous applause whenever we've presented them to developers!

In addition to all the great features provided directly by ASP.NET, one of the best things about it is that it is part of a much larger initiative for Microsoft, called "The .NET Framework." The .NET Framework is a remarkably rich platform for building applications and services that provides a number of compelling advantages for developers.

The Common Language Runtime, for example, is a key part of the .NET Framework. It provides an execution environment that increases developer productivity by removing the housekeeping and plumbing details. It shields developers from common programming errors and versioning problems, and it provides an advanced object-oriented architecture with features such as implementation inheritance. And most impressively, it does this across many languages. So, for example, you can implement an object in C# and then inherit from it in Visual Basic (yes, VB now has inheritance!).

The .NET Framework also contains a rich set of class libraries that enable developers to build richer applications with less code. There are object libraries for consuming and manipulating XML and relational data, for doing file and network I/O, and for creating and manipulating images. In addition, there are general purpose data structures such as hash tables and lists.

To top it all off, Visual Studio.NET is an incredibly powerful tool that directly targets ASP.NET and the .NET Framework. Therefore, developers can use the world's most popular development tool when developing, debugging, and deploying Web services and applications.

Of course, with all these fantastic features, there is still a key question: What is the best way to learn about ASP.NET? Although we did make it so that developers could just "climb aboard and start riding," I believe that the best way is to have a good teacher, and that's where *ASP.NET: Tips, Tutorials, and Code* comes in. This book brings together some of the world's best, most experienced ASP.NET developers and lets them teach you some of their best "licks" by taking you through key areas of both ASP.NET and the .NET Framework and showing you practical examples of how to use them to solve real-world problems in the applications that you're building.

The original concept for the book actually started with the ASP.NET team. Over the past three and a half years, I and other members of the team have done hundreds of presentations on ASP.NET, both within Microsoft and at conferences around the world. One of the best talks was "ASP.NET Tips and Tricks," by Scott Guthrie, with whom I started the ASP.NET team. In it, he walked through a number of cool features of ASP.NET and the .NET Framework. With almost all the features, you could hear developers say "Wow, I didn't know you could do that!"

In talking with the publishers at Sams, we mentioned that it would be great to have a book in a similar format, and we assisted them in finding the best people to write it. Scott Mitchell, Steve Walther, Doug Seven, Donny Mack, Dan Wahlin, and Chris Payne are among the most experienced ASP.NET developers and community "gurus." Adam Nathan works here on the Common Language Runtime team at Microsoft, and Billy Anders was one of the first inside Microsoft to put together solutions with ASP.NET. And unlike Jimi Hendrix, Eddie Van Halen, and Eric Clapton, I have met them all personally!

I think you will find *ASP.NET: Tips, Tutorials, and Code* a worthwhile resource in helping you get the most out of ASP.NET. Enjoy!

Mark Anders
Product Unit Manager
.NET Framework

Microsoft Corporation

INTRODUCTION

At the Professional Developer's Conference (PDC) in July 2000, Microsoft officially introduced the world to its .NET initiative, a business strategy focusing on providing software as a service hosted on the Internet. For end users, .NET aims to simplify the process of accessing and storing information by describing data in a platform-independent way (via XML) on a universally accessible medium (the Internet). For developers, .NET brings with it an entirely new framework, along with new languages and programming tools.

At the PDC conference where Microsoft introduced .NET, one of its forerunning .NET applications, Active Server Pages.NET (ASP.NET) was showcased. ASP.NET, which is the .NET predecessor to Active Server Pages (ASP, a technology for creating scriptable dynamic Web pages), provides significant and exciting changes and enhancements.

To assist with the creation of .NET applications, Microsoft has released the .NET Framework SDK, a collection of hundreds of classes arranged in logical namespaces. These classes provide the functionality needed for .NET application development. For example, the `System.Diagnostics` namespace contains classes for performing diagnostic functionality through a .NET application, such as reading from and writing to the Windows Event Log, and the `System.Data` namespace contains a number of classes for accessing and working with a vast array of databases.

When creating ASP.NET Web pages, you are, in essence, creating .NET applications. Therefore, ASP.NET pages can access the rich functionality of the .NET Framework, meaning that, from an ASP.NET page, you can do things that were only possible in ASP through the use of COM components (or were not possible at all).

Due to the many development changes in creating .NET applications, it's not surprising that building a dynamic Web site using ASP.NET is strikingly different from building the same site using classic ASP. For example, whereas classic ASP pages were created with scripting languages, ASP.NET Web pages are created using compiled, .NET-compatible programming languages, such as Visual Basic.NET and C#. ASP.NET Web pages, like any .NET application, are created using event-driven, object-oriented programming techniques.

Those developers who have worked with classic ASP will find ASP.NET radically different. There is a bit of a learning curve associated with any new technology, and ASP.NET is no exception. However, once classic ASP developers become familiar with ASP.NET, they will come to quickly enjoy its functionality and ease of use. Not only does ASP.NET provide more features and better performance than classic ASP, but creating ASP.NET pages usually requires far less code and development time than comparable classic ASP pages.

This book explores the many exciting advantages ASP.NET offers over classic ASP. Some of the advantages that are immediately available once you begin working with ASP.NET include the following:

- An event-driven programming interface (Chapter 1, "Common ASP.NET Page Techniques")

- Programmatic access to the plethora of classes in the .NET Framework (Chapter 2, "Common ASP.NET Code Techniques")

- Rich server-side and client-side form field validation (Chapter 3, "Form Field Input Validation")

- Easy development and deployment of reusable user interface controls (Chapter 5, "Creating and Using User Controls")

- Tight integration with Active Data Objects.NET (ADO.NET), the .NET predecessor to Microsoft's Active Data Objects (ADO), used for accessing databases. (Chapter 6, "Data Manipulation with ADO.NET")

- The capability to create rich data controls and bind the results of database queries to these controls (Chapter 7, "Data Presentation")

- Simple deployment of ASP.NET Web sites and custom components (Chapter 11, "ASP.NET Deployment and Configuration")

- The deployment of components (Web services) on the Internet so that other Web sites can use them (Chapter 13, "Web Services")

- The capability for an ASP.NET Web page to easily utilize a Web service, a component deployed on the Internet. (Chapter 13, "Web Services")

- A rich Caching API for increased Web page performance (Chapter 15, "ASP.NET Performance Tips")

- The capability to easily create Web controls that will render in mobile devices (Chapter 17, "Mobile Controls")

- Backward compatibility with pre-.NET COM components (Chapter 19, "COM and Win32 in ASP.NET Web Pages")

This list of advantages just scratches the surface! ASP.NET provides a wealth of enhancements and improvements over classic ASP pages and will truly take the Web programming world by storm. If you are excited and interested in learning about ASP.NET in detail, let this comprehensive book serve as your guide.

Conventions Used in This Book

The people at Sams Publishing have spent many years developing and publishing computer books designed for ease of use and containing the most up-to-date information available.

With that experience, we've learned what features help you the most. Look for these features throughout the book to help enhance your learning experience and get the most out of HTML.

- Screen messages, code listings, and command samples appear in `monospace type`.
- Uniform Resource Locators (URLs) used to identify pages on the Web and values for HTML attributes also appear in `monospace type`.
- Terms that are defined in the text appear in italics. *Italics* are sometimes used for emphasis, too.
- In code lines, placeholders for variables are indicated by using `italic monospace type`.

Tip
Tips give you advice on quick or overlooked procedures, including shortcuts.

Note
Notes present useful or interesting information that isn't necessarily essential to the current discussion, but might augment your understanding with background material or advice relating to the topic.

Caution
Cautions warn you about potential problems a procedure might cause, unexpected results, or mistakes that could prove costly.

Who Should Read This Book?

This book is intended for intermediate to advanced Web developers who are interested in learning the many ins and outs of ASP.NET. ASP.NET offers so many new features and enhancements over classic ASP that even the most proficient ASP developer will find the entirety of this book invaluable.

Due to the many radical changes to ASP.NET, having experience with classic ASP is not a prerequisite for this book. The reader should, however, have programming experience, preferably in VBScript, Visual Basic, Java, or some other high-level programming language.

CHAPTER 1

COMMON ASP.NET PAGE TECHNIQUES

by Scott Mitchell

In this chapter we will examine:
- The events of the Page object
- How to use the `Page_Load` event handler
- Using post-back forms
- Different methods for determining when a form has been posted-back successfully
- Creating custom event handlers for ASP.NET Web control events

Development of ASP.NET Web pages differs wildly from development of classic ASP Web pages. Classic ASP pages were composed of procedural-based script; ASP.NET pages, on the other hand, can consist of numerous Web controls that can be programmatically accessed by both procedural-based code and event handlers. Event handlers are custom functions that are executed when a particular event occurs for a particular object on the ASP.NET page, such as the user entering text into a textbox Web control, or clicking a button Web control. (This style of programming should feel very familiar for Visual Basic developers.)

ASP.NET provides an object-oriented approach to Web development. Each ASP.NET Web page can contain numerous objects (Web controls) that expose properties, methods, and events. In fact, each ASP.NET Web page itself is, in actuality, an object! The .NET Framework consists of a `Page` class (found in the `System.UI.Web` namespace) that serves as an abstraction for an actual ASP.NET Web page, containing events, properties, and methods that represent an ASP.NET Web page.

Since classic ASP and ASP.NET development differs so greatly, it is important to have a chapter that explains the underlying theory of ASP.NET Web page development. In this chapter we'll examine the techniques new to ASP.NET Web page development and look at how they differ from classic ASP development.

1. Using `Page_Load`: Executing Code When a Page Is Loaded

As we discussed earlier in this chapter, each ASP.NET page is actually an instance of the `Page` class (found in the `System.UI.Web` namespace). The `Page` class contains a number of events that are fired each time an ASP.NET Web page is visited. The page-level events that fire occur in the following sequence:

1. `Init`—This event is defined in the `Control` class from which the `Page` class is derived. This event is to be used to perform an initialization needed for the control. When this event fires, the view state hasn't been populated yet, so the user-entered values of controls on the page have not been populated yet either. Furthermore, you should not access Web controls in the ASP.NET page through this event handler. Because of these restrictions, you will rarely need to write an event handler for this event for the `Page` class.

2. `Load`—This is the event for which you'll most often create an event handler. When the `Page_Load` event fires, the view state has been populated and you can access other Web controls on the ASP.NET Web page.

3. `PreRender`—This event fires before the `Page` object renders the ASP.NET page. If you need to perform any prerendering tasks, here is where to place them.

Listing 1.1.1 illustrates these three event handlers and the order of their execution when an ASP.NET Web page is visited.

LISTING 1.1.1 Each Time an ASP.NET Page Is Visited, a Number of Events Are Fired

```
 1: <%@Page Trace="True" %>
 2: <script language="vb" runat="server">
 3:    Sub Page_Init(sender as Object, e as EventArgs)
 4:      Trace.Write("Page_Init Event Handler", "Currently in the Page_Init
 ➥event handler!")
 5:    End Sub
 6:
 7:    Sub Page_Load(sender as Object, e as EventArgs)
 8:      Trace.Write("Page_Load Event Handler", "Currently in the
 ➥ Page_Load event handler!")
 9:    End Sub
10:
11:    Sub Page_PreRender(sender as Object, e as EventArgs)
12:      Trace.Write("Page_PreRender Event Handler", "Currently in the
 ➥ Page_PreRender event handler!")
13:    End Sub
14: </script>
```

In Listing 1.1.1, the Tracing features have been turned on in line 1 with the `Trace="True"` page directive. (ASP.NET's tracing features are discussed in detail in Chapter 10, "Debugging ASP.NET Applications.") Then, an event handler is created for each page-level event; in each event handler, a single `Trace.Write` is executed, outputting a statement to the Trace

Information section. This output, which helps illustrate the order of the page-level events, can be seen in Figure 1.1.

Note

`Trace.Write` allows developers to output information that may be helpful for debugging. A single page-level directive (`<% @Page Trace="[True|False]" %>`) determines if the output from `Trace.Write` is displayed on the ASP.NET page. (With classic ASP, developers often inserted `Response.Write`s throughout their pages for debugging purposes. `Trace.Write` is the preferred option for ASP.NET since the output can be turned on and off through a single directive.)

FIGURE 1.1
The Tracing features inherent with ASP.NET help to illustrate when various page-level events fire.

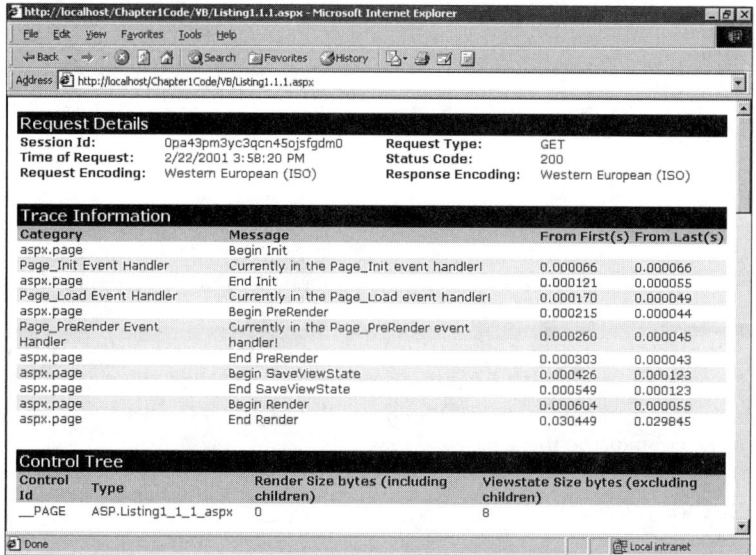

After the `PreRender` event handler fires, the `Page` class instance saves its state information in the view state. After the view state has been saved, the `Page` object is ready to render itself, and does so via the protected `Render` method. Finally, when the page has completed rendering, the `Unload` event fires. If you need to complete any clean-up tasks (perhaps the ASP.NET page created a temporary file on the Web server's file system and you want to delete it), place them in the `Page_Unload` event handler.

The `Page_Load` event handler is the place to set, check, or modify any properties of the Web controls in the ASP.NET page. Additionally, the `Page_Load` event handler is the place for code that should execute on every Web request for the page. A very simple example of using the `Page_Load` event handler can be seen in Listing 1.1.2. The ASP.NET page in Listing 1.1.2 contains a single text box in a postback form; the `Page_Load` event handler simply displays the current value of the text box. (In the next section, "2. Using Forms in ASP.NET," we'll look at using postback forms in more detail.)

LISTING 1.1.2 The `Page_Load` Event Handler Can Read, Set, and Alter the Values of Web Controls on the ASP.NET Page

```
 1: <script language="vb" runat="server">
 2:   Sub Page_Load(sender as Object, e as EventArgs)
 3:     'Output the value of the txtSomething text box
 4:     Response.Write("The text box contains the value: " & txtSomething.Text)
 5:   End Sub
 6: </script>
 7:
 8: <html>
 9: <body>
10:   <form runat="server">
11:     Enter something:
12:     <asp:textbox runat="server" id="txtSomething" />
13:     <p>
14:     <asp:button runat="server" Text="Submit!" />
15:   </form>
16: </body>
17: </html>
```

Listing 1.1.2 contains a simple postback form with a text box (line 12) and a button control (line 14). When the page is first loaded, the `Page_Load` event handler fires. Because the `txtSomething` text box doesn't contain any initial value, line 4 outputs: `"The text box contains the value: "` When the user enters a value into the text box and submits the form (by clicking the button), the form will be posted back, the page reloaded, and the `Page_Load` event handler fired again. Again, the value of the `txtSomething` text box is outputted. Figure 1.2 illustrates the output of Listing 1.1.2 when the user enters a value in to the text box and submits the form.

FIGURE 1.2
The value the user has entered into the text box is outputted in the `Page_Load` event handler.

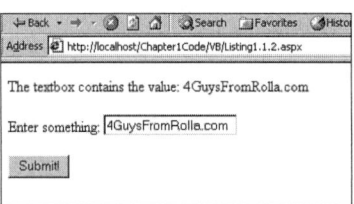

With classic ASP, if you want some script to run prior to the display of the HTML, you'd simply place it before the HTML content in the ASP page. With ASP.NET, however, the `Page_Load` event handler should be used instead. For example, if you want to display information from a database table, the `Page_Load` event handler could contain the code to establish a connection to the database, to query the data, and to display it.

Or, the `Page_Load` event handler could simply establish a connection to the database, while other, user-defined functions in the ASP.NET page could query different data, or display the same data differently. These user-defined functions could be fired as a result of user input, such as clicking a particular button or hyperlink on the ASP.NET page. (For more information on working with databases through an ASP.NET page, be sure to refer to Chapter 6, "Data Manipulation with ADO.NET.")

2. Using Forms in ASP.NET

With classic ASP, two common techniques were used by developers to obtain their users' inputs through forms. The first technique involved a two-page system. The first Web page would simply present the HTML code for the form. The form would contain in its `ACTION` parameter the URL for the *form processing script*, an ASP page that would be directed to when the user submitted the form. From this second page, the values entered into the form by the user could be extracted via the `QueryString` or `Form` collections from the `Request` object.

The second technique involved using a postback form. In the postback scenario, the form, when submitted, reloads itself as opposed to redirecting to a different URL. With classic ASP development, when using a postback form, the developer was responsible for determining whether the form had been posted back or not. If the page had *not* been posted back, the HTML form display code would be run; if it had been posted back, form processing code would execute instead.

Next, we'll briefly examine how the two-page form technique was used in classic ASP and how it can be used in ASP.NET. In the following section, we'll look how the postback form technique was employed using classic ASP and how to accomplish the same results with ASP.NET. ASP.NET was designed to handle postback forms with extreme ease; therefore, it is recommended that when developing interactive ASP.NET pages, you rely on postback forms.

Using the Two-Page Form Processing Technique

Listing 1.2.1 and Listing 1.2.2 illustrate this technique in progress. (Note that Listing 1.2.1 and Listing 1.2.2 are classic ASP pages, not ASP.NET pages.)

Note

Over the next few pages, we're going to examine how forms were handled with classic ASP. Don't worry, though, we'll soon tackle using postback forms in ASP.NET pages!

LISTING 1.2.1 The First Page in the Two-Page Form Processing Scenario Creates the HTML Form

```
 1: <%@ Language="VBScript" %>
 2: <html>
 3: <body>
 4:   <form method="post" action="Listing1.2.2.asp">
 5:     <h1>Personal Information</h1>
 6:     Name: <input type="text" name="txtName"><br>
 7:     Phone: <input type="text" name="txtPhone"><br>
 8:     Address: <textarea name="txtAddress" wrap="virtual"></textarea><br>
 9:     City/State/Zip: <input type="text" name="txtCity">,
10:     <input type="text" name="txtState" size="2">
11:         
```

LISTING 1.2.1 Continued

```
12:     <input type="text" name="txtZIP" size="5">
13:     <p>
14:     <input type="submit" value="Submit Information">
15:  </form>
16: </body>
17: </html>
```

The code in Listing 1.2.1 is fairly straightforward. It creates text boxes for the user to enter personal information. Note the `form` tag on line 4; the `action` property specifies the URL to load when the user submits the form: `Listing1.2.2.asp`, which can be seen in Listing 1.2.2. Figure 1.3 contains a screenshot of the code in Listing 1.2.1 when viewed through a browser.

FIGURE 1.3
Listing 1.2.1, when viewed through a browser, produces a form for the user to enter personal information.

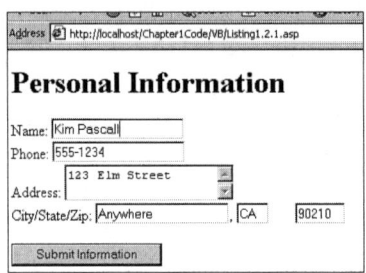

When the form in Listing 1.2.1 is submitted, the user is directed to the form processing script, `Listing1.2.2.asp`. From this ASP page, the user can access the values entered by the user via the `Form` collection of the `Request` object.

LISTING 1.2.2 The User's Entered Values Are Read Through the Second Page, the Form Processing Script

```
 1: <%@ Language="VBScript" %>
 2: <% Option Explicit %>
 3: <%
 4:    'Read in the form field values
 5:    Dim strName, strPhone, strAddress, strCity, strState, strZip
 6:    strName = Request.Form("txtName")
 7:    strPhone = Request.Form("txtPhone")
 8:    strAddress = Request.Form("txtAddress")
 9:    strCity = Request.Form("txtCity")
10:    strState = Request.Form("txtState")
11:    strZip = Request.Form("txtZip")
12:
13:    'Display user form values
14: %>
15:    Hello <%=strName%>!  A representative will call you at <%=strPhone%>
16:    and we will mail you some information.  This will be sent to:
17:    <p><ul>
18:      <%=strName%><br>
```

LISTING 1.2.2   Continued

```
19:       <%=strAddress%><br>
20:       <%=strCity%>, <%=strState%>    <%=strZip%>
21:     </ul><p>
22:     Thanks for your interest in our company!
```

The form values entered by the user in the code in Listing 1.2.1 can be read in the form processing script using the **Form** collection of the **Request** method. The output of Listing 1.2.2 can be seen Figure 1.4.

FIGURE 1.4
The form processing script can read the values entered by the user in the previous page.

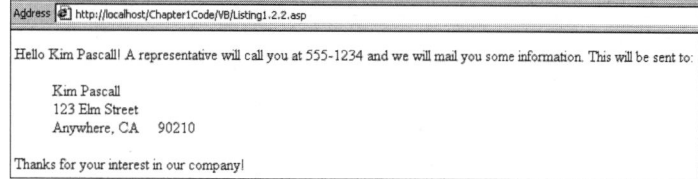

The code in Listings 1.2.1 and 1.2.2 illustrate the two-page form processing system commonly used with classic ASP. This system can also be used with ASP.NET pages. The **Request** object in ASP.NET contains both **QueryString** and **Form** collections, similar to the **Request** object in classic ASP. Listings 1.2.3 and 1.2.4 illustrate how this two-page form system can work with ASP.NET.

LISTING 1.2.3   Again, the First Page in the Two-Page Form Processing Scenario Creates the HTML Form

```
 1: <html>
 2: <body>
 3:   <form method="post" action="Listing1.2.4.aspx">
 4:     <h1>Personal Information</h1>
 5:     Name: <input type="text" name="txtName"><br>
 6:     Phone: <input type="text" name="txtPhone"><br>
 7:     Address: <textarea name="txtAddress" wrap="virtual"></textarea><br>
 8:     City/State/Zip: <input type="text" name="txtCity">,
 9:     <input type="text" name="txtState" size="2">
10:          
11:     <input type="text" name="txtZIP" size="5">
12:     <p>
13:     <input type="submit" value="Submit Information">
14:   </form>
15: </body>
16: </html>
```

As with Listing 1.2.1, the code in Listing 1.2.3 is fairly straightforward. It also creates text boxes for the user to enter personal information. Note the **form** tag on line 4; the **action** property specifies the ASP.NET page to load when the user submits the form: **Listing1.2.4.aspx**, which can be seen in Listing 1.2.4. Because the output of Listing 1.2.1 and Listing 1.2.3 are identical, refer to Figure 1.3 for a screenshot of the code in Listing 1.2.3 when viewed through a browser.

When the form in Listing 1.2.3 is submitted, the user is directed to the form processing script, an ASP.NET page, Listing1.2.4.aspx. From this page, the user can access the values entered by the user via the Form collection of the Request object, similar to the method in Listing 1.2.2.

LISTING 1.2.4 As Before, the User's Entered Values Are Read Through the Second Page, the Form Processing Script

```
 1: <script language="vb" runat="server">
 2:   Sub Page_Load(sender as Object, e as EventArgs)
 3:     'Read in the form field values
 4:     Dim strName, strPhone, strAddress, strCity, _
 5:       strState, strZip as String
 6:
 7:     strName = Request.Form("txtName")
 8:     strPhone = Request.Form("txtPhone")
 9:     strAddress = Request.Form("txtAddress")
10:     strCity = Request.Form("txtCity")
11:     strState = Request.Form("txtState")
12:     strZip = Request.Form("txtZip")
13:
14:     'Display user form values
15:
16:     Response.Write("Hello " & strName & "!  A representative " & _
17:       "will call you at " & strPhone & " and we will mail you " & _
18:       "some information.  This will be sent to:<p><ul>" & _
19:       strName & "<br>" & strAddress & "<br>" & _
20:       strCity & ", " & strState & "     " & _
21:       strZip & "</ul><p>Thanks for your interest in our company!")
22:   End Sub
23: </script>
```

The form values entered by the user in the code in Listing 1.2.3 can be read in the form processing script using the Form collection of the Request method. Note that there is only a slight difference between the code in Listing 1.2.2 and Listing 1.2.4. Also note that we placed all our form processing logic in Listing 1.2.4 in the Page_Load event handler. Because the output of Listing 1.2.4 is synonymous with the output of Listing 1.2.2, refer back to Figure 1.4 for a screenshot of Listing 1.2.4 when viewed through a browser.

Note

This two-page form processing technique has become obsolete with ASP.NET's more useful postback forms. This two-page form processing technique was shown for two reasons: to illustrate that the two-page form processing technique, which was very popular among classic ASP developers, still works in ASP.NET; and to provide a means to compare the amount of code that must be written to utilize the two-page form processing technique as compared to the postback form processing technique.

The next section, "Using the Postback Form Processing Technique," examines using postback forms in both classic ASP and ASP.NET.

Using the Postback Form Processing Technique

The second technique to handle forms involves a single Web page. This sole Web page is responsible for both displaying the HTML form (when appropriate) and processing the user-submitted form data (again, when appropriate). To have a form reload the same page when it is submitted, the ACTION property of the FORM tag can either be explicitly set to the URL of the Web page or not specified at all. This method is referred to as a *postback form* because the HTML form, when submitted, posts the user's responses back to the same Web page.

Listing 1.2.5 presents a classic ASP page that uses the postback form technique. Note the If ... Then ... Else logic that must be applied to determine whether the ASP page should display the HTML form or process it.

LISTING 1.2.5 A Postback Form Uses a Single Page Displaying Both the HTML Form and the Form Processing Script

```
 1: <%@ Language="VBScript" %>
 2: <html>
 3: <body>
 4: <% If Len(Request.Form("btnSubmit")) = 0 then
 5:      'Display the form %>
 6:    <form method="post">
 7:      <h1>Personal Information</h1>
 8:      Name: <input type="text" name="txtName"><br>
 9:      Phone: <input type="text" name="txtPhone"><br>
10:      Address: <textarea name="txtAddress" wrap="virtual"></textarea><br>
11:      City/State/Zip: <input type="text" name="txtCity">,
12:      <input type="text" name="txtState" size="2">
13:           
14:      <input type="text" name="txtZIP" size="5">
15:      <p>
16:      <input name="btnSubmit" type="submit" value="Submit Information">
17:    </form>
18: <% Else
19:      'The user has submitted the form
20:    'Read in the form field values
21:    Dim strName, strPhone, strAddress, strCity, strState, strZip
22:    strName = Request.Form("txtName")
23:    strPhone = Request.Form("txtPhone")
24:    strAddress = Request.Form("txtAddress")
25:    strCity = Request.Form("txtCity")
26:    strState = Request.Form("txtState")
27:    strZip = Request.Form("txtZip")
28:
```

LISTING 1.2.5   Continued

```
29:    'Display user form values  %>
30:    Hello <%=strName%>!  A representative will call you at <%=strPhone%> and
31:    we will mail you some information.  This will be sent to:
32:    <p><ul>
33:      <%=strName%><br>
34:      <%=strAddress%><br>
35:      <%=strCity%>, <%=strState%>     <%=strZip%>
36:    </ul><p>
37:    Thanks for your interest in our company!
38: <% End If %>
39: </body>
40: </html>
```

The code in Listing 1.2.5 begins by determining whether to display the HTML form. The `If` statement on line 4 checks to see if the `btnSubmit` button (created on line 16) contains any value. If it does, the form has been submitted. If it has not, though, the length of the value of the `btnSubmit` button would be zero, and the code from lines 5 through 17 would be executed. This code creates a postback form.

Note

Note that the `form` tag on line 6 does *not* contain an `ACTION` property. This will cause the form to reload the current URL when submitted. We could have also received the same results by specifying the `action` property as: `action="Listing1.2.5.asp"`.

When the page is submitted, the form processing script section (lines 19 through 37) is executed. This section reads the user-entered form values and displays a message. Note that when the code in Listing 1.2.5 is first visited through a Web browser, the output is identical to that in Figure 1.3. When the user enters information and submits the form, the same page is reloaded, but the output displayed is similar to that in Figure 1.4.

As the code in Listing 1.2.5 illustrates, postback forms in classic ASP were messy at best, resulting in spaghetti code from the `If ... Then ... Else` blocks nested in the ASP page. Furthermore, to read the values entered by the user, the developer has to explicitly read values from the `Form` (or `QueryString`) collections of the `Request` object.

ASP.NET aims at providing the developer with a different experience when working with forms in general. Before we delve into the specifics, let's look at a postback form example in ASP.NET that takes advantage of the new Web programming paradigm offered by ASP.NET. Listing 1.2.6 creates a similar postback form to the one in Listing 1.2.5.

LISTING 1.2.6 ASP.NET Post-Back Forms Offer Several Advantages Over Classic ASP Form Handling Techniques

```
 1: <script language="vb" runat="server">
 2:   Sub Page_Load(sender as Object, e as EventArgs)
 3:     If Page.IsPostBack then
 4:       Response.Write("Hello " & txtName.Value & "!  A representative " & _
 5:         "will call you at " & txtPhone.Value & " and we will
 mail you " & _
 6:         "some information.  This will be sent to:<p><ul>" & _
 7:         txtName.Value & "<br>" & txtAddress.Value & "<br>" & _
 8:         txtCity.Value & ", " & txtState.Value & " 
    " & _
 9:         txtZip.Value & "</ul><p>Thanks for your information in
 our company!")
10:     End If
11:   End Sub
12: </script>
13:
14: <html>
15: <body>
16:   <form runat="server" id="frmSurvey">
17:     <h1>Personal Information</h1>
18:     Name: <input type="text" id="txtName" runat="server"><br>
19:     Phone: <input type="text" id="txtPhone" runat="server"><br>
20:     Address: <textarea wrap="virtual" id="txtAddress" runat="server">
 </textarea><br>
21:     City/State/Zip: <input type="text" id="txtCity" runat="server">,
22:     <input type="text" id="txtState" size="2" runat="server">
23:          
24:     <input type="text" id="txtZIP" size="5" runat="server">
25:     <p>
26:     <input type="submit" value="Submit Information" runat="server">
27:   </form>
28: </body>
29: </html>
```

The code in Listing 1.2.6 is a bit familiar to the code in Listing 1.2.5, except that Listing 1.2.6 does not contain any sort of sloppy `If ... Then ... Else` block to determine whether to display the form. Rather, the `Page.IsPostBack` property (line 3) is used to determine whether or not the form has been posted back. (The `Page.IsPostBack` property is discussed in further detail in the next section, "Responding to a Form Postback.") There are a couple of changes to the HTML tags in Listing 1.2.6. First, note that the `form` tag on line 16 has the `runat="server"` attribute set. This informs the ASP.NET engine that we want to create a postback form and have the state (the user-entered values) of the form field elements inside the form maintained for us automatically.

Also note that each of the form field element tags also contain a `runat="server"` attribute (see lines 18, 19, 20, 21, 22, 24, and 26). By specifying the `runat="server"` attribute, we are indicating to the ASP.NET engine that these are not mere HTML, but HTMLControls, rich controls that contain properties, events, and methods. Also note that instead of using the `name` property to identify each of our form field elements, we used the `id` property.

When the ASP.NET page in Listing 1.2.6 is first visited the user is presented with the HTML form show back in Figure 1.3. However, the actual HTML that generates the form is not the same as the HTML content in Listing 1.2.6. Listing 1.2.7 contains the actual HTML code returned when Listing 1.2.6 is visited via a Web browser. (I used the View/Source option of my Web browser to view the HTML content of `Listing1.2.6.aspx` when viewed through a browser.)

LISTING 1.2.7 The HTML Received by the Browser When `Listing1.2.6.aspx` Is Visited Differs Slightly from the Actual Code in Listing 1.2.6

```
 1: <html>
 2: <body>
 3:   <form name="frmSurvey" method="post" action="Listing1.2.6.aspx"
➥ id="frmSurvey">
 4: <input type="hidden" name="__
➥ VIEWSTATE" value="YTB6LTc5MDI2MzkxM19fX3g=4573fad6" />
 5:
 6:     <h1>Personal Information</h1>
 7:     Name: <input name="txtName" id="txtName" type="text" /><br>
 8:     Phone: <input name="txtPhone" id="txtPhone" type="text" /><br>
 9:     Address: <textarea name="txtAddress" id="txtAddress" wrap="virtual">
➥ </textarea><br>
10:     City/State/Zip: <input name="txtCity" id="txtCity" type="text" />,
11:     <input name="txtState" id="txtState" type="text" size="2" />
12:          
13:     <input name="txtZIP" id="txtZIP" type="text" size="5" />
14:     <p>
15:     <input name="ctrl10" type="submit" value="Submit Information" />
16:   </form>
17: </body>
18: </html>
```

Note that the `form` tag (seen on line 3 in Listing 1.2.7) has changed a bit, automatically specifying a `method` and `action` attribute for us. On line 4, a hidden `input` tag that we did not create is presented. This hidden `input` tag is known as the *viewstate*; the `value` of the hidden tag contains information about the state of each of the controls present in the postback form.

When the user first visits the ASP.NET page in Listing 1.2.6, she is presented with an HTML form identical to that in Figure 1.3. After filling in the form field values and submitting the form, the page is reloaded. Both times the page is loaded the `Page_Load` event handler is fired (see lines 2 through 11 in Listing 1.2.6). The first thing the `Page_Load` event handler does is check the `Page.IsPostBack` property (line 3). This property returns a Boolean value: True if the page has been posted back to (by a postback form), False otherwise.

After the user posts the form back (by filling in the form and submitting it), the code inside the `If` statement will execute (lines 4 through 9). This code displays the user-entered form values. Instead of using the `Form` collection of the `Request` object, the values of the HTMLControls in Listing 1.2.6 can be accessed programmatically. This is because each HTMLControl (each form field element in the postback form with a `runat="server"` attribute specified) is actually an object; the `Value` property of the HTMLControls returns the user-entered value.

After the user enters values into the HTMLControls and submits the form, the ASP.NET page is posted back and the user's input is displayed. Figure 1.5 contains a screenshot of Listing 1.2.6 when viewed through a browser *after* the user has filled out and submitted the form.

FIGURE 1.5
The form processing script can read the values entered by the user in the previous page.

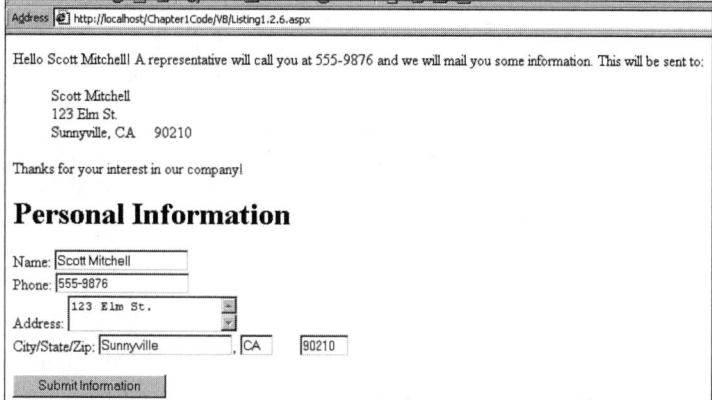

Note

The HTML form is still displayed even after the form has been submitted. This is a slight break from the postback form example in Listing 1.2.5. Because the postback form itself is also an object, you could easily hide the form after it had been submitted by adding `frmSurvey.Visible = False` immediately following line 3 in Listing 1.2.6.

3. Responding to a Form Postback

As we examined in the previous section, a developer can programmatically determine when an ASP.NET page has been posted back to by checking the `Page.IsPostBack` property. If this property returns `True`, the page has received the postback. Often you will want to take some different course of action *after* the postback.

For example, you might have a search page on your Web site that accepts search terms from a user and then, based on the search terms, returns URLs to relevant content on your site. This can be easily handled with a postback form. You'd initially want to create a postback form that contained a text box for the user to enter his search terms; you'd also want to include a submit button that will post the form back once clicked.

Listing 1.3.1 contains an ASP.NET page that displays a simple search form.

LISTING 1.3.1   A Simple Search Form

```
 1: <html>
 2: <body>
 3:    <form runat="server" id="frmSearch">
 4:      <h1>Search the Site</h1>
 5:      <b>Search Terms:</b>
 6:      <asp:text box runat="server" id="txtSearchTerms" />
 7:      <p>
 8:      <asp:button runat="server" id="btnSubmit" Text="Start Search!" />
 9:    </form>
10: </body>
11: </html>
```

The search text box in Listing 1.3.1 is created slightly different from the `input` text boxes in Listing 1.2.6. ASP.NET contains two incarnations of form field controls. The first type, known as HTMLControls, resemble HTML input tag syntax. In fact, their only distinction is the addition of the (very important) `runat="server"` attribute. Web controls, on the other hand, are created with a unique syntax, a tag in the form of `<asp:WebControlName ... >  </asp:WebControlName>` (or, in a shorthand way: `<asp:WebControlName ... />`).

Both HTMLControls (controls created like regular HTML controls with the `runat="server" attribute included`) and Web controls (controls created with the `asp:` prefix, such as `<asp:textbox ... />`) produce browser-independent HTML. When a user visits the ASP.NET page created by the code in Listing 1.3.1, the Web controls are converted into standard HTML-compliant form field tags, which are returned to the browser as plain HTML. Listing 1.3.2 displays the HTML returned when `Listing1.3.1.aspx` is viewed through a Web browser.

LISTING 1.3.2   When a Browser Requests an ASP.NET Page with Web Controls, These Controls Are Converted into Compliant HTML

```
 1: <html>
 2: <body>
 3:    <form name="frmSearch" method="post" action="Listing1.3.1.aspx"
➥ id="frmSearch">
 4: <input type="hidden" name="__VIEWSTATE"
➥ value="YTB6MTk1NDExNjQxNl9fX3g=e92c2469" />
 5:
 6:      <h1>Search the Site</h1>
 7:      <b>Search Terms:</b>
 8:      <input name="txtSearchTerms" type="text" id="txtSearchTerms" />
 9:      <p>
10:      <input type="submit" name="btnSubmit" value="Start Search!"
➥ id="btnSubmit" />
11:    </form>
12: </body>
13: </html>
```

Note that, as with Listing 1.2.7, Listing 1.3.2 contains some HTML code that we did not enter ourselves. The `form` tag on line 3 has been expanded and the viewstate `input` control (line 4)

has been tacked on as well. Our text box Web control on line 6 in Listing 1.3.1 has been converted into a standard `input` tag on line 8 in Listing 1.3.2. Additionally, the button Web control on line 8 in Listing 1.3.1 is converted into an `input` tag on line 10 in Listing 1.3.2.

Although the ASP.NET page created by Listing 1.3.1 might look fine and dandy, it is pretty worthless. When the user submits the form we'd want to have the site searched, but how can we tell when the form has been posted back? There are a couple of common techniques that can be used and that we will be using throughout this book.

The first technique is to place the code that should fire when the form is posted back in the `Page_Load` event handler. Because this event handler fires *every* time the page is visited, we must be certain to place the postback–specific code within an `If` block that checks to ensure that the `Page.IsPostBack` property is `True`. We illustrated how to accomplish this in Listing 1.2.6.

Listing 1.3.3 contains another working example of this method. Note that in Listing 1.3.3 we've simply taken the code from Listing 1.3.1 and added a server-side script block with a `Page_Load` event handler.

LISTING 1.3.3 A Check of the `Page.IsPostBack` Property in the `Page_Load` Event Handler Can Be Used to Determine When the ASP.NET Page Has Been Posted Back

```
 1: <script language="vb" runat="server">
 2:   Sub Page_Load(sender as Object, e as EventArgs)
 3:     'Check to see if the form has been posted-back
 4:     If Page.IsPostBack Then
 5:       '*** Perform the search (enter your code here) ***
 6:
 7:       Response.Write("Display search terms for " & txtSearchTerms.Text)
 8:     End If
 9:   End Sub
10: </script>
11:
12: <html>
13: <body>
14:   <form runat="server" id="frmSearch">
15:     <h1>Search the Site</h1>
16:     <b>Search Terms:</b>
17:     <asp:text box runat="server" id="txtSearchTerms" />
18:     <p>
19:     <asp:button runat="server" id="btnSubmit" Text="Start Search!" />
20:   </form>
21: </body>
22: </html>
```

When the ASP.NET page is initially visited, the `Page_Load` event handler is executed. However, because the `Page.IsPostBack` property is `False` at this time, no code is executed (see line 4). After the user submits the form, the ASP.NET page is posted back, the `Page_Load` event handler fires again (as it does every time the page is loaded) and, this time, the code from lines 5 through 7 will be executed because the `Page.IsPostBack` property is `True`.

Figure 1.6 shows a screenshot of the code in Listing 1.3.3 when viewed through a browser *after* the user has entered a search term and submitted it.

FIGURE 1.6
When the user has entered some search terms and submitted the form, the page is posted back and the search code is ready to be executed

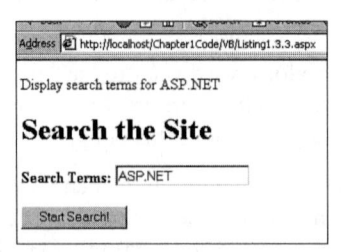

Checking the `Page.IsPostBack` property in the `Page_Load` event handler is one method of running specific code when the ASP.NET page has been posted back. Another solution is to wire up the submit button's `OnClick` event to an event handler function. This method is demonstrated in Listing 1.3.4.

LISTING 1.3.4 Creating an Event Handler for the Submit Button's `OnClick` Event

```
 1: <script language="vb" runat="server">
 2:   Sub btnSubmit_Click(sender as Object, e as EventArgs)
 3:     ' *** Perform the search ***
 4:
 5:     Response.Write("Display search terms for " & txtSearchTerms.Text)
 6:   End Sub
 7: </script>
 8:
 9: <html>
10: <body>
11:   <form runat="server" id="frmSearch">
12:     <h1>Search the Site</h1>
13:     <b>Search Terms:</b>
14:     <asp:text box runat="server" id="txtSearchTerms" />
15:     <p>
16:     <asp:button runat="server" id="btnSubmit" Text="Start Search!"
17:         OnClick="btnSubmit_Click" />
18:   </form>
19: </body>
20: </html>
```

When the user submits the form (by clicking the submit button), the form is posted back and the `btnSubmit_Click` event handler is fired. This event handler fires because we explicitly wired it up through the button Web control's `OnClick` event (line 17). So, when the user clicks the Start Search button, the form is posted back, the page is reloaded, and the `btnSubmit_Click` event handler is fired.

Note that the `btnSubmit_Click` event handler doesn't check the `Page.IsPostBack` property such as the `Page_Load` event handler did in Listing 1.3.3. This is because the `btnSubmit_Click` event handler will only fire when the Start Search submit button is clicked, and therefore we will know that the form would have been posted-back.

In this section we examined how to use either the `Page_Load` event handler or a custom event handler to run certain code when a form has been posted back. In the next section, we'll take a closer look at how to create event handlers for Web controls.

4. Creating Event Handlers for Web Control Events

In "Using `Page_Load`: Executing Code When a Page is First Visited," we examined how a developer could create event handlers for the `Page` class's events. The `Page` class, which represents an ASP.NET Web page, contains events similar to every other class in the .NET Framework. Because the ASP.NET Web controls (`<asp:textbox ... />`, `<asp:button ... />`, and so on) are all classes in the .NET Framework, they each have their own events. These events can be wired up to custom event handlers in an ASP.NET page.

Listing 1.4.1 contains a simple example of an event handler for a Web control event.

LISTING 1.4.1 The `CheckboxChanged` Event Handler Is Executed When the Check Box's `CheckedChanged` Event Fires

```
 1: <script language="c#" runat="server">
 2:   void CheckboxValueChanged(Object sender, EventArgs e)
 3:   {
 4:     if (chkInfo.Checked)
 5:       Response.Write("<i>You have just checked the text box</i>");
 6:     else
 7:       Response.Write("<i>You have just unchecked the text box</i>");
 8:   }
 9: </script>
10:
11: <html>
12: <body>
13:   <form runat="server">
14:     Send me information about Acme Widgets:
15:     <asp:CheckBox id="chkInfo" runat="server"
16:              OnCheckedChanged="CheckboxValueChanged" />
17:     <p>
18:     <asp:button id="btnSubmit" Text="Submit" runat="server" />
19:   </form>
20: </body>
21: </html>
```

Listing 1.4.1 illustrates how to wire up an event handler to a Web control event. Before we examine the event handler, though, let's look at the HTML section of Listing 1.4.1 (lines 11 through 21). On lines 15 and 16, a check box Web control is created. Line 18 contains a submit button Web control.

The check box Web control contains an event named `CheckedChanged`. To create an event handler for this Web control event, we need to do two things:

1. Create an event handler function in a server-side script block (see the `CheckboxValueChanged` function from lines 2 through 8).

2. Specify the event handler in the Web control using the `OnEventName` syntax (line 16).

For step 1, note that the event handler must conform to a certain declaration. Event handler functions must be functions that do not return any value and accept two parameters: an Object and an `EventArgs` parameter. In C#, this is declared in the following form:

`void EventHandlerName(Object objectName, EventArgs eventArgsName)`

In VB.NET, an event handler must be defined in the following form:

`Sub EventHandlerName(objectName as Object, eventArgsName as EventArgs)`

The `EventHandlerName` can be any valid function name. Often it helps to use a special naming scheme, such as `WebControlID_EventName`. For a text box Web control's `TextChanged` event handler, you might want to use an event handler name such as `txtName_TextChanged`. Additionally, the `objectName` and `eventArgsName` are simple variable names, but, throughout this book, we will be using `sender` and `e` for the `objectName` and `eventArgsName` variables, respectively.

In Listing 1.4.1 we create our event handler function in C#, spanning lines 2 through 8. This event handler is named `CheckboxValueChanged`, but could have been named `chkInfo_Changed`, `FooBar`, or any other legal function name. This code in `CheckboxValueChanged` is painfully simple. On line 4 the `Checked` property is examined and, if it is `True`, we display a message that the user just checked the check box; if it is `False`, we display a message that the user just unchecked the check box.

At this point we need to wire up the `CheckboxChanged` event of the `chkInfo` check box Web control to the `CheckboxValueChanged` event handler. This is accomplished in the check box Web control declaration (line 16). The syntax for wiring up an event to an event handler in a Web control is

`<asp:WebControlName ... OnEventName="EventHandlerName" ... />`

On line 16, note that this is accomplished with the following code:

`OnCheckChanged="CheckboxValueChanged"`

When working with Web controls events, it is often a bit misleading when trying to determine when a particular event will fire. For example, Listing 1.4.1 illustrates how to wire up an event handler to the `CheckboxChanged` event of the check box Web control. But when does the `CheckboxChanged` event fire? One might conclude that it fires immediately whenever the user clicks the check box, but this would be an incorrect assumption. All the Web control events can't fire until the ASP.NET page is posted back. Therefore, the `CheckboxChanged` event only fires if the user submits the postback form and, upon submitting the form, the checked status of the check box control was different than it was last time the user posted-back the page.

This might all sound a little bit confusing, so let's step through this process. Figure 1.7 contains a screenshot of Listing 1.4.1 when visited for the first time.

FIGURE 1.7
The user is initially presented with a postback form containing an unchecked check box and a Submit button.

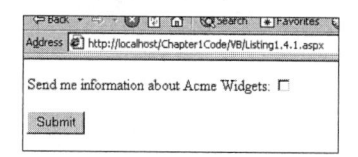

If, at this point, we check the check box, nothing happens: no event handlers are fired, and the form is automatically posted back. After we submit the form by clicking the submit button, the form is posted back. Because the check box was initially unchecked, if it is checked when the form is submitted, the `CheckboxValueChecked` event handler will execute and a message will be displayed (see Figure 1.8).

FIGURE 1.8
If the check box's checked status has changed since the last form postback, the `CheckboxChanged` event will fire, executing the `CheckboxValueChecked` event handler.

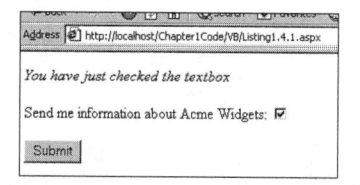

Summary

In this chapter, we looked at some of the basics of an ASP.NET page and how the nature of ASP.NET programming differs from classic ASP programming. Whereas classic ASP development focused on sequential, procedural-based coding techniques, ASP.NET encourages object-oriented techniques and event-based programming. For example, the .NET Framework contains a `Page` class that represents an ASP.NET Web page. This class contains properties, methods, and events that are indicative of a Web page. As a developer, you can have certain code execute when various page-level events occur. In the section "1. Using `Page_Load`: Executing Code When a Page Is Loaded," we looked at how to use the `Load` event of the `Page` object to execute code when an ASP.NET page is first loaded.

ASP.NET development is geared toward using postback forms. These postback forms, when specified with the `runat="server"` attribute, can maintain the state of the Web controls contained in the form. The `Page` class contains an `IsPostBack` property that you can programmatically check to determine whether a page has been posted back. Postback forms in ASP.NET provide enhanced functionality and cleaner code than their equivalents in classic ASP. With postback forms, the code for ASP.NET pages start looking similar to VisualBasic forms.

This chapter concludes with an examination of creating event handlers for ASP.NET Web control events. Event handlers are created in a two-step process: First you must create an event handler function, which has particular requirements in its form; second, you must wire up an event to the created event handler through the `OnEventHandlerName` syntax in the Web control.

Throughout the remainder of this book you will see the code techniques discussed in this chapter used again and again. If you are a previous ASP/VBScript developer, these changes are quite awesome ones, providing an entirely new programming paradigm that will likely take some getting used to. If you are a VB developer, you will probably feel more comfortable with ASP.NET development, with its object-oriented and event-based approach as opposed to classic ASP development.

Other Resources

At the end of each chapter you'll find an "Other Resources" section with links, books, magazine articles, and other pertinent information. These auxiliary readings provide additional information on various chapter topics and also provide a next step for learning about a particular chapter topic in greater detail.

In this chapter, we introduced ASP.NET and examined the new programming paradigm. Gone are the days of Web pages with intermingled code and content; gone are the days of inefficient, procedural-based spaghetti code. To help with that transition to ASP.NET and the new event-driven/object-oriented approach, be sure to check out these great ASP.NET Web resources for more information:

- www.ASP.NET—This Microsoft-run ASP.NET Web site serves as a great starting place for new ASP.NET developers. It provides quick access to the latest ASP.NET bits, links to popular ASP.NET resource sites on the Web, a list of newsgroups and ListServs for ASP.NET-focused discussions, and ASP.NET books.

- www.ASPNG.com—This ASP.NET-dedicated Web site contains dozens of very active ASP.NET-related ListServs as well as a number of great tutorials and code examples.

- www.ASPNextGen.com—This ASP.NET-focused site, authored and maintained by authors Doug Seven and Don Wolthuis, provides a plethora of information about ASP.NET for developers of any skill level. The site includes tutorials on getting started with ASP.NET and a repository for Web services and .NET components.

- www.IBuySpy.com—For a real-world example of ASP.NET look no further than Microsoft's IbuySpy.com Web site. This site, which contains an eCommerce storefront, a Portal, and a News section, was built entirely with ASP.NET. Best of all, the code for this entire Web application (in both C# and VB.NET) is freely available from the site.

CHAPTER 2

COMMON ASP.NET CODE TECHNIQUES

by Scott Mitchell

In this chapter we will examine many topics, including the following:

- Working with the many collections available in the .NET Framework
- Reading and writing to the Web server's file system
- Using regular expressions
- Generating graphs and custom images on-the-fly through an ASP.NET Web page
- Sending email through an ASP.NET Web page
- Grabbing HTML content from another Web site through an ASP.NET Web page
- Performing advanced networking features
- Uploading files from the client's browser to the Web server
- Retrieving low-level system information about the ASP.NET engine
- Reading and writing to the Windows Event Log through an ASP.NET Web page
- Reading and displaying various Windows performance counters through an ASP.NET Web page

---

One of the things that I personally found frustrating with classic ASP was the difficulty associated with completing many common Web-related tasks. For example, the need to allow Web visitors to upload files to the Web server is fairly common for Web developers; however, with classic ASP the only way to accomplish this without much difficulty was through the use of a third-party COM component. Similarly, common tasks such as sending emails, reading and writing to the Windows Event Log, working with the Web server's file system, and dynamically generating images based on database information were all tricky, if not impossible, without the aid of a COM component.

Thankfully this has all changed with ASP.NET. Now Web developers can easily accomplish a plethora of common tasks without the need to create or buy a third-party component thanks in large part to ASP.NET being part of the robust .NET Framework. When you install the ASP.NET software on your computer from the CD accompanying this book, in addition to the ASP.NET engine, the entire .NET Framework will be installed. The .NET Framework consists of hundreds of classes broken down into a number of logical namespaces. These classes provide the methods and properties needed to create powerful Windows applications, from standalone desktop apps to Internet applications.

ASP.NET Web pages can utilize any of these hundreds of classes, giving ASP.NET Web pages the power and flexibility that classic ASP developers could only receive with the use of bulky COM components. In this chapter we will examine many of the new features that were difficult to implement with classic ASP but can be easily performed with an ASP.NET Web page.

1. Using Collections

Most modern programming languages provide support for some type of object that can hold a variable number of elements. These objects are referred to as collections, and they can have elements added and removed with ease without having to worry about proper memory allocation. If you've programmed with classic ASP before, you're probably familiar with the `Scripting.Dictionary` object, a collection object that references each element with a textual key. A collection that stores objects in this fashion is known as a *hash* table.

There are many types of collections in addition to the hash table. Each type of collection is similar in purpose: It serves as a means to store a varying number of elements, providing an easy way, at a minimum, to add and remove elements. Each different type of collection is unique in its method of storing, retrieving, and referencing its various elements.

The .NET Framework provides a number of collection types for the developer to use. In fact, an entire namespace, `System.Collections`, is dedicated to collection types and helper classes. Each of these collection types can store elements of type Object. Because in .NET all primitive data types—string, integers, date/times, arrays, and so on—are derived from the Object class, these collections can literally store anything! For example, you could use a single collection to store a couple of integers, an instance of a classic COM component, a string, a date/time, and two instances of a custom-written .NET component. Most of the examples in this section use collections to house primitive data types (strings, integers, doubles). However, Listing 2.1.8 (which appears in the "Similarities Among the Collection Types" section) illustrates a collection of collections—that is, a collection type that stores entire collections as each of its elements!

Throughout this section we'll examine five collections the .NET Framework offers developers: the `ArrayList`, the `Hashtable`, the `SortedList`, the `Queue`, and the `Stack`. As you study each of these collections, realize that they all have many similarities. For example, each type of collection can be iterated through element-by-element using a `For Each ... Next` loop in VB (or a `foreach` loop in C#). Each collection type has a number of similarly named functions that perform the same tasks. For example, each collection type has a `Clear` method that removes all elements from the collection, and a `Count` property that returns the number of elements in the collection. In fact, the last subsection "Similarities Among the Collection Types" examines the common traits found among the collection types.

Working with the `ArrayList` Class

The first type of collection we'll look at is the `ArrayList`. With an `ArrayList`, each item is stored in sequential order and is indexed numerically. In our following examples, keep in mind that the developer need not worry himself with memory allocation. With the standard array, the developer cannot easily add and remove elements without concerning himself with the size and makeup of the array. With all the collections we'll examine in this chapter, this is no longer a concern.

Adding, Removing, and Indexing Elements in an `ArrayList`

The `ArrayList` class contains a number of methods for adding and removing Objects from the collection. These include `Add`, `AddRange`, `Insert`, `Remove`, `RemoveAt`, `RemoveRange`, and `Clear`, all of which we'll examine in Listing 2.1.1. The output is shown in Figure 2.1.

LISTING 2.1.1 For Sequentially Accessed Collections, Use the `ArrayList`

```
 1:  <script language="vb" runat="server">
 2:
 3:    Sub Page_Load(sender as Object, e as EventArgs)
 4:      ' Create two ArrayLists, aTerritories and aStates
 5:      Dim aTerritories as New ArrayList
 6:      Dim aStates as New ArrayList
 7:
 8:      ' Use the Add method to add the 50 states of the US
 9:      aStates.Add("Alabama")
10:      aStates.Add("Alaska")
11:      aStates.Add("Arkansas")
12:      ' ...
13:      aStates.Add("Wyoming")
14:
15:      ' Build up our list of territories, which includes
16:      ' all 50 states plus some additional countries
17:      aTerritories.AddRange(aStates)   ' add all 50 states
18:      aTerritories.Add("Guam")
19:      aTerritories.Add("Puerto Rico")
20:
21:      ' We'd like the first territory to be the District of Columbia,
22:      ' so we'll explicitly add it to the beginning of the ArrayList
23:      aTerritories.Insert(0, "District of Columbia")
24:
25:      ' Display all of the territories with a for loop
26:      lblTerritories.Text = "<i>There are " & aTerritories.Count & _
27:                            "territories...</i><br>"
28:
```

LISTING 2.1.1 Continued

```
29:    Dim i as Integer
30:    For i = 0 to aTerritories.Count - 1
31:      lblTerritories.Text = lblTerritories.Text & _
32:                    aTerritories(i) & "<br>"
33:    Next
34:
35:    ' We can remove objects in one of four ways:
36:    '   ... We can remove a specific item
37:    aTerritories.Remove("Wyoming")
38:
39:    '   ... We can remove an element at a specific position
40:    aTerritories.RemoveAt(0)   ' will get rid of District
41:                               ' of Columbia,
42:                               ' the first element
43:
44:    ' Display all of the territories with foreach loop
45:    lblFewerTerritories.Text = "<i>There are now " & _
46:             aTerritories.Count & " territories...</i><br>"
47:
48:    Dim s as String
49:    For Each s in aTerritories
50:      lblFewerTerritories.Text = lblFewerTerritories.Text & _
51:                    s & "<br>"
52:    Next
53:
54:    '   ... we can remove a chunk of elements from the
55:    '       array with RemoveRange
56:    aTerritories.RemoveRange(0, 2)  ' will get rid of the
57:                                    ' first two elements
58:
59:    ' Display all of the territories with foreach loop
60:    lblEvenFewerTerritories.Text = "<i>There are now " & _
61:             aTerritories.Count & " territories...</i><br>"
62:
63:    For Each s in aTerritories
64:      lblEvenFewerTerritories.Text = lblEvenFewerTerritories.Text & _
65:                    s & "<br>"
66:    Next
67:
68:    ' Finally, we can clear the ENTIRE array using the clear method
69:    aTerritories.Clear()
70:  End Sub
71:
72: </script>
73:
74: <html>
75: <body>
76:   <b>The Territories of the United States:</b><br>
77:   <asp:label id="lblTerritories" runat="server" />
78:
79:   <p>
80:
```

LISTING 2.1.1 Continued

```
81:    <b>After some working with the Territories ArrayList:</b><br>
82:    <asp:label id="lblFewerTerritories" runat="server" />
83:
84:    <p>
85:
86:    <b>After further working with the Territories ArrayList:</b><br>
87:    <asp:label id="lblEvenFewerTerritories" runat="server" />
88:  </body>
89:  </html>
```

FIGURE 2.1
Output of Listing 2.1.1 when viewed through a browser.

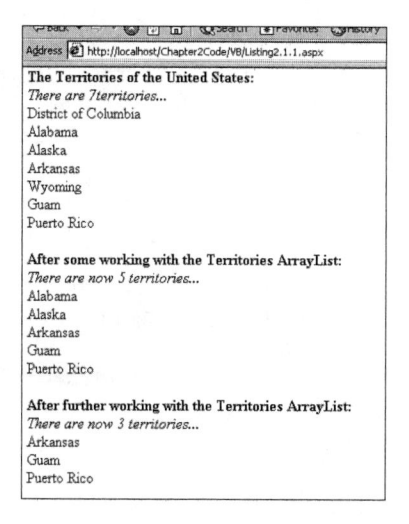

Adding Elements to an `ArrayList`

In Listing 2.1.1 we create two `ArrayList` class instances, `aTerritories` and `aStates`, on lines 5 and 6, respectively. We then populate the `aStates ArrayList` with a small subset of the 50 states of the United States using the `Add` method (lines 9 through 13). The `Add` method takes one parameter, the element to add to the array, which needs to be of type Object. This Object instance is then appended to the end of the `ArrayList`. In this example we are simply adding elements of type String to the `ArrayList aStates` and `aTerritories`.

The `Add` method is useful for adding one element at a time to the end of the array, but what if we want to add a number of elements to an `ArrayList` at once? The `ArrayList` class provides the `AddRange` method to do just this. `AddRange` expects a single parameter that supports the `ICollection` interface. A wide number of .NET Framework classes—such as the `Array`, `ArrayList`, `DataView`, `DataSetView`, and others—support this interface. On line 18 in Listing 2.1.1, we use the `AddRange` method to add each element of the `aStates ArrayList` to the end of the `aTerritories ArrayList`. (To add a range of elements starting at a specific index in an `ArrayList`, use the `InsertRange` method.) On lines 18 and 19, we add two more strings to the end of the `aTerritories ArrayList`.

Because `ArrayList`s are ordered sequentially, there might be times when we want to add an element to a particular position. The `Insert` method of the `ArrayList` class provides this capability, allowing the developer to add an element to a specific spot in the `ArrayList` collection. The `Insert` method takes two parameters: an integer representing the index in which you want to add the new element, and the new element, which needs to be of type Object. In line 23 we add a new string to the start of the `aTerritories ArrayList`. Note that if we had simply used the `Add` method, `"District of Columbia"` would have been added to the end of `aTerritories`. Using Insert, however, we can specify exactly where in the `ArrayList` this new element should reside.

Removing Elements from an `ArrayList`

The `ArrayList` class also provides a number of methods for removing elements. We can remove a specific element from an `ArrayList` with the `Remove` method. On line 37 we remove the String `"Wyoming"` from the `aTerritories ArrayList`. (If you attempt to remove an element that does not exist, an `ArgumentException` exception will be thrown.) `Remove` allows you to take out a particular element from an `ArrayList`; `RemoveAt`, used on line 40, allows the developer to remove an element at a specific position in the `ArrayList`.

Both `Remove` and `RemoveAt` dissect only one element from the `ArrayList` at a time. We can remove a chunk of elements in one fell swoop by using the `RemoveRange` method. This method expects two parameters: an index to start at and a count of total elements to remove. In line 56 we remove the first two elements in `aTerritories` with the statement: `aTerritories.RemoveRange(0, 2)`. Finally, to remove all the contents of an `ArrayList`, use the `Clear` method (refer to Line 69 in Listing 2.1.1).

Referencing `ArrayList` Elements

Note that in our code example, we used two different techniques to iterate through the contents of our `ArrayList`. Because an `ArrayList` stores items sequentially, we can iterate through an `ArrayList` by looping from its lowest bound through its upper bound, referencing each element by its integral index. The following code snippet is taken from lines 30 through 33 in Listing 2.1.1:

```
For i = 0 to aTerritories.Count - 1
   lblTerritories.Text = lblTerritories.Text & _
                      aTerritories(i) & "<br>"
Next
```

The `Count` property returns the number of elements in our `ArrayList`. We start our loop at 0 because all collections are indexed starting at 0. We can reference an `ArrayList` element with: `aArrayListInstance(index)`, as we do on line 32 in Listing 2.1.1.

We can also step through the elements of any of the collection types we'll be looking at in this chapter using a `For Each ... Next` loop with VB.NET (or a `foreach` loop with C#). A simple example of this approach can be seen in the following code snippet from lines 48 through 52:

```
Dim s as String
For Each s in aTerritories
    lblFewerTerritories.Text = lblFewerTerritories.Text & _
                                s & "<br>"
Next
```

This method is useful for stepping through all the elements in a collection. In the future section "Similarities Among the Collection Types," we'll examine a third way to step through each element of a collection: using an enumerator.

If we wanted to grab a specific element from an `ArrayList`, it would make sense to reference it in the *aArrayListInstance(index)* format. If, however, you are looking for a particular element in the `ArrayList`, you can use the `IndexOf` method to quickly find its index. For example,

```
Dim iPos as Integer
iPos = aTerritories.IndexOf("Illinois")
```

would set `iPos` to the location of Illinois in the `ArrayList aTerritories`. (If Illinois did not exist in `aTerritories`, `iPos` would be set to -1.) Two other forms of `IndexOf` can be used to specify a range for which to search for an element in the `ArrayList`. For more information on those methods, refer to the .NET Framework SDK documentation.

Working with the `Hashtable` Class

The type of collection most developers are used to working with is the hash table collection. Whereas the `ArrayList` indexes each element numerically, a hash table indexes each element by an alphanumeric key. The `Collection` data type in Visual Basic is a hash table; the `Scripting.Dictionary` object, used commonly in classic ASP pages, is a simple hash table. The .NET Framework provides developers with a powerful hash table class, `Hashtable`.

When working with the `Hashtable` class, keep in mind that the ordering of elements in the collection are irrespective of the order in which they are entered. The `Hashtable` class employs its own hashing algorithm to efficiently order the key/value pairs in the collection. If it is essential that a collection's elements be ordered alphabetically by the value of their keys, use the `SortedList` class, which is discussed in the next section, "Working with the `SortedList` Class."

Adding, Removing, and Indexing Elements in a `Hashtable`

With the `ArrayList` class, there were a number of ways to add various elements to various positions in the `ArrayList`. With the `Hashtable` class, there aren't nearly as many options because there is no sequential ordering of elements. To add new elements to a `Hashtable` use the `Add` method.

Not surprisingly, there are also fewer methods to remove elements from a `Hashtable`. The `Remove` method dissects a single element, whereas the `Clear` method removes all elements from a `Hashtable`. Examples of both of these methods can be seen in Listing 2.1.2. The output is shown in Figure 2.2.

LISTING 2.1.2 For Sequentially Accessed Collections, Use the `ArrayList`

```
 1: <script language="VB" runat="server">
 2:
 3:   Sub Page_Load(sender as Object, e as EventArgs)
 4:     ' Create a HashTable
 5:     Dim htSalaries As New Hashtable()
 6:
 7:     ' Use the Add method to add Employee Salary Information
 8:     htSalaries.Add("Bob", 40000)
 9:     htSalaries.Add("John", 65000)
10:     htSalaries.Add("Dilbert", 25000)
11:     htSalaries.Add("Scott", 85000)
12:     htSalaries.Add("BillG", 90000000)
13:
14:     ' Now, display a list of employees and their salaries
15:     lblSalary.Text = "<i>There are " & htSalaries.Count & _
16:                     " Employees...</i><br>"
17:
18:     Dim s as String
19:     For Each s in htSalaries.Keys
20:       lblSalary.Text &= s & " - " & htSalaries(s) & "<br>"
21:     Next
22:
23:     ' Is BillG an Employee?  If so, FIRE HIM!
24:     If htSalaries.ContainsKey("BillG") Then
25:       htSalaries.Remove("BillG")
26:     End If
27:
28:
29:     ' List the remaining employees (using databinding)
30:     dgEmployees.DataSource = htSalaries.Keys
31:     dgEmployees.DataBind()
32:
33:
34:     htSalaries.Clear()   ' remove all entries in hash table...
35:   End Sub
36:
37: </script>
38:
39: <html>
40: <body>
41:   <b>Employee Salary Information:</b><br>
42:   <asp:label id="lblSalary" runat="server" />
43:   <p>
44:
45:   <b>Remaining Employees After Round One of Firings:</b><br>
46:   <asp:datagrid runat="server" id="dgEmployees"
47:                 AutoGenerateColumns="True" ShowHeader="False"
48:                 CellSpacing="1" CellPadding="4" />
49: </body>
50: </html>
```

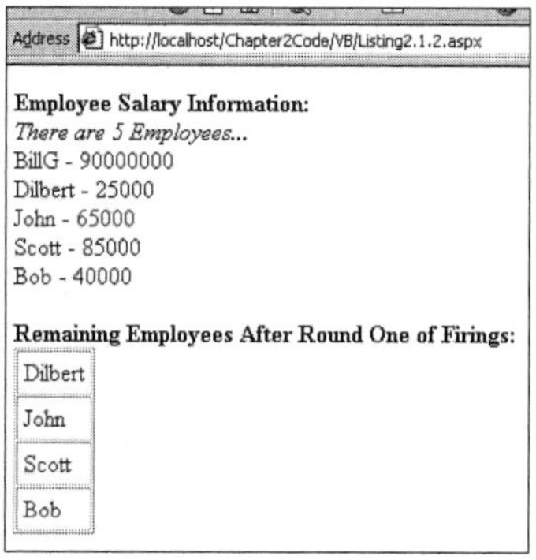

FIGURE 2.2
Output of Listing 2.1.2 when viewed through a browser.

Adding Elements to a `Hashtable`

In Listing 2.1.2, we begin by creating an instance of the `Hashtable` class, `htSalaries`, on line 5. Next, we populate this hash table with our various employees and their respective salaries on lines 7 through 12. Note that the `Add` method, which adds an element to the `Hashtable` collection, takes two parameters: the first is an alphanumeric key by which the element will be referenced, and the second is the element itself, which needs to be of type Object.

In Listing 2.1.2, we are storing integer values in our `Hashtable` class. Of course we are not limited to storing just simple data types; rather, we can store any type of Object. As we'll see in an example later in this chapter, we can even create collections of collections (collections whose elements are also collections)!

Removing Elements from a `Hashtable`

The `Hashtable` class contains two methods to remove elements: `Remove` and `Clear`. `Remove` expects a single parameter, the alphanumeric key of the element to be removed. Line 25 demonstrates this behavior, removing the element referred to as `"BillG"` in the hash table. On line 34 we remove all the elements of the hash table via the `Clear` method. (Recall that all collection types contain a `Clear` method that demonstrates identical functionality.)

The `Hashtable` class contains two handy methods for determining whether a key or value exists. The first function, `ContainsKey`, takes a single parameter, the alphanumeric key to search for. If the key is found within the hash table, `ContainsKey` returns `True`. If the key is not found, `ContainsKey` returns `False`. In Listing 2.1.2, this method is used on line 24. The `Hashtable` class also supports a method called `ContainsValue`. This method accepts a single parameter of type Object and searches the hash table to see if any element contains that particular value. If it finds such an element, `ContainsValue` will return `True`; otherwise, it will return `False`. The `ContainsKey` and `ContainsValue` methods are used primarily for quickly determining whether a particular key or element exists in a `Hashtable`.

On line 24, a check was made to see if the key `"BillG"` existed before the `Remove` method was used. Checking to make sure an item exists before removing it is not required. If you use the

`Remove` method to try to remove an element that does not exist (for example, if we had `Remove("Homer")` in Listing 2.2.1), no error or exception will occur.

The `Keys` and `Values` Collections

The `Hashtable` class exposes two collections as properties: `Keys` and `Values`. The `Keys` collection is, as its name suggests, a collection of all the alphanumeric key values in a `Hashtable`. Likewise, the `Values` collection is a collection of all the element values in a `Hashtable`. These two properties can be useful if you are only interested in, say, listing the various keys.

On line 30 in Listing 2.1.2, the `DataSource` property of the `dgEmployees` DataGrid is set to the `Keys` collection of the `hySalaries Hashtable` instance. Because the `Keys` property of the `Hashtable` class returns an `ICollection` interface, it can be bound to a DataGrid using data binding. For more information on data binding and using the DataGrid, refer to Chapter 7, "Data Presentation."

Working with the `SortedList` Class

So far we've examined two collections provided by the .NET Framework: the `Hashtable` class and the `ArrayList` class. Each of these collections indexes elements in a different manner. The `ArrayList` indexes each element numerically, whereas the `Hashtable` indexes each element with an alphanumeric key. The `ArrayList` orders each element sequentially, based on its numerical index; the `Hashtable` applies a seemingly random ordering (because the order is determined by a hashing algorithm).

What if you need a collection, though, that allows access to elements by both an alphanumeric key and a numerical index? The .NET Framework includes a class that permits both types of access, the `SortedList` class. This class internally maintains two arrays: a sorted array of the keys and an array of the values.

Adding, Removing, and Indexing Elements in a `SortedList`

Because the `SortedList` orders its elements based on the key, there are no methods that insert elements in a particular spot. Rather, similar to the `Hashtable` class, there is only a single method to add elements to the collection: `Add`. However, because the `SortedList` can be indexed by both key and value, the class contains both `Remove` and `RemoveAt` methods. As with all the other collection types, the `SortedList` also contains a `Clear` method that removes all elements.

Because a `SortedList` encapsulates the functionality of both the `Hashtable` and `ArrayList` classes, it's no wonder that the class provides a number of methods to access its elements. As with a `Hashtable`, `SortedList` elements can be accessed via their keys. A `SortedList` that stored Integer values could have an element accessed similar to the following:

```
Dim SortedListValue as Integer
SortedListValue = slSortedListInstance(key)
```

The `SortedList` also can access elements through an integral index, like with the `ArrayList` class. To get the value at a particular index, you can use the `GetByIndex` method as follows:

```
Dim SortedListValue as Integer
SortedListValue = slSortedListInstance.GetByIndex(iPosition)
```

iPosition represents the zero-based ordinal index for the element to retrieve from *slSortedListInstance*. Additionally, elements can be accessed by index using the `GetValueList` method to return a collection of values, which can then be accessed by index:

```
Dim SortedListValue as Integer
SortedListVluae = slSortedListInstance.GetValueList(iPosition)
```

Listing 2.1.3 illustrates a number of ways to retrieve both the keys and values for elements of a `SortedList`. The output is shown in Figure 2.3.

LISTING 2.1.3 A `SortedList` Combines the Functionality of a `Hashtable` and `ArrayList`

```
 1: <script language="VB" runat="server">
 2:   Sub Page_Load(sender as Object, e as EventArgs)
 3:     ' Create a SortedList
 4:     Dim slTestScores As New SortedList()
 5:
 6:     ' Use the Add method to add students' Test Scores
 7:     slTestScores.Add("Judy", 87.8)
 8:     slTestScores.Add("John", 79.3)
 9:     slTestScores.Add("Sally", 94.0)
10:     slTestScores.Add("Scott", 91.5)
11:     slTestScores.Add("Edward", 76.3)
12:
13:     ' Display a list of test scores
14:     lblScores.Text = "<i>There are " & slTestScores.Count & _
15:                     " Students...</i><br>"
16:     Dim dictEntry as DictionaryEntry
17:     For Each dictEntry in slTestScores
18:       lblScores.Text &= dictEntry.Key & " - " & dictEntry.Value & "<br>"
19:     Next
20:
21:     'Has Edward taken the test?  If so, reduce his grade by 10 points
22:     If slTestScores.ContainsKey("Edward") then
23:       slTestScores("Edward") = slTestScores("Edward") - 10
24:     End If
25:
26:     'Assume Sally Cheated and remove her score from the list
27:     slTestScores.Remove("Sally")
28:
29:     'Grade on the curve - up everyone's score by 5 percent
30:     Dim iLoop as Integer
31:     For iLoop = 0 to slTestScores.Count - 1
32:       slTestScores.GetValueList(iLoop) = _
33:                   slTestScores.GetValueList(iLoop) * 1.05
34:     Next
35:
```

LISTING 2.1.3 Continued

```
36:      'Display the new grades
37:      For iLoop = 0 to slTestScores.Count - 1
38:        lblCurvedScores.Text &= slTestScores.GetKeyList(iLoop) & " - " & _
39:                    String.Format("{0:#.#}", slTestScores.GetByIndex(iLoop))
➥ & "<br>"
40:      Next
41:
42:      slTestScores.Clear()   ' remove all entries in the sorted list...
43:    End Sub
44:  </script>
45:
46:  <html>
47:  <body>
48:    <b>Raw Test Results:</b><br>
49:    <asp:label id="lblScores" runat="server" />
50:    <p>
51:
52:    <b>Curved Test Results:</b><br>
53:    <asp:label id="lblCurvedScores" runat="server" />
54:  </body>
55:  </html>
```

FIGURE 2.3
Output of Listing 2.1.3 when viewed through a browser.

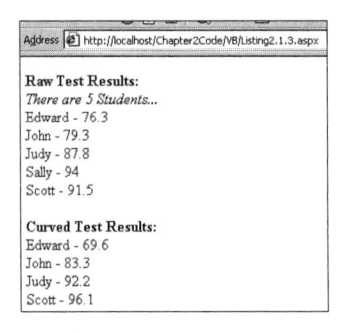

Listing 2.1.3 begins with the instantiation of the `SortedList` class (line 4). `slTestScores`, the `SortedList` instance, contains the test scores from five students (see lines 7 through 11). Each element of a `SortedList` really is represented by the `DictionaryEntry` structure. This simple structure contains two public fields: `Key` and `Value`. Starting at line 17, we use a `For Each ... Next` loop to step through each `DictionaryEntry` element in our `SortedList` `slTestScores`. On line 18, we output the `Key` and `Value`, displaying the student's name and test score. Be sure to examine Figure 2.3 and notice that the displayed results are ordered by the value of the key.

On line 22, the `ContainsKey` method is used to see if Edward's score has been recorded; if so, it's reduced by ten points. (Poor Edward.) Note that we access the value of Edward's test score using the element's key—`slTestScores("Edward")`—just as if `slTestScores` were a `Hashtable` (line 23). On line 27, Sally's test score is removed from the `SortedList` via the `Remove` method.

Next, each remaining student's test score is upped by 5 percent. On lines 31 through 34, each test score is visited via a `For ... Next` loop (which is possible because `SortedList` elements can be accessed by an index). Because .NET collections are zero-based, notice that we loop from `0` to `slTestScores.Count - 1` (line 31). On line 32, the value of each element is accessed via the `GetValueList` method, which returns a collection of values; this collection can then be indexed numerically.

On lines 37 through 40, another `For ... Next` loop is used to display the curved test results. On line 38, the `GetKeyList` method is used to return a collection of keys (which is then accessed by index); on line 39, the test results are outputted using the `String.Format` function. The format string passed to the `String.Format` function (`"{0:#.#}"`) specifies that the first parameter following the format string (`slTestScores.GetByIndex(iLoop)`, the test results) should only display one decimal place. Finally, on line 42, all the test results are erased with a single call to the `Clear` method.

Working with the `Queue` Class

`ArrayLists`, `Hashtables`, and `SortedLists` all have one thing in common—they allow random access to their elements. That is, a developer can programmatically read, write, or remove any element in the collection, regardless of its position. However, the `Queue` and `Stack` classes (the remaining two collections we'll examine) are unique in that they provide sequential access only. Specifically, the `Queue` class can only access and remove elements in the order they were inserted.

Adding, Removing, and Accessing Elements in a `Queue`

Queues are often referred to as *First In, First Out (FIFO)* data structures because the Nth element inserted will be the Nth element removed or accessed. It helps to think of the queue data structure as a line of people. There are two parts to a queue as there are two parts to any line up: the tail of the queue, where people new to the line start waiting, and the head of the queue, where the next person in line waits to be served. In a line, the person who is standing in line first will be first served; the person standing second will be served second, and so on. In a queue, the element that is added first will be the element that is removed or accessed first, whereas the second element added will be the second element removed or accessed.

The .NET Framework provides support for the queue data structure with the `Queue` class. To add an element to the tail, use the `Enqueue` method. To retrieve and remove an element from the head of a queue, use `Dequeue`. As with the other collection types we've examined thus far, the `Queue` class contains a `Clear` method to remove all elements. To simply examine the element at the head without altering the queue, use the `Peek` method. As with all the other collections, the elements of a `Queue` can be iterated through using an enumerator or a `For Each ... Next` loop. Listing 2.1.4 illustrates some simple queue operations. The output is shown in Figure 2.4.

LISTING 2.1.4 A Queue Supports First In, First Out Element Access and Removal

```
 1: <script language="VB" runat="server">
 2:
 3:   Sub Page_Load(sender as Object, e as EventArgs)
 4:     ' Create a Queue
 5:     Dim qTasks as New Queue()
 6:
 7:     qTasks.Enqueue("Wake Up")
 8:     qTasks.Enqueue("Shower")
 9:     qTasks.Enqueue("Get Dressed")
10:     qTasks.Enqueue("Go to Work")
11:     qTasks.Enqueue("Work")
12:     qTasks.Enqueue("Come Home")
13:     qTasks.Enqueue("Eat Dinner")
14:     qTasks.Enqueue("Go to Sleep")
15:
16:     ' To determine if an element exists in the Queue,
17:     ' use the Contains method
18:     If Not qTasks.Contains("Shower") Then
19:       ' Forgot to bathe!
20:       Response.Write("<b><i>Stinky!</i></b>")
21:     End If
22:
23:     ' Output the list of tasks
24:     lblTaskList.Text &= "<i>There are " & qTasks.Count & _
25:                         " tasks for today...</i><br>"
26:
27:     Dim iCount as Integer = 1
28:     Do While qTasks.Count > 0
29:       lblTaskList.Text &= iCount.ToString() & ".) " & _
30:                           qTasks.Dequeue() & "<br>"
31:       iCount += 1
32:     Loop
33:
34:
35:     ' At this point the queue is empty, since we've
36:     ' Dequeued all of the elements.
37:   End Sub
38:
39: </script>
40:
41: <html>
42: <body>
43:
44:   <b>An In-Order List of Tasks for the Day:</b><br>
45:   <asp:label runat="server" id="lblTaskList" />
46:
47: </body>
48: </html>
```

FIGURE 2.4
Output of Listing 2.1.4 when viewed through a browser.

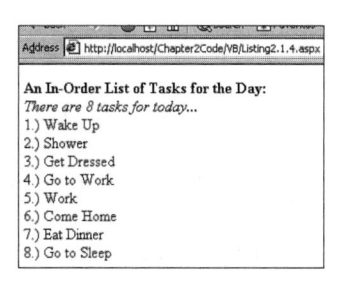

```
Address  http://localhost/Chapter2Code/VB/Listing2.1.4.aspx

An In-Order List of Tasks for the Day:
There are 8 tasks for today...
1.) Wake Up
2.) Shower
3.) Get Dressed
4.) Go to Work
5.) Work
6.) Come Home
7.) Eat Dinner
8.) Go to Sleep
```

Adding Elements to a `Queue`

In Listing 2.1.4, we begin by creating an instance of the `Queue` class, `qTasks` (line 5). In line 7 through 14, we add eight new elements to `qTasks` using the `Enqueue` method. Recall that a queue supports First In, First Out ordering, so when we get ready to remove these elements, the first element to be removed will be `"Wake Up"`, which was the first element added.

To quickly check if a particular element is an element of the queue, you can use the `Contains` method. Line 18 demonstrates usage of the `Contains` method. Note that it takes a single parameter, the element to search for, and returns `True` if the element is found in the queue and `False` otherwise.

Removing Elements from a `Queue`

With a `Queue`, you can only remove the element at the head. With such a constraint, it's no wonder that the `Queue` class only has a single member to remove an element: `Dequeue`. `Dequeue` not only removes the element at the head of the queue, but it also returns the element just removed.

If you attempt to remove an element from an empty `Queue`, the `InvalidOperationException` exception will be thrown and you will receive an error. Therefore, to prevent producing a run-time error in your ASP.NET page, be sure to either place the `Dequeue` statement in a `Try ... Catch ... Finally` block or ensure that the `Count` property is greater than zero (`0`) *before* using `Dequeue`. (For more information on `Try ... Catch ... Finally` blocks, refer to Chapter 9, "ASP.NET Error Handling." For an example of checking the `Count` property prior to using `Dequeue`, see lines 28 through 32 in Listing 2.1.4.) As with all the other collection types, you can remove all the `Queue` elements with a single call to the `Clear` method (line 36).

There might be times when you want to access the element at the head of the `Queue` without removing it from the `Queue`. This is possible via the `Peek` method, which returns the element at the head of the `Queue` without removing it. As with the `Dequeue` method, if you try to `Peek` an empty `Queue`, an `InvalidOperationException` exception will be thrown.

Iterating Through the Elements of a `Queue`

One way to iterate through the elements of a `Queue` is to simply use `Dequeue` to successively grab each item off the head. This approach can be seen in lines 27 through 32 in Listing 2.1.4.

The major disadvantage of this approach is that, after iteration is complete, the `Queue` is empty!

As with every other collection type, the `Queue` can be iterated via a `For Each ... Next` loop or through the use of an enumerator. The following code snippet illustrates using the C# `foreach` statement to iterate through all the elements of a `Queue` without affecting the structure:

```
Queue qMyQueue = new Queue();    // Create a Queue

qMyQueue.Enqueue(5);
qMyQueue.Enqueue(62);    // Add some elements to the Queue
qMyQueue.Enqueue(-7);

// Iterate through each element of the Queue, displaying it
foreach (int i in qMyQueue)
  Response.Write("Visiting Queue Element with Value: " + i + "<br>");
```

Working with the `Stack` Class

A *stack* is a data structure similar to a queue in that it supports only sequential access. However, a stack does bear one major difference from a queue: Rather than storing elements with a First In, First Out (FIFO) semantic, a stack uses *Last In, First Out (LIFO)*. A crowded elevator behaves similar to a stack: The first person who enters the crowded elevator is the last person to leave, whereas the last person to board the elevator is the first out when it reaches its destination.

Adding, Removing, and Accessing Elements in a `Stack`

The .NET Framework provides an implementation of the stack data type with the `Stack` class. A stack has two basic operations: adding an element to the top of the stack, which is accomplished with the `Push` method, and removing an element from the top of the stack, accomplished via the `Pop` method. Similar to the `Queue` class, the `Stack` class also contains a `Peek` method to permit developers to access the top of the stack without removing the element.

Up until this point, the code provided in the previous listings has just given you a feel for the syntax of the various collections. Listing 2.1.5, however, contains a handy little piece of reusable code that can be placed on each page of your Web site to provide a set of navigation history links for your visitors.

The code in Listing 2.1.5 uses a session-level `Stack` class instance that is used to store the links that a Web visitor has traversed on your site since the start of his session. Each time a user visits a Web page, the stack is displayed in a history label and the page's URL is pushed onto the stack. As the user visits various pages on your Web site, his navigation history stack will continue to grow and he will be able to quickly jump back to previous pages on your site. Basically, this is mimicking the functionality of a browser's Back button. The output is shown in Figure 2.5.

LISTING 2.1.5 A Stack Is Ideal for Keeping Track of a User's Navigation History

```
 1: <script language="c#" runat="server">
 2:
 3:   void Page_Load(Object sender, EventArgs e)
 4:   {
 5:     // See if we have a stack created or not:
 6:     if (Session["History"] == null)
 7:     {
 8:       // the history stack has not been created, so create it now.
 9:       Session["History"] = new Stack();
10:     } else {
11:       // we already have a history stack.  Display the history:
12:       IEnumerator enumHistory =
13:               ((Stack) Session["History"]).GetEnumerator();
14:       while (enumHistory.MoveNext())
15:         lblStackHistory.Text += "<a href=\"" + enumHistory.Current +
16:                                 "\">" + enumHistory.Current +
17:                                 "</a><br>";
18:     }
19:
20:     // Push current URL onto Stack IF it is not already on the top
21:     if (((Stack) Session["History"]).Count > 0)
22:     {
23:       if(((Stack) Session["History"]).Peek().ToString() !=
24:                                 Request.Url.PathAndQuery.ToString())
25:         ((Stack) Session["History"]).Push(Request.Url.PathAndQuery);
26:     } else
27:       ((Stack) Session["History"]).Push(Request.Url.PathAndQuery);
28:   }
29:
30: </script>
31:
32: <html>
33: <body>
34:     <b>Session History</b><br>
35:     <asp:label runat=server id="lblStackHistory" /><br>
36:
37:     <a href="ClearStackHistory.CSharp.aspx">Clear Stack History</a><br>
38:     <a href="Back.CSharp.aspx">Back</a>
39:
40:     <p>
41:     <b>Links:</b><br>
42:     <li><a href="Listing2.1.5.aspx">Listing2.1.5.aspx</a><br>
43:     <li><a href="Listing2.1.5.b.aspx">Listing2.1.5.b.aspx</a><br>
44: </body>
45: </html>
```

FIGURE 2.5
Output of Listing 2.1.5 when viewed through a browser.

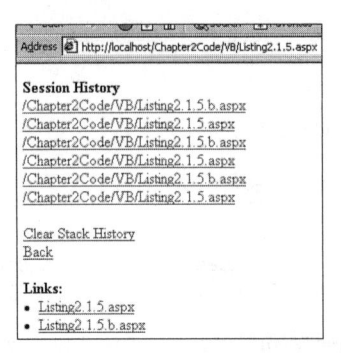

If you've worked with classic ASP, you are likely familiar with the concept of session-level variables. These variables are defined on a per-user basis and last for the duration of the user's visit to the site. These variables are synonymous with global variables in that their values can be accessed across multiple ASP pages. Session-level variables, which are discussed in greater detail in Chapter 14, "Managing State," are a simple way to maintain state on a per-user basis. Because we want the user's navigation history stack to persist as the user bounces around our site, we will store the **Stack** class instance in a session-level variable.

To implement a navigation history stack as a session-level variable, we must make sure that we have created such a variable before trying to reference it. Keep in mind that when a visitor first comes to our site and visits that first page, the session-level variable will not be instantiated. Therefore, on each page, before we refer to the navigation history stack, it is essential that we check to ensure that our session-variable, **Session["History"]**, has been assigned to an instance of the **Stack** class.

> **Note**
>
> To access a session variable using C#, the braces are used around the session variable name. For example, to retrieve the value of the **History** session variable with C# we'd use:
>
> Session["History"]
>
> With VB.NET, however, parentheses are used in place of the brackets:
>
> Session("History")

Line 6 in Listing 2.1.5 checks **Session["History"]** to determine whether it references a **Stack** object instance. If **Session["History"]** has not been assigned an object instance, it will equal **null** (or **Nothing**, in VB). If **Session["History"]** is **null**, we need to set it to a newly created instance of the **Stack** class (line 9).

However, if **Session["History"]** is *not* **null**, we know that the user has already visited at least one other page on our site. Therefore, we can display the contents of the

`Session["History"]` `Stack`. This is accomplished in lines 12 through 17 with the use of an enumerator. We'll discuss iteration through collections via enumerators in the next section, "Similarities Among the Collection Types." With C#, as opposed to VB, explicit casting must be done when working with the `Session` object. For example, on line 13, before we can call the `GetEnumerator()` method (a method of the `Stack` class), we must cast the `Session["History"]` variable to a `Stack`:

```
// C# code must use an explicit cast
IEnumerator enumHistory = ((Stack) Session["History"]).GetEnumerator();

'VB code, however, does not require an explicit cast
Dim enumHistory As IEnumerator = Session("History").GetEnumerator()
```

With VB, however, such a cast is not necessary. Casting issues with the `Session` object are discussed in more detail in Chapter 14.

After either creating a new session-level `Stack` instance or displaying the `Stack`'s contents, we're ready to add the current URL to the navigation history stack. This could be accomplished with the following simple line of code:

```
((Stack) Session["History"]).Push(Request.Url.PathAndQuery);
```

However, if the user refreshed the current page, it would, again, get added to the navigation history stack. It would be nice not to have the same page repeatedly appear in the navigation history stack. Therefore, on line 23, we use the `Peek` method to see if the top-most element in the `Stack` is not equal to the current URL. If the top-most element of the stack is not equal to the current URL, we `Push` the current URL onto the top of the stack, otherwise we do nothing.

Before we use the `Peek` method, we first determine whether the `Stack` is empty. Recall from the previous section, "Working with the `Queue` Class," using the `Peek` method on an empty `Queue` will raise an `InvalidOperationException` exception. This is the same case with the `Stack` class; therefore, on line 21, we first check to ensure that at least one element is in the `Stack` before using the `Peek` method.

Two useful utility ASP.NET pages have been created to provide some extra functionality for our navigation history stack. The fist page, `ClearStackHistory.Csharp.aspx`, erases the contents of the history stack and is presented in Listing 2.1.6. The second page, `Back.Csharp.aspx`, serves like a back button in the user's browser, taking him to the previously visited page. The code for `Back.Csharp.aspx` is given in Listing 2.1.7. We'll examine these two code listings momentarily.

Listing 2.1.5 also contains a link to another ASP.NET page, `Listing2.1.5.b.aspx`. This page is identical to `Listing2.1.5.aspx`. In your Web site, you would need to, at a minimum, include the code in Listing 2.1.5 in each ASP.NET page to correctly keep the navigation history up-to-date.

LISTING 2.1.6 `ClearStackHistory.CSharp.aspx` Erases the Contents of the Navigation History Stack

```
 1: <script language="c#" runat="server">
 2:
 3:   void Page_Load(Object sender, EventArgs e)
 4:   {
 5:     // See if we have a stack created or not:
 6:     if (Session["History"] == null)
 7:     {
 8:       // There's no Stack, so we don't need to do anything!
 9:     } else {
10:       // we need to clear the stack
11:       ((Stack) Session["History"]).Clear();
12:     }
13:   }
14:
15: </script>
16:
17: <html>
18: <body>
19:    Your navigation history has been cleared!
20: </body>
21: </html>
```

Listing 2.1.6 contains the code for `ClearStackHistory.CSharp.aspx`. This code only has a single task—clear the contents of the navigation history stack—and therefore is fairly straightforward. The ASP.NET page starts by checking to determine if `Session["History"]` refers to a `Stack` object instance (line 6). If it does, the `Clear` method is used to erase all the stack's elements (line 11).

The code for the second utility page, `Back.CSharp.aspx`, can be seen in Listing 2.1.7.

LISTING 2.1.7 `Back.CSharp.aspx` Sends the User to the Previous Page in His Navigation History Stack

```
 1: <script language="c#" runat="server">
 2:   void Page_Load(Object sender, EventArgs e)
 3:   {
 4:     // See if we have a stack created or not:
 5:     if (Session["History"] == null ||
 6:         ((Stack) Session["History"]).Count < 2)
 7:     {
 8:       // There's no Stack, so we can't go back!
 9:       Response.Write("Egad, I can't go back!");
10:     } else {
11:       // we need to go back to the prev. page
12:       ((Stack) Session["History"]).Pop();
13:       Response.Redirect(((Stack) Session["History"]).Pop().ToString());
14:     }
15:   }
16: </script>
```

As with `ClearStackHistory.CSharp.aspx`, `Back.CSharp.aspx` starts by checking to determine if `Session["History"]` is `null`. If that is the case, a warning message is displayed because we can't possibly step back through our navigation history stack if it doesn't exist!

Take a moment to briefly look over Listing 2.1.5 again. Note that on each page we visit, we add the current URL to the stack. Therefore, if we want to go back to the previous page, we can't just pluck off the top element from the stack (because that contains the current URL). Rather, we must pluck off the top-most item, dispose of it, and then visit the next item on the top of the stack. For that reason, our stack must have at least two elements to be able to traverse back to the previous page. On line 6, we check to make sure that the navigation history stack contains at least two elements.

Given that we have a properly defined navigation history stack—that is, `Session["History"]` is not `null` and there are at least two elements in the `Stack`—we will reach lines 12 and 13, which do the actual work of sending the user back to the previous page. Line 12 simply disposes of the top-most `Stack` element; line 13 uses the `Redirect` method of the `Response` object to send the user to the next element at the top of the stack.

That wraps up our examination of the navigation history stack example. The code samples spanned three listings: Listing 2.1.5, Listing 2.1.6, and Listing 2.1.7. If you decide to use this code on your Web site, there are a couple of things to keep in mind:

- First, because our implementation of the navigation history stack is a code snippet in an ASP.NET page, the code in Listing 2.1.5 would need to appear in every Web page on your site. This, of course, is a ridiculous requirement; it would make sense to encapsulate the code and functionality in a user control to allow for easy code reuse. (For more information on user controls, refer to Chapter 5, "Creating and Using User Controls.")
- Second, remember that in `Back.CSharp.aspx` we are `Pop`ping off the top two URLs. Because `Pop` removes these elements from the `Stack` altogether, the navigation history stack cannot contain any sort of Forward link.

Similarities Among the Collection Types

Because each collection has the same basic functionality—to serve as a variable-sized storage medium for Objects—it is not surprising that the collection types have much in common with one another. All have methods to add and remove elements from the collection. The `Count` property, which returns the total number of elements in the collection, is common among all collection types.

Each collection also has a means to iterate through each element. This can be accomplished in VB using a `For Each ... Next` loop or, in C#, a `foreach` loop, as follows:

```
'With VB, use a For Each ... Next Loop
Dim qTasks as Queue = New Queue()

' ... Populate the Queue ...

Dim s as String
For Each s in qTasks
```

```
    's represents the current element in qTasks
    Response.Write(s + "<br>")
Next


// In C#, a foreach construct can be used to iterate
// through each element
Queue qTasks = new Queue();

// … Populate the Queue …

foreach (String s in qTasks)
{
    // s represents the current element in qTasks
    Response.Write(s + "<br>");
}
```

Although each collection can be iterated via a `For Each ... Next` or `foreach` loop, each collection can also have its elements iterated with an enumerator. Enumerators are small classes that provide a simple functionality: to serve as a (read-only) cursor to allow the developer to step through the elements of a collection.

The .NET Framework provides a number of specific enumerators for specific collection types. For example, the `IDictionaryElement` enumerator is useful for iterating through a `Hashtable`. The `IList` enumerator is handy for stepping through the elements of an `ArrayList`. All these specialized enumerators are derived from a base enumerator interface, `IEnumerator`. Because of this fact, all the collection types can be iterated via the `IEnumerator` enumerator as well.

Because an enumerator's most basic purpose is to serve as a cursor for a collection, the `IEnumerator` class contains only a single property that returns the element in the collection to which the enumerator is currently pointing. (More specialized enumerators, such as `IDictionaryElement`, contain multiple properties.) `IEnumerator` contains just two methods: `MoveNext`, which advances the enumerator to the next element in the collection, and `Reset`, which returns the enumerator to its starting position—the position immediately before the first element in the collection.

Listing 2.1.8 contains a simple ASP.NET page that illustrates iteration through both an `ArrayList` and `Hashtable` with the `IEnumerator` enumerator. The output is shown in Figure 2.6.

LISTING 2.1.8 To Step Through Each Element of a Collection, an Enumerator Can Be Used

```
1: <script language="VB" runat="server">
2:
3:   Sub Page_Load(sender as Object, e as EventArgs)
4:     ' Create some Collections
5:     Dim aTeam1 as New ArrayList(), _
6:         aTeam2 as New ArrayList(), _
7:         aTeam3 as New ArrayList()
8:
```

LISTING 2.1.8 Continued

```
 9:      Dim htProjects as New Hashtable()
10:
11:      ' Assign memebers to the various teams
12:      aTeam1.Add("Scott")
13:      aTeam1.Add("Rob")
14:      aTeam1.Add("Chris")
15:
16:      aTeam2.Add("Doug")
17:      aTeam2.Add("Don")
18:
19:      aTeam3.Add("Billy")
20:      aTeam3.Add("Mark")
21:      aTeam3.Add("Charles")
22:      aTeam3.Add("Steve")
23:
24:
25:      ' Add each team to the htProjects HashTable
26:      htProjects.Add("Prototyping", aTeam1)
27:      htProjects.Add("Coding", aTeam2)
28:      htProjects.Add("Testing", aTeam3)
29:
30:      ' Now, list each project
31:      Dim enumProjects as IEnumerator = htProjects.GetEnumerator()
32:      Do While enumProjects.MoveNext()
33:        lblProjectListing.Text &= enumProjects.Current.Key & "<br>"
34:      Loop
35:
36:      ' Now list each team
37:      Dim enumTeam as IEnumerator
38:      enumProjects.Reset()
39:      Do While enumProjects.MoveNext()
40:        lblDetailedListing.Text &= "<b>" & enumProjects.Current.Key
➥ & ":</b><ul>"
41:
42:        enumTeam = enumProjects.Current.Value.GetEnumerator()
43:        Do While enumTeam.MoveNext()
44:          lblDetailedListing.Text &= enumTeam.Current & "<br>"
45:        Loop
46:
47:        lblDetailedListing.Text &= "</ul><p>"
48:      Loop
49:    End Sub
50:
51:  </script>
52:
53:  <html>
54:  <body>
55:
56:    <font size=+1><b><u>Project Listing:</u></b></font><br>
57:    <asp:label runat="server" id="lblProjectListing" />
58:    <p>
59:
```

LISTING 2.1.8 Continued

```
60:     <font size=+1><b><u>Detailed Project Listing</u>:</b></font><br>
61:     <asp:label runat="server" id="lblDetailedListing" />
62:
63: </body>
64: </html>
```

FIGURE 2.6
Output of Listing 2.1.8 when viewed through a browser.

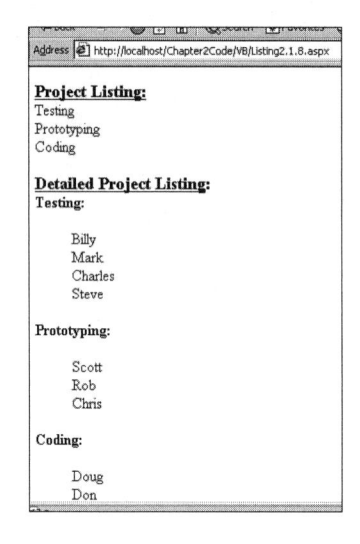

The code in Listing 2.1.8 begins by creating three `ArrayList` collections: `aTeam1`, `aTeam2`, and `aTeam3` (lines 5, 6, and 7, respectively). These three `ArrayList`s are then populated with various strings in lines 12 through 22. Each of these `ArrayList`s is added to the `htProjects` `HashTable` on lines 26 through 28. As pointed out earlier, collection types can hold any Object, not just simple data types such as integers and strings.

On line 31, an instance of the `IEnumerator` interface is created and assigned to the enumerator for `htProjects`. (Each of the collection types contains a `GetEnumerator()` method that returns a read-only enumerator for the collection.) From lines 32 to 34, the `enumProjects` enumerator is stepped through, visiting each element in the `Hashtable` collection.

Note that each element returned to the enumerator from a `Hashtable` is an instance of the `DictionaryEntry` object. The `DictionaryEntry` object contains two public fields: `Key` and `Value`. Therefore, on line 33, to obtain the key of the current `Hashtable` element, we need to specify that we want the `Key` field of the current element. We could have created a `DictionaryEntry` instance and referenced the `Key` field in a more explicit manner as follows:

```
Dim dictEntry as DictionaryEntry
Do While enumProjects.MoveNext()
  dictEntry = enumProjects.Current
  lblProjectListing.Text &= dictEntry.Key & "<br>"
Loop
```

Because each entry in `htProjects` is an `ArrayList` collection itself, we need to create another enumerator to step through each element in each `ArrayList`. This is accomplished on line 37. At the end of our iteration through `htProjects` in lines 32 through 34, the enumerator `enumProjects` is positioned at the end of the collection. Because we are going to iterate through the `htProjects` collection again, we need to reposition the enumerator back to before the first element. This is accomplished with the `Reset` method of the `IEnumerator` interface (line 38).

In lines 39 through 48, the `htProjects` collection is enumerated through again. This time, each element of `htProjects` is also iterated through itself. On line 42, the `enumTeam` enumerator is assigned via the `GetEnumerator()` method of the current `ArrayList` collection. Next, the `enumTeam` enumerator is stepped through in lines 43 through 45, outputting each `ArrayList` element (line 44).

Conclusion

The .NET Framework provides developers with a number of powerful collection-type classes, greatly extending the functionality of the `Scripting.Dictionary` object, the sole collection type available for classic ASP developers. These collections, although each have unique capabilities, are more alike than they are different. All of them share similar methods and properties, and can have their elements iterated through using a number of techniques.

> **Note**
> All of the collection types we've examined in this chapter inherit from the `ICollection` interface. This interface is responsible for providing the size, enumeration, and synchronization methods for collection types. All of the classes in the .NET Framework that inherit the `ICollection` interface support the basic collection functionality discussed in this section, "Similarities Among the Collection Types."

2. Working with the File System

Very often Web application developers need to have the ability to access the file system on the Web server. Perhaps they need to list the contents of a particular text file, remove a temporary directory or file, or copy a file from one location to another.

Classic ASP provided adequate support for working with the Web server's file system. The `FileSystemObject` object—along with its accompanying objects such as the `File`, `Folder`, and `TextStream` objects—permitted the classic ASP developer to perform rudimentary tasks with the Web server's file system. One serious shortcoming of the `FileSystemObject` was that the developer, without having to jump through hoops, could only read and write text files; reading and writing binary files with the `FileSystemObject` was possible, but a pain.

The .NET Framework provides a number of classes for working with the file system. These classes are much more robust and have greater functionality than their `FileSystemObject` counterparts. In this section, we'll look at how to accomplish some common file system tasks:

- Reading, creating, and deleting directories
- Reading, writing, and creating files

Reading, Creating, and Deleting Directories

In classic ASP, developers could access directory information with the `Folder` object, one of the many useful `FileSystemObject` objects. The .NET Framework provides a plethora of file system–accessing classes in the `System.IO` namespace, including a `DirectoryInfo` class. This class will be examined in this section.

Listing 2.2.1 illustrates the `DirectoryInfo` class in action! From `Listing2.2.1.aspx`, the user can enter the name of a directory on the Web server. The page will then list the properties of that directory (if it exists), along with the directory's subdirectories. The output is shown in Figure 2.7.

LISTING 2.2.1 The `DirectoryInfo` Class Provides Information About a Particular Directory

```
 1: <%@ Import Namespace="System.IO" %>
 2: <script language="VB" runat="server">
 3: Sub Page_Load(sender as Object, e as EventArgs)
 4:   If Not Page.IsPostBack then
 5:     lblDirInfo.Text = "Enter the fully qualified name of the " & _
 6:             "directory that you're interested in (<i>i.e., C:\</i>)"
 7:   Else
 8:     ' a postback, so get the directory information
 9:     Dim dirInfo as DirectoryInfo = new DirectoryInfo(txtDirectoryName.Text)
10:
11:     Try
12:       ' Display the directory properties
13:       lblDirInfo.Text = "<b>Information for " & txtDirectoryName.Text & _
14:          "</b><br> Attributes: " & _
15:          DisplayAttributes(dirInfo.Attributes) & "<br>Creation Time:" & _
16:          dirInfo.CreationTime.ToShortDateString() & _
17:          ", " & dirInfo.CreationTime.ToLongTimeString() & _
18:          "<br>Full Name: " & dirInfo.FullName & "<br>" & _
19:          "Root Drive: " & dirInfo.Root.Name & "<br>" & _
20:          "Parent Directory Name: " & dirInfo.Parent.Name & "<br>" & _
21:          "Directory Name: " & dirInfo.Name & "<br>Last Access Time: " & _
22:          dirInfo.LastAccessTime.ToShortDateString() & ", " & _
23:          dirInfo.LastAccessTime.ToLongTimeString() & "<br>" & _
24:          "Last Write Time: " & dirInfo.LastWriteTime.ToShortDateString() & _
25:          ", " & dirInfo.LastWriteTime.ToLongTimeString() & "<br>"
26:
27:       ' List all of the subdirectories for the current directory:
28:       lblSubDirectories.Text = "<b>Subdirectories of " & _
```

LISTING 2.2.1 Continued

```
29:                          dirInfo.FullName & "</b><br>"
30:     Dim dirSubDirectory as DirectoryInfo
31:     For Each dirSubDirectory in dirInfo.GetDirectories()
32:       lblSubDirectories.Text &= dirSubDirectory.FullName & "<br>"
33:     Next
34:    Catch dnfException as DirectoryNotFoundException
35:     ' Whoops!  A directoryNotFound Exception has been raised!
36:     ' The user entered an invalid directory name!
37:     lblDirInfo.Text = "<font color=red><b>" & _
38:                       dnfException.Message & "</b></font>"
39:    End Try
40:   End If
41: End Sub
42:
43:
44: Function DisplayAttributes(fsa as FileAttributes) as String
45: 'Display the file attributes
46:    Dim strOutput as String = ""
47:
48:    if (fsa And FileAttributes.Archive) > 0 Then
➥ strOutput &= "Archived, "
49:    if (fsa And FileAttributes.Compressed) > 0 Then
➥ strOutput &= "Compressed, "
50:    if (fsa And FileAttributes.Directory) > 0 Then
➥ strOutput &= "Directory, "
51:    if (fsa And FileAttributes.Encrypted) > 0 Then
➥ strOutput &= "Encrypted, "
52:    if (fsa And FileAttributes.Hidden) > 0 Then
➥ strOutput &= "Hidden, "
53:    if (fsa And FileAttributes.Normal) > 0 Then
➥ strOutput &= "Normal, "
54:    if (fsa And FileAttributes.NotContentIndexed) > 0 Then _
55:                                       strOutput &= "Not Content Indexed, "
56:    if (fsa And FileAttributes.Offline) > 0 Then
➥ strOutput &= "Offline, "
57:    if (fsa And FileAttributes.ReadOnly) > 0 Then
➥ strOutput &= "Read Only, "
58:    if (fsa And FileAttributes.ReparsePoint) > 0 Then
➥ strOutput &= "Reparse Point, "
59:    if (fsa And FileAttributes.SparseFile) > 0 Then
➥ strOutput &= "Sparse File, "
60:    if (fsa And FileAttributes.System) > 0 Then
➥ strOutput &= "System, "
61:    if (fsa And FileAttributes.Temporary) > 0 Then
➥ strOutput &= "Temporary, "
62:
63:    ' whack off the trailing ", "
64:    If strOutput.Length > 0 Then
65:      DisplayAttributes = strOutput.Substring(0, strOutput.Length - 2)
66:    Else
```

LISTING 2.2.1 Continued

```
67:      DisplayAttributes = "No attributes found..."
68:    End If
69: End Function
70: </script>
71:
72: <html>
73: <body>
74:    <form method="post" runat="server">
75:       <b>Get Information on Directory:</b><br>
76:       <asp:textbox runat="server" id="txtDirectoryName" /><p>
77:       <asp:button id="btnSubmit" runat="server" type="Submit" text="Go!" />
78:       <p><hr><p>
79:       <asp:label runat="server" id="lblDirInfo" /><p>
80:       <asp:label runat="server" id="lblSubDirectories" />
81:    </form>
82: </body>
83: </html>
```

FIGURE 2.7
Output of Listing 2.2.1 when viewed through a browser.

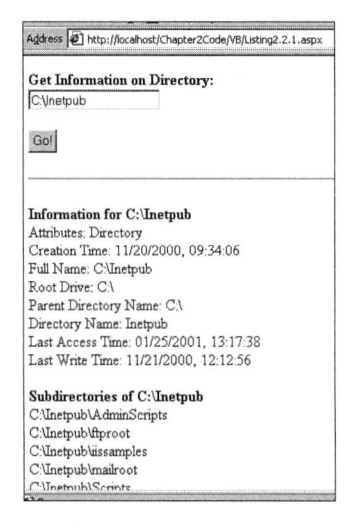

When working with the various file system classes, it is often handy to import the `System.IO` namespace to save unneeded typing (line 1).

Listing 2.2.1 uses the postback form technique we discussed in Chapter 1, "Common ASP.NET Page Techniques." On line 74, a form with the `runat="server"` attribute is created. In the form, there is an `asp:textbox` control and a submit button (`btnSubmit`, line 77). When a user first visits the page, `Page.IsPostBack` is `False` and lines 5 and 6 in the `Page_Load` event handler are executed, displaying an instructional message.

After the user enters a directory name and submits the form, the `Page.IsPostBack` property is set to `True` and the code from lines 8 through 39 is executed. On line 9, a `DirectoryInfo` object, `dirInfo`, is created. Because the `DirectoryInfo` class is useful for retrieving information on a particular directory, including the files and subdirectories of a particular directory, it isn't surprising that the `DirectoryInfo` constructor requires, as a parameter, the path of the directory with which the developer is interested in working. In this case, we are interested in the directory specified by the user in the `txtDirectoryName` text box.

> **Note**
>
> The `DirectoryInfo` class represents a specific directory on the Web server's file system; the `DirectoryInfo` constructor requires that you specify a valid directory path. However, there may be times when you don't want to have to go through the steps of creating an instance of the `DirectoryInfo` class just to, say, delete a directory. The .NET Framework contains a `Directory` class for this purpose. This class cannot be instantiated and, instead, contains a number of static methods that can be used to work with any directory. We'll examine this class later in this section.

After we've created an instance of the `DirectoryInfo` class, we can access its methods and properties. However, what if the user specified a directory that does not exist? Such a case would generate an unsightly runtime error. To compensate for this, we use a `Try ... Catch` block, nesting the calls to the `DirectoryInfo` classes properties and methods inside the `Try` block (lines 13 through 33). If the directory specified by the user doesn't exist, a `DirectoryNotFoundException` exception will be thrown. The `Catch` block starting on line 34 will then catch this exception and an error message will be displayed. Figure 2.8 shows the browser output when a user enters a nonexistent directory name.

FIGURE 2.8
An attractive error message is displayed if the user enters an invalid directory name.

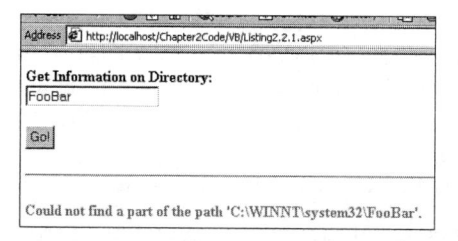

A useful property of the `DirectoryInfo` class (and the `FileInfo` class, which we'll examine in the next section, "Reading, Writing, and Creating Files") that deserves further attention is the `Attributes` property. This property is of type `FileAttributes`, an enumeration also found in the `System.IO` namespace. The `FileAttributes` enumeration lists the various attributes a directory (or file) can have. Table 2.1 lists these attributes.

TABLE 2.1 Available Attributes in the `FileAttributes` Enumeration

Attribute	Description
Archive	Indicates the file system entity's archive status
Compressed	Indicates the file system entity's compression status
Directory	Indicates if the file system entity is a directory
Encrypted	Indicates whether the file system entity is encrypted
Hidden	Indicates if the file system entity is hidden
Normal	If the file system entity has no other attributes set, it is labeled as Normal
NotContentIndexed	Indicates whether the file system entity will be indexed by the operating system's indexing service
Offline	Indicates if the file system entity is offline
ReadOnly	Indicates whether the file system entity is read-only
ReparsePoint	Indicates if the file system entity contains a reparse point (a block of user-defined data)
SparseFile	Indicates if a file is defined as a sparse file
System	Indicates if the file is a system file
Temporary	Indicates whether the file system entity is temporary or not

Because each directory (or file) can have a number of attributes (such as a file being both hidden and a system file), the single `Attributes` property has the capability of housing multiple pieces of information. To pick out the individual attributes represented by the `Attributes` property, a bit-wise `AND` can be used (see lines 48 through 61). To properly display the attributes for a directory in Listing 2.2.1, a helper function, `DisplayAttributes`, is called from line 15, passing to it the `FileAttributes` enumeration returned by the `Attributes` property.

The `DisplayAttributes` function, spanning lines 44 through 69, returns a nicely formatted display listing the various attributes indicated by the `FileAttributes` enumeration passed in (`fsa`). On lines 48 through 61, a check is performed to determine if `fsa` contains a particular attribute; if it does, the textual description of the attribute is appended to `strOutput`, which will be returned by `DisplayAttributes` at the end of the function.

The `DirectoryInfo` class contains two useful methods for retrieving a list of a directory's subdirectories and folders. These two methods are `GetDirectories()`, which returns an array of `DirectoryInfo` objects representing the subdirectories, and `GetFiles()`, which returns an array of `FileInfo` objects representing the list of files in the directory. (We'll examine the

`FileInfo` object in detail in the next section, "Reading, Writing, and Creating Files." In lines 31 through 33, the array returned by the `GetDirectories()` method is iterated using a `For Each ... Next` loop, displaying the subdirectories for the directory represented by `dirInfo`.

Listing 2.2.1 demonstrates how to list the properties of a directory (such as its attributes, creation date, last accessed date, and so on) and how to retrieve the subdirectories for a given directory. However, we have not examined how to create and delete directories.

Recall that the `DirectoryInfo` class represents a specific directory (after all, the `DirectoryInfo` constructor requires a directory path). Therefore, it makes sense that the `DirectoryInfo` class can only be used to create subdirectories of the physical directory represented by the `DirectoryInfo` instance. To create a subdirectory use the `CreateSubdirectory` method:

```
Dim dirInfo as DirectoryInfo = new DirectoryInfo("C:\Inetpub\wwwroot\")

'Create a subdirectory
dirInfo.CreateSubdirectory("images")
```

The preceding script creates an `images` subdirectory in the directory in the `C:\Inetput\wwwroot\` directory. There are a number of exceptions that the `CreateSubdirectory` method can throw if something goes awry.

- `ArgumentException`—This exception will be thrown if you try to create a subdirectory that contains invalid directory characters (such as \, /, :, *, ?, ", <, >, and |).

- `IOException`—This exception is thrown if you attempt to create a subdirectory that already exists.

- `PathTooLongException`—This exception is thrown if the subdirectory you attempt to create contains too long a path. (At the time of writing this path length limitation was set at 248 characters.)

- `SecurityException`—This exception occurs if the caller does not have sufficient permissions.

To delete a directory, use the `DirectoryInfo` class's `Delete` method. The `Delete` method will delete the directory represented by the `DirectoryInfo` instance. The `Delete` method can accept an optional Boolean parameter *RecurseDirs*, which if `True`, will delete the directory, all its files, and all its subdirectories and their files. If *RecurseDir* is `False` (or not specified at all) and you attempt to delete a directory that contains any files or subdirectories, an `IOException` exception will be thrown:

```
'Delete C:\ASP and all its subdirectories with the Delete method
Dim dirASP as New Directory("C:\ASP")
dirASP.Delete(True)
```

While the `CreateSubdirectory` and `Delete` methods of the `DirectoryInfo` class can be used to create or delete any directory on the file system, it's a bit verbose if all you want to do is quickly create a new directory. The .NET Framework provides another class, `Directory`, which you can use if you do not want to go through the trouble of creating an instance of the `DirectoryInfo` class.

The `Directory` class contains a number of static methods (methods that can be called without creating a new instance of the `Directory` class). (In fact, you cannot create an instance of the `Directory` method—if you try you will receive a "'`System.IO.Directory.Directory()`' is inaccessible due to its protection level" error.) One of these static methods of the `Directory` class is `CreateDirectory`, which, as its name suggests, creates a directory! Simply use the following syntax:

`Directory.CreateDirectory(DirectoryPath)`

The CreateDirectory method will throw an IOException exception if the directory DirectoryPath already exists.

To delete a directory with the `Directory class`, use the `Delete` method. The `Delete` method has two forms:

`Directory.Delete(DirectoryPath)`
`Directory.Delete(DirectoryPath, RecurseDirs)`

The *DirectoryPath* is the path of the directory that you want to delete. As with the `DirectoryInfo` class's `Delete` method, *RecurseDirs* is a Boolean value, which if `True`, will delete the directory, all its files, and all its subdirectories and their files. If *RecurseDir* is `False` (or not specified at all) and you attempt to delete a directory that contains any files or subdirectories, an `IOException` exception will be thrown.

Caution
When working with the file system using C#, keep in mind that the string escape sequence for C# is the backslash (\). To insert a literal backslash into a string, you must use two consecutive backslashes. For example, to delete a directory, use `Directory.Delete("C:\\ASP");`.

Reading, Writing, and Creating Files

Because the .NET Framework provides a class for retrieving information about a particular directory (the `DirectoryInfo` class), it should come as no surprise that it also provides a class for accessing file information. This class, aptly named `FileInfo`, contains a number of properties similar to the `DirectoryInfo` class. For example, the `Attributes`, `CreationTime`, `Exists`, `FullName`, `LastAccessedTime`, `LastWriteTime`, and `Name` properties are common to both the `FileInfo` and `DirectoryInfo` classes.

The methods of the `FileInfo` class are fairly straightforward; they provide the basic functionality for files. The methods to open a file are `Open`, `OpenRead`, `OpenText`, and `OpenWrite`. The methods to create a file are `Create` and `CreateText`. The methods to delete and do miscellaneous file-related tasks are `CopyTo`, `Delete`, and `MoveTo`.

> **Note**
>
> The .NET Framework also includes a `File` class, which is strikingly similar to the `Directory` class. As with the `DirectoryInfo` and `Directory` classes, the `FileInfo` class allows for actions on a specific file while the `File` class contains a number of static methods for use with any generic file.

Listing 2.2.2 illustrates how to read (and display) the contents of a text file, as well as how to use a DataList and databinding to display the contents of an array. A thorough examination of databinding and use of the DataList can be found in Chapter 7.

LISTING 2.2.2 The `FileInfo` Class Can Be Used to Retrieve Properties or the Contents of a File on the Web Server

```
 1: <%@ Import Namespace="System.IO" %>
 2: <script language="VB" runat="server">
 3: Sub Page_Load(sender as Object, e as EventArgs)
 4:    If Not Page.IsPostBack then
 5:       ' What directory are we interested in?
 6:       const strDir = "C:\My Projects\ASP.NET Book\Chapter 2\Code\VB"
 7:       lblHeader.Text = "<b><u>File Listing for " & strDir & ":</u></b>"
 8:
 9:       Dim dirInfo as New DirectoryInfo(strDir)
10:       ' Get the files for the directory strDir
11:          Dim aFiles as FileInfo() = dirInfo.GetFiles ("*.aspx")
12:       dlFileList.DataSource = aFiles
13:          dlFileList.DataBind()
14:    End If
15: End Sub
16:
17: Sub dlFileList_Select(sender as Object, e as EventArgs)
18:    Dim strFilePath as String = _
19:       dlFileList.DataKeys(dlFileList.SelectedItem.ItemIndex).ToString()
20:    Dim objFile as FileInfo = new FileInfo(strFilePath)
21:    Dim objStream as StreamReader = objFile.OpenText()
22:    Dim strContents as String = objStream.ReadToEnd()
23:    objStream.Close()
24:    lblFileContents.Text = "<b>Contents of " & objFile.Name & ":</b>" & _
25:                           "<xmp>" & vbCrLf & strContents & vbCrLf & "</xmp>"
26: End Sub
27: </script>
28: <html>
29: <body>
```

LISTING 2.2.2 Continued

```
30:     <form runat="server">
31:       <asp:label id="lblHeader" runat="server" /><br>
32:       <asp:DataList runat="server" id="dlFileList"
33:                   OnSelectedIndexChanged="dlFileList_Select"
34:                   DataKeyField="FullName" >
35:        <ItemTemplate>
36:          <li><%# DataBinder.Eval(Container.DataItem, "Name") %><br>
37:          <font size=-1>
38:            [<asp:linkbutton Text="View Contents"
39:                 CommandName="Select" runat="server"/>] |
40:            [<%# DataBinder.Eval(Container.DataItem, "Length") %> bytes]
41:          </font>
42:          <p>
43:        </ItemTemplate>
44:       </asp:DataList>
45:       <p><hr><p>
46:       <asp:label runat="server" id="lblFileContents" />
47: <form>
48: <body>
49: <html>
```

The code in Listing 2.2.2 serves a very simple purpose: to list the ASP.NET pages in a particular directory and to allow the user to view the source code for any one of these pages. This can be thought of as two separate tasks:

1. Listing the files in a particular directory
2. Displaying the contents of the selected file

The first task is handled by the `Page_Load` event handler (lines 3 through 15) and the DataList control (lines 32 through 44). The first line of the `Page_Load` event handler checks to determine if the page is being visited for the first time (if so, `Page.IsPostBack` will be `False`, and the code from lines 5 through 13 will be executed). In such a case, we want to display the files for a particular directory. On line 6, the directory path whose files will be displayed has been hard coded and stored in the constant `strDir`. By using concepts from Listing 2.2.1, however, Listing 2.2.2 could be expanded to allow the user to specify the directory.

Next, those files in the directory `strDir` that end with the `.aspx` extension are returned (line 11). The `GetFiles` method of the `DirectoryInfo` class can accept an optional parameter indicating that only a subset of files should be returned from the directory. This optional parameter, if specified, is a search criteria field in which wildcards can be used to limit the files returned. Because we are only interested in listing ASP.NET pages, we want to grab only those files that have the `.aspx` extension. The `GetFiles` method returns an array of `FileInfo` objects, which we assign to our variable `aFiles` (line 11).

On lines 12 and 13, we bind this array to `dlFileList`, our DataList whose definition begins on line 36. The DataList uses databinding syntax to display the `Name` property of each `FileInfo` object in the `aFiles` array (line 36) along with the `Length` property, which indicates the file's size in bytes (line 40). In the DataList heading (lines 32 through 34), the `SelectedIndexChanged` event is wired up to the `dlFileList_Select` event handler;

furthermore, the DataList specifies the `FullName` property of the `FileInfo` class as its `DataKeyField` (line 34).

A LinkButton server control is created on lines 38 and 39 with a `CommandName` of `Select`. When this LinkButton is clicked, the page will be reposted and the `dlFileList_Select` event handler will be called. From the `dlFileList_Select` event handler, the `FullName` of the file clicked can be programmatically determined because of the `DataKeyField` property on line 34. If you are unfamiliar with the DataList control and databinding, this might be a bit overwhelming to you. Don't worry, though; databinding will be discussed thoroughly in Chapter 7.

After a View Contents link is clicked, the page will be reloaded and we're on to the second task: displaying the contents of the selected file. This is handled in the `dlFileList_Select` event handler. On line 19, the clicked LinkButton's `DataKeyField` is extracted and stored in the variable `strFilePath`. This contains the full path to the file that we want to display.

Next, on line 20, a `FileInfo` object is instantiated and the constructor is called, passing it the path of the file we are interested in. To simply read the contents of a text file, the `FileInfo` class provides an `OpenText` method, which returns a `StreamReader` instance that can be used to step through the contents of the file. On line 21, a `StreamReader` instance is created and assigned to the object returned by the `OpenText` method. Next, the entire stream is read into a string variable, `strContents` (line 22), and the stream is closed (line 23).

On line 24 and 25, the contents of the selected file are displayed in the `lblFileContents` label server control. Because we are displaying the contents of a file that likely contains HTML and script-block code, the contents are surrounded by a pair of `XMP` tags. (The `XMP` tag is a standard HTML tag that displays text ignoring all HTML tags.)

Figure 2.9 shows the output of the code in Listing 2.2.2 when we first visit the page. Note that the contents of the specified directory are displayed with a link to view the source and a note on their file size.

FIGURE 2.9
When the user first visits the page, she is shown a listing of files.

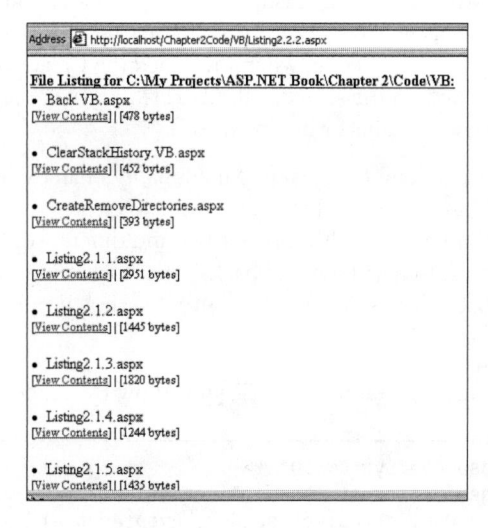

When the user clicks the View Contents link for a particular file, the page is reloaded and the file's contents are displayed beneath the file listing. Figure 2.10 shows what a user would see after clicking on a particular file in the listing.

FIGURE 2.10
Clicking on a particular file displays its contents beneath the file listing.

In Listing 2.2.2 we examined how to list the contents of a directory, how to list certain `FileInfo` class properties, and how to read the contents of a text file. However, we've yet to look at how to create a file and how to work with binary files (a task that was difficult in classic ASP with the `FileSystemObject`).

Creating Text Files

Let's first examine how to create a file. Listing 2.2.3 demonstrates an ASP.NET page that serves as a very basic Create your own Web Page utility. From the page, users can enter a filename for their HTML page and the HTML code; when they click the Create HTML Page button, a new HTML page will be created on the server with the HTML syntax they entered. After this file is created, anyone can view it via his or her browser.

The script in Listing 2.2.3 demonstrates the functionality of an extremely simple HTML file editor that might be found on a site that allows users to create personal home pages. Listing 2.2.3 is written in C#; note some of the similarities and differences between C#'s syntax and VB's syntax. For example, to insert a literal backslash into a string, when using C# you must use two consecutive backslashes (line 6). The output is shown in Figure 2.11.

LISTING 2.2.3 The `File` and `StreamWriter` Classes Allow Developers to Create Files on the Web Server

```
1: <%@ Import Namespace="System.IO" %>
2: <script language="C#" runat="server">
3:   void btnSubmit_OnClick(Object sender, EventArgs e)
```

LISTING 2.2.3 *Continued*

```
 4:    {
 5:      // Create an HTML file in the directory strDir
 6:      const String strDir = "C:\\Inetpub\\wwwroot\\UserPages\\";
 7:
 8:      String strFileName = strDir + txtPageName.Text;
 9:
10:      // Create the file using the static method CreateText
11:      StreamWriter objStream = File.CreateText(strFileName);
12:
13:      // Write the contents of the txtContents textarea to the stream
14:      objStream.Write(txtContents.Text);
15:
16:      // Close the stream, saving the file...
17:      objStream.Close();
18:
19:      // Display a link to the newly created HTML page.
20:      lblLink.Text = "Page created!<br><a href=\"/UserPages/" +
21:                     txtPageName.Text + "\">View New Page!</a>";
22:    }
23: </script>
24:
25: <html>
26: <body>
27:   <form runat="server">
28:     <font size=+2><b>Create your own HTML page!</b></font>
29:     <p>
30:     <b>Name:</b> <asp:textbox id="txtPageName" runat="server" /><br>
31:     <b>Contents:</b><br>
32:     <asp:textbox id="txtContents" runat="server" TextMode="MultiLine"
33:                  Columns="40" Rows="5" />
34:     <p>
35:     <asp:button id="btnSubmit" runat="server" text="Create HTML Page!"
36:                 OnClick="btnSubmit_OnClick" />
37:     <p>
38:     <asp:label id="lblLink" runat="server" />
39:   </form>
40: </body>
41: </html>
```

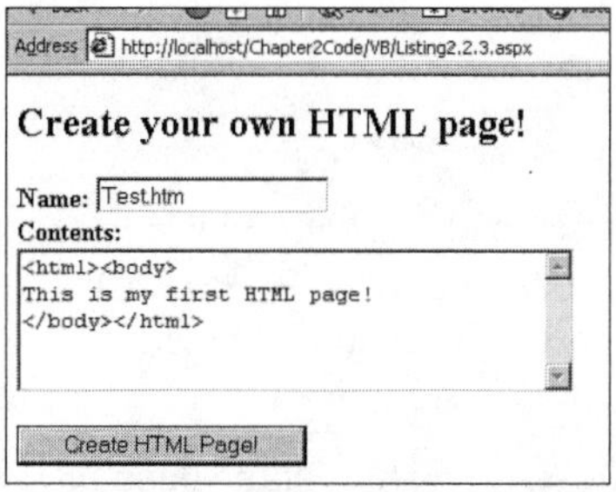

FIGURE 2.11
The user can enter HTML and a filename and the ASP.NET page will generate a file on the Web server with the proper name and contents!

Listing 2.2.3 is the first code sample we've looked at in this chapter that did not include the `Page_Load` event handler. Therefore, before looking at the C# code, let's turn our attention to the HTML portion first (lines 25 through 41). First, note that we are using postback forms, so we must create a form with the `runat="server"` attribute (line 27). Next, we need two text boxes: one for the user to enter the filename of the HTML page he wants to create and another for the HTML contents for the page.

The text box for the filename, `txtPageName`, is created on line 30. The text box for the HTML contents, `txtContents`, is created as a multiline text box with 40 columns and 5 rows (lines 32 and 33). A multiline text box is, in HTML terms, a `TEXTAREA`. Next, we create a button and wire up its click event to the `btnSubmit_OnClick` event handler (lines 35 and 36). The last server control is a label, `lblLink`, which we'll use to display a link to the newly created HTML page.

When the Create HTML Page! button is clicked, the postback form is submitted and the `btnSubmit_OnClick` event handler is called. This event handler's task is to create the file specified by the user with the HTML contents specified by the user. All the HTML files created by the user will be placed in the directory specified by the string constant `strDir` (line 6). The actual filename for the file to be created is the concatenation of `strDir` and the value the user entered in the `txtPageName` text box (line 8).

On line 11 the static version of the `CreateText` method is used to create a new text file. The static version of the `CreateText` method expects a single parameter, the path to the file to create, and returns a `StreamWriter` object that can be used to write the contents to the newly created file. On line 14, the `Write` method of the `StreamWriter` class is used to write the HTML contents entered by the user to the file. This file is saved on line 17, when the `Close` method is called. Finally, a link to the newly created file is displayed on lines 20 and 21.

Caution

The code in Listing 2.2.3 does not contain any sort of error-handling code. If the user doesn't enter a filename, an exception will be thrown. Additionally, if the `C:\Inetpub\wwwroot\UserPages\` directory does not exist an exception will be thrown. Either of these errors could be remedied via a `try ... catch` block, an `if` statement in `btnSubmit_OnClick` to check if `txtPageName` contains a valid value, or through a validation control. (For more information on `try ... catch` blocks, be sure to read Chapter 9, "ASP.NET Error Handling." For information on validation controls, refer to Chapter 3, "Form Field Input Validation.")

Working with Binary Files

The `FileSystemObject` objects used with classic ASP were designed to work with text files. The file system objects in the .NET Framework, however, were designed to be much more flexible, able to easily work with binary or text files alike. So far, we've examined how to read and create text files. It's time that we took a quick look at how binary files are handled.

The code in Listing 2.2.4 uses the static version of the `Open` method of the `File` class to open a binary file (in this case, a GIF file). The binary data is then squirted to the user's browser via the `Response.BinaryWrite` method. Because browsers can inherently display GIF files, the user ends up seeing the image file as though he had directed his browser directly to the image file on the Web server (as opposed to an ASP.NET page).

LISTING 2.2.4 The .NET Framework Can Easily Handle Both Binary and Text Files

```
 1: <%@ Page ContentType="image/gif" %>
 2: <%@ Import Namespace="System.IO" %>
 3: <script language="vb" runat="server">
 4:   Sub Page_Load(sender as Object, e as EventArgs)
 5:     Const strFileName as String = "C:\Inetpub\wwwroot\Web.gif"
 6:
 7:     ' Read the contents of a binary file
 8:     Dim objStream as Stream = File.Open(strFileName, FileMode.Open)
 9:
10:     Dim buffer(objStream.Length) as Byte
11:     objStream.Read(buffer, 0, objStream.Length)
12:     objStream.Close()
13:
14:     Response.BinaryWrite(buffer)
15:   End Sub
16: </script>
```

Listing 2.2.4 displays a GIF in the users browser specified by the hard-coded file path on line 5. Next, on line 8, the **Open** method is used to retrieve a **Stream** object to the GIF file's contents. There are many variations of the **Open** method; in this example we pass the **Open** method two parameters: the path to the file to open and the **FileMode** access to use. **FileMode** is an enumeration with its various entries representing various modes of which a file can be accessed. Table 2.2 lists these various file modes.

TABLE 2.2 The **FileMode** Enumeration Contains the Various Modes through which a File Can Be Accessed

Attribute	Description
Append	If the files exists, it is opened and the stream is positioned at the end of the file; if the file does not exist, it is created.
Create	Creates a new file if the file does not exist; if the file does exist, it is overwritten.
CreateNew	Specifies that a new file should be created.
Open	Opens an existing file.
OpenOrCreate	Specifies that the file should be opened if it exists, and created if it does not currently exist.
Truncate	Opens an existing file and positions the stream at the beginning of the file to overwrite existing data.

The `Open` method returns a `Stream` object that we can use to read from the file. The `Stream` class contains a `Read` method that takes three parameters: a buffer as a byte array, an integral offset, and an integral count, in the following format:

`Stream.Read(buffer(), offset, count)`

The `Read` method will then dump `count` bytes from the stream into the `buffer` array starting at a specified `offset` in the array. Before we execute this statement, though, we need to create and initialize a buffer array. Because we want to read the entire contents of the GIF file into our array, we need to create an array the size of the GIF file. This size can be retrieved from the `Length` property of the `Stream` class (line 10).

When we have this array properly initialized, we can go ahead and dump all the contents of the GIF file into the buffer using the `Read` method (line 11). Note that we are beginning the dump into the start of the buffer (hence `offset` is set to zero) and we are reading the entire stream (hence `count` is set to the length of the stream—`objStream.Length`).

Finally, the byte array is squirted to the browser using the `BinaryWrite` method of the Response object. The code in Listing 2.2.4, when viewed through a browser, will display the GIF specified by `strFileName` (line 5). Figure 2.12 is a screenshot of the browser visiting `Listing2.2.4.aspx`.

FIGURE 2.12
Use the `Stream` object to read binary files.

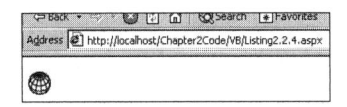

> **Note**
>
> Note that on line 1 of Listing 2.2.4 we used the page-level directive `ContentType`, setting it to `image/gif`. This `ContentType` setting is sent along as an HTTP header to the browser, indicating the type of binary content being sent. Note that we could have experienced the same results by inserting the following line before line 14 in Listing 2.2.4:
>
> `Response.ContentType = "image/gif"`

3. Using Regular Expressions

Regular expressions are a neat and efficient way to perform extremely powerful string pattern matching and replacing. For example, imagine that you had an HTML document and you wanted to pick through it to retrieve all the text between any bold tags (between `<b>` and `</b>`). Although this can be done with `String` class methods such as `IndexOf` and `Substring`, it would involve an unnecessarily complex loop with some ugly code. Instead, a relatively simple regular expression could be used.

Originally with classic ASP, regular expression support was a language-specific feature. That is, it was up to the syntax language being used to support regular expressions. With the release of the Microsoft Scripting Engine Version 5.0, Microsoft released a regular expression COM component to handle regular expression support in the same manner regardless of the scripting language.

With the .NET Framework, regular expressions are supported via a number of classes in the `System.Text.RegularExpressions` namespace. In this section we will examine these classes and look at some code samples. This section is not intended to teach regular expressions fundamentals—rather, it aims to illustrate how to work with regular expressions using the classes in the `System.Text.RegularExpressions` namespace.

> **Tip**
>
> For some very useful, very handy, real-world regular expressions, be sure to check out Chapter 3 which has a section on common regular expression validations for the `RegularExpressionValidator` validation control. Also take a peek at Appendix B, "Commonly Used Regular Expression Templates."

The class in the `System.Text.RegularExpressions` namespace that handles the bulk of the regular expression work is the `Regex` class. The constructor for this class is very important because it requires the most essential part of a regular expression: the pattern. Three forms of the constructor are as follows:

```
'Parameterless constructor
Regex()

'Requires the string pattern
Regex(pattern)

'Requires the string pattern and regular expression options
Regex(pattern, options)
```

The *pattern* parameter, if specified, needs to be of type String. The *options* parameter, if specified, needs to be a member of the `RegexOptions` enumeration. The `RegexOptions` enumeration (also found in the `System.Text.RegularExpressions` namespace), contains a number of options you can set when creating a `Regex` object instance. Some of the more useful `RegexOptions` enumeration members include:

- `Compiled`—If you are going to use a specific regular expression repeatedly in a single ASP.NET Web page you can achieve a small performance gain by having set the `Compiled` option. With this option set, the regular expression will be compiled once when it is first used rather than being recompiled for each instance of the regular expression on the page.

- `IgnoreCase`—By default, regular expressions are case-sensitive. Include this option if you wish to have a case-insensitive regular expression.

- `RightToLeft`—By default regular expressions parse through the input string in a left-to-right manner. If you wish to reverse this order, specify this option.

To specify multiple RegexOptions options in the Regex constructor, use a bit-wise OR to string together multiple options (in C#, bit-wise Ors are specified with the pipe (|)). For example, to create a regular expression instance that is both compiled and case insensitive, we could use the following statements:

```
'In VB.NET
Dim objRegex as Regex = New Regex(pattern,
➥ RegexOptions.IgnoreCase Or RegexOptions.Compiled)

// in C#
Regex objRegex = new Regex(pattern,
➥ RegexOptions.IgnoreCase | RegexOptions.Compiled);
```

The `Regex` class contains a number of methods for finding matches to a pattern in a string, replacing instances of the matching pattern with another string and testing to see if a matching pattern exists in a string. Let's look at the `IsMatch` method, which tests to see if a pattern is found in a string.

There are both static and nonstatic versions of the `IsMatch` method. The nonstatic version, which requires a `Regex` instance, requires only one parameter, the string to search for the pattern. (Recall that you must supply the pattern for the regular expression in the constructor.) A very simple `IsMatch` example can be seen in Listing 2.3.1.

LISTING 2.3.1   The `IsMatch` Method Determines if a Pattern Is Found in a String

```
 1: <%@ Import Namespace="System.Text.RegularExpressions" %>
 2: <script language="VB" runat="server">
 3: Sub Page_Load(sender as Object, e as EventArgs)
 4:   Dim str as String = "Reality, the external world, exists " & _
 5:     "independent of man's consciousness, independent of any " & _
 6:     "observer's knowledge, beliefs, feelings, desires or fears.
➥ This means that A is A..."
 7:
 8:   ' Check to see if the string str contains the pattern 'A is A'
 9:   Dim regexp as Regex = new Regex("A is A", RegexOptions.IgnoreCase)
10:
11:   If regexp.IsMatch(str) then
12:     Response.Write("This is an Ayn Rand quote.")
13:   Else
14:     Response.Write("I don't know who said this.")
15:   End If
16: End Sub
17: </script>
```

Because the `Regex` class exists in the `System.Text.RegularExpressions` namespace, our first line of code imports the proper namespace so that we can refer to the `Regex` class without fully qualifying it (line 1). On lines 4 through 6, a string, `str`, is hard-coded with a quote from Ayn Rand. Next, on line 9, an instance of the `Regex` class is created. This instance, `regexp`, is created with the `Regex` constructor that takes two parameters, the pattern and options strings. The pattern `"A is A"` will simply match the substring `"A is A"`; the option `RegexOptions.IgnoreCase` indicates that the search should not be case sensitive.

On line 11, the `IsMatch` method is used to check if the substring "A is A" exists in the string `str` (line 11). `IsMatch` returns a Boolean value: `True` if the pattern is found in the passed-in string, `False` otherwise. If the substring "A is A" is found in `str`, "This is an Ayn Rand quote." is displayed; otherwise "I don't know who said this." is displayed. As you might have guessed, the output of Listing 2.3.1, when viewed through a browser, is "This is an Ayn Rand quote.".

As mentioned earlier, there is also a static version of the `IsMatch` method. The static version takes either two or three parameters. The first parameter is the input string, the second is the regular expression pattern, and the third option parameter is the options string for the regular expression. In Listing 2.3.1, line 9 could be snipped and line 11 replaced with the following:

```
If Regex.IsMatch(str, "A is A", RegexOptions.IgnoreCase) then
```

Finding out whether a regular expression pattern exists in a string is all well and good, but being able to grab a listing of substrings that matched would be ideal. The `Matches` method of the `Regex` has such functionality. The non-static version of the method expects a single parameter, the string to search, and returns the resulting matches as a `MatchCollection`.

Listing 2.3.2 uses the `Matches` method to list all the text between the bold tags in an HTML document. This code borrows some file-reading code from Listing 2.2.2 to read in the contents of a text file on the Web server. The output is shown in Figure 2.13.

LISTING 2.3.2 The `Matches` Method Will Return All the Matching Regular Expression Patterns in a String

```
 1: <%@ Import Namespace="System.IO" %>
 2: <%@ Import Namespace="System.Text.RegularExpressions" %>
 3: <script language="VB" runat="server">
 4:   Sub Page_Load(sender as Object, e as EventArgs)
 5:     'Read in the contents of the file strFilePath
 6:     Dim strFilePath as String = "C:\Inetpub\wwwroot\Index.htm"
 7:     Dim objFileInfo as FileInfo = new FileInfo(strFilePath)
 8:     Dim objStream as StreamReader = objFileInfo.OpenText()
 9:     Dim strContents as String = objStream.ReadToEnd()
10:     objStream.Close()
11:
12:     'List the text between the bold tags:
13:     Dim regexp as Regex = New Regex("<b>((.|\n)*?)</b>",
➥ RegexOptions.IgnoreCase)
14:
15:     Response.Write("<u><b>Items Between Bold Tags in the HTML page " & _
16:                    strFilePath & ":</b></u><br>")
17:
18:     'Create a Match object instance / iterate through the MatchCollection
19:     Dim objMatch as Match
20:     For Each objMatch in regexp.Matches(strContents)
21:        Response.Write("<li>" & objMatch.ToString() & "<br>")
22:     Next
23:   End Sub
24: </script>
```

FIGURE 2.13
The HTML text between (and including) each bold tag pair is returned as its own Match object.

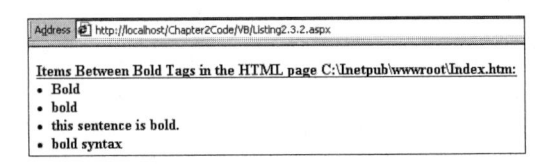

Listing 2.3.2 begins with two `Import` directives: the first imports the `System.IO` namespace to assist with our use of the `FileInfo` class (line 1); the second imports the `System.Text.RegularExpressions` namespace to assist with our use of the `Regex` and `Match` classes (line 2).

When the `Imports` are out of the way, Listing 2.3.2 starts by opening and reading the contents of a hard coded HTML file (lines 6 through 10). The contents of this HTML file are stored in the variable `strContents`. (This code snippet should look familiar—it's taken directly from Listing 2.2.2!)

Next, a regular expression instance is created with a pattern set to `<b>((.|\n)*?)</b>`. This might seem a bit confusing, especially if you are not very familiar with regular expressions. Translated to English, the pattern would read: "Find a bold tag (`<b>`), find zero or more characters, and then find a closing bold tag (`</b>`)." The period (`.`) is a special character in regular expressions, meaning, "Match any character except the new line character." The new line character is represented by `\n`, the asterisk (`*`) means to match zero or more characters, and the question mark following the asterisk means to perform "nongreedy" matching. For a more thorough explanation of all these terms, be sure to read *Picking Out Delimited Text with Regular Expressions*, available at `http://www.4guysfromrolla.com/webtech/103100-1.shtml`.

Note

If you are new to regular expressions the above regular expression may look quite confusing. To learn more about the basics of regular expressions be sure to check out Appendix B, and the "Other Resources" section at the end of this chapter.

When we have our regular expression object instance, we're ready to call the `Matches` method. The `Matches` method returns a `MatchCollection` class instance, which is, essentially, a collection of `Match` objects. The `Match` class contains various properties and methods that provide information on a particular match of a regular expression pattern in a string.

To iterate through the `MatchCollection`, we first create a `Match` instance, `objMatch`, on line 19. Next, a `For Each ... Next` loop is used to iterate through each resulting `Match` returned by the `Matches` method on the HTML contents of the file (line 20). On line 21, the matched text is outputted. Figure 2.13 shows the output of Listing 2.3.2 when the file `C:\Inetpub\wwwroot\Index.htm` contains the following text:

```
<html>
<head><title>Hello, World!</title></head>
<body bgcolor=white text=black>

    <b>Bold</b> text in HTML is defined using the <b>bold</b> tags:
    <code>&lt;b&gt; ... &lt;/b&gt;</code>.  For example, <b>this
```

```
sentence is bold.</b>  This sentence is not bold.  <i>This sentence
is in italics!</i>
<p>
To learn more about the <b>bold syntax</b>, read a book covering
HTML syntax in-depth!

</body>
</html>
```

Another useful task of regular expressions is their capability of doing powerful string replacements. For example, many Web sites have a searching feature in which the user enters a keyword on which to search and various results are returned. Wouldn't it be nice to have the words in the results that matched the search keyword to be highlighted?

Listing 2.3.3 contains the code for an ASP.NET page that allows the user to enter both a search term and some text that the search term will be applied to. Any instances of the search term are highlighted. The output is shown in Figure 2.14.

LISTING 2.3.3 Regular Expressions Perform Search and Replace Features on Complex Patterns

```
 1: <%@ Import Namespace="System.Text.RegularExpressions" %>
 2: <script language="VB" runat="server">
 3:   Sub btnSubmit_OnClick(sender as Object, e as EventArgs)
 4:     'Create a regex object
 5:     Dim strTerms as String = txtSearchTerms.Text
 6:     Dim regexp as Regex = new Regex("\b" & strTerms & "\b",
➥ RegexOptions.IgnoreCase)
 7:
 8:     'Replace all search terms in txtText
 9:     Dim strNewText as String = regexp.Replace(txtText.Text, _
10:       "<span style='color:black;background-color:yellow'>" &
➥ strTerms & "</span>")
11:
12:     lblResults.Text = "<p><hr><p><b><u>Search Results:</u></b><br>" &
➥ strNewText
13:   End Sub
14: </script>
15:
16: <html>
17: <body>
18:   <form runat="server">
19:     <b>Enter a search term:</b><br>
20:     <asp:textbox id="txtSearchTerms" runat="server" />
21:     <p>
22:     <b>Enter some text:</b><br>
23:     <asp:textbox id="txtText" runat="server" TextMode="MultiLine"
24:             Cols="50" Rows="6" />
25:     <p>
26:     <asp:button id="btnSubmit" runat="server" OnClick="btnSubmit_OnClick"
27:             text="Search Entered Text For Keyword" />
28:     <p><asp:label id="lblResults" runat="server" />
29:   </form>
30: </body>
31: </html>
```

FIGURE 2.14
Search terms found in the text are highlighted.

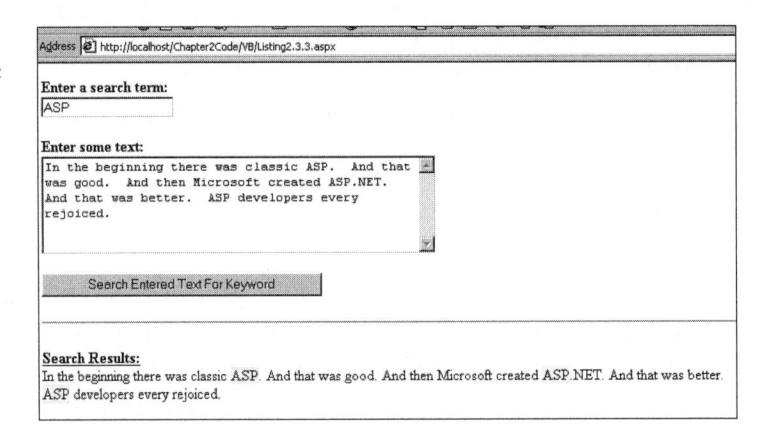

Listing 2.3.3 is another code example that doesn't contain a `Page_Load` event handler. Therefore, let's begin our examination with the HTML portion of the script (lines 16 through 31). Because Listing 2.3.3 uses postback forms, a server-side form is created on line 18. Next, a pair of text boxes are created: The first, `txtSearchTerms`, will be the text box the user enters his search term in (line 20); the second, `txtText`, is a multilined text box in which the user will enter the text to search (lines 23 and 24). On lines 26 and 27, a button control is created that, when clicked, will fire the `btnSubmit_OnClick` event handler. Finally, on line 28 a label control, `lblResults`, is created; this label control will display the user's text entered in `txtTerms` with all instances of the search term entered in `txtSearchTerms` highlighted.

The `btnSubmit_OnClick` function, starting at line 3, begins by reading in the value of the `txtSearchTerms` text box into a string variable, `strTerms` (line 5). Next, a `Regex` object instance is created with a pattern of the user-entered search term surrounded by `\b`. In regular expressions, `\b` is a special character representing a word boundary. Adding this both before and after the search term will have the effect of only highlighting search terms in the user-entered text that are their own words. That is, if the user enters a search term of "in" and the text, "I sleep in the incinerator," the word "in" will be highlighted, but the "in" in "incinerator" will not. Also, the `RegexOptions.IgnoreCase` option is specified, indicating that the search and replace will be non case-sensitive (line 6).

On lines 9 and 10, the `Replace` method of the `Regex` class is used. The `Replace` method accepts two parameters: the string to search for the pattern and the string to replace any found matches. In English, lines 9 and 10 say, "Search the contents of `txtText.Text` looking for any matches to the pattern (the search term as its own word). If you find any, replace it with a highlighted version of the search term."

The `Replace` method returns a string that has had all matches in its first parameter replaced by the second. On line 9 we set this return string equal to the variable `strNewText`. Finally, line 12 outputs the highlighted results, `strNewText`.

The `Regex` class contains a number of other useful methods. One really neat method that I encourage you to examine in detail on your own is the `Split` method. This method is similar to the `Split` method of the `String` class, except that instead of taking a string delimiter to split a string into an array, it accepts a regular expression as a delimiter!

4. Generating Images Dynamically

There are many real-world scenarios in which the ability to create graphic images on-the-fly is needed. For example, imagine that you had a database table with monthly profits. It would be nice to be able to allow a user to visit a reporting page and have a chart dynamically created as a GIF file on the Web server and seamlessly embedded into the reports ASP.NET page.

This was an impossible task in classic ASP without the use of a third-party component (or without some very ugly and hacked-together code). With ASP.NET, though, creating images on-the-fly in a wide variety of formats is quite possible and easy, thanks to the inherent support of image generation in the .NET Framework.

The .NET Framework contains an extensive drawing API, offering a multitude of classes with an array of methods and properties for drawing all sorts of shapes and figures. In fact, there is such an assortment of drawing functions that an entire book could be dedicated to the topic. Therefore, we will only look at a few of the more useful drawing functions. I highly suggest that you take ample time to root through all the classes in the `System.Drawing` and its derivative namespaces. There are many classes within these namespaces with literally hundreds of methods and properties!

When an image is dynamically created using the .NET Framework, it is created as an in-memory image. Methods can be used to send this in-memory image to disk on the Web server or to a stream (such as the Response stream). In this section we'll examine both how to save an image to file on the Web server and how to send a dynamically created image to the user's browser!

Saving Dynamically Created Images on the Web Server

When creating images on-the-fly, the two most useful classes are the `Bitmap` and `Graphics` classes. The `Bitmap` class represents an instance of an image. The `Graphics` class contains the various methods for drawing lines, curves, ellipses, rectangles, and other geometric shapes.

Rather than presenting a lengthy tutorial on these two classes, let's look at a code example and then examine the methods and properties used to create a dynamic image. We will, of course, only be looking at a small subset of all the graphic functions. To learn more about the numerous graphic functions, refer to the `System.Drawing` namespace documentation in the .NET Framework Reference.

Listing 2.4.1 contains the code for a function that creates a very rudimentary bar chart and saves it as a file on the server. The function, `DrawBarGraph`, has the following definition:

```
DrawBarGraph(title, X_Data, Y_Data)
```

76 ASP.NET: TIPS, TUTORIALS, AND CODE

The first parameter, *title*, is of type String and is used to give a title to the chart. *X_Data* and *Y_Data* are both `ArrayLists`: *X_Data* contains the X-axis labels for each data point, whereas *Y_Data* contains each data point (and needs to be an integral value). Lines 57 through 72 in Listing 2.4.1 illustrate how to set up the data points and call the `DrawBarGraph` function. Although Listing 2.4.1 uses hard-coded values for the X and Y axes, these values could have been easily pulled from a database. The output is shown in Figure 2.15.

LISTING 2.4.1 With the .NET Framework You Can Create a Bar Chart On-the-Fly

```
 1: <%@ Import Namespace="System.Drawing" %>
 2: <%@ Import Namespace="System.Drawing.Imaging" %>
 3: <script language="VB" runat="server">
 4:   Sub DrawBarGraph(strTitle as String, aX as ArrayList, aY as ArrayList)
 5:     Const iColWidth as Integer = 60, iColSpace as Integer = 25, _
 6:           iMaxHeight as Integer = 400, iHeightSpace as Integer = 25, _
 7:           iXLegendSpace as Integer = 30, iTitleSpace as Integer = 50
 8:     Dim iMaxWidth as Integer = (iColWidth + iColSpace) *
➥ aX.Count + iColSpace, _
 9:           iMaxColHeight as Integer = 0, _
10:           iTotalHeight as Integer = iMaxHeight + iXLegendSpace + iTitleSpace
11:
12:     Dim objBitmap as Bitmap = new Bitmap(iMaxWidth, iTotalHeight)
13:     Dim objGraphics as Graphics = Graphics.FromImage(objBitmap)
14:
15:     objGraphics.FillRectangle(new SolidBrush(Color.White), _
16:                               0, 0, iMaxWidth, iTotalHeight)
17:     objGraphics.FillRectangle(new SolidBrush(Color.Ivory), _
18:                               0, 0, iMaxWidth, iMaxHeight)
19:
20:     ' find the maximum value
21:     Dim iValue as Integer
22:     For Each iValue in aY
23:       If iValue > iMaxColHeight then iMaxColHeight = iValue
24:     Next
25:
26:     Dim iBarX as Integer = iColSpace, iCurrentHeight as Integer
27:     Dim objBrush as SolidBrush = new SolidBrush(Color.FromArgb(70,20,20))
28:     Dim fontLegend as Font = new Font("Arial", 11), _
29:         fontValues as Font = new Font("Arial", 8), _
30:         fontTitle as Font = new Font("Arial", 24)
31:
32:     ' loop through and draw each bar
33:     Dim iLoop as Integer
34:     For iLoop = 0 to aX.Count - 1
35:       iCurrentHeight = ((Convert.ToDouble(aY(iLoop)) /
➥ Convert.ToDouble(iMaxColHeight)) * _
36:                        Convert.ToDouble(iMaxHeight - iHeightSpace))
37:
38:       objGraphics.FillRectangle(objBrush, iBarX, _
39:             iMaxHeight - iCurrentHeight, iColWidth, iCurrentHeight)
```

LISTING 2.4.1 *Continued*

```
40:        objGraphics.DrawString(aX(iLoop), fontLegend, objBrush, _
➥ iBarX, iMaxHeight)
41:        objGraphics.DrawString(String.Format("{0:#,###}", aY(iLoop)), _
➥ fontValues, objBrush, iBarX, _
42:                              iMaxHeight - iCurrentHeight - 15)
43:
44:        iBarX += (iColSpace + iColWidth)
45:     Next
46:
47:     objGraphics.DrawString(strTitle, fontTitle, objBrush, _
48:              (iMaxWidth / 2) - strTitle.Length * 6, _
➥ iMaxHeight + iXLegendSpace)
49:     objBitmap.Save("C:\inetpub\wwwroot\graph.gif", ImageFormat.Gif)
50:
51:     objGraphics.Dispose()
52:     objBitmap.Dispose()
53:  End Sub
54:
55:
56:  Sub Page_Load(sender as Object, e as EventArgs)
57:     Dim aMonths as ArrayList = new ArrayList(), _
58:         aProfits as ArrayList = new ArrayList()
59:
60:     aMonths.Add("January")
61:     aMonths.Add("February")
62:     aMonths.Add("March")
63:     aMonths.Add("April")
64:     aMonths.Add("May")
65:
66:     aProfits.Add(240500)
67:     aProfits.Add(220950)
68:     aProfits.Add(283500)
69:     aProfits.Add(340000)
70:     aProfits.Add(325750)
71:
72:     DrawBarGraph("Profits!", aMonths, aProfits)
73:  End Sub
74: </script>
```

Listing 2.4.1 begins with two `Import` directives that are useful when creating images on-the-fly. Line 1 imports the `System.Drawing` namespace, which contains most of the many classes we use in the code: `Bitmap`, `Graphics`, `Font`, `SolidBrush`, and so on. Line 2 imports the `System.Drawing.Imaging` namespace, which contains the `ImageFormat` class that we use on line 49 to save the bar chart as a GIF image file.

The `DrawBarGraph` function begins on line 4, defined to accept three parameters: a string title, an `ArrayList` of labels for the X axis, and an `ArrayList` of data points. Next, on lines 5 through 7, a number of useful constants are defined, and on lines 8 through 10, the variables we'll need for this function are created and assigned values.

FIGURE 2.15
A bar chart with company profits has been dynamically created.

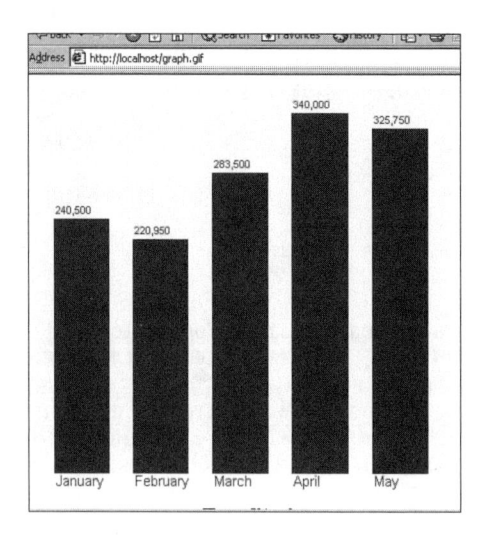

On line 12, an instance of the `Bitmap` class is created. The version of the `Bitmap` constructor we've used in this example expects two integer values, a width and a height, which are defined by `iMaxWidth` and `iTotalHeight` in our example. Next, on line 13, an instance of the `Graphics` class is created. The `Graphics` class does not contain a constructor; rather, to get an instance of the `Graphics` class, we must use the static method `FromImage`. `FromImage` expects an `Image` object as its lone parameter and returns a `Graphics` object. (Because the `Bitmap` class is derived from the `Image` class, we can simply pass our `Bitmap` instance, `objBitmap`, to the `FromImage` method.)

On line 15, the entire image is painted white using the `FillRectangle` method of the `Graphics` class. Keep in mind that the `Graphics` class contains the various functions to draw lines, rectangles, ellipses, and other geometric shapes. All these functions require either a `Pen` or `Brush` instance, depending on whether a line or filled image is being drawn. On line 17 another rectangle is drawn with the `FillRectangle` method, this one serving as the backdrop for the graphed data. For more information on the `FillRectangle` method (or for information on the `Brush` and `SolidBrush` classes), be sure to refer to the .NET Framework Documentation.

Because we only have a fixed height to draw all the bars in the bar graph, we must first determine the largest value in our set of data points so that we can scale all the data points relative to the largest one. On lines 21 through 24, a simple `For Each ... Next` loop is used to iterate through the `ArrayList` of data points to find the largest value. This largest value is stored in `iMaxColHeight` (line 23).

Lines 26 through 30 define the variables we'll need for the actual graphing of the bar chart. Line 27 creates a dark red solid brush; lines 28 through 30 create three instances of the `Font` class, each of the Arial font family with varying point sizes. The font instances `fontLegend`, `fontValues`, and `fontTitle` are used to write the X-axis labels (represented by the values in `aX`), the data point values, and the title of the chart, respectively.

The code in lines 34 through 45 does the actual work of creating the graph. Line 34 starts a `For ... Next` loop to iterate through each element of the `aX ArrayList`. It is essential that the X-axis label `ArrayList` (aX) and the data points `ArrayList` (aY) contain the same number of elements. Furthermore, realize that `aX(N)` represents the X-axis label for data point `aY(N)`.

With each iteration of the loop, we will be drawing a particular bar in the bar chart. Lines 35 and 36 calculate the height for the current bar; this height is relative to the tallest bar in the bar chart. A ratio is derived with `Convert.ToDouble(aY(iLoop)) / Convert.ToDouble(iMaxColHeight)`, which is then multiplied with the highest bar chart value to obtain the scaled height for the current bar.

On lines 38 and 39, the actual bar is drawn with the `FillRectangle` method. Line 40 draws the X-axis label at the bottom of the bar, whereas lines 41 and 42 draw the data point value at the top of the bar. This function assumes that the values of the data points are going to be numeric and, based on that assumption, formats the value using the `String.Format` method (line 41). Finally, line 44 increments the current x position, `iBarX`.

By the time the code execution reaches line 47, all the bars have been drawn and labeled. Line 47 simply adds the bar chart title to the image. Line 49 uses the `Save` method of the `Image` class (which the `Bitmap` class inherits). In Listing 2.4.1, the `Save` method expects two parameters: The first parameter it expects needs to be a string that represents the full path of the file to save to image to; the second parameter must be an instance of the `ImageFormat` class. The `ImageFormat` class defines the low-level details on how an image is to be physically stored. A number of static properties of the `ImageFormat` class return `ImageFormat` instances. A listing of these image formats can be seen in Table 2.3.

TABLE 2.3 The `ImageFormat` Class Contains a Number of Properties Representing Various Image Formats

Property	Description
Bmp	Specifies a bitmap image
Emf	Specifies the Windows enhanced metafile image format
Exif	Specifies the Exchangeable Image Format
Gif	Specifies the GIF image format
Icon	Specifies a Windows icon image format
Jpeg	Specifies the JPEG image format
MemoryBmp	Specifies the memory bitmap image format
Png	Specifies the PNG image format
Tiff	Specifies the TIFF image format
Wmf	Specifies the Windows metafile image format

After line 49 has executed, the bar chart has been saved as a file to the Web server, indicated by the path specified as the first parameter to the `Save` method. To conclude our `DrawBarChart` function, we clean up the resources used by calling the `Dispose` method for the `Graphics` class and `Bitmap` class instances.

In Listing 2.4.1, the `DrawBarChart` function is called from the `Page_Load` event handler. Before calling the function, however, two `ArrayList`s must be built and populated with the X-axis labels and data points. These two `ArrayList`s are created in Listing 2.4.1 on lines 57 and 58. The X-axis labels are populated in lines 60 through 64; the data points are assigned in lines 66 through 70. On line 72, the `DrawBarChart` function is called and passed the two `ArrayList`s along with the chart's title, "Profits!"

Sending Dynamically Created Images to the Browser

In the previous section, we examined how to create and save a dynamic image to the Web server's file system through an ASP.NET page. Although this capability is quite useful, at times it would be nice to bypass this step and stream the dynamically created image directly to the Web visitor's browser.

Fortunately, this is possible with the `Save` method of the `Image` class. In Listing 2.4.1, we looked at one use of the `Save` method, passing it a file path on the Web server and an `ImageFormat`. The `Save` method can also accept a `Stream` object as its first parameter; in doing so, the `Save` method will send the output of the image to the stream as opposed to disk.

With ASP.NET, the `Response` object has a number of new properties and methods. One such property is the `OutputStream` property, which provides programmatic access to the binary data being sent to the client's browser. The `Save` method of the `Image` class can use the `Response` object's `OutputStream` property to send a dynamically created, in-memory image directly to the client! Listing 2.4.2 contains a short code example in which a standard advertising banner is created on-the-fly and squirted to the user's browser.

LISTING 2.4.2 Dynamically Created Images Can Be Sent Directly to the User's Browser

```
 1: <%@ Import Namespace="System.Drawing" %>
 2: <%@ Import Namespace="System.Drawing.Imaging" %>
 3: <script language="VB" runat="server">
 4: Sub Page_Load(sender as Object, e as EventArgs)
 5:    Dim objBitmap as Bitmap = new Bitmap(468, 60)
 6:    Dim objGraphics as Graphics = Graphics.FromImage(objBitmap)
 7:    Dim objBrush as SolidBrush = new SolidBrush(Color.FromArgb(0,80,80)), _
 8:       objBlackBrush as SolidBrush = new SolidBrush(Color.Black), _
 9:       objYellowBrush as SolidBrush = new SolidBrush(Color.Yellow)
10:
11:    Dim fontTitle as Font = new Font("Arial", 24), _
12:       fontSubtitle as Font = new Font("Arial Black", 9)
13:
14:    objGraphics.FillRectangle(new SolidBrush(Color.Ivory), 0, 0, 468, 60)
15:    objGraphics.DrawString("When you think ASP, think...", _
```

LISTING 2.4.2   Continued

```
16:                           fontSubtitle, objBlackBrush, 5, 8)
17:    objGraphics.DrawString("4GuysFromRolla.com", fontTitle, objBrush, 10, 20)
18:
19:    ' Draw a smiley face.. first draw the yellow circle!
20:    objGraphics.FillEllipse(objYellowBrush, 375, 5, 50, 50)
21:
22:    ' Now create the eyes.
23:    objGraphics.FillEllipse(objBlackBrush, 387, 20, 6, 6)
24:    objGraphics.FillEllipse(objBlackBrush, 407, 20, 6, 6)
25:
26:    ' And finally the smile.
27:    Dim aPoints(3) as Point
28:    aPoints(0).X = 383 : aPoints(0).Y = 35
29:    aPoints(1).X = 395 : aPoints(1).Y = 45
30:    aPoints(2).X = 405 : aPoints(2).Y = 45
31:    aPoints(3).X = 417 : aPoints(3).Y = 35
32:    objGraphics.DrawCurve(new Pen(Color.Black), aPoints)
33:
34:    Response.ContentType = "image/jpeg"
35:    objBitmap.Save(Response.OutputStream, ImageFormat.JPEG)
36:
37:    objGraphics.Dispose()
38:    objBitmap.Dispose()
39: End Sub
40: </script>
```

Listing 2.4.2 begins as Listing 2.4.1 did: by Importing the System.Drawing and System.Drawing.Imaging namespaces. Next, in the Page_Load event handler, a 468×60 Bitmap instance is created (the dimensions of the standard advertising banner; on line 5). On line 6, a Graphics instance is created and instantiated with the Graphics.FromImage method. On lines 7 through 9, a number of SolidBrushes are created and instantiated; lines 11 and 12 create the two Fonts we'll be using.

From lines 14 through 32, a number of Graphics methods are called to create the image. Finally, after the image is created, it's time to send it to the browser. Before we send the actual binary content to the browser, however, we set the binary data's ContentType as "image/jpeg" (line 34). This ContentType informs the browser how to display the binary information that it is receiving.

To actually send the binary data of the image, we use the Save method. Note that, on line 35, instead of specifying a filename as the first parameter, we specify the Stream to write the image to. Because we want to send the image to the browser, we specify that the OutputStream of the Response object be used. Also, the image should be converted and sent as a JPEG. Listing 2.4.2 concludes with a little housecleaning on lines 37 and 38.

One way to view the dynamically created image in Listing 2.4.2 is to visit the ASP.NET page that creates it and squirts it out to the OutputStream of the Response object. Figure 2.16 depicts a browser visiting the ASP.NET page directly.

FIGURE 2.16
The dynamically created image can be viewed by directly visiting the ASP.NET page.

Ideally, it would be nice to be able to display both content and the dynamically generated graphic on the same page. This, however, cannot be done through the same ASP.NET page; for example, if you were to add `Response.Write("Hello, World!")` in line 33 of Listing 2.4.2, instead of seeing an image when visiting the ASP.NET page, you'd see a broken image link. Essentially, this is because the browser is being sent `"Hello, World!"` and then the binary data for the image, and it assumes that the `"Hello, World"` is part of the binary data for the image.

If you want to display both textual content and a dynamically created image, you must create a standard HTML or ASP.NET page and then refer to the dynamic image content using HTML `IMG` tags. Listing 2.4.3 contains a very short example of an ASP.NET page that displays HTML content and the dynamic image created in Listing 2.4.2. `Listing2.4.2.aspx`, the ASP.NET page that creates the image, is referred to in the `IMG` tag as if it were a JPG image itself. Figure 2.17 contains a screenshot of Listing 2.4.3 when viewed through a browser.

LISTING 2.4.3 To View a Dynamically Created Image from an HTML Page, Use the `IMG` tag

```
 1: <html>
 2: <body>
 3:    <h1>Hello, World!</h1>
 4:    Here is a picture of my banner!
 5:    <p>
 6:    <img src="Listing2.4.2.aspx" border="1"
 7:         alt="Dynamically created banner!">
 8: </body>
 9: </html>
```

FIGURE 2.17
The output of Listing 2.4.3, when viewed through a browser.

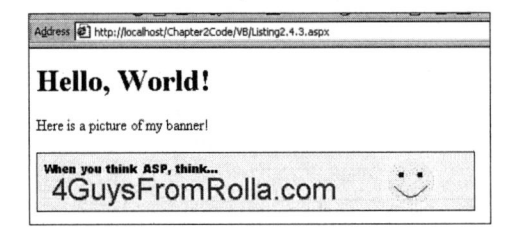

> **Tip**
>
> When viewing a dynamically created image from an ASP.NET page through an `IMG` tag, you can pass parameters through the QueryString such as: `<img src="`*`ASP.NET_Page`*`.aspx?id=4">`. The ASP.NET page can then read the QueryString value and alter its actions based on such information!

5. Sending Email from an ASP.NET Page

With classic ASP, there were a variety of ways to send an email from an ASP page. Microsoft included its own free component, *CDONTS (Collaborative Data Object for NT Server)*, but there were also a number of commercially (and freely) available third-party emailing components.

The .NET Framework contains two classes (found in the `System.Web.Mail` namespace) to assist with sending email. The first class, `MailMessage`, defines the various properties of the email message itself, such as the email message body, the sender, the receiver, the subject, the priority, and so on. The second class, `SmtpMail`, performs the work of actually sending the email message. To send emails through an ASP.NET page, you will need to have the SMTP Service installed on your Web server. This is a standard installation option when installing IIS.

Listing 2.5.1 depicts a very simple product information request form. The user can enter his name and email address to receive further product information by email. Upon submission of the form, an email is sent to the user providing information on the various product lines.

LISTING 2.5.1 The .NET Framework Provides Inherent Email-Sending Support

```
 1: <%@ Import Namespace="System.Web.Mail" %>
 2: <script language="VB" runat="server">
 3: Sub btnSubmit_OnClick(sender as Object, e as EventArgs)
 4:    'Send an email address with product information
 5:    Dim objMessage as New MailMessage
 6:    objMessage.BodyFormat = MailFormat.Html
 7:    objMessage.To = txtEmail.Text & " (" & txtName.Text & ")"
 8:    objMessage.From = "webmaster@acme.com (Product Information)"
 9:    objMessage.Headers.Add("Reply-To", "questions@acme.com")
10:    objMessage.Priority = MailPriority.High
11:    objMessage.Subject = "Product Information Request"
12:
13:    objMessage.Body = "<i>Hello " & txtName.Text & "</i>!  To learn more
➥ about our " & _
14:                    "various products, visit the following URLs:<p><ul>" & _
15:                    "<li><a href=""http://www.acme.com/Widgets.htm"">
➥ Widgets</a>" & _
```

LISTING 2.5.1 Continued

```
16:                    "<li><a href=""http://www.acme.com/DooHickies.htm"">
➥ DooHickies</a>" & _
17:                    "<li><a href=""http://www.acme.com/TAMB.htm"">
➥ Thning-a-ma-Bobs</a>" & _
18:                    "</ul><p> If you have any " & _
19:                    "questions, please simply reply to this email!
➥ <p><hr><p>" & _
20:                    "<font color=red size=-1><i>Thank you for choosing Acme!
➥ </i></font>"
21:
22:
23:     'Send the message
24:     SmtpMail.Send(objMessage)
25:
26:     'Display notification of mail being sent
27:     Response.Write("<font color=red><b>You have been sent " & _
28:                    "product information!  Thank you!</b></font>")
29: End Sub
30: </script>
31:
32: <html>
33: <body>
34:   <form method=post runat=server>
35:     <h1>Information Request</h1>
36:     <b>Your Name:</b>
37:     <asp:textbox id="txtName" runat="server" /><br>
38:     <b>Your Email Address:</b>
39:     <asp:textbox id="txtEmail" runat="server" /><p>
40:
41:     <asp:button id="btnSubmit" runat="server" OnClick="btnSubmit_OnClick"
42:                 text="Send me Product Information" />
43:   </form>
44: </body>
45: </html>
```

Listing 2.5.1 starts by importing the namespace that the `MailMessage` and `SmtpMail` classes exist under: `System.Web.Mail`. Because there is no `Page_Load` event handler, let's next move on to examining the HTML content from line 32 through line 45. Note that a postback, server-side form control is used (line 34). Next, two text boxes are created: The first, `txtName`, is for the user's name (line 37), whereas the second, `txtEmail` is for the user's email address (line 39). Finally, a button control is used on lines 41 and 42. When clicked, the form will be posted back and the `btnSubmit_OnClick` event handler will fire.

The `btnSubmit_OnClick` event handler (lines 3 through 29), sends an email to the email address specified by the user in the `txtEmail` text box. As mentioned earlier, sending emails involves two classes, `MailMessage` and `SmtpMail`. On line 5 a new instance of the `MailMessage` class is created and, in lines 6 through 20, some of its many properties are set.

Some of the properties for the `MailMessage` include a `BodyFormat` property (line 6), which can be set to either `MailFormat.Text` or `MailFormat.Html`. On line 7 and 8, we set the `To` and `From` email addresses using the following format:

```
Email-address (Display Name)
```

Many email clients will pick out the text between the parentheses and display that in the From section of the email message as opposed to the actual email address itself. On line 9 we access the `Headers` property of the `MailMessage` class. This property is an `IDictionary` interface, meaning that it can be treated similar to a `Hashtable`. On line 9 we add the `Reply-To` header to the outgoing email address so that if the user replies to the product information-request email, it will be sent to questions@acme.com as opposed to webmaster@acme.com. Next, the `Priority` of the message is set. This property can be set to one of three values: `MailPriority.Low`, `MailPriority.Normal` (the default), or `MailPriority.High`. Line 11 sets the email's subject, whereas line 13 defines the HTML-formatted body for the email message.

If you've worked with the CDONTS component with classic ASP, you'll no doubt feel at home with the properties of the `MailMessage` class. The `MailMessage` and CDONTS component are almost syntactically identical. One major difference, however, is that the `MailMessage` class does not encompass any functionality for sending a message. That, instead, is left up to the `SmtpMail` class.

The `SmtpMail` class is a very bare-bones class. It's sole purpose is to send a `MailMessage` instance using the SMTP protocol. It contains a single shared function, `Send`, which expects a `MailMessage` object instance. Line 24 illustrates the use of the `Send` method.

Finally, on lines 27 and 28, a message is displayed indicating to the user that he can expect to receive an email with product information. Figure 2.18 contains a screenshot of Listing 2.5.1 after the user has entered his name and email address. Figure 2.19 contains a screenshot of the email received by the user. Note that a high priority is set; the email is displayed as coming from Product Information as opposed to just webmaster@acme.com; the email is addressed to the user's name, not to his email address; and the email is HTML-formatted.

FIGURE 2.18
The output of Listing 2.5.1, when viewed through a browser.

FIGURE 2.19
An HTML-formatted, high priority email is sent to the user with information on Acme products.

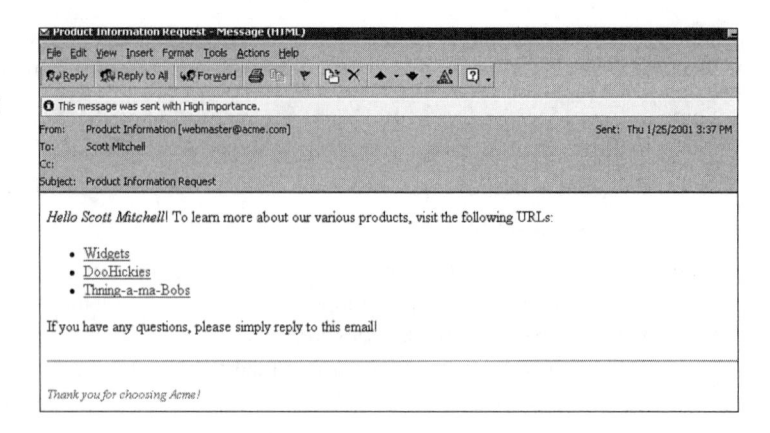

6. Network Access via an ASP.NET Page

With classic ASP, performing network access through an ASP page was impossible without the use of a third-party or custom-developed COM component. For example, grabbing the HTML output of a Web page on a remote Web server via an ASP page was only possible with a component of some kind, such as ASPHTTP from ServerObjects.com. The .NET Framework, however, contains a plethora of classes to assist with network access. These numerous classes are all located in the `System.Net` namespace.

A very common need for Web developers is the ability to grab the HTML content of a Web page on a remote server. Perhaps the developer wants to perform a *screen scrape*, grabbing specific portions of the HTML output to integrate into his own Web page. To assist in this task, the .NET Framework provides an easy-to-use class—`WebClient`—that can be used for accessing information over the Internet.

Listing 2.6.1 contains a "Poor Man's Internet Explorer," a browser within a browser. The code in Listing 2.6.1, when viewed through a browser presents the user with a text box in to which he can enter a fully qualified URL (such as `http://www.4GuysFromRolla.com`). After the user enters a URL and clicks the Go button, the Web page he entered is displayed along with the Response and Request headers. Output is shown in Figure 2.20.

LISTING 2.6.1   The .NET Framework Provides Internet Access from an ASP.NET Page

```
1: <%@ Import Namespace="System.Net" %>
2: <script language="VB" runat="server">
3:    Sub btnSubmit_OnClick(sender as Object, e as EventArgs)
4:       'Create a WebClient instance
5:       Dim objWebClient as New WebClient()
6:
```

LISTING 2.6.1 Continued

```
 7:    Dim strHeader as String
 8:    lblHTML.Text = "<b>Request Header Information:</b><br>"
 9:    For Each strHeader in objWebClient.Headers
10:      lblHTML.Text &= strHeader & " - " & _
11:                     objWebClient.Headers(strHeader) & "<br>"
12:    Next
13:
14:    'Read the Response into an array of bytes, but use the UTF8Encoding
15:    'class to convert the byte array into a string
16:    Dim objUTF8 as New UTF8Encoding()
17:    Dim strRequestedHTML as String
18:    strRequestedHTML =
➥ objUTF8.GetString(objWebClient.DownloadData(txtURL.Text))
19:
20:
21:    lblHTML.Text &= "<p><b>Response Header Information:</b><br>"
22:    For Each strHeader in objWebClient.ResponseHeaders
23:      lblHTML.Text &= strHeader & " - " & _
24:                     objWebClient.ResponseHeaders(strHeader) & "<br>"
25:    Next
26:
27:    'Output the contents of the Web request
28:    lblHTML.Text &= strRequestedHTML
29:
30:  End Sub
31: </script>
32:
33: <html>
34: <body>
35:   <form runat="server">
36:     <font size=+1><b>Poor Man's Internet Explorer</b></font>
37:     <br>Browse the Web:
38:     <asp:textbox id="txtURL" runat="server" /><br>
39:     <i>Enter a URL starting with <code>http://</code></i><br>
40:     <asp:button id="btnSubmit" runat="server" Text="  Go!  "
41:                 OnClick="btnSubmit_OnClick" />
42:
43:     <p><hr><p>
44:     <asp:label id="lblHTML" runat="server" />
45:   </form>
46: </body>
47: </html>
```

Listing 2.6.1 starts out with some familiar lines of code. Line 1 `Imports` the `System.Net` namespace, which contains the `WebClient` class that we'll be using.

FIGURE 2.20
This ASP.NET page acts like an extremely simple browser.

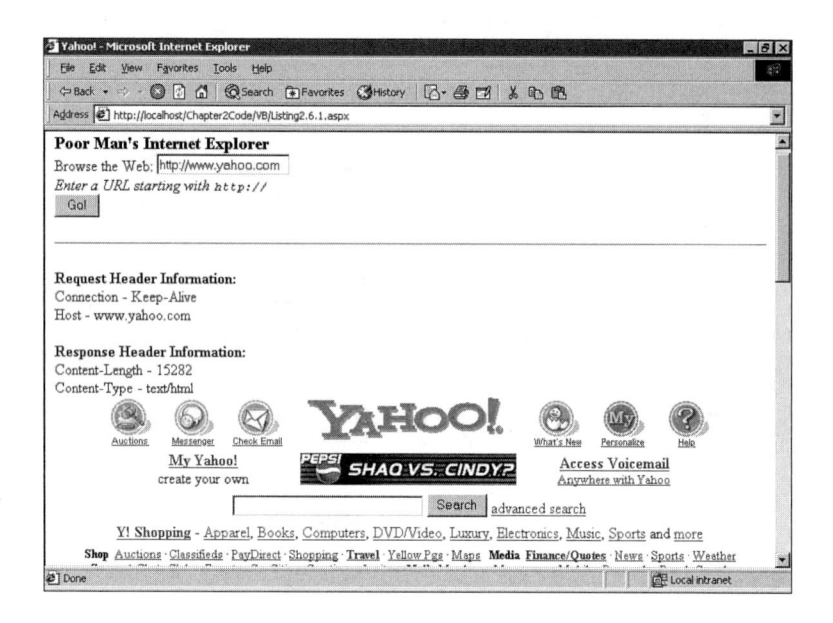

Because Listing 2.6.1 contains no `Page_Load` event handler, let's start our examination of the code with the HTML content. On line 35 a postback form is created. Inside this form are two form elements: a text box, `txtURL`, into which the user will enter the URL she wants to visit (line 38); and a Go button, `btnSubmit`, for the user to click to load the entered URL (lines 40 and 41). Note that the button has its `OnClick` event wired up to the `btnSubmit_OnClick` event handler. When this button is clicked, the form will be submitted; when the page reloads, the `btnSubmit_OnClick` event handler will execute.

The `btnSubmit_OnClick` event handler, starting on line 3, is responsible for grabbing the HTML from the URL entered by the user in the `txtURL` text box. To grab the HTML at the URL specified by the user, we need to simply create an instance of the `WebClient` class and call its `DownloadData` method.

Whenever a client sends an HTTP request to the server, a number of optional headers are usually passed along with various bits of information. Likewise, when the server returns the content to the client, a number of headers can be sent along with the data. (These headers are referred to as request headers and response headers, respectively.) The `WebClient` class has both `Headers` and `ResponseHeaders` properties, for reading the request and response headers, respectively. These properties are instances of the `WebHeadersCollection` class, which represents a collection of `WebHeaders` classes. Through this property, a developer can programmatically send request headers and iterate through the response headers.

To explicitly send a header to the server when making a Web request from an ASP.NET page, simply use the `Add` method of the `WebHeadersCollection` class to add a new request header:

`WebClientInstance.Headers.Add(HeaderName, HeaderValue);`

Therefore, if you wanted to add the specific request header `Foo: Bar`, in Listing 2.6.1 you would need to add the following line of code before line 18 (where the actual Web request is initiated).

`ObjWebClient.Headers.Add("Foo", "Bar");`

Recall that the `Headers` property returns a `WebHeadersCollection` class instance. The `WebHeadersCollection` class is derived from the `NameValueCollection` class, which means that we can treat the `Headers` property similar to an ordinary `Hashtable` collection. On lines 9 through 12, the request headers are displayed using a `For Each` loop. On lines 22 through 25, the response headers are displayed in a similar fashion.

> **Note**
>
> Take a moment to examine Figure 2.20. Note that there are no request headers being sent. This is because the `WebClient` class does not implicitly set any request headers. That is, if you wish any request headers to be sent along, you must explicitly supply them.

Next, we need to actually do the work of downloading the HTML for the requested URL. This is accomplished via the `WebClient` class's `DownloadData` method (line 18). This method accepts a single parameter, the URL of the content to retrieve, and returns an array of bytes containing the result of the Web request. Since we'd rather deal with a String than an array of bytes, on line 16 a `UTF8Encoding` class is instantiated and, on line 18, the `GetString` method is used to convert the array of bytes returned by `DownloadData` into a String, which is then assigned to the variable `strRequestedHTML` (line 18). Listing 2.6.1 concludes by listing the response headers (lines 22 through 25) and *then* outputting `strRequestedHTML` (line 28).

Another useful class in the `System.Net` namespace is the `DNS` class. (This capability was not possible in classic ASP without the use of a third-party component.) This class can be used to resolve DNS hostnames into IP addresses. Such a technique could be used to verify email addresses by ensuring that the domain name specified by the user actually resolved to an existing domain name.

Listing 2.6.2 illustrates how to use the `DNS` classes `Resolve` method, along with a regular expression, to build a fairly reliable email address validation ASP.NET page. Of course the only way to *truly guarantee* that a user has entered his own valid email address is to require him to respond to a confirmation email message. However, the technique shown in Listing 2.6.2 is more reliable than *just* checking the email address against a regular expression.

LISTING 2.6.2 ASP.NET Provides Built-In DNS Resolving Support

```
 1: <%@ Import Namespace="System.Net" %>
 2: <%@ Import Namespace="System.Net.Sockets" %>
 3: <%@ Import Namespace="System.Text.RegularExpressions" %>
 4: <script language="VB" runat="server">
 5:   Sub btnSubmit_OnClick(sender as Object, e as EventArgs)
 6:     'Check to make sure that the email addy is in the right form
 7:     Dim strEmail as String, strPattern as String
 8:     strEmail = txtEmail.Text
 9:     strPattern = "^[\w-_\.]+\@([\w]+\.)+\w+$"
10:
11:     If Not Regex.IsMatch(strEmail, strPattern,
➥ RegexOptions.IgnoreCase) then
12:       'Invalid email address form!
13:       Response.Write("<font color=red><i>Your email address is in an" & _
14:                      " illegal format.</i></font><p>")
15:     Else
16:       'Check to see if the domain name entered in the email address exists
17:       Dim strDomain as String
18:       strDomain = strEmail.Substring(strEmail.IndexOf("@") + 1)
19:
20:       'Attempt to Resolve the hostname
21:       Dim strIP as String
22:       try
23:         strIP = DNS.Resolve(strDomain).AddressList(0)ToString()
24:
25:         'If we reach here, we have a valid email address, so do whatever
26:         'processing or whatnot needs to be done...
27:         Response.Write("<b>Valid email address.  Your domain name has " & _
28:                        "an IP of " & strIP & ".  Thank you!</b>")
29:       catch se as SocketException
30:         'The DNS resolve was unsuccessful...
31:         strIP = se.Message
32:
33:         Response.Write("<font color=red><i>" & strIP & "</i></font><p>")
35:       end try
36:     End If
37:   End Sub
38: </script>
39:
40: <html>
41: <body>
42:   <form runat="server">
43:     <br><b>Enter your Email address:</b>
44:     <asp:textbox id="txtEmail" runat="server" />
45:     <p>
46:     <asp:button id="btnSubmit" runat="server" Text="Check Email"
47:                 OnClick="btnSubmit_OnClick" />
48:   </form>
49: </body>
50: </html>
```

Listing 2.6.2 begins by `Import`ing three namespaces: `System.Net`, which contains the definition for the `DNS` class; `System.Net.Sockets`, which contains the definition for the `SocketException` class that we'll need to use if the user enters an email address with an invalid domain name; and `System.Text.RegularExpressions` because we are going to use a regular expression to ensure that the email address is in the proper format.

The code in Listing 2.6.2 creates a postback form with a text box, `txtEmail`, for the user to enter his email address (lines 42 and 44, respectively). The page also displays a button titled Check Email, which, when clicked, will submit the form, causing the `btnSubmit_OnClick` event handler to fire. This button, `btnSubmit`, is created on lines 46 and 47.

The task of the `btnSubmit_OnClick` event handler is to ensure that the user has entered a valid email address. We begin by reading the value of the `txtEmail` text box in to a String variable, `strEmail` (line 8). Then, on line 9, we create a regular expression pattern, `strPattern`, which, in short, looks for one or more characters preceding the @ sign, followed by one or more of a number of characters followed by a period, and then followed by another grouping of one or more characters. Whew, that sounds overly complex! Basically we are trying to ensure that the user has entered the following:

SomeCharacters@(SomeCharacters.(ONE OR MORE TIMES))SomeCharacters

Next, on line 11, we call the static version of the `IsMatch` method of the `Regex` class to determine if our pattern is found in the email address. If it is *not*, lines 12 through 14 are executed, which displays an error message. If the pattern is found, the code following the `Else` statement on line 15 is executed.

> **Note**
>
> We could have simply used a `RegularExpressionValidator` control in our HTML document to ensure that the email address was valid. For more information on the `RegularExpressionValidator` control, refer to Chapter 3.

If the email address is in the proper format, all that is left to do is ensure that the domain name portion of the email address is valid. To do this, we must first snip out the domain name from the email address, which we do on line 18 using the `Substring` and `IndexOf` methods of the `String` class. When we have the domain name, we are ready to try to resolve it in to an IP address—if we can resolve the domain name in to an IP address, the domain name is valid; otherwise it is invalid.

The `Resolve` method of the `DNS` class resolves a domain name (in the form of a string) into an instance of the `IPHostEntry` class, which contains a list of `IPAddress` class instances (`AddressList`) that express the domain name in an IP address. If the domain name cannot be resolved into an IP address, a `SocketException` is thrown. For that reason, we must have the call to the `Resolve` method in a `Try ... Catch` block. On line 22 we begin the `Try ... Catch` block and, on line 23, make a call to `Resolve`, a static method. Because the `Resolve` method returns an `IPAddress` instance, we must call the `ToString()` method of the `IPAddress` class before assigning it to our string variable, `strIP`.

If the domain name is successfully resolved into an IP address, line 27 will be reached, where a message is displayed informing the user that his email address is valid (and also displaying the resolved IP address). If, however, the domain name was not resolved to an IP address, the `Catch` portion of the `Try ... Catch` block will be reached (line 29). On line 31, `strIP` is assigned to the value of the `Message` property of the `SocketException` exception. On line 33, this `Message` is displayed as an error message to the user.

Figures 2.21, 2.22, and 2.23 show the output of Listing 2.6.2 for various scenarios. Figure 2.21 shows the error message a user will receive if she enters her email address in an invalid format. Figure 2.22 depicts the output the user will be presented with if he enters an invalid domain name in his email address. Finally, Figure 2.23 shows the output of Listing 2.6.2 when the user enters an email address in a valid format with a valid domain name.

FIGURE 2.21
The user has entered an invalid email address.

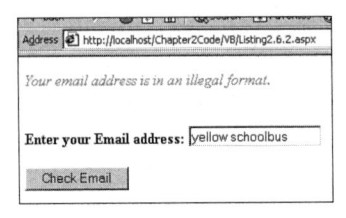

FIGURE 2.22
This user has entered an invalid domain name in her email address.

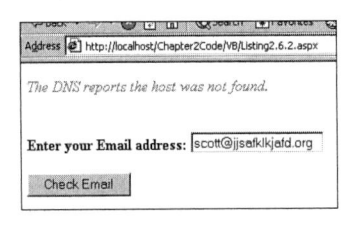

FIGURE 2.23
The user has entered a valid email address.

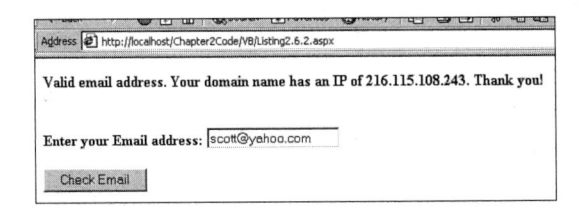

Understand that a clever user could easily bypass this check system by entering an invalid username portion of his email address with a valid domain name. For example, the domain name `yahoo.com` is, of course, valid. However, I suspect the username `ThisIsAReallyLongNameAndIAmTryingToProveAPoint` is not a registered `@yahoo` email address. Therefore, if a user were to enter the following:

`ThisIsAReallyLongNameAndIAmTryingToProveAPoint@yahoo.com`

the script would identify that email address as valid, even though it clearly does not really exist. As aforementioned, if you must guarantee that a user enters a valid email address, it is imperative that you send him a confirmation email and require him to respond.

7. Uploading Files from the Browser to the Web Server via an ASP.NET Page

Whether a user on Monster.com needs to upload her resume, or a GeoCities member wants to upload his personal Web site, there are a vast number of practical scenarios in which the ability for a visitor to upload a file (or files) from his computer to the Web site is essential. With classic ASP, this task usually fell on the shoulders of a third-party component, such as ASPUpload (`http://www.aspupload.com/`) or SoftArtisan's SA-FileUp (`http://www.softartisans.com/`). With ASP.NET, however, file upload capabilities are available without the need for any third-party component.

> **Note**
> To learn more about file uploading, make sure to check out the "Other Resources" section at the end of this chapter!

When uploading a file from an HTML form, there are a few guidelines you must follow. First, and most importantly, you must specify the `multipart/form-data` encoding type in the form tag. This encoding type is specified in the form tag in the following syntax:

```
<form ... enctype="multipart/form-data" ...>
```

Next, you must provide an `INPUT` form element that has its `TYPE` property set to `FILE`. These types of `INPUT` form elements are displayed in a user's browser as a text box that contains a Browse button next to it. If the user clicks the Browse button, she will be able to select a file from her hard drive. When she does, the filename will appear in the associated text box. The following HTML would generate such a file upload text box with an accompanying Browse button:

```
<form enctype="multipart/form-data" method="post">
    <input type="file" name="fupUpload">
</form>
```

Because the previous snippet of code is simply HTML, you could easily add such code to a classic ASP page. The problem was actually retrieving the contents of the uploaded file and saving it to the Web server. Although this could be done with script alone, the implementation was usually difficult and messy enough to warrant the use of a third-party component. (For information on a script-only upload scenario with classic ASP, be sure to read `http://www.asp101.com/articles/jacob/scriptupload.asp`.)

94 ASP.NET: TIPS, TUTORIALS, AND CODE

> **Note**
> The complete documentation for uploading files through an HTML form can be found in RFC 1867, "Form-based File Upload in HTML," at http://www.ietf.org/rfc/rfc1867.txt.

With ASP.NET, an entire class exists to handle the uploaded file and its contents. This class, `HttpPostedFile`, enables a developer to either programmatically save the uploaded file on the Web server's file system or to access the contents of the uploaded file via a `Stream`. In this section we'll look at two examples: The first example demonstrates how to provide a form to allow the user to upload a file and have it saved on the Web server; the second example illustrates an ASP.NET page that accepts an uploaded image and reports the image's properties. (When examining the second example, note that the image is never saved to the Web server's file system.)

Saving an Uploaded File to the Web Server's File System

When viewed through a browser, Listing 2.7.1 presents the user with a text box and Browse button, enabling the user to select a file from her hard drive that she wanted to upload to the Web server. If the user attempts to upload a file that does not exist, a warning message will be displayed. If, however, the user enters a valid filename (either by typing it in the text box or selecting the file via the Browse button) and the file is successfully saved on the Web server, a confirmation message will be displayed, and the user will be presented with a link to view the uploaded content through the Web server. (Refer to Figure 2.24 to see a screenshot of the user's browser after successfully uploading a file.)

LISTING 2.7.1 Component-less File Upload Is Possible via an ASP.NET Page

```
 1:  <%@ Import Namespace="System.IO" %>
 2:  <script language="VB" runat="server">
 3:    Sub btnSubmit(sender as Object, e as EventArgs)
 4:      'Has the file been uploaded properly?
 5:      If Not fupUpload.PostedFile Is Nothing Then
 6:        'Save the file if it has a filename and exists...
 7:        If fupUpload.PostedFile.FileName.Trim().Length > 0 AND _
 8:           fupUpload.PostedFile.ContentLength > 0 then
 9:
10:          Const strBaseDir as String = "C:\My Projects\Uploaded Files\"
11:          Dim strFileName as String = _
12:                Path.GetFileName(fupUpload.PostedFile.FileName)
13:
14:          fupUpload.PostedFile.SaveAs(strBaseDir & strFileName)
15:
16:          'File has been saved!
17:          lblResults.Text = "<hr><p>Your file, " & _
➥ fupUpload.PostedFile.FileName & _
18:                           ", has been saved to the Web server!<br>" & _
```

LISTING 2.7.1 Continued

```
19:                           "[<a href=""/Upload/" & strFileName & """>
➥ View File</a>]"
20:        End If
21:      Else
22:        lblResults.Text = "<hr><p>Enter a filename to upload!"
23:      End If
24:    End Sub
25: </script>
26:
27: <html>
28: <body>
29:    <form runat="server" EncType="multipart/form-data">
30:      <h1>File Upload</h1>
31:      <b>Select the file to upload:</b><br>
32:      <input runat="server" id="fupUpload" type="file" >
33:      <p>
34:      <asp:button id="btnSubmit" runat="server" Text="Upload File"
➥OnClick="btnSubmit_Click"/>
35:      <p><asp:label runat="server" id="lblResults" />
36:    </form>
37: </body>
38: </html>
```

FIGURE 2.24
A file has been uploaded from the user's hard drive to the Web server's hard drive.

Listing 2.7.1 begins by Importing the System.IO namespace. This namespace is imported because, on line 12, the GetFileName method of the Path class is used to snip out the filename of the uploaded file. No namespaces need to be imported to use those classes that assist with browser-based file uploads.

We have a btnSubmit_Click event handler in this ASP.NET page that runs when the btnSubmit button has been clicked. Before we discuss this event handler, let's first examine the HTML content from lines 27 through 38. This content begins with form tag that has both the runat="server" attribute set as well as the enctype="multipart/form-data" setting (line 29). It is vitally important that this enctype parameter be included in the form tag, or else the file upload will not work.

Next, on line 32, a file upload HTML control is created with the `id fupUpload`. Note that its `type` property is set to `file`; again, it is essential that this `INPUT` tag have its `type` property set to `file` for the file upload to work properly. It is important to set the `runat="server"` property of the `INPUT` tag so that you can programmatically access the uploaded file. On line 34 a button control, `btnSubmit`, exists. When this is clicked, the form will be submitted. Finally, on line 35, a label control, `lblResults`, is created, which will display a success message after the file is uploaded from the client's machine to the Web server.

The `btnSubmit_Click` event handler begins on line 3 and immediately checks to ensure that the `PostedFile` property of the `fupUpload` file upload control is assigned a value. `PostedFile` is a property of the `HtmlInputFile` class and represents the file uploaded from the client to the Web server.

This `PostedFile` property is an instance of the `HttpPostedFile` class. The `HttpPostedFile` class has four very useful properties:

- `ContentLength`—Represents the size, in bytes, of the uploaded file.
- `ContentType`—Represents the MIME content type of the uploaded file.
- `FileName`—Represents the full path and filename on the client's computer of the uploaded file.
- `InputStream`—Provides a `Stream` instance for access to the uploaded file's bits.

If the form has been posted back and the `PostedFile` property is not equal to `Nothing`, the code between lines 6 and 20 will execute. If either of these conditions is `False`, line 22 will execute, displaying a message to the user to enter a filename to upload.

Line 7 performs one more check on the validity of the file selected by the user for uploading. It checks to ensure that the user has not typed in a filename that does not correspond to a file on his hard drive (by checking that the `ContentLength` property of the `PostedFile` property is greater than zero). Furthermore, line 7 checks to ensure that the user did not enter a blank filename in the file upload text box. Assuming that these conditions are met, the code from lines 10 through 19 is executed. This is the code that performs the actual work of saving the uploaded file to the Web server's file system.

On line 10 the constant `strBaseDir` is assigned the directory to save the uploaded files in. Next, on lines 11 and 12, the filename portion of the uploaded file is snipped out from the `FileName` property of the `PostedFile` property and assigned to the variable `strFileName`. If the user selected to upload the file `C:\Resume\MyResume.doc`, the `FileName` property would be equal to `C:\Resume\MyResume.doc`. Because we already know what directory in which we want to save the file, we simply want just the name of the file (without the path). The `System.IO` namespace contains a `Path` class that contains a number of static methods to extract various bits of information from a file or directory path. One of these methods, `GetFileName`, can be used to quickly snare this portion of the `FileName` property (line 12).

Next, on line 14, the uploaded file is saved to the Web server's file system. The `SaveAs` method of the `HttpPostedFile` class expects a single parameter: the physical path to upload the file to (directory name and file name). Finally, we want to display a message to the user letting him know that his file has been successfully uploaded. Lines 17 through 19 accomplish this task, providing a link to the uploaded file.

> **Note**
>
> If you want the uploaded files to be Web accessible, you must upload them to a Web accessible directory. For this example, I created a virtual directory named `/Upload` that pointed to `C:\My Projects\Uploaded Files\`.

Working Directly with an Uploaded File

Listing 2.7.1 illustrated how to upload a file from the client to the Web server and then save this file to the Web server's file system. This is useful for scenarios in which you want the user and, perhaps, other visitors to be able to access the uploaded content at a later date. But what if you only needed to perform some task with the uploaded data and then no longer needed it? Why bother saving it to the file system at all?

The `InputStream` property of the `HttpPostedFile` class provides direct access to the contents of the uploaded file in the form of a `Stream`. Therefore, a developer can programmatically access this information as opposed to saving the file first, if he so desires.

Listing 2.7.2 illustrates accessing an uploaded file via the `InputStream`. Listing 2.7.2 allows the user to upload an image file and then displays information about the image, such as its dimensions, resolution, and file type.

LISTING 2.7.2   Developers Can Programmatically Access the Uploaded File's Contents

```
 1: <%@ Import Namespace="System.IO" %>
 2: <%@ Import Namespace="System.Drawing" %>
 3: <%@ Import Namespace="System.Drawing.Imaging" %>
 4: <script language="VB" runat="server">
 5: Sub btnSubmit_OnClick(sender as Object, e as EventArgs)
 6:    'Read in the uploaded file into a Stream
 7:    Dim objStream as Stream = fupUpload.PostedFile.InputStream
 8:    Dim objImage as System.Drawing.Image = _
 9:             System.Drawing.Image.FromStream(objStream)
10:
11:    'List the properties of the Image
12:    Dim strFileName as String = fupUpload.PostedFile.FileName
13:    lblImageProps.Text = "<hr><p><b>Uploaded File:</b> " & strFileName & _
14:       "<br><b>Type:</b> "
15:
16:    'Determine the file type
17:    If objImage.RawFormat.Equals(ImageFormat.Gif) then
➥ lblImageProps.Text &= "GIF"
18:    If objImage.RawFormat.Equals(ImageFormat.Bmp) then
➥ lblImageProps.Text &= "BMP"
```

LISTING 2.7.2 Continued

```
19:    If objImage.RawFormat.Equals(ImageFormat.Jpeg) then
➥ lblImageProps.Text &= "JPEG"
20:    If objImage.RawFormat.Equals(ImageFormat.Icon) then
➥ lblImageProps.Text &= "Icon"
21:    If objImage.RawFormat.Equals(ImageFormat.Tiff) then
➥ lblImageProps.Text &= "TIFF"
22:
23:    lblImageProps.Text &= "<br><b>Dimensions:</b> " & objImage.Width & _
24:        " x " & objImage.Height & " pixels<br><b>Size:</b> " & _
25:        objStream.Length & " bytes<br>" & "<b>Horizontal
➥ Resolution:</b> " & _
26:        objImage.HorizontalResolution & _
27:        " pixels per inch<br><b>Vertical Resolution:</b> " & _
28:        objImage.VerticalResolution & " pixels per inch" & _
29:        "<p><img src=""" & strFileName & """>"
30:
31:    objImage.Dispose()
32: End Sub
33: </script>
34:
35: <html>
36: <body>
37:    <form runat="server" EncType="multipart/form-data">
38:      <h1>Image Converter</h1>
39:      <b>Select an image file:</b><br>
40:      <input runat="server" id="fupUpload" type="file">
41:      <p>
42:      <asp:button id="btnSubmit" runat="server" Text="Get Image Info"
43:              OnClick="btnSubmit_OnClick" />
44:
45:      <p><asp:label id="lblImageProps" runat="server" />
46:    </form>
47: </body>
48: </html>
```

Listing 2.7.2 begins, as many of our examples have thus far, with a number of `Import` directives. Because we will be dealing with the `Stream` class, the `System.IO` namespace is imported (line 1). Likewise, because Listing 2.7.2 will need to be able to determine an image's various properties, we will need to work with the `Image` and `ImageFormat` classes, which require the `System.Drawing` and `System.Drawing.Imaging` namespaces, respectively.

Because Listing 2.7.2 does not contain the `Page_Load` event handler, let's begin our examination of the code starting with the HTML content (lines 35 through 48). (This HTML content is very similar to the HTML content presented in the earlier listing.) We start by creating a postback form that contains the always important `enctype="multipart/form-data"` property (line 37). Next, a file upload HTML control is created on line 40. A button control, `btnSubmit`, is created on lines 42 and 43; note that the button's `OnClick` event is wired up to the `btnSubmit_OnClick` event handler, which we'll examine shortly. Finally, on line 45, there is a label control that will be used to display the uploaded image file's properties.

The HTML content defined from line 35 through line 48 will present the user with an upload form field (a text box with the accompanying Browse button). After the user selects a file and clicks the Get Image Info button, the form will be submitted, the selected image file will be uploaded to the server, and the `btnSubmit_OnClick` event handler will fire, displaying the properties of the uploaded image file.

The `btnSubmit_OnClick` event handler begins on line 5 and starts by assigning a `Stream` variable, `objStream`, to the `Stream` instance returned by the `InputStream` property (line 7). At this point, the contents of the uploaded file are accessible via the `objStream` variable. Next, on line 8, an `Image` class variable is created and assigned the value returned from the `FromStream` method of the `Image` class. (Recall that the `Image` class is abstract, and therefore cannot be instantiated with the `new` keyword.)

Now that we have an `Image` class instance representing the uploaded image file, we can go ahead and list its properties. On line 12 we assign the `FileName` property of the `PostedFile` property to the variable `strFileName`. Next, this variable is displayed in the `lblImageProps` label control (lines 13 and 14).

Next, on lines 16 through 21, we check to determine the file type of the uploaded image. The `RawFormat` property of the `Image` class returns an instance of the `ImageFormat` class that represents the file format of the image. The `Equals` method is a method of the `Image` class (inherited from the `Object` class) that checks to determine if two `Objects` are equivalent. We check the return value of the `RawFormat` property against the various `ImageFormat` types to determine the file type of the upload image.

In lines 23 through 29, we output the various properties of the `Image` class: the `Height`, `Width`, file size (`Length` property of the `Stream` class), `HorizontalResolution`, and `VerticalResolution`. We also output an `IMG` tag with the `SRC` property specifying the path to the image on the client's computer. Finally, on line 31, we clean up the resources claimed by the `objImage` class.

Figure 2.25 shows the output of Listing 2.7.2 after a user has selected an image file from his hard drive. Keep in mind that the uploaded image file is never saved to the Web server's file system.

FIGURE 2.25
This ASP.NET page provides information about an image on the user's hard drive.

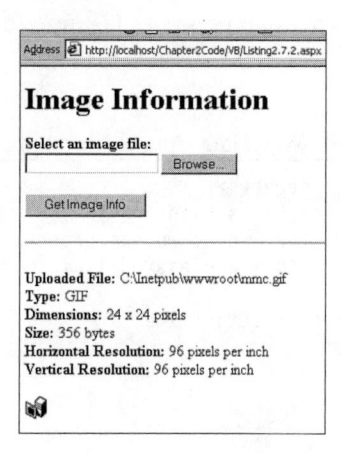

8. Using `ProcessInfo`: Retrieving Information About a Process

One of the biggest benefits of ASP.NET over classic ASP, in my opinion, is ASP.NET's capability to automatically restart itself based on programmatically defined conditions. With classic ASP, developers often felt the need to reboot the Web server once a day (or week, or whatever) to ensure that things chunked along smoothly, free of any dreaded Server Too Busy errors.

Not only does ASP.NET allow the developer to set conditions on when to have the Web service restarted, but it also provides access to information on both the state of the currently running `aspnet_wp.exe` process and previously running instances! (The `aspnet_wp.exe` process is the process that is responsible for handling calls to ASP.NET pages, similar to `asp.dll` with classic ASP.) This means that, through an ASP.NET page, you can determine your Web site's uptime, find out why the `aspnet_wp.exe` process might have restarted itself, or see how much memory the current `aspnet_wp.exe` process has consumed.

> **Note**
> To learn more about configuring ASP.NET to automatically restart itself when certain criteria are met be sure to read Chapter 11, "ASP.NET Deployment and Configuration."

All these tasks are handled through a pair of classes: `ProcessInfo` and `ProcessModelInfo`. The `ProcessInfo` class handles information about a specific instance of the `aspnet_wp.exe` process, whereas the `ProcessModelInfo` class provides access to information on both current and past instances of the process.

Displaying Information for the Currently Executing `aspnet_wp.exe` Process

Listing 2.8.1 shows how to use these two classes to retrieve information about the currently executing `aspnet_wp.exe` process. Because this ASP.NET page returns information such as memory consumed by the `aspnet_wp.exe` process (see Figure 2.26) and the current uptime, it could be used as a monitoring page for the site's Web master.

LISTING 2.8.1 Gather Information on the Web Site's Uptime Through an ASP.NET Page

```
1: <script language="VB" runat="server">
2: Sub Page_Load(sender as Object, e as EventArgs)
3:   'Display information about the aspnet_wp.exe process
4:   Dim objProcInfo as ProcessInfo = ProcessModelInfo.GetCurrentProcessInfo()
5:
6:   lblStartTime.Text = objProcInfo.StartTime
```

LISTING 2.8.1 Continued

```
 7:    lblAge.Text = String.Format("{0:0.##}", objProcInfo.Age.TotalHours) & " hours"
 8:    Select Case objProcInfo.Status
 9:      Case ProcessStatus.Alive:
10:        lblStatus.Text = "Alive"
11:      Case ProcessStatus.ShutDown:
12:        lblStatus.Text = "Shut down"
13:      Case ProcessStatus.ShuttingDown:
14:        lblStatus.Text = "Currently shutting down"
15:      Case ProcessStatus.Terminated:
16:        lblStatus.Text = "Terminated"
17:    End Select
18:
19:    lblProcessID.Text = objProcInfo.ProcessID
20:    lblPeakMemoryUsed.Text = String.Format("{0:#,###}",
➥ objProcInfo.PeakMemoryUsed) & " K"
21: End Sub
22: </script>
23:
24: <html>
25: <body>
26:    <table align="center" border="1" cellspacing="0" cellpadding="5">
27:      <tr>
28:        <th colspan=2>
29:          <code>aspnet_wp.exe</code> Process Information
30:        </th>
31:      </tr>
32:      <tr>
33:        <td>Start Time</td>
34:        <td><asp:label runat="server" id="lblStartTime" /></td>
35:      </tr>
36:      <tr>
37:        <td>Age</td>
38:        <td><asp:label runat="server" id="lblAge" /></td>
39:      </tr>
40:      <tr>
41:        <td>Status</td>
42:        <td><asp:label runat="server" id="lblStatus" /></td>
43:      </tr>
44:      <tr>
45:        <td>ProcessID</td>
46:        <td><asp:label runat="server" id="lblProcessID" /></td>
47:      </tr>
48:      <tr>
49:        <td>Peak Memory Used</td>
50:        <td><asp:label runat="server" id="lblPeakMemoryUsed" /></td>
51:      </tr>
52:    </table>
53: </body>
54: </html>
```

FIGURE 2.26
Information about the currently executing `aspnet_wp.exe` process is displayed.

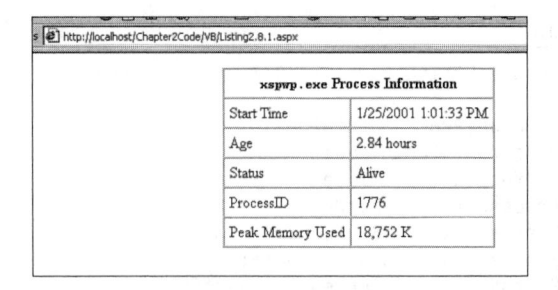

xspwp.exe Process Information	
Start Time	1/25/2001 1:01:33 PM
Age	2.84 hours
Status	Alive
ProcessID	1776
Peak Memory Used	18,752 K

The code in Listing 2.8.1 is fairly straightforward. It simply grabs the information about the currently executing `aspnet_wp.exe` process and displays its information in an HTML table. To accomplish this, we must first create an instance of the `ProcessInfo` class (line 4). To get information about the currently executing `aspnet_wp.exe` process, though, we must make a call to the `GetCurrentProcessInfo` method of the `ProcessModelInfo` class (line 4). After line 4 has executed, the `objProcInfo` variable has been assigned to a `ProcessInfo` instance populated with the information on the currently executing `aspnet_wp.exe` process.

Lines 7 through 20 simply display the various properties of the `ProcessInfo` class. On line 6, the start time of the currently executing `aspnet_wp.exe` process is displayed; next, on line 7, the number of hours the process has been running is displayed. The `Status` property of the `ProcessInfo` class returns a `ProcessStatus` enumeration representing the status of the currently executing process. On lines 8 through 17, a `Select Case` is used to display an English representation of this numeric property. Finally, on lines 19 and 20, the `ProcessID` and `PeakMemoryUsed` properties are displayed. The HTML from lines 24 through 54 simply display an HTML table with a number of label controls to represent the various properties of the `ProcessInfo` class.

Displaying Information for Past Instances of the `aspnet_wp.exe` Process

The `ProcessModelInfo` has another handy method, `GetHistory`, which returns information on a specified number of past instances of the `aspnet_wp.exe` process. This means that you can, after a Web service restart, view the cause of the restart from an ASP.NET page! The `GetHistory` method expects one parameter, an integer representing the number of past instances to return; the method returns an array of `ProcessInfo` instances.

Listing 2.8.2 provides an ASP.NET page in which the user can enter how many Web service restarts back he wants to view. The past (and current) processes are listed displaying when they started, how long they ran for, and why they were shut down. As with Listing 2.8.2, this ASP.NET page would make a very handy tool for a Web site's administrator. The output is shown in Figure 2.27.

LISTING 2.8.2 The `ProcessModelInfo` Class Can Provide Information on Past Instances of the `aspnet_wp.exe` Process

```vb
 1: <script language="VB" runat="server">
 2:   Sub Page_Load(sender as Object, e as EventArgs)
 3:     Dim iCount as Integer = 10
 4:
 5:     If Not Page.IsPostBack Then
 6:       'View the last 10 restart reasons
 7:       txtCount.Text = iCount
 8:     Else
 9:       'View the recounts defined by txtCount
10:       iCount = txtCount.Text.ToInt32()
11:     End If
12:
13:     'Display the reasons for the last iCount restarts
14:     Dim aProcInfos() as ProcessInfo = ProcessModelInfo.GetHistory(iCount)
15:     Dim objProcInfo as ProcessInfo
16:
17:     lblProcHistory.Text = ""
18:     For Each objProcInfo in aProcInfos
19:       lblProcHistory.Text &= "<b>Process " & objProcInfo.ProcessID & _
20:         "</b><br><li>Started At: " & objProcInfo.StartTime & "<br>" & _
21:         "<li>Duration: " & _
22:         String.Format("{0:0.##}", 
➥ objProcInfo.Age.TotalHours) &
➥ " hours<br>" & _
23:         "<li>Shutdown Reason: " & 
➥ DisplayReason(objProcInfo.ShutdownReason) & _
24:         "<p>"
25:     Next
26:
27:     Dim objCurrentProc as ProcessInfo = 
➥ ProcessModelInfo.GetCurrentProcessInfo()
28:     lblCurrentProc.Text = "<i>The current process is running 
➥ under Process ID " & _
29:       objCurrentProc.ProcessID & "</i>"
30:   End Sub
31:
32:   Function DisplayReason(enumReason as ProcessShutdownReason) as String
33:     Select Case enumReason
34:       Case ProcessShutdownReason.IdleTimeout:
35:         DisplayReason = "Idle Timeout"
36:       Case ProcessShutdownReason.MemoryLimitExceeded:
37:         DisplayReason = "Memory Limit Exceeded"
38:       Case ProcessShutdownReason.None:
39:         DisplayReason = "None"
40:       Case ProcessShutdownReason.RequestQueueLimit:
41:         DisplayReason = "Request Queue Limit"
42:       Case ProcessShutdownReason.RequestsLimit:
43:         DisplayReason = "Requests Limit"
44:       Case ProcessShutdownReason.Timeout:
45:         DisplayReason = "Timeout"
```

LISTING 2.8.2 Continued

```
46:        Case ProcessShutdownReason.Unexpected:
47:            DisplayReason = "Unknown"
48:      End Select
49:   End Function
50: </script>
51:
52: <html>
53: <body>
54:    <form runat="server">
55:       <h1>Process Restart Reasons</h1>
56:       View last
57:       <asp:textbox id="txtCount" runat="server" Size="3" />
58:       restart reasons.
59:       <asp:button id="btnSubmit" runat="server" Text="View Reasons" />
60:       <hr>
61:       <asp:label runat="server" id="lblProcHistory" />
62:       <hr><asp:label id="lblCurrentProc" runat="server" />
63:    </form>
64: </body>
65: </html>
```

FIGURE 2.27
View information on the last N process invocations of **aspnet_wp.exe**.

Listing 2.8.2 begins by determining how many Web service restarts back to view information on. The variable `iCount` represents how many Web service restarts back to display. If the page is loaded for the first time, `iCount` will have a value of `10`. Otherwise, `iCount` will be set equal to the value specified by the user in the `txtCount` text box.

Next, on line 14, an array of `ProcessInfo` instances are retrieved by the `GetHistory` method of the `ProcessModelInfo` class. This array of `ProcessInfo` instances is then assigned to the variable `aProcInfos`. On lines 18 through 25, a `For Each ... Next` loop is used to iterate through each element of the array `aProcInfos`. Similar to the `Status` property we examined in Listing 2.8.1, the `ShutdownReason` property of the `ProcessInfo` class is an enumeration. Therefore, rather than displaying the numerical representation of the enumeration, we use a helper function, `DisplayReason`, that will provide an English-readable explanation of why the previous Web service restart occurred.

The HTML content, spanning lines 52 through 65, creates a postback form with a text box (line 57), a submit button (line 59), and a label control to display the process information (line 62). The text box, `txtCount`, allows the user to enter an exact number of past `aspnet_wp.exe` processes to review. When the button `btnSubmit` is clicked, the form is posted back; the `Page_Load` event handler will fire and set `iCount` to the value of `txtCount` (see line 10).

9. Accessing the Windows Event Log

Hopefully, by now you realize that there are a plethora of tasks you can do with ASP.NET which, with classic ASP, were impossible or extremely difficult without the use of a COM component. One such task that was not possible with just classic ASP was the ability to access the Windows event log. The .NET Framework, however, contains a number of classes that allow developers to both read and write to the event log!

This means that you can create an ASP.NET page through which a user could view event log history. Such functionality, coupled with the `ProcessInfo` ASP.NET page discussed in "Using `ProcessInfo`: Retrieving Information about a Process," could be used to create a very powerful remote administration tool for site information and maintenance purposes. Additionally, because an ASP.NET page can write entries to the event log, you could have various ASP.NET errors recorded to the Windows event log.

This section is broken down into two parts. In the first part, "Reading from the Event Log," we'll look at an ASP.NET page that displays the current entries from a selected log. In the second part, "Writing to the Event Log," we'll examine how to record events to the event log.

Reading from the Event Log

The .NET Framework contains a number of classes to read and write to the event log, all of which reside in the `System.Diagnostics` namespace. The main class that provides access to the event log is aptly named `EventLog`. Keep in mind that the Windows event log can contain many logs itself. Windows 2000 comes with three default logs: the Application log, the Security log, and the System log. The `EventLog` class can read and write to any of these various logs. In fact, the `EventLog` class can even be used to create new logs in the Windows event log.

> **Note**
>
> The `EventLog` class can be used to read and write to remote computers' Windows event logs as well as for the Web server's Windows event log. For more information on accessing remote event logs, refer to the documentation for the `EventLog` class.

Listing 2.9.1 shows a very simple ASP.NET page that displays the event log entries in the System event log that have been registered as errors. The output of Listing 2.9.1, when viewed through a browser, can be seen in Figure 2.28.

LISTING 2.9.1 The `EventLog` Class Provides Access to the Windows Event Log

```
 1: <%@ Import Namespace="System.Diagnostics" %>
 2: <script language="VB" runat="server">
 3:   Sub Page_Load(sender as Object, e as EventArgs)
 4:     Dim objEventLog as EventLog = New EventLog("System")
 5:
 6:     Dim objEntry as EventLogEntry
 7:     For Each objEntry in objEventLog.Entries
 8:       If objEntry.EntryType = EventLogEntryType.Error then
 9:         Response.Write(objEntry.TimeGenerated & " - " & _
10:                        objEntry.Source & " - " & _
11:                        objEntry.Message & "<br>")
12:       End If
13:     Next
14:   End Sub
15: </script>
```

FIGURE 2.28
Displays the error entries in the System log.

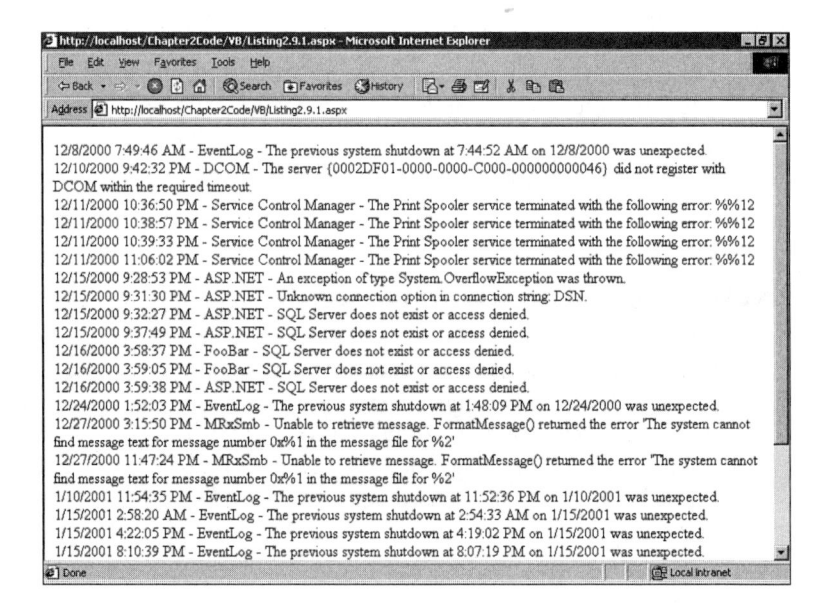

Listing 2.9.1 begins with an `Import` directive to include the namespace of the `EventLog` class, `System.Diagnostics`. In the `Page_Load` event handler, an instance of the `EventLog` class, `objEventLog`, is created (line 4). There are many forms of the `EventLog` constructor; on line 4, we used the one that expects a single String parameter specifying the log filename to open.

Each log in the Windows event log is composed of a number of entries. The .NET Framework provides an abstraction of each event log entry as a class, `EventLogEntry`. The `EventLog` class contains an `Entries` property that exposes a collection of `EventLogEntry` instances representing all the entries for a specific event log. On lines 7 through 13, we iterate through this collection using a `For Each ... Next` loop (line 7).

The `EventLogEntry` class contains a number of properties that represent an entry in the event log. One of these properties is `EntryType`, which indicates the type of event log entry. The possible values for this property are defined by the `EventLogEntryType` enumeration, and include values such as `Error`, `Information`, `Warning`, and others. One line 8, we check to determine if the current `EventLogEntry` instance in our `For Each ... Next` loop is an error entry. If it is, we display additional information about the entry (lines 9 through 11); otherwise, we skip on to the next entry.

Although viewing all the error entries for a particular log file might have plausible uses, we could easily create a much more graphically pleasing and easier-to-use interface without much effort. Listing 2.9.2 contains the code for an ASP.NET page that lists all the entries for a user-chosen log file. Furthermore, these event log entries are displayed through the creation of a dynamic HTML table using the various ASP.NET table controls. Figure 2.29 contains a screenshot of Listing 2.9.2 when viewed through a browser.

LISTING 2.9.2 The Complete Contents of a User-Chosen Event Log Are Displayed with Pretty Formatting

```
 1: <%@ Import Namespace="System.Diagnostics" %>
 2: <%@ Import Namespace="System.Drawing" %>
 3: <script language="VB" runat="server">
 4:   Sub Page_Load(sender as Object, e as EventArgs)
 5:     If Not Page.IsPostBack Then
 6:       DisplayEventLog("System")
 7:     End If
 8:   End Sub
 9:
10:   Sub btnSubmit_OnClick(sender as Object, e as EventArgs)
11:     DisplayEventLog(lstLog.SelectedItem.Value)
12:   End Sub
13:
14:   Sub btnClear_OnClick(sender as Object, e as EventArgs)
15:     'Clear all of the event log entries
16:     Dim objEventLog as New EventLog(lstLog.SelectedItem.Value)
17:     objEventLog.Clear()
18:   End Sub
19:
20:   Sub DisplayEventLog(strLogName as String)
21:     Dim objRow as New TableRow
22:     Dim objCell as New TableCell
23:
24:     objCell.BackColor = Color.Bisque
25:     objCell.HorizontalAlign = HorizontalAlign.Center
```

LISTING 2.9.2 *Continued*

```
26:       objCell.Text = "Type"
27:       objRow.Cells.Add(objCell)
28:
29:       objCell = New TableCell
30:       objCell.BackColor = Color.Bisque
31:       objCell.HorizontalAlign = HorizontalAlign.Center
32:       objCell.Text = "Date"
33:       objRow.Cells.Add(objCell)
34:
35:       objCell = New TableCell
36:       objCell.BackColor = Color.Bisque
37:       objCell.HorizontalAlign = HorizontalAlign.Center
38:       objCell.Text = "Time"
39:       objRow.Cells.Add(objCell)
40:
41:       objCell = New TableCell
42:       objCell.BackColor = Color.Bisque
43:       objCell.HorizontalAlign = HorizontalAlign.Center
44:       objCell.Text = "Source"
45:       objRow.Cells.Add(objCell)
46:
47:       objCell = New TableCell
48:       objCell.BackColor = Color.Bisque
49:       objCell.HorizontalAlign = HorizontalAlign.Center
50:       objCell.Text = "User"
51:       objRow.Cells.Add(objCell)
52:
53:       objCell = New TableCell
54:       objCell.BackColor = Color.Bisque
55:       objCell.HorizontalAlign = HorizontalAlign.Center
56:       objCell.Text = "Computer"
57:       objRow.Cells.Add(objCell)
58:
59:       tblLog.Rows.Add(objRow)
60:
61:
62:       Dim objEventLog as EventLog = New EventLog(strLogName)
63:       Dim objEntry as EventLogEntry
64:
65:       For Each objEntry in objEventLog.Entries
66:         objRow = New TableRow
67:         objCell = New TableCell
68:
69:         'Determine the type of error
70:         If objEntry.EntryType = EventLogEntryType.Error Then
71:           objCell.BackColor = Color.Red
72:           objCell.ForeColor = Color.White
73:           objCell.Text = "Error"
74:         ElseIf objEntry.EntryType = EventLogEntryType.Information Then
75:           objCell.Text = "Information"
76:         ElseIf objEntry.EntryType = EventLogEntryType.Warning Then
```

LISTING 2.9.2 *Continued*

```
 77:            objCell.BackColor = Color.Yellow
 78:            objCell.Text = "Warning"
 79:         ElseIf objEntry.EntryType = EventLogEntryType.SuccessAudit Then
 80:            objCell.Text = "Success Audit"
 81:         ElseIf objEntry.EntryType = EventLogEntryType.FailureAudit Then
 82:            objCell.ForeColor = Color.Red
 83:            objCell.Text = "Failure Audit"
 84:         End If
 85:         objCell.HorizontalAlign = HorizontalAlign.Center
 86:         objRow.Cells.Add(objCell)
 87:
 88:         objCell = New TableCell
 89:         objCell.Text = objEntry.TimeGenerated.ToShortDateString()
 90:         objRow.Cells.Add(objCell)
 91:
 92:         objCell = New TableCell
 93:         objCell.Text = objEntry.TimeGenerated.ToLongTimeString()
 94:         objRow.Cells.Add(objCell)
 95:
 96:         objCell = New TableCell
 97:         objCell.Text = objEntry.Source
 98:         objRow.Cells.Add(objCell)
 99:
100:         objCell = New TableCell
101:         If objEntry.UserName <> Nothing then
102:            objCell.Text = objEntry.UserName
103:         Else
104:            objCell.Text = "N/A"
105:         End If
106:         objRow.Cells.Add(objCell)
107:
108:         objCell = New TableCell
109:         objCell.Text = objEntry.MachineName
110:         objRow.Cells.Add(objCell)
111:
112:
113:         tblLog.Rows.Add(objRow)
114:      Next
115:   End Sub
116: </script>
117:
118: <html>
119: <body>
120:   <form runat="server">
121:     <h1>Event Log Viewer</h1>
122:     <asp:listbox runat="server" id="lstLog" Rows="1">
123:       <asp:listitem>Application</asp:listitem>
124:       <asp:listitem>Security</asp:listitem>
125:       <asp:listitem Selected="True">System</asp:listitem>
126:     </asp:listbox>
127:     <asp:button runat="server" id="btnSubmit" Text="Display Event Log"
```

LISTING 2.9.2   Continued

```
128:                        OnClick="btnSubmit_OnClick" />
129:     <hr>
130:     <asp:table runat="server" id="tblLog" CellPadding="5"
131:                CellSpacing="0" GridLines="Both" Font-Size="10pt"
132:                Font-Name="Verdana" />
133:     <hr>
134:     <asp:button runat="server" id="btnClear" Text="Clear Event Log"
135:                 OnClick="btnClear_OnClick" />
136:   </form>
137: </body>
138: </html>
```

FIGURE 2.29
Listing 2.9.2 displays an event log's entries through an ASP.NET page.

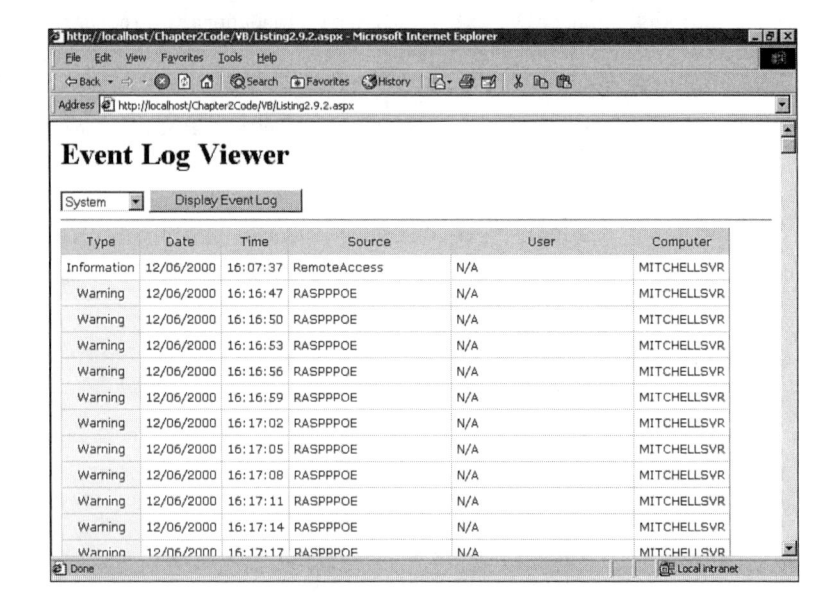

Listing 2.9.2 begins by Importing two namespaces: System.Diagnositics, for the EventLog and EventLogEntry classes (line 1); and System.Drawing, for the Color structure that is used to set the foreground and background colors of the table cells (line 2). When the page is loaded for the first time, the Page_Load event handler will fire and line 6 will be reached, in which case the DisplayEventLog subroutine will be called to display the entries in the System log.

The DisplayEventLog subroutine, spanning from line 20 through line 115, displays all the entries for the event log specified by strLogName in a nice format. This format is in the form of an HTML table and created via the ASP.NET table controls (the Table, TableRow, and TableCell Web controls). (For more information on these controls, refer to the .NET Framework Documentation.)

The HTML section for the page, found in lines 118 through 138, starts by defining a postback form (line 120). Next, a list box control is created on line 122 and hard-coded with the three default Windows 2000 event logs: Application, Security, and System (lines 123 through 125). Next, a button, `btnSubmit`, is created on lines 127 and 128. This button, when clicked, will postback the form and cause the `btnSubmit_OnClick` event handler to fire. Next, on lines 130, 131, and 132, a table control is created. This is the table control that is dynamically built-up in the `DisplayEventLog` subroutine. Finally, on lines 134 and 135, another button control is created. When clicked, this button, `btnClear`, will cause all the event log entries for the selected event log to be cleared.

The `btnSubmit_OnClick` event handler can be found from lines 10 through 12. It is very simple, containing only one line of code. All it needs to do is display the event log selected by the user. This is accomplished by calling the `DisplayEventLog` subroutine and passing the `Value` of the selected list box item (line 11).

The `btnClear_OnClick` event handler is called when the `btnClear` button is clicked (see lines 134 and 135). This event handler is responsible for clearing all the event log entries, which is accomplished with the `Clear` method of the `EventLog` class (line 17).

> **Note**
>
> Notice that in Listing 2.9.2 we invest nearly 100 lines of code to display the Event Log in an HTML table. We could have used data binding with the DataList control to display this information in far fewer lines of code. However, I wanted to examine code to dynamically build an HTML table. For information on data binding be sure to check out Chapter 7.

Writing to the Event Log

The `EventLog` class also provides the ability for developers to have information written to the event log. There are a number of real-world situations in which it might be advantageous for an ASP.NET page to be able to make an entry to the Windows event log. In an article on ASPFree.com (`http://aspfree.com/asp+/eventlog2.aspx`), Steve Schofield demonstrates how to create a global error-handling page so that no matter when or where an ASP.NET error occurs, it is logged to a custom created error log.

Listing 2.9.3 provides similar functionality to Steve Schofield's event log article. Rather than recording any error in any ASP.NET Web page, however, Listing 2.9.3 provides a simple function that can be included in certain ASP.NET pages and called when an error occurs. Furthermore, rather than writing errors to a custom event log, Listing 2.9.3 records errors to the System event log.

LISTING 2.9.3 With the .NET Framework, a Developer Can Add Entries to an Event Log via an ASP.NET Page

```
 1: <%@ Import Namespace="System.Data" %>
 2: <%@ Import Namespace="System.Data.SqlClient" %>
 3: <%@ Import Namespace="System.Diagnostics" %>
 4: <script language="c#" runat="server">
 5:   void Page_Load(Object sender, EventArgs e)
 6:   {
 7:     // Perform some type of illegal operation
 8:     try {
 9:       SqlConnection objConn;
10:       objConn = new SqlConnection("server=localhost;uid=foo;
➥ pwd=bar;database=pubs");
11:       objConn.Open();
12:       // ...
13:     }
14:     catch (Exception eError)
15:     {
16:       RecordError(eError, EventLogEntryType.Error);
17:     }
18:   }
19:
20:
21:   void RecordError(Exception eError, EventLogEntryType enumType)
22:   {
23:     const String strSource = "ASP.NET",
24:           strLogName = "System";
25:
26:     // Add the strMessage entry to the ASPX event log
27:     EventLog objLog = new EventLog(strLogName);
28:     objLog.Source = strSource;
29:     objLog.WriteEntry(eError.Message, enumType);
30:   }
31: </script>
```

Listing 2.9.3 demonstrates how an entry can be written to the event log when an error occurs. Although the code in the **try** block from lines 9 through 11 might seem valid, the connection string specified on line 10 is not. This will cause an error to be thrown on line 11, when attempting to **Open** the connection. At this point, the **catch** block will catch the exception and make a call to the **RecordError** function, which will add an entry to the System event log indicating the error (line 16).

The **RecordError** function, stretching from line 21 through line 30, adds an entry to the System event log. First, on lines 23 and 24, two constants are defined: **strSource**, specifying the source of the error, and **strLogName**, specifying the event log that is to record the error. Next, on line 27, an **EventLog** instance representing the System event log is created. On line 28, the **Source** property is set to the constant **strSource**. Finally, on line 29, an entry is added to the event log. This entry's **Message** is identical to the **Message** property of the thrown **Exception**. The entry type is specified by the developer, passed in as the second parameter to the **RecordError** function. In Listing 2.9.3, an **Error** entry type is specified (see line 16).

> **Note**
>
> The `Source` of the entry added to the event log is used to specify the application or service that caused the error.

Figure 2.30 displays the detailed information for the entry added to the System event log for the error caused by Listing 2.9.2. Note that the event log entry has its source set to `"ASP.NET"` and indicates that there was an error in accessing the specified database. The `RecordError` function could be improved to add more detailed error messages, such as the ASP.NET page that threw the error and other relevant information.

FIGURE 2.30
A new error entry has been added to the System event log.

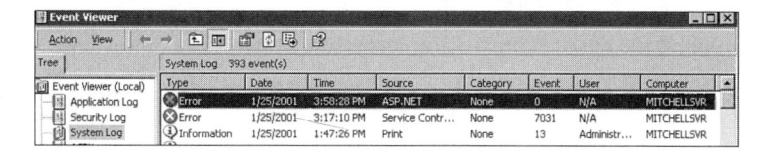

10. Working with Server Performance Counters

As we examined in "Accessing the Windows Event Log," the .NET Framework contains a `System.Diagnostics` namespace that houses classes which can be used for diagnostic information. One such class is the `EventLog` class, which we just looked at in the previous section; another useful diagnostics class is the `PerformanceCounter` class. This class gives the developer direct read access to the existing Windows Performance counters and provides the capability to create new performance counters!

Because this functionality is encapsulated in the .NET Framework, these techniques can be used through an ASP.NET page. That means you can create an ASP.NET page that reports information on the Web server's various resources! Talk about a remote administrator's dream!

Performance counters, which are represented by the `PerformanceCounter` class, are defined by at least two required properties. The first two required properties are `CategoryName` and `CounterName`; these represent the category and counter one sees when selecting a performance monitor through the Administrative Performance tool (see Figure 2.31). For example, to view the percentage of the processor's power being used, you'd be interested in the `"% Processor Time"` counter of the `"Processor"` category.

For certain performance counters, a third property, `InstanceName`, is required. Specifically, the `InstanceName` is needed for counters that monitor a metric with multiple instances, such as Web server information. Because a single Web server can run many different Web sites, we must specify the Web site if we want to view specific Web server–related information (such as total number of requests). Figure 2.31, for example, shows three options for the Web Services Bytes Total/sec performance counter, a `_Total` instance and an instance for each of the Web sites configured on my server.

FIGURE 2.31
When choosing a performance counter through the administrative interface, a category and counter are selected.

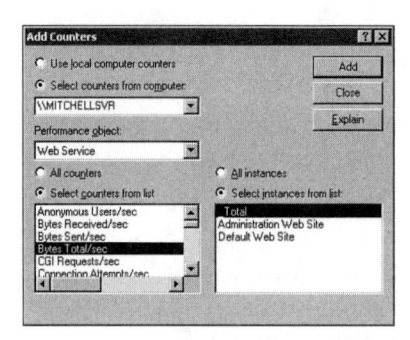

When creating an instance of the `PerformanceCounter`, you can specify these two (or three) properties in the constructor. For example, to create an instance of the `PerformanceCounter` class that could be used to report the total number of threads, the following code could be used:

```
Dim objPerf as New PerformanceCounter("System", "Threads")
```

The previous snippet creates an instance of the `PerformanceCounter` class named `objPerf`. This instance represents the performance counter `"Threads"` found in the `"System"` category.

To read the performance counter's value, simply use the `NextValue()` method. `NextValue()` returns the value of the next performance counter's sample. Therefore, we could amend our previous code to display the total number of threads with a simple call to `NextValue()`:

```
Dim objPerf as New PerformanceCounter("System", "Threads")
Response.Write("There are " & objPerf.NextValue() & " threads.")
```

Listing 2.10.1 illustrates a very simple ASP.NET page that could possibly serve as a handy tool for an off-site Web site administrator. The code for Listing 2.10.1, when viewed through a browser, will display the total available memory for the Web server, the number of processes currently running on the Web server, and the total number of anonymous page requests for the particular Web application in which the ASP.NET page resides. The output is shown in Figure 2.32.

LISTING 2.10.1 Gather System Information about the Web Server via an ASP.NET Page

```
 1: <%@ Import Namespace="System.Diagnostics" %>
 2: <script language="VB" runat="server">
 3: Sub Page_Load(sender as Object, e as EventArgs)
 4:   Dim objMemPerf as New PerformanceCounter("Memory", "Available Bytes")
 5:   lblFreeMemory.Text = String.Format("{0:#,###}",
➥ objMemPerf.NextValue()) & " bytes"
 6:
 7:   Dim objProcPerf as New PerformanceCounter("System", "Processes")
 8:   lblProcesses.Text = objProcPerf.NextValue().ToString()
 9:
10:   Dim strAppName as String = Request.ServerVariables("APPL_MD_PATH")
11:   strAppName = strAppName.Replace("/", "_")
```

LISTING 2.10.1 *Continued*

```
12:    Dim objCompPerf as New PerformanceCounter("ASP.NET Applications", _
13:                                     "Page Compilations", strAppName)
14:
15:    lblPageReqs.Text = objCompPerf.NextValue().ToString()
16: End Sub
17: </script>
18:
19: <html>
20: <body>
21:    <h1>Web Server Stats </h1>
22:    <i>These stats were taken as of <%=Now().ToLongDateString()%> at
23:    <%=Now().ToLongTimeString()%>...</i><p>
24:
25:    <b>Available Memory:</b> <asp:label id="lblFreeMemory"
➥ runat="server" /><br>
26:    <b>Processes:</b> <asp:label id="lblProcesses" runat="server" /><br>
27:    <b>ASP.NET Page Requests:</b>
28:        <asp:label id="lblPageReq" runat="server" /><br>
29: </body>
30: </html>
```

FIGURE 2.32
Performance counter values can be displayed through an ASP.NET page.

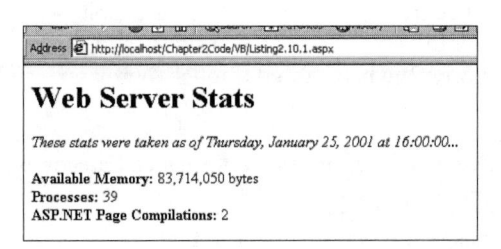

In Listing 2.10.1 we begin by importing the `System.Diagnostics` namespace (line 1). Next, in the `Page_Load` event handler, three `PerformanceCounter` class instances are created. The first one, `objMemPerf`, determines the amount of free memory in bytes available (line 4). On line 5, this value is output into the `lblFreeMemory` label control. The `objProcPerf` performance counter on line 7 determines the total number of currently running processes and displays this value in the `lblProcesses` label control (line 8).

The third performance counter displays the total number of anonymous requests (lines 12 and 13). For this metric, we must specify what Web application to use. To accomplish this, we can either hard-code a value for the `InstanceName` property, or we can dynamically determine it through the `APPL_MD_PATH` server variable. This server variable has values such as `/LM/W3SVC/1/Root`, for example. The `PerformanceCounter` class, however, prefers the `InstanceName` in the following format: `_LM_W3SVC_1_Root`, so, on line 11, all the forward slashes (/) are replaced with underscores (_). Finally, on line 15, the value of the page compilations performance counter is output.

Lines 19 through 30 define the HTML content of the page. Lines 22 and 23 output the current system time that the stats were monitored, whereas lines 25, 27, and 28 create the three performance counter label controls. These three label controls are populated with the values from their respective `PerformanceCounter` instances in the `Page_Load` event handler.

> **Caution**
>
> On line 12 of Listing 2.10.1 the performance counter category "ASP.NET Applications" is used to retrieve the Page Compilations counter. At the time of writing, this performance category and counter existed. However, since this is Beta software, these values may change. Refer to the Windows Performance Counter program to see a listing of existing performance categories and counters.

Although being able to view a particular performance counter through an ASP.NET page is an amazing feat in itself, it's only the tip of the iceberg! The .NET Framework provides an additional class, `PerformanceCounterCategory`, that can be used to iterate through the Web server's available performance categories and counters. This means that you can provide a remote administrator with an ASP.NET page that lists the entire contents set of performance counters for the administrator to choose from. After a performance counter has been selected, its current value can be displayed.

Listing 2.10.2 illustrates how to use the `PerformanceCounterCategory` class—in conjunction with the `PerformanceCounter` class—to list all the available performance categories and counters, permitting the user to select a particular category and counter and view its current value. The output of Listing 2.10.2, when viewed through a browser, can be seen in Figure 2.33.

LISTING 2.10.2 Iterate Through the Available Performance Categories and Counters with the `PerformanceCounterCategory` Class

```
 1: <%@ Import Namespace="System.Diagnostics" %>
 2: <script language="c#" runat="server">
 3:   void Page_Load(Object sender, EventArgs e)
 4:   {
 5:     if (!Page.IsPostBack)
 6:     {
 7:       foreach (PerformanceCounterCategory objPerfCounterCat in
➥ PerformanceCounterCategory.GetCategories())
 8:         lstCategories.Items.Add(new
➥ ListItem(objPerfCounterCat.CategoryName));
 9:
10:       //Add the counters for the first category
11:       PopulateCounters(PerformanceCounterCategory.GetCategories()[0]);
12:     }
13:   }
14:
15:
16:   void PopulateCounters(PerformanceCounterCategory objPerfCat)
17:   {
18:     // Populates the lstCounters list box with the counters for the
19:     // selected performance category (objPerfCat)...
20:
21:     lstCounters.Items.Clear();
22:
```

LISTING 2.10.2 *Continued*

```csharp
23:      PopulateInstances(objPerfCat);
24:
25:      if (lstInstances.Items.Count > 0)
26:      {
27:        foreach (PerformanceCounter objCounter in
➥ objPerfCat.GetCounters(lstInstances.Items[0].Value))
28:          lstCounters.Items.Add(new ListItem(objCounter.CounterName));
29:
30:        DisplayCounter(objPerfCat.GetCounters(
➥ lstInstances.Items[0].Value)[0]);
31:      } else {
32:
33:        foreach (PerformanceCounter objCounter in objPerfCat.GetCounters())
34:          lstCounters.Items.Add(new ListItem(objCounter.CounterName));
35:
36:        DisplayCounter(objPerfCat.GetCounters()[0]);
37:      }
38:    }
39:
40:
41:    void PopulateInstances(PerformanceCounterCategory objPerfCat)
42:    {
43:      // Populates the lstInstances list box with the counters for the
44:      // selected performance category (objPerfCat)...
45:
46:      lstInstances.Items.Clear();
47:
48:      foreach (String strInstanceName in objPerfCat.GetInstanceNames())
49:        lstInstances.Items.Add(new ListItem(strInstanceName));
50:    }
51:
52:
53:
54:    void lstCategories_OnChange(Object sender, EventArgs e)
55:    {
56:      PerformanceCounterCategory objPerfCat;
57:      objPerfCat = new PerformanceCounterCategory(
➥ lstCategories.SelectedItem.Value);
58:
59:      PopulateCounters(objPerfCat);
60:    }
61:
62:
63:    void lstCounters_OnChange(Object sender, EventArgs e)
64:    {
65:      // Display counter information for the selected counter and category
66:      if (lstCounters.SelectedItem != null)
67:      {
68:        PerformanceCounter objPerf = new PerformanceCounter();
69:        objPerf.CategoryName = lstCategories.SelectedItem.Value;
70:        objPerf.CounterName = lstCounters.SelectedItem.Value;
71:        if (lstInstances.SelectedItem != null) objPerf.InstanceName =
➥ lstInstances.SelectedItem.Value;
```

LISTING 2.10.2 *Continued*

```
 72:
 73:       DisplayCounter(objPerf);
 74:     }
 75:   }
 76:
 77:
 78:   void lstInstances_OnChange(Object sender, EventArgs e)
 79:   {
 80:     // Display counter information for the selected counter and category
 81:     if (lstCounters.SelectedItem != null)
 82:     {
 83:       PerformanceCounter objPerf = new PerformanceCounter();
 84:       objPerf.CategoryName = lstCategories.SelectedItem.Value;
 85:       objPerf.CounterName = lstCounters.SelectedItem.Value;
 86:       if (lstInstances.SelectedItem != null) objPerf.InstanceName =
➥ lstInstances.SelectedItem.Value;
 87:
 88:       DisplayCounter(objPerf);
 89:     }
 90:   }
 91:
 92:   void DisplayCounter(PerformanceCounter objPerf)
 93:   {
 94:     try {
 95:       objPerf.NextValue();
 96:       lblLastValue.Text = objPerf.NextValue().ToString();
 97:     }
 98:     catch (Exception e)
 99:     {
100:       try {
101:         PerformanceCounterCategory tmpCat = new
➥PerformanceCounterCategory(lstCategories.SelectedItem.Value);
102:         objPerf.InstanceName = tmpCat.GetInstanceNames()[0];
103:         objPerf.NextValue();
104:         lblLastValue.Text = objPerf.NextValue().ToString();
105:       }
106:       catch (Exception e2)
107:       {
108:         lblLastValue.Text = "<font color=red>ERROR: " +
➥ e.Message + "</font>";
109:       }
110:     }
111:   }
112: </script>
113:
114: <html>
115: <body>
116:   <form runat="server">
117:     <h1>Performance Counter Display</h1>
118:     <asp:listbox runat="server" id="lstCategories"
➥ Rows="1" AutoPostBack="True"
119:                  OnSelectedIndexChanged="lstCategories_OnChange" />
```

LISTING 2.10.2 Continued

```
120:      <asp:listbox runat="server" id="lstCounters"
➥ Rows="1" AutoPostBack="True"
121:               OnSelectedIndexChanged="lstCounters_OnChange" />
122:      <asp:listbox runat="server" id="lstInstances"
➥ Rows="1" AutoPostBack="True"
123:               OnSelectedIndexChanged="lstInstances_OnChange" />
124:      <p>
125:      <b>Current Value:</b>
126:      <asp:label id="lblLastValue" runat="server" />
127:    </form>
128:  </body>
129: </html>
```

FIGURE 2.33
A list of available performance categories and counters are presented to the user.

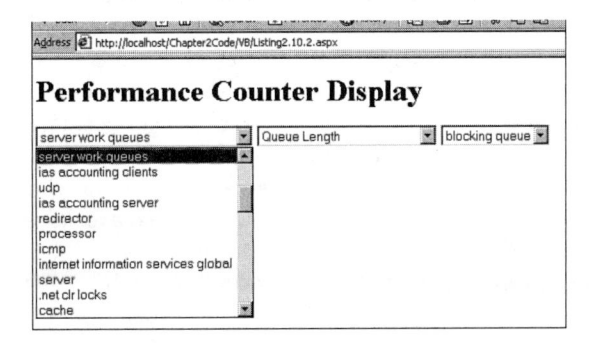

Before examining the `script` block in Listing 2.10.2, let's first turn our attention to the HTML section of the page (lines 114 through 129). Keep in mind the intended functionality for the code: to list the available performance categories and counters on the Web server. To accomplish this, we'll use three list boxes: The first list box will list the available performance categories; the second will list the available performance counters for the selected performance category; the third will list the available instance values for the selected performance category.

These three list boxes are created on lines 118 through 123. The performance category list box, `lstCategories`, has the `OnSelectedIndexChanged` event wired up to the `lstCategories_OnChange` event handler (defined from lines 54 through 60). When this list box's currently selected item is changed, the form will be posted back and the `lstCategories_OnChange` event handler will fire. The list box for each counter, `lstCounters`, is defined on lines 120 and 121. This list box, too, has an event handler (`lstCounters_OnChange`) wired up to the `OnSelectedIndexChanged` event handler. Finally, `lstInstances`, the last list box, is defined on lines 122 and 123.

The final server control is a label control, defined on line 126. Its purpose is to display the current value of the selected performance counter. All these controls are encased by a postback form control (defined on line 116).

The `Page_Load` event handler, found spanning lines 3 through 13, only executes code the first time the page is visited. This is because of the conditional on line 5 that checks to determine whether the form has been posted back. If it is the first visit to the page (that is, the form has not been posted back), all the available performance categories are iterated through. The `PerformanceCounterCategory` class contains a static method `GetCategories()`, which will return an array of `PerformanceCounterCategory` instances that represent the available performance categories on the machine. A `foreach` loop is used to iterate through all these categories, adding a new item to the `lstCategories` list box at each iteration (line 8). On line 11, the `PopulateCounters` function is called, which populates the `lstCounters` list box with the applicable counters for the selected category.

The `PopulateCounters` function begins by clearing out all the items in the `lstCounters` list box (line 21). Next, the `PopulateInstances` function is called to load the instance values for the performance category into the `lstInstance` list box. Keep in mind that only certain performance counters have Instance values. Therefore, when control returns to the `PopulateCounters` function, an `if` statement is used on line 25 to check if any instances exist for the performance category. If the performance category contains any instances, a `foreach` loop is used to iterate through each of the counters in the performance category for the default instance (line 27). The `GetCounters(InstanceName)` method returns all the available counters for the performance category for the given instance *InstanceName* (see line 27). Each of these counter names are then added to the `lstCounters` list box (line 28). If the performance category does not contain any instances, the code following the `else` statement on line 31 is executed. The only difference in this code is that the `GetCounters()` method does not specify an *InstanceName* (line 33). Finally, before the `PopulateCounters` function terminates, the `DisplayCounter` function is called; this function displays the current value of the selected performance counter.

The `DisplayCounter` function (defined from lines 92 through 111) lists the current value of the passed-in `PerformanceCounter`, `objPerf`. A `try ... catch` block is used on line 94 to ensure that the performance counter can be successfully read. If an error occurs, we assume that it is because the instance name hasn't been specified. In such a case, the `catch` block starting on line 98 will begin executing, and another `try ... catch` block ensues (line 100). Here, the default instance name for the selected performance category is selected and used and the performance counter's value is output. The `GetInstanceNames()` method of the `PerformanceCounterCategory` class will return a String array of available instance names; on line 102 we simply choose the first available instance name. Again, if an error occurs, the `catch` block on line 106 will begin executing; at this point, we don't know how to handle the error, and the `Message` property of the exception is displayed (line 108). Because some performance counters require two consecutive reads to the `NextValue()` method to retrieve a meaningful value, two calls are made (lines 95 and 96, and lines 103 and 104).

Whenever the user changes the currently selected performance category in the `lstCategories` list box, the form is posted back and the `lstCategories_OnChange` event handler fires (see lines 54 through 60). This event handler creates a `PerformanceCounterCategory` instance representing the currently selected performance category (lines 56 and 57). Next, the

`PopulateCounters` method is called (line 59), thereby populating the `lstCounters` list box with the appropriate counters for the selected performance category.

When the user selects a performance counter from the `lstCounters` list box, the form is posted back and the `lstCounters_OnChange` event handler is executed (see lines 63 through 75). This event handler begins by ensuring that a valid selection in the `lstCounters` list box has been made (line 65). Next, a `PerformanceCounter` instance is created (line 68), and its `CategoryName`, `CounterName`, and `InstanceName` properties are set based on the selected values in the corresponding list boxes. Finally, on line 73, the `DisplayCounter` method is called, displaying the current value for the selected performance counter. The `lstInstances_OnChange` event handler (lines 78 through 90), which fires when the user changes the current selection in the `lstInstances` list box, contains identical code to the `lstCounters_OnChange` list box.

To see Listing 2.10.2 in action, refer back to Figure 2.33. Using some enhancements we discussed earlier in this chapter (see the section "Generating Images Dynamically"), one could conceivably create an on-the-fly chart that would display the current (and past) status of one or more performance counters through an ASP.NET page, similar to the Performance tool in Windows NT/2000.

Summary

In this chapter we examined a number of common tasks that Web developers face and illustrated how to accomplish them through an ASP.NET page using the .NET Framework. Clearly the robust .NET Framework enables ASP.NET Web pages a degree of power that was only possible in classic ASP with clunky COM components.

If you have developed classic ASP Web pages in the past you will no doubt be impressed by ASP.NET's new capabilities. Just imagine, with ASP.NET you can dynamically create rich reports with graphs based on database data—no need for an expensive third-party component! With the `System.Net` classes you can seamlessly make HTTP requests through an ASP.NET Web page, access DNS information, and use with low-level socket programming techniques. Accepting and working with uploaded files from your Web visitors is now a breeze, no longer requiring a third-party component. With ASP.NET accomplishing common Web-related tasks is simple, easy, and built-in.

Despite this chapter's great length, it covered only a small handful of the capabilities of the .NET Framework. To get a full grasp of the capabilities, you should take a moment to poke through the .NET Framework Documentation (this documentation is included in the installation of this book's accompanying CD). The majority of these numerous classes can be used through an ASP.NET page just as they could through a VB.NET or C# standalone application.

This chapter provides a mere taste of the ASP.NET and .NET Framework's capabilities. As you work through the coming chapters you will soon appreciate the multitude of improvements and the ease with which you can create truly powerful Web applications!

Other Resources

Due to the extensive number of subjects this chapter covered, an in-depth examination of each subject was not possible. These supplemental readings, though, should provide a starting place for you to learn more about the topics in this chapter that piqued your interest.

- Mastering Regular Expressions—This book is a must have for anyone who wishes to become truly proficient at regular expressions. While the book presents most of its examples using Perl, it still does a fantastic job of explaining regular expressions. *Authored by: Friedl, Jeffrey E. F. Published By: O'Reilly Press, 1997*

- Form-Based File Upload in HTML—This RFC contains the gory technical details for uploading a file from a client's Web browser to the Web server.
  http://www.ietf.org/rfc/rfc1867.txt?number=1867

- Using Cookies with ASP.NET—One common Web developer task we did not have time to examine in this chapter was using Cookies through ASP.NET. With VB.NET the syntax is nearly identical to Cookie usage in classic ASP, but if you're making the switch to C# there are some things you should be aware of.
  http://www.asp101.com/samples/cookie_aspx.asp

- Fun ASP.NET Code Examples—This collection of useful ASP.NET code examples comes from Scott Guthrie, lead program manager and co-creator of ASP.NET!
  http://www.eraserver.net/scottgu/

- Validating Emails Against a Mail Server—This article takes a more in-depth look at validating email address through a mail server. In this chapter we examined validating the domain—this article shows how to validate *both* the domain and mail account!
  http://www.aspnextgen.com/tutorials.aspx?tutorialid=64

- Logging Unhandled Page Exceptions to the System Event Log—This article goes a bit beyond the "Writing to the Event Log" section in this chapter, showing how to record errors to a custom Windows Event Log category.
  http://www.aspnextgen.com/tutorials.aspx?tutorialid=42

CHAPTER 3

FORM FIELD INPUT VALIDATION

by Scott Mitchell

In this chapter you will learn

- How to use the `RequiredFieldValidator` control
- How to use the `CompareValidator` control
- How to use the `RangeValidator` control
- How to use the `RegularExpressionValidator` control
- How to use the `CustomValidator` control
- How to use the `ValidationSummary` control

*I*f you're reading this book, you've no doubt created HTML forms to collect information from the users visiting your Web site. For example, if you want to create a form for a user to send feedback to the Webmaster, you might create a form with two text boxes: one for the user's email address (so the Webmaster can reply to the user's feedback), and another for the user's comments.

Unfortunately, HTML form field elements provide no sort of inherent data validation. That is, when you create a text box with the following code, the user can enter any sort of value, from something valid (such as `Mitchell@ASP.NET`) to something nonsensical (such as `76!r.2`):

`Enter your Email Address: <input type="text" name="txtEmail">`

With classic ASP, the developer would have had to create some sort of form-validation routine to ensure that the email address text box contains a valid email address.

The process of creating form-validation routines for every form on a Web site is both tiresome and error prone. Because no form-validation library shipped with classic ASP, developers were on their own to create their form-validation functions.

Fortunately, with ASP.NET, form validation is a breeze. ASP.NET pages can include *validation controls*, which are Web controls used to ensure that the entered values in form fields meet developer-defined criteria. Validation controls "point" to other Web controls, automatically verifying that these other Web controls contain valid entries. Since these validation controls are Web controls they can be added to your ASP.NET pages just like other Web controls, in the declarative `asp:WebControlName` format. For all these reasons (and others we'll examine in this chapter), these validation controls are incredibly powerful and useful, and, best of all, easy to use, requiring only a few lines of code!

1. Validating Form Field Input with ASP.NET's Validation Controls

To help with form validation, ASP.NET ships with five validation controls (and a `ValidationSummary` control). Over the next six sections, we'll examine these five controls and the `ValidationSummary` control, looking at how they can be used to provide extensive form validation with just a few lines of code!

Before we delve into the validation controls, let's take a step back and look at fundamentals of form validation. Form validation can take one of two forms:

- Client-side form validation
- Server-side form validation

In client-side form validation, the HTML page contains client-side JavaScript code that is executed on the client's Web browser. This code is usually executed when the user attempts to submit a form: If the form fields are valid, the form submits; otherwise, the user is usually shown some message regarding his invalid form information. The nice thing about client-side form validation is that it executes entirely on the client's machine and doesn't require a roundtrip to the Web server. It can be used, then, to quickly detect any validation errors and alert the user of such errors. Client-side form validation has its downsides, though. For starters, it requires that the visitor be able to execute client-side JavaScript code on his browser. Some older browsers don't have this feature, and some Web surfers explicitly turn off JavaScript support in their Web browsers.

Server-side form validation, on the other hand, takes place *after* the user submits the form but before any action is done on the submitted data. The main advantage of server-side form validation is that it will work regardless of the user's browser or browser configuration. Additionally, clever visitors can easily bypass any sort of client-side form validation. With server-side form validation, however, it is impossible for users to circumvent the validation process altogether.

When developing forms in classic ASP, developers were highly encouraged to use *both* client-side and server-side form validation because both have advantages. In my experiences, I found that most classic ASP developers just used server-side form validation (if any form validation at all). Using *just* client-side form validation should be avoided unless your Web application will be used in an environment where you know none of the users to be malicious and you are certain that they are all using modern browsers with client-side scripting features enabled.

The ASP.NET validation controls *always* use server-side form validation. However, if the user's browser can support DHTML features, client-side form validation is automatically included as well! In fact, the validation controls will automatically determine whether or not the requesting Web browser supports the needed client-side technologies to handle client-side form validation.

You can explicitly specify that the validation controls should *never* use client-side form validation on a page-by-page basis. Simply set the `ClientTarget` property to `Downlevel` using the `@Page` directive at the top of your ASP.NET page:

```
<%@ Page ClientTarget="Downlevel" %>
```

This will cause *all* the validation controls on the Web page to not use client-side form validation, regardless of the visitor's browser. Unfortunately you cannot specify client-side form validation on a validation control–by–validation control basis.

> **Note**
> Again, regardless of whether client-side form validation is used, server-side form validation will *always* be employed by the ASP.NET validation controls. Requiring server-side form validation is important since client-side form validation can be diverted by clever and malicious users.

2. Using the `RequiredFieldValidator` Control

The `RequiredFieldValidator` control, as its name implies, is useful when you have a form field that the user must enter before she can successfully submit the form.

There are many situations in which a form field requires an entry before processing can continue. For example, many Web sites have a "members-only" area, where a visitor must supply his username and password to proceed to a particular area of the Web site. With such a login form, both the username and password fields would be required fields. Listing 3.2.1 contains the code for an ASP.NET page that, when first loaded, presents the user with two text boxes for her username and password.

LISTING 3.2.1 Using a `RequiredFieldValidator` Control Ensures That the User Enters a Value for a Form Field

```
 1: <script language="vb" runat="server">
 2:   Sub btnSubmit_Click(sender as Object, e as EventArgs)
 3:
 4:     ' The User has submitted the form.  Is it valid?
 5:     If Page.IsValid then
 6:       ' Yes it is, check to make sure password/username are valid
 7:       ' Then do whatever you intended on doing if they're login
 8:       ' credentials were (or were not) valid.
 9:     Else
10:       ' The page is not valid, meaning they either didn't enter
11:       ' the username or password
12:       Response.Write("You must enter both the username and password.")
13:     End If
14:
15:   End Sub
16: </script>
17:
18: <html>
```

LISTING 3.2.1 Continued

```
19: <body>
20:    <form method="post" runat="server">
21:      <b>UserName:</b>
22:      <asp:textbox runat="server" id="txtUserName" />
23:      <!-- Create a RequiredFieldValidator Control for txtUserName -->
24:      <asp:RequiredFieldValidator runat="server"
25:          id="reqUserName" ControlToValidate="txtUserName"
26:          Display="Dynamic">
27:        Enter your UserName!
28:      </asp:RequiredFieldValidator>
29:
30:      <br><b>Password:</b>
31:      <asp:textbox runat="server" id="txtPassword" TextMode="Password" />
32:      <!-- Create a RequiredFieldValidator Control for txtPassword -->
33:      <asp:RequiredFieldValidator runat="server"
34:          id="reqPassword" ControlToValidate="txtPassword"
35:          Display="Dynamic">
36:        Enter your Password!
37:      </asp:RequiredFieldValidator>
38:
39:      <p><asp:button runat="server" id="btnSubmit" Text="Login!"
➥OnClick="btnSubmit_Click"/>
40:    </form>
41: </body>
42: </html>
```

Let's begin our examination of Listing 3.2.1 at line 18, where the HTML section begins. On line 20, a postback form is created. On line 22, a text box, `txtUserName`, is created for the visitor to enter her username into. Next, a `RequiredFieldValidator` control is created (lines 24 through 26).

This `RequiredFieldValidator` requires a couple properties that must be supplied by the developer. First, it must contain the `runat="server"` attribute (line 24). Second, it should contain a value for the `id` property; in Listing 3.2.1 this `RequiredFieldValidator` control is given the name `reqUserName`. The `ControlToValidate` property specifies the required form field. Because we want to ensure that the user enters a value in the `txtUserName` text box, the `reqUserName` control specifies `txtUserName` as its `ControlToValidate` property. The final property, `Display` (line 26), determines how the validation control should be displayed (refer to Table 3.1 for a list of legal `Display` values).

On line 27, we have specified the message that should be supplied if the user doesn't enter a value for the `txtUserName` form field (or, more generally, the message that is displayed if the validation control reports an invalid state). You can also achieve the same effect by explicitly setting the `ErrorMessage` property of the validation control. For examples of explicitly setting the `ErrorMessage` property, refer to Listing 3.2.3, line 24.

Next, we create the Password text box and its associated `RequiredFieldValidator` control. On line 31, the Password text box, `txtPassword`, is created. On lines 33 through 37, the `RequiredFieldValidator` control for `txtPassword` is created. It is strikingly similar to the `RequiredFieldValidator` control for `txtUserName`—the only differences being the `id` and `ControlToValidate` properties (line 34) as well as the error message (line 36).

Our form also contains a submit button on line 39, called `btnSubmit`, which, when clicked, fires the `btnSubmit_Click` event handler. Figure 3.1 shows the result of the code in Listing 3.2.1 when first viewed through a browser. The form contains two text boxes, for the username and password, and a button.

FIGURE 3.1
A simple HTML form is presented for the visitor to enter her username and password.

When the user enters her logon information and clicks the submit button, the form will be posted back and the `btnSubmit_Click` event handler will fire (spanning lines 2 through line 15).

The `IsValid` property of the `Page` object is checked on line 5 to determine whether the form fields in the posted back form are valid. The `IsValid` property will be True if all validation controls report that the controls they represent contain valid information. Because we have two `RequiredFieldValidator` controls, `Page.IsValid` will be True only if the user has entered data into *both* the `txtUserName` and `txtPassword` text boxes.

FIGURE 3.2
An error message is displayed from the `RequiredFieldValidator` control if the user fails to enter a value for the form field.

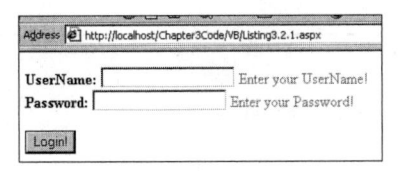

> **Note**
>
> The output of Listing 3.2.1 will depend, in large part, on the browser you use. If ASP.NET identifies your browser as an "uplevel" browser (IE 4.0 and up, at the time of this writing), client-side JavaScript and DHTML code will be used to provide client-side form validation as well. In such a case, you may not be able to submit the form to the Web server until all of the form fields are valid. In such a case, you will never see the error message output on line 12, since that only is displayed when the page is posted back *and* the page is not valid.

All the validation controls contain `Display` properties, which can have one of three values. For example, in Listing 3.2.1 (lines 26 and 35), we set the `RequiredFieldValidator` controls' `Display` properties to `Dynamic`. Table 3.1 contains the three legal values for the `Display` property and a brief explanation.

TABLE 3.1 The *Display* Properties of the ASP.NET Validation Controls Can Accept the Following Values

Value	Description
Dynamic	When validation fails, the error message is displayed. However, when validation succeeds (that is, when the validation control is hidden), the control takes up no space on the Web page.
Static	Like the Dynamic setting, when validation fails using the Static setting, the error message is displayed. However, even when validation succeeds, the control does takes up space on the Web page.
None	The error message of the validation control is never displayed.

The difference between the **Dynamic** and **Static** settings might not be entirely clear; therefore, an example will help. Listing 3.2.2 contains two text boxes and two validation controls. The first validation control has its **Display** property set to **Static**, whereas the second validation control has its **Display** property set to **Dynamic**. Each control also has text immediately following it. You can see how this text is displayed in Figure 3.3.

LISTING 3.2.2 The *Display* Property Determines Whether a "Hidden" Validation Control Takes Up Space on the Web Page

```
 1: <html>
 2: <body>
 3:   <form method="post" runat="server">
 4:     <b>UserName:</b>
 5:     <asp:textbox runat="server" id="txtUserName" />
 6:     <asp:RequiredFieldValidator runat="server"
 7:         id="reqUserName" ControlToValidate="txtUserName"
 8:         Display="Static">
 9:       Enter your UserName!
10:     </asp:RequiredFieldValidator><i>Text following control...</i>
11:
12:     <br><b>Password:</b>
13:     <asp:textbox runat="server" id="txtPassword" TextMode="Password" />
14:     <asp:RequiredFieldValidator runat="server"
15:         id="reqPassword" ControlToValidate="txtPassword"
16:         Display="Dynamic">
17:       Enter your Password!
18:     </asp:RequiredFieldValidator><i>Text following control...</i>
19:   </form>
20: </body>
21: </html>
```

Note that each validation control in Listing 3.2.2 has some text immediately following it (lines 10 and 18). The first validation control, **reqUserName**, has its **Display** property set to **Static**, whereas the second validation control, **reqPassword**, has its **Display** property set to **Dynamic** (lines 8 and 16, respectively). Figure 3.3 illustrates how the **Static** setting has even the "hidden" validation control take up space, whereas the **Dynamic** setting does not.

FIGURE 3.3
The `Display` property determines how the validation control is displayed in the Web page.

| UserName: | | Text following control... |
| Password: | | Text following control... |

(Address: http://localhost/Chapter3Code/VB/Listing3.2.2.aspx)

`RequiredFieldValidator` controls can also be used for radio button, check box, and list box form fields. Many developers create list boxes that have, as their initial value, some nonsensical choice so that the user must make a conscious selection from the list box, as opposed to just skipping over it and leaving the default choice selected.

For example, in Listing 3.2.3 the user is presented with a list box containing a number of foods. If this were for some survey, the user might, in his haste, skip over this list box, accepting the default value. If we want users to more accurately fill out the survey, we might decide to make them consciously choose an item from the list box by making the default choice an instruction, such as "--Select a Favorite Food--." We could then use a `RequiredFieldValidator` control to ensure that the user did indeed select a value from the list box (other than the default value, which serves only an instructional purpose). Listing 3.2.3 sets up such a form.

LISTING 3.2.3 The `RequiredFieldValidator` Control Can Also Be Used on List Boxes

```
 1: <script language="vb" runat="server">
 2:   Sub btnSubmit_Click(sender as Object, e as EventArgs)
 3:     If Page.IsValid Then
 4:       Response.Write("<i><b>Your favorite food is " & _
 5:              lstFood.SelectedItem.Value & "!!</b></i>")
 6:     End If
 7:   End Sub
 8: </script>
 9:
10: <html>
11: <body>
12:   <form method="post" runat="server">
13:     What is your favorite food?
14:     <asp:DropDownList id="lstFood" runat="server">
15:       <asp:ListItem>--Select a Food--</asp:ListItem>
16:       <asp:ListItem>Cookies</asp:ListItem>
17:       <asp:ListItem>Tuna Roll</asp:ListItem>
18:       <asp:ListItem>Popcorn Shrimp</asp:ListItem>
19:       <asp:ListItem>Liver and Onions</asp:ListItem>
20:     </asp:DropDownList>
21:
22:     <asp:RequiredFieldValidator runat="server"
23:         id="reqFood" ControlToValidate="lstFood"
24:         ErrorMessage="You must select a favorite food!"
25:         InitialValue="--Select a Food--" />
26:
```

LISTING 3.2.3 Continued

```
27:     <p><asp:button id="btnSubmit" runat="server"
28:            OnClick="btnSubmit_Click" Text="Next -->" />
29:   </form>
30: </body>
31: </html>
```

Listing 3.2.3 does not contain a `Page_Load` event handler, so let's begin our examination in the HTML section. On line 12, a postback form is created. Next, on lines 14 through 20, a `DropDownList` Web control is created and populated with five items. The first item serves as an instructional bit to the user, informing him to select his favorite food from the list (line 15).

Next, a `RequiredFieldValidator` control is created (lines 22 through 26). Because we want the user to select an item from the `lstFood` list box, we specify the `lstFood` list box in the `ControlToValidate` property (line 23). On line 24, we specify the `ErrorMessage` property; recall that in Listing 3.2.1 and Listing 3.2.2 we specified this in between the `<asp:RequiredFieldValidator>` and `</asp:RequiredFieldValidator>` tags. Finally, on line 25, we specify the `InitialValue` property. This tells the `RequiredFieldValidator` control what the initial value of the list box was. When the form is submitted, the `RequiredFieldValidator` checks to ensure that the value submitted is *not* the same as the `InitialValue`.

Finally, on lines 27 and 28, a button control is created, `btnSubmit`, which, when clicked, will cause the `btnSubmit_Click` event handler to fire. (Recall that in Listing 3.2.1 we used an alternative approach: We didn't wire up any event handler to the button's `OnClick` event; rather, we checked in the `Page_Load` event handler to determine whether the form had been posted back.)

When the button is clicked and the form submitted, the `btnSubmit_Click` event handler will fire. This event handler immediately checks to determine whether the page is valid (line 3). If it is—meaning that the user did indeed select a favorite food—the user's favorite food is displayed. Figure 3.4 shows the result of the code in Listing 3.2.3 when viewed through a browser.

FIGURE 3.4
The page is not valid until the user selects a food item from the list other than the first, instructional item.

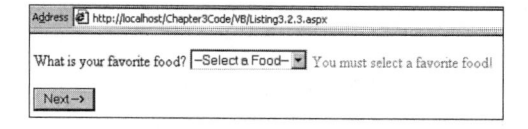

3. Using the `CompareValidator` Control

The `CompareValidator` validation control is useful for comparing the value of a form field to a static, hard-coded value or to the value of another form field. For example, you may present a user with a text box and ask him to enter the number of cars he owns. Clearly, no one could own less than zero cars, so you could use a `CompareValidator` on the text box control to ensure that the value entered is greater than or equal to zero.

> **Note**
>
> If you want to restrict a value between a certain range, you can use two `CompareValidator` controls—one for the lower bound and another for the upper bound. However, a wiser choice would be to use the `RangeValidator` validation control, which we'll examine in the next section.

The `CompareValidator` control can also be used to ensure that a form field entry is of a certain data type. For example, if you have a text box that asks a user to enter her birth date, you would not want to allow the user to submit a value of "purple" or some other nonsensical value. A `CompareValidator` control can be used to ensure that a form field entry can map to a particular data type.

Listing 3.3.1 presents an HTML form with three text boxes. These text boxes use one or more `CompareValidator` validation controls. The small code section in Listing 3.3.1 is presented in C#.

LISTING 3.3.1 CompareValidator Controls Can Be Used to Compare Values Between Form Fields

```
 1: <script language="c#" runat="server">
 2:    void btnSubmit_Click(Object sender, EventArgs e)
 3:    {
 4:      if (Page.IsValid)
 5:        if (Convert.ToSingle(txtSavings.Text) / Convert.ToSingle(txtSalary.Text)
            ➥> 0.1)
 6:          lblResults.Text = "<hr><p>You are saving enough!";
 7:        else
 8:          lblResults.Text = "<hr><p>You are <b>NOT</b> saving enough!";
 9:    }
10: </script>
11:
12: <html>
13: <body>
14:    <form method="post" runat="server">
15:      <h1>Savings Survey</h1>
16:      How old are you?
17:      <asp:textbox id="txtAge" runat="server" Columns="3" />
18:      <asp:CompareValidator runat="server"
19:           id="compAge" Type="Integer" Operator="DataTypeCheck"
20:           ControlToValidate="txtAge" Display="Dynamic"
21:           ErrorMessage="Age must be an integer value." />
22:
23:      <br>What is your salary?
24:      $<asp:textbox id="txtSalary" runat="server" />
25:      <asp:CompareValidator runat="server"
26:           id="compSalary" Type="Currency" Operator="DataTypeCheck"
27:           ControlToValidate="txtSalary" Display="Dynamic"
28:           ErrorMessage="Salary must be an currency value." />
```

LISTING 3.3.1 Continued

```
29:     <asp:CompareValidator runat="server"
30:             id="compPositiveSalary" Type="Currency"
31:             ControlToValidate="txtSalary" Display="Dynamic"
32:             ValueToCompare="0" Operator="GreaterThanEqual"
33:             ErrorMessage="You can't make less than $0.00!" />
34:
35:     <br>How much do you save each year?
36:     $<asp:textbox id="txtSavings" runat="server" />
37:     <asp:CompareValidator runat="server"
38:             id="compSavigs" Type="Currency" Operator="DataTypeCheck"
39:             ControlToValidate="txtSavings" Display="Dynamic"
40:             ErrorMessage="Savings must be an currency value." />
41:     <asp:CompareValidator runat="server"
42:             id="compSavigsSalary" Type="Currency" Operator="LessThanEqual"
43:             ControlToValidate="txtSavings" ControlToCompare="txtSalary"
44:             Display="Dynamic"
45:             ErrorMessage="You cannot save more than you earn!" />
46:
47:     <p><asp:button id="btnSubmit" runat="server"
48:             OnClick="btnSubmit_Click" Text="Next -->" />
49:     <p><asp:label runat="server" id="lblResults" />
50:     </form>
51: </body>
52: </html>
```

Because Listing 3.3.1 doesn't contain a `Page_Load` event handler, let's begin by examining the HTML section, starting on line 12. As expected, we start by creating a postback form (line 14). Next, a text box for the user to enter his age is created (line 17). On lines 18 through 21, a `CompareValidator` control is created to ensure that the age entered by the user is an integer. One of the important properties here is the `Type` property (line 19), which specifies what data type the value of `txtAge` needs to be (see Table 3.2 for a complete list of legal data types). The `Operator` property (line 19) specifies what check the `CompareValidator` control should make (see Table 3.3 for a list of legal `Operator` values). A value of `DataTypeCheck` specifies that the `CompareValidator` should ensure that the control specified by the `ControlToValidate` property is of the data type specified by the `Type` property. The `ErrorMessage` property (line 21) is the string that will be displayed if the user enters an invalid entry into the `txtAge` text box (a noninteger value).

> **Note**
>
> Checking to see whether the user's entered age is an integer is not very thorough because values such as 4,500 and –9 are legal integers. A `RangeValidator` control would be a wiser choice to use in this situation. We'll examine this control in the next section, "Using the `RangeValidator` Control."

On line 24, another text box is created—this one for the user to enter his salary. This control has two `CompareValidator` controls: the first, `compSalary` (lines 25 through 28), ensures that the value entered into the text box is of type `Currency`; the second, `compPositiveSalary` (lines 29 through 33), ensures that the value entered is greater than or equal to zero, because a negative salary is (hopefully) impossible. The `compSalary` `CompareValidator` control sets the `Type` property to `Currency` and the `Operator` property to `DataTypeCheck` (line 26). Both `CompareValidator` controls specify the `ControlToValidate` property as `txtSalary`, the ID of the salary text box. The `compSalary` `CompareValidator` control will be valid if the user's entered salary is of type `Currency`.

Because the second `CompareValidator` control is comparing the value of the `txtSalary` text box to a static value, the `Operator` property is changed from `DataTypeCheck` to `GreaterThanEqual`. Furthermore, the `ValueToCompare` property is set to the hard-coded value to compare—in this case, `0`. This `CompareValidator` control will be valid only if the user's entered salary is greater than or equal to zero.

The final text box appears on line 36 and asks the user to enter how much money he saves each year. This value must be of type `Currency` and must be less than the user's salary. Therefore, two `CompareValidator` controls are used. The first, `compSavings` (lines 37 through 40), checks to ensure that the value entered into the `txtSavings` text box is of type `Currency`. The second, `compSavingsSalary` (lines 41 through 45), compares the value of the `txtSavings` text box (specified in the `ControlToValidate` property, line 43) to the value in the `txtSalary` text box (specified in the `ControlToCompare` property, line 43). Because we only want `compSavingsSalary` to be valid if the savings is less than or equal to the salary, we set the `Operator` property to `LessThanEqual` (line 42). With these settings, the `compSavingsSalary` `CompareValidator` control will be valid only if the value of `txtSavings` is less than or equal to the value of `txtSalary`.

The HTML section ends with a submit button (lines 47 and 48) that has its `OnClick` event wired up to the `btnSubmit_Click` event handler. On line 49, a label control, `lblResults`, is created. An analysis of the user's saving habits will be output to this label control when the form is submitted (assuming the form data is valid).

When the button is clicked, the form will be reposted and the `btnSubmit_Click` event handler will fire. This event handler (spanning lines 2 through 9) immediately checks to determine whether the page is valid (line 4). If it is (meaning that all the validation controls have reported that their respective controls have valid data), a quick check is made to determine whether the user is saving at least 10 percent of his income. If he is, a message is outputted that the user is saving enough; otherwise, the user is encouraged to save more of his income.

Figure 3.5 shows the result of the code in Listing 3.4 when the user has entered some invalid entries into the text boxes. Figure 3.6 shows the result of the form when the user has entered legal values into the three text boxes.

In Listing 3.3.1 a number of `CompareValidator` controls were created to check the data type of a form field. To accomplish this with the `CompareValidator`, we needed to set the `Operator` property to `DataTypeCheck` and the `Type` property to the required data type. The legal values for the `Type` property are specified by the `ValidationDataType` enumeration (found in the `System.Web.UI.WebControls` namespace) and are listed in Table 3.2.

FIGURE 3.5
Error messages are displayed if the user enters invalid information.

FIGURE 3.6
Once legitimate values have been entered into all the form fields, the user is presented with an analysis of his saving habits.

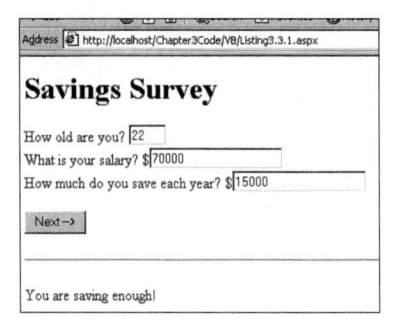

TABLE 3.2 The `Type` Property Can Accept the Following Values of the `ValidationDataType` Enumeration

Value	Description
Currency	Ensures that the form field is of type `Currency`
Date	Ensures that the form field is a legal `DateTime` value
Double	Ensures that the form field is of type `Double` (a numeric data type that accepts decimals, negative numbers, and so on)
Integer	Ensures that the form field is of type `Integer` (a negative or positive whole number)
String	Ensures that the form field is of type `String`

The `CompareValidator` control also contains an `Operator` property that determines what sort of comparison should be performed. This property can accept values from the `ValidationCompareOperator` enumeration (also found in the `System.Web.UI.WebControls` namespace). The members of the `ValidationCompareOperator` enumeration are listed in Table 3.3.

TABLE 3.3 The `Operator` Property Can Accept the Following Values of the `ValidationCompareOperator` Enumeration

Value	Description
`DataTypeCheck`	Checks to ensure that the `ControlToValidate` control is of the data type specified by the `Type` property.
`Equal`	An equality (=) comparison is performed.
`GreaterThan`	A greater-than (>) comparison is performed.
`GreaterThanEqual`	A greater-than-or-equal (>=) comparison is performed.
`LessThan`	A less-than (<) comparison is performed.
`LessThanEqual`	A less-than-or-equal (<=) comparison is performed.
`NotEqual`	An inequality (<>) comparison is performed.

4. Using the `RangeValidator` Control

As you saw in the previous section, the `CompareValidator` is a useful validation control when you need to ensure that a form field entry is greater than, equal to, or less than some static value or user-entered value. What if, however, a form field's value needs to fall between a certain range of values? For example, when asking the user for her age, you might want to restrict the user to entering an integral value between 0 and 90. Although this can be accomplished with a pair of `CompareValidator` controls, ASP.NET provides a more succinct approach through the use of the `RangeValidator` control.

The `RangeValidator` control, as its name suggests, ensures that a form field entry is between two values. These two values must be static, hard-coded values. To check if a value exists between two dynamic values – that is, values entered by the user into another form field element on the ASP.NET page – you must use a `CompareValidator` control.

The `RangeValidator` control, like the `CompareValidator` control, contains a `Type` property that specifies the expected data type of the validation control (see Table 3.2 for a list of legal `Type` values). Like all the other validation controls, the `RangeValidator` also contains a `ControlToValidate` property.

Listing 3.4.1 contains code that presents the user with a retirement savings calculator of sorts. The user is asked to enter her age, the age at which she wishes to retire, and her current savings. The amount that her savings would be worth at retirement, assuming it is placed in a CD with a 6-percent interest rate, is calculated and displayed once the form is submitted. `RangeValidator` controls are used to ensure that valid entries are entered for the user's current age and expected retirement age. A `CompareValidator` is used to ensure that the user enters an acceptable value for her current savings.

LISTING 3.4.1 RangeValidator Controls Ensure That a Form Field's Value is Between an Acceptable Range

```
 1: <script language="vb" runat="server">
 2:   Sub btnSubmit_Click(sender as Object, e as EventArgs)
 3:     Dim dblValue as Double = 0.0, dblPrincipal as Double = 0.0
 4:     Dim iYears as Integer = 0
 5:
 6:     If Page.IsValid Then
 7:       iYears = CInt(txtRetireAge.Text) - CInt(txtAge.Text)
 8:       dblPrincipal = CSng(txtSavings.Text)
 9:       dblValue = dblPrincipal * Math.Exp(CSng(iYears) * 0.06)
10:
11:       lblResults.Text = "Your savings will be worth $" & _
12:             String.Format("{0:c}", dblValue) & " when you retire."
13:     End If
14:   End Sub
15: </script>
16:
17: <html>
18: <body>
19:   <form method="post" runat="server">
20:     <h1>Retirement Calculator</h1>
21:     How old are you?
22:     <asp:textbox id="txtAge" runat="server" Columns="3" />
23:     <asp:RangeValidator runat="server"
24:         id="rngAge" Type="Integer" MinimumValue="0"
25:         MaximumValue="90"
26:         ControlToValidate="txtAge" Display="Dynamic"
27:         ErrorMessage="Age must be between 0 and 90." />
28:
29:     <br>When do you expect to retire?
30:     <asp:textbox id="txtRetireAge" runat="server" Columns="3" />
31:     <asp:RangeValidator runat="server"
32:         id="rngRetireAge" Type="Integer"
33:         ControlToValidate="txtRetireAge" Display="Dynamic"
34:         MinimumValue="0" MaximumValue="100"
35:         ErrorMessage="Retirement age must be between current
➥ age and 100." />
36:     <asp:CompareValidator runat="server"
37:         id="compRetireAge" Type="Integer" Operator="GreaterThanEqual"
38:         ControlToValidate="txtRetireAge" Display="Dynamic"
39:         ControlToCompare="txtAge"
40:         ErrorMessage="Your projected retirement age must
➥be >= to your Age." />
41:
42:     <br>How much do you have in a 6% CD?
43:     $<asp:textbox id="txtSavings" runat="server" />
44:     <asp:CompareValidator runat="server"
45:         id="compSavigs" Type="Currency" Operator="DataTypeCheck"
46:         ControlToValidate="txtSavings" Display="Dynamic"
47:         ErrorMessage="Savings must be an currency value." />
48:     <asp:CompareValidator runat="server"
```

LISTING 3.4.1 Continued

```
49:              id="compSavigsMinimum" Type="Currency"
➥Operator="GreaterThanEqual"
50:              ControlToValidate="txtSavings" ValueToCompare="0"
51:              Display="Dynamic"
52:              ErrorMessage="You must have at least 0 dollars saved!" />
53:
54:     <p><asp:button id="btnSubmit" runat="server"
55:            OnClick="btnSubmit_Click"
56:              Text="Calculate Retirement Monies" />
57:     <p><asp:label runat="server" id="lblResults" />
58:   </form>
59: </body>
60: </html>
```

The HTML section for Listing 3.4.1 (starting on line 17) begins by creating a postback form (line 19). Next, a text box (`txtAge`) is presented for the user to enter her age (line 22). This is immediately followed by a `RangeValidator` control that is used to ensure that the age entered by the user is between 0 and 90 (lines 23 through 27). Note that these range values are specified with the `MinimumValue` and `MaximumValue` properties (lines 24 and 25, respectively). The `ControlToValidate` property on line 26 refers to the `txtAge` text box; the `Type` property (line 24) is set to `Integer`. If the user enters an age outside of the legal bounds, the error message on line 27 will be displayed.

On line 30, the `txtRetireAge` text box is created. In this text box, the user will enter the age she intends on retiring. A `RangeValidator` control is then created to ensure that this age is between 0 and 100 (lines 31 through 35). Since we also want to ensure that the user's desired retirement age is greater than or equal to their current age, we use a `CompareValidator` immediately following the `RangeValidator` (see lines 36 through 40). This `CompareValidator` specifies that the `ControlToValidate` (`txtRetireAge`) must be greater than or equal to the `ControlToCompare` (`txtAge`).

The final text box, `txtSavings`, prompts the user to enter the amount of money she currently has saved (line 43). Two `CompareValidator` controls follow: The first one (`compSavings`) ensures that the data entered is of type `Currency`, whereas the second (`compSavingsMinimum`) ensures that the user entered a positive value. This is all followed by a submit button (lines 54 through 56) and a label control (`lblResults`) for the calculated output (line 57).

When the user enters legal values for all the form fields and submits the form, the form is posted back and the `btnSubmit_Click` event handler is fired. This event handler begins by creating some variables (line 3 and 4) and then checks to ensure that all the validation controls have reported back as valid (line 6). If the page is valid, the difference in years between the user's current age and intended retirement age are calculated (line 7). The value of the investment in a 6-percent CD is then determined on line 9 with the formula `InvestmentValue = Principal * exp(Rate * Time)`. This value is then output to the `lblResults` label (lines 11 and 12).

> **Note**
>
> Keep in mind that with the current code found in Listing 3.4.1 the user is not required to enter any values. That is, if the user submits the form without entering values for her age, expected retirement age, and savings, the page will be considered valid. As we examined earlier in this chapter, to make a form field a required field, use the `RequiredFieldValidator` control. (Note that multiple validation controls can serve to validate a single Web control.)

Figure 3.7 shows the result of the code in Listing 3.4.1 when the user has entered some invalid entries into the text boxes. Figure 3.8 shows the result of the form when the user has entered legal values into the three text boxes.

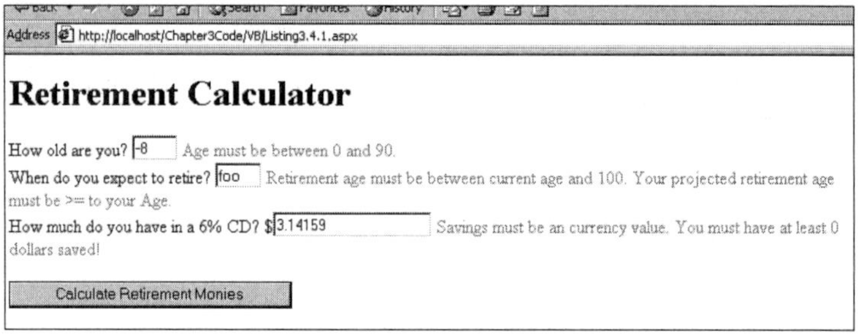

FIGURE 3.7
Error messages are displayed if the user enters invalid information.

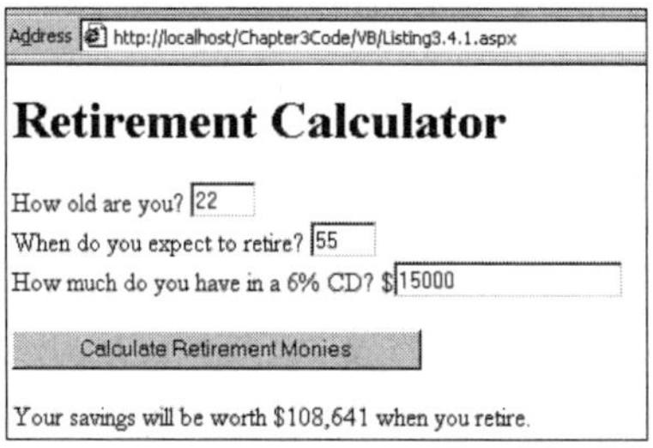

FIGURE 3.8
Once legitimate values have been entered into all the form fields, the user is presented with her investment's value upon reaching retirement age.

5. Using the `RegularExpressionValidator` Control

The validation controls that we've examined thus far all serve a fairly specific purpose. The `RequiredFieldValidator` control is designed for ensuring that the user enters a value into a form field; the `CompareValidator` is useful for comparing a form field value with either a static value or the value of another form field; the `RangeValidator` is handy for requiring that a form field's value be between two values.

The `RegularExpressionValidator`, on the other hand, is the most flexible and generic validation control. As its name implies, the `RegularExpressionValidator` checks a form field entry against a developer-defined regular expression. A *regular expression* is a special string that can be used to efficiently check for patterns in another string. For more information on regular expressions, refer to "3.Using Regular Expressions," in Chapter 2, "Common ASP.NET Code Techniques."

The `RegularExpressionValidator` control is most handy for ensuring that a user-entered form field value meets a certain formatting criteria. social security numbers, zip codes, telephone numbers, email addresses, and URLs are all commonly requested pieces of information that must conform to a particular format. When collecting such information from your users, it behooves you to use a `RegularExpressionValidator` to ensure that your users are supplying the information in the proper format.

Listing 3.5.1 contains a very simple ASP.NET page that inquires the user for his social security number and zip code. A `RegularExpressionValidator` control is used for each text box in Listing 3.5.1.

LISTING 3.5.1 Use a `RegularExpressionValidator` Control to Ask Your Users for Information in a Particular Format

```
 1: <script language="vb" runat="server">
 2:    Sub btnSubmit_Click(sender as Object, e as EventArgs)
 3:
 4:        If Page.IsValid Then
 5:           'Page is valid...
 6:           Response.Write("<font color=red><b>Valid form field entries!
➥ </b></font>")
 7:        Else
 8:           'Page is NOT valid
 9:           Response.Write("<font color=red><b>Not yet valid!</b></font>")
10:        End If
11:
12:    End Sub
13: </script>
14:
15: <html>
16: <body>
17:    <form method="post" runat="server">
18:      <h1>Give Us Your Personal Information, Please</h1>
19:      Social Security Number (###-##-####):
20:      <asp:textbox id="txtSSN" runat="server" />
21:      <asp:RegularExpressionValidator runat="server"
22:           id="regexpSSN" ValidationExpression="^\d{3}\-\d{2}\-\d{4}$"
23:           ControlToValidate="txtSSN" Display="Dynamic"
24:           ErrorMessage="SSN must be in ###-##-#### format." />
25:      <asp:RequiredFieldValidator runat="server"
26:           id="reqSSN"
27:           ControlToValidate="txtSSN" Display="Dynamic"
28:           ErrorMessage="You must supply an SSN." />
29:
30:      <br>ZIP Code:
31:      <asp:textbox id="txtZip" runat="server" />
```

LISTING 3.5.1 Continued

```
32:      <asp:RegularExpressionValidator runat="server"
33:         id="regexpZip" ValidationExpression="^\d{4}(\d|\d\-\d{4})$"
34:         ControlToValidate="txtZip" Display="Dynamic"
35:         ErrorMessage="Zip must be in ##### or #####-#### format." />
36:      <asp:RequiredFieldValidator runat="server"
37:         id="reqZip"
38:         ControlToValidate="txtZip" Display="Dynamic"
39:         ErrorMessage="You must supply a Zip Code." />
40:      <p><asp:button id="btnSubmit" runat="server"
41:             Text="Submit" OnClick="btnSubmit_Click" />
42:   </form>
43: </body>
44: </html>
```

The HTML section for Listing 3.5.1 starts on line 15. A postback form is created on line 17, followed by a text box (`txtSSN`) for the user's social security number (line 19). Social security numbers, for those outside of the U.S., are nine-digit numbers usually represented as ###-##-####, where each # is represented by a number (such as 123-12-1234).

A `RegularExpressionValidator` control is created on lines 21 through 24 to ensure that the user's entered social security number matches the specified format. The `RegularExpressionValidator` control only has a couple required properties: `ControlToValidate`, like any other validation control, specifies the form field to validate (line 23). The other important property is `ValidationExpression`, which specifies the regular expression pattern to validate the form field against (line 22).

Regardless of the regular expression pattern, `RegularExpressionValidator` controls report as valid if the user does not supply an entry into the form field. If you want to require that the user enter a value into the form field and have it match the regular expression specified in the `RegularExpressionValidator`, you must also use a `RequiredFieldValidator` control. Because we want to require the user to enter a social security number in Listing 3.5.1, we use a `RequiredFieldValidator` control (lines 25 through 28).

The second text box created in Listing 3.5.1 is the `txtZip` text box, which appears on line 31. This text box is for the user's zip code, which can either be in the format ##### or #####-#### (replacing each # with a number). A `RegularExpressionValidator` control is created from lines 32 through 35 to ensure that the user's entry in the `txtZip` text box conforms to the accepted format. Because we also want to require the user to enter his zip code, a `RequiredFieldValidator` (lines 36 through 39) is also included.

The HTML section in Listing 3.5.1 concludes on lines 40 and 41 with the creation of a submit button (`btnSubmit`). When this button is clicked, the form will be posted back, the page will be reloaded, and the `Page_Load` event handler will fire. The `Page_Load` event handler is very simple: It first checks to ensure that the page has been posted back (line 3); if it has, the `Page_Load` event checks to determine whether the page is valid and outputs a message indicating the validity of the form fields (lines 4 through 10).

Figure 3.9 shows the result of the code in Listing 3.5.1 when the user has entered some invalid entries into the text boxes. Figure 3.10 shows the result of the form when the user has entered legal values into the three text boxes.

FIGURE 3.9
Error messages are displayed if the user enters invalid information.

FIGURE 3.10
A simple message is displayed once the form fields contain legal values.

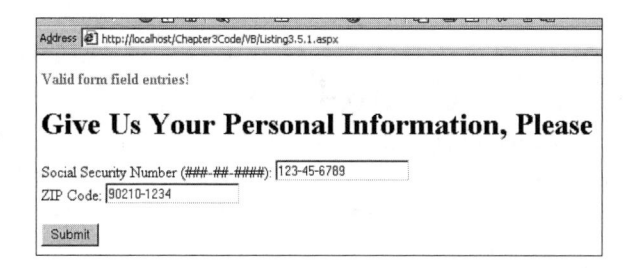

> **Tip**
>
> For a listing of useful regular expressions for use with the RegularExpressionValidation control be sure to refer to Appendix B, "Commonly Used Regular Expressions."

6. Using the `CustomValidator` Control

Although there are a number of validation controls for you to use in your ASP.NET pages to validate form field values, there will inevitably come a time where one of the existing validation controls just won't cut it for you. For example, all valid credit card numbers, when entered into what is known as the *Luhn formula*, will return a value that is evenly divisible by 10. The Luhn formula is a two-step process: First, every alternating digit, starting from the second-to-the-right digit, has its value doubled; next, the individual digits in each of these doublings are summed up along with those digits *not* doubled. If the final summation returns a value that is divisible by 10, the credit card number is a valid card number; otherwise, it is not.

> **Note**
>
> If you know the credit card company (MasterCard, Visa, American Express, and so on), there are more accurate tests that can be performed. To learn more, visit `http://perl.miningco.com/compute/perl/library/weekly/aa073000a.htm`. Note that any such validation routine just ensures that the credit card number presented *could* be a valid credit card number. To completely ensure that a credit card number exists and is in good standing, you must run the credit card number through some sort of Web server setup to validate credit card information and transactions.

When the form is submitted and validation needs to occur, the `CustomValidator` control's `ServerValidate` event is fired. For the `CustomValidator`, you must create an event handler for this event. The `CustomValidator` control can also contain a reference to a client-side function that will fire if the user's browser can handle client-side form validation.

In this section, we'll examine first how to create just the server-side validation event handler and then look at how to create a client-side form-validation function for the `CustomValidator` control. Because ASP.NET validation controls *always* perform server-side validation, it is *required* that you provide a server-side validation function for the `CustomValidator` control. The client-side validation function, however, is completely optional.

Creating Server-Side Validation Functions for the `CustomValidator` Control

Because we've already discussed the Luhn function and how it can be used to validate credit card numbers, let's go ahead and create a `CustomValidator` control that provides such functionality. Recall that `CustomValidator` controls must supply a server-side event handler that will perform the actual work of determining whether or not the user's entry was valid. This event handler must use the following specific definition:

```
'In VB.NET:
Sub CustomValidator(sender as Object, args as ServerValidateEventArgs)

// In C#
void CustomValidator(Object sender, ServerValidateEventArgs args)
```

Keep in mind that the purpose of the `CustomValidator` control is to validate some other Web control. So in our event handler we'll need to do two things:

1. Retrieve the value entered into the Web control that we wish to validate.
2. Let the `CustomValidator` control know if the user's entry was valid or invalid.

We can accomplish these two tasks by using the `ServerValidateEventArgs` parameter that is passed into our event handler. The `ServerValidateEventArgs` class contains two useful properties that we'll need to use. The property `Value` returns the String value entered by the user into the Web control that we wish to validate. Inside the event handler we must properly set the Boolean property `IsValid` indicating whether or not the user's entry was valid. (For examples on working with the `Value` and `IsValid` properties of the `ServerValidateEventArgs` class, see lines 13 and 16 in Listing 3.6.1, respectively.)

Listing 3.6.1 contains an ASP.NET page that displays a form with a single text box for the user's credit card number. This form field is validated by a `CustomValidator` control and its accompanying server-side validation function, `CreditCardCheck`.

LISTING 3.6.1 A `CustomValidator` Control Can Be Used to Perform Miscellaneous Validation Tasks, Such As Validating a Credit Card Number

```
 1: <script language="vb" runat="server">
 2:   Sub btnSubmit_Click(sender as Object, e as EventArgs)
 3:     If Page.IsValid then
 4:       Response.Write("You entered a valid credit card number.")
 5:     Else
```

LISTING 3.6.1 *Continued*

```
 6:          Response.Write("You entered an <b>invalid</b> credit card number.")
 7:       End If
 8:    End Sub
 9:
10:
11:    Sub CreditCardCheck(sender as Object, args as ServerValidateEventArgs)
↪ as Boolean
12:       Dim iLoop, iTotal, iTmpDoubling as Integer
13:       Dim strCreditCard as String = args.value
14:       'Make sure we're between 13 and 16 digits
15:       If strCreditCard.Length < 13 or strCreditCard.Length > 16 then
16:         args.IsValid = False
17:         Exit Sub
18:       End If
19:
20:       iLoop = strCreditCard.Length - 2
21:       iTotal += CInt(strCreditCard.Substring(iLoop+1,1))
22:       While iLoop >= 0
23:         'Double the current digit
24:         iTmpDoubling = CInt(strCreditCard.Substring(iLoop,1)) * 2
25:
26:         iTotal += iTmpDoubling mod 10
27:         If iTmpDoubling >= 10 then iTotal += 1
28:
29:         iLoop -= 1    'Move one digit to the left
30:
31:         If iLoop >= 0 Then
32:           iTotal += CInt(strCreditCard.Substring(iLoop,1))
33:           iLoop -= 1    'Move one digit to the left
34:         End If
35:       End While
36:
37:       'Return true if the number is evenly divisible by 10, false otherwise
38:       args.IsValid = (iTotal mod 10 = 0)
39:    End Function
40: </script>
41:
42: <html>
43: <body>
44:   <form method="post" runat="server">
45:     <h1>Enter Your Credit Card Information</h1>
46:     Enter your Credit Card Number:
47:     <asp:textbox id="txtCreditCardNumber" runat="server" />
48:     <asp:CustomValidator runat="server" id="custCreditCardVal"
49:         ControlToValidate="txtCreditCardNumber"
50:         OnServerValidate="CreditCardCheck" Display="Dynamic"
51:         ErrorMessage="Invalid Credit Card Number" />
52:
53:     <p><asp:button id="btnSubmit" runat="server"
54:           OnClick="btnSubmit_Click" Text="Calculate Retirement Monies" />
55:     <p><asp:label runat="server" id="lblResults" />
56:   </form>
57: </body>
58: </html>
```

The HTML section for Listing 3.6.1 is very straightforward: It creates a single text box in a postback form. This text box, `txtCreditCardNumber`, is created on line 47 and, as its name suggests, is for the user's credit card number. Validating this credit card number is not a task that any of the validation controls we've examined so far is up to. Rather, we will have to write our own validation function and wire it up to the form field via the `CustomValidator` control.

A `CustomValidator` control is created spanning lines 48 through 51. On line 49, the `ControlToValidate` property is set to the text box created on line 47. The `ControlToValidate` property for the `CustomValidator` control, like every other validation control we've looked at so far, specifies the form field control the validation control is responsible for validating. On line 50, the `OnServerValidate` event is wired up to the `CreditCardCheck` event handler (defined starting at line 11). The HTML section of Listing 3.6.1 ends with a submit button (`btnSubmit`) that, when clicked, posts back the form and fires the `btnSubmit_Click` event handler.

When the form is submitted, the custom validation event hanlder (`CreditCardCheck`, in Listing 3.6.1) is executed. This event handler's purpose is to determine whether or not the user's entry is valid. If the user's entry is valid, `args.IsValid` should be set to True; otherwise, it should be set to False.

In the `CreditCardCheck` function, the Luhn function is applied to the value entered by the user in the `txtCreditCardNumber` text box. On line 15, a quick check is made to ensure that the value of the text box, represented by the `Value` property of the `ServerValidateEventArgs` parameter (`args`) (see line 13), is 13, 14, 15, or 16 digits long. If it is not, `args.IsValid` is set to False and the event handler exits (lines 16 and 17). The Luhn function is applied in lines 20 through 35. Finally, on line 38, the summation value (`iTotal`) is checked to see whether it is evenly divisible by 10. If it is, `IsValid` is set to True; otherwise, it is set to False. For more information on the Luhn function, be sure to check out http://perl.miningco.com/compute/perl/library/weekly/aa073000a.htm.

> **Note**
> Rather than just performing a simple Luhn validation, `CreditCardCheck` could make a Web Services call to a credit card–validation server. For more information on Web Services, be sure to read Chapter 13, "Web Services."

When the user enters his credit card number and submits the form, the `btnSubmit_Click` event handler is fired. It immediately checks to determine whether the page is valid (line 3) and displays a message accordingly. The validity status of the `CustomValidator` control we created depends on the Boolean value returned by our custom function `CreditCardCheck`.

Figure 3.11 shows the result of the code in Listing 3.6.1 when viewed through a browser.

FIGURE 3.11
The user has entered an invalid credit card number and is not allowed to proceed.

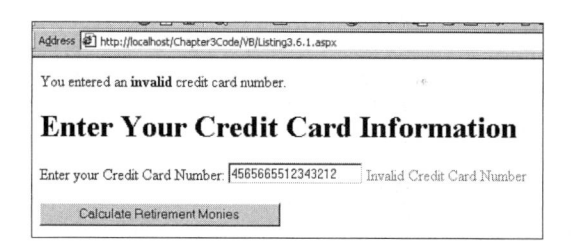

Creating Client-Side Validation Functions for the `CustomValidator` Control

As mentioned earlier in this chapter, it is always best to provide your users with *both* client-side and server-side form validation. The ASP.NET validation controls we've examined so far provide both forms of validation (assuming that the user's browser can support such client-side validation). With the `CustomValidator` control, you are responsible for providing any sort of client-side validation function.

Adding client-side validation support for the `CustomValidator` control is fairly simple. All you need to do is create a client-side function that accepts two parameters, just like the server-side event handler. This function name should then be specified in the `CustomValidator` control's `ClientValidationFunction` property. That's all there is to it! Because the client-side and server-side validation functions both have the same task—validating a form field entry's data—you can oftentimes simply cut and paste the server-side function to the client-side function. Although a few syntactical changes will need to be made from the server-side version to the client-side version, these changes should only take a few minutes.

Listing 3.6.2 contains the code for a simple ASP.NET page. This page displays a single text box into which the user is asked to enter her favorite prime number. (A prime number is a whole number that is divisible only by 1 and itself.) Both server-side and client-side validation functions exist.

LISTING 3.6.2 `CustomValidator` Controls Can Contain a Client-Side Validation Function As Well As a Server-Side One

```
 1: <script language="vb" runat="server">
 2:   Sub btnSubmit_Click(sender as Object, e as EventArgs)
 3:     If Page.IsValid then
 4:       Response.Write(txtPrimeNumber.Text & " is, indeed, a good
➥ prime number.")
 5:     Else
 6:       Response.Write(txtPrimeNumber.Text & " is <b>not</b> a
➥ prime number.")
 7:     End If
 8:   End Sub
 9:
```

LISTING 3.6.2 Continued

```
10:    Sub PrimeNumberCheck(sender as Object, args as ServerValidateEventArgs)
11:      Dim iPrime as Integer = CInt(args.value), iLoop as Integer, _
12:         iSqrt as Integer = CInt(Math.Sqrt(iPrime))
13:
14:      For iLoop = 2 to iSqrt
15:        If iPrime mod iLoop = 0 then
16:          args.IsValid = False
17:          Exit Function
18:        End If
19:      Next
20:
21:      args.IsValid = True     'Number is prime
22:    End Function
23: </script>
24:
25: <html>
26: <head>
27:    <script language="JavaScript">
28:    <!--
29:      function CheckPrime(source, args)
30:      {
31:        var iPrime = parseInt(args.Value);
32:        var iSqrt = parseInt(Math.sqrt(iPrime));
33:
34:        for (var iLoop=2; iLoop <= iSqrt; iLoop++)
35:          if (iPrime % iLoop == 0) {args.IsValid=false;return;}
36:
37:        args.IsValid= true;
38:      }
39:    // -->
40:    </script>
41: </head>
42: <body>
43:    <form method="post" runat="server">
44:      <h1>Enter Your Credit Card Information</h1>
45:      Enter your favorite prime number:
46:      <asp:textbox id="txtPrimeNumber" runat="server" />
47:      <asp:CustomValidator runat="server" id="custPrimeCheck"
48:          ControlToValidate="txtPrimeNumber"
49:          OnServerValidate="PrimeNumberCheck" Display="Dynamic"
50:          ClientValidationFunction="CheckPrime"
51:          ErrorMessage="Invalid Prime Number" />
52:      <asp:CompareValidator runat="server" id="compPrimeNumber"
53:          Operator="DataTypeCheck" Type="Integer"
54:          Display="Dynamic" ControlToValidate="txtPrimeNumber"
55:          ErrorMessage = "You must enter an integer value." />
56:      <asp:CompareValidator runat="server" id="compPrimeNumberPositive"
57:          Operator="GreaterThan" Type="Integer"
58:          Display="Dynamic" ValueToCompare="0"
59:          ControlToValidate="txtPrimeNumber"
```

LISTING 3.6.2   Continued

```
60:              ErrorMessage = "You must enter a value greater than zero." />
61:
62:     <p><asp:button id="btnSubmit" runat="server"
63:              OnClick="btnSubmit_Click" Text="Submit" />
64:   </form>
65: </body>
66: </html>
```

The HTML section for Listing 3.6.2 contains a postback form (line 43) with a single text box, `txtPrimeNumber` (line 46). This text box is for the user to enter her favorite prime number. Because prime numbers must be whole numbers (integer values greater than zero), two `CompareValidator` controls are used. The first, `compPrimeNumber`, spans lines 52 through 55 and ensures that the `txtPrimeNumber` text box value is an integer. The second, `compPrimeNumberPositive`, spans lines 56 through 60 and ensures that `txtPrimeNumber` contains a value greater than zero.

The `CustomValidator` control `custPrimeCheck`, spanning lines 47 through 51, does the actual prime number verification. It specifies a server-side event handler for the `OnServerValidate` function (line 49) as well as a client-side function. Users who visit with a browser capable of client-side validation will utilize the client-side function specified by the `ClientValidationFunction` property on line 50. This function, `CheckPrime`, is defined from lines 29 through 38, ensuring that the number entered into the `txtPrimeNumber` text box is indeed prime.

Note that this client-side function accepts two parameters, just like the server-side version. Also, like the server-side event handler, the client-side event handler needs to set the `IsValid` property of the second parameter (this parameter was named `args` on line 29 in Listing 3.6.2). The `CheckPrime` and `PrimeNumberCheck` functions work in a similar fashion: They loop from 2 through the square root of the number in the `txtPrimeNumber` text box. At each iteration, a check is done to determine whether the number entered by the user is divisible by the current value of the loop iteration. If it is evenly divisible, the `IsValid` property is set to False because, clearly, the number is not a prime. If this loop completes, however, the number is prime.

> **Note**
>
> In Listing 3.6.2 the client-side validation function is written using JavaScript. Client-side form validations for Internet Explorer can be written using VBScript. However, it's recommended that you use JavaScript because that's the only supported scripting language by both Netscape and IE.

Figure 3.12 shows the result of the code in Listing 3.6.2 when viewed through a browser.

FIGURE 3.12
The user has entered a non-prime number.

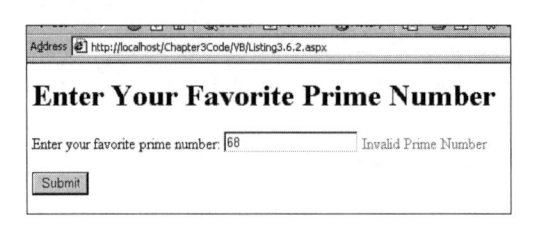

Take a moment to look at Figure 3.12 and Figure 3.11. Recall that Figure 3.11 depicts the `CustomValidator` control's output when using *just* a server-side form-validation function. Unfortunately, the screenshots do not clearly reveal the benefit of having a client-side validation function. Rather, you have to actually try out the demos that are downloadable from the Web site to note the differences.

With just the server-side validation, the form must be submitted and a roundtrip to the Web server must occur for the form field to be validated. With a supplied client-side validation function, however, all the validation can be performed on the client's Web browser. Therefore, in Figure 3.12, if the user were to enter a non-prime number and then move focus from the text box (for example, by tabbing out of the text box), the validation error message would be displayed immediately, as opposed to requiring the user to actually submit the form before seeing the validation error.

7. Using the `ValidationSummary` Control

In the numerous code listings throughout this chapter, we examined how an error message can be displayed from a validation control when the control reports an invalid state. (In case you need a refresher, all you need to do is set the validation control's `Display` property to either `Dynamic` or `Static` and set the `ErrorMessage` property to the message you want to have displayed when the user enters invalid data.) Clearly, displaying error information for each validation control is simple, requiring just a few lines of code. But what if you want to display a summary of the errors in one convenient location, as opposed to an error near each form field?

This can be done by programmatically accessing each validation control, checking its `IsValid` property and, if it's invalid, displaying the validation control's `ErrorMessage` value. Writing such a validation summary function wouldn't be incredibly difficult, but it would be a bulky chunk of code that needs to appear in each ASP.NET page that needed to display a validation summary. Additionally, each developer would be on his own to create this functionality. To accommodate the anticipated need for a validation summary, the ASP.NET team created the `ValidationSummary` control.

This control, like the other validation controls, requires only a few lines of code. Because the `ValidationSummary` control is responsible for summarizing the state of the validation controls on the ASP.NET page, it does not contain any sort of `ControlToValidate` property. Rather, all its properties reflect settings on how the validation summary report should be displayed.

In Listing 3.7.1, the form from Listing 3.4.1 is enhanced by adding a validation summary report. Note that each of the existing validation controls has had its `Display` property changed to None. This change is purely a cosmetic one: Because we have created a validation summary for the page, there's no need to have each form field element *also* display its error message.

LISTING 3.7.1 To Display a Summary Report of the Validation Controls on an ASP.NET Page, Use the ValidationSummary Control

```
 1: <script language="c#" runat="server">
 2:   void btnSubmit_Click(Object sender, EventArgs e)
 3:   {
 4:     Double dblValue = 0.0, dblPrincipal = 0.0;
 5:     int iYears = 0;
 6:
 7:     if (Page.IsValid) {
 8:       iYears = Convert.ToInt32(txtRetireAge.Text) -
➥ Convert.ToInt32(txtAge.Text);
 9:       dblPrincipal = Convert.ToSingle(txtSavings.Text);
10:       dblValue = dblPrincipal * Math.Exp(Convert.ToSingle(iYears) * 0.06);
11:
12:       lblResults.Text = "Your savings will be worth $" +
13:                 String.Format("{0:c}", dblValue) +
➥ " when you retire.";
14:     }
15:   }
16: </script>
17:
18: <html>
19: <body>
20:   <form method="post" runat="server">
21:     <h1>Retirement Calculator</h1>
22:     <asp:ValidationSummary runat="server" id="ValSummary"
23:           HeaderText="Validation Summary"
24:           DisplayMode="BulletList" />
25:
26:     How old are you?
27:     <asp:textbox id="txtAge" runat="server" Columns="3" />
28:     <asp:RangeValidator runat="server"
29:           id="rngAge" Type="Integer" MinimumValue="0"
30:           MaximumValue="90"
31:           ControlToValidate="txtAge" Display="None"
32:           ErrorMessage="Age must be between 0 and 90." />
33:
34:     <br>When do you expect to retire?
35:     <asp:textbox id="txtRetireAge" runat="server" Columns="3" />
36:     <asp:RangeValidator runat="server"
37:           id="rngRetireAge" Type="Integer"
38:           ControlToValidate="txtRetireAge" Display="None"
39:           MinimumValue="0" MaximumValue="100"
40:           ErrorMessage = "Retirement age must be between 0
➥ and 100." />
41:     <asp:CompareValidator runat="server"
42:           id="compRetireAge" Type="Integer" Operator="GreaterThanEqual"
43:           ControlToValidate="txtRetireAge" Display="Dynamic"
```

LISTING 3.7.1 *Continued*

```
44:            ControlToCompare="txtAge"
45:            ErrorMessage="Your projected retirement age must be >= to your Age."
➥/>
46:
47:     <br>How much do you have in a 6% CD?
48:     $<asp:textbox id="txtSavings" runat="server" />
49:     <asp:CompareValidator runat="server"
50:            id="compSavigs" Type="Currency" Operator="DataTypeCheck"
51:            ControlToValidate="txtSavings" Display="None"
52:            ErrorMessage="Savings must be an currency value." />
53:     <asp:CompareValidator runat="server"
54:            id="compSavigsMinimum" Type="Currency" Operator="GreaterThanEqual"
55:            ControlToValidate="txtSavings" ValueToCompare="0"
56:            Display="None"
57:            ErrorMessage="You must have at least 0 dollars saved!" />
58:
59:     <p><asp:button id="btnSubmit" runat="server"
60:            OnClick="btnSubmit_Click" Text="Calculate Retirement Monies" />
61:     <p><asp:label runat="server" id="lblResults" />
62:   </form>
63: </body>
64: </html>
```

Because Listing 3.7.1 contains a lot of code from Listing 3.4.1, I won't delve into the details of the retirement savings calculator code. Rather, we'll just look at the `ValidationSummary` control (lines 22 through 24). In this control, we set two properties: `HeaderText` and `DisplayMode`. `HeaderText` indicates the title that should be used when displaying the validation summary report; `DisplayMode` indicates how the report should be displayed. `DisplayMode` expects a value from the `ValidationSummaryDisplayMode` enumeration (found in the `System.Web.UI.WebControls` namespace). The members of this enumeration can be found in Table 3.4.

When the page is first loaded, the validation summary report is not displayed because the page is considered valid at that point. If the user enters any invalid form field data, the validation summary report will be displayed once the form is submitted. Figure 3.13 shows the result of the code in Listing 3.7.1 when viewed through a browser with various illegal form fields.

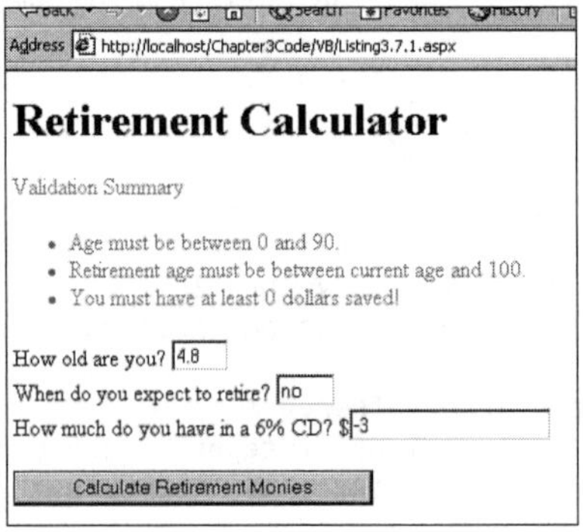

FIGURE 3.13
A validation summary report can be displayed as a bulleted list.

Some of the optional `ValidationSummary` properties that were not utilized in Listing 3.7.1 include the following:

- `ForeColor`—Specifies the text color that should be used when displaying the validation summary (defaults to Red). Legal values for this property include those in the `System.Drawing.Color` structure.

- `ShowMessageBox`—A Boolean value indicating whether or not the validation summary report should be displayed in a pop-up message box. The default value is False.

- `ShowSummary`—A Boolean value indicating whether or not the validation summary report should be displayed at all. The default value is True.

In Listing 3.7.1 the `ValidationSummary` control had its `DisplayMode` property set to `BulletList`, which, as its name implies, displays the validation summary report in a bulleted list. The other legal `DisplayMode` options can be seen in Table 3.4.

TABLE 3.4 The Values of the `ValidationSummaryDisplayMode` Enumeration That the `DisplayMode` Property of the `ValidationSummary` Control Can Accept

Value	Description
BulletList	Each invalid validation control's error message is displayed on its own line with a bullet point.
List	Each invalid validation control's error message is displayed on its own line.
SingleParagraph	Each invalid validation control's error message is displayed in a single paragraph.

Figure 3.14 shows a screenshot of a slightly modified Listing 3.7.1, one that has had the `DisplayMode` property changed from `BulletList` to `List` (the `DisplayMode` property is set on line 24 of Listing 3.7.1). Finally, Figure 3.15 shows the output of the validation summary report when `DisplayMode` is set to `SingleParagraph`.

FIGURE 3.14
The validation summary report can also be displayed as a simple list.

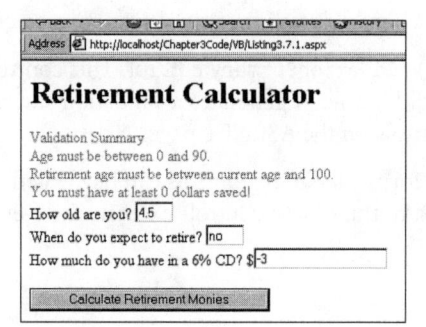

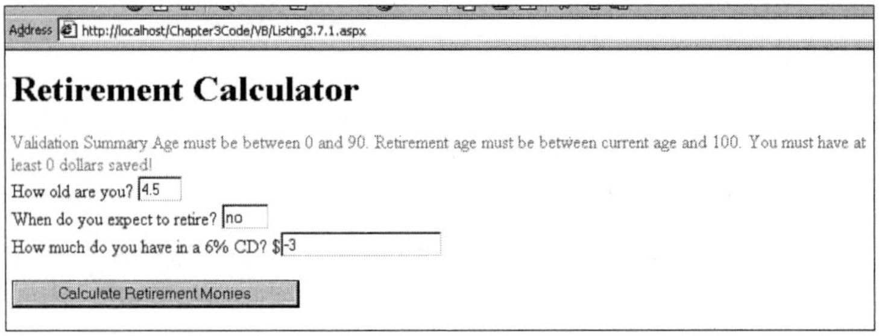

FIGURE 3.15
Additionally, the validation report summary can be displayed as a single paragraph.

Summary

One of the most useful (and coolest) new features of ASP.NET is the ability to use the validation controls. These controls provide developers with a reusable means to create powerful client- and server-side validation checks with just a few lines of code. ASP.NET contains a number of existing validation controls for common validation needs.

The `RequiredFieldValidator` control is useful when a user *must* enter a value for a particular form field, whether it be a text box, list box, radio button, or check box. The `CompareValidator` is useful for comparing the value of a form field against the value of another form field or against a hard-coded value. Furthermore, the `CompareValidator` can be used to ensure that a form field's value is of a particular data type. The `RangeValidator` control is handy for ensuring that the value of a form field falls within a certain range. The bounds for the range can be determined by a hard-coded value, a form field value, or a combination of the two.

The two most powerful validation controls, in my opinion, are the `RegularExpressionValidator` and `CustomValidator` controls. The `RegularExpressionValidator` control enables developers to quickly check a form field entry against a regular expression pattern. This can be handy for checking data that must be presented in a certain format, such as a social security number or phone number. The `CustomValidator` control grants the developer the ability to create his own validation functions. Both server-side and client-side validation functions can be created.

ASP.NET also includes the `ValidationSummary` control. This control is not responsible for validating a particular form field; rather, it generates a validation summary report based on the status of the validation controls on the ASP.NET page.

Given the ease with which form-validation controls can be created, there's no excuse why ASP.NET developers should not use these controls extensively to ensure that their form fields have valid entries.

Other Resources

This chapter focused on examining the various ASP.NET form validation controls and how to use them. We did not, however, delve into creating client-side form validation routines for the

`CustomValidator`; nor did we look at the rules behind creating and using regular expressions. In these recommended readings you will find information on JavaScript client-side form validation techniques as well as information on creating and using regular expressions.

- The JavaScript Source—There are a plethora of Web sites available with oodles of client-side JavaScript functions that can be easily cut and pasted into your Web pages. One of the best sites is The JavaScript Source. `http://javascript.internet.com/`

- JavaScript Articles and Tutorials—If you have not had much experience with client-side JavaScript programming in the past, a great place to get started is WebReference.com's JavaScript Tutorials and Article Index. `http://webreference.com/programming/javascript/`

- QuickStart Documentation—The QuickStart documentation (which you can install on your computer from the CD included in this book) contains a full section on the various form validation controls with examples and a technical discussion. Visit the QuickStart documentation online at: `http://www.gotdotnet.com/quickstart/aspplus/doc/webvalidation.aspx`

- Commonly Used Regular Expressions—Appendix B of this book contains a handy list of useful regular expressions that you can start using with the `RegularExpressionValidation` control. Refer to Appendix B, "Commonly Used Regular Expressions."

- Mastering Regular Expressions—This book is a must have for anyone who wishes to become truly proficient at regular expressions. While the book presents most of its examples using Perl, it still does a fantastic job of explaining regular expressions. *Authored by: Friedl, Jeffrey E. F. Published By: O'Reilly Press, 1997*

CHAPTER 4

ENABLING BETTER BROWSER SUPPORT

by Doug Seven

> **In this chapter you will learn**
> - About the `HttpBrowserCapabilities` class
> - How to determine the requesting browser's capabilities in an ASP.NET Web Form
> - How to redirect page requests based on the requesting browser's capabilities
> - How the `ClientTarget` property affects the rendered output of an ASP.NET Web Form

ASP.NET brings with it a number of new features and functions that enable you to build Web applications suitable for any browser. Many of these new features, such as expression validator controls and data controls, can be rendered by the .NET Framework as either HTML 3.2, or HTML 4.0 with JavaScript support. The decision on how to render the page is dependent on the browser type and version making the request. The .NET Framework evaluates the browser and renders content appropriately.

At the time this book was written the factors the .NET Framework used to make a rendering decision were are based around:

- For validation controls, the .NET Framework evaluates whether the browser is Microsoft Internet Explorer 4.0 DHTML compatible or better, higher for up-level, or any other browser for down-level.

- Many of the rich controls and properties render based on the browsers CSS support.

There will likely be situations when you will want to evaluate a browser and its capabilities and generate output accordingly. In previous versions of ASP, you could use the Browser Capabilities component to find out information about the requesting browser. The classic ASP version of the Browser Capabilities provided attributes for checking things such as the browser name, version, if frames or tables were supported, etc. In ASP.NET, the functionality of the Browser Capabilities component has been encapsulated and expanded in the `HttpBrowserCapabilities` class.

The `HttpBrowserCapabilities` class enables a server to compile information on the capabilities of a browser making a request. It is part of the `System.Web` namespace.

> **Note**
> The `System.Web` namespace is automatically imported for all ASP.NET Web Forms, so there is no need to explicitly import the namespace.

1. Determining a Visitor's Browser Capabilities with the `HttpBrowserCapabilities` Class

The `HttpBrowserCapabilities` class provides the same base functionality as the Browser Capabilities component that shipped with classic ASP.

The Browser Capabilities component exposed the attributes listed in Table 4.1.

TABLE 4.1 The Attributes of the Browser Capabilities Component

Attribute	Description
ActiveXControls	Specifies whether the browser supports ActiveX controls.
Backgroundsounds	Specifies whether the browser supports background sounds.
Beta	Specifies whether the browser is beta software.
Browser	Specifies the name of the browser.
Cdf	Specifies whether the browser supports the Channel Definition Format for Web casting.
Cookies	Specifies whether the browser supports cookies.
Frames	Specifies whether the browser supports frames.
Javaapplets	Specifies whether the browser supports Java applets.
Javascript	Specifies whether the browser supports JavaScript or JScript.
Platform	Specifies the platform the browser runs on.
Tables	Specifies whether the browser supports tables.
Vbscript	Specifies whether the browser supports VBScript.
Version	Specifies the version number of the browser.

Along with this base functionality, the `HttpBrowserCapabilities` class provides some new properties not previously found in the Browser Capabilities component. The full set of properties in the `HttpBrowserCapabilities` class are listed in Table 4.2.

> **Note**
> When using C# as the programming language to author ASP.NET applications, case sensitivity becomes an issue. The full set of `HttpBrowserCapabilities`' properties are listed in Table 4.2 to ensure we have the correct capitalization.

TABLE 4.2 The Properties of the `HttpBrowserCapabilities` Class

Property	Description
`ActiveXControls`	Gets a value indicating whether the client browser supports ActiveX controls.
`AOL`	Gets a value indicating whether the client is an America Online (AOL) browser.
`BackgroundSounds`	Gets a value indicating whether the client browser supports background sounds.
`Beta`	Gets a value indicating whether the browser is a beta release.
`Browser`	Gets the browser string (if any) that was transmitted in the `User-Agent` header.
`CDF`	Gets a value indicating whether the client browser supports Channel Definition Format (CDF) for Web casting.
`Cookies`	Gets a value indicating whether the client browser supports cookies.
`Crawler`	Gets a value indicating whether the client browser is a Web crawler search engine.
`EcmaScriptVersion`	Gets the version number of ECMA script that the client browser supports.
`Frames`	Gets a value indicating whether the client browser supports HTML frames.
`Item`	Allows access to individual dictionary values. In C#, this property is the indexer for the `HttpBrowserCapabilities` class.
`JavaApplets`	Gets a value indicating whether the client browser supports Java applets.
`JavaScript`	Gets a value indicating whether the client browser supports JavaScript.
`MajorVersion`	Gets the major version number of the client browser.
`MinorVersion`	Gets the minor version number of the client browser.

TABLE 4.2 Continued

Property	Description
MSDomVersion	Gets the version of Microsoft XML Document Object Model (DOM) that the client browser supports.
Platform	Gets the name of the platform that the client uses.
Tables	Gets a value indicating whether the client browser supports HTML tables.
Type	Gets the name and major version number of the client browser.
VBScript	Gets a value indicating whether the client browser supports VBScript.
Version	Gets the full (major and minor) version number of the client browser.
W3CdomVersion	Gets the version of the World Wide Web Consortium (W3C) XML Document Object Model (DOM) that the client browser supports.
Win16	Gets a value indicating whether the client is a Win16-based machine.
Win32	Gets a value indicating whether the client is a Win32-based machine.

To use the `HttpBrowserCapabilities` class, you must instantiate it as an instance of the current `Request.Browser` object. This enables you to access all the class's properties and evaluate them.

`Dim bc As HttpBrowserCapabilities = Request.Browser`

Once you have an instance of the `HttpBrowserCapabilities` class, you can use the properties to perform evaluations, make decisions, or simply list the capabilities. Listing 4.1.1 shows the ASP.NET Web Form that renders a table listing all the capabilities of the current browser.

LISTING 4.1.1 Displaying the Capabilities of a Browser

```
 1: <script runat="server" language="vb">
 2:   Protected css As String
 3:   Protected Sub Page_Load(Sender As Object, E As EventArgs)
 4:     Dim bc As HttpBrowserCapabilities = Request.Browser
 5:     If bc.Browser = "IE" Then
 6:       css = "<LINK rel='stylesheet' type='text/css' href='4.1.2.css'>"
 7:     Else
 8:       css = "<LINK rel='stylesheet' type='text/css' href='4.1.2.nonie.css'>"
 9:     End If
10:
11:     Welcome.Text = "Welcome! You are using " & bc.Browser & " v." & _
12:       bc.Version & " on a " & bc.Platform & " machine."
13:     ActiveXControls.Text = bc.ActiveXControls
14:     AOL.Text = bc.AOL
15:     BackgroundSounds.Text = bc.BackgroundSounds
16:     Beta.Text = bc.Beta
17:     Browser.Text = bc.Browser
18:     CDF.Text = bc.CDF
```

LISTING 4.1.1 *Continued*

```
19:     Cookies.Text = bc.Cookies
20:     Crawler.Text = bc.Crawler
21:     EcmaScriptVersion.Text = bc.EcmaScriptVersion.ToString()
22:     Frames.Text = bc.Frames
23:     JavaApplets.Text = bc.JavaApplets
24:     JavaScript.Text = bc.JavaScript
25:     MajorVersion.Text = bc.MajorVersion.ToString()
26:     MinorVersion.Text = bc.MinorVersion.ToString()
27:     MSDomVersion.Text = bc.MSDomVersion.ToString()
28:     Platform.Text = bc.Platform
29:     Tables.Text = bc.Tables
30:     Type.Text = bc.Type
31:     VBScript.Text = bc.VBScript
32:     Version.Text = bc.Version.ToString()
33:     W3CDomVersion.Text = bc.W3CDomVersion.ToString()
34:     Win16.Text = bc.Win16
35:     Win32.Text = bc.Win32
36:   End Sub
37: </script>
38: <html>
39: <head>
40:   <title>DotNetJunkies.com - HttpBrowserCapabilities</title>
41:   <%= css %>
42: </head>
43: <body>
44: <form runat="server" method="post">
45: <p><asp:Label runat="server" id="Welcome" Font-Bold="True" /></p>
46:
47: <asp:Table runat="server" id="myTable" BorderWidth="1" Width="400"
48:   BorderColor="Black" BorderStyle="Solid" Gridlines="Horizontal"
49:   CellPadding="4" CellSpacing="0">
50:
51: <asp:TableRow runat="server" CssClass="EvenRow">
52:   <asp:TableCell runat="server" Text="Propety" Width="50%" />
53:   <asp:TableCell runat="server" Text="Value" Width="50%" />
54: </asp:TableRow>
55:
56: <asp:TableRow runat="server" CssClass="OddRow">
57:   <asp:TableCell runat="server" Text="ActiveXControls:" Width="50%" />
58:   <asp:TableCell runat="server" ID="ActiveXControls" Width="50%" />
59: </asp:TableRow>
60:
61: <asp:TableRow runat="server" CssClass="EvenRow">
62:   <asp:TableCell runat="server" Text="AOL:" Width="50%" />
63:   <asp:TableCell runat="server" ID="AOL" Width="50%" />
64: </asp:TableRow>
65:
66: <asp:TableRow runat="server" CssClass="OddRow">
67:   <asp:TableCell runat="server" Text="BackgroundSounds:" Width="50%" />
68:   <asp:TableCell runat="server" ID="BackgroundSounds" Width="50%" />
69: </asp:TableRow>
70:
```

LISTING 4.1.1 *Continued*

```
 71:     <asp:TableRow runat="server" CssClass="EvenRow">
 72:       <asp:TableCell runat="server" Text="Beta:" Width="50%" />
 73:       <asp:TableCell runat="server" ID="Beta" Width="50%" />
 74:     </asp:TableRow>
 75:
 76:     <asp:TableRow runat="server" CssClass="OddRow">
 77:       <asp:TableCell runat="server" Text="Browser:" Width="50%" />
 78:       <asp:TableCell runat="server" ID="Browser" Width="50%" />
 79:     </asp:TableRow>
 80:
 81:     <asp:TableRow runat="server" CssClass="EvenRow">
 82:       <asp:TableCell runat="server" Text="CDF:" Width="50%" />
 83:       <asp:TableCell runat="server" ID="CDF" Width="50%" />
 84:     </asp:TableRow>
 85:
 86:     <asp:TableRow runat="server" CssClass="OddRow">
 87:       <asp:TableCell runat="server" Text="Cookies:" Width="50%" />
 88:       <asp:TableCell runat="server" ID="Cookies" Width="50%" />
 89:     </asp:TableRow>
 90:
 91:     <asp:TableRow runat="server" CssClass="EvenRow">
 92:       <asp:TableCell runat="server" Text="Crawler:" Width="50%" />
 93:       <asp:TableCell runat="server" ID="Crawler" Width="50%" />
 94:     </asp:TableRow>
 95:
 96:
 97:     <asp:TableRow runat="server" CssClass="OddRow">
 98:       <asp:TableCell runat="server" Text="EcmaScriptVersion:" Width="50%" />
 99:       <asp:TableCell runat="server" ID="EcmaScriptVersion" Width="50%" />
100:     </asp:TableRow>
101:
102:     <asp:TableRow runat="server" CssClass="EvenRow">
103:       <asp:TableCell runat="server" Text="Frames:" Width="50%" />
104:       <asp:TableCell runat="server" ID="Frames" Width="50%" />
105:     </asp:TableRow>
106:
107:     <asp:TableRow runat="server" CssClass="OddRow">
108:       <asp:TableCell runat="server" Text="JavaApplets:" Width="50%" />
109:       <asp:TableCell runat="server" ID="JavaApplets" Width="50%" />
110:     </asp:TableRow>
111:
112:     <asp:TableRow runat="server" CssClass="EvenRow">
113:       <asp:TableCell runat="server" Text="JavaScript:" Width="50%" />
114:       <asp:TableCell runat="server" ID="JavaScript" Width="50%" />
115:     </asp:TableRow>
116:
117:     <asp:TableRow runat="server" CssClass="OddRow">
118:       <asp:TableCell runat="server" Text="MajorVersion:" Width="50%" />
```

LISTING 4.1.1 *Continued*

```
119:      <asp:TableCell runat="server" ID="MajorVersion" Width="50%" />
120:    </asp:TableRow>
121:
122:    <asp:TableRow runat="server" CssClass="EvenRow">
123:      <asp:TableCell runat="server" Text="MinorVersion:" Width="50%" />
124:      <asp:TableCell runat="server" ID="MinorVersion" Width="50%" />
125:    </asp:TableRow>
126:
127:    <asp:TableRow runat="server" CssClass="OddRow">
128:      <asp:TableCell runat="server" Text="MSDomVersion:" Width="50%" />
129:      <asp:TableCell runat="server" ID="MSDomVersion" Width="50%" />
130:    </asp:TableRow>
131:
132:    <asp:TableRow runat="server" CssClass="EvenRow">
133:      <asp:TableCell runat="server" Text="Platform:" Width="50%" />
134:      <asp:TableCell runat="server" ID="Platform" Width="50%" />
135:    </asp:TableRow>
136:
137:    <asp:TableRow runat="server" CssClass="OddRow">
138:      <asp:TableCell runat="server" Text="Tables:" Width="50%" />
139:      <asp:TableCell runat="server" ID="Tables" Width="50%" />
140:    </asp:TableRow>
141:
142:    <asp:TableRow runat="server" CssClass="EvenRow">
143:      <asp:TableCell runat="server" Text="Type:" Width="50%" />
144:      <asp:TableCell runat="server" ID="Type" Width="50%" />
145:    </asp:TableRow>
146:
147:    <asp:TableRow runat="server" CssClass="OddRow">
148:      <asp:TableCell runat="server" Text="VBScript:" Width="50%" />
149:      <asp:TableCell runat="server" ID="VBScript" Width="50%" />
150:    </asp:TableRow>
151:
152:    <asp:TableRow runat="server" CssClass="EvenRow">
153:      <asp:TableCell runat="server" Text="Version:" Width="50%" />
154:      <asp:TableCell runat="server" ID="Version" Width="50%" />
155:    </asp:TableRow>
156:
157:    <asp:TableRow runat="server" CssClass="OddRow">
158:      <asp:TableCell runat="server" Text="W3CDomVersion:" Width="50%" />
159:      <asp:TableCell runat="server" ID="W3CDomVersion" Width="50%" />
160:    </asp:TableRow>
161:
162:    <asp:TableRow runat="server" CssClass="EvenRow">
163:      <asp:TableCell runat="server" Text="Win16:" Width="50%" />
164:      <asp:TableCell runat="server" ID="Win16" Width="50%" />
165:    </asp:TableRow>
166:
167:    <asp:TableRow runat="server" CssClass="OddRow">
168:      <asp:TableCell runat="server" Text="Win32:" Width="50%" />
```

LISTING 4.1.1 Continued

```
169:      <asp:TableCell runat="server" ID="Win32" Width="50%" />
170:    </asp:TableRow>
171: </asp:Table>
172:
173: </form>
174: </body>
175: </html>
```

Listing 4.1.1 is rather long, but the majority of it is the code for an ASP.NET Table server control. The core of the functionality is in the first 37 lines.

On line 4, you instantiate the `HttpBrowserCapabilities` class as an instance of the `Request.Browser`. In lines 5–9, you use a basic `If...Then...Else` statement to evaluate the `Browser` property of the `HttpBrowserCapabilities` class. If the `Browser` property is the string "IE" (Microsoft Internet Explorer), you set a variable that will be used to render a link to a Cascading Stylesheet specifically designed for Internet Explorer. Otherwise, you set the variable to render a link to a non-Internet Explorer style sheet.

> **Note**
> The CSS style sheets used in Listing 4.1.1 can be found on the CD-ROM that came with this book, in the Chapter 4 directory.

Lines 5–9 demonstrate the basic functionality required to evaluate and make dynamic decisions based on the requesting browser's capabilities. Lines 11–12 dynamically assemble a "Welcome" line of text and set it to a Label control's `Text` property. The welcome text specifies the `Browser` property, the `MajorVersion` and `MinorVersion` properties, and the `Platform` property. Lines 13–35 apply each one of the `HttpBrowserCapabilities` properties to a separate TableRow control embedded in an ASP.NET Table server control.

> **Note**
> Visual Basic.NET does not require explicit conversions from Boolean data types to String data types. However, C# *does* require explicit conversions. Therefore, with C# code, all Boolean data types must be explicitly converted to String types using the `ToString()` method.
>
> `ActiveXControls.Text = bc.ActiveXControls.ToString();`

Figure 4.1 shows the rendered output of Listing 4.1.1 in Microsoft Internet Explorer 5.5 on a Windows 2000 Server machine.

Figure 4.2 shows the same ASP.NET Web Form rendered in Netscape 6.01.

FIGURE 4.1
The `HttpBrowser-Capabilities` properties can be displayed as text on an ASP.NET Web Form or evaluated and used to make dynamic decisions about how to process the page.

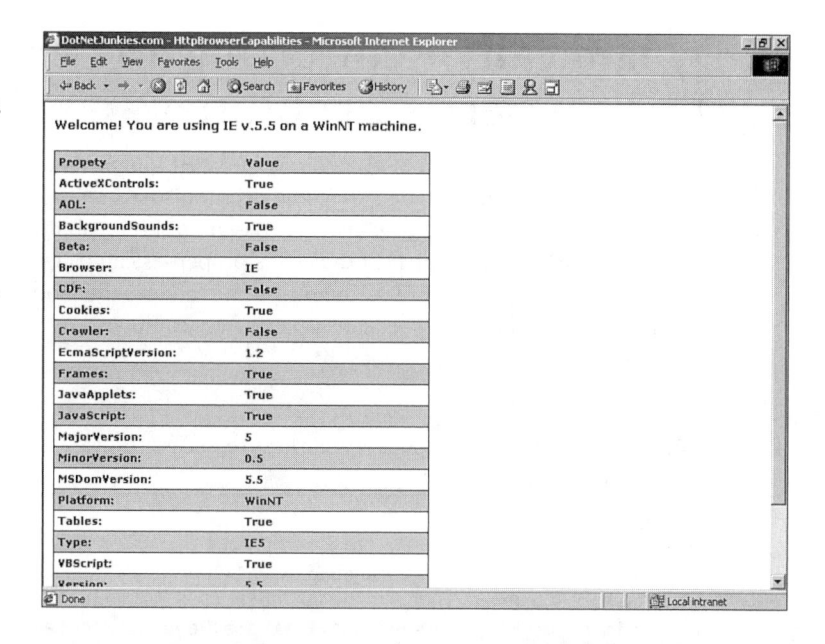

FIGURE 4.2
The `HttpBrowserCapabilities` properties are evaluated based on the requesting browser.

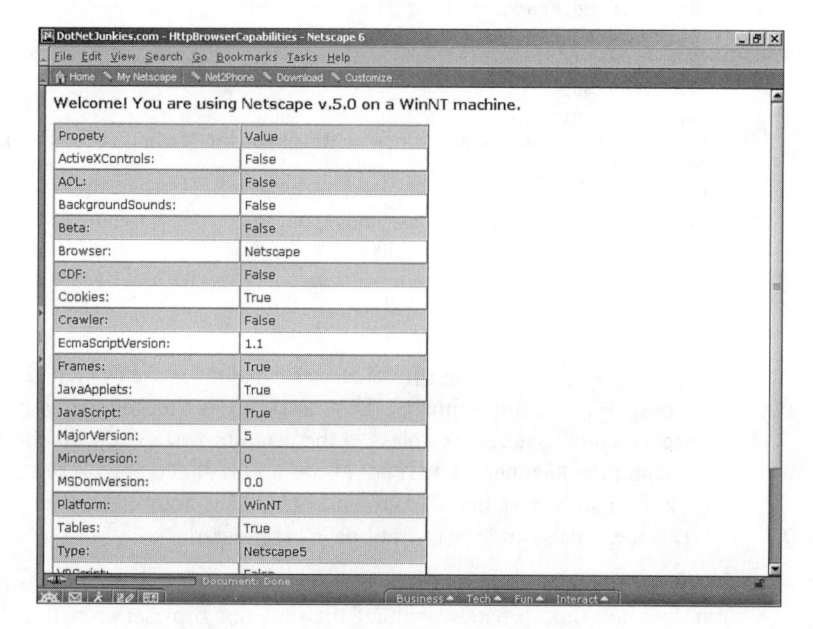

2. Dynamically Redirecting a User Based on His Browser's Capabilities

In the previous examples you evaluated one of the `HttpBrowserCapabilies` class's properties, the `Browser` property, and made a dynamic decision based on the result. Using similar logic, you can dynamically redirect page requests based on the capabilities of the requesting browser. Any of the `HttpBrowserCapabilities` class's properties can be evaluated and used as criteria. Listing 4.2.1 shows an ASP.NET Web Form that evaluates the requesting browser's capability to use HTML frames. If the browser can support frames, the user is automatically redirected to a frames-capable page (`4.2.1.frames.htm`).

LISTING 4.2.1 Using the `HttpBrowserCapabilities` Class to Evaluate the Requesting Browser's Capabilities and Redirect a Request

```
 1: <html>
 2: <head>
 3:   <script runat="server" language="vb">
 4:     Public Sub Page_Load(Sender As Object, E As EventArgs)
 5:       Dim bc As HttpBrowserCapabilities = Request.Browser
 6:       If bc.Frames = True Then
 7:         Response.Redirect("4.2.1.frames.htm")
 8:       End If
 9:     End Sub
10:   </script>
11:   <title>DotNetJunkies.com - HttpBrowserCapabilities</title>
12: </head>
13: <body>
14: <form runat="server" method="post">
15:   <p>This page does not use frames.</p>
16: </form>
17: </body>
18: </html>
```

In Listing 4.2.1, the requesting browser's capabilities are evaluated to determine whether it supports HTML frames (line 6). This capability is checked using the `Frames` property of the `HttpBrowserCapabilities` class. If the user's browser supports frames, the code on line 7 executes and the `Response.Redirect()` method redirects the user to a frame-enabled Web page (`4.2.1.frames.htm`, line 7). If the user's browser does *not* support frames, the `Frames` property returns False and the current page is rendered.

The `HttpBrowserCapabilities` class is limited to evaluating a browser's built-in functionality. It does not, unfortunately, evaluate the state of a browser's functionality. For example, Internet Explorer 4.0 and greater (IE4.0+) all support client-side JavaScript or JScript. If the requesting browser is IE4.0+, the `HttpBrowserCapabilities.JavaScript` property returns True; JavaScript is supported by this browser. However, if the user has the scripting capabilities of the browser turned off, the `JavaScript` property still returns True.

3. Testing Various Types of Server Control Output Through the `ClientTarget` Property

The ASP.NET `Page` class contains the `ClientTarget` property. The `ClientTarget` property indicates whether the requesting browser is an uplevel or downlevel browser. *Uplevel* browsers are currently defined (as of this writing) as Microsoft Internet Explorer 4.0 and greater. *Downlevel* browsers are all other browsers, including Netscape Navigator.

For uplevel browsers, the .NET Framework renders Web Forms using HTML 4.0 and client-side JavaScript support. For downlevel browsers, HTML 3.2 is rendered without client-side JavaScript support.

To understand how this affects the output result, let's look at a couple examples. Listing 4.3.1 shows an ASP.NET Web Form that uses a `RequiredFieldValidator` server control on an input form.

LISTING 4.3.1 Using a `RequiredFieldValidator` Server Control

```
 1: <html>
 2: <head>
 3:   <script runat="server" language="vb">
 4:   Public Sub Page_Load(Source As Object, E As EventArgs)
 5:     If Page.IsPostBack and Page.IsValid Then
 6:       Success.Text = "Welcome " & Name.Text
 7:     End If
 8:   End Sub
 9:   </script>
10:   <title>DotNetJunkies.com - HttpBrowserCapabilities</title>
11: </head>
12: <body>
13: <form runat="server" method="post">
14:   <asp:Label runat="server" id="Success" /><br>
15:   <b>Name:</b><br>
16:   <asp:TextBox runat="server" id="Name" /><br>
17:   <asp:RequiredFieldValidator runat="server"
18:     ControlToValidate="Name"
19:     ErrorMessage="Name is required." /><br>
20:   <input type="submit" value="Submit">
21: </form>
22: </body>
23: </html>
```

In Listing 4.3.1, you create an ASP.NET Web Form that uses a `RequiredFieldValidator` server control. In uplevel browsers, this will render in the HTML page using client-side JavaScript to provide the validation on the client without a roundtrip to the server. Downlevel browsers will not have the client-side JavaScript, thus requiring a roundtrip to validate the form submission. Listing 4.3.2 shows the rendered HTML in an uplevel browser.

LISTING 4.3.2 The Rendered HTML in an Uplevel Browser

```
 1: <html>
 2: <head>
 3:
 4:  <title>DotNetJunkies.com - HttpBrowserCapabilities</title>
 5: </head>
 6: <body>
 7: <form name="ctrl2" method="post" action="4.3.1.aspx" language="javascript"
        onsubmit="ValidatorOnSubmit();" id="ctrl2">
 8: <input type="hidden" name="__VIEWSTATE"
        value="dDw0MzU0NjY5NTc7Oz42FlJ7xXR6heX045SIUINEwLzwtQ==" />
 9:
10: <script language="javascript"
        src="/_aspx/1.0.2523/script/WebUIValidation.js"></script>
11:
12:
13:  <span id="Success"></span><br>
14:  <b>Name:</b><br>
15:  <input name="Name" type="text" id="Name" /><br>
16:  <span id="ctrl7" controltovalidate="Name" errormessage="Name is required."
        evaluationfunction="RequiredFieldValidatorEvaluateIsValid"
        initialvalue="" style="color:Red;visibility:hidden;">Name
        is required.</span><br>
17:  <input type="submit" value="Submit">
18:
19: <script language="javascript">
20: <!--
21:     var Page_Validators =  new Array(document.all["ctrl7"]);
22:         // -->
23: </script>
24:
25:
26: <script language="javascript">
27: <!--
28: var Page_ValidationErrorPrefix = "Validation script error: ";
29: var Page_ValidationBadID = "Client ID is not unique: ";
30: var Page_ValidationBadFunction = "Invalid ClientValidationFunction: ";
31: var Page_ValidationActive = false;
32: if (typeof(Page_ValidationVer) == "undefined")
33:     alert("Warning! Unable to find script library 'WebUIValidation.js'.");
34: else if (Page_ValidationVer != "116")
35:     alert("Warning! This page is using the wrong version of
        'WebUIValidation.js'. Page expects version '116'.
        Script library is '" + Page_ValidationVer + "'.");
36: else
37:     ValidatorOnLoad();
38:
39: function ValidatorOnSubmit() {
40:     if (Page_ValidationActive) {
41:         ValidatorCommonOnSubmit();
42:     }
43: }
44: // -->
```

LISTING 4.3.2 Continued

```
45: </script>
46:
47:
48:         </form>
49: </body>
50: </html>
```

In Listing 4.3.2, the HTML output is sprinkled with JavaScript functions that enable client-side validation of the form. All the JavaScript in Listing 4.3.2 was dynamically created by the .NET Framework.

Listing 4.3.3 shows the same ASP.NET Web Form rendered in a downlevel browser.

LISTING 4.3.3 The Rendered HTML in a Downlevel Browser

```
 1: <html>
 2: <head>
 3:
 4:   <title>DotNetJunkies.com - HttpBrowserCapabilities</title>
 5: </head>
 6: <body>
 7: <form name="ctrl2" method="post" action="4.3.1.aspx" id="ctrl2">
 8: <input type="hidden" name="__VIEWSTATE"
        value="YTB6NDM1NDY2OTU3X19feA==a9530e44" />
 9:
10:   <span id="Success"></span><br>
11:   <b>Name:</b><br>
12:   <input name="Name" type="text" id="Name" /><br>
13:    <br>
14:   <input type="submit" value="Submit">
15: </form>
16: </body>
17: </html>
```

In Listing 4.3.3 none of the JavaScript found in Listing 4.3.2 is rendered to the client. Although the HTML output is much smaller, a downlevel browser requires a round-trip to the server to validate the input.

Many of the ASP.NET server controls will render JavaScript for uplevel browsers, including all the validation controls and the data controls that use paging or sorting. In some instances you may want to have more control over how the output is rendered. The **Page** class allows you to set the **ClientTarget** property so all requests are rendered for a specified browser type, either **UpLevel** or **DownLevel**. The following code snippet shows how to manually set the **ClientTarget** property of the page (this will override the .NET Framework from doing the uplevel/downlevel evaluation):

```
<%@ Page ClientTarget="[ DownLevel | UpLevel ]" %>
```

Setting **ClientTarget** to **DownLevel** will force all browsers to receive HTML 3.2 with no JavaScript, even if the browser is an uplevel browser. This may be useful if you want to ensure all browsers have the same interaction with your Web application. It is not advisable to set the `ClientTarget` property to `UpLevel` unless you know that all the browsers using your Web application will be able to support the uplevel functionality (such as in an intranet environment).

If, for example, we want to ensure that all of our Web site visitors have the exact same experience, we must build our site for the lowest common denominator, in other words, for a downlevel browser. We can tell the .NET Framework to render the pages in our Web site as downlevel, with HTML 3.2 and no client-side JavaScript support, by specifying the `ClientTarget` property in the `@ Page` directive, as seen here:

```
<%@ Page ClientTarget="DownLevel" %>
```

Summary

Having the capability to discover and evaluate a requesting browser's capabilities and react dynamically based on what you find has become an important part of Web development. There are many browsers available to users, and not being able to react appropriately can render your Web application useless to a particular user. Traditional ASP provides various means for discovering the capabilities of requesting browsers, and ASP.NET continues on this path, with the `HttpBrowserCapabilities` class. As with all things that evolve in this manner, the `HttpBrowserCapabilities` class provides all the properties we have been using with classic ASP as well as a set of new properties to enable us to discover more about a requesting browser.

In this chapter you learned:

- What the `HttpBrowserCapabilities` class is
- How to determine a requesting browser's capabilities in an ASP.NET Web Form
- How to redirect a page request based on a requesting browser's capabilities
- How the `ClientTarget` property affects the rendered output of an ASP.NET Web Form

In part 1 of this chapter we looked at what the `HttpBrowserCapabilities` class is and the properties it exposes. We saw how the Browser Capabilities component was expanded on with new properties, such as `AOL`, `Crawler`, `EcmaScriptVersion`, `MajorVersion`, `MinorVersion`, `MSDomVersion`, `Type`, `W3CDomVersion`, `Win16`, and `Win32`.

In part 2, we looked at how we can use the `HttpBrowserCapabilities` class to evaluate the browser's capabilities and react. In one of the examples, we built a page that evaluated the Frames property and redirected the browser request. Unfortunately, the `HttpBrowserCapabilities` class cannot evaluate the current state of the capabilities. In other words, if the browser is capable of supporting client-side JavaScript, the `JavaScript` property returns True even if the user has disabled JavaScript.

In part 3, we saw how the `ClientTarget` property of the Page class can be used to mandate how the ASP.NET Web Form is rendered to the client. Currently, two values are available for the `ClientTarget` property, `UpLevel` and `DownLevel`. `UpLevel` is defined as Microsoft Internet Explorer 4.0 or greater, while `DownLevel` is everything else.

Other Resources

In this chapter, we learned how to detect browser capabilities with ASP.NET, and how to use the `ClientTarget` property of the Page class to force rendering of the Web Form as either HTML 3.2 or HTML 4.0 with JavaScript support. Be sure to check out these other great resources for more information on using the `HttpBrowserCapabilities` class.

- `www.DotNetJunkies.com`—This ASP.NET-focused site, authored and maintained by authors Doug Seven and Don Wolthuis, provides a plethora of information about ASP.NET for developers of any skill level. The site includes tutorials on getting started with ASP.NET and a repository for Web services and .NET components!

  http://www.DotNetJunkies.com

- `www.GotDotNet.com`—This .NET Framework-focused site is run by Microsoft and contains articles and tutorials written by many .NET community gurus and Microsoft developers. The site includes a library of user-uploaded components and articles, as well as many third-party samples.

  http://www.GotDotNet.com

- `www.ASP.NET`—This Microsoft-run ASP.NET Web site serves as a great starting place for new ASP.NET developers. It provides quick access to the latest ASP.NET bits, links to popular ASP.NET resource sites on the Web, a list of newsgroups and ListServs for ASP.NET-focused discussions, and ASP.NET books!

  http://www.ASP.NET

CHAPTER 5

CREATING AND USING USER CONTROLS

by Doug Seven

In this chapter you will
- Create a user control
- Register a user control on an ASP.NET page
- Expose properties and methods of a user control
- Dynamically load user controls

One of the many tools that ASP developers have come to rely on is the *include file*—a separate file that can be dynamically included in a page when a request is made. Include files can contain script for processing, HTML output, or both. With classic ASP, include files have served as a means of providing reusable code without the use of a COM component. A classic example of the include file is an HTML menu that is displayed on every page or a script block for recognizing and authenticating users. Unfortunately, when used in abundance, include files can lead to confusing code situations. I recall the days of working in an ASP development shop where ASP pages included files that included files that included files, and so on. Debugging such ASP applications was anything but easy.

Another disadvantage of using include files is that when a page request is made, the script engine includes all the included files as one continuous page while processing. This entire package is processed in the same *sandbox*, or processing space. That means that, for example, every include file has to use unique variables to prevent a naming conflict. Additionally, include files cannot be loaded dynamically–either you include the file or you don't, but you cannot have code that decides whether a file should be included. Of course, include files cannot expose any properties or methods like a COM component can. Clearly, include files did not provide the ideal solution for code reuse and code encapsulation, but using them was one of the best (and easiest) solutions offered by classic ASP.

Although include files can still be used in ASP.NET, ASP.NET contains the concept of a *custom control*, which compensates for many of the weaknesses inherent in include files. Custom controls have the capability to be dynamically loaded and expose rich properties and events. Furthermore, each custom control processes in its own sandbox, enabling each control to use any variable name without the possibility of naming conflicts with other controls.

ASP.NET custom controls sound a lot like ActiveX controls, but they are quite different. ActiveX controls are built as separate files (.ocx) and made available to users for download. The controls typically encompass rich functionality that is too complex to do with HTML. The greatest downfall of ActiveX controls was that every visitor had to download the .ocx file to his computer before he could view the Web page it was on. Additionally, ActiveX controls are only supported by Internet Explorer, without a plug-in.

ASP.NET custom controls, on the other hand, are compiled either manually by the developer or using Just-In-Time (JIT) compilation on the Web server. The control's output is rendered by the .NET Framework on the Web server as HTML, so there is no file for the Web site visitor to download. Since they render HTML output, there is no browser compatibility to worry about, and no plug-ins to install. As you can see, ASP.NET controls immediately demonstrate their superiority by compiling on the server side and rendering standard HTML output, thus alleviating the need for users to download a custom control.

Two types of custom controls exist in ASP.NET:

- *Custom server controls*—Custom server controls are precompiled. They can expose properties and methods and can render HTML output, although they do not have to—a custom control may simply do some processing without rendering anything to the client. Custom sever controls are closer in relation to COM components than to include files.

- *User controls*—User controls comprise the happy median between server controls and include files. User controls process in their own sandbox but are compiled and rendered on demand, like an ASP.NET page. User controls can expose rich properties and methods and can include HTML and .NET programmatic code.

1. Creating User Controls

In its simplest form, a user control is nothing more than HTML contained in a separate file that is dynamically included in an ASP.NET page when the page request is processed. The most basic user control would simply contain text to be displayed on the screen when the page is rendered. This is remarkably similar to include files. They can simply be files of text or HTML that are included dynamically at run-time.

> **Note**
> User controls are identified by the .NET Framework with an `.ascx` extension. No other extension is allowed for user controls.

A real-world example of a basic user control is the copyright line you see at the bottom of most Web pages. On DotNetJunkies.com, for example, we have a copyright line at the bottom of every page. Rather than duplicating this HTML and text on every ASP.NET page, we put it into a user control, much like an include file. This HTML content now exists in only one file. Updates or changes to the HTML content can be made in the user control and all pages are updated simultaneously. Listing 5.1.1 shows the `copyright.ascx` user control from DotNetJunkies.com.

LISTING 5.1.1 The `copyright.ascx` User Control from DotNetJunkies.com

```
 1: <table cellpadding="0" cellspacing="0" width="100%" border="0">
 2: <tr align="center">
 3:    <td><img src="images/trans.gif" width="1" height="10"></td>
 4: </tr>
 5: <tr align="center">
 6:    <td>
 7:     <font size="1"
 8:     face="Verdana, Arial, Helvetica, sans-serif">
 9:     Copyright 2001
10:     <a href="http://www.dotnetjunkies.com">dotnetjunkies.com</a>
11:     All rights reserved.
12:     <a href="privacy.aspx">Privacy Policy</a>.
13:    </font>
14:    </td>
15: </tr>
16: <tr align="center">
17:    <td><img src="images/trans.gif" width="1" height="5"></td>
18: </tr>
19: </table>
```

The HTML in Listing 5.1.1 simply creates a table to show a copyright line (lines 9–12) and a link to a privacy statement (line 12). Figure 5.1 shows the bottom of the DotNetJunkies.com front page. For this figure, I greyed-out everything except the copyright user control to help identify it.

As you can see, building a user control is very similar to building an ASP.NET Web Form. Any Web Form can easily be converted to a user control. As you can see in Listing 5.1.1, user controls do not include the `<html>` and `<body>` tags because they will be included in a Web Form that already has these tags. Additionally, server-side `<form runat="server"></form>` tags should not be included. A Web Form is only allowed one server-side form, so these tags should be included in the Web Form that the user control is placed on. If you need to take advantage of `PostBack` functionality of server-side form handling in your user control, declare an instance of your user control between the `<form runat="server"></form>` tags on the Web Form.

If the Web Form you are converting to a user control has an `@ Page` directive, it must be changed to the `@ Control` directive. The `@ Control` directive supports all the functionality that the `@ Page` directive supports, except for the `Trace` attribute. Tracing cannot be enabled for user controls.

FIGURE 5.1
The `copyright.ascx` user control on DotNetJunkies.com.

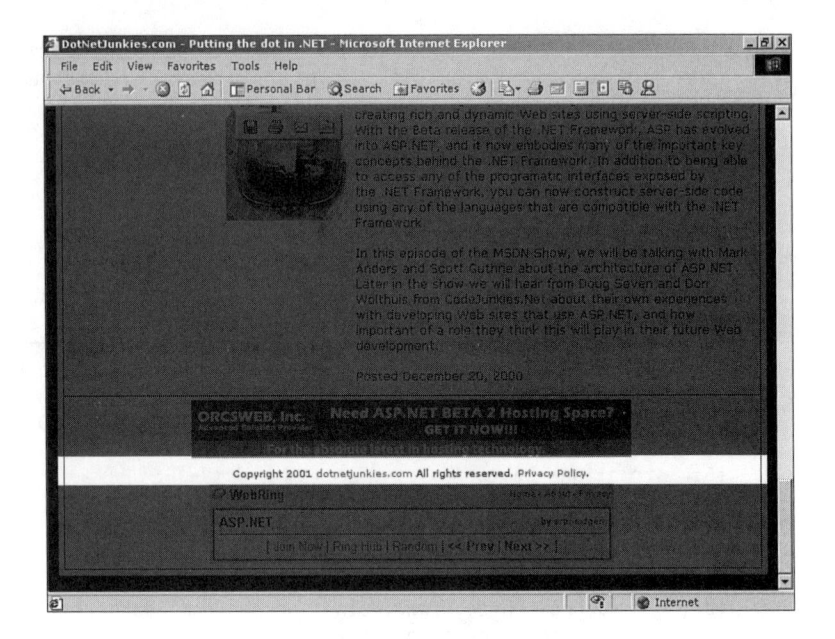

> **Note**
>
> If you wish to have tracing information for a user control, you must turn on the tracing information for an ASP.NET page that uses the user control.

2. Registering a User Control

In Listing 5.1.1 I demonstrated a very basic user control—it simply contains some HTML content. It really isn't anything you couldn't do with an include file, but it demonstrates how a basic user control works. However, there is one piece missing. For a user control to be used on an ASP.NET Web Form, it must be registered.

Registering a user control means adding the `@ Register` directive to identify the user control with a prefix and name as well as defining the path to the source file (`copyright.ascx`, in the preceding example).

To register a user control at the page level, you use the `@ Register` directive. The `@ Register` directive contains three properties: `TagPrefix`, which is the prefix used when adding the user control on a Web Form (similar to the `asp` prefix for the built ASP.NET server controls, i.e.: `<asp:Label>`); `TagName`, the name the user control is identified with; and `Src`, the relative path to the `.ascx` file.

The `@ Register` directive for the `copyright.ascx` user control is shown here:

```
<%@ Register TagPrefix="dnj" TagName="copyright"
➥     src="/controls/copyright.ascx" %>
```

The preceding code is added to the top of any Web Form in the Web application that will have the copyright.ascx user control as part of its output.

Once the user control is registered with the Web Form, it can be placed anywhere on the Web Form in the same fashion an intrinsic server control is placed, using the following syntax:

```
<tagprefix:tagname id="idName" runat="server" />
```

To place the DotNetJunkies.com copyright user control, I added the following code to my Web Form:

```
<dnj:copyright id="copyright1" runat="server" />
```

A user control can have any number of instances in a single Web Form. Each instance runs in its own sandbox, protecting the Web Form from any variable-, property-, method-, or event-naming conflicts. We could easily create a user control for a basic purpose that needs to be included several times on a page. For example, on DotNetJunkies.com, there is a `rating.ascx` user control that displays a small "visitor rating" input form. On some pages this control may appear as many as 20 times. Each instance of this user control is protected from the others, even though they all share common attributes. This is much like having multiple ASP.NET `Label` controls on one Web Form. Although they are all the same control, each instance of the control is a separate object and treated independently by the .NET Framework.

3. Properties and Methods

Although we have seen a few strengths user controls have over include files, such as independent sandboxes to protect conflicts, we really haven't seen the true power of user controls yet. The strength of user controls really comes in their capability to expose properties and methods in a true object-oriented manner. Like any .NET object, each user control can expose either inherent properties and methods or custom properties and methods.

Inherent Properties and Methods

The `UserControl` class, which is the base class for all user controls, is derived from the `TemplateControl` class, which is derived from the `Control` class, which is derived from the `Object` class. As a result of this class "family tree", the `UserControl` class has a rich set of inherent properties and methods. These properties and methods are exposed on every user control without any code having to be written by you. In Listing 5.3.1 we build a Web Form that has a simple user control on it, and use a `Button` control to fire an event that alters a property of the user control.

LISTING 5.3.1 Working with Intrinsic User Control Properties

```
 1: <%@ Page Language="VB" %>
 2: <%@ Register TagPrefix="dotnetjunkies" TagName="test"
        src="user_control.ascx" %>
 3: <html>
 4: <head>
 5: <script runat="server">
 6:   Public Sub Go_OnClick(Source As Object, E As EventArgs)
 7:     If myUserControl.Visible = True Then
 8:       myUserControl.Visible = False
 9:     Else
10:       myUserControl.Visible = True
11:     End If
12:   End Sub
13: </script>
14: </head>
15: <body>
16: <form runat="server" method="post">
17:   <dotnetjunkies:test id="myUserControl" runat="server" />
18: <p>
19:   <asp:Button runat="server" Text="Go" OnClick="Go_OnClick" />
20: </p>
21: </form>
22: </body>
23: </html>
```

In Listing 5.3.1, we have a Web Form that includes a user control, `user_control.ascx`. This user control has only one line of text in it:

`My user control.`

On line 2, we register the user control, specifying its `TagPrefix`, `TagName`, and `SRC` (source) attributes. The user control is instantiated inside the server-side form tags on line 17. We added an ASP.NET `Button` control and set the `OnClick` attribute to point to the `Go_OnClick()` event handler on lines 6–12.

When the page is first requested, the user control is visible, as is the Go button, as shown in Figure 5.2.

When the Go button is clicked, the `Go_OnClick()` event handler is fired and the user control's `Visible` property is evaluated and set to its opposite value. The `PostBack` result is shown in Figure 5.3.

Although we wrote no code in the user control for the `Visible` property, the user control understands what this property is. This is due to the `UserControl` class inheriting from multiple other classes, particularly the `Control` class. Figure 5.4 shows the hierarchy of inheritance for the `UserControl` class.

FIGURE 5.2
When the page is first loaded, the user control is visible.

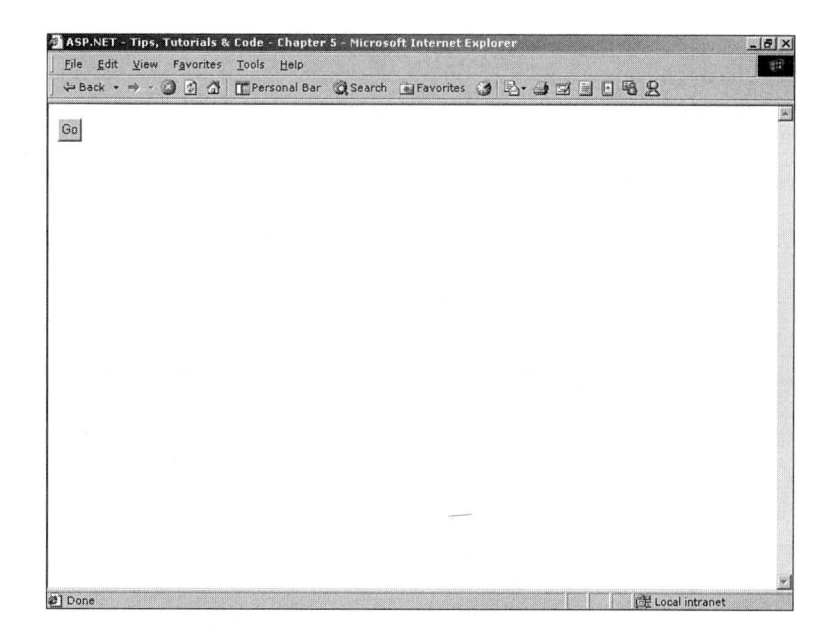

FIGURE 5.3
The user control's `Visible` property is reset when the `Go_OnClick()` even handler is fired.

FIGURE 5.4
The hierarchy of inheritance for the `UserControl` class.

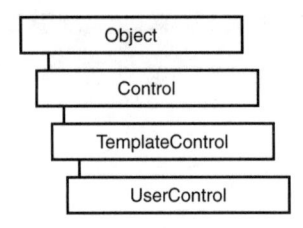

Custom Properties and Methods

A user control has stock properties and methods, but you can also write your own custom properties and methods for your user control to expose. Custom properties can be used to set or retrieve (*get*) text of a control in the user control, change a color, hide or show a control, or do just about anything you can think of (for a control, that is).

A user control can expose properties in two ways:

- As public variables
- As `Property` objects

User Control Properties as Public Variables

You can expose simple properties as public variables in the user control. As public variables, other objects have access to these properties. Listing 5.3.2 demonstrates using a public variable as a property.

LISTING 5.3.2 A User Control Exposing a Public Variable

```
 1: <%@ Control %>
 2: <script runat="server" Language="VB">
 3: Public myText As String
 4:
 5: Sub Page_Load(Source As Object, E As EventArgs)
 6:    myLabel.Text = myText
 7: End Sub
 8: </script>
 9:
10:<asp:Label id="myLabel" runat="server" />
```

We expose a public variable, `myText`, as a string on line 3. On line 10, we add an ASP.NET `Label` control named `myLabel`. In the `Page_Load()` event handler, lines 5–7, we set `myLabel`'s `Text` property to the value of the public variable, `myText`. If we register and instantiate this control on a Web Form, we have programmatic access to the `myText` variable, which in turn enables us to set the `myLabel.Text` property.

On a Web Form, the public variable can be accessed in two ways:

- Declaratively
- Programmatically

As a property of the user control, the value of a public variable can be set in the same manner as the value of a server control property—*declaratively*. When we place an instance of the user control on the page, we can set the value of **myText** inline by declaring the property/value pair:

```
<dotnetjunkies:C5_3_2 runat="server" id="myUserControl"
  myText="This is set for the first page load" />
```

Unless we provide any programmatic code to alter the **myText** property of my user control, it will maintain the value we assigned it declaratively when it was instantiated.

We can also access the public variable and change its value programmatically in code. Listing 5.3.3 contains the code for a Web Form that utilizes the user control presented in Listing 5.3.2.

LISTING 5.3.3 Programmatically Accessing the Public Variable

```
 1: <%@ Register TagPrefix="dotnetjunkies" TagName="C5_3_2"
        src="5.3.2.ascx" %>
 2: <script runat="server" Language="VB">
 3:   Public Sub Page_Load(Sender As Object, E As EventArgs)
 4:     If Page.IsPostBack Then
 5:       myUserControl.myText = myValue.Text
 6:     End If
 7:   End Sub
 8: </script>
 9: <html>
10: <head>
11: <title>ASP.NET - Tips, Tutorials & Code - Chapter 5</title>
12: </head>
13: <body>
14: <form runat="server" method="post">
15:   <dotnetjunkies:C5_3_2 runat="server" id="myUserControl"
16:     myText="This is set for the first page load" />
17: <p>
18:   <asp:TextBox id="myValue" runat="server" /><br>
19:   <asp:Button runat="server" Text="Go" />
20: </p>
21: </form>
22: </body>
23: </html>
```

In Listing 5.3.3 we created a Web Form that uses our user control, a **TextBox** control, and a **Button** control. The **Button** control triggers a **PostBack** event, captured inside the **Page_Load()** event handler on line 3. If the **Page_Load()** event is the result of a **PostBack** event, myUserControl's **myText** property is set to the **Text** property of the **TextBox** control (line 5).

The value of the **myText** property that is displayed when the page is first requested is the value that we set declaratively when we placed the user control on the Web Form, as shown in Figure 5.5.

FIGURE 5.5
When the page first loads, the inline value of the user control's public variable is used.

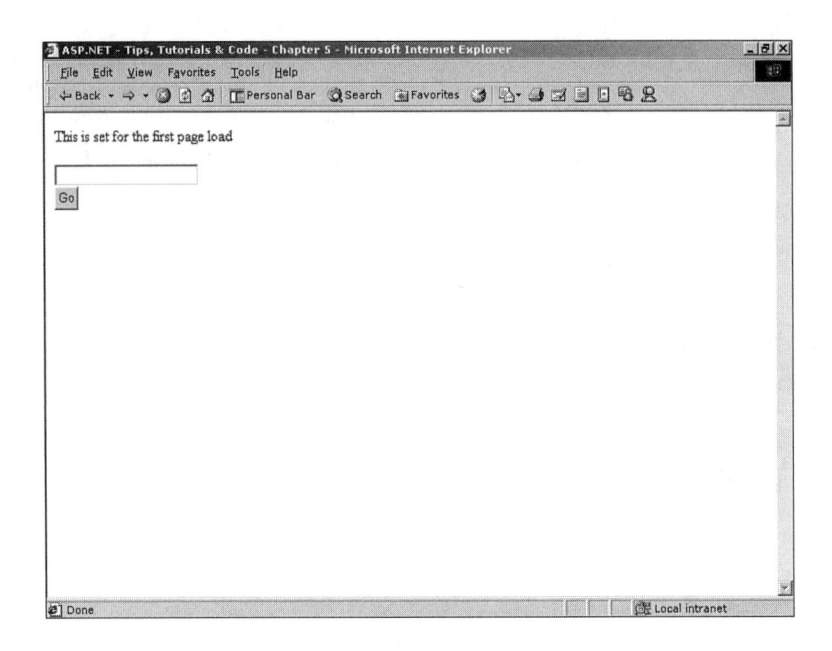

[Screenshot: Browser showing "This is set for the first page load" with a TextBox and Go button]

When I enter a value in the `TextBox` control and click the `Button` control, the `PostBack` event is fired, the value of the public variable in the user control is changed, and the page is rendered as shown in Figure 5.6.

FIGURE 5.6
When the Web Form posts back, the value of the public variable is set to the value of the `TextBox` control.

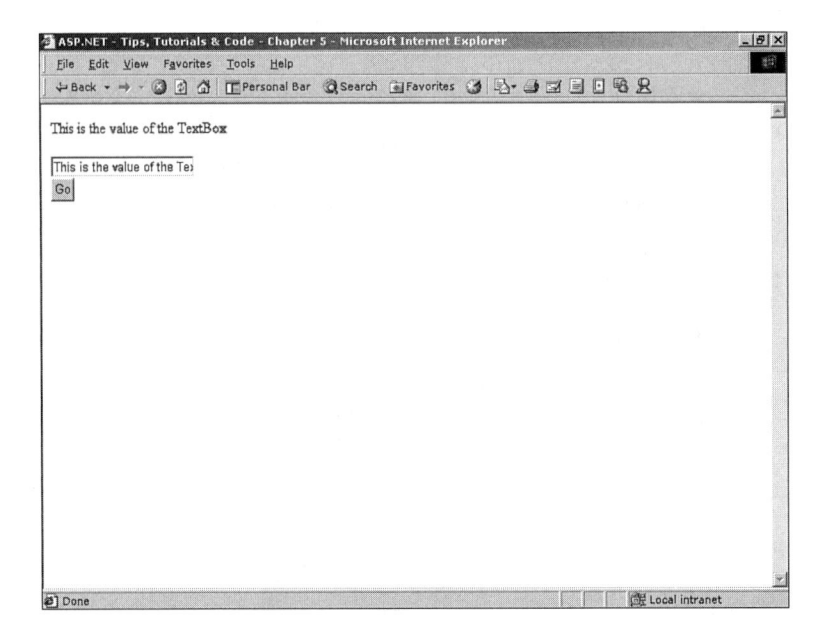

[Screenshot: Browser showing "This is the value of the TextBox" with a TextBox containing "This is the value of the Te)" and Go button]

User Control Properties as Property Objects

Although public variables are easy to use, they provide only a limited value. They are great for assigning values to and getting values from a user control. However, they do not provide any means for programmatically working with a property when it is set. User controls can have `Property` objects that have `Set` and `Get` methods exposed. In either of these methods, you can add code to perform functions, call other functions, or simply assign or retrieve the value of the property (much like you saw with public variables). One of the distinct values of the `Property` object is that it allows you to add code to the Set method to validate property value assignments before using them. An example of this is a property of a user control that accepts a `DateTime` object as its value. In the Set method of the property you can add code to validate the `DataTime` value passed in to ensure it is a date after the current date, for example.

A distinct advantage in this model is that you can create rich functionality that only executes when the property's `Set` or `Get` methods are fired. An example of this is retrieving product information from a database only when the `Product_ID` property of a user control is set. Rather than having the data-access code in the `Page_Load()` event handler and evaluating the property to see whether there is a value, you can put the data-access code inside the `Set...End Set` block of the property.

To demonstrate this, we are going to build a user control that exposes the `ProductId` property as an `integer`. When the property is set, we'll access the Northwind database on a SQL Server and retrieve the detail information for the `ProductId` given. The benefit here is that the data-access code will not execute when the page is loaded, unless the `ProductId` property has been set.

Listing 5.3.4 shows the code for the `GetSingleProduct` user control.

LISTING 5.3.4 The `GetSingleProduct` User Control

```
 1: <%@ Import Namespace="System.Data" %>
 2: <%@ Import Namespace="System.Data.SqlClient" %>
 3: <script runat="server" language="vb">
 4: Public Property ProductId As Integer
 5:    Get
 6:      Return Int32.Parse(txtProductID.Text)
 7:    End Get
 8:
 9:    Set
10:      txtProductID.Text = value
11:
12:      Dim con As SqlConnection = New
         SqlConnection("server=localhost;database=Northwind;uid=sa;pwd=;")
13:      Dim cmd As SqlCommand = New SqlCommand("SELECT * FROM
         Products Where ProductID = " & value, con)
14:
15:      con.Open()
16:
```

LISTING 5.3.4 Continued

```
17:        ProductDetail.DataSource = cmd.ExecuteReader()
18:        ProductDetail.DataBind()
19:
20:        con.Close()
21:    End Set
22: End Property
23: </script>
24:
25: <asp:Label id="txtProductID" runat="server" Visible="False" />
26:
27: <asp:DataGrid runat="server" id="ProductDetail"
28:     AutoGenerateColumns="False"
29:     ShowHeader="False">
30:     <Columns>
31:       <asp:TemplateColumn>
32:         <ItemTemplate>
33:         <table border="0" cellpadding="4" cellspacing="0" width="100%">
34:         <tr>
35:         <td><b><%# Container.DataItem("ProductName") %></b></td>
36:         </tr>
37:         <tr>
38:         <td><b>Quantity per Unit:</b></td>
39:         <td><%# Container.DataItem("QuantityPerUnit") %></td>
40:         <td><b>Unit Price:</b></td>
41:         <td><%# DataBinder.Eval(Container.DataItem,
     "UnitPrice", "{0:c}") %></td>
42:         </tr>
43:         <tr>
44:         <td><b>Units In Stock:</b></td>
45:         <td><%# Container.DataItem("UnitsInStock") %></td>
46:         <td><b>Units on Order:</b></td>
47:         <td><%# Container.DataItem("UnitsOnOrder") %></td>
48:         </tr>
49:         </table>
50:         </ItemTemplate>
51:       </asp:TemplateColumn>
52:     </Columns>
53: </asp:DataGrid>
```

On lines 1–2, we include the directives necessary to use a `DataSet` (`System.Data`) object and the SQL Managed Provider (`System.Data.SqlClient`). We declare a public property (`ProductId`), on line 4, as an `Integer`. I added a `Get...End Get` block to provide the capability for a Web Form to retrieve the current value of the property. I retrieve the value from an ASP.NET `Label` control on line 25. We set the `Visible` property of the `Label` control to `false`, so no HTML output is rendered.

The `Set...End Set` block that starts on line 9 is the more interesting part of this control. We added code to create a `SqlConnection` (line 12) and `SqlCommand` (line 13), which are used to retrieve the product information from the database and bind it to a `DataGrid` (lines 17–18). The `DataGrid` uses an ASP.NET `TemplateColumn` to create a more interesting layout on the page than a basic grid.

Listing 5.3.5 shows the other half of this equation: the Web Form that includes the user control.

LISTING 5.3.5 Including the `GetSingleProduct` User Control on a Web Form

```
 1: <%@ Register TagPrefix="dotnetjunkies" TagName="GetSingleProduct"
➥    src="5.3.4.ascx" %>
 2: <script runat="server" language="vb">
 3:   Public Sub Page_Load(Source As Object, E As EventArgs)
 4:     If Page.IsPostBack Then
 5:        myUserControl.ProductId = Int32.Parse(txtID.Text)
 6:     End If
 7:   End Sub
 8: </script>
 9: <html>
10: <head>
11:   <title>ASP.NET - Tips, Tutorials & Code - Chapter 5</title>
12: </head>
13: <body>
14: <form runat="server" method="post">
15:    <dotnetjunkies:GetSingleProduct id="myUserControl" runat="server" />
16:
17:    Enter a Product ID: <br>
18:    <asp:TextBox id="txtID" runat="server" />
19:    <input type="submit" value="Go">
20: </form>
21: </body>
22: </html>
```

In Listing 5.3.5 we create a Web Form to include the `GetSingleProduct` user control. On line 1, we register the user control.

The `Page_Load()` event handler (lines 4–7) evaluates the request to see whether it is a `PostBack` event. If it is, the value of the `TextBox` control on line 15 is passed to the user control's `ProductId` property. Once a value is passed to the `ProductId` property, the code in the `SET...END SET` block of the user control (lines 9–21 of Listing 5.3.4) is executed.

Figure 5.7 shows the page when it is first loaded. None of the data-access code has been executed yet.

After you enter a product ID number (such as 67, the product number for the delicious-but-potent Laughing Lumberjack Lager) the `SET` event of the property is fired, and the data-access code is executed. Figure 5.8 shows the result of requesting the product detail for Laughing Lumberjack Lager...looks like there is enough for everyone!

Of course, an advantage to using a user control to perform this functionality is its reusability. If we want to display multiple products on this page, we can add multiple instances of the same `GetSingleProduct` user control. In Listing 5.3.6 we modify the Web Form in Listing 5.3.5 to render multiple instances of the `GetSingleProduct` user control to display three products (in case you want to do any comparison-shopping).

FIGURE 5.7
When the page is loaded, none of the data-access code is fired because the `Set` event of the user control's `ProductId` property has not been fired.

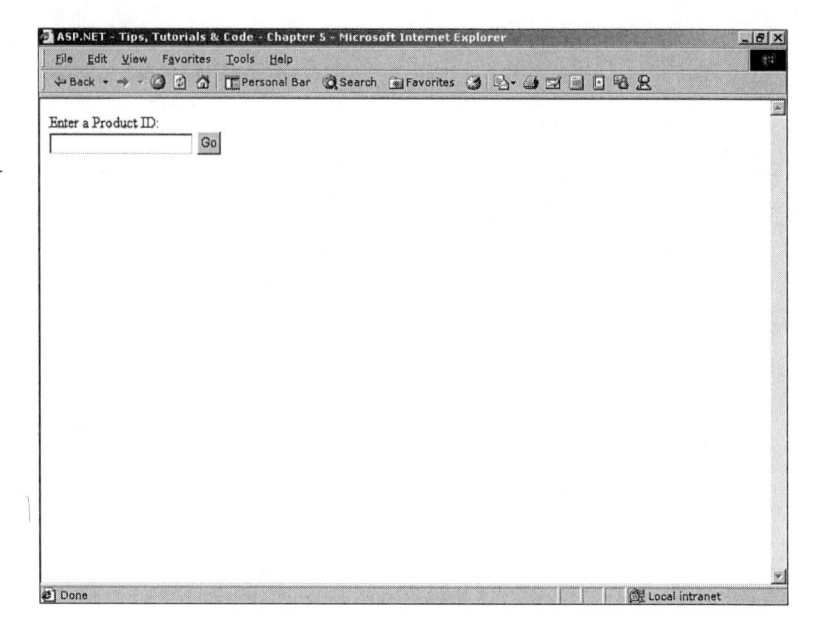

FIGURE 5.8
When the Web Form's `PostBack` event occurs, the value in the `TexBox` control is passed to the `ProductId` property, causing the data-access code to execute.

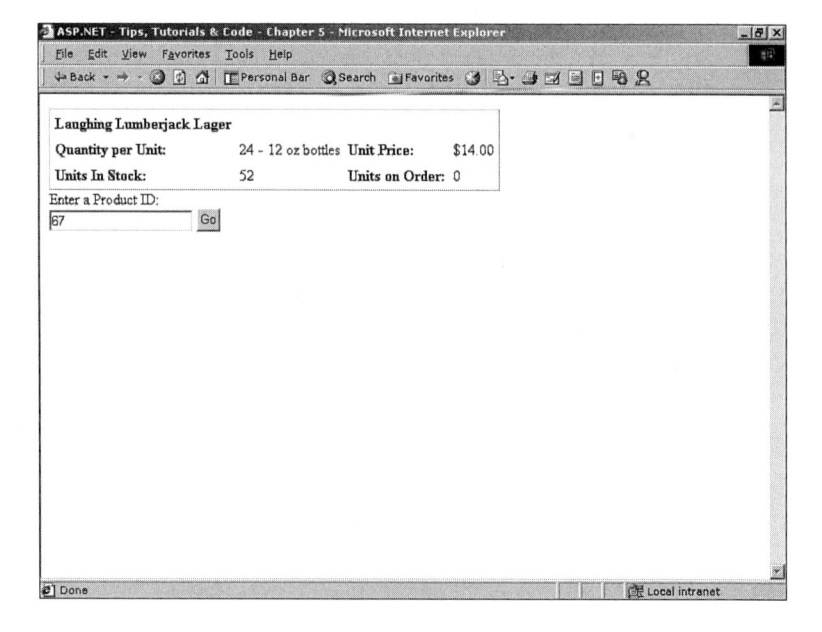

LISTING 5.3.6 Reusing a User Control on a Web Form

```
 1: <%@ Register TagPrefix="dotnetjunkies" TagName="GetSingleProduct"
      src="5.3.4.ascx" %>
 2: <script runat="server" Language="VB">
 3:   Public Sub Page_Load(Source As Object, E As EventArgs)
 4:     If Page.IsPostBack Then
 5:       myUserControl1.ProductId = Int32.Parse(txtID.Text) -1
 6:       myUserControl2.ProductId = Int32.Parse(txtID.Text)
 7:       myUserControl3.ProductId = Int32.Parse(txtID.Text) +1
 8:     End If
 9:   End Sub
10: </script>
11: <html>
12: <head>
13:   <title>ASP.NET - Tips, Tutorials & Code - Chapter 5</title>
14: </head>
15: <body>
16: <form runat="server" method="post">
17:   <p><dotnetjunkies:GetSingleProduct id="myUserControl1"
        runat="server" /></p>
18:   <p><dotnetjunkies:GetSingleProduct id="myUserControl2"
        runat="server" /></p>
19:   <p><dotnetjunkies:GetSingleProduct id="myUserControl3"
        runat="server" /></p>
20:   <p>
21:     Enter a Product ID: <br>
22:     <asp:TextBox id="txtID" runat="server" />
23:     <input type="submit" value="Go">
24:   </p>
25: </form>
26: </body>
27: </html>
```

In Listing 5.3.6 we modified the Web Form from Listing 5.3.5 to include three instances of the `GetSingleProduct` user control. Each instance is given a unique `ID` value, but they are all instances of the same user control declared on line 1 in the `@ Register` directive. In the `PostBack` event handler, we set the `ProductId` property of each user control to a separate value based on the number input in the `TextBox` control. As a result, each user control renders a different set of detail about a different product, as shown in Figure 5.9.

Retrieving a property from a user control is done in the same way you set a property. When you add code to retrieve (or *get*) a user control property, any code in the `GET...END GET` block of the user control executes. In the case of the `GetSingleProduct` user control (Listing 5.3.4), we return the value of the invisible `Label` control converted to an `Integer`. In Listing 5.3.7 we have added three ASP.NET `Label` controls to the Web Form, each directly above a user control instance. In the `PostBack` handler, we set the `Text` property of the `Label` controls to the `ProductId` property value of their respective user controls.

FIGURE 5.9
Although three instances of the `GetSingleProduct` user control are rendered on the same page, each instance maintains its own value and does not conflict with the others.

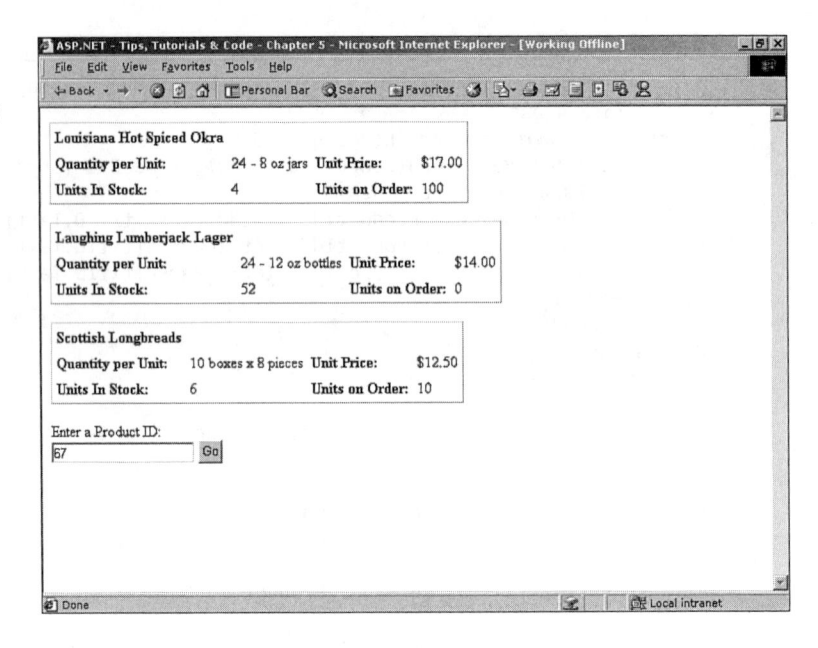

LISTING 5.3.7 Retrieving User Control Properties

```
 1: <%@ Register TagPrefix="dotnetjunkies" TagName="GetSingleProduct"
➥    src="5.3.4.ascx" %>
 2: <script runat="server" Language="VB">
 3:   Public Sub Page_Load(Source As Object, E As EventArgs)
 4:     If Page.IsPostBack Then
 5:       myUserControl1.ProductId = Int32.Parse(txtID.Text) -1
 6:       myUserControl2.ProductId = Int32.Parse(txtID.Text)
 7:       myUserControl3.ProductId = Int32.Parse(txtID.Text) +1
 8:
 9:       Product1.Text = "Product ID: " & myUserControl1.ProductId
10:       Product2.Text = "Product ID: " & myUserControl2.ProductId
11:       Product3.Text = "Product ID: " & myUserControl3.ProductId
12:     End If
13:   End Sub
14: </script>
15: <html>
16: <head>
17:   <title>ASP.NET - Tips, Tutorials & Code - Chapter 5</title>
18: </head>
19: <body>
20: <form runat="server" method="post">
21:   <p><asp:Label id="Product1" runat="server" /><br>
22:     <dotnetjunkies:GetSingleProduct id="myUserControl1"
➥      runat="server" /></p>
23:   <p><asp:Label id="Product2" runat="server" /><br>
24:     <dotnetjunkies:GetSingleProduct id="myUserControl2"
➥      runat="server" /></p>
```

LISTING 5.3.7 Continued

```
25:     <p><asp:Label id="Product3" runat="server" /><br>
26:       <dotnetjunkies:GetSingleProduct id="myUserControl3"
➥   runat="server" /></p>
27:     <p>
28:       Enter a Product ID: <br>
29:       <asp:TextBox id="txtID" runat="server" />
30:       <input type="submit" value="Go">
31:     </p>
32: </form>
33: </body>
34: </html>
```

In Listing 5.3.7, on lines 21, 23, and 25, we added ASP.NET `Label` controls. In the `PostBack` handler, we set their `Text` properties to a string ("Product ID: ") concatenated with the `ProductId` property of each user control (lines 9–11). Figure 5.10 shows the Web Form after a product ID is input.

FIGURE 5.10
The ASP.NET Label properties get the `ProductId` property from each user control and concatenate it with the text "Product ID:."

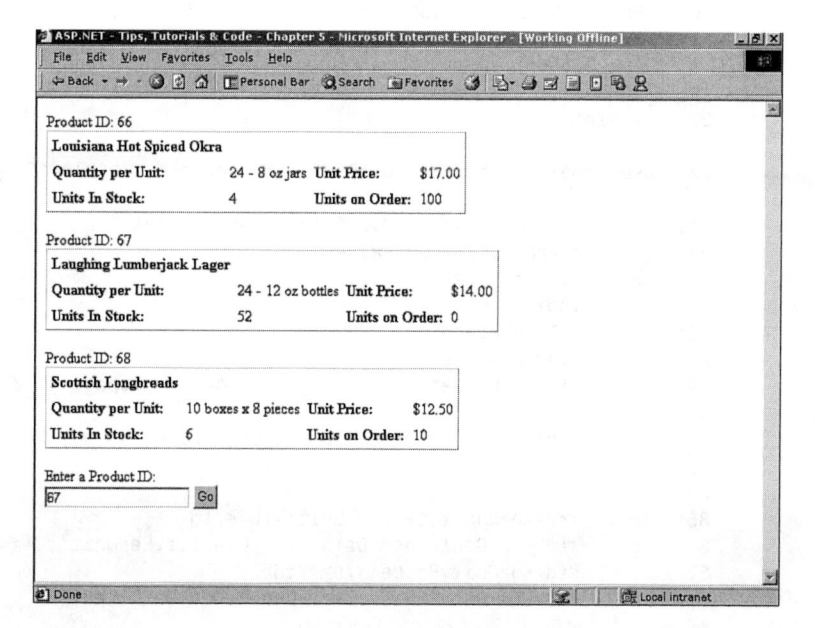

User Control Methods

Just as user controls can expose properties, they can also expose methods. Any subprocedure or function in a user control declared as `Public` is automatically exposed as a method of the user control. In the previous examples, I could have just as easily created a `GetNewProduct()` method that accepted a single parameter, a product ID. Listing 5.3.8 shows the `GetSingleProduct` user control rewritten to expose the `GetNewProduct()` public method rather than a property.

LISTING 5.3.8 Exposing a User Control Public Method

```vb
 1: <%@ Import Namespace="System.Data" %>
 2: <%@ Import Namespace="System.Data.SqlClient" %>
 3: <script runat="server" Language="VB">
 4: Public ReadOnly Property ProductId As Integer
 5:   Get
 6:     Return Int32.Parse(txtProductID.Text)
 7:   End Get
 8: End Property
 9:
10: Public Sub GetNewProduct(_productId As Integer)
11:   txtProductID.Text = _productId
12:   Dim con As SqlConnection = new
➥     SqlConnection("server=localhost;database=Northwind;uid=sa;pwd=;")
13:   Dim cmd As SqlCommand = new SqlCommand("SELECT * FROM Products
➥     Where ProductID = " & _productId, con)
14:
15:   con.Open()
16:   ProductDetail.DataSource = cmd.ExecuteReader()
17:   ProductDetail.DataBind()
18:   con.Close()
19: End Sub
20: </script>
21:
22: <asp:Label id="txtProductID" runat="server" Visible="False" />
23:
24: <asp:DataGrid runat="server" id="ProductDetail"
25:   AutoGenerateColumns="False"
26:   ShowHeader="False">
27:   <Columns>
28:     <asp:TemplateColumn>
29:       <ItemTemplate>
30:         <table border="0" cellpadding="4" cellspacing="0" width="100%">
31:         <tr>
32:         <td><b><%# Container.DataItem("ProductName") %></b></td>
33:         </tr>
34:         <tr>
35:         <td><b>Quantity per Unit:</b></td>
36:         <td><%# Container.DataItem("QuantityPerUnit") %></td>
37:         <td><b>Unit Price:</b></td>
38:         <td><%# DataBinder.Eval(Container.DataItem,
➥     "UnitPrice", "{0:c}") %></td>
39:         </tr>
40:         <tr>
41:         <td><b>Units In Stock:</b></td>
42:         <td><%# Container.DataItem("UnitsInStock") %></td>
43:         <td><b>Units on Order:</b></td>
44:         <td><%# Container.DataItem("UnitsOnOrder") %></td>
45:         </tr>
46:         </table>
47:       </ItemTemplate>
48:     </asp:TemplateColumn>
49:   </Columns>
50: </asp:DataGrid>
```

Listing 5.3.8 is roughly the same as Listing 5.3.4. In both listings, we have created the `GetSingleProduct` user control. The difference is how we actually exposed the means to get the product information. In Listing 5.3.4 we used a public property and encapsulated the functionality in the `SET...END SET` block of the user control's `ProductId` property. In Listing 5.3.8 we changed our approach and put the functionality in a public method. Some points of interest involve how we modified the `ProductId` property and how the Web Form works with the user control.

On line 5 of Listing 5.3.8 we added the `ReadOnly` attribute to the `ProductId` property declaration. This attribute eliminates (and actually prevents) the use of the `SET...END SET` block in the property. The `SET` method is no longer available because the property is declared as `ReadOnly`.

In the Web Form that includes the user control, we had to make a slight modification. Rather than setting a property value of the user control, we now call a method of the user control. Listing 5.3.9 shows only the code block of the Web Form in Listing 5.3.7 because that is the only part of the page that required a change.

LISTING 5.3.9 Calling a User Control Public Method

```
 1: <script runat="server" Language="VB">
 2:    Public Sub Page_Load(Source As Object, E As EventArgs)
 3:      If Page.IsPostBack Then
 4:        myUserControl1.GetNewProduct(Int32.Parse(txtID.Text)-1)
 5:        myUserControl2.GetNewProduct(Int32.Parse(txtID.Text))
 6:        myUserControl3.GetNewProduct(Int32.Parse(txtID.Text)+1)
 7:
 8:        Product1.Text = "Product ID: " & myUserControl1.ProductId
 9:        Product2.Text = "Product ID: " & myUserControl2.ProductId
10:        Product3.Text = "Product ID: " & myUserControl3.ProductId
11:      End If
12:    End Sub
13: </script>
```

In Listing 5.3.9 we changed lines 4–6 to make a call to the user control's `GetNewProduct()` method. The method requires one input parameter, the product ID, as an `Integer`. We didn't change the way we captured the value; we only changed the property reference to a method call. In lines 8–10, we still retrieve the `ProductId` property value (remember, it is still there, but it is read-only now). Figure 5.11 shows the Web Form output using method calls instead of properties.

Although the examples used in this chapter are easily interchangeable between property references and method calls, you will find that given different scenarios, one way is better than another. For instance, in a user control you may expose a `BackgroundColor` property rather than a method, and a `GetData()` method rather than a property, and so on. Typically active tasks (`GetData()`, `Open()`, `Close()`) are methods, while descriptive attributes (`BackgroundColor`, `Visible`, `Width`) are properties.

FIGURE 5.11
The Web Form renders the same when the property references are changed to method calls.

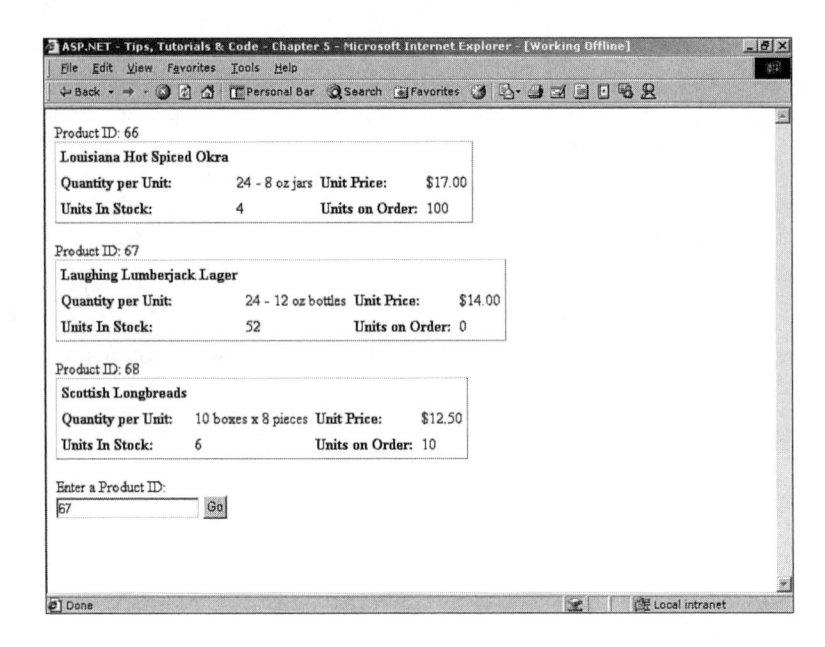

4. Dynamically Loading User Controls

User controls, as you have seen in this chapter, are simply object instances of the `UserControl` class. Like other objects in ASP.NET, user controls can be dynamically loaded. With dynamic loading, you can essentially build a Web Form on the fly, based on any parameters you see fit.

Any object that has a `Controls` collection can have controls added to it dynamically. In other words, an object that can have child controls, such as the `Page`, `Form`, or `PlaceHolder` objects, can have user controls added to its `Controls` collection dynamically. By accessing the `Add()` method of the `Controls` collection, you can add a control to the end of the collection.

The `Add()` method takes only one parameter–the object to add to the collection:

`Object.Controls.Add(Object)`

In Listing 5.4.1 we create a user control that displays a DataGrid of customers from the Northwind database. For this user control we are using a Code-Behind class for all of the code. This allows us to pre-compile the DLL and have access to the user control's class at compile time. Code behind concepts and practices will be covered in depth in Chapter 16, "Separating Code from Content."

The code behind file (`5.4.1.vb`) is listed first, followed by the presentation file (`5.4.1.ascx`).

LISTING 5.4.1 CustomerList User Control

[5.4.1.vb]

```vb
 1: Imports System
 2: Imports System.Web
 3: Imports System.Web.UI
 4: Imports System.Web.UI.WebControls
 5: Imports System.Data
 6:
 7: Public Class C5_4_1 : Inherits UserControl
 8:
 9:   Protected myGrid As DataGrid
10:
11:   Public Property DataSource As DataView
12:     Set
13:       myGrid.DataSource = value
14:       myGrid.DataBind()
15:     End Set
16:
17:     Get
18:       Return myGrid.DataSource
19:     End Get
20:   End Property
21:
22: End Class
```

[5.4.1.ascx]

```aspx
 1: <%@ Control Inherits="C5_4_1" %>
 2:
 3: <asp:DataGrid runat="server" id="myGrid"
 4:    AutoGenerateColumns="False"
 5:    Width="100%"
 6:    BorderWidth="1"
 7:    BorderColor="Black"
 8:    Gridlines="Horizontal"
 9:    HeaderStyle-Font-Size="9pt"
10:    HeaderStyle-Font-Bold="True"
11:    HeaderStyle-Font-Name="Verdana"
12:    HeaderStyle-BackColor="Maroon"
13:    HeaderStyle-ForeColor="White"
14:    ItemStyle-Font-Size="8pt"
15:    ItemStyle-Font-Name="Verdana"
16:    AlternatingItemStyle-BackColor="Tan"
17: >
18:    <Columns>
19:      <asp:BoundColumn DataField="CompanyName" HeaderText="Company" />
20:      <asp:BoundColumn DataField="ContactName" HeaderText="Contact" />
21:      <asp:BoundColumn DataField="City" HeaderText="City" />
22:      <asp:BoundColumn DataField="Country" HeaderText="Country" />
23:    </Columns>
24: </asp:DataGrid>
```

In the `Code-Behind` class in Listing 5.4.1 we create a class named `C5_4_1` that inherits from the `UserControl` class. On line 9 we declare an instance of the `DataGrid` class that will map to an instance of the `DataGrid` in the .ascx file. On lines 11-20 we create a `DataSource` property as an instance of the `System.Data.DataView` class. When this property is set, the `DataView` will be bound to the `DataGrid`.

In the presentation file (`5.4.1.ascx`) we inherit the Code-Behind class (`C5_4_1`) on line 1. On lines 3-24 we create a `DataGrid` for rendering four columns of data about a customer.

Once the `Code-Behind` class is created, we must compile it into a DLL. If you are using Visual Studio.NET, you can build this project and a DLL will be created. If you are using a command line compiler, run the following code from the command line (change the file system path as appropriate for your machine):

```
vbc.exe /t:library
 /out:[path to application root]\bin\C5_4_1.dll
  [path to code behind file]\5.4.1.vb
 /r:System.dll /r:System.Web.dll /r:System.Data.dll /r:System.Xml.dll
```

After running the preceding code, you should have a DLL named `C5_4_1.dll` in your application's `\bin` directory. We are now ready to use this user control in a Web Form. Listing 5.4.2 shows a Web Form that retrieves customer information from the Northwind database, and loads two instances of the `CustomerList` user control.

LISTING 5.4.2 Dynamically Loading User Controls

```
 1: <%@ Import Namespace="System.Data" %>
 2: <%@ Import Namespace="System.Data.SqlClient" %>
 3: <script runat="server" language="vb">
 4:   Protected Sub Page_Load(Sender As Object, E As EventArgs)
 5:     Dim SqlStmt As String
 6:
 7:     SqlStmt = "SELECT CompanyName, ContactName, City, Country FROM Customers"
 8:
 9:     Dim sda As SqlDataAdapter = new SqlDataAdapter(SqlStmt, _
10:       "server=localhost;Database=Northwind;uid=sa;pwd=;")
11:     Dim ds As New DataSet()
12:     sda.Fill(ds, "Customers")
13:
14:     ' Load a user control for customers in Mexico
15:     Dim dvMexico As DataView
16:     dvMexico = ds.Tables("Customers").DefaultView
17:     dvMexico.RowFilter = "Country = 'Mexico'"
18:
19:     If dvMexico.Count > 0 Then
20:       Dim MexicoUC As C5_4_1 = LoadControl("5.4.1.ascx")
```

LISTING 5.4.2 *Continued*

```
21:        MexicoUC.DataSource = dvMexico
22:        myForm.Controls.Add(MexicoUC)
23:     End If
24:
25:     ' Load a user control for customers in Tanzania
26:     Dim dvTanzania As DataView
27:     dvTanzania = ds.Tables("Customers").DefaultView
28:     dvTanzania.RowFilter = "Country = 'Tanzania'"
29:
30:     If dvTanzania.Count > 0 Then
31:        Dim TanzaniaUC As C5_4_1 = LoadControl("5.4.1.ascx")
32:        TanzaniaUC.DataSource = dvTanzania
33:        myForm.Controls.Add(TanzaniaUC)
34:     End If
35:
36:   End Sub
37: </script>
38: <html>
39: <head>
40:   <title>ASP.NET - Tips, Tutorials & Code - Chapter 5</title>
41: </head>
42: <body>
43: <form runat="server" method="post" id="myForm">
44:   <%-- User Controls will be added here --%>
45: </form>
46: </body>
47: </html>
```

In Listing 5.4.2 we create a Web Form that dynamically loads instances of the user control from Listing 5.4.1 based on information retrieved from the Customers table in the Northwind database.

On line 12 we use a `SqlDataAdapter` to fill a `DataTable` in a `DataSet` with data from the Customers table in Northwind. On lines 15-17 we create a `DataView` representation of that data and use the `DataView.RowFilter` property to filter out all customers except those whose Country field is "Mexico." On line 19 we evaluate the number of rows in the `DataView` using the `DataView.Count` property. If there are customers in Mexico (rows in the filtered `DataView`), then we create an instance of the `C5_4_1` class (our user control class), and use the `LoadControl()` method to load the `5.4.2.ascx` user control into that class instance. We then set the `DataView` as the `DataSource` property of the user control, and use the `Form.Add()` method to add the user control to the `Form.Controls` collection.

On lines 25-34 we do the same thing as we did for Mexico, but the second time around we filter for customers in Tanzania. Since there are no customers from Tanzania, only one user control instance will be loaded. Figure 5.12 shows the rendered Web Form from Listing 5.4.2.

FIGURE 5.12
We can dynamically load user controls using the `LoadControl()` and `Add()` methods.

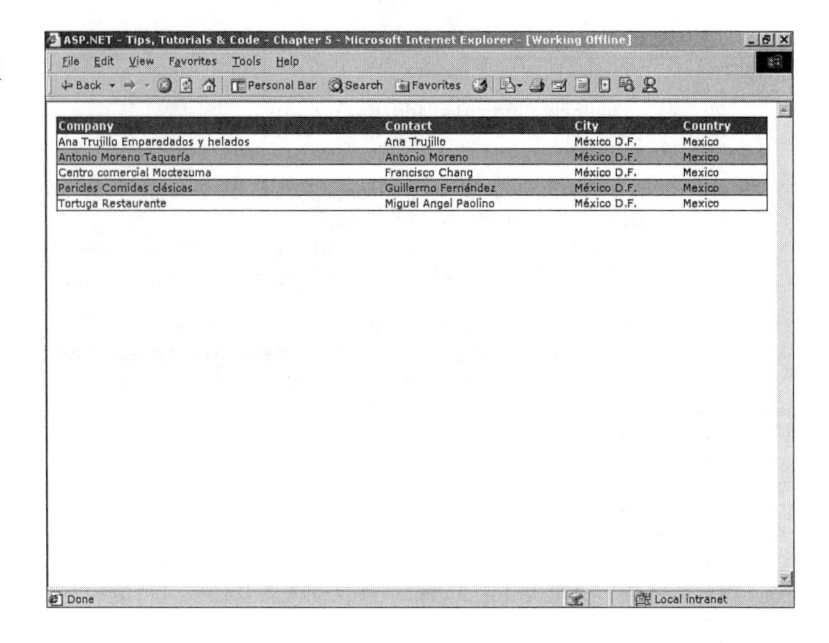

Summary

User controls can truly add a new level of development to Web applications. As you have seen in this chapter, user controls can be everything from basic HTML output, to very complex functionality with or without output. User controls truly comprise the middle ground between include files and custom server controls. As a page developer, you can work with user controls in the same manner as any server control, using the `TagPrefix` and `TagName` format. As a middle-tier developer, user controls enable an easy means of encapsulating code that you need to use in a Web application more than once.

Other Resources

- `www.DotNetJunkies.com`—This ASP.NET-focused site, authored and maintained by authors Doug Seven and Donny Mack, provides a plethora of information about ASP.NET for developers of any skill level. The site includes tutorials on getting started with ASP.NET and a repository for Web services and .NET components!
  `http://www.DotNetJunkies.com`

- Web Forms User Controls—Microsoft's MSDN Web site offers tips and examples for creating user controls. `http://msdn.microsoft.com/library/default.asp?url=/library/en-us/cpguidnf/html/cpconwebformsusercontrols.asp`

CHAPTER 6

DATA MANIPULATION WITH ADO.NET

by Steve Walther

In this chapter you will learn the following:

- How to open a database connection and perform common database operations such as inserting, updating, and deleting database records.
- How to use a DataReader to represent records retrieved from a database table.
- How to use parameters and execute stored procedures from an ASP.NET page.
- How to create a memory resident database using DataSets and DataTables.

Database access is a crucial component of almost any ASP.NET application. Fortunately, the .NET framework contains a rich set of classes and controls for working with database data in your ASP.NET pages.

We'll approach the subject of database access by dividing the topic into two chapters. In this chapter, you'll be given an overview of ADO.NET, the data access technology built into the .NET framework. You'll learn how to use the ADO.NET classes to perform standard database tasks such as modifying and accessing database data. We'll also cover some of the more advanced features of ADO.NET, such as stored procedure support and filtering and sorting data.

In the next chapter, "Data Presentation," you'll learn how to use ADO.NET with ASP.NET controls. You'll learn how to use ADO.NET to bind database data to standard Web Controls, such as the `DropDownList` and `RadioButtonList` controls. You'll also learn how to display and edit database data using the more specialized data controls such as the `Repeater`, `DataList`, and `DataGrid` controls.

1. Overview of ADO.NET

Let's begin with a quick tour of ADO.NET. The .NET Framework contains several namespaces with dozens of classes devoted to database access. However, for the purposes of explaining ADO.NET in this chapter, I'll make a rough division of these classes into three groups.

The first group consists of the following three classes:

- SqlConnection
- SqlCommand
- SqlDataReader

If you plan to build your ASP.NET application with Microsoft SQL Server (version 7.0 or greater), these are the classes you'll use most often. These classes enable you to execute SQL statements and quickly retrieve data from a database query.

The SqlConnection class represents an open connection to a Microsoft SQL Server database. The SqlCommand class represents a SQL statement or stored procedure. Finally, the SqlDataReader class represents the results from a database query. We'll go into the details of using each of these classes in the next section of this chapter.

> **Note**
>
> If you have used the ActiveX Data Objects (ADO), these three classes should be very familiar. The SqlConnection and SqlCommand classes are similar to the ADO Connection and Command objects, with the important exception that they work only with Microsoft SQL Server.
>
> The SqlDataReader class is similar to an ADO Recordset object opened with a fast, forward-only cursor. However, unlike a Recordset object, the SqlDataReader class does not support alternative cursor types and it only works with Microsoft SQL Server.

These classes work only with Microsoft SQL Server. If you need to work with another type of database, such as an Access or Oracle database, you will need to use the following classes:

- OleDbConnection
- OleDbCommand
- OleDbDataReader

Notice that these classes have the same names as the ones in the previous group, except these classes start with OleDb rather than Sql.

Why did Microsoft duplicate these classes, creating one version specifically for SQL Server and one version for non–SQL Server databases? By creating two sets of classes, Microsoft was able to optimize the performance of the first set of classes specifically for SQL Server.

The OleDb classes use OLEDB providers to connect to a database. The Sql classes, on the other hand, communicate with Microsoft SQL Server directly on the level of the Tabular Data Stream

(TDS) protocol. TDS is the low-level proprietary protocol used by SQL Server to handle client and server communication. By bypassing OLEDB and ODBC and working directly with TDS, you get dramatic performance benefits.

There's one last group of classes that we'll work with in this chapter. This group contains the following classes:

- `SqlDataAdapter`
- `OleDbDataAdapter`
- `DataSet`
- `DataTable`
- `DataRelation`
- `DataView`

You can use the classes in this group to build a memory-resident representation of a database (an in-memory database). A `DataSet` represents the in-memory database itself. Once you create a `DataSet`, you can populate it with one or more `DataTables` that represent database tables. You create the `DataTables` with the help of either the `SqlDataAdapter` or `OleDbDataAdapter` class. You can then define various relationships between the tables with the `DataRelation` class and create filtered or sorted views on the `DataTables` with `DataViews`.

Why would you want to build an in-memory database? In certain situations, it is useful to have all the data from a database table available to your ASP.NET application in such a way that it is disconnected from the underlying database. For example, using the classes from this group, you can cache one or more database tables in your server's memory and use the same data in multiple ASP.NET pages. You'll see some other applications of these classes in the final section of this chapter.

> **Note**
>
> If you are an experienced ADO developer, it might be helpful to think of a DataTable as a disconnected, client-side, static Recordset.

2. Using ADO.NET to Accomplish Common Database Tasks

In this section, you'll learn how to use ADO.NET classes to perform common database tasks, such as retrieving database data, inserting new data, updating data, and deleting data. We'll focus on the ADO.NET classes for performing these tasks in this chapter and worry about constructing a friendly user interface for performing these tasks in the following chapter.

Whenever you need to work with database data in an ASP.NET page, you should import the proper namespaces so you can easily access the ADO.NET classes in your page. There are three namespaces that you'll use:

- `System.Data`
- `System.Data.SqlClient`
- `System.Data.OleDb`

If you are accessing a SQL Server database (version 7.0 or greater), you'll need to include these two `Import` statements:

```
<%@ Import Namespace="System.Data" %>
<%@ Import NameSpace="System.Data.SqlClient" %>
```

If you are accessing a database other than Microsoft SQL Server 7.0 or greater (for example, Microsoft Access, Oracle, Microsoft SQL Server 6.5 or just about any data source that has an OLE DB Provider), you would use the following two `Import` statements:

```
<%@ Import Namespace="System.Data" %>
<%@ Import NameSpace="System.Data.OleDb" %>
```

> **Note**
>
> You *can* use the classes from the `System.Data.OleDb` namespace with Microsoft SQL Server. You might want to do this if you want your ASP.NET page to be compatible with any database. For example, you might want your page to work with both Microsoft SQL Server and Oracle. However, you will lose all the speed advantages of the SQL-specific classes if you use the `System.Data.OleDb` namespace.

Opening a Database Connection

The first thing you'll need to do in order to access a database is create and open a database connection. Once again, you'll create the connection in different ways, depending on the type of database that you want to access.

Listing 6.2.1 shows how you would create and open a connection for a Microsoft SQL Server database (this page is included on the CD as `SQLConnection.aspx`).

LISTING 6.2.1 Opening a Connection to SQL Server

```
1: <%@ Import Namespace="System.Data" %>
2: <%@ Import NameSpace="System.Data.SqlClient" %>
3: <%
4: Dim myConnection As SqlConnection
5: myConnection = New SqlConnection( "server=localhost;database=Pubs;uid=sa" )
6:
7: myConnection.Open()
8: %>
9: Connection Opened!
```

The first two lines in Listing 6.2.1 import the necessary namespaces for working with SQL Server. Next, in lines 4 and 5, an instance of the `SqlConnection` class is created named `myConnection`. The `myConnection` class is initialized by passing a connection string as a parameter to the constructor for the `SqlConnection` class. Finally, the connection is actually opened by calling the `Open()` method of the `SqlConnection` class.

The connection string contains all the necessary location and authentication information to connect to SQL Server. In the code in Listing 6.2.1, the connection string contains the name of the server, the name of the database, and the SQL Server login and password.

> **Note**
>
> Notice that you do not specify a provider parameter for the connection string when using the `SqlConnection` class. The classes in the `System.Data.SqlClient` namespace do not use an OLEDB provider, ADO, ODBC, or any other intermediate interface to SQL Server. The classes work directly with the TDS (Tabular Data Stream) protocol.
>
> Furthermore, you cannot use a data source name (DSN) when opening a connection with the `SqlConnection` class. If you really want to use a DSN with SQL Server, you must use the classes in the `System.Data.OleDb` namespace instead.

You would use similar code to create a connection to a Microsoft Access database. In Listing 6.2.2, a database connection is created and opened for a Microsoft Access database named `Authors` (this page is included on the CD as `OleDbConnection.aspx`).

LISTING 6.2.2 Opening a Connection to Microsoft Access

```
1: <%@ Import Namespace="System.Data" %>
2: <%@ Import NameSpace="System.Data.OleDb" %>
3: <%
4: Dim myConnection As OleDbConnection
5: myConnection = New OleDbConnection( "PROVIDER=Microsoft.Jet.OLEDB.4.0;DATA
➥Source=c:\authors.mdb" )
6:
7: myConnection.Open()
8: %>
9: Connection Opened!
```

Because we are creating a connection for Microsoft Access, we must import the `System.Data.OleDb` namespace rather than the `System.Data.SqlClient` namespace. Next, we must create an instance of the `OleDbConnection` class and initialize it with a connection string appropriate for Microsoft Access. Finally, calling the `Open()` method of the `OleDbConnection` class actually opens the database connection.

In the code contained in Listing 6.2.2, we pass the name of the OLEDB provider for Microsoft Access (`Microsoft.Jet.OLEDB.4.0`) and the path to the Access database on the server. If you wanted to connect to another type of database, you would need to specify a different provider. For example, to connect to an Oracle database, you would use the MSDAORA provider. (This provider is automatically installed as part of the Microsoft Data Access Components.)

> **Note**
>
> If you prefer, you can use a data source name (DSN) with the `OleDbConnection` class to open a database connection. For example, after you create a System DSN named myDSN, you can connect using this:
>
> `myConnection = New OleDbConnection( "DSN=myDSN" )`
>
> Realize, however, that opening a connection in this way forces you to use the OLEDB for ODBC provider rather than the native OLEDB provider for your database. Typically, but not always, this will result in slower performance.

By default, when you call the `Open()` method with either the `SqlConnection` or the `OleDbConnection` classes, the connection is given 15 seconds to open before timing out. You can override this default behavior by setting the `ConnectionTimeout` property before you open the database connection. For example, to allow up to 90 seconds to open a connection, you would use a statement like the following:

`MyConnection.ConnectionTimeout = 90`

Inserting Data Using ADO.NET

Now that you know how to create and open a database connection, we can use this connection to add new data to a database table. We'll add the new data with the SQL `INSERT` command. Here's the syntax for a basic `INSERT` command:

`INSERT tablename ( column1, column2... ) VALUES ( value1, value2... )`

You insert new records into a table by listing the table columns and listing the values that you want to insert into the columns. For example, imagine that you have a table named Authors that has both a `FirstName` and a `LastName` column. The following statement inserts a new author named Ralph Ellison:

`INSERT Authors ( FirstName, LastName ) VALUES ( 'Ralph', 'Ellison' )`

Three steps are required for executing a SQL `INSERT` command in an ASP.NET page:

1. Create and open a database connection.
2. Create a database command that represents the SQL `INSERT` statement to execute.
3. Execute the command.

The ASP.NET page in Listing 6.2.3 uses the classes from the `System.Data.SqlClient` namespace to insert a new record into a SQL Server database table (this page is included on the CD as `SQLINSERTcommand.aspx`).

LISTING 6.2.3 Executing an `INSERT` Command

```
1: <%@ Import Namespace="System.Data" %>
2: <%@ Import NameSpace="System.Data.SqlClient" %>
3:
```

LISTING 6.2.3 Continued

```
 4: <%
 5: Dim myConnection As SqlConnection
 6: Dim myCommand As SqlCommand
 7:
 8: myConnection = New SqlConnection( "server=localhost;uid=sa;
➥pwd=secret;database=myDataPubs" )
 9: myConnection.Open()
10: myCommand = New SqlCommand( "Insert testTable ( col1 )
➥Values ( 'Hello' )", myConnection )
11: myCommand.ExecuteNonQuery()
12: myConnection.Close()
13: %>
14: New Record Inserted!
15:
```

The first two statements in Listing 6.2.3 are used to import the necessary namespaces. Next, in lines 8 and 9, a connection to a SQL database is created. An instance of the `SQLConnection` class is initialized with a connection string for the myData database located on the local server. Next, the `SqlConnection` is opened with the `Open()` method.

In the statement that follows, an instance of the `SqlCommand` class is created. The `SqlCommand` class is initialized with two parameters: the command to execute and the connection to use for executing the command.

In line 10, a string containing an `INSERT` statement is passed to the instance of the `SqlCommand` class. The `INSERT` statement inserts a new record into a table named `testTable` with a single column named `col1`.

Finally, the command is executed by calling the `ExecuteNonQuery()` method of the `SqlCommand` class. The `ExecuteNonQuery()` method sends the SQL command to the database server. The method is called the `ExecuteNonQuery()` method because it is used to execute non-row-returning SQL commands.

The code in Listing 6.2.3 works only with Microsoft SQL Server (version 7.0 or greater). To work with other databases, you would need to modify the code to use the classes from the `System.Data.OleDb` namespace rather than the `System.Data.SqlClient` namespace. The ASP.NET page in Listing 6.2.4 demonstrates how you would add a new record to a Microsoft Access database table (this page is included on the CD as `OleDbINSERTcommand.aspx`).

LISTING 6.2.4 Adding a Record to Access

```
1: <%@ Import Namespace="System.Data" %>
2: <%@ Import NameSpace="System.Data.OleDb" %>
3:
4: <%
5: Dim myConnection As OleDbConnection
6: Dim myCommand As OleDbCommand
7:
8: myConnection = New OleDbConnection( "PROVIDER=Microsoft.Jet.OLEDB.4.0;DATA
➥Source=c:authors.mdb" )
```

LISTING 6.2.4   Continued

```
 9: myConnection.Open()
10: myCommand = New OleDbCommand( "Insert INTO Authors ( Author ) Values
➥ ( 'Simpson' )", myConnection )
11: myCommand.ExecuteNonQuery()
12: myConnection.Close()
13: %>
14: New Record Inserted!
15:
```

The code in Listing 6.2.4 executes an `INSERT` statement that adds a new record to a Microsoft Access table named `authors.mdb`. Notice that Microsoft Access requires you to use the keyword `INTO` with the `INSERT` statement (you use `INSERT INTO Authors` rather than `INSERT Authors`).

> **Note**
>
> The apostrophe character (') can cause problems when you're inserting data into a database table. For example, imagine that you want to add a new author named O'Leary to the Authors table. You might try to execute the following statement:
>
> `INSERT INTO Authors ( Author ) Values ( 'O'Leary' )`
>
> This statement will generate an error because the apostrophe in O'Leary will be interpreted as marking the end of the SQL string. To get around this problem, you'll need to double up your apostrophes. For example, use the following statement to add O'Leary to a database table:
>
> `INSERT INTO Authors ( Author ) Values ( 'O''Leary' )`

Updating Data Using ADO.NET

To update existing records in a database table, you use the SQL `UPDATE` command. Here's the syntax for the basic `UPDATE` command:

```
UPDATE tablename SET column1 = value1, column2 = value2...
WHERE search condition
```

You update a table by setting certain columns to certain values where a certain search condition is true. For example, imagine that you have a database table named `Authors` that has a column named `LastName`. The following statement sets the value of the `LastName` column to `'Smith'` wherever the column has a value of `'Bennet'`:

```
UPDATE Authors SET LastName = 'Smith'
WHERE LastName = 'Bennet'
```

You execute an `UPDATE` command within an ASP.NET page by completing the following steps:

1. Create and open a database connection.
2. Create a database command that represents the SQL `UPDATE` statement to execute.
3. Execute the command.

For example, the ASP.NET page contained in Listing 6.2.5 updates a record in a SQL Server database (this page is included on the CD as `SQLUPDATEcommand.aspx`).

LISTING 6.2.5 Updating a SQL Database

```
 1: <%@ Import Namespace="System.Data" %>
 2: <%@ Import NameSpace="System.Data.SqlClient" %>
 3:
 4: <%
 5: Dim myConnection As SqlConnection
 6: Dim myCommand As SqlCommand
 7:
 8: myConnection = New SqlConnection( "server=localhost;uid=sa;
➥pwd=secret;database=myDataPubs" )
 9: myConnection.Open()
10: myCommand = New SqlCommand( "UPDATE Authors SET LastName='Smith'
➥WHERE LastName='Bennett'", myConnection )
11: myCommand.ExecuteNonQuery()
12: myConnection.Close()
13: %>
14: Record Updated!
15:
```

The first two statements in Listing 6.2.5 import the necessary namespaces for working with the SQL ADO.NET classes. Next, in lines 8 and 9, a database connection is created and opened for the local server. In the statement that follows, an instance of the `SqlCommand` class is created by passing a SQL command and `SqlConnection` to the constructor for the class.

The SQL **UPDATE** command is executed when the `ExecuteNonQuery()` method of the `SqlCommand` class is called. At this point, the **UPDATE** statement is transmitted to SQL Server and executed.

The code in Listing 6.2.5 will only work with Microsoft SQL Server (version 7.0 and greater). If you want to update a record in another type of database, you will need to use the ADO.NET classes from the `System.Data.OleDb` namespace rather than the `System.Data.SqlClient` namespace.

The ASP.NET page contained in Listing 6.2.6 modifies a record in a Microsoft Access database (the page is included on the CD as `OleDbUPDATEcommand.aspx`).

LISTING 6.2.6 Updating an Access Database

```
 1: <%@ Import Namespace="System.Data" %>
 2: <%@ Import NameSpace="System.Data.OleDb" %>
 3:
 4: <%
 5: Dim myConnection As OleDbConnection
 6: Dim myCommand As OleDbCommand
 7:
 8: myConnection = New OleDbConnection( "PROVIDER=Microsoft.Jet.OLEDB.4.0;DATA
➥Source=c:\authors.mdb" )
```

LISTING 6.2.6 Continued

```
 9: myConnection.Open()
10: myCommand = New OleDbCommand( "UPDATE Authors SET Author='Bennett'
➥WHERE Author = 'Simpson'", myConnection )
11: myCommand.ExecuteNonQuery()
12: myConnection.Close
13: %>
14: Record Updated!
15:
```

One difference between the SQL UPDATE command and the SQL INSERT command is that the SQL UPDATE command might affect more than one record at a time. When you execute an UPDATE command, the command changes every record that satisfies the UPDATE command's WHERE clause.

You can determine the number of records affected by an UPDATE command within an ASP.NET page by grabbing the value returned by the ExecuteNonQuery() method. The page contained in Listing 6.2.7 illustrates this method (this page is included on the CD as SQLUPDATERecordsAffected.aspx).

LISTING 6.2.7 Records Affected by the UPDATE Command

```
 1: <%@ Import Namespace="System.Data" %>
 2: <%@ Import NameSpace="System.Data.SqlClient" %>
 3:
 4: <%
 5: Dim myConnection As SqlConnection
 6: Dim myCommand As SqlCommand
 7: Dim recordsAffected As Integer
 8:
 9: myConnection = New SqlConnection( "server=localhost;uid=sa;
➥pwd=secret;database=myDataPubs" )
10: myConnection.Open()
11: myCommand = New SqlCommand( "UPDATE testTable SET col1='hello'
➥WHERE col1='fred'", myConnection )
12: recordsAffected = myCommand.ExecuteNonQuery()
13: Response.Write( "The UPDATE statement modified " &
➥recordsAffected.toString() & " records!" )
14: myConnection.Close
15: %>
16:
```

Deleting Data Using ADO.NET

You can delete data from a database by using the SQL DELETE command. The syntax for a basic DELETE command takes the following form:

```
DELETE tablename WHERE search condition
```

For example, if you want to delete all the rows from a table named Authors in which the LastName column has the value 'Bennet', use the following statement:

```
DELETE Authors WHERE LastName = 'Bennet'
```

Chapter 6 • DATA MANIPULATION WITH ADO.NET

To execute a **DELETE** command from within an ASP.NET page, you must complete the following steps:

1. Create and open a database connection.
2. Create a database command that represents the SQL **DELETE** statement to execute.
3. Execute the command.

For example, the ASP.NET page in Listing 6.2.8 demonstrates how you can delete a record from a SQL Server database table (this page is included on the CD as `SQLDELETEcommand.aspx`).

LISTING 6.2.8 *Deleting a Record from SQL Server*

```
 1: <%@ Import Namespace="System.Data" %>
 2: <%@ Import NameSpace="System.Data.SqlClient" %>
 3:
 4: <%
 5: Dim myConnection As SqlConnection
 6: Dim myCommand As SqlCommand
 7:
 8: myConnection = New SqlConnection( "server=localhost;uid=sa;
➥pwd=secret;database=myDataPubs" )
 9: myConnection.Open()
10: myCommand = New SqlCommand( "DELETE testTable WHERE col1='fred'", myConnection )
11: myCommand.ExecuteNonQuery()
12: myConnection.Close()
13: %>
14: Record Deleted!
15:
```

The first two lines in Listing 6.2.8 are used to import the necessary namespaces to work with SQL Server. Next, a connection to the SQL Server running on the local machine is opened.

In line 10, the `SqlCommand` class is initialized with two parameters: a SQL **DELETE** command and the `SqlConnection` class. Next, the command is executed, and the connection is closed.

If you need to work with a database other than Microsoft SQL Server, you would use similar code. However, you must use the classes from the `System.Data.OleDb` namespace rather than the classes from `System.Data.SqlClient`.

The page contained in Listing 6.2.9 illustrates how you would delete a record from a Microsoft Access database table named **Authors** (this page is included on the CD as `OleDbDELETEcommand.aspx`).

LISTING 6.2.9 *Deleting a Record from an Access Database*

```
1: <%@ Import Namespace="System.Data" %>
2: <%@ Import NameSpace="System.Data.OleDb" %>
3:
4: <%
```

LISTING 6.2.9 Continued

```
 5: Dim myConnection As OleDbConnection
 6: Dim myCommand As OleDbCommand
 7:
 8: myConnection = New OleDbConnection( "PROVIDER=Microsoft.Jet.OLEDB.4.0;DATA
➥Source=c:\authors.mdb" )
 9: myConnection.Open()
10: myCommand = New OleDbCommand( "DELETE FROM Authors
➥WHERE Author = 'Simpson'", myConnection )
11: myCommand.ExecuteNonQuery()
12: myConnection.Close()
13: %>
14: Record Deleted!
15:
16:
```

Notice that you must use **DELETE FROM** rather than just **DELETE** when working with a Microsoft Access database.

A SQL **DELETE** command is similar to a SQL **UPDATE** command in that it might affect an unknown number of records. A SQL **DELETE** command deletes all the records that match the condition specified by the command's **WHERE** clause.

If you need to determine the number of records affected by a **DELETE** command, you can grab the value returned by the **ExecuteNonQuery()** method. The page contained in Listing 6.2.10 illustrates how you would do this (this page is included on the CD as **SQLDELETERecordsAffected.aspx**).

LISTING 6.2.10 Records Affected by **DELETE**

```
 1: <%@ Import Namespace="System.Data" %>
 2: <%@ Import NameSpace="System.Data.SqlClient" %>
 3:
 4: <%
 5: Dim myConnection As SQLConnection
 6: Dim myCommand As SQLCommand
 7: Dim recordsAffected As Integer
 8:
 9: myConnection = New SqlConnection( "server=localhost;uid=sa;
➥pwd=secret;database=myDataPubs" )
10: myConnection.Open()
11: myCommand = New SqlCommand( "DELETE Authors2
➥WHERE LastName='Smith'", myConnection )
12: recordsAffected = myCommand.ExecuteNonQuery()
13: Response.Write( "The DELETE statement modified "
➥& recordsAffected.toString() & " records!" )
14: myConnection.Close
15: %>
16:
17:
```

Querying Data Using ADO.NET

The SQL command that you will use most often in your ASP.NET pages is the `SELECT` command. The `SELECT` command enables you to retrieve records from a database table that match a certain condition. Here's the syntax for a basic `SELECT` command:

```
SELECT column1, column2...
FROM tablename1, tablname2...
WHERE search condition
```

For example, if you wanted to retrieve the `FirstName` and `LastName` columns from the `Authors` table, where the LastName column has the value `'Smith'`, you would use the following `SELECT` command:

```
SELECT FirstName, LastName
FROM Authors
WHERE LastName = 'Smith'
```

If you simply want to retrieve all the columns and all the rows from the Authors table, use the following `SELECT` statement:

```
SELECT * FROM Authors
```

The asterisk (*) is a wildcard character that represents all the columns. Without a `WHERE` clause, all the rows from the `Authors` table are automatically returned.

> **Note**
> For performance reasons, you should avoid using the * wildcard character in the `SELECT` statement.

Four steps are involved in executing a `SELECT` command in an ASP.NET page:

1. Create and open a database connection.
2. Create a database command that represents the SQL `SELECT` statement to execute.
3. Execute the command returning a DataReader.
4. Loop through the DataReader, displaying the results of the query.

When you execute a query using ADO.NET, the results of the query are returned in a `DataReader`. More accurately, the results of a query are represented by either the `SqlDataReader` or the `OleDbDataReader`, depending on the database from which you are retrieving the records.

A `DataReader` represents a forward-only stream of database records. This means that the `DataReader` only represents a single record at a time. To fetch the next record in the stream, you must call the `Read()` method. To display all the records returned from a query, you must call the `Read()` method again and again until you read the end of the stream.

> **Note**
>
> If you have used earlier versions of ADO, it may be helpful to think of a `DataReader` as a `Recordset` opened with a forward-only cursor.

For example, the ASP.NET page in Listing 6.2.11 displays all the records from a SQL Server database table named `Authors;`. (This page is included on the CD as `SQLDataReader.aspx`.)

LISTING 6.2.11 Using the SQLDataReader

```
 1: <%@ Import Namespace="System.Data" %>
 2: <%@ Import NameSpace="System.Data.SqlClient" %>
 3:
 4: <%
 5: Dim myConnection As SqlConnection
 6: Dim myCommand As SqlCommand
 7: Dim myDataReader As SqlDataReader
 8:
 9: myConnection = New SqlConnection( "server=localhost;uid=sa;
➥pwd=secret;database=Pubs" )
10: myConnection.Open()
11: myCommand = New SqlCommand( "Select * from Authors", myConnection )
12: myDataReader = myCommand.ExecuteReader()
13: While myDataReader.Read()
14:    Response.Write( myDataReader.Item( "au_lname" ) )
15: End While
16: myDataReader.Close()
17: myConnection.Close()
18: %>
19:
```

The first two lines in Listing 6.2.11 are used to import the necessary namespaces to use the ADO.NET classes for SQL Server. Next, in lines 9 and 10, a connection is created and opened for the database located on the local server named **Pubs**.

Next, a `SqlCommand` object is initialized with a SQL string that contains a SQL **SELECT** command. The SQL **SELECT** command retrieves all the records from a database table named **Authors**.

Next, the command is executed by calling the `ExecuteReader()` method of the `SqlCommand` class. In this case, we want to call the `ExecuteReader()` method rather than the `ExecuteNonQuery()` method because we need to retrieve the results of a query. The `ExecuteReader()` method returns a SQLDataReader that represents the results of executing the SQL **SELECT** statement.

Once we have a `SQLDataReader`, we need to loop through its contents to display all the records returned by the query. In Listing 6.2.11, this is accomplished with a **WHILE...END WHILE** loop. All the records returned by the **SELECT** command are displayed with the following block of code:

```
While myDataReader.Read
   Response.Write( myDataReader.Item( "au_lname" ) )
End While
```

The `Read()` method of the `SqlDataReader` class does two things whenever it is called. First, the method returns the value `TRUE` if there is another record; otherwise, it returns `FALSE`. Second, the method advances the `DataReader` to the next record if a next record exists. By combining these functions, the `Read()` method makes it very easy to quickly loop through the contents of a `DataReader`.

> **Caution**
>
> Remember to call the `Read()` method at least once before displaying a record with the `DataReader`. When a `DataReader` is first returned, the first record is not retrieved until you call the `Read()` method.

The value of a returned column is displayed by using the `Item` property of the `DataReader`. For example, in the code in Listing 6.2.11, the value of the `au_lname` column is displayed.

> **Note**
>
> The `Item` property will automatically convert the value returned to the proper .NET data type. The value of a SQL Varchar column is returned as a String, the value of a SQL Int column is returned as an Int32 value, the value of a SQL Money column is returned as a Decimal, and so on.

The page in Listing 6.2.11 was written using Visual Basic.NET. The page in Listing 6.2.12 does the same thing using the C# language (this page is included on the CD as `SqlDataReader.aspx` in the C# folder).

LISTING 6.2.12 Using the SqlDataReader with C#

```
 1: <%@ Page Language="C#" %>
 2: <%@ Import Namespace="System.Data" %>
 3: <%@ Import NameSpace="System.Data.SqlClient" %>
 4:
 5: <%
 6: SqlDataReader myDataReader;
 7: SqlConnection myConnection = new
➥SqlConnection( "server=localhost;uid=sa;
➥pwd=secret;database=Pubs" );
 8: myConnection.Open();
 9: SqlCommand myCommand = new SqlCommand( "Select * from
➥Authors", myConnection );
10: myDataReader = myCommand.ExecuteReader();
11: while ( myDataReader.Read() )
12: {
13:   Response.Write( myDataReader[ "au_lname" ].ToString() );
14: }
15: myDataReader.Close();
16: myConnection.Close();
17: %>
18:
```

The ASP.NET pages in Listing 6.2.11 and 6.2.12 will only work with Microsoft SQL Server. To use other databases, you must use the `System.Data.OleDb` classes rather than the `System.Data.SqlClient` classes.

The page in Listing 6.2.13 illustrates how you would execute a query against a Microsoft Access database (this page is included on the CD as `OleDbDataReader.aspx`).

LISTING 6.2.13   Using the OleDbDataReader

```
 1: <%@ Import Namespace="System.Data" %>
 2: <%@ Import NameSpace="System.Data.OleDb" %>
 3:
 4: <%
 5: Dim myConnection As OleDbConnection
 6: Dim myCommand As OleDbCommand
 7: Dim myDataReader As OleDbDataReader
 8:
 9: myConnection = New OleDbConnection( "PROVIDER=Microsoft.Jet.OLEDB.4.0;DATA
➥Source=c:\authors.mdb" )
10: myConnection.Open()
11: myCommand = New OleDbCommand( "Select * from Authors", myConnection )
12: myDataReader = myCommand.ExecuteReader()
13: While myDataReader.Read
14:   Response.Write( myDataReader.Item( "author" ) )
15: End While
16: myDataReader.Close()
17: myConnection.Close
18: %>
19:
```

After you finish displaying the records from a `DataReader`, it is important that you explicitly close it (using the `Close()` method). If you neglect to close the `DataReader`, you might encounter problems when attempting to reuse the conncetion later in the page.

3. Using Parameters with SQL Commands

When building your ASP.NET pages, you'll need to use variables when working with SQL commands. Otherwise, you will insert the very same data every time a page is executed.

For example, if you retrieve data from a form, you'll need to use variables in your `INSERT` command to insert the values retrieved from the form. So far, we have not discussed how you can use variables with SQL commands.

The simplest way to use variables when working with SQL commands is to build up the command string itself with variables. An example of this can be found in Listing 6.3.1.

LISTING 6.3.1   Inserting Data with Variables

```
 1: <%@ Import Namespace="System.Data" %>
 2: <%@ Import NameSpace="System.Data.SqlClient" %>
 3:
```

LISTING 6.3.1 Continued

```
 4: <%
 5: Dim myConnection As SqlConnection
 6: Dim myCommand As SqlCommand
 7: Dim sqlString As String
 8:
 9: Dim FirstName As String = "Robert"
10: Dim LastName As String = "Johnson"
11:
12: myConnection = New SQLConnection(
"server=localhost;uid=sa;pwd=secret;database=myData" )
13: myConnection.Open()
14: sqlString = "Insert Authors ( FirstName, LastName ) Values
➥('" & FirstName & "','" & LastName & "')"
15: myCommand = New SqlCommand( sqlString, myConnection )
16: myCommand.ExecuteNonQuery()
17: myConnection.Close()
18: %>
19: New Record Inserted!
20:
```

The page in Listing 6.3.1 contains two variables named `FirstName` and `LastName`. You could imagine that these variables represent information retrieved from an HTML form. The variables are used to build the contents of another variable called `sqlString`. The `sqlString` variable contains a standard SQL `INSERT` command.

Notice that the `sqlString` variable is used in line 15 when initializing the `SqlCommand` class. When the `SqlCommand` is executed, the SQL command contained in the `sqlString` variable is executed. When the page is executed, the new author, Robert Johnson, is added to the Authors table.

The page in Listing 6.3.1 will execute without generating an error. However, it has some limitations. You will encounter three types of problems when taking this approach of using variables with SQL commands.

First, building a SQL string with variables in this manner will produce errors when the variables contain apostrophes. For example, if the value of the `LastName` variable is "O'Leary," SQL Server will generate an error when you attempt to execute the SQL string. SQL Server generates this error because it interprets the apostrophe as marking the end of a SQL string.

> **Note**
>
> One way to get around this problem with the apostrophe character is to write a function that automatically doubles up every apostrophe in a string. SQL Server will automatically interpret two apostrophes in a row as a single apostrophe.

Second, imagine that you have a very large HTML form that has, for example, 50 form fields. Building a SQL string with this number of variables would be a very tedious and error-prone operation. You'll end up with a massive string as the value of the `sqlString` variable.

Finally, building SQL strings out of variables in this manner makes it difficult to convert your code to use stored procedures (stored procedures are discussed in the next section, "Using Stored Procedures with ADO.NET"). You cannot use this method of building SQL strings when working with stored procedures.

Fortunately, there is a better method for using variables with SQL commands: You can explicitly create parameters for a SQL command to represent variable information.

The ASP.NET page in Listing 6.2.15 illustrates how you can use parameters with the `SqlCommand` class (this page is included on the CD with the name `SQLParameters.aspx`).

LISTING 6.3.2   Using SQL Parameters

```
 1: <%@ Import Namespace="System.Data" %>
 2: <%@ Import NameSpace="System.Data.SqlClient" %>
 3:
 4: <%
 5: Dim myConnection As SqlConnection
 6: Dim myCommand As SqlCommand
 7: Dim FirstName As String = "Robert"
 8: Dim LastName As String = "Johnson"
 9:
10: myConnection = New SqlConnection(
"server=localhost;uid=sa;pwd=secret;database=myData" )
11: myConnection.Open()
12: myCommand = New SQLCommand( "Insert Authors ( FirstName, LastName )
➥Values ( @FirstName, @LastName )", myConnection )
13:
14: myCommand.Parameters.Add( New SqlParameter( "@FirstName",
➥SqlDbType.Varchar, 30 ))
15: myCommand.Parameters( "@FirstName" ).Value = FirstName
16:
17: myCommand.Parameters.Add( New SqlParameter( "@LastName",
➥SqlDbType.Varchar, 30 ))
18: myCommand.Parameters( "@LastName" ).Value = LastName
19:
20: myCommand.ExecuteNonQuery()
21: myConnection.Close()
22: %>
23: Record Inserted!
```

In Listing 6.3.2, two parameters are created: `@FirstName` and `@LastName`. These parameters are used within the SQL `INSERT` command as placeholders for the values of the `FirstName` and `LastName` string variables. The SQL `INSERT` statement looks like this:

```
Insert Authors ( FirstName, LastName ) Values ( @FirstName, @LastName )
```

Next, the parameters are created and added to the `Parameters` collection of the `SqlCommand` class. For example, the `@LastName` parameter is created and added with the following statement:

```
myCommand.Parameters.Add( New
➥SqlParameter( "@FirstName", SqlDbType.Varchar, 30 ))
```

The parameter is initialized with the name of the parameter (`@FirstName`), the data type of the parameter (`SqlDbType.Varchar`), and the maximum size of the value of the parameter (30 characters).

The name of the parameter must match the name that you used for the parameter placeholder in the SQL string. The name must also start with the `@` character.

The data type should be a valid Microsoft SQL Server data type. When using variable-length data types, such as Varchar and VarBinary, you can also list the maximum size of the parameter. This size should match the size of the column in the underlying database table.

The value of the parameter is assigned with the following line of code:

`myCommand.Parameters( "@FirstName" ).Value = FirstName`

This statement assigns the value of the `FirstName` variable to the `SqlCommand` parameter named `@FirstName`.

The code in Listing 6.3.2 will only work with Microsoft SQL Server because it uses the classes from the `System.Data.SqlClient` namespace. The page in Listing 6.3.3 uses the classes from the `System.Data.OleDb` namespace to work with Microsoft Access (this page is included on the CD as `OleDbParameters.aspx`).

LISTING 6.3.3 Using Parameters with Microsoft Access

```
 1: <%@ Import Namespace="System.Data" %>
 2: <%@ Import NameSpace="System.Data.OleDb" %>
 3:
 4: <%
 5: Dim myConnection As OleDbConnection
 6: Dim myCommand As OleDbCommand
 7: Dim FirstName As String = "Robert"
 8: Dim LastName As String = "Johnson"
 9:
10: myConnection = New OleDbConnection( "PROVIDER=Microsoft.Jet.OLEDB.4.0;
➥DATA Source=c:\author2.mdb" )
11: myConnection.Open()
12: myCommand = New OleDbCommand( "Insert INTO Authors ( FirstName, LastName )
➥ Values ( @FirstName, @LastName )", myConnection )
13:
14: myCommand.Parameters.Add( New OleDbParameter( "@FirstName",
➥OleDbType.Varchar, 30 ))
15: myCommand.Parameters( "@FirstName" ).Value = FirstName
16:
17: myCommand.Parameters.Add( New OleDbParameter( "@LastName",
➥OleDbType.Varchar, 30 ))
18: myCommand.Parameters( "@LastName" ).Value = LastName
19:
20: myCommand.ExecuteNonQuery()
21: myConnection.Close()
22: %>
23: Record Inserted!
24:
```

Notice that the data types used for initializing the `OleDbParameter` class are different from those used for the `SqlParameter` class. When working with the `OleDbParameter` class, you must use values from the `OleDbType` enumeration. So, to represent an Access Text column, you must use the value `OleDbType.Varchar`.

> **Note**
>
> The `SqlDbType` enumeration can be found in the `System.Data` namespace, and the `OleDbType` enumeration can be found in the `System.Data.OleDb` namespace.

4. Using Stored Procedures with ADO.NET

There are two ways of executing a SQL command from within an ASP.NET page. You can execute the command directly from code in the page, or you can package the SQL command as a stored procedure and execute the stored procedure from the page.

Building stored procedures takes a little more work than executing commands directly on a page. However, you can significantly increase the performance of a database-driven Web site by using stored procedures. A SQL statement must be parsed, compiled, and optimized by SQL Server whenever it is executed from an ASP.NET page. A stored procedure, on the other hand, needs to be parsed, compiled, and optimized only once.

Another advantage of using stored procedures is that they enable you to reuse the same SQL statements in multiple ASP.NET pages. If, at some later date, you need to make changes to your code, you can change it in only one place rather than in every page.

In any case, after you have set up the parameters for a SQL command (as you did in the previous section), executing the command as a stored procedure requires a trivial amount of work. For example, Listing 6.4.1 illustrates how you can convert the code in Listing 6.3.1 to use a stored procedure (this page is included on the CD as `SQLStoredProcedure.aspx`).

LISTING 6.4.1 Using Stored Procedures

```
 1: <%@ Import Namespace="System.Data" %>
 2: <%@ Import NameSpace="System.Data.SqlClient" %>
 3:
 4: <%
 5: Dim myConnection As SqlConnection
 6: Dim myCommand As SqlCommand
 7: Dim FirstName As String = "Robert"
 8: Dim LastName As String = "Johnson"
 9:
10: myConnection = New SqlConnection(
➥"server=localhost;uid=sa;pwd=secret;database=myData" )
11: myConnection.Open()
12: myCommand = New SqlCommand( "InsertAuthors", myConnection )
```

LISTING 6.4.1 Continued

```
13: myCommand.CommandType = CommandType.StoredProcedure
14:
15: myCommand.Parameters.Add( New SqlParameter( "@FirstName",
➥SqlDbType.Varchar, 30 ))
16: myCommand.Parameters( "@FirstName" ).Value = FirstName
17:
18: myCommand.Parameters.Add( New SqlParameter( "@LastName",
➥SqlDbType.Varchar, 30 ))
19: myCommand.Parameters( "@LastName" ).Value = LastName
20:
21: myCommand.ExecuteNonQuery()
22: myConnection.Close
23: %>
24: Record Inserted!
25:
26:
```

When you execute the page contained in Listing 6.4.1, a new record is added to the `Authors` table with the following stored procedure named `InsertAuthors`:

```
create procedure InsertAuthors
(
  @FirstName Varchar( 50 ),
  @LastName Varchar( 50 )
)
AS
Insert Authors ( FirstName, LastName )
  VALUES ( @FirstName, @LastName )
```

To create this stored procedure in Microsoft SQL Server, launch the SQL Query Analyzer by going to Start, Programs, Microsoft SQL Server, Query Analyzer. Enter the preceding stored procedure and click Execute (the green VCR play button).

This stored procedure accepts two input parameters: `@FirstName` and `@LastName`. The input parameters are used in the SQL `INSERT` command to add a new record to the Authors table.

Two modifications were made to the ASP.NET page in Listing 6.2.17 to enable the page to execute the `InsertAuthors` stored procedure. First, instead of a SQL statement being passed to the `SqlCommand` object, the name of the stored procedure (`InsertAuthors`) is passed instead:

```
myCommand = New SqlCommand( "InsertAuthors", myConnection )
```

An additional line of code was also added to Listing 6.2.17. The following statement was added to set the `CommandType` property of the `SQLCommand` class to the value `StoredProcedure`:

```
myCommand.CommandType = CommandType.StoredProcedure
```

Using Output Parameters

The code in Listing 6.4.1 demonstrates how you can pass input parameters to a stored procedure. However, stored procedures can also have output parameters and return values. You can use both output parameters and return values to return information from a stored procedure.

Output parameters and return values return different types of data. A return value can only return an integer value. Whenever you execute a stored procedure, the stored procedure has a return value. By default, the return value is 0.

Output parameters can return values of most data types. For example, you can use an output parameter to return a Varchar, Money, or Integer value. However, all versions of SQL Server, including the current version (SQL Server 2000), do not support returning TEXT values as output parameters.

For example, the following stored procedure has an input parameter, an output parameter, and Listing 6.4.1 demonstrates a return value:

```
create procedure getLastName
(
  @FirstName Varchar( 50 ),
  @LastName Varchar( 50 ) Output
)
As
Select @LastName = LastName
From Authors
WHERE FirstName = @FirstName

IF @LastName is Null
 Return( 0 )
ELSE
 Return( 1 )
```

The `getLastName` stored procedure accepts an input parameter named `@FirstName` and returns an output parameter named `@LastName`. If an author with the first name exists in the `Authors` table, a return value of 1 is retrieved. Otherwise, the stored procedure sends back a return value of 0.

The ASP.NET page in Listing 6.4.2 illustrates how you can use the `getLastName` stored procedure from within an ASP.NET page (this page is included on the CD as `SQLInputOutput.aspx`).

LISTING 6.4.2 Retrieving Output Parameters and Return Values

```
1: <%@ Import Namespace="System.Data" %>
2: <%@ Import NameSpace="System.Data.SqlClient" %>
3:Listing 6.4.1 demonstrates
4: <%
```

LISTING 6.4.2 *Continued*

```
 5: Dim myConnection As SqlConnection
 6: Dim myCommand As SqlCommand
 7: Dim myParam As SqlParameter
 8:
 9: myConnection = New SqlConnection( "server=localhost;uid=sa;
➥pwd=secret;database=myDataPubs" )
10: myConnection.Open()
11:
12: myCommand = New SqlCommand( "getLastName", myConnection )
13: myCommand.CommandType = CommandType.StoredProcedure
14:
15: myParam = myCommand.Parameters.Add( New
➥SqlParameter( "RETURN VALUE", SqlDbType.INT ))
16: myParam.Direction = ParameterDirection.ReturnValue
17:
18: myParam = myCommand.Parameters.Add( New
➥SqlParameter( "@FirstName", SqlDbType.Varchar, 50 ))
19: myParam.Direction = ParameterDirection.Input
20: myParam.Value = "Robert"
21:
22: myParam = myCommand.Parameters.Add( New
➥SqlParameter( "@LastName", SqlDbType.Varchar, 50 ))
23: myParam.Direction = ParameterDirection.Output
24:
25: myCommand.ExecuteNonQuery()
26: If myCommand.Parameters( "RETURN VALUE" ).Value Then
27:   Response.Write( "The last name is " &
➥MyCommand.Parameters( "@LastName" ).Value )
28: Else
29:   Response.Write( "No author found!" )
30: END If
31: myConnection.Close()
32: %>
33:
```

In Listing 6.4.2, a return value parameter, input parameter, and output parameter are added to the `Parameters` collection of the `SqlCommand` class. The direction of the parameter is set with the `Direction` property of the `SqlParameter` class. For example, the following two statements are used to create the output parameter that Listing 6.4.1 demonstrates:

```
myParam = myCommand.Parameters.Add( New
➥SqlParameter( "@LastName", SqlDbType.Varchar, 50 ))
myParam.Direction = ParameterDirection.Output
```

After the command has been executed, the value of the parameters can be retrieved. The value of the output parameter is displayed in the following `Response.Write()` statement:

```
Response.Write( "The last name is " & Listing 6.4.1 demonstrates
➥MyCommand.Parameters( "@LastName" ).Value )
```

5. Retrieving Data with DataSets

In previous sections, we examined how to use the ADO.NET classes to access and modify data from a database table. However, ADO.NET includes another group of classes that provides you with an alternative method of working with data. The classes in this group include `DataSet`, `DataTable`, and `DataView`. In this section, you learn how to use these classes in your ASP.NET pages.

Why are there two groups of classes? These two groups of classes represent database data in different ways, and they are appropriate for different types of applications. The first group of classes enables you to work with database data with an open database connection. The second group of classes enables you to work with a disconnected set of database data.

For example, we've looked at how to use the `DataReader` to represent the results of a database query. The `DataReader` enables you to quickly retrieve a set of records from a database and display the records in an ASP.NET page.

However, the `DataReader` has a limitation that's important to note: It can retrieve only a single database record into memory at a time. Because the `DataReader` fetches only a single record at a time, you cannot use it to work with the results of a query as a whole. For example, you cannot use a `DataReader` to retrieve a count of the number of records returned or to filter or sort the records. You also cannot cache a `DataReader` in your server's memory.

> **Note**
> It's worth emphasizing that retrieving data with the `DataReader` is typically much faster than with a `DataSet`. Under the hood, the `Dataset` class uses the `DataReader` class to retrieve data.

Because of these limitations, Microsoft has introduced an alternative group of classes for working with data. These classes enable you to build a memory-resident, disconnected representation of data. Because the data is held in memory, you have more options for manipulating the data in your ASP.NET applications. Because the data is disconnected from the underlying data source, you can easily cache the data.

There are six important classes in this group:

- `DataSet`
- `DataTable`
- `DataRelation`
- `DataView`
- `SQLDataAdapter`
- `OleDbDataAdapter`

The `DataSet` class represents a memory-resident database. It is a container for the `DataTable` and `DataRelation` classes.

The `DataTable` class represents a memory-resident database table. You can create a `DataTable` from an existing database, or you can programmatically build a `DataTable` from scratch.

You can define relationships between `DataTables` by using the `DataRelation` class. Once you define a relationship between tables with the `DataRelation` class, you can navigate through the records contained in the two tables and return related values.

Finally, you can filter and sort the contents of a DataTable by using the `DataView` class. The `DataView` class also includes methods for searching a `DataTable`.

The `SQLDataAdapter` and `OleDbDataAdapter` classes are used for creating a `DataTable` from an existing database table. The `SQLDataAdapter` class enables you to build a DataTable from a Microsoft SQL Server database table. The `OleDbDataAdapter` class enables you to build a DataTable from other types of databases, such as Microsoft Access and Oracle databases.

The ASP.NET page in Listing 6.5.1 illustrates how you can use these classes to build a memory-resident database table and display all the records from the table (this page is included on the CD as `SQLDataTable.aspx`).

LISTING 6.5.1   Using a DataTable

```
 1: <%@ Import Namespace="System.Data" %>
 2: <%@ Import NameSpace="System.Data.SqlClient" %>
 3:
 4: <%
 5: Dim myConnection As SqlConnection
 6: Dim myDataAdapter As SqlDataAdapter
 7: Dim myDataSet As DataSet
 8: Dim myDataTable As DataTable
 9: Dim myRow As DataRow
10:
11: myConnection = New SqlConnection( "server=localhost;uid=sa;
➥pwd=secret;database=Pubs" )
12: myDataAdapter = New SqlDataAdapter( "Select * From Authors", myConnection )
13: myDataSet = New DataSet()
14: myDataAdapter.Fill( myDataSet, "Authors" )
15:
16: For each myRow in myDataSet.Tables( "Authors" ).Rows
17:   Response.Write( myRow( "au_lname" ) )DataTable

18: Next
19:
20: %>
21:
```

The first two lines in Listing 6.5.1 are used to import the necessary namespaces to work with the ADO.NET classes. Next, after some variables are declared, a connection to a Microsoft SQL Server database is created.

The database connection is used when initializing the `SqlDataAdapter` class. An instance of the `SqlDataAdapter` class is initialized by passing a SQL `SELECT` command and the database connection.

Next, the `DataSet` is initialized. The `DataSet` will be used to contain the `DataTable`.

The `DataTable` itself is created in the next line (line 14). The `DataTable` is created by calling the `Fill()` method of the `SqlDataAdapter` class. When the `Fill()` method is called, the records from the `Authors` table are copied from the Microsoft SQL Server database table into the `DataSet`.

> **Note**
>
> Notice that you never need to explicitly open a database connection when adding DataTables to a DataSet. When you call the `Fill()` method, a connection is opened automatically to the underlying database.

The final three lines of code are used to loop through the rows of the memory-resident `DataTable`. The `Rows` property represents all the rows in the `DataTable`. The FOR...EACH loop walks through all the rows displaying the value of the au_lname column.

Because the page in Listing 6.5.1 uses the classes from the `System.Data.SqlClient` namespace, it will not work with other databases such as Microsoft Access and Oracle. The ASP.NET page contained in Listing 6.5.2 demonstrates how you would rewrite the page to work with a Microsoft Access database (this page is included on the CD as `OleDbDataTable.aspx`).

LISTING 6.5.2 Using a DataTable with Microsoft Access

```
 1: <%@ Import Namespace="System.Data" %>
 2: <%@ Import NameSpace="System.Data.OleDb" %>
 3:
 4: <%
 5: Dim myConnection As OleDbConnection
 6: Dim myDataAdapter As OleDbDataAdapter
 7: Dim myDataSet As DataSet
 8: Dim myDataTable As DataTable
 9: Dim myRow As DataRow
10:
11: myConnection = New OleDbConnection( "PROVIDER=Microsoft.Jet.OLEDB.4.0;DATA
➥Source=c:\authors.mdb" )
12: myDataAdapter = New OleDbDataAdapter( "Select * From Authors", myConnection )
13: myDataSet = New DataSet()
14: myDataAdapter.Fill( myDataSet, "Authors" )
15:
16: For each myRow in myDataSet.Tables( "Authors" ).Rows
17:   Response.Write( myRow( "Author" ) )
18: Next
19:
20: %>
21:
```

6. Understanding DataTables

A DataTable represents a table of data in a DataSet. There are two ways to create a DataTable: by using the `Fill()` method of the `DataAdapter` class and by building the DataTable programmatically.

It is important to understand that all the data in a DataTable is copied into your server's memory after you call the `Fill()` method. This means that if you have a database with two million records, all these records will be placed in your server's memory. Therefore, be cautious about opening large DataTables.

A DataTable has both a `Columns` property, which represents a collection of columns, and a `Rows` property, which represents a collection of rows. You can display the value for a particular column in a particular row by using a statement like the following:

```
Response.Write( myDataSet.Tables( "Authors" ).Rows( 2 ).Item( "au_lname",
↪DataRowVersion.Current ) )
```

This statement displays the value of the au_lname column for the indicated row in the DataTable. The statement displays the current value of the row. Instead of referring to the column by name, you can also use an integer index to indicate the column, like this:

```
Response.Write( myDataSet.Tables( "Titles" ).Rows( 2 ).Item( 1,
↪DataRowVersion.Current ) )
```

This statement displays the value of the column with index 1 and the row with index 2 (both collections are zero based). In addition, the statement retrieves the current version of the row by passing the value `DataRowVersion.Current` to the `Item` property.

Because you can display any column in any row by supplying the proper indexes, you can write an ASP.NET page that automatically displays the contents of a table without knowing anything about the columns in the DataTable beforehand. The ASP.NET page in Listing 6.6.1 illustrates how you can automatically display a table named Authors from the Pubs database table (this page is included on the CD as `SQLShowTable.aspx`).

LISTING 6.6.1 Automatically Displaying a Table

```
 1: <%@ Import Namespace="System.Data" %>
 2: <%@ Import NameSpace="System.Data.SqlClient" %>
 3:
 4: <%
 5: Dim myConnection As SqlConnection
 6: Dim myDataAdapter As SQLDataAdapter
 7: Dim myDataSet As DataSet
 8: Dim myDataTable As DataTable
 9:
10: Dim RowCount As Integer
11: Dim ColCount As Integer
12: Dim i, k As Integer
13:
14: myConnection = New SqlConnection( "server=localhost;uid=sa;
↪pwd=secret;database=Pubs" )
```

LISTING 6.6.1 Continued

```
15: myDataAdapter = New SQLDataAdapter( "Select * From Authors", myConnection )
16: myDataSet = New DataSet()
17: myDataAdapter.Fill( myDataSet, "Authors" )
18:
19: RowCount = myDataSet.Tables( "Authors" ).Rows.Count
20: ColCount = myDataSet.Tables( "Authors" ).Columns.Count
21:
22: Response.Write( "<table border=1>" )
23: For i = 0 To RowCount - 1
24:   Response.Write( "<tr>" )
25:   For k = 0 To ColCount - 1
26:     Response.WRite( "<td>" )
27:     Response.Write( myDataSet.Tables( "Authors" ).Rows( i ).Item( k,
➥DataRowVersion.Current ).toString() )
28:     Response.Write( "</td>" )
29:   Next
30:   Response.WRite( "</tr>" )
31: Next
32: Response.Write( "</table>" )
33: %>
34:
```

In Listing 6.6.1, the Authors database table is automatically displayed (see Figure 6.1). A count of the number of rows and columns in the Authors table is retrieved by using the `Count` property of the `Rows` and `Columns` collections. Next, a `FOR...NEXT` loop is used to iterate through each of the rows, and a second `FOR...NEXT` loop is used to display the value of each column in each row. The Authors table is displayed in an HTML table.

FIGURE 6.1
Automatically displaying a database table.

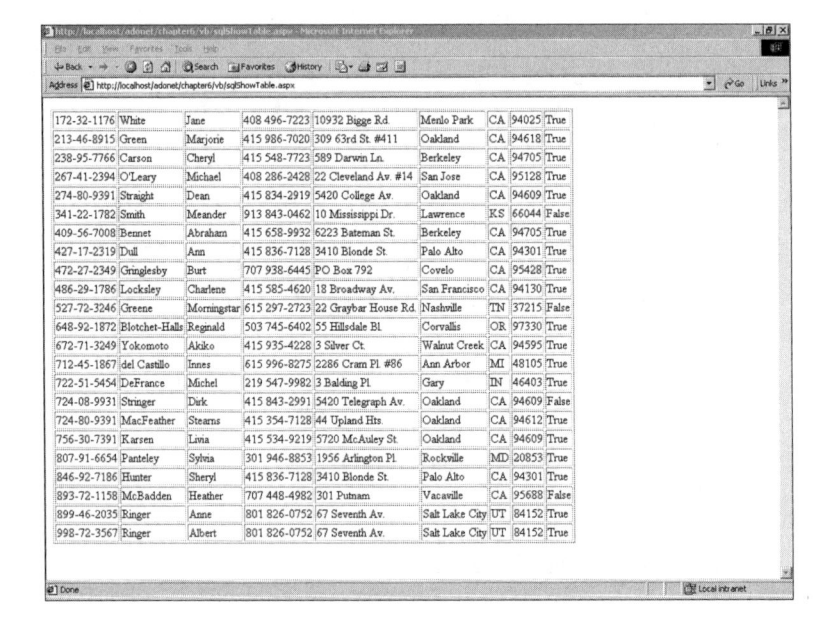

Building a DataTable Programmatically

Instead of creating a `DataTable` from existing data in a database, you can make one from thin air. Why would you want to do this? A `DataTable` can be a convenient container for information. For example, the code in Listing 6.6.2 demonstrates how you can create a `DataTable` that represents a shopping cart (this page is included on the CD as `buildDataTable.aspx`).

LISTING 6.6.2   Building a DataTable

```
 1: <%@ Import Namespace="System.Data" %>
 2: <%
 3: Dim myDataTable as DataTable
 4: Dim myColumn as DataColumn
 5: Dim myRow As DataRow
 6: Dim i As Integer
 7: Dim myRand As System.Random
 8: Dim productID As Integer
 9:
10: ' Create a DataTable
11: myDataTable = new DataTable("ShoppingCart")
12: myDataTable.MinimumCapacity = 50
13: myDataTable.CaseSensitive = False
14:
15: ' Add an AutoIncrement (Identity) Column
16: myColumn = myDataTable.Columns.Add("ID",
➥System.Type.GetType("System.Int32") )
17: myColumn.AutoIncrement = TRUE
18: myColumn.AllowDBNull = false
19:
20: ' Add an Integer Column
21: myColumn = myDataTable.Columns.Add("UserID",
➥System.Type.GetType("System.Int32") )
22: myColumn.AllowDBNull = false
23:
24: ' Add an Integer Column
25: myColumn = myDataTable.Columns.Add("ProductID",
➥System.Type.GetType("System.Int32") )
26: myColumn.AllowDBNull = false
27:
28: ' Add a String Column
29: myColumn = myDataTable.Columns.Add( "ProductName",
➥System.Type.GetType("System.String") )
30: myColumn.AllowDBNull = false
31:
32: ' Add a Decimal Column
33: myColumn = myDataTable.Columns.Add("ProductPrice",
➥System.Type.GetType("System.Decimal") )
34: myColumn.AllowDBNull = false
35:
36: ' Add Some Data
37: myRand = New Random
38: For i = 0 To 20
39:    productID = myRand.Next( 5 )
```

LISTING 6.6.2 Continued

```
40:    myRow = myDataTable.NewRow()
41:    myRow( "UserID" ) = myRand.Next( 3 )
42:    myRow( "ProductID" ) = productID
43:    myRow( "ProductName" ) = "Product " & productID.toString()
44:    myRow( "ProductPrice" ) = 10.25
45:    myDataTable.Rows.Add( myRow )
46: Next
47:
48: ' Display All the Rows
49: For each myRow in myDataTable.Rows
50:    Response.Write( "<hr>" )
51:    For each myColumn in myDataTable.Columns
52:      Response.Write( myRow.Item( myColumn ).toString() & " / " )
53:    Next
54: Next
55: %>
56:
57:
```

In the first part of Listing 6.6.2, a new `DataTable` named `ShoppingCart` is created. The DataTable is created with a minimum capacity of 20 rows by setting the `MinimumCapacity` property. You're not required to set the minimum capacity, but you can optimize the performance of the `DataTable` by doing so. By default, the `MinimumCapacity` property has a value of 25 rows.

The `DataTable` is created in such a way that string comparisons are case insensitive. This is accomplished by setting the `CaseSensitive` property to `False`. Because this is the default value of the `CaseSensitive` property, we really did not need to set the property here.

Next, five columns are added to the `DataTable`. The first column added is an autoincrement column. Every time a new row is added to the `DataTable`, this column is automatically assigned a new integer value. This column is the same as an Identity column in SQL Server.

The other four columns represent information about the items in the shopping cart. The `UserID` column represents the user with which the item in the shopping cart is associated. The `ProductID` column represents the unique integer `ID` for each product in the shopping cart. The `ProductName` column represents the name of the product in the shopping cart. Finally, the `ProductPrice` column represents the price of the item.

Next, 21 rows of data are added to the shopping cart. A new row is created by calling the `NewRow()` method of the DataTable. Each of the columns of the new row are assigned a value. Finally, the new row of data is added back to the DataTable by using the `Add()` method of the DataTable.

The final section of Listing 6.6.2 simply displays all 21 rows from the DataTable. Each row is displayed by looping through the `Rows` collection of the DataTable, and the value of each column is displayed by looping through the `Columns` collection.

Filtering and Sorting Data in a DataTable

There are two ways that you can filter and sort the data in a `DataTable`. You can either use the `Select()` method of the `DataTable` class or use the `RowFilter` and `Sort` properties of a DataView.

First, the `Select()` method of the `DataTable` class enables you to filter and sort data by returning an array of `DataRows`. The `Select()` method returns an array of `DataRows` that represent the selected rows in a `DataTable`. For example, the ASP.NET page in Listing 6.6.3 uses the `Select()` method to return all the rows from the Titles table where the Type column has the value popular_comp (popular computing). The `Select()` method is also used to order the rows returned by title (in descending order). Finally, the `CurrentRows` value is passed to the `Select()` statement so that only the current rows are returned. (The file is included on the CD with the name `SQLSelectFilter.aspx`.)

LISTING 6.6.3 Selecting DataRows

```
 1: <%@ Import Namespace="System.Data" %>
 2: <%@ Import NameSpace="System.Data.SqlClient" %>
 3:
 4: <%
 5: Dim myConnection As SqlConnection
 6: Dim myDataAdapter As SqlDataAdapter
 7: Dim myDataSet As DataSet
 8: Dim myDataTable As DataTable
 9: Dim myRow As DataRow
10: Dim selectRows() As DataRow
11:
12: myConnection = New SqlConnection(
"server=localhost;uid=sa;pwd=secret;database=Pubs" )
13: myDataAdapter = New SqlDataAdapter( "Select * From Titles", myConnection )
14: myDataSet = New DataSet()
15: myDataAdapter.Fill( myDataSet, "Titles" )
16: selectRows = myDataSet.Tables( "Titles" ).Select( "type='popular_comp'",
➥"title DESC", DataViewRowState.CurrentRows )
17:
18: For each myRow in selectRows
19:    Response.Write( myRow.Item( "title" ) )
20: Next
21: %>
```

When you use the `Select()` method, an array of `DataRows` is returned. Instead of filtering and sorting the rows from a `DataTable` with the `Select()` method, you can use the `RowFilter` and `Sort` properties of a `DataView` without returning an array. The page in Listing 6.6.4 illustrates how to use the `RowFilter` and `Sort` properties (this page is included on the CD as `SQLDataViewFilter.aspx`).

LISTING 6.6.4 DataView Filter

```
 1: <%@ Import Namespace="System.Data" %>
 2: <%@ Import NameSpace="System.Data.SqlClient" %>
 3: <%
 4: Dim myConnection As SqlConnection
 5: Dim myDataAdapter As SqlDataAdapter
 6: Dim myDataSet As DataSet
 7: Dim myDataTable As DataTable
 8: Dim myDataView As DataView
 9: Dim myRow As DataRowView
10:
11: myConnection = New SqlConnection(
"server=localhost;uid=sa;pwd=secret;database=Pubs" )
12: myDataAdapter = New SqlDataAdapter( "Select * From Titles", myConnection )
13: myDataSet = New DataSet()
14: myDataAdapter.Fill( myDataSet, "Titles" )
15: myDataView = myDataSet.Tables( "Titles" ).DefaultView
16: myDataView.RowFilter = "type='popular_comp'"
17: myDataView.Sort = "title DESC"
18:
19: For each myRow in myDataView
20:   Response.Write( myRow( "title" ) )
21: Next
22: %>
23:
```

In Listing 6.6.4, a DataView is returned from the `DefaultView` property of a DataTable. Next, the `RowFilter` and `Sort` properties of the `DataView` are set. Finally, all the sorted and filtered rows from the `DataView` are displayed.

Understanding DataRelations

A `DataSet` can contain multiple `DataTables`. You can relate the columns in separate DataTables by creating instances of the `DataRelation` class. All the `DataRelations` for a particular DataSet are contained in the DataSet's `Relations` collection.

For example, the most common type of relation between two tables is a master/detail relation. For each row in the master table, one or more rows exist in the detail table. To create a master/detail relationship between two tables, the tables must share a common key.

The page in Listing 6.6.5 demonstrates how you can create an association between two tables in a `DataSet` with a `DataRelation`. The `DataRelation` is used to associate the `Publishers` table with the `Titles` table in a master/detail relationship. The common key shared by both tables is the `pub_id` column (this page is included on the CD as `SQLDataRelation.aspx`).

LISTING 6.6.5 Creating a Master/Detail Relationship

```
1: <%@ Import Namespace="System.Data" %>
2: <%@ Import NameSpace="System.Data.SqlClient" %>
3:
```

LISTING 6.6.5 Continued

```
 4: <%
 5: Dim myConnection As SqlConnection
 6: Dim myDataAdapter As SqlDataAdapter
 7: Dim myDataSet As DataSet
 8: Dim myDataTable As DataTable
 9: Dim Publisher As DataRow
10: Dim Title As DataRow
11:
12: myConnection = New SqlConnection(
"server=localhost;uid=sa;pwd=secret;database=Pubs" )
13: myDataSet = New DataSet()
14: myDataAdapter = New SQLDataAdapter( "Select * From Publishers",
➥myConnection )
15: myDataAdapter.Fill( myDataSet, "Publishers" )
16: myDataAdapter.SelectCommand = New SqlCommand( "Select * From Titles",
➥myConnection )
17: myDataAdapter.Fill( myDataSet, "Titles" )
18:
19: myDataSet.Relations.Add( "PubTitles",
➥myDataSet.Tables( "Publishers" ).Columns( "pub_id" ),
➥myDataSet.Tables( "Titles" ).Columns( "pub_id" ) )
20:
21: For Each Publisher in myDataSet.Tables( "Publishers" ).Rows
22:    Response.Write( "<p>" & Publisher( "pub_name" ) & ":" )
23:    For Each Title In Publisher.GetChildRows( "PubTitles" )
24:       Response.Write("<li>" & Title( "title" ) )
25:    Next
26: Next
27:
28: %>
29:
```

The `DataRelation` is both created and added to the `Relations` collection of the `DataSet` class with the following statement:

```
myDataSet.Relations.Add( "PubTitles",
➥myDataSet.Tables( "Publishers" ).Columns( "pub_id" ),
➥myDataSet.Tables( "Titles" ).Columns( "pub_id" ) )
```

This statement creates a new `DataRelation` named `PubTitles` that associates the `pub_id` column in the `Publishers` table with the column with the same name in the Titles table.

After the `DataRelation` is added to the `DataSet`, related rows from the `Publishers` and `Titles` `DataTables` can be retrieved and displayed. For each row in the `Publishers` `DataTable`, the corresponding rows in the `Titles` `DataTable` are returned by using the `GetChildRows()` method:

```
For Each Title In Publisher.GetChildRows( "PubTitles" )
```

The `GetChildRows()` method returns an array of `DataRows`. The method accepts one parameter: the name of the `DataRelation` to use when returning the child rows. You can, of course, create multiple `DataRelations` between one `DataTable` and another.

7. Understanding the DataAdapter

In previous sections, we've used the `Fill()` method of the `DataAdapter` to add new `DataTables` to a `DataSet`. However, we really haven't gotten into the details of how the `DataAdapter` works.

A `DataAdapter` contains a collection of four instances of the `Command` class: `SelectCommand`, `InsertCommand`, `UpdateCommand`, and `DeleteCommand`. When you use the `SqlDataAdapter`, these four commands are `SqlCommand` classes. When you use the `OleDbDataAdapter`, these four commands are `OleDbCommand` classes.

We've been using the `SelectCommand` class of the `DataAdapter` to indicate the rows that we want to retrieve when adding a `DataTable`. For example, we've been using code like this:

```
myDataSet = New DataSet()
myDataAdapter = New SqlDataAdapter( "Select * From Publishers", myConnection )
myDataAdapter.Fill( myDataSet, "Publishers" )
```

This code is actually equivalent to creating an instance of a `SelectCommand` class for the `DataAdapter`. For example, we could use the following code instead:

```
myDataSet = New DataSet()
myDataAdapter = New SqlDataAdapter
myDataAdapter.SelectCommand = New SqlCommand( "Select * From Publishers",
➥myConnection )
myDataAdapter.Fill( myDataSet, "Publishers" )
```

The `DataAdapter` can be used for operations other than simply retrieving data from a database table. You can also use the `DataAdapter` to update a database table after the data in a `DataTable` has been modified.

For example, the code in Listing 6.7.1 demonstrates how you can update data in the `Authors` database table after the data has been modified in the `Authors` `DataTable` (this page is included on the CD as `SQLDataAdapterUpdate.aspx`).

LISTING 6.7.1 Using the DataAdapter `Update` Method

```
 1: <%@ Import Namespace="System.Data" %>
 2: <%@ Import NameSpace="System.Data.SqlClient" %>
 3:
 4: <%
 5: Dim myConnection As SqlConnection
 6: Dim myDataAdapter As SqlDataAdapter
 7: Dim myBuilder As SqlCommandBuilder
 8: Dim myDataSet As DataSet
 9: Dim myDataTable As DataTable
10: Dim Author As DataRow
11:
12: ' Create the DataSet and DataAdapter
13: myConnection = New SqlConnection(
"server=localhost;uid=sa;pwd=secret;database=Pubs" )
14: myDataSet = New DataSet()
15: myDataAdapter = New SqlDataAdapter( "Select * From Author", myConnection )
```

LISTING 6.7.1 Continued

```
16: myDataAdapter.Fill( myDataSet, "Authors" )
17:
18: ' Change value of first row
19: myDataSet.Tables( "Authors" ).Rows( 0 ).Item( "au_fname" ) = "Jane"
20:
21: ' Update the Database Table
22: myBuilder = New SqlCommandBuilder( myDataAdapter )
23: myDataAdapter.Update( myDataSet, "Authors" )
24:
25: ' Display the Records
26: For Each Author in myDataSet.Tables( "Authors" ).Rows
27:   Response.Write( "<p>" & Author( "au_fname" ) & " "
➥& Author( "au_lname" ) )
28: Next
29: %>
30:
```

In Listing 6.7.1, the `au_fname` column contained in the first row of the DataTable is assigned the value `Jane`. Next, an instance of the `SqlCommandBuilder` class is used to automatically generate UPDATE, DELETE, and INSERT commands for the `DataAdapter`. The `SqlCommandBuilder` automatically builds these commands when a `DataAdapter` is passed to it.

After the `SqlCommandBuilder` has done its work, the `Update()` method of the `DataAdapter` class is called. The `Update` method modifies the records in the underlying database table to reflect the changes made to the `DataSet`.

It's worth emphasizing that you do not need to explicitly create the UPDATE, DELETE, and INSERT commands when working with the `DataAdapter`. The `SqlCommandBuilder` will automatically generate these commands for you. As long as you specify a `SelectCommand`, and the underlying table has a primary key or unique column, the other three commands are generated automatically.

> **Note**
> The primary key or unique column requirement is important. The `UpdateCommand`, `InsertCommand`, and `DeleteCommand` classes require a primary key in order to be automatically generated. Furthermore, the commands can apply to only one table.

The page in Listing 6.7.2 does the same thing as the page in Listing 6.7.1, except it is written in C#.

LISTING 6.7.2 Using the DataAdapter `Update` Method in C#

```
1: <%@ Page Language="C#" %>
2: <%@ Import Namespace="System.Data" %>
3: <%@ Import NameSpace="System.Data.SqlClient" %>
4:
```

LISTING 6.7.2 *Continued*

```
 5: <%
 6: // Create the DataSet and DataAdapter
 7: SqlConnection myConnection = new
➥SqlConnection( "server=localhost;uid=sa;pwd=secret;database=Pubs" );
 8: DataSet myDataSet = new DataSet();
 9: SqlDataAdapter myDataAdapter = new SqlDataAdapter(
➥"Select * From Authors3", myConnection );
10: myDataAdapter.Fill( myDataSet, "Authors" );
11:
12: // Change value of first row
13: myDataSet.Tables[ "Authors" ].Rows[ 0 ][ "au_fname" ] = "Jane";
14:
15: // Update the Database Table
16: SqlCommandBuilder myBuilder = new SqlCommandBuilder( myDataAdapter );
17: myDataAdapter.Update( myDataSet, "Authors" );
18:
19: // Display the Records
20: foreach ( DataRow Author in myDataSet.Tables[ "Authors" ].Rows )
21: {
22:    Response.Write( "<p>" + Author[ "au_fname" ] + " "
➥+ Author[ "au_lname" ] );
23: }
24: %>
25:
```

Summary

We've covered a lot of material in this chapter. You've been provided with an overview of all the major classes contained in ADO.NET.

In the first part of this chapter, you learned how to use the `Connection`, `Command`, and `DataReader` classes to access and modify data in a database table. You learned how to create and open a database connection to both a Microsoft SQL Server and a Microsoft Access database. You also learned how to use the `Command` class to represent parameterized queries and work with SQL stored procedures.

In the last part of this chapter, you learned how to represent disconnected data with the `DataSet`, `DataTable`, `DataRelation`, and `DataView` classes. You learned how to create `DataTables` from existing database tables and how to create `DataTables` programmatically. You also learned how to sort and filter a DataTable as well as how to create Master/Detail relationships between DataTables by using the `DataRelation` class. Finally, you learned how to synchronize a DataTable and an underlying database table with the `DataAdapter` class.

Other Resources

For more information on the material covered in this chapter:

- To view updated code samples and post questions about the topics covered in this chapter visit the ASP.NET community at www.superexpert.com.

- For more information on using ADO.NET with ASP.NET Applications see *ASP.NET Unleashed* (also published by SAMS Publishing). Six chapters in *ASP.NET Unleashed* are devoted to working with ADO.NET.

- For information on ADO.NET and ASP.NET training, visit www.AspWorkshops.com.

CHAPTER 7

DATA PRESENTATION

by Steve Walther

In this chapter you will learn

- How to save data entered into a form to a database table
- How to bind database data to basic HTML and Web controls such as the `DropDownList` and `Hyperlink`
- How to bind database data to a `Repeater` control and format the data by using templates
- How to use the `DataList` control to display data in multiple columns and edit data
- How to use the DataGrid control to sort, page through, and edit database data

*I*n the previous chapter, you were provided with an overview of the most important classes contained in ADO.NET. You learned how to use these classes to access and modify database data. In this chapter, you'll learn how to use these classes with ASP.NET controls.

In the first section, you'll learn how to perform one of the most common activities in your Web applications: how to save the information entered into a Web Form to a database table.

Next, you'll be introduced to the topics of data binding and templates. You'll learn how to bind database data to a `Repeater` control and customize the manner in which the data is displayed by using a template. You'll also learn how to bind data to basic HTML and Web controls, such as the `DropDownList`, `HTMLSelect`, and `RadioButtonList` controls. For example, you'll learn how to display a drop-down list that contains a list of records from a database table.

Finally, you'll learn how to use two of the more specialized data controls. You'll learn how to display and modify data using both the `DataList` and `DataGrid` controls. At the end of the chapter, you'll also learn how to use the advanced features of the `DataGrid` control to enable you to sort and page through database records.

1. Saving Form Data

We start with an activity that you'll perform often with ADO.NET. In this section, you learn how to retrieve the information a user enters into an HTML form and save the data to a database table.

In this section, we build a customer survey form. You can use this form to retrieve a customer's first name, last name, and favorite color. The form for retrieving this information is contained in Listing 7.1.1.

LISTING 7.1.1 Customer Survey Form

```
 1: <html>
 2: <head><title>Customer Survey</title></head>
 3: <body>
 4:
 5: Please complete the following form:
 6:
 7: <form runat="Server">
 8:
 9: <p>First Name:
10: <br><asp:TextBox id="firstname" Runat="Server"/>
11: <asp:RequiredFieldValidator
12:     ControlToValidate="firstname"
13:     Runat="Server">
14:     You must enter your first name!
15: </asp:RequiredFieldValidator>
16:
17: <p>Last Name:
18: <br><asp:TextBox id="lastname" Runat="Server"/>
19: <asp:RequiredFieldValidator
20:     ControlToValidate="lastname"
21:     Runat="Server">
22:     You must enter your last name!
23: </asp:RequiredFieldValidator>
24:
25: <p>Favorite Color:
26: <br><asp:DropDownList id="favColor" Runat="Server">
27:       <asp:ListItem>Red</asp:ListItem>
28:       <asp:ListItem>Green</asp:ListItem>
29:       <asp:ListItem>Blue</asp:ListItem>
30:     </asp:DropDownList>
31: <p>
32: <asp:button text="Submit Survey!" Runat="Server"/>
33:
34: </form>
35:
36: </body>
37: </html>
```

Listing 7.1.1 shows a Web Form that contains two `TextBox` controls, named `firstname` and `lastname`, and a `DropDownList` control, named `favColor` (for the customer's favorite color). The form also includes two `RequiredFieldValidator` controls to prevent the form from being submitted when no data is entered into the `lastname` and `firstname` `TextBox` controls.

> **Note**
> To learn more about the `RequiredFieldValidator` and other form-validation controls, be sure to refer back to Chapter 3, "Form Field Input Validation."

We'll lbe storing the data that a user enters into a database table named *surveys*. The following statement can be used to create the surveys table when using Microsoft SQL Server:

```
Create Table surveys (
  s_id INT NOT NULL IDENTITY,
  s_firstname Varchar( 50 ),
  s_lastname Varchar( 50 ),
  s_favColor Varchar( 10 )
)
```

Listing 7.1.1 does not contain the necessary application logic to save the form information to the surveys database table. To save the information that a user enters, we'll need to execute a SQL `INSERT` command to add the data to the surveys table.

The code in Listing 7.1.2 can be used to add the form data to a Microsoft SQL Server database table.

LISTING 7.1.2 SQL Save Form

```
 1: <%@ Import Namespace="System.Data" %>
 2: <%@ Import Namespace="System.Data.SqlClient" %>
 3:
 4: <Script Runat="Server">1
 5: Sub SQLSaveForm( s As Object, e As EventArgs )
 6:    Dim myConnection As SQLConnection
 7:    Dim myCommand As SQLCommand
 8:    Dim sqlString As String
 9:    If isValid Then
10:      ' Save Form Data
11:      myConnection = New SQLConnection( "server=localhost;uid=sa;pwd=secret" )
12:      SQLString = "Insert surveys ( s_firstname, s_lastname, s_favColor ) " _
13:        & "Values ( @firstname, @lastname, @favColor )"
14:      myCommand = New SQLCommand( SQLString, myConnection )
15:      myCommand.Parameters.Add( New SQLParameter( "@FirstName",
16: ➥SqlDbType.Varchar, 50 ))
17:      myCommand.Parameters( "@FirstName" ).Value = FirstName.Text
18:      myCommand.Parameters.Add( New SQLParameter( "@LastName",
19: ➥SqlDbType.Varchar, 50 ))
20:      myCommand.Parameters( "@LastName" ).Value = LastName.Text
```

LISTING 7.1.2 *Continued*

```
21:     myCommand.Parameters.Add( New SQLParameter( "@favColor",
22: ↪SqlDbType.Varchar, 10 ))
23:     myCommand.Parameters( "@favColor" ).Value = favColor.SelectedItem.Text
24:     myConnection.Open()
25:     myCommand.ExecuteNonQuery()
26:     myConnection.Close()
27:     ' Transfer to Thank You Page
28:     Response.Redirect( "Thankyou.aspx" )
29:
30:   End If
31: End Sub1
32: </Script>
```

The first two statements in Listing 7.1.2 are used to import the necessary ADO.NET namespaces to work with Microsoft SQL Server. The bulk of Listing 7.1.2 consists of a single subroutine named `SQLSaveForm`. This subroutine is called when the user submits the form.

The subroutine starts by checking whether the form is valid by using the `IsValid` property. If the user has not entered required form field information, we do not lwant to add the form data to the database table.

> **Note**
>
> One common mistake made by developers new to ASP.NET concerns the proper use of the `IsValid` property. It's easy to forget to check the `IsValid` property before adding data to a database table. Beware of this mistake, especially if you are developing your ASP.NET application exclusively with Internet Explorer.
>
> When you use Internet Explorer (an uplevel browser), you can't submit a form to the server without completing all the required form fields. Internet Explorer uses JavaScript code on the browser to prevent the form from being submitted.
>
> However, if you use a downlevel browser such as Netscape Navigator, which does not use JavaScript code on the client, a form can be submitted even if all the form fields are not completed.
>
> Therefore, you should always check the `IsValid` property before adding data to a database table. For more information on form validation and using the `IsValid` property, refer back to Chapter 3, "Form Field Input Validation."

Next, in line 14, an instance of the `SQLCommand` class is instantiated. Two parameters are passed to the `SQLCommand` class: an instance of the `SQLConnection` class and a SQL string that contains an `INSERT` statement.

The `INSERT` statement contains parameters that represent the data for each of the form fields. Each of the parameters is created from the `SQLParameter` class and added to the `SQLCommand` class's `Parameters` collection. A value is assigned to each parameter from each of the three form controls (the `lastname`, `firstname`, and `favColor` Web Form controls).

After the database connection is opened in line 24, the `INSERT` statement is actually executed by calling the `ExecuteNonQuery()` method of the `SQLCommand` class. When `SQLCommand` is executed, the `INSERT` statement is passed to Microsoft SQL Server and the form data is added to the database.

Finally, after the data has been successfully added to the database, the `Response.Redirect` method is called to transfer the user to the `thankyou.aspx` page. The code for the `thankyou.aspx` page is shown in Listing 7.1.3.

> **Note**
> One nice thing about using the `Response.Redirect` method to transfer a user automatically to another page is that it prevents users from entering duplicate database data by hitting the Reload/Refresh button on their browser. When a user clicks the Reload/Refresh button, the `thankyou.aspx` page is reloaded and not the `surveyForm.aspx` page. Therefore, the database information is not entered twice.

LISTING 7.1.3 The Thank-You Page

```
<html>
<head><title>Thank You!</title></head>
<body>

Thank you for completing
our survey!

</body>1
</html>
```

Because saving form information is such an important activity, I also want to show you how you would do this with databases other than Microsoft SQL Server. If you need to save form data with a Microsoft Access or Oracle database (or practically any other database), you need to use the `OleDbSaveForm` subroutine contained in Listing 7.1.4.

LISTING 7.1.4 The `OleDb` Save Form

```
 1: <%@ Import Namespace="System.Data" %>
 2: <%@ Import Namespace="System.Data.OleDb" %>
 3:
 4: <Script Runat="Server">
 5: Sub OleDbSaveForm( s As Object, e As EventArgs )
 6:    Dim myConnection As OleDbConnection
 7:    Dim myCommand As OleDbCommand
 8:    Dim sqlString As String
 9:    If isValid Then
10:      ' Save Form Data
11:      myConnection = New OleDbConnection( "PROVIDER=Microsoft.Jet.OLEDB.4.0;DATA
         ➥Source=C:\customers.mdb" )
12:      SQLString = "Insert Into surveys ( s_firstname, s_lastname, s_favColor ) "
13:         & "Values ( @firstname, @lastname, @favColor )"
```

LISTING 7.1.4 Continued

```
14:    myCommand = New OleDbCommand( SQLString, myConnection )
15:    myCommand.Parameters.Add( New OleDbParameter( "@FirstName",
       ➥OleDbType.Varchar, 50 ))
16:    myCommand.Parameters( "@FirstName" ).Value = FirstName.Text
17:    myCommand.Parameters.Add( New OleDbParameter( "@LastName",
       ➥OleDbType.Varchar, 50 ))
18:    myCommand.Parameters( "@LastName" ).Value = LastName.Text
19:    myCommand.Parameters.Add( New OleDbParameter( "@favColor",
       ➥OleDbType.Varchar, 10 ))
20:    myCommand.Parameters( "@favColor" ).Value = favColor.SelectedItem.Text
21:    myConnection.Open()
22:    myCommand.ExecuteNonQuery()
23:    myConnection.Close()
24:    ' Transfer to Thank You Page
25:    Response.Redirect( "Thankyou.aspx" )
26:
27:   End If
28: End Sub
29: </Script>
```

The `OleDbSaveForm` subroutine is very similar to the `SQLSaveForm` subroutine, except that it uses the classes from the `System.Data.OleDb` namespace rather than the `System.Data.SqlClient` namespace. The first two lines in Listing 7.1.4 are used to import the necessary ADO.NET namespaces for working with a database such as Microsoft Access. The `OleDbSaveForm` subroutine is used to save the form data. The subroutine is called when the user clicks the form's submit button.

The complete listing for the Microsoft SQL Server version of the customer survey form is contained in Listing 7.1.5. This page is also included on the CD as `SqlSurveyForm.aspx`. The complete listing for the Microsoft Access version of the customer survey form is contained in Listing 7.1.6. This page is included on the CD as `OleDbSurveyForm.aspx`.

LISTING 7.1.5 The SQL Survey Form

```
 1: <%@ Import Namespace="System.Data" %>
 2: <%@ Import Namespace="System.Data.SqlClient" %>
 3:
 4: <Script Runat="Server">
 5: Sub SqlSaveForm( s As Object, e As EventArgs )
 6:   Dim myConnection As SqlConnection
 7:   Dim myCommand As SqlCommand
 8:   Dim sqlString As String
 9:   If isValid Then
10:     ' Save Form Data
11:     myConnection = New SqlConnection( "Server=localhost;uid=sa;PWD=secret" )
12:     SQLString = "Insert Into surveys ( s_firstname, s_lastname, s_favColor ) "
       ➥_
13:       & "Values ( @firstname, @lastname, @favColor )"
14:     myCommand = New SqlCommand( SQLString, myConnection )
```

LISTING 7.1.5 Continued

```
15:     myCommand.Parameters.Add( New SqlParameter( "@FirstName",
16: ➥SqlDbType.Varchar, 50 ))
17:     myCommand.Parameters( "@FirstName" ).Value = FirstName.Text
18:     myCommand.Parameters.Add( New SqlParameter( "@LastName",
19: ➥SqlDbType.Varchar, 50 ))
20:     myCommand.Parameters( "@LastName" ).Value = LastName.Text
21:     myCommand.Parameters.Add( New SqlParameter( "@favColor",
22: ➥SqlDbType.Varchar, 10 ))
23:     myCommand.Parameters( "@favColor" ).Value = favColor.SelectedItem.Text
24:     myConnection.Open()
25:     myCommand.ExecuteNonQuery()
26:     myConnection.Close()
27:     ' Transfer to Thank You Page
28:     Response.Redirect( "Thankyou.aspx" )
29:
30:   End If
31: End Sub
32: </Script>
33:
34:
35: <html>
36: <head><title>Customer Survey</title></head>
37: <body>
38:
39: Please complete the following form:
40:
41: <form runat="Server">
42:
43: <p>First Name:
44: <br><asp:TextBox id="firstname" Runat="Server"/>
45: <asp:RequiredFieldValidator
46:    ControlToValidate="firstname"
47:    Runat="Server">
48:    You must enter your first name!
49: </asp:RequiredFieldValidator>
50:
51: <p>Last Name:
52: <br><asp:TextBox id="lastname" Runat="Server"/>
53: <asp:RequiredFieldValidator
54:    ControlToValidate="lastname"
55:    Runat="Server">
56:    You must enter your last name!
57: </asp:RequiredFieldValidator>
58:
59: <p>Favorite Color:
60: <br><asp:DropDownList id="favColor" Runat="Server">
61:      <asp:ListItem>Red</asp:ListItem>
62:      <asp:ListItem>Green</asp:ListItem>
63:      <asp:ListItem>Blue</asp:ListItem>
64:    </asp:DropDownList>
65: <p>
```

LISTING 7.1.5 Continued

```
66: <asp:button text="Submit Survey!" OnClick="SqlSaveForm" Runat="Server"/>
67:
68: </form>
69:
70: </body>
71: </html>
```

LISTING 7.1.6 The `OleDb` Survey Form

```
 1: <%@ Import Namespace="System.Data" %>
 2: <%@ Import Namespace="System.Data.OleDb" %>
 3:
 4: <Script Runat="Server">
 5: Sub OleDbSaveForm( s As Object, e As EventArgs )
 6:   Dim myConnection As OleDbConnection
 7:   Dim myCommand As OleDbCommand
 8:   Dim sqlString As String
 9:   If isValid Then
10:     ' Save Form Data
11:     myConnection = New OleDbConnection( "PROVIDER=Microsoft.Jet.OLEDB.4.0;
12: ➥DATA Source=C:\customers.mdb" )
13:     SQLString = "Insert Into surveys ( s_firstname, s_lastname, s_favColor ) "
➥_
14:       & "Values ( @firstname, @lastname, @favColor )"
15:     myCommand = New OleDbCommand( SQLString, myConnection )
16:     myCommand.Parameters.Add( New OleDbParameter( "@FirstName",
17: ➥OleDbType.Varchar, 50 ))
18:     myCommand.Parameters( "@FirstName" ).Value = FirstName.Text
19:     myCommand.Parameters.Add( New OleDbParameter( "@LastName",
20: ➥OleDbType.Varchar, 50 ))
21:     myCommand.Parameters( "@LastName" ).Value = LastName.Text
22:     myCommand.Parameters.Add( New OleDbParameter( "@favColor",
23: ➥OleDbType.Varchar, 10 ))
24:     myCommand.Parameters( "@favColor" ).Value = favColor.SelectedItem.Text
25:     myConnection.Open()
26:     myCommand.ExecuteNonQuery()
27:     myConnection.Close()
28:     ' Transfer to Thank You Page
29:     Response.Redirect( "Thankyou.aspx" )
30:
31:   End If
32: End Sub
33: </Script>
34:
35: <html>
36: <head><title>Customer Survey</title></head>
37: <body>
38:
39: Please complete the following form:
40:
```

LISTING 7.1.6 Continued

```
41: <form runat="Server">
42:
43: <p>First Name:
44: <br><asp:TextBox id="firstname" Runat="Server"/>
45: <asp:RequiredFieldValidator
46:    ControlToValidate="firstname"
47:    Runat="Server">
48:    You must enter your first name!
49: </asp:RequiredFieldValidator>
50:
51: <p>Last Name:
52: <br><asp:TextBox id="lastname" Runat="Server"/>
53: <asp:RequiredFieldValidator
54:    ControlToValidate="lastname"
55:    Runat="Server">
56:    You must enter your last name!
57: </asp:RequiredFieldValidator>
58:
59: <p>Favorite Color:
60: <br><asp:DropDownList id="favColor" Runat="Server">
61:       <asp:ListItem>Red</asp:ListItem>
62:       <asp:ListItem>Green</asp:ListItem>
63:       <asp:ListItem>Blue</asp:ListItem>
64:    </asp:DropDownList>
65: <p>
66: <asp:button text="Submit Survey!" OnClick="OleDbsaveform" Runat="Server"/>
67:
68: </form>
69:
70: </body>
71: </html>
```

2. Displaying Database Information in ASP.NET Server Controls

In this section, you'll learn how to bind database data to an ASP.NET control. You'll need to bind data to a control when you want to apply fancy formatting to the data, display database data in a drop-down list, or perform complicated tasks with the data, such as sorting and paging through the data.

Not all controls support the capability to databind directly to database data. To bind database data to a control, the control must have a `DataSource` property. Here's a list of all the controls that support a `DataSource` property:

- CheckBoxList (`<asp:CheckboxList runat="Server" />`)
- DataGrid (`<asp:DataGrid runat="Server" />`)
- DataList (`<asp:DataList runat="Server" />`)

- DropDownList (`<asp:DropDownList runat="Server" />`)
- HTMLSelect (`<select runat="Server">`)
- ListBox (`<asp:ListBox runat="Server"/>`)
- RadioButtonList (`<asp:RadioButtonList runat="Server" />`)
- Repeater (`<asp:Repeater runat="Server" />`)

You can use the `DataSource` property of any of these controls to associate the control with database data. For example, you can assign a `DataReader` or a `DataView` as the value of the `DataSource` property. When the control is displayed, the records from the underlying `DataSource` property are also displayed.

It is important to understand that you can bind other types of data to a data-binding control. You can also bind collections such as `ArrayLists` and `HashTables`.

Binding Data to the Repeater Control

The simplest data-binding control to work with is the `Repeater` control, so we'll start with this control. You can use the `Repeater` control to display a list of records from a database table and apply custom formatting to the way each record is displayed.

For example, the ASP.NET page in Listing 7.2.1 displays all the records from a table named *Titles* in the Pubs database (this page is included on the CD as `SqlRepeaterSimple.aspx`).

LISTING 7.2.1 Using the `Repeater` Control

```
 1: <%@ Import Namespace="System.Data" %>
 2: <%@ Import Namespace="System.Data.SqlClient" %>
 3:
 4: <Script Runat="Server">
 5:   Sub Page_Load( s As Object, e As EventArgs )
 6:     Dim myConnection As SqlConnection
 7:     Dim myCommand As SqlCommand
 8:
 9:     myConnection = New SqlConnection( "Server=Localhost;uid=sa;
        ➥pwd=secret;Database=Pubs" )
10:     myCommand = New SqlCommand( "Select title, notes From Titles",
        ➥ myConnection )
11:     myConnection.Open()
12:     myRepeater.DataSource = myCommand.ExecuteReader()
13:     myRepeater.DataBind()
14:     myConnection.Close()
15:   End Sub
16: </Script>
17:
18: <html>
19: <head><title>Titles</title></head>
20: <body>
21:
```

LISTING 7.2.1 *Continued*

```
22: <form Runat="Server">
23:
24: <asp:Repeater
25:    id="myRepeater"
26:    Runat="Server">
27:    <ItemTemplate>
28:    <hr>
29:    <%# Container.DataItem( "title" ) %>
30:    <blockquote>
31:    <%# Container.DataItem( "notes" ) %>
32:    </blockquote>
33:    </Itemtemplate>
34: </asp:Repeater>
35:
36: </form>
37:
38: </body>
39: </html>
```

The `Page_Load` subroutine in Listing 7.2.1 is used to associate the `Titles` database table with the `Repeater` control. This is accomplished by creating an instance of the `SQLDataReader` class that represents the `Titles` table and associating the `SQLDataReader` class with the `Repeater` control by using the following two statements:

```
myRepeater.DataSource = myCommand.ExecuteReader()
myRepeater.DataBind()
```

The first statement associates the `SqlDataReader` class (returned by the `ExecuteReader()` method of the SqlCommand class) with the Repeater control, and the second statement actually loads the records from the `DataReader` into the control.

The database records are displayed within the `Repeater` control. The `Repeater` control is created with the following tags:

```
<asp:Repeater
  id="myRepeater"
  Runat="Server">
  <ItemTemplate>
  <hr>
  <%# Container.DataItem( "title" ) %>
  <blockquote>
  <%# Container.DataItem( "notes" ) %>
  </blockquote>
  </Itemtemplate>
</asp:Repeater>
```

Notice the `ItemTemplate` tag within the `Repeater` tag. The `ItemTemplate` specifies how each of the database records should be displayed when rendered in the `Repeater` control. In this case, a horizontal rule is displayed before each record and the `notes` field is displayed inside a `<blockquote>` tag (see Figure 7.1).

FIGURE 7.1

Using templates with the `Repeater` control.

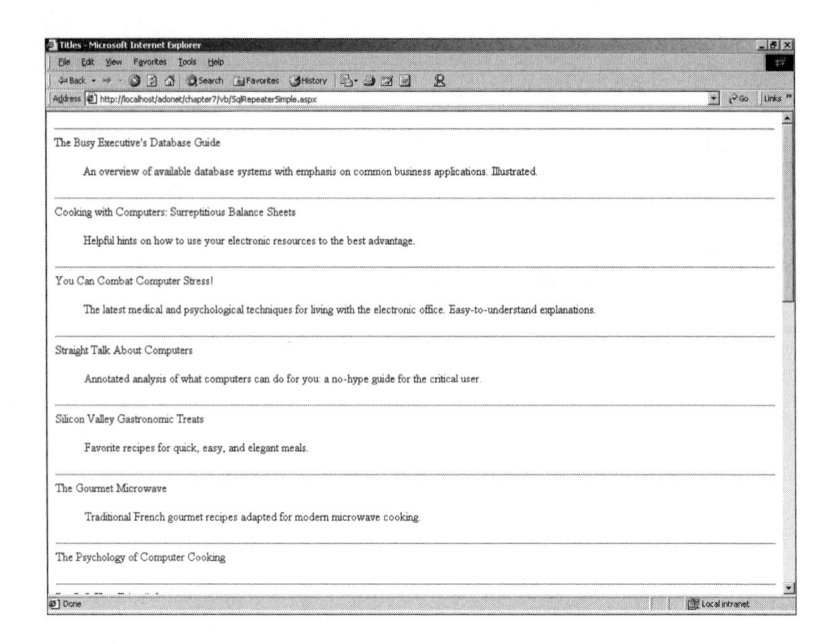

You can place anything you please within a template: HTML tags, controls, literal text, whatever. The contents of the template are displayed for each record in the `DataSource`. You can use a template to control the layout of your data when it is displayed.

Notice that the database fields are displayed by using statements such as:

```
<%# Container.DataItem( "title" )%>
```

This statement displays the title field from the `Titles` database table. The `Container` part of the statement refers to the control that contains the statement. In this case, the container is an instance of the `RepeaterItem` class. The `DataItem` property represents one of the items from the `Repeater` control's `DataSource` property. In this case, the `DataItem` represents the title field.

Notice the `#` character used when displaying the value of the title field. All data-binding expressions must appear within `<%#` and `%>` characters. Data-binding expressions are special. They do not have a value until the `DataBind()` method of the containing control (or page) is called.

> **Note**
>
> It's a good idea when displaying text from a database to use `Server.HTMLEncode` to HTML encode the text before you display it. If you don't use `HTMLEncode`, special characters such as the < and > characters can cause problems. Browsers can become confused by these characters and interpret them as marking the beginning and end of an HTML tag.

To get around this problem, you'll need to replace every statement that looks like this:

```
<%# Container.DataItem( "notes" ) %>
```

Here's the replacement statement you'll use:

```
<%# Server.HTMLEncode( Container.DataItem( "notes" ) )%>
```

Each record is formatted in Listing 7.2.1 by using an `ItemTemplate` template. A `Repeater` control actually supports more than one type of template:

- `HeaderTemplate`—Anything you place within the `HeaderTemplate` template is only rendered once before anything else is rendered by the Repeater control.
- `ItemTemplate`—Specifies the formatting for each item from the underlying data source.
- `AlternatingItemTemplate`—Used for controlling the formatting for alternating items.
- `SeparatorTemplate`—Enables you to specify content that is displayed between each item.
- `FooterTemplate`—Anything you place within the `FooterTemplate` template is only rendered once after everything else has been rendered by the `Repeater` control.

The other templates are useful when performing more complicated formatting. For example, suppose you want to display a list of database records within an HTML table, and you want to display each row of database data within a `<TR>` tag. Furthermore, suppose you want alternating rows in the table to be displayed with different background colors (see Figure 7.2).

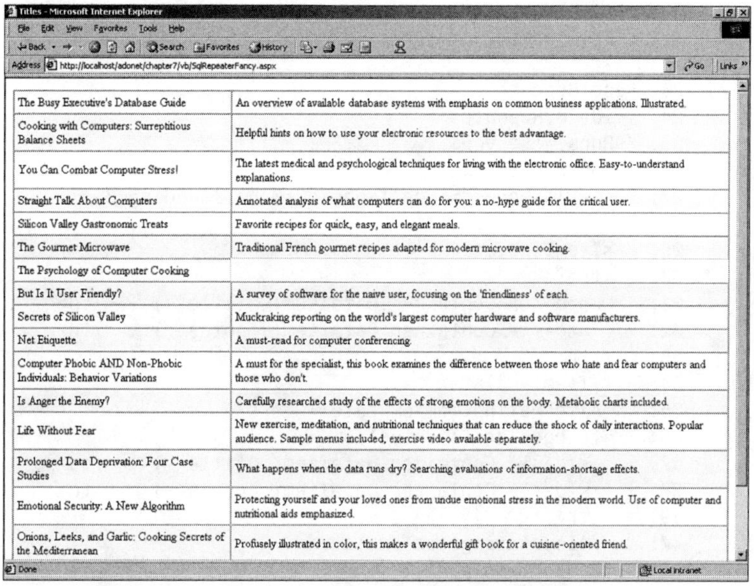

The Busy Executive's Database Guide	An overview of available database systems with emphasis on common business applications. Illustrated.
Cooking with Computers: Surreptitious Balance Sheets	Helpful hints on how to use your electronic resources to the best advantage.
You Can Combat Computer Stress!	The latest medical and psychological techniques for living with the electronic office. Easy-to-understand explanations.
Straight Talk About Computers	Annotated analysis of what computers can do for you: a no-hype guide for the critical user.
Silicon Valley Gastronomic Treats	Favorite recipes for quick, easy, and elegant meals.
The Gourmet Microwave	Traditional French gourmet recipes adapted for modern microwave cooking.
The Psychology of Computer Cooking	
But Is It User Friendly?	A survey of software for the naive user, focusing on the 'friendliness' of each.
Secrets of Silicon Valley	Muckraking reporting on the world's largest computer hardware and software manufacturers.
Net Etiquette	A must-read for computer conferencing.
Computer Phobic AND Non-Phobic Individuals: Behavior Variations	A must for the specialist, this book examines the difference between those who hate and fear computers and those who don't.
Is Anger the Enemy?	Carefully researched study of the effects of strong emotions on the body. Metabolic charts included.
Life Without Fear	New exercise, meditation, and nutritional techniques that can reduce the shock of daily interactions. Popular audience. Sample menus included, exercise video available separately.
Prolonged Data Deprivation: Four Case Studies	What happens when the data runs dry? Searching evaluations of information-shortage effects.
Emotional Security: A New Algorithm	Protecting yourself and your loved ones from undue emotional stress in the modern world. Use of computer and nutritional aids emphasized.
Onions, Leeks, and Garlic: Cooking Secrets of the Mediterranean	Profusely illustrated in color, this makes a wonderful gift book for a cuisine-oriented friend.

FIGURE 7.2
Using multiple templates with the `Repeater` control.

The page in Listing 7.2.2 illustrates how you could do this using the `HeaderTemplate`, `ItemTemplate`, `AlternatingItemTemplate`, and `FooterTemplate` templates (this page is included on the CD as `SQLRepeaterFancy.aspx`).

LISTING 7.2.2 Fancy Repeater

```
 1: <%@ Import Namespace="System.Data" %>
 2: <%@ Import Namespace="System.Data.SqlClient" %>
 3:
 4: <Script Runat="Server">
 5:   Sub Page_Load( s As Object, e As EventArgs )
 6:     Dim myConnection As SQLConnection
 7:     Dim myCommand As SQLCommand
 8:     myConnection = New SQLConnection( "Server=Localhost;uid=sa;
        ↪pwd=secret;Database=Pubs" )
 9:     myCommand = New SQLCommand( "Select title, notes From Titles",
        ↪myConnection )
10:     myConnection.Open()
11:     myRepeater.DataSource = myCommand.ExecuteReader()
12:     myRepeater.DataBind()
13:     myConnection.Close()
14:   End Sub
15: </Script>
16:
17: <html>
18: <head><title>Titles</title></head>
19: <body>
20:
21: <form Runat="Server">
22:
23: <asp:Repeater
24:   id="myRepeater"
25:   Runat="Server">
26:   <HeaderTemplate>
27:   <table border=1 cellspacing=0 cellpadding=5>
28:   </HeaderTemplate>
29:   <ItemTemplate>
30:   <tr>
31:     <td><%# Container.DataItem( "title" ) %></td>
32:     <td><%# Container.DataItem( "notes" ) %></td>
33:   </tr>
34:   </ItemTemplate>
35:   <AlternatingItemTemplate>
36:   <tr bgcolor="lightyellow">
37:     <td><%# Container.DataItem( "title" ) %></td>
38:     <td><%# Container.DataItem( "notes" ) %></td>
39:   </tr>
40:   </AlternatingItemTemplate>
41:   <FooterTemplate>
42:   </table>
43:   </FooterTemplate>
```

LISTING 7.2.2   Continued

```
44:    </asp:Repeater>
45:
46:  </form>
47:
48:  </body>
49:  </html>
```

The `Repeater` control in Listing 7.2.2 contains four templates. The `HeaderTemplate` is used to display an opening `<table>` tag, the `ItemTemplate` is used to display a row of data with a white background, the `AlternatingItemTemplate` is used to display a row of data with a light yellow background, and the `FooterTemplate` is used to display the closing `</table>` tag (see Figure 7.2).

Binding to a Function

One problem with how the records are displayed in the page contained in the previous section (Listing 7.8) concerns `Null` values. Instead of showing nothing when a database field has the value `Null`, you might want to display text such as "No Value" or "Nothing There!".

The page in Listing 7.2.3 illustrates how you can display the text "[Null]" whenever a field has the value `Null` (this page is included on the CD as `SQLRepeaterFixNulls.aspx`).

LISTING 7.2.3   Binding to a Function

```
 1:  <%@ Import Namespace="System.Data" %>
 2:  <%@ Import Namespace="System.Data.SqlClient" %>
 3:
 4:  <Script Runat="Server">
 5:    Sub Page_Load( s As Object, e As EventArgs )
 6:      Dim myConnection As SQLConnection
 7:      Dim myCommand As SQLCommand
 8:
 9:      myConnection = New SQLConnection( "Server=Localhost;uid=sa;
         ➥pwd=secret;Database=Pubs" )
10:      myCommand = New SQLCommand( "Select title, notes From Titles",
         ➥ myConnection )
11:      myConnection.Open()
12:      myRepeater.DataSource = myCommand.ExecuteReader()
13:      myRepeater.DataBind()
14:      myConnection.Close()
15:    End Sub
16:
17:    Function fixNulls( theString As String ) As String
18:      If theString = "" Then
19:        fixNulls = "[NULL]"
20:      Else
21:        fixNulls = theString
22:      End If
23:    End Function
24:  </Script>
```

LISTING 7.2.3 *Continued*

```
25: <html>
26: <head><title>Titles</title></head>
27: <body>
28:
29: <form Runat="Server">
30:
31: <asp:Repeater
32:   id="myRepeater"
33:   Runat="Server">
34:   <HeaderTemplate>
35:   <table border=1 cellspacing=0 cellpadding=5>
36:   </HeaderTemplate>
37:   <ItemTemplate>
38:   <tr>
39:     <td><%# fixNulls( Container.DataItem( "title" ).ToString() ) %></td>
40:     <td><%# fixNulls( Container.DataItem( "notes" ).ToString() ) %></td>
41:   </tr>
42:   </ItemTemplate>
43:   <AlternatingItemTemplate>
44:   <tr bgcolor="lightyellow">
45:     <td><%# fixNulls( Container.DataItem( "title" ).ToString() ) %></td>
46:     <td><%# fixNulls( Container.DataItem( "notes" ).ToString() ) %></td>
47:   </tr>
48:   </AlternatingItemTemplate>
49:   <FooterTemplate>
50:   </table>
51:   </FooterTemplate>
52: </asp:Repeater>
53: </form>
54:
55: </body>
56: </html>
```

In Listing 7.2.3, the `fixNulls()` function is used when displaying each database field. The `fixNulls()` function displays the value of a database field when it is not `Null` and displays the text "[Null]" otherwise (see Figure 7.3).

Using a `Repeater` Control to Display a Numbered List

I want to show you one more example of how you can use the `Repeater` control. Suppose you want to display a numbered list of items. For example, a Top 10 list or a list of the last 20 messages posted at your Web site.

One way you could display a numbered list is by using the HTML `<OL>` tag. For example, you could create your `Repeater` control like this:

```
<asp:Repeater
  id="myRepeater"
  Runat="Server">
  <HeaderTemplate>
  <OL>
  </HeaderTemplate>
```

```
    <ItemTemplate>
      <LI> <%# Container.DataItem( "title" ) %>
    </ItemTemplate>
    <FooterTemplate>
    </OL>
    </FooterTemplate>
</asp:Repeater>
```

FIGURE 7.3
Binding to a function.

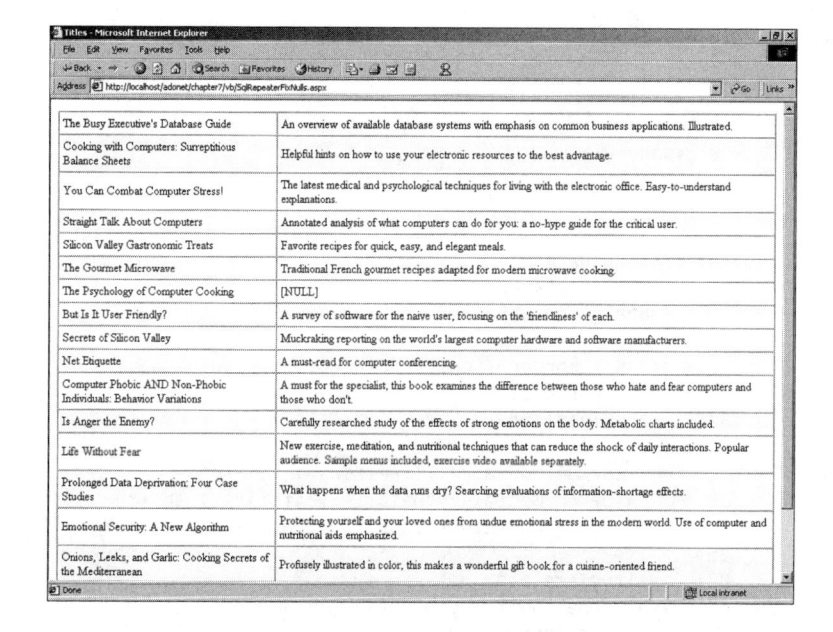

This approach works perfectly fine, but suppose you want to display each row from the database table in a separate HTML table row. In that case, you could no longer use the <OL> tag because it does not span across table rows.

An alternative approach to numbering items displayed by a `Repeater` control is demonstrated in Listing 7.2.4 (this page is included on the CD as `SQLRepeaterIndex.aspx`).

LISTING 7.2.4 The `ItemIndex` Property

```
1: <%@ Import Namespace="System.Data" %>
2: <%@ Import Namespace="System.Data.SqlClient" %>
3:
4: <Script Runat="Server">
5:   Sub Page_Load( s As Object, e As EventArgs )
6:     Dim myConnection As SqlConnection
7:     Dim myCommand As SqlCommand
8:
9:     myConnection = New SQLConnection( "Server=Localhost;uid=sa;
       ➥pwd=secret;Database=Pubs" )
```

LISTING 7.2.4 Continued

```
10:      myCommand = New SqlCommand( "Select title, notes From Titles",
           ↪myConnection )
11:      myConnection.Open()
12:      myRepeater.DataSource = myCommand.ExecuteReader()
13:      myRepeater.DataBind()
14:      myConnection.Close()
15:    End Sub
16: </Script>
17:
18: <html>
19: <head><title>Titles</title></head>
20: <body>
21:
22: <form Runat="Server">
23:
24: <asp:Repeater
25:   id="myRepeater"
26:   Runat="Server">
27:   <HeaderTemplate>
28:   <table border=1 cellspacing=0 cellpadding=5>
29:   </HeaderTemplate>
30:   <ItemTemplate>
31:   <tr>
32:      <td><%# Container.ItemIndex + 1 %></td>
33:      <td><%# Container.DataItem( "title" ) %></td>
34:      <td><%# Container.DataItem( "notes" ) %></td>
35:   </tr>
36:   </ItemTemplate>
37:   <AlternatingItemTemplate>
38:   <tr bgcolor="lightyellow">
39:      <td><%# Container.ItemIndex + 1 %></td>
40:      <td><%# Container.DataItem( "title" ) %></td>
41:      <td><%# Container.DataItem( "notes" ) %></td>
42:   </tr>
43:   </AlternatingItemTemplate>
44:   <FooterTemplate>
45:   </table>
46:   </FooterTemplate>
47: </asp:Repeater>
48:
49: </form>
50:
51: </body>
52: </html>
```

In Listing 7.2.4, the `ItemIndex` property of the `RepeaterItem` class is used to display a number next to each record displayed (see Figure 7.4). The `ItemIndex` property contains the index of the particular `RepeaterItem` being displayed.

FIGURE 7.4
Using the `DataItem ItemIndex` property.

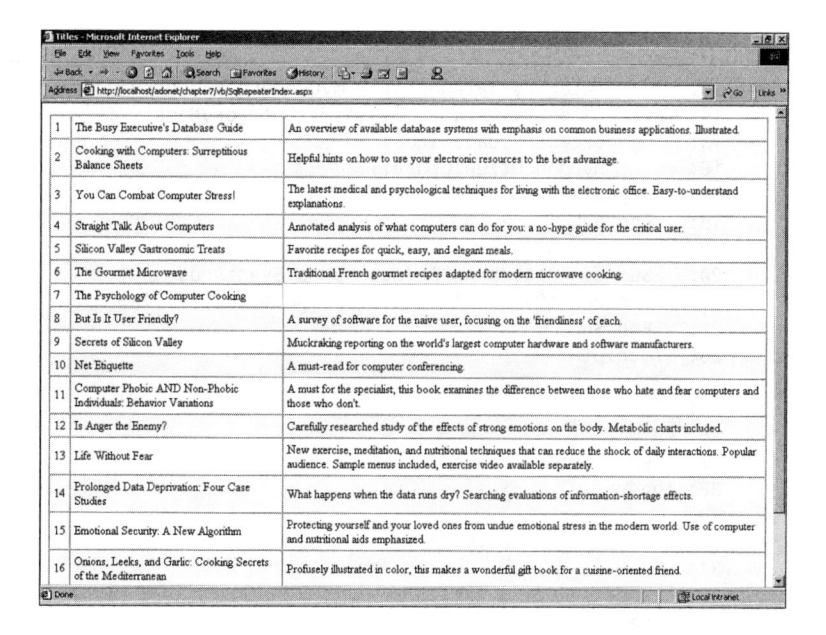

Binding Data to the `DropDownList` Control

You can also bind database data to Web Form controls, such as the `DropDownList`, `ListBox`, and `RadioButtonList` controls. You bind data to these controls in the same way you bind data to a Repeater control. You set the `DataSource` property of the control and then call `DataBind()`.

For example, suppose you want to bind records from a database table to a `DropDownList` control. You might want to do this to enable a user to pick a country, a product category, or a job type. The page in Listing 7.2.5 illustrates how you can bind a list of product categories to a DropDownList control (this page is included on the CD as `SqlDropDownList.aspx`).

LISTING 7.2.5 Binding to a `DropDownList` Control

```
 1: <%@ Import Namespace="System.Data" %>
 2: <%@ Import Namespace="System.Data.SqlClient" %>
 3:
 4: <Script Runat="Server">
 5:   Sub Page_Load( s As Object, e As EventArgs )
 6:     Dim myConnection As SqlConnection
 7:     Dim myCommand As SqlCommand
 8:     If Not isPostBack Then
 9:       ' Get List of Categories From Database
10:       myConnection = New SQLConnection( "Server=Localhost;uid=sa;
          ↪pwd=secret;Database=Northwind" )
11:       myCommand = New SqlCommand( "Select CategoryName From Categories",
          ↪myConnection )
12:       myConnection.Open()
```

LISTING 7.2.5 *Continued*

```
13:         category.DataSource = myCommand.ExecuteReader()
14:         category.DataTextField = "CategoryName"
15:         category.DataBind()
16:         myConnection.Close()
17:     End If
18:   End Sub
19:
20:   Sub pickCat( s As Object, e As EventArgs )
21:     currentCat.Text = category.SelectedItem.Text
22:   End Sub
23: </Script>
24:
25:
26: <html>
27: <head><title>Categories</title></head>
28: <body>
29:
30: <form Runat="Server">
31:
32: Please select a category:
33: <br>
34: <asp:DropDownList
35:     id="category"
36:     Runat="Server" />
37:
38: <asp:button
39:     Text="Select!"
40:     onClick="pickCat"
41:     Runat="Server" />
42:
43: <p>
44:
45: Current Category:
46: <asp:Label
47:     id="currentCat"
48:     Runat="Server" />
49:
50: </form>
51:
52:
53: </body>
54: </html>
```

The page in Listing 7.2.5 contains two subroutines. The first subroutine, **Page_Load**, is used to load the list of product categories into the **DropDownList** control. A **DataReader** is created and associated with the **DropDownList** control with the following three statements:

```
category.DataSource = myCommand.ExecuteReader()
category.DataTextField = "CategoryName"
category.DataBind()
```

The first statement assigns the `DataReader` returned by the `ExecuteReader()` method to the `DataSource` property of the `DropDownList` control. The second statement picks a field from the `DataSource` property to display as the text field in the `DropDownList` control. The final statement actually loads all the records from the `DataReader` into the `DropDownList` control.

The second subroutine in Listing 7.2.5, named `pickCat`, is executed when a category is chosen from the `DropDownList` control. The subroutine simply displays the selected category in a Label control named `currentCat` (see Figure 7.5).

FIGURE 7.5
Binding to a `DropDownList` control.

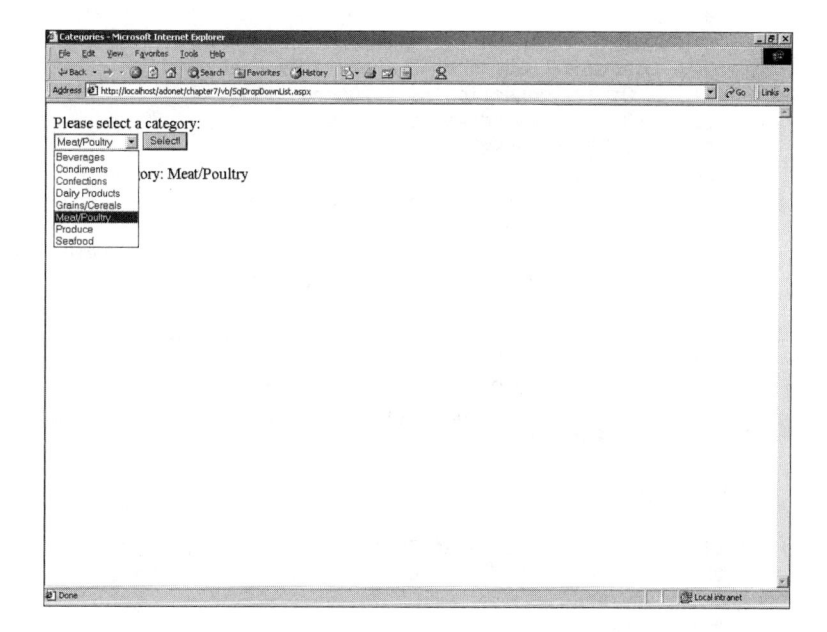

One important thing you should notice about Listing 7.11 is that the `DataReader` is bound to the `DropDownList` control only once, when the page is first loaded. Notice that the data-binding code executes in the `Page_Load` subroutine only when the `IsPostBack` property is not true.

The `DropDownList` control will automatically remember the list of product categories. The list of product categories is preserved in the page's view state (a big hidden form field that you can see if you use your browser's `View Source` command). So, when you click the button to select a category and the page is redisplayed, all the categories are automatically redisplayed in the `DropDownList` control without going to the database.

In Listing 7.2.5, we bound the `CategoryName` field to the `DropDownList` control. When the user selects a category, the category name is returned. Typically, however, you'll want to return the `CategoryID` field rather than the `CategoryName` field. For example, if you want to get a list of products from the database for a particular category, you'll need to perform a query with the `category ID`.

You can bind the `category ID` to the `DropDownList` control by using its `DataValueField` property. The page in Listing 7.2.6 illustrates how to use the `DataValueField` property (this page is included on the CD as `SqlDropDownListValue.aspx`).

LISTING 7.2.6 Using the `DataValueField` Property

```
 1: <%@ Import Namespace="System.Data" %>
 2: <%@ Import Namespace="System.Data.SqlClient" %>
 3:
 4: <Script Runat="Server">
 5:   Sub Page_Load( s As Object, e As EventArgs )
 6:     Dim myConnection As SqlConnection
 7:     Dim myCommand As SqlCommand
 8:     If Not isPostBack Then
 9:       ' Get List of Categories From Database
10:       myConnection = New SQLConnection( "Server=Localhost;uid=sa;
          ➥pwd=secret;Database=Northwind" )
11:       myCommand = New SqlCommand( "Select CategoryID, CategoryName
          ➥From Categories", myConnection )
12:       myConnection.Open()
13:       category.DataSource = myCommand.ExecuteReader()
14:       category.DataTextField = "CategoryName"
15:       category.DataValueField = "CategoryID"
16:       category.DataBind()
17:       myConnection.Close()
18:     End If
19:   End Sub
20:
21:   Sub pickCatID( s As Object, e As EventArgs )
22:     currentCat.Text = category.SelectedItem.Value
23:   End Sub
24: </Script>
25:
26: <html>
27: <head><title>Categories</title></head>
28: <body>
29:
30: <form Runat="Server">
31:
32: Please select a category:
33: <br>
34: <asp:DropDownList
35:   id="category"
36:   Runat="Server" />
37:
38: <asp:button
39:   Text="Select!"
40:   onClick="pickCatID"
41:   Runat="Server" />
42:
43: <p>
44:
```

LISTING 7.2.6 *Continued*

```
45: Current Category:
46: <asp:Label
47:   id="currentCat"
48:   Runat="Server" />
49:
50: </form>
51:
52: </body>
53: </html>
```

The `SQLDataReader` that represents the list of categories is bound to the `DropDownList` control with the following four statements:

```
category.DataSource = myCommand.ExecuteReader()
category.DataTextField = "CategoryName"
category.DataValueField = "CategoryID"
category.DataBind()
```

When the `DropDownList` control is displayed, the `CategoryName` field is displayed in the `DropDownList` control. However, when a user picks a category, the `category ID` is returned.

> **Note**
>
> You can also specify the `DataTextField` and `DataValueField` properties of a `DropDownList` control when you declare the control like this:
>
> ```
> <asp:DropDownList
>   id="category"
>   DataTextField="CategoryName"
>   DataValueField="CategoryID"
>   Runat="Server" />
> ```
>
> The choice of whether to assign these properties declaritively or programmatically is purely a matter of preference.

Binding Data to the `HyperLink` Control

Controls such as the `HyperLink`, `Button`, `Label`, and `Image` do not have a `DataSource` property. That means that you cannot bind these controls directly to a data source such as a `DataReader`. For example, you cannot bind a `DataReader` directly to an `Image` control to create a list of images. However, you can indirectly bind these controls to a data source by embedding these controls inside other controls that do support data binding.

For example, in Listing 7.2.7, a `HyperLink` control is embedded in a `Repeater` control (this page is included on the CD as `SqlHyperLink.aspx`).

LISTING 7.2.7 Binding a `HyperLink` Control to a Data Source

```
 1: <%@ Import Namespace="System.Data" %>
 2: <%@ Import Namespace="System.Data.SqlClient" %>
 3:
 4: <Script Runat="Server">
 5:   Sub Page_Load( s As Object, e As EventArgs )
 6:     Dim myConnection As SqlConnection
 7:     Dim myCommand As SqlCommand
 8:
 9:     myConnection = New SqlConnection( "Server=Localhost;uid=sa;
        ➥pwd=secret;Database=Northwind" )
10:     myCommand = New SqlCommand( "Select CategoryID, CategoryName
        ➥From Categories", myConnection )
11:     myConnection.Open()
12:     myRepeater.DataSource = myCommand.ExecuteReader()
13:     myRepeater.DataBind()
14:     myConnection.Close()
15:   End Sub
16: </Script>
17:
18: <html>
19: <head><title>Categories</title></head>
20: <body>
21:
22: <form Runat="Server">
23:
24: <asp:Repeater
25:   id="myRepeater"
26:   Runat="Server">
27:   <ItemTemplate>
28:   <li><asp:Hyperlink
29:        id="myLink"
30:        Text='<%# Container.DataItem( "CategoryName" ) %>'
31:        NavigateURL='<%# String.Format( "catpage.aspx?id={0}",
            ➥Container.DataItem( "CategoryID" ) )%>'
32:        Runat="Server" />
33:   </ItemTemplate>
34: </asp:Repeater>
35:
36: </form>
37:
38: </body>
39: </html>
```

The `HyperLink` control appears within the `ItemTemplate` template of the `Repeater` control. Both the `Text` and `NavigateURL` properties of the `HyperLink` control are bound to the `DataItem` of the current `RepeaterItem`. This creates a list of category links (see Figure 7.6).

FIGURE 7.6
Displaying hyperlinks in a `Repeater` control.

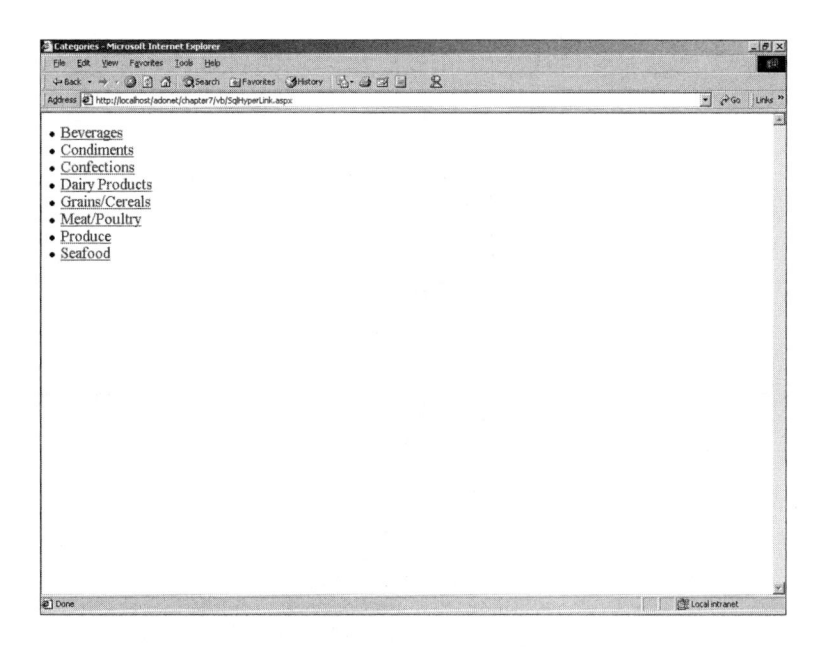

Notice that single apostrophes (') are used around the data-binding expressions rather than the normal quotation marks ("). For example, the following code isn't used:

`Text="<%# Container.DataItem( "CategoryName" ) %>"`

Instead, this code is used:

`Text='<%# Container.DataItem( "CategoryName" ) %>'`

It's a good idea to use apostrophes rather than quotation marks because the data-binding expression itself may return a string that contains a quotation mark. If you use quotation marks, and the data-binding expression generates quotation marks, an error will be raised.

Finally, notice how the `Format` method of the `String` class is used when formatting the value of the `NavigateURL` property:

```
NavigateURL='<%# String.Format( "catpage.aspx?id={0}",
➥Container.DataItem( "CategoryID" ) )%>'
```

When each `HyperLink` control is displayed, it will link to the `catpage.aspx` page and pass a `category ID` to the page. You could use the `catpage.aspx` page, for example, to display all the products for the particular category selected.

Instead of using the `Format` method of the `String` class to format the value of the `NavigateURL` property, you could use the `Eval` method of the `DataBinder` class instead:

`<%# DataBinder.Eval( Container.DataItem,"CategoryID","catpage.aspx?id={0}" )%>`

In general, however, you should not use the `Eval` method because using this method results in slower performance. When the `Eval` method is used, the data type of the evaluated expression must be determined at runtime.

3. Using the `DataList` Control

In this section, you'll learn how to use the `DataList` control. Like the `Repeater` control, the `DataList` control can be used to display and format database data. However, unlike the `Repeater` control, the `DataList` control has several advanced properties for controlling layout and editing data.

The ASP.NET page in Listing 7.3.1 illustrates how to use the `DataList` control (this page is included on the CD as `SqlDataList.aspx`).

LISTING 7.3.1 Using the `DataList` Control

```
 1: <%@ Import Namespace="System.Data" %>
 2: <%@ Import Namespace="System.Data.SqlClient" %>
 3:
 4: <Script Runat="Server">
 5:   Sub Page_Load( s As Object, e As EventArgs )
 6:     Dim myConnection As SQLConnection
 7:     Dim myCommand As SQLCommand
 8:     myConnection = New SQLConnection( "Server=Localhost;uid=sa;
        ➥pwd=secret;Database=Northwind" )
 9:     myCommand = New SQLCommand( "Select CategoryName
        ➥from Categories", myConnection )
10:     myConnection.Open()
11:     myDataList.DataSource = myCommand.ExecuteReader()
12:     myDataList.DataBind()
13:     myConnection.Close()
14:   End Sub
15: </Script>
16:
17: <html>
18: <head><title>Categories</title></head>
19: <body>
20:
21: <form Runat="Server">
22: <asp:DataList
23:   id="myDataList"
24:   Runat="Server">
25:   <ItemTemplate>
26:     <%# Container.DataItem( "CategoryName" ) %>
27:   </ItemTemplate>
28: </asp:DataList>
29: </form>
30:
31: </body>
32: </html>
```

Controlling `DataList` Table Properties

By default, the `DataList` control displays data in an HTML table. The `DataList` control in Listing 7.3.1 displays each category name in a separate table row. You can modify the appearance of the table by assigning values to the `Cellpadding`, `Cellspacing`, and `GridLines` properties. For example, in Listing 7.3.2, grid lines are displayed around each cell in the `DataList` control as you can see in Figure 7.7 (this page is included on the CD as `SqlDataListGrid.aspx`).

FIGURE 7.7
Binding to a `DataList` control.

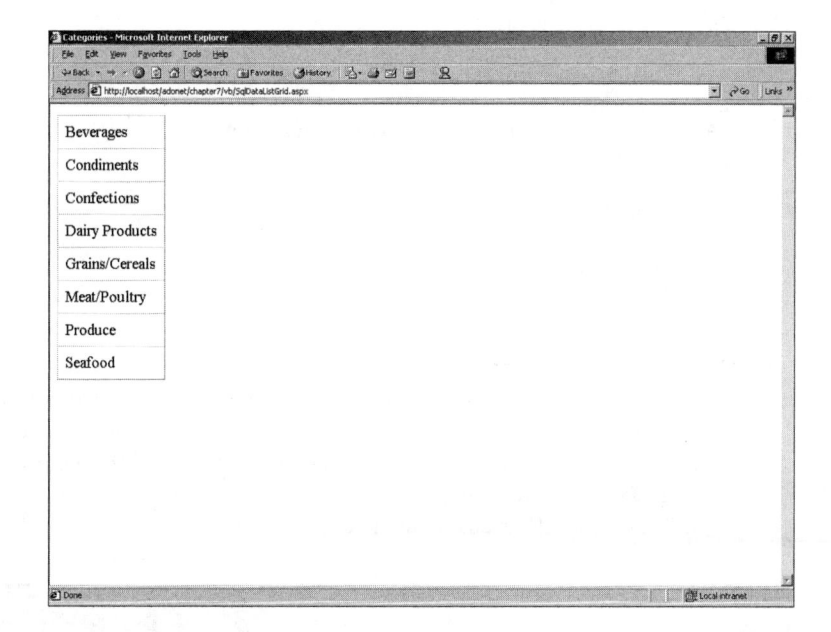

LISTING 7.3.2 Displaying Grid Lines in a `DataList`

```
 1: <%@ Import Namespace="System.Data" %>
 2: <%@ Import Namespace="System.Data.SqlClient" %>
 3:
 4: <Script Runat="Server">
 5:   Sub Page_Load( s As Object, e As EventArgs )
 6:     Dim myConnection As SqlConnection
 7:     Dim myCommand As SqlCommand
 8:     myConnection = New SqlConnection( "Server=Localhost;uid=sa;
        ➥pwd=secret;Database=Northwind" )
 9:     myCommand = New SqlCommand( "Select CategoryName
        ➥from Categories", myConnection )
10:     myConnection.Open()
11:     myDataList.DataSource = myCommand.ExecuteReader()
12:     myDataList.DataBind()
13:     myConnection.Close()
14:   End Sub
15: </Script>
16:
17: <html>
18: <head><title>Categories</title></head>
19: <body>
20:
```

LISTING 7.3.2 Continued

```
21: <form Runat="Server">
22: <asp:DataList
23:   id="myDataList"
24:   cellpadding=10
25:   cellspacing=0
26:   gridlines="both"
27:   Runat="Server">
28:   <ItemTemplate>
29:     <%# Container.DataItem( "CategoryName" ) %>
30:   </ItemTemplate>
31: </asp:DataList>
32: </form>
33:
34: </body>
35: </html>
```

Controlling `DataList` Column Layout

One thing that you can do with a `DataList` control that you cannot do with a `Repeater` control is display data in multiple columns (see Figure 7.8). You can control the columns in a `DataList` control by setting the `RepeatColumns` and `RepeatDirection` properties. The page in Listing 7.3.3 takes advantage of these properties to display data in three columns (this page is included on the CD as `SqlDataListLayout.aspx`).

FIGURE 7.8
Displaying a multi-column `DataList` control.

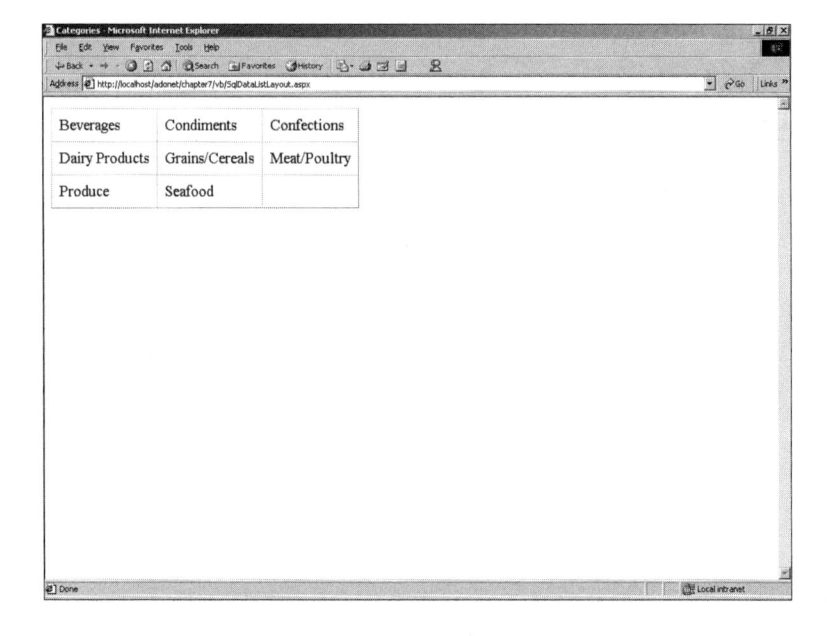

LISTING 7.3.3 Controlling Columns in a `DataList` Control

```
 1: <%@ Import Namespace="System.Data" %>
 2: <%@ Import Namespace="System.Data.SqlClient" %>
 3:
 4: <Script Runat="Server">
 5:   Sub Page_Load( s As Object, e As EventArgs )
 6:     Dim myConnection As SQLConnection
 7:     Dim myCommand As SQLCommand
 8:     myConnection = New SQLConnection( "Server=Localhost;uid=sa;
          ➥pwd=secret;Database=Northwind" )
 9:     myCommand = New SQLCommand( "Select CategoryName
          ➥from Categories", myConnection )
10:     myConnection.Open()
11:     myDataList.DataSource = myCommand.ExecuteReader()
12:     myDataList.DataBind()
13:     myConnection.Close()
14:   End Sub
15: </Script>
16:
17: <html>
18: <head><title>Categories</title></head>
19: <body>
20:
21: <form Runat="Server">
22: <asp:DataList
23:   id="myDataList"
24:   cellpadding=10
25:   cellspacing=0
26:   gridlines="both"
27:   RepeatColumns="3"
28:   RepeatDirection="Horizontal"
29:   Runat="Server">
30:   <ItemTemplate>
31:      <%# Container.DataItem( "CategoryName" ) %>
32:   </ItemTemplate>
33: </asp:DataList>
34: </form>
35:
36: </body>
37: </html>
```

Displaying a `DataList` Control Without a Table

By default, a `DataList` control displays data in an HTML table. You might not always want to display the data in a `DataList` control in an HTML table. If you want more control over the layout of a `DataList` control, you can change its `RepeatLayout` property. If you assign the value `Flow` to `RepeatLayout`, each row is displayed inside a `<SPAN>` tag. Here's an example:

```
<asp:DataList
  id="myDataList"
  RepeatLayout="Flow"
  Runat="Server">

  <ItemTemplate>
     <%# Container.DataItem( "CategoryName" ) %>
  </ItemTemplate>

</asp:DataList>
```

Event Bubbling in a DataList Control

Unlike any of the other controls discussed so far in this chapter, the DataList control supports event bubbling. By taking advantage of event bubbling, you can create subroutines to handle the events raised by controls embedded in a DataList control.

You can capture five types of events in a DataList control:

- OnItemCommand—This event is raised by a control contained in a DataList control that raises an event that is not captured by the OnEditCommand, OnUpdateCommand, OnDeleteCommand, and OnCancelCommand events.

- OnEditCommand—This event is raised by a control contained in a DataList control that has a Command property set to the value Edit.

- OnUpdateCommand—This event is raised by a control contained in a DataList control that has a Command property set to the value Update.

- OnDeleteCommand—This event is raised by a control contained in a DataList control that has a Command property set to the value Delete.

- OnCancelCommand—This event is raised by a control contained in a DataList control that has a Command property set to the value Cancel.

You can associate any of these events with a subroutine. For example, you can associate a subroutine with the OnEditCommand event by assigning the name of the subroutine to the OnEditCommand property of the DataList control.

Certain controls—such as the Button, LinkButton, and ImageButton controls—support the Command property. If you display a Button control in a DataList control and set its Command property to the value Edit, the OnEditCommand event will be raised whenever the button is clicked.

In the following sections, you'll see examples of how each of these events can be used.

Selecting an Item in a DataList Control

A DataList control can be used to display a menu of options. For example, you might want to display a multicolumn list of product categories on each page of your Web site (see Figure 7.9). You can display the list of categories by displaying a list of LinkButton controls within a DataList control.

FIGURE 7.9
Displaying a menu with a `DataList` control.

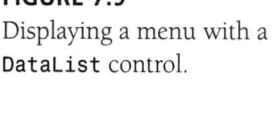

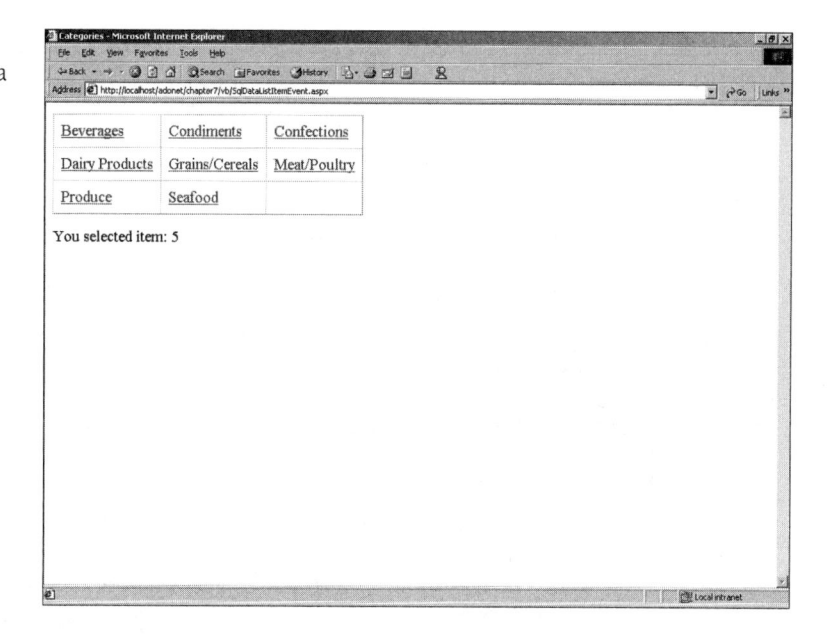

The page in Listing 7.3.4 illustrates how you can display a list of `LinkButton` controls and identity when a `LinkButton` has been clicked (this page is included on the CD as `SqlDataListItemEvent.aspx`).

LISTING 7.3.4 Capturing the `OnItemCommand` Event

```
 1: <%@ Import Namespace="System.Data" %>
 2: <%@ Import Namespace="System.Data.SqlClient" %>
 3:
 4: <Script Runat="Server">
 5:   Sub Page_Load( s As Object, e As EventArgs )
 6:     Dim myConnection As SqlConnection
 7:     Dim myCommand As SqlCommand
 8:     If Not isPostBack Then
 9:       myConnection = New SqlConnection( "Server=Localhost;uid=sa;
          ➥pwd=secret;Database=Northwind" )
10:       myCommand = New SqlCommand( "Select CategoryName
          ➥from Categories", myConnection )
11:       myConnection.Open()
12:       myDataList.DataSource = myCommand.ExecuteReader()
13:       myDataList.DataBind()
14:       myConnection.Close()
15:     End If
16:   End Sub
17:
18:   Sub pickCat( s As Object, e As DataListCommandEventArgs )
19:     currentCatIndex.Text = e.Item.ItemIndex.toString()
20:   End Sub
```

LISTING 7.3.4 Continued

```
21: </Script>
22:
23: <html>
24: <head><title>Categories</title></head>
25: <body>
26:
27: <form Runat="Server">
28: <asp:DataList
29:    id="myDataList"
30:    cellpadding=10
31:    cellspacing=0
32:    gridlines="both"
33:    RepeatColumns="3"
34:    RepeatDirection="Horizontal"
35:    OnItemCommand="pickCat"
36:    Runat="Server">
37:    <ItemTemplate>
38:      <asp:LinkButton
39:        id="myLink"
40:        Text='<%# Container.DataItem( "CategoryName" ) %>'
41:        Runat="Server" />
42:    </ItemTemplate>
43: </asp:DataList>
44:
45: <p>
46: You selected item:
47: <asp:Label id="currentCatIndex" Runat="Server" />
48:
49: </form>
50:
51: </body>
52: </html>
```

When someone clicks one of the `LinkButton` controls contained in the `DataList` control, a `Click` event is raised. The `Click` event, in turn, raises an `OnItemCommand` event in the containing `DataList` control. Because the `OnItemCommand` event is associated with the `pickCat` subroutine, the `pickCat` subroutine is executed whenever a `LinkButton` control is clicked.

In Listing 7.3.4, the `pickCat` subroutine simply assigns the index of whatever `LinkButton` control the user clicked to a label named `currentCatIndex`. Therefore, if someone clicks the first link displayed by the `DataList` control, the value `0` is displayed in the `currentCatIndex` label.

> **Note**
>
> When viewing the page from Listing 7.17 through a Web browser, you may notice a double-click sound when you click a `LinkButton` control contained in the `DataList` control. When you click a `LinkButton` control, a JavaScript function is called that actually submits the form. The first click sound is caused by the link being clicked; the second click sound is caused by the JavaScript function. The sound is annoying, and potentially confusing, but there is no way around this problem when using a `LinkButton`. (You can, of course, use the `Button` or `ImageButton` control instead.)

Using the `SelectedItemTemplate` Template

Instead of displaying the index of the `LinkButton` control that was clicked in a `Label` control, you can highlight the selected link in the `DataList` control. The `DataList` control has a template, named the `SelectedItemTemplate`, which controls how a selected item in the `DataList` control appears.

For example, when you click a `LinkButton` control within the `DataList` control in the page in Listing 7.3.5, the cell containing the link is automatically formatted with `SelectedItemTemplate` (this page is included on the CD as `SqlDataListItemEventSelect.aspx`).

LISTING 7.3.5 Using the `SelectedItemTemplate` Template

```
 1: <%@ Import Namespace="System.Data" %>
 2: <%@ Import Namespace="System.Data.SqlClient" %>
 3:
 4: <Script Runat="Server">
 5:   Sub Page_Load( s As Object, e As EventArgs )
 6:     If Not isPostBack Then
 7:       BindData
 8:     End If
 9:   End Sub
10:
11:   Sub BindData
12:     Dim myConnection As SQLConnection
13:     Dim myCommand As SQLCommand
14:     myConnection = New SQLConnection( "Server=Localhost;uid=sa;
        ↪pwd=secret;Database=Northwind" )
15:     myCommand = New SQLCommand( "Select CategoryName
        ↪from Categories", myConnection )
16:     myConnection.Open()
17:     myDataList.DataSource = myCommand.ExecuteReader()
18:     myDataList.DataBind()
19:     myConnection.Close()
20:   End Sub
21:
22:   Sub pickCat( s As Object, e As DataListCommandEventArgs )
23:     myDataList.SelectedIndex = e.Item.ItemIndex
24:     BindData
25:   End Sub
26: </Script>
27:
28: <html>
29: <head><title>Categories</title></head>
30: <body>
31:
32: <form Runat="Server">
33:
34: <asp:DataList
35:   id="myDataList"
36:   cellpadding=10
37:   cellspacing=0
```

LISTING 7.3.5 Continued

```
38:    gridlines="both"
39:    RepeatColumns="3"
40:    RepeatDirection="Horizontal"
41:    OnItemCommand="pickCat"
42:    Runat="Server">
43:
44:    <ItemTemplate>
45:      <asp:LinkButton
46:        id="myLink"
47:        Text='<%# Container.DataItem( "CategoryName" ) %>'
48:        Runat="Server"/>
49:    </ItemTemplate>
50:
51:    <SelectedItemTemplate>
52:      <b><%# Container.DataItem( "CategoryName" ) %></b>
53:    </SelectedItemTemplate>
54:
55: </asp:DataList>
56:
57: </form>
58:
59: </body>
60: </html>
```

In Listing 7.3.5, `ItemTemplate` is used to display a list of product categories as `LinkButton` controls. When you click any of the `LinkButton` controls, the `OnItemCommand` event is raised. This event executes the `pickCat` subroutine.

The `pickCat` subroutine assigns the index of the `LinkButton` control that was clicked to the `SelectedIndex` property of the `DataList` control. When the `DataList` control is displayed, the item in the `DataList` control with the `SelectedIndex` property will be formatted with the `SelectedItemTemplate` template rather than the normal `ItemTemplate` template. The name of the selected category will appear bold.

Retrieving the Category Name

You can use the page described in the previous section (Listing 7.3.5) to enable a user to select a product category from a menu. However, you may need to retrieve the name of the category that the user selected so you can display the category name in your page.

When you click a `LinkButton` control, you can determine the index of the `LinkButton` control selected by examining its `itemIndex` property of the item selected. However, the actual name of the category is not passed.

To pass the name of the category, you need to use the `CommandArgument` property of the `LinkButton` control. You can assign any value you please to the `CommandArgument` property. When the `LinkButton` control is clicked, the value of the `CommandArgument` property is also passed.

FIGURE 7.10
Using the `SelectedItemTemplate` with the `DataList` control.

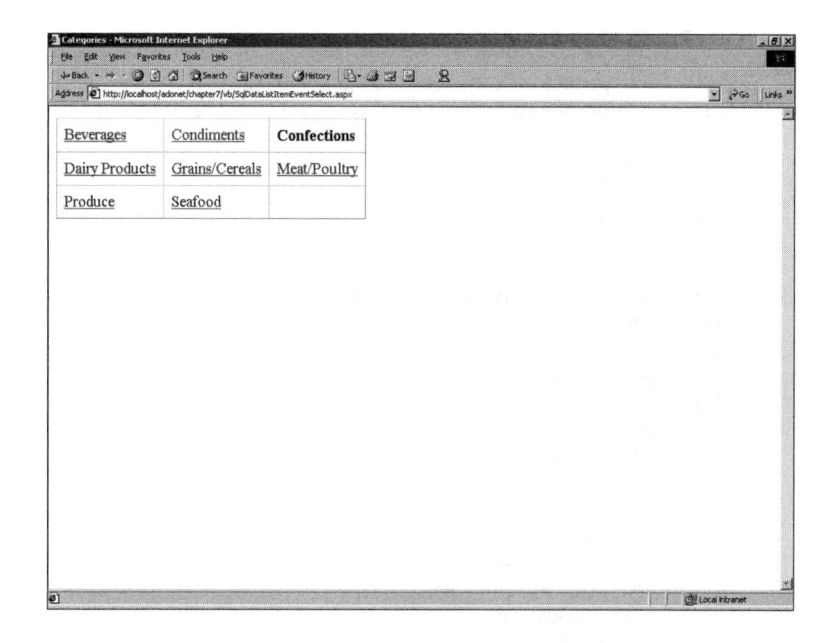

In Listing 7.3.6, the `CommandArgument` property is used to pass the name of the selected category (this page is included on the CD as `SqlDataListItemEventSelect2.aspx`).

LISTING 7.3.6 Using the `CommandArgument` Property

```
 1: <%@ Import Namespace="System.Data" %>
 2: <%@ Import Namespace="System.Data.SqlClient" %>
 3:
 4: <Script Runat="Server">
 5:   Sub Page_Load( s As Object, e As EventArgs )
 6:     If Not isPostBack Then
 7:       BindData
 8:     End If
 9:   End Sub
10:
11:   Sub BindData
12:     Dim myConnection As SQLConnection
13:     Dim myCommand As SQLCommand
14:     myConnection = New SQLConnection( "Server=Localhost;uid=sa;
        ↪pwd=secret;Database=Northwind" )
15:     myCommand = New SQLCommand( "Select CategoryName
        ↪from Categories", myConnection )
16:     myConnection.Open()
17:     myDataList.DataSource = myCommand.ExecuteReader()
18:     myDataList.DataBind()
19:     myConnection.Close()
20:   End Sub
21:
```

LISTING 7.3.6 Continued

```
22:    Sub pickCat( s As Object, e As DataListCommandEventArgs )
23:       myDataList.SelectedIndex = e.Item.ItemIndex
24:       currentCat.Text = e.CommandArgument
25:       BindData
26:    End Sub
27: </Script>
28:
29: <html>
30: <head><title>Categories</title></head>
31: <body>
32:
33: <form Runat="Server">
34:
35: <asp:DataList
36:    id="myDataList"
37:    cellpadding=10
38:    cellspacing=0
39:    gridlines="both"
40:    RepeatColumns="3"
41:    RepeatDirection="Horizontal"
42:    OnItemCommand="pickCat"
43:    Runat="Server">
44:    <ItemTemplate>
45:      <asp:LinkButton
46:        id="myLink"
47:        Text='<%# Container.DataItem( "CategoryName" ) %>'
48:        CommandArgument='<%# Container.DataItem( "CategoryName" ) %>'
49:        Runat="Server"/>
50:    </ItemTemplate>
51:    <SelectedItemTemplate>
52:      <b><%# Container.DataItem( "CategoryName" ) %></b>
53:    </SelectedItemTemplate>
54: </asp:DataList>
55:
56: The Current Category is:
57: <asp:Label id="currentCat" Runat="Server"/>
58:
59: </form>
60:
61: </body>
62: </html>
```

Notice that the name of the current product category is assigned to the `CommandArgument` property of each of the `LinkButton` controls displayed in the `DataList` control. When a `LinkButton` is clicked, the `CommandArgument` property is passed to the `pickCat` subroutine as part of the `DataListCommandEventArgs` parameter. The name of the selected category is then assigned to the `currentCat` `Label` control.

Retrieving the Category ID

There is one last bit of information that you might need to retrieve when working with a list of product categories in a `DataList` control. You know how to retrieve the index of the category selected, and you know how to retrieve the name of the category selected, but we haven't discussed any method for retrieving the category ID for the category selected (the value of the primary key of the `Category` table).

For example, in the sample Northwind database included with Microsoft SQL Server, there are two tables: `Categories` and `Products`. Each product in the `Products` table is associated with a category in the `Categories` table through the `CategoryID` column shared by both tables. If you want to enable a user to click the name of a product category and retrieve a list of products in that category, you'll need a method of retrieving the category ID.

The page contained in Listing 7.3.7 demonstrates how you can retrieve the category ID when a user clicks a category name in a `DataList` control (this page is included on the CD as `SqlDataListItemEventSelect3.aspx`).

LISTING 7.3.7 The `DataKeyField` Property

```
 1: <%@ Import Namespace="System.Data" %>
 2: <%@ Import Namespace="System.Data.SqlClient" %>
 3:
 4: <Script Runat="Server">
 5:   Sub Page_Load( s As Object, e As EventArgs )
 6:     If Not isPostBack Then
 7:       BindData
 8:     End If
 9:   End Sub
10:
11:   Sub BindData
12:     Dim myConnection As SQLConnection
13:     Dim myCommand As SQLCommand
14:     myConnection = New SQLConnection( "Server=Localhost;uid=sa;
          ➥pwd=secret;Database=Northwind" )
15:     myCommand = New SQLCommand( "Select CategoryID, CategoryName
          ➥from Categories", myConnection )
16:     myConnection.Open()
17:     myDataList.DataSource = myCommand.ExecuteReader()
18:     myDataList.DataBind()
19:     myConnection.Close()
20:   End Sub
21:
22:   Sub pickCat( s As Object, e As DataListCommandEventArgs )
23:     myDataList.SelectedIndex = e.Item.ItemIndex
24:     currentCat.Text = e.CommandArgument
25:     currentCatIndex.Text = e.Item.ItemIndex
26:     currentCatID.Text = myDataList.DataKeys.Item( e.Item.ItemIndex ).toString()
27:     BindData
28:   End Sub
29: </Script>
30:
31: <html>
32: <head><title>Categories</title></head>
33: <body>
34:
```

LISTING 7.3.7   Continued

```
35: <form Runat="Server">
36:
37: <asp:DataList
38:    id="myDataList"
39:    cellpadding=10
40:    cellspacing=0
41:    gridlines="both"
42:    RepeatColumns="3"
43:    RepeatDirection="Horizontal"
44:    DataKeyField="CategoryID"
45:    OnItemCommand="pickCat"
46:    Runat="Server">
47:    <ItemTemplate>
48:      <asp:LinkButton
49:        id="myLink"
50:        Text='<%# Container.DataItem( "CategoryName" ) %>'
51:        CommandArgument='<%# Container.DataItem( "CategoryName" ) %>'
52:        Runat="Server"/>
53:    </Itemtemplate>
54:    <SelectedItemTemplate>
55:       <b><%# Container.DataItem( "CategoryName" ) %></b>
56:    </SelectedItemTemplate>
57: </asp:DataList>
58:
59: <p>
60: The Current Category is:
61: <asp:Label id="currentCat" Runat="Server"/>
62:
63: <p>
64: The Current Category Index is:
65: <asp:Label id="currentCatIndex" Runat="Server"/>
66:
67: <p>
68: The Current Category ID is:
69: <asp:Label id="currentCatID" Runat="Server"/>
70:
71: </form>
72:
73: </body>
74: </html>
```

In Listing 7.3.7, the `DataKeyField` property is assigned the name of the primary key field for the `DataSource` property. In this case, the `DataKeyField` property is assigned the value `CategoryID`. After the `DataKeyField` property is set, a `DataKeys` collection that contains the values of the primary keys is automatically created for the `DataList` control.

The value of `CategoryID` for the selected category is retrieved in the `pickCat` subroutine. The category ID is retrieved by passing the index of the selected category to the `DataKeys` collection. Finally, the category ID is assigned to a `Label` control named `currentCatID` and displayed (see Figure 7.11).

FIGURE 7.11
Retrieving the `DataKeyField` with a `DataList` control.

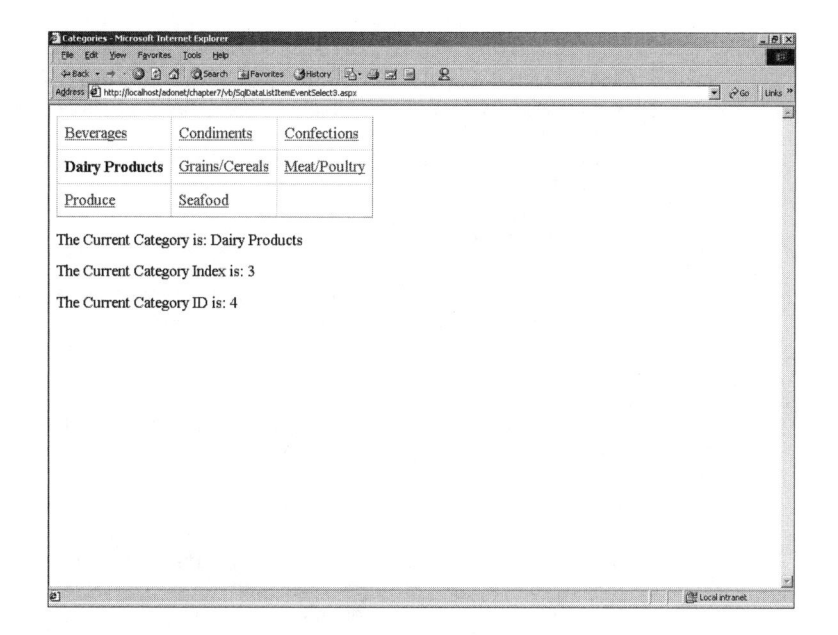

[Screenshot: Categories - Microsoft Internet Explorer showing a table with categories: Beverages, Condiments, Confections, Dairy Products (bold), Grains/Cereals, Meat/Poultry, Produce, Seafood. Below:
The Current Category is: Dairy Products
The Current Category Index is: 3
The Current Category ID is: 4]

Editing an Item in a `DataList` Control

You can edit the items listed in a `DataList` control. The `DataList` control has a template named `EditItemTemplate` that you can display when you want to edit a particular item.

For example, suppose you want to edit a list of authors that you retrieve from a database table named `Authors`. You want the ability to update or delete particular entries in this table. The page in Listing 7.3.8 illustrates how you could do this with the `DataList` control (this page is included on the CD as `SqlDataListEdit.aspx`).

LISTING 7.3.8 Editing Items in a `DataList` Control

```
 1: <%@ Import Namespace="System.Data" %>
 2: <%@ Import Namespace="System.Data.SqlClient" %>
 3:
 4: <Script Runat="Server">
 5:   Sub Page_Load( s As Object, e As EventArgs )
 6:     If Not isPostBack Then
 7:       BindData
 8:     End If
 9:   End Sub
10:
11:   Sub BindData
12:     Dim myConnection As SqlConnection
13:     Dim myCommand As SQLCommand
14:     myConnection = New SqlConnection( "Server=Localhost;uid=sa;
        ➥pwd=secret;Database=Pubs" )
```

LISTING 7.3.8 *Continued*

```
15:      myCommand = New SqlCommand( "Select au_id, au_lname,
         ↪au_fname, phone from Authors order by au_lname", myConnection )
16:      myConnection.Open()
17:      myDataList.DataSource = myCommand.ExecuteReader()
18:      myDataList.DataBind()
19:      myConnection.Close()
20:    End Sub
21:
22:    Sub editAuthor( s As Object, e As DataListCommandEventArgs )
23:      myDataList.EditItemIndex = e.Item.ItemIndex
24:      BindData
25:    End Sub
26:
27:    Sub cancelEdit( s As Object, e As DataListCommandEventArgs )
28:      myDataList.EditItemIndex = -1
29:      BindData
30:    End Sub
31:
32:    Sub deleteAuthor( s As Object, e As DataListCommandEventArgs )
33:      Dim myConnection As SqlConnection
34:      Dim myCommand As SqlCommand
35:      Dim sqlString As String
36:      myConnection = New SqlConnection( "Server=Localhost;uid=sa;
         ↪pwd=secret;Database=Pubs" )
37:      sqlString = "Delete Authors Where au_id=@authorID"
38:      myCommand = New SqlCommand( sqlString, myConnection )
39:      myCommand.Parameters.Add( New SQLParameter( "@authorID",
         ↪SqlDbType.VarChar, 11 ))
40:      myCommand.Parameters( "@authorID" ).Value =
         ↪myDataList.DataKeys.Item( e.Item.ItemIndex )
41:      myConnection.Open()
42:      myCommand.ExecuteNonQuery
43:      myDataList.DataBind()
44:      myConnection.Close()
45:      myDataList.EditItemIndex = -1
46:      BindData
47:    End Sub
48:
49:    Sub updateAuthor( s As Object, e As DataListCommandEventArgs )
50:      Dim myConnection As SQLConnection
51:      Dim myCommand As SQLCommand
52:      Dim sqlString As String
53:      myConnection = New SQLConnection( "Server=Localhost;uid=sa;
         ↪pwd=secret;Database=Pubs" )
54:      sqlString = "Update Authors Set au_lname=@lastname,
         ↪au_fname=@firstname, phone=@phone" _
55:        & " Where au_id=@authorID"
56:      myCommand = New SQLCommand( sqlString, myConnection )
57:      myCommand.Parameters.Add( New SQLParameter( "@lastname",
         ↪SqlDbType.VarChar, 40 ))
58:      myCommand.Parameters( "@lastname" ).Value =
         ↪cTYPE( e.Item.FindControl( "lastname" ), textBox ).Text
```

LISTING 7.3.8 *Continued*

```
59:        myCommand.Parameters.Add( New SQLParameter( "@firstname",
           ➥SqlDbType.VarChar, 20 ))
60:        myCommand.Parameters( "@firstname" ).Value =
           ➥cTYPE( e.Item.FindControl( "firstname" ), textBox ).Text
61:        myCommand.Parameters.Add( New SQLParameter( "@phone",
           ➥SqlDbType.Char, 12 ))
62:        myCommand.Parameters( "@phone" ).Value =
           ➥cTYPE( e.Item.FindControl( "phone" ), textBox ).Text
63:        myCommand.Parameters.Add( New SQLParameter( "@authorID",
           ➥SqlDbType.VarChar, 11 ))
64:        myCommand.Parameters( "@authorID" ).Value =
           ➥myDataList.DataKeys.Item( e.Item.ItemIndex )
65:        myConnection.Open()
66:        myCommand.ExecuteNonQuery
67:        myDataList.DataBind()
68:        myConnection.Close()
69:        myDataList.EditItemIndex = -1
70:        BindData
71:     End Sub
72: </Script>
73:
74: <html>
75: <head><title>Edit Authors</title></head>
76: <body>
77:
78: <form Runat="Server">
79:
80: <asp:DataList
81:    id="myDataList"
82:    cellpadding=10
83:    cellspacing=0
84:    gridlines="both"
85:    RepeatColumns="3"
86:    RepeatDirection="Horizontal"
87:    DataKeyField="au_id"
88:    OnEditCommand="editAuthor"
89:    OnDeleteCommand="deleteAuthor"
90:    OnUpdateCommand="updateAuthor"
91:    OnCancelCommand="cancelEdit"
92:    Runat="Server">
93:
94:    <ItemTemplate>
95:      <asp:LinkButton
96:        Text="Edit"
97:        CommandName="edit"
98:        Runat="Server"/>
99:      <%# Container.DataItem( "au_lname" )%>
100:   </ItemTemplate>
101:
102:   <EditItemTemplate>
103:     <b>Last Name:</b>
104:     <br><asp:TextBox
```

LISTING 7.3.8 Continued

```
105:        id="lastname"
106:        text='<%# Container.DataItem( "au_lname" ) %>'
107:        Runat="Server"/>
108:      <p>
109:      <b>First Name:</b>
110:      <br><asp:TextBox
111:        id="firstname"
112:        text='<%# Container.DataItem( "au_fname" ) %>'
113:        Runat="Server"/>
114:      <p>
115:      <b>Phone:</b>
116:      <br><asp:TextBox
117:        id="phone"
118:        text='<%# Container.DataItem( "phone" ) %>'
119:        Runat="Server"/>
120:      <p>
121:      <asp:Button
122:        Text="Update"
123:        CommandName="update"
124:        Runat="Server"/>
125:      <asp:Button
126:        Text="Delete"
127:        CommandName="delete"
128:        Runat="Server"/>
129:      <asp:Button
130:        Text="Cancel"
131:        CommandName="cancel"
132:        Runat="Server"/>
133:    </EditItemTemplate>
134:
135: </asp:DataList>
136:
137: </form>
138:
139: </body>
140: </html>
```

The output of the page in Listing 7.3.8 is illustrated in Figure 7.12. The page contained in Listing 7.3.8 is complicated, but we'll go over how it works step by step.

First, you should notice that each **LinkButton** control displayed by the **ItemTemplate** has the value **Edit** assigned to its **Command** property. When you click any of the links displayed by the **ItemTemplate**, the **DataList** control's **OnEditCommand** event is raised. This event triggers the **editAuthor** subroutine.

The **editAuthor** subroutine assigns the index of the selected author to the **EditItemIndex** property of the **DataList** control. When the **DataList** control is rendered, the **EditItemTemplate** template is rendered for this item rather than the normal **ItemTemplate** template.

FIGURE 7.12
Editing items with the `DataList` control.

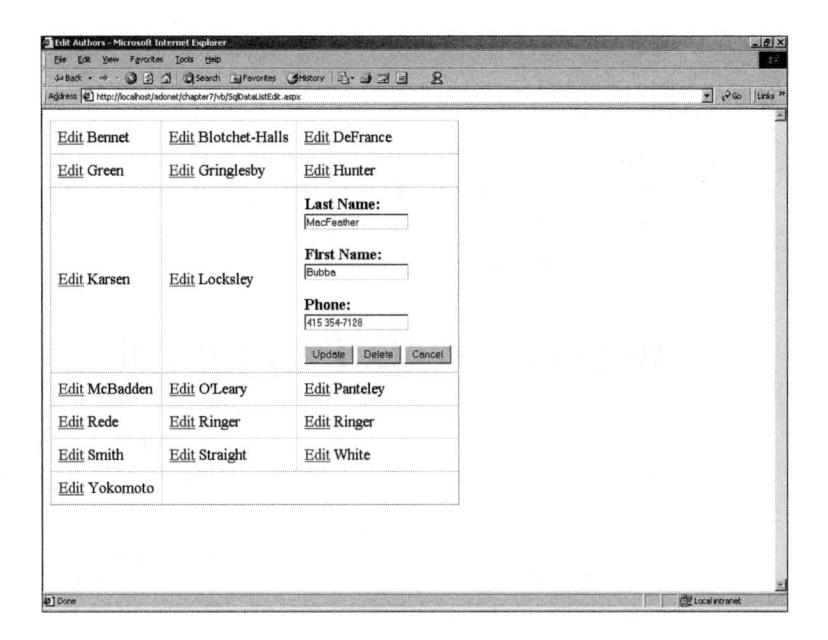

`EditItemTemplate` contains three `TextBox` controls for the author's last name, first name, and phone number. The template also contains three `Button` controls: one labeled "Update," one labeled "Delete," and one labeled "Cancel."

When a user clicks the `Update` control, the `DataList` control's `OnUpdateCommand` event is raised. When this event is raised, the `updateAuthor` subroutine is executed.

The `updateAuthor` subroutine updates the information for the selected author in the `Authors` database table. This is accomplished with an instance of the `SqlCommand` class. The `SqlCommand` class has three parameters that correspond to the `lastname`, `firstname`, and `phone` `TextBox` controls contained in `EditItemTemplate`.

For example, the value entered into the `lastname` `TextBox` control is retrieved and assigned to the `SQLCommand` class's `@lastname` parameter with the following statement:

```
myCommand.Parameters( "@lastname" ).Value =
➥cTYPE( e.Item.FindControl( "lastname" ), textBox ).Text
```

This statement uses the `FindControl()` method to retrieve the value of the `lastname` `TextBox` control for the selected item. The `FindControl()` method returns the actual `TextBox` control. The `Text` property of the control returned by `FindControl()` contains the actual text assigned to the `lastname` `TextBox` control.

Finally, the `@authorID` parameter is assigned with the following statement:

```
myCommand.Parameters( "@authorID" ).Value = myDataList.DataKeys.
➥Item( e.Item.ItemIndex )
```

This statement assigns the primary key of the selected item to the `@authorID` parameter by retrieving the primary key from the `DataKeys` collection of the `DataList` control.

The `deleteAuthor` subroutine deletes the selected author from the `Authors` database table. The correct author is identified by using the primary key of the author from the `DataKeys` collection.

The `cancelEdit` subroutine cancels any modifications made to an item. This subroutine simply assigns the value `-1` to the `EditItemIndex` property of the `DataList` control. When the `EditItemIndex` property has the value `-1`, none of the items in the `DataList` control are selected for editing.

4. Using the `DataGrid` Control

The `DataGrid` control is the most feature-rich (and complicated) data control included with ASP.NET. Despite the complexity of the control, when it is used for the simple task of displaying a database table, it is actually much easier to use than the `Repeater` or `DataList` controls.

You can use the `DataGrid` control, like the `Repeater` and `DataList` controls, to display and format data from a database table. You can also use the `DataGrid` control, like the `DataList` control, to edit particular items in a database table. However, the `DataGrid` control has some advanced features that it does not share with either the `Repeater` or `DataList` control. For example, you can use the `DataGrid` control to sort and page through database data.

The page in Listing 7.4.1 demonstrates a simple application of the `DataGrid` control (see Figure 7.13). In this page, the `DataGrid` control is used to automatically display all the columns and all the rows from a database table (this page is included on the CD as `SqlDataGrid.aspx`).

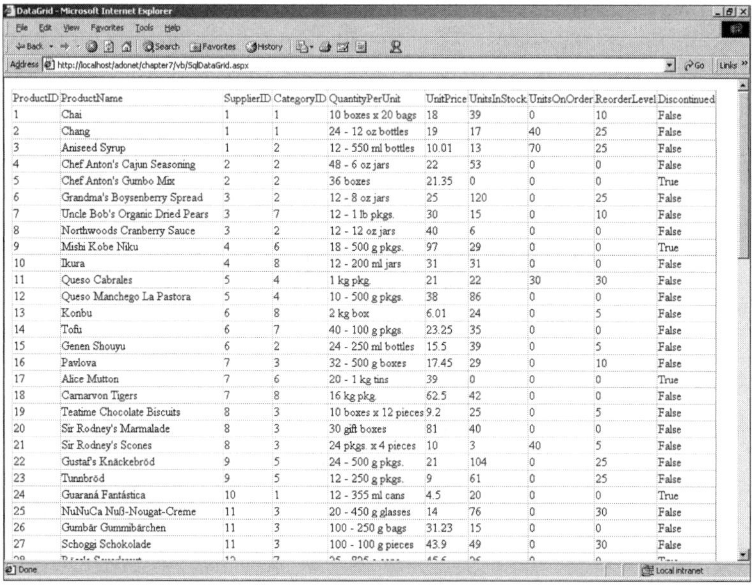

ProductID	ProductName	SupplierID	CategoryID	QuantityPerUnit	UnitPrice	UnitsInStock	UnitsOnOrder	ReorderLevel	Discontinued
1	Chai	1	1	10 boxes x 20 bags	18	39	0	10	False
2	Chang	1	1	24 - 12 oz bottles	19	17	40	25	False
3	Aniseed Syrup	1	2	12 - 550 ml bottles	10.01	13	70	25	False
4	Chef Anton's Cajun Seasoning	2	2	48 - 6 oz jars	22	53	0	0	False
5	Chef Anton's Gumbo Mix	2	2	36 boxes	21.35	0	0	0	True
6	Grandma's Boysenberry Spread	3	2	12 - 8 oz jars	25	120	0	25	False
7	Uncle Bob's Organic Dried Pears	3	7	12 - 1 lb pkgs.	30	15	0	10	False
8	Northwoods Cranberry Sauce	3	2	12 - 12 oz jars	40	6	0	0	False
9	Mishi Kobe Niku	4	6	18 - 500 g pkgs.	97	29	0	0	True
10	Ikura	4	8	12 - 200 ml jars	31	31	0	0	False
11	Queso Cabrales	5	4	1 kg pkg.	21	22	30	30	False
12	Queso Manchego La Pastora	5	4	10 - 500 g pkgs.	38	86	0	0	False
13	Konbu	6	8	2 kg box	6.01	24	0	5	False
14	Tofu	6	7	40 - 100 g pkgs.	23.25	35	0	0	False
15	Genen Shouyu	6	2	24 - 250 ml bottles	15.5	39	0	5	False
16	Pavlova	7	3	32 - 500 g boxes	17.45	29	0	10	False
17	Alice Mutton	7	6	20 - 1 kg tins	39	0	0	0	True
18	Carnarvon Tigers	7	8	16 kg pkg.	62.5	42	0	0	False
19	Teatime Chocolate Biscuits	8	3	10 boxes x 12 pieces	9.2	25	0	5	False
20	Sir Rodney's Marmalade	8	3	30 gift boxes	81	40	0	0	False
21	Sir Rodney's Scones	8	3	24 pkgs. x 4 pieces	10	3	40	5	False
22	Gustaf's Knäckebröd	9	5	24 - 500 g pkgs.	21	104	0	25	False
23	Tunnbröd	9	5	12 - 250 g pkgs.	9	61	0	25	False
24	Guaraná Fantástica	10	1	12 - 355 ml cans	4.5	20	0	0	True
25	NuNuCa Nuß-Nougat-Creme	11	3	20 - 450 g glasses	14	76	0	30	False
26	Gumbär Gummibärchen	11	3	100 - 250 g bags	31.23	15	0	0	False
27	Schoggi Schokolade	11	3	100 - 100 g pieces	43.9	49	0	30	False

FIGURE 7.13
Displaying items with the `DataGrid` control.

LISTING 7.4.1 Using the `DataGrid` Control

```
 1: <%@ Import Namespace="System.Data" %>
 2: <%@ Import Namespace="System.Data.SqlClient" %>
 3:
 4: <Script Runat="Server">
 5:   Sub Page_Load( s As Object, e As EventArgs )
 6:     Dim myConnection As SqlConnection
 7:     Dim myCommand As SqlCommand
 8:     myConnection = New SqlConnection( "Server=Localhost;uid=sa;
        ➥pwd=secret;Database=Northwind" )
 9:     myCommand = New SqlCommand( "Select * from Products", myConnection )
10:     myConnection.Open()
11:     myDataGrid.DataSource = myCommand.ExecuteReader()
12:     myDataGrid.DataBind()
13:     myConnection.Close()
14:   End Sub
15: </Script>
16:
17: <html>
18: <head><title>DataGrid</title></head>
19: <body>
20:
21: <form Runat="Server">
22:
23: <asp:DataGrid
24:   id="myDataGrid"
25:   Runat="Server" />
26:
27: </form>
28:
29: </body>
30: </html>
```

The `DataGrid` control in Listing 7.4.1 is used to display all the rows from a database table named `Products`. Notice that a template was not created for the `DataGrid` control. The `DataGrid` control automatically displays all the rows from its data source in an HTML table.

Controlling Which Columns Are Displayed in a `DataGrid` Control

Typically, you will not want to display all the columns from a database table when you display the table in a `DataGrid` control. You can specify the columns that you want to display in a `DataGrid` control by assigning the value `False` to the `AutoGenerateColumns` property of the `DataGrid` control and listing the names of each of the columns you want to display.

The page in Listing 7.4.2 displays only two columns from the Products database table (this page is included on the CD as `SqlDataGridBoundCols.aspx`).

LISTING 7.4.2 The BoundColumn Property

```
 1: <%@ Import Namespace="System.Data" %>
 2: <%@ Import Namespace="System.Data.SqlClient" %>
 3:
 4: <Script Runat="Server">
 5:   Sub Page_Load( s As Object, e As EventArgs )
 6:     Dim myConnection As SqlConnection
 7:     Dim myCommand As SqlCommand
 8:     myConnection = New SQLConnection( "Server=Localhost;uid=sa;
         ↪pwd=secret;Database=Northwind" )
 9:     myCommand = New SQLCommand( "Select * from Products", myConnection )
10:     myConnection.Open()
11:     myDataGrid.DataSource = myCommand.ExecuteReader()
12:     myDataGrid.DataBind()
13:     myConnection.Close()
14:   End Sub
15: </Script>
16:
17: <html>
18: <head><title>DataGrid</title></head>
19: <body>
20:
21: <form Runat="Server">
22:
23: <asp:DataGrid
24:   id="myDataGrid"
25:   AutoGenerateColumns="False"
26:   Runat="Server">
27:   <Columns>
28:     <asp:BoundColumn HeaderText="Product Name" DataField="ProductName" />
29:     <asp:BoundColumn HeaderText="Price" DataField="UnitPrice"
30:       DataFormatString="{0:c}" />
31:   </Columns>
32: </asp:DataGrid>
33:
34: </form>
35:
36: </body>
37: </html>
```

The page in Listing 7.4.2 displays the `ProductName` and `UnitPrice` columns from the `Products` database table (see Figure 7.14). These two columns are added to the `Columns` collection of the `DataGrid` control by using two instances of the `BoundColumn` class.

For example, the `ProductName` column is added with this statement:

`<asp:BoundColumn HeaderText="Product Name" DataField="ProductName" />`

This statement displays the `ProductName` column in the `DataGrid` control and places the label `Product Name` in the heading for the column.

FIGURE 7.14
Using `BoundColumns` with the `DataGrid` control.

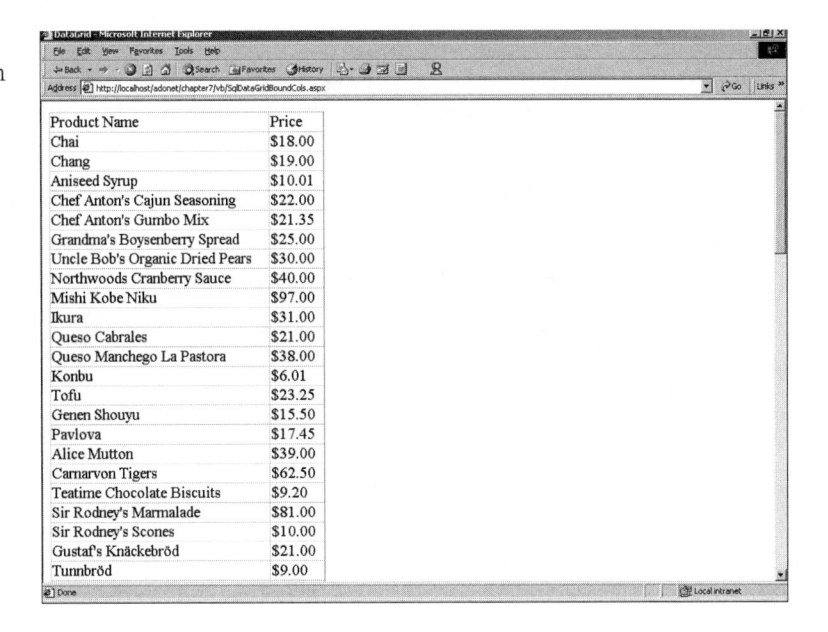

Product Name	Price
Chai	$18.00
Chang	$19.00
Aniseed Syrup	$10.01
Chef Anton's Cajun Seasoning	$22.00
Chef Anton's Gumbo Mix	$21.35
Grandma's Boysenberry Spread	$25.00
Uncle Bob's Organic Dried Pears	$30.00
Northwoods Cranberry Sauce	$40.00
Mishi Kobe Niku	$97.00
Ikura	$31.00
Queso Cabrales	$21.00
Queso Manchego La Pastora	$38.00
Konbu	$6.01
Tofu	$23.25
Genen Shouyu	$15.50
Pavlova	$17.45
Alice Mutton	$39.00
Carnarvon Tigers	$62.50
Teatime Chocolate Biscuits	$9.20
Sir Rodney's Marmalade	$81.00
Sir Rodney's Scones	$10.00
Gustaf's Knäckebröd	$21.00
Tunnbröd	$9.00

Showing and Hiding Columns

You can display and hide particular columns in a `DataGrid` control by using a column's `Visible` property. For example, the `UnitPrice` and `QuantityPerUnit` columns are hidden when the `DataGrid` control in Listing 7.4.3 is first displayed. However, if you click the Show `Details` button, these columns are displayed (this page is included on the CD as `SqlDataGridVisible.aspx`).

LISTING 7.4.3   Hiding Columns in a `DataGrid` Control

```
 1: <%@ Import Namespace="System.Data" %>
 2: <%@ Import Namespace="System.Data.SqlClient" %>
 3:
 4: <Script Runat="Server">
 5:   Sub Page_Load( s As Object, e As EventArgs )
 6:     If Not isPostBack Then
 7:       BindData
 8:     End If
 9:   End Sub
10:
11:   Sub BindData
12:     Dim myConnection As SQLConnection
13:     Dim myCommand As SqlCommand
14:     myConnection = New SqlConnection( "Server=Localhost;uid=sa;
       ➥pwd=secret;Database=Northwind" )
```

LISTING 7.4.3 Continued

```
15:      myCommand = New SqlCommand( "Select * from Products", myConnection )
16:      myConnection.Open()
17:      myDataGrid.DataSource = myCommand.ExecuteReader()
18:      myDataGrid.DataBind()
19:      myConnection.Close()
20:    End Sub
21:
22:    Sub showDetails( s As Object, e As EventArgs )
23:      Dim colCounter As Integer
24:      For colCounter = 1 to myDataGrid.Columns.Count - 1
25:        myDataGrid.Columns( colCounter ).Visible = True
26:      Next
27:    End Sub
28:
29:    Sub hideDetails( s As Object, e As EventArgs )
30:      Dim colCounter As Integer
31:      For colCounter = 1 to myDataGrid.Columns.Count - 1
32:        myDataGrid.Columns( colCounter ).Visible = False
33:      Next
34:    End Sub
35:  </Script>
36:
37:  <html>
38:  <head><title>DataGrid</title></head>
39:  <body>
40:
41:  <form Runat="Server">
42:
43:  <asp:Button
44:    Text="Show Details"
45:    onClick="showDetails"
46:    Runat="Server"/>
47:
48:  <asp:Button
49:    Text="Hide Details"
50:    onClick="hideDetails"
51:    Runat="Server"/>
52:  <p>
53:
54:  <asp:DataGrid
55:    id="myDataGrid"
56:    AutoGenerateColumns="False"
57:    Runat="Server">
58:    <Columns>
59:      <asp:BoundColumn HeaderText="Product Name" DataField="ProductName"/>
60:      <asp:BoundColumn HeaderText="Price" DataField="UnitPrice"
61:        DataFormatString="{0:c}" Visible="False"/>
62:      <asp:BoundColumn HeaderText="Quantity Per Unit"
63:        DataField="QuantityPerUnit" Visible="False"/>
64:    </Columns>
```

LISTING 7.4.3 Continued

```
65: </asp:DataGrid>
66:
67: </form>
68:
69: </body>
70: </html>
```

The page in Listing 7.4.3 contains two subroutines: `showDetails` and `hideDetails`. When the `showDetails` subroutine is executed, the `Visible` property for each column (other than the first column) is set to `True`. When the `hideDetails` subroutine is executed, the `Visible` property for each column (other than the first column) is set to `False` (see Figure 7.15).

FIGURE 7.15
Hiding and displaying `DataGrid` control.

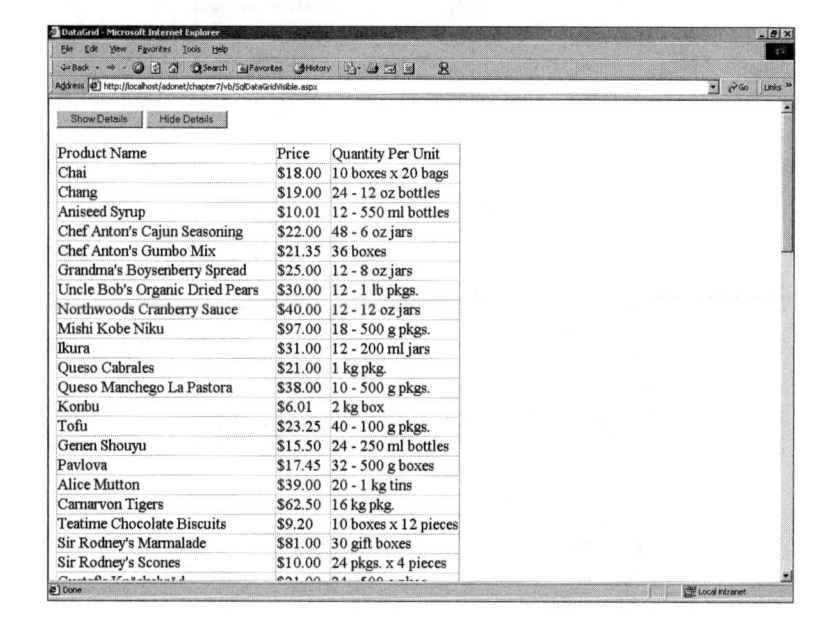

Editing Data in a `DataGrid` Control

You can edit individual items in a `DataGrid` control. You do this by assigning the index number of the item that you want to edit to the `EditItemIndex` property. When an item in a `DataGrid` control is selected for editing, the text contained in all the item's bound columns is automatically displayed within `TextBox` controls (see Figure 7.16).

For example, you can use the page in Listing 7.4.4 to edit records in a database table named `Products` (this page is included on the CD as `SqlDataGridEdit.aspx`).

FIGURE 7.16
Editing items with the `DataGrid` control.

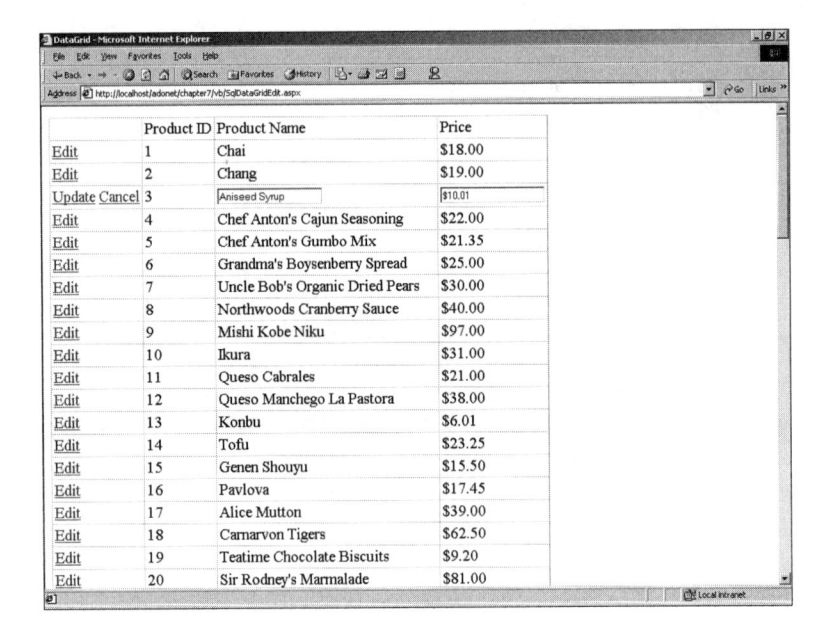

LISTING 7.4.4 Editing Items in a `DataGrid` Control

```
 1: <%@ Import Namespace="System.Data" %>
 2: <%@ Import Namespace="System.Data.SqlClient" %>
 3:
 4: <Script Runat="Server">
 5:   Sub Page_Load( s As Object, e As EventArgs )
 6:     If Not isPostBack Then
 7:       BindData
 8:     End If
 9:   End Sub
10:
11:   Sub BindData
12:     Dim myConnection As SQLConnection
13:     Dim myCommand As SQLCommand
14:     myConnection = New SQLConnection( "Server=Localhost;uid=sa;
        ➥pwd=secret;Database=Northwind" )
15:     myCommand = New SQLCommand( _
16:       "Select * from Products", myConnection )
17:     myConnection.Open()
18:     myDataGrid.DataSource = myCommand.ExecuteReader()
19:     myDataGrid.DataBind()
20:     myConnection.Close()
21:   End Sub
22:
23:   Sub editProduct( s As Object, e As DataGridCommandEventArgs )
24:     myDataGrid.EditItemIndex = e.Item.ItemIndex
25:     BindData
26:   End Sub
27:
```

LISTING 7.4.4 Continued

```
28:    Sub cancelEdit( s As Object, e As DataGridCommandEventArgs )
29:      myDataGrid.EditItemIndex = -1
30:      BindData
31:    End Sub
32:
33:    Sub updateProduct( s As Object, e As DataGridCommandEventArgs )
34:
35:      ' Get New Values
36:      Dim productName As TextBox
37:      productName = e.Item.Cells( 2 ).Controls( 0 )
38:      Dim unitPrice As TextBox
39:      unitPrice = e.Item.Cells( 3 ).Controls( 0 )
40:
41:      ' Update Database
42:      Dim myConnection As SqlConnection
43:      Dim myCommand As SqlCommand
44:      Dim sqlString As String
45:
46:      myConnection = New SqlConnection( "Server=Localhost;uid=sa;
         ➥pwd=secret;Database=Northwind" )
47:      sqlString = "Update Products Set ProductName = " & _
48:        "@productName, UnitPrice=@unitPrice Where ProductID=@productID"
49:      myCommand = New SQLCommand( sqlString, myConnection )
50:      myCommand.Parameters.Add( _
51:        New SQLParameter( "@ProductName", SqlDbType.NVarChar, 80 ))
52:      myCommand.Parameters( "@ProductName" ).Value = productName.Text
53:      myCommand.Parameters.Add( _
54:        New SQLParameter( "@unitprice", SqlDbType.Money ))
55:      myCommand.Parameters( "@unitPrice" ).Value = _
56:        cType( unitPrice.Text, Decimal )
57:      myCommand.Parameters.Add( _
58:        New SQLParameter( "@productID", SqlDbType.INT ))
59:      myCommand.Parameters( "@productID" ).Value = _
60:        myDataGrid.DataKeys.Item( e.Item.ItemIndex )
61:      myConnection.Open()
62:      myCommand.ExecuteNonQuery
63:      myConnection.Close()
64:      myDataGrid.EditItemIndex = -1
65:      BindData
66:    End Sub
67: </Script>
68:
69: <html>
70: <head><title>DataGrid</title></head>
71: <body>
72:
73: <form Runat="Server">
74:
75: <asp:DataGrid
76:   id="myDataGrid"
77:   cellpadding=3
78:   AutoGenerateColumns="False"
```

LISTING 7.4.4 *Continued*

```
 79:    DataKeyField="ProductID"
 80:    OnEditCommand="editProduct"
 81:    OnCancelCommand="cancelEdit"
 82:    OnUpdateCommand="updateProduct"
 83:    Runat="Server">
 84:    <Columns>
 85:      <asp:EditCommandColumn
 86:        EditText="Edit"
 87:        CancelText="Cancel"
 88:        UpdateText="Update" />
 89:      <asp:BoundColumn HeaderText="Product ID"
 90:        DataField="ProductID" ReadOnly="True"/>
 91:      <asp:BoundColumn HeaderText="Product Name"
 92:        DataField="ProductName" />
 93:      <asp:BoundColumn HeaderText="Price"
 94:        DataField="UnitPrice" DataFormatString="{0:c}" />
 95:    </Columns>
 96: </asp:DataGrid>
 97:
 98: </form>
 99:
100: </body>
101: </html>
```

The `DataGrid` control in Listing 7.4.4 contains a column named `EditCommandColumn`. This column automatically displays `LinkButton` controls for common editing tasks. When a row is not selected for editing, the `EditCommandColumn` displays a `LinkButton` control labeled "Edit." When a user clicks the Edit link and selects the row for editing, the `EditCommandColumn` displays `LinkButton` controls labeled "Update" and "Cancel."

When the Update `LinkButton` control is clicked, the `updateProduct` subroutine is called. This subroutine updates the `ProductName` and `UnitPrice` columns in the `Products` table for the particular product selected.

For example, the new value for the `ProductName` column is retrieved using the following two statements:

```
Dim productName As TextBox

productName = e.Item.Cells( 2 ).Controls( 0 )
```

The first statement declares a variable named `productName`. Next, the `TextBox` control used to edit the `ProductName` column is retrieved from the `DataGrid` control and assigned to the `productName` variable.

The `TextBox` control is retrieved from the third cell of the `DataGrid` control (the cell with index number 2). The first cell of the `DataGrid` control contains the `EditCommandColumn` column, the second cell contains the `ProductID` column, and the third cell contains the `ProductName` column.

When a `BoundColumn DataGrid` cell is selected for editing, the cell will contain a single `TextBox` control. Therefore, by retrieving the first control from the cell, you will retrieve the `TextBox` control from the cell.

Next, the `updateProduct` subroutine creates an instance of the `SQLCommand` class that contains an `UPDATE` command. The `SQLCommand` class is executed, and the underlying database table is updated with the new values.

Using Templates When Editing

One problem with the page contained in Listing 7.4.5 is that it does not prevent you from entering bad data when updating the items in the `DataGrid` control. For example, there is nothing to prevent you from entering the word *Apple* as the value for the `UnitPrice` field. To prevent this type of mischief, you need to use validation controls.

The page contained in Listing 7.4.5 illustrates how you can use validation controls when editing data in a `DataGrid` control (this page is included on the CD as `SqlDataGridEditTemplate.aspx`).

LISTING 7.4.5 Using Template Columns with a `DataGrid` Control

```
 1: <%@ Import Namespace="System.Data" %>
 2: <%@ Import Namespace="System.Data.SqlClient" %>
 3:
 4: <Script Runat="Server">
 5:  Sub Page_Load( s As Object, e As EventArgs )
 6:    If Not isPostBack Then
 7:      BindData
 8:    End If
 9:  End Sub
10:
11:  Sub BindData
12:    Dim myConnection As SQLConnection
13:    Dim myCommand As SQLCommand
14:    myConnection = New SQLConnection( "Server=Localhost;uid=sa;
       ➥pwd=secret;Database=Northwind" )
15:    myCommand = New SQLCommand( "Select * from Products", _
16:      myConnection )
17:    myConnection.Open()
18:    myDataGrid.DataSource = myCommand.ExecuteReader()
19:    myDataGrid.DataBind()
20:    myConnection.Close()
21:  End Sub
22:
23:  Sub editProduct( s As Object, e As DataGridCommandEventArgs )
24:    myDataGrid.EditItemIndex = e.Item.ItemIndex
25:    BindData
26:  End Sub
27:
28:  Sub cancelEdit( s As Object, e As DataGridCommandEventArgs )
29:    myDataGrid.EditItemIndex = -1
```

LISTING 7.4.5 *Continued*

```
30:     BindData
31:   End Sub
32:
33:   Sub updateProduct( s As Object, e As DataGridCommandEventArgs )
34:     If isValid Then
35:     ' Get New Values
36:     Dim productName As TextBox
37:     productName = e.Item.FindControl( "ProductName" )
38:     Dim unitPrice As TextBox
39:     unitPrice = e.Item.FindControl( "UnitPrice" )
40:
41:     ' Update Database
42:     Dim myConnection As SQLConnection
43:     Dim myCommand As SQLCommand
44:     Dim sqlString As String
45:
46:     myConnection = New SQLConnection( "Server=Localhost;uid=sa;
➥pwd=secret;Database=Northwind" )
47:     sqlString = "Update Products Set ProductName=@productName, " & _
48:       "UnitPrice=@unitPrice Where ProductID=@productID"
49:     myCommand = New SQLCommand( sqlString, myConnection )
50:     myCommand.Parameters.Add( _
51:       New SQLParameter( "@ProductName", SqlDbType.NVarChar, 80 ))
52:     myCommand.Parameters( "@ProductName" ).Value = _
53:       productName.Text
54:     myCommand.Parameters.Add( _
55:       New SQLParameter( "@unitprice", SqlDbType.Money ))
56:     myCommand.Parameters( "@unitPrice" ).Value = _
57:       CType( unitPrice.Text, Decimal )
58:     myCommand.Parameters.Add( _
59:       New SQLParameter( "@productID", SqlDbType.INT ))
60:     myCommand.Parameters( "@productID" ).Value = _
61:       myDataGrid.DataKeys.Item( e.Item.ItemIndex )
62:     myConnection.Open()
63:     myCommand.ExecuteNonQuery
64:     myConnection.Close()
65:     myDataGrid.EditItemIndex = -1
66:     BindData
67:     End If
68:   End Sub
69: </Script>
70:
71: <html>
72: <head><title>DataGrid</title></head>
73: <body>
74:
75: <form Runat="Server">
76:
77: <asp:DataGrid
78:   id="myDataGrid"
79:   cellpadding=3
80:   AutoGenerateColumns="False"
```

LISTING 7.4.5 *Continued*

```
 81:    DataKeyField="ProductID"
 82:    OnEditCommand="editProduct"
 83:    OnCancelCommand="cancelEdit"
 84:    OnUpdateCommand="updateProduct"
 85:    Runat="Server">
 86:    <Columns>
 87:      <asp:EditCommandColumn
 88:        EditText="Edit"
 89:        CancelText="Cancel"
 90:        UpdateText="Update" />
 91:      <asp:TemplateColumn>
 92:        <ItemTemplate>
 93:          <%# Container.DataItem( "ProductID" )%>
 94:        </ItemTemplate>
 95:      </asp:TemplateColumn>
 96:      <asp:TemplateColumn>
 97:        <ItemTemplate>
 98:          <%# Container.DataItem( "ProductName" )%>
 99:        </ItemTemplate>
100:        <EditItemTemplate>
101:        <asp:TextBox
102:          id="ProductName"
103:          Text='<%# Container.DataItem( "ProductName" )%>'
104:          Runat="Server"/>
105:        <asp:RequiredFieldValidator
106:           ControlToValidate="ProductName"
107:           Display="Dynamic"
108:           Runat="Server">
109:          You must enter a product name!
110:        </asp:RequiredFieldValidator>
111:        </EditItemTemplate>
112:      </asp:TemplateColumn>
113:      <asp:TemplateColumn>
114:        <ItemTemplate>
115:          <%# String.Format( "{0:c}", Container.DataItem( "UnitPrice" ) ) %>
116:        </ItemTemplate>
117:        <EditItemTemplate>
118:        <asp:TextBox
119:          id="UnitPrice"
120:          Text='<%# Container.DataItem( "UnitPrice" )%>'
121:          Runat="Server"/>
122:        <asp:RequiredFieldValidator
123:           ControlToValidate="UnitPrice"
124:           Display="Dynamic"
125:           Runat="Server">
126:          You must enter a unit price!
127:        </asp:RequiredFieldValidator>
128:        <asp:CompareValidator
129:           ControlToValidate="UnitPrice"
130:           Display="Dynamic"
131:           Type="Currency"
132:           Operator="DataTypeCheck"
```

LISTING 7.4.5 Continued

```
133:            Runat="Server">
134:            The unit price must be a money amount!
135:          </asp:CompareValidator>
136:        </EditItemTemplate>
137:      </asp:TemplateColumn>
138:    </Columns>
139: </asp:DataGrid>
140:
141: </form>
142:
143: </body>
144: </html>
```

The trick in Listing 7.4.5 is to use `TemplateColumns` rather than `BoundColumns`. A `TemplateColumn` can contain both an `ItemTemplate` template and an `EditItemTemplate` template. `EditItemTemplate` displays an item from a `DataGrid` control when the item is selected for editing.

For example, the `EditItemTemplate` template for `UnitPrice` contains two validation controls: a `RequiredFieldValidator` control and a `CompareValidator` control. The `RequiredFieldValidator` control is used to prevent a blank unit price from being entered into the database. The `CompareValidator` control performs a Currency data type check to prevent "Apple" from being entered as a unit price (see Figure 7.17).

FIGURE 7.17
Editing items using a template with the `DataGrid` control.

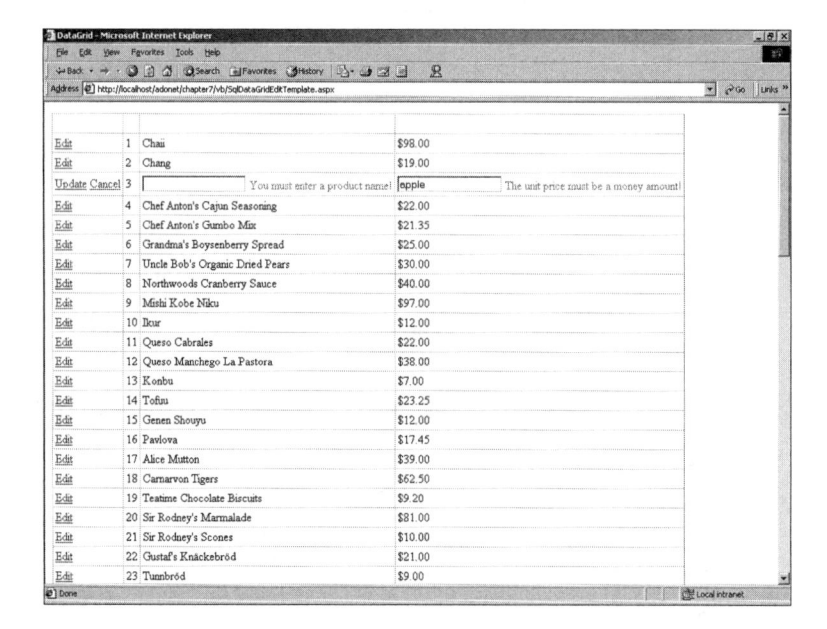

Sorting Data in a `DataGrid` Control

The `DataGrid` control has a property named `AllowSorting` that enables you to sort the columns contained in the `DataGrid`. The `DataGrid` control does not contain the actual application logic for sorting the records. You must add the code to perform the sorting yourself. However, when the `AllowSorting` property is set to `True`, the `DataGrid` control will automatically display the proper links for sorting columns and raise an `OnSortCommand` event when one of the links is clicked (see Figure 7.18).

FIGURE 7.18
Sorting columns with the `DataGrid` control.

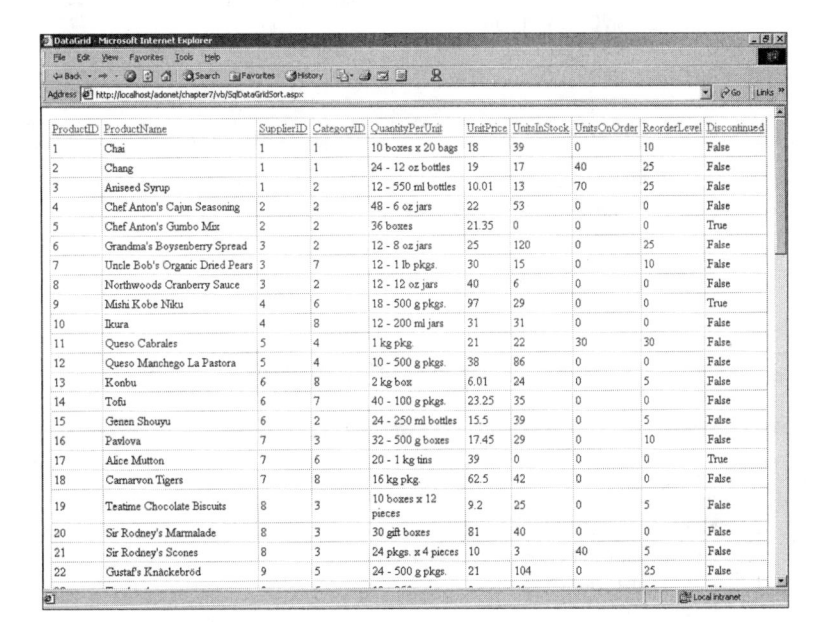

The page in Listing 7.4.6 demonstrates how you can add sorting capabilities to a `DataGrid` control (this page is included on the CD as `SqlDataGridSort.aspx`).

LISTING 7.4.6 Sorting Data in a `DataGrid`

```
 1: <%@ Import Namespace="System.Data" %>
 2: <%@ Import Namespace="System.Data.SqlClient" %>
 3:
 4: <Script Runat="Server">
 5:   Dim sortField As String = "ProductID"
 6:
 7:   Sub Page_Load( s As Object, e As EventArgs )
 8:     If Not isPostBack Then
 9:       BindData
10:     End If
11:   End Sub
12:
13:   Sub BindData
```

LISTING 7.4.6 *Continued*

```
14:      Dim myConnection As SqlConnection
15:      Dim myCommand As SqlCommand
16:      Dim sqlString As String
17:      ' Get Records From Database
18:      myConnection = New SQLConnection( "Server=Localhost;uid=sa;
         ➥pwd=secret;Database=Northwind" )
19:      sqlString = "Select * from Products Order By " & sortfield
20:      myCommand = New SQLCommand( sqlString, myConnection )
21:      myConnection.Open()
22:      myDataGrid.DataSource = myCommand.ExecuteReader()
23:      myDataGrid.DataBind()
24:      myConnection.Close()
25:    End Sub
26:
27:    Sub SortGrid( s As Object, e As DataGridSortCommandEventArgs )
28:       sortField = e.SortExpression
29:       BindData
30:    End Sub
31: </Script>
32:
33: <html>
34: <head><title>DataGrid</title></head>
35: <body>
36:
37: <form Runat="Server">
38: <asp:DataGrid
39:   id="myDataGrid"
40:   AllowSorting="True"
41:   onSortCommand="SortGrid"
42:   cellpadding=3
43:   Runat="Server" />
44: </form>
45:
46: </body>
47: </html>
```

The page in Listing 7.4.6 displays a `DataGrid` control in which you can sort all the columns. The header text for each column appears as a hypertext link. When you click the link for a column, the rows in the `DataGrid` control are sorted by that column.

When you click a link, the `OnSortCommand` event is raised. This event triggers the execution of a subroutine named `SortGrid`. The `SortGrid` subroutine simply assigns the name of the column clicked to a variable named `sortField`.

The `sortField` variable is used in the `BindData` subroutine when retrieving the database rows for the `DataGrid` control. The `sortField` variable is used in the `Order By` clause of the SQL `SELECT` statement used to retrieve the database records.

One problem with the page contained in Listing 7.4.6 is that it enables you to sort all the columns contained in the `DataGrid` control. You might, however, want to sort only certain columns.

To sort only a limited number of columns in a `DataGrid` control, you can use the `SortExpression` property of the `BoundColumn` class. For example, in the page contained in Listing 7.4.7, (see Figure 7.19) you can sort the `ProductName` and `UnitPrice` columns but not the `ProductID` column (this page is included on the CD as `SqlDataGridSortCustom.aspx`).

FIGURE 7.19
Custom column sorting with the `DataGrid` control.

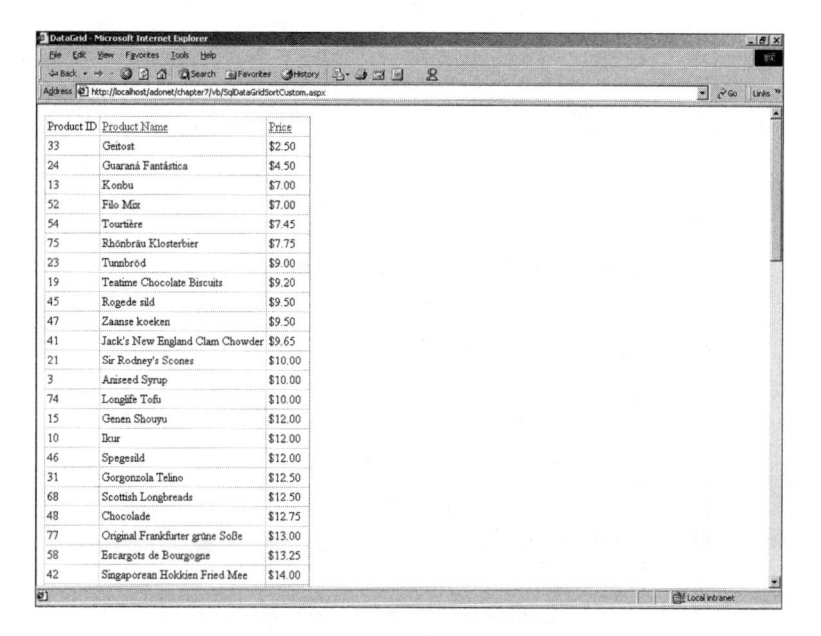

LISTING 7.4.7   Sorting Only Certain Columns

```
 1: <%@ Import Namespace="System.Data" %>
 2: <%@ Import Namespace="System.Data.SqlClient" %>
 3:
 4: <Script Runat="Server">
 5:   Dim sortField As String = "ProductID"
 6:
 7:   Sub Page_Load( s As Object, e As EventArgs )
 8:     If Not isPostBack Then
 9:       BindData
10:     End If
11:   End Sub
12:
13:   Sub BindData
14:     Dim myConnection As SqlConnection
15:     Dim myCommand As SqlCommand
16:     Dim sqlString As String
17:     myConnection = New SqlConnection( "Server=Localhost;uid=sa;
         ➥pwd=secret;Database=Northwind" )
18:     sqlString = "Select * from Products Order By " & sortfield
19:     myCommand = New SQLCommand( sqlString, myConnection )
20:     myConnection.Open()
```

LISTING 7.4.7 *Continued*

```
21:       myDataGrid.DataSource = myCommand.ExecuteReader()
22:       myDataGrid.DataBind()
23:       myConnection.Close()
24:    End Sub
25:
26:    Sub SortGrid( s As Object, e As DataGridSortCommandEventArgs )
27:       sortField = e.SortExpression
28:       BindData
29:    End Sub
30:
31: </Script>
32:
33: <html>
34: <head><title>DataGrid</title></head>
35: <body>
36:
37: <form Runat="Server">
38:
39: <asp:DataGrid
40:    id="myDataGrid"
41:    AutoGenerateColumns="False"
42:    AllowSorting="True"
43:    onSortCommand="SortGrid"
44:    cellpadding=3
45:    Runat="Server">
46:    <Columns>
47:      <asp:BoundColumn HeaderText="Product ID"
48:        DataField="ProductID"/>
49:      <asp:BoundColumn HeaderText="Product Name"
50:        DataField="ProductName" SortExpression="ProductName"/>
51:      <asp:BoundColumn HeaderText="Price"
52:        DataField="UnitPrice" DataFormatString="{0:c}"
53:        SortExpression="UnitPrice"/>
54:    </Columns>
55: </asp:DataGrid>
56:
57: </form>
58:
59: </body>
60: </html>
```

Paging Through a `DataGrid`

Suppose that you want to display a list of your products in a `DataGrid` control. However, suppose that you have thousands of products. You would not want to display a complete list of your products in the `DataGrid` control at once. Instead, you would want to enable users to view the list of your products in multiple pages.

The `DataGrid` control supports paging. You can retrieve a set of records from a database table and logically divide the records into multiple pages. You can use the `DataGrid` control's paging properties to enable a user to jump directly to a particular page. Alternatively, a user can click "next" and "previous" links to go forward and backward through the pages represented by a `DataGrid` control (see Figure 7.20).

FIGURE 7.20
Paging through data with the `DataGrid` control.

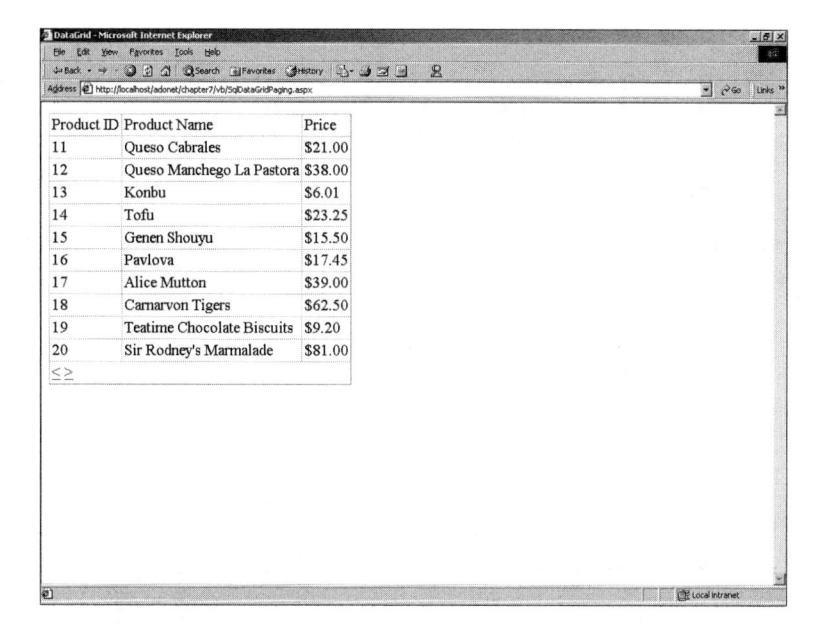

There are, however, some important limitations in how you can use a `DataGrid` control's paging properties. First, you cannot use a `DataGrid` control's paging properties when binding to a `DataReader`. For paging to work, all the records must be loaded into memory. Therefore, you can only page through database records in a `DataGrid` control when you bind it to a `DataSet`.

Second, all the records must be loaded into memory every time you move to a new page. For example, if you view the first page of a database table that contains 2 billion records, all 2 billion records must be loaded into memory even if you are viewing just the first page of 10 records.

Keeping these warnings in mind. The page in Listing 7.4.8 illustrates how you can use a `DataGrid` control's paging properties to view the records from the `Products` database table in multiple pages (the page is included on the CD with the name `SqlDataGridPaging.aspx`).

LISTING 7.4.8 Paging Through a `DataGrid`

```
1: <%@ Import Namespace="System.Data" %>
2: <%@ Import Namespace="System.Data.SqlClient" %>
3:
4: <Script Runat="Server">
5:
6:   Sub Page_Load( s As Object, e As EventArgs )
```

LISTING 7.4.8 *Continued*

```
 7:     If Not isPostBack Then
 8:       BindData
 9:     End If
10:   End Sub
11:
12:   Sub BindData
13:     Dim myConnection As SqlConnection
14:     Dim myAdapter As SqlDataAdapter
15:     Dim sqlString As String
16:     Dim myDataSet As DataSet
17:     ' Get Records From Database
18:     myConnection = New SqlConnection( "Server=Localhost;uid=sa;
19:  ➥pwd=secret;Database=Northwind" )
20:     sqlString = "Select * from Products"
21:     myAdapter = New SQLDataAdapter( sqlString, myConnection )
22:     myDataSet = New DataSet
23:     myAdapter.Fill( myDataSet, "Products" )
24:     myDataGrid.DataSource = myDataSet
25:     myDataGrid.DataBind()
26:   End Sub
27:
28:   Sub pageGrid( s As Object, e As DataGridPageChangedEventArgs )
29:     myDataGrid.CurrentPageIndex = e.NewPageIndex
30:     BindData
31:   End Sub
32:
33: </Script>
34:
35: <html>
36: <head><title>DataGrid</title></head>
37: <body>
38:
39: <form Runat="Server">
40:
41: <asp:DataGrid
42:   id="myDataGrid"
43:   AutoGenerateColumns="False"
44:   AllowPaging="True"
45:   onPageIndexChanged="pageGrid"
46:   cellpadding=3
47:   Runat="Server">
48:   <Columns>
49:     <asp:BoundColumn HeaderText="Product ID"
50:       DataField="ProductID"/>
51:     <asp:BoundColumn HeaderText="Product Name"
52:       DataField="ProductName"/>
53:     <asp:BoundColumn HeaderText="Price"
54:       DataField="UnitPrice" DataFormatString="{0:c}"/>
55:   </Columns>
56: </asp:DataGrid>
57:
```

LISTING 7.4.8 *Continued*

```
58:    </form>
59:
60:  </body>
61: </html>
```

Paging is enabled for the `DataGrid` control in Listing 7.4.8 by enabling its `AllowPaging` property. When this property is enabled, "next" and "previous" links are automatically displayed in the DataGrid control. When these links are clicked, the `OnPageIndexChanged` event is raised and the `pageGrid` subroutine is executed.

The `pageGrid` subroutine does two things. First, it updates the `CurrentPageIndex` property with the index number of the new page. Next, the subroutine rebinds the data source to the `DataGrid` control.

Notice that the `DataGrid` control is bound to a `DataSet` rather than a `SQLDataReader`. You'll receive an error if you attempt to bind a `DataGrid` control that has paging enabled to a `DataReader`. All the records in the data source must be available in memory for the paging to work.

Controlling Paging Properties

The `DataGrid` control in Listing 7.4.8 contains "previous" and "next" links. Instead of using "previous" and "next" links to enable a user to move from one page to another, you can simply display a list of page numbers.

FIGURE 7.21
Displaying page numbers with the `DataGrid` control.

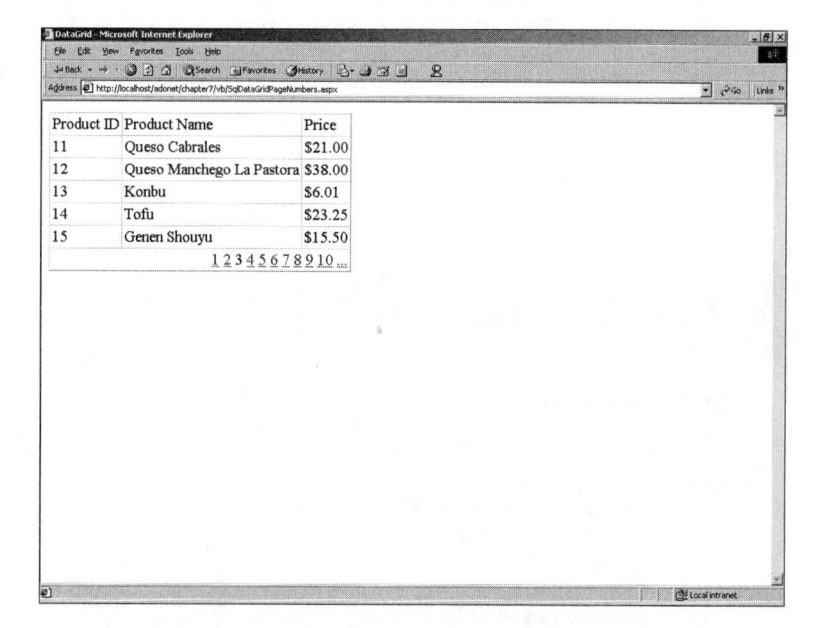

The page in Listing 7.4.9 illustrates how you can page through records in a `DataGrid` control by using page numbers (this page is included on the CD as `SqlDataGridPageNumbers.aspx`).

LISTING 7.4.9 Numeric Paging Through a `DataGrid` Control

```
 1: <%@ Import Namespace="System.Data" %>
 2: <%@ Import Namespace="System.Data.SqlClient" %>
 3:
 4: <Script Runat="Server">
 5: Sub Page_Load( s As Object, e As EventArgs )
 6:    If Not isPostBack Then
 7:       BindData
 8:    End If
 9: End Sub
10:
11: Sub BindData
12:    Dim myConnection As SqlConnection
13:    Dim myAdapter As SqlDataAdapter
14:    Dim sqlString As String
15:    Dim myDataSet
16:    ' Get Records From Database
17:    myConnection = New SqlConnection( "Server=Localhost;uid=sa;
18:    ↪pwd=secret;Database=Northwind" )
19:    sqlString = "Select * from Products"
20:    myAdapter = New SqlDataAdapter( sqlString, myConnection )
21:    myDataSet = New DataSet
22:    myAdapter.Fill( myDataSet, "Products" )
23:    myDataGrid.DataSource = myDataSet
24:    myDataGrid.DataBind()
25: End Sub
26:
27: Sub pageGrid( s As Object, e As DataGridPageChangedEventArgs )
28:    myDataGrid.CurrentPageIndex = e.NewPageIndex
29:    BindData
30: End Sub
31: </Script>
32:
33: <html>
34: <head><title>DataGrid</title></head>
35: <body>
36:
37: <form Runat="Server">
38:
39: <asp:DataGrid
40:    id="myDataGrid"
41:    AutoGenerateColumns="False"
42:    AllowPaging="True"
43:    PageSize="5"
44:    PagerStyle-Mode="NumericPages"
45:    PagerStyle-HorizontalAlign="Right"
46:    onPageIndexChanged="pageGrid"
47:    cellpadding=3
```

LISTING 7.4.9 Continued

```
48:      Runat="Server">
49:      <Columns>
50:        <asp:BoundColumn HeaderText="Product ID"
51:          DataField="ProductID"/>
52:        <asp:BoundColumn HeaderText="Product Name"
53:          DataField="ProductName"/>
54:        <asp:BoundColumn HeaderText="Price"
55:          DataField="UnitPrice" DataFormatString="{0:c}"/>
56:      </Columns>
57: </asp:DataGrid>
58:
59:
60: </form>
61:
62: </body>
63: </html>
```

A `DataGrid` control displays page numbers when the `PagerStyle-Mode` property is assigned the value `NumericPages`. You can control a number of other aspects of the appearance of the paging interface by modifying properties of the `DataGridPagerStyle` class:

- `HorizontalAlign`—Possible values are `Center`, `Justify`, `Left`, and `Right`.

- `Mode`—When `Mode` has the value `NextPrev`, "previous" and "next" links are displayed. When `Mode` has the value `NumericPages`, page numbers are displayed.

- `NextPageText`—The text used for the next page link. The default value is >.

- `PageButtonCount`—The number of page numbers to show at a time (the default value is `10`). Additional pages are indicated by an ellipsis (...).

- `Position`—The position on the `DataGrid` control where the paging user interface should be displayed. Possible values are `Bottom`, `Top`, and `TopAndBottom`.

- `PrevPageText`—The text used for the previous page link. The default value is <.

Custom Paging in Chunks

You were warned that the paging properties of the `DataGrid` control have some serious limitations. The most significant limitation is that the paging properties do not work well with large data sources. All the records from the data source must be loaded for every page whenever you view any single page.

In this section, you'll learn one way to get around this limitation. We'll build some custom application logic that will enable us to retrieve pages a single page at a time.

Let's imagine that we have a database table named `Products` that contains 2 million records. Let's also suppose that we want to view only five records from the table at a time. How can we efficiently move through the records in the database table?

Imagine that the first 15 rows look like this (these rows are taken from the sample **Products** table in the Northwind database, with some modifications):

ProductID	ProductName
1	Chai
3	Aniseed Syrup
4	Chef Anton's Cajun Seasoning
5	Chef Anton's Gumbo Mix
6	Grandma's Boysenberry Spread
7	Uncle Bob's Organic Dried Pears
8	Northwoods Cranberry Sauce
9	Mishi Kobe Niku
10	Ikura
11	Queso Cabrales
13	Konbu
14	Tofu
15	Genen Shouyu
16	Pavlova
18	Carnarvon Tigers

If we want to display the first five rows, we'll need to display the rows with **ProductID** values 1–6 (the row with **ProductID** value 2 has been deleted from the table). We can do this by using the following SQL statement:

```
Select TOP 5 * From Products
Order By ProductID
```

If we want to display the next five rows, we could use the following SQL statement:

```
Select TOP 5 * From Products
Where ProductID > 6
Order By ProductID
```

In general, we can keep retrieving the next five rows by finding the top five rows greater than the last **ProductID** value returned from the previous query.

If we want to retrieve the previous five rows, then we need to get the top five rows less than the **ProductID** retrieved from the previous query (in descending order).

By using this method, we can move through the database records forward and backward five records a time (see Figure 7.22).

FIGURE 7.22
Using Custom Paging with the `DataGrid` control.

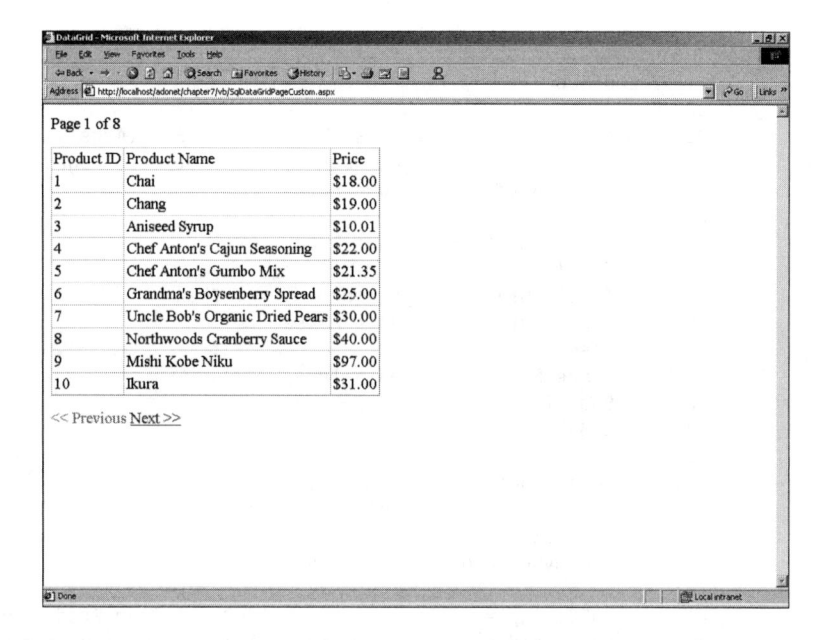

The page in Listing 7.4.10 illustrates how you can use this method of moving through database records with a `DataGrid` control. This page enables a user to move through the Products table in the Northwind database 10 records a time (the page is included on the CD as `SqlDataGridPageCustom.aspx`).

LISTING 7.4.10 Paging in Chunks

```
 1: <%@ Import Namespace="System.Data" %>
 2: <%@ Import Namespace="System.Data.SqlClient" %>
 3:
 4: <Script Runat="Server">
 5:   Const PageSize = 10
 6:   Dim myConnection As SqlConnection
 7:   Dim myAdapter As SqlDataAdapter
 8:   Dim sqlString As String
 9:   Dim myDataSet As DataSet
10:
11:   Sub Page_Load( s As Object, e As EventArgs )
12:     myConnection = New SQLConnection( "Server=Localhost;uid=sa;
13:     ➥pwd=secret;Database=Northwind" )
14:     If Not isPostBack Then
15:       ViewState( "PageNumber" ) = 0
16:       ViewState( "PageCount" ) = getPageCount()
17:       ViewState( "startProductID" ) = -1
18:       ViewState( "endProductID" ) = -1
19:       moveNext
20:     End If
```

LISTING 7.4.10 Continued

```
 21:    End Sub
 22:
 23:    Sub Page_PreRender( s As Object, e As EventArgs )
 24:      If ViewState( "PageNumber" ) = ViewState( "PageCount" ) Then
 25:        nextButton.Enabled = False
 26:      Else
 27:        nextButton.Enabled = True
 28:      End If
 29:      If ViewState( "PageNumber" ) = 1 Then
 30:        prevButton.Enabled = False
 31:      Else
 32:        prevButton.Enabled = True
 33:      End If
 34:    End Sub
 35:
 36:    Function getPageCount As Integer
 37:      Dim theCount As Double
 38:      Dim sqlString As String
 39:      Dim myCommand As SQLCommand
 40:
 41:      sqlString = "Select Count(*) theCount From Products"
 42:      myCommand = New SQLCommand( sqlString, myConnection )
 43:      myConnection.Open()
 44:      theCount = myCommand.ExecuteScalar()
 45:      myConnection.Close()
 46:      Return Math.Ceiling( theCount / PageSize )
 47:    End Function
 48:
 49:    Sub pageGrid( s As Object, e As EventArgs )
 50:      If s.CommandArgument = "Next" Then
 51:        moveNext
 52:      Else
 53:        movePrevious
 54:      End If
 55:    End Sub
 56:
 57:    Sub moveNext
 58:      Dim lastRowIndex As Integer
 59:      sqlString = "Select Top " & PageSize.toString() & " * from Products " _
 60:        & "Where ProductID > " & ViewState( "endProductID" ).toString()
 61:      myAdapter = New SQLDataAdapter( sqlString, myConnection )
 62:      myDataSet = New DataSet
 63:      myAdapter.Fill( myDataSet, "Products" )
 64:      myDataGrid.DataSource = myDataSet
 65:      myDataGrid.DataBind()
 66:      ViewState( "PageNumber" ) = ViewState( "PageNumber" ) + 1
 67:      ViewState( "startProductID" ) = MyDataSet.Tables( "Products" ).
 68: ➥Rows( 0 ).Item( "ProductID", DataRowVersion.Current )
 69:      lastRowIndex = myDataSet.Tables( "Products" ).Rows.Count - 1
 70:      ViewState( "endProductID" ) = MyDataSet.Tables( "Products" ).
 71: ➥Rows( lastRowIndex ).Item( "ProductID", DataRowVersion.Current )
```

LISTING 7.4.10 *Continued*

```
 72:    End Sub
 73:
 74:    Sub movePrevious
 75:      Dim myDataView As DataView
 76:      Dim lastRowIndex As Integer
 77:      sqlString = "Select Top " & PageSize.toString() & " * from Products " _
 78:        & " Where ProductID < " & ViewState( "startProductID" ).toString() _
 79:        & " Order By ProductID DESC"
 80:      myAdapter = New SQLDataAdapter( sqlString, myConnection )
 81:      myDataSet = New DataSet
 82:      myAdapter.Fill( myDataSet, "Products" )
 83:      myDataView = myDataSet.Tables( "Products" ).DefaultView
 84:      myDataView.Sort = "ProductID"
 85:      myDataGrid.DataSource = myDataView
 86:      myDataGrid.DataBind()
 87:      lastRowIndex = myDataSet.Tables( "Products" ).Rows.Count - 1
 88:      ViewState( "PageNumber" ) = ViewState( "PageNumber" ) - 1
 89:      ViewState( "startProductID" ) = MyDataSet.Tables( "Products" ).
 90:    ➥Rows( lastRowIndex ).Item( "ProductID", DataRowVersion.Current )
 91:      ViewState( "endProductID" ) = MyDataSet.Tables( "Products" ).
 92:    ➥Rows( 0 ).Item( "ProductID", DataRowVersion.Current )
 93:    End Sub
 94: </Script>
 95:
 96: <html>
 97: <head><title>DataGrid</title></head>
 98: <body>
 99:
100: Page <%=ViewState( "PageNumber" ) %> of <%=ViewState( "PageCount" ) %>
101:
102: <form Runat="Server">
103:
104: <asp:DataGrid
105:   id="myDataGrid"
106:   AutoGenerateColumns="False"
107:   cellpadding=3
108:   Runat="Server">
109:   <Columns>
110:     <asp:BoundColumn HeaderText="Product ID" DataField="ProductID"/>
111:     <asp:BoundColumn HeaderText="Product Name" DataField="ProductName"/>
112:     <asp:BoundColumn HeaderText="Price"
113:       DataField="UnitPrice" DataFormatString="{0:c}"/>
114:   </Columns>
115: </asp:DataGrid>
116: <p>
117: <asp:LinkButton
118:   id="prevButton"
119:   Text="<< Previous"
120:   onClick="pageGrid"
121:   commandArgument="Previous"
122:   Runat="Server"/>
123:
```

LISTING 7.4.10 Continued

```
124: <asp:LinkButton
125:    id="nextButton"
126:    Text="Next >>"
127:    onClick="pageGrid"
128:    commandArgument="Next"
129:    Runat="Server" />
130:
131: </form>
132:
133: </body>
134: </html>
```

You can use this custom technique of paging through a set of records with any table that has a column that you order the rows by. For example, you can use this technique with a table that contains a `DateTime` column to page through the records in order of date and time.

Summary

In this chapter, you learned how to use ADO.NET classes with ASP.NET controls. In the first section, you learned how to save form data to a database table.

You then learned how to use the `Repeater` control to display database records. You learned how to use templates to control how each record is formatted in a `Repeater` control. You also learned how to bind database data to controls such as the `DropDownList` and `HyperLink` controls.

Finally, you learned how to use several advanced properties of the `DataList` and `DataGrid` controls. You learned how to edit data contained in `DataList` and `DataGrid` controls. You also learned how to sort and page through database records displayed in a `DataGrid` control.

Other Resources

For more information on the material covered in this chapter

- To view updated code samples and post questions about the topics covered in this chapter visit the ASP.NET community at `www.superexpert.com`.

- For more information on using ADO.NET with ASP.NET applications see *ASP.NET Unleashed* (also published by SAMS). Six chapters in *ASP.NET Unleashed* are devoted to working with ADO.NET.

- For information on ADO.NET and ASP.NET training, visit `www.AspWorkshops.com`.

CHAPTER 8

USING XML

by Dan Wahlin

In this chapter, the following topics will be covered:

- What's in the `System.Xml` assembly?
- Reading XML documents using the `XmlTextReader` class
- Validating XML documents against XML schemas
- Creating XML documents using the `XmlTextWriter` class
- Working with XML documents using the Document Object Model (DOM)
- Transforming XML documents with XSLT
- XML support in ADO.NET

This chapter will provide you with a look at the different ways XML can be created, manipulated, and used in ASP.NET applications. The chapter assumes that you have a general understanding of the XML rules as well as the characteristics associated with XML schemas.

1. XML Support in .NET

Unless you've been on a secluded island for the past several years, it would be difficult to miss all the hype surrounding Extensible Markup Language (XML). Product vendors, CEOs, journalists, and technology evangelists alike have proclaimed that XML is *the* next big programming paradigm shift that will revolutionize computing. Although some of this hype is certainly not justified, much of it has been realized by early prototype applications developed to simplify document management, data exchange, and application integration issues. These applications have shown that XML can play a powerful role in making applications more flexible, maintainable, and accessible in today's distributed world.

Microsoft has been supportive of XML for many years now and has taken advantage of its benefits in different applications, including BizTalk Server, Internet Explorer, and SQL Server 2000 (to name a few). Microsoft's support for XML continues with the release of the .NET platform, which provides excellent end-to-end XML support. Microsoft built in this support when developing .NET (as opposed to adding it at the end), so XML is truly integrated into the platform from the ground-up. As a result, programmers have unparalleled flexibility and power in developing .NET applications that leverage XML.

2. Why Use XML?

With all the different programming languages available today, you may wonder why we need another one just to mark up data. Although many languages allow for programming different interfaces and interacting with remote computers, few provide a platform-neutral way to share data between disparate systems. Fewer yet allow this data to pass through firewalls or other security-related mechanisms or provide a format that is easy to work with by individuals with varying levels of technical skill.

To get a good feel for one of the reasons why XML is needed, take a look at the following comma-delimited flat file:

```
Elbow Joint,12930430,6,25,06/28/2000,1238 Van Buren,B2B Supply,1111236894,Walters
Valve,39405938,3,40,06/20/2000,4568 Arizona Ave.,A+ Supply,2221236894,Tammy
PVC,234954048,6,20,06/14/2000,49032 S. 51,A+ Supply,2221236894,Walters
```

Although some assumptions can be made about what some of the data elements are within the file, many of the elements provide you with no way of knowing what they represent. For example, does the field **06/28/2000** (shown in the first line) represent a date? If so, what type of date? How about the **234954048** field in the third line? Is it a part number, a customer number, or something totally unrelated? Now take a look at Listing 8.2.1, which is this same file converted into XML.

Listing 8.2.1 Marking Up a Comma-Delimited File Using XML

```
 1:  <?xml version="1.0"?>
 2:  <supplies>
 3:      <item supplier="1">
 4:          <description>Elbow Joint</description>
 5:          <partID>12930430</partID>
 6:          <numberInStock>6</numberInStock>
 7:          <numberOnOrder>25</numberOnOrder>
 8:          <deliveryDate>06/28/2000</deliveryDate>
 9:          <supplier>
10:              <street>1238 Van Buren</street>
11:              <company>B2B Supply</company>
12:              <phone>1111236894</phone>
```

Listing 8.2.1 Continued

```
13:            </supplier>
14:            <orderedBy>Walters</orderedBy>
15:       </item>
16:       <item supplier="2">
17:            <description>Valve</description>
18:            <partID>39405938</partID>
19:            <numberInStock>3</numberInStock>
20:            <numberOnOrder>40</numberOnOrder>
21:            <deliveryDate>06/20/2000</deliveryDate>
22:            <supplier>
23:                <street>4568 Arizona Ave.</street>
24:                <company>A+ Supply</company>
25:                <phone>2221236894</phone>
26:            </supplier>
27:            <orderedBy>Tammy</orderedBy>
28:       </item>
29:       <item supplier="3">
30:            <description>PVC</description>
31:            <partID>234954048</partID>
32:            <numberInStock>6</numberInStock>
33:            <numberOnOrder>20</numberOnOrder>
34:            <deliveryDate>06/14/2000</deliveryDate>
35:            <supplier>
36:                <street>49032 S. 51</street>
37:                <company>A+ Supply</company>
38:                <phone>2221236894</phone>
39:            </supplier>
40:            <orderedBy>Walters</orderedBy>
41:       </item>
42: </supplies>
```

With XML, each data item can easily be recognized and understood because all the data has been described using XML markup tags. Using these tags, humans and computers can more easily process the data.

Although it's true that computers normally take care of automating many data-intensive applications, programs based on files such as the flat file shown earlier have little flexibility concerning changes in the data's structure. On the other hand, XML presents applications with an opportunity to access data based on descriptive tags rather than by position. This presents a great opportunity to increase an application's flexibility toward changes in data structure.

XML also presents a great opportunity to be able to share data among applications and even components within an application. By knowing an XML file's structure in advance, a component within an application can work with data contained in the XML file and perform different tasks. In some cases, the data may represent information about a customer or business scenario. In other cases, the XML file may simply represent object property values that an ASP.NET component can use to make programming more simple and efficient.

XML also benefits from the ability to determine in advance what structure the file must follow through incorporating Document Type Definition (DTD) and schema files. Defining this structure allows for companies with differing systems to exchange data without worrying about what system the data was originally stored in. As long as both companies know what the XML document's structure will be, they can exchange data using XML syntax. Applications based on XML, such as BizTalk Server and SQL Server 2000, help to make this process even easier, and when they are combined with the power of .NET, very advanced applications can be created.

Finally, as has been referenced several times, XML does not require an advanced degree in computer science to use it. Looking at the preceding XML code in Listing 8.2.1, you can see that there's no intimidating characters or syntax being used. In fact, the XML file could be read and understood by an individual with no technical experience at all. Once the syntax, structural, and programmatic rules are learned, XML documents can be created and manipulated in both simple and complex applications.

3. What's in the `System.Xml` Assembly

Much of the .NET platform's XML support can be found in an assembly named `System.Xml.dll`. Other assemblies, such as `System.Data.dll`, contain other XML features.

The `System.Xml` assembly encapsulates many of the classes that provide XML functionality in the .NET platform. The following list contains some of the *main* classes you'll find yourself using in ASP.NET/XML applications:

- `XmlAttribute`
- `XmlDocument`
- `XmlElement`
- `XmlNode`
- `XmlNamedNodeMap`
- `XmlNodeList`
- `XmlNodeReader`
- `XmlTextReader`
- `XmlTextWriter`
- `XmlValidatingReader`
- `XPathDocument`
- `XslTransform`

In the next few sections, you'll see how to use these and other classes in your ASP.NET applications.

4. Reading XML Documents Using the XmlTextReader Class

XML documents can be large, small, and anywhere in between as far as size is concerned. In cases where XML documents need to be read quickly and efficiently with little overhead, the .NET platform provides the `XmlTextReader` class. This class reads documents in a forward-only, noncached manner.

Rather than loading the entire document into memory, as is the case with the Document Object Model (covered later in section 7, "Working with XML Documents Using the Document Object Model (DOM)"), `XmlTextReader` provides a stream API that allows XML tokens to be "pulled" one node at a time from the stream. The pull model exposed by `XmlTextReader` offers many benefits over the standard push model found in other XML readers, as you'll see next.

Pull Versus Push Models

There is more than one way to parse an XML document in a forward-only manner. If you've worked with XML much in the past, you're more than likely familiar with the Simple API for XML (SAX), which relies on an event-based push model. SAX has become popular for parsing XML documents in a fast and efficient manner. Microsoft's MSXML3 parser contains SAX support that can be used in Visual Basic and C++ applications.

Although SAX is not a W3C recommendation and is not even maintained by the W3C, it has become a *de facto* standard throughout the world when XML documents must be read in a forward-only manner. SAX is actually maintained and developed by David Megginson and several others who belong to an XML-DEV mailing list. SAX is an event-based model that works by "pushing out" information about different XML nodes it finds in a document to a content handler. The content handler can then process the data it receives as appropriate. If you're interested in learning more about SAX and how it works, you can find more information at http://www.megginson.com/SAX/index.html.

With the widespread use of SAX throughout the world, you're probably thinking that .NET must surely include SAX support Actually, SAX is not "officially" supported in .NET. As mentioned earlier, the .NET platform provides an alternative pull model for parsing an XML document rather than the push model found in SAX. Why, you ask? There are actually several reasons, most of which focus on performance gains. Table 8.1 lists many of these reasons.

Table 8.1 Benefits of the Pull Model Found in .NET

Comparison	Description
State management	Push model content handlers must build complex state machines that a pull model client can simplify by managing the state with natural top-down procedural refinement.
Multiple input streams	A pull model allows a client to splice together multiple input streams. Doing this with a push model can be difficult.
Layering test	You can easily build a push model on top of a pull model, whereas the reverse isn't true.
Hints from client	You can design a pull model API to allow the client to give hints to the parser about what the client expects next. For example, in data type support, when a client knows the next item to process is supposed to be an integer, the parser can parse the integer right out of the parser buffer instead of returning a string that's subsequently thrown away.
Avoids extra copy	A pull model allows the client to give the parser the buffer to write the strings into. This technique avoids the extra copy from the parser buffer to the string object, which is then pushed to the client buffer.
Skipping items	The push model must push everything, including the attributes, comments, text, whitespace, and so on. With a pull model, the client pulls only what it's interested in. If, for example, the client doesn't read the attributes, those attribute values don't need to be entity expanded, values "stringized," names atomized, and so on. This model allows for more efficient messaging-level applications of XML.

Now that you're familiar with the differences between pull and push models and have seen some of the advantages of the `XmlTextReader` class, let's take a look at how to use this class to read an XML document.

Using the `XmlTextReader` Class to Read an XML Document

To use the `XmlTextReader` class, the `System.Xml` namespace must be referenced in your ASP.NET applications. Once this namespace is referenced, the class can be instantiated by calling one of its constructors, as follows:

```
<%@ Import Namespace="System.Xml" %>
<script language="C#" runat=server>
    public void Page_Load(Object sender,EventArgs e) {
        string xmlDocPath = Server.MapPath("golfers.xml");
        XmlTextReader xmlReader = new XmlTextReader(xmlDocPath);
        // More code would follow....
    }
</script>
```

This version of the constructor allows the file path (a string) to the XML document to be passed as an argument. Several other constructors can be used while instantiating `XmlTextReader`, as well. For example, `TextReader` or `Stream` can also be passed in as arguments. See the .NET SDK for more details on the different `XmlTextReader` constructors.

Once the `XmlTextReader` object is instantiated, parsing can then begin on the XML document stream in a forward-only manner. This process is started by calling the `Read()` method, as shown in Listing 8.4.1.

Listing 8.4.1 Calling the `XmlTextReader` Class's `Read()` Method

```
 1: <%@ Import Namespace="System.Xml" %>
 2: <script language="VB" runat="server">
 3:     public sub Page_Load(sender as Object,e as EventArgs)
 4:         Dim xmlDocPath as string = Server.MapPath("golfers.xml")
 5:         Dim xmlReader as XmlTextReader = new XmlTextReader(xmlDocPath)
 6:         while (xmlReader.Read())
 7:             'Process XML tokens found in Stream
 8:             Response.Write(xmlReader.Name)
 9:             Response.Write("<br />")
10:         end while
11:         xmlReader.Close()
12:     end sub
13: </script>
```

After the `XmlTextReader` class is instantiated in line 5, its `Read()` method is called in line 6. This method returns `True` until the end of the stream is reached. As the XML stream is being read, the name of each XML token pulled from the stream is written out to the browser using the `XmlTextReader` class's `Name` property (line 8).

`XmlTextReader` has many different properties and methods that can be used to move through the stream and access different tokens. One of the more useful properties is named `NodeType`. This property returns an `XmlNodeType` enumeration member value. Table 8.2 shows the different `XmlNodeType` enumeration members, as defined in the .NET SDK.

Table 8.2 `XmlNodeType` Enumeration Members

Member Name	Description
All	All node types.
Attribute	An attribute (for example, `id='123'`). An Attribute node can have the following child node types: Text and EntityReference. The Attribute node does not appear as the child node of any other node type; note that it is not considered a child node of an Element node.

Table 8.2 Continued

Member Name	Description
CDATA	A CDATA section (for example, `<![CDATA[my escaped text]]>`). CDATA sections are used to escape blocks of text that would otherwise be recognized as markup. A CDATASection node cannot have any child nodes. The CDATASection node can appear as the child of the DocumentFragment, EntityReference, and Element nodes.
Comment	A comment (for example, `<!-- my comment -->`). A Comment node cannot have any child nodes. The Comment node can appear as the child of the Document, DocumentFragment, Element, and EntityReference nodes.
Document	A document object, which, as the root of the document tree, provides access to the entire XML document. A Document node can have the following child node types: Element (maximum of one), ProcessingInstruction, Comment, and DocumentType. The Document node cannot appear as the child of any node types.
DocumentFragment	A document fragment. The DocumentFragment node associates a node or sub-tree with a document without actually being contained within the document. A DocumentFragment node can have the following child node types: Element, ProcessingInstruction, Comment, Text, CDATASection, and EntityReference. The DocumentFragment node cannot appear as the child of any node types.
DocumentType	The document type declaration, indicated by the `<!DOCTYPE>` tag (for example, `<!DOCTYPE ...>`). A DocumentType node can have the following child node types: Notation and Entity. The DocumentType node can appear as the child of the Document node.
Element	An element (for example, `<Name>`). An Element node can have the following child node types: Element, Text, Comment, ProcessingInstruction, CDATA, and EntityReference. The Element node can be the child of the Document, DocumentFragment, EntityReference, and Element nodes.
EndElement	Returned when `XmlReader` gets to the end of an element (for example, `</item>`).
EndEntity	Returned when `XmlReader` gets to the end of the entity replacement as a result of a call to `ResolveEntity`.
Entity	An entity declaration (for example, `<!ENTITY ...>`). An Entity node can have child nodes that represent the expanded entity (for example, Text and EntityReference nodes). The Entity node can appear as the child of the DocumentType node.

Table 8.2 Continued

Member Name	Description
EntityReference	A reference to an entity (for example, #). This applies to all entities, including character entity references. An EntityReference node can have the following child node types: Element, ProcessingInstruction, Comment, Text, CDATASection, and EntityReference. The EntityReference node can appear as the child of the Attribute, DocumentFragment, Element, and EntityReference nodes.
None	This is returned by the XmlReader if a Read method has not been called.
Notation	A notation in the document type declaration (for example, <!NOTATION ...>). A Notation node cannot have any child nodes. The Notation node can appear as the child of the DocumentType node.
ProcessingInstruction	A processing instruction (PI); an example is <?pi test?>. A PI node cannot have any child nodes. The PI node can appear as the child of the Document, DocumentFragment, Element, and EntityReference nodes.
SignificantWhitespace	The whitespace between markup in a mixed-content model.
Text	The text content of an element. A Text node cannot have any child nodes. The Text node can appear as the child node of the Attribute, DocumentFragment, Element, and EntityReference nodes.
Whitespace	The whitespace between markup.
XmlDeclaration	The XML declaration node (for example, <?xml version='1.0'?>;). This has to be the first node in the document, and it can have no children. It is a child of the root node, and it can have attributes that provide version and encoding information.

As different XML tokens are encountered while reading the stream, the `NodeType` property of each token can be checked so that additional information can be pulled if necessary. For example, to get to the attributes located on a particular Element node, it's important to know when Element-type nodes are found.

Listing 8.4.2 shows how the `NodeType` property can be used, as well as several other properties and methods of the `XmlTextReader` class, to read through an XML document and write each XML token found in the stream back to the browser. Although this example doesn't have much utility on its own, it would be rather trivial to change the code to dynamically create SQL statements to update a database with the data found in the XML document.

Listing 8.4.2 Reading an XML Document with the `XmlTextReader` Class

```vb
 1: <%@ Import Namespace="System.Xml" %>
 2: <%@ Import Namespace="System.Text" %>
 3: <script language="VB" runat="server">
 4: public class ReadXmlFileVB
 5:     Dim output as StringBuilder = new StringBuilder()
 6:     public function ReadDoc(doc as string) as string
 7:         Dim m_Document as string = doc
 8:         Dim xmlReader as XmlTextReader
 9:         try
10:             xmlReader = new XmlTextReader(m_Document)
11:             Call WriteXml(xmlReader)
12:         catch e as Exception
13:             output.Append("Error Occured While Reading " & m_Document & _
14:                 " " & e.ToString())
15:         finally
16:             if (NOT xmlReader Is Nothing) then
17:                 xmlReader.Close()
18:             end if
19:         end try
20:         return output.ToString()
21:     end function
22:     private sub WriteXml(xmlReader as XmlTextReader)
23:         do while (xmlReader.Read())
24:             if (xmlReader.NodeType = XmlNodeType.Element) then
25:                 output.Append(indent(xmlReader.Depth*4))
26:                 output.Append("<b>&lt;" & xmlReader.Name & "</b>")
27:                 do while (xmlReader.MoveToNextAttribute())
28:                     output.Append(" <i>" & xmlReader.Name & "=""" & _
29:                                   xmlReader.Value & """</i> ")
30:                 loop
31:                 if (xmlReader.IsEmptyElement) then
32:                     output.Append("<b>/&gt;</b><br>")
33:                 else
34:                     output.Append("<b>&gt;</b><br>")
35:                 end if
36:             else if (xmlReader.NodeType = XmlNodeType.EndElement) then
37:                 output.Append(indent(xmlReader.Depth*4))
38:                 output.Append("<b>&lt;/" & xmlReader.Name & "&gt;</b><br>")
39:             else if (xmlReader.NodeType = XmlNodeType.Text)
40:                 if (xmlReader.Value.Length <> 0) then
41:                     output.Append(indent(xmlReader.Depth*4))
42:                     output.Append("<font color=#ff0000>" & _
43:                                   xmlReader.Value & "<br></font>")
44:                 end if
45:             end if
46:         loop
47:     end sub
48:     private function indent(number as integer) as string
49:         Dim spaces as string = ""
50:         Dim i as integer
51:         for i=0 to number
52:             spaces = spaces & " "
```

Listing 8.4.2 Continued

```
53:            next
54:            return spaces
55:        end function
56: end class
57:
58: private sub Page_Load(sender as Object, e as EventArgs)
59:     Dim readXmlFileSample as ReadXmlFileVB = new ReadXmlFileVB()
60:     output.InnerHtml = _
61:         readXmlFileSample.ReadDoc(Server.MapPath("golfers.xml"))
62: end sub
63: </script>
64: <html>
65:     <body>
66:         <font size="5" color="#02027a">
67:             Reading XML Documents with the XmlTextReader Class
68:         </font>
69:         <p />
70:         <div id="output" runat="server" />
71:     </body>
72: </html>
```

This example starts by referencing the `System.Xml` assembly in line 1. Doing this allows access to all the classes found within the assembly, including the `XmlTextReader` class needed for this application. Once the page is hit, the `Page_Load()` event takes care of instantiating the `ReadXmlFile` class (line 59). Once the class is instantiated, the `ReadDoc()` method is called and the path to the XML document is passed in as an argument (lines 60–61).

The `ReadDoc()` method takes care of instantiating the reader by passing the file path to its constructor. It then passes the newly create `XmlTextReader` object to the `WriteXml()` method (line 22). Each node in the XML document is processed as it is reached. This processing begins with a call to the `XmlTextReader`'s `Read()` method. As each token in the stream is read, the node type is checked. If the node type is equal to `XmlNodeType.Element`, the `MoveToNextAttribute()` method is called within a `while` loop (lines 27–30). Any existing attributes are iterated through and displayed as appropriate.

If the node is not an element but is instead an element end tag (`XmlNodeType.EndElement`), the appropriate closing tag is included (line 38). If the node is actually a text node (`XmlNodeType.Text`), the text is included but the font color is set to red so that the data stands out more (lines 40–44). The text is read by calling the `Value` property.

Each node is indented a specified amount by checking `XmlTextReader`'s `Depth` property. This property automatically tracks how deep you are into an XML document's hierarchical structure, making it very easy to display the document in a properly formatted manner or to simply track parent/child relationships. Once the entire document has been parsed, it is written out to the browser.

Note that the attributes are not automatically passed to you, as is the case with SAX. For example, if you don't want to work with any attributes, they can simply be skipped over. The same logic follows for text nodes, processing instructions, comments, and so on. Until you tell the code to pull these different node types from the stream, they are simply ignored, which keeps buffer sizes minimal, thus resulting in very fast and efficient XML document parsing.

Associating `XmlTextReader` with the `XmlNameTable` Class

`XmlTextReader` can also be associated with the `XmlNameTable` class to increase efficiency even more in certain scenarios. The `XmlNameTable` class is capable of holding a table of atomized string values and is useful when the same element, namespace, or attribute name is compared multiple times while the XML document stream is being read. Instead of performing costly string comparisons, `XmlNameTable` can do object pointer comparisons. For example, if a conditional check is done on a particular namespace Uniform Resource Identifier (URI) many times during a parsing operation, the URI can be added to the `XmlNameTable` object, as shown here, to increase efficiency:

```
XmlTextReader reader = new XmlTextReader(url);
object myUri = reader.NameTable.Add("http://www.SomeServer.com/namespaceURI");
```

As the stream of XML tokens is read, a direct object pointer comparison can then be made against the `XmlNameTable` object:

```
if (reader.NamespaceURI == myUri) {
  //Do special processing if the two URI values are equal
}
```

This method of testing for a URI value is opposed to the following less-efficient way of doing the same conditional test:

```
if (reader.NamespaceURI == "http://www.SomeServer.com/namespaceURI") {
  //Do special processing if the two URI values are equal
}
```

5. Validating XML Documents Against XML Schemas

XML provides a very useful and extensible framework for marking up data that can be exchanged between applications in a platform-neutral manner. However, the ability to create your own XML element and attribute names does come with a price. This price comes into play when you want to exchange XML documents with other people or applications not familiar with your document structure.

If you've worked with MSXML3, you're probably familiar with using the `validateOnParse` property or the `validate()` method to validate XML documents against DTDs or XML Data-Reduced (XDR) schemas. With the `validateOnParse` property, a document can be validated as it is parsed into the DOM structure, while the `validate()` method allows for runtime validation of a document that has already been parsed and loaded. Although validating XML documents in .NET applications is quite a bit different from doing so using the MSXML3 mechanism, the manner in which documents are validated is much more efficient and flexible now.

The validation process involves `XmlTextReader` because it provides fast, forward-only, non-cached access to XML documents. However, `XmlTextReader` doesn't have any properties or methods that can handle the validation process. Instead, `XmlTextReader` is used in conjunction with another class, named `XmlValidatingReader`. This class inherits from the abstract `XmlReader` class just as the `XmlTextReader` does. In fact, almost all the properties and methods found in `XmlTextReader` are also found in `XmlValidatingReader`. However, `XmlValidatingReader` is designed specifically to validate XML documents or read XML fragments.

`XmlValidatingReader` has three different constructors that can be used to initialize it. The first one accepts an `XmlTextReader` object as an argument, whereas the remaining two accept several different arguments and handle XML fragments, such as those returned from SQL Server 2000. To validate XML documents, you'll want to use the first constructor, as shown here:

```
XmlValidatingReader vReader = new XmlValidatingReader(reader);
```

The XML document that is parsed by the `reader` object (an `XmlTextReader` object) is used by `XmlValidatingReader` as it performs comparisons of the XML document against DTDs or schemas.

After `XmlValidatingReader` is instantiated, the type of validation to perform must be specified. This is accomplished by using the `ValidationType` property along with the `ValidationType` enumeration. The different members of this enumeration are shown in Table 8.3.

Table 8.3 `ValidationType` Enumerations

Member Name	Description
Auto	If `XmlValidatingReader`'s `ValidationType` property is not set, this member will be used as the default. The .NET SDK lists the following rules about the Auto member:
	If there is no DTD or schema, the Auto member will parse the XML without validation.
	If there is a DTD defined in a <!DOCTYPE ...> declaration, the Auto member will load the DTD and process the DTD declarations such that default attributes and general entities will be made available. General entities are only loaded and parsed if they are used (expanded).
	If there is no <!DOCTYPE ...> declaration but there is an XSD `schemaLocation` attribute, the Auto member will load and process those XSD schemas and it will return any default attributes defined in those schemas.

Table 8.3 Continued

Member Name	Description
	If there is no `<!DOCTYPE ...>` declaration and no XSD or XDR schema information, the parser is a nonvalidating parser (for example, `ValidationType=ValidationType.None`).
	If there is no `<!DOCTYPE ...>` declaration and no XSD `schemaLocation` attribute, but there are some namespaces using the MSXML "x-schema:" URN prefix, the Auto member will load and process those schemas and it will return any default attributes defined in those schemas.
	If there is no `<!DOCTYPE ...>` declaration but there is a schema declaration (`<schema>`), the Auto member will validate using the inline schema.
DTD	Allows for validation against a DTD only.
None	Creates the equivalent of a nonvalidating parser. No validation errors will be thrown when this member is used.
Schema	Validates against XSD schemas.
XDR	Validates against XDR schemas.

Once `XmlValidatingReader` has been instantiated and its properties have been set, the reader must be hooked up to an event handler that will be called if an error occurs during the validation process. In .NET, event handlers can be attached to an object by using the += syntax and subtracted by using the -= syntax. `XmlValidatingReader` has one event, named `ValidationEventHandler`, that can be attached in order to catch errors that may arise. Attaching to the event involves using the += syntax along with specifying the callback handler that should be called if a validation error occurs. Once the event handler is attached, the `Read()` method is called on the `XmlValidatingReader` object to start validating the XML document. Here's an example:

```
vReader.ValidationEventHandler +=
                    new ValidationEventHandler(this.ValidationCallBack);
// Parse through XML
while (vReader.Read()){}
```

The callback handler, named `ValidationCallBack()`, is shown in the following code segment (note that an external class with specific error-handling capabilities could be referenced as well):

```
private void ValidationCallBack(object sender, ValidationEventArgs args) {
    //Deal with any errors here
}
```

Listing 8.5.1 shows how to use the `XmlValidatingReader` class along with its properties, methods, and event handler to validate against an XSD Schema.

Listing 8.5.1 Using `XmlValidatingReader` to Validate an XML Document

```
 1: <%@ Import Namespace="System.Xml" %>
 2: <%@ Import Namespace="System.Xml.Schema" %>
 3: <%@ Import Namespace="System.Text" %>
 4: <%@ Import Namespace="System.IO" %>
 5: <script language="C#" runat="server">
 6:     private void Page_Load(Object sender, EventArgs e) {
 7:         bool status;
 8:         string xmlFilePath = Server.MapPath("golfersNotValid(XSD).xml");
 9:         string logFile = Server.MapPath("validationErrors.log");
10:         Validator objValidate = new Validator(xmlFilePath,logFile,true);
11:         status = objValidate.Validate();
12:         if (status) {
13:             Response.Write("Validation of golfersNotValid(XSD).xml " +
14:                         "was SUCCESSFUL!");
15:             //Call method to process XML document
16:         } else {
17:             Response.Write("Validation of golfersNotValid(XSD).xml " +
18:                         " failed! Check the log file for information "+
19:                         " on the failure.");
20:         }
21:     }
22:     public class Validator {
23:         bool _valid = true;
24:         bool _logError = true;
25:         string _logFile = "";
26:         string _xmlFilePath = "";
27:         XmlTextReader xmlReader = null;
28:         XmlValidatingReader vReader = null;
29:
30:         public Validator(string xmlFilePath,string logFile,
31:                         bool logError) {
32:             xmlFilePath = xmlFilePath;
33:             logFile = logFile;
34:             logError = logError;
35:         }
36:
37:         public bool Validate() {
38:             try {
39:                 xmlReader = new XmlTextReader(xmlFilePath);
40:                 vReader = new XmlValidatingReader(xmlReader);
41:                 vReader.ValidationType = ValidationType.Schema;
42:                 vReader.ValidationEventHandler +=
43:                     new ValidationEventHandler(this.ValidationCallBack);
44:                 // Parse through XML
45:                 while (vReader.Read()){}
46:             } catch {
47:                 valid = false;
48:             } finally {  //Close our readers
49:                 if (xmlReader.ReadState != ReadState.Closed) {
50:                     xmlReader.Close();
51:                 }
52:                 if (vReader.ReadState != ReadState.Closed) {
53:                     vReader.Close();
```

Listing 8.5.1 Continued

```
54:            }
55:        }
56:        return _valid;
57:    } //Validate()
58:
59:    private void ValidationCallBack(object sender,
60:                                      ValidationEventArgs args) {
61:        valid = false;   //hit callback so document has a problem
62:        DateTime today = DateTime.Now;
63:        StreamWriter writer = null;
64:        try {
65:            if (_logError) {
66:                writer = new StreamWriter(_logFile,true,Encoding.ASCII);
67:                writer.WriteLine("Validation error in: " +_xmlFilePath);
68:                writer.WriteLine();
69:                writer.WriteLine(args.Message + " " + today.ToString());
70:                writer.WriteLine();
71:                if (xmlReader.LineNumber > 0) {
72:                    writer.WriteLine("Line: "+ xmlReader.LineNumber +
73:                                     " Position: " +
74:                                     xmlReader.LinePosition);
75:                }
76:                writer.WriteLine();
77:            }
78:            writer.Flush();
79:        }
80:        catch {}
81:        finally {
82:            if (writer != null) {
83:                writer.Close();
84:            }
85:        }
86:    } //ValidationCallBack()
87: } //Validator
88: </script>
```

The code in Listing 8.5.1 takes care of passing an `XmlTextReader` object to an instance of the `XmlValidatingReader` class. It then calls the `Read()` method of `XmlValidatingReader` to begin parsing the XML document. As it does this, the validating reader compares what it finds in the XML document to an XML Schema document. If anything invalid is found, the `ValidationCallBack()` method is called and any errors are logged to a file.

6. Creating XML Documents Using the `XmlTextWriter` Class

Up to this point in the chapter, you've seen how the `XmlTextReader` class can be used along with different supporting classes to parse XML in a forward-only, noncached manner. In this section, you'll see how this same concept can be used to dynamically create XML documents. Later in the chapter, you'll see how the same thing can be done using DOM classes.

The `XmlTextWriter` class performs the task of writing to an XML document in a forward-only/cursor-style manner. Although all the properties and methods associated with the class won't be listed here, they are extremely simple to use once you've seen an example. To introduce you to how the `XmlTextWriter` class works, Listing 8.6.1 shows how to use several of its properties and methods.

Listing 8.6.1 Generating XML with the `XmlTextWriter` Class

```
 1: <%@ Import Namespace="System.Xml" %>
 2: <script language="VB" runat="server">
 3:     public sub Page_Load(Src as Object, e as EventArgs)
 4:       Dim xmlDoc as string = Server.MapPath("xmltextwriter.xml")
 5:       Dim writer as XmlTextWriter
 6:       try
 7:           writer = new XmlTextWriter(xmlDoc,Encoding.UTF8)
 8:           writer.Formatting = Formatting.Indented
 9:           writer.WriteStartDocument(true)
10:           writer.WriteComment("XML Nodes added using the XmlTextWriter")
11:           writer.WriteStartElement("customers")
12:              writer.WriteStartElement("customer")
13:                 writer.WriteAttributeString("id","123456789")
14:                 writer.WriteStartElement("info")
15:                    writer.WriteStartElement("name")
16:                       writer.WriteAttributeString("firstName","John")
17:                       writer.WriteAttributeString("lastName","Doe")
18:                    writer.WriteEndElement()
19:                    writer.WriteStartElement("address")
20:                       writer.WriteAttributeString("street","1234 Anywhere")
21:                       writer.WriteAttributeString("city","Tempe")
22:                       writer.WriteAttributeString("state","Arizona")
23:                       writer.WriteAttributeString("zip","85255")
24:                    writer.WriteEndElement()
25:                 writer.WriteEndElement() 'info
26:              writer.WriteEndElement() 'customer
27:           writer.WriteEndElement() 'customers
28:           writer.Flush()
29:           writer.Close()
30:           Dim doc as XmlDocument = new XmlDocument()
31:           doc.Load(xmlDoc)
32:           Response.ContentType = "text/xml"
33:           doc.Save(Response.Output)
34:
35:       catch exp as Exception
36:           Response.Write(exp.ToString())
37:
38:       finally
39:           if (NOT writer is Nothing) then
40:               writer.Close()
41:           end if
42:       end try
43:     end sub
44: </script>
```

The `XmlTextWriter` constructor accepts several different arguments. This example passes in a document name (`xmltextwriter.xml`) to which all output can be written. It also passes in the desired encoding type for the document by using the `Encoding` enumeration. Once the class is instantiated, several methods, including `WriteStartElement()`, `WriteEndElement()`, and `WriteAttributeString()`, are called that allow for customization over what is included in the XML document.

The `XmlTextWriter` class is very useful when non-XML documents need to be converted to XML. For example, the flat file from the beginning of the chapter (also shown here) could be converted to XML quickly and efficiently using this class:

```
Elbow Joint,12930430,6,25,06/28/2000,1238 Van Buren,B2B Supply,1111236894,Walters
Valve,39405938,3,40,06/20/2000,4568 Arizona Ave.,A+ Supply,2221236894,Tammy
PVC,234954048,6,20,06/14/2000,49032 S. 51,A+ Supply,2221236894,Walters
```

Listing 8.6.2 provides an example of a C# module that can be called from an ASP.NET page or other .NET application to handle converting the flat file to XML.

Listing 8.6.2 Converting CSV Flat Files to XML with the `XmlTextWriter` Class (`FlatFileModule.cs`)

```
 1: namespace FlatFile.Converter {
 2:     using System;
 3:     using System.Xml;
 4:     using System.IO;
 5:     using System.Text;
 6:
 7:     /// <summary>
 8:     ///         CSV to XML Converter
 9:     /// </summary>
10:     public class PartsCSVToXml {
11:         string _csvPath;
12:         XmlTextWriter writer;
13:         int counter = 0;
14:         public PartsCSVToXml(string csvPath,string xmlPath) {
15:             _csvPath = csvPath;
16:             writer = new XmlTextWriter(xmlPath,Encoding.UTF8);
17:         }
18:         public bool Convert() {
19:             FileStream fs = null;
20:             StreamReader reader = null;
21:             string csvLine;
22:             try {
23:                 writer.WriteStartDocument();
24:                 writer.WriteStartElement("supplies");
25:                 fs = new FileStream(_csvPath,FileMode.Open,
26:                                     FileAccess.Read);
27:                 reader = new StreamReader(fs);
28:                 while ((csvLine = reader.ReadLine()) != null) {
29:                     string[] tokens = csvLine.Split(new char[]{','});
30:                     counter++;
```

Listing 8.6.2 Continued

```
31:                    GenerateXml(tokens);
32:                }
33:                writer.WriteEndElement(); //Close supplies element
34:                return true;
35:            }
36:            catch {
37:                return false;
38:            }
39:            finally {
40:                if (fs != null) {
41:                    fs.Close();
42:                }
43:                if (reader != null) {
44:                    reader.Close();
45:                }
46:                if (writer != null) {
47:                    writer.Close();
48:                }
49:            }
50:        }
51:        private void GenerateXml(string[] tokens) {
52:            if (tokens[0] != null) {
53:                writer.WriteStartElement("item");
54:                writer.WriteAttributeString("supplier",
55:                                             counter.ToString());
56:                writer.WriteStartElement("description");
57:                    writer.WriteString(tokens[0].ToString());
58:                writer.WriteEndElement();
59:                writer.WriteStartElement("partID");
60:                    writer.WriteString(tokens[1].ToString());
61:                writer.WriteEndElement();
62:                writer.WriteStartElement("numberInStock");
63:                    writer.WriteString(tokens[2].ToString());
64:                writer.WriteEndElement();
65:                writer.WriteStartElement("numberOnOrder");
66:                    writer.WriteString(tokens[3].ToString());
67:                writer.WriteEndElement();
68:                writer.WriteStartElement("deliveryDate");
69:                    writer.WriteString(tokens[4].ToString());
70:                writer.WriteEndElement();
71:                writer.WriteStartElement("supplier");
72:                    writer.WriteStartElement("street");
73:                        writer.WriteString(tokens[5].ToString());
74:                    writer.WriteEndElement();
75:                    writer.WriteStartElement("company");
76:                        writer.WriteString(tokens[6].ToString());
77:                    writer.WriteEndElement();
78:                    writer.WriteStartElement("phone");
79:                        writer.WriteString(tokens[7].ToString());
80:                    writer.WriteEndElement();
81:                    writer.WriteEndElement(); //supplier
82:                writer.WriteStartElement("orderedBy");
```

Listing 8.6.2 *Continued*

```
83:                         writer.WriteString(tokens[8].ToString());
84:                     writer.WriteEndElement();
85:                 writer.WriteEndElement(); //item
86:             }
87:         }
88:     }
89: }
```

Executing this code results in the XML document shown in Figure 8.1.

FIGURE 8.1
Converting flat files to XML.

7. Working with XML Documents Using the Document Object Model (DOM)

You may not realize it, but you're probably already familiar with the concept of the DOM. If you've done any type of Dynamic HTML (DHTML) development in Internet Explorer 4 or higher, you have used a Document Object Model that was created by the browser. You may have used it to change a heading color or dynamically show or hide specific content. When a browser loads a page in IE4+, the various parts that make up the page are loaded into a structure and placed in memory. Accessing this structure using DHTML is as easy as knowing what part of the document you want to gain access to. By using the `window.document.all` collection, you have access to all the HTML page's objects and content through client-side code written in JavaScript (officially called *ECMAScript*; `http://www.ecma.ch/ecma1/stand/ecma-262.htm`) or VBScript. For example, changing the text color of a particular section located within a `<div>` tag having an `ID` attribute equal to `"mainContent"` can be accomplished with the following code in IE4+:

```
<html>
    <head>
        <Script Language="JavaScript">
            function changeColor(color,div) {
                window.document.all(div).style.color=color
            }
        </Script>
    </head>

    <body bgcolor="#FFFFFF">
        <div id="mainContent"
         onMouseOver="changeColor('#ff0000','mainContent')"
         onMouseOut="changeColor('#000000','mainContent')"
        >
            Testing this out
        </div>
    </body>
</html>
```

If you have done much DHTML programming, you're probably painfully aware that the DOM used in IE4+ is very different from the one used in Netscape Navigator 4. Unfortunately, the two browsers are so different that a page that works perfectly fine in one is very unlikely to work in the other. The W3C recognized the problems caused by inconsistencies between DOMs and issued a DOM Level 1 recommendation back in 1998. More information about this can be found at `http://www.w3.org/TR/REC-DOM-Level-1/introduction.html`. Since releasing the DOM Level 1 recommendation, the W3C has also released DOM Level 2 and is currently starting work on DOM Level 3. The W3C states the following:

> "The DOM Level 2 is made of a set of core interfaces to create and manipulate the structure and contents of a document and a set of optional modules. These modules contain specialized interfaces dedicated to XML, HTML, an abstract view, generic style sheets, Cascading Style Sheets, Events, traversing the document structure, and a Range object."

Note

Many of the concepts mentioned in the W3C statement are new additions to the DOM specification. Some of these include a style sheet object model, namespace support, an event model, and support for text ranges. More information about the DOM Level 2 specification can be found at `http://www.w3.org/TR/DOM-Level-2/`.

So what does all this have to do with XML, you ask? Actually, everything. Although the DOM created by the browser isn't exactly the same due to form collections, image collections, and so on, many of the same concepts apply to an XML document's DOM. When an XML document is first loaded and parsed, an internal representation (similar to a tree structure) of the document is placed in memory. This structure is based on the concept of nodes, with the root node being followed by other children nodes. As with the DOM the browser creates, the DOM created by a DOM-compatible XML parser is programmatically accessible using classes that help you access specific nodes within the DOM structure. Once these classes and their associated properties and methods are understood, virtually any node within an XML document can be accessed, updated, inserted, or deleted.

To gain a better understanding of how the DOM works, Figure 8.2 shows a visual representation of the following XML document's DOM:

```xml
<?xml version="1.0"?>
<golfer>
        <name>Dan Wahlin</name>
        <courses>
            <course>Pinetop Lakes CC</course>
            <course>Ocotillo</course>
        </courses>
</golfer>
```

FIGURE 8.2
A representation of the Document Object Model (DOM).

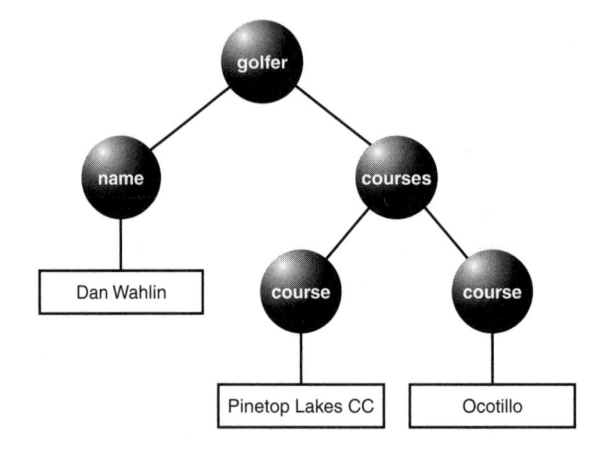

As shown in Figure 8.2, the DOM is composed of the various items found within the XML document. Each of these items is a node in the DOM structure. This means that the text under the two course nodes is actually represented in the DOM by a text node. The example shown is very basic and doesn't include many of the nodes that could exist in a given XML DOM (attribute nodes, comment nodes, and so on), but it does give you a visual overview of how the DOM is structured.

The next sections explains how you can gain access to an XML document's DOM, both on the server side with ASP.NET and on the client side with JavaScript. Before covering those topics, however, let's first revisit the differences between in-memory and forward-only parsing.

In-Memory Versus Forward Only Cursor-Based Parsing

The Document Object Model (DOM) is very efficient at allowing access to specific XML document nodes. It allows complete flexibility in updating, inserting, deleting, and moving nodes. However, as with most things, this power does come with a price. One of the problems associated with the DOM concerns memory consumption. Because an entire XML document's structure is loaded into memory after being parsed, a large document could potentially consume a lot of memory. A smarter implementation of an XML DOM might behave more like a database system and page nodes in and out from disk to conserve memory. In fact, some object database vendors have put DOM wrappers on their systems, thereby achieving this sort of hybrid XML database.

Earlier in the chapter, you saw how the DOM memory limitations can be overcome by using the `XmlTextReader` class (and helper classes). Rather than loading the entire document into memory, as with the DOM, the reader processes one node at a time by creating a stream that XML tokens can be read from. This forward-only stream means that when the document's root element is reached, very little data is buffered in memory at any given time. When a child node is reached, its ancestors have been parsed, but they are not in memory and going back to them is not an option. This type of functionality allows one item at a time to be checked and processed rather than everything being loaded into memory. It provides a low-memory alternative that is capable of working with large XML documents.

So when should you use the DOM instead of the forward-only parsing model exhibited by the `XmlTextReader` class? Unfortunately, the answer to this question isn't a simple one because each application has unique requirements. In general, XML documents that simply need to be read and not updated should leverage the speed and efficiency provided by the `XmlTextReader` class. Doing this helps ensure that the application remains scalable. On the other hand, an XML document that needs modification in the form of updates, inserts, or deletes will benefit from the flexibility of having the document's structure in memory and should therefore use classes associated with the DOM. Although this is a less-scalable solution, it is certainly needed in many situations. Let's take a look at some of the classes that can be used to manipulate the DOM.

DOM Classes

The DOM support found in .NET is based on the W3C DOM Level 2 Core XML specification (http://www.w3.org/TR/DOM-Level-2/core.html). Understanding the classes that provide this support as well as how they work together is very straightforward once you learn a few basics. To start things off, examine the classes listed in Table 8.4.

Table 8.4 DOM Classes

Class Name	Description
XmlNode	The `XmlNode` class is the principle object used in the DOM. It is an abstract class, meaning that it is not instantiated directly but is implemented and extended by many other classes in the `System.Xml` namespace. It is used to manipulate a particular node type located within an XML document or to access a node's attributes.
XmlElement	The `XmlElement` class is used with Element-type nodes within an XML document.

Table 8.4 Continued

Class Name	Description
XmlAttribute	The `XmlAttribute` class is used with Attribute-type nodes within an XML document.
XmlDocument	The `XmlDocument` class is used to access XML documents and identify the root element. It acts as the gateway to an XML document's DOM. Instantiating an instance of the `XmlDocument` class in ASP.NET is accomplished by the following code:
	`XmlDocument xmlDoc = new XmlDocument();`
	The `XmlDocument` class can also be used to create any node that can exist in an XML document. This will be shown later.
XmlNodeList	The `XmlNodeList` class provides access to a collection of nodes that can be iterated through. Calls to the `XmlDocument` class's `ChildNodes` property or `GetElementsByTagName()` method return an `XmlNodeList` object.
XmlNamedNodeMap	The `XmlNamedNodeMap` class provides access to a collection of nodes (attributes, for instance) that can be called by name or iterated through on a given `XmlNode` object.
XmlNodeReader	The `XmlNodeReader` class can be used to turn a DOM structure into a stream.
XMLHTTPRequest	Although *not* part of the `System.Xml` namespace, the `XMLHttpRequest` object (installed with IE5+) can be used for sending and receiving XML content over HTTP from the client browser.

Through instantiating the classes shown in Table 8.4, the DOM can be accessed and manipulated as desired. In order for you to better understand how some of these classes can be used, here's a step-by-step look at the process of creating the DOM structure:

1. An XML document is loaded using the `XmlDocument` class:

   ```
   XmlDocument doc = new XmlDocument();
   doc.Load("golfers.xml");
   ```

2. The root node is found and assigned to an `XmlNode` object:

   ```
   XmlNode node = doc.DocumentElement;
   ```

3. The child nodes of the root node are accessed and assigned to a `XmlNodeList` collection class:

   ```
   XmlNodeList nodeList = node.ChildNodes;
   ```

4. While you're working with a particular node, the node's attributes are assigned to an `XmlNamedNodeMap` collection class:

   ```
   XmlNameNodeMap namedNodeMap = node.Attributes;
   ```

Adding Nodes to an XML Document Using the DOM

Adding nodes into an empty or existing XML document using the DOM is a fairly straightforward process. This task can be accomplished by using the XmlDocument class because it exposes several different methods that can be used to create any node that can exist in an XML document. Listing 8.7.1 shows a simple example of creating elements and attributes and then adding them into a DOM structure.

Listing 8.7.1 Adding Nodes to an XML Document

```
 1: <%@ Import Namespace="System.Xml" %>
 2: <script language="VB" runat="Server">
 3:    public sub Page_Load(sender as object, e as EventArgs)
 4:        Dim sXML as string = "<?xml version=""1.0""?><root><testA>"
 5:        sXML += "<testChild>Testing!</testChild></testA></root>"
 6:        Dim oDocument as XmlDocument= new XmlDocument()
 7:        oDocument.LoadXml(sXML)
 8:        Dim oRoot as XmlNode = oDocument.DocumentElement
 9:        try
10:            Dim oElement1 as XmlElement = oDocument.CreateElement("testB")
11:            oElement1.SetAttribute("testBAtt","Testing B")
12:            Dim oElement2 as XmlElement = oDocument.CreateElement("testC")
13:            oElement2.AppendChild(oDocument.CreateTextNode("Text Node"))
14:            oElement2.SetAttribute("testCAtt","Testing C")
15:            oRoot.AppendChild(oElement1)
16:            oRoot.AppendChild(oElement2)
17:
18:        catch exc as Exception
19:            Response.Write(exc.ToString())
20:        end try
21:        Response.ContentType ="text/xml"
22:        oDocument.Save(Response.Output)
23:    end sub
24: </script>
```

The code starts by loading a string into the DOM using the LoadXml() method of XmlDocument (line 7). After this string is loaded, the root node is identified (line 8) and assigned to a variable named oRoot. From there, two XmlElement-type nodes are created and attributes are added to the nodes using the SetAttribute() method (lines 10–14). A Text node is also added to the oElement2 node. These nodes are then appended to the root node via a call to the AppendChild() method. Many different types of nodes can be added to the DOM using similar coding techniques.

Recursion in the DOM

One of the most powerful features of the DOM is *recursion*. Because the DOM provides a hierarchical structure that can be accessed programmatically, you can parse the DOM tree from top to bottom by calling methods recursively. This allows a lot of work to be done in relatively few lines of code. Listing 8.7.2 shows how different nodes in the DOM can be "walked" through programmatically.

Listing 8.7.2 Walking the DOM Using Recursive Techniques

```vb
 1: <%@ Import Namespace="System.Text" %>
 2: <%@ Import Namespace="System.Xml" %>
 3: <script language="VB" runat="server">
 4:     public class XmlDocumentTestVB
 5:         Dim output as StringBuilder = new StringBuilder()
 6:         Dim indent as integer = 1
 7:
 8:         public function ParseDoc(xmlFilePath as string) as string
 9:             Dim xmlReader as XmlTextReader
10:
11:             try
12:                 xmlReader = new XmlTextReader(xmlFilePath)
13:                 Dim xmlDoc as XmlDocument = new XmlDocument()
14:                 xmlDoc.Load(xmlReader)
15:                 Dim oNode as XmlNode = xmlDoc.DocumentElement
16:
17:                 Call WriteNodeName(oNode,0)
18:                 Dim oNodeList as XmlNodeList = oNode.ChildNodes
19:                 Dim node as XmlNode
20:                 Dim oCurrentNode as XmlNode
21:                 for each node in oNodeList
22:                     oCurrentNode = node
23:                     if (oCurrentNode.HasChildNodes) then
24:                         WriteNodeName(oCurrentNode,indent)
25:                         WalkTheTree(oCurrentNode)
26:                         indent = indent - 1
27:                     else
28:                         WriteNodeName(oCurrentNode,indent)
29:                     end if
30:                 next
31:
32:             catch exp as Exception
33:                 output.Append(exp.ToString())
34:             finally
35:                 if (NOT xmlReader Is Nothing) then
36:                     xmlReader.Close()
37:                 end if
38:             end try
39:             return output.ToString()
40:         end function
41:
42:         private sub WalkTheTree(oNodeToWalk as XmlNode)
43:             indent = indent + 1
44:             Dim j as integer
45:             Dim oNodeList as XmlNodeList = oNodeToWalk.ChildNodes
46:             Dim oCurrentNode as XmlNode
47:             for j=0 to oNodeList.Count -1
48:                 oCurrentNode = oNodeList(j)
49:                 if (oCurrentNode.HasChildNodes) then
50:                     Call WriteNodeName(oCurrentNode,indent)
51:                     Call WalkTheTree(oCurrentNode)
52:                     indent = indent - 1
```

Listing 8.7.2   Continued

```
53:                    else
54:                        Call WriteNodeName(oCurrentNode,indent)
55:                    end if
56:                next
57:            end sub
58:
59:            private sub WriteNodeName(node as XmlNode,iIndent as integer)
60:                Dim h as integer= 0
61:                Dim k as integer
62:                for k=0 to (iIndent * 10)
63:                    output.Append(" ")
64:                next
65:                if (node.NodeType = XmlNodeType.Text) then ' Text node
66:                    output.Append("<font color='#ff0000'>" & node.Value & _
67:                                "</font><br>")
68:                else
69:                    if (node.Attributes.Count > 0) then
70:                        Dim oNamedNodeMap as XmlNamedNodeMap = node.Attributes
71:                        output.Append("<b>" & node.Name & "</b> (")
72:                        Dim att as XmlAttribute
73:                        for each att in oNamedNodeMap
74:                            if (h<>0) then output.Append("  ")
75:                            h = h + 1
76:                            output.Append("<i>" & att.Name & "</i>=""" & _
77:                                        att.Value & """")
78:                        next
79:                        output.Append(")<br>")
80:                    else
81:                        output.Append("<b>" & node.Name & "</b><br>")
82:                    end if
83:                end if ' end if
84:            end sub ' WriteNodeName
85:        end class
86:
87:        public sub Page_Load(sender as Object, e as EventArgs)
88:            Dim xmlFilePath as string = Server.MapPath("golfers.xml")
89:            Dim xmlDocument as XmlDocumentTestVB = new XmlDocumentTestVB()
90:            xml.InnerHtml = xmlDocument.ParseDoc(xmlFilePath)
91:        end sub
92: </script>
93: <html>
94:     <body>
95:         <font size="5" color="#02027a">Working with XML Objects</font>
96:         <p />
97:         <div id="xml" runat="server" />
98:     </body>
99: </html>
```

The code starts off by loading the XML document into the DOM (lines 12-14) via an **XmlTextReader**. Once the document is loaded into memory, the root node is accessed and its node name is written out. The code then proceeds to check if the root node has any child nodes. If it does, they are assigned to an **XmlNodeList** type variable named **oNodeList** (line

18). Any nodes within `oNodeList` are iterated through in lines 21-30. During the iterative process, each node is examined and checked to see if it has any child nodes of its own. If it does, a method named `WalkTheTree()` is called to process these child nodes. The `WalkTheTree()` method is the workhorse of the ASP.NET page(lines 42–57). It accepts a node as an argument and then checks whether the node has child nodes of its own. If it does, this method calls itself recursively until all the child nodes have been processed.

Looking through this code listing, you'll see how several different DOM classes can be used, including `XmlTextReader`, `XmlDocument`, `XmlNode`, `XmlNodeList`, `XmlNamedNodeMap`, and `XmlAttribute`. Figure 8.3 shows the results of using these classes to walk through the DOM structure.

FIGURE 8.3
Using recursion to walk the DOM tree.

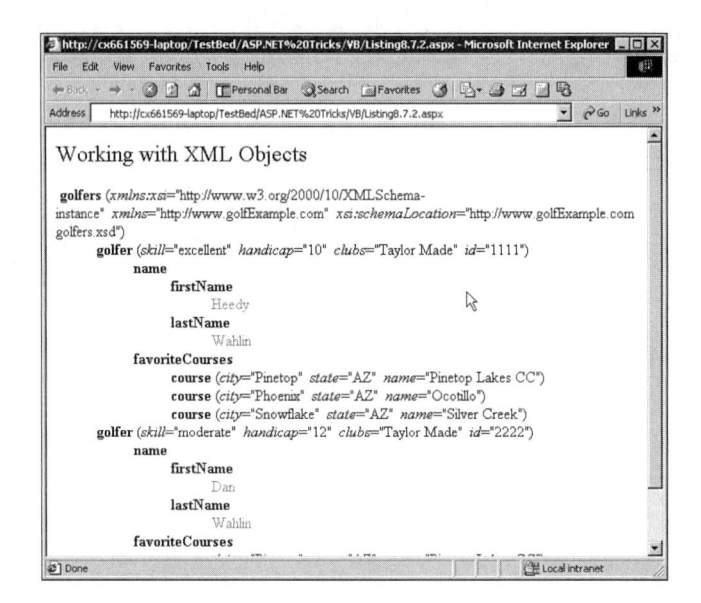

Selecting Nodes in the DOM Using XPath

`XmlDocument` has two methods—`SelectNodes()` and `SelectSingleNode()`—that can be very useful in selecting specific XML nodes using XPath statements. Although a full discussion on XPath is beyond the scope of this chapter, you should know that it provides a way to programmatically access any node in an XML document.

> **Note**
> More information about the XPath language can be obtained from `http://www.w3.org/TR/xpath`.

Listing 8.7.3 shows how the `SelectNodes()` and `SelectSingleNode()` methods can be used to access nodes in the DOM using XPath statements.

Listing 8.7.3   Accessing DOM Nodes Using XPath

```
 1: <%@ Import Namespace="System.Xml" %>
 2: <script language="VB" runat="Server">
 3:     public sub Page_Load(sender as Object, e as EventArgs)
 4:         Dim filePath as string = Server.MapPath("requests.xml")
 5:         Dim i as integer
 6:         Dim doc as XmlDocument = new XmlDocument()
 7:         doc.Load(filePath)
 8:         Dim xpath as string = "//contactName"
 9:         Dim contactNodes as XmlNodeList = doc.SelectNodes(xpath)
10:         Dim count as integer = contactNodes.Count
11:         Response.Write("<b>Using SelectNodes()</b><br />")
12:         for i=0 to count -1
13:             Response.Write(contactNodes.Item(i).Name & " = ")
14:             Response.Write(contactNodes.Item(i).InnerText & "<br />")
15:         next
16:
17:         xpath = "//request[@id='462001|32633|PM']/contactName"
18:         Response.Write("<p /><b>Using SelectSingleNode()</b><br />")
19:         Dim contactNode as XmlNode = doc.SelectSingleNode(xpath)
20:         if (NOT contactNode Is Nothing) then
21:            Response.Write(contactNode.Name & " = " & contactNode.InnerText)
22:         end if
23:     end sub
24: </script>
```

You can see that the DOM offers a lot of powerful ways to access and manipulate nodes in an XML document. In cases where XML documents need updating, you'll want to get to know the different DOM classes and their associated properties and methods well.

8. Transforming XML Documents with XSLT

XML represents an excellent mechanism for marking up data in a platform-neutral manner. However, what if the data marked up in an XML document needs to be transformed into a different format to be viewed more easily? The W3C realized early on that for XML to reach its full potential, it would need to be transformed into other structures and formats. Therefore, the W3C has developed a language named *Extensible Stylesheet Language Transformations* (XSLT) to perform this task.

With the release of XSLT in November of 1999, an XML-based language became available that could transform XML into HTML, Wireless Markup Language (WML), flat file, EDI, other forms of XML, and many other structures. XSLT is a template-based language that works in conjunction with the XPath language to allow XML documents to be transformed into a variety of structures. The ability to transform XML using XSLT makes it perfect for applications that require different views of the same data. Although a full discussion of the XSLT language will not be given here, Listing 8.8.1 shows a simple XSLT style sheet that could be used to transform XML into HTML.

Listing 8.8.1 An XSLT Style Sheet

```xml
 1: <?xml version="1.0" encoding="UTF-8" ?>
 2: <xsl:stylesheet xmlns:xsl="http://www.w3.org/1999/XSL/Transform" version="1.0">
 3:     <xsl:output method="html" indent="yes"/>
 4:     <xsl:template match="/">
 5:         <html>
 6:             <body>
 7:                 <xsl:apply-templates />
 8:             </body>
 9:         </html>
10:     </xsl:template>
11:     <xsl:template match="golfers">
12:         <b>Golfer Names:</b>
13:         <xsl:apply-templates />
14:     </xsl:template>
15:     <xsl:template match="golfer">
16:         <br />
17:         <xsl:number format="1" />.
18:         <xsl:value-of select="name/firstName" />
19:     </xsl:template>
20: </xsl:stylesheet>
```

When this XSLT style sheet is used to transform the XML document in Listing 8.8.2, the HTML document shown in Listing 8.8.3 results.

Listing 8.8.2 The XML Document to Transform to EDI

```xml
 1: <?xml version="1.0" encoding="UTF-8"?>
 2: <golfers>
 3:     <golfer skill="excellent" handicap="10" clubs="Taylor Made" id="1111">
 4:         <name>
 5:             <firstName>Kevin</firstName>
 6:             <lastName>Trainer</lastName>
 7:         </name>
 8:         <favoriteCourses>
 9:             <course city="Pinetop" state="AZ" name="Pinetop Lakes CC"/>
10:             <course city="Phoenix" state="AZ" name="Ocotillo"/>
11:             <course city="Snowflake" state="AZ" name="Silver Creek"/>
12:         </favoriteCourses>
13:     </golfer>
14:     <golfer skill="moderate" handicap="12" clubs="Taylor Made" id="2222">
15:         <name>
16:             <firstName>Dan</firstName>
17:             <lastName>Wahlin</lastName>
18:         </name>
19:         <favoriteCourses>
20:             <course city="Pinetop" state="AZ" name="Pinetop Lakes CC"/>
21:             <course city="Pinetop" state="AZ" name="White Mountain CC"/>
22:             <course city="Springville" state="UT" name="Hobble Creek"/>
23:         </favoriteCourses>
24:     </golfer>
25: </golfers>
```

Listing 8.8.3 The Result of the XML Transformation

```
<html>
    <body>
        <b>Golfer Names:</b>
        <br>
        1. Kevin
        <br>
        2. Dan
    </body>
</html>
```

So how does the data within the XML document shown in Listing 8.8.2 actually get transformed into the HTML structure shown in Listing 8.8.3 using XSLT? Figure 8.4 shows the different pieces involved in the transformation process.

FIGURE 8.4
The transformation process.

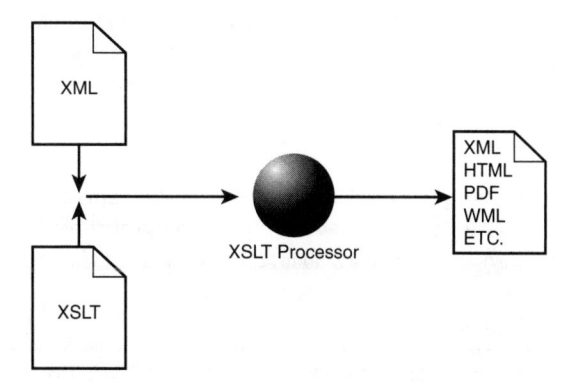

Looking at this figure, you can see that at the center of all XML transformations is an XSLT processor. The processor accepts an XML document and an XSLT document as inputs. By matching up nodes found in the XML document with templates in the XSLT document, the XSLT processor transforms the XML into the desired output structure. The XSLT style sheet shown in Listing 8.8.1 was designed to generate HTML. It can easily be changed to generate a variety of other structures as well. You may be wondering where you get an XSLT processor. Fortunately, the .NET platform provides a robust XSLT processor that can be used in ASP.NET applications to transform XML.

XSLT Classes in the .NET Platform

The `System.Xml` assembly contains different namespaces and classes that can be used with XSLT transformations. Table 8.5 provides a description of each of these classes.

Table 8.5 NET Classes Used in XSL Transformations

Class	Description
XmlDocument	The XmlDocument class implements the IXPathNavigable interface and extends the XmlNode class, which provides the ability to create nodes within a DOM structure. Because the XmlDocument class provides node-creation capabilities, it will not provide the fastest throughput in XSL transformations. However, in cases where a DOM structure must be edited first before being transformed, this class can be used.
XmlDataDocument	The XmlDataDocument class extends the XmlDocument class. The XmlDataDocument class can be used when working with DataSet objects in ADO.NET. This topic will be covered in section 9, "XML Support in ADO.NET."
XPathDocument	The XPathDocument class implements the IXPathNavigable interface like the XmlDocument class does. However, the XPathDocument class does not extend the XmlNode class (as the XmlDocument class does) and therefore provides the fastest option for transforming XML via XSLT. You'll see this class used in the examples that follow.
	Because the XPathDocument class implements the IXPathNavigable interface, it is able to leverage features built in to the abstract XPathNavigator class (which, in turn, uses the XPathNodeIterator abstract class for iteration over node sets) to provide cursor-style access to XML data, resulting in fast and efficient XSL transformations.
XslTransform	The XslTransform class is used to transform XML data into other structures. Using the XslTransform class involves instantiating it, loading the proper style sheet with the Load() method, and then passing specific parameters to its Transform() method. This process will be detailed in the next few sections.
XsltArgumentList	The XsltArgumentList class is used to provide parameters needed by an XSLT style sheet and can be passed as a parameter to the XslTransform class's Transform() method.

Then next sections discusses a few of these classes in detail.

The XPathDocument Class

Before looking at the XslTransform class, which serves as the XSLT processor, you need to familiarize yourself with the XPathDocument class. To use this class, you must reference the System.Xml.XPath namespace in your ASP.NET applications. As mentioned in Table 8.5, this class provides the most efficient way to transform an XML document using XSLT because it provides a read-only representation of a DOM structure. The XPathDocument class is very simple to use because it has no public properties or methods. However, it does have several different constructors that are worth mentioning. Table 8.6 shows the different constructors.

Table 8.6 XPathDocument Constructors

Constructor	Description
Public XPathDocument(XmlTextReader, XmlSpace)	Accepts an XmlTextReader object as well as an XmlSpace enumeration
Public XPathDocument(XmlTextReader)	Accepts an XmlTextReader object
Public XPathDocument(TextReader)	Accepts a TextReader object
Public XPathDocument(Stream)	Accepts a Stream object
Public XPathDocument(string)	Accepts the string value of the path to an XML document

You can load the XPathDocument class with XML data contained in a Stream object (a FileStream object, for instance), an XmlTextReader object, a TextReader object, or a file path. Having these different constructors offers you complete control over how transformations will be carried out in your ASP.NET applications. Which one you use will depend on how you choose to access your application's XML documents. Listing 8.8.4 instantiates an XPathDocument class by passing in an XmlTextReader object.

Listing 8.8.4 Instantiating an XPathDocument Class

```
 1: <%@ Import Namespace="System.Xml" %>
 2: <%@ Import Namespace="System.Xml.Xsl" %>
 3: <%@ Import Namespace="System.Xml.XPath" %>
 4: <%@ Import Namespace="System.IO" %>
 5: <%@ Import Namespace="System.Text" %>
 6: <script language="VB" runat="server">
 7:     public sub Page_Load(sender as Object, e as EventArgs)
 8:         Dim xmlPath as string = Server.MapPath("listing8.8.2.xml")
 9:         Dim xslPath as string = Server.MapPath("listing8.8.1.xsl")
10:
11:         Dim fs as FileStream = new FileStream(xmlPath, _
12:                                 FileMode.Open,FileAccess.Read)
13:         Dim reader as StreamReader = _
14:                                 new StreamReader(fs,Encoding.UTF8)
15:         Dim xmlReader as XmlTextReader = new XmlTextReader(reader)
16:
17:         'Instantiate the XPathDocument Class
18:         Dim doc as XPathDocument = new XPathDocument(xmlReader)
19:         Response.Write("XPathDocument successfully created!")
20:
21:         'Close Readers
22:         reader.Close()
23:         xmlReader.Close()
24:     end sub
25: </script>
```

This code loads an XML document into a `StreamReader` object named `fs` by using the `FileStream` object. The `FileStream` object (`fs`) is then passed to an `XmlTextReader`'s constructor. This `XmlTextReader` is then passed to the `XpathDocument`'s constructor and the document is loaded into the DOM.

Running this code will write out "XPathDocument successfully created!" to the browser. You'll certainly agree that this code doesn't buy you much because it has simply readied the XML document for transformation. To actually transform the XML document using XSLT, you'll need to use another class, named `XslTranform`.

The `XslTransform` Class

The `XslTransform` class is found in the `System.Xml.Xsl` namespace. Using it is as easy as instantiating it, loading the XSLT document, and then calling its `Transform()` method. Listing 8.8.5 builds on Listing 8.8.4 by adding in the `XslTransform` class.

Listing 8.8.5 Using the `XslTransform` Class

```
 1: <%@ Import Namespace="System.Xml" %>
 2: <%@ Import Namespace="System.Xml.Xsl" %>
 3: <%@ Import Namespace="System.Xml.XPath" %>
 4: <%@ Import Namespace="System.IO" %>
 5: <script language="C#" runat="server">
 6:     public void Page_Load(Object sender, EventArgs E) {
 7:         string xmlPath = Server.MapPath("listing8.11.xml");
 8:         string xslPath = Server.MapPath("listing8.10.xsl");
 9:
10:         FileStream fs = new FileStream(xmlPath,FileMode.Open,
11:                                        FileAccess.Read);
12:         StreamReader reader = new StreamReader(fs,Encoding.UTF8);
13:         XmlTextReader xmlReader = new XmlTextReader(reader);
14:
15:         //Instantiate the XPathDocument Class
16:         XPathDocument doc = new XPathDocument(xmlReader);
17:
18:         //Instantiate the XslTransform Class
19:         XslTransform xslDoc = new XslTransform();
20:         xslDoc.Load(xslPath);
21:         xslDoc.Transform(doc,null,Response.Output);
22:
23:         //Close Readers
24:         reader.Close();
25:         xmlReader.Close();
26:     }
27: </script>
```

Looking at the code you'll see that after the `XPathDocument` class is created, the `XslTransform` class is created (line 19) so that the transformation can be performed. After the `XslTransform` object is ready to use, it's `Load()` method is called and the path of the XSLT document is passed in as an argument. The `Transform()` method is then called and the result of the transformation is written to the `Response` object's output stream (line 21).

For a full listing of the properties and methods of the `XslTransform` class, refer to the .NET SDK documentation.

Passing Parameters into XSLT Style Sheets

The XSLT language defines an `xsl:param` element that can be used to hold parameter information passed into the XSLT style sheet from the XSLT processor. The use of parameters provides XSLT style sheets with more flexibility in transforming data. Listing 8.8.6 adds an XSLT parameter element to the original XSLT style sheet shown earlier in Listing 8.8.1. This parameter holds the last name of the specific golfer to select from the XML document.

Listing 8.8.6 Using the `xsl:param` Element

```
 1: <?xml version="1.0" encoding="UTF-8" ?>
 2: <xsl:stylesheet xmlns:xsl="http://www.w3.org/1999/XSL/Transform"
 3:     version="1.0">
 4:     <xsl:output method="html" indent="yes" />
 5:     <xsl:param name="golferLastName" />
 6:     <xsl:template match="/">
 7:         <html>
 8:             <body>
 9:                 <xsl:apply-templates />
10:             </body>
11:         </html>
12:     </xsl:template>
13:     <xsl:template match="golfers">
14:         <b>Golfer Information:</b>
15:         <br />
16:         <b>Name:</b>
17:         <xsl:value-of
18:           select="golfer[name/lastName=$golferLastName]/name/firstName" />
19:          
20:         <xsl:value-of
21:           select="golfer[name/lastName=$golferLastName]/name/lastName" />
22:     </xsl:template>
23: </xsl:stylesheet>
```

To pass a value into the `xsl:param` element named `golferLastName` shown in line 5, the `XsltArgumentList` class must be instantiated and passed to the `XslTransform` class's `Transform()` method. Listing 8.8.7 shows this process.

Listing 8.8.7 Using the `XsltArgumentList` Class

```
1: <%@ Import Namespace="System.Xml" %>
2: <%@ Import Namespace="System.Xml.Xsl" %>
3: <%@ Import Namespace="System.Xml.XPath" %>
4: <%@ Import Namespace="System.IO" %>
5: <script language="VB" runat="server">
6:     public sub Page_Load(sender as Object, e as EventArgs)
7:         Dim xmlPath as string = Server.MapPath("listing8.8.2.xml")
```

Listing 8.8.7 *Continued*

```
 8:         Dim xslPath as string = Server.MapPath("listing8.8.6.xsl")
 9:
10:         Dim fs as FileStream = new FileStream(xmlPath,FileMode.Open, _
11:                                           FileAccess.Read)
12:         Dim reader as StreamReader = new StreamReader(fs,Encoding.UTF8)
13:         Dim xmlReader as XmlTextReader= new XmlTextReader(reader)
14:
15:         'Instantiate the XPathDocument Class
16:         Dim doc as XPathDocument = new XPathDocument(xmlReader)
17:
18:         'Instantiate the XslTransform Class and XsltArgumentList
19:         Dim args as XsltArgumentList = new XsltArgumentList()
20:         args.AddParam("golferLastName","","Trainor")
21:
22:         Dim xslDoc as XslTransform = new XslTransform()
23:         xslDoc.Load(xslPath)
24:         xslDoc.Transform(doc,args,Response.Output)
25:
26:         'Close Readers
27:         reader.Close()
28:         xmlReader.Close()
29:     end sub
30: </script>
```

After the `XPathDocument` class is loaded with the XML document to transform in line 16, the `XsltArgumentList` class is instantiated (line 19). This class has several different methods that can be called, but to pass parameter values to XSLT stylesheets the `AddParam()` method must be used. It accepts the name of the parameter, any namespace URI associated with the parameter, and the value to pass.

Once the `AddParam()` method is called, the `XsltArgumentList` object (named `args`) is passed to the `XslTransform` class's `Transform()` method. This will cause the parameter named `golferLastName` to be updated with a value of `Trainor`.

Using the `Asp:Xml` Web Control

The .NET framework also comes with a prebuilt Web control that can be used for performing simple XSL transformations in ASP.NET pages. This control allows the XML document source and XSLT style sheet source to be set using attributes, as shown here:

```
<html>
    <body>
        <asp:Xml ID="xslTransform" Runat="server"
            DocumentSource="Listing7.1.xml"
            TransformSource="Listing7.2.xsl">
        </asp:Xml>
    </body>
</html>
```

In situations where the values of the `DocumentSource` and/or `TransformSource` attributes are not known until runtime, they can be assigned dynamically, as Listing 8.8.8 shows.

Listing 8.8.8 Dynamically Assigning Source Documents to the `asp:Xml` Web Control

```
 1: <script language="C#" runat="server">
 2:     void Page_Load(object sender, System.EventArgs e) {
 3:         xslTransform.DocumentSource = "Listing8.11.xml";
 4:         xslTransform.TransformSource = "Listing8.10.xsl";
 5:     }
 6: </script>
 7: <html>
 8:     <body>
 9:         <asp:Xml ID="xslTransform" Runat="server"></asp:Xml>
10:     </body>
11: </html>
```

> **Note**
> The output for Listing 8.8.8 can be seen in Listing 8.8.3.

Although there's much more that can be done with XSLT in the .NET platform, you should now have a good feel for which classes to use and how to use them. Before ending the chapter, let's take a quick look at how XML is supported in ADO.NET.

9. XML Support in ADO.NET

When ADO version 2.5 was released, it provided the ability to work with ADO `Recordset` objects as XML by using the `adPersistXml` keyword along with the `Stream` object. Although this was a welcome addition, it was simply an add-on to ADO rather than an integrated feature. Passing ADO `Recordset` objects through a firewall with tight security was still problematic and creating custom-shaped `Recordset` objects still required `Shape` commands.

ADO.NET tips the scale as far as XML integration goes. No longer are you restricted to converting a `Recordset` object to XML using `adPersistXml` or some other manual means. In ADO.NET, XML is a first-class citizen and its integration is apparent from the start. What does this mean for your ASP.NET projects? Quite simply, you no longer have to worry about which way you'd like to work with data. If you would rather work with a standard relational view, you can. If you need to work with XML natively, you can do that as well. Changing between these different views can be accomplished with a call to a single property. You'll learn more about this in a moment.

Introducing the `DataSet` Class

The `Recordset` object found in classic ADO has been replaced with a new breed of class in ADO.NET: `DataSet`. The `DataSet` class shifts ADO.NET away from the connection-based model exposed by ADO and toward a more message-like model. This change offers many improvements, including the ability send data through firewalls, the elimination of type conversions in COM, and a truly disconnected way of working with data. ADO.NET's basis in

XML means that virtually any data type can now be supported and passed. This is opposed to the limited set of data types exposed by COM marshaling. The elimination of type conversions results in an increase in scalability and efficiency.

Another important point that can be made about ADO.NET is that data sets are always disconnected, which results in connections being released earlier. Looping through a data set can be done without any connection being open to the data source. Although this can be done using the disconnected `Recordset` object in ADO, disconnected recordsets are still subject to the inefficiencies found in COM marshaling, as mentioned earlier.

The following list details some of the improvements found in the `DataSet` class:

- The data set is completely disconnected and has no knowledge of the data source. All communication with the data source is done through the managed provider.
- The data set can easily be viewed as an XML document and queried using XPath. This XML basis means that it can pass through firewalls by riding on top of the HTTP protocol.
- The data set allows multiple tables to be added along with relationships and constraints between the tables.
- Because data sets are XML aware, more-robust data types can be described. Also, inefficiencies associated with COM marshaling are eliminated.
- Data sets can be mapped to XML schemas that can be used to create an initial structure.

Chapter 6, "Data Manipulation with ADO.NET," provided you with a look at how ADO.NET can be used with different managed providers. As a quick review, Listing 8.9.1 provides an example of loading a DataSet by using the `Fill()` method of the `SqlDataAdapter` class.

Listing 8.9.1 Filling a DataSet Using the `SqlDataAdapter` Class

```
 1: <%@ Import Namespace="System.Data"%>
 2: <%@ Import Namespace="System.Data.SqlClient"%>
 3: <script language="C#" runat="server">
 4:    public void Page_Load(Object Src, EventArgs E) {
 5:        string connStr = "server=localhost;uid=sa;pwd=;database=Northwind";
 6:        string sql = "SELECT * FROM Customers";
 7:        SqlConnection dataConn = new SqlConnection(connStr);
 8:        SqlDataAdapter adap = new SqlDataAdapter(sql,dataConn);
 9:        DataSet ds = new DataSet();
10:        adap.Fill(ds,"Customers");
11:        foreach (DataRow row in ds.Tables["Customers"].Rows) {
12:            Response.Write(row["ContactName"].ToString() + "<br />");
13:        }
14:        if (dataConn != null) dataConn.Close();
15:    }
16: </script>
```

Once the DataSet is loaded, the records it contains can be accessed as relational data, as shown in the previous listing, or as an XML structure. To write the contents of the DataSet out as XML, the DataSet's `GetXml()` method can be used. The XML schema that describes the structure of the XML can also be accessed by calling the `GetXmlSchema()` method. Listing 8.9.2 shows these methods in action.

Listing 8.9.2 Using the DataSet's `GetXmlSchema()` and `GetXml()` Methods

```
 1: <%@ Import Namespace="System.Data"%>
 2: <%@ Import Namespace="System.Data.SqlClient"%>
 3: <%@ Import Namespace="System.Xml"%>
 4: <script language="C#" runat="server">
 5:     public void Page_Load(Object Src, EventArgs E) {
 6:         string connStr ="server=localhost;uid=sa;pwd=;database=Northwind";
 7:         string sql = "SELECT * FROM Customers";
 8:         SqlConnection dataConn = new SqlConnection(connStr);
 9:         SqlDataAdapter adap = new SqlDataAdapter(sql,dataConn);
10:         DataSet ds = new DataSet();
11:         ds.DataSetName = "CustomerRecords";
12:         adap.Fill(ds,"Customers");
13:         xmlSchema.Text = ds.GetXmlSchema();
14:         xml.Text = ds.GetXml();
15:         if (dataConn != null) dataConn.Close();
16:     }
17: </script>
18: <html>
19:     <body>
20:         <b>DataSet XML Schema:</b><br />
21:         <asp:TextBox id="xmlSchema" Runat="server" Columns="90"
22:             Rows="20" TextMode="MultiLine" />
23:         <p />
24:         <b>DataSet XML:</b><br />
25:         <asp:TextBox id="xml" Runat="server" Columns="90"
26:             Rows="20" TextMode="MultiLine" /></body>
27: </html>
```

Figure 8.5 shows the results of running this code.

To query the data within a DataSet using XPath, the DataSet can be passed into the `XmlDataDocument` class's constructor. `XmlDataDocument` is designed to work hand in hand with the `DataSet` class. It extends the `XmlDocument` class shown earlier so that all the normal properties and methods of the DOM are available to use.

Listing 8.9.3 shows how to load a DataSet into `XmlDataDocument` and then use XPath to perform a query.

FIGURE 8.5
Viewing a DataSet's XML and schema.

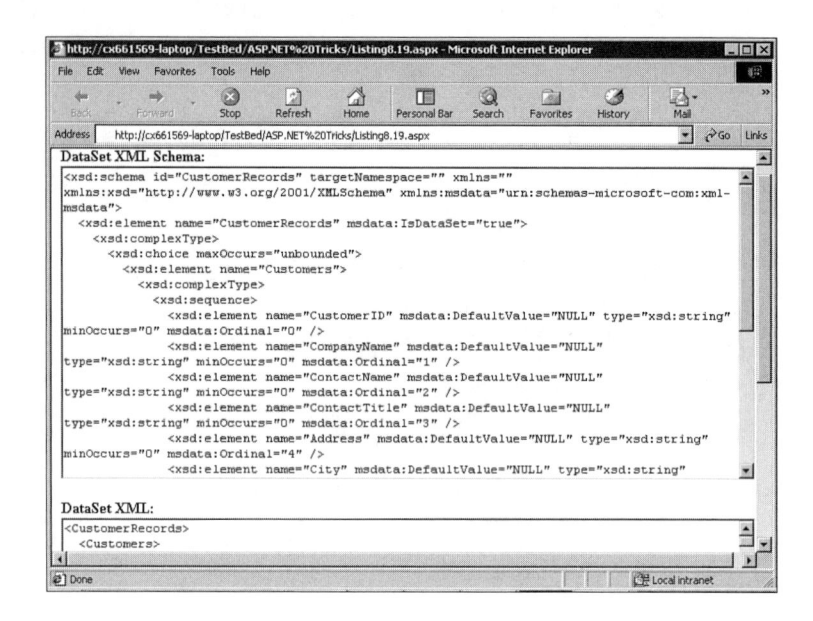

Listing 8.9.3 Using `XmlDataDocument` with the `DataSet` Class

```
 1: <%@ Import Namespace="System.Data"%>
 2: <%@ Import Namespace="System.Data.SqlClient"%>
 3: <%@ Import Namespace="System.Xml"%>
 4: <script language="VB" runat="server">
 5:     public sub Page_Load(sender as Object, e as EventArgs)
 6:         Dim connStr as string = "server=localhost;uid=sa;" & _
 7:                                 "pwd=;database=Northwind"
 8:         Dim sql as string = "SELECT * FROM Customers"
 9:         Dim dataConn as SqlConnection = new SqlConnection(connStr)
10:         Dim adap as SqlDataAdapter = new SqlDataAdapter(sql,dataConn)
11:         Dim ds as DataSet = new DataSet()
12:         ds.DataSetName = "CustomerRecords"
13:         adap.Fill(ds,"Customers")
14:         Dim dataDoc as XmlDataDocument = new XmlDataDocument(ds)
15:         Dim xpath as string = _
16:             "/CustomerRecords/Customers[CustomerID='ALFKI']/ContactName"
17:         Dim customer as XmlNode = dataDoc.SelectSingleNode(xpath)
18:         if (NOT customer Is Nothing) then
19:             Response.Write(customer.InnerText)
20:         end if
21:         if (NOT dataConn Is Nothing) then dataConn.Close()
22:     end sub
23: </script>
```

Notice that the XPath methods shown with the `XmlDocument` class earlier in section 7 (`SelectNode()` and `SelectSingleNode()`) can also be used with the `XmlDataDocument` class since it extends `XmlDocument`.

Reading and Writing XML Using the `DataSet` Class

DataSets can load XML data directly by calling the `ReadXml()` method. This method accepts a variety of input parameters, including the path to the XML document. After the XML is loaded into the DataSet, the data can be treated as relational data or XML data, as desired. This is a very powerful feature because XML data can be loaded into the DataSet and then updated in a data store using the proper data adapter class. Listing 8.9.4 shows how XML can be loaded into a DataSet using the ReadXml() method.

Listing 8.9.4 Loading XML into a DataSet

```
 1: <%@ Import Namespace="System.Data"%>
 2: <script language="C#" runat="server">
 3:    public void Page_Load(Object Src, EventArgs E) {
 4:        DataSet ds = new DataSet();
 5:        ds.ReadXml(Server.MapPath("golfers.xml"));
 6:        foreach (DataRow row in ds.Tables["name"].Rows) {
 7:            Response.Write(row["firstName"].ToString() + "<br />");
 8:        }
 9:    }
10: </script>
```

The DataSet also has a `WriteXml()` method that can be used to save the XML structure within a DataSet to a file, `Stream` object, `TextWriter` object, and so on.

Mapping XSD Schemas to a DataSet

XSD schemas can be loaded into a DataSet via calls to the `ReadXmlSchema()` method. Why would you want to load an XML schema in the first place? One potential answer is that it can save you a lot of work!

When you first create a DataSet, it is completely empty. In order for you to add rows of data to it, tables with columns must be programmatically added first. By you loading a schema from a file, tables and columns are loaded for you, along with their appropriate data types. Also, any relationships specified between tables are also loaded for you. This means that you can easily add new records and then persist them to a data source at a later time. It also means that a schema can be used in different capacities. It can be used to validate an XML document or to create the shell structure for a DataSet table (or tables). Listing 8.9.5 shows how an XML schema can be used to provide the shell structure for a DataSet using the DataSet's `ReadXmlSchema() method`. Once this structure is created, rows of data can be added to the table.

Listing 8.9.5 Mapping an XSD Schema to a DataSet

```
1: <%@ Import Namespace="System.Data"%>
2: <%@ Import Namespace="System.Data.SqlClient"%>
3: <%@ Import Namespace="System.Xml"%>
4: <%@ Import Namespace="System.IO"%>
```

Listing 8.9.5 Continued

```
 5: <html>
 6: <script language="C#" runat="server">
 7: public void Page_Load(Object Src, EventArgs E) {
 8:     DataSet ds = new DataSet();
 9:     //**** Load the Schema File
10:     ds.ReadXmlSchema(new StreamReader(Server.MapPath("schema.xsd")));
11:     //**** Add Row to the Empty DataSet
12:     DataRow row = ds.Tables["Customers"].NewRow();
13:     row["CustomerID"] = "DLWID";
14:     row["CompanyName"] = "Wahlin Consulting";
15:     row["ContactName"] = "Dan Wahlin";
16:     row["ContactTitle"] = "Programmer/Author";
17:
18:     //****** Let's see how well the schema validates
19:     try {
20:         row["test"] = "Testing Schema";
21:     }
22:     catch (Exception exc) {
23:         //Don't do the insert because column["test"] doesn't really exist
24:     }
25:     ds.Tables["Customers"].Rows.Add(row);
26:     // Code to actually insert the row into a data source would go here
27:
28:     BeforeDataGrid.DataSource = ds.Tables["Customers"].DefaultView;
29:     BeforeDataGrid.DataBind();
30: }
31: </script>
32: </head>
33: <body bgcolor="#ffffff">
34:   <form runat="server">
35:   <h2>Data Loaded into a DataSet and Validated by a Schema</h2>
36:   <ASP:DataGrid id="BeforeDataGrid" runat="server"
37:     Width="700"
38:     BackColor="#E6E6CC"
39:     BorderColor="#000000"
40:     ShowFooter="false"
41:     CellPadding=5
42:     CellSpacing="0"
43:     Font-Name="Arial"
44:     Font-Size="8pt"
45:     HeaderStyle-BackColor="#6C0A00"
46:     HeaderStyle-ForeColor="#ffffff"
47:     EnableViewState="false"
48:   />
49:   </form>
50: </body>
51: </html>
```

Line 10 takes care of creating the structure that the data set should follow for you. Once the structure has been established using the schema, rows can be added and saved to a remote data source. In cases where an XML document containing the new records needs to be returned to the end user's application, the data set can return an XML document, as shown earlier. This is a very powerful feature that can be leveraged when you're working with Web services.

In cases where an XML schema is not available, the structure that the DataSet should follow can be inferred from an existing XML document. This is accomplished by using the `InferXmlSchema()` method.

Although this section has only skimmed the surface of XML features found in ADO.NET, you can see that when compared to "classic" ADO, ADO.NET makes working with data in different forms very easy.

Summary

As XML becomes more and more popular as a mechanism for data exchange and application integration, your choice of development platform will greatly influence how robust and flexible your applications are. Fortunately, the .NET platform provides numerous features that can be used to work with XML and relational data. Whether you need to manipulate XML or simply read large XML documents, classes within the `System.Xml` assembly will provide you with the power you need when building ASP.NET applications.

For a more detailed look at how XML can be used in the .NET platform, consult the book *XML for ASP.NET Developers* (Sams Publishing; ISBN 0672320398), by Dan Wahlin.

Other Resources

This chapter has shown how XML can be used in a variety of ways with the .NET platform. From reading large documents to editing smaller ones, to turning relational data into XML, the classes found within the System.Xml assembly provide a host of features to meet any XML requirement. For additional .NET/XML information, visit the resources listed below.

- `www.TomorrowsLearning.com`. This site focuses specifically on .NET/XML topics and Web Services. At the site you'll find numerous demos (with downloadable code) that show how XML can be used in .NET. The site is always expanding its samples and methods for providing .NET/XML training.

- `www.dotnet101.com`. This site provides different articles on a variety of .NET topics including XML. It's an excellent source for staying up-to-speed on all things .NET.

- `www.c-sharpcorner.com`. Although this site focuses specifically on C#, it has several different articles related to using XML in the .NET platform.

CHAPTER 9

ASP.NET ERROR HANDLING TECHNIQUES

by Donny Mack

> **This chapter will cover the following:**
> - Using Option Explicit and Option Strict
> - Structured Error handling
> - Throwing Exceptions
> - Creating Custom Exceptions
> - Page level Exception handling
> - Application level Exception handling

There is one thing that I can predict in the utmost confidence: Your application, no matter what type it is, will not be error free. We all know this from work we have done in the past. There are two ways to deal with this, let the error happen and potentially cause damage to the computer the application is running on, or recover gracefully from the error, thereby limiting the frustration level of the user, or recover gracefully from the error, thereby limiting the frustration level of the user. In this chapter, we will examine the options that developers have for catching and handling errors on both an application and a page-level basis. The chapter also covers how to catch many errors before they happen. We will first go into how the .NET runtime error-handling environment is different from what you are accustomed to, and how it makes handling errors a very easy task by doing most of the work for you behind the scenes.

1. Error Handling and the .NET Runtime

Error handling has always been a fundamental part of application development. Traditionally, the way you handled errors or exceptions depended on the programming language and operating system on which you were developing. The Common Language Runtime (CLR), a primary piece of the .NET Framework, implements exception handling as one of its fundamental features. Another benefit is that the CLR is language independent, so it doesn't care what language the exception was thrown by. For example, a `NullReferenceException` thrown by a C# application is the same as a `NullReferenceException` thrown by a VB application. We can now write universal exception handlers for entire applications. Regardless of whether you are writing in C#, Visual Basic.Net, or any other of .NET's supported languages, the exception object being thrown is derived from the same primitive type, the Exceptions type. Each programming language has its own set of errors and ways of handling errors, so there is a need to create a uniform way to handle these errors across languages. The CLR uses exceptions. Exceptions are thrown when an error occurs; the type of exception depends on the type of base error that occurred. So when an error occurs because of a null reference in a Visual Basic application a `NullReferenceException` is thrown, as with a Jscript or C# application and even though each of the three language would traditionally handle this error differently they can handle the `NullReferenceException` the uniformly. Of course there are differences in the language syntax to handle these exceptions once they are thrown, but the concept of what exceptions are and how they occur are the same across every language.

2. Stopping Errors Before They Occur

One of the best ways to combat errors is to catch them at design time, stopping them before they start. In this section, I'll cover Visual Basic.NET's `Option Strict` and `Option Explicit` Statements and illustrate how you can use these two statements to prevent potential error code from creeping into your runtime applications.

Option Explicit

Most traditional ASP VBScript developers are familiar with the `Option Explicit` statement.

`Option Explicit` forces explicit declaration of all variables at a module level. When used, `Option Explicit`'s declaration must appear in the module before any procedures.

> **Note**
> In ASP.NET pages you must declare `Option Explicit` within the `@ Page` directive. We will go over how to do this shortly.

In addition, when `Option Explicit` is turned `On`, you must declare all variables using `Public`, `Private`, `Dim`, or `Redim`. A great benefit of the `Option Explicit` statement is that it catches a simple mistake that is easy to make, saving you some heartache in the future. The `Option Explicit` displays a "Variable Name Is Defined Multiple Times" compilation error if you accidentally name one variable the same as another variable within the same scope.

Surprisingly, in many Web applications I have seen the developer has failed to declare the `Option Explicit` statement. I suggest you should always use the `Option Explicit` statement because it will solve many design time syntax errors that can ultimately cause runtime errors. Luckily, in ASP.NET and VB.NET `Option Explicit` is set to `On` by default.

I highly recommend you not turn `Option Explicit Off`, but if the need arises you can optionally set it to `Off` by writing the following code (Listing 9.2.1) at the top of your code module or ASP.NET page.

Listing 9.2.1 Turning `Option Explicit` On or Off

[Code Module]

```
Option Explicit Off

All Other Code Below…
```

[Web Form]

```
<%@ Page Explicit="False" %>
```

Listing 9.2.2 demonstrates some of the errors `Option Explicit` can catch for you:

Listing 9.2.2 Using `Option Explicit` to Combat Syntax Errors

```
 1: <%@ Page language="vb" Explicit="true" %>
 2: <script runat="server">
 3:   public sub Page_Load(sender as Object, e as EventArgs)
 4:
 5:   dim var1,var1 as string
 6:
 7:   var1 = "This is a declared variable"
 8:   var2 = "This is a undeclared variable"
 9:
10:   end sub
11: </script>
12:
13: <html>
14: <body>
15: </body>
16: </html>
```

In Listing 9.2.2, using `Option Explicit` catches two errors. The first one caught appears on line 5 in which I declare two variables that share the same name. In this case, the "The local variable 'var1' is defined multiple times in the same method" error message displays. The second error would occur on line 8 because I did not name my second variable correctly when I declared it. I get an error message that states "The name var2 is not declared". Figure 9.1 illustrates the page when the first error occurs. Following that in Figure 9.2 is an illustration after that problem is fixed and the second error occurs.

Option Strict

When working with an application that requires precise values, you receive an error or will lose data if you attempt to convert a value of one data type to another. Visual Basic generally allows conversions from one data type to another without a problem. However, if the result of the conversion results in a loss of data, then your application will throw an exception. The use of `Option Strict` prevents you from making such errors.

FIGURE 9.1
Error occurs because a variable was defined multiple times within the same method.

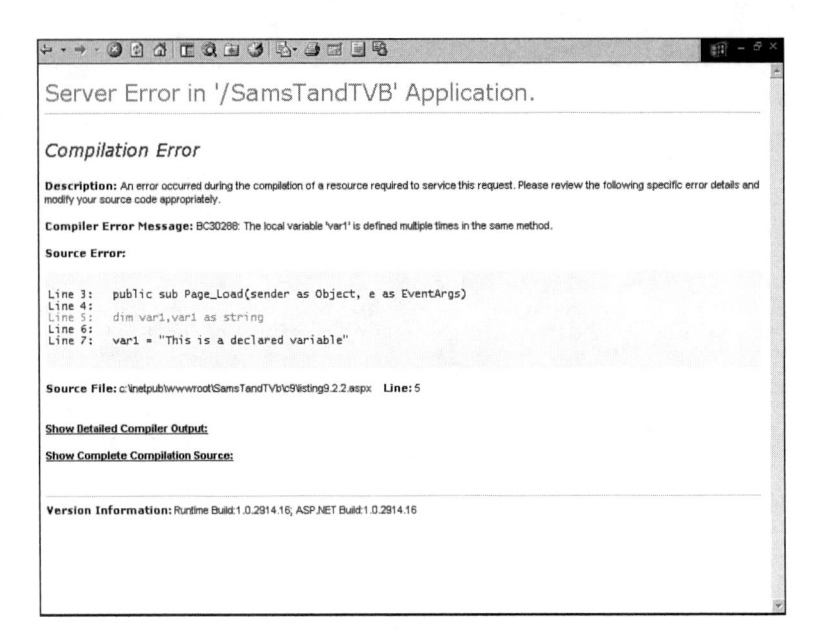

FIGURE 9.2
Error occurs because a variable that has not been declared is used.

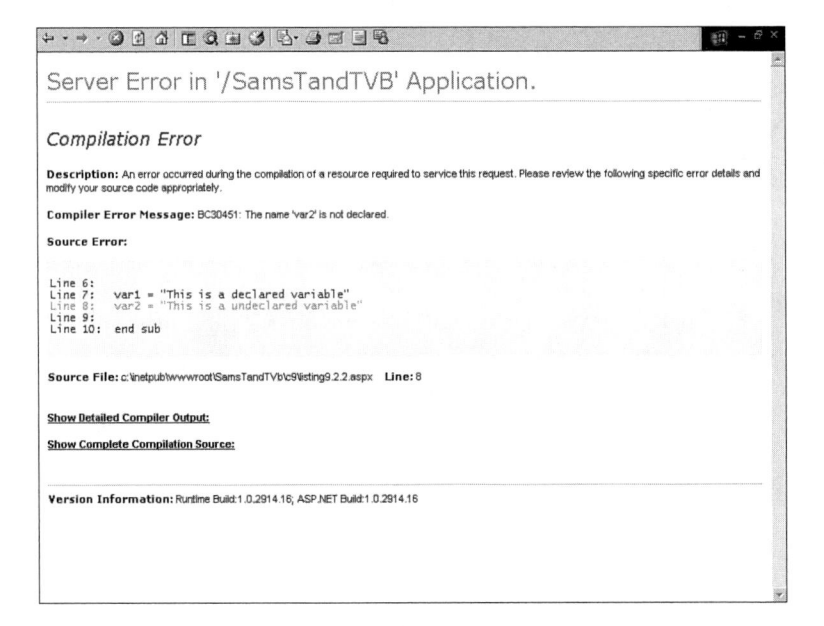

`Option Strict` restricts the conversion of data types to only *widening conversions* (see Table 9.1). You can only convert from one data type to another if the data type being converted too can accommodate the same or greater amount of data than the data type being converted from hence there is no chance for data loss. Table 9.1 is a list of acceptable widening conventions. At compile time, you are notified of improper conversions if `Option Strict` is set to `On`. Additionally, `Option Strict` generates an error for any undeclared variable, because setting `Option Strict On` implicitly means `Option Explicit` is also `On`. In addition, late binding is also prohibited because the run-time cannot determine what data type will be used when the object is created.

Table 9.1 List of Acceptable `Widening` Conventions

Type	Widens to
Byte	Byte, Short, Integer, Long, Decimal, Single, Double, Object
Char	Char, Integer, Long, Decimal, Single, Double, String, Object
Short	Short, Integer, Long, Decimal, Single, Double, Object
Integer	Integer, Long, Decimal, Single, Double, Object
Long	Long, Single, Decimal, Double, Object
Single	Single, Double, Object
Double	Double, Object
Date	Date, String, Object
String	String, Object
Nothing	Byte, Short, Integer, Long, Decimal, Single, Double, String, Object
Fixed-length	String, Object, String
Class	Object; any of the classes that it inherits from; any of the interfaces that it implements (for .NET Runtime defined classes, this will include only the interfaces listed in the class's definition within its type library).
Interface	Object; any of the interfaces that it inherits from.
Structure	Object
Array	Object

Like the `Option Explicit` statement, the `Option Strict` statement must be declared before any other code. You can set `Option Strict` statement `On` or `Off` by using the code shown in Listing 9.2.3 at the top of your code module:

Listing 9.2.3 Setting `Option Strict On` or `Off`

[Code Module]

```
Option Strict On
Option Strict Off
```

[Web Form]

```
<%@ Page Strict="true" %>
<%@ Page Strict="false" %>
```

Listing 9.2.4 demonstrates some of the errors that `Option Strict` catches at compile time:

Listing 9.2.4 Using `Option Strict` to Combat Data Type Conversion Errors

```
 1: <%@ Page language="vb" Strict="true" %>
 2:
 3: <script runat="server">
 4: public sub Page_Load(sender as Object, e as EventArgs)
 5:
 6:    dim int1 as Integer
 7:    dim obj1 as Object
 8:    int1 = 1000
 9:    int1 = 1234567891.98765
10:    int2 = 10
11:    obj1.CallMethod()
12:
13: end sub
14: </script>
15: <html>
16: <body>
17: </body>
18: </html>
```

In Listing 9.2.4, you receive three different exceptions. The first exception occurs at line 9 with an "Option Strict disallows implicit conversions from System.Double to System.Integer" error. The second exception occurs at line 10. `Option Strict` is `On`, so all variables must be declared. In our example, however, `int2` has not been declared so we'll receive an error stating "The name 'int2' is not declared." The third error happens on line 12. Here an error message occurs because the use of late binding is prohibited. The error that occurs is, "Option Strict disallows late binding". Figure 9.3 illustrates the page from Listing 9.2.4 after the second exception is thrown.

The Exception Class

Before we get into how to handle exceptions we need to discuss what an exception is. The `Exception` class is found in the `System` namespace and is the base class for all exceptions. Under the Exception base class resides two base categories for all exceptions in .NET, the `SystemException` class and the `ApplicationException` class.

FIGURE 9.3
Exception occurs converting a Double to Integer.

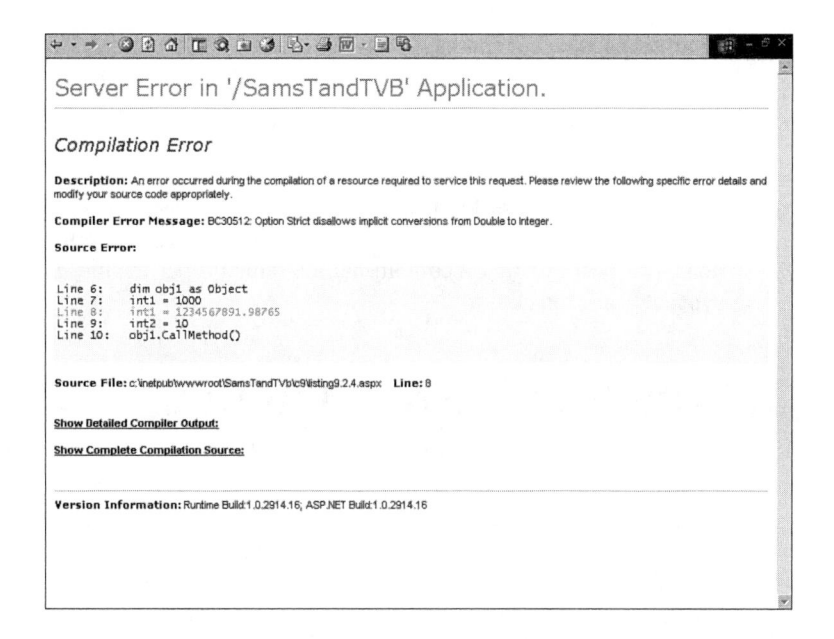

[Screenshot of a browser showing:]

Server Error in '/SamsTandTVB' Application.

Compilation Error

Description: An error occurred during the compilation of a resource required to service this request. Please review the following specific error details and modify your source code appropriately.

Compiler Error Message: BC30512: Option Strict disallows implicit conversions from Double to Integer.

Source Error:

```
Line 6:     dim obj1 as Object
Line 7:     int1 = 1000
Line 8:     int1 = 1234567891.98765
Line 9:     int2 = 10
Line 10:    obj1.CallMethod()
```

Source File: c:\inetpub\wwwroot\SamsTandTVb\c9\listing9.2.4.aspx   **Line:** 8

Show Detailed Compiler Output:

Show Complete Compilation Source:

Version Information: Runtime Build:1.0.2914.16; ASP.NET Build:1.0.2914.16

The `SystemException` class defines the base class for all .NET predefined exceptions. For example, if look up the `SqlException` class in the SDK help files you will see that it is derived from the `SystemException` class:

`public sealed class SqlException : SystemException`

On the other hand if you look up the `OleDbException` you'll notice that it isn't derived from `SystemException`, rather it is derived from `ExternalException`. According to this fact my prior statement must be incorrect that all predefined exceptions are derived from the `SystemException` class. Well follow `ExternalException` back and see where it is derived from. That's right it is derived from the `SystemException` class.

When an exception object is thrown that is derived from the `SystemException` class you can obtain vital information from it regarding the exception that occurred. The following list contains some of the `SystemException`'s properties and methods:

- `Helplink` Property—Gets information about a possible help file associated with the exception
- `InnerException` Property—Gets a reference to the inner exception. The inner exception is the very first exception to occur within the stack. This is useful because the initial exception may be 20 calls within a routine.
- `Message` Property—Gets the exceptions error message.
- `StackTrace` Property—Gets the stack trace back to the point the exception occurred.
- `TargetSite` Property—Gets the method name that threw the exception.

- **GetBaseException** Method—Returns a reference to the inner most exception in the stack. (see InnerException for more detail on inner exception)
- **ToString** Method—Returns the full name of the exception, error message, inner exception name, and the stack trace as a string.

The `ApplicationException` class defines the base class in which all user-defined exceptions are derived from. Later in this chapter we will be going over how to create your own exceptions. Just be aware that it contains all the same properties and methods as the `SystemException` class.

3. Structured Error Handling

Visual Basic.NET introduces structured error handling. Previous versions of Visual Basic had only unstructured error handling. For those not familiar with the term unstructured error handling it is the method of using a single error handler (see the following list) within a method that catches all exceptions. There are obvious limitations to using unstructured error handling. One is the lack of the ability to use multiple handlers within a single method. Another is its very messy. The following is a list of Visual Basics unstructured error handlers:

- **On Error GoTo** *line[or]label*—If a run-time error occurs. the error handling routine starts at the line or label specified.
- **On Error Resume Next**—If a run-time error occurs, code execution goes to the statement immediately following the statement where the error occurred.
- **On Error GoTo 0**—Disables error handling in the current procedure, resetting it to Nothing.
- **On Error GoTo -1**—Like **On Error GoTo 0**, Disables any enabled exception in the current procedure, resetting it to Nothing.

Visual Basic.NET still supports unstructured error handling, but has also introduced structured exception handling to its arsenal. Structured exception handling in VB.NET is derived from Visual C++. It is called the `Try...Catch...Finally` statement, and its structure is listed in Listing 9.3.1. It provides a control structure similar to a `Select Case` or a `While` to provide you with ways to handle exceptions, protected blocks of code, and filters.

Listing 9.3.1   A `Try...Catch...Finally` Block

```
1: try
2:    'code to try
3: catch Variable as ExceptionType
4:    'code to execute if exception occurs
5: finally
6:    'cleanup code (ex: close a file)
7: end try
```

You always begin a `Try...Catch...Finally` statement with the `Try` block as seen on line 1 of Listing 9.3.1. The `Try` block code execution continues until the first `Catch` statement (line 3) and any code within the `Try` block will be executed unless an exception occurs. If an exception occurs code execution halts in the `Try` block and control switches to a `Catch` block (line 3). You can have one or more `Catch` blocks within a `Try...Catch...Finally` statement and it is good form to do so. So when you create `Catch` blocks you must first determine what type of exception you want to `Catch` and its priority within the group of `Catch` blocks. The Catch block that is executed is dependent on what type of exception has been thrown, but also its placement within a group of `Catch` blocks. For instance, you have three Catch blocks in your `Try...Catch` statement (`Exception`, `SqlException`, and `FileNotFoundException`) and a `FileNotFoundException` occurs. The exception object will be passed up the stack and all three `Catch` statements will have a chance to handle the exception starting at the first `Catch` block (see Listing 9.3.2):

Listing 9.3.2 `Try...Catch...Finally` Example

```
1: try
2:   'code to open non-existent file
3: catch SqlEx As SqlException
4:   'Code to execute
5: catch Ex As Exception
6:   'Code to execute
7: catch FNFEx As FileNotFoundException
8:   'Code to execute
9: end try
```

The `SqlException` Catch block is first in the chain (line 3) since it wasn't a `SqlException` that was thrown it is passed by. The second `Catch` block handles general exceptions (line 5) so this block will be executed even though there is a `FileNotFoundException` handler (line 7) because the `Exception Catch` block is ahead of the `FileNotFoundException` block. The `Finally` block in Listing 9.3.1 is used to perform any code cleanup such as closing a database connection or an open file.

There are three different forms to the `Try` Statement:

- A `Try` block followed by one or more `Catch` block
- A `Try` block followed by one or more `Catch` block followed by a `Finnally` block
- A `Try` block followed by only a `Finally` block

In the following sections, I'll be going over how to use the `Try...Catch...Finally` exception handler, how to catch general and specific exceptions, and how to throw exceptions.

Catching General Exceptions

In the previous section we went over a situation where a specific exception occurred, but instead of the `Catch` block designed to handle that exception being executed the general exception `Catch` block was executed. Only using a general exception handler is not recommended. Instead you should always try to write `Catch` blocks for specific exceptions that may occur first. Then end the group of `Catch` blocks with a general exception handler as a last ditch effort to gracefully recover from an exception. The syntax of a general `Try...Catch...Finally` exception handler is demonstrated in Listing 9.3.3:

Listing 9.3.3 Code Demonstrating How to Catch General Exceptions

```
 1: <%@ Page Language="vb" Strict="False" %>
 2: <html>
 3:  <script runat="server">
 4:  public sub Page_Load(sender as Object, e as EventArgs)
 5:    try
 6:
 7:      Response.Write("1: Try Block Executes<br>")
 8:      dim obj1 as Object
 9:      obj1.CallUknownMethod()
10:
11:    Catch ex As Exception
12:      Response.Write("2: Catch Block Execute<br>")
13:      Response.Write(ex.ToString & "<br>")
14:
15:    Finally
16:
17:      Response.Write("3: Finally Block Executes")
18:
19:    End Try
20: End Sub
21: </script>
22: <body>
23: </body>
24: </html>
```

Figure 9.4 illustrates the output when this code is executed to the page. I had to turn off `Option Strict` because of the use of the late bound object. On line 5, I start the `Try` block and within the `Try` block I create an object and invokea non-existent `method name` `"CallUnknownMethod"`. When I try to invoke this method, an Exception is thrown (raised), I catch (handle) it and use the `Exception.ToString` method to retrieve information about the exception and write it out to the page. I also write a message out to the page in each of the three blocks so you can see the course of code execution.

Catching Specific Exceptions

As previously mentioned you should always try to predict what exceptions might occur and create `Catch` blocks to handle those specific exceptions. For instance, if you know that an object may return a null value and will cause an exception, you can handle it gracefully by writing a specific catch statement for a `NullReferenceException`. Listing 9.3.4 demonstrates how to use the `SQLException` object to handle a "SQL Server Not Found" error:

FIGURE 9.4
General exception handler example page after exception is thrown with information about code execution and exception information written out to the page.

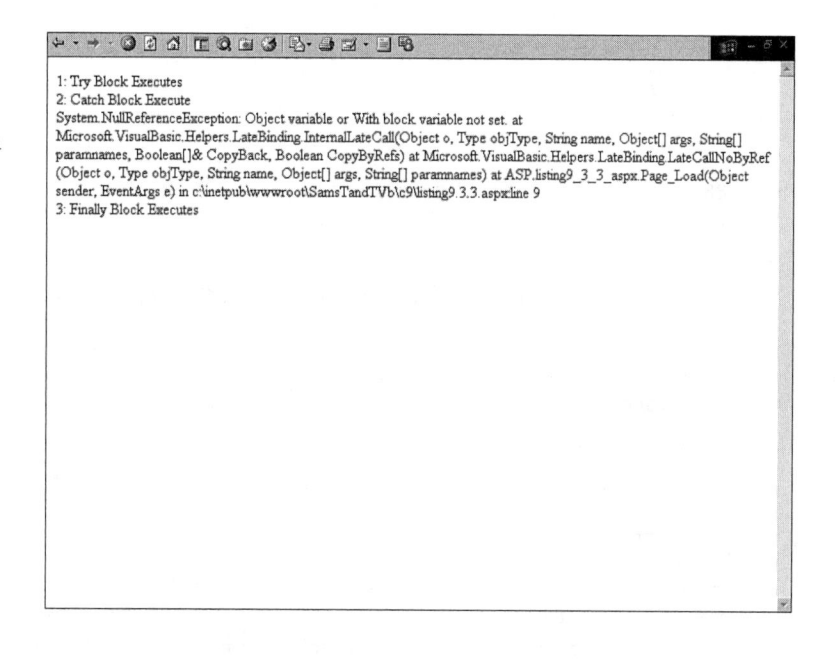

```
1: Try Block Executes
2: Catch Block Execute
System.NullReferenceException: Object variable or With block variable not set. at
Microsoft.VisualBasic.Helpers.LateBinding.InternalLateCall(Object o, Type objType, String name, Object[] args, String[]
paramnames, Boolean[]& CopyBack, Boolean CopyByRefs) at Microsoft.VisualBasic.Helpers.LateBinding.LateCallNoByRef
(Object o, Type objType, String name, Object[] args, String[] paramnames) at ASP.listing9_3_3_aspx.Page_Load(Object
sender, EventArgs e) in c:\inetpub\wwwroot\SamsTandTVb\c9\listing9.3.3.aspx:line 9
3: Finally Block Executes
```

Listing 9.3.4   Handling a "SQL Server Not Found" Error

```
 1: <%@ Import Namespace="System.Data" %>
 2: <%@ Import Namespace="System.Data.SqlClient" %>
 3: <script language="c#" runat="server">
 4:  void Page_Load(Object sender, EventArgs e) {
 5:
 6:   try {
 7:
 8:    Response.Write("<b>1:</b> Try block executed<p>");
 9:    SqlConnection SqlCon = new SqlConnection("server=donnymack;" +
10:     "uid=sa;pwd=;database=Northwind");
11:    SqlCommand SqlCmd = new SqlCommand("SELECT TOP 10 * " +
12:     "FROM Products", SqlCon);
13:    SqlCon.Open();
14:    dg.DataSource = SqlCmd.ExecuteReader(CommandBehavior.CloseConnection);
15:    dg.DataBind();
16:
17:   } catch (SqlException SqlEx) {
18:
19:    Response.Write("<b>2:</b> SqlException Catch block executed<br>");
20:    Response.Write(SqlEx.ToString() + "<p>");
21:    SqlConnection SqlCon = new SqlConnection("server=localhost;" +
22:     "uid=sa;pwd=;database=Northwind");
23:    SqlCommand SqlCmd = new SqlCommand("SELECT TOP 10 * " +
24:     "FROM Products", SqlCon);
25:    SqlCon.Open();
26:    dg.DataSource = SqlCmd.ExecuteReader(CommandBehavior.CloseConnection);
27:    dg.DataBind();
28:
```

Listing 9.3.4 Continued

```
29:    }
30:
31:    catch (Exception ex) {
32:
33:      Response.Write("General Exception,<p>");
34:
35:    } finally {
36:
37:      Response.Write("<b>3:</b> Clean up code executed<p>");
38:
39:    }
40:  }
41: </script>
42: <html>
43:   <body>
44:     <asp:datagrid runat="server" id="dg" font-size="10" />
45:   </body>
46: </html>
```

When the code in Listing 9.3.4 executes and a connection is attempted to the SQL Server named *donnymack* (see lines 9–10) an exception is thrown because that server does not exist. Code execution resumes at the first Catch statement within the `Try...Catch...Finally` block and will go through each of the `Catch` statements starting at the top. The runtime will searches for a catch statement for the specific exception that was thrown. In this example, an `SqlException` was thrown. When the `SqlException Catch` block is found, any statements within its block will be executed. In this example, the same code is re-executed (lines 19–31), but instead of using the server named *donnymack*, localhost is used. Because this is the correct server, no exception is thrown. On lines 35-39 I inserted a `Finally` block strictly for demonstration purposes. After the `Finally` block is executed the page renders, as it should. An ASP.NET `DataGrid` server control is rendered with the contents of the `Products` table. Figure 9.5 contains the executed page. You will see a numbered list at the top of the page. This list illustrates code execution within the `Try...Catch...Finally` block.

A list of standard predefined exception types provided by the .NET runtime can be found in Table 9.2.

Table 9.2 List of Standard Exceptions

Exception	Description
Exception	The base class for all exceptions
SystemException	The base class for all runtime generated errors
CoreException	The base class for all fatal runtime errors
IndexOutOfRangeException	Thrown by the runtime when an Array is improperly indexed

Table 9.2 Continued

Exception	Description
`NullReferenceException`	Thrown by the runtime when a null object if referenced
`InvalidOperationException`	Thrown by Methods when they are in an invalid state
`ArgumentException`	The base class for all argument exceptions
`ArgumentNullException`	Thrown by methods that do not allow null arguments
`ArgumentOutOfRangeException`	Thrown by methods that have arguments that must be within a particular range
`InteropException`	The base class for exceptions that occur outside the .NET Runtime environment
`ComException`	Thrown by encapsulating Classic COM (Component Object Model) Components Hresult information
`SEHException`	Thrown by encapsulating Win32 structured error handling information
Other Common Types Of Exceptions	
`SqlException`	Thrown when an error occurs from the SQL Server adapter
`OleDbException`	Thrown when an error occurs from the OleDb adapter

FIGURE 9.5

Notice the list at the top of the page. The `Try` block is executed first, then the `SqlException` `Catch` block, ending with the `Finally` block.

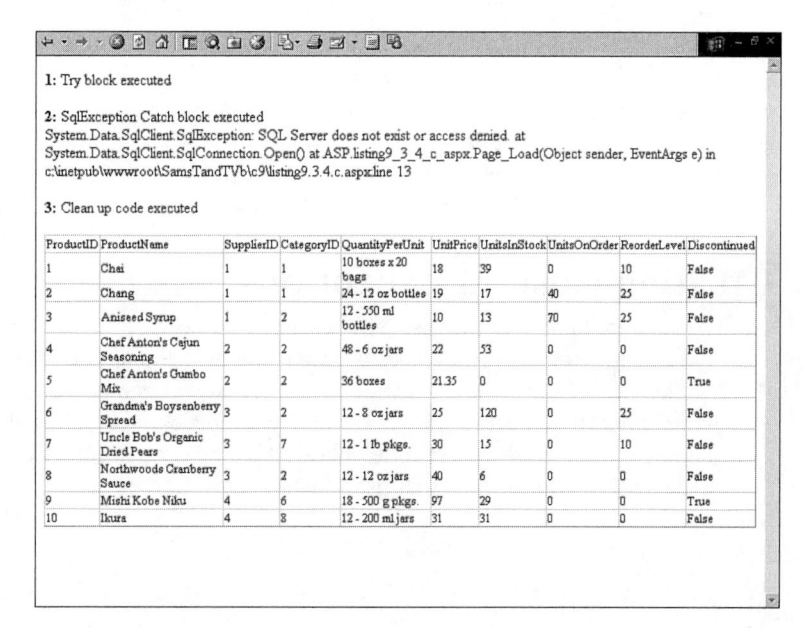

Throwing Exceptions

The .NET Runtime gives you the capability to throw exceptions when needed. For example, you may wish to re-throw an exception after catching it and not recovering from the exception. Then your application-level error handling can handle browser redirection.

Listing 9.3.5 demonstrates how to throw an exception by using the `Throw` keyword.

Listing 9.3.5 Using the `Throw` Statement to Throw an Exception

```
 1: <script runat="server" language="vb">
 2:
 3:  public sub Page_Load(sender as Object, e as EventArgs)
 4:
 5:    try
 6:
 7:      throw new DivideByZeroException()
 8:
 9:    catch DBZEx As DivideByZeroException
10:
11:      Response.Write(DBZEx.Message)
12:
13:    end try
14:
15:  end sub
16: </script>
17: <html>
18: <body>
19: </body>
20: </html>
```

In Listing 9.3.5, I have a `Try...Catch` block. In the `Try` block I throw (raise) a `DivideByZeroException` (line 7). On line 9 there is a Catch block to handle that specific error. In the Catch block I write out the error message (line 11). Figure 9.6 contains the rendered page with the error message "Attempted to divide by zero."

Creating Custom Exceptions

You are not limited to the base .NET exception objects. You have the capability to make and utilize your own exception types by inheriting from the `ApplicationException` class. This section demonstrates how to create your own exception object and how to make use of it in your application. Listing 9.3.6 contains the sample code for a Visual Basic class file server containing the exception object code, followed by the code to compile the file, ending with the code for a web form client that uses the new exception object.

FIGURE 9.6
Page with "Attempted to divide by zero" error message.

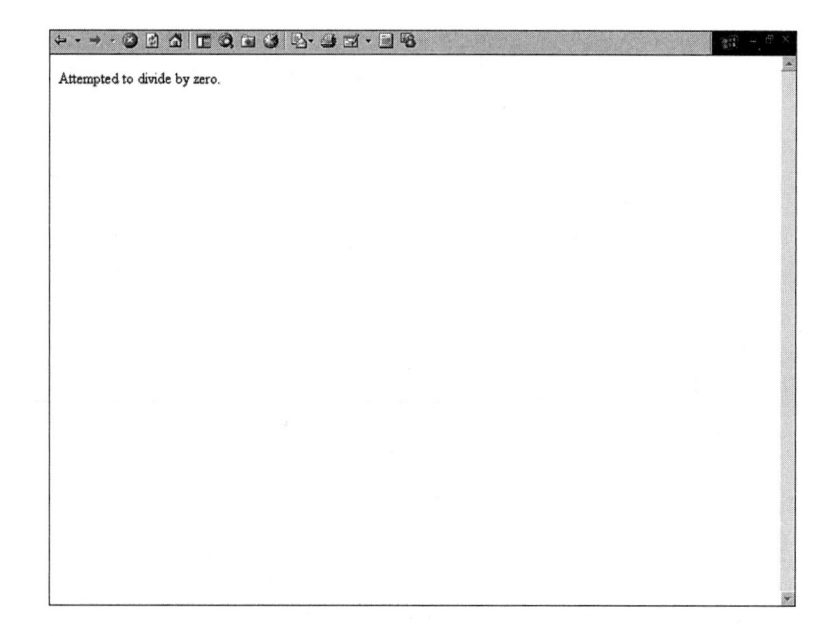

> Attempted to divide by zero.

Listing 9.3.6 Sample Code for Making, Compiling, and Using a Custom Exception [VB Server Class–Name: `CustomEx.vb`]

```
 1: imports System
 2: imports System.Text
 3:
 4:   namespace CustomExceptions
 5:
 6:    public class DrinkBoyException : Inherits ApplicationException
 7:
 8:     public sub New()
 9:
10:      MyBase.New("<H3><B>DrinkBoy Exception</B></H3><BR>")
11:      dim sBuild as new StringBuilder()
12:       sBuild.Append("<FONT COLOR=""RED"">")
13:       sBuild.Append("<B>For more information ")
14:       sBuild.Append("please visit: ")
15:       sBuild.Append("<a href=""http://www.drinkboy.com"" Target=""_Blank"">")
16:       sBuild.Append("DrinkBoy.com</a></b></FONT>")
17:      MyBase.HelpLink = sBuild.ToString()
18:
19:     end sub
20:
21:    end class
22:
23:   end namespace
```

When you make a custom exception you must inherit the `ApplicationException` class as seen on line 6. On line 10 I initialize a new instance of the `ApplicationException` class by MyBase.New instance constructor. Since this class implements the `ApplicationException` class that is what is initialized. I passed in a string when it was initialized; this will be the `Message` property of the `DrinkBoyException` (see `ApplicationException` overload list for other constructors). I set the `HelpLink` property for the `DrinkBoyException` by constructing a `StringBuilder` object appending a user friendly message together for the client to read (lines 11–17). Listing 9.3.7 contains the code necessary to compile this class. Following that in Listing 9.3.8 is code you can use in a web form to test out the `DrinkBoyException`.

Listing 9.3.7 Make File for Class File

```
vbc /t:library /out:C:\TipsAndTricks\bin\ExceptionObjects.dll
➥C:\TipsAndTricks\CustomEx.vb /r:System.dll
```

Listing 9.3.8 Web Form Client Code to Implement Custom `DrinkBoyException`

```
 1: <%@ Import Namespace="CustomExceptions" %>
 2: <script language="vb" runat="server">
 3: public sub Page_Load(sender as Object, e as EventArgs)
 4:   try
 5:
 6:     throw new DrinkBoyException
 7:
 8:   catch ex As DrinkBoyException
 9:
10:     Response.Write(ex.Message & "   " & ex.HelpLink)
11:
12:   end try
13: end sub
14: </script>
15: <html>
16: <body>
17: </body>
18: </html>
```

After importing the `CustomExceptions` namespace we can throw the new exception just as though it is a `SystemException` by using the `throw` statement (line 6). I am also able to create a `Catch` block for the `DrinkBoyException` (line 8). Figure 9.7 contains the web form client from Listing 9.3.8 after the `DrinkBoyException` has been thrown and handled by the `Catch` block.

FIGURE 9.7
Web form with DrinkBoyException `Message` property written out to the page.

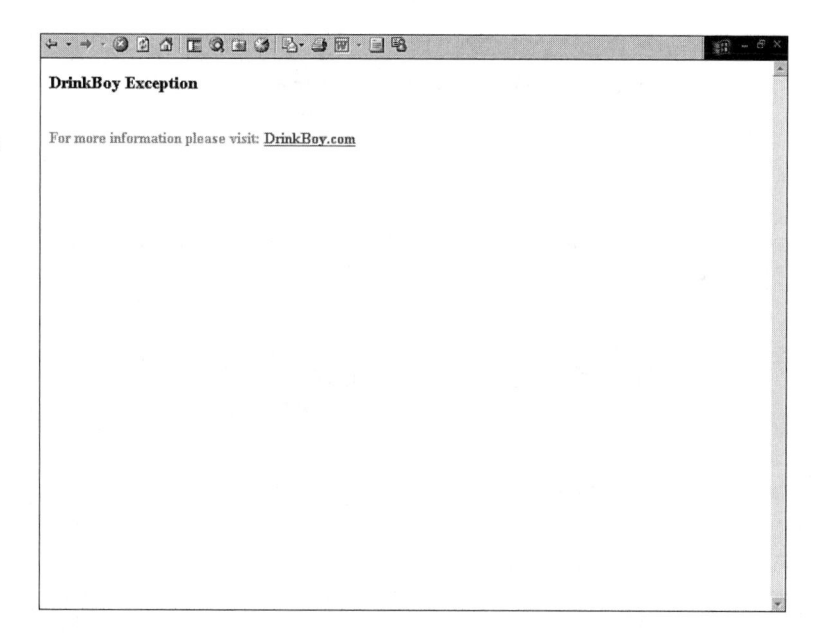

4. Page Level Error Handling

Beyond the use of the inline error handling, ASP.NET enables you to handle exceptions on a page-level basis. In this section I'll discuss using an attribute of the `@Page` directive to redirect a user to a custom error page in the event of an un-handled exception. Also in this section I'll explain how to use the `Page` objects `Error` event to handle uncaught exceptions. Unfortunately, you cannot use either of the two to directly handle exceptions. They are more or less used to recover from un-handled exceptions. For instance, if an un-handled exception occurs you can use these methods to redirect the user to a user-friendly page rather than having a nasty error message printed out to the screen. Other uses may be error logging or debugging.

Using the Page Objects Error Event

The `Page` object has an `Error event` that is fired when an un-handled exception occurs within a page. You can handle this method and use it for various functions such as page redirection or debugging. If an exception occurs and is handled within an exception handler such as a `Try...Catch....Finally` this event will not be raised. Listing 9.4.1 demonstrates how you can use this method to display an error message in the event of an error.

Listing 9.4.1 Code Example of How to Use the **Page** Objects **Error** Method

```
1:  <script language="vb" runat="server">
2:
3:   public sub Page_Load(sender as Object, e as EventArgs)
4:
5:    try
6:
7:     throw new ApplicationException("An unhandled exception")
8:
9:    catch ex as Exception
10:
11:    dim PageException as string = ex.ToString()
12:    dim sBuilder as new StringBuilder()
13:    sBuilder.Append("<b>1: This exception was caught:</b><br>")
14:    sBuilder.Append(PageException)
15:    sBuilder.Append("</br>")
16:    Response.Write(sBuilder.ToString())
17:
18:    finally
19:
20:     throw new ApplicationException("An unhandled exception")
21:    end try
22:
23:   end sub
24:
25:  protected sub Page_Error(sender as Object, e as EventArgs)
26:
27:    dim PageException as string = Server.GetLastError().ToString()
28:    dim sBuilder as new StringBuilder()
29:    sBuilder.Append("<b>2: This exception was not caught:</b><br>")
30:    sBuilder.Append(PageException)
31:
32:    Response.Write(sBuilder.ToString())
33:    Context.ClearError()
34:
35:   end sub
36:
37:  </script>
38:  <html>
39:  <body>
40:    Regular Page Processing
41:  </body>
42:  </html>
```

I added a little extra code to Listing 9.4.1 to demonstrate the string of events that occur when this page is executed. First, during the **Page_Load** event (lines 3–23) I create a **Try...Catch...Finally** block. Within the Try block I throw a new **ApplicationException** object (line 7). This exception is caught in the **Catch** block on line 9. In lines 11–16 I create a string to information regarding the exception thrown out to the page. In the finally block (lines 18–21) I throw another **ApplicationException** and since this exception is not caught it is considered un-handled and the **Page** objects **Error** event is fired (line 20). Within the **Error** event I use the `GetLastError` method from the `HttpServerUtility` class (discussed later in this chapter) to obtain a reference to the last exception thrown for the request and construct a message to write out to the page containing information regarding the thrown exception (lines 27–31). Line 40 contains some text that should be written out to the page, but you will notice that it is not, this is because after the un-handled exception is thrown, page processing halts. You can see the final page from Listing 9.4.1 in Figure 9.8.

FIGURE 9.8
Code from the Catch block and `Page_Error` event is written out to the page, but no HTML code is.

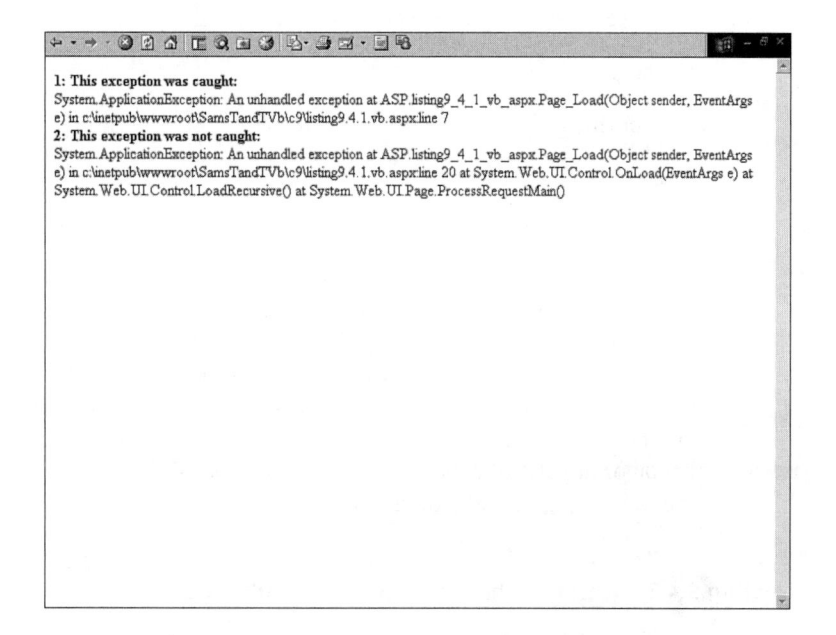

```
1: This exception was caught:
System.ApplicationException: An unhandled exception at ASP.listing9_4_1_vb_aspx.Page_Load(Object sender, EventArgs e) in c:\inetpub\wwwroot\SamsTandTVb\c9\listing9.4.1.vb.aspx:line 7
2: This exception was not caught:
System.ApplicationException: An unhandled exception at ASP.listing9_4_1_vb_aspx.Page_Load(Object sender, EventArgs e) in c:\inetpub\wwwroot\SamsTandTVb\c9\listing9.4.1.vb.aspx:line 20 at System.Web.UI.Control.OnLoad(EventArgs e) at System.Web.UI.Control.LoadRecursive() at System.Web.UI.Page.ProcessRequestMain()
```

Using the `@Page` Directive To Handle Page Redirection

You will not be able to plan for, catch, and recover from every exception that may occur in your ASP.NET application. ASP.NET helps us out in this situation by giving us a couple of options on how to deal with these unpredictable exceptions. The `Page` object offers us ways to capture errors and work around them.

One way to handle errors at the page level is to use the `@Page` directive. The `@Page` directive defines page-specific attributes used by the ASP.NET parser and compiler. Among these attributes are page-level `Language` preference, `Buffer`, `ContentType`, and the `ErrorPage`. In this section I'll be discussing the `ErrorPage` attribute. The `ErrorPage` attribute defines a target URL for redirection in the event of an un-handled exception. An illustration of how to use this attribute can be found in Listing 9.4.2.

Listing 9.4.2 Illustration of How to Use the `ErrorPage` Attribute of the `@Page` Directive

```
 1: <%@ Page ErrorPage="http://www.dotnetjunkies.com/GenericError.htm" %>
 2: <%@ Import Namespace="CustomExceptions" %>
 3: <script language="vb" runat="server">
 4:
 5:   public sub Page_Load(sender as Object, e as EventArgs)
 6:
 7:     throw new DrinkBoyException
 8:
 9:   end sub
10:
11: </script>
12: <html>
13: <body>
14: </body>
15: </html>
```

On line 1 of Listing 9.4.2 I insert the `@Page` directive and set the `ErrorPage` attribute to a `URL`. Within the `Page_Load` event I throw our `DrinkBoyException` (line 7). Since there are now exception handlers within the page the runtime will handle the error and the user will receive a very unfriendly page. In order to overcome this undesired behavior we must also make a change to the web.config file. The specific section of the web.config file we want to edit or add is the `<customErrors>` section. The `<customErrors>` section mode attribute must be set to either `On` or `RemoteOnly` for page redirection to occur. Listing 9.4.3 illustrates what this section of the web.config should look like.

Listing 9.4.3 Changing the web.config File to Allow Custom Errors

```
1: <configuration>
2:    <system.web>
3:       <customErrors mode="On">
4:       </customErrors>
5:    </system.web>
6: </configuration>
```

If the `mode` attribute is set to `On` in the `<customErrors>` section, as it is in Listing 9.4.3, any time there is an un-handled exception on a page that has the `ErrorPage` attribute set to a value, the browser will redirect to the specified page. If the `mode` attribute is set to `RemoteOnly`, then anytime there is an un-handled exception from anywhere other than the local computer the web application is running on, the browser will redirect to the page specified in the `ErrorPage` attribute. If the requesting browser is on the same computer as the ASP.NET web application, then the actual error message will be displayed in the browser. To illustrate how changing the `mode` value in the `<customErrors>` section, see the following examples.

Our first example found in Figure 9.9 illustrates the result of a `DrinkBoyException` being thrown with `mode` set to off and the `ErrorPage` attribute in the page is set to a value.

Chapter 9 • ASP.NET ERROR HANDLING TECHNIQUES 367

FIGURE 9.9
Web form with `DrinkBoyException` `Message` property written out to the page.

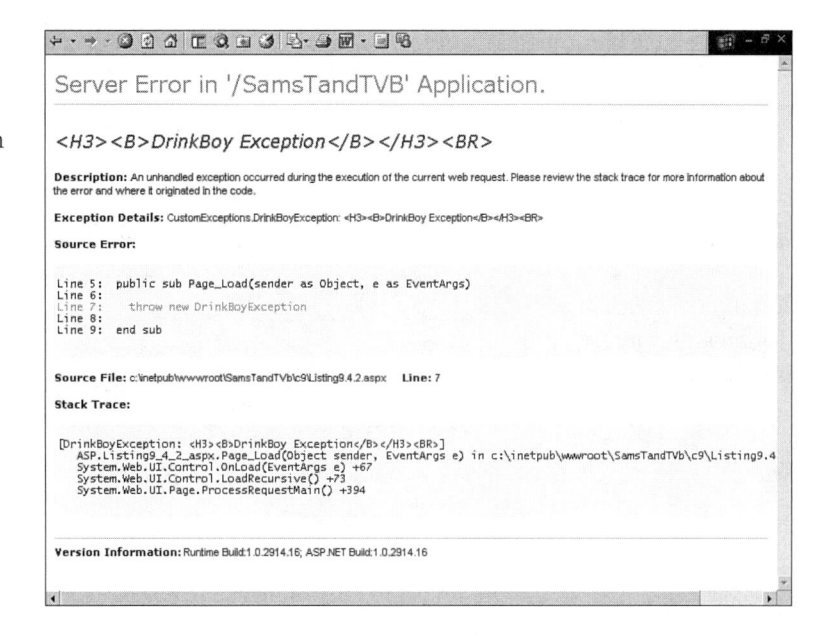

![Figure 9.9: Browser screenshot showing Server Error in '/SamsTandTVB' Application with DrinkBoy Exception details, source error lines, source file path, stack trace, and version information.]

The second example found in Figure 9.10 illustrates the result of a `DrinkBoyException` being thrown with `mode` set to `On` with the `ErrorPage` attribute set to a value.

FIGURE 9.10
Page gets redirected to custom error page.

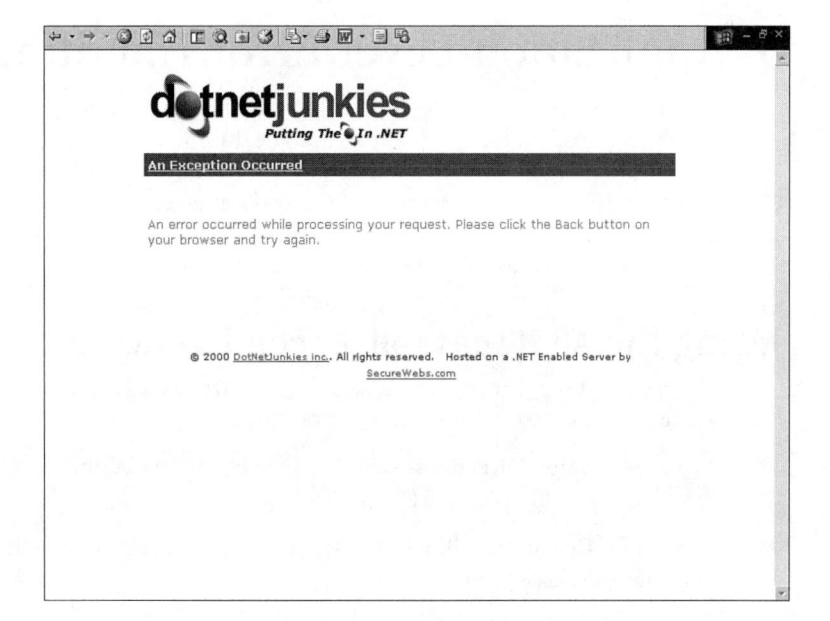

![Figure 9.10: Browser screenshot showing dotnetjunkies custom error page with "An Exception Occurred" heading and message "An error occurred while processing your request. Please click the Back button on your browser and try again." Footer reads "© 2000 DotNetJunkies Inc. All rights reserved. Hosted on a .NET Enabled Server by SecureWebs.com".]

Figure 9.11 illustrates the result of a `DrinkBoyException` being thrown with `mode` set to `remoteonly` with and the `ErrorPage` attribute set to a value.

FIGURE 9.11
Web form with `DrinkBoyException` `Message` property written out to the page since I am running this Web application on my local machine.

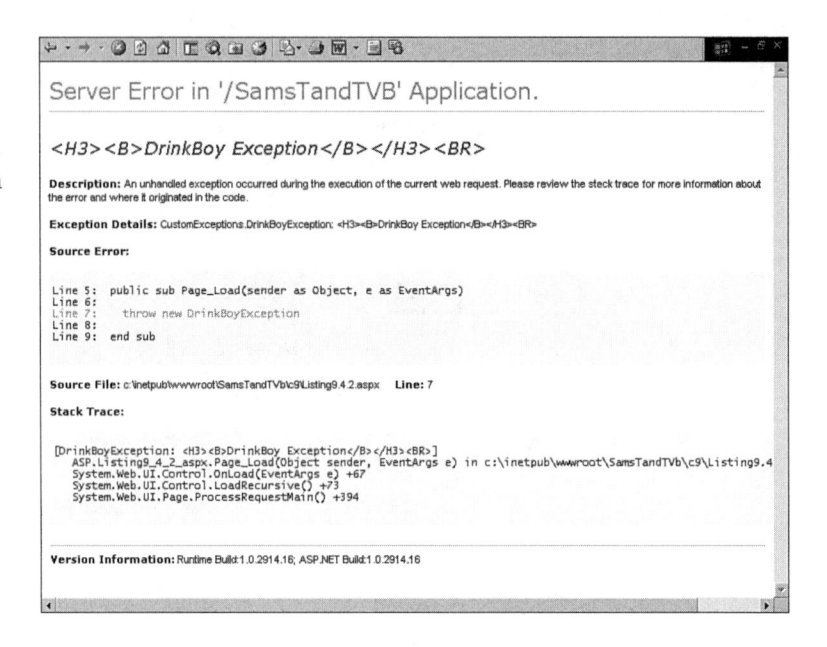

5. Application-Level Error Handling

Page-level exception handling is great for specific page-level situations, such as invalid use of null exceptions. But this method can become quite cumbersome and complicated especially if you are developing a couple hundred pages for your site. ASP.NET saves you time by giving you the capability to handle errors at the application level. In this section I'll go over how to implement application wide page redirect in the event of an un-handled exception, and how to use the `HttpApplication` objects `Error` event to catch all un-handled exceptions.

Using the `Application_Error` Event

The `Application_Error` event is found in the `Global.asax` file of your web application. The `Global.asax` is used for the following purposes:

- **Application Directives**—Used to specify optional settings used by the ASP.NET runtime when handling ASP.NET files

- **Code Declaration Blocks**—Used to define variables and methods to be compiled into the `Page` class

- **Server Side Object Tag**—Used to declare and create new instances of objects

- **Server Side Include Directives**—Used to insert the contents of another file into the Global.asax file

In this section of the chapter, we'll concentrate on code declaration blocks. Code declaration blocks are located in the global.asax are defined exactly the same as they are within web forms. There are a couple different event handlers available to you in the global.asax; for instance, the `Application_OnStart`, `Application_OnEnd`, `Session_OnStart`, and `Session_OnEnd` events. You can comfortably assume that any events that were in ASP X.0's global.asa are still available in ASP.NET's global.asax plus many new ones. We'll be going over the `Application_Error` event in this section.

The `Application_Error` event fires when an exception occurs in the web application. You can find the syntax for using the `Application_Error` event within the *Global.asax* in Listing 9.5.1.

Listing 9.5.1 Code Block to Use `Application_Error` Event Within the `global.asax`

```
1: <script runat="server" language="c#">
2:   void Application_Error(Object sender, EventArgs e) {
3:     //Do Something
4:   }
5: </script>
```

The `EventArgs` parameter contains data related to the error event, but unfortunately nothing about the exception itself. Luckily, there are a couple different methods you can use to determine what exception was thrown despite the lack of it as a parameter for the event.

The first method is to use the `HttpServerUtility.GetLastError` method. The `GetLastError` method returns a reference to the last exception thrown in the web application. In Listing 9.5.2 is a code example illustrating how to use the `GetLastError` method to retrieve a reference to an un-handled exception. You can use the page we created in Listing 9.4.2 as the test page to throw an exception. In this example I catch the exception, clear all errors from the request, and write the exception which occurred out to the page being requested.

Listing 9.5.2 Code Example Using the `HttpServerUtility`'s `GetLastError` Method

```
 1: <script runat="server" language="c#">
 2:
 3: void Application_Error(Object sender, EventArgs e) {
 4:
 5:   string LastException = Server.GetLastError().ToString();
 6:
 7:   Context.ClearError();
 8:
 9:   Response.Write(LastException);
10:
11:     }
12:
13: </script>
```

On line 5 I put the exception details into a local string by calling the `ToString` method of the `Exception` class. After which I call the `HttpContext`'s class `ClearError` method. This clears all exceptions from the current request (line 7). Finally, on line 9 I write the exception that occurred out to the page. Figure 9.12 contains the page that throws the exception after it is processed.

FIGURE 9.12
Page after exception was thrown and page was processed.

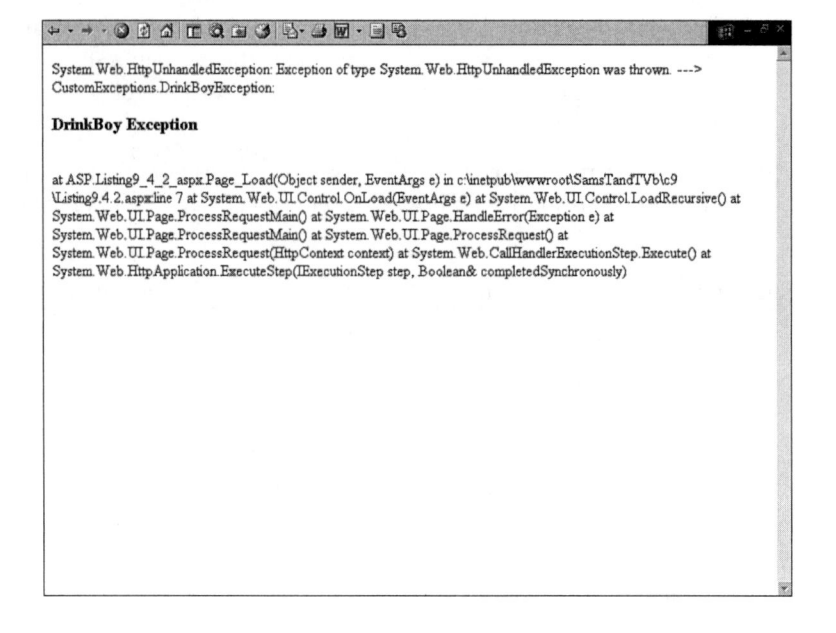

The next method you can use to determine the last exception thrown is to use the `HttpContext`'s class `Error` property. The `Error` property also returns a reference to the first exception object thrown for the current HTTP request/response. Listing 9.5.3 has a code example on using this property. In this example instead of writing out the exception details to the requested page we will redirect the user to a custom error page. The code for the custom error page can be found in Listing 9.5.4.

Listing 9.5.3 Code Example Illustrating How to Use the `HttpContext`'s `Error` Property to Get a Reference to an Un-Handled Exception

```
 1: <script runat="server" language="c#">
 2:
 3: void Application_Error(Object sender, EventArgs e) {
 4:
 5:   string LastException = Context.Error.ToString();
 6:
 7:   Context.ClearError();
 8:
 9:   Response.Redirect("CustomErrors.aspx?Err=" +
10:     Server.UrlEncode(LastException));
11:
12: }
13:
14: </script>
```

Listing 9.5.4 `CustomErrors.aspx` Page Used to Redirect User When an Un-Handled Exception Occurs—the Label Control Displays the Exception Details

```
 1: <script runat="server" language="Vb">
 2: public sub Page_Load(sender as Object, e as EventArgs)
 3:   ErrorMessage.Text = Request.QueryString("Err")
 4: end sub
 5: </script>
 6: <html>
 7:   <body>
 8:     <table width="50%" align="center" cellpadding="3"
 9:       border="0" cellspacing="3">
10:       <tr>
11:         <td>
12:           <h3>
13:           <font color="red">
14:           Sorry....</font>
15:           </h3>
16:         </td>
17:       </tr>
18:       <tr>
19:         <td>
20:           <h4>
21:           <font color="navy">
22:           The page you have requested
23:           has experienced problems, please try again later!
24:           </h4>
25:           </font>
26:         </td>
27:       </tr>
28:       <tr>
29:         <td bgcolor="navy">
30:           <font color="white">
31:           <b>
32:           <h3>
33:            Exception Details:<br>
34:           </h3>
35:           </b>
36:           <asp:label runat="server" id="ErrorMessage" />
37:           </font>
38:         </td>
39:       </tr>
40:     </table>
41:   </body>
42: </html>
```

Now when an exception occurs within the Web application. The `Application.Error` event handles the expectation by putting it into a local string (line 5), clears all exceptions from the request (line 7), and then redirects to a custom error page (lines 9 and 10). The exception details are also passed to the custom error page so it can be displayed to the user. Figure 9.13 contains an illustration of the custom error page after an exception has occurred.

FIGURE 9.13
Page after exception was thrown and page was processed.

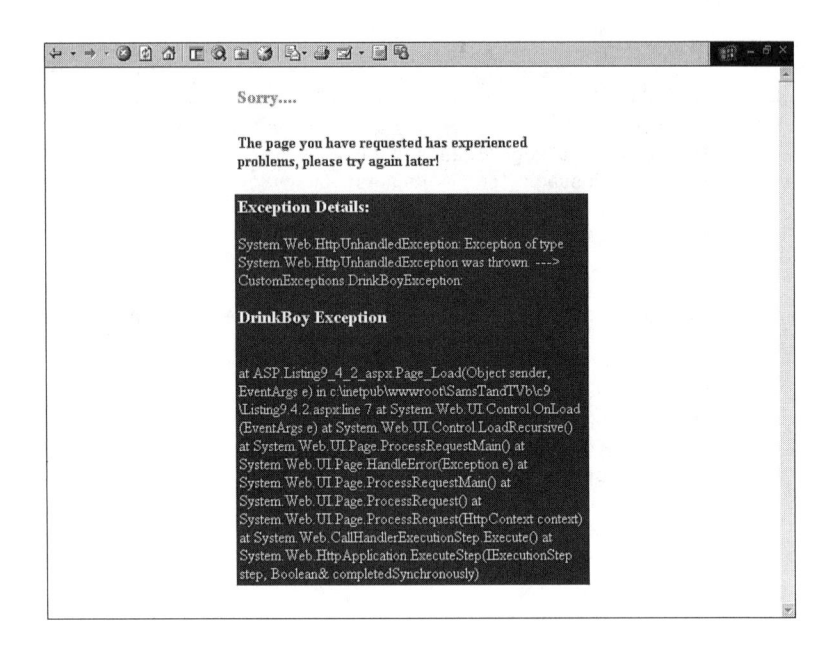

You will notice in all of the code examples demonstrating how to user the `Application_Error` event I called the Context classes `ClearError` method. The `ClearError` method clears all exceptions from the current request. If the `ClearError` is not called the exception which occurred will still show up in the clients browser unless other actions are taken.

One great use of the `Application_Error` event is to use it to exceptions. On DotNetJunkies.com we use the `Application_Error` event to log exceptions to the system event log. See Chapter 2 for information on how to create *Event Log* entries with ASP.NET. You can implement the same kind of logging within individual web forms either in a `Catch` block or the `Error` event, but putting it into the `global.asax` file eliminates the need to write repetitive code and centralizes the process of error logging within your application.

Implementing an Application-Wide Error Page Redirect

The Web.Config file contains all the configuration information about your ASP.NET Web application. As stated in the previous section, there is a `<customErrors>` section of this file. You can use this section to turn on `<customErrors>` as we demonstrated in the previous section; additionally you customize error pages for certain errors that may occur. For instance, you can redirect to one page if error 404 occurs and to another if error 405 occurs.

> **Note**
> Web.Config attributes are case sensitive. For instance, `<customErrors>` is correct, but `<customerrors>` (small "e" in errors) will cause an exception.

You can create a default error page, which will be directed to when any error occurs by using the `defaultRedirect` attribute. A code example can be found in Listing 9.5.2 demonstrating the use of the `defaultRedirect` attribute:

Listing 9.5.2 Using the `defaultredirect` Attribute of `<customerrors>`

```
1: <configuration>
2:    <system.web>
3:       <customErrors mode="On" defaultredirect="
➥customerrors.aspx?err=Unspecified">
4:       </customErrors>
5:    </system.web>
6: </configuration>
```

The default error page in Listing 9.5.2 is the `CustomErrors.aspx` page from Listing 9.5.3. Because this is a catch all exception handler I use *"Unspecified"* as the value of err. Although, if the `<customErrors>` attribute is your only error handler in your application you can obtain the exception information on the `CustomErrors.aspx` page by using the `GetLastError` method or `Error` property we discussed in the previous section to retrieve it.

You can customize the page that is redirected to by using one or more `<error>` sub-elements. The `<error>` sub-element supports two attributes:

- `statuscode`—The error status code that should occur before redirecting the clients browser to the new page

- `redirect`—The URL which the browser should be redirected to if the error that occurred matches that of the status Code

Listing 9.5.3 is an example of how to implement the `<error>` sub-element in the `<customerrors>` section of the `web.config`.

Listing 9.5.3 Implementing the `<error>` Sub-Element

```
1: <configuration>
2:    <system.web>
3:    <customErrors mode="on" defaultRedirect="
➥customerrors.aspx?err=Unspecified">
4:    <error statuscode="404" redirect="customerrors.aspx?err=File+Not+Found" />
5:    </customErrors>
6:    </system.web>
7: </configuration>
```

In Listing 9.5.3, I not only have the `defaultRedirect` attribute set, but I added an `<error>` sub-element for errors with the `statuscode` equal to 404. HTTP error code 404 means that the requested file cannot be found (see Table 9.5.1). If this error occurs, the client's browser is redirected to the `CustomErrors.aspx` page with a custom message to display to the user to read as you can see in Figure 9.14. You can test this out by requesting a page within your web application that does not exist.

Table 9.5.1 contains a list of status codes found in the `HttpStatusCode` enumeration. The `HttpStatusCode` enumeration is found in the `System.Net` namespace. Some of the listed status codes are not applicable to make an error handler.

FIGURE 9.14
`CustomErrors.aspx` after a page is requested that doesn't exist.

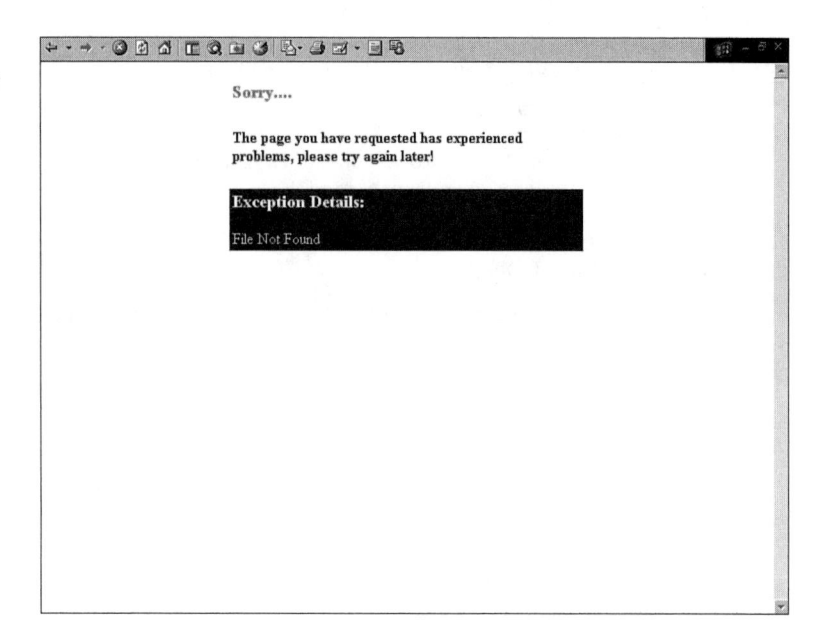

TABLE 9.5.1 Codes You Can Create Custom Error Pages For

Status code	Name	Description
100	`Continue`	The client can continue with a request.
101	`SwitchingProtocols`	The protocal version is being changed.
200	`OK`	The request succeeded.
201	`Created`	The request resulted in a new resource that was sent to the requestor.
202	`Accepted`	A request has been accepted for further processing.
203	`NonAuthoritativeInformation`	The returned meta-information is a cached copy and may be incorrect.
204	`NoContent`	The request was completed successfully and the response is blank.
205	`ResetContent`	Indicates the client should reset the current resource.

TABLE 9.5.1 Continued

Status code	Name	Description
206	PartialContent	The content is a partial response by using a get request that includes a byte range.
300	Ambiguous	The requested information has multiple representations.
300	MultipleChoices	(see: Ambiguous).
301	Moved	The requested information has been moved to the URI specified in the Location header.
301	MovedPermanently	(see: Moved).
302	Found	The URI located in the Location header is available.
302	Redirect	The requested information is at the URI specified in the Location header. The client shall go to this URI using the GET method.
303	RedirectMethod	Automatically redirects client to the URI specified in the Location header. The client shall go to this URI using the GET method.
303	SeeOther	(see: RedirectMethod).
304	NotModified	Indicates the requestors cached copy is up to date and new.
305	UseProxy	The request should use the proxy server specified in the Location header.
306	Unused	A proposed extension to HTTP 1.1 specification is not fully specified.
307	RedirectKeepVerb	The requested information is at the URI specified in the Location header. The client shall go to this URI using the POST method if the original request used the POST method.
307	TemporaryRedirect	(see: RedirectKeepVerb)
400	BadRequest	The request wasn't understood by the server and no other error is applicable (catch all).
401	Unauthorized	The requested resource requires authentication.
402	PaymentRequired	Not yet implemented.
403	Forbidden	The server will not fulfil a request.

TABLE 9.5.1 Continued

Status code	Name	Description
404	NotFound	The resource doesn't exist on the server.
405	MethodNotAllowed	Indicates that either a POST or GET or both is not allowed.
406	NotAcceptable	The client indicated in the Accept header that it will not accept the resource.
407	ProxyAuthenticationRequired	The requested proxy requires authentication.
408	RequestTimeout	The client did not send a request within the time the server was expecting one.
409	Conflict	The request couldn't be carried out due to a conflict on the server.
410	Gone	Requested resource is no longer available.
411	LengthRequired	Content-Length header is missing.
412	PreconditionFailed	A condition set in the request failed and the request cannot be completed.
413	RequestEntityTooLarge	The request is too large for the server to process.
414	RequestUriTooLong	Indicates the URI is too long.
415	UnsupportedMediaType	The request is for an unsupported type.
416	RequestedRangeNotSatisfiable	The range of data requested from a resource cannot be returned because the range of data requested either begins too early or too late.
417	ExpectationFailed	A expectation requested in the Except header couldn't be met by the server.
500	InternalServerError	Generic error.
501	NotImplemented	The server doesn't support the requested function.
502	BadGateway	The intermediate proxy server received a bad response from another proxy server.
503	ServiceUnavailable	The server is currently unavailable.
504	GatewayTimeout	The intermediate proxy timed out waiting for a response from another proxy server.
505	HttpVersionNotSupported	The requested HTTP version isn't supported by the server.

Summary

ASP.NET, VB.NET, and the .NET Framework brings a rich set of objects and language enhancements that if used will enable you to build highly stable web applications. In this chapter, we discussed methods you can use to help eliminate runtime errors at design time by using the `Option Explicit` and `Option Strict` statements. Then we discussed structured exception handling using the `Try...Catch...Finally` statement and how to use it to catch general and specific exceptions. We also discussed how you could create your own custom exceptions by inheriting the `ApplicationException` class. We ended the chapter by discussing how you to implement Page- and Application-wide exception handling to prevent users from seeing nasty error messages. Specifically we discussed the following:

- Using `Option Explicit` and `Option Strict` to catch potential errors at design time
- Structured error handling
- How to throw exceptions
- How to create custom exceptions
- Page level exception handling
- Application level exception handling

Other Resources

Probably the best place to find an example of application exception handling is in Microsoft's Duwamish Books Inc. online store example. It is an online eCommerce bookstore built entirely using the .NET Framework and architecture. The Duwamish design and development teams did a superb job on utilizing nearly all aspects of the .NET Framework. You can find more information on the Duwamish example at `http://msdn.microsoft.com/library/default.asp?URL=/library/techart/d4root.htm&RLD=598` and a live sample of the final web site at `http://www.duwamishonline.com`. Complete sample code in both Visual Basic.NET and C# come with VisualStudio.NET, and are found in the Enterprise Samples folder.

Other great resources are the .NET SDK help files, MSDN.NET, and Web sites like DotNetJunkies.com and GotDotNet.com.

SDK Help Files Suggested Reading:

- `Exception` Class
- `SystemException` Class
- `ApplicationException` Class
- `HttpStatusCode` Class
- Structured Error Handling

CHAPTER 10

DEBUGGING ASP.NET APPLICATIONS

by Multiple Authors

> **In this chapter you will learn**
> - How to use the `Trace` directive
> - How to add to the trace output
> - How to use the GUI debugger
> - How to work with breakpoints
> - How to view and modify variables of debugged applications
> - How to debug across language boundaries

A rule of thumb states that for every 50 lines of code, there is at least one error or bug. This is a good reason to debug your code. However, with classic ASP, debugging always ends up being a royal pain in the neck.

With ASP.NET, the debugging process is changing dramatically. For example, we can now use the Visual Studio debugger, which enables us to see call stacks, debug across language boundaries, and deal with exceptions like never before.

Even if you don't want to start a debugger for every little problem, ASP.NET provides a number of other simple debugging tools, such as trace output, which allows you to trace page execution and measure performance, among other things.

1. Tracing Code Execution

It is always a good idea to know what your code is doing and in which order various code snippets are being executed. With classic ASP, developers are forced to use `Response.Write` statements when they are interested in a particular variable's value at a particular point in a script. ASP.NET, however, provides you with a tracing functionality that enables you to forget about the hacks of the past.

In this section, I'm going to present the following topics:

- Page-Level Tracing
- Adding to the Trace Output
- Application-Level Tracing

Page-Level Tracing

With classic ASP, how often have you added code to your pages to output query string parameters, server variables, cookie contents, or dynamic SQL strings? I attest that I have used this technique many times, just to find out that the problem I was experiencing on an ASP page was a simple bug. Adding `Response.Write` code over and over again can be slightly annoying, and it's certainly a sloppy way to perform debugging.

With ASP.NET, inspecting page information is a snap with its tracing feature. Turning on this tracing functionality is a snap, too—all you have to do is modify the `@Page` directive in the ASP.NET Web page you want to trace:

```
<% @Page Language="VB" Trace="True" %>
```

Figure 10.1 contains the output of a "full-blown" ASP.NET page that has tracing enabled. Note that the tracing feature outputs a multitude of important information.

FIGURE 10.1
Trace output for the simplest possible ASP.NET page.

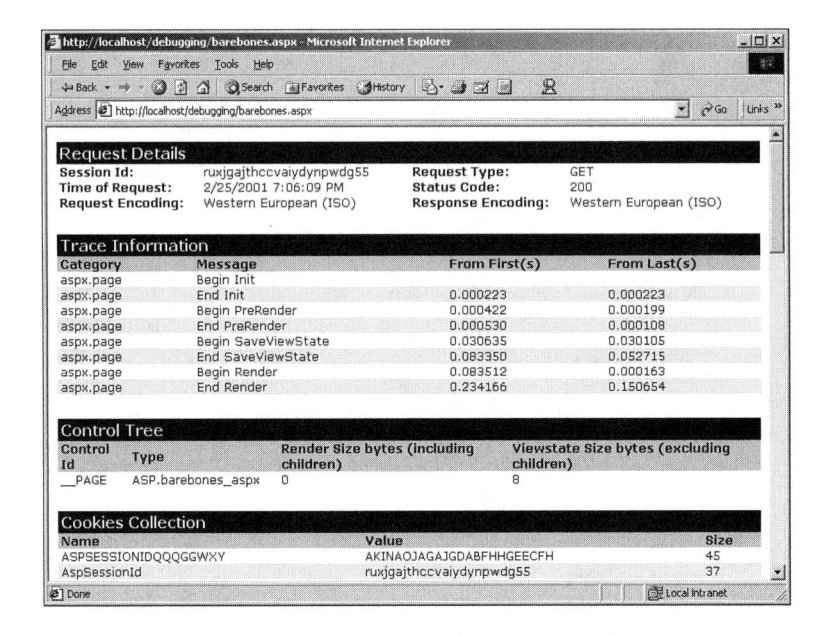

By simply adding the `Trace="True"` attribute to the `@Page` directive in an ASP.NET Web page, you get the following information in a trace output:

- Request Details. This information pertains to the request, such as status, session ID, encoding, and time of request.

- Trace Information. This section shows the time taken by specific events. You can add your own trace information, which is shown in the next section. You can use this timing information to measure the performance of your code.

- Control Tree. This section shows control dependencies on the page. This control tree is extremely helpful when you're examining which controls were created as server controls. It's also useful for determining which controls are the parents of other controls.

> **Tip**
>
> Control Tree is also a good point of reference to find out where you forgot to add a `RUNAT=SERVER` tag for a control.

- Cookies Collection. This section shows the cookie names, values, and sizes. It's important for tracking down cookie issues.

- Headers Collection. This section shows (client-sent) HTTP header names and values.

- Server Variables. This section lists all server variable names and values.

The trace output really contains a wealth of information that, in itself, can help you quickly identify and sort out problems. With page-level tracing, you can also include your own trace messages, which we will examine in the next section. When tracing is turned on, these tracing messages appear in the Trace Information section.

Adding to the Trace Output

In the previous section, we looked at how, by just specifying `Trace="True"` in the `@Page` directive, a plethora of technical information is presented to you when viewing an ASP.NET Web page. In this section, we'll look at how to get the most out of the Trace Information section that is shown in the trace output. For example, you can add your own messages to the Trace Information section. In addition to your tracing message, timing information is included as well.

Listing 10.1.1 contains a simple ASP.NET Web page that has page-level tracing enabled. It uses the `Trace.Write` and `Trace.Warn` methods to write information and warnings to the Tracing Information section.

LISTING 10.1.1 Using `Trace.Warn` and `Trace.Write`

```vb
 1: <% @Page Language="VB" Trace=True %>
 2: <% @Import Namespace="System.IO" %>
 3:
 4: <script language="VB" runat="server">
 5:
 6:   Sub Page_Load(sender as Object, e as EventArgs)
 7:
 8:     Dim StmReader As StreamReader
 9:     Dim strLine As String
10:
11:     Trace.Warn("Reading hard-coded file", "Test Setup")
12:     StmReader = File.OpenText(Server.MapPath("web.config"))
13:
14:     Trace.Write("Reading started","File IO")
15:
16:     While (StmReader.Peek() <> -1)
17:       strLine = StmReader.ReadLine()
18:       strLine = Server.HtmlEncode(strLine)
19:       Response.Write(strLine & "<br>" & vbCrLf)
20:     End While
21:
22:     Trace.Write("Reading done","File IO")
23:
24:     StmReader.Close()
25:
26:   End Sub
27: </script>
```

There are two `Trace` statements in this code: `Trace.Write` (lines 14 and 22) and `Trace.Warn` (line 11). Both methods take two `String` parameters: a message and a category.

The `Trace.Warn` method notifies testers of this page that there is a hard-coded string on line 12. The two `Trace.Write` statements measure the performance of the entire read and dump process—all you have to do is subtract the times (see Figure 10.2).

FIGURE 10.2

The Trace Information section shows `Trace.Warn` information in red.

Category	Message	From First(s)	From Last(s)
aspx.page	Begin Init		
aspx.page	End Init	0.000463	0.000463
aspx.page	Begin PreRender	0.000588	0.000125
aspx.page	End PreRender	0.000696	0.000108
aspx.page	Begin SaveViewState	0.000941	0.000245
aspx.page	End SaveViewState	0.001716	0.000775
aspx.page	Begin Render	0.001832	0.000116
Reading hard-coded file	Test Setup	0.005276	0.003444
Reading started	File IO	0.006928	0.001652
Reading done	File IO	0.018787	0.011859
aspx.page	End Render	0.019181	0.000395

These two methods are your first steps into debugging and performance testing your application. When you start adding more `Trace.Warn` and `Trace.Write` statements to your code, the Trace Information section grows. The default sort order of messages is by time—sometimes, however, you might want to sort the Trace Information output by categories. To accomplish this, set the `TraceMode` attribute to `SortByCategory`, like so:

```
<% @Page Language="VB" Trace="True" TraceMode="SortByCategory" %>
```

This sorts the output by category. (As you might have guessed already, the time-sorted default for `TraceMode` is `SortByTime`.)

Suppose you want all your ASP.NET Web pages to output tracing information. It would be a headache to go to each file and add the `Trace="True"` attribute to each Web page's `@Page` directive. Fortunately, using the `web.config` file, you can control tracing settings from a central location. In the next section, we'll examine how to turn on page-level tracing for an entire Web application. Additionally, we'll look at how to view tracing information for an entire Web application from one central, special Web page!

Application-Level Tracing

You can define trace settings per Web application in the configuration file, `Web.config`. The tracing features you can set in `Web.config` are actually richer than those you can set in the `@Page` directive.

Listing 10.1.2 shows a `Web.config` file that enables some of the more interesting features of tracing.

LISTING 10.1.2 A Sample `Web.config` File That Enables Tracing for an Application

```
 1: <configuration>
 2:   <system.web>
 3:      <trace
 4:          enabled="true"
 5:          requestLimit="10"
 6:          pageOutput="true"
 7:          traceMode="SortByTime"
 8:          />
 9:   </system.web>
10: </configuration>
```

Four settings define how tracing is handled:

- `enabled`—This setting enables or disables tracing for the entire application. The default is `False`.
- `requestLimit`—This setting defines the number of page traces to be cached. The default is `10`.
- `pageOutput`—When set to `True`, this setting automatically appends the trace output to every page processed in the application. The default is `False`.
- `traceMode`—This setting defines the sort order of the trace information. The default `SortByTime`, but you can also set it to `SortByCategory`.

All of these default settings are configurable through the `machine.config` file. For more information on `machine.config` refer to Chapter 11, "ASP.NET Deployment and Configuration."

> **Note**
>
> Even if `enabled` is set to `False` in `Web.config`, the `Trace` statement can be used to turn on tracing on a per-page basis.

Viewing an Entire Application's Trace Information in One Place

In Listing 10.1.2 we looked at how to enable tracing for the entire application. All that is needed, essentially, is the addition of the `<trace enabled="true">` attribute in `Web.config`. Once application-level tracing is turned on, you can view the entire application's trace information from a single Web-accessible file: `trace.axd`.

To visit `trace.axd`, simply point your Web browser to the file `trace.axd` for the appropriate Web application. For example, to view the tracing information for our default Web application we could point our browsers to `http://localhost/trace.axd`, as shown in Figure 10.3.

FIGURE 10.3
The `trace.axd` file is located at the same level as the `Web.config` file.

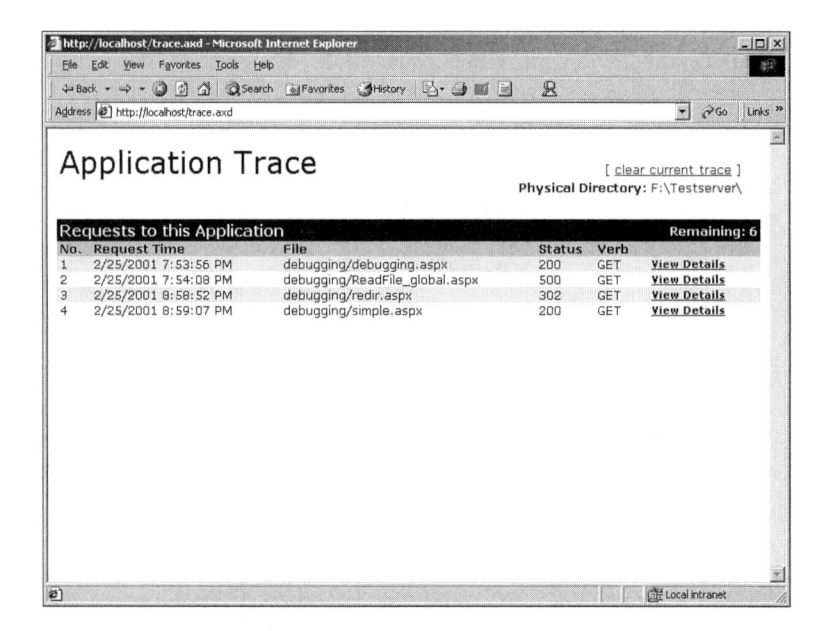

> **Note**
>
> Notice the `View Details` link next to each application request. By clicking on this hyperlink you will be taken to a page that shows the trace output for that request. This output is identical to what you would see if page-level tracing were turned on.

`trace.axd` offers a number of advantages. If you wish to examine trace information for the entire application for a live site you would not, obviously, want to have page-level tracing enabled, but you would still want to view the application-wide tracing information through `trace.axd`. You can accomplish this through the `trace` attribute in your `Web.config` file: simply set `enabled` to `true` and `pageOutput` to `false`.

One other important setting in the `trace` attribute is `localOnly`. This setting accepts either a `true` or `false` value and indicates if `trace.axd` can be viewed only from the local Web server machine or if *anyone* can view it. The default for this setting is `true`.

2. Debugging with the CLR Debugger

When debugging, you cannot prove the absence of bugs in your application—you can only prove the existence of bugs. This is why debugging and testing code are so important.

In this section, we will look at how to enable debugging for your ASP.NET Web pages. We'll examine how to use the GUI debugger the .NET Framework ships with. (Note that you can also use Visual Studio.NET as the ASP.NET debugger.) In examining this GUI debugger, we'll look at how to set breakpoints, step through your ASP.NET application, examine variables, and other common debugger tasks.

Enabling Debugging

To use the GUI debugger you have to prepare your application for debugging. To effectively work in the debugger, you need to provide additional information about the code—the so-called *program database*. Because providing this information carries a speed penalty, you have to explicitly request the VB.NET or C# compiler for debuggable versions of your code.

Providing this information for debugging an ASP.NET page can be enabled in one of two ways: for a single page only or for the entire ASP.NET application.

The easiest way, of course, is on a per-page basis. All you have to do is add one more property to the `@Page` directive:

```
<% @Page Debug="True" %>
```

This approach, however, has advantages as well as disadvantages. For example, it is really convenient and effortless to use. However, the downside is that when you ship your application, you have to check each and every page to make sure that you didn't forget one of these performance killers in your pages.

Therefore, the better approach is to enable debugging per application because then it can easily be turned on and off for the entire application. Turning on debuggin for the application can be done in `Web.config` (see Listing 10.2.1).

LISTING 10.2.1 A Sample `Web.config` File That Enables Debugging for an Entire Application

```
1: <configuration>
2:   <system.web>
3:     <compilation debug="true" />
4:   </system.web>
5: </configuration>
```

Now every ASP.NET page will be compiled with debugging information, which enables you to track down bugs in your application.

Now that we've looked at how to prepare our ASP.NET pages (or applications) for debugging, we need to examine how to attach our ASP.NET application to our debugger of choice.

Attaching to Your Application

Usually the first step in debugging is to define which application you want to debug. For a command-line or Windows Forms application, you normally select the executable to start the debugging session with. For ASP.NET, however, you do it a bit differently:

First, you have to start the GUI debugger. You can find the debugger in the directory `\Program Files\Microsoft.NET\FrameworkSDK\GuiDebug`. The executable is named `DbgCLR.exe`—double-click it to start the GUI debugger. Better yet, right-click and drag `DbgCLR.exe` to your Desktop to create a shortcut. This will save you time in the future.

> **Note**
>
> The `DbgCLR.exe` debugger is a stand-alone debugging application that ships with the .NET Framework. It is, essentially, a watered-down version of the Visual Studio.NET debugger. If you own a copy of Visual Studio.NET, you may wish to use its more feature-rich debugger.

To attach the debugger to ASP.NET, select Debug Processes from the Tools menu. When you open the debugger, you will see a list of processes currently running on your machine. However, you won't see the ASP.NET process at first because it is a system process, and system processes aren't shown the first time you start the debugger. You have to select the check box Show System Processes (see Figure 10.4).

The good news, however, is that the GUI debugger remembers this setting in the future.

> **Caution**
>
> You will see the `aspnet_wp.exe` process only if it is running—obviously. However, not so obvious is the fact that this process is started only after the very first ASP.NET page is executed on the server. Therefore, if it doesn't show up, execute any ASP.NET page and refresh the processes list.

FIGURE 10.4
ASP.NET is listed as a system process.

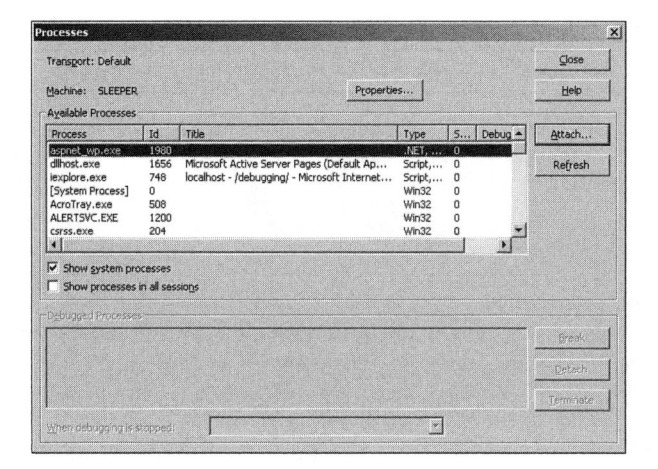

From the Processes dialog box, select the `aspnet_wp.exe` process and click Attach. Click Close to leave the Processes dialog box. At this point we're ready to begin debugging an ASP.NET application!

> **Note**
>
> You can also detach from a currently attached process at any time. You can bring up the Processes dialog box by clicking on the Tools, Debug Processes menu option.
>
> Detaching from a managed application (such as ASP.NET) allows it to continue to execute—in the unmanaged world, however, detaching from a process terminates it.

Working with Breakpoints

One of the most useful tools any decent debugger provides is the ability to set breakpoints. Breakpoints serve as markers in the code, indicating to the debugger locations it should stall the executing application, allowing the developer to view the values of variables, object properties, and other relevant debugging information. In this section we'll examine how to set breakpoints in an ASP.NET Web page, allowing us to step through the Web page's execution.

Before we can set breakpoints for an ASP.NET Web page, though, we must load a Web page into the debugger. Listing 10.2.2 provides an extremely simplistic example.

LISTING 10.2.2 A Simple Example of Setting a Breakpoint—`SetAbreakpoint.aspx`

```
1: <% @Page Language="C#" Debug=True %>
2: <script language="C#" runat="server">
3:
4:    void Page_Load(Object sender, EventArgs e)
5:    {
```

LISTING 10.2.2 Continued

```
 6:     int nVar = 10;
 7:
 8:     for (int iLoop=1; iLoop <= nVar; iLoop++)
 9:       Response.Write("Hello, World!<br>");
10:
11:   }
</script>
```

Here, we want to set a breakpoint for line 9. To do this, start the CLR Debugger, as shown in the previous section, and attach to the ASP.NET process. Then choose Open File and open the file `SetABreakpoint.aspx`. The file is opened as read-only in the debugger.

To set a breakpoint, you have multiple options. The easiest way is to click the gray bar next to line 9. You can also right-click and select Insert Breakpoint from the context menu. Regardless of how you add the breakpoint, you get a red circle, denoting the new breakpoint (see Figure 10.5).

FIGURE 10.5
The new breakpoint is set.

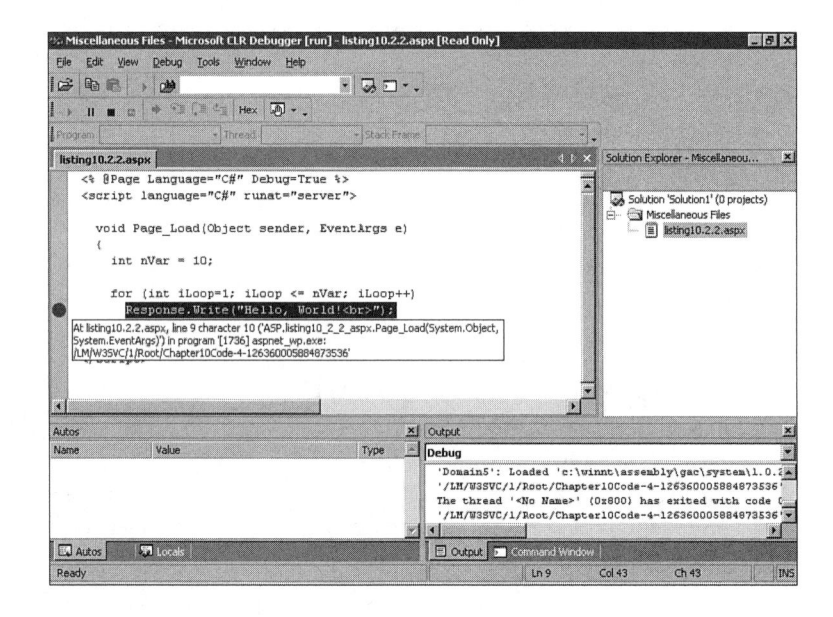

At this point you may be wondering how to "execute" the ASP.NET page we examined in Listing 10.2.2. At this point, we simply need to have the ASP.NET engine compile our page into a DLL containing managed code. This is accomplished by simply visiting the page in a Web browser!

As soon as you access the page via a Web browser, the page gets compiled and the debugger picks up the code processing, stopping at the breakpoint we set (see Figure 10.6).

FIGURE 10.6
The breakpoint is hit on the first execution of the ASP.NET page.

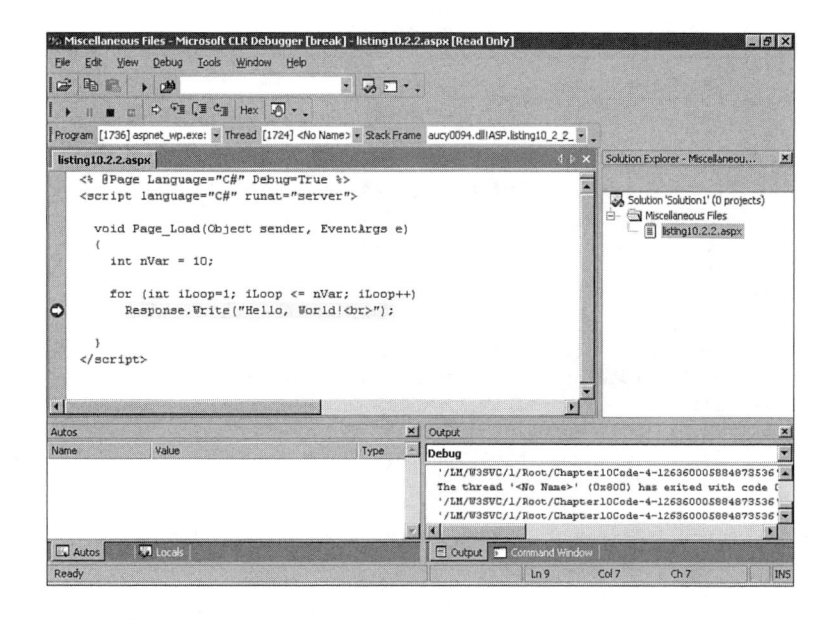

At this point, the execution of the page is halted, and now you are in charge of stepping through your application.

> **Note**
>
> The breakpoint we have added is of the type "break at line." The GUI debugger sports some other breakpoint types; however, these are more advanced and seldom used for debugging ASP.NET pages. Please consult the .NET SDK documentation for how to use the other types of breakpoints.

Stepping Through Your Application

Once you are in break mode, you can step through your application, controlling how the statements are being executed. To illustrate the actions you can perform, Listing 10.2.3 demonstrates a binary image read. Notice that Listing 10.2.3 assumes that you have a file named `bannerad.jpg` in the same directory as Listing 10.2.3.

LISTING 10.2.3 `BinaryWrite.aspx` Is Used to Send an Image to the Client

```
1: <% @Page Language="VB" Debug=True %>
2: <% @Import Namespace="System.IO" %>
3: <%
4: Response.Buffer = True
5:
6: Dim StmRead As Stream = File.OpenRead(Server.MapPath("bannerad.jpg"))
7:
8: Dim nBufferSize As Integer = 255
```

LISTING 10.2.3 *Continued*

```
 9: Dim nReadBytes As Integer = 0
10: Dim nTotalBytes As Integer = 0
11:
12:
13: Dim arrByte(nBufferSize) As Byte
14: Response.ClearContent()
15: Response.ContentType = "image/jpeg"
16:
17:
18: While (StmRead.Position < StmRead.Length)
19:    nReadBytes = StmRead.Read(arrByte, 0 , nBufferSize-1)
20:    nTotalBytes = nTotalBytes + nReadBytes
21:
22:    If (nReadBytes = nBufferSize) Then
23:      Response.BinaryWrite(arrByte)
24:    Else
25:      Dim arrCopy(nReadBytes) As Byte
26:      Array.Copy(arrByte, 0, arrCopy, 0, nReadBytes)
27:      Response.BinaryWrite(arrCopy)
28:    End If
29: End While
30:
31: StmRead.Close()
32: Response.End()
33: %>
```

Set the breakpoint to line 6, which opens the file for reading. Now execute the page in your browser, and the debugger will stop at this line, as shown in Figure 10.7.

FIGURE 10.7
The debugger stops execution at the line where you set the breakpoint.

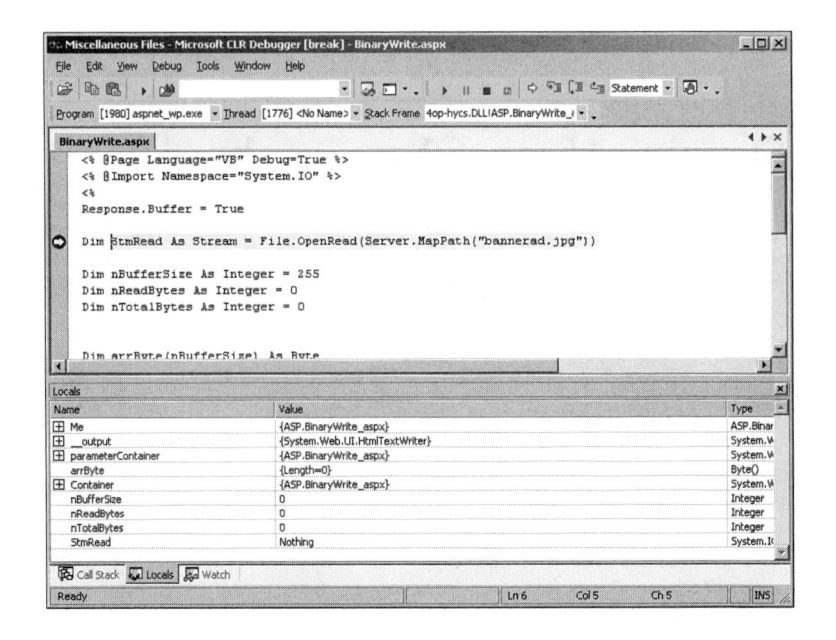

You can start to step through your code using the following commands:

- **Step Over (F10)**—Executes the current line of code. This is the most commonly used command.

- **Step Into (F11)**—Allows you to step into a method that is being called on the current line. We use this feature in the section "Cross-Language Debugging," later in this chapter.

- **Step Out (Shift+F11)**—When you have entered a method using Step Into, you can go back to the calling statement at any time using Step Out. The code in the method you were in is completely executed, though.

- **Run to Cursor (Ctrl+F10)**—All code between the current break line and the cursor position is being executed. This provides a dynamic breakpoint of sorts during debugging.

These commands are accessible via their keyboard shortcuts, the Debug menu, and the Debug toolbar.

However, stepping through code without actually examining any interesting data isn't exactly what you'd call debugging. More important information can be gleaned by examining the current values of variables, the values of object properties, and so on. Accessing such important debugging information is covered in the next section.

Examining Variables

Now is the time to examine what the GUI debugger really can do for you—most of it is hidden in the submenu Debug, Windows.

At first, this seems to be overwhelming, but the good news is that, for the average ASP.NET programmer, only a few of those are really important:

- **Locals**—Displays the variables in the scope of the current method.

- **Me**—Displays the current object's properties. Me is also available in Locals.

- **Call Stack**—Displays a hierarchy of methods that called the method you are currently in. This allows you to examine where the call to your method came from.

- **Watch**—Displays variables and their values you want to watch specifically. This feature comes in handy when you have too many local variables to effectively keep track of them in the Locals window.

Now let's see how all this works in real life using the `BinaryWrite.aspx` example (Listing 10.2.3), starting at line 6. To get some interesting information into the Locals window, select Step Over from the Debug menu. The StreamReader is now opened for the file `bannerad.jpg`.

> **Note**
>
> For more information on working with the Web server's file system, refer to Chapter 2, "Common ASP.NET Code Techniques."

To verify what happened in that line of code, expand the variable `StmRead` in the Locals window, and you'll also get an interesting tree view, as shown in Figure 10.8.

FIGURE 10.8
A `StreamReader` expanded.

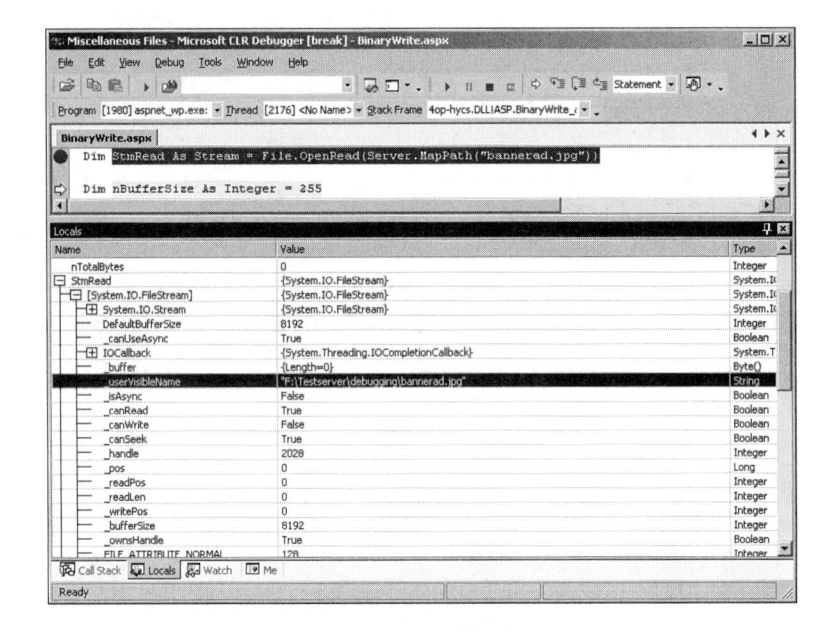

You have access to all properties of the `StreamReader` object as well as its parent objects. You are able to verify that all settings are as expected.

However, there's more thing you can do in the Locals window. First, step over the initialization of the `nBufferSize` variable. Notice that as the value changes, this change is shown in a different color. To make things interesting, double-click the value. You'll noticed that it changes to an edit field. Type in a different value and press the Enter key—you've just changed the value of the variable.

We are now at line 8. Spend some time with this ASP.NET page to play with the different stepping features as well as the Locals window. The source code only reads files, so you can safely do about anything you like in the Locals window. Every minute you spend learning how to use the GUI debugger with this rather simple example will pay off later when you start to debug more complex solutions.

Cross-Language Debugging

Have you ever had to debug a C++ transacted component inside an ASP application? Or perhaps you've had a Java component used through an ASP page? Maybe it was a VB component and your ASP developers used JScript as the scripting language? With classic ASP, there did not exist any sort of integrated debugger that could seamlessly debug parts of an application written in different languages.

The good news with ASP.NET is that, as long as you stay in the managed code arena, debugging code in different programming languages is not complicated at all—in fact, it's a snap. To illustrate this, I'll walk you through an ASP.NET page written in VB that calls a component written in C#.

The component used in this example is one that many businesses (at least in Europe) need: a component that converts the new Euro currency to "old" European currencies, and vice versa. This component conforms to all regulations regarding Euro money conversion, which includes a special rounding functionality as well as certain triangulation rules. You can see the entire source code in Listing 10.2.4.

LISTING 10.2.4 Source Code for the Euro Conversion Component—`EuroConv.cs`.

```
 1: // Christoph Wille, christophw@alphasierrapapa.com
 2: // 22.01.2001
 3: // conversion rates from http://europa.eu.int/euro/html/home5.html?lang=5
 4:
 5: using System;
 6: using System.Collections;
 7:
 8: namespace AlphaSierraPapa.Utilities
 9: {
10: public class EuroConverter
11: {
12:    protected Hashtable m_MapCurrencySymbol2Factor;
13:
14:    public EuroConverter()
15:    {
16:      m_MapCurrencySymbol2Factor = new Hashtable();
17:      m_MapCurrencySymbol2Factor.Add("ATS", 13.7603);   // Austria
18:      m_MapCurrencySymbol2Factor.Add("BEF", 40.3399);   // Belgium
19:      m_MapCurrencySymbol2Factor.Add("LUF", 40.3399);   // Luxemburg
20:      m_MapCurrencySymbol2Factor.Add("FIM", 5.94573);   // Finland
21:      m_MapCurrencySymbol2Factor.Add("FRF", 6.55957);   // France
22:      m_MapCurrencySymbol2Factor.Add("DEM", 1.95583);   // Germany
23:      m_MapCurrencySymbol2Factor.Add("IEP", 0.787564);  // Ireland
24:      m_MapCurrencySymbol2Factor.Add("ITL", 1936.27);   // Italy
25:      m_MapCurrencySymbol2Factor.Add("NLG", 2.20371);   // Netherlands
26:      m_MapCurrencySymbol2Factor.Add("PTE", 200.482);   // Portugal
27:      m_MapCurrencySymbol2Factor.Add("ESP", 166.386);   // Spain
28:      m_MapCurrencySymbol2Factor.Add("GRD", 340.750);   // Greece
29:    }
30:
31:    public double GetExchangeRate(String strCurrencySymbol)
32:    {
33:      if (m_MapCurrencySymbol2Factor.ContainsKey(strCurrencySymbol))
34:      {
35:        return (double)m_MapCurrencySymbol2Factor[strCurrencySymbol];
36:      }
37:
38:      throw new ArgumentException("Currency not defined!");
```

LISTING 10.2.4 *Continued*

```
39:      return -1;  // unreachable code; intentionally
40:    }
41:
42:    public double ConvertToEuro(double dVal2Convert, string strCurrencyFrom)
43:    {
44:    if (!m_MapCurrencySymbol2Factor.ContainsKey(strCurrencyFrom))
45:    {
46:      throw new ArgumentException("Lookup of currency symbol failed!");
47:    }
48:
49:    double dRate = (double)m_MapCurrencySymbol2Factor[strCurrencyFrom];
50:    return Round((dVal2Convert / dRate));
51:    }
52:
53:    public double ConvertFromEuro(double dVal2Convert, string strCurrencyTo)
54:    {
55:      if (!m_MapCurrencySymbol2Factor.ContainsKey(strCurrencyTo))
56:    {
57:      throw new ArgumentException("Lookup of currency symbol failed!");
58:    }
59:
60:    double dRate = (double)m_MapCurrencySymbol2Factor[strCurrencyTo];
61:    return Round((dVal2Convert * dRate));
62:    }
63:
64:    public double Triangulate(double dVal2Convert, string strCurrencyFrom,
➥string strCurrencyTo)
65:    {
66:    if (!m_MapCurrencySymbol2Factor.ContainsKey(strCurrencyFrom) ||
67:       !m_MapCurrencySymbol2Factor.ContainsKey(strCurrencyTo))
68:    {
69:      throw new ArgumentException("Lookup of currency symbol failed!");
70:    }
71:
72:    double dRateFrom =(double)m_MapCurrencySymbol2Factor[strCurrencyFrom];
73:    double dRateTo = (double)m_MapCurrencySymbol2Factor[strCurrencyTo];
74:
75:    // do the conversion
76:    double dHelper = dVal2Convert / dRateFrom;
77:    dHelper *= dRateTo;
78:
79:    return Round(dHelper);
80:    }
81:
82:    // our EMU compliant rounding function
83:    protected double Round(double dVal2Round)
84:    {
85:    // first, strip off everything after third decimal
86:    double dVal2 = 0.0;
87:    dVal2Round *= 1000;
88:    dVal2 = Fix(dVal2Round);
89:
```

LISTING 10.2.4 Continued

```
90:      // now, round the result
91:      dVal2 /= 10;
92:      dVal2Round = Fix(dVal2 + (dVal2 > 0 ? 0.5 : -0.5));
93:
94:      // we are done.
95:      return (dVal2Round/100);
96:    }
97:
98:    protected double Fix(double dVarIn)
99:    {
100:     if (Math.Sign(dVarIn) < 0)
101:     {
102:       // less than 0, negative values
103:       return Math.Ceiling(dVarIn);
104:     }
105:     else
106:     {
107:       return Math.Floor(dVarIn);
108:     }
109:     return -1;   // unreachable code; intentionally
110:   }
111: }
112: }  // end of namespace AlphaSierraPapa.Utilities
```

This component employs a hashtable as a map between the currency symbol and exchange rate. Because the exchange rates of the 12 Euro participant countries are set in stone, I can easily hard-code these in the constructor.

The code, itself, and the calculations aren't complicated. So, let's see how we can use them in ASP.NET in a debugging scenario.

First, we need to compile the component into an assembly; however, we must not forget that we need debug information. This is done with the **debug+** switch for `csc.exe`:

`csc.exe /target:library /out:euroconv.dll EuroConv.cs /debug+`

The compiler generates one DLL and one PDB file. Copy both to the `bin` directory of the application. Now we can use the component in ASP.NET and debug it.

The public methods we'll call from the VB ASP.NET page are `ConvertFromEuro`, `ConvertToEuro`, `Triangulate`, and `GetExchangeRate`. Because we're doing this for debugging purposes only, we are not going to add any user interface (see Listing 10.2.5).

LISTING 10.2.5 `Simple.aspx` Uses the Methods Provided by the Euro Conversion Component

```
1: <% @Page Language= "VB" Debug=True %>
2: <% @Import Namespace="AlphaSierraPapa.Utilities" %>
3:
4: <script language="VB" runat="server">
5:
6:   Sub Page_Load(sender as Object, e as EventArgs)
7:
```

LISTING 10.2.5 Continued

```
 8:     Dim ecuConv As EuroConverter = new EuroConverter()
 9:     Response.Write(ecuConv.ConvertToEuro(100, "ATS") & "<br>")
10:     Response.Write(ecuConv.ConvertFromEuro(100, "ATS") & "<br>")
11:     Response.Write(ecuConv.Triangulate(100, "ATS", "DEM") & "<br>")
12:     Response.Write(ecuConv.GetExchangeRate("ESP") & "<br>")
13:
14: End Sub
15:
16: </script>
```

Open `Listing 10.2.5` in the GUI debugger and set a breakpoint at line 9. To start the debugging process, execute `simple.aspx` in the browser. At line 9, if you click Step Over, the statement is executed.

Now let's try a different command—Step Into. Without any hassle, you are inside the component's `ConvertFromEuro` method, and you are still in the same debugger and still have full access to Locals, Call Stack, and Watch (see Figure 10.9).

FIGURE 10.9
You can seamlessly step from VB to C# code in the same debugging session.

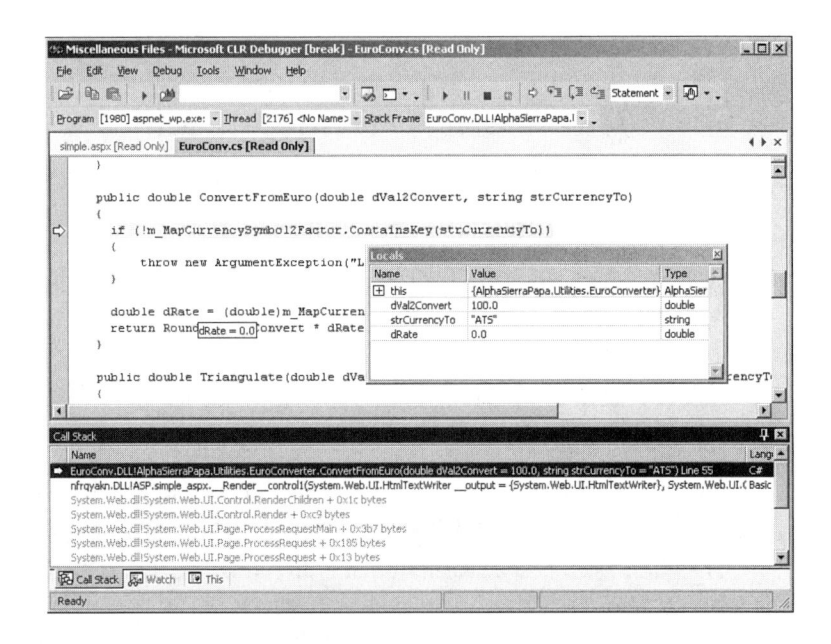

Debugging Exceptions

I've kept this goodie for last. One "exceptional" feature of the GUI debugger is that you can break into the debugger when an exception is thrown in an ASP.NET page. With this technique, you can easily debug your exception-handler code in the `Catch` block.

All you have to do is slightly modify the settings in Debug, Exceptions—set the Common Language Runtime Exceptions to "Break into debugger all the time" (see Figure 10.10).

FIGURE 10.10
Breaking into the debugger on any exception.

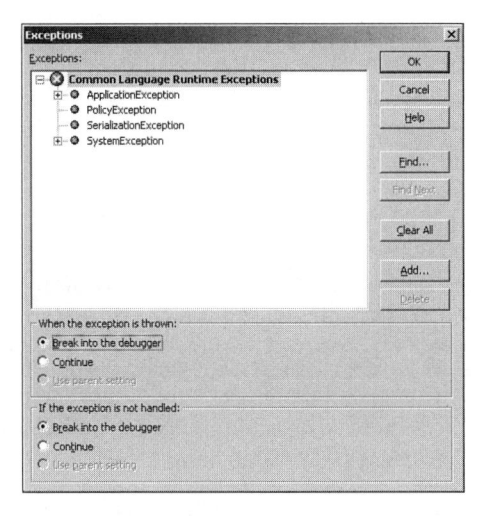

Now all we need is some code that throws an exception. In Listing 10.2.3 we looked at some code that would send binary content to the browser, specifically the binary content of the file `bannerad.jpg` (refer back to line 6). If you change that file name on line 6 to a file name that does not exist, a `FileNotFoundException` exception will be thrown.

Once an exception is thrown, the debugger will kick in, as shown in Figure 10.11.

FIGURE 10.11
The debugger tells you that an exception was thrown.

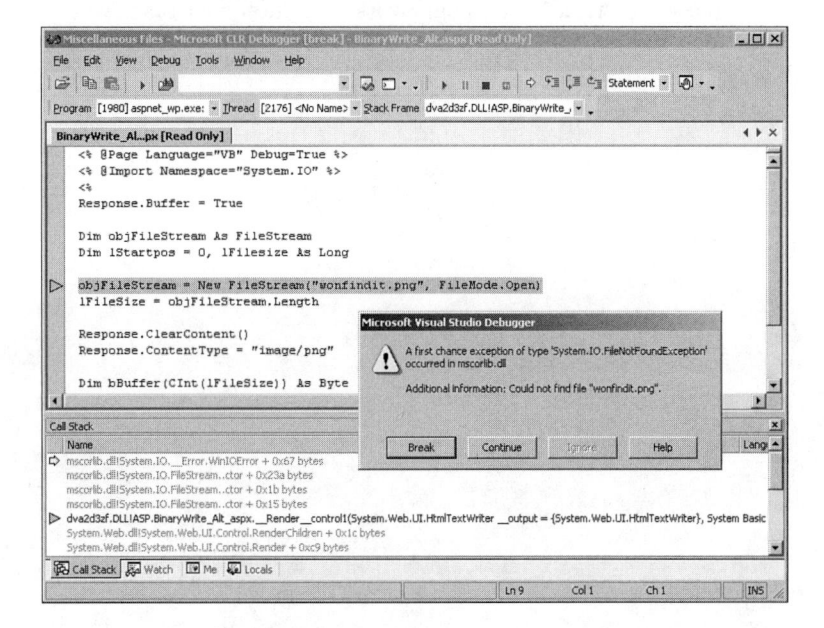

You are in the debugger at the very point the problem has occurred. You can examine the call stack, manipulate variables, and even continue execution.

Summary

This chapter started with a discussion of tracing, which provides a simple way of debugging your ASP.NET pages. You learned how to enable tracing per page as well as for an entire application. You also learned what kind of information you can glean from the trace output. We looked at the kind of performance monitoring you can do with page tracing as well.

The remainder of this chapter dealt with the debugging procedures that you, as an ASP.NET programmer, will be using most of the time. We toured breakpoints and various information windows, and we dealt with more advanced tricks of the trade, such as debugging code from multiple programming languages and breaking into the debugger on exceptions.

Take a moment to compare these powerful and very useful features of ASP.NET to classic ASP. In classic ASP, there was no such debugger, and tracing meant inserting `Response.Write`s throughout your code.

Other Resources

You can learn more about debugging and the GUI debugger in the .NET SDK documentation, the section titled ".NET Framework Reference/.NET Framework Tools and Debugger/Debugging."

CHAPTER 11

ASP.NET DEPLOYMENT AND CONFIGURATION

Doug Seven

In this chapter you will learn how to:

- Deploy components to the bin directory
- Set common `web.config` configuration settings
- Read settings from web.config
- Add application configuration settings
- Read application configuration settings
- Add custom configuration settings
- Read custom configuration settings
- Enable worker process restarts
- Enable Web Gardens (multiprocessor functionality)

ASP.NET allows for multiple Web applications to run on the same system with each Web application running independently of the others. Each Web application has its own directory for components (the `\bin` directory) and its own XML-based configuration file. This allows you to build robust Web applications using custom components (even different versions of components), and have different configuration settings for each application.

1. Deploying Components to the `\bin` Directory

Each ASP.NET Web application uses a local assembly cache to hold application-specific logic. The application logic, known as assemblies, are contained in compiled DLLs. Since each Web application hosts its own application-specific logic, multiple applications on one server can use different versions of the same application logic. Copying the necessary version of the DLL to the Web application's local assembly cache does this. When the .NET Framework is installed on a server, IIS is configured to use the `\bin` subdirectory of the Web application as its local application cache, as seen in Figure 11.1. The `\bin` directory is located immediately under the Web application's root directory, and is automatically configured to deny browser access. This prevents users from accessing the `\bin` directory and downloading any DLLs contained in it.

FIGURE 11.1
ASP.NET applications are configured to use the `\bin` directory, immediately below the root directory, as its local application cache directory.

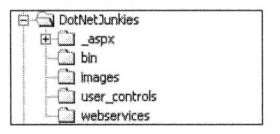

When the Web application is started, the .NET Framework constructs a new instance of the `System.AppDomain` class. The `AppDomain` class enables multiple Web applications to run in the same process, and manages the isolation of each Web application. The `AppDomain` class performs the following functions:

- Enumerates the assemblies and threads in a domain.
- Defines dynamic assemblies in a domain.
- Specifies assembly loading and domain termination events.
- Loads assemblies and types into the domain.
- Terminates the domain.

When the `AppDomain` instance is constructed it creates in-memory shadow copies of the DLLs that are in the `\bin` directory. This allows the Web application to use the assemblies without locking the actual DLL files. The .NET Framework monitors the original DLLs. If any changes are made to the original DLL, all requests currently using the shadow copy are completed, and a new shadow copy is created for the new requests to use. Because the actual DLL is not locked on the server, you can replace the DLL simply by replacing the DLL with a different version. A shadow copy of the new DLL is created, and new requests use the new shadow copy. As soon as the old requests are done using the original shadow copy, it is destroyed and all requests use the new shadow copy.

Because ASP.NET tracks any new DLLs or changes in existing DLLs, deploying DLLs to a Web application is dramatically simplified compared to classic ASP. In classic ASP, deploying a DLL to a Web server involved stopping the Web server, copying the DLL to the Web server, registering the DLL with `RegServ32.exe`, and restarting the Web server. In ASP.NET you do not need to stop the Web server, nor do you need to explicitly register the DLL. Simply copying the DLL to the `\bin` directory will successfully add the assembly to the Web application. ASP.NET, which constantly monitors the `\bin` directory, will register the new DLL and make a make a shadow copy of it. The shadow copy is then loaded into the local application cache.

If the DLL is changed, as soon as the new version is copied to the `\bin` directory, the Web application is updated to use the new assembly.

2. Configuring Applications to Use Specific Component Versions

The .NET Framework enables multiple versions of the same assembly to exist on the same machine, and it allows different applications to use different versions of the same assembly. Gone are the days of "DLL Hell," where loading a new version of an assembly on a machine meant that applications built with the older version might break. With the .NET Framework we have two ways to allow applications to use version specific assemblies.

The first is by putting the DLL in the `\bin` directory of an application. The DLL and all of its namespaces and classes will be available only to that application. This allows for each application on a machine to have different versions of the same assembly in their `\bin` directory, with no DLL version conflicts.

The second is by registering each version of an assembly with the global assembly cache and doing assembly redirecting at the application level.

The Global Assembly Cache

The *global assembly cache* is a machine-wide code cache where assemblies designed to be shared by multiple applications are stored. The DLL is stored on the file system and is registered with the global assembly cache using the `GacUtil.exe` utility. The utility registers the assembly, and keeps track of its version. Using the global assembly cache we can have two DLLs with the same name, but separate version numbers, on our file system. At the machine-level we can specify which assembly version is the default version to be used. This can then be overridden at the application level.

A scenario where this type of versioning is applicable is on a Web server hosted by an Internet Service Provider (ISP). An ISP may host several applications on one server, and likely a separate customer owns each application. As an added feature the ISP may have a third-party assembly that it makes available to customers. Each customer can implement the functionality of the assembly in his or her application. If the third-party ships a newer version of the assembly that has a breaking change in it, the ISP would not want to load this assembly on the server because it would break the customers' applications. With the versioning support provided by the .NET Framework, the ISP can load the new assembly on the Web server and register it with the global assembly cache. The existing applications will continue to use the original version of the assembly, while any customer who wanted to could add an assembly redirect to his or her application's configuration file, and use the new version of the assembly. The net result is different applications on one machine using multiple versions of the same assembly.

Building a Versioned Assembly

To illustrate this we are going to build a versioned assembly called **myData**, which will expose a single class with a single method that binds a `DataGrid` to the results of a stored procedure, and returns the number of customers in the Northwind Customers table. In version 1.0.0.0 the return data type will be a `string`, and in version 2.0.0.0 the return data type will be an `integer`. Since explicit data type conversions are not allowed in C#, or in Visual Basic.NET with `Option Strict` turned on, this is a breaking change.

In Listing 11.2.1 we build the class file for **myData.myDataClass**.

LISTING 11.2.1 Building the myData.myDataClass—myDataClass.vb

```
 1: Imports System
 2: Imports System.Web.UI.WebControls
 3: Imports System.Data
 4: Imports System.Data.SqlClient
 5:
 6: Namespace myData
 7:
 8:   Public Class myDataClass
 9:
10:     Public Function getData( ByVal _myGrid As DataGrid ) As String
11:       Dim con As SqlConnection = New
        SqlConnection("server=localhost;database=Northwind;uid=sa;pwd=;")
12:       Dim cmd As SqlCommand = New
        SqlCommand("sp_GetTenCustAndOutputParam", con)
13:       cmd.CommandType = CommandType.StoredProcedure
14:       cmd.Parameters.Add(New SqlParameter("@count", SqlDbType.Int, 4))
15:       cmd.Parameters.Item("@count").Direction = ParameterDirection.Output
16:       'Open the connection
17:       con.Open()
18:
19:       'Set the grid data source to the DataReader returned by ExecuteReader
20:       myGrid.DataSource =
        cmd.ExecuteReader(CommandBehavior.CloseConnection)
21:       myGrid.DataBind()
22:
23:       'Close the DataReader returned by ExecuteReader()
24:       CType(_myGrid.DataSource, SqlDataReader).Close()
25:
26:       Return cmd.Parameters.Item("@count").Value.ToString()
27:     End Function
28:
29:   End Class
30:
31: End Namespace
```

In Listing 11.2.1 we build the **myData.myDataClass** file. On line 6 we declare the namespace (**myData**), followed on line 8 by the class declaration. On lines 10–27 we create a method that executes a stored procedure against the Northwind database. The method takes in a `DataGrid` as its only argument, and, on lines 20–21 binds the `DataGrid` to data returned from our `SqlCommand`. The `SqlCommand` has one parameter that returns the total number of records in the Customers table as a string.

The `getData()` method executes the `sp_GetTenCustAndOutputParam` stored procedure. This stored procedure is shown in Listing 11.2.2.

LISTING 11.2.2   The `sp_GetTenCustAndOutputParam` Stored Procedure

```
1: CREATE PROCEDURE [sp_GetTenCustAndOutputParam]
2: @count int output
3: AS
4: SELECT @count=COUNT(*) FROM Customers
5: SELECT TOP 5 * FROM Customers
6: GO
```

To add this stored procedure to your SQL Server installation do one of the following:

1. Copy this code into the SQL Server Query Analyzer and press F5 to execute it.

2. Open the SQL Server Enterprise Manager and navigate to the **Stored Procedures** node under the Northwind database. Right-click on the node and choose **New Stored Procedure**. Copy the code in Listing 11.2.2 into the stored procedure window and click OK.

To compile this class into a versioned assembly we must define the assembly attributes. This can be done in the same file as the class, but I prefer to keep it in a separate file and compile them together. Listing 11.2.3 shows the code to define the assembly.

LISTING 11.2.3   Building the Assembly Info—`myDataAssemblyInfo.vb`

```
 1: Imports System.Reflection
 2: Imports System.Runtime.CompilerServices
 3:
 4: <Assembly: AssemblyTitle("ASP.NET Tips Tutorials & Code")>
 5: <Assembly: AssemblyDescription("Data Access for my application")>
 6: <Assembly: AssemblyCompany("DotNetJunkies.com")>
 7: <Assembly: AssemblyProduct("myData")>
 8: <Assembly: AssemblyCopyright("Copyright 2001. All rights reserved.")>
 9: <Assembly: AssemblyVersion("1.0.0.0")>
10: <Assembly: AssemblyDelaySign(false)>
11: <Assembly: AssemblyKeyFile("[path to application directory]\myKey.snk")>
```

In Listing 11.2.3 we create the `myDataAssemblyInfo.vb` file. This file will be compiled with the `myDataClass.vb` file to create an assembly (`myData.dll`). On line 4 we define an assembly title. This can be anything we want it to be. On line 5 we define the assembly description. Each of the attributes follows the same format, and is used to define the assembly, such as the name of the company that produced the assembly.

On line 9 we define the assembly version. The version numbering follows the following structure:

[major].[minor].[build].[revision]

For example, a version number of 1.0.2914.16 indicates that the assembly is major version 1, minor version 0, build 2914, and revision 16.

On line 10 we use the `AssemblyDelaySign(false)` attribute to indicate that we do not want to delay applying a signature to our assembly. A signature is required in our assembly to be allowed to register it with the global assembly cache. The signature is generated when the assembly is compiled based on a private key. On line 11 we define the path to the key file.

Creating a Key File for Strong Named Assemblies

A strong named assembly is identified by its text name, version number, and culture information (if provided), plus a public key and a digital signature. The .NET Framework provides a tool, `sn.exe`, for generating keys used to generate digital signatures when the assembly is compiled.

The key that is generated ensures that the assembly name is unique, hence the term strong named. When an assembly is registered with the global assembly cache, its human readable name becomes irrelevant. The assembly is kept track of by its strong name. Since no two keys are generated the same, two different assemblies cannot have the same name.

To generate a private key pair that will be used when compiling the `myData` assembly, open a command line prompt and execute the following code:

```
sn.exe -k [path to application directory]\myKey.snk
```

A file, `myKey.snk`, will be added to the directory you specified.

> **Note**
> The `-k` option we used indicates that a new key file should be created. To see other options for the `sn.exe` utility, execute the following command from the command line:
> ```
> sn.exe /?
> ```

Compiling a Strong Named Assembly

Now that we have all of the pieces in place—the assembly info file, the class file, and the key file—we can compile the assembly into a DLL. To compile a strong named assembly, the assembly info file (`myDataAssemblyInfo.vb`) and the class file (`myDataClass.vb`) have to be compiled together.

> **Caution**
>
> The `myKey.snk` file must be at the path specified in the `AssemblyKeyFile` attribute of `myDataAssemblyInfo.vb`, as it is grabbed by the compiler to generate the digital signature.

To compile the DLL, open a command prompt and navigate to the directory the assembly files are in by using the `CD` command. Execute the following command:

```
vbc.exe /target:library /out:myData.dll myDataClass.vb myDataAssemblyInfo.vb
➥/r:System.dll /r:System.Web.dll /r:System.Data.dll
```

A new file, `myData.dll` will be added to the directory you navigated to.

If you right-click on the DLL and click on **Properties**, you can verify that the assembly information was compiled into the DLL. Click on the **Version** tab. Figure 11.2 shows the property window you will see.

FIGURE 11.2
You can view the DLL properties to verify the assembly information was compiled into the DLL.

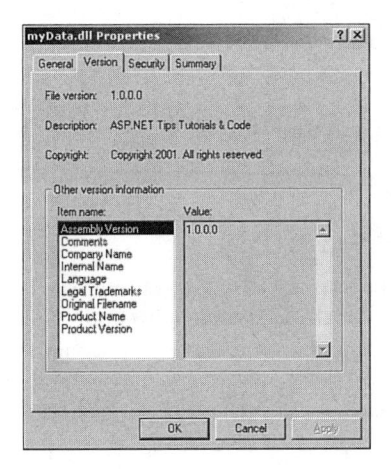

Registering an Assembly with the Global Assembly Cache

To register an assembly with the global assembly cache you use the `GacUtil.exe` tool. The tool adds the assembly to the global assembly cache, using its strong name. Before we do that, lets move the DLL to a different directory. For this example we are going to create a `3rdPartyDll` directory with subdirectories for different DLL versions.

Create a `3rdPartyDll` directory, and a `myDataV1` subdirectory, such as `C:\3rdPartyDll\myDataV1`. Move the `myData.dll` to this new directory. When we create a `myData.dll` version 2.0.0.0 DLL we will add a `myDataV2` subdirectory, so we do not inadvertently overwrite the original DLL.

Once the DLL is in place, open a command prompt and execute the following command:

```
gacutil.exe /i C:\3rdPartyDll\myDataV1\myData.dll
```

The /i option used in the preceding command tells the `GacUtil.exe` tool to install the assembly in the DLL into the global assembly cache. You can verify that the assembly was added by executing the following command:

```
gacutil.exe /l
```

The /l option tells the tool to list all of the assemblies in the global assembly cache. They are listed alphabetically, so you may have to scroll through the list to find the `myData` assembly. Figure 11.3 shows the output of the preceding command.

FIGURE 11.3
You can verify the assembly was added to the global assembly cache by using the GacUtil tool.

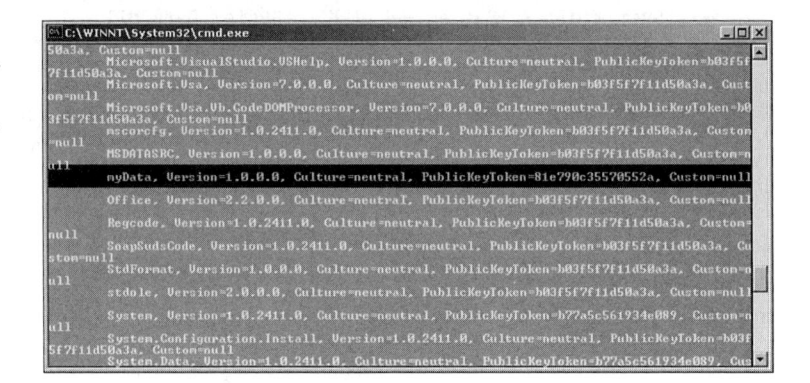

Using a Registered Assembly

Before we can use the `myData` namespace in our applications, we need to add a reference to it in the `machine.config` file. This is the machine-wide configuration file, and all of its settings affect every application on the machine. We will cover the `machine.config` file later in this chapter. For now, simply open the `machine.config` file and add the following code to the `<configuration><system.web><compilation><assemblies>` section.

```
<add assembly="myData, Version=1.0.0.0, Culture=neutral,
  PublicKeyToken=[value from GacUtil /l]"/>
```

> **Note**
> By default, the `machine.config` file is installed at
> C:\WINNT\Microsoft.NET\Framework*[version number]*\CONFIG\machine.config
> Depending on your installation, the location of the `machine.config` file may vary.

> **Caution**
> After making a change to the `machine.config` file, you must restart IIS for the changes to take effect. Execute an `IISRESET` at the command prompt to do this.

In the preceding code you are adding the `myData` namespace to the `machine.config` configuration file. This makes the `myData` namespace available to all applications on the machine, without the `myData.dll` having to be in each application's `\bin` directory.

The `PublicKeyToken` is an 8-byte hash in hexadecimal format of the key used to build the assembly. Use the `PublicKeyToken` value that is associated with the `myData` assembly (found by running `GacUtil.exe /l` at the command line).

Once an assembly is registered with the global assembly cache, and added in the `<assemblies>` section of `machine.config`, you can import its namespace and use it in your application. In Listing 11.2.4 we create a Web Form that creates an instance of the `myDataClass` class, calls the `getData()` method (passing in a `DataGrid`), and displays the return result in a `Label` on the page.

LISTING 11.2.4 Using a Registered Assembly on a Web Form

```
 1: <%@ Page Language="VB" Strict="True" %>
 2: <%@ Import Namespace="myData" %>
 3: <script runat="server">
 4:  Protected Sub Page_Load(Sender As Object, E As EventArgs)
 5:    Dim mdc As myDataClass = New myDataClass()
 6:    myLabel.Text = mdc.getData(myGrid)
 7:  End Sub
 8: </script>
 9: <html>
10: <body style="font: x-small Verdana;">
11: <form runat="server">
12:    <h4>myDataV1</h4>
13:    <b>Total Number of Customers:</b>
14:    <asp:Label Runat="server" ID="myLabel" />
15:    <br>
16:    <asp:DataGrid Runat="server" ID="myGrid"
17:      HeaderStyle-Font-Size="10pt"
18:      ItemStyle-Font-Size="8pt" />
19: </form>
20: </body>
21: </html>
```

In Listing 11.2.4 we create a Web Form that uses the `myData` namespace. On line 1 we add the Visual Basic.NET `Strict="True"` attribute to the `@ Page` directive. The `Strict="True"` attribute prevents implicit data type conversions in Visual Basic.NET (implicit data type conversions are not allowed at all in C#). We did this so that we can test how a breaking change in the `myData` assembly affects this application.

On line 2 we import the `myData` namespace, giving us access to the `myDataClass` class and its method. In the `Page_Load()` event handler we create an instance of `myDataClass`, and call the `getData()` method, passing it `myGrid`. A reference to the `DataGrid` will be passed into the method. In the `getData()` method we bind the top ten records from the Customers table in the Northwind database to the `DataGrid`. On line 6 we set the `Text` property of the `myLabel` control to the return value of the `getData()` method. The return value is the total number of records in the Customers table, as a string data type.

Figure 11.4 shows the Web Form in the browser.

FIGURE 11.4
The Web Form uses the `getData()` method to populate a `Label` and `DataGrid`.

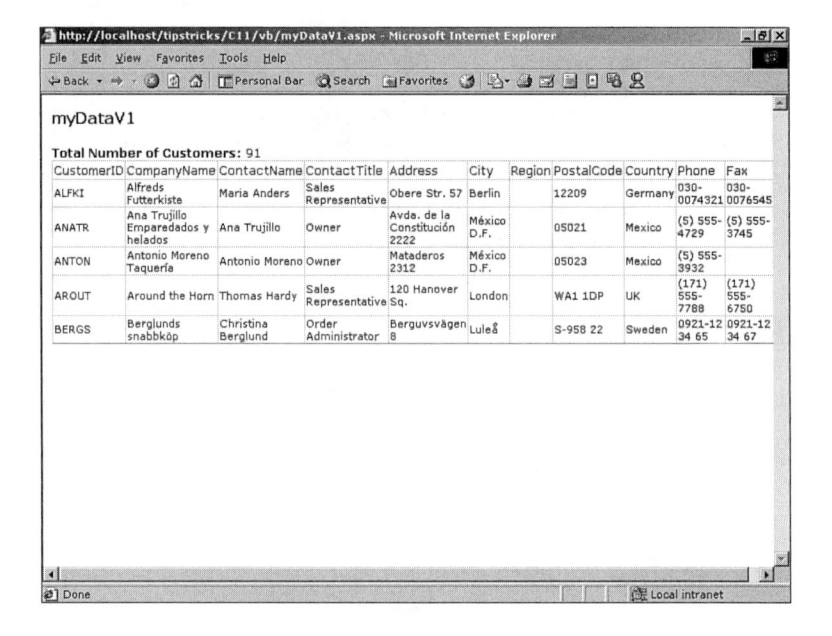

Adding a New Assembly Version to the Global Assembly Cache

To create a breaking version of the `myData` assembly we will modify the `getData()` method to return an `integer` instead of a `string`. Since we set `Strict="True"` on our Web Form, an implicit data type conversion is not allowed. By returning an `integer`, any existing code will break.

Listing 11.2.5 shows the code for a new class file, `myDataClassV2.vb`. The code that changed from `myDataClass.vb` is indicated in **bold**.

LISTING 11.2.5 Building the `myDataClassV2.vb` File

```
 1: Imports System
 2: Imports System.Web.UI.WebControls
 3: Imports System.Data
 4: Imports System.Data.SqlClient
 5:
 6: Namespace myData
 7:
 8:     Public Class myDataClass
 9:
```

Chapter 11 • ASP.NET DEPLOYMENT AND CONFIGURATION

LISTING 11.2.5 Continued

```
10:    Public Function getData( ByVal _myGrid As DataGrid ) As Integer
11:       Dim con As SqlConnection = New
➥ SqlConnection("server=localhost;database=Northwind;uid=sa;pwd=;")
12:       Dim cmd As SqlCommand = New
➥ SqlCommand("sp_GetTenCustAndOutputParam", con)
13:       cmd.CommandType = CommandType.StoredProcedure
14:       cmd.Parameters.Add(New SqlParameter("@count", SqlDbType.Int, 4))
15:       cmd.Parameters.Item("@count").Direction = ParameterDirection.Output
16:       'Open the connection
17:       con.Open()
18:
19:       'Set the grid data source to the DataReader returned by ExecuteReader
20:       myGrid.DataSource =
➥ cmd.ExecuteReader(CommandBehavior.CloseConnection)
21:       myGrid.DataBind()
22:
23:       'Close the DataReader returned by ExecuteReader()
24:       CType(_myGrid.DataSource, SqlDataReader).Close()
25:
26:       Return Int32.Parse(cmd.Parameters.Item("@count").Value.ToString())
27:    End Function
28:
29:  End Class
30:
31: End Namespace
```

Next, create a new file named `myDataAssemblyInfoV2.vb`. The code for this file is shown in Listing 11.2.6. The code that changed from `myDataAssemblyInfo.vb` is indicated in **bold**.

LISTING 11.2.6 Building the `myDataAssemblyInfoV2.vb` File

```
1: Imports System.Reflection
2: Imports System.Runtime.CompilerServices
3:
4: <Assembly: AssemblyTitle("ASP.NET Tips Tutorials & Code")>
5: <Assembly: AssemblyDescription("Data Access for my application")>
6: <Assembly: AssemblyCompany("DotNetJunkies.com")>
7: <Assembly: AssemblyProduct("myData")>
8: <Assembly: AssemblyCopyright("Copyright 2001. All rights reserved.")>
9: <Assembly: AssemblyVersion("2.0.0.0")>
10: <Assembly: AssemblyDelaySign(false)>
11: <Assembly: AssemblyKeyFile("[path to application directory]\myKey.snk")>
```

> **Note**
>
> Both version 1.0.0.0 and version 2.0.0.0 of `myData` use the same private key (`myKey.snk`) to create the strong named assembly. By using the same private key, both assemblies will have the same `PublicKeyToken`, and will be distinguished only by their version number.

To compile the `myData.dll` (version 2.0.0.0), open a command prompt and navigate to the directory the assembly files are in using the `CD` command. Execute the following command:

```
vbc.exe /target:library /out:myData.dll myDataClassV2.vb
➥myDataAssemblyInfoV2.vb
➥/r:System.dll /r:System.Web.dll /r:System.Data.dll
```

Create a subdirectory of the `3rdPartyDll` directory, named `myDataV2` (for example, `C:\3rdPartyDll\myDataV2`) and move the new `myData.dll` file there.

Use the `GacUtil.exe` tool to register the new `myData.dll` in the global assembly cache.

```
gacutil.exe /i C:\3rdPartyDll\myDataV2\myData.dll
```

Now if you run the `GacUtil.exe` with the `/l` option you will see both version 1.0.0.0 and version 2.0.0.0 in the global assembly cache. This is shown in Figure 11.5.

FIGURE 11.5
Running the `GacUtil.exe` tool with the list option reveals that both versions of `myData` are in the global assembly cache.

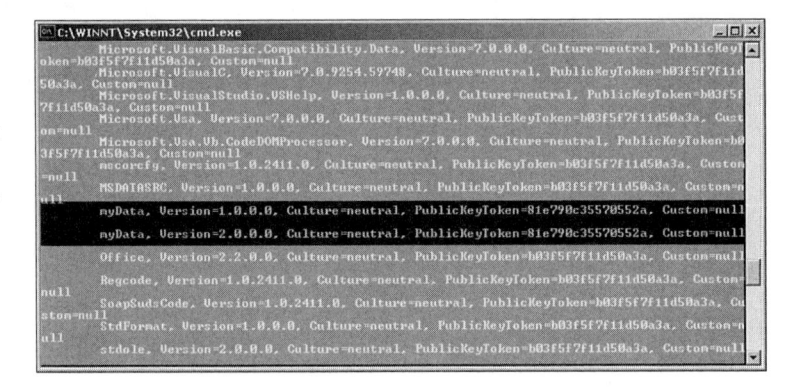

Using Multiple Assembly Versions

If you open the Web Form we created in Listing 11.2.4 in a browser, you will find that even though we registered the new version of `myData`, which included a breaking change, the Web Form still works. This is because the `machine.config` configuration file specifies that version 1.0.0.0 is the default version of this assembly. If we were to change the `machine.config` file to reference version 2.0.0.0, any existing application using the `myDataClass.getData()` method would break, as it is expecting a string data type to be returned, and the new assembly returns an integer. For that reason, we should not update the `machine.config` file. Instead, applications that want to use the new version of the `myData` assembly can do so by adding an assembly redirect to the application configuration file (`web.config`).

In the `web.config` file of your application, add the section shown in listing 11.2.7 between the `<configuration></configuration>` elements.

LISTING 11.2.7 Adding an Assembly Redirect to an Application

```
1: <runtime>
2:    <assemblyBinding xmlns="urn:schemas-microsoft-com:asm.v1">
3:      <dependentAssembly>
```

LISTING 11.2.7   Continued

```
 4:        <assemblyIdentity name="myData"
 5:          publicKeyToken="[value from GacUtil /l]" />
 6:        <bindingRedirect
 7:           oldVersion="1.0.0.0"
 8:           newVersion="2.0.0.0"/>
 9:      </dependentAssembly>
10:    </assemblyBinding>
11: </runtime>
```

In Listing 11.2.7 you add a `<runtime>` element to the Web application's configuration file. In this section you specify the `<assemblyBinding>` settings—the settings for assembly redirection. On line 2 we specify the `xmlns` namespace. This is a required attribute, and must be set to `urn:schemas-microsoft-com:asm.v1`.

The `<dependentAssembly>` element encapsulates assembly-binding policies. Each assembly we are binding in your application should have its own `<dependentAssembly>` element. On lines 4–5 we create an `<assemblyIdentity>` element to specify the assembly we are redirecting. The `name` attribute is simply the assembly name, and the `publicKeyToken` is the value found when executing the `GacUtil.exe` tool with the list (`/l`) option.

On lines 6–8 we create a `<bindingRedirect>` element to indicate which versions of the assembly we are working with. The `oldVersion` attribute specifies the version of the assembly that was originally requested by the application. In this example, that is version 1.0.0.0, since that is what was specified in the `machine.config` file. The `newVersion` attribute specifies which version of the assembly should be used by the application.

> **Note**
>
> Since other assemblies can be compiled with a reference to our assembly, the `oldVersion` attribute becomes more important to us. Even if we changed the `machine.config` file to use version 2.0.0.0 of the `myData` assembly, the existing assemblies that referenced `myData` would still look for version 1.0.0.0. To overcome this, we can use the same assembly redirection syntax in the `machine.config` file to provide assembly-redirecting machine-wide.

With these settings in the Web application's configuration file, any request for the `myData` assembly will automatically be redirected to the version 2.0.0.0 assembly. All other applications on the Web server will continue to use version 1.0.0.0. We can test this by browsing to the Web Form we created in Listing 11.2.4. Figure 11.6 shows the result of browsing to this Web Form.

Of course, we can update our Web Form to use the newer version of `myData` (v 2.0.0.0), while all the other applications on the Web server continue to use the older version (v 1.0.0.0). Listing 11.2.8 shows the revised Web Form.

FIGURE 11.6
The request for the `myData` assembly is redirected to version 2.0.0.0, which has a breaking change.

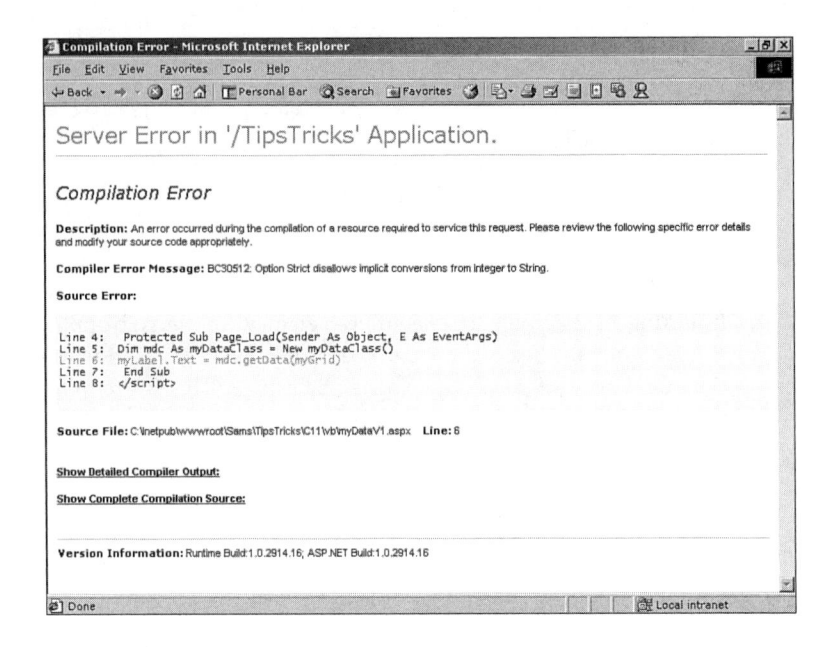

LISTING 11.2.8 Updating the Web Form to use `myData` v 2.0.0.0

```
 1: <%@ Page Language="VB" Strict="True" %>
 2: <%@ Import Namespace="myData" %>
 3: <script runat="server">
 4:  Protected Sub Page_Load(Sender As Object, E As EventArgs)
 5:    Dim mdc As myDataClass = New myDataClass()
 6:    Dim totalCustomers As Integer = mdc.getData(myGrid)
 7:    myLabel.Text = totalCustomers.ToString()
 8:  End Sub
 9: </script>
10: <html>
11: <body style="font: x-small Verdana;">
12: <form runat="server">
13:   <h4>myDataV1</h4>
14:   <b>Total Number of Customers:</b>
15:   <asp:Label Runat="server" ID="myLabel" />
16:   <br>
17:   <asp:DataGrid Runat="server" ID="myGrid"
18:     HeaderStyle-Font-Size="10pt"
19:     ItemStyle-Font-Size="8pt" />
20: </form>
21: </body>
22: </html>
```

3. Common `web.config` Configuration Settings

ASP.NET Web applications use an XML-based file, named `web.config`, to maintain application configuration settings. The `web.config` file is optional, and multiple configurations files can exist in an application, in separate directories (one per directory). The configuration file in the root directory is considered the primary configuration file. Subdirectories in the application can have configuration files as well, although the settings in the sub-configuration files are limited. The configuration files in subdirectories will override any settings in the root configuration file, and their settings will be applied to not only the subdirectory, but they will be extended to any child directories as well. With this model in mind, we could have a Web application with a root configuration file and a subdirectory with a configuration file that overrides the primary configuration. The subdirectory could have two child directories, one of which inherits the configuration settings from the second-level directory, and the other of which also has a configuration file that overrides the second-level configuration settings.

The `web.config` file is used to set application configuration settings that we used to have to set by altering the settings for the application in the IIS MMC. The use of XML-based configuration files allows us to change the application settings simply by changing the values in the `web.config` file. This is a much better model than in the past. Now we can make the changes to the file and FTP it to the Web server, where we used to have to track down the Web site administrator and have them make the changes in the IIS MMC. As soon as the `web.config` file is uploaded, or changed, the .NET Framework detects the change, and the new configuration settings are used. The Web application does not need to be restarted for the configuration settings to take effect.

A machine-wide configuration file is installed when the .NET Framework is installed. The `machine.config` file sets the base-configuration settings for the machine. All Web applications inherit the base-configuration settings from the `machine.config` file. These settings can be overridden in any `web.config` file. The `machine.config` file can be found at

C:\WINNT\Microsoft.NET\Framework*[version]*\CONFIG\machine.config

machine.config Sections

The `machine.config` file is the sever-wide configuration file. The `machine.config` settings affect every .NET application running on the server. It also defines the sections of the `web.config` files that we use in our applications. While it is out of the scope of this chapter to go over all the sections of the `machine.config` file, it is important we understand the role that it plays in our applications.

Each `web.config` section is defined in the `machine.config` file. In Listing 11.3.1 we see the `<configSections>` element of the `machine.config` file. This is where the sections of the `web.config` file are defined.

LISTING 11.3.1 The `<configSections>` Element of the `machine.config` File

```
1: <?xml version="1.0" encoding="UTF-8" ?>
2:
3: <configuration>
4:
5:     <configSections>
```

LISTING 11.3.1 *Continued*

```
 6:         <section name="appSettings"
➥ type="System.Configuration.NameValueFileSectionHandler,
➥ System, Version=1.0.2411.0, Culture=neutral,
➥ PublicKeyToken=b77a5c561934e089" />
 7:
 8:         <sectionGroup name="system.web">
 9:             <section name="browserCaps"
➥ type="System.Web.Configuration.HttpCapabilitiesSectionHandler,
➥ System.Web, Version=1.0.2411.0, Culture=neutral,
➥ PublicKeyToken=b03f5f7f11d50a3a" />
10:             <section name="clientTarget"
➥ type="System.Web.Configuration.ClientTargetSectionHandler,
➥ System.Web, Version=1.0.2411.0, Culture=neutral,
➥ PublicKeyToken=b03f5f7f11d50a3a" />
11:             <section name="compilation"
➥ type="System.Web.UI.CompilationConfigurationHandler,
➥ System.Web, Version=1.0.2411.0, Culture=neutral,
➥ PublicKeyToken=b03f5f7f11d50a3a" />
12:             <section name="pages"
➥ type="System.Web.UI.PagesConfigurationHandler,
➥ System.Web, Version=1.0.2411.0, Culture=neutral,
➥ PublicKeyToken=b03f5f7f11d50a3a" />
13:             <section name="customErrors"
➥ type="System.Web.Configuration.CustomErrorsConfigHandler,
➥ System.Web, Version=1.0.2411.0, Culture=neutral,
➥ PublicKeyToken=b03f5f7f11d50a3a" />
14:             <section name="httpRuntime"
➥ type="System.Web.Configuration.HttpRuntimeConfigurationHandler,
➥ System.Web, Version=1.0.2411.0, Culture=neutral,
➥ PublicKeyToken=b03f5f7f11d50a3a" />
15:             <section name="globalization"
➥ type="System.Web.Configuration.GlobalizationConfigurationHandler,
➥ System.Web, Version=1.0.2411.0, Culture=neutral,
➥ PublicKeyToken=b03f5f7f11d50a3a" />
16:             <section name="httpHandlers"
➥ type="System.Web.Configuration.HttpHandlersSectionHandler,
➥ System.Web, Version=1.0.2411.0, Culture=neutral,
➥ PublicKeyToken=b03f5f7f11d50a3a" />
17:             <section name="httpModules"
➥ type="System.Web.Configuration.HttpModulesConfigurationHandler,
➥ System.Web, Version=1.0.2411.0, Culture=neutral,
➥ PublicKeyToken=b03f5f7f11d50a3a" />
18:             <section name="iisFilter"
➥ type="System.Web.Configuration.IisFilterConfigurationHandler,
➥ System.Web, Version=1.0.2411.0, Culture=neutral,
➥ PublicKeyToken=b03f5f7f11d50a3a" allowDefinition="MachineOnly" />
19:             <section name="processModel"
➥ type="System.Web.Configuration.ProcessModelConfigurationHandler,
➥ System.Web, Version=1.0.2411.0, Culture=neutral,
➥ PublicKeyToken=b03f5f7f11d50a3a" allowDefinition="MachineOnly" />
20:             <!-- security -->
```

LISTING 11.3.1 *Continued*

```
21:            <section name="identity"
➥ type="System.Web.Configuration.IdentityConfigHandler,
➥ System.Web, Version=1.0.2411.0, Culture=neutral,
➥ PublicKeyToken=b03f5f7f11d50a3a" />
22:            <section name="authorization"
➥ type="System.Web.Configuration.AuthorizationConfigHandler,
➥ System.Web, Version=1.0.2411.0, Culture=neutral,
➥ PublicKeyToken=b03f5f7f11d50a3a" />
23:            <section name="authentication"
➥ type="System.Web.Configuration.AuthenticationConfigHandler,
➥ System.Web, Version=1.0.2411.0, Culture=neutral,
➥ PublicKeyToken=b03f5f7f11d50a3a"
➥ allowDefinition="MachineToApplication" />
24:            <section name="machineKey"
➥ type="System.Web.Configuration.MachineKeyConfigHandler,
➥ System.Web, Version=1.0.2411.0, Culture=neutral,
➥ PublicKeyToken=b03f5f7f11d50a3a" />
25:            <!-- /security -->
26:            <section name="sessionState"
➥ type="System.Web.SessionState.SessionStateSectionHandler,
➥ System.Web, Version=1.0.2411.0, Culture=neutral,
➥ PublicKeyToken=b03f5f7f11d50a3a"
➥ allowDefinition="MachineToApplication" />
27:            <section name="trace"
➥ type="System.Web.Configuration.TraceConfigurationHandler,
➥ System.Web, Version=1.0.2411.0, Culture=neutral,
➥ PublicKeyToken=b03f5f7f11d50a3a" />
28:            <section name="trust"
➥ type="System.Web.Security.CodeAccessSecurityHandler,
➥ System.Web, Version=1.0.2411.0, Culture=neutral,
➥ PublicKeyToken=b03f5f7f11d50a3a"
➥ allowDefinition="MachineToApplication" />
29:            <section name="securityPolicy"
➥ type="System.Web.Configuration.SecurityPolicyConfigHandler,
➥ System.Web, Version=1.0.2411.0, Culture=neutral,
➥ PublicKeyToken=b03f5f7f11d50a3a"
➥ allowDefinition="MachineToApplication" />
30:            <section name="webControls"
➥ type="System.Configuration.SingleTagSectionHandler,
➥ System, Version=1.0.2411.0, Culture=neutral,
➥ PublicKeyToken=b77a5c561934e089" />
31:            <section name="webServices"
➥ type="System.Web.Services.Configuration.
➥WebServicesConfigurationSectionHandler,
➥ System.Web.Services, Version=1.0.2411.0, Culture=neutral,
➥ PublicKeyToken=b03f5f7f11d50a3a" />
32:        </sectionGroup>
33:    </configSections>
```

As we look at the sections in Listing 11.3.1 we can see how our `web.config` file is defined. On line 6 a section named `<appSettings>` is defined as a name/value dictionary object (`System.Configuration.NameValueFileSectionHandler`). Later in this chapter we will look at how we can use the `<appSettings>` section to store name/value pairs, such as database connection strings.

Lines 8–32 define the subsections of the `system.web` section. These include all of the `web.config` sections you will learn about in the next section of this chapter. We can go through each subsection of the `<system.web>` element and see what type each section is. For example, on line 15 we can see that the `<processModel>` section of our `web.config` file will be a `System.Web.Configuration.ProcessModelConfigurationHandler` type.

web.config Sections

The `web.config` file has a base set of possible settings, all of which are optional, and as we learned previously, they are defined in the `machine.config` file. Each of the settings falls under a specified section of the `web.config` file. The configuration file is built as an XML document, with sections for different settings inside a `<configuration>` element.

Configuration settings are nested together under grouping tags that typically represent the namespace that the settings apply to. For example, the core ASP.NET configuration settings are nested together inside the `<system.web></system.web>` tags.

```
<?xml version="1.0" encoding="utf-8" ?>
<configuration>
 <system.web>
  <!-- ASP.NET configuration settings go here -->
 </system.web>
</configuration>
```

Table 11.1 shows the various `web.config` sections.

TABLE 11.1 web.config Sections

Section	Description
`<appSettings>`	Configures custom settings for an application. This section can be declared at the machine, site, application, and subdirectory levels.
`<authentication>`	Configures the Web application's Authentication schema.
`<authorization>`	Configures the Web application's Authorization schema.
`<browserCaps>`	Configures the Web application's settings for `HttpBrowserCapabilities`.
`<compilation>`	Configures the Web application's compilation settings.
`<customErrors>`	Configures the Web application's custom error handling settings.
`<globalization>`	Configures the Web application's globalization settings.
`<httpHandlers>`	Configures the Web application's handlers to map incoming URL requests to `IhttpHandler` classes.

TABLE 11.1 Continued

Section	Description
`<httpModules>`	Adds, removes, or clears HTTP modules within the Web application.
`<httpRuntime>`	Configures ASP.NET HTTP runtime settings. This section can be declared at the machine, site, application, and subdirectory level.
`<identity>`	Configures the identity of the Web application.
`<machineKey>`	Configures keys to use for encryption and decryption of forms authentication cookie data. This section allows developers to configure a validation key that performs message authentication checks on view state data and forms authentication tickets. It can be declared at the machine, site, and application levels, but not at the subdirectory level.
`<pages>`	Configures page-specific configuration settings.
`<processModel>`	Configures the Web server's process model settings (can only be set at the machine level).
`<securityPolicy>`	Defines valid mappings of named security levels to policy files. This section can be declared at the machine, site, and application levels.
`<sessionState>`	Configures the session state `HttpModule` for the Web application.
`<trace>`	Configures the Web application's trace settings.
`<webServices>`	Configures the Web application's Web services settings.

Since the `web.config` file is XML-based, it can be written using any text editor. Let's take a look at a typical `web.config` file, and then dissect it. Listing 11.3.2 shows a typical `web.config` file.

LISTING 11.3.2 A Typical `web.config` file

```
 1: <?xml version="1.0" encoding="utf-8" ?>
 2: <configuration>
 3:
 4:   <system.web>
 5:     <compilation debug="false" defaultLanguage="VB" />
 6:     <customErrors mode="On" defaultRedirect="GenericError.htm">
 7:       <error statusCode="404" redirect="FileNotFound.htm"/>
 8:     </customErrors>
 9:
10:     <authentication mode="Forms">
11:       <forms loginUrl="login_page.aspx" name="NORTHWIND">
12:         <credentials passwordFormat="Clear">
13:           <user name="WillyWonka" password="OompaLoompa"/>
14:         </credentials>
```

LISTING 11.3.2 Continued

```
15:      </forms>
16:    </authentication>
17:
18:    <authorization>
19:      <allow users="*" />
20:    </authorization>
21:
22:    <trace
23:      enabled="true"
24:      requestLimit="0"
25:      pageOutput="true" />
26:
27:    <globalization
28:      requestEncoding="utf-8"
29:      responseEncoding="utf-8"  />
30:
31:  </system.web>
32:
33: </configuration>
```

In Listing 11.3.2 we create a typical `web.config` file. This is our primary configuration file and should be saved in the root directory of our Web application. In this `web.config` file we are setting the configuration settings within the `System.Web` namespace. This is done by putting all of our section handlers inside the `<system.web>` and `</system.web>` tags on lines 4 and 31.

The first section, `<compilation>` on line 5, is used to set the compilation settings for use when the .NET Framework dynamically compiles resources. The debug attribute specifies whether the framework should compile debug binaries or retail binaries. In a production environment we should set debug to false for increased performance.

The `<customErrors>` section (lines 6–8) is used to specify settings for handling Web application errors, such as 404–File Not Found. The mode attribute specifies how custom error handling is enabled. Possible values are

- `On`: Specifies that custom error handling is enabled for all requests.
- `Off`: Specifies that custom error handling is not enabled.
- `RemoteOnly`: Specifies that custom error handling is enabled only for remote clients. Errors that occur in requests from the local machine will not be handled by the custom error settings.

The `defaultRedirect` attribute specifies a page to redirect to for unhandled errors.

Within the `<customErrors>` section we can specify error codes and how they are handled. In Listing 11.3.1 we specify that 404 errors should be redirected to a "File Not Found" page. Specifying the `redirect` attribute of an `<error>` child element does this. We can have as many `<error>` child elements as we need.

The `<authentication>` section (lines 10–16) specifies how ASP.NET authentication will be handled. This can be set to use Forms authentication, Windows authentication, or no authentication. The next chapter, Security with ASP.NET, will cover authentication in more detail.

The `<authorization>` section (lines 18–20) specifies who is authorized to access files and directories in the Web application. Authorization is part of the ASP.NET security model, and will also be covered in detail in the next chapter.

The `<trace>` section (lines 22–25) specifies how the .NET Framework will enable tracing for the Web application. In this example we have enabled tracing and specified that trace output should be rendered at the bottom of a page when the `Trace` attribute of the `@ Page` directive is set to `True`. See Chapter 10, "Debugging ASP.NET Applications," for more information on tracing.

The `<globalization>` section specifies how the Web application will handle globalization. In this example we have specified that the assumed request encoding will be utf-8 (Unicode) and that the response encoding will also be utf-8. See Chapter 16, "Separating Code from Content," for more information on globalization and localization.

> **Note**
> Each of the sections we have added to our `web.config` file has more attributes and elements available. See the .NET Reference Documentation for details on possible settings for each of these sections. The `web.config` file shown in Listing 11.3.2 is simply a sample of a typical configuration file.

4. Reading Custom Configuration Settings from `web.config`

The `web.config` file format is extensible; we can add our own custom sections to the configuration file. This allows us to add application specific settings to the configuration file. One typical example of this is storing a database connection string in the configuration file. This allows us to specify the connection string in one place, and access it from anywhere in our application. If the connection string changes, we only need to update it in one place, and the entire application is updated.

Adding Application Configuration Settings

The `web.config` file specifies a section for storing application settings. The `<appSettings>` section is an optional section outside of the `<system.web>` class that we can use to specify our own application settings. Listing 11.4.1 shows the same configuration file from Listing 11.3.2, with the `<appSettings>` section added.

LISTING 11.4.1 Adding Custom Configuration Settings

```
 1:  <?xml version="1.0" encoding="utf-8" ?>
 2:  <configuration>
 3:   <appSettings>
 4:    <add key="constring"
 5:     value="server=localhost;database=Northwind;uid=sa;password=;"/>
 6:   </appSettings>
 7:
 8:   <system.web>
 9:    <compilation debug="false" defaultLanguage="VB" />
10:    <customErrors mode="On" defaultRedirect="GenericError.htm">
11:     <error statusCode="404" redirect="FileNotFound.htm"/>
12:    </customErrors>
13:
14:    <authentication mode="Forms">
15:     <forms loginUrl="login_page.aspx" name="NORTHWIND">
16:      <credentials passwordFormat="Clear">
17:       <user name="WillyWonka" password="OompaLoompa"/>
18:      </credentials>
19:     </forms>
20:    </authentication>
21:
22:    <authorization>
23:     <allow users="*" />
24:    </authorization>
25:
26:    <trace
27:     enabled="true"
28:     requestLimit="0"
29:     pageOutput="true" />
30:
31:    <globalization
32:     requestEncoding="utf-8"
33:     responseEncoding="utf-8"  />
34:
35:   </system.web>
36:
37:  </configuration>
```

The `<appSettings>` section on lines 3–6 is used to specify custom configurations settings for our application. Custom `appSettings` are added as key/value pairs. In Listing 11.4.1 we have added a custom `appSetting` key, `constring`. This custom key has a value of `"server=localhost;database=Northwind;uid=sa;password=;"`.

Reading Application Configuration Settings

By declaring a custom application setting in the `web.config` file, we can access it from anywhere in our application. Listing 11.4.2 shows how we can use the `constring` key from a Web Form.

LISTING 11.4.2 Using a Custom Application Setting from a Web Form

```
 1: <%@ Page Language="VB" %>
 2: <%@ Import Namespace="System.Data.SqlClient" %>
 3: <%@ Import Namespace="System.Configuration" %>
 4: <script runat="server">
 5:   Protected Sub Page_Load(Sender As Object, E As EventArgs)
 6:     If Not Page.IsPostBack Then
 7:       Dim myDataReader As SqlDataReader
 8:       Dim myCommand As SqlCommand
 9:       Dim myConnection As SqlConnection
10:       Dim conString As String
11:
12:       ' Get the appSettings constring value
13:       conString = ConfigurationSettings.AppSettings("constring")
14:
15:       myConnection = new SqlConnection(conString)
16:       myCommand = new SqlCommand("SELECT TOP 10 CompanyName, ContactName,
➥ContactTitle From Customers", myConnection)
17:       myCommand.Connection.Open()
18:       myDataReader = myCommand.ExecuteReader()
19:       myDataGrid.DataSource = myDataReader
20:       Page.DataBind()
21:       myDataReader.Close()
22:       myCommand.Connection.Close()
23:     End If
24:   End Sub
25: </script>
26: <html>
27: <head>
28:  <title>Using Custom AppSettings in a Web Form</title>
29: </head>
30: <body>
31: <form method="post" runat="server">
32:   <asp:DataGrid runat="server" id="myDataGrid" Width="100%" />
33: </form>
34: </body>
35: </html>
```

In Listing 11.4.2 we render a page that displays a DataGrid showing ten customers from the Northwind database. The connection string for our `SqlConnection` is retrieved from the `web.config` file. On line 3 we import the `System.Configuration` namespace. This provides access to the `ConfigurationSettings` class, which we use on line 13 to gain access to the `appSettings` section of the `web.config` file.

Adding Custom Configuration Sections

We are not limited to the predefined configuration section, `appSettings`. The `web.config`'s extensible format allows us to add new custom configuration sections by simply adding a `<configSections>` element. Within this element we can define new configuration sections. Listing 11.4.3 shows a modified `web.config` file where we add a new configuration section, named `mySettings`.

LISTING 11.4.3   Adding a Custom Configuration Section

```
 1: <?xml version="1.0" encoding="utf-8" ?>
 2: <configuration>
 3:   <configSections>
 4:     <section name="mySettings"
 5:       type="System.Configuration.NameValueSectionHandler,System" />
 6:   </configSections>
 7:
 8:   <mySettings>
 9:     <add key="constring"
10:       value="server=localhost;database=Northwind;uid=sa;password=;"/>
11:   </mySettings>
12: </configuration>
```

In Listing 11.4.3 we define a new configuration section named `<mySettings>` using the `<configSections>` element. This element is used to define custom configuration sections. Note that we did not have to have this element in the previous examples because the default configuration sections we were working with are defined in the `machine.config` file. Since `<mySettings>` is a custom section we have to define what type of configuration section it is. Using the `<section>` child element on line 4 we define the section name, and the type. In this example we use the `System.Configuration.NameValueSectionHandler` type (which is the same type that `<appSettings>` is defined as). This allows us to add key/value pairs to our new configuration section, which we can read from anywhere in our application. We can define custom configuration sections of any type the `System.Configuration` class supports.

Reading Custom Configuration Sections

Reading custom configuration settings is similar to reading the applications settings in Listing 11.4.2—we use the `System.ConfigurationSettings` class to access the configuration settings. The `GetConfig()` method of the class enables access to the custom sections of the configuration file. This is shown in Listing 11.4.4.

LISTING 11.4.4   Reading Custom Configuration Settings

```
 1: <%@ Page Language="VB" %>
 2: <%@ Import Namespace="System.Data.SqlClient" %>
 3: <%@ Import Namespace="System.Configuration" %>
 4: <script runat="server">
 5:   Protected Sub Page_Load(Sender As Object, E As EventArgs)
 6:     If Not Page.IsPostBack Then
 7:       Dim myDataReader As SqlDataReader
 8:       Dim myCommand As SqlCommand
 9:       Dim myConnection As SqlConnection
10:       Dim conString As String
11:
12:       conString = ConfigurationSettings.GetConfig("mySettings")("constring")
13:
14:       myConnection = new SqlConnection(conString)
15:       myCommand = new SqlCommand("SELECT TOP 10 CompanyName, ContactName,
➥ContactTitle From Customers", myConnection)
```

Chapter 11 • ASP.NET DEPLOYMENT AND CONFIGURATION

LISTING 11.4.4 *Continued*

```
16:        myCommand.Connection.Open()
17:        myDataReader = myCommand.ExecuteReader()
18:        myDataGrid.DataSource = myDataReader
19:        Page.DataBind()
20:        myDataReader.Close()
21:        myCommand.Connection.Close()
22:      End If
23:    End Sub
24: </script>
25: <html>
26: <head>
27:   <title>Using Custom AppSettings in a Web Form</title>
28: </head>
29: <body>
30: <form method="post" runat="server">
31:   <asp:DataGrid runat="server" id="myDataGrid" Width="100%" />
32: </form>
33: </body>
34: </html>
```

On line 12 of Listing 11.4.4 we use the `ConfigurationSettings.GetConfig()` method to gain access to our custom configuration section. The `GetConfig()` method takes the name of the custom configuration section as an argument, and the name of the key we are accessing is passed as a property of the custom configuration section.

Caution

The code we use on line 12 is specific to Visual Basic.NET. If you are using C# then you must make a slight code change to line 12.

```
conString =
➥((NameValueCollection)
➥ConfigurationSettings.GetConfig
➥("mySettings"))["constring"];
```

In C# we must cast the results of `ConfigurationSettings.GetConfig("mySettings")` as a `NameValueCollection` type, then access it's `constring` property, which returns a `string` type.

5. Enabling Worker Process Restarts

The ASP.NET configuration format enables settings for managing worker processes. A variety of possible scenarios could lead to situations where the `aspnet_wp.exe` process (the ASP.NET process) could get locked up, and hang the Web applications. These range from memory leaks to deadlocks, to any number of possible scenarios. In the past this meant that the Web site administrator had to shut down and restart IIS, or even worse, cycle the physical server. If the Web application was hanging, the Web site was inaccessible until the Web site administrator was able to get to the machine to cycle it. For some e-commerce sites, this downtime could equate to thousands of dollars in lost business.

The ASP.NET configuration file format includes a `<processModel>` section. In this configuration element you can configure settings for how often, or in what situations a new worker process should be spun up and the existing process should be killed. The `<processModel>` settings are machine-wide, and can only be set in the `machine.config` file (`C:\WINNT\Microsoft.NET\Framework\[version]\CONFIG\macine.config`). The `<processModel>` configuration section has nine attributes as seen in Table 11.2.

TABLE 11.2 `<processModel>` Settings

Setting	Description
enable = *true*	*false*	Specifies whether the process model is enabled.
timeout = *[secs]*	Specifies the number of seconds until ASP.NET launches a new worker process to take the place of the current one. The default is infinite.
idleTimeout = *[secs]*	Specifies the number of seconds of inactivity until ASP.NET automatically shuts down the worker process. The default is infinite.
shutdownTimeout = *[hrs:mins:secs]*	Specifies the number of minutes allowed for the worker process to shut itself down. When the time-out expires, ASP.NET shuts down the worker process. The time is expressed in hr:min:sec format, so 0:00:05 is 5 seconds. The default is 5 seconds, or 0:00:05.
requestLimit = *[number of requests]*	Specifies the number of requests allowed before ASP.NET automatically launches a new worker process to take the place of the current one. The default is infinite.
requestQueueLimit = *[number of requests]*	Specifies the number of requests allowed in the queue before ASP.NET launches a new worker process and reassigns the requests. The default is 5000.
memoryLimit = *[percent of memory]*	Specifies the maximum allowed memory size, as a percentage of total system memory that the worker process can consume before ASP.NET launches a new process and reassigns existing requests. The default is 40%.

TABLE 11.2 Continued

Setting	Description
cpuMask = [DWORD value – bit mask]	Specifies which processors on a multi-processor server are eligible to run ASP.NET processes. The cpuMask value specifies a bit pattern that indicates the CPUs eligible to run ASP.NET threads. For example, the cpuMask value 13 represents the bit pattern 1101. On a computer with four CPUs, this indicates ASP.NET processes can be scheduled on CPUs 0, 2, and 3, but not on CPU 1. ASP.NET launches one worker process for each eligible CPU. If the webGarden attribute (see below) is set to false, the cpuMask limits worker processes to the number of eligible CPUs. (The maximum allowed number of worker processes is equal to the number of CPUs). By default all CPUs are enabled and ASP.NET launches one process for each CPU.
webGarden = true	false	Controls CPU multi-affinity when used in conjunction with the cpuMask attribute. (A multi-processor Web server is called a Web garden).

Listing 11.5.1 shows the default set-up for the `<processModel>` section of the `machine.config` file.

LISTING 11.5.1 The `<processModel>` Section of `machine.config`

```
 1: <processModel
 2:   enable="true"
 3:   timeout="Infinite"
 4:   idleTimeout="Infinite"
 5:   shutdownTimeout="0:00:05"
 6:   requestLimit="Infinite"
 7:   requestQueueLimit="5000"
 8:   restartQueueLimit="10"
 9:   memoryLimit="60"
10:   webGarden="false"
11:   cpuMask="0xffffffff"
12:   userName="SYSTEM"
13:   password="AutoGenerate"
14:   logLevel="Errors"
15:   clientConnectedCheck="0:00:05"
16:   comAuthenticationLevel="Connect"
17:   comImpersonationLevel="Impersonate"
18:   />
```

The default `<processModel>` settings seen in Listing 11.5.1 define how IIS will handle process restarts. On line 3 the `timeout` attribute specifies that the process will not automatically restart at periodic time intervals. Changing this to a time value (seconds) will cause the process to restart periodically, regardless of performance. The same is true for `idleTimeout`, on line 4. `idleTimeout` specifies a how long (in seconds) to allow the process to be idle before the existing process is shutdown. The `shutdownTimeout` attribute on line 5 indicates that if the process does not gracefully shut down in five seconds it will be killed.

The `requestLimit` attribute on line 6 is set to infinite by default. If a value is set for the `requestLimit`, the process will restart after the number of requests is equal to the `requestLimit` value. For example, if `requestLimit="10000"` then the process will automatically restart every 10,000 requests, regardless of the process performance. The `requestQueueLimit` on line 7 is set to 5,000 by default. This indicates that when the request queue reaches 5,000 requests pending, the process will restart. This setting proactively responds to deadlocks by restarting the process when a resource is locked, preventing other requests from being processed.

The `memoryLimit` attribute on line 8 is set to 80 by default. This indicates that if the ASP.NET process uses up 80% of the available memory on the server, the process should be restarted. This setting proactively responds to memory leaks. If memory is being consumed at an accelerated rate, this limit will be reached and the process will be restarted.

Listing 11.5.2 shows a modified `<processModel>` section for the `machine.config` file.

LISTING 11.5.2 Modified `<processModel>` Section of `machine.config`

```
 1: <processModel
 2:   enable="true"
 3:   timeout="30"
 4:   idleTimeout="30"
 5:   shutdownTimeout="0:00:05"
 6:   requestLimit="5"
 7:   requestQueueLimit="5000"
 8:   restartQueueLimit="10"
 9:   memoryLimit="60"
10:   webGarden="false"
11:   cpuMask="0xffffffff"
12:   userName="SYSTEM"
13:   password="AutoGenerate"
14:   logLevel="Errors"
15:   clientConnectedCheck="0:00:05"
16:   comAuthenticationLevel="Connect"
17:   comImpersonationLevel="Impersonate"
18: />
```

In Listing 11.5.2 we modify the `machine.config` file to use custom process restart settings. On line 3 we set the timeout attribute to restart the process every 30 seconds, and the same on the next line for the `idleTimeout` attribute. On line 6 we set the `requestLimit` to 5. These settings will cause the process to restart every 30 seconds (idle or active) or every 5 requests whichever comes first.

Chapter 11 • ASP.NET DEPLOYMENT AND CONFIGURATION 427

> **Caution**
> The settings in Listing 11.5.2 are for demonstration purposes, and should not be used on a production machine. We really do not want the ASP.NET process restarting every 30 seconds, or 5 requests.

We can test the `<processModel>` settings using the Web Form shown in Listing 11.5.3.

LISTING 11.5.3 Testing the `<processModel>` Settings

```
 1: <%@ Page Language="VB" %>
 2: <%@ Import Namespace="System.Diagnostics" %>
 3: <script runat="server">
 4:   Protected Sub Page_Load(Sender As Object, E As EventArgs)
 5:     Dim proc As Process = Process.GetCurrentProcess()
 6:     Dim dt As DateTime = DateTime.Now
 7:     Dim ts As TimeSpan = dt.TimeOfDay
 8:     processID.Text = proc.Id.ToString()
 9:     processTime.Text = proc.TotalProcessorTime.ToString()
10:     currentRequest.Text = ts.ToString()
11:   End Sub
12: </script>
13: <html>
14: <body style="font: bold x-small Verdana">
15: <form method="post" runat="server">
16:   Current Process Id: <asp:Label runat="server" id="processID"
➥EnableViewState="False" /><br/>
17:   Process Active Time: <asp:Label runat="server" id="processTime"
➥EnableViewState="False" /><br/>
18:   Current Request Time: <asp:Label runat="server" id="currentRequest" />
19: </form>
20: </body>
21: </html>
```

In Listing 11.5.3 we create a Web Form that displays the current process information. On line 5 we create a new instance of the `System.Diagnostics.Process` class, and set it to the current process. The `Process.ID` property is displayed in an ASP.NET Label control, and the `TotalProcessorTime` and `System.DateTime.TimeOfDay` are displayed below it. Figure 11.7 shows the output from the Web Form in Listing 11.5.3.

Based on the `<processModel>` settings in Listing 11.5.2 the process will restart every 5 requests. Test this by refreshing the page 5 times. On the last refresh the `Process.ID` will change, showing that the old process has shut down and a new process has started.

FIGURE 11.7

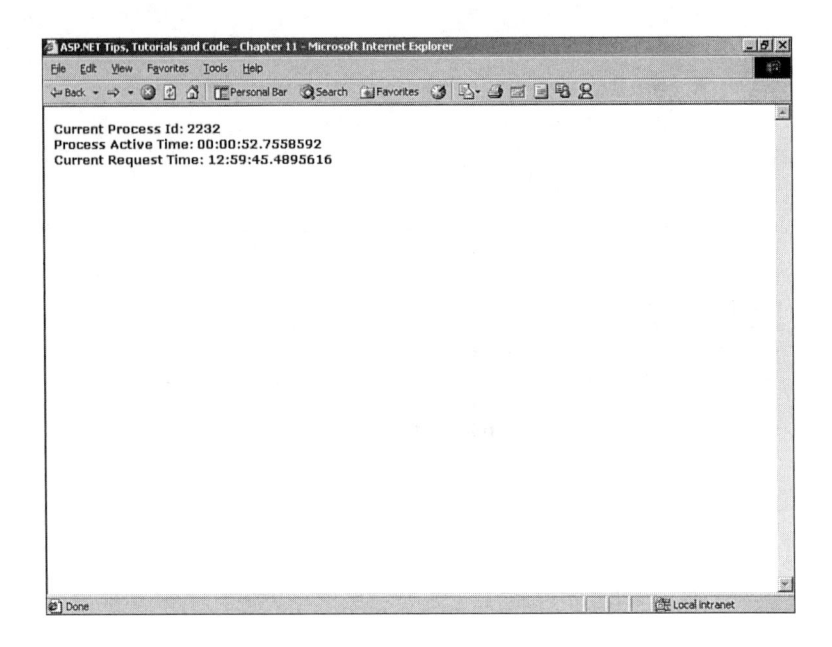

Testing the `<processModel>` Settings with the `System.Diagnostics.Process` Class in a Web Form.

```
Current Process Id: 2232
Process Active Time: 00:00:52.7558592
Current Request Time: 12:59:45.4895616
```

6. Using Web Gardens: Enabling Multiprocessor Functionality

The .NET Framework is designed with performance in mind. One means of increasing performance on a machine is to add multiple processors. The .NET Framework is capable of running a separate, isolated ASP.NET process on each of the processors. This is referred to as *Web Gardening* (you know...smaller than a Web Farm).

When Web Gardening is enabled (via the `<processModel>` section of the `machine.config` file) each processor runs an ASP.NET process independent of the others. This means that each process has its own session state, application state and caching. Session state can be run out-of-process and shared across the processors (see Chapter 14, "Managing State"), but the application state and caching are always independent.

CPU affinity refers to the marriage of an application process, such as the ASP.NET process (`aspnet_wp.exe`), to one or more specific CPUs. When we discuss setting CPU affinity, what we are discussing is how we determine which application processes run on which CPUs in a multiple processor computer. The use of multiple processors enables us to isolate CPU-intensive processes so they do not contend with other processes that are running. An example would be using a four CPU server with the ASP.NET process isolated on two CPUs, the SQL Server process isolated on a single CPU, and the forth CPU available for all other applications.

ASP.NET will automatically take advantage of multiple processors. The `<processModel>` section of the `machine.config` file has setting to allow you to determine the CPU affinity for the ASP.NET process. This is done with the `webGarden` and `cpuMask` attributes.

The `cpuMask` is a DWORD value representing a bit mask. The DWORD value specifies a bit pattern indicating which processors are allowed to run ASP.NET processes. The bit pattern is read from right to left (that is, processor 0 is the right-most mask position). The maximum number of processes is the number of CPUs in the machine. An ASP.NET process will be launched for every CPU unless otherwise specified. You can control this by changing the value of the `cpuMask`.

If we have eight processors on our machine, but we do not want the third processor to run ASP.NET processes, we simply switch the bit mask in the third position:

11111011

This bit mask indicates that all processors except the third one should run ASP.NET processes. The DWORD value for this is `0x0000007B`. Listing 11.8.1 shows the modified `machine.config` file enabling our defined CPU affinity for an eight-processor machine.

LISTING 11.6.1 Enabling Web Gardening in the `machine.config` for an Eight-Processor Machine with the Third Processor Not ASP.NET Enabled

```
 1: <processModel
 2:    enable="true"
 3:    timeout="Infinite"
 4:    idleTimeout="Infinite"
 5:    shutdownTimeout="0:00:05"
 6:    requestLimit="Infinite"
 7:    requestQueueLimit="5000"
 8:    restartQueueLimit="10"
 9:    memoryLimit="60"
10:    webGarden="false"
11:    cpuMask="0x0000007B"
12:    userName="SYSTEM"
13:    password="AutoGenerate"
14:    logLevel="Errors"
15:    clientConnectedCheck="0:00:05"
16:    comAuthenticationLevel="Connect"
17:    comImpersonationLevel="Impersonate"
18:    />
```

The DWORD value `0x0000007B`, on line 11, translates to a bit mask of 1111011. This will allow ASP.NET processes on all processors but the third one.

The `webGarden` attribute of the `<processModel>` element determines if Windows manages CPU affinity, or you define CPU affinity in the `cpuMask` attribute. The default value is `False`, allowing Windows to manage CPU affinity. When the `webGarden` attribute is set to `True`, CPU affinity is managed according to the settings in the `cpuMask` attribute.

On line 10 of Listing 11.6.1 we set the `webGarden` attribute to `True`. This overrides Windows CPU management and allows us to define the CPU affinity with the `cpuMask` attribute.

> **Note**
> Changes to the `webGarden` and `cpuMask` attributes will only take effect after a server restart.

Summary

ASP.NET is certainly a powerful tool, built on a powerful framework. New functionality in ASP.NET enables much easier management of Web applications than in previous versions of ASP.

Each Web application on a server is an isolated application capable of having a set of components not accessible to other applications on the server. By deploying components to the `\bin` directory of the Web application we can enable use of the components, while keeping them isolated from other Web applications. For an ISP this means that each client on a server can upload their own components with no impact on other clients. Additionally, two applications on the same server can use different versions of the same component without any contention. XCopy deployment makes adding components easy—no `RegServ32.exe` required. Literally drag and drop (or FTP as the case may be) the component into the `\bin` directory, and it is ready to go. We no longer have to cycle IIS, or manually register the component.

Additionally, we can set the configuration settings for each Web application in an XML-based configuration file, named `web.config`. This allows us to change configuration settings that used to require accessing the IIS MMC. We can change the settings in the `web.config` file with any text editor, and when the file is saved, the changes are made.

Using the configuration file we can set application-level settings, such as the database connection string example we saw in this chapter. Using the `System.Configuration.ConfigurationSettings` class we can extract the values and use them in our application. We can also create custom configuration settings. This gives us quite a bit of flexibility in setting up our Web applications.

At the machine level there is a configuration file that spans all Web applications, `machine.config`. This configuration file provides default values for all configuration settings, so a `web.config` is not required in any Web application. If a Web application does not have a `web.config` file, the default values provided in `machine.config` will be used.

In the `machine.config` file we can also set the values to handle process restart settings, including time frames for active and idle time restarts, and request limit restarts. Even memory threshold restarts are support, to proactively address memory leaks.

The `machine.config` configuration file has settings for enabling custom CPU affinity in a multiprocessor machine.

Other Resources

The ASP.NET configuration settings are very flexible. In this chapter we looked at a couple samples of configuration settings. For more information check out these resources:

- www.DotNetJunkies.com—This ASP.NET-focused site, authored and maintained by authors Doug Seven and Don Wolthuis, provides a plethora of information about ASP.NET for developers of any skill level. The site includes tutorials on getting started with ASP.NET and a repository for Web services and .NET components!
  http://www.DotNetJunkies.com

- Redirecting Assembly Versions—This section of the .NET Developer Reference Guide covers how to build versioned assemblies and redirect assembly requests based on the versions. http://msdn.microsoft.com/library/default.asp?url=/library/en-us/cpguidnf/html/cpconassemblyversionredirection.asp

- Format of ASP.NET Configuration Files—The Microsoft MSDN Web site contains full ASP.NET documentation. Here you will find a detailed breakdown of the ASP.NET configuration file structure.
  http://msdn.microsoft.com/library/default.asp?url=/library/en-us/cpguidnf/html/cpconformatofconfigurationfiles.asp

CHAPTER 12

SECURITY WITH ASP.NET

by Billy Anders

This chapter will cover the following items:

- Integrated Windows Authentication
- Forms-based Authentication
- Authorization
- Role based Security

This chapter concentrates on the application-level security features available with ASP.NET. It does not look at page-level functionality but rather focuses on application-wide authorization and authentication.

ASP.NET provides robust, extensible authentication and authorization services for Web-based applications. Although extremely flexible, the authentication services provided by ASP.NET are easy to use.

An Overview of Authentication and Authorization

In many web applications, the architect needs to decide on the type of access that the application will need. Some sites are purely public and therefore want to make sure that all web pages are accessible by all visitors. Other sites are purely private and want only particular individuals and groups of individuals to have access to the resources of the site. The more common style of site is the one where some resources are available to all visitors and other resources are reserved only for certain, known visitors. The process of "knowing" your visitors is authentication.

Authentication is the process of accepting credentials from a user and validating those credentials against some authority. Here where the word Authority is used we are referring to a service or data store, where credentials can be validated against. This validating authority can be as simple as a text file or as robust and extensible as the Microsoft Active Directory. In versions of Windows prior to Windows 2000, this domain authority was the Security Accounts Manager (SAM). In Windows 2000 and Windows XP domains, the domain authority is Active Directory. These domain authorities are used for validating user credentials. Once validated, a user is said to have an authenticated identity. However, just because a user is authenticated does not necessarily mean that the user is authorized to do anything. In order to actually access a resource the user must also be authorized.

Authorization is the process of determining whether the authenticated user has access to a given resource. ASP.NET provides authorization services using both the URL and the file of the resource. If both the URL and the file-access checks are successful, the user is considered authorized to access the resource.

1. Authentication

ASP.NET provides a variety of methods to authenticate requests. The methods are implemented as providers. ASP.NET ships with the following authentication providers:

- Integrated Windows authentication using Windows NT Challenge/Response (NTLM) and Microsoft Kerberos
- Forms-based authentication
- Passport authentication

Configuring ASP.NET to use a particular authentication method involves editing the configuration file of the application. Along with most other configurable aspects of ASP.NET, the declarative, XML-based configuration files can control security settings such as which authentication method the application is to use, the users that are authorized to use the application and how sensitive information such as passwords should be encrypted.

> **Note**
>
> For more information on using the configuration files of ASP.NET, please see Chapter 11, "ASP.NET Deployment and Configuration."

Listing 12.1.1 shows an example application configuration file (`Web.config`) that enables the Forms-based authentication method of authentication.

LISTING 12.1.1 Forms-based Authentication Can Be Specified Through a Setting in the `Web.config` File

```
1: <configuration>
2:     <system.web>
3:         <authentication mode="Forms" />
4:     </system.web>
5: </configuration>
```

This listing from the `web.config` file shows how to configure an ASP.NET application for Forms-based authentication. Forms-based authentication will be discussed in detail later in this chapter.

Integrated Windows Authentication

Integrated Windows authentication involves authenticating against a Windows domain authority such as Active Directory or the Security Accounts Manager (SAM) using Windows NT Challenge/Response (NTLM). Although Integrated Windows authentication is a secure authentication method, it is only supported in Microsoft Internet Explorer browsers and therefore is most suitable in intranet scenarios.

Integrated Windows authentication is a two-phase challenge/response authentication protocol. A user requests a protected resource, and the server responds with a 401 HTTP status code and a `WWW-Authenticate:` header with NTLM as the authentication scheme. The client then responds with a username, computer name, and the domain. The server uses those three pieces of information to generate a challenge for the client. The newly generated challenge is returned to the client within the `WWW-Authenticate:` header. Upon receiving the challenge from the server, the client uses its password to compute and send a response to the server in the `Authorization:` header. This process is illustrated in Figure 12.1.

FIGURE 12.1 Integrated Windows Authentication in IIS.

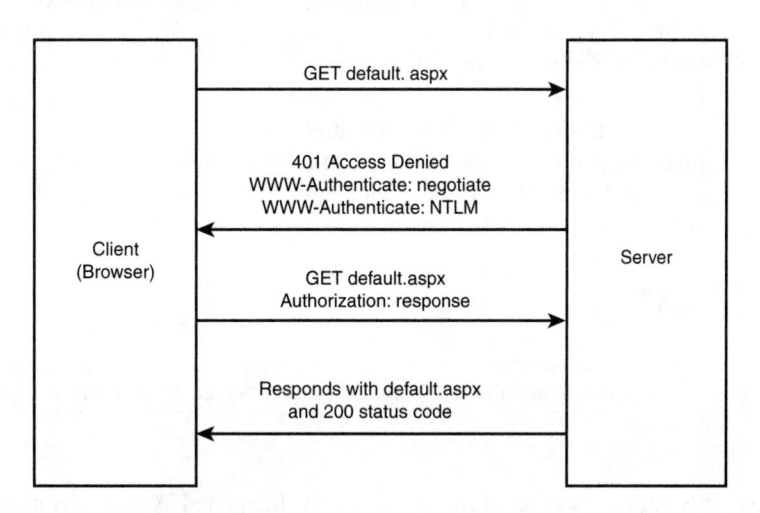

Under Windows authentication, Listing 12.1.2 will display the domain\username of the user accessing the page.

LISTING 12.1.2 Using the `Identity` Object to Display the Name of the User

```
1: <html>
2: <head>
3:     <title>Show Windows User Name</title>
4:
```

LISTING 12.1.2 Continued

```
 5:        <script language="VB" runat=server>
 6:
 7:        Sub Page_Load(Src As Object, E As EventArgs)
 8:            AuthUser.Text = User.Identity.Name
 9:        End Sub
10:
11:        </script>
12: </head>
13: <body>
14:        <h2>
15:            <font face="Verdana">
16:                <asp:label id=AuthUser runat=server/>
17:            </font>
18:        </h2>
19: </body>
20: </html>
```

Line 8 of listing 12.1.2 displays the name of the user by getting the `Identity` associated with the request and using its `Name` property. With Anonymous access enabled on the site in IIS, the page will display the Anonymous user account. Typically this account is `IUSR_COMPUTERNAME`.

Listings 12.1.3 and 12.1.4 demonstrate how to use the Windows authentication services of ASP.NET to retrieve the name of the user. In order for you to use Windows authentication, the application must be properly configured using the IIS Administration tool (MMC snap-in). Using the IIS Administration tool, you should configure the directory where the files are stored as an application. In addition, the directory security needs to be configured with the Windows Authentication check box selected and the Anonymous check box unselected. If Anonymous is selected, the application will not authenticate users; instead, all requests will run under the `IUSR_MACHINENAME` guest account.

> **Note**
>
> `IUSR_MACHINENAME` will vary depending on the name of your machine. For instance, my machine is named `WEBSKILLZ`; therefore, `IUSR_WEBSKILLZ` is the default anonymous user.

LISTING 12.1.3 `Web.config` Configured for Integrated Windows Authentication

```
1: <configuration>
2:     <system.web>
3:         <authentication mode="Windows" />
4:     </system.web>
5: </configuration>
```

Line 3 of listing 12.1.3 shows a `Web.config` file configured for Integrated Windows authentication.

LISTING 12.1.4 Displays the Name of the User and the Authentication Type Being Used

```
 1: <html>
 2:
 3: <script language="VB" runat=server>
 4:
 5: Sub Page_Load(Src As Object, E As EventArgs)
 6:     AuthUser.Text = User.Identity.Name
 7:     AuthType.Text = User.Identity.AuthenticationType
 8: End Sub
 9:
10: </script>
11:
12: <body>
13: <h3><font face="Verdana">Using Windows Authentication</font></h3>
14:
15: <table Width="700" rules="all"
16:     style="background-color:#ccccff;
17:     bordercolor:black;
18:     font-family:Verdana;
19:     font-size:8pt;
20:     border-collapse:collapse;">
21: <tr>
22: <td>User:</td>
23: <td><asp:label id=AuthUser runat=server/>
24: </tr>
25: <tr>
26: <td>Authentication Type:</td>
27: <td><asp:label id=AuthType runat=server/>
28: </tr>
29: </table>
30:
31: </body>
32:
33: </html>
```

Listing 12.1.4 shows both the name of the user and the authentication method being used. Lines 5-8 shows the `Page_Load` event handler using the `Identity` object, made available via the `User` object for requesting both the `Name` and `AuthenticationType` of the User. These values are then set to the `Text` properties of the `AuthUser` and `AuthType` label.

Forms-based Authentication

Forms-based authentication, also sometimes referred to as *cookie-based authentication*, is commonly used on large, public Internet sites. Forms authentication works by redirecting unauthenticated requests to a user-defined Web page for collecting and validating the credentials of the user. The collected credentials, which are typically in the form of a username and password, are then submitted for validation by ASP.NET. If the credentials are valid, ASP.NET issues an authorization ticket in the cookie that contains either the username or a key for reacquiring the identity. Subsequent requests from the browser are issued with the authorization ticket in the request headers and are authenticated and authorized by an ASP.NET module using the validation method configured. Figure 12.2 illustrates this process.

FIGURE 12.2
IIS snap-in configured for integrated Windows authentication.

Whereas Windows authentication validates against a domain authority, such as the Windows SAM or Active Directory, Forms-based authentication can validate credentials against other, nontraditional authentication authorities, such as a relational database, a text file, or even a remote Web service.

An advantage of the Forms-based authentication method (versus that of methods such as basic authentication) is that it gives the site creator control over the look and feel of the authentication user interface. Whereas basic authentication uses a standard, non-customizable, pop-up message prompt for the user to enter credentials, Forms-based authentication uses a Web page that gives the developer full control over how the page should look. This allows a Web page designer to create a page that gives instructions on what is being asked of the end user instead of just a generic prompts asking for a username and password.

Many public sites, from MSN to Yahoo!, use some derivative of Forms-based authentication for authenticating users.

The following source code demonstrates how to use Forms-based authentication in ASP.NET to authenticate users' credentials against an XML file. The XML file holds both the users' names and passwords. Because the text file contains the passwords in clear text, this type of system would not be used for much more than the simplest of Web applications. Listing 12.1.5 shows the `users.xml` file that contains all the users and their corresponding passwords.

LISTING 12.1.5 *Users.xml*

```
 1: <root>
 2:     <User>
 3:         <UserEmail>jane.user@company.com</UserEmail>
 4:         <UserPassword>janespassword</UserPassword>
 5:     </User>
 6:     <User>
 7:         <UserEmail>joe.user@company.com</UserEmail>
 8:         <UserPassword>joespassword</UserPassword>
 9:     </User>
10: </root>
```

Listing 12.1.6 shows the contents of the `web.config` file. The `web.config` file of the application needs to be configured for Forms-based authentication. The mode attribute of the `<authentication>` subsection is set to `Cookie`. The `decryptionkey` attribute of the `<cookie>` subsection is set to `autogenerate`. Using the `loginurl` attribute, we inform ASP.NET that our authentication page is `login.aspx`. Unauthenticated requests will automatically be sent to the `login.aspx` page. The `<deny users="?">` element specifies that we want to deny access to the anonymous user. The question mark (?) is a special character that means the anonymous user. An asterisk (*) means all or everyone.

LISTING 12.1.6 `Web.config` File for Enabling Forms Authentication and Disallowing Unauthenticated Users

```
 1: <configuration>
 2:     <system.web>
 3:
 4: <authentication mode="Forms">
 5:
 6: <forms name=".AUTHCOOKIE"
 7:                 loginUrl="login.aspx"
 8:                 protection="All" />
 9:     </authentication>
10:
11: <machineKey validationKey="AutoGenerate"
12:             decryptionKey="AutoGenerate"
13:     validation="SHA1"/>
14:
15: <authorization>
16:         <deny users="?" />
17:     </authorization>
18:
19:     </system.web>
20: </configuration>
```

Listing 12.1.6 shows a `Web.config` file that is used for enabling authentication and disallowing unauthenticated users. Line 4 enables Forms-based authentication for the application. Lines 11-12 allow ASP.NET to control the decryption key that is used. If this were a web-farm scenario where users will be served by multiple servers, this value should be hard-coded with a shared decryption key. Line 7 establishes `login.aspx` as our login page. Unauthenticated users that attempt to request a protected file will automatically be redirected to the `login.aspx` page.

Listing 12.1.7 presents the user with a login page. After the user enters a username and a password, the page authenticates the users' credentials against an XML file.

LISTING 12.1.7 Authenticating Users Against an XML File

```
 1: <%@ Page Language="VB" %>
 2: <%@ Import Namespace="System.Data" %>
 3: <%@ Import Namespace="System.Data.SqlClient" %>
 4: <%@ Import Namespace="System.Web.Security " %>
 5: <%@ Import Namespace="System.IO" %>
 6:
 7: <html>
 8: <head>
 9: <title>Cookie Authentication</title>
10:
11: <script runat=server>
12:
13: Private Sub Login_Click(sender As Object, E As EventArgs)
14: If Not Page.IsValid Then
15: Msg.Text = "Some required fields are missing"
16: End If
17:
18: Dim cmd As String = "UserEmail='" & UserEmail.Value & "'"
19: Dim ds As DataSet = New DataSet()
20: Dim fs As FileStream = New FileStream(Server.MapPath("users_encrypted.xml"),
➥FileMode.Open,FileAccess.Read)
21: Dim reader As StreamReader = New StreamReader(fs)
22:
23: ds.ReadXml(reader)
24: fs.Close()
25:
26: Dim users As DataTable = ds.Tables(0)
27:
28: Dim matches() As DataRow = users.Select(cmd)
29:
30: If (Not IsDBNull(matches)) And (matches.Length > 0) Then
31: Dim row As DataRow = matches(0)
32: Dim pass As String = CStr(row("UserPassword"))
33:
34: If (0 <> String.Compare(pass, UserPass.Value, false)) Then
35: Msg.Text = "Invalid Password: Please try again"
36: Else
37: FormsAuthentication.RedirectFromLoginPage(UserEmail.Value,
➥PersistCookie.Checked)
38: End If
39: End If
40: End Sub
41:
42: </script>
43: <body>
44:
45: <form runat=server>
46:     <h3><font face="Verdana">Login Page</font></h3>
47:
```

LISTING 12.1.7 Continued

```
48:        <table>
49:           <tr>
50:
51:        <td>Email:</td>
52:        <td><input id="UserEmail" type="text" runat=server/></td>
53:        <td><ASP:RequiredFieldValidator
54:            ControlToValidate="UserEmail"
55:            Display="Static"
56:            ErrorMessage="*"
57:            runat=server/>
58:        </td>
59:
60:        </tr>
61:        <tr>
62:
63:        <td>Password:</td>
64:        <td><input id="UserPass" type=password runat=server/></td>
65:        <td><ASP:RequiredFieldValidator
66:            ControlToValidate="UserPass"
67:            Display="Static"
68:            ErrorMessage="*"
69:            runat=server/>
70:        </td>
71:        </tr>
72:        <tr>
73:
74:        <td>Persistent Cookie:</td>
75:        <td><ASP:CheckBox id=PersistCookie runat="server"
76:            autopostback="true" />
77:        </td>
78:        <td></td>
79:        </tr>
80:
81: </table>
82:
83:
84: <input type="submit" OnServerClick="Login_Click" Value="Login"
85:                                        runat="server"/><p>
86:     <asp:Label id="Msg" ForeColor="red" Font-Name="Verdana"
87:                        Font-Size="10" runat=server />
88:
89: </form>
90: </body>
91: </html>
```

Listing 12.1.7 is responsible for presenting the Web page that allows the user to enter a username and password and then authenticates the credentials against the `users.xml` file. Line 1 establishes Visual Basic as the programming language for this page. Lines 2–5 import the Data, SqlClient, Security, and IO namespaces into our `Page` class. The `Click` event handler for the Login button checks the `IsValid` property of the `Page` object. The `RequiredFieldValidator` controls of the page will set the `IsValid` property of the page to `False` if the controls discover that the user failed to properly enter a username and/or password. If the `IsValid` property returns `True`, the `Text` property of the `Msg` label is set to "Some required fields are missing." If the `IsValid` property of the page is true, line 18 builds a string (`cmd`) that will be used to search for the user's email address in the `users.xml` file. Line 19 creates a new `DataSet` object. Line 20 open a new `FileStream` object on the `users.xml` file. Next we create a `StreamReader` and assign our `FileStream` (`fs`) to it. Line 24 reads the XML of the `StreamReader` into the `DataSet`. Since we now have all of the XML data from the file, we close the file on line 24. Line 26 creates a `DataTable` object. Line 28 uses the Select method of the `DataTable` (users) to select all rows that match the string that was created on line 18. If there are matches, line 30 succeeds. Once inside of the conditional at lines 31-32, we select the "UserPassword" of the first matched row. Line 34 compares the password found in the `users.xml` file with the password submitted on the web page. If the passwords match, the `RedirectFromLoginPage` method of the `FormsAuthentication` object is called. If the passwords do not match, the user will receive the message "Invalid Password: Please try again." If the username was not found in the `users.xml` file, the message "Invalid User: Please try again" is displayed to the user.

Although the code in Listing 12.1.8 is relatively straightforward, ASP.NET provides an even simpler approach for accomplishing the same goals. This approach involves storing user credentials directly in the `Web.config` file of the application. Listing 12.1.8 illustrates a valid credentials section for a `Web.config` file.

LISTING 12.1.8 Sample Credentials Section of a `Web.config` File

```
1:  <credentials passwordFormat="Clear">
2:      <user name="John" password="Foo"/>
3:      <user name="Mary" password="Bar"/>
4:  </credentials>
```

A complete `Web.config` file will look similar to the one shown in Listing 12.1.9.

LISTING 12.1.9 A Complete `Web.config` File with Credentials Section

```
 1:  <configuration>
 2:  <system.web>
 3:          <authentication mode="Forms">
 4:              <forms name=".AUTHCOOKIE"
 5:                  loginUrl="login.aspx"
 6:          protection="All">
 7:
 8:                  <credentials passwordFormat="Clear">
 9:                      <user name="John" password="Foo"/>
10:  <user name="Mary" password="Bar"/>
11:                  </credentials>
12:
13:          </forms>
14:              </authentication>
15:
```

LISTING 12.1.9 Continued

```
16: <machinekey validationKey="AutoGenerate" decryptionKey="AutoGenerate" />
17:
18: <authorization>
19:         <deny users="?" />
20:     </authorization>
21:
22:     </system.web>
23: </configuration>
```

In listing 12.1.9 the authentication mode of the application is set to Forms. All unauthenticated requests will be redirected to `login.aspx` for authentication. In this example, only John and Mary have access to the application.

The next step is to create a `login.aspx` page that uses the helper methods provided by the `System.Web.Security.FormsAuthentication` class. The code in our `login.aspx` page needs to authenticate the credentials provided by the user. If the credentials are valid, the user will be redirected to the initially requested page. Listing 12.1.10 achieves these goals with very little user code.

LISTING 12.1.10 Authenticating Against the Credentials Section of the `Web.config` File

```
 1: <html>
 2: <head>
 3: <script runat=server Language="VB">
 4:
 5: Sub SubmitBtn_Click(ByVal Source as Object, ByVal E as EventArgs)
 6:     If FormsAuthentication.Authenticate(
 7:        ➥UserName.Value, UserPassword.Value) Then
 8:        FormsAuthentication.RedirectFromLoginPage (UserName.Value, false)
 9:     Else
10:        Message.Text = "The credentials are not valid."
11:     End If
12: End Sub
13:
14: </script>
15: </head>
16:
17: <body>
18:
19: <form method=post runat=server>
20: <table>
21:     <tr>
22:        <td>Name:</td>
23:        <td><input type="text" id="UserName" runat=server/></td>
24:     </tr>
25:     <tr>
26:        <td>Password:</td>
27:        <td><input type="password" id="UserPassword" runat=server/></td>
28:     </tr>
29:     <tr>
```

LISTING 12.1.10 *Continued*

```
30:            <td colspan=2>
31:                <asp:Label id=Message runat=server />
32:            </td>
33:        </tr>
34: </table>
35:
36: <input type="submit"
37:     id="SubmitBtn"
38:     OnServerClick="SubmitBtn_Click"
39:     runat=server />
40:
41: </form>
42:
43: </body>
44: </html>
```

The developer has very little coding to do when using the approach in Listing 12.1.10. A walkthrough of the code shows that during the `Click` event of `SubmitBtn`, the `Authenticate` method of the `FormsAuthentication` object is called. The `Authenticate` method returns `True` (boolean value) if the credentials are valid. If the credentials are valid, we call the `Redirect` method of the `FormsAuthentication` object, passing in the username and the value `False`. The second parameter indicates whether we want ASP.NET to send a persistent cookie to the browser. After the cookie is set with the authentication ticket, the browser is redirected to the page initially requested or `default.aspx` if the `RedirectURL` query string parameter is missing. If the credentials submitted were invalid, we simply display a message informing the user.

> **Note**
>
> As I briefly touched on in the previous discussion of Listing 12.1.10, users will be redirected to the `default.aspx` page in the root of the application if the `RedirectURL` query string parameter is missing. For this reason, you may want to consider using `default.aspx` as the default page for your application.

Just by leveraging more of the built-in functionality of ASP.NET, we have saved ourselves quite a bit of coding. However, there is still a key piece of functionality missing from this example—password security. As luck would have it, ASP.NET has even made securing passwords clean and straightforward. The preceding example can be made secure by encrypting the passwords stored in the `web.config` file. ASP.NET supports encrypted passwords using both the MD5 (Message Digest version 5) and the SHA1 (Secure Hash Algorithm version 1) algorithms.

The code in listings 12.1.11 and 12.1.12 can be used to encrypt passwords using an SHA1 hash for storage in the `users.xml` file.

LISTING 12.1.11 The Password Utility Is Used for Encrypting Passwords Using the SHA1 Algorithm

```
 1: 'vbc /r:System.dll /r:System.Web.dll PasswordUtil.vb
 2:
 3: Imports System
 4: Imports System.Web.Security
 5:
 6: Public Class PasswordUtil
 7:     Public Shared Sub Main()
 8:         Passwords(System.Environment.GetCommandLineArgs())
 9:     End Sub
10:
11:     Public Shared Sub Passwords(args() as String)
12: Dim password As String
13: Dim clearpw As String
14: Dim iLoop As Integer
15:
16: If args.Length > 1 Then
17: For iLoop = 1 to args.Length - 1
18:     password = FormsAuthentication.HashPasswordForStoringInConfigFile(args(iLoop), "SHA1")
19:     Console.WriteLine("{0}={1}", args(iLoop), password)
20: Next iLoop
21: End If
22:
23:     End Sub
24: End Class
```

LISTING 12.1.12 PasswordUtil Compile

```
vbc /r:System.dll /r:System.Web.dll PasswordUtil.vb
```

After compiling the code for `PasswordUtil`, we run the executable from a command window, passing in the two passwords that need to be encrypted:

`PasswordUtil Foo Bar`

The `PasswordUtil` executable returns the following to the console:

Foo=AC8E6B90D7BB18294ABEF9E37EDD2A37BEA8979E

Bar=18297FD1478A81EEA4FC93D24F4650FB193BCAEF

We use the values to the right of the equal signs (=) as our SHA1 encrypted passwords. Listing 12.1.13 shows what the `web.config` file now looks like.

LISTING 12.1.13 Web.config File with SHA1 Encrypted Passwords

```
1: <configuration>
2: <system.web>
3:     <authentication mode="Forms">
4:         <forms name=".AUTHCOOKIE"
```

LISTING 12.1.13   Continued

```
 5:              loginUrl="login.aspx"
 6:              protection="All">
 7:              <credentials passwordFormat="SHA1">
 8:                  <user name="John"
 9:                      password="AC8E6B90D7BB18294ABEF9E37EDD2A37BEA8979E" />
10:                  <user name="Mary"
11:                      password="18297FD1478A81EEA4FC93D24F4650FB193BCAEF" />
12:              </credentials>
13:          </forms>
14:      </authentication>
15:      <machinekey validationKey="AutoGenerate" decryptionKey="AutoGenerate" />
16:      <authorization>
17:          <deny users="?" />
18:      </authorization>
19:      </system.web>
20: </configuration>
21:
```

After editing the `Web.config` file with the new SHA1 encrypted passwords, we change the `passwordformat` attribute of the credentials subsection on line 7 to the value `SHA1`. The passwords for John and Mary are now encrypted. Now when the `Authenticate` method is called on the `CookieAuthentication` object, ASP.NET will first hash the submitted password using SHA1 and then compare the value to the value stored in the `Web.config` file. For more information on encryption in ASP.Net, please see Chapter 2, "Common ASP.NET Code Techniques."

Forms Authentication Using SQL Server

Another advantage of Forms Authentication beyond user interface control is flexibility in choosing your data store. Integrated Windows Authentication and Basic Authentication both use domain authorities such as the Windows SAM or Active Directory for authenticating users. Although these authorities work well for thousands, and maybe even hundreds of thousands, of users, they are not ideal for sites that have, or plan on having, millions of users. Forms authentication in ASP.NET is flexible enough to use any data source as its authentication provider. The authentication provider can be anything—a text file, mainframe system, Microsoft's Active Directory, or relational database. Because of its performance, reliability, and scalability, Microsoft's SQL Server is one of the most popular data stores on Windows. ADO.NET makes the choice of authenticating against SQL Server a straightforward decision and implementation. Just as it did when we authenticated using the `users.xml` file earlier, Forms authentication provides the cookie and authorization facilities. The developer simply needs to write the code for validating user credentials against SQL Server.

The code listings that follow create a simple SQL-backed, Forms-authentication system.

In order to store credentials in our database, we first need to create the necessary database and table in SQL. For this application, only one table, called Logins, is needed. Listing 12.1.14 shows the script that can be used to create the `SamsBook` database and `Logins` table.

LISTING 12.1.14 This Script Creates the `SamsBook` Database and the `Logins` Table

```
 1: CREATE DATABASE SamsBook
 2: GO
 3: USE SamsBook
 4: GO
 5: CREATE TABLE [Logins] (
 6: [UserID] [int] IDENTITY (1, 1) NOT NULL ,
 7: [EmailAddress] [nvarchar] (50) COLLATE SQL_Latin1_General_CP1_CI_AS NULL ,
 8: [Password] [nvarchar] (50) COLLATE SQL_Latin1_General_CP1_CI_AS NULL ,
 9: CONSTRAINT [PK_Logins] PRIMARY KEY  CLUSTERED
10: (
11: [UserID]
12: )  ON [PRIMARY]
13: ) ON [PRIMARY]
14: GO
15:
```

To validate the username and password of our users, we will use the `ValidateUser` stored procedure. The script for creating the `ValidateUser` stored procedure is shown in Listing 12.1.15.

LISTING 12.1.15 The create Script for the *ValidateUser* Stored Procedure

```
 1: CREATE PROCEDURE ValidateUser
 2:      @Email nvarchar(50),
 3:      @Password nvarchar(50),
 4:      @LoginID int = 0 OUTPUT
 5: AS
 6:
 7:      SELECT @LoginID = UserID From Logins
 8:      WHERE EmailAddress = @Email And Password = @Password
 9:
10: If @@RowCount < 1
11:      SELECT @LoginID = 0
```

The `register.aspx` page and `CreateUser` stored procedure of our application allow new users to register themselves. The `CreateUser` stored procedure in Llisting 12.1.16 accepts an e-mail address and password as input parameters and checks to see whether the email address already exists in the Logins table. If the email address does not exist, `CreateUser` inserts a new row with the email address and password and then returns the newly created user ID as an output parameter. If the email address already exists in the `Logins` table, the returned `UserID` parameter will have the value `0` (zero).

LISTING 12.1.16 The create Script for the *CreateUser* Stored Procedure

```
 1: CREATE PROCEDURE CreateUser
 2:     @Email nvarchar(50),
 3:     @Password nvarchar(50),
 4:     @UserID int = 0 OUTPUT
 5: AS
 6:     SELECT
 7:         UserID from Logins
 8:     WHERE
 9:         EmailAddress = @Email
10:
11:     IF @@ROWCOUNT > 0
12:         SELECT @UserID = 0
13:     ELSE
14:         BEGIN
15:         INSERT INTO Logins
16:             (EmailAddress, Password)
17:         VALUES
18:             (@Email, @Password)
19:
20:         SELECT @UserID = @@IDENTITY
21:         END
22: GO
```

The configuration file enables Forms authentication for the application and denies access to all un-authenticated users. The configuration file also contains two separate `<system.web>` sections for the `register.aspx` and `admin.aspx` pages. Because we want all users to be able to register with the application, the configuration file gives all users—authenticated and unauthenticated—access to the `register.aspx` file. Without this, unauthenticated users would not be able to register with the application. The `web.config` file in listing 12.1.17, however, denies access to all users (*) except BillyAnders@hotmail.com from accessing the `admin.aspx` page. The reason for this is that the `admin.aspx` page shows the email address and password for all users of our application. This type of information should only be viewable by a select number of people.

LISTING 12.1.17 Configuration File That Contains Two Separate `<system.web>` Sections

```
 1: <configuration>
 2:     <system.web>
 3:
 4:     <authentication mode="Forms">
 5:         <forms loginUrl="login.aspx"
 6:             name=".AUTHCOOKIE"
 7:             protection="All"
 8:             timeout="15" />
 9:     </authentication>
10:
11:     <authorization>
12:         <deny users="?" />
13:     </authorization>
14:
```

LISTING 12.1.17 Continued

```
15:         </system.web>
16:
17:         <location path="register.aspx">
18:             <system.web>
19:                 <authorization>
20:                     <allow users="*,?" />
21:                 </authorization>
22:             </system.web>
23:         </location>
24:
25:         <location path="admin.aspx">
26:             <system.web>
27:                 <authorization>
28:                     <allow users="BillyAnders@hotmail.com" />
29:                     <deny users="*" />
30:                 </authorization>
31:             </system.web>
32:         </location>
33:
34:
35:         <appSettings>
36:             <add key="dsn"
37:                 value="server=localhost;
38:                 uid=loginuser;
39:                 pwd=password;
40:                 database=SamsBook;" />
41:         </appSettings>
42: </configuration>
```

Now that we have our database created and configuration file inplace, we need to create an ASP.NET page to allow users to register with the site. The code in Listing 12.1.18 shows a page that allows users to log-in to the site using their email address and password.

LISTING 12.1.18 `Login.aspx` for Authenticating User Credentials Against SQL Server

```
 1: <%@ Import Namespace="System.Data" %>
 2: <%@ Import Namespace="System.Data.SqlTypes" %>
 3: <%@ Import Namespace="System.Data.SqlClient" %>
 4:
 5: <script Language="C#" runat=server>
 6:
 7:     public void Login_Click(Object sender, EventArgs E) {
 8:
 9:         String dsn = (String) ((Hashtable)
➥Context.GetConfig("custom"))["dsn"];
10:
11:         SqlConnection conn = new SqlConnection(dsn);
12:         SqlCommand cmd = new SqlCommand("ValidateUser", conn);
13:
```

LISTING 12.1.18 Continued

```
14:          cmd.CommandType = CommandType.StoredProcedure;
15:
16:          SqlParameter prmEmail = new SqlParameter("@Email", SqlDbType.NVarChar,
➥50);
17:          prmEmail.Value = UserEmail.Text;
18:          cmd.Parameters.Add(prmEmail);
19:
20:          SqlParameter prmPassword = new SqlParameter("@Password",
➥SqlDbType.NVarChar, 50);
21:          prmPassword.Value = UserPass.Text;
22:          cmd.Parameters.Add(prmPassword);
23:
24:          SqlParameter prmUserID = new SqlParameter("@LoginID", SqlDbType.Int,
➥4);
25:          prmUserID.Direction = ParameterDirection.Output;
26:          cmd.Parameters.Add(prmUserID);
27:
28:          try {
29:              conn.Open();
30:              cmd.ExecuteRow();
31:          }
32:          catch (Exception e) {
33:              Msg.Text = e.ToString();
34:          }
35:          finally {
36:              if (conn.State == ConnectionState.Open)
37:                  conn.Close();
38:          }
39:
40:          if ((int) prmUserID.Value > 0 ) {
41:              // The User ID was found, validate the user
42:              FormsAuthentication.RedirectFromLoginPage(
43:                  UserEmail.Text, PersistCookie.Checked);
44:          }
45:          else {
46:              // Not found or incorrect
47:              Msg.Text = "Invalid Credentials!<br>Please try again.";
48:          }
49:      }
50:
51:
52:
53: </script>
54: <html>
55:     <head>
56:     <title>Forms Authentication with SQL</title>
57:     </head>
58: <body>
59:
60: <form runat=server>
61:     <h3><font face="Verdana">Login Page</font></h3>
62:
```

LISTING 12.1.18   Continued

```
63:        <table>
64:           <tr>
65:
66:           <td>Email:</td>
67:           <td><ASP:TextBox id="UserEmail" runat=server/></td>
68:           <td><ASP:RequiredFieldValidator
69:              ControlToValidate="UserEmail"
70:              Display="Static"
71:              ErrorMessage="* - Please enter your email address."
72:              runat=server/>
73:           </td>
74:
75:        </tr>
76:        <tr>
77:
78:           <td>Password:</td>
79:           <td><ASP:TextBox id="UserPass" TextMode="password" runat=server/></td>
80:           <td><ASP:RequiredFieldValidator
81:              ControlToValidate="UserPass"
82:              Display="Static"
83:              ErrorMessage="* - Please enter your password."
84:              runat=server/>
85:           </td>
86:        </tr>
87:        <tr>
88:
89:           <td>Persistent Cookie:</td>
90:           <td><ASP:CheckBox id=PersistCookie runat="server"
91:              autopostback="true" />
92:           </td>
93:           <td></td>
94:        </tr>
95:
96: </table>
97:
98:
99: <input type="submit" OnServerClick="Login_Click" Value="Login"
100:                                         runat="server"/><p>
101:    <asp:Label id="Msg" ForeColor="red" Font-Name="Verdana"
102:                            Font-Size="10" runat=server />
103:
104: </form>
105: </body>
106: </html>
```

The `login.aspx` file, shown in Listing 12.1.18, is where the custom authorization code lives for the login functionality of our application. Inside of the `Login_Click` event handler is where we check the credentials submitted by the user against the credentials stored in our SQL Server database. The `login.aspx` file uses ADO.NET and the `ValidateUser` stored procedure for validating the credentials. If the credentials are valid, we authenticate the user using the

RedirectFromLoginPage method of the **FormsAuthentication** object. If the email address and password do not match the values stored in our database, the `login.aspx` page is shown to the user again, this time with the message "Invalid Credentials. Please try again." on the page.

The `register.aspx` file in Listing 12.1.19 is used by users for registering for access to the application.

Three ASP.NET validation controls are used on the `register.aspx` page in Listing 12.1.19. The **RegularExpressionValidator** control checks for the presence of a valid-looking email address. The **RequiredFieldValidator** control checks for the existence of a non-blank value in the password field. Finally, the **CompareValidator** control is used to compare the values of the two password fields. For more information on the validation controls, please see Chapter 3, "Form Field Input Validation."

LISTING 12.1.19 The `register.aspx` File Is Used for Creating New Users in the Database

```
 1: <%@ Import Namespace="System.Collections" %>
 2: <%@ Import Namespace="System.Data" %>
 3: <%@ Import Namespace="System.Data.SqlClient" %>
 4: <%@ Import Namespace="System.Web.Security" %>
 5:
 6: <Script Language="C#" Runat=server >
 7:
 8:
 9:     public void Page_Load(Object sender, EventArgs E) {
10:
11:         if (User.Identity.Name != "")
12:         {
13:             CurrentUser.Text = "You are currently logged on as: " +
➥User.Identity.Name;
14:         }
15:     }
16:
17:     public void Register_Click(Object sender, EventArgs E) {
18:
19:         if(!Page.IsValid)
20:         {
21:             Msg.Text = "Page is invalid.<br>Please try again.";
22:
23:             //Cancel further processing.
24:             return;
25:         }
26:
27:         String dsn = (String) ((Hashtable)
➥Context.GetConfig("custom"))["dsn"];
28:
29:         SqlConnection conn = new SqlConnection(dsn);
30:         SqlCommand cmd = new SqlCommand("CreateUser", conn);
31:
```

LISTING 12.1.19 Continued

```
32:            cmd.CommandType = CommandType.StoredProcedure;
33:
34:            SqlParameter prmEmail = new SqlParameter("@Email", SqlDbType.NVarChar,
➥50);
35:            prmEmail.Value = UserEmail.Text;
36:            cmd.Parameters.Add(prmEmail);
37:
38:            SqlParameter prmPassword = new SqlParameter("@Password",
➥SqlDbType.NVarChar, 50);
39:            prmPassword.Value = UserPass.Text;
40:            cmd.Parameters.Add(prmPassword);
41:
42:            SqlParameter prmUserID = new SqlParameter("@UserID", SqlDbType.Int,
➥4);
43:            prmUserID.Direction = ParameterDirection.Output;
44:            cmd.Parameters.Add(prmUserID);
45:
46:            try {
47:                conn.Open();
48:                cmd.ExecuteRow();
49:            }
50:            catch (Exception e) {
51:                Msg.Text = e.ToString();
52:            }
53:            finally {
54:                if (conn.State == ConnectionState.Open)
55:                    conn.Close();
56:            }
57:
58:            if ((int) prmUserID.Value > 0 ) {
59:                // The User ID has been created
60:                if (User.Identity.Name != "")
61:                    FormsAuthentication.SignOut();
62:
63:                FormsAuthentication.RedirectFromLoginPage(UserEmail.Text, false);
64:            }
65:            else {
66:                // Not found or incorrect
67:                Msg.Text = "User has <b>not</b> been created.";
68:            }
69:
70:        }
71:
72:
73: </Script>
74: <html>
75: <head>
76:     <title>Forms Authentication with SQL</title>
77:
```

LISTING 12.1.19 Continued

```
 78: <body>
 79:
 80: <form runat=server>
 81:     <h3><font face="Verdana">Registration Page</font></h3>
 82:
 83:     <table>
 84:
 85:     <tr>
 86:         <td>Email:</td>
 87:         <td><ASP:TextBox id="UserEmail" runat=server/></td>
 88:         <td><asp:RegularExpressionValidator id="RegularExpressionValidator1"
➥runat="server"
 89:             ControlToValidate="UserEmail"
 90:             ValidationExpression="^[\w-]+@[\w-]+\.(com|net|org|edu|mil)$"
 91:             Display="Static">Please enter a valid e-mail address
 92:         </asp:RegularExpressionValidator>
 93:
 94:         </td>
 95:     </tr>
 96:
 97:     <tr>
 98:         <td>Password:</td>
 99:         <td><ASP:TextBox id="UserPass" TextMode="password" runat=server/></td>
100:         <td><ASP:RequiredFieldValidator
101:             ControlToValidate="UserPass"
102:             Display="Static"
103:             ErrorMessage="* - Please enter a password."
104:             runat=server/>
105:         </td>
106:     </tr>
107:
108:     <tr>
109:         <td>Password (confirm):</td>
110:         <td><ASP:TextBox id="UserConfirmPass" TextMode="password"
➥runat=server/></td>
111:         <td><ASP:RequiredFieldValidator
112:             ControlToValidate="UserPass"
113:             Display="Dynamic"
114:             ErrorMessage="* - Please re-enter your password."
115:             runat=server/>
116:         <asp:CompareValidator
117:             id="PassComps"
118:             ControlToValidate="UserPass"
119:             ControlToCompare="UserConfirmPass"
120:             Text="Passwords do not match."
121:             Type="String"
122:             runat="server"/>
123:         </td>
124:     </tr>
125:
```

LISTING 12.1.19 Continued

```
126: </table>
127:
128:
129:
130: <br>
131: <input type="submit"
132:     OnServerClick="Register_Click"
133:     Value="Register/Update"
134:     runat="server"/><p>
135:
136: <p>
137: <asp:Label id="CurrentUser"
138:     ForeColor="red"
139:     Font-Name="Verdana"
140:     MaintainState="False"
141:     Font-Size="10"
142:     runat=server />
143: </p>
144:
145: <p>
146: <asp:Label id="Msg"
147:     ForeColor="red"
148:     Font-Name="Verdana"
149:     MaintainState="False"
150:     Font-Size="10"
151:     runat=server />
152: </p>
153:
154: </form>
155: </body>
156: </html>
```

The `register.aspx` file, shown in Listing 12.1.19, contains our C# code for new user registration. The `Page_Load` event handler is being used to inform the user of the user account they are currently logged into the system with. In the `Page_Load method`, we check the `Name` property of the `Identity` object for any value. If a value exists, we inform the user of his current email address. The `Register_Click` event handler is called when the user clicks the Register button on the `register.aspx` page. The event handler first checks the `IsValid` property of the `Page` object. This property will be set to `False` if any of the validation controls have invalid values. If the value is `False`, a message will be displayed to the user and the method will return without further processing. If the property is valid, we use the email address and passwords submitted by the user and execute the `CreateUser` stored procedure in SQL. If the stored procedure returns a non-zero number, we know that the user has been created successfully. We then authenticate the user using the `RedirectFromLoginPage` method of the `FormsAuthentication` object. This method sets an authentication ticket in the user's cookie and redirects him to the `default.aspx` page. In the case where the value zero (`0`) is returned from the stored procedure, we inform the user that his account has not been created.

The `default.aspx` page shown in Listing 12.1.20 welcomes the user using the authenticated email address. The page also displays a Signout button that can be used to log out of the application.

LISTING 12.1.20   Welcome Page for Authenticated Users

```
 1: <%@ Page EnableSessionState="False" %>
 2: <html>
 3: <head>
 4: <title>Forms Authentication with SQL</title>
 5:
 6: <Script Language="C#" runat=server>
 7:
 8: private void Page_Load(Object src, EventArgs E) {
 9:     Welcome.InnerHtml = "Hello, " + Context.User.Identity.Name;
10: }
11:
12: private void Signout_Click(Object src, EventArgs E) {
13:     FormsAuthentication.SignOut();
14:     Response.Redirect("login.aspx");
15: }
16:
17: </script>
18:
19: <body>
20: <h3><font face="Verdana">Forms Authentication with SQL</font></h3>
21:
22: <span id="Welcome" runat=server/>
23: <form runat=server>
24:     <input type="submit"
25:         OnServerClick="Signout_Click"
26:         Value="Signout"
27:         runat="server"/>
28: </form>
29: </body>
30: </html>
```

Listing 12.1.20 is our welcome page. This page displays a greeting to the newly authenticated user in the `Page_Load` method. The text is written to the `Welcome` label using its `InnerHtml` property. Listing 12.1.20 also shows how to sign a user out of the system. To sign a user out, we use the `SignOut()` method of the `FormsAuthentication` object. The `SignOut()` method expires the authentication ticket in the user's browser, thereby making the user unknown to the system and therefore un-authenticated. Next, we `Redirect` the user to the `login.aspx` page where they can sign in again if they choose to do so.

The `admin.aspx` page, shown in Listing 12.1.21, is only available to a subset of users listed in the `web.config` configuration file. This page uses the ASP.NET `DataGrid` control and ADO.NET to list all the registered users.

LISTING 12.1.21 A Simple Read-Only Administration Page for Viewing Registered Users

```
 1: <%@ Import Namespace="System.Data" %>
 2: <%@ Import Namespace="System.Data.SqlClient" %>
 3: <%@ Import Namespace="System.Configuration" %>
 4:
 5: <html>
 6: <script language="C#" runat="server">
 7:
 8: protected void Page_Load(Object Src, EventArgs E)
 9: {
10: String dsn = ConfigurationSettings.AppSettings["dsn"];
11:
12: SqlConnection myConnection = new SqlConnection(dsn);
13: SqlCommand myCommand = new SqlCommand("SELECT * FROM Logins Order By UserID", ➥myConnection);
14:
15: myConnection.Open();
16:
17: SqlDataReader dr = myCommand.ExecuteReader();
18:
19: MyDataGrid.DataSource = dr;
20: MyDataGrid.DataBind();
21:
22: myConnection.Close();
23: }
24: </script>
25:
26: <body>
27:
28: <h3><font face="Verdana">Administrator's Page</font></h3>
29:
30:     <ASP:DataGrid id="MyDataGrid" runat="server"
31:       Width="400"
32:       BackColor="#ccccff"
33:       BorderColor="black"
34:       ShowFooter="false"
35:       CellPadding=3
36:       CellSpacing="0"
37:       Font-Name="Verdana"
38:       Font-Size="8pt"
39:       HeaderStyle-BackColor="#aaaadd"
40:       MaintainState="false"
41:     />
42:
43: </body>
44: </html>
```

Our `admin.aspx` page in Listing 12.1.21 uses ADO.NET to bind the results from a query to a `DataGrid`. Line 10 requests the "dsn" value from our `web.config` file and places the value into a string named `dsn`. Line 12 creates a connection to our SQL database using the `dsn` variable. Line 13 creates a `SqlCommand` object with the SQL statement needed for retrieving user data from the `Logins` database. Once our `SqlConnection` and `SqlCommand` objects are created, we

458 ASP.NET: TIPS, TUTORIALS, AND CODE

Open the Connection on line 15. Line 17 uses the `ExecuteRead` method of the `SqlCommand` object for reading the user data into the `SqlDataReader`. A `SqlDataReader` is a forward-only, stream of data records. Line 19 sets the `DataSource` of our `DataGrid` to the `SqlDataReader` (`dr`). And line 20 instructs the `DataGrid` to bind itself to the data in the `SqlDataReader`. Finally on line 22, we close our Connection to the database using the `Close()` method of the `SqlConnection` object.

Forms Authentication Using a Web Service

As I hinted to earlier, Forms authentication in ASP.NET can authenticate against a remote Web service. Validating credentials against a Web service could prove useful in cases where the validating authority is outside of your control or outside of your physical environment. Another benefit is that, by default, Web services use well-known (and often trusted) TCP/IP ports and the HTTP protocol. This would allow a centralized authority to authenticate for any number of clients without opening more ports on the firewall. Although our authentication Web service is potentially located outside our physical network, secure communications with the service need not be sacrificed.

Authenticating against a Web service is a straightforward process using ASP.NET. First off, we need to create a Web service to authenticate against. Listing 12.1.22 creates the Web service that we will use.

LISTING 12.1.22   WebAuth.asmx Remote Authentication Service

```
 1: <%@ WebService Language="C#" Class="WebAuth" %>
 2:
 3: using System;
 4: using System.Web;
 5: using System.Web.Services;
 6: using System.Data;
 7: using System.Collections;
 8: using System.Data.SqlClient;
 9: using System.Configuration;
10:
11:
12: class WebAuth : WebService {
13:
14:     [WebMethod] public bool Authenticate (string UserEmail, string UserPass) {
15:
16: String dsn = ConfigurationSettings.AppSettings["dsn"];
17:
18:         SqlConnection conn = new SqlConnection(dsn);
19:         SqlCommand cmd = new SqlCommand("ValidateUser", conn);
20:
21:         cmd.CommandType = CommandType.StoredProcedure;
22:
23:         SqlParameter prmEmail = new SqlParameter("@Email", SqlDbType.NVarChar, 50);
24:         prmEmail.Value = UserEmail;
```

LISTING 12.1.22 Continued

```
25:            cmd.Parameters.Add(prmEmail);
26:
27:            SqlParameter prmPassword = new SqlParameter("@Password",
➥SqlDbType.NVarChar, 50);
28:            prmPassword.Value = UserPass;
29:            cmd.Parameters.Add(prmPassword);
30:
31:            SqlParameter prmUserID = new SqlParameter("@LoginID", SqlDbType.Int,
4);
32:            prmUserID.Direction = ParameterDirection.Output;
33:            cmd.Parameters.Add(prmUserID);
34:
35:        try {
36:            conn.Open();
37:            cmd.ExecuteRow();
38:        }
39:        catch (Exception e) {
40:            //Eat the exception and return false
41:     return false;
42:        }
43:        finally {
44:            if (conn.State == ConnectionState.Open)
45:                conn.Close();
46:        }
47:
48:        if ((int) prmUserID.Value > 0 ) {
49:            // The credentials are valid.
50:            return true;
51:        }
52:        else {
53:            // The credentials are invalid.
54:            return false;
55:            }
56:        }
57: }
```

Listing 12.1.22 leverages the code in the previous SQL authentication example. The authentication service is secured using SSL (Secured Sockets Layer). To make certain that users of our service send and receive information in a secure fashion, we configure the Web service to only allow secure communications. This is achieved using the MMC snap-in for IIS.

If a client tries to access the `WebAuth.asmx` file without using SSL, it receives a 403.3 error that states "SSL is required." Figure 12.4 shows what the screen looks like.

Instead of the standard `.aspx` page file extension, the code for our Web service resides in a file with the extension `.asmx`. When this file is requested using a browser, the following screen is shown.

FIGURE 12.3
Forms-based authentication redirection process.

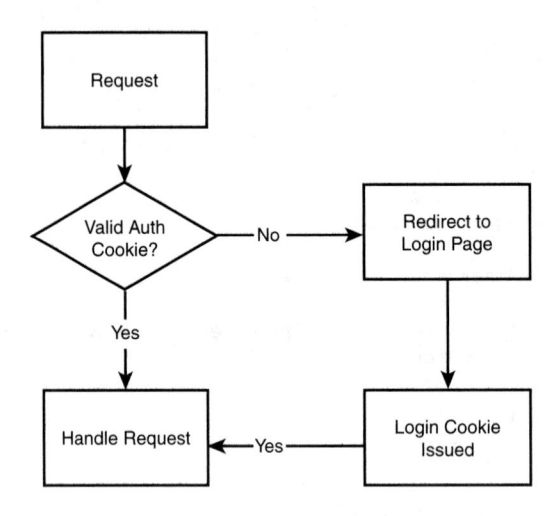

FIGURE 12.4
SSL required error screen.

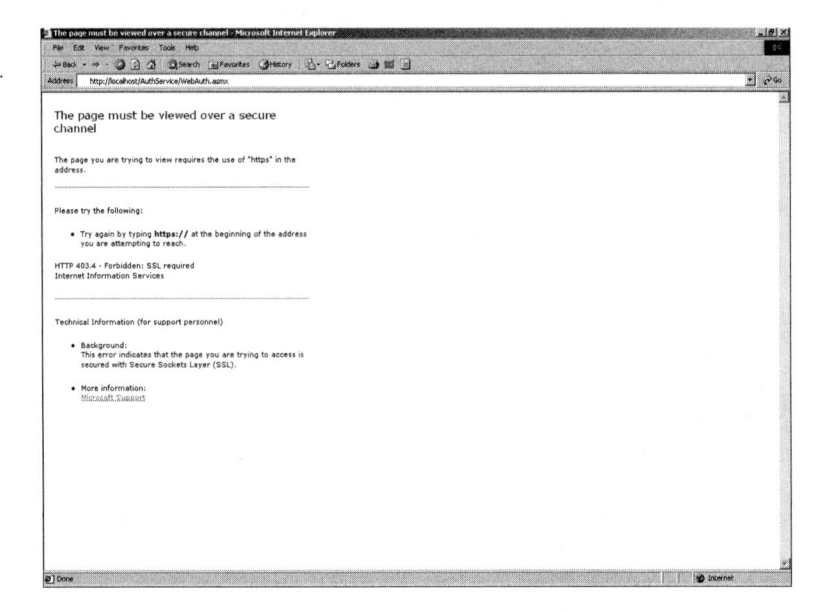

The page in Figure 12.4 is automatically generated by ASP.NET. This gives us a simple way in which to test our service via the Web.

In order to use our new authentication service, we need to create a proxy object to the service. To create a proxy object, we use the command line–based Web Service Description Language Utility provided in the .NET Frameworks SDK. The syntax for creating a proxy using `wsdl` follows:

`wsdl https://localhost/AuthService/WebAuth.asmx?WSDL`

The Web Service Utility application requests the contract for the Web service via HTTP and then creates a proxy class in C#.

> **Note**
> To create proxy classes in other languages with `wsdl`, use the `/l:` switch.
> For instance, to create another proxy for our Web Authentication service in VB.NET, use
> `wsdl https://localhost/AuthService/WebAuth.asmx?WSDL/l:VB`

Unless specified otherwise, the proxy class will use the name of the Web service. In our case, the file that is saved by `WSDL` is named `WebAuth.cs`. Listing 12.1.23 shows the proxy class that was generated by the wsdl utility.

LISTING 12.1.23 `WebAuth.cs` Proxy Class Generated by the WSDL Utility

```
 1: //------------------------------------------------------------
 2: // <autogenerated>
 3: //     This code was generated by a tool.
 4: //     Runtime Version: 1.0.2914.16
 5: //
 6: //     Changes to this file may cause incorrect behavior and will be lost if
 7: //     the code is regenerated.
 8: // </autogenerated>
 9: //------------------------------------------------------------
10:
11: //
12: // This source code was auto-generated by wsdl, Version=1.0.2914.16.
13: //
14: using System.Diagnostics;
15: using System.Xml.Serialization;
16: using System;
17: using System.Web.Services.Protocols;
18: using System.Web.Services;
19:
20:
21: [System.Web.Services.WebServiceBindingAttribute(Name="WebAuthSoap",
➥Namespace="http://tempuri.org/")]
22: public class WebAuth : System.Web.Services.Protocols.SoapHttpClientProtocol {
23:
```

LISTING 12.1.23 Continued

```
24:        [System.Diagnostics.DebuggerStepThroughAttribute()]
25:        public WebAuth() {
26:            this.Url = "http://localhost/testapp/webauth.asmx";
27:        }
28:
29:        [System.Diagnostics.DebuggerStepThroughAttribute()]
30:        [System.Web.Services.Protocols.SoapDocumentMethodAttribute("http://tempuri.
➥org/Authenticate", Use=System.Web.Services.Description.SoapBindingUse.Literal,
➥ParameterStyle=System.Web.Services.Protocols.SoapParameterStyle.Wrapped)]
31:        public bool Authenticate(string UserEmail, string UserPass) {
32:            object[] results = this.Invoke("Authenticate", new object[] {
33:                        UserEmail,
34:                        UserPass});
35:            return ((bool)(results[0]));
36:        }
37:
38:        [System.Diagnostics.DebuggerStepThroughAttribute()]
39:        public System.IAsyncResult BeginAuthenticate(string UserEmail, string
➥UserPass, System.AsyncCallback callback, object asyncState) {
40:            return this.BeginInvoke("Authenticate", new object[] {
41:                        UserEmail,
42:                        UserPass}, callback, asyncState);
43:        }
44:
45:        [System.Diagnostics.DebuggerStepThroughAttribute()]
46:        public bool EndAuthenticate(System.IAsyncResult asyncResult) {
47:            object[] results = this.EndInvoke(asyncResult);
48:            return ((bool)(results[0]));
49:        }
50: }
```

To use our proxy class (`WebAuth.cs`), we must compile the source file using the following command (in C#):

```
csc /t:library /r:System.dll
    ➥/r:System.Web.Services.dll
    ➥/r:System.xml.dll WebAuth.cs
```

This command runs the command-line C# compiler and creates a DLL named `WebAuth.dll`, which should be copied to the `bin` directory within the ASP.NET application that will use the proxy.

We can create a console application to demonstrate that the authentication service works even outside of an ASP.NET authentication scenario. The code for this console-based test application is shown in Listing 12.1.24.

LISTING 12.1.24 Console-Based Remote Authentication Test Application

```
1: //Compile using:
2: //csc /r:System.dll /r:WebAuth.dll /r:System.Web.Services.dll TestAuthApp.cs
3:
```

LISTING 12.1.24 Continued

```
 4: using System;
 5:
 6: class MyClass {
 7:
 8:     static void Main(string[] args) {
 9:
10:         if (args.Length == 2)
11:         {
12:
13:             WebAuth wa = new WebAuth();
14:
15:             if (wa.Authenticate(args[0], args[1]))
16:                 Console.WriteLine("The credentials are VALID!");
17:             else
18:                 Console.WriteLine("The credentials are INVALID!");
19:         }
20:         else
21:         {
22:             Console.WriteLine ("Usage: TestAuth [Email Address] [Password]");
23:             Console.WriteLine ("Sample: TestAuth joeuser@somewhere.com
24:                 ➥joespassword");
25:         }
26:     }
27: }
```

The application in listing 12.1.24 uses our remote Web service via the local proxy class for authenticating email addresses and passwords sent to the application on the command line. A screenshot of the application is shown in Figure 12.5.

FIGURE 12.5
Console-based Test Authentication Application.

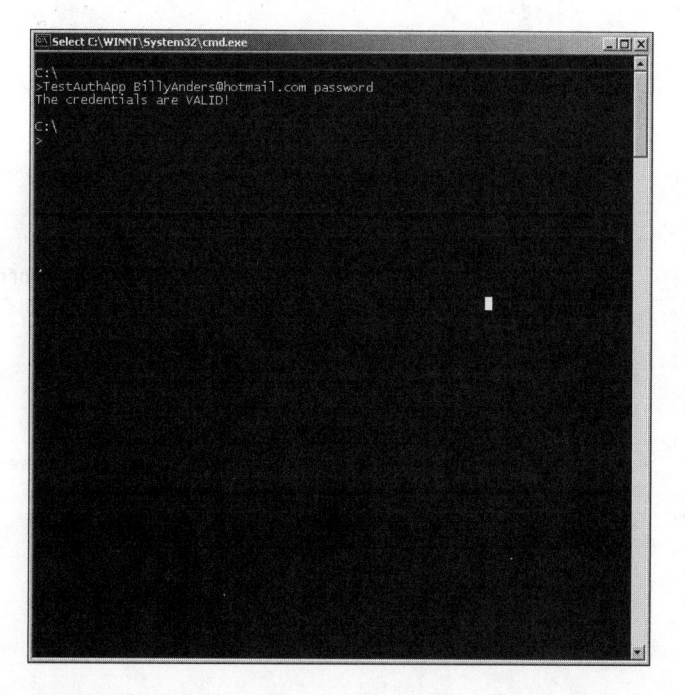

Now that we have tested our application from both the ASP.NET-provided test page and our console-based application, we need to incorporate the authentication service into our Web application.

The application in Listing 12.1.25 again leverages the user interface introduced earlier in this chapter.

LISTING 12.1.25 Forms Authentication Using a Remote Web Service

```
 1: <%@ Page Inherits="SQLLogin" Debug="True" Src="login.cs" %>
 2:
 3: <html>
 4: <head>
 5:     <title>Forms Authentication using a Web Service</title>
 6: <body>
 7:
 8: <form runat=server>
 9:     <h3><font face="Verdana">Login Page</font></h3>
10:
11:     <table>
12:        <tr>
13:
14:          <td>Email:</td>
15:          <td><ASP:TextBox id="UserEmail" runat=server/></td>
16:          <td><ASP:RequiredFieldValidator
17:             ControlToValidate="UserEmail"
18:             Display="Static"
19:             ErrorMessage="* - Please enter your email address."
20:             runat=server/>
21:          </td>
22:
23:        </tr>
24:        <tr>
25:
26:          <td>Password:</td>
27:          <td><ASP:TextBox id="UserPass" TextMode="password" runat=server/></td>
28:          <td><ASP:RequiredFieldValidator
29:             ControlToValidate="UserPass"
30:             Display="Static"
31:             ErrorMessage="* - Please enter your password."
32:             runat=server/>
33:          </td>
34:        </tr>
35:        <tr>
36:
37:          <td>Persistent Cookie:</td>
38:          <td><ASP:CheckBox id=PersistCookie runat="server"
39:             autopostback="true" />
40:          </td>
41:          <td></td>
42:        </tr>
43:
```

LISTING 12.1.25 Continued

```
44: </table>
45:
46:
47: <input type="submit" OnServerClick="Login_Click" Value="Login"
48:                                  runat="server"/><p>
49:     <asp:Label id="Msg" ForeColor="red" Font-Name="Verdana"
50:                                  Font-Size="10" runat=server />
51:
52: </form>
53: </body>
54: </html>
```

This is the same page used earlier in the chapter and therefore does not need further explaining. However, the following `login.cs` page is different. Because we have outsourced our authentication to the remote Web service, we now have significantly less coding work in the `login.cs` file. Our `login.cs` page effectively does the same work as the previous versions. The `Login_Click` event handler is again called when the user clicks the Login button. When the `Click` event of the Login button is called, two variables are created. The `IsValid` variable is a Boolean that will contain the result of the Web service method call. The `wa` variable is the instance of our Web service proxy object. The login page uses this object instance as though it were the Web service. Method calls are turned into SOAP calls and sent to the remote Web service over HTTP. When the call is returned from the remote Web service, the returned SOAP value is unwrapped and returned to our `login.cs` page as though everything was done locally. The rest of `login.cs` remains consistent with the previous examples and either issues an authentication ticket upon success or informs the user of a failure.

Listing 12.1.26 uses the remote web service for authenticating users.

LISTING 12.1.26 `Login.aspx` Page for Authenticating User Credentials Against a Remote Web Service

```
 1: <%@ Import Namespace="System.Collections" %>
 2: <%@ Import Namespace="System.Data" %>
 3: <%@ Import Namespace="System.Web.Security" %>
 4: <Script Language="C#" Runat=Server >
 5:
 6:     public void Login_Click(Object sender, EventArgs E) {
 7:
 8:         bool IsValid = false;
 9:         WebAuth wa = new WebAuth();
10:
11:         try {
12:             IsValid = wa.Authenticate(UserEmail.Text, UserPass.Text);
13:         }
14:         catch {
15:             Msg.Text = "There was a problem validating your credentials.";
16:         }
17:
18:         if (IsValid) {
19:
```

LISTING 12.1.26   Continued

```
20:              // The credentials were valid
21:              FormsAuthentication.RedirectFromLoginPage(UserEmail.Text,
➥PersistCookie.Checked);
22:
23:         } else {
24:
25:              // The credentials were invalid
26:              Msg.Text = "Invalid Credentials!<br>Please try again.";
27:         }
28:     }
29:
30: </Script>
31:
32: <html>
33: <head>
34:     <title>Forms Authentication using a Web Service</title>
35: </head>
36: <body>
37:
38: <form runat=server>
39:     <h3><font face="Verdana">Login Page</font></h3>
40:
41:     <table>
42:         <tr>
43:
44:         <td>Email:</td>
45:         <td><ASP:TextBox id="UserEmail" runat=server/></td>
46:         <td><ASP:RequiredFieldValidator
47:             ControlToValidate="UserEmail"
48:             Display="Static"
49:             ErrorMessage="* - Please enter your email address."
50:             runat=server/>
51:         </td>
52:
53:     </tr>
54:     <tr>
55:
56:         <td>Password:</td>
57:         <td><ASP:TextBox id="UserPass"
58:                 ➥TextMode="password"
59:                 ➥runat=server/></td>
60:         <td><ASP:RequiredFieldValidator
61:             ControlToValidate="UserPass"
62:             Display="Static"
63:             ErrorMessage="* - Please enter your password."
64:             runat=server/>
65:         </td>
66:     </tr>
67:     <tr>
68:
69:         <td>Persistent Cookie:</td>
70:         <td><ASP:CheckBox id=PersistCookie runat="server"
```

LISTING 12.1.26 Continued

```
71:                autopostback="true" />
72:            </td>
73:            <td></td>
74:        </tr>
75:
76: </table>
77:
78:
79: <input type="submit" OnServerClick="Login_Click" Value="Login"
80:                                     runat="server"/><p>
81:     <asp:Label id="Msg" ForeColor="red" Font-Name="Verdana"
82:                                 Font-Size="10" runat=server />
83:
84: </form>
85: </body>
86: </html>
```

The code in Listing 12.1.26 accomplishes the same goals as in earlier samples. The page presents the user with an HTML page that allows them to enter their username and password. However, instead of going against a local data store, we have outsourced the authentication responsibilities to a web service. Line 8 creates a `Boolean` variable `IsValid`. This variable will contain the final answer as to whether the user credentials are valid or not. On line 9 we create an instance of our `WebAuth` class and place the instance in our `wa` variable. Lines 11-16 setup a try-catch block. There may be a problem when validating against the remote service and we want to be sure to catch any exceptions. Line 12 is where we call the `Authenticate` method provided by our remote Web Service. The service returns a `Boolean` that we place into our `IsValid` variable. If everything works as expected, line 18 checks the value of `IsValid`. If `IsValid` is true on line 18, we use the `RedirectFromLoginPage` method provided by the `FormsAuthentication` object to place an authentication ticket in the browser of the user and redirect them to the page they originally requested or `default.aspx`.

Passport Authentication

Microsoft's Passport is another authentication method provided in ASP.NET. Passport is Microsoft's single sign-on service. Using Passport, users can use one sign-in name and password at any participating Web site. This has the advantage of allowing members to save time by creating a single sign-in profile of basic demographic information that can be shared with participating sites.

Passport uses standard Web technologies such as SSL, cookies, and JavaScript version 1.2. In addition, Passport uses strong symmetric key encryption using Triple DES (sometimes referred to as 3DES) to deliver the single sign-in service. You must first install the Passport SDK and register your site with the Passport service in order to use Passport authentication from ASP.NET. The SDK can be downloaded from the Microsoft Passport site (www.passport.com).

Among other things, registering with the Passport service provides members with a site-specific key based on the Triple DES data-encryption scheme. Both the member site and the Passport login server use this key for encrypting and decrypting the query strings passed between sites.

Passport is, in effect, a cookie-based authentication service. Using cookies, encrypted query string information, and redirects, the Passport service is able to authenticate users for any number of Passport member sites.

A passport authentication conversation is typically comprised of several steps. A typical Passport authentication conversation will go through these steps:

1. A client browser issues a `GET` request over HTTP for a resource that requires authentication.
2. If the headers sent by the client do not contain a valid Passport cookie, the server returns a 302 response and redirects the client to the Passport login service, sending encrypted information about the original request in the query string.
3. The client then issues a `GET` request to the Passport login server with the supplied query string.
4. The Passport service presents the client with a login form.
5. The user fills in the login form with his email address and password and submits the credentials over SSL back to the Passport service for verification.
6. If the credentials are valid, the login server authenticates the user and redirects the client back to the originally requested URL with the authentication ticket encrypted in the query string.
7. The client follows the redirect and makes a request for the original protected resource with the ticket encrypted on the query string.
8. The `FormsAuthenticationModule`, which is an instance of `System.Web.IHttpModule`, first checks for the presence of the authentication ticket in headers, and then in the query string. If the authentication ticket is found on the query string, the `FormsAuthenticationModule` issues a cookie-based authentication ticket. The authentication ticket consists of both the authentication information and a path of /. The user is now authenticated.

Figure 12.6 gives a high-level graphical representation of the interactions involved in a typical Passport authentication dialogue.

Subsequent requests for protected resources are authenticated at the local server using the supplied authentication ticket. Passport also provides other facilities, such as ticket expiration and reusing tickets across other member sites.

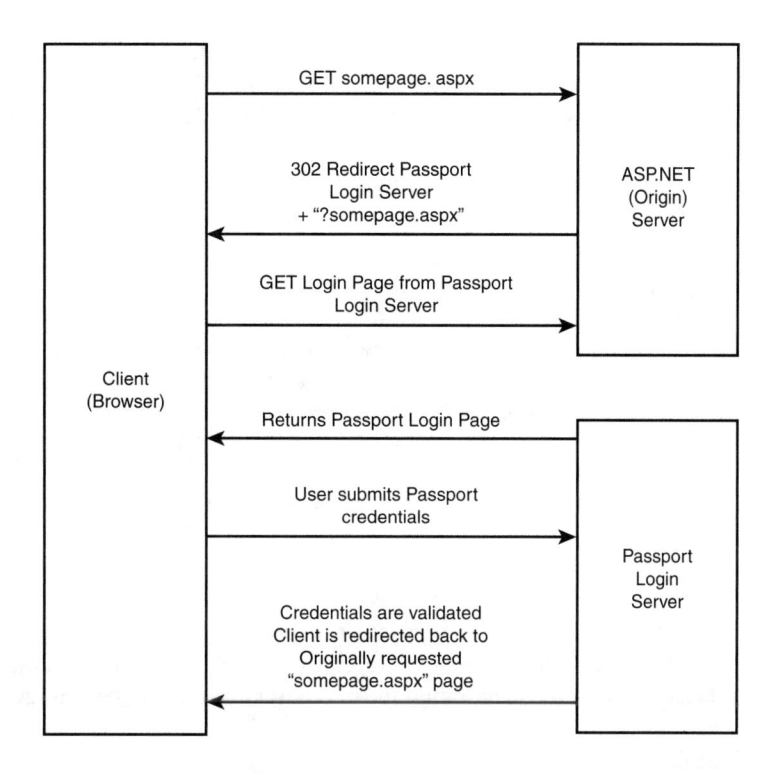

FIGURE 12.6
High-Level Passport Authentication flow.

Using the `PassportAuthenticationModule`

The `PassportAuthenticationModule` provides an ASP.NET wrapper around the Passport SDK. The `PassportAuthenticationModule` provides both Passport authentication services as well as profile information from the `PassportIdentity` class. The `PassportIdentity` class is derived from the `System.Security.Principal.IIdentity` interface. The `IIdentity` interface defines three properties: `IsAuthenticated`, `Name`, and `Type`. In addition to the properties required by the `IIdentity` interface, the derived `PassportIdentity` class provides a number of facilities, such as the following:

- Requesting the age of the authentication ticket
- Receiving time since the user signed into Passport
- Verifying whether the user uses the Save Password feature of Passport
- Signing the user out of Passport

You may want to see how long the user has been signed in to the Passport service. If he has been signed in for 24 hours and has the Save Password feature enabled, you may want to have him re-authenticate with the Passport service.

In order to begin using Passport authentication on your site you must download the Passport SDK from `http://www.passport.com`. Once the Passport SDK is downloaded and installed, you will have a couple of Passport supplied test sites on your server. One of the sites is an electronic commerce site in a virtual directory named `/PassportExample`, the other a simple test site named `/PassportTest`. The `/PassportExample` application is used as an example application to help the developer see how Passport works when used with a full-blown site. The `/PassportTest` application is simply used to see if Passport has been installed and configured correctly.

> **Note**
>
> In order to develop and test your site with Passport authentication, all that is needed is the Passport SDK.
>
> However, until your site is registered with Passport as a Passport Partner site, you will have limited Passport functionality. Functionality such as signing out of passport is not available until your site is registered.
>
> Until your site is registered as a Passport Partner site, you will need to close all browser instances and delete the Passport cookies from your user directory in order to sign-out of.

Once Passport is installed and has been verified using the two sample sites, we can begin to use Passport Authentication from within our own ASP.NET application. To use Passport we use the IIS Administration tool to configure our application with "Anonymous" authentication. The `web.config` configuration file of our application will be configured with the "`authentication mode`" set to `passport`. Listing 12.1.27 shows an example configuration file for enabling passport authentication.

LISTING 12.1.27 `Web.config` File for Enabling Passport Authentication

```
 1: <configuration>
 2:
 3: <system.web>
 4: <authentication mode="Passport" />
 5:
 6: <authorization>
 7:     <deny users="?"/>
 8: </authorization>
 9: </system.web>
10:
11: </configuration>
```

A walk-thru of Listing 12.1.27 shows that we are establishing "`passport`" as our authentication mode on line 4. The "`<authorization>`" section on lines 6-8 only allow authenticated users and deny access to all unauthenticated (anonymous) users. This makes sure that all users who use this site will be authenticated by passport before they are allowed to proceed.

The way the `web.config` file in 12.1.27 is configured only allows users that have been authenticated with passport access to any part of our site. Depending on the needs of your site, this level of security may or may not be desired. In order to give unauthenticated users a means in which to sign-in with Passport, we need to make a change to our configuration file and provide an ASP.NET page that allows signing users into Passport. Listing 12.1.28 shows how to use a location element to change the behavior of a particular section of a site. In our case, we are changing the security of ASP.NET to allow unauthenticated (anonymous) users access to the `SignIn.aspx` page.

LISTING 12.1.28 `Web.config` File for Enabling Passport Authentication and Allowing Anonymous Access to `SignIn.aspx`

```
 1: <configuration>
 2:
 3: <system.web>
 4:
 5: <authentication mode="Passport">
 6:     <passport redirectUrl="SignIn.aspx"/>
 7: </authentication>
 8:
 9: </system.web>
10:
11: <location path="SignIn.aspx">
12:
13:     <system.web>
14:     <authorization>
15:         <allow users="?"/>
16:     </authorization>
17:     </system.web>
18:
19: </location>
20:
21: </configuration>
```

The code Listing in 12.1.28 now allows anonymous to the "`Signin.aspx`" page. Line 6 uses the `redirectUrl` parameter of the `Passport` element for establishing "`PleaseSignIn.aspx`" as the page that unauthenticated users should be sent to. Normally the page listing in the `redirectURL` parameter will provide information to the user concerning the need for them to sign in using their Passport. The page does not accept credentials on behalf of passport. Accepting passport credentials is the responsibility of login servers hosted and maintained by Passport (http://www.passport.com/). Another difference between the `web.config` listing of 12.1.28 from 12.1.27 is that 12.1.28 now includes a `<location>` section which allows changing a particular area of the site independently from the rest of the site from within the same `web.config` file. In our case, lines 14-16 allow the anonymous (**?**) account to access "`SignIn.aspx`". This is necessary in order to allow unauthenticated users to access the "`SignIn.aspx`" page of our application.

Now that we have our application correctly configured to use Passport authentication, we need to see some of the information that is provided to use. In order to show some of the information provided by passport we will use the code in Listings 12.1.29 and 12.1.30. Listing 12.1.29 welcomes users using the nickname in their Passport profile.

LISTING 12.1.29 Simple Page That Welcomes Users Using Their Nickname

```
 1: <%@ Register TagName="PassportLogo"
 2:     ➥TagPrefix="Sams"
 3:     ➥src="PassportLogo.ascx" %>
 4:
 5: <Script Language="C#" Runat="Server" >
 6:
 7: protected void Page_Load(Object o, EventArgs e) {
 8:
 9: System.Web.Security.PassportIdentity id =
10: ➥(System.Web.Security.PassportIdentity)
11:     ➥Context.User.Identity;
12:
13: Nickname.Text = id["Nickname"];
14: }
15:
16: </Script>
17:
18: <html>
19: <head>
20: <title>Welcome</title>
21: </head>
22:
23: <body>
24: <h2>
25: Welcome <font color="green">
26:     ➥<asp:Label id="Nickname" Runat="Server" />
27:     ➥</font>!
28: </h2>
29:
30: <Sams:PassportLogo Runat="Server" />
31:
32: </body>
33: </html>
```

Lines 1-3 register a custom user control that helps with displaying the Passport sign-in and sign-out logo. The source for the control is in Listing 12.1.32. Lines 9-11 cast the generic `Context.User.Identity` object to the more specific Passport identity (`PassportIdentity`) object named `id`. After the case to the `PassportIdentity` object we have access to the profile information provided by the object. Line 13 sets the `Text` property of the `Nickname` label control to the `Nickname` property of the `PassportIdentity` object.

Listing 12.1.30 uses an HTML table format for displaying various pieces of information provided by Passport and the .NET `System.Web.Security.PassportIdentity` object.

LISTING 12.1.30 Passport Information Page Shows Some of the Information Provided by the `System.Web.Security.PassportIdentity` Object

```
 1: <%@ Register TagName="PassportLogo"
 2:     ➥TagPrefix="Sams"
 3:     ➥src="PassportLogo.ascx" %>
```

LISTING 12.1.30 *Continued*

```
 4:
 5: <%@ Import Namespace="System.Collections" %>
 6: <%@ Import Namespace="System.ComponentModel" %>
 7: <%@ Import Namespace="System.Data" %>
 8: <%@ Import Namespace="System.Web.SessionState" %>
 9:
10:
11: <Script Language="C#" Runat="Server" >
12:
13: protected void Page_Load(object sender, EventArgs e)
14: {
15:
16: if (!(Context.User.Identity is
17:     ➥System.Web.Security.PassportIdentity)) {
18:
19: Message.Text = "Error: Passport authentication failed.
20:     ➥ Make sure that the passport auth module has
21:     ➥ been added to the pipeline and this server
22:     ➥is configured to use passport authentication.";
23:
24: return;
25: }
26:
27: System.Web.Security.PassportIdentity id =
28: (System.Web.Security.PassportIdentity)
29:     ➥Context.User.Identity;
30:
31:
32: if (!id.IsAuthenticated) {
33:
34: passportInfo.Visible = false;
35:
36: Message.Text = "Although you have access to this page,
37:     ➥ there is nothing to see without
38:     ➥ first signing in with your Passport.";
39:
40: return;
41: }
42: else
43: {
44: passportInfo.Visible = true;
45: }
46:
47:
48: identity.Text= Context.User.Identity.Name;
49: accessibility.Text= id["Accessibility"];
50: birthdate.Text= id["BirthDate"];
51: birthdate_precisison.Text= id["BDay_precision"];
52: city.Text= id["city"];
53: country.Text= id["country"];
54: directory.Text= id["Directory"];
55: flags.Text= id["flags"];
```

LISTING 12.1.30 Continued

```
56: gender.Text= id["gender"];
57: language.Text= id["Lang_Preference"];
58: member_id_high.Text= id["memberIDHigh"];
59: member_id_low.Text= id["memberIDLow"];
60: member_name.Text= id["memberName"];
61: nick_name.Text= id["Nickname"];
62: postal_code.Text= id["postalCode"];
63: email.Text= id["PreferredEmail"];
64: profile_version.Text= id["profileVersion"];
65: region.Text= id["region"];
66:
67: Message.Text = "You've been signed in for: " +
68:     ➥id.TimeSinceSignIn + " seconds.";
69:
70: }
71:
72:
73:
74: </Script>
75:
76: <html>
77:   <head>
78: <title>Test Page for Passport</title>
79:   </head>
80:
81:   <body>
82:       <h2>Passport Information Page for ASP.NET</h2>
83:
84: <Sams:PassportLogo Runat="Server" />
85:
86: <br><br>
87:
88: <font color="red"><asp:Label id="Message" Runat="Server" /></font>
89:
90:     <div id="passportInfo" align="left" runat="Server" >
91:       <table border="0" cellpadding="0"
92: ➥cellspacing="0"
93: ➥style="border-collapse: collapse"
94: ➥bordercolor="#111111"
95: ➥width="100%"
96: ➥id="AutoNumber1"
97: ➥runat="Server">
98:       <tr>
99:         <td width="13%" align="right"> </td>
100:         <td width="2%"> </td>
101:         <td width="85%"> </td>
102:       </tr>
103:       <tr>
104:         <td width="13%" align="right">Passport Identity:</td>
105:         <td width="2%"> </td>
106:         <td width="85%"><asp:Label id="identity"
107:     ➥runat="server"
```

LISTING 12.1.30 Continued

```
108:        ➥size="50"
109:        ➥name="identity" /></td>
110:          </tr>
111:          <tr>
112:            <td width="13%" align="right">Accessibility</td>
113:            <td width="2%"> </td>
114:            <td width="85%">
115:              <asp:Label id="accessibility"
116:        ➥runat="server"
117:        ➥size="50"
118:        ➥name="accessibility" /></td>
119:          </tr>
120:          <tr>
121:            <td width="13%" align="right">Birthdate</td>
122:            <td width="2%"> </td>
123:            <td width="85%">
124:              <asp:Label id="birthdate"
125:        ➥runat="server"
126:        ➥size="50"
127:        ➥name="birthdate" /></td>
128:          </tr>
129:          <tr>
130:            <td width="13%" align="right">Birthdate Precision</td>
131:            <td width="2%"> </td>
132:            <td width="85%">
133:              <asp:Label id="birthdate_precisison"
134:        ➥runat="server"
135:        ➥size="50"
136:        ➥name="birthdate_precisison" /></td>
137:          </tr>
138:          <tr>
139:            <td width="13%" align="right">City</td>
140:            <td width="2%"> </td>
141:            <td width="85%">
142:              <asp:Label id="city"
143:        ➥runat="server"
144:        ➥size="50"
145:        ➥name="city" /></td>
146:          </tr>
147:          <tr>
148:            <td width="13%" align="right">Country</td>
149:            <td width="2%"> </td>
150:            <td width="85%">
151:              <asp:Label id="country"
152:        ➥runat="server"
153:        ➥size="50"
154:        ➥name="country" /></td>
155:          </tr>
156:          <tr>
157:            <td width="13%" align="right">Directory</td>
158:            <td width="2%"> </td>
159:            <td width="85%">
```

LISTING 12.1.30 Continued

```
160:              <asp:Label id="directory"
161:         ↪runat="server"
162:         ↪size="50"
163:         ↪name="directory" /></td>
164:            </tr>
165:            <tr>
166:              <td width="13%" align="right"> </td>
167:              <td width="2%"> </td>
168:              <td width="85%">
169:               </td>
170:            </tr>
171:            <tr>
172:              <td width="13%" align="right">Flags</td>
173:              <td width="2%"> </td>
174:              <td width="85%">
175:              <asp:Label id="flags"
176:         ↪runat="server"
177:         ↪size="50"
178:         ↪name="flags" /></td>
179:            </tr>
180:            <tr>
181:              <td width="13%" align="right">Gender</td>
182:              <td width="2%"> </td>
183:              <td width="85%">
184:              <asp:Label id="gender"
185:         ↪runat="server"
186:         ↪size="50"
187:         ↪name="gender" /></td>
188:            </tr>
189:            <tr>
190:              <td width="13%" align="right">Language Preference</td>
191:              <td width="2%"> </td>
192:              <td width="85%">
193:              <asp:Label id="language"
194:         ↪runat="server"
195:         ↪size="50"
196:         ↪name="language" /></td>
197:            </tr>
198:            <tr>
199:              <td width="13%" align="right">Member ID High</td>
200:              <td width="2%"> </td>
201:              <td width="85%">
202:              <asp:Label id="member_id_high"
203:         ↪runat="server"
204:         ↪size="50"
205:         ↪name="member_id_high" /></td>
206:            </tr>
207:            <tr>
208:              <td width="13%" align="right">Member ID Low</td>
209:              <td width="2%"> </td>
210:              <td width="85%">
211:              <asp:Label id="member_id_low"
212:         ↪runat="server"
```

LISTING 12.1.30 *Continued*

```
213:    ➥size="50"
214:    ➥name="member_id_low" /></td>
215:       </tr>
216:       <tr>
217:         <td width="13%" align="right">Member Name</td>
218:         <td width="2%"> </td>
219:         <td width="85%">
220:         <asp:Label id="member_name"
221:    ➥runat="server"
222:    ➥size="50"
223:    ➥name="member_name" /></td>
224:       </tr>
225:       <tr>
226:         <td width="13%" align="right">Nick Name</td>
227:         <td width="2%"> </td>
228:         <td width="85%">
229:         <asp:Label id="nick_name"
230:    ➥runat="server"
231:    ➥size="50"
232:    ➥name="nick_name" /></td>
233:       </tr>
234:       <tr>
235:         <td width="13%" align="right">Postal Code</td>
236:         <td width="2%"> </td>
237:         <td width="85%">
238:         <asp:Label id="postal_code"
239:    ➥runat="server"
240:    ➥size="50"
241:    ➥name="postal_code" /></td>
242:       </tr>
243:       <tr>
244:         <td width="13%" align="right">Preferred Email</td>
245:         <td width="2%"> </td>
246:         <td width="85%">
247:         <asp:Label id="email"
248:    ➥runat="server"
249:    ➥size="50"
250:    ➥name="email" /></td>
251:       </tr>
252:       <tr>
253:         <td width="13%" align="right">Profile Version</td>
254:         <td width="2%"> </td>
255:         <td width="85%">
256:         <asp:Label id="profile_version"
257:    ➥runat="server"
258:    ➥size="50"
259:    ➥name="profile_version" /></td>
260:       </tr>
261:       <tr>
262:         <td width="13%" align="right">Region</td>
263:         <td width="2%"> </td>
264:         <td width="85%">
```

LISTING 12.1.30   Continued

```
265:                <asp:Label id="region"
266:        ↪runat="server"
267:        ↪size="50"
268:        ↪name="region" /></td>
269:           </tr>
270:         </table>
271: </div>
272:
273:     </body>
274: </html>
```

Listing 12.1.30 starts off by registering a simple page control named "`Sams:PassportLogo`." The source for the control is in listing 12.1.31. Next on lines 5-8 we import the `System.Collections`, `System.ComoponentModel`, `System.Data` and `System.Web.SessionState` namespaces. Inside of the `Page_Load` event handler we check to see if the `Context.User.Identity` object is of type `System.Web.Security.PassportIdentity`. This does not ensure that the user has been authenticated using Passport, only that Passport authentication is correctly configured. Now that we know that the `Context.User.Identity` object is of type `PassportIdentity`, on lines 27-29 we can safely cast the generic `Identity` object to its specific `PassportIdentity` object. Line 32 uses the `IsAuthenticated` method available to all classes derived from the `System.Web.Security.Identity` base class to check whether the user is authenticated. If the user is not authenticated with Passport, they will receive the message from lines 36-38. If the user has been authenticated by Passport, line 44 sets the `Visible` property of our `passportInfo` HTML DIV element to true. Once the DIV and its contents are visible we begin to set the `Text` properties of our various Label controls to the properties from our `PassportIdentity` (`id`) object.

As mentioned earlier, Listing 12.1.31 shows the code to the `PassportLogo` user control. The `PassportLogo` user control would be placed everywhere you want to show the Passport image that allows user to use Passport to log-in and log-out of your site.

LISTING 12.1.31   `PassportLogo` Control

```
1: <%@ Language="C#" %>
2: <%
3:    PassportIdentity id = (PassportIdentity)
4:    ↪    Page.User.Identity;
5:    logoControl.Text = id.LogoTag();
6: %>
7: <asp:Label id="logoControl" Runat="Server" />
```

The control in Listing 12.1.31 uses the `LogoTag()` method available through the `System.Web.Security.PassportIdentity` object. The `LogoTag()` method contains the HTML necessary to construct an HTML image (`<img>`) tag for users to log-in and log-out of the system. Lines 4-5 show that we are casting the `Page.User.Identity` object to a `PassportIdentity` object. If the cast was successful, we will have an instance of the `PassportIdentity` object in our id variable. Line 5 invokes the `LogoTag()` method of the `PassportIdentity` object. The `LogoTag()` method returns a complete HTML image tag that the Text property of the `logoControl` Label control is set to.

2. Authorization

Authorization is the process of determining whether an authenticated identity has access to a resource. ASP.NET provides two types of authorization services: file authorization and URL authorization.

File Authorization

File authorization uses the authorized identity and HTTP request method for determining which access control lists (ACLs) are required for access to a given resource. ASP.NET file authorization is hard-coded to require read permission for the `GET`, `POST`, and `HEAD` methods.

File authorization works using the Windows security services for resources such as files. For instance, if a file resource only allows members of the Administrators group, ASP.NET will honor those settings and only members belonging to that group will have access to the file.

To demonstrate file authorization with ASP.NET, we will place different permissions on a simple ASP.NET file.

Listing 12.2.1 shows the code for `file_auth.aspx`.

LISTING 12.2.1 A Very Simple Welcome Page That Displays the Name by Which the User is Accessing the Page

```
 1: <html>
 2: <head>
 3:     <title>Welcome</title>
 4: </head>
 5:
 6: <body>
 7:     <h2>
 8:         <font face="Verdana">
 9:             <%= User.Identity.Name %>, welcome to the page!
10:         </font>
11:     </h2>
12: </body>
13: </html>
```

This straightforward piece of code simply outputs a welcome message using the `Name` property of the `Identity` object.

We will configure the file for only members of the Administrators group to access the file. To configure the permissions right-click and choose properties on the file in the Windows Explorer. Once the properties dialog is open, choose the Security tab. From the Security tab, you can add and remove users and groups at will. Figure 12.7 shows the security tab only allowing access by members of the Administrators group.

FIGURE 12.7
Administrators group only having file access.

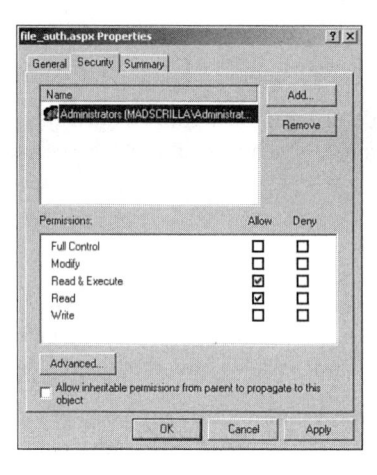

Members of the Administrators group of the machine will receive a response similar to screenshot in Figure 12.8.

FIGURE 12.8
Access granted to members of the Administrators group.

Next, by removing the Administrators group and adding only the Guests group to the file, we deny administrators access while allowing guests.

When a user who is not a member of the Guests group requests the file, the result will be an "Access Denied" error as shown in Figure 12.9.

FIGURE 12.9
Access denied due to ACL permissions screen.

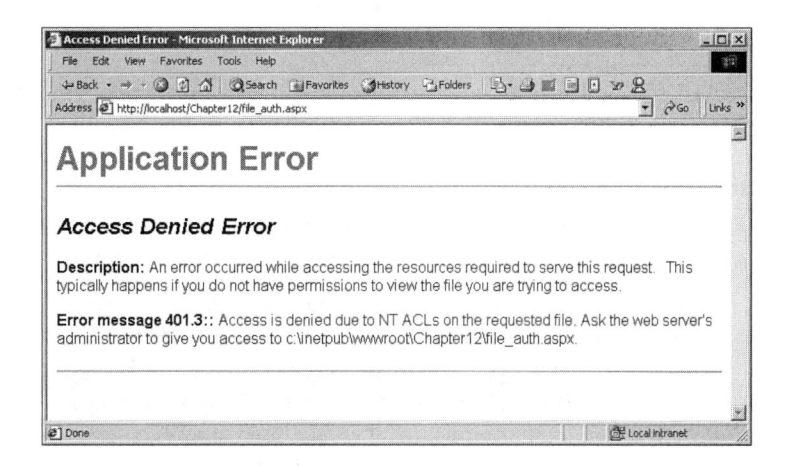

URL Authorization

The code in listing 12.2.2 grants access to Mary while denying it to everyone else.

LISTING 12.2.2 Granting Access to Individuals Using the `Web.config` File

```
1: <configuration>
2: <system.web>
3:     <authorization>
4:         <allow users="Mary" />
5:         <deny users="*" />
6:     <authorization>
7: </system.web>
8: <configuration>
```

There are two special characters for the `<allow>` and `<deny>` subsections. The first character, the asterisk (*), effectively means *everyone*. The second character, the questions mark (?), represents the anonymous user.

The `<authorization>` tag supports only two subelements: `<allow>` and `<deny>`. The `<allow>` and `<deny>` elements support three attributes. These attributes are defined in the following list:

Attribute	Description
Users	Identifies the targeted identities for this element
Roles	Identifies a targeted role for this element.
Verbs	Defines the HTTP verbs to which the action applies (for example, *, GET, HEAD, POST). An asterisk (*) denotes *all*.

Users

The users attribute contains the names of one or more users that are allowed or denied access to the resource. Multiple names should be separated by commas.

Roles

The roles attribute contains the names of one or more roles that are allowed or denied access to the resource. Multiple names should be separated by commas.

The associated `IPrincipal` object determines role membership. The `IPrincipal` interface defines the basic functionality of a principal object. The principal object contains the security context and identity of the user for which the request is being processed. In the case of the default principal class for a Windows user, the `WindowsPrincipal` class uses Windows (NT) groups for determining role membership. Developers can create custom principal objects by implementing the `System.Security.Principal.IPrincipal` interface themselves. From here, the `IPrincipal` object instance can be attached to the context for a given request and roles can be mapped as the developers see fit.

Verbs

The verbs attribute specifies for which of the HTTP verbs the `<allow>` or `<deny>` tag applies. Valid values for the verbs attribute are `*`, `GET`, `HEAD`, and `POST`.

The `<allow>` and `<deny>` subsections work from the bottom up. The example shown in Listing 12.2.3 identifies two users: Bob and Mary. The `<authorization>` subsection both grants and denies access to the Mary account.

LISTING 12.2.3 Demonstration of Allow/Disallow Precedence

```
 1: <configuration>
 2:     <system.web>
 3:
 4:         <authentication mode="Forms">
 5:         <forms loginUrl="login.asp"
 6:             name=".AUTHCOOKIE"
 7:             protection="All"
 8:             timeout="15">
 9:
10:         <credentials passwordFormat="Clear">
11:             <user name="Bob" password="bob" />
12:             <user name="Mary" password="mary" />
13:         </credentials>
14:
15:         </forms>
16:     </authentication>
17:
18:     <authorization>
19:         <allow users="Mary" />
20:         <deny users="Mary" />
21:         <deny users="*" />
```

LISTING 12.2.3 Continued

```
22:        </authorization>
23:
24:     </system.web>
25: </configuration>
```

Although redundant in appearance, Listing 12.2.3 demonstrates how ASP.NET grants access from the configuration file. Reading the contents of this configuration file, you will notice that the Mary account is first granted access using the `<allow>` tag and then denied access using the `<deny>` tag. The ASP.NET configuration system rolls the access rights up, meaning that where there is a potential conflict of user rights, the declaration earlier (or higher) in the configuration file will be used. In the case of this example, although Mary is both granted and denied permission, she will be granted permission because the `<allow>` tag is declared earlier (and higher) in the file.

LISTING 12.2.4 Simple Login Page

```
 1: <html>
 2: <head>
 3: <script runat=server Language="VB">
 4:
 5: Sub SubmitBtn_Click(ByVal Source as Object, ByVal E as EventArgs)
 6:     If FormsAuthentication.Authenticate(
 7: ➥        UserName.Value, UserPassword.Value) Then
 8:        FormsAuthentication.RedirectFromLoginPage (
 9: ➥        UserName.Value, false)
10:     End If
11: End Sub
12:
13: </script>
14: </head>
15:
16: <body>
17:
18: <form method=post runat=server>
19: <table>
20:     <tr>
21:        <td>Name:</td>
22:        <td><input type="text"
23:            id="UserName" runat=server/>
24:     </tr>
25:     <tr>
26:        <td>Password:</td>
27:        <td><input type="password"
28:            id="UserPassword" runat=server/>
29:     </td>
30: </table>
31: <input type="submit"
32:        OnServerClick="SubmitBtn_Click"
33:        runat=server />
34:
```

LISTING 12.2.4 Continued

```
35: </form>
36:
37: </body>
38: </html>
```

Using Role-Based Security

Roles work in a similar fashion as roles. The example shown in Listing 12.2.5 uses Windows authentication and grants access to members of the Administrators and Power Users groups. All other users are denied access.

LISTING 12.2.5 Using Roles to Grant/Deny Permission

```
 1: <configuration>
 2:     <system.web>
 3:
 4:     <authentication mode="Windows" />
 5:
 6:     <authorization>
 7:         <allow roles="Administrators, Power Users" />
 8:         <deny users="*" />
 9:     </authorization>
10:
11:     </system.web>
12: </configuration>
```

The page shown in Listing 12.2.6 simply displays the name of the user if he is allowed access.

LISTING 12.2.6 Welcome Page After Validating Role Membership

```
 1: <html>
 2: <head>
 3: <title>Roles with Windows Authentication</title>
 4:
 5: <Script Language="VB" runat=server>
 6:     Private Sub Page_Load(Src As Object, E As EventArgs)
 7:         Welcome.InnerHtml = "Hello, " & Context.User.Identity.Name
 8:     End Sub
 9: </script>
10:
11: <body>
12:     <h3>
13:         <font face="Verdana">
14:             Using Roles with Windows Authentication
15:         </font>
16:     </h3>
17:
18:     <span id="Welcome" runat=server/>
19: </body>
20: </html>
```

If users are denied access because they are not members of either the Administrators or Power Users group, they will receive an "Access Denied" error. This error can be trapped in the application file or in an `IHttpModule` class. The error is a standard 401 error and therefore can be configured to redirect to another page in the case of the error by using the IIS Administration tool.

Impersonation

Impersonation is the concept whereby an application executes with the identity of the client in which is accessing the application.

By default, ASP.NET does not perform impersonation on a per-request basis. Instead, ASP.NET executes under the process token provided by IIS.

	Windows Authentication	Non-Windows Authentication
ACL Check	Yes	No
URL Check	Yes	Yes

When impersonation is enabled for an application, ASP.NET uses the token provided by IIS for executing the request.

Access Tokens

Access tokens contain user information such as the security identifier (SID) and access control entries (ACEs) for the user.

Impersonation Disabled

While ASP.NET is executing under the process token, it performs a URL access check using the access token provided by IIS. If the URL access check is successful, the request handler is executed using the process token.

Impersonation Enabled

While ASP.NET is executing under the process token, it performs a URL access check using the access token provided by IIS. If the URL access check is successful, ASP.NET then impersonates the user and executes the request handler. Immediately after executing the request handler, ASP.NET reverts back to the identity of the process token.

> **Note**
> Regardless of whether impersonation is enabled, when Windows authentication is being used, ASP.NET performs both URL and ACL (access control list) checks.

Impersonation enables the security context to "flow" throughout an application even if the application goes beyond the ASP.NET world. This means that, with impersonation, if a user makes a request to an ASP.NET page that instantiates a .NET DLL that calls a COM+ object, the security context can flow to all parts of your application. Listing 12.2.7 enables impersonation in an application.

LISTING 12.2.7 Enabling Impersonation in an ASP.NET Application

```
1: <configuration>
2:     <system.web>
3:         <identity impersonate="true" />
4:     </system.web>
5: </configuration>
```

To enable impersonation, you simply need to set the `impersonate` attribute of the `<identity>` tag to `True`. Setting this attribute to `False` will disable impersonation. By default, ASP.NET is configured to not impersonate individual requests. This setting is in the machine-wide `machine.config` file.

> **Note**
> ASP.NET only impersonates application code during the request handler. Tasks such as executing the compiler and reading configuration data occur as the default process account.

Enabling Fixed NT Account Execution

An application can also be configured to run under a particular identity. To configure the application to use a particular set of credentials, you need to edit the configuration file of the application. Listing 12.2.8 shows what a `web.config` file looks like when enabled for fixed NT account execution.

LISTING 12.2.8 Enabling Fixed NT Account Execution

```
1: <configuration>
2: <system.web>
3:     <identity impersonate="false"
4:         userName="MyDomain\Bob"
5:         password="password" />
6: </system.web>
7: </configuration>
```

Listing 12.2.8 disables per-request impersonation and uses a fixed Windows account (`MyDomain\Bob`) for execution. After the URL access check, the request will be executed using the fixed account, `MyDomain\Bob`.

As the following table shows, when an ASP.NET application is configured for fixed-account execution, it will always use the configured credentials, regardless of the authentication model.

Impersonation	Anonymous On	Anonymous Off State
On	IUSR_COMPUTERNAME	Remote User Identity
Off	Process ID	Process ID
Configured Identity	Configured Identity	Configured Identity

However, when ASP.NET is not configured to use a fixed account and impersonation is also disabled, each request will execute using the account of the process (the default is `LocalSystem`), regardless of the authentication model (anonymous, Windows, and so on). When impersonation is enabled and the application allows anonymous access, the request will execute using the account configured in IIS as the anonymous account (by default, this is `IUSR_COMPUTERNAME`). If anonymous is disabled in the application, the request will run using the identity of the client user.

UNC Shares

Impersonation works slightly different with Universal Naming Convention (UNC) shares and mapped drives (for example, `\\thatcomputer\thatshare`). In cases where an ASP.NET application is being accessed via a network share, the share will always be accessed using the identity of the request. If the application is configured to allow anonymous access, the application will, by default, use the `IUSR_COMPUTERNAME` account. In cases where anonymous access is not allowed, the identity of the client making the request will be used. This is true even in cases where the drive is mapped to a share on the local computer. For example, let's assume that my computer is named `billyw2k` and has a folder shared using the name `401kApp`. If, while at `billyw2k`, I map a drive to `\\billyw2k\401kApp` (for example, `NET USE Z: \\billyw2k\401kApp`), the mapped drive will still be treated as though it were a remote UNC share. Network shares, whether mapped or using the UNC, are always accessed as though impersonation were enabled.

> **Note**
> Running ASP.NET applications on remote shares is not recommended.

Summary

In this chapter we covered application-level security using both Integrated Windows authenticated and Forms authentication. We learned that although Windows authentication is a secure and powerful authentication scheme, forms authentication is flexible enough to use any data store that you can program against. We also covered role-based security which allows administrators to assign users to groups and then work with the groups as a collective unit. In addition to the items we also learned how impersonation and fixed-account execution allows an administrator to select under what user-context requests execute under.

Other Resources

In this chapter we learned about the various ASP.NET authentication and authorization methods. We also briefly introduced some of the encryption methods that are provided by the .NET Frameworks. For more information on these items, please see these detailed resources available on the Internet.

- **MD5 RFC (Request For Comments)**   For detailed information on the MD5 hashing algorithm, please see RFC 1321 at `ftp://ftp.isi.edu/in-notes/rfc1321.txt`.

- **SHA1 RFC**   For detailed information on the SHA1 hashing algorithm, please see RFC 2841 at `ftp://ftp.isi.edu/in-notes/rfc2841.txt`.

- **Basic Authentication**   For detailed information on Basic Authentication in HTTP, please see the Basic Authentication section of RFC 2617 at `ftp://ftp.isi.edu/in-notes/rfc2617.txt`.

- **Digest Authentication**   For detailed information on Digest Authentication in HTTP, please see the Digest Authentication section of RFC 2617 at `ftp://ftp.isi.edu/in-notes/rfc2617.txt`.

- **NTLM**   For detailed information on NTLM, please see `http://msdn.microsoft.com/library/psdk/secpack/ntlmssp_0k19.htm`.

- **Kerberos**   For a detailed explanation of the Kerberos authentication scheme, please see `http://xyw.com`.

- `http://www.passport.com`   The Microsoft Passport site not only provides users a place in which to sign-up for a passport, but also provides developers with an SDK (Software Development Kit) and documentation for creating Passport partner sites.

- `www.GotDotNet.com`   This Web site is run by the ASP.NET team and provides articles, user-submitted code contributions and the ASP.NET quickstarts. In addition, this site uses Passport authentication.

CHAPTER 13

WEB SERVICES

by Chris Payne

In this chapter you will learn

- What a Web service is
- How to create a simple Web service
- How to use Web Services in the client portion of your .NET applications (that is, how to "consume" Web Services)
- How to make synchronous and asynchronous calls to a Web Service
- How to create a Web service that accesses and returns data stored in a database
- How to publish a Web service so that others can use it in their applications
- How to secure a Web service using a variety of security standards
- How to avoid pitfalls when designing a Web service implementation

E-business is in a huge explosion. Within and among companies, processes are being electronically automated. The number of e-business connections between computer systems is increasing at an ever-increasing rate. The desire to connect many computers is fueled by dramatic improvements in business due to these links; e-business connections allow companies to be more efficient, thus reducing costs and allowing companies to react quicker to changes in the business marketplace.

For example, a retailer can reduce inventory costs by electronically linking its inventory system with the production-management applications of its products' providers. The retailer can keep less inventory on hand because the electronic links between systems allow the manufacturing companies to realize when the retailer's inventory is low and send it a new supply just in time.

Electronic links between applications have existed before, but they suffered from several problems. Up until now, electronic links between companies' systems were typically provided using a technology called *Electronic Data Interchange*, or *EDI* for short. These EDI connections have always been expensive and time-consuming to set up, and they require companies to use specific computer hardware and software. Therefore, the number of connections has remained small, mostly limited to large companies that have very large transaction volumes for specific processes that change infrequently.

These limitations must be overcome for eBusiness to thrive. Luckily, Microsoft's new Web Services portion of the .NET Framework is built specifically to solve these problems. Microsoft's Web Services can be built and deployed quickly, making them appropriate even for connections with small transaction volumes. They are flexible in their implementation, allowing many different types of systems to be linked together. Also, they run on inexpensive, widely available hardware (Windows-based systems and potentially many others), making them a good option for small companies. Finally, they utilize open standards, making them potentially available to any system that can support the standards.

In this chapter, we will look in detail at all you need to know to put Microsoft Web Services to work for you!

1. What Is a Web Service?

A *Web service* is a piece of executable code with a special interface that makes it available for access by other programs through an HTTP-based request. In .NET, a Web service is typically implemented as an object that is created and used just as any other object, and has additions to its binary COM interfaces so that it can be called through an HTTP-based request. In other words, a Web service is used by an application from across the Internet, and acts as a black box, hiding complex functionality behind an easy to use interface. The only difference between a Web service and a normal object is that the former is accessible over the Internet using standardized protocols.

These standardized protocols include Http-Get, Http-Post, and the Simple Object Access Protocol (SOAP). The first two you should be familiar with. The third is something familiar in a different guise. SOAP is simply a format for structuring XML data so that it can represent requests and responses from an application. In other words, SOAP is XML with a specific schema. The beauty of SOAP is that, because it is based on XML, it can represent many complex forms of data, and send them anywhere that plain text can go (even through firewalls!). Because it is standards-based, any application can take advantage of it without having to rely on proprietary systems.

So why should Web developers be interested in Web services? The main reason is that they enable you to use components from disparate systems and locations in your applications as though they are installed on the local system. Previously, this was nearly impossible. Components used in an application needed to be local to work. Now you can assemble parts from all around the Web and create a unique application, and your clients wouldn't know any different. (Web services also open up a new realm of software-pricing schemes; for example, you could build a component and charge clients a monthly fee for its use.) And with SOAP, any type of data can be sent easily around the Web.

Let's take a high-level look at a client call to a Web service to get a sense of all the steps involved in the roundtrip between the client and the Web service:

1. A Web service is deployed on a Web server, waiting for a call to action. This typically involves creating the functionality and copying appropriate files into an assembly cache; no registration or other installation required (we'll examine this further later in the chapter).

2. A client application that knows of the Web service generates a method call destined for the Web service.

3. The method invocation message is passed along the client's binary network (COM+ in the case of .NET) to a SOAP client.

4. The SOAP client converts the binary invocation request into a SOAP message. SOAP stands for *Simple Object Access Protocol* and is a special XML (Extensible Markup Language) format used to call methods on a Web service. We'll take a detailed look at the composition of SOAP messages later in the chapter, but for now just remember that the SOAP message is a piece of XML that will be sent to the Web service.

5. The SOAP client passes the SOAP message via an HTTP connection to the Web server, where the Web service resides.

6. The SOAP server converts the SOAP message into the appropriate binary format for that network operating system (such as COM+, J2EE, and so on), and passes the message along in the appropriate format.

7. The binary message reaches the object implementing the Web service.

8. This object performs the appropriate method and then passes the results back to the SOAP server using a response message in binary format.

9. The SOAP server converts the binary response into a SOAP message and passes it back to the calling SOAP client, again via HTTP.

10. The SOAP client converts the response into a binary response message and passes it back to the client application. At this point, the client application is able to use the information in the response to continue its processing.

Figure 13.1 depicts this series of events graphically.

FIGURE 13.1
An overview of a SOAP call to a Web service.

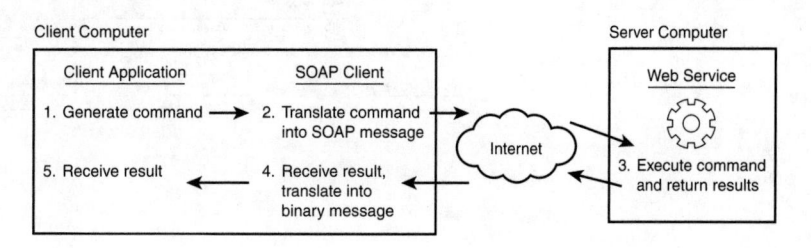

> **Note**
>
> This sounds like a universally acceptable procedure, but you may be wondering how Web services are truly supported on non-Microsoft operating systems. The beauty of Web services, is that *any* computer that has access to the Internet and can understand XML can be a client to a Web service. This includes operating systems such as Unix, Windows, and Mac OS —all of these can connect to the Internet and send and receive XML, so they can all be clients.
>
> A Web service server, on the other hand, is a bit more restrictive; it must support the .NET Framework.

This may seem like a lot of work just to make a simple method call! Don't worry, though. The .NET Framework and Visual Studio 7 will do the lion's share of the work for us in setting up Web services and configuring calls to them. Let's take a look at how easy it is to create a simple Web service.

2. Creating and Exposing a Simple Web Service

In this section, we will build a simple Web service example. We'll keep it intentionally simple so that you can see all the new aspects of Web service programming and won't be distracted with anything else.

Begin by opening Visual Studio 7. Open a new Web Services project by doing the following:

1. From the menu bar in the main Visual Studio window, select File, New, Project.

2. The New Project dialog box appears (see Figure 13.2). Make sure the Visual Basic Projects folder is selected in the Project Types pane (the left pane). In the Templates pane (the right pane), single-click the Web Service option.

FIGURE 13.2
The New Project dialog box.

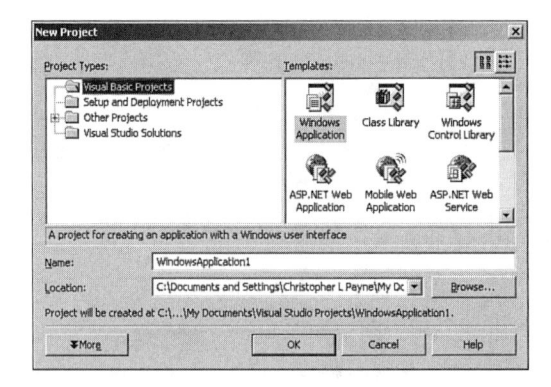

3. In the Name text box, enter a name for your Web service project. For this first example, use the name "Example1" for the project title.

4. Set the location for your project. For this example, I will use the default location, the root Web directory for my machine. (Note that my machine is named "beta2," so this designation refers to the machine name, not the version of .NET running on the computer.) If your development Web server is elsewhere on the network, click the Browse button and locate the physical directory associated with the appropriate virtual directory.

5. Click OK to dismiss the New Project dialog box.

At this point, Visual Studio will spend a little time generating default project files for us. When Visual Studio is done generating files, your Solution Explorer window will look something like the one shown in Figure 13.3.

FIGURE 13.3
Default files generated for a new Web service project.

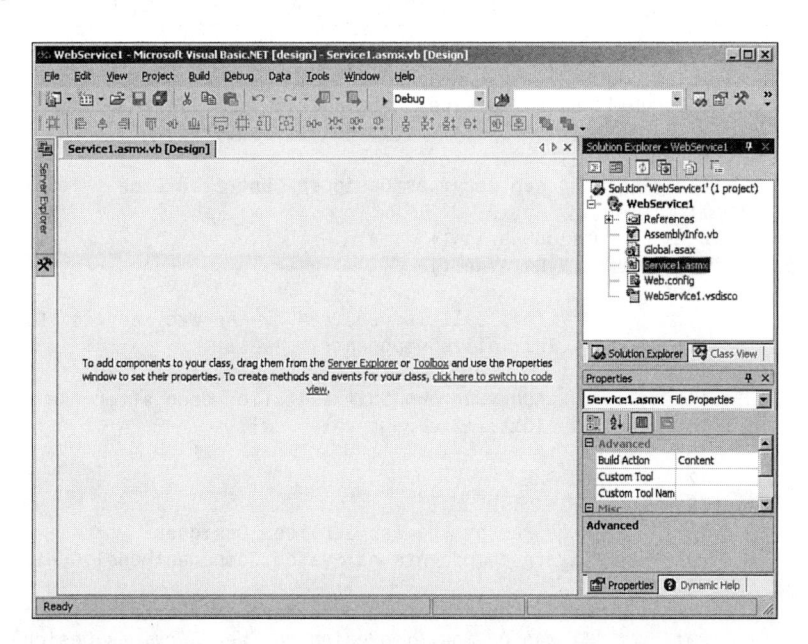

> **Note**
> Note that Visual Studio is not necessary to create a Web service. You can use any text editor to do the same, such as Notepad. In the following examples, all code can just as easily be placed in text files with the appropriate extensions.

Some of these files may look familiar: You learned earlier in this book that `Web.config` holds the configuration information for a project/application. `Global.asax` also should look familiar. It plays the role of handling initialization and cessation events for your Web service, just as it does in a regular Web Forms application. The final similarity is the References folder, which holds all the project's references for the base class libraries used.

The new files in this project type are the `.disco` file (in this example, `Example1.disco`) and the `.asmx` file (in this example, `Service1.asmx`). We will be looking in detail at `.disco` files later in the chapter; for now, though, just keep in mind that developers use this file type at design time to discover the existence of our Web service. (If you're not using Visual Studio, the `.disco` file isn't created automatically, but it's unnecessary for now, so we won't cover it here.) The `.asmx` file is the one we're most interested in at the moment. This is where we will add code to build the Web service.

Right-click the `Service1.asmx` icon in the Solution Explorer window and then choose View Code from the context list (or simply open the text file if using another editor). Your main code window should now contain code similar to the code shown in Listing 13.2.1.

LISTING 13.2.1 Autogenerated Code for a New Web Service Project

```
 1:  Imports System.Web.Services
 2:
 3:  Public Class Service1
 4:      Inherits System.Web.Services.WebService
 5:
 6:  #Region " Web Services Designer Generated Code "
 7:
 8:      Public Sub New()
 9:          MyBase.New()
10:
11:          'This call is required by the Web Services Designer.
12:          InitializeComponent()
13:
14:          'Add your own initialization code after the
15:          'InitializeComponent() call
16:
17:      End Sub
18:
19:      'Required by the Web Services Designer
20:      Private components As System.ComponentModel.Container
21:
22:      'NOTE: The following procedure is required by the Web Services Designer
23:      'It can be modified using the Web Services Designer.
24:      'Do not modify it using the code editor.
25:      <System.Diagnostics.DebuggerStepThrough()> Private Sub _
26:          InitializeComponent()
27:          components = New System.ComponentModel.Container()
28:      End Sub
29:
30:      Protected Overloads Overrides Sub Dispose(ByVal disposing As Boolean)
31:          'CODEGEN: This procedure is required by the Web Services Designer
32:          'Do not modify it using the code editor.
33:      End Sub
34:
35:  #End Region
36:
37:      ' WEB SERVICE EXAMPLE
```

LISTING 13.2.1 Continued

```
38:        ' The HelloWorld() example service returns the string Hello World.
39:        ' To build, uncomment the following lines then save and build the
40:        ' project. To test this web service, ensure that the .asmx file is the
41:        'start page and press F5.
42:        '
43:        '<WebMethod()> Public Function HelloWorld() As String
44:        ':   HelloWorld = "Hello World"
45:        ' End Function
46:
47:    End Class
```

Line 1 specifies the import of the different base class files used in a Web service. On line 3, our new Web service class is actually created. Line 4 specifies that this class inherits from the `System.Web.Services` base classes. All the methods for a Web service should be added between this line and the `End Class` statement (now found on line 47).

> **Note**
>
> Now is a good time to turn on the line-numbering feature in Visual Studio, if it's not already on. To make this change, select Tools, Options, Text Editor, All Languages, General. Then check the Line Numbers check box and click OK.

Type the following code into the code window on the line just above the `End Class` statement:

```
<WebMethod()> Public Function  TestString(ByVal x As String) As String
        TestString = "TestString received the following as input:" & x
    End Function

    <WebMethod()> Public Function TestMath(ByVal y As Integer, ByVal z As
➥Integer) As Integer
        TestMath = y + z
    End Function
```

These two functions will be the core of our Web service. Note the `<WebMethod()>` syntax in the declaration line for each function. By adding this syntax mark to the declaration of a function or method, we signal to the .NET Framework to allow the function or method to be called using the SOAP communication format. Behind the scenes, the framework adds information about marked functions or methods to the Web service's SOAP contract. The SOAP contract is an XML document that describes the interface a Web service exposes over the SOAP communication format. We'll take a look at SOAP contracts later in the chapter. For now, remember that all functions marked with the `<WebMethod()>` syntax will be callable over the Web.

Other than the Web service interfaces syntax, the two functions we've added are pretty simple. The first takes one string parameter and joins it with some other text to create a string return value. The second function takes in two integer values and passes the sum back as an integer.

Now that we have a complete Web service, we need to run it in debug mode to try it out. If the Debug toolbar is not already visible, right-click anywhere on the toolbar portion of the

Visual Studio window and then select the Debug toolbar. Next, click the Start button (the rightmost button on the Debug toolbar).

As you can see, several things happen. Visual Studio brings up the Output window, which reports on all the activities of the runtime as it loads base class files. The Autos, Call Stack, Breakpoints, Command, Locals, and Watch windows also are opened. Assuming you typed (or copied) the code additions correctly into the code window of the Web service, there shouldn't be anything interesting to see in any of these other windows, so we'll move on to the Web browser, which should have been opened by Visual Studio (if not, you can request the `.asmx` file from your browser directly).

Your browser should now look something like the one shown in Figure 13.4.

FIGURE 13.4
The HTML view of a Web service's interface.

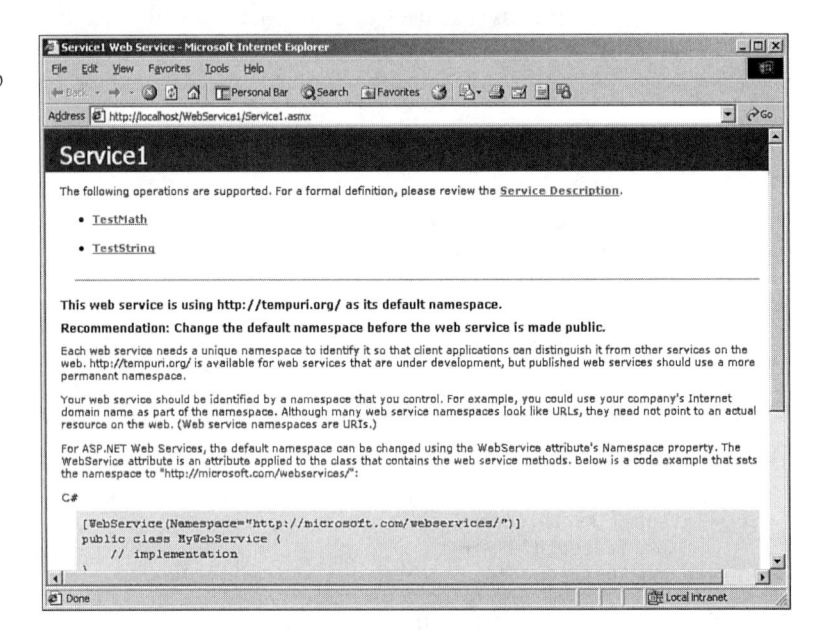

The browser is now displaying the HTML view of the Web service's interface that .NET assembles for you when you call the Web service directly from your browser. As you can see, the name of the Web service is displayed at the top of the page (in this case, Service1). Below that, the methods of the Web service are listed. In this example, we built two methods: `TestString` and `TestMath`. Each is listed as a link to a more detailed description of the method's interface. Below these methods are the detailed method descriptions.

Each method description lists the inputs and outputs of the method and provides form fields needed to invoke the Web service from the HTML view page. Try this out on the first method, `TestString`. Type any string value into the text box labeled "x" (for example, enter the string **Web Services are fun!**) and then click the Invoke button. You should see a result that looks similar to what's shown in Figure 13.5.

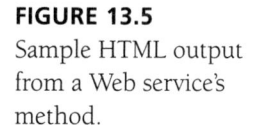

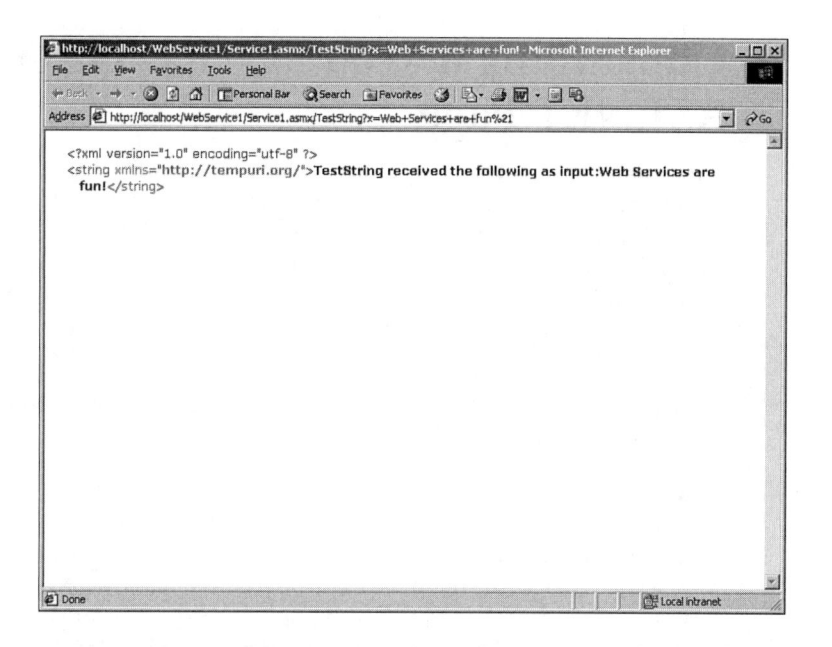

FIGURE 13.5
Sample HTML output from a Web service's method.

```
<?xml version="1.0" encoding="utf-8" ?>
<string xmlns="http://tempuri.org/">TestString received the following as input:Web Services are
   fun!</string>
```

When you press the Invoke button, your browser posts (via an Http-Post operation) any user-entered information to the Web service. The service then executes the appropriate method, and spits the answer out in an XML-formatted message (shown in Figure 13.5). We're simplifying the process here by interacting directly with the service through the browser, but applications can potentially retrieve this XML output and utilize it from across the Web (as we'll show later in the chapter).

> **Note**
>
> Note that by testing the service through the HTML view you're not actually using SOAP to send the commands; there's no need to as commands can be sent directly to the service. Rather, you're using Http-Post; Web services also can communicate via Http-Get operations as well. The SOAP protocol will be very useful, however, when using a more formal service client.

Congratulations! You've just successfully built and ran your first Web service. Adding more functionality to the Web service is as simple as copying and pasting code into the Web service class, and making sure to add the appropriate attributes (such as `<WebMethod()>`).

You may notice that the results we receive back from the function come wrapped in some extra XML syntax. This is actually some of the code involved in the SOAP formatting of the response to our call. For now, you can ignore it. Later in the chapter, we'll go over what this XML means and how it's used.

3. Consuming a Web Service Through an ASP.NET Page

Now that we have successfully created a basic Web service, the next thing we need to cover is how to access a Web service from a client application (an ASP.NET page in this case). In this section, we'll walk through all the steps involved in building a Web Forms application that uses a Web service (or in Microsoft terminology, *consumes* a Web service). Consuming a Web service involves three steps: discovery, creating a proxy class of the Web service, and actual usage of the service from a client.

Discovery is an optional step that involves examining a Web service's SOAP contract to determine what methods and data formats are supported. It can be combined with the second step of creating a proxy class.

Because you are accessing the service over the Internet, your application must provide some additional capabilities, such as sending and receiving XML messages. You can build this yourself, of course, but that involves additional hassle. Also remember that the goal of consuming a Web service is to allow you to use the service as though it were a component residing on your local system. The .NET Framework can build a proxy class for you, which encapsulates all of the functionality needed to send and receive messages, and additionally allows you to use the service easily.

Finally, once the first two steps are accomplished, using the service from a client is as easy as using a regular compiled object. Let's examine each of these steps in detail.

Creating a Proxy Class

To call a Web service from an ASP.NET Web page, we need to create a client application project and then add a reference to the Web service. Adding a reference to a Web service causes Visual Studio to get a copy of the Web service's SOAP contract, which describes the service's interface. Visual Studio uses the SOAP contract at design time to help developers make syntactically correct calls to the Web service (using IIntellisense), and at runtime Visual Studio uses the contract to create a proxy class on the client machine that acts as a go-between for all communication between the client application and the Web service. If you have worked with Visual Basic version 6 or earlier, you will recognize that SOAP contracts are very similar to COM object Type Libraries. Indeed, they are functionally the same, except that SOAP contracts are described in a variant of XML (called *Web Services Description Language*, or *WSDL*) and, therefore, can potentially be read and used by any development tool that understands WSDL.

Even if you're not using Visual Studio, the SOAP contract is used by the proxy class at runtime for the same reasons. To view this contract in the browser, tack a `?WSDL` to the end of the URL of the page. For example

`http://localhost/Service1.asmx?WSDL`

This page shows all of the XML used to describe the service completely, including the input it expects and the output it sends. Listing 13.3.1 shows a partial contract (using Listing 13.2.1 as an example).

LISTING 13.3.1 The XML Service Contract

```
 1:  <?xml version="1.0"?>
 2:  <definitions xmlns:s="http://www.w3.org/2000/10/XMLSchema"
     ➥xmlns:http="http://schemas.xmlsoap.org/wsdl/http/"
     ➥xmlns:mime="http://schemas.xmlsoap.org/wsdl/mime/"
     ➥xmlns:urt="http://microsoft.com/urt/wsdl/text/"
     ➥xmlns:soap="http://schemas.xmlsoap.org/wsdl/soap/"
     ➥xmlns:soapenc="http://schemas.xmlsoap.org/soap/encoding/"
     ➥xmlns:s0="http://tempuri.org/" targetNamespace="http://tempuri.org/"
     ➥xmlns="http://schemas.xmlsoap.org/wsdl/">
 3:    <types>
 4:      <s:schema attributeFormDefault="qualified" elementFormDefault="qualified"
         ➥targetNamespace="http://tempuri.org/">
 5:        <s:element name="TestString">
 6:          <s:complexType>
 7:            <s:sequence>
 8:              <s:element name="x" nullable="true" type="s:string"/>
 9:            </s:sequence>
10:          </s:complexType>
11:        </s:element>
12:        <s:element name="TestStringResponse">
13:          <s:complexType>
14:            <s:sequence>
15:              <s:element name="TestStringResult" nullable="true"
     ➥type="s:string"/>
16:            </s:sequence>
17:          </s:complexType>
18:        </s:element>
19:        <s:element name="TestMath">
20:          <s:complexType>
21:            <s:sequence>
22:              <s:element name="y" type="s:int"/>
23:              <s:element name="z" type="s:int"/>
24:            </s:sequence>
25:          </s:complexType>
26:        </s:element>
27:        <s:element name="TestMathResponse">
28:          <s:complexType>
29:            <s:sequence>
30:              <s:element name="TestMathResult" type="s:int"/>
31:            </s:sequence>
32:          </s:complexType>
33:        </s:element>
34:        <s:element name="string" nullable="true" type="s:string"/>
35:        <s:element name="int" type="s:int"/>
36:      </s:schema>
37:    </types>
```

LISTING 13.3.1 Continued

```
38:      <message name="TestStringSoapIn">
39:        <part name="parameters" element="s0:TestString"/>
40:      </message>
41:      <message name="TestStringSoapOut">
42:        <part name="parameters" element="s0:TestStringResponse"/>
43:      </message>
44:      <message name="TestMathSoapIn">
45:        <part name="parameters" element="s0:TestMath"/>
46:      </message>
47:      <message name="TestMathSoapOut">
48:        <part name="parameters" element="s0:TestMathResponse"/>
49:      </message>
50:      <message name="TestStringHttpGetIn">
51:        <part name="x" type="s:string"/>
52:      </message>
```

Even if you aren't familiar with XML, you'll see quite a few familiar names, such as the parameters *y* and *z* on lines 22-23. We won't go into detail here (the WSDL is a very large topic!) but it is useful to know how to get to it if necessary.

We'll start by opening a new Web Application project in Visual Studio 7 (see section 2, "Creating and Exposing a Simple Web Service" for details on creating a new project, but note that here we are creating a Web Application type project, whereas in section 2 we created a Web Service type project.). For this example, I will use the name ClientApp1 for the project title. If you're creating a copy of this example as we go along, you may want to use the same name to keep all the names and references synchronized with this text.

Next, we need to add a reference to our Web service to get its SOAP contract. Note that if you're not using Visual Studio, you'll have to perform each of the following steps manually, as we'll discuss in a moment.

To get the SOAP contract for the Web service we created in section 2, click the Add Web Reference option in the Project menu. This will bring up the Add Web Reference window (see Figure 13.6).

This window allows us to search for Web services on any Web site we want to explore. For example, if you want to search for Web services on Microsoft.com, enter **www.microsoft.com** in the Address line at the top of the window and then click the Go To arrow to the right of the Address box. However, right now we are interested in getting a contract for the Example1 Web service, so we will fire off a contract search by clicking the link Web References on Local Web Server in the window on the left.

> **Note**
>
> The Microsoft UDDI link listed in the left pane above the link to the local server connects to a list of available Web services. UDDI stands for *Universal Description, Discovery, and Integration* and is the method Microsoft has constructed for Web service developers to advertise their offerings.

FIGURE 13.6
The Add Web Reference window before searching for Web services.

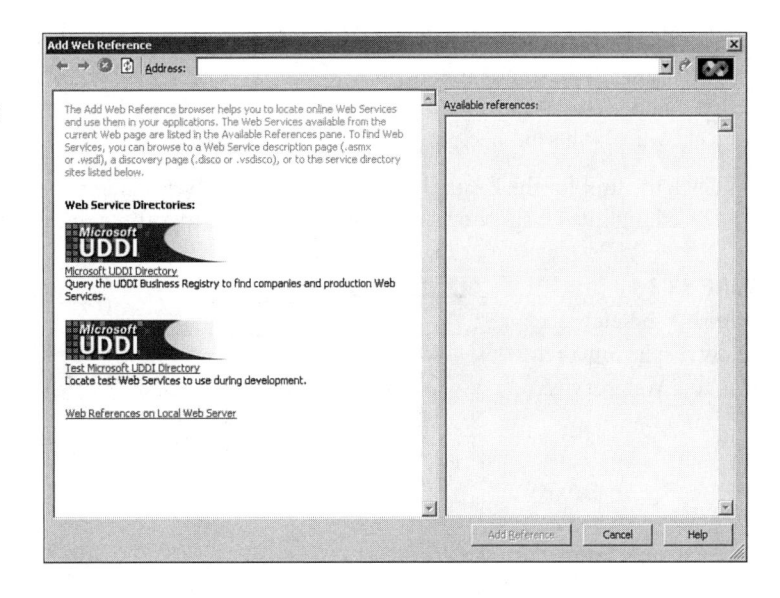

As you can see in Figure 13.7, the search comes back with two hits (you may have more hits in your results window if you have created other VS7 projects). There is a list for the Web Forms application we are building, ClientApp1, and one for the Web service we built earlier, Example1.

FIGURE 13.7
The Add Web Reference window showing Web services "discovered" on the local Web server.

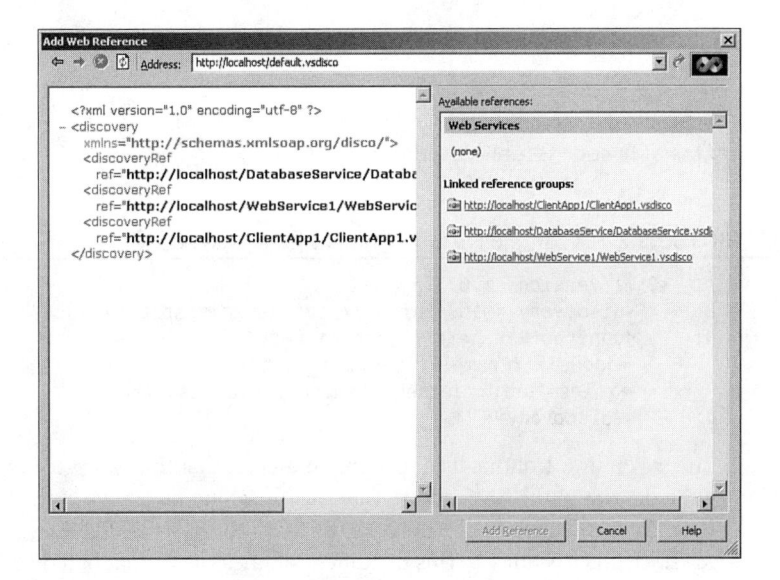

Notice the filename that is listed in each hit. It is the name of the project with a `.disco` file extension. Disco stands for *discovery of Web services*. Therefore, a disco file is *not* the SOAP contract of a Web service. Instead, it is a pointer to the location for the Web services in that project, which will send back their contracts if contacted.

Click the link for the Example1 project. The Add Web Reference window will change to look something like what's shown in Figure 13.8. Note that three things have changed.

FIGURE 13.8
The Add Web Reference window displaying a reference to a Web service.

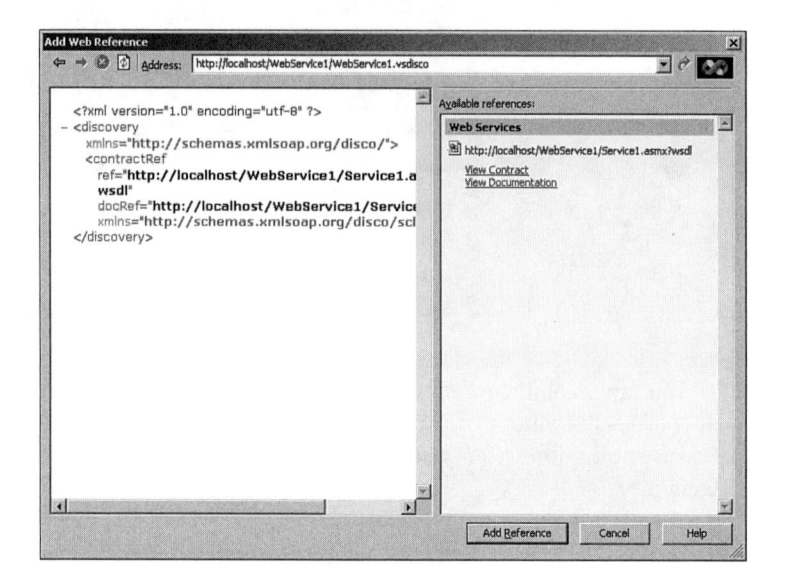

First, the left pane has changed to show the XML syntax of the disco file for the Web service. This XML code is reproduced in Listing 13.3.2.

LISTING 13.3.2 A Sample Disco Document for a Web Service

```
1:   <?xml version="1.0" ?>
2:      <discovery xmlns="http://schemas.xmlsoap.org/disco/">
3:      <contractRef ref="/Example1/Service1.asmx?wsdl"
     ➥docRef="/Example1/Service1.asmx"
     ➥xmlns="http://schemas.xmlsoap.org/disco/scl/" />
4:      </discovery>
```

The tag on line 1 of this listing simply indicates that this is a piece of XML code. Lines 2 and 6 wrap the rest of the XML and signify that this content represents a Web service discovery file. Line 2 also includes an attribute, `xmlns`, that points to a URL where an XML parser can find an XML schema document. This document defines the format of a disco document. Using the schema found at this URL, an XML parser program can determine whether a disco document, like the one in Listing 13.3.1, is correctly constructed in both structure and syntax. For more about validating XML documents, refer to Chapter 8, "Using XML."

Lines 3 to 5 comprise the interesting part of this document. The `docRef` attribute on line 4 specifies the Web service that this information applies to. The `ref` attribute specifies the URL location of the Web service's contract. Notice the syntax. It is simply the path to the Web service (not the path to the project's disco file) with `?wsdl` added to the end. Adding `?wsdl` is the standard syntax for retrieving a Web service's contract. Any Web service will return its contract if you enter the Web service's URL path and add `?wsdl` into a browser's Address line. This is true only if you have permissions to see the contract.

Second, the Available References pane has changed its links to display links to Example1's documentation and contract. The Documentation link is to the HTML interface that the Web service produces to allow manual calls to methods on the Web service. We used the HTML interface for the Example1 Web service in section 2. Flip back to Figure 13.4 if you'd like to review what the interface looks like.

The Contract link, as you might guess, displays the Web service's SOAP contract in the left pane. As we've discussed, viewing the contract is the definitive way to be sure you have located a Web service that does what you want it to. In practice, if I need to look at a contract in any detail, I click the Contract link and then copy the contract's address from the Address line into a browser window so that I can scroll through the entire contract. Third, the Add Reference button has become active (it's no longer grayed out). Click the button to complete the process of adding a Web reference. Visual Studio will add a Web References folder in the Solution Explorer window (see Figure 13.9).

FIGURE 13.9
The Solution Explorer window displaying a Web reference to a Web service.

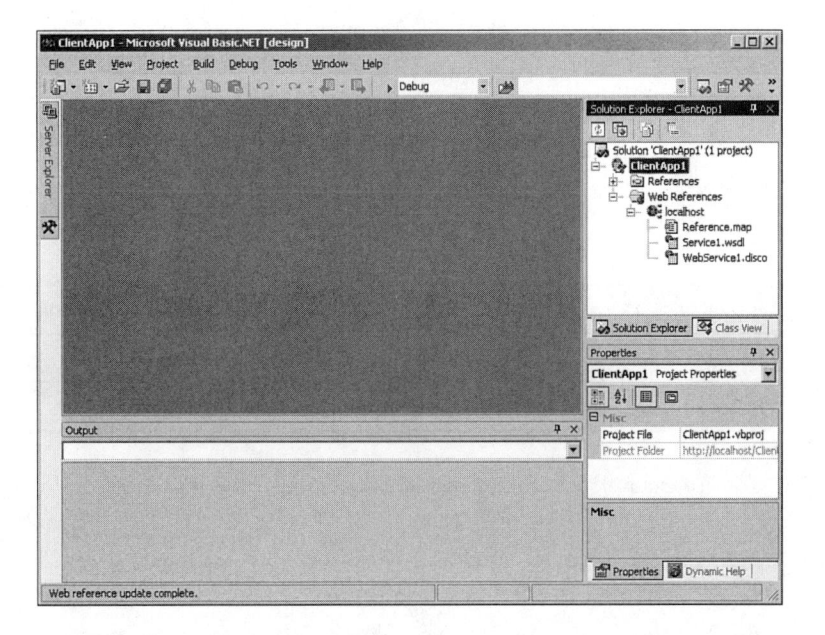

The `Service1.sdl` file is the actual SOAP contract for our Web service. With the Web service's contract now part of the client project, Visual Studio will be able to provide Intellisense for all the Web service's methods. Also notice that the new reference is organized under the Web service's location (localhost). If Web references are added from other Web sites, they would be added to the Web References folder under a different division at this level. Finally, note that the Example1 project's disco document was added to the Web references for the client application project. There is only one disco document per Web service project, but there may be several Web services in one project, so one disco document can potentially point to several Web services.

If you're not using Visual Studio, the process isn't quite as simple. You'll have to make use of a couple of command line tools to generate your proxy class: `disco.exe` and `wsdl.exe` (and optionally `vbc.exe` or `csc.exe` to compile the proxy class).

The first tool, as you may have guessed, is responsible for examining a Web service's `.disco` files. It is helpful if you want to know about a Web service, but doesn't provide much additional functionality. The syntax is simple; from the command prompt, simply type `disco` followed by the URL of the service to examine. For example, using Listing 13.2.1 as the example:

```
disco http://localhost/Service1.disco
```

The `disco.exe` tool has six command-line options, shown in Table 13.1.

TABLE 13.1 The `disco.exe` Tool Options

Option	Description
/nologo	Suppresses the proprietary Microsoft message displayed when using this tool.
/nosave	Specifies that the results of the discovery process shouldn't be saved to a file.
/out	Specifies the directory that you should save the results to. The default value is the current directory.
/username	Specifies the username needed to access the server.
/password	The password needed to access the server.
/domain	The domain needed to access the server.

For example, the following command suppresses the Microsoft logo, and saves the results in the `c:\temp\disco` folder:

```
disco /nologo /out:c:\temp\disco http://localhost/
➥tyaspnet21days/services.disco
```

This tool outputs two different files by default: *service*`.disco` (where *service* is the name of the service being examined) and `results.discomap`. The first file is a duplicate of the `.disco` file on the server, and the second is an XML file that provides additional information about where the output is stored.

The next tool, `wsdl.exe`, examines a Web service's contract, and generates a proxy class based upon it. This proxy will have methods with identical names as the ones in the service, so that implementers need not worry about remembering which local method maps to which service method. We'll examine these methods in the next two sections in depth.

The syntax for this tool is nearly identical to `disco.exe`. From the command prompt type

`wsdl /language:VB http://localhost/Service1.asmx?WSDL`

The `language` attribute can be set to `CS` (C#) or `VB` depending on your preferences. Then follows the URL of the service description. Note that the `?WSDL` is tacked onto the URL; `wsdl.exe` requires the contract to generate the proxy, and won't work with the service directly. This tool generates a file with VB (or C#) code, shown in Listing 13.2.3.

LISTING 13.2.3 The Generated Proxy Class, `Service1.vb`

```
 1:  '------------------------------------------------------------
 2:  ' <autogenerated>
 3:  '     This code was generated by a tool.
 4:  '     Runtime Version: 1.0.2914.16
 5:  '
 6:  '     Changes to this file may cause incorrect behavior and will be lost if
 7:  '     the code is regenerated.
 8:  ' </autogenerated>
 9:  '------------------------------------------------------------
10:
11:  Option Strict Off
12:  Option Explicit On
13:
14:  Imports System
15:  Imports System.Diagnostics
16:  Imports System.Web.Services
17:  Imports System.Web.Services.Protocols
18:  Imports System.Xml.Serialization
19:
20:  '
21:  'This source code was auto-generated by wsdl, Version=1.0.2914.16.
22:  '
23:
24:  <System.Web.Services.WebServiceBindingAttribute(Name:="Service1Soap", _
25:   [Namespace]:="http://tempuri.org/")> _
26:  Public Class Service1
27:      Inherits System.Web.Services.Protocols.SoapHttpClientProtocol
28:
29:      <System.Diagnostics.DebuggerStepThroughAttribute()> _
30:      Public Sub New()
31:          MyBase.New
32:          Me.Url = "http://localhost/WebService1/Service1.asmx"
33:      End Sub
34:
35:      <System.Diagnostics.DebuggerStepThroughAttribute(), _
36:       System.Web.Services.Protocols.SoapDocumentMethodAttribute( _
```

LISTING 13.2.3 *Continued*

```
37:            "http://tempuri.org/TestString", Use:=System.Web.Services. _
38:            Description.SoapBindingUse.Literal, ParameterStyle:=System.Web. _
39:            Services.Protocols.SoapParameterStyle.Wrapped)> _
40:        Public Function TestString(ByVal x As String) As String
41:            Dim results() As Object = Me.Invoke("TestString", New Object() {x})
42:            Return CType(results(0),String)
43:        End Function
44:
45:        <System.Diagnostics.DebuggerStepThroughAttribute()> _
46:        Public Function BeginTestString(ByVal x As String, ByVal callback As _
47:          System.AsyncCallback, ByVal asyncState As Object) As _
48:          System.IAsyncResult
49:            Return Me.BeginInvoke("TestString", New Object() {x}, callback, _
50:                asyncState)
51:        End Function
52:
53:        <System.Diagnostics.DebuggerStepThroughAttribute()> _
54:        Public Function EndTestString(ByVal asyncResult As System.IAsyncResult) _
55:            As String
56:            Dim results() As Object = Me.EndInvoke(asyncResult)
57:            Return CType(results(0),String)
58:        End Function
59:
60:        <System.Diagnostics.DebuggerStepThroughAttribute(), _
61:          System.Web.Services.Protocols.SoapDocumentMethodAttribute( _
62:            "http://tempuri.org/TestMath", Use:=System.Web.Services. _
63:            Description.SoapBindingUse.Literal, ParameterStyle:=System.Web. _
64:            Services.Protocols.SoapParameterStyle.Wrapped)> _
65:        Public Function TestMath(ByVal y As Integer, ByVal z As Integer) _
66:            As Integer
67:            Dim results() As Object = Me.Invoke("TestMath", New Object() {y, z})
68:            Return CType(results(0),Integer)
69:        End Function
70:
71:        <System.Diagnostics.DebuggerStepThroughAttribute()> _
72:        Public Function BeginTestMath(ByVal y As Integer, ByVal z As Integer, _
73:          ByVal callback As System.AsyncCallback, ByVal asyncState As Object) _
74:          As System.IAsyncResult
75:            Return Me.BeginInvoke("TestMath", New Object() {y, z}, callback, _
76:                asyncState)
77:        End Function
78:
79:        <System.Diagnostics.DebuggerStepThroughAttribute()> _
80:        Public Function EndTestMath(ByVal asyncResult As System.IAsyncResult) _
81:            As Integer
82:            Dim results() As Object = Me.EndInvoke(asyncResult)
83:            Return CType(results(0),Integer)
84:        End Function
85:    End Class
```

This file looks similar to the service you created earlier in the chapter, with quite a few more attributes and parameters. We won't examine these in detail here (after all, **wsdl.exe** was supposed to save us the hassle of dealing with this code), but know that these are responsible for allowing the proxy class to send and receive commands and data.

The `wsdl.exe` utility has a few more options that you can specify to generate different types of proxies. It supports all the options in Table 13.1 (with the exception of `/nosave`), in addition to those shown in Table 13.2.

TABLE 13.2 `wsdl.exe` Options

Option	Description
/language	The language used to generate the proxy class. The default is C#.
/namespace	The namespace to use for the generated proxy. The default is the global namespace.
/protocol	The protocol to use for communication with the service. Can be SOAP, HttpGet, or HttpPost. The default is SOAP.

> **Tip**
> Many of the options for `wsdl.exe` and `disco.exe` have shortcuts. For instance, instead of typing `/language:`, you can use `/l:`. For more information, type `wsdl.exe /?` or `disco.exe /?` at the command line.

The following line creates a proxy class in VB.NET, using a custom namespace, and the SOAP protocol:

```
wsdl /l:VB /namespace:MyWebServiceConsumer /protocol:SOAP
➥http://localhost/Service1.asmx?WSDL
```

Now that you have a generated class, you need to compile it and place it in your assembly cache for use. This can be done either through your favorite IDE environment in Visual Studio, or again from the command line, using the `vbc.exe` or `csc.exe` compilers. The syntax for these two compilers are identical. For example, use the following command to compile the previously generated proxy into a DLL, placed in the assembly cache:

```
vbc /t:library /out:bin\Service1Client.dll
➥/r:System.dll /r:System.XML.dll
➥/r:System.Web.Services.dll Service1.vb
```

Making Synchronous Calls to the Web Service

Now that we have completed the addition of a Web reference to our Web service, we're almost ready to call methods on the Web service.

At this point, we just need to decide *how* we want to make the call. Should we do it synchronously or asynchronously? A synchronous call to the Web service will stop all execution on the client application while it waits for a response from the Web service. An asynchronous call to the Web service will allow the client application to continue processing while it waits for a response from the Web service. The only complication with an asynchronous call is that we have to provide some sort of handler code in the client application to handle the response from the Web service when it does come back. We'll look at how to implement asynchronous call response handlers in the next section, but for now, think about the decision on a program-flow basis.

Web service calls can take a relatively long time to return to the client. This is due to three factors that can vary in significance. First, the translation of the call between binary and SOAP format must be done four times during a roundtrip call: binary to SOAP on the client for the invocation request, SOAP to binary on the server for the invocation request, binary to SOAP on the server for the invocation response, and SOAP to binary on the client for the invocation response. Second, the invocation request and response may have to be transmitted over great distances through the Internet. Third, the Web service method being called can involve lots of calculations, database activity, file system activity, or even an internal transaction, requiring lots of processing time.

If our client application *must* wait for the results of the call, it is simple to decide to use a synchronous call. For example, we would use a synchronous call to a Web service if the results of the call update the client program's interface in a way that determines the behavior of other UI controls. Think of the situation where the results of a database lookup by a Web service would affect whether buttons on the UI are enabled.

If, however, it is possible to wait for the Web service's response while doing something else, an asynchronous call is possible. It may even be preferable because it allows the user to continue doing at least some things with the client application while the Web service call is processed.

A good example of this is the validation of a credit card by a Web service when processing an order on an e-commerce site. Very few e-commerce sites do credit card validation internally. Instead, most pass the account and purchase information to computers at financial institutions, which in turn do the validation and return the results. It can take considerable time to perform the validation check: The validation service must be contacted, perform the validation, and then return the results over the Internet. Although it might be technically possible to synchronously call the credit card–validation Web service, this would mean that the Web site visitor would have to wait for the entire validation process to complete before the e-commerce site could return a page to the visitor. In many cases, this would be too long a wait, and the visitor would abandon his shopping to go shop at a faster site.

A much better way to do this is to collect the credit card information on the initial page of the check-out phase and asynchronously call the validation Web service as soon as the credit card information has been received. The e-commerce Web site then can collect the rest of the visitor's information needed to complete the transaction (name, mailing address, promotion code, and so on) while waiting for the validation results.

Now that we've looked at the considerations involved in deciding between a synchronous and asynchronous call to a Web service, let's go ahead and step through the process of actually making a synchronous call to a Web service. For this example, we'll use the Example1 Web service that we built in section 2.

Create a new file in the same directory as your Service1 service (i.e. `c:\inetpub\wwwroot\WebService1`) named `Listing13.3.4.aspx`, and insert the code in Listing 13.3.4.

LISTING 13.3.4 Client Code for a Synchronous Call to a Function on a Web Service

```
1:  <%@ Page Language="VB" %>
2:
3:  <script runat="server">
4:     sub ExecuteService(sender as Object, args as EventArgs)
5:        dim objService as new WebService1.Service1
6:
7:        lblMessage.Text = objService.TestString(tb1.Text)
8:
9:     end sub
10: </script>
11:
12: <html><body>
13:    <form runat="server">
14:       <asp:TextBox id="tb1" runat="server"
15:          OnTextChanged="ExecuteService"
16:          AutoPostBack="true" />
17:       <p>
18:       <asp:Label id="lblMessage" runat="server"/>
19:    </form>
20: </body></html>
```

Listing 13.3.4 is clearly not very long, and that's the point! It takes only two lines of code to call a Web service synchronously. In line 1, we create a new proxy object that will represent the Web service to the client application. Note the syntax `[Website address].[Web service name]`. On line 2, we call the `TestString` function, pass it the value in the text box, and print the return value in the label.

Go ahead and request this page from the browse and you should see something that looks like the window shown in Figure 13.10.

Enter some text and then click the button. For example, enter **Web Services are cool!!!**. When the page refreshes, it should look something like the one shown in Figure 13.11.

Let's examine the workflow. When this ASP.NET page is requested, it creates an instance of the proxy class you built (or generated), as indicated by Listing 13.2.4. When you call a method from this proxy class, it invisibly makes a call across the Internet to the Web service's corresponding method, which, in turn, executes and returns the appropriate information to the proxy class. The result can be used in the ASP.NET page just as a result returned from an arbitrary function. The developer, if aware of the Web service, thinks that he is interacting with the service directly—he can't tell the difference between the proxy's methods and the service's methods. On the other hand, if the developer isn't aware that a service is being used, it appears that the proxy class is doing all the computational work. Thus, you see the beauty of using a proxy class; all technical details are hidden and allow the service to interact directly with a client.

FIGURE 13.10
The Web Form client application when it's first run.

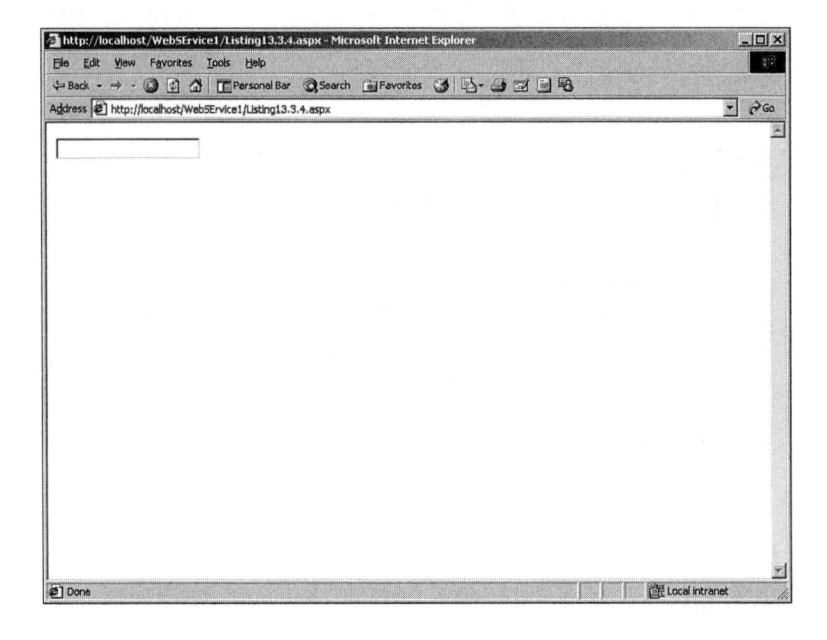

FIGURE 13.11
The Web Form client application after a call the Web service.

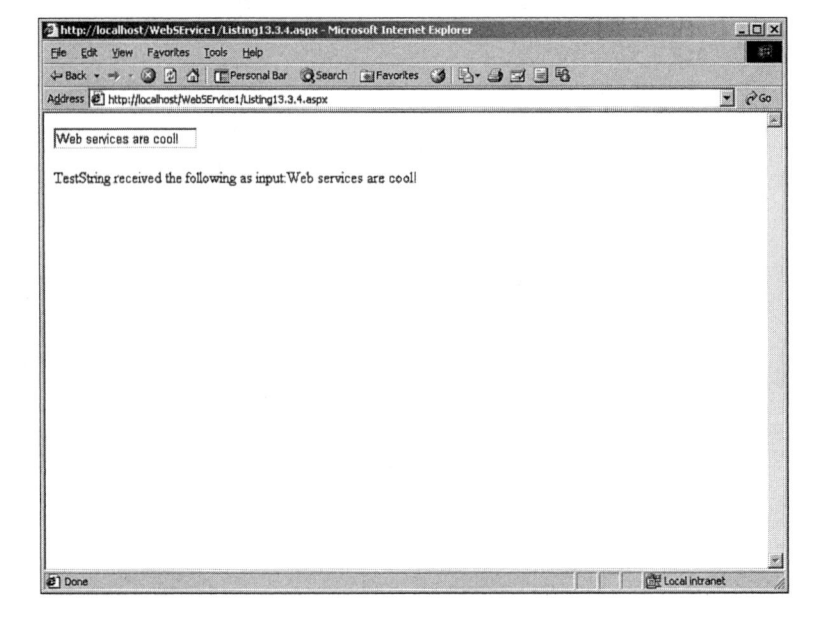

Making Asynchronous Calls to the Web Service

Now that we've made a synchronous call to the Web service, let's add to our client application so that it can make an asynchronous call to the Web service.

Let's examine this process in a bit more detail. Use the `wsdl.exe` tool on your `Service1` Web service with the following command:

`C:\Inetpub\wwwroot\WebService1>wsdl /l:VB http://localhost/WebService1/Service1.`
➥`asmx?WSDL`

`wsdl.exe` should generate a file `Service1.vb`, which contains the proxy class for the `Service1` Web service. You needn't analyze this whole file, but several lines in particular are interesting. Note that there are, in addition to the `TestString` and `TestMath` functions, four additional functions named `BeginTestString`, `EndTestString`, `BeginTestMath`, and `EndTestMath`. These are all asynchronous functions, and you'll be calling these from your client ASP.NET pages. Compile this proxy class with the command:

`vbc /t:library /out:bin\Service1.dll /r:System.dll /r:System.web.dll`
➥`/r:System.Web.SErvices.dll /r:System.xml.dll Service1.vb`

Let's take a look at the ASP.NET file that calls the Web service, shown in Listing 13.3.5.

LISTING 13.3.5 Client Code for an Asynchronous Call to a Function on a Web Service

```
 1:    <%@ Page Language="VB" %>
 2:
 3:    <script runat="server">
 4:       sub Page_Load(sender as Object, args as EventArgs)
 5:          dim objService as new Service1.Service1
 6:
 7:          Dim ar As IAsyncResult = objService.BeginTestString( _
 8:             "Async Web services rock!", nothing, nothing)
 9:
10:          ar.AsyncWaitHandle.WaitOne()
11:
12:          lblMessage.Text =objService.EndTestString(ar)
13:       end sub
14:    </script>
15:
16:    <html><body>
17:       <form runat="server">
18:          <asp:Label id="lblMessage" runat="server"/>
19:       </form>
20:    </body></html>
```

This file is almost as simple as Listing 13.3.4. The first 5 lines are identical. On line 7 we create an instance of an `IAsyncResult` object, which will be responsible for watching the call to the Web service and determining when the process has completed. The asynchronous method, `BeginTestString` is then called with three parameters: the argument to the method, a reference to an `ASyncCallBack` object (if you want another method to handle the returned results, as opposed to handling them all in the `Page_Load` method), and a reference to the proxy Web service you created. These last two parameters aren't necessary for our purposes here, so we set them to `Nothing`.

On line 10, we instruct the `AsyncResult` object to wait with the `WaitOne` method, and then simply display the results on line 12. The `EndTestString` method causes the asynchronous method call to complete and return results. The result is shown in Figure 13.12.

FIGURE 13.12
The Web Form client application after a call the Web service.

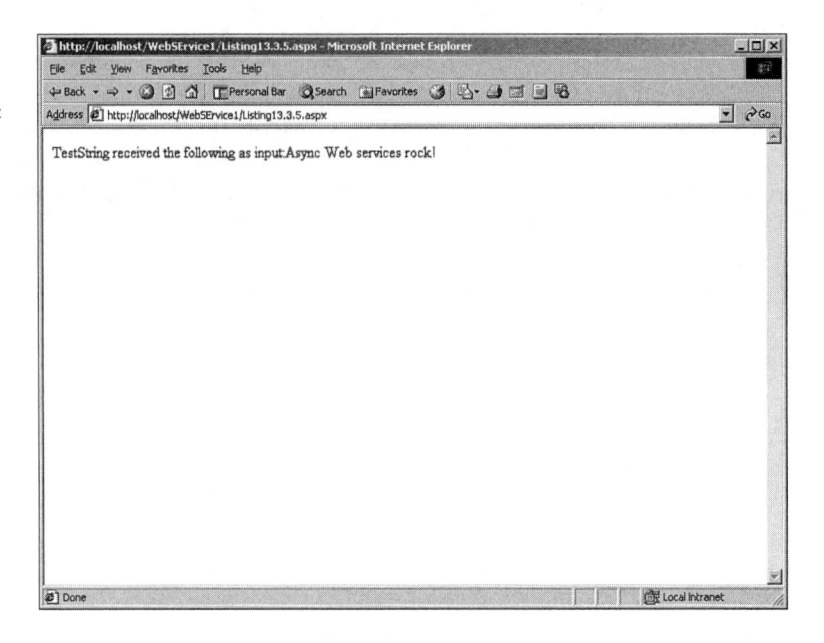

This example shows a simple method for executing asynchronous calls to Web services, but as you can imagine, async calls can get much more complex. Most async calls will be performed from regular .NET applications, due to the fact that ASP.NET pages typically complete execution before asynchronous results can be returned. For more information, see the .NET SDK Documentation.

4. Returning Database Data from a Web Service

Now that we've built both Web services and client applications that call Web services, let's focus on making a Web service do something really useful—return data from a database.

As we'll see in the next section, accessing a database from a Web service is identical to accessing one from an ASP.NET page; simply include the necessary namespaces and create the appropriate objects. In subsequent sections, we'll examine more about what type of data can be sent with Web services.

Using Database Data in a Web Service to Make Decisions

To build the first example, we need to create a database. For this example, we will use SQL Server 2000. Open the SQL Server Enterprise Manager from the SQL Server program group. When the administrative tool opens, drill down in the left pane from Console Root to Databases. Right-click the folder icon next to the Databases label and choose New Database. Name the database "Sample" and then click OK. After Enterprise Manager finishes creating the database, drill down to the Sample database listing in the left pane.

Right-click the Table icon and select New Table. You now have an opportunity to specify the columns in the new table. Name the first column colAlpha and make it a `VarChar` data type. Similarly, name the second column colInteger and make it an `Integer` data type. Click the disk image in the upper-left corner of the window to save and close the table. When the dialog box prompts you, save the table with the name tblSample.

The one remaining task to complete our database setup is to add some test data to our simple database table. Right-click the `tblSample` table's icon, and choose Open Table, Return All Rows. In this screen, enter the following pairs of values for four rows: [A,1], [B,2], [C,3], [D,4].

Now that we have the database set up, let's create a Web service that accesses this data. Start by opening a new Visual Studio Web Service project. Name this project "WS Data Access."

Open the code window for the new Web service file created, `Service1.asmx` (right-click the file's icon in the Solution Explorer and choose View Code). Rename this file to `SimpleExample.asmx`. The entire file, (excluding the generated code), appears in Listing 13.4.1 (Note that if you're not using Visual Studio, you can simply copy the code in Listing 13.4.1 into the appropriate file).

LISTING 13.4.1 Simple Data-Access Code for a Web Service

```
 1:  <%@ WebService Language="VB" Class="SimpleExample" %>
 2:
 3:  Imports System
 4:  Imports System.Data
 5:  Imports System.Data.SqlClient
 6:  Imports System.Web.Services
 7:
 8:  Public Class SimpleExample : Inherits WebService
 9:      private objConn as SqlConnection
10:      private objCmd as SqlCommand
11:
12:      public function <WebMethod()> GetValue(intInteger as Integer) as String
13:          dim strChar as String
14:          try
15:              objConn = new SqlConnection("server=localhost;uid=sa;pwd=;" & _
16:                  "database=sample")
17:              objCmd = new SqlCommand("SELECT colAlpha FROM tblSample WHERE " & _
```

LISTING 13.4.1 *Continued*

```
18:                "colInteger = " & intInteger, objConn)
19:            objCmd.Connection.Open()
20:            strChar = CType(objCmd.ExecuteScalar, String)
21:            objCmd.Connection.Close()
22:            return strChar
23:        catch ex as SqlException
24:            'do nothing
25:        end try
26:    end function
27: End Class
```

This listing is very simple, and since we've already examined both how to create Web services and access data, there should be nothing new here. Lines 3-6 import the necessary namespaces for use with SQL data sources and Web services. The class, `SimpleExample`, is declared on line 8, and some variables are declared on lines 9-10. Inside the `try` block, you try to execute the SQL statement, `SELECT colAlpha FROM tblSample WHERE colInteger = intInteger`, where `intInteger` is a number supplied by the user. The effect is that the corresponding letter will be returned.

Now that we've looked over the code in the Web service, go ahead and run it by clicking the Run button, located at the extreme left of the Debug toolbar (or simply request the page from the browser). At this point, the project will produce the by-now familiar HTML interface, describing its interface. In the text box for the `GetValue` function, go ahead and enter 2 and then click the Invoke button.

After you execute the code, if no errors are encountered, the Web service will return an XML string with the value "B" at its core. Although the scenario of this example is a little unrealistic, you now have a Web service that makes a decision at runtime based on database data.

Creating Web Services That Return Datasets

Now it's time to look at a Web service example that returns a dataset to the calling client. The previous example showed us how simple data can be returned from a Web service. What happens when you need more data though?

For example, in the e-commerce application described earlier in this chapter, suppose a user wanted to retrieve their credit information, such as ratings, outstanding inquiries, and so on. The ASP.NET pages make calls to a Web service that has access to this information. In this situation, you'd want to return quite a bit of information; simply returning one field from the data would be inadequate.

Recall that the data in a dataset is internally represented in ADO.NET via XML. Since all Web service data is sent as XML anyway, it is logical that a dataset can be sent along as well. (A DataReader, on the other hand, can't be sent from a Web service because it can't be easily translated to XML.)

We'll use the Sample database created in "Using Database Data in a Web Service to Make Decisions," so we can move on to creating a new Web service. Name your new Web service "WS Data Access 2." Name your file `DatasetExample.asmx`, and add the code in Listing 13.4.2.

LISTING 13.4.2 Web Service Method That Returns an ADO.NET Dataset

```
 1:  <%@ WebService Language="VB" Class="DataSetExample" %>
 2:
 3:  Imports System
 4:  Imports System.Data
 5:  Imports System.Data.SqlClient
 6:  Imports System.Web.Services
 7:
 8:  Public Class DataSetExample : Inherits WebService
 9:     private objConn as SqlConnection
10:     private objCmd as SqlCommand
11:
12:     public function <WebMethod()> SelectSQL(strSelect as _
13:        string) as DataSet
14:        try
15:           objConn = new SqlConnection("server=localhost;uid=sa;pwd=;" & _
16:              "database=sample")
17:           dim objDataCmd as SqlDataAdapter = new _
18:              SqlDataAdapter(strSelect, objConn)
19:
20:           Dim objDS as new DataSet
21:           objDataCmd.Fill(objDS, "tblSample")
22:           return objDS
23:        catch ex as SqlException
24:           return nothing
25:        end try
26:     end function
27:  End Class
```

Again, all of this code should look familiar so we won't spend too much time examining it. Note our sole function, `SelectSQL`, beginning on line 12. This method takes a string (that will contain a user specified SQL statement) and returns a `DataSet` object. The rest of the code is similar to Listing 13.4.1, except that we're using an `SqlDataAdapter` and `DataSet` instead of an `SqlCommand` object. The `SqlDataAdapter` executes the statement passed from the client, fills a dataset on line 21, and then returns the result on line 22.

Go ahead and run the project. When the HTML interface to the Web service comes up in the browser window, enter an SQL `SELECT` statement into the text input box for the `SelectSQL` function, such as `SELECT * FROM tblSample,` and then click the Invoke button. Listing 13.4.3 is a copy of the XML that is returned from the Web service. Notice how the entire dataset is represented in XML (in this case, it is just one table with four rows). Near the start of the XML (lines 3-19) is information about the origin of the data and its structure (data types for fields and so on). In the lower part of the XML (lines 20-37) is the actual representation of the data.

LISTING 13.4.3 The returned XML data containing a `DataSet`

```xml
 1:  <?xml version="1.0"?>
 2:  <DataSet xmlns="http://tempuri.org/">
 3:     <xsd:schema id="NewDataSet" targetNamespace="" xmlns=""
        ➥xmlns:xsd="http://www.w3.org/2000/10/XMLSchema"
        ➥xmlns:msdata="urn:schemas-microsoft-com:xml-msdata">
 4:        <xsd:element name="tblSample">
 5:           <xsd:complexType>
 6:              <xsd:all>
 7:                 <xsd:element name="colAlpha" minOccurs="0" type="xsd:string"/>
 8:                 <xsd:element name="colInteger" minOccurs="0" type="xsd:int"/>
 9:              </xsd:all>
10:           </xsd:complexType>
11:        </xsd:element>
12:        <xsd:element name="NewDataSet" msdata:IsDataSet="true">
13:           <xsd:complexType>
14:              <xsd:choice maxOccurs="unbounded">
15:                 <xsd:element ref="tblSample"/>
16:              </xsd:choice>
17:           </xsd:complexType>
18:        </xsd:element>
19:     </xsd:schema>
20:     <NewDataSet xmlns="">
21:        <tblSample>
22:           <colAlpha>A</colAlpha>
23:           <colInteger>1</colInteger>
24:        </tblSample>
25:        <tblSample>
26:           <colAlpha>B</colAlpha>
27:           <colInteger>2</colInteger>
28:        </tblSample>
29:        <tblSample>
30:           <colAlpha>C</colAlpha>
31:           <colInteger>3</colInteger>
32:        </tblSample>
33:        <tblSample>
34:           <colAlpha>D</colAlpha>
35:           <colInteger>4</colInteger>
36:        </tblSample>
37:     </NewDataSet>
38:  </DataSet>
```

Once the client has received this data, the proxy class will convert it back into a dataset so that your applications will never know the data was transmitted as XML. Thus, you can send entire database tables across the Internet easily and flexibly, without worrying about transfer mechanisms or converting data.

5. Security and Web Services

Security with Web services can be implemented in a number of ways. Since they are simply ASP.NET pages, you can secure them just as regular `.aspx` files, using IIS or the `Web.config` file (see Chapter 12, "Security with ASP.NET"). However, there is a method particular to Web services that provides tight security for your files: SOAP headers.

SOAP headers are packets of information sent along with regular communications with Web services; they "tag along" silently with commands. When a Web service class uses a SOAP header, the additional information must be present or any methods will fail; thus, SOAP headers needn't be used only for security, but lend themselves well to this application.

To pass a SOAP header along with the regular communication, you must create a class that inherits from the `System.Web.Services.Protocols.SoapHeader` class. If you are familiar with OOP, then you should know that a class can only inherit from one other class. If our Web service class inherits from the `SoapHeader` class, then how can it inherit from the `WebService` class?

The key is that the class to inherit from `SoapHeader` only contains properties that are required for security, for example, a username and password. Another class that derives from `WebService` then implements the first class to ensure that SOAP headers are passed along. Listing 13.5.1 shows an example of a class used for security.

LISTING 13.5.1 Using SOAP Headers

```
1:  Imports System.Web.Services
2:  Imports System.Web.Services.Protocols
3:
4:  Public Class Authenticator : Inherits SoapHeader
5:     Public Username as string
6:     Public Password as string
7:  End Class
```

This class is very simple. The `Username` and `Password` properties will be used by the Web service class to provide authentication. Also note that the `System.Web.Services.Protocols` namespace must be imported as well.

The Web service class to be secured, then, must create an instance of this `Authenticator` class. Additionally, each secure method must use the `<SoapHeader>` attribute (similar to `<WebMethod>`). Let's modify the dataset example you created in Listing 13.4.2 to add security and SOAP headers, shown in Listing 13.5.2.

LISTING 13.5.2 Securing the Dataset Web Service Example

```
1:  <%@ WebService Language="VB" Class="TipsTricks.SecureDataSetExample" %>
2:
3:  Imports System
4:  Imports System.Data
5:  Imports System.Data.SqlClient
6:  Imports System.Web.Services
7:  Imports System.Web.Services.Protocols
8:
9:  Namespace TipsTricks
10:
```

LISTING 13.5.2 Continued

```
11:    Public Class Authenticator : Inherits SoapHeader
12:       Public Username as string
13:       Public Password as string
14:    End Class
15:
16:    Public Class SecureDataSetExample : Inherits WebService
17:       private objConn as SqlConnection
18:       private objCmd as SqlCommand
19:       public objAuth as Authenticator
20:
21:       public function <WebMethod(), SoapHeader("objAuth")> _
22:          SelectSQL(strSelect as String) as DataSet
23:
24:          if objAuth.Username = "Rob" and objAuth.Password = "hello!" then
25:             try
26:                objConn = new SqlConnection("server=localhost;uid=sa;pwd=;" & _
27:                   "database=sample")
28:                dim objDataCmd as SqlDataAdapter = new _
29:                   SqlDataAdapter(strSelect, objConn)
30:
31:                Dim objDS as new DataSet
32:                objDataCmd.Fill(objDS, "tblSample")
33:                return objDS
34:             catch ex as SqlException
35:                return nothing
36:             end try
37:          end if
38:       end function
39:    End Class
40:
41:    End Namespace
```

Save this listing as `SecureDataSetExample.asmx`. Notice on lines 11-14, the new `Authenticator` class that inherits from `SoapHeader`. This is the same as from Listing 13.5.1. The `SecureDataSetExample` class on lines 16-39 is the same as the `DataSetExample` class you built in the previous section, with a few differences.

First, notice the publicly declared variable of type `Authenticator` on line 19. This variable will be used by secure methods. On line 21 you declare the `SelectSQL` method, with a new attribute, `<SoapHeader>`, which uses the public variable you just declared. This method now expects a SOAP header to be sent in addition to the commands. On line 24, you check the properties of the SOAP header, `Username` and `Password`, for the correct credentials. Note that though we've hard-coded the values here, you can authenticate the user however you wish, including via a database pull. The rest of the method is the same as the `SelectSQL` method from the previous section.

Recall that if your Web service specifies the use of a SOAP header, one must be sent or the service will not work. Therefore, the Http-Post and Http-Get protocols (and thus the HTML view that you've been using to test your services) will not work because these protocols cannot send

SOAP headers. You must, therefore, build a client capable of sending SOAP headers, which means creating a proxy class, and using it from an ASP.NET page.

To generate the proxy, use the following command from the command prompt:

```
wsdl /l:VB /namespace:TipsTricks
↪http://localhost/tipstricks/SecureDatasetExample.asmx?WSDL
```

Note that we've specified an additional namespace parameter; this is so we easily can keep track of our objects (this namespace is also declared on line 9 of Listing 13.5.2). The generated proxy class, `SecureDataSetExample.vb`, can be compiled using the following command:

```
vbc /t:library /out:..\bin\SecureDatasetExample.dll /r:System.dll
↪/r:System.Data.dll /r:System.XML.dll /r:System.web.dll
↪/r:System.Web.Services.dll SecureDataSetExample.vb
```

This command assumes your assembly cache (the `\bin` directory) is one level below the current directory. Remember to update this command and the previous one to include the directory structure used on your system.

Finally, you must build an ASP.NET page to use this proxy class, and the Web service. This page can be very simple, and is shown in Listing 13.5.3.

LISTING 13.5.3 Using the Secure service from an ASP.NET Page

```
 1:  <%@ Page Language="VB" Debug="true" %>
 2:  <%@ Import Namespace="System.Data" %>
 3:
 4:  <script runat="server">
 5:     sub Submit(Sender as Object, E as Eventargs)
 6:         dim objService as new TipsTricks.SecureDataSetExample
 7:         dim sHeader as new TipsTricks.Authenticator
 8:         dim objDS as new DataSet
 9:
10:         sHeader.Username = tbUser.Text
11:         sHeader.Password = tbPass.Text
12:         objService.Authenticator = sHeader
13:
14:         try
15:            objDS = objService.SelectSQL(tbQuery.Text)
16:
17:            DataGrid1.DataSource = objDS
18:  :         DataGrid1.DataMember = "tblSample"
19:            DataGrid1.Databind()
20:         catch ex as exception
21:            Response.Write("Invalid username or password")
22:         end try
23:     end sub
24:  </script>
25:
26:  <html><body>
27:     <form runat="server">
28:         Username:
```

LISTING 13.5.3 Continued

```
29:        <asp:Textbox id="tbUser" runat="server"/><br>
30:        Password:
31:        <asp:Textbox id="tbPass" runat="server"
32:           TextMode="password" /><p>
33:        Enter a query:
34:        <asp:Textbox id="tbQuery" runat="server"/>
35:        <asp:Button id="btSubmit" runat="server"
36:           text="Submit"
37:           OnClick="Submit" />
38:        <p>
39:        <asp:DataGrid id="DataGrid1"
40:           runat="server" BorderColor="black"
41:           GridLines="Vertical" cellpadding="4"
42:           cellspacing="0" width="100%"
43:           Font-Name="Arial" Font-Size="8pt" />
44:     </form>
45: </body></html>
```

This page will produce the image shown in Figure 13.13.

FIGURE 13.13
A simple interface to test the secure Web service.

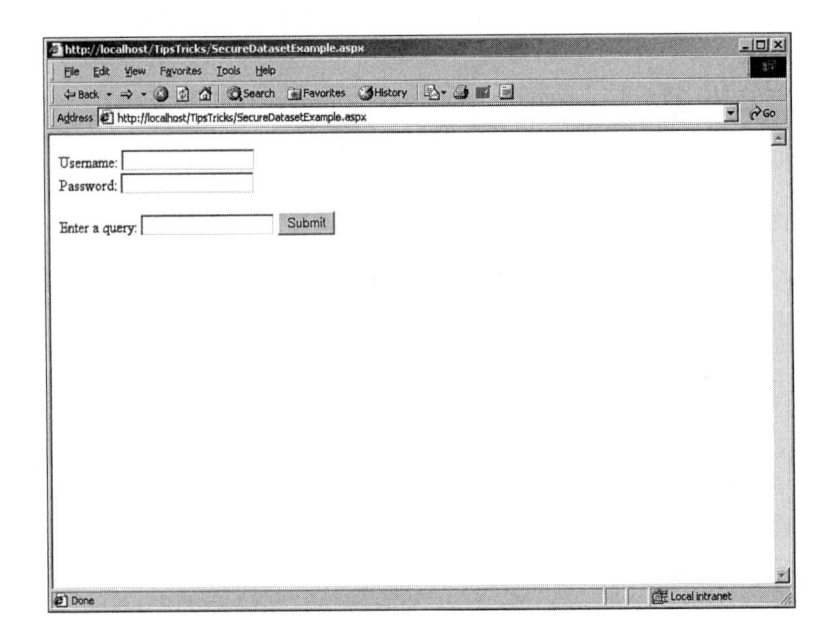

Try entering values in each of the textboxes, and examine the results. If the username and password you enter do not match those specified in the Web service (the .asmx file), or you leave these fields blank, then you shouldn't receive any output; the service is denying you access. The SQL statement you enter in the third textbox will be executed only if the proper credentials are supplied, and thus, your Web service is secure from unauthorized users.

6. Design Considerations When Creating and Using Web Services

Web services must be implemented wisely to make use of their full potential. If they are implemented poorly, they can cause problems, ranging from mild problems to extremely severe ones. On the mild end of the scale, it may be clumsy and slow for people to integrate your Web services into their applications. For example, methods may be named poorly, or returned data is sent in abnormal formats. On the severe end, the problems might range from security breaches to threats to the stability of your business's critical infrastructure.

Now that the stakes are laid out, let's look at some of the areas to consider when you're designing Web services and applications that use Web services.

Security Concerns

We've already looked at the details of setting up security in the section "Security and Web Services," but it's valuable here to discuss a couple of security design considerations.

First, keep security in balance with usability. In general, the more secure a system is, the less useable that system is, and the more difficult it is for your intended audience to access it. For example, using Secure Sockets Layer (SSL) encryption on communication between a client application and a Web service makes it much harder for a third party to read the communication if it is intercepted. However, it also requires more processing on both ends of the communication to handle the SSL keys, making the communication slower. If this makes the client application too slow, the application can become hard to use. In general, the more sensitive the data being passed, the more secure the communication should be—but don't forget usability in the rush to secure your applications.

Second, think about the tradeoffs of each security method. There are several ways to secure Web services. Before deciding on one, think about the positives and negatives of each of your options. For example, if you require Digest authentication, will there be client applications that would like to use your secure Web service but can't? Recall that Digest authentication is easy and fast to configure but is commonly supported only on Windows-based operating systems. Is it worth using Basic authentication over SSL to make your Web service accessible by a larger variety of platforms, even though the SSL will take longer to set up and will increase the processing load on the Web server? The answers to these questions will be very different, depending on whether your Web service will be accessible over the Internet or only within a Windows-based LAN. There is no one perfect security method for all cases. Each situation should be evaluated on its own.

With that said, the third idea is that the Web service security method should be picked to integrate with the security of other systems in your IT infrastructure. For example, a client application using application-level security will have to have some special (and tricky) code added to use a Web service that relies on operating system–level security. In this case, the application would have to use the username and password it receives from the logged-on user to obtain the appropriate OS-level security credential and pass that to the Web service in a process termed *impersonation*. This is a hassle at best. To avoid this type of situation, plan your development ahead of time to make sure it integrates with the security already in place.

Responding to Web Service Failures

The second major Web service design consideration involves the dependencies client applications have on Web services. How should a client application respond if a Web service it depends on is suddenly no longer available? Should it simply report an error to the user (and hopefully the administrator as well) and then wait for the Web service to become available again before allowing the user to continue? Should the client application instead remember its need to talk to the Web service, allow the user to continue working, and try the Web service procedure call again later when the Web service is back online? Should the client application be set up to immediately switch to a different Web service to get the needed work done? Or is there another way to solve this problem?

The short answer to these questions is, "It depends." It depends on at least two factors. First, how urgent is the need for the call to the Web service? The need is urgent if the client application will have to stop performing an important business function until it can complete its interaction with the Web service. Notice that urgency is a combination of two subfactors: whether there are no alternative ways to continue performing the business function and whether this function has a significant impact on a company's business.

The second factor to weigh in designing a client's response to a nonfunctioning Web service is the importance of connecting to that *specific* Web service. Does the connection between the client application and the Web service fulfill a link between tight business partners, or is it more of a generic link? Asked another way, is there a business requirement mandating that the client application use a specific Web service with no options for substituting others in its place?

These two factors come together to provide four scenarios a client application can follow in responding to a nonresponsive Web service. Let's look at each of them in turn.

First, when a client application consumes a generic Web service and the need for the Web service is urgent, it is worth building the client application so that it can automatically switch to a backup Web service if the primary Web service is down for some reason.

For example, suppose we are building a business-to-consumer Web site. Our Web site (the client application) relies on a credit card–validation Web service provided by a major bank to handle card validation. If the Web service is unavailable for some reason, credit cards can no longer be validated, and therefore, sales drop to zero until the problem is fixed. The impact on the business is high, so there is a business justification to do extra work to avoid this problem. The best solution is to build our Web site so that it can switch to another bank's credit card–validation Web service if the first bank's Web site goes down, shown in Figure 13.14. Think of this as fail-over in the Web service consumption layer of the application.

FIGURE 13.14

When the connection to one Web service is interrupted or severed, another service can be used immediately as a fail-over.

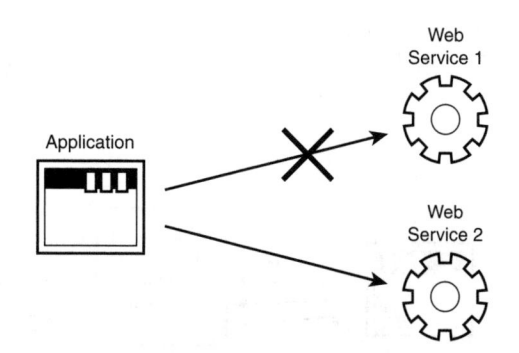

The second scenario is when a client application consumes a generic Web service, but the need is not urgent. In this case, it is not worth the cost of the extra development and maintenance time to build the client application so that it can switch to a different company's Web service when the first provider's Web service is not working.

Think of a company that has negotiated special rates with a printing company to do printing on demand. The client company sends the documents to be printed to a Web service on the printing company's Web server. The client company needs the printed materials delivered quickly, but if there is a problem, it will not be a catastrophe. In this example, if the printing company's Web service is unavailable, the best response for the client application to make is to report the problem to the user and the system administrator and then pause and wait for the Web service to become available again. The administrator can contact the printing company to resolve the problem. Although it is possible to build the client application to fail over to another printing company's Web service, the extra development and maintenance effort required is likely not worth the return.

The third scenario is when a client application consumes a specific Web service, and the need for that Web service is urgent. For example, a retail company could provide access to its inventory database for its suppliers through a Web service. The supplier companies are able to keep the retailer in stock with its products by tying production to the retailer's inventory levels. The retailer and its suppliers are tightly connected business partners, and this link is urgently needed. In this case, there is no wiggle room for the client application to respond to a down Web service. The only way to protect against problems is to invest extra effort into making the Web service super reliable.

The final scenario involves a client application that consumes a specific Web service, but there is not the urgency of the first or third examples. In this case, the client application can record the need to talk to the Web service when the user generates the request. Then, later, it can contact the Web service to process the request. This is message queue programming applied to Web services.

For example, consider an intranet application that records registrations for the monthly company offsite strategy meeting. The application (in this case, the client application) records the details of each person's registration. Once registration has closed, the application contacts the catering company's Web service and orders box lunches for everyone in the amounts specified. In this example, the client application can continue performing its primary task without problems, even if the Web service is busy or offline for long periods of time. Figure 13.15 illustrates this concept.

FIGURE 13.15
An application stores requests to the Web service in a queue, and makes the actual call when it is convenient.

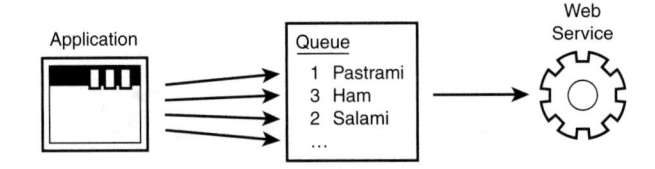

> **Note**
> Web services are focused on remote procedure calls, not so much on queued messaging. Other tools, such as Microsoft Biztalk Server, may be more appropriate here. I mention message queuing simply to illustrate the flexibility of the Web services concept.

Interface-Based Programming Challenges

Web services are exciting, but they are susceptible to the traditional problems that come with interface-based programming. *Interface-based programming* is a technique of programming where code is grouped into blocks that can be called from other blocks. The goal of the grouping is to reuse whole blocks of code. This idea has been around since the earliest days of programming and is now expressed in several layers of computer architecture, from functions written within a program, to operating system APIs (application programming interfaces), and more recently with software objects that support binary interfaces (for example, COM/COM+ objects). In this section, we'll cover two challenges of interface-based programming that are important when designing Web services.

The first challenge of interface-based programming that's important for Web services is that interfaces are hard to change once client applications have been written to use them. Changing the interface for a block of code (including a Web service) potentially requires rework in all the client applications that talk to the block of code through the interface. This can be tremendously expensive and can create lots of confusion.

There is little flexibility for responding to this problem with simple interfaces (functions inside programs and APIs), so they are changed very infrequently. The problem is simply avoided for as long as possible.

However, objects that have binary interfaces have the capability for one block of code to implement (support) multiple, different interfaces. This capability provides a powerful option for object programmers to use in managing changes to interfaces. They can build new interfaces for an object, as needed, and at the same time keep the object's old interface(s) so that client applications relying on those interfaces can continue using the object without any rework or updates. A single Web service can support multiple SOAP interfaces; therefore, Web service programmers can make use of the same flexibility in versioning their interfaces when handling needed interface changes.

FIGURE 13.16 Support for multiple interfaces allows developers to modify their applications without breaking client support.

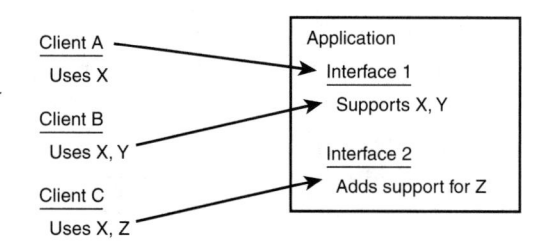

```
Client A ─────────────►  Application
Uses X                    Interface 1
                          Supports X, Y
Client B ─────────────►
Uses X, Y                 Interface 2
                          Adds support for Z
Client C ─────────────►
Uses X, Z
```

Versioning interfaces, although initially an attractive solution to problems with changing interfaces, has a problem that may be particularly acute for Web services. The problem is due to the goal of Web services—to connect many different systems, where the transaction volumes on the new links will be small (compared with EDI links) and where the systems being connected will likely be changed, replaced, or upgraded frequently. It is the number of Web service links and the number of changes constantly happening to the connected systems that poses the challenge to Web service interface versioning. Consider, for example, the following scenario.

Your company has set up a Web service that 20 or so business partner companies use to get information to and from your company's systems. The exact number and names of companies using your Web service fluctuate month to month because business partnerships between companies are constantly changing in your company's marketplace.

Everything is going great. Then one day your company's public Web site is the victim of a Distributed Denial-of-Service attack (DDS). Your Web service was not the target of the attack, and the company survives the attack. However, the CEO and CIO agree to perform an independent security audit of your company's systems to calm investors' fears of IT security risks at your company. The report recommends tightening security at all openings of the LAN to the Internet, and your Web service must be upgraded quickly to support SSL encryption.

No problem! SSL is relatively easy to add to a new SOAP interface that is otherwise identical to the old one for your Web service. But that's not where the problem lies. The real problem is that you must now, in a short amount of time, get all the companies that use your Web service to upgrade their systems to work with SSL. If you are using Web services as they are envisioned, you will likely have some small companies that are using your Web service as trading partners. They may have very limited IT budgets and personnel to do the upgrade. They may tell you that they have to continue using the old interface for six months before they can upgrade, but your CIO is pushing you to drop the old non-SSL interface so your company can report full compliance with the security audit's recommendations at the next shareholder's meeting, which is only three months away.

You get the picture. Because Web services involve negotiating the content of a Web service's interface (it's service "contract"), you will constantly have to be working with interface versioning issues.

The second problem with interface-based programming, that is an issue with Web services, is how generic to make a Web service interface. The more generic and "low level" the service the interface provides, the easier it will be to use the Web service in a wide variety of applications. However, more work will be required in the client applications to make use of the information returned from a call to the Web service.

An example will help describe this issue. Suppose we are building a Web service for a municipal school district's IT shop, and the goal for the service is to allow other applications used in the schools to easily ask for attendance records from a central database holding all students' attendance records. Let's say that most client applications will be concerned with whether a student has surpassed a threshold of absences for the semester. Because this is the most common request concerning the attendance data, we build a method on our Web service's interface that will accept a student's ID number and return a binary "yes" or "no" answer to whether the student is over the threshold number.

That's a great initial interface design because it meets all the needs of applications currently being developed, and it certainly is easy to program against this method's simple interface. But what happens when a client application comes along that would like to show the user whether the student has crossed the limit as well as the dates when the student was absent?

At that time, we could add another method to the Web service's interface that would return an array with the dates of the absences. The new client application could call the new method and use the array of data returned to both display the absence dates and calculate whether the student was over the threshold number. Now, at this point you might be thinking, "Why don't we just build the second method in the first place?" If we had, we would be able to keep the number of methods on the interface to a smaller number and generally avoid a situation that could confuse developers who come along later and want to build yet another application that leverages the Web service.

In general, you need to decide what the goal is for a Web service's interface and then stick with that goal throughout the life of the interface. Is your Web service designed to provide a high-level interface (for example, it provides a yes-or-no answer as to whether the student has too many absences) or a low-level interface (for example, it provides the absence dates and lets the client application calculate whether there are too many)? A Web service that provides a high-level interface saves the client application developers from having to build the same code many times (for example, the code that counts the number of absences to determine whether it is too many can be built just once inside the Web service, instead of once in *every* client that uses the Web service). However, the high-level interface restricts flexibility in the client application (for example, the client can only find out whether there are too many absences, not when the absences occurred).

Both goals are appropriate for Web service interfaces, depending on the situation. The key is to be consistent with each interface's goal and implementation. If you need the other level of service at some point in development, consider building a separate interface to the same Web service to provide for the need. The topic of interface composition is discussed extensively in the object-oriented development community. You should read about design patterns in object-oriented development for more on this topic (see the "Other Resources" section for other sources of information pertaining to this discussion).

The problems we've just explored may be more common in Web service development than in other types of interface-base programming because the teams developing the client applications and the Web services are not likely to initially be knowledgeable about each others' needs. This is possible because the goal of Web services is to integrate "loosely coupled" systems from different companies and/or far different parts of a big company.

Fortunately, this problem can be minimized with communication between the different development teams. If you're developing and supporting a Web service, make sure other developers can easily contact you about the needs of their client applications. These are your customers in the world of the "programmable Web." Do everything you can to meet their needs.

Likewise, if you are developing client applications that consume Web services, talk with the people who provide the Web services you plan to use. A Web service feature that you would like to have to simplify and speed your client application development may be easy to add. The feature may be something already being planned for an upgrade to the Web service, or it might be something that other consumers of that Web service could use.

Summary

Web services provide an exciting new direction for application development, promising an easy way to connect many disparate applications through "loose coupling." In this chapter, you learned what Web services are, how to build them, how to call them synchronously and asynchronously, and how to secure them.

Creating a Web service is just like creating any other class for use with ASP.NET. Web service files end in a `.asmx` file extension, and are plain text, just as `.aspx` files. There are two caveats to make a regular class a Web service: the class must inherit from the `System.Web.Services.WebService` class, and any methods that will be exposed to clients must use the `<WebMethod()>` attribute. Everything else works the same as in ASP.NET pages, including session state and database functions.

Consuming a Web service from any client (such as an ASP.NET page as we showed in this chapter) involves discovery, building a proxy class, and implementation of that proxy class. Discovery is used to determine what a Web service is capable of and what data it expects and returns, and can be accomplished either via Visual Studio or the `disco.exe` tool. Build a proxy class so that the complex functionality of dealing with Internet calls are encapsulated in an object, allowing you to interact with the service as though it were local. Again, this can be accomplished with Visual Studio or through the `wsdl.exe` tool. Finally, you can compile and then use the proxy in your ASP.NET pages like any other object. The proxy will act on your behalf to communicate with the Web service, and provide you with the returned data.

SOAP headers can be used to add security to your Web services. The process is simple: create a new class that inherits from the `System.Web.Services.Protocols.SoapHeader` class, create an instance of that class in your Web service class, and add the `<SoapHeader>` attribute to any methods that need to be secured. The SOAP header class should contain only the properties necessary for the security of the service, such as a username and password. You then can use these properties in your Web methods to implement authentication in any way you choose.

Finally, you learned several points to keep in mind when planning Web service–oriented development, including design techniques and security measures. This new area promises to continue to grow and evolve very quickly. Have fun!

Other Resources

As you can imagine, Web services are quite a large topic, and we just touched the tip of the iceberg in this chapter. They have many, many applications, from uniting disparate systems and architectures, to sending stock quotes directly to your desktop. The following resources will help you apply your Web service skills and forge ahead in the new era of Internet-based applications.

- `http://msdn.microsoft.com/webservices`—This site should be your first stop for Web services. It contains beaucoup links for Web service resources around the Web, including many excellent Microsoft sites.

- `http://msdn.microsoft.com/workshop/essentials/hess/hess01082001.asp`—This article, entitled "Software as a Service," provides a very good explanation on the theory behind Web services, that is, to deliver software over the Internet.

- `http://msdn.microsoft.com/library/techart/Hawksoap.htm`— This article explains how SOAP fits into the Microsoft .NET Framework, and how it fits into various developer scenarios.

CHAPTER 14

MANAGING STATE

by Chris Payne

In this chapter you will learn

- How to use ViewState to maintain page-level information
- How to take advantage of SQL Server to store session information
- How cookies are used with session state
- How to use cookieless sessions
- How to use the Session State Server in and out of process
- How to maintain application state

We all know the Web is a stateless medium, meaning that there is no inherent way for servers to keep track of multiple requests from the same client.

ASP.NET seeks to counteract the statelessness of the Web by providing support for several different mechanisms to manage state. For example, HTML form information is automatically maintained and persisted across form submissions by ASP.NET's ViewState, so it is no longer necessary to perform tedious requests of the **Response** object, as in classic ASP, to retrieve information.

This chapter takes a look at the different ways to manage state in ASP.NET—from ViewState to cookies to ASP.NET's Session State Server, which allows us to persist session information indefinitely and safely.

1. Managing Page-Level State with ViewState

State is managed on a number of different levels in ASP.NET: page, application, and session-level. Page-level state generally keeps track of user input in ASP.NET Web Forms and any other UI elements that are displayed to a user. This state management only keeps track of the information per page—it doesn't care what happened on another page or where the user came from. Once the user leaves the page, the state information is lost.

With ASP.NET Web Forms, page-level state is automatically maintained across roundtrips to the server. As this information is generally shown to the user directly, it is appropriately called *ViewState*. We don't have to take any explicit action to retrieve user input values from Web controls or refill form fields after a form post.

There are two methods associated with ViewState information that occur during a page load: `LoadViewState` and `SaveViewState`. The `SaveViewState` method saves any Web Form state information for use later with the `LoadViewState` method. Let's look at an example. Listing 14.1.1 shows a simple page that uses the ASP.NET trace feature to pick apart the loading process.

Listing 14.1.1 Information Is Saved in ViewState with the `SaveViewState` Method

```
 1: <%@ Page Language="VB" Trace="true" %>
 2:
 3: <script runat="server">
 4:    sub Submit(sender as Object, e as EventArgs)
 5:       Trace.Write("Submit button handler", "Submit button clicked")
 6:    end sub
 7: </script>
 8:
 9: <html><body>
10:    <form runat="server">
11:       Please enter your name:
12:       <asp:TextBox id="tbName" runat="server"/>
13:       <p>
14:       <asp:Button id="btSubmit" text="Submit"
15:          runat="server" OnClick="Submit" />
16:    </form>
17: </body></html>
```

On line 1, the tracing features have been turned on using the directive `Trace="True"`. The script block contains one method, `Submit`, that handles the event of the button on line 14 being clicked. This method writes a message to the trace output to help us discover the order of events. Figure 14.1 depicts the output from this listing.

After the `PreRender` event, the page-level state information is saved to ViewState. Recall from Chapter 1, "Common ASP.NET Page Techniques," that the ViewState information is saved using the protected `SavePageStateToPersistentMedium` member of the `Page` class instance. This information can now be retrieved when the page is reloaded.

Scrolling down to the Control Tree section (shown in Figure 14.1), we can see just how many resources are required for maintaining this state information. In this case, only 20 bytes are needed to maintain the state for the entire page. Now enter some text into the text box of Listing 14.1.1 and click the Submit button. You should see Figure 14.2.

FIGURE 14.1
The `SaveViewState` method saves page-level state information to ViewState.

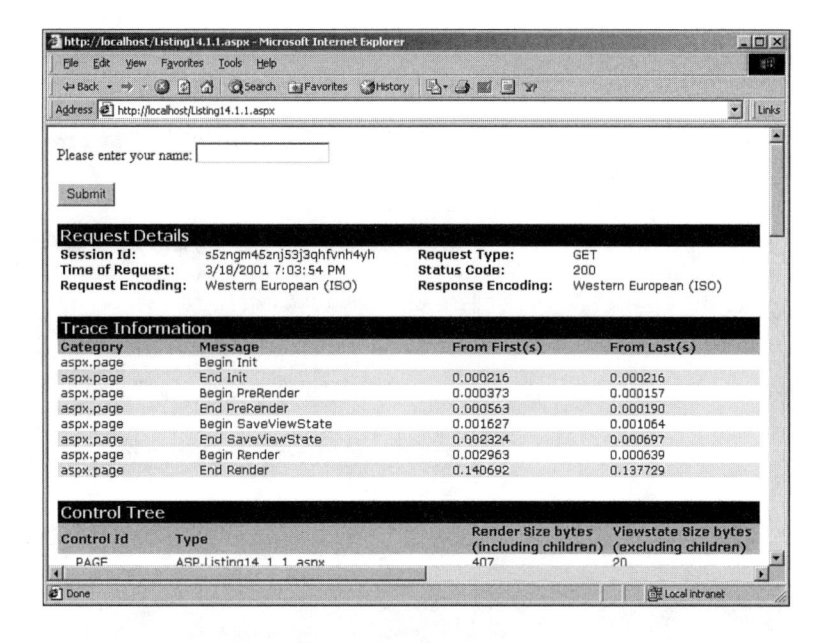

FIGURE 14.2
The `LoadViewState` information retrieves state information saved earlier using `SaveViewState`.

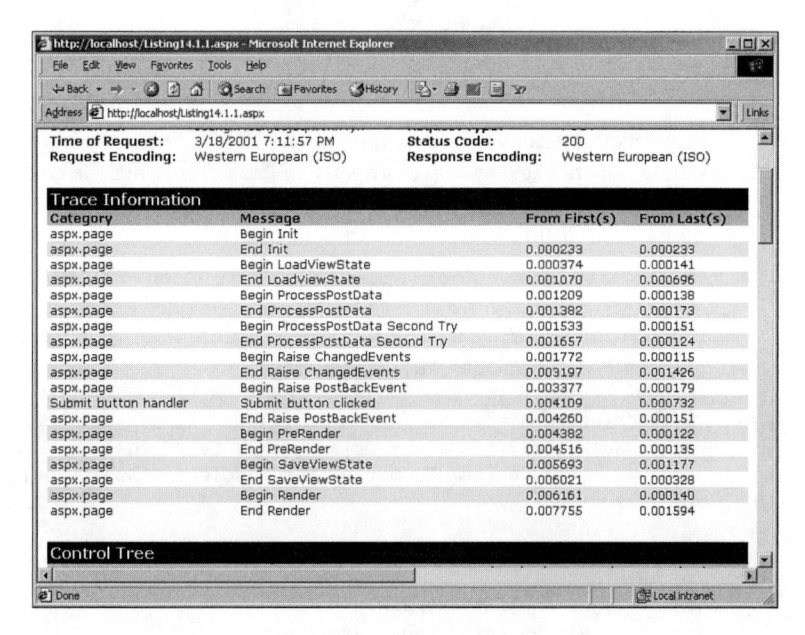

In Figure 14.2, notice the addition of the `LoadViewState` method executed immediately after the `Page` class's `Init` method. This method retrieves the saved state information to be used to repopulate the Web Form's controls. Scrolling down to the Control Tree section again (shown in Figure 14.3), we see that some additional memory resources are required on the client to maintain the information you typed into the text box (it is important to note that no state information is saved on the server).

FIGURE 14.3
The Control Tree section outlines the memory resources required to maintain state for the page.

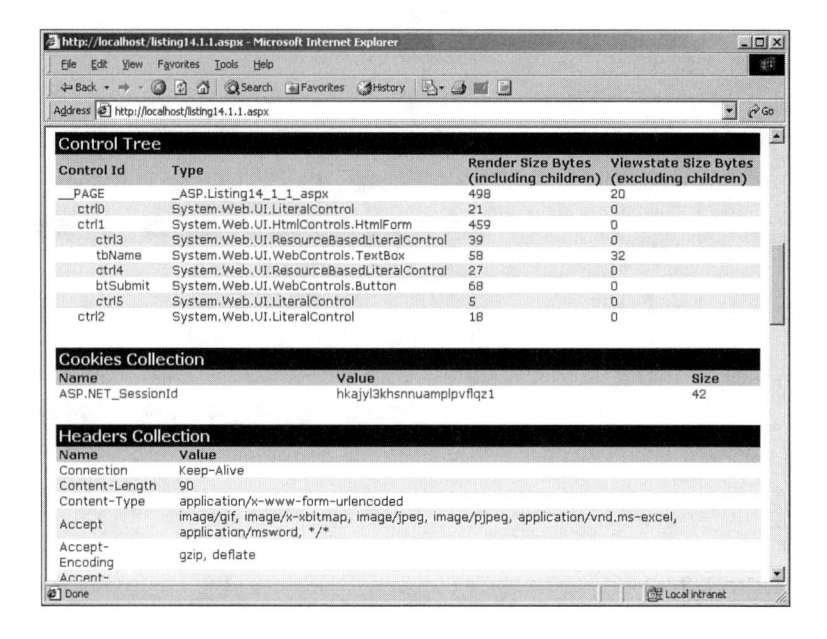

Page-level state is maintained automatically by ASP.NET, but you can disable it, if necessary, by setting the `EnableViewState` property to `False` for either the controls whose state doesn't need to be maintained or the page as a whole. Listing 14.1.2 illustrates using this property to disable state maintenance for a particular control.

Listing 14.1.2 `EnableViewState` Can Be Used to Disable Automatic Page-Level State Management

```
 1: <%@ Page Language="VB" Trace="true" %>
 2:
 3: <script runat="server">
 4:    sub Submit(sender as Object, e as EventArgs)
 5:        Trace.Write("Submit button handler", "Submit button clicked")
 6:    end sub
 7: </script>
 8:
 9: <html><body>
10:    <form runat="server">
11:        Please enter your name:
12:        <asp:TextBox id="tbName" runat="server"
13:            EnableViewState="false" />
14:
15:        <p>
16:        <asp:Button id="btSubmit" text="Submit"
17:            runat="server" OnClick="Submit" />
18:    </form>
19: </body></html>
```

This listing is very similar to Listing 14.1.1. Notice, however, the addition of `EnableViewState="false"` on line 13. State information for this TextBox control will no longer be maintained. View this page with tracing still enabled, enter some information into the text box, and click Submit. When the page reloads, scroll down to the Control Tree section. Notice that resources are no longer being used to maintain the state of the control in question.

When you disable ViewState, ASP.NET will no longer fill the control with the data maintained in state during a request. While this will speed performance slightly, you won't be able to access that control's state upon subsequent requests to the page. Thus, you should only disable ViewState for controls that won't require any state manipulation.

You can also disable state management for the entire page at once by using the following directive:

```
<%@ Page EnableViewState="false" %>
```

This ensures that no controls in the page use resources to maintain their state. Imagine you have a page with data-bound controls; when the page is loaded, data is retrieved from a database to fill the controls. In this situation, it may be beneficial to disable ViewState. Since the controls will be populated from a database upon every request, there is no reason to have ASP.NET spend the time to repopulate them from ViewState.

You can save custom information in ViewState, as well, using the ASP.NET State Bag. This structure stores any type of data for retrieval after roundtrips to the server, allowing you to save information other than that entered into Web Forms. The syntax is simple:

```
ViewState(key) = value
```

Storing information in the State Bag is very similar to using other dictionary collections, such as the `Session` object. Listing 14.1.3 shows an example of using the State Bag.

Listing 14.1.3 The State Bag Saves Custom Information in ViewState

```
 1: <%@ Page Language="VB" %>
 2:
 3: <script runat="server">
 4:    sub Page_Load(sender as Object, e as EventArgs)
 5:       if not Page.IsPostBack then
 6:          ViewState("Time") = DateTime.Now.ToString("G")
 7:          lblTime.Text = ViewState("Time")
 8:       end if
 9:    end sub
10:
11:    sub Submit(sender as Object, e as EventArgs)
12:       lblTime.Text = ViewState("Time")
13:       lblTime.Text += "<p>The time is now " & DateTime.Now.ToString("G")
14:    end sub
15: </script>
16:
17: <html><body>
```

Listing 14.1.3 Continued

```
18:     <form runat="server">
19:         This form was first loaded at:
20:         <asp:Label id="lblTime" runat="server" />
21:         <p>
22:         <asp:Button id="btSubmit" runat="server"
23:             Text="Refresh" OnClick="Submit" />
24:     </form>
25: </body></html>
```

In this script block, we have two methods: the `Page_Load` event handler and a method to handle the form submission. If the form has not been posted back, the `Page_Load` event saves the current time in the State Bag on line 6. Notice that this is very similar to using the `Session` object. On line 7, we output the time to a Label control on line 20.

When the button on line 22 is clicked, the form is posted, resulting in a roundtrip to the server, and the `Submit` method displays the time saved in the State Bag in the Label control once again. It also displays the new current time in the same Label control. Because we saved the original time in ViewState, the current time shown by line 13 should be later than the time stored on line 6. Figure 14.4 shows the output of this listing after the Submit button is clicked.

FIGURE 14.4
The time saved in the State Bag is different from the current time.

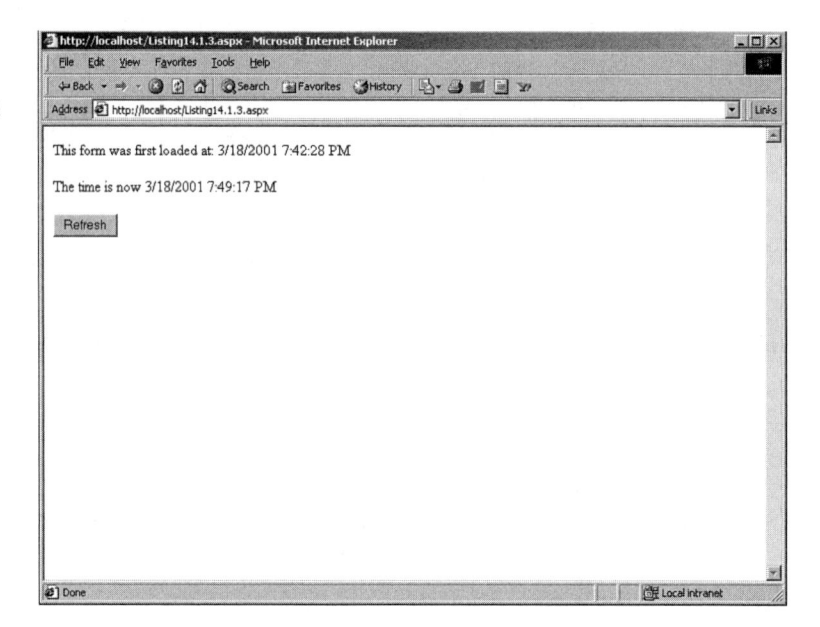

> **Caution**
>
> The State Bag only saves information on a single page between roundtrips. This means that once you leave the page, the saved information is discarded by ASP.NET. If you need to persist information for longer periods, use Session variables or cookies for more control.

2. Managing ASP.NET Session State

Session-level state management deals with information that is stored throughout a user's entire session, typically defined as his or her entire visit to a site. Let's examine for a moment why session state is needed.

The Web is a stateless medium, meaning no information is maintained about your activities on the net. When you request a page from a server, the server responds by sending it back to you. After that occurs, as far as the server is concerned, you never existed; it doesn't care what you do after that, and if you request another page, the server won't recognize you from your first request. This makes iT a bit difficult to build applications over the Internet. For example, in an e-commerce site, a typical application would be to maintain a shopping cart for each user. But how can the server keep track of which items a user has in the cart if it can't match a cart to a user?

Enter ASP.NET session state. ASP.NET creates a session (it reserves a piece of the server's memory) for a user upon their first visit to your site, and assigns that user a unique session ID. A session ID is tied to a specific piece of memory. By default, ASP.NET then creates a cookie on the client that contains this ID. Now, whenever a user makes a request of the server, ASP.NET retrieves this ID and knows who is making the request. You can store data that is specific to that user by placing it in the memory location linked to that user. Thus, your server can keep track of each user's actions, even as they move from page to page. Note that each user has their own session store; no two users share the same session ID or information. This session, or piece of memory, is kept alive while the user is moving through your site. By default, it expires after 20 minutes of idle time (we'll examine how to change this value in a moment). After this time, the server discards any information that was particular to that user and frees up the associated memory. If that same user returns to the page, another session will be created.

Storing information in session variables is very simple. The following code snippet stores the string "Hello World!" in a session variable named `Greeting`:

```
Session("Greeting") = "Hello World!"
```

To retrieve this variable is equally simple. The following code would write "Hello World!" to the browser:

```
Response.Write(Session("Greeting"))
```

This variable will be persisted for as long as the session is valid.

Controlling Session Expiration

There are two ways to control the amount of time a session is kept alive. You can do so from your ASP.NET pages, programmatically with the `Timeout` property. For example, the following code causes the session to expire after 5 minutes of user inactivity:

```
Session.Timeout = 5
```

The second method is through the `web.config` file. The following code shows an example:

```
<configuration>
   <system.web>
      <sessionState timeout=5 />
   </system.web>
</configuration>
```

> **Note**
>
> The `<sessionState>` section in `Web.config` also has the following properties: `mode`, `cookieless`, `connectionString`, and `sqlConnectionString`. We'll discuss all of these in subsequent sections.

The difference between these two methods is that the first causes the timeout value to change for only the current user; that user that requested that ASP.NET page. The latter method applies to all users and pages.

There is an important factor to be aware of when setting timeout values: server resources. Let's imagine, for example, that a user comes to your site and leaves after one minute. The server has created a session in memory for that user, which won't (by default) expire for another twenty minutes. The server's resources then are wasted for nineteen minutes; valuable resources that could be put to use for other purposes are left sitting idle. When you have many users on your site at once, this kind of behavior can lead to reduced performance.

On the other hand, you don't want to set the timeout value too low. Imagine that, trying to combat the previous scenario, you set the timeout to two minutes. In an e-commerce site, a user may let the page idle for longer than two minutes trying to decide on a product. If you've stored the user's shopping cart in session variables, then this information will be lost while the user is trying to decide. Thus, your session timeout is set too low.

Twenty minutes is ideal for many situations, but you may need to tweak this setting depending on your circumstances. A secure banking Web site may want a smaller value, while an online e-mail site may want a bigger one.

You can manually cause the session to expire with the `Abandon` method:

`Session.Abandon`

This is useful when a user wishes to "log out" of your site. Rather than keeping the valuable server resources tied up and potentially leaving the information there for hackers to see, you can dispose of the session immediately when the user logs off.

Controlling Session Initialization

Let's take a look at the initialization process of ASP.NET session state.

1. A user makes a request from the server.

2. ASP.NET retrieves the session ID from a cookie stored on the user's computer. If one does not exist, ASP.NET creates a new one and raises the `SessionStart` event.

3. ASP.NET retrieves any session data associated with the session ID from a session store (note that this data can be retrieved from a number of different places; see subsequent sections for more details).

4. A `System.Web.SessionState.SessionState` object is created and is populated with the data retrieved from step 3. It is this object that you are accessing when you use the `Session` variable:

   ```
   Session("Greeting") = "Hello World!"
   ```

Note that this process occurs each time a user makes a request. When the request ends, the data is stored back in the session store, and the `SessionEnd` event is raised. This all happens automatically, so you needn't worry about the process too much. However, you can provide a handler for the `SessionStart` and `SessionEnd` events in your `global.asax` file, as shown in Listing 14.2.1. This allows you greater control over what happens the first time a session is created and when it is abandoned.

Listing 14.2.1 Using `global.asax` to Handle the `SessionStart` and `SessionEnd` Events

```
 1:   <script language="VB" runat="server">
 2:      Sub Session_Start(Sender As Object, E As EventArgs)
 3:         Session("Start") = DateTime.Now.ToString
 4:         Response.Write("Session is starting...<br>")
 5:      End Sub
 6:
 7:      Sub Session_End(Sender As Object, E As EventArgs)
 8:            'do nothing
 9:      End Sub
10:   </script>
```

Save this in your `global.asax` file in the root directory of this application. When a session is created, the time is stored in a session variable on line 3, and a message is displayed in the browser on line 4. Now create a simple ASP.NET page with the following code, and request it from the browser:

```
<%@ Page Language="VB" %>
<script Language="VB" runat="server">
   Sub Page_Load(Sender as Object, E as EventArgs)
      lblTime.Text = Session("Start")
   end sub
</script>
<html><body>
   <asp:Label id="lblTime" runat="server"/>
</body></html>
```

This page simply displays the time stored in the session variable `Start` and displays it in a label. Upon first request, you should see something similar to Figure 14.5.

Request this page again and "Session is starting..." should disappear, but the time should stay the same.

FIGURE 14.5
The `SessionStart` event allows you to write data to an ASP.NET page.

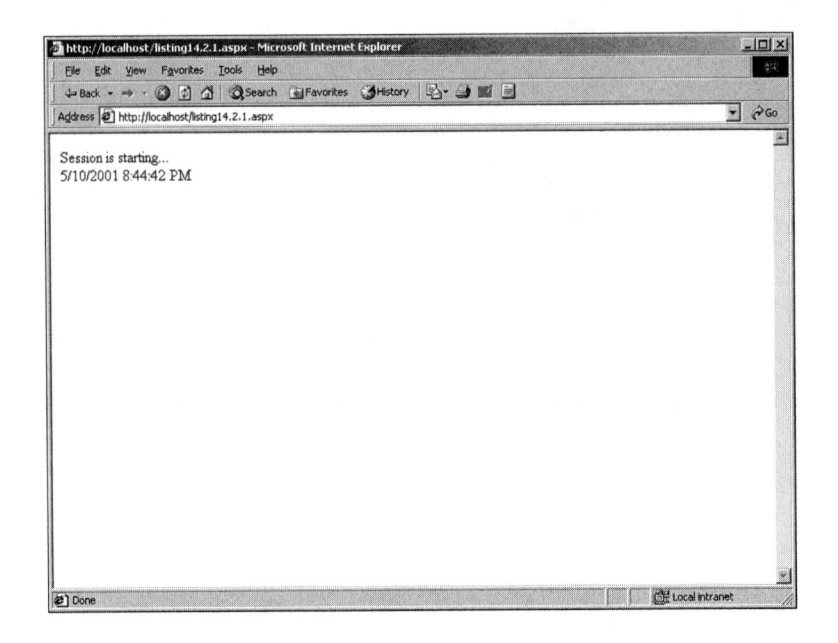

Using the `SessionStart` method is useful when you need to store data that will be applicable across an entire user's visit. For example, their user name or site style preferences.

In the next few sections, we'll examine some more advanced features of ASP.NET session management, such as controlling where session variables are stored and how to keep track of sessions without cookies.

3. Managing Session State with SQL Server

SQL Server is a robust database system that efficiently represents many different types of data. It is used in many high-end performance-critical Web applications with both classic ASP and ASP.NET.

ASP.NET allows you to store user session information separately from your ASP.NET applications in SQL Server. To do so, we must first create the necessary tables and stored procedures that ASP.NET will use to persist the session information. Luckily, Microsoft has provided the necessary tools for us.

> **Note**
> Note that the following section is only supported in SQL Server 7 or later.

The `InstallSQLState.sql` file (typically located in the `c:\WinNT\Microsoft.NET\Framework\version` directory) contains SQL statements that will properly set up SQL Server for use with ASP.NET session state. This is quite a large file, so we won't cover the entire listing here. However, Listing 14.3.1 highlights the first portion of the file.

Listing 14.3.1 The `InstallSQLState.sql` File Contains the Necessary SQL Statements to Set Up SQL Server for Use with ASP.NET Session State

```
 1: /* First uninstall - this section is exactly the same as uninstall.sql */
 2: USE master
 3: GO
 4:
 5: /* Drop the database containing our sprocs */
 6: IF DB_ID('ASPState') IS NOT NULL BEGIN
 7:     DROP DATABASE ASPState
 8: END
 9: GO
10:
11: /* Drop temporary tables */
12: IF EXISTS (SELECT * FROM tempdb..sysobjects WHERE name =
➥'ASPStateTempSessions' AND type = 'U') BEGIN
13:     DROP TABLE tempdb..ASPStateTempSessions
14: END
15: GO
16:
17: IF EXISTS (SELECT * FROM tempdb..sysobjects WHERE name =
➥'ASPStateTempApplications' AND type = 'U') BEGIN
18:     DROP TABLE tempdb..ASPStateTempApplications
19: END
20: GO
21:
22: /* Drop the startup procedure */
23: DECLARE @PROCID int
24: SET @PROCID = OBJECT_ID('ASPState_Startup')
25: IF @PROCID IS NOT NULL AND OBJECTPROPERTY(@PROCID, 'IsProcedure') = 1 BEGIN
26:     DROP PROCEDURE ASPState_Startup
27: END
28: GO
29:
30: /* Drop the obsolete startup enabler */
31: DECLARE @PROCID int
32: SET @PROCID = OBJECT_ID('EnableASPStateStartup')
33: IF @PROCID IS NOT NULL AND OBJECTPROPERTY(@PROCID, 'IsProcedure') = 1 BEGIN
34:     DROP PROCEDURE EnableASPStateStartup
35: END
36: GO
```

If you are familiar with the SQL language, you'll notice that this first part of the file removes any tables and stored procedures that contain the same names as the ones we'll be using for ASP.NET. The file also contains commands to generate tables and stored procedures, not shown here.

To execute this SQL script, open the SQL Server Query Analyzer and copy and paste the script into the window. Execute the query (press F5) and allow it to complete. Now open SQL Server Enterprise Manager and expand the Databases node. You should see a new database named ASPState. This database contains stored procedures used to retrieve and insert session data into the database, as shown in Figure 14.6.

FIGURE 14.6
The newly inserted stored procedures created by `InstallSQLState.sql`.

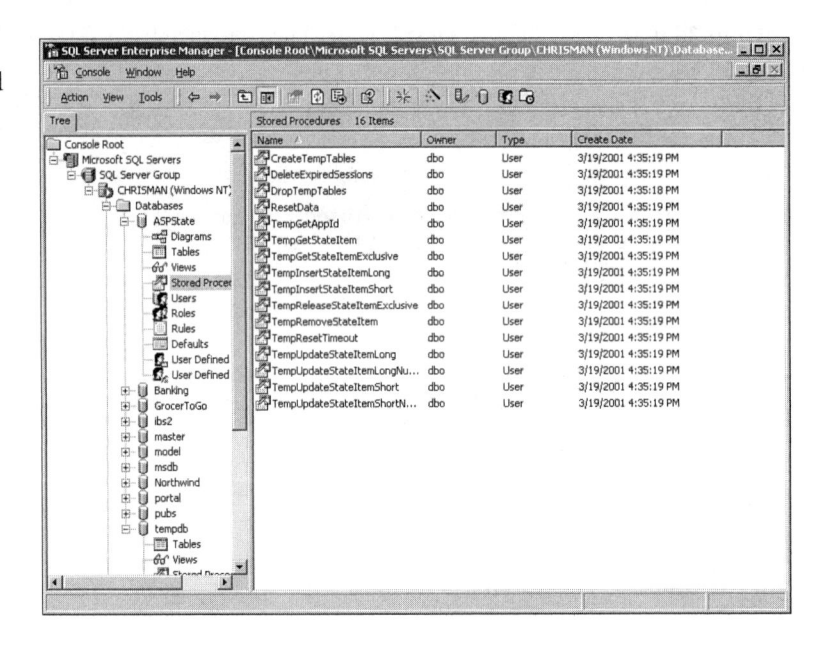

Click the Tables element. Notice that this script did not insert any new tables to store information, so where are they? All the tables are stored in the tempdb database. Scroll down in Enterprise Manager, expand the tempdb database, and click the Tables element. You should see two new tables: ASPStateTempApplications and ASPStateTempSessions. These tables will hold all the necessary information for our session state.

Now that our database is properly set up, we need to modify the `Web.config` file to take advantage of SQL Server. Modify this file to read as follows:

```
<configuration>
  <system.web>
    <sessionState mode="sqlserver" sqlConnectionString="connectionString" />
  </system.web>
</configuration>
```

The mode for the `sessionState` setting must be set to `sqlserver`. `sqlConnectionString` is a string that tells ASP.NET which database to use and how to connect to it. For example, the following string tells ASP.NET to use a database stored on the local server, with the user ID "sa" and a blank password:

```
"server=localhost;user id=sa;pwd=;"
```

To test this functionality, let's build a simple ASP.NET page that reads and writes to session state. Listing 14.3.2 shows a simple page that stores and retrieves information from session state.

Listing 14.3.2 Adding Information to Session State

```
 1: <%@ Page Language="VB" %>
 2:
 3: <script runat=server>
 4:    Sub AddSession(sender As Object, e As EventArgs)
 5:       Session("MySession") = tbText.Text
 6:       lblMessage.Text = "Session data updated! <P>" & _
 7:          "Your session contains: <font color=red>" & _
 8:          Session("MySession").ToString() & "</font>"
 9:    End Sub
10:
11:    Sub CheckSession(sender As Object, e As EventArgs)
12:       If (Session("MySession") is nothing) Then
13:          lblMessage.Text = "Nothing, session data lost!"
14:       Else
15:          lblMessage.Text = "Your session contains: " & _
16:             "<font color=red>" & _
17:             Session("MySession").ToString() & "</font>"
18:       End If
19:    End Sub
20: </script>
21:
22: <html><body>
23:    <form runat=server>
24:       <asp:TextBox id="tbText" runat=server />
25:       <asp:Button id="btAdd" runat=server
26:          OnClick="AddSession" Text="Add to Session State"/>
27:       <asp:Button id="btView" runat=server
28:          OnClick="CheckSession" Text="View Session State"/>
29:    </form>
30:
31:    <asp:Label id="lblMessage" runat="server" />
32: </body></html>
```

When the page first loads, the user is presented with a text box and two buttons, as shown on lines 24, 25, and 27. When the first button is clicked, the method **AddSession** is executed, which adds the text contained in the text box to session state, as shown on line 5. A message is then printed out to the user describing the contents of the session.

When the second button is clicked, the session state is evaluated and a message is displayed, depending on whether anything is contained within session state. Figure 14.7 shows an example after a name is entered into the text box and the first button is clicked.

FIGURE 14.7
The information contained in the text box is added to the session state.

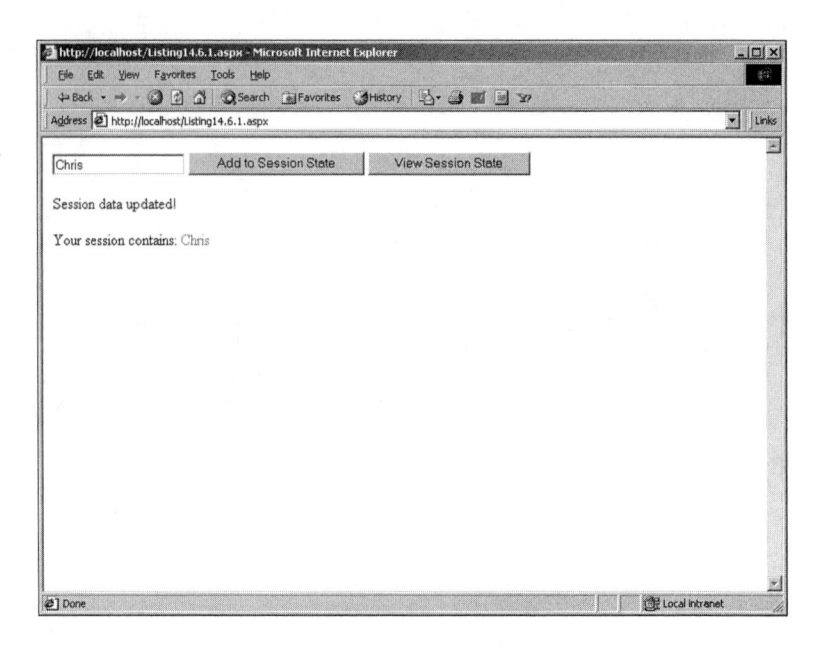

Now that we've stored a variable in session, let's return to SQL Server and examine the database entries. Navigate to the tempdb database and open and return all rows from the ASPStateTempApplications and ASPStateTempSessions tables. The data should be similar to Figure 14.8.

FIGURE 14.8
Session information is inserted into SQL Server.

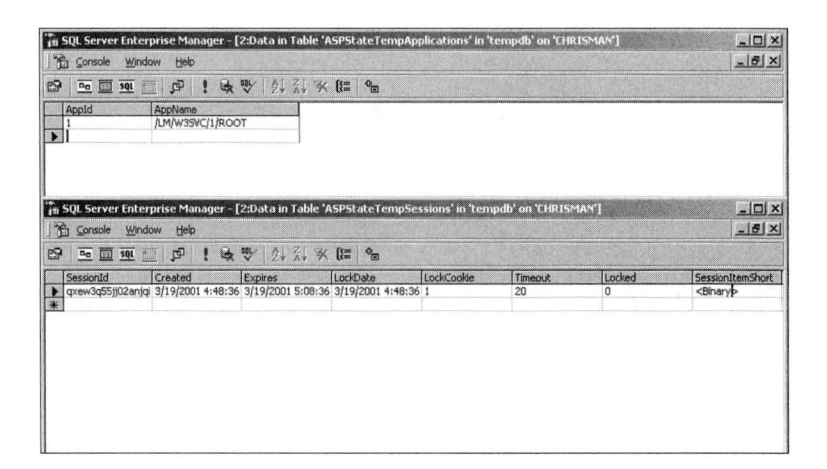

In the ASPStateTempApplications table, ASP.NET has inserted a row describing which application is currently using SQL Server for its session store. In this case, it happens to be the root application. The more applications that use SQL Server for their state stores, the more entries there will be in this table.

In the ASPStateTempSessions table, we see detailed information about the session we just created, including the session ID, creation time, expiration time, and timeout values. The session variables are stored in binary format in the database.

The session information is now stored separately from the ASP.NET process. Even if we restart the Web server (see "Running the Session State Server InProc," later in this chapter), this information will remain in the database for use later.

> **Note**
>
> If you ever want to remove the tables and data created in SQL Server by ASP.NET, there is an easy way to do so. Microsoft has provided another SQL script that does just that: `UninstallSqlState.sql`. This file is stored in the same directory as `InstallSqlState.sql` and can be executed in the same fashion.

4. Managing Session State with Cookies

Session state in ASP.NET is, by default, managed with session IDs communicated from the client to server via HTTP cookies. If session state is enabled when a user comes to your Web site for the first time, ASP.NET generates a unique session ID with which to identify the user during subsequent requests. This ID is stored in a temporary file, known as a *cookie*, on the user's machine. Whenever the user makes a request of the Web server, ASP.NET reads the session ID from this cookie and can associate it with any session data stored on the server. Once the user's session is over, the cookie is deleted from the computer.

Cookies open up a wide range of possibilities for ASP.NET Web sites. We can store nearly any type of data in a cookie, and because it is stored on the user's computer, we don't have to worry about using up valuable resources on the server. Each cookie is unique to the visitor and the Web site—cookies cannot be shared across Web sites, so personalized information can safely be stored in cookies.

Cookies make an excellent place to store custom session information. Because they are unique to each user, we can be sure that any session information placed in a cookie is applicable to only that user. For example, you can store username and ID information in a cookie. When that user returns to your Web site, it is a simple matter to retrieve that cookie and determine which user is making the request.

Cookies in the .NET Framework are represented by the `HttpCookie` object. This object contains all the necessary members to create, set, and retrieve values for and otherwise manipulate cookies. Though this object provides the necessary functionality, it is rather awkward to use. The most common way to manipulate cookies is through the `Response` and `Request` ASP.NET objects. Working with cookies through these objects is intuitive, because cookies are communicated from client to server (and vice versa) with HTTP requests and responses, which these objects represent.

544 ASP.NET: TIPS, TUTORIALS, AND CODE

The `Response` and `Request` objects each contain a `Cookies` property that returns an instance of an `HttpCookie` object, with which we can set and retrieve custom values, respectively. We can perform all the functionality necessary through the `Cookies` property. Listing 14.4.1 shows an example of setting and retrieving values from a cookie.

Listing 14.4.1   Using the `Cookies` Property of the `Request` and `Response` Objects to Store Custom Information

```
 1: <%@ Page Language="VB" %>
 2:
 3: <script runat=server>
 4:    Sub AddCookie(sender As Object, e As EventArgs)
 5:       Response.Cookies("MyCookie")("Data") = tbText.Text
 6:       Response.Cookies("MyCookie")("Time") = DateTime.Now.ToString("G")
 7:       lblMessage.Text = "Cookie created! <P>" & _
 8:          "Your cookie contains: <font color=red>" & _
 9:          Request.Cookies("MyCookie")("Data") & "<br>" & _
10:          Request.Cookies("MyCookie")("Time") & "</font>"
11:    End Sub
12:
13:    Sub CheckCookie(sender As Object, e As EventArgs)
14:       If (Request.Cookies("MyCookie") is nothing) Then
15:          lblMessage.Text = "There is no cookie!"
16:       Else
17:          lblMessage.Text = "Your cookie contains: " & _
18:             "<font color=red>" & _
19:             Request.Cookies("MyCookie")("Data") & "<br>" & _
20:             Request.COokies("MyCookie")("Time") & "</font>"
21:       End If
22:    End Sub
23: </script>
24:
25: <html><body>
26:    <form runat=server>
27:       <asp:TextBox id="tbText" runat=server />
28:       <asp:Button id="btAdd" runat=server
29:          OnClick="AddCookie" Text="Add Cookie"/>
30:       <asp:Button id="btView" runat=server
31:          OnClick="CheckCookie" Text="View Cookie"/>
32:    </form>
33:
34:    <asp:Label id="lblMessage" runat="server"/>
35: </body></html>
```

The HTML portion of this page is similar to Listing 14.3.2; it contains a text box (line 27), two buttons (lines 28 through 31), and a label (line 34). When a user enters information into the text box and clicks the "Add Cookie" button, the `AddCookie` event handler on line 4 takes over. This method creates a new cookie named `MyCookie` through the `Response` object (line 5). Each cookie can contain multiple key/value pairs, so on lines 5 and 6 we create two keys named `Data` and `Time`. These keys are accessed by adding a second parameter to the `Cookies` property. The general syntax is as follows:

```
Response.Cookies("CookieName")("keyName") = value
```

Our `Data` and `Time` keys contain the data entered into the text box and the current time, respectively.

The `CheckCookie` method handles the processing when the "View Cookie" button is clicked. It simply outputs the values contained in the cookie to the browser. Figure 14.9 illustrates the output from this listing.

FIGURE 14.9
Creating cookies to store custom session information is easy.

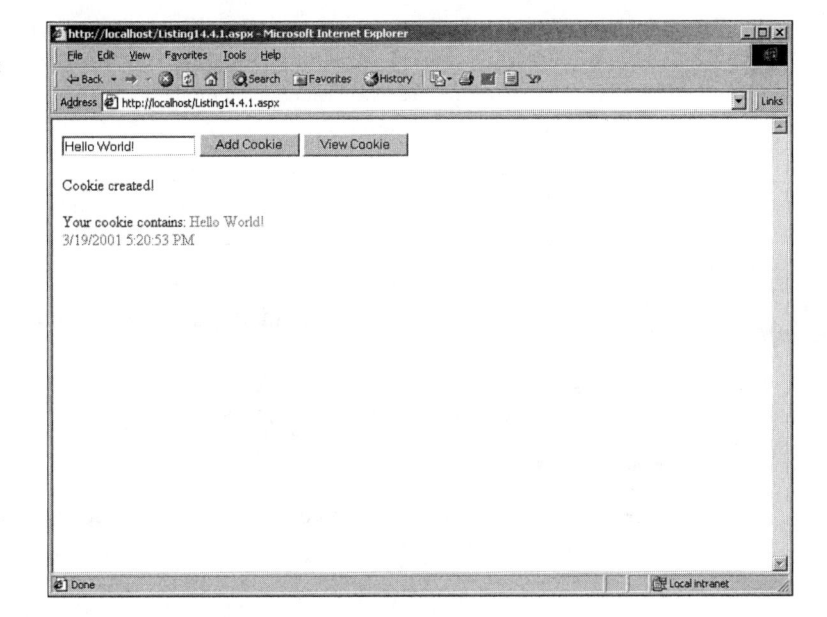

The `Cookies` property of the `Response` object contains another member, `Expires`, that tells the cookie when its content should be rendered invalid. This property can be set either to an absolute date in the future or to a time relative to the current date. For example, the following line tells `MyCookie` to expire on January 1, 2002:

```
Response.Cookies("MyCookie").Expires = DateTime.FromString("1/1/2002")
```

We can use the `DateTime` object to set a relative time for the expiration. The following line instructs the cookie to expire one month from now:

```
Response.Cookies("MyCookie").Expires = DateTime.Now.AddMonths(1)
```

> **Tip**
> To delete a cookie or render it invalid immediately, set the `Expires` property to some time in the past. Setting it to zero may not work as expected because time settings may be different on the server and the client. Setting it to a significant amount of time in the past ensures that the data will be invalidated.

5. Cookieless Session State Management

Sometimes you'll want to manage session state without relying on cookies (for instance, if your application is targeted toward older browsers that may not support cookies). It is easy to configure ASP.NET to use a process known as *cookie munging*, which provides session state without relying on the client accepting cookies.

Cookie munging is a process by which ASP.NET tacks the session ID to URLs within the page, such as in HTML anchors. When the user clicks such a link, the server retrieves the session ID stored in the link and can use it to determine a client's session identity, and consequently, session state information.

To enable cookieless session management, modify your `Web.config` file to read as follows:

```
<configuration>
   <system.web>
      <sessionState cookieless="true" />
   </system.web>
</configuration>
```

Listing 14.5.1 shows a simple page demonstrating cookie munging, whereas Figure 14.10 shows the output in a browser.

Listing 14.5.1 Cookie Munging Adds the session ID to the URL

```
 1: <%@ Page Language="VB" %>
 2:
 3: <script runat="server">
 4:    sub Page_Load(sender as Object, e as EventArgs)
 5:       Response.Write("Your ID is: " & Session.SessionID & "<p>")
 6:    end sub
 7: </script>
 8:
 9: <html><body>
10:    <a href="Listing14.5.1.aspx">Click me!</a>
11: </body></html>
```

The `Page_Load` method displays the session ID, `vjj2v3m0mr4tnp45qCt12oav`, to the user. Notice in Figure 14.10 that this ID is also contained in the address bar of Internet Explorer and the `href` tag of the link:

```
http://localhost/(vjj2v3m0mr4tnp45qCt12oav)/Listing14.5.1.aspx
```

FIGURE 14.10
The munged session ID is placed in the URL of the page and in any links within the page.

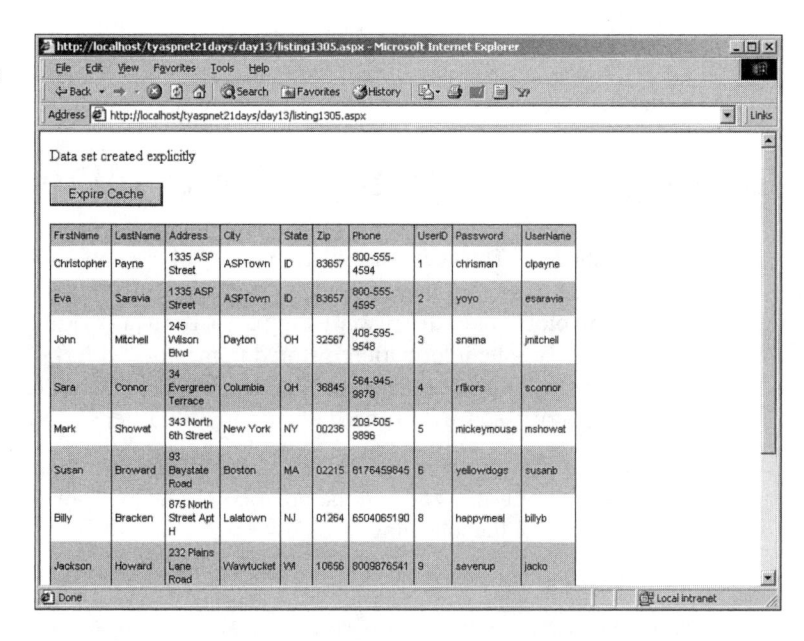

As a user moves from page to page following the links, this value is retrieved by ASP.NET to determine where each request is from. However, if the URL of the page is manipulated manually by the user, session information may be lost, specifically if the session ID is changed.

Cookie-less sessions are a great way to maintain session information if there is a possibility that the audience for your site won't have support for cookies. It is, unfortunately, a rather insecure method of using sessions. For example, anyone can access the session IDs from the address bar, which potentially could allow one user to impersonate another. Additionally, you have to place faith in your users that they won't modify the URL of the page manually; another security problem. In general, try not to use cookie-less sessions unless necessary.

6. Using the Session State Server

One major drawback of classic ASP was that session information was tied to the ASP process. If the Web server or ASP application crashed or had to be restarted, all session information would be lost. Also, there was no way to know how much of the server's resources were being devoted to each user session.

ASP.NET changes this method of operation by introducing the Session State Server. The Session State Server runs independently of any application or Web server, meaning that a server crash will not result in a loss of session data. This State Server is highly protected to prevent data corruption, and no end-user code is allowed to run within this process. The State Server also allows us to deploy session information anywhere we wish: on a single Web server, on a server across a network, or even across Web farms.

Next, we'll examine two different methods of using the Session State Server to provide different degrees of security. As you'll see, configuring the State Server is very simple through the `Web.config` file.

Running the Session State Server InProc

The Session State Server can be run *InProc*, or in process, meaning it can run in the same process as ASP.NET. This means it is tied to the ASP.NET application—similar to the way classic ASP worked. Why, you may ask, would we want to use this dated mechanism when it contains so many problems? The answer is simple: performance. Running the Session State Server InProc means that state information is stored in memory with ASP.NET, and any overhead caused by reaching across application boundaries is avoided. InProc is the default mode for the Session State Server, so we don't need to take any extra steps to set it up.

Let's attempt to manipulate the ASP.NET process to see what happens with the session data. Open a command prompt and run the program `iisreset`. Your command window should look something like the following:

```
C:\>iisreset

Attempting stop...
Internet services successfully stopped
Attempting start...
Internet services successfully restarted
```

Now go back to the page generated by Listing 14.3.2 and click the "View Session State" button. You should see "Nothing, session data lost!" displayed in the window.

What happened to our data? The session information, when run InProc, is tied to the ASP.NET process. By us executing `iisreset`, the ASP.NET process (as well as the Web server) was restarted, and all information associated with that process (such as session data) was discarded. Therefore, when running InProc, the Session State Server data depends on the ASP.NET process. Any complications or crashes in the latter will result in loss of data in the former. Running the State Server Out-of-Proc will prevent this.

Running the Session State Server Out-of-Proc

The Session State Server can also be run Out-of-Proc. This means that the session data is stored separately from the ASP.NET process, even on a separate computer if we so desire! This has one major benefit over running the State Server InProc: data security. If, for any reason, the Web server containing the ASP.NET application goes offline (due to a crash or a forced restart, or even a hardware failure, for instance), the session data is safely stored in another process or on another computer, and it can be accessed once the Web server returns online.

For example, suppose you are running an e-commerce site where visitors are allowed to add items to a shopping cart. This information for each user's cart is stored in session variables (running InProc). If, for whatever reason, your site went down (application crash, power failure, and so on) all the information in your session variables—and thus your shopping carts—would be lost. Your users may become irate wondering where their shopping cart items are.

When you store session information Out-of-Proc, you can keep the data safe, separate from the Web server or ASP.NET application. Thus, crashes or restarts in the server won't affect the session information.

The Out-of-Proc server is handled with the `ASPNETState` process (`aspnet_state.exe`). This process runs independently from any other application as a Windows NT/2000 service, and it stores session data in memory. Before we can run the Session State Server Out-of-Proc, we must start the `aspnet_state` process. Open a command prompt and type **net start aspnet_state**. Your command window should look something like this:

```
C:\>net start aspnet_state
The ASP.NET State service is starting.
The ASP.NET State service was started successfully.
```

This command will start the `ASPNETState` process, but if you happen to restart your server, you'll have to retype this command. For a more permanent method, go to Start, Settings, Control Panel, Administrative Tools, Services. You should see the `ASPNETState` process in the list in the right window. Double click on it and change the startup type to Automatic. This ensures that the process is started every time the computer is started.

Now open the Windows 2000 (or NT) task manager (Ctrl+Shift+Escape). You should now see the Session State Server process, `aspnet_state.exe`, running, as shown in Figure 14.11.

FIGURE 14.11
The Session State Server process is named `aspnet_state.exe`.

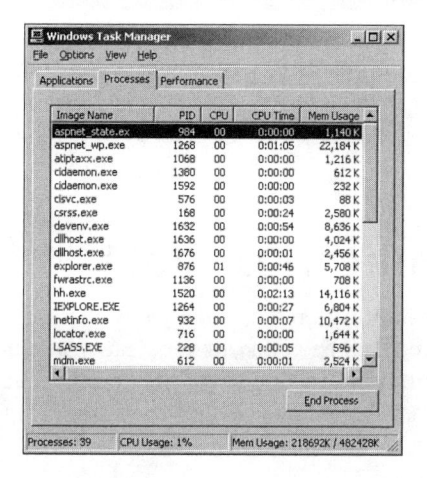

Now that the `ASPNETState` process is running, we need to configure ASP.NET to use this process. Listing 14.6.1 shows the necessary settings that should be applied in our `Web.config` file.

Listing 14.6.1 Setting Up the Session State Server to Run Out-of-Proc

```
1: <configuration>
2:    <system.web>
3:       <sessionState mode="stateserver"
➥stateConnectionString="tcpip=127.0.0.1:42424" />
4:    </system.web>
5: </configuration>
```

There are two important elements in this `Web.config` file. The first is setting the mode to *stateserver*, which indicates that our application should use a separate process to handle our session state. This process will also hold any session data. The second element is the `stateConnectionString` property. This string specifies the server and port that should manage the State Server. It must follow this format:

`stateConnectionString="tcpip=server:port"`

`stateConnectionString` is not required when the mode is set to `stateserver`, but it allows you to specify a remote computer to handle your session information. Using a remote computer adds an additional security measure; the session information no longer is dependent on the Web server machine at all. By default, the local computer is used (IP address 127.0.0.1, port 80).

Note

The default port 80 will work well for most applications. However, there may be some times that you may want to change this port number.

Port 80 is the default for all HTTP traffic, which means it is susceptible to a lot of—potentially harmful (hacker)— requests. By changing the port to another, little known one, such as 454545, you can further protect your session data. (See your operating system documentation for information on setting/retrieving port numbers.)

Let's go back to Listing 14.3.2. Use it to set a session variable, and restart the Web server once again by using `iisreset`. Once the Internet services are restarted, click the "View Session State" button again. The session information you entered is still there, even after the Web server was restarted!

7. Managing Application State

Application state represents information that is shared by all users accessing your application. It is data that is applicable to an entire application, not any particular user. Typical uses of application state include storing connection strings that can be used to access databases or other global variables that may be required by your application. Figure 14.12 illustrates the difference between application state and session state.

Using application state is very similar to using session state. The `HttpApplicatonState` object contains an `Application` property that provides a dictionary-like interface to manipulate variables contained in application state. The syntax is simple:

`Application("key") = value`

Because application state is used by your entire application, you'll typically want to set this information up as soon as your application starts by using the `global.asax` file. This file allows you to respond to application events, much as ASPX files allow you to respond to user events in ASP.NET pages. Listing 14.7.1 shows a sample `global.asax` file that sets up some global variables, and Listing 14.7.2 shows a typical ASP.NET page that uses this application information.

FIGURE 14.12
Session state uses one session object per user; application state uses one application object for all users.

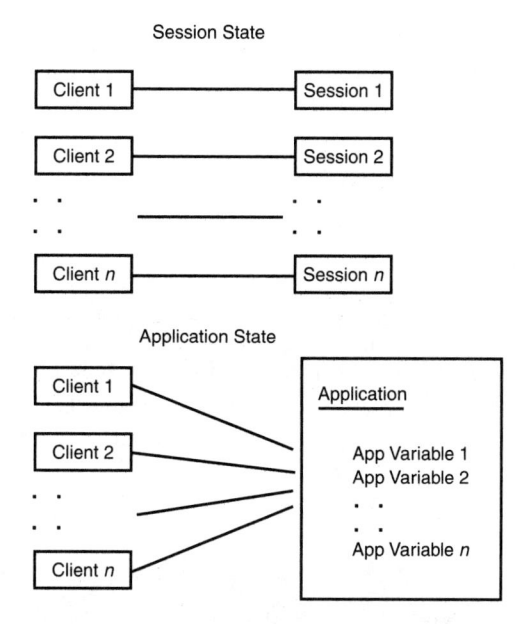

Session State

Client 1 ——— Session 1
Client 2 ——— Session 2
⋮   ⋮
Client *n* ——— Session *n*

Application State

Client 1 ⎫
Client 2 ⎬—→ Application
⋮   ⎪   App Variable 1
Client *n* ⎭   App Variable 2
                ⋮
                App Variable *n*

Listing 14.7.1 Using the `Application_Start` Event to Initialize

```
1: <script language="VB" runat="server">
2:    Sub Application_Start(Sender As Object, E As EventArgs)
3:        Application("ConnectionString") = "Data Source=CHRISMAN;Initial
➥Catalog=MyDatabase;user id=sa;pwd="
4:    End Sub
5: </script>
```

The `Application_Start` event handler executes as soon as your application starts; that is, upon the first request to your application. On line 3, we set up an application variable named `ConnectionString` that contains a SQL connection string used to connect to a database associated with your application. Let's look at Listing 14.7.2 next.

Listing 14.7.2 Retrieving Information from Application State

```
1: <%@ Page Language="VB" %>
2: <%@ Import Namespace="System.Data" %>
3: <%@ Import Namespace="System.Data.SqlClient" %>
4:
5: <script runat=server>
6:    Sub Page_Load(sender As Object, e As EventArgs)
7:        dim strConnectionString = Application("ConnectionString")
8:
9:        dim objConn as new SqlConnection(strConnectionString)
10:       'open database and retrieve information here
11:
12:       lblMessage.Text = "Data successfully retrieved using the string: " &
➥Application("ConnectionString")
```

Listing 14.7.2 Continued

```
13:      End Sub
14: </script>
15:
16: <html><body>
17:     <form runat=server>
18:         <asp:Label id="lblMessage" runat="server" />
19:     </form>
20: </body></html>
```

This page uses the connection string stored in application state to connect to a database. On lines 2 and 3, we import additional namespaces used for connecting to SQL Server. In the `Page_Load` event, we retrieve the string from application state and store it in a local variable on line 7. On line 9, we create a `SqlConnection` object, and we leave the actual data-retrieval code out, as shown on line 10. Assuming all goes well, line 12 outputs a success message to the label on line 18. This success message retrieves the information from application state for display to the user, as shown in Figure 14.13.

FIGURE 14.13
Application state information can be retrieved from any page in the application.

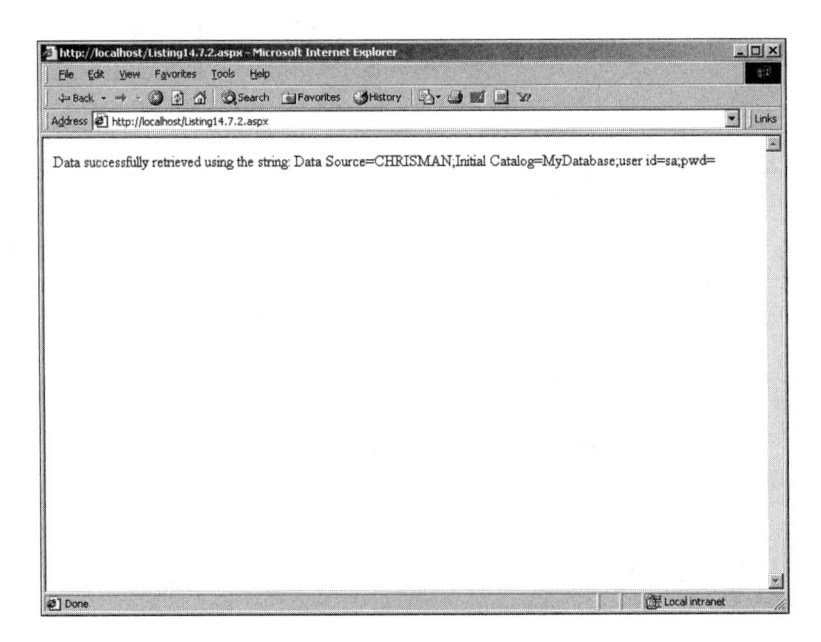

Setting application state information is not limited to the `global.asax` file; you can set and retrieve this information from any page in the application. However, there is an issue with doing it this way. Imagine you've created a page that sets a counter in application state based on the number of requests to that page. Every time the page is requested, you'll want to increment the counter. However, application variables are global, meaning they are available to all threads within the application (a thread is an application process). If another process accesses the application variable at the same time as the current thread, it may result in data corruption or, potentially, an application crash.

The `HttpApplicationState` object provides a method to prevent this situation: `Lock`. This method ensures that only one thread is accessing the application state object at a time, by assigning a lock to the thread currently accessing the state. No other threads can access the state variables until the lock is released, at which point it may be assigned to another thread. For example, the following code snippet demonstrates locking on the request counter from the previous paragraph:

```
Application.Lock
Application("RequestCounter") = Application("RequestCounter") + 1
Application.Unlock
```

The `UnLock` method releases the lock on the `HttpApplicationState` instance. If this method is not explicitly called, ASP.NET will automatically unlock the lock when the request ends or an error occurs, thereby preventing a permanent lock.

Summary

In this chapter, you learned about several different ways to maintain and manipulate state information. ASP.NET provides several solutions for combating the statelessness of the Web, allowing developers to keep track of users as they move through our sites and enabling seemingly unconnected client requests to be strung together accurately.

Page-level state information is maintained automatically by the ViewState. This mechanism keeps track of user input in Web Forms and the state of controls in these forms in general. ASP.NET uses the `SaveViewState` and `LoadViewState` methods to save and retrieve this information. We can disable ViewState management by setting the `EnableViewState` property to `False` for the controls that don't require state management. Alternatively, we can set this property in the `@Page` directive to disable ViewState for the page as a whole. Disabling ViewState affords us a slight performance advantage, because server resources are not required to maintain state information. Finally, we can store custom information in the State Bag as well. This object allows us to store state information that will be maintained across roundtrips to the server, but not across different pages.

ASP.NET can store state information separately from the ASP.NET process in SQL Server. To enable this mechanism, we first had to create the necessary tables and stored procedures by using the `InstallSqlState.sql` SQL script. We then modified our `Web.config` file to set the `sessionState` mode to `sqlserver`, and we included a `sqlConnectionString` attribute with the information needed to connect to the SQL database. Any session information is then automatically stored in SQL Server. This provides an additional security feature for the session data; the information is persisted to a separate medium that is independent of the Web server or ASP.NET process.

ASP.NET, by default, identifies clients with session IDs stored in cookies located on the clients' computers. We can manually store session information in cookies as well, through the `Cookies` property of the `Response` object, and retrieve that information through the same property in the `Request` object. Cookies can contain many different data types and are unique to each user and Web site, so they provide an excellent way to maintain session information without using any of the server's resources.

We can also disable cookie state management, if necessary, by setting the `cookieLess` property of `sessionState` to `True`. ASP.NET will use a process known as *cookie munging* to keep track of clients. This process places the session ID of each user in the URL of every link in a page. As long as the user follows only these links, session information can easily be maintained.

By default, session state information is run InProc, meaning in the same process as ASP.NET and its applications. This provides a large performance benefit, but it can result in data loss in your application; if the ASP.NET process crashes or is restarted, the session information is lost. To combat this, ASP.NET allows us to run the session state information Out-of-Proc, meaning in a separate process, independent of the ASP.NET Web server. This process, `aspnet_state.exe`, can even be maintained on a completely different computer. To run the Session State Server Out-of-Proc, we must first start the `ASPNETState` Windows NT/2000 service, with the command `net start aspnet_state`. We then modify our `Web.config` file to set the mode of the `sessionState` element to `stateserver`. Optionally, we can provide a `stateConnectionString` string that describes a separate computer to maintain the state information. The result is that if ASP.NET crashes in any way, session information is still safely persisted in another process.

Finally, you learned how to maintain application state. Setting application state information is very similar to setting session state information. This information is used across your entire application, and its contents are shared by all users. Application state is a great tool for storing global data.

Other Resources

ASP.NET provides much stronger state-management capabilities than did classic ASP. Learning about and taking advantage of these new methods may take some time, but these resources should help expedite the process:

- *Nothin' but ASP.NET: ASP.NET Session State*—This Microsoft article provides a great intermediate-level introduction to managing state with ASP.NET, including some of the methods we talked about in this chapter. Go to `http://msdn.microsoft.com/voices/aspnet.asp`.

- *ASP.NET State Management*—This is the official ASP.NET SDK Documentation detailing state management in ASP.NET. It discusses both session and application state management in great detail. Go to `http://msdn.microsoft.com/library/default.asp?URL=/library/dotnet/cpguide/cpconaspstatemanagement.htm`

CHAPTER 15

ASP.NET PERFORMANCE TIPS

by Donny Mack

In this chapter you will learn
- Page output caching
- Partial page or fragment caching
- Caching in Web Services
- How to use lower-level Cache APIs
- Performance tips for Web forms
- Performance tips for data access
- Performance tips for Web Services

Comparing ASP.NET to other Web development platforms is like comparing a Ferrari to a Yugo. They both have a lot of the similar features—tires, steering wheels, and engines—but one always outperforms the other. Even with third-party components installed on your Yugo, the Ferrari will always be the better performer due to its original design and features. As with the Yugo, there are things you can do to the Ferrari to make it perform even better, such as changing fuels, keeping it tuned correctly, and upgrading the spark plug wires with custom high-performance ones you've developed. Along the same lines, you can increase ASP.NET's performance. In this chapter, I discuss the different features and tools available to you in ASP.NET that can increase the performance of your ASP.NET Web applications. I'll also provide some tips on how to tune your Web applications to gain even more performance.

1. What Is Caching?

Caching is a programming technique to keep frequently used data in memory for quick access by programs. For example, let's say you have a page that, each time it's requested, queries a database and then displays this data to the user. If the data in the database changes only one or two times a day, you can use caching to store the results of the database query into memory and display the data from the cache rather than querying the database every time it is needed and thus saving computer resources. Many performance advantages are gained from using this technique—the biggest being the savings in time and resources used to query the database. In this case, your database is queried twice a day, rather than every time a user visits the particular page.

ASP.NET offers a couple different methods of implementing caching in your ASP.NET applications. This chapter introduces you to each of them.

2. Caching Entire ASP.NET Web Forms with Page Output Caching

Page output caching is the easiest way to start taking advantage of caching in ASP.NET. By default, the ability to use output caching is enabled, but you must add code to have it applied to a particular ASP.NET Web page or user control. To do this, you must specify at least two things:

- A valid expiration or validation policy
- Public cache visibility

The following code example illustrates the most basic things you need to do to enable page caching in your Web form or user control. This example uses the `@ OutputCache` directive. When using the `@ OutputCache` directive you must set two attributes: `Duration`, which is the number of seconds the document should remain in the cache, and `VaryByParam`, which is used to vary the number of documents that should be cached for the page based on query string parameters and FORM post parameters.

LISTING 15.2.1 Code Example Illustrating How to Enable Page Caching

```
 1: <%@ OutputCache Duration="60" VaryByParam="none" %>
 2: <script language="vb" runat="server">
 3:
 4:   public sub Page_Load(Sender as Object, E as EventArgs)
 5:
 6:     Time.Text = "Time Is: " + DateTime.Now.TimeOfDay.ToString()
 7:
 8:   end sub
 9: </script>
10:
11: <html>
12:   <head></head>
13:   <body>
14:     <asp:Label id="Time" runat="server" />
15:   </body>
16: </html>
```

or:

```
17: <script language="vb" runat="server">
18:
19:   public sub Page_Load(Sender as Object, E as EventArgs)
20:
21:     Response.Cache.SetExpires(DateTime.Now.AddMinutes(1))
22:     Response.Cache.SetCacheability(HttpCacheability.Public)
```

LISTING 15.2.1 *Continued*

```
23:    Time.Text = "Time Is: " + DateTime.Now.TimeOfDay.ToString()
24:
25:  end sub
26: </script>
27:
28: <html>
29:   <head></head>
30:   <body>
31:     <asp:Label id="Time" runat="server" />
32:   </body>
33: </html>
```

Listing 15.2.1 contains two different methods of enabling page caching. The first method uses the `@OutputCache` directive and the second uses the `HttpResponse` classes `Cache` property. We will be going into greater detail of both later in the chapter, but for now you'll notice that both code examples have an expiration policy set (lines 1 and 21) and are public cache visible (lines 1 and 22). Even though the two look very different, both have the same end result—this entire Web form will be cached for 60 seconds.

When output caching is enabled, the first time there is a request for a page, a cache entry is made on the response for that document. All subsequent requests for that page will be served to the requester from the cache until the specified expiration time. When the expiration time has passed, the page is removed from the cache. The page is then recompiled and cached on the next request for the page. All `POST` requests that serve dynamic data dependent on the `POST` must explicitly be generated and will not be served up from the cache using output caching. Dynamic, data-driven pages often vary from one request to another based on query string values. Query strings are made up as named pairs (Key/Value). Using the `@ OutputCache VaryByParam`, which we will discuss in a moment, you can create multiple representations of the same document based on these parameters. For example, if you have a Web Form named `default.aspx` with caching enabled and the `VaryByParam` attribute set to `Mode` (`VaryByParam="Mode"`) and a request is made for it, `default.aspx` is cached for the duration specified. If another request is made to the same page, but a query string parameter has been added (something like `default.aspx?Mode=2`), another version of the same document will be put into the cache. Now you have two different cache entries for the same page; each will have different expiration times since each was put into the cache at different times.

In Listing 15.2.1, I demonstrated two methods you can use to implement page output caching. The first used the `@OutputCache` directive. The second used members of the `HttpCachePolicy` class exposed through the `HttpResponse.Cache` property. The following list contains some of the differences between the two:

- `HttpCachePolicy` settings are set in code rather than a directive so it would be useful to use if the cache settings need to be dynamically set.

- You have more control over setting the expiration time with the `HttpCachePolicy`. You can set it to either an absolute expiration time (DateTime.Parse(12:00:00PM)) or time from last cache (DateTime.Now.AddSeconds(60)))—while you can only specify time from last cache in seconds with the `@ OutputCache` directive.

In this section, I'll demonstrate how to use the `@OutputCache` directive. I'll be providing examples illustrating various implementations and some common situations in which you can benefit from page caching. I'll be going into the `HttpCachePolicy` class in detail later in this chapter.

The `@OutputCache` directive declaratively controls output caching for an entire page and is the quickest and easiest way to implement page caching. Listing 15.2.2 is a code example illustrating how to implement page caching using the `@OutputCache` directive.

LISTING 15.2.2 Code Example Using the `@OutputCache` Directive

```
1: <%@ OutputCache Duration="10" VaryByParam="none" %>
2: <html>
3:  <body>
4:   Cache Time:   <%= DateTime.Now.TimeOfDay.ToString() %>
5:  </body>
6: </html>
```

When the page from Listing 15.2.2 is first rendered, the current server time is printed to the page. If you refresh the page within ten seconds you will notice that the time printed to the page does not change. However, if you wait for eleven seconds and refresh the page, a new current time will be rendered to the page. The reason for this is because we set the `Duration` attribute of the `@OutputCache` directive to expire in 10 seconds (line 1). The `VaryByParam` attribute (line 1) is set to `none`; setting this attributes value to `none` means that there will only be one copy of this document cached. Listing 15.2.2 contains a code example that is easy to use and understand, but tremendously powerful because using this alone can increase your sites performance dramatically.

In Listing 15.2.3 I'll illustrate what caching is best for: caching dynamic database driven pages. In this example I use the `Northwind` database to return 20 rows from the `Products` table and use the `DataGrid` control to display the data.

LISTING 15.2.3 Code Example Using Page Caching with Data Access Pages

```
 1: <%@ OutputCache Duration = "10" VaryByParam="None" %>
 2: <%@ Import Namespace="System.Data" %>
 3: <%@ Import Namespace="System.Data.SqlClient" %>
 4:
 5: <script runat="server" language="c#">
 6:
 7: void Page_Load(Object Sender, EventArgs E) {
 8:
 9:   SqlConnection sCon = new SqlConnection("server=localhost;" +
10:    "uid=sa;pwd=;database=northwind");
11:   SqlCommand SqlCmd = new SqlCommand("SELECT TOP 20 * " +
12:    "FROM Products",sCon);
13:   SqlCon.Open();
14:
```

LISTING 15.2.3 *Continued*

```
15: dg1.DataSource = SqlCmd.ExecuteReader(CommandBehavior.CloseConnection);
16: dg1.DataBind();
17:
18: }
19: </script>
20: <html>
21: <body>
22: <b>Cache Time: <%= DateTime.Now.TimeOfDay.ToString() %></b><p>
23: <asp:datagrid runat="server" id="dg1" />
24: </body>
25: </html>
```

An illustration of the page in Listing 15.2.3 on first request can be scene in Figure 15.1. Figure 15.2 is an illustration after a refresh of the page after only a five second duration. You will notice that the time printed out the page in both figures is the same. This is because upon the first request a cache of the page was made, and on the second request the page was pulled (or served) from the cache. Try waiting 11 seconds and refreshing and you will see that the time refreshes also.

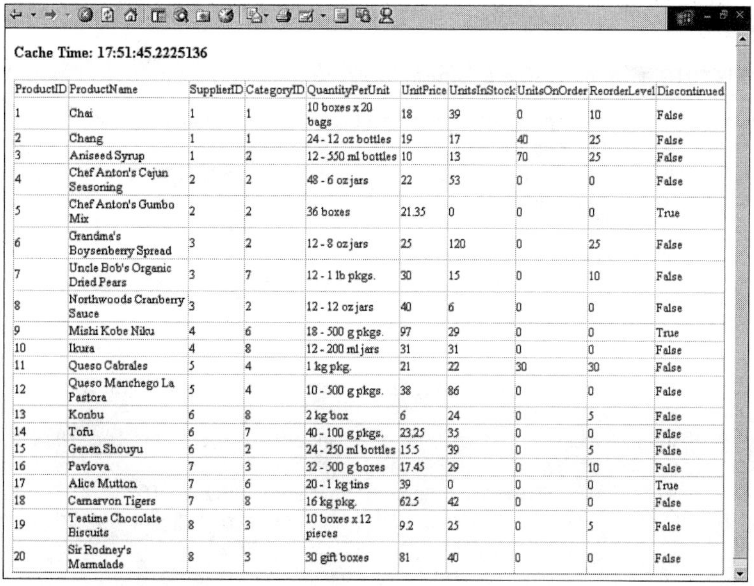

FIGURE 15.1
The page on the first page request. The cache is created.

The final example, shown in Listing 15.2.4, illustrates how query string values are used to cache the same page multiple times based on different query string named pair values. Listing 15.4 uses the `Products` table from the `Northwind` database.

Located at the top of the page is a list of hyperlinks. Each hyperlink navigates to the same page and has one query string named pair. The key is number and the value is an integer. The integer value determines the number of rows shown on the page at any one time.

FIGURE 15.2
The page on the second page request. The page is served to the client from the cache.

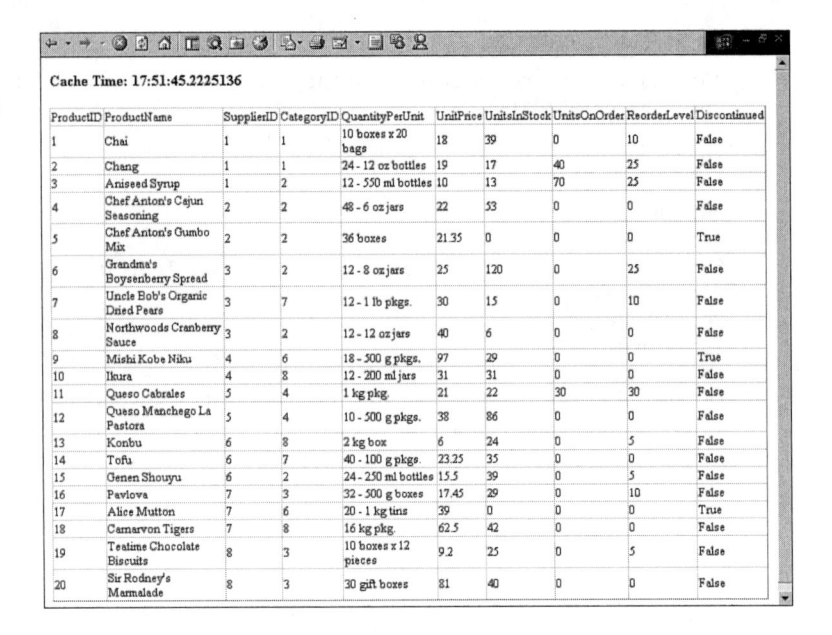

LISTING 15.2.4 Code Example Illustrating Caching Based on Query String Parameters

```
 1: <%@ OutputCache Duration="61" VaryByParam="number" %>
 2: <%@ Import Namespace="System.Data" %>
 3: <%@ Import Namespace="System.Data.SqlClient" %>
 4:
 5: <script language="vb" runat="server">
 6:
 7:  Sub Page_Load(sender as Object, e As EventArgs)
 8:
 9:   If Not Request.QueryString("number") = Nothing Then
10:
11:    time.Text = DateTime.Now.TimeOfDay.ToString()
12:
13:    dim SqlCon as new SqlConnection("server=localhost;" & _
14:     "uid=sa;pwd=;database=Northwind")
15:    dim SqlCmd as new SqlCommand("SELECT TOP " & _
16:     Request.QueryString("number") & " * FROM Products", SqlCon)
17:    SqlCon.Open()
18:
19:    dg1.DataSource = SqlCmd.ExecuteReader(CommandBehavior.CloseConnection)
20:    Page.DataBind()
21:
22:   End If
23:  End Sub
24:
25: </script>
26: <html>
27:  <body>
28:
```

LISTING 15.2.4 *Continued*

```
29:    <a href="listing15.2.4.aspx?number=2">Show 2</a> 
30:    <a href="listing15.2.4.aspx?number=4">Show 4</a> 
31:    <a href="listing15.2.4.aspx?number=6">Show 6</a> 
32:    <a href="listing15.2.4.aspx?number=8">Show 8</a> 
33:    <a href="listing15.2.4.aspx?number=10">Show 10</a> 
34:    <a href="listing15.2.4.aspx?number=12">Show 12</a><br>
35:    <a href="listing15.2.4.aspx?number=14">Show 14</a> 
36:    <a href="listing15.2.4.aspx?number=16">Show 16</a> 
37:    <a href="listing15.2.4.aspx?number=18">Show 18</a> 
38:    <a href="listing15.2.4.aspx?number=20">Show 20</a> 
39:    <a href="listing15.2.4.aspx?number=22">Show 22</a> 
40:    <a href="listing15.2.4.aspx?number=24">Show 24</a> <p>
41:
42:    <asp:Label id="time" runat="server" maintainstate="false" /><p>
43:
44:    <asp:DataGrid id="dg1" runat="server"
➥ maintainstate="false" font-size="10" />
45:
46:  </body>
47:  </html>
```

When the code from listing 15.2.4 first executes, you'll have a page with two lines of hyperlinks rendered across the top of the page. After a hyperlink is clicked, the page reloads and a `Label` control with a time value and a `DataGrid` is additionally rendered to the page. The time value in the `Label` control is set to the time that the page was put into the cache and the `DataGrid` has (n)number of rows from the `Products` table. Figures 15.3 and 15.4 contains illustrations of the page after the "Show 6" and "Show 8" hyperlinks are clicked.

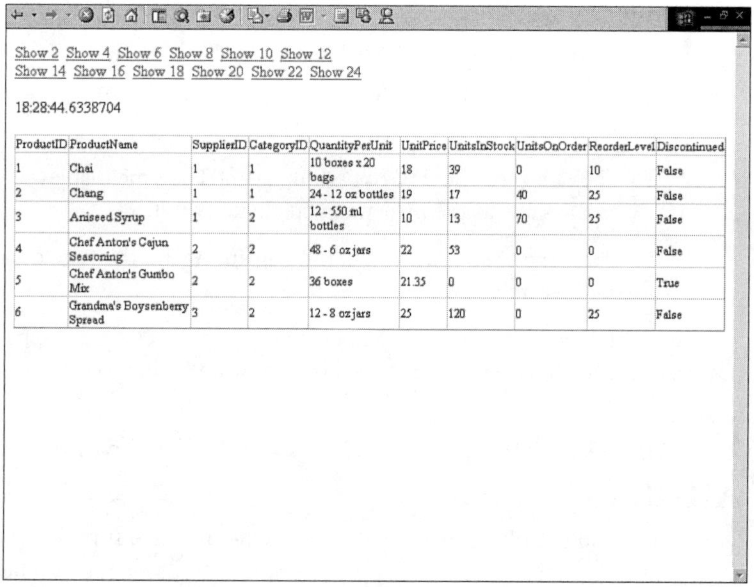

FIGURE 15.3
Page after "Show 6" is clicked. Note the time difference with Figure 15.4.

FIGURE 15.4
Page after "Show 8" is clicked.

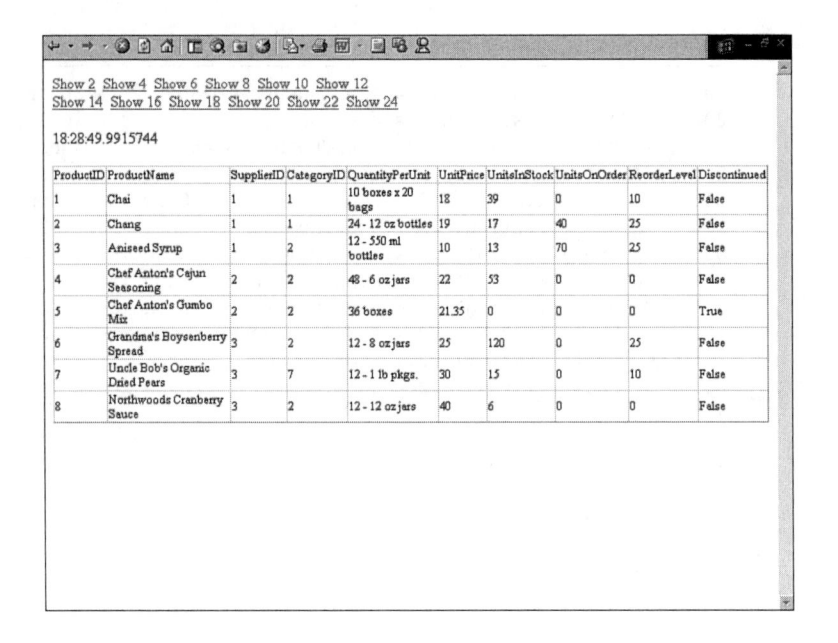

ProductID	ProductName	SupplierID	CategoryID	QuantityPerUnit	UnitPrice	UnitsInStock	UnitsOnOrder	ReorderLevel	Discontinued
1	Chai	1	1	10 boxes x 20 bags	18	39	0	10	False
2	Chang	1	1	24 - 12 oz bottles	19	17	40	25	False
3	Aniseed Syrup	1	2	12 - 550 ml bottles	10	13	70	25	False
4	Chef Anton's Cajun Seasoning	2	2	48 - 6 oz jars	22	53	0	0	False
5	Chef Anton's Gumbo Mix	2	2	36 boxes	21.35	0	0	0	True
6	Grandma's Boysenberry Spread	3	2	12 - 8 oz jars	25	120	0	25	False
7	Uncle Bob's Organic Dried Pears	3	7	12 - 1 lb pkgs.	30	15	0	10	False
8	Northwoods Cranberry Sauce	3	2	12 - 12 oz jars	40	6	0	0	False

Notice the time displayed on the `Label` control—it is different in both views of the page even though it is the same page. After selecting the second link, click on the first link you selected again. You will notice that the time in the `Label` control for that link has not changed. If you would like to replicate this example, follow the following list:

1. Open up page from Listing 15.2.4 in your browser.

2. Click on the "Show 6" hyperlink (make a note of the time displayed in the `Label` control).

3. Click on the "Show 8" hyperlink (make a note of the time displayed in the `Label` control).

4. Click on the "Show 6" hyperlink again. The time displayed in the `Label` control should be the same as the first time you clicked on it.

5. Click on the "Show 8" hyperlink again. Again, the time displayed should be the same as the first time.

In the following sections we will be going over the `@OutputCache`'s other attributes that you can use to gain even more control over how and when your pages are cached.

Using the `@OutputCache` Directive's `VaryByParam` Attribute

The second attribute that the `@OutputCache` directive supports is the `VaryByParam` attribute. You can use this attribute to selectively cache multiple representations of documents based on query string GET parameter values and form POST parameter values. An example of where using the VaryByParam attribute would be if you have an online store and in your query string you always pass two keys: a `MemberID` key and `CategoryID` key. Because personal information may be contained on a page, you would not want to serve up a page cache created by one user on your site to another user. By using the `VaryByParam` attribute, you can cache pages based on the `MemberID` and `CategoryID`. Now when *User1* visits and looks at a category with an ID of 5, *User2* will not receive that cache if they request the same page; instead, a new cache will be created for them. However, if *User1* navigates around a little and then navigates back to that page it will now be served from the cache to them.

You can use the `VaryByParam` attribute by inserting it in your `@OutputCache` declaration, as follows:

`<%@ OutputCache Duration="Seconds" VaryByParam="Key" %>`

You can cache every possible query string key and value and form POST parameter for a given page by setting the `VaryByParam` attribute equal to `*`:

`<%@ OutputCache Duration="Seconds" VaryByParam="*" %>`

You can alternatively select which parameters to use by separating each value given for the `VaryByParam` attribute with a semicolon (;):

`<%@ OutputCache Duration="Seconds" VaryByParam="Mode;Area" %>`

Finally, you can specify that only one representation of the page should exist in the cache by using `none` as the value:

`%@ OutputCache Duration="Seconds" VaryByParam="none" %>`

The following example demonstrates how to use the `VaryByParam` attribute. It also demonstrates how adding or removing a value from the list of keys affects how the document is cached. This example uses four URLs, each with a varying set of query string values and keys:

a. http://www.ASPNextGen.com/default.aspx?Key1=Value1&Key2=Value2
b. http://www.ASPNextGen.com/default.aspx?Key2=Value2&Key1=Value2
c. http://www.ASPNextGen.com/default.aspx?Key2=Value2&Key4=Value4
d. http://www.ASPNextGen.com/default.aspx?Key3=Value3

Table 15.1 shows how changing the value of the `VaryByParam` attribute affects how documents are cached and when.

TABLE 15.2.1 Breakdown from `VaryByParam` Example

VaryByParam Setting	URL(s) Cached	Reason
VaryByParam="*"	4 - A, B, C, D	When * is specified, all pages are cached.
VaryByParam="Key1"	2 - A, B	Key1 is in both URLs, but the value is different for each. Both A and B are cached. C and D do not contain Key1, so they are not cached.

TABLE 15.2.1 Continued

VaryByParam Setting	URL(s) Cached	Reason
VaryByParam="Key2"	1 – The first requested out of A, B, and C	Key2 is located in A, B, and C, but the value of each is the same. After the first URL is requested for the first time, all subsequent URLs with Key2 are served up. D doesn't contain Key2, so it is not cached.
VaryByParam="Key2;Key1"	2 – a, b	A has a unique value of Value1 for Key1, so it is cached. B's Key2 value matches A, but its Key1 value has a different value, so it also is cached. C's Key2 value is a duplicate, and because Key4 is not specified as a VaryByParam value, it is not cached. D's Key4 isn't specified in the query string as a value, so it is not cached.
VaryByParam="Key3"	d	D is the only URL containing Key3, so it is the only one cached.

Using the @OutputCache Directive's Location Attribute

The next attribute @OutputCache has available is the Location attribute. The Location attribute enables you to control where the client receives the cached document. For example, you can control whether a client receives a page from his or her own client side cache (if available) or if it should always be served from the server cache.

This section discusses the different values available for use in the Location attribute and how cached documents are affected by setting this attribute. You can enable the Location attribute as follows:

`<%@ OutputCache Duration="Seconds" Location="Value" %>`

Five values are available for the Location attribute: Any, Client, Downstream, Server, and None. The default value is Any. Below is a list containing a description of each:

- **Any**—Any and all applications capable of caching will cache the requested document for the specified time. Again, Any is the default value, so if you don't specify a Location attribute in your directive, Any will be enabled by default. Here's an example of using the Any value:
  `<%@ OutputCache Duration="Seconds" Location="Any" %>`

- **Client**—Only the client will be allowed to cache the document. When you're developing ASP.NET applications, the typical client will be a browser (for example, Microsoft's Internet Explorer):
  `<%@ OutputCache Duration="Seconds" Location="Client" %>`

- **Downstream**—Each time a document is requested from the server, a new document is generated for the requester. The document created will be a cacheable item by the requester (another server downstream from the server that processed the request):
  `<%@ OutputCache Duration="Seconds" Location="Downstream" %>`

- **Server**—If `Server` is specified as the `Location` value, only the server that served up the document is able to cache it. Clients must retrieve a new document from the server each time a document is requested. This is the exact opposite of the `Downstream` value. Here's an example:
  `<%@ OutputCache Duration="Seconds" Location="Server" %>`

- **None**—Disables caching for the page:
  `<%@ OutputCache Duration="Seconds" Location="None" %>`

Using the `@OutputCache` Directive's `VaryByCustom` Attribute

The next attribute `@OutputCache` has is `VaryByCustom`. This attribute is deceiving because it does have one built-in value—`Browser`. Besides `Browser`, you can create custom strings to determine whether a page should be cached and when. You can enable the `VaryByCustom` attribute by using the following code:

`<%@ OutputCache Duration="Seconds" VaryByCustom="String Value" %>`

If you set the value of `VaryByCustom` to `Browser`, a new cache item is created for each type of browser that requests a document. For instance, if I go to the ASPNextGen.com Web site and request `default.aspx` using Internet Explorer 5.5, a cache item for that document is created. If I again request the same page with Internet Explorer 5.0, another item for the same page is created, as is the case if I again request `default.aspx` with Navigator 4.0. Therefore, a total of three cache items are created—one for each type of browser. The cache is created based on the type of browser and its major version. Here's an example of using the `VaryByCustom` attribute with `Browser` as its value:

`<%@ OutputCache Duration="Seconds" VaryByCustom="Browser" %>`

The second value that can be applied to `VaryByCustom` is a custom attribute. By itself, this means nothing to the compiler or output cache. Take for example the following directive:

`<%@ OutputCache Duration="Seconds" VaryByCustom="Platform" %>`

At this point, `Platform` means absolutely nothing, and caching will not take place in the desired manner. We know what it means: We want a different cache item created for each type of platform that requests the page, but in its default form, `VaryByCustom` only recognizes the value of `Browser`. You can override this functionality in the `global.asax` file for the application. The method you need to override is the `GetVaryByCustomString` method. Listing 15.2.5 demonstrates how you override this method and implement the `VaryByCusom` attribute.

LISTING 15.2.5 Code Example Illustrating How to Override the `GetVaryByCustomString` Method in the `global.asax` File

```
 1: <script runat="server" language="vb">
 2: Public overrides function GetVaryByCustomString(Context As HttpContext, _
 3:    Args As String) As String
 4: Select Case Args
 5:   Case "Platform"
 6:     Return "Platform =" & Context.Request.Browser.Platform
 7:   Case "Browser"
 8:     Return "Browser =" & Context.Request.Browser.Browser
 9: End Select
10: End Function
11: </script>
```

With this code, two users request the same page, with one user having Windows 2000 as a platform, and the other uses Apple Macintosh. What results is that two cache entries are made for the same page—one for the Macintosh user and one for the Windows 2000 user.

> **Note**
> If a value is specified in the VaryByCustom attribute that doesn't exist the default value will be used (Browser) and caching will still take place.

Using the `@OutputCache` Directive's `VaryByHeader` Attribute

The last attribute available when using the `@OutputCache` directive is the `VaryByHeader` attribute. The `VaryByHeader` attribute enables you to control caching based on HTTP headers. You can use the `VaryByParam` attribute by inserting it in your `@OutputCache` declaration, as follows:

`<%@ OutputCache Duration="`*Seconds*`" VaryByHeader="`*semi-colon separated list*`" %>`

As you might imagine, the list could be quite long. The VarybyHeader attribute gives you precise control for caching based on client and server data. The following is a short list of available values:

- Accept
- Accept-Charset
- Accept-Encoding
- Accept-Language
- Authorization
- Content-Encoding

- Expect
- From
- Host
- If-Match
- If-Modified-Since
- If-None-Match
- If-Range
- If-Unmodified-Since
- Max-Forwards
- Proxy-Authorization
- Range
- Referer
- TE
- User-Agent

3. Caching Portions of ASP.NET Web Forms—Fragment Caching

ASP.NET offers the capability to cache portions or regions of Web forms. You can use this technique when you want more control over the way items are cached on particular pages. The term *fragment caching* is somewhat deceiving in that you don't actually cache a portion of a single page. Instead, you cache one or more user controls included on a base Web form. For example, if you have a page named `sample1.aspx` with 200 lines of code, you cannot cache just lines 50–100. However, you can pull out lines 50–100 of that page, create a user control, enable caching in it, and then include that user control in `sample1.aspx`.

There is not a limit to the amount of user controls you can include in Web forms—at least not one that I have reached. So you can have (n)amount of user controls and each one can have different cache durations. For instance, you can cache items that don't change often such as navigation bars, but also continue to dynamically create items on every request such as banner advertisements.

Listing 15.3.1 and Listing 15.3.2 contain a code example illustrating how to implement partial page caching. Listing 15.3.1 contains the code for a user control, and Listing 15.3.3 contains the Web form the user control is contained in. In Listings 15.8–15.10 I'll demonstrate how to include multiple user controls within the same page.

LISTING 15.3.1 User Control for Partial Page Caching Example

```
1: <%@ OutputCache Duration="10" VaryByParam="none" %>
2: Cache time from user control: <%= DateTime.Now.TimeOfDay.ToString() %>
```

LISTING 15.3.2 Web Form for Partial Page Caching Example

```
 1: <%@ Register TagPrefix="DotNetJunkiesControls"
➥   TagName="CacheTime" Src="listing15.3.1.ascx" %>
 2: <html>
 3: <body>
 4: <table>
 5:   <tr>
 6:     <td>
 7: <DotNetJunkiesControls:CacheTime runat="server" />
 8:     </td>
 9:   </tr>
10: </table>
11: </body>
12: </html>
```

Inside the Web form from Listing 15.3.2, I include my custom user control from Listing 15.3.1 that writes out the current time. When executed, you will get a page similar to Figure 15.5. If you refresh the page, you will notice that the time printed out doesn't change for a 10 second duration.

FIGURE 15.5
The time is written to the page from the custom user control.

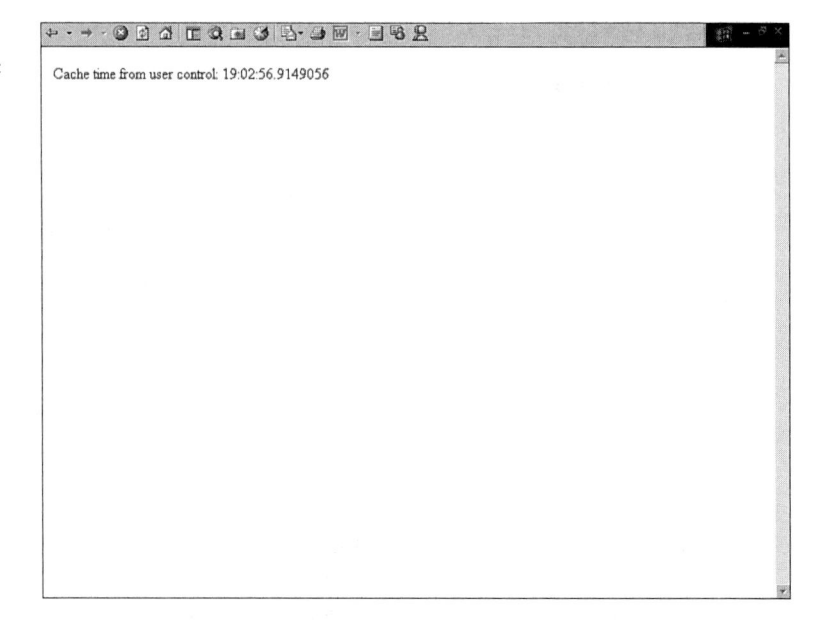

The power comes in when you add more than one user control to the page. Let's say you have a user control that gets news and displays it in a `DataGrid` control on your site. However, the news is updated only three times a day. Instead of querying your database every time the page loads, you can set that user control to cache every 28,800 seconds (that is, three times a day). You may also have an ad banner on the page that you only want to cache for a 10 second duration. Using partial page caching you can accomplish this very easily by setting different expiration policies for the two different controls.

In listing 15.3.3, 15.3.4, and 15.3.5 I'll be demonstrating how you can use partial page caching to cache the results of two database queries for different intervals.

LISTING 15.3.3 Code for First User Control

```
 1: <%@ OutputCache Duration="10" VaryByParam="none" %>
 2: <%@ Import Namespace="System.Data.SqlClient" %>
 3: <%@ Import Namespace="System.Data" %>
 4:
 5: <script language="c#" runat="server">
 6:
 7:   void Page_Load(Object sender, EventArgs e) {
 8:
 9:     SqlConnection SqlCon = new SqlConnection("server=localhost;" +
10:       "uid=sa;pwd=;database=northwind");
11:     SqlCommand SqlCmd = new SqlCommand(
➥"select top 5 * from Suppliers", SqlCon);
12:     SqlCon.Open();
13:
14:     dg1.DataSource = SqlCmd.ExecuteReader(CommandBehavior.CloseConnection);
15:     dg1.DataBind();
16:
17:     CacheTime.Text = DateTime.Now.TimeOfDay.ToString();
18:
19:   }
20:
21: </script>
22:
23: <b>User Control 1 Cache Time: <asp:Label
24:   id="CacheTime" runat="server" /></b>
25: <asp:DataGrid runat="server" Font-Size="10" id="dg1" />
```

LISTING 15.3.4 Code for Second User Control

```
 1: <%@ OutputCache Duration="20" VaryByParam="none" %>
 2: <%@ Import Namespace="System.Data.SqlClient" %>
 3: <%@ Import Namespace="System.Data" %>
 4:
 5: <script language="c#" runat="server">
 6:
 7:   void Page_Load(Object sender, EventArgs e) {
 8:
```

LISTING 15.3.4 Continued

```
 9:    SqlConnection SqlCon = new SqlConnection("server=localhost;" +
10:      "uid=sa;pwd=;database=northwind");
11:    SqlCommand SqlCmd = new SqlCommand(
➥      "select top 5 * from Products", SqlCon);
12:    SqlCon.Open();
13:
14:    dg1.DataSource = SqlCmd.ExecuteReader(CommandBehavior.CloseConnection);
15:    dg1.DataBind();
16:
17:    CacheTime.Text = DateTime.Now.TimeOfDay.ToString();
18:
19:  }
20:
21: </script>
22:
23: <b>User Control 1 Cache Time: <asp:Label
24:   id="CacheTime" runat="server" /></b>
25: <asp:DataGrid runat="server" Font-Size="10" id="dg1" />
```

LISTING 15.3.5 Code for Web for with Both User Controls Included

```
 1: <%@ Register TagPrefix="DotNetJunkiesControls"
➥TagName="SuppliersDG" Src="listing15.3.3.ascx" %>
 2: <%@ Register TagPrefix="DotNetJunkiesControls"
➥TagName="ProductsDG" Src="listing15.3.4.ascx" %>
 3: <html>
 4: <body>
 5: <table>
 6: <tr>
 7: <td>
 8: <DotNetJunkiesControls:SuppliersDG runat="server" id="SDG" />
 9: </td>
10: </tr>
11: <tr>
12: <td>
13: <DotNetJunkiesControls:SuppliersDG runat="server" id="PDG" />
14: </td>
15: </tr>
16: </table>
17: </body>
18: </html>
```

What we have are two user controls (Listing 15.3.3 and Listing 15.3.4) included in our Web form (Listing 15.3.5). The user control from Listing 15.3.3 gets and displays the top 5 rows from the `Suppliers` table and displays the current time. I set it to cache for a duration of 10 seconds. The second user control from Listing 15.3.4 gets and displays the top 5 rows from the `Products` table and also displays the current time. This user control is set to cache for a duration of 20 seconds.

When the Web form from Listing 15.3.5 is rendered, you will see a page similar to Figure 15.6. You'll notice that the times of the two user controls are not exactly the same: This is by design because controls are rendered in a tree and not at the same time. If you wait 11 seconds and refresh the page, you'll see that only the top user controls time changes, and the gap between the times in the first user control and the second user control widens (see Figure 15.7).

> **Caution**
>
> If you enable caching in a Web form that contains user controls that have caching enabled, and the Duration in the Web form exceeds that of the user control, the user control will not refresh until the *Web* forms cache duration expires. The *Web* forms CacheDuration effectively over writes that of the user control.

> **Tip**
>
> To work around the previous warning, you can use a *Web* form template and merely include multiple user controls to design your *Web* sites UI. For instance, you can have a `"NavigationBar"` user control and a `"Content"` user control included on a bare bones *Web* form. You can then cache `"NavigationBar"` for a particular duration and `"Content"` for another or not at all.

FIGURE 15.6
Both user controls are rendered to the page. Cache time for both is very close.

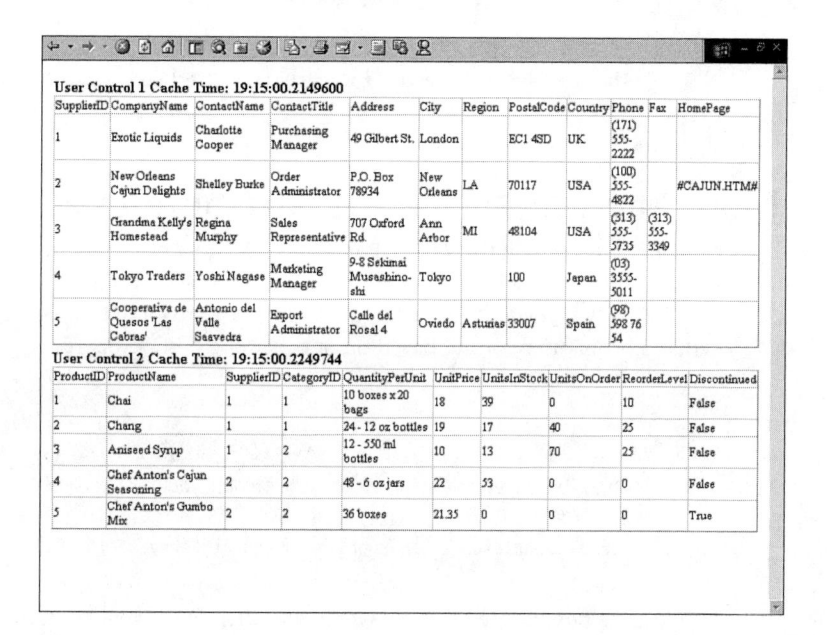

FIGURE 15.7
The bottom user control is served from the cache while the top is dynamically created. Cache time for both is spreading apart.

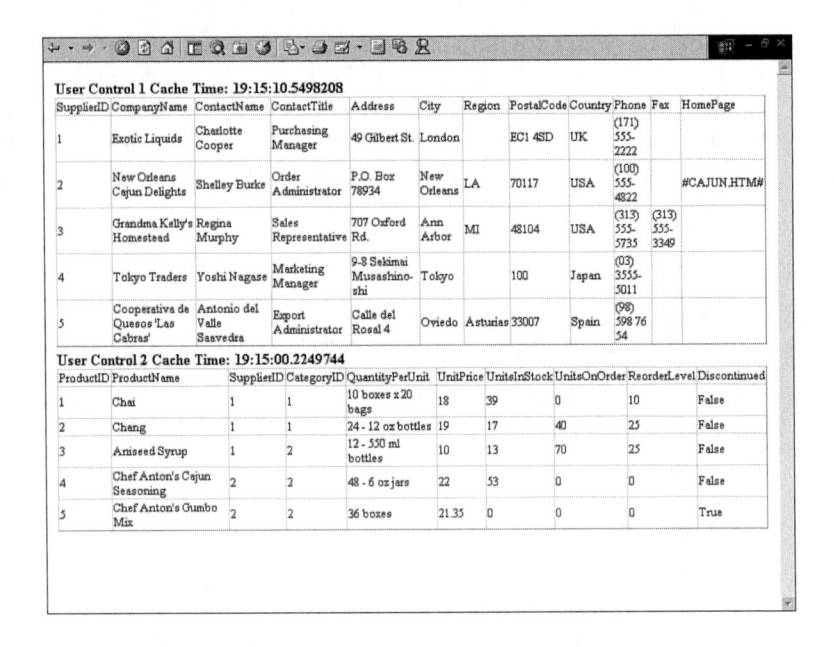

> **Note**
>
> The `@CacheDuration` and `HttpCachePolicy` object behave exactly the same regardless of whether they used in a *Web* form or user control.

Using the `VaryByControl` Attribute in a User Control

Not only can you use the `VaryByParam` attribute in a user control to vary how many versions of the control are cached, but also you have another attribute available that's not available in a web form—`VaryByControl`. The `VaryByControl` attribute enables you to have multiple representations of a user control based on one or more of its properties.

> **Note**
>
> To enable multiple versions user control caching you must apply an ID attribute to the user control in your web form:
>
> `<DotNetJunkiesControls:SuppliersDG runat="server" ID="SDG" />`

To illustrate how to use the `VaryByControl` attribute to make multiple representation of user controls we will be using the user control and web form created in listings 15.3.1 and 15.3.2. Make changes found in listing 15.3.6 and 15.3.7:

LISTING 15.3.6 User Control with Two Properties

```
 1: <%@ OutputCache Duration="120" VaryByParam="*"
➥    VaryByControl="BackColor;ForeColor" %>
 2: <script language="VB" runat="server">
 3:
 4:   private _BackColor as string = System.Drawing.Color.White.ToString()
 5:   public ForeColor as string = System.Drawing.Color.Black.ToString()
 6:
 7:   Public Property BackColor() As String
 8:
 9:     Get
10:       Return _BackColor
11:     End Get
12:
13:     Set
14:       _BackColor = value
15:     End Set
16:
17:   End Property
18:
19:   protected sub Page_Load(sender as Object, e as EventArgs)
20:
21:     lblMessage.BackColor = System.Drawing.Color.FromName(BackColor)
22:     lblMessage.ForeColor = System.Drawing.Color.FromName(ForeColor)
23:
24:   end sub
25:
26: </script>
27: <asp:Label id="lblMessage"
➥    runat="server" Text="Cache time from user control: " />
28: <%= DateTime.Now.TimeOfDay.ToString() %>
```

LISTING 15.3.7 Web Form with User Control Added Twice, Each with Different Property Values

```
 1: <%@ Register TagPrefix="DotNetJunkiesControls"
➥    TagName="CacheTime" Src="listing15.3.6.ascx" %>
 2: <html>
 3: <body>
 4: <table>
 5:   <tr>
 6:     <td>
 7:     <DotNetJunkiesControls:CacheTime runat="server"
 8:     BackColor="Yellow" ForeColor="black"/>
 9:     </td>
10:   </tr>
11:   <tr>
12:     <td>
13:     <DotNetJunkiesControls:CacheTime runat="server"
14:     BackColor="Red" ForeColor="black"/>
15:     </td>
```

LISTING 15.3.7   Continued

```
16:        </tr>
17:    </table>
18:  </body>
19: </html>
```

The user control in listing 15.3.6 has two properties—`ForeColor` and `BackColor`. These properties are used to set the Label controls `ForeColor` and `BackColor` attributes. Listing 15.3.7 has two of these user controls included in it each with different values for the properties. When this page renders two different versions of the user control from listing 15.3.6 are added to the fragment cache. The first has `ForeColor` set to Black and `BackColor` set to Yellow. The second has `BackColor` set to Red and `ForeColor` set to Black. You can test this out by opening two browser windows and requesting the same page from both.

Not only can you vary the fragment cache based on properties you enable users of the control to set (that is, `BackColor` and `ForeColor`), you can vary it on properties that are set programmatically. For instance, a property that is set as a result of a database query from within the user control itself. We will not be giving an example on how to do this, because it is done exactly the same as the previous example except the property value changes programmatically.

4. Obtaining Page-Level Information with `Response.Cache`

Recall that earlier in the chapter we had an example illustrating two ways to enable output caching in *Web* forms and user control. The first way was through the use of the `@OutputCache` directive. The second way is to use the caching APIs exposed through the `System.Web.HttpResponse` class's cache property. This class exposes the `HttpCachePolicy` class, which provides a low-level interface for setting caching information for the current response. The `@OutputCache` directive is simply a high-level wrapper for this class. In the following sections I illustrate how to control output caching using this object.

You have the option to enable caching in your code by using the `HttpCachePolicy` class rather than using the `@OutputCache` directive in your Web Forms. The `HttpCachePolicy` class contains all the methods and properties for controlling the output cache in ASP.NET Web Forms and user controls and is found in the `System.Web` namespace. This section discusses how to use this class in your Web Forms to set the output cache for your page, and how using this class rather than the `@OutputCache` directive gives you greater control over how and when a page is cached.

This section consists of one full code example illustrating how to enable output caching with the `HttpCachePolicy` class. We will go through some of its important properties and methods. Because we have gone over many of these already in the previous section, we will not be spending much time explaining each one in detail.

LISTING 15.4.1 Code Example Illustrating Page Caching Using the `HttpCachePolicy` Class

```
 1: <%@ Import Namespace="System.Data" %>
 2: <%@ Import Namespace="System.Data.SqlClient" %>
 3:
 4: <script language="vb" runat="server">
 5:
 6:  public sub Page_Load(sender as Object, e as EventArgs)
 7:
 8:    Response.Cache.SetExpires(DateTime.Now.AddSeconds(10))
 9:    Response.Cache.SetCacheability(HttpCacheability.Public)
10:    Response.Write("<b>Cache Time: " & _
11:     DateTime.Now.TimeOfDay.ToString() & "</b>")
12:
13:    dim SqlCon as new SqlConnection("server=localhost;" & _
14:     "uid=sa;pwd=;database=Northwind")
15:    dim SqlCmd as new SqlCommand("select top 5 * from products", SqlCon)
16:    SqlCon.Open()
17:
18:    dg1.DataSource = SqlCmd.ExecuteReader(CommandBehavior.CloseConnection)
19:    dg1.DataBind()
20:  end sub
21:
22: </script>
23:
24: <html>
25: <body>
26: <asp:DataGrid id="dg1" runat="server" font-size="10"/>
27: </body>
28: </html>
```

A `DataGrid` and the cache time are rendered when the code from Listing 15.4.1 is executed. If the page is refreshed, you'll notice the time doesn't change this indicates it is being served to you via the cache. Lines 8 and 9 are where caching for the page is enabled. This code produces the same effect as using the following `@OutputCache` directive:

`<%@ OutputCache Duration="10" VaryByParam="none" %>`

On line 8 I set the expiration time of the cache using the `SetExpires` method that expects a `DateTime` as a parameter. On line 9 I use the `SetCacheability` method and `HttpCacheability` enumeration to set the cache to `Public`.

The following list contains the most important members of the `HttpCachePolicy` class that you'll use to enable caching:

- `SetExpires`—Similar to the `Duration` attribute of the `@OutputCache` directive and sets the expiration time of the cache. This method expects a DateTime as a parameter.

    Ex: `Response.Cache.SetExpires(DateTime)`

- `SetCacheability`—Method used to set a cache's visibility. The value passed in must be a member of the `HttpCacheability` enumeration: `NoCache`, `Private`, `Public`, or `Server`.

  `Ex: Response.Cache.SetCacheability(HttpCacheability.Public)`

- `SetVaryByCustom`—This method expects a string as a parameter. We discussed the `VaryByCustom` attribute in the `@OutputCache` section of this chapter. This method allows you to set this in code.

  `Ex: Response.Cache.SetVaryByCustom("Platform")`

You'll notice that this class doesn't contain any members similar to the `@OutputCache`'s `VaryByParam` or `VaryByHeader` attributes. If you want to implement either of these two caching features, you must use their respective classes.

The `HttpCacheVaryByHeaders` class is used to vary the cache by header information. The following list contains the `HttpCacheVaryByHeaders` classes built in properties and methods available to you:

- `AcceptTypes`—Boolean value indicating that caching should vary by Accept types.

  `Ex: Response.Cache.Vary.AcceptTypes = true`

- `UserAgent`—Boolean value indicating that caching should vary based by user agent.

  `Ex: Response.Cache.Vary.UserAgent = true`

- `UserCharSet`—Boolean value indicating that caching should vary by the client browsers character set.

  `Ex: Response.Cache.Vary.UserCharSet = true`

- UserLanguage—Boolean value indicating that caching should vary by user language.

  `Ex: Response.Cache.Vary.UserLanguage = true`

- `VaryByUnspecifiedParameters`—A method that when called varies the cache on all headers. This is similar to using * as a value in the `VaryByHeader` attribute of the `@OutputCache` directive.

  `Ex: Response.Cache.Vary.VaryByUnspecifiedParameters()`

Alternatively you can use the `HttpCacheVaryByHeaders` Item indexer to define your own headers to vary the cache by

`Ex: Response.Cache.Vary.Item(Header) = true`

The `HttpCacheVaryByParams` is used to vary the cache based on named pairs. `HttpCacheVaryByParams` can be implemented by using the following code:

`Ex: Response.Cache.Vary.VaryByParams.Item(Key)`

5. Enabling Output Caching with Web Services

Up to this point we have covered how to enable caching in Web forms and user controls by use of the `HttpCachePolicy` class and its higher level wrapper counterpart; the `@OutputCache` directive. In this section we will be demonstrating the ease of enabling caching in your Web services. As you may or may not know, for a method to be callable from remote Web clients in a Web service it must have a `WebMethod` attribute assigned to it. The `WebMethodAttribute` class has six different properties you can take advantage of. We will only be going over one of these six different attributes in this section: `CacheDuration`. This property may seem familiar to you from the previous sections and functions the same way.

Listing 15.5.1 is an example of how to implement the `CacheDuration` attribute of the `WebMethodAttribute` class in a Web service.

LISTING 15.5.1   Code Example Illustrating How to Use the `CacheDuration` Attribute

```
 1: <%@ WebService Language="VB" Class="Products" %>
 2:
 3: Imports System
 4: Imports System.Web.Services
 5: Imports System.Data
 6: Imports System.Data.SqlClient
 7:
 8: public class Products : inherits WebService
 9:
10:    <WebMethod( _
11:     CacheDuration:=60, _
12:     Description:="<h3>-Gets a list of
       products from Northwind database</h3>")> _
13:    public function GetProducts(RecordCount As Integer) As DataSet
14:
15:    dim sCon as new SqlConnection("server=localhost;" & _
16:      "uid=sa;pwd=;database=Northwind")
17:    dim sda as new SqlDataAdapter("select top " & _
18:      RecordCount & " * from Products", sCon)
19:    dim ds as new DataSet()
20:    sda.Fill(ds, "Products")
21:    return ds
22:
23:   end function
24:
25:    <WebMethod( _
26:     CacheDuration:=60, _
27:     Description:="<h3>-Gets cache time</h3>")> _
28:    public function GetCacheTime() as String
29:
30:    return "Web Method Cached: " & DateTime.Now
31:
32:   end function
33:
34: end class
```

The Web service from Listing 15.5.1 has two methods. The first method (`GetProducts`) returns a `DataSet` object, and the second (`GetCacheTime`) returns a string indicating the cache time. Figure 15.8 contains two different browser's results after a request for the `GetCacheTime` function at different times.

FIGURE 15.8
The top browser was executed first. The results in both are identical.

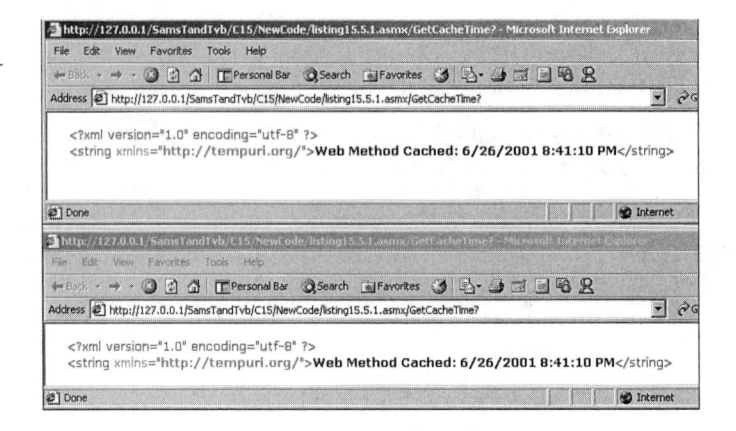

If you choose to build this Web service, execute the `GetProducts` method. You will notice a huge difference in response time between the first request and the second request served from the cache.

Beyond output caching you also have access to the cache API's, which we discuss in the next section, within web services. We won't be giving an example because the technology is the API's are the same whether you're using it within a Web Form, Class, or Web Service.

6. Programmatically Caching Using the `Cache` Class

ASP.NET output caching is a great way to increase performance in your web applications. The downside is that output caching doesn't give you control over caching data or objects that can be shared. For example, there are no mechanisms to allow you to share commonly used `DataSets` from page to page. The `Cache` class opens this door to you and enables you to take advantage of data caching. The `Cache` class, part of the `System.Web.Caching` namespace, enables you to implement application-wide caching of objects rather than page wide as with the `HttpCachePolicy` class.

In this section, I cover how to implement data caching in a few different situations. I illustrate how to cache data sets derived from a database, XML file, and array list as well as how to share this data across an application with relatively little coding. Beyond how to implement data caching, I also cover how to set different validation and expiration policies for the cached data.

The `Insert` Method

Let's first go through the different ways to insert data into the cache. The method used to insert data into the cache is the `Cache.Insert` method. Presently, the `Cache.Insert` method has four overload methods:

- `Cache.Insert(String, Object)`
- `Cache.Insert(String, Object, CacheDependency)`
- `Cache.Insert(String, Object, CacheDependency, DateTime, TimeSpan)`
- `Cache.Insert(String, Object, CacheDependency, DateTime, TimeSpan, CacheItemPriorities, CacheItemPriorityDecay, CacheItemRemovedCallback)`

The following list contains a description of each parameter from the above list.

- `String`—The data you give the cached object.
- `Object`—The object you want to cache.
- `CacheDependency`—File or cache key dependencies for the new cache item. If the file or cache key changes or is invalidated, the object is removed from the cache. An example is an XML file. If there are no dependencies, specify null or nothing.
- `DateTime`—A date/time value indicating the time the cache expires. This is called the *absolute expiration*. If there is no absolute expiration, you can use `DateTime.MaxValue` or the constant `NoAbsoluteExpiration`.
- `TimeSpan`—A time span value indicating the length of time an item should remain in the cache after it is last accessed. This is called the *sliding expiration*. If there is no sliding expiration, you can use `TimeSpan.Zero` or the constant `NoSlidingExpiration`.
- `CacheItemPriorities`—An enumeration value. Items with lower priorities are removed before ones with higher priorities when the system is under a heavy load and is forced to release resources.
- `CacheItemPriorityDecay`—An enumeration value. Items with a fast decay value are removed when they are not used frequently. For example, if you have a cache item that is accessed frequently during the day, you don't want it removed from cache that often. However, if at night the cache item is rarely accessed, you can refresh the cache more often.
- `CachItemRemovedCallback`—A delegate that is called when an item is removed from the cache.

The first of the following three examples shows how to cache an `ArrayList` object. Listing 15.6.1 illustrates a very basic way to cache data.

LISTING 15.6.1 Caching an `ArrayList`

```vb
 1: <script language="vb" runat="server">
 2:
 3:  public sub Page_Load(sender as Object, e as EventArgs)
 4:
 5:    dim CacheItemArrayList as object = Cache.Get("CacheItemArrayList")
 6:
 7:    if CacheItemArrayList is nothing then
 8:
 9:      Response.Write("Created Dynamically")
10:      dim ar as new ArrayList
11:
12:      dim i as integer
13:      for i = 0 to 9
14:        ar.Add("Item " & i)
15:      next i
16:
17:      ddl.DataSource = ar
18:      Cache.Insert("CacheItemArrayList", ar)
19:
20:    else
21:
22:      Response.Write("Created from cache")
23:      ddl.DataSource = CacheItemArrayList
24:
25:    end if
26:
27:    DataBind()
28:
29:  end sub
30:
31: </script>
32:
33: <html>
34: <body>
35:
36:   <asp:dropdownlist id="ddl" runat="server" />
37:
38: </body>
39: </html>
```

Listing 15.6.1 demonstrates the very simplest form of data caching because an object is put into the cache without an expiration time and with no dependencies. When inserting an item into the cache in this way you are allowing the runtime to regulate when to take out the cache.

On line 5, I invoke the `Cache.Get` method to verify whether or not the cache item I want to use already exists. Starting on line 7 and proceeding to line 25 I have an `if...then` statement where I do all the work. First, I check if the `CacheItemArrayList` object is null. If so, then I must create the cache item again (lines 10–15). After creating my `ArrayList` I invoke the `Cache.Insert` method passing in the name I want for the cache item and the object I want to be cached as parameters. If the `CacheItemArrayList` is not found to be empty, I can proceed to bind the `DropDownList` control to the cache item.

In both sections of the `if...then` statement I write out whether or not the `DropDownList` was populated from the cache or dynamically so we can tell where the `ArrayList` is coming from. Figure 15.9 is an illustration of the first request of the page when the `ArrayList` is dynamically populated and the second request when the `DropDownList` is bound to the cached `ArrayList`:

FIGURE 15.9
The top browser is bound to the dynamically created `ArrayList` and the bottom browser is bound to the `ArrayList` from the cache.

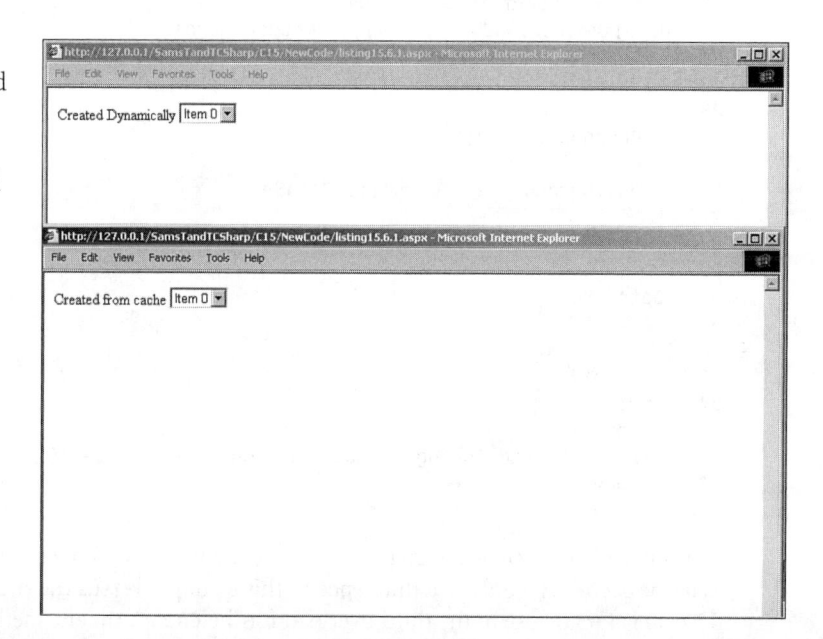

Listing 15.6.2 contains an example of caching a `DataSet` object. In this example we are going to add an expiration time.

LISTING 15.6.2 DataSet Cache Example

```
1: <%@ Import Namespace="System.Data" %>
2: <%@ Import Namespace="System.Data.SqlClient" %>
3:
4: <script language="c#" runat="server">
5:
6:  void Page_Load(Object sender, EventArgs e) {
7:
```

LISTING 15.6.2 Continued

```csharp
 8:    DataSet CacheItemDataSet = (DataSet) Cache.Get("CacheItemDataSet");
 9:
10:    if (CacheItemDataSet == null) {
11:
12:      Response.Write("Dynamic");
13:      DataSet ds = new DataSet();
14:      SqlConnection sCon = new SqlConnection("server=localhost;" +
15:        "uid=sa;pwd=;database=Northwind");
16:      SqlDataAdapter sda = new SqlDataAdapter(
➥     "select Top 10 * from products", sCon);
17:      sda.Fill(ds, "Products");
18:      dg1.DataSource = ds.Tables["Products"];
19:
20:      Cache.Insert("CacheItemDataSet", ds, null,
➥     DateTime.Now.AddMinutes(1), TimeSpan.Zero);
21:
22:    } else {
23:
24:      Response.Write("Cached");
25:
26:      dg1.DataSource = CacheItemDataSet;
27:
28:    }
29:
30:    DataBind();
31:
32:  }
33: </script>
34: <html>
35:   <body>
36:     <asp:datagrid id="dg1" runat="server" Font-Size="10" />
37:   </body>
38: </html>
```

In Listing 15.6.2, I basically go through the same validation concerning making sure the item is in the cache. The only real difference in this example versus the previous example (Listing 15.6.1) is I made use of the third overload for the `Cache.Insert` method (line 20). Starting from left separated by commas: the name for the new cache item, the object to be cached, dependencies (there were none so I specified `nothing` (VB) or `null` (C#)), the expiration time for the cache (I set to one minute from the current time), and finally for the sliding expiration time I specify `TimeSpan.Zero` (no sliding expiration).

Figure 15.10 is an illustration of the first request of the page when the `DataSet` was dynamically populated and the second request when the `DataGrid` was bound to the cached `DataSet`:

Our last example will illustrate how to cache an item that has a dependent XML file. An important thing to note is if the file you are using as a dependency changes in any way, the cache item becomes invalid and taken out of the cache automatically.

Chapter 15 • ASP.NET PERFORMANCE TIPS 583

FIGURE 15.10
The top browser is bound to the dynamically created `DataSet` and the bottom browser is bound to the `DataSet` from the cache.

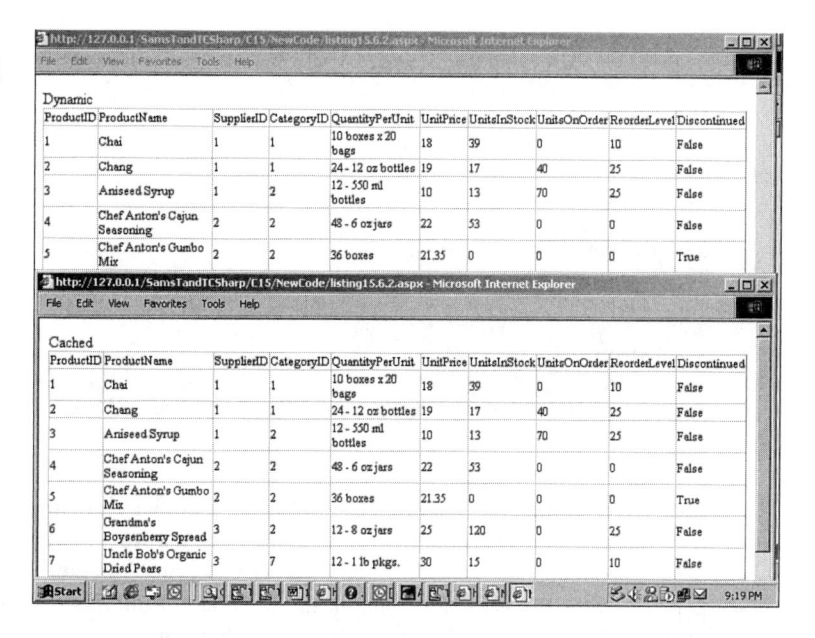

LISTING 15.6.3 Caching XML Data

```
 1: <%@ Import Namespace="System.IO" %>
 2: <%@ Import Namespace="System.Data" %>
 3:
 4: <script language="vb" runat="server">
 5:
 6:  public sub Page_Load(sender as Object, e as EventArgs)
 7:
 8:   dim CacheItemDataSetXml as object = Cache.Get("CacheItemDataSetXml")
 9:
10:   if CacheItemDataSetXml is nothing then
11:
12:    Response.Write("Dynamic")
13:    dim ds as new DataSet()
14:    dim FStream as new FileStream(Server.MapPath("authors.xml"), _
15:     FileMode.Open, FileAccess.Read)
16:    dim SReader as new StreamReader(FStream)
17:    ds.ReadXml(SReader)
18:    FStream.Close()
19:
20:    dg1.DataSource = ds
21:
22:    Cache.Insert("CacheItemDataSetXml", ds, _
23:     new CacheDependency(Server.MapPath("authors.xml")), _
24:     DateTime.Now.AddMinutes(1), TimeSpan.Zero)
25:
26:   else
27:
28:    Response.Write("Cache")
```

584 ASP.NET: TIPS, TUTORIALS, AND CODE

LISTING 15.6.3 Continued

```
29:    dg1.DataSource = CacheItemDataSetXml
30:
31:  end if
32:
33: DataBind()
34:
35: end sub
36:
37: </script>
38:
39: <html>
40:  <body>
41:    <asp:datagrid id="dg1" runat="server" Font-Size="10" />
42:  </body>
43: </html>
```

Again you'll notice similarities between Listing 15.6.3 and the previous two examples. But in this `Cache.Insert` method, instead of using `nothing` we are providing a dependency (line 25) using the `CacheDependency` object. Figure 15.11 is an illustration of the first request of the page when the `DataSet` was dynamically populated from the XML file and the second request when the `DataGrid` was bound to the cached `DataSet`:

FIGURE 15.11
Top browser is bound to the dynamically created `DataSet` and the bottom browser is bound to the `DataSet` from the cache.

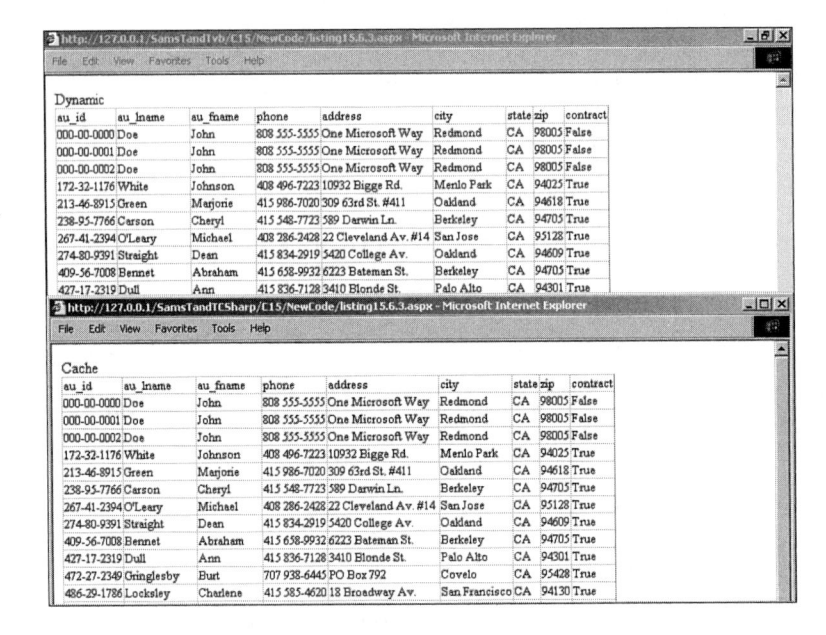

If you have done this example on your computer, try changing some data in the XML file after it has been cached. Then refresh the page before the cache items expiration time. The page will again be dynamically created because the XML file has been manipulated. The `CacheDependency` object keeps track of such changes for us.

The Remove Method

You can remove items from the cache using the `Cache.Remove` method. The `Cache.Remove` method expects one parameter: the string value of the key for the cached item. Listing 15.16 illustrates how to use the `Remove` method.

LISTING 15.6.4 Code Example Illustrating the `Cache.Remove` Method

```
 1: <%@ Import Namespace="System.Data" %>
 2: <%@ Import Namespace="System.Data.SqlClient" %>
 3:
 4: <script language="vb" runat="server">
 5:
 6:  public sub Page_Load(sender as Object, e as EventArgs)
 7:
 8:    if not IsPostBack then Bind()
 9:
10:  end sub
11:
12:  sub Bind()
13:
14:    dim CacheItemDataSet as object = Cache.Get("CacheItemDataSet")
15:
16:    if CacheItemDataSet is nothing then
17:
18:      Response.Write("Dynamic")
19:      dim ds as new DataSet()
20:      dim SqlCon as new SqlConnection("server=localhost;" & _
21:        "uid=sa;pwd=;database=Northwind")
22:      dim sda as new SqlDataAdapter(
➥     "select Top 10 * from products", SqlCon)
23:      sda.Fill(ds, "Products")
24:
25:      dg1.DataSource = ds.Tables("Products")
26:
27:      Cache.Insert("CacheItemDataSet", ds, nothing, _
28:        DateTime.Now.AddMinutes(1), TimeSpan.Zero)
29:
30:    else
31:
32:      Response.Write("Cached")
33:
34:      dg1.DataSource = CacheItemDataSet
35:
36:    end if
37:
38:    DataBind()
39:
40:  end sub
41:
42:  public sub Remove(sender as Object, e as EventArgs)
43:
```

LISTING 15.6.4 Continued

```
44:    if not Cache.Get("CacheItemDataSet") is nothing then
45:
46:      Cache.Remove("CacheItemDataSet")
47:      Response.Redirect("listing15.6.4.aspx")
48:
49:    end if
50:
51:  end sub
52:
53: </script>
54:
55: <html>
56:  <body>
57:    <form runat="server">
58:      <asp:datagrid id="dg1" runat="server" Font-Size="10" />
59:      <p>
60:      <asp:button runat="server"
➥     text="Remove Cached Item" OnClick="Remove" />
61:    </form>
62:  </body>
63: </html>
```

Listing 15.6.4 generates a `DataSet` that populates a `DataGrid` either dynamically or from the cache. At the bottom of the page is a button that the user can press to rremove the `DataSet` from the cache. When the Remove button is clicked the `Remove` method is invoked and checks if the cache item named `CacheItemDataSet` exists, and, if so, the item is removed from the cache and a redirection occurs back to the same page. If you call the `Cache.Remove` method and the item doesn't exist in the cache, the method returns `null`. If, on the other hand, the item is found, the method removes the object and returns the cached item.

The Get Method

The `Get` method can be used to get an item from the cache. This method expects one parameter: the string value of the key for the cached item. Getting an object from the cache can be done in two ways. One way involves explicitly calling the `Get` method. The other way is just to use `Cache("Key")`. Listing 15.6.5 provides an example of using both methods.

LISTING 15.6.5 Code Example Illustrating How to Use the `Cache.Get` Method

```
1: Cache.Insert("MyCacheItem", Object)
2: Dim obj AsObject
3: Obj = Cache.Get("MyCacheItem")
4: Obj = Cache("MyCacheItem")
```

On line 1 of Listing 15.6.5, a new item is inserted into the cache. On line 3 I use the `Cache.Get` method to retrieve the item. On line 4 I do the same thing but leave off the `Get`.

The GetEnumerator Method

The `Cache.GetEnumerator` method returns a dictionary enumerator containing the key/value of all the currently cached items. Because the cache is constantly changing, you will not be able to rely on the returned object containing every cache item. You can add and remove items from the cache during the enumeration. Listing 15.6.6 illustrates how to use the `Cache.GetEnumerator` method to retrieve and list all currently cached items.

LISTING 15.6.6 Code Example Illustrating How to Retrieve All Cache Items from the Cache Using the GetEnumerator Method

```vb
 1: <script language="vb" runat="server">
 2:
 3:  Sub Page_Load(SRC As System.Object, E As System.EventArgs)
 4:
 5:    Dim myEnumerater As IDictionaryEnumerator
 6:    myEnumerater = Cache.GetEnumerator()
 7:
 8:    While (myEnumerater.MoveNext)
 9:      Response.Write(myEnumerater.Key.ToString() & "<BR>")
10:    End While
11:
12:  End Sub
13: </script>
14: <html><body></body></html>
```

On line 4, I call the `GetEnumerator` method to return all the values. Then in lines 5-7 I write them out to the page by looping through the returned collection. Figure 15.12 shows what is currently in my cache—notice the user controls, Web forms, config file, global.asax, and so on.

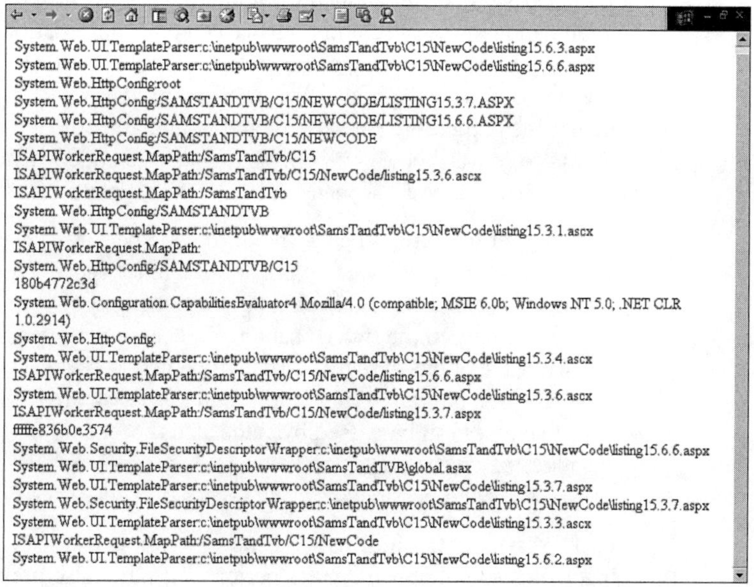

FIGURE 15.12
Result of Listing 15.6.6—all the items in my cache.

7. ASP.NET Web Forms Performance Checklist

When you are building Web applications—or for that matter, any application—performance is always a concern. Building a high-performance Web application takes extensive planning, great programmers, and good software. The following sections provide a performance checklist to help you optimize your Web applications. Of course, there are always situations in which you must take a performance hit to implement certain features. However, if you can speed up processing even a little, overall you will be better off.

- **String Manipulation**—You might be thinking this couldn't possibly affect the performance of an application, but it can. You will use strings in your applications, and you will probably use a lot of them. When you create a string and assign a value to it, a piece of memory is allocated for it. This is not negotiable. However, did you know that if you change or modify the string, a new string is created? Now you have two string objects instead of just one modified string, as you would think. For example

    ```
    dim x as string
    x="Foo"
    x = x & "Bar"
    ```

    The proceeding code will actually create two string objects. With the .NET Framework comes the `StringBuilder` object, which is a constructor for strings and is designed for runtime string manipulation. This means that if you don't plan on ever changing the value of a string during runtime execution, then just use a string otherwise, use `StringBuilder`. The following example illustrates how to use `StringBuilder` to concatenate two strings together.

    ```
    Dim x As New StringBuilder("Foo")
    x.Append("Bar")
    ```

- **Managed Versus Unmanaged Code**—The second code performance tip deals with the combination of managed and unmanaged code—for example, in a situation when you're calling a classic COM component method using a Runtime Callable Wrapper (COM Interop). For every method call to the unmanaged COM component from a managed code environment, there are between 10 and 50 more instruction calls. It is recommended that you try to convert these components to managed code whenever possible. If this is not possible, try to convert as many tasks as possible per method call to the COM component.

- **Working with Value Types**—The third code performance tip deals with types. There are two kinds of types: value types and reference types. Types can be used to describe data as it is passed around from method to method in your code (`ByVal` or `ByRef`). The difference between the two is that a reference type describes a value or data as a *location* of a sequence of bits, whereas a value type describes a value or data as a sequence of bits. Objects types, interface types, and pointer types all are passed by reference, whereas all primitive types can be passed by value. This speeds up performance because value types are allocated on the stack, whereas reference types are allocated on the garbage collection heap. When possible, use value types over reference types.

- **Early Versus Late Binding**—Whenever possible use early binding rather than late binding. Doing so not only increases performance, but also prevents runtime exceptions from occurring (refer to the `Option Strict` and `Option Explicit` sections of Chapter 9, "ASP.NET Error Handling"). The following is a sample of each.

Late Binding:

```
dim x
x = "late bound"
```

Early Binding:

```
dim y as string
y = "early bound"
```

- **Avoiding Roundtrips to the Server**—Even though ASP.NET has made it incredibly easy to work with objects on the server, you should still try to avoid excessive trips to it! For example, before a form is submitted to the server you should, if possible, validate the data on the client side before submitting to the server. Sure the data is revalidated on the server, but what if the user submits the form 5+ times to the server before they fill the form out correctly. A perfect way to accomplish this task would be to use the ASP.NET Validation controls, which can perform client side validation with very little work.

- **Use Server Controls only when necessary**—Server controls are incredibly easy to use and implement, but on the flip side they add overhead to page processing. If you do not need programmatic access to the data or controls, then you should opt to use traditional methods. For example

```
<script Language="vb" runat="server" >
sub Page_Load(source As Object, e as System.EventArgs)
 txtdate.Text = DateTime.Now.ToString()
end sub
</script>
<html>
<body>
<asp:Label runat="server" id="txtdate" /> **Expensive
<br>
<%=DateTime.Now.ToString()%> **Less Expensive
</body>
</html>
```

- **Disable `Viewstate` if it's not needed**—When dealing with a heavily data driven applications that use server controls, `ViewState` is enabled by default. However, if the page is not going to be posted back to the server or the server controls are re-bound on every request, then you are unnecessarily sending a lot of information back to the client that is never used. You can disable `ViewState` for individual server controls or page wide by using the following code:

Page:

```
<%@ Page MaintainState="false" %>
```

Server Control:

```
<asp:DataList runat="server" MaintainState="false" />
```

- **Disable `SessionState` if it's not needed**—If you do not use sessions in your web application or on a particular page, then turn `SessionState` off and increase performance!

There are two ways you can disable `SessionState`. The first is for a particular page using the `@Page` directive:

```
<%@ Page EnableSessionState="false" %>
```

The second is application-wide in your Web applications configuration file (`Web.config`).

```
<configuration>
   <system.web>
      <sessionstate
         mode="off"
      />
      </sessionstate>
   </system.web>
</configuration>
```

- **Turn of `Debug` Mode**—If your site is in production turn debug mode off for you application. Not doing so will significantly slow it down (`Web.config`).

  ```
  <compilation debugmode="false" />
  ```

- **Caching**—Whenever possible, you should implement either output caching or data caching in your application. Even if you only cache a page or item for 2 seconds, you will see increased performance. Use user controls to separate content so that you can cache items for different durations.

Using ASP.NET Performance Counters

No matter how much planning you do or how well you write your code, the only sure way to test the performance of your application is to test-drive it. When you install the .NET SDK, a set of .NET performance counters and performance counter APIs are also installed. You can use these counters to monitor all aspects of your Web application's performance. What's more, you can monitor a single Web application or all Web applications on the machine. The data obtained from the counters include errors per second and cache page hits and much more detailed statistical data. In this section, I discuss how to set up Microsoft NT/2000 Performance Monitor to view your application's performance data.

Setting up performance monitor to monitor ASP.NET applications:

1. Open up Performance Monitor (`perfmon`): Start | Programs | Administration Tools | Performance.

2. Select "View Report."

3. Either click the Add "+" button or....

4. Select Computer to run performance monitor on.

5. Under "Performance object" select "ASP.NET Applications."

6. You now have the option to use all counters or select counters. If you would like to view all counters select the "All Counters" radio button and the other if you want to select from the list.

7. Finally, select which application you would like to use. For all applications select the "All Instances" radio button otherwise select from the list. Press "Add" button and "Close" button (see Figure 15.13).

Obviously, this report isn't from our Web site—http://www.DotNetJunkies.com—our site gets at least twice as many hits as are showing here! But really, personal computer just happens to be called DotNetJunkies.

You can also access these performance counter API's programmatically, but that goes beyond the scope of this book, bit for more information see the System.Diagnostics Namespace. Additionally, you may want to test your site against a heavy payload. Microsoft offers a free tool to simulate multiple clients hitting your site. It is called "*Web Application Stress Tool*" and can be downloaded at http://webtool.rte.microsoft.com/download.asp.

FIGURE 15.13
Add Counters dialog box.

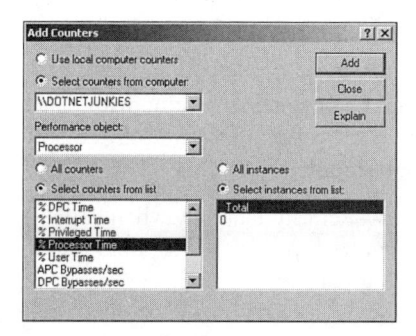

You will then see a report of all counters data similar to that in Figure 15.14.

FIGURE 15.14
ASP.NET Performance report.

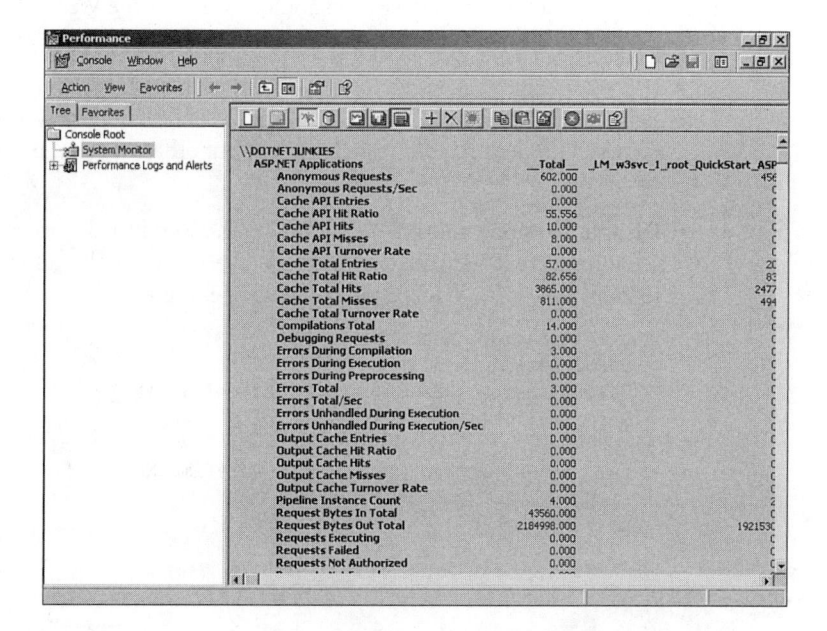

8. Database Performance Checklist

In this section, I give you tips on increasing database performance in your ASP.NET applications. Many of the traditional performance tips still apply, such as using `SQL` stored procedures instead of inline `SQL` statements in your code. In addition, proper database design is crucial. But beyond that, you can use certain techniques to increase performance even further.

- **Use SQL Stored Procedures**—`SQL` Stored procedures should be used over dynamic `SQL` statements whenever possible. SQL Stored procedures increase performance because they are compiled on the server and therefore are executed more quickly.

- **Cache Data When You Can**—When applicable, you should try to cache commonly used data. Each query to the database adds overhead to your application. If you can limit the number of queries to your database, your overall application will speed up. On a high-traffic site, even a five-second data cache will speed up overall performance dramatically.

- **Use Correct Data Objects**—If you are working with data pick your data objects correctly. For instance, if you only need a forward only cursor, use the `SqlDataReader` and not the more expensive `DataSet`.

- **Limit Database Queries**—Refresh data only when you need to. If you are only returning a small amount of data from your database, hold it in `ViewState` on page `PostBack`'s instead of re-querying your database if you can.

9. Web Services Performance Checklist

The following is a short checklist you should review for the Web services you provide:

- **Caching**—If your web service doesn't provide real-time data, then enable caching in it and serve clients cached objects instead of dynamically creating them on each request. Remember, you can still take advantage of data caching in web services. So if portions of your service does rely on real-time data, but others do not, then take advantage of data caching.

- **Disable Sessions**—As we mentioned in the web forms performance checklist, disabling session state will increase performance. Web services also allow you to disable sessions to increase your web method's performance. For example

```
public function <WebMethod( _
  EnableSession:=false, _
  Description:="<h3>-Gets cache time</h3>")> _
  GetCacheTime() as String

  return "Web Method Cached: " & DateTime.Now

end function
```

Summary

In this chapter we discussed many different caching techniques available in ASP.NET. We discussed how to implement page output caching using both the `HttpCachePolicy` class and its higher-level counterpart the `@OutputCache` directive. We then went over how to implement caching in web services using the `CacheDuration` web method attribute. We ended the caching sections by discussing the `Cache` class and its various methods and properties you can use to enable data caching for application wide objects. We ended the chapter by going over some performance tips for web forms, data access, and web services. Specifically we discussed the following subjects in this chapter:

- Page output caching
- Partial page or fragment caching
- Caching in Web services
- How to use lower-level cache APIs
- Performance tips for Web forms
- Performance tips for data access
- Performance tips for Web services

Other Resources

For more information on the subjects discussed in this chapter please see the following:

- **Output Caching**—`@OutputCache`, `HttpCachePolicy` class, `HttpCacheability` enumeration, `HttpCacheVaryByHeaders` class, `HttpCacheVaryByParams` class, and the `DateTime` class, and the `System.Web` namespace in the SDK help files or MSDN. Also see the Quickstart tutorials that come with the SDK.

- **Data Caching**—`System.Web.Caching` namespace, `Cache` class, `DateTime` class, `CacheDependency` class, `CacheItemPriority` class, and `HttpContext` class in the SDK help files or MSDN. Also see the Quickstart tutorials that come with the SDK.

- **Caching in Web Services**—`WebMethodAttribute` class from in the SDK help files. Also see the Quickstart tutorials that come with the SDK.

- **Performance Tuning All**—See Quickstart tutorials that come with the SDK.

- **General**—Check out *DotNetJunkies.com* for a series of articles and samples related to caching and performance tuning.

CHAPTER 16

SEPARATING CODE FROM CONTENT

by Doug Seven

In this chapter you will learn
- Code-Behind techniques for ASP.NET Web Forms
- Code-Behind techniques for user controls
- How to localize a Web application
- How to specify character encoding
- How to use resource files for localization

One of the drawbacks to traditional ASP development has been that it encourages spaghetti-like code. For example, when HTML tags and ASP scripts are intermixed, the manageability and readability of the code is seriously hampered. In larger companies where there are separate teams of ASP developers and HTML developers, the ASP developers often have to insert script code throughout pages that the HTML developers have put together. This intermingling of HTML and ASP scripts makes it difficult sometimes for the HTML developers to go back and make aesthetic changes to the Web page, and it opens up a Pandora's box of presentation problems when an experienced business-layer developer with little HTML experience needs to modify the logic of the page.

The developers of ASP.NET sought to remedy this nightmare by providing an easy means of separating the code and the HTML content of an ASP.NET Web page. Such techniques for separation of code and content can be found in some of the earlier chapters in this book. For example, the use of custom controls and user controls provides encapsulated functionality in the form of controls that can be used in a similar manner to that of HTML elements. Another powerful method of separating code and content with ASP.NET is through the use of a technology called *Code Behind*, which we'll examine in detail in this chapter.

1. Using Code Behind

ASP.NET Web Forms are divided into two sections: the user interface and the logic (or code). The user interface comprises HTML markup and ASP.NET Web controls, whereas the logic is the programmatic code that interacts with the user interface. You can choose to have the user interface and the logic in the same file as you have seen in previous chapters. Although placing the code and content in the same file may seem natural for classic ASP developers, you should strive to keep the code and content as separate as possible.

Thankfully ASP.NET provides a mechanism known as *Code Behind*, which you can use to separate the user interface and logic, placing each in its own file.

The user interface file is the Web Form and associated HTML and Web controls. This file should be created with an `.aspx` extension.

The logic file, referred to as the *Code-Behind file*, ends with an extension appropriate for the language it is written in, such as `.vb` for Visual Basic or `.cs` for C#. The Code-Behind file can be written using any programming language for which there is a .NET compiler.

Code-Behind Techniques for ASP.NET Web Forms

Since an ASP.NET Web Form is compiled into an object and a tree of controls is built, the user interface and logic can exist separately. The logic, a class file, is then compiled into an object on the tree when the page is requested. The logic class is then just another object on the execution tree, and all its properties, methods, and event handlers are exposed like any object. To build the structure for this object tree to work, you must create a Web Form that inherits from a "base class." In other words, the Code-Behind file is a class file that defines the base class for the Web Form. This is illustrated in Figure 16.1.

FIGURE 16.1
When a Web Form is compiled, the Web Form inherits from the Code-Behind class, which in turn inherits from the Page class.

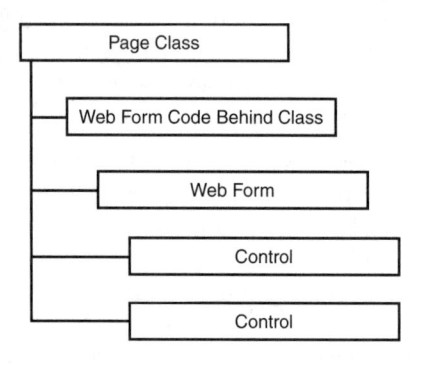

The logic in the Code-Behind file looks, works, and performs similarly to the code you have been writing directly into a Web Form. The primary difference is that an ASP.NET Web Form (`.aspx` files) automatically inherits common classes in the .NET Framework, such as the `System.Web.UI.Page` class. Code-Behind class files do not have any automatic inheritance, so some special care must be taken to ensure all the necessary classes are imported into the Code-Behind class.

In Listing 16.1.1, we build the Code-Behind file (16.1.1.vb) for an ASP.NET Web Form that uses the `DataGrid` server control to render a table of customers from the Northwind Customers table.

LISTING 16.1.1 Using Code Behind with an ASP.NET Web Form (16.1.1.vb)

```
 1: Imports System
 2: Imports System.Data
 3: Imports System.Data.SqlClient
 4: Imports System.Web
 5: Imports System.Web.UI
 6: Imports System.Web.UI.WebControls
 7: Imports System.Web.UI.HtmlControls
 8:
 9: Public Class myCodeBehind_1611
10:    Inherits Page
11:
12:    Public myDataGrid As DataGrid
13:
14:    Public Sub Page_Load(Sender As Object, E As EventArgs)
15:       Dim myDataAdapter As SqlDataAdapter
16:       Dim myDataSet As New DataSet
17:
18:       myDataAdapter = New SqlDataAdapter("SELECT TOP 10 CustomerID, _
    CompanyName, ContactName, ContactTitle FROM Customers", _
19:          "server=localhost;database=Northwind;uid=sa;pwd=;")
20:       myDataAdapter.Fill(myDataSet, "Customers")
21:
22:       myDataGrid.DataSource = myDataSet.Tables("Customers")
23:       myDataGrid.DataBind()
24:    End Sub
25:
26: End Class
```

One of the first and notably one of the most important things to point out in Listing 16.1.1 is the first seven lines of code, where we import all the namespaces necessary to interact with the Web Form. As I mentioned previously, ASP.NET Web Forms automatically inherit from many of these namespaces, but in a Code-Behind file we must explicitly import the necessary namespaces. On lines 2 and 3, the `System.Data` and `System.Data.SqlClient` namespaces are imported to provide access to the ADO.NET classes (such as `DataSet`) and the SQL Managed Provider. The `System.Web` and `System.Web.UI` namespaces enable access to Web classes such as the `Page` class. The two `System.Web.UI` namespaces, on lines 6 and 7, are provided to enable access to classes for the various server controls. In Listing 16.1.1, we only reference one server control, a `DataGrid` control, but importing both the `WebControls` and `HtmlControls` namespaces is a good habit to get into. If we forget to import one of these namespaces and later write code that references a server control, we could end up spending unnecessary time trying to figure out why we are getting a "User type not defined" error on a line that references an HTML table, for example.

On line 9 of Listing 16.1.1 we define the class `myCodeBehind_1611`, and on line 10 we inherit from the `Page` class. By inheriting from the `Page` class, we are enabling the typical Page class properties, methods and events to be a part of our Code-Behind class. On line 12 we define the variable `myDataGrid` as an instance of the `System.Web.UI.WebControls.DataGrid` class. This class instance will be matched to a `DataGrid` control, named `myDataGrid`, in the Web Form.

On lines 14-24, we define the `Page_Load()` event handler. On the `Load` event, we retrieve data from the Northwind Customers table and apply the data to the `myDataGrid` instance of the `DataGrid` class (which will be matched to a `DataGrid` control on the Web Form).

Listing 16.1.2 shows the Web Form, 16.1.1.aspx, that will use the Code-Behind class (`myCodeBehind_1611`) created in Listing 16.1.1.

LISTING 16.1.2 An ASP.NET Web Form, 16.1.1.aspx, Using Code Behind

```
 1: <%@ Page Inherits="myCodeBehind_1611" Src="16.1.1.vb" %>
 2: <html>
 3: <head>
 4: <title>ASP.NET Tips, Tutorials and Code -
        Chapter 16: Using Code Behind</title>
 5: </head>
 6: <body>
 7: <asp:DataGrid runat="server" id="myDataGrid"
 8:     Width="740"
 9:     BorderColor="black"
10:     ShowFooter="false"
11:     Font-Name="Verdana"
12:     Font-Size="10pt"
13:     HeaderStyle-BackColor="Black"
14:     HeaderStyle-ForeColor="White"
15: />
16: </body>
17: </html>
```

On line 1 of Listing 16.1.2, we use the `@ Page` directive to inherit for the Code-Behind base class. We specify the class we defined in the Code-Behind file as the class to inherit from. We also provide an `Src` (source) attribute that has as its value the relative path to the Code-Behind file. The `Src` attribute is optional. If an `Src` value is provided, the .NET Framework will look for the file and compile the class on the first request. If the `Src` attribute is left off, the .NET Framework will look for a compiled DLL in the `bin` directory that contains the Code-Behind class.

Caution

If the Code-Behind file is not on the Web server and the `Src` attribute is used, you will get an error that a resource required for the requested page could not be found. Because the Code-Behind class is compiled on demand when using the `Src` attribute, the Code-Behind file must be available on the Web server. If the Code-Behind class is compiled into a DLL in the `bin` directory, the Code-Behind file does not need to be deployed to the Web server because the class will be read from the DLL.

> **Note**
>
> If you are using Visual Studio.NET to build your Web Forms, a Code-Behind file will be created for you when you create a new Web Form. The Web Form's @ `Page` directive will have the `INHERITS` attribute referencing the class name in the Code-Behind file and a `CODEBEHIND` attribute. Visual Studio.NET uses the `CODEBEHIND` attribute to track the Code-Behind file—it is not actually used by the .NET Framework. Visual Studio.NET requires that all Code-Behind classes be precompiled into a DLL in the `bin` directory. You can supercede this by adding the `Src` attribute to the @ `Page` directive.

On line 7 of Listing 16.1.2, we place a `DataGrid` server control. The `ID` property of the server control is `myDataGrid`, the same name as the `DataGrid` class instantiated in the `myCodeBehind_1611` Code-Behind class. Since the server control's `ID` property is the same as the object in the Code-Behind class, when the Web Form is compiled, the `myDataGrid` object will be matched up to the `myDataGrid` server control. When the page is requested, the `Page_Load()` event is triggered and the handler in the Code-Behind class retrieves data from the database and binds it to the `myDataGrid` server control. Figure 16.2 shows the rendered page created from Listings 16.1.1 and 16.1.2.

FIGURE 16.2
A Web Form inherits from a base class defined in a Code-Behind file.

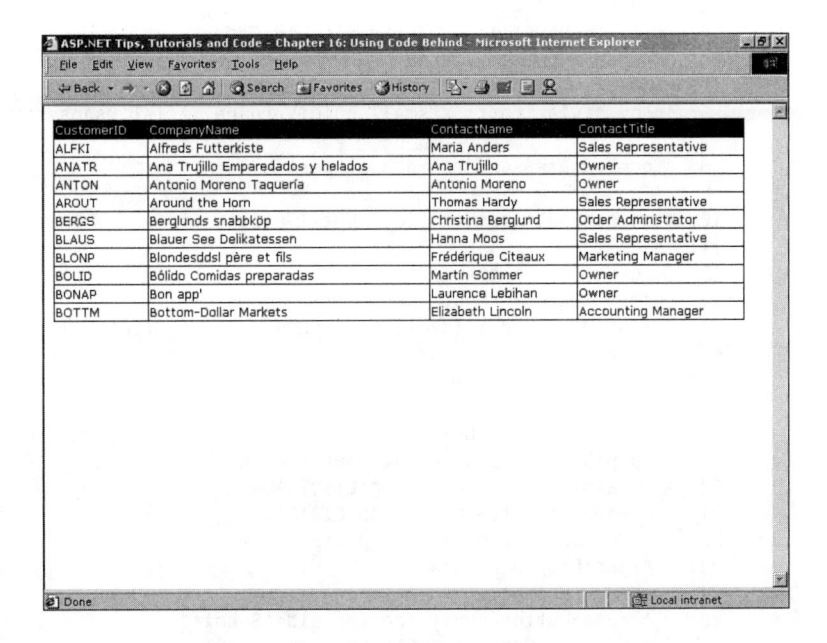

In the preceding examples, we created a Web Form that used a Code-Behind class to render a table filled with data from a database. All in all, this was a rather simple operation; we dealt with one event, the `Page_Load()` event, and one control, the `DataGrid` server control. We are not limited to one event or one control when using Code-Behind technology. We can use Code Behind to provide all the same functionality we have been using in previous chapters directly in the Web Form. By instantiating an object of the appropriate class for each control we need programmatic access to and creating event handlers or methods for all the functionality we need, we can use Code Behind to completely separate our logic code from our presentation markup.

Not every control needs to be declared as an object in our Code Behind, and we are not limited to ASP.NET server controls. Only controls we need programmatic access to must be instantiated as objects in the Code-Behind class. Because we are getting into the (good) habit of always importing the `System.Web.UI.HtmlControls` namespace, HTML controls (HTML elements that have the `runat="server"` attribute) may also be accessed from the Code-Behind class.

Listing 16.1.3 shows a Web Form, 16.1.3.aspx, that uses an HTML `<table>` element to hold a form made up of a `TextBox`, a `DropDownList` and a `Button` control. Outside of the `<table>`, we have a `Label` control.

LISTING 16.1.3 Working with Code Behind and Multiple Events and Controls

```
 1: <%@ Page Inherits="Welcome" Src="16.1.4.vb"  %>
 2: <html>
 3: <head>
 4: <title>ASP.NET Tips, Tutorials and Code -
        Chapter 16: Using Code Behind</title>
 5: </head>
 6: <body style="font: x-small bold Verdana, Arial, sans-serif">
 7:
 8: <form runat="server" method="post">
 9:
10: <table runat="server" id="myHtmlTable">
11:   <tr><td>
12:     <b>Name:</b><br>
13:     <asp:TextBox runat="server" id="Name" />
14:     <asp:RequiredFieldValidator runat="server" ControlToValidate="Name"
15:       ErrorMessage="Name is required" />
16:     <br>
17:
18:     <b>Prefix:</b><br>
19:     <asp:DropDownList runat="server" id="Prefix">
20:       <asp:ListItem>Mr.</asp:ListItem>
21:       <asp:ListItem>Mrs.</asp:ListItem>
22:       <asp:ListItem>Ms..</asp:ListItem>
23:     </asp:DropDownList>
24:     <p>
25:       <asp:Button runat="server" id="Submit"
26:         Text="Submit" OnClick="Submit_OnClick" />
27:     </p>
28:   </td></tr>
29: </table>
30:
31: <asp:Label runat="server" id="WelcomeMsg" />
32:
33: </form>
34: </body>
35: </html>
```

In Listing 16.1.3, we added the `runat="server"` attribute to the `<table>` element to convert it to an ASP.NET HTML control. We also gave it an `ID` attribute so we can access it by name. On line 1, we used the `@ Page` directive to inherit from the `Welcome` class in a file named `16.1.4.vb`. The Code-Behind file is shown in Listing 16.1.4.

LISTING 16.1.4 The Code-Behind File for 16.1.3.aspx

```
 1: Imports System
 2: Imports System.Web
 3: Imports System.Web.UI
 4: Imports System.Web.UI.WebControls
 5: Imports System.Web.UI.HtmlControls
 6:
 7: Public Class Welcome
 8:    Inherits Page
 9:
10:    Public Name As TextBox
11:    Public Prefix As DropDownList
12:    Public WelcomeMsg As Label
13:    Public myHtmlTable As HtmlTable
14:
15:    Public Sub Page_Load(Sender As Object, E As EventArgs)
16:      If Not Page.IsPostBack Then
17:        myHtmlTable.Visible = True
18:      End If
19:    End Sub
20:
21:    Public Sub Submit_OnClick(Sender As Object, E As EventArgs)
22:      myHtmlTable.Visible = False
23:      WelcomeMsg.Text = "Welcome, " & _
24:        Prefix.SelectedItem.Text & " " & _
25:        Name.Text & "!"
26:    End Sub
27:
28: End Class
```

In Listing 16.1.4, we create the `Welcome` class (16.1.4.vb) that the Web Form in Listing 16.1.3 (16.1.3.aspx) inherits from. We import all the necessary namespaces to provide the functionality we are building. Inside of the class definition, we declare objects for only the server controls we need programmatic access to. You will notice in Listing 16.1.3 that we have a `RequiredFieldValidator` control, on line 14, but we do not declare an object for it in the Code-Behind class. This is because we have no need to access the `RequiredFieldValidator` control programmatically.

In the `Page_Load()` event handler on lines 15–19, we set the `<table>` element's `Visible` property to `True` if the request is not the result of a form post (`Page.IsPostBack`).

In Listing 16.1.3 on lines 25 and 26, we created an ASP.NET `Button` control that references the `Submit_OnClick()` method as its event handler. In the Code-Behind class, we created a `Submit_OnClick()` event handler (lines 21–26). In the `Submit_OnClick()` event handler, we set the `HtmlTable` control's `Visible` property to `False` (to prevent it from rendering to the client) and use the `TextBox` and `DropDownList` values to create a "Welcome" message. The message is rendered to the client in a `Label` control on lines 23–25. Figure 16.3 shows the Web Form when it is first requested and a postback is attempted without filling in the `Name` value.

FIGURE 16.3
When the Web Form is first requested, the `Page_Load()` event handler is triggered and the `HtmlTable` control's `Visible` property is set to `True` (the default) and the Name text box is empty.

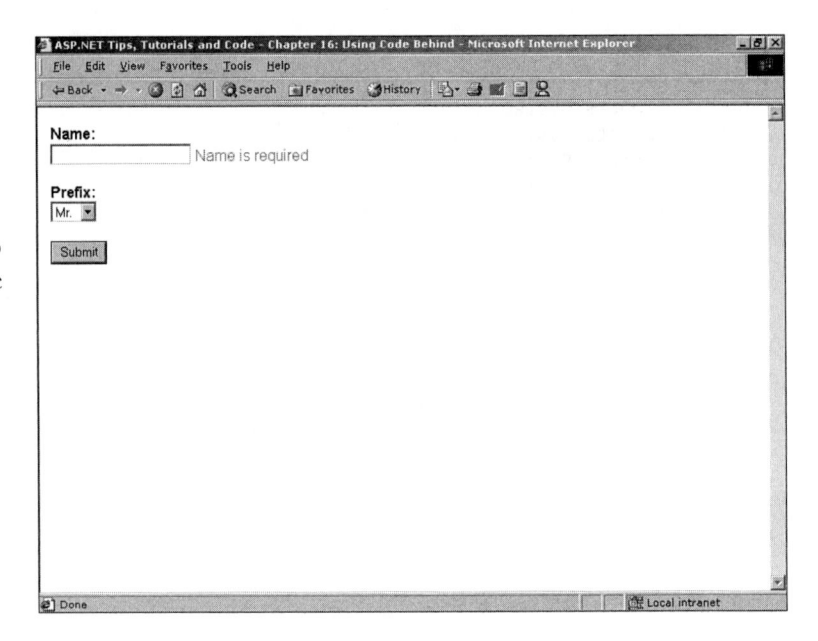

Even though we never referenced the `RequiredFieldValidator` control for the Code-Behind class, it still performs its built-in functions. Not every control needs to be declared in the Code-Behind file—only those we need programmatic access to.

Once the form is filled out and a form post occurs when the submit button is clicked, the `Submit_OnClick()` event handler is triggered. The `HtmlTable` control is not rendered and a welcome message is displayed. This is shown in Figure 16.4.

Code-Behind Techniques for User Controls

Using Code Behind with a user control is nearly identical to using Code Behind with a Web Form. All the same rules apply, such as declaring objects for each control we want programmatic access to. The primary differences are as follows:

- Using the `@ Control` directive instead of `@ Page`
- Inheriting from the `UserControl` class rather than the `Page` class
- Declaring objects in Code Behind for user controls that expose properties

FIGURE 16.4
When the Web Form is filled in correctly and submitted, the `Submit_OnClick()` event handler in the Code-Behind class is triggered.

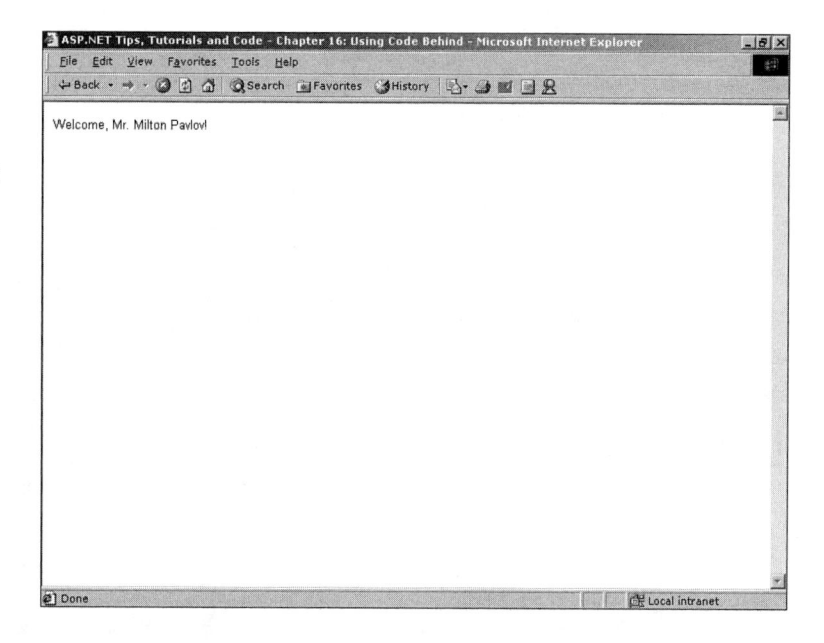

Using the `@ Control` Directive with User Controls

When we were building Web Forms using the Code-Behind technique, we used the `@ Page` directive to specify the Code-Behind class and the optional `Src` attribute to specify the path to the Code-Behind file. With a user control, the `Inherits` and `Src` attributes are still used, but they are used with the `@ Control` directive. Here's an example:

```
<%@ Control Inherits="[className]" Src="[path to class file]" %>
```

The `@ Control` directive is used with user controls to indicate to the .NET Framework that the file being parsed and compiled is a `Control` rather than a `Page`.

Inheriting from the `UserControl` Class

In the Code-Behind class of a Web Form, we inherited the `Page` class to give our Code-Behind class all the functionality of the `Page` class. In a user control's Code Behind, the same principal applies; however, we inherit the `UserControl` class to give our class all the functionality of that class.

Listing 16.1.5 shows a Web Form, 16.1.5.aspx, that, using the `@ Register` directive, has a user control as its only control.

LISTING 16.1.5 Using Code Behind with a User Control—Part 1

```
 1: <%@ Register TagPrefix="dotnetjunkies" TagName="myUserControl"
➥       src="16.1.6.ascx" %>
 2: <html>
 3: <body>
 4: <dotnetjunkies:myUserControl runat="server" />
 5: </body>
 6: </html>
```

In Listing 16.1.5, we create a Web Form, 16.1.5.aspx, that registers a user control from a file (`16.1.6.ascx`) in the same directory. Listing 16.1.6 shows the user control's presentation file, 16.1.6.ascx.

LISTING 16.1.6 Using Code Behind with a User Control—Part 2

```
 1: <%@ Control Inherits="myCodeBehind_1617" Src="16.1.7.vb" %>
 2: <asp:DataGrid runat="server" id="myDataGrid"
 3:     Width="740"
 4:     BorderColor="black"
 5:     ShowFooter="false"
 6:     Font-Name="Verdana"
 7:     Font-Size="10pt"
 8:     HeaderStyle-BackColor="Black"
 9:     HeaderStyle-ForeColor="White"
10: />
```

In Listing 16.1.6, we create the user control, 16.1.6.ascx, that is used in the Web Form in Listing 16.1.5. On line 1 of the user control, we use the `@ Control` directive to inherit the `myCodeBehind_1617` class defined in the Code-Behind file `16.1.7.vb` (as defined in the `Src` attribute). Listing 16.1.7 shows the Code-Behind file (`16.1.7.vb`).

LISTING 16.1.7 Using Code Behind with a User Control—Part 3

```
 1: Imports System
 2: Imports System.Data
 3: Imports System.Data.SqlClient
 4: Imports System.Web
 5: Imports System.Web.UI
 6: Imports System.Web.UI.WebControls
 7: Imports System.Web.UI.HtmlControls
 8:
 9: Public Class myCodeBehind_1617 : Inherits UserControl
10:
11:     Public myDataGrid As DataGrid
12:
13:     Public Sub Page_Load(Sender As Object, E As EventArgs)
14:        Dim myDataAdapter As SqlDataAdapter
15:        Dim myDataSet As New DataSet
16:
17:        myDataAdapter = New SqlDataAdapter("SELECT TOP 10 CustomerID,
➥   CompanyName, ContactName, ContactTitle FROM Customers", _
```

LISTING 16.1.7 Continued

```
18:            "server=localhost;database=Northwind;uid=sa;pwd=;")
19:        myDataAdapter.Fill(myDataSet, "Customers")
20:
21:        myDataGrid.DataSource = myDataSet.Tables("Customers")
22:        myDataGrid.DataBind()
23:     End Sub
24:
25: End Class
```

The class in our Code-Behind file is nearly identical to the Code-Behind class we created in Listing 16.1.1 for our Web Form in the previous examples. The only difference is on line 9 of Listing 16.1.7, where we inherit the `UserControl` class rather than the `Page` class. The remainder of the code works the same way. The result of requesting the Web Form (16.1.5.aspx) from Listing 16.1.5 is shown in Figure 16.4.

FIGURE 16.5
Code Behind for a user control works the same as Code Behind with a Web Form.

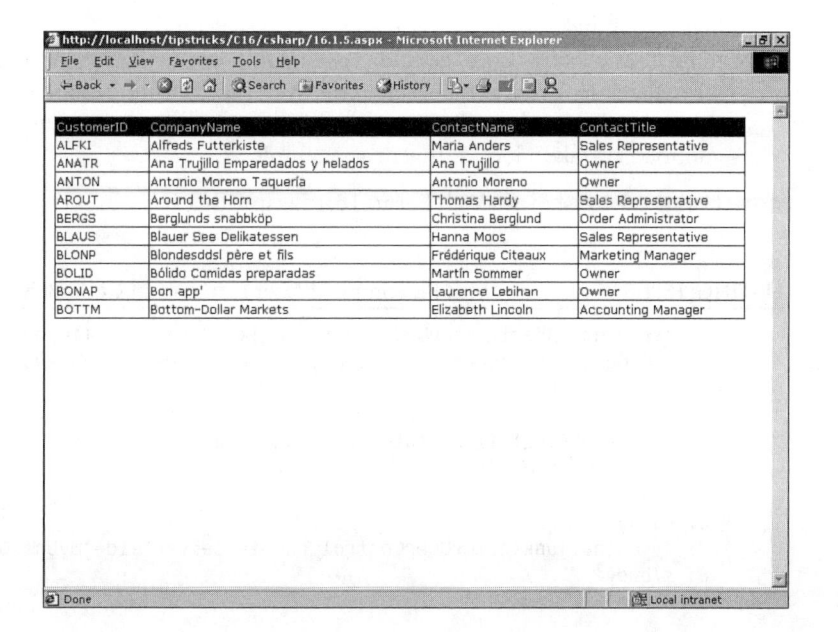

Declaring Objects in Code Behind for User Controls That Expose Properties

In the preceding example, we created a Web Form that has an instance of a user control built using a Code-Behind class. This works fine for basic user controls, but it does not provide us access to any custom properties or methods exposed by our user control. Like with a standard server control, we must create an instance of the user control class in our Web Form's Code-Behind class to gain access to the user control's properties and methods.

We can create an instance of a user control in one of two ways depending on the circumstances. If the user control is precompiled into a DLL, then at compile-time we know the class name of the user control, and the .NET Framework can identify it. With a precompiled user control we can create an instance of the user control's class, like we would any server control, as shown here:

```
Public myUserControl As MyApp.myCodeBehindClass
```

If the user control uses the `Src` attribute, and is not precompiled, then the .NET Framework cannot identify the properties and methods of the user control at compile-time, since the class definition is unknown until it is compiled. In this scenario we must use reflection to discover the properties and methods of the user control. At compile-time the user control does not have a custom class; it is simply an instance of the `UserControl` class. The user control in the Web Form Code-Behind class is instantiated as a `UserControl`, as shown here:

```
Public myUserControl As UserControl
```

Working with Precompiled User Controls

When we build a user control that uses a Code-Behind class, and precompile it we have access to the user control's Code-Behind class at compile time for the Web Form. This means we can instantiate the user control's class in the Web Form's Code-Behind class. By instantiating the user control's class we are given access to any properties and methods exposed by the user control. Lets take a look at this in an example.

Listing 16.1.8 shows a Web Form, 16.1.8.aspx, that has a user control registered.

LISTING 16.1.8 Working With Precompiled User Controls in Code Behind—Part 1

```
1: <%@ Page Inherits="myCodeBehind_16111" Src="16.1.11.vb" %>
2: <%@ Register TagPrefix="dotnetjunkies" TagName="myUserControl"
➥     src="16.1.9.ascx" %>
3: <head>
4: <title>ASP.NET Tips, Tutorials and Code -
➥     Chapter 16: Using Code Behind</title>
5: </head>
6: <body>
7:   <dotnetjunkies:myUserControl runat="server" id="myUserControl1" />
8: </body>
9: </html>
```

In Listing 16.1.8 we create a Web Form that uses a JIT compiled Code-Behind class. On line 2 we register a user control using the `@ Register` directive. On line 7 we place the user control.

Listing 16.1.9 shows the user controls `.ascx` file (`16.1.9.ascx`).

LISTING 16.1.9 Working With Precompiled User Controls in Code Behind—Part 2

```
1: <%@ Control Inherits="myCodeBehind_16110" %>
2: <%-- This User Control's Code-Behind class was precompiled --%>
3: <asp:DataGrid runat="server" id="myDataGrid"
4:   Width="740"
5:   BorderColor="black"
```

LISTING 16.1.9 Continued

```
 6:     ShowFooter="false"
 7:     Font-Name="Verdana"
 8:     Font-Size="10pt"
 9:     HeaderStyle-BackColor="Black"
10:     HeaderStyle-ForeColor="White"
11: />
```

In Listing 16.1.9 we create a user control that renders a `DataGrid`. Note that on line 1 we use the `@ Control` directive to inherit the `myCodeBehind_16110` class. We don't use the `Src` directive because we will be precompiling the user control's Code-Behind class. The user control's Code-Behind class (`16.1.10.vb`) is shown in listing 16.1.10.

LISTING 16.1.10 Working With Precompiled User Controls in Code Behind—Part 3

```
 1: Imports System
 2: Imports System.Data
 3: Imports System.Data.SqlClient
 4: Imports System.Web
 5: Imports System.Web.UI
 6: Imports System.Web.UI.WebControls
 7: Imports System.Web.UI.HtmlControls
 8: Imports System.Drawing
 9:
10: Public Class myCodeBehind_16110 : Inherits UserControl
11:
12:    Public myDataGrid As DataGrid
13:
14:    Public Property GridBackColor As Color
15:       Get
16:          Return myDataGrid.BackColor
17:       End Get
18:
19:       Set
20:          myDataGrid.BackColor = Value
21:       End Set
22:    End Property
23:
23:    Public Sub Page_Load(Sender As Object, E As EventArgs)
25:       Dim myConnection As SqlConnection = New
➡         SqlConnection("server=localhost;database=Northwind;uid=sa;pwd=;")
26:       Dim myCommand As SqlCommand = New
➡         SqlCommand("SELECT TOP 10 CustomerID, CompanyName, ContactName,
➡         ContactTitle FROM Customers", myConnection)
27:       myConnection.Open()
28:       myDataGrid.DataSource = myCommand.ExecuteReader()
29:       myDataGrid.DataBind()
30:       myConnection.Close()
31:    End Sub
32:
33: End Class
```

In Listing 16.1.10 we create the Code-Behind class that the user control (`16.1.9.ascx`) in Listing 16.1.9 uses. In the Code-Behind class we create one public property, `GridBackColor`, on lines 14-22. The `GridBackColor` property takes a `Color` value and applies it to the `BackColor` property of the `DataGrid` server control in the 16.1.9.ascx user control. In the `Page_Load()` event handler on lines 23-31 we retrieve 10 records from the Northwind Customers table. Note this is the same data access code from the previous examples.

To precompile this Code-Behind class into a DLL, open a command line prompt, navigate to the directory that the Code-Behind file (`16.1.10.vb`) is in and execute the following command:

```
vbc.exe /target:library 16.1.10.vb /r:System.dll /r:System.Web.dll
       /r:System.Drawing.dll /r:System.Data.dll /r:System.Xml.dll
```

Executing the Visual Basic.NET command line compiler (`vbc.exe`) will create a DLL named `16.1.10.Dll`. Move this DLL to the `\bin` directory of your Web application.

Now that the DLL is compiled, the `myCodeBehind_16110` Code-Behind class can be referenced directly in the Web Form's Code-Behind class. Listing 16.1.11 shows the Code-Behind class (`16.1.10.vb`) for the Web Form in Listing 16.1.8 (`16.1.8.aspx`)

LISTING 16.1.11 Working With Precompiled User Controls in Code Behind—Part 4

```
 1: Imports System
 2: Imports System.Web
 3: Imports System.Web.UI
 4: Imports System.Web.UI.WebControls
 5: Imports System.Web.UI.HtmlControls
 6: Imports System.Drawing
 7:
 8: Public Class myCodeBehind_16111 : Inherits Page
 9:
10:    Public myUserControl1 As myCodeBehind_16110
11:
12:    Public Sub Page_Load(Sender As Object, E As EventArgs)
13:       myUserControl1.GridBackColor = Color.FromName("LightBlue")
14:    End Sub
15:
16: End Class
```

In Listing 16.1.11 we create the Code-Behind class for the Web Form in Listing 16.1.8. On line 10 we create an instance of the user control's class, `myCodeBehind_16110`. This instance is mapped to the user control in the Web Form, on line 7 of Listing 16.1.8(`myUserControl1`). Since we create an instance of the `myCodeBehind_16110` class, we have direct access to all of its exposed properties and methods, like the `GridBackColor` property. On line 13 we set the `GridBackColor` property using the `Color.FromName()` method.

Working with User Controls That Are JIT Compiled

When we build a user control that uses JIT compilers at run time, we have to use reflection to discover its properties and methods. *Reflection* is the process of discovering object types, properties, and methods. We can use the `System.Reflection` namespace to discover this information about our user control.

In Listing 16.1.12 you create a Web Form (`16.1.12.aspx`) that has one user control and a Code-Behind class.

LISTING 16.1.12 (`16.1.12.aspx`)   Working With JIT Compiled User Controls in Code Behind—Part 1

```
 1: <%@ Page Inherits="myCodeBehind_16115" Src="16.1.15.vb" %>
 2: <%@ Register TagPrefix="dotnetjunkies" TagName="myUserControl"
➥ src="16.1.13.ascx" %>
 3: <head>
 4: <title>ASP.NET Tips, Tutorials and Code -
➥ Chapter 16: Using Code Behind</title>
 5: </head>
 6: <body>
 7:   <dotnetjunkies:myUserControl runat="server" id="myUserControl1" />
 8: </body>
 9: </html>
```

Before we build the Code-Behind class for Listing 16.1.12 (line 01), we'll build the user control. In Listing 16.1.13 you build a user control (`16.1.13.ascx`) similar to the one you built in the previous examples.

LISTING 16.1.13 (`16.1.13.ascx`)   Working With JIT Compiled User Controls in Code Behind—Part 2

```
 1: <%@ Control Inherits="myCodeBehind_16114" Src="16.1.14.vb" %>
 2: <%-- This User Control's Code-Behind class is not precompiled --%>
 3: <asp:DataGrid runat="server" id="myDataGrid"
 4:   Width="740"
 5:   BorderColor="black"
 6:   ShowFooter="false"
 7:   Font-Name="Verdana"
 8:   Font-Size="10pt"
 9:   HeaderStyle-BackColor="Black"
10:   HeaderStyle-ForeColor="White"
11: />
```

In Listing 16.1.13 you build a user control similar to the one you built in previous examples. On line 01 you specify the `Src` attribute of the `@ Control` directive. In Listing 16.1.14 you build the Code-Behind class (16.1.14.vb) for the user control in Listing 16.1.13.

LISTING 16.1.14 (16.1.14.vb)   Working With JIT Compiled User Controls in Code Behind—Part 3

```
 1: Imports System
 2: Imports System.Data
 3: Imports System.Data.SqlClient
 4: Imports System.Web
 5: Imports System.Web.UI
 6: Imports System.Web.UI.WebControls
 7: Imports System.Web.UI.HtmlControls
 8: Imports System.Drawing
 9:
10: Public Class myCodeBehind_16114 : Inherits UserControl
11:
12:    Public myDataGrid As DataGrid
13:
14:    Public Property GridBackColor As Color
15:      Get
16:        Return myDataGrid.BackColor
17:      End Get
18:
19:      Set
20:        myDataGrid.BackColor = Value
21:      End Set
22:    End Property
23:
24:    Public Sub Page_Load(Sender As Object, E As EventArgs)
25:      Dim myConnection As SqlConnection = New
         SqlConnection("server=localhost;database=Northwind;uid=sa;pwd=;")
26:      Dim myCommand As SqlCommand = New
         SqlCommand("SELECT TOP 10 CustomerID, CompanyName, ContactName,
         ContactTitle FROM Customers", myConnection)
27:      myConnection.Open()
28:      myDataGrid.DataSource = myCommand.ExecuteReader()
29:      myDataGrid.DataBind()
30:      myConnection.Close()
31:    End Sub
32:
33: End Class
```

In Listing 16.1.14 you create the Code-Behind class for the user control in Listing 16.1.13. This is the same data access code from Listing 16.1.10.

Now lets get to the guts of this thing. In the Code-Behind class for the Web Form in Listing 16.1.12 you will use reflection to discover the properties of the user control at run-time. In Listing 16.1.15 you build the Code-Behind class (`16.1.15.vb`) for the Web Form.

LISTING 16.1.15 (16.1.15.vb) Working With JIT Compiled User Controls in Code Behind—Part 4

```
 1: Imports System
 2: Imports System.Web
 3: Imports System.Web.UI
 4: Imports System.Web.UI.WebControls
 5: Imports System.Web.UI.HtmlControls
 6: Imports System.Drawing
 7: Imports System.Reflection
 8:
 9: public class myCodeBehind_16115
10:   Inherits Page
11:
12:   Public Sub Page_Load(Sender As Object, E As EventArgs)
13:     Dim myUC As Control = Page.FindControl("myUserControl1")
14:     ' Use the type object from the System.Reflection Namespace
15:     ' to create an object of the user control type
16:     Dim ucType As Type = myUC.GetType()
17:     ' Use the PropertyInfo class to create an object out of the
18:     ' GridBackColor property
19:     Dim uc_GridBackColorProperty As PropertyInfo =
➥       ucType.GetProperty("GridBackColor")
20:     ' Use reflection to set the value of the GridBackColor property
21:     ' and apply it to the user control
22:     uc_GridBackColorProperty.SetValue(myUC,
➥       Color.FromName("LightBlue"), Nothing)
23:   End Sub
24:
25: End Class
```

> **Note**
>
> The files used in Listings 16.1.12–16.1.15 have been duplicated in the C# directory for this chapter. The files in the C# directory use Code Behind written in C#.

In Listing 16.1.15, we dynamically load the user control and use reflection to gain access to its custom `GridBackColor` property. On Line 13 we load the user control into a type-defined variable; we create an instance of a variable, `myUserControl`, as an instance of the `Control` class. We load our user control into the variable. On line 16, we create an instance of the `Type` class and use the `GetType()` method to load the type of the user control into the variable. This loads the class of the user control, `myUserControl_16114`, including custom properties and methods.

The `Type` class exposes a method, `GetProperty()`, which returns a `PropertyInfo` class instance. Using this method on line 19, we create a `PropertyInfo` object for the `GridBackColor` property. We then use the `SetValue()` method of the `PropertyInfo` class, on line 22, to reflect the property value onto the user control.

2. Localization

The .NET Framework provides built-in mechanisms for localizing applications. *Localization* is the process of customizing or translating the separated data and resources needed for a specific region or language. Since the Internet reaches all corners of the world, it may be important for you to create localized versions of some of your content. This may be as simple as ensuring dates and times are presented in a format appropriate for the user, or it may be as much as providing a translated version of your content.

ASP.NET internally uses Unicode, and the `String` class of the .NET Framework also uses Unicode. The use of Unicode enables us to easily specify different localized, culture encoding types, such as `de-DE` for German, for the response data sent to the client. Although the .NET Framework will not translate our documents from the language they are written in to a different language, the built-in mechanisms will reconfigure output, such as `DateTime` objects, to their appropriate format.

Localization is managed through the `System.Globalization` and `System.Threading` namespaces. Culture encoding can be set for an application, for a directory of an application, or for a specific Web Form in an application.

Using the `System.Globalization` Namespace

The `System.Globalization` namespace houses the class libraries for all localization functionality. These class libraries include the various calendar classes, such as `GregorianCalendar`, `HebrewCalendar`, `JulianCalendar`, and so on, as well as the `CultureInfo` class. The latter of these classes is the one we'll be most concerned with.

The `CultureInfo` class provides all the basic functionality for changing the response-encoding format, which manages the various localization structures, such as the language, writing system, and calendar used by a particular culture. As a developer of a Web application that will have a global audience, response-encoding will be very important to you. This will allow you to specify different encoding types for different locales. A locale refers to a collection of rules and data specific to a language and a geographic area. Locales include information on sorting rules, date and time formatting, numeric and monetary conventions, and character classification. For example, you may want to ensure that dates and times are formatted appropriately for each locale that your application caters to. Dates are formatted differently in the USA than they are in many European countries, for example.

The `CultureInfo` class maintains the values for `CurrentCulture` and `CurrentUICulture`.

- `CurrentCulture` indicates the encoding culture used for locale-dependent formatting, such as with dates.

- `CurrentUICulture` indicates the encoding culture used for resource lookups.

The browser's culture settings can be displayed on a Web Form by importing the `System.Globalization` namespace and calling the `EnglishName` property of the `CurrentCulture` and `CurrentUICulture` classes.

```
<%@ Import Namespace="System.Globalization" %>
<%= CultureInfo.CurrentCulture.EnglishName %>
<%= CultureInfo.CurrentUICulture.EnglishName %>
```

The preceding code uses the `Response.Write` shortcut (`<%=...%>`) to render the values of the `CultureInfo.CurrentCulture.EnglishName` property and the `CultureInfo.CurrentUICulture.EnglishName` property. Figure 16.6 shows the result of browsing to this Web Form.

FIGURE 16.6
The `CultureInfo.CurrentCulture.EnglishName` and `CultureInfo.CurrentUICulture.EnglishName` properties indicate the current culture encoding.

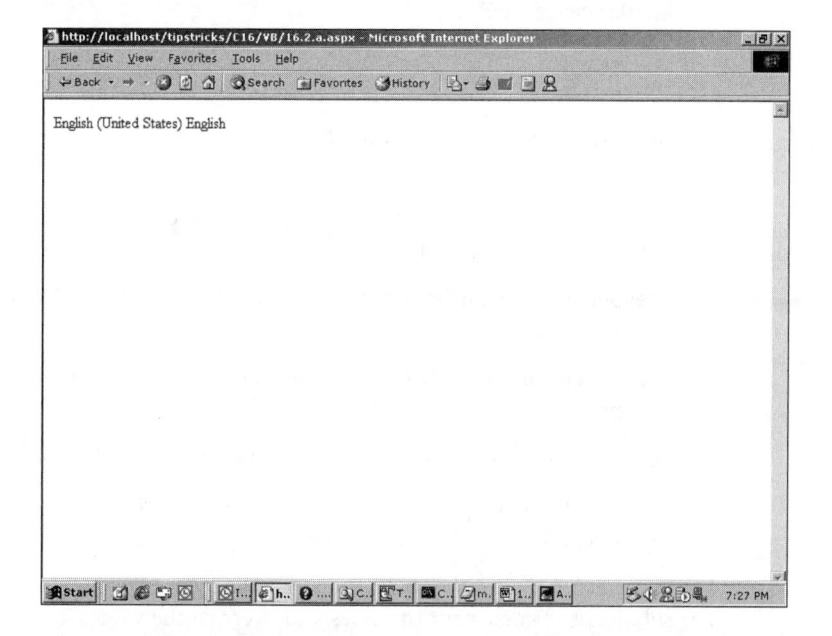

Specifying Character Encodings

Typically when localizing a Web application, you will create duplicate pages for each locale you are catering to. Using the .NET localization functionality, you can format data appropriately. Localization uses standardized character encoding codes, as specified by the Internet RFC 1766, "Tags for the Identification of Languages." The codes are defined by two ISO standards:

- ISO 639, "Code for the representation of names of languages."
- ISO 3166, "Codes for the representation of names of countries."

The character encoding codes are formatted in a culture-region format. English is specified as `en`, and the USA is specified as `US`. To specify the character encoding for the USA we would use `en-US`.

Specification of the character encoding can be managed at an application level by specifying the localization culture in the `Web.config` file, in the `<globalization>` section.

```
<configuration>
  <system.web>
    <globalization
      requestEncoding="utf-8"
      responseEncoding="utf-8"
      fileEncoding="utf-8"
      culture="de-DE"
      uiCulture="de" />
  </system.web>
</configuration>
```

The `<globalization>` section of the `Web.config` file specifies the various encoding options available:

- `requestEncoding`. This specifies the assumed encoding of each incoming request. The default value is "us-ascii."
- `responseEncoding`. This specifies the content encoding of responses. The default value is "iso-8859-1."
- `fileEncoding`. This specifies the default encoding for `.aspx`, `.asmx`, and `.asax` file parsing.
- `culture`. This specifies the default culture for processing incoming Web requests.
- `uiCulture`. This specifies the default culture for processing locale-dependent resource searches.

Any subdirectory below the root can have a `Web.config` file with a `<globalization>` section. The subdirectory's `Web.config` values will override the values in the root directory's `Web.config` file.

To override or set the culture encoding at the page level, we use the `@ Page` directive:

```
<%@ Page Culture="ja-JP" UICulture="ja" ResponseEncoding="utf-8"%>
```

Caution

The same elements used in the `<globalization>` section of the `Web.config` file can be used as attributes of the `@ Page` directive, except `FileEncoding` and `RequestEncoding`. These attributes are default values for the application or a subdirectory of the application and cannot be set at the page level.

Culture encoding can also be set programmatically. By creating an instance of the `CultureInfo` class, we can programmatically change the culture encoding. To send new encoding information to the client, we must import the `System.Threading` namespace. The `System.Threading` namespace gives us access to the `CurrentCulture` property of the `CurrentThread` object:

`Thread.CurrentThread.CurrentCulture = [CultureInfo instance]`

Listing 16.2.1 shows the presentation file (`.aspx`) for a Web Form that we will use to implement the `CultureInfo` class.

LISTING 16.2.1 Implementing the `CultureInfo` Class—Part 1

```
 1: <%@ Page Inherits="myCodeBehind_1622" Src="16.2.2.vb"
        ResponseEncoding="utf-8" %>
 2: <html>
 3: <head>
 4:  <title>Using Localization in ASP.NET</title>
 5: </head>
 6: <body style="font: x-small Verdana, Arial, sans-serif;">
 7: <form runat="server" method="post">
 8:    <b>The Current Culture is:</b>
 9:    <asp:Label runat="server" id="cultureType" />
10:
11:    <p><b>Choose your encoding:</b>
12:    <asp:DropDownList runat="server" id="EncodType" AutoPostBack="True">
13:      <asp:ListItem Value="en-US" Text="English" />
14:      <asp:ListItem Value="fr-FR" Text="French" />
15:      <asp:ListItem Value="de-DE" Text="German" />
16:      <asp:ListItem Value="ja-JP" Text="Japanese" />
17:      <asp:ListItem Value="es-MX" Text="Spanish (Mexican)" />
18:      <asp:ListItem Value="zh-TW" Text="Chinese (Taiwan)" />
19:      <asp:ListItem Value="uk-UA" Text="Ukrainian (Ukraine)" />
20:    </asp:DropDownList>
21:    </p>
22:
23:    <asp:DataGrid runat="server" id="myDataGrid"
24:      Width="740"
25:      BorderColor="black"
26:      ShowFooter="false"
27:      Font-Name="Verdana"
28:      Font-Size="8pt"
29:      HeaderStyle-BackColor="Black"
30:      HeaderStyle-ForeColor="White"
31:      AutoGenerateColumns="False">
32:
```

LISTING 16.2.1 Continued

```
33:     <Columns>
34:       <asp:BoundColumn DataField="FirstName" HeaderText="First Name" />
35:       <asp:BoundColumn DataField="LastName" HeaderText="Last Name" />
36:       <asp:BoundColumn DataField="BirthDate" DataFormatString="{0:D}"
37:         HeaderText="Birth Date" />
38:       <asp:BoundColumn DataField="HireDate" DataFormatString="{0:D}"
39:         HeaderText="Hire Date" />
40:     </Columns>
41:   </asp:DataGrid>
42: </form>
43: </body>
44: </html>
```

In Listing 16.2.1, we create the presentation file for a Web Form that will display a label (line 9), a drop-down list (lines 12–20), and a data grid (lines 23–41). The data grid will display information from the Employees table of the Northwind database. The information displayed includes both birth date and hire date. We will use the `CultureInfo` class to programmatically alter the format of the two date fields.

Listing 16.2.2 shows the Code-Behind file that accompanies the Web Form.

LISTING 16.2.2 Implementing the `CultureInfo` Class—Part 2

```
 1: Imports System
 2: Imports System.Data
 3: Imports System.Data.SqlClient
 4: Imports System.Web
 5: Imports System.Web.UI
 6: Imports System.Web.UI.WebControls
 7: Imports System.Web.UI.HtmlControls
 8: Imports System.Globalization
 9: Imports System.Threading
10:
11: Public Class myCodeBehind_1622 : Inherits Page
12:
13:   Public myDataGrid As DataGrid
14:   Public EncodType As DropDownList
15:   Public cultureType As Label
16:
17:   Public Sub Page_Load(Sender As Object, E As EventArgs)
18:     Dim culture As CultureInfo
19:     Dim myDataAdapter As SqlDataAdapter
20:     Dim myDataSet As New DataSet
21:
22:     If Not Page.IsPostBack Then
23:       culture = CultureInfo.CurrentCulture
```

LISTING 16.2.2 Continued

```
24:      Else
25:        culture = New CultureInfo(EncodType.SelectedItem.Value)
26:        Thread.CurrentThread.CurrentCulture = culture
27:      End If
28:
29:      cultureType.Text = culture.EnglishName
30:
31:      myDataAdapter = New SqlDataAdapter("Select LastName, FirstName,
➥          BirthDate, HireDate From Employees", _
32:         "server=localhost;database=Northwind;uid=sa;pwd=;")
33:      myDataAdapter.Fill(myDataSet, "Employees")
34:
35:      myDataGrid.DataSource = myDataSet.Tables("Employees")
36:      myDataGrid.DataBind()
37:    End Sub
38:
39: End Class
```

On line 8 of Listing 16.2.2, we import the `System.Globalization` namespace to gain access to the `CultureInfo` class. The `System.Threading` namespace is imported on line 9 to gain access to the `Thread` class. We create an instance of the `CultureInfo` class on line 18. Using an If...Then statement on lines 22–27, we set the instance of the `CultureInfo` class to either the default culture (on the first page request) by using the `CurrentCulture` property or to the culture specified in the drop-down list on a form post.

On line 25, we set the instance of the `CultureInfo` class to a new instance of the `CultureInfo` class (using the `CultureInfo` constructor) defined by the encoding type selected in the drop-down list. To set this new `CultureInfo` object as the current culture used for the response to the client, we must access the current thread and set the value there. This is done on line 26 by accessing the `Thread` class's `CurrentThread` class. In the `CurrentThread` class, we set the `CurrentCulture` property to our new instance of the `CultureInfo` class.

Lastly, on line 29, we set the `Label.Text` property to display the `CultureInfo.CurrentCulture.EnglishName` property. This displays the culture value in English.

Figure 16.7 shows the Web Form created in Listings 16.2.1 and 16.2.2 after a form post has occurred, changing the current culture to Hebrew (Israel).

FIGURE 16.7
Using the `Threading` namespace, we set the new culture info for the request.

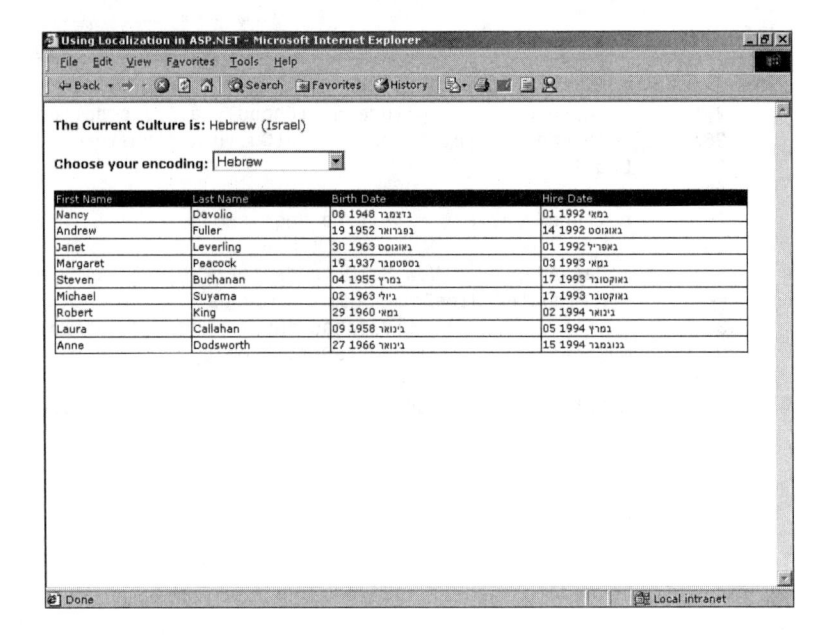

3. Using Resource Files

In the previous section, we looked at implementing localization in ASP.NET through the `System.Globalization` namespace and through character encodings. ASP.NET can also use resource files to customize Web Form output for a specific culture encoding. *Resource files* are files of non-executable data. Resource files can contain key/value pairs of data, such as strings, images, or other data types, that render differently depending on the culture encoding of the requesting client.

In the previous examples, we used the `CultureInfo` class to localize a Web Form and alter the rendering of `DateTime` objects. This was all managed for us by the .NET Framework once we specified the current culture value. Although the `DateTime` objects were rendered appropriately for the requesting client, other parts of the Web Form remained unchanged. Items such as column headings in the data grid remained in English even when, as in Figure 16.7, the Hebrew encoding was used.

Resource files provide a means for managing key/value pairs of data that are to be displayed differently based on the culture encoding specified. This is done by creating separate `.resources` files. A base `.resources` file is created specifying all the key/value pairs defined in the application. Separate `.resources` files are created for each separate culture encoding that will be handled. For instance, we may have a base `.resources` file with key/value pairs in English. We would also have `.resources` files for de-DE (German) encoding, es-MX (Spanish-Mexican) encoding, and so on. To create a `.resources` file, you use the ResGen utility shipped with the .NET Framework SDK. The ResGen utility takes a `.txt` (text) or a `.resx` (XML-based) resource file and creates a `.resources` file.

Let's start by creating a basic text resource file. Listing 16.3.1 shows a resource file in English.

LISTING 16.3.1   A Base Resource File, `myResourceFile.txt`

```
 1: [strings]
 2: ;
 3: ; lines beginning with semi-colons are treated as comments
 4: ;
 5: ; Specify a locale-specific welcome message
 6: Greeting = Welcome!
 7: ;
 8: ; Create locale-specific header text for our DataGrid
 9: FirstName = First Name
10: LastName = Last Name
11: BirthDate = Birth Date
12: HireDate = Hire Date
13: ;
14: ; Create locale-specific text for our Label
15: EncMessage = Choose your encoding:
```

Save the code from Listing 16.3.1 as `myResourceFile.txt` to a subdirectory named `resources` just below your root directory.

Next, to create a `.resources` file from the `myResourceFile.txt` file created in Listing 16.3.1, use the ResGen utility. From a command-line prompt, navigate to the `/resources` directory (`cd [path to resources sub-directory]`) and execute the following command:

`resgen myResourceFile.txt`

ResGen takes in the `.txt` (or `.resx`) file and creates a binary file with the same name, using the extension `.resources`.

Now that we have a `.resources` file, we can we build a Web Form that will use the key/value pairs created in that file. To bring in these values, we use an instance of the **ResourceManager** class. The **ResourceManager** class will be constructed with a reference to the name of our base resource file and its path. As we add new resource files for different encoding types (such as de-DE or es-MX) the **ResourceManager** class will adapt and provide the appropriate values with no additional coding from us.

Listing 16.3.2 shows the Web Form presentation file that utilizes our `.resources` file.

LISTING 16.3.2   Using a Resource File from a Web Form

```
 1: <%@ Page Inherits="myCodeBehind_1633" Src="16.3.3.vb"
➥    ResponseEncoding="utf-8" %>
 2: <html>
 3: <head>
 4:    <title>Using Resource Files in ASP.NET</title>
 5: </head>
 6: <body style="font: x-small Verdana, Arial, sans-serif;">
 7: <form runat="server" method="post">
 8:    <b>The Current Culture is:</b>
 9:    <asp:Label runat="server" id="CultureType" />
10:    <hr>
11:
```

LISTING 16.3.2 *Continued*

```
12:     <p><b><asp:Label runat="server" id="Welcome" /></b></p>
13:     <p><b><asp:Label runat="server" id="Choose" /></b>
14:
15:     <asp:DropDownList runat="server" id="EncodType" AutoPostBack="True">
16:       <asp:ListItem Value="en-US" Text="English" />
17:       <asp:ListItem Value="en-NZ" Text="English (New Zealand)" />
18:       <asp:ListItem Value="fr-FR" Text="French" />
19:       <asp:ListItem Value="de-DE" Text="German" />
20:       <asp:ListItem Value="he-IL" Text="Hebrew" />
21:       <asp:ListItem Value="ja-JP" Text="Japanese" />
22:       <asp:ListItem Value="es-MX" Text="Spanish (Mexican)" />
23:       <asp:ListItem Value="uk-UA" Text="Ukrainian (Ukraine)" />
24:     </asp:DropDownList>
25:     </p>
26:
27:     <asp:DataGrid runat="server" id="myDataGrid"
28:       Width="740"
29:       BorderColor="black"
30:       ShowFooter="false"
31:       Font-Name="Verdana"
32:       Font-Size="8pt"
33:       HeaderStyle-BackColor="Black"
34:       HeaderStyle-ForeColor="White"
35:       AutoGenerateColumns="False">
36:
37:     <Columns>
38:       <asp:BoundColumn DataField="FirstName" />
39:       <asp:BoundColumn DataField="LastName" />
40:       <asp:BoundColumn DataField="BirthDate" DataFormatString="{0:D}" />
41:       <asp:BoundColumn DataField="HireDate" DataFormatString="{0:D}" />
42:     </Columns>
43:     </asp:DataGrid>
44: </form>
45: </body>
46: </html>
```

On line 1 of Listing 16.3.2, we use the `ResponseEncoding` attribute of the `@ Page` directive, setting `ResponseEncoding` to `utf-8` to encode Unicode characters with the UTF8 encoding scheme (UCS Transformation Format, 8-bit form). UTF8 encoding will allow us to render foreign language characters, such as Japanese or Hebrew characters. On line 9, we placed a Label control that will display the current culture encoding type. On lines 12 and 13, we placed two Label controls that will render culture-specific information.

On the DataGrid server control, we have used the `<Columns>` element to create a custom column layout. This is primarily so we can alter the header text of each column for the appropriate culture encoding.

Listing 16.3.3 shows the Code-Behind file associated with the Web Form in Listing 16.3.2.

LISTING 16.3.3 Using Resource Files in Code Behind

```vb
 1: Imports System
 2: Imports System.Data
 3: Imports System.Data.SqlClient
 4: Imports System.Web
 5: Imports System.Web.UI
 6: Imports System.Web.UI.WebControls
 7: Imports System.Web.UI.HtmlControls
 8: Imports System.Globalization
 9: Imports System.Threading
10: Imports System.Resources
11: Imports System.IO
12:
13: Public Class myCodeBehind_1633 : Inherits Page
14:
15:    Public myDataGrid As DataGrid
16:    Public EncodType As DropDownList
17:    Public CultureType As Label
18:    Public Choose As Label
19:    Public Welcome As Label
20:    Public rm As ResourceManager = _
       ResourceManager.CreateFileBasedResourceManager("myResourceFile", _
       Server.MapPath("/resources") & Path.DirectorySeparatorChar, _
       Nothing)
21:
22:    Public Sub Page_Load(Sender As Object, E As EventArgs)
23:       Dim culture As CultureInfo
24:       Dim myDataAdapter As SqlDataAdapter
25:       Dim myDataSet As New DataSet
26:
27:       If Not Page.IsPostBack Then
28:          culture = CultureInfo.CurrentCulture
28:       Else
29:          culture = New CultureInfo(EncodType.SelectedItem.Value)
30:          Thread.CurrentThread.CurrentCulture = culture
31:       End If
32:
33:       CultureType.Text = culture.EnglishName
34:       Welcome.Text = rm.GetString("Greeting", culture)
35:       Choose.Text = rm.GetString("EncMessage", culture)
36:
37:       myDataGrid.Columns(0).HeaderText = rm.GetString("FirstName", culture)
38:       myDataGrid.Columns(1).HeaderText = rm.GetString("LastName", culture)
39:       myDataGrid.Columns(2).HeaderText = rm.GetString("BirthDate", culture)
40:       myDataGrid.Columns(3).HeaderText = rm.GetString("HireDate", culture)
41:
42:       myDataAdapter = New SqlDataAdapter("Select LastName, FirstName, _
          BirthDate, HireDate From Employees", _
43:          "server=localhost;database=Northwind;uid=sa;pwd=;")
44:       myDataAdapter.Fill(myDataSet, "Employees")
45:
46:       myDataGrid.DataSource = myDataSet.Tables("Employees")
47:       myDataGrid.DataBind()
```

LISTING 16.3.3 Continued

```
48:     End Sub
49:
50: End Class
```

In Listing 16.3.3, we build off the examples used previously in the "Localization" section of this chapter. On line 10, we import the `System.Resources` namespace to gain access to the `ResourceManager` class, followed by the `System.IO` namespace for access to the `Path` class. On line 20, we create a class-level instance of the `ResourceManager` class. When using the `ResourceManager` constructor, we create a `ResourceManager` object that looks to a specific directory for .resources files rather than referencing an assembly manifest. This is done with the `CreateFileBasedResourceManager()` shared method. We pass in the base resource filename (or the *root name* of the resource files), the path to the resource files, and the type of a custom resource set (`Null` or `Nothing` cause the default runtime resource set to be used).

Once we have a `ResourceManager` object, we can retrieve values from our resource files using the `GetString()` method. The `GetString()` method can take one or two parameters: a string value that is the name of the key to retrieve or a `CultureInfo` object for the requested culture encoding. If no `CultureInfo` object is passed in, the current `UICulture` will be used.

On line 34, we set the Welcome label's `Text` property to the return value of `ResourceManager.GetString("Greeting", culture)`, where *culture* is a `CultureInfo` object built on the selected culture encoding. The result of this method call is a string value from the appropriate resource file. So far we have only created one resource file—our base resource file. At this point, if we browse to the Web Form and choose a language from the drop-down list, the only thing that would change is the `DataTime` objects in the data grid. They are, after all, handled by the localization code from previous examples. Figure 16.8 shows the requested Web Form.

FIGURE 16.8
When the Web Form is requested, the `ResourceManager` object retrieves the key/value pairs from the resource files based on the requested encoding.

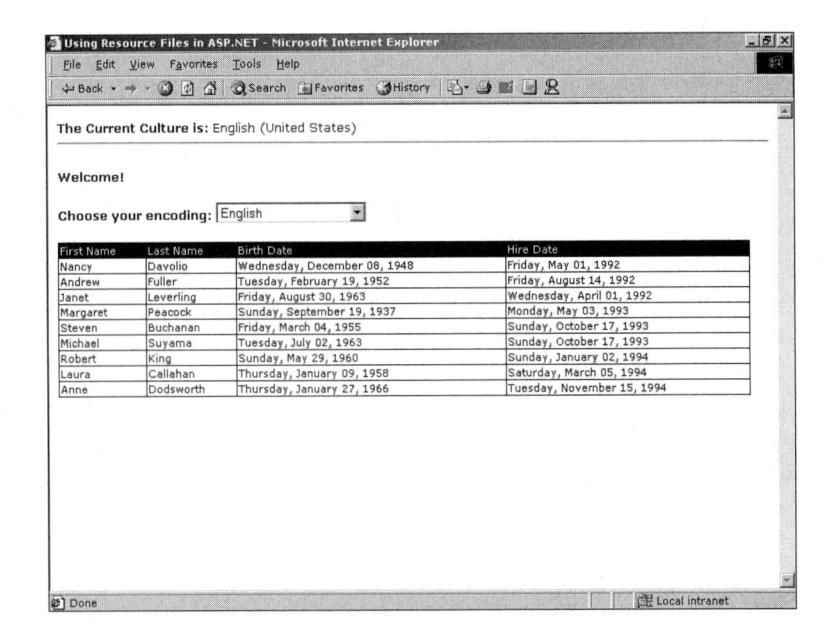

In Listing 16.3.4, we create another resource file. This resource file will be used for the de-DE (German) encoding.

LISTING 16.3.4 A Resource File for de-DE (German) Encoding, `myResourceFile.de-DE.txt`

```
1: [strings]
2: Greeting = Willkommen!
3: FirstName = Vorname
4: LastName = Familienname
5: BirthDate = Geburtsdatum
6: HireDate = Miete-Datum
7: EncMessage = Wählen Sie Ihre Verschlüsselung:
```

Save the de-DE resource file as `myResourceFile.de-DE.txt` in the `/resources` directory of your Web application.

> **Note**
>
> For resource files to work, they must all use the same base name—the name of the base resource file. They should then be appended with a second node specifying the culture encoding, such as "de-DE" for German.

Use the ResGen utility to create a `.resources` file:

`resgen myResourceFile.de-DE.txt`

Now when you browse to the Web Form and select German from the drop-down list, the `CultureInfo` class is constructed using the de-DE encoding, and the `ResourceManager` class automatically knows to retrieve the string values from the `myResourceFile.de-DE.resources` file rather than from the base resource file. The result is that all the key/value pairs in the resource file are used to render localized content on the Web Form. Additional resource files can be added and no additional code is necessary to enable them.

> **Note**
>
> Additional resource files for es-MX (Spanish-Mexican), en-NZ (English-New Zealand), and fr-FR (French) are available in the Chapter 16 directory on the CD.

Figure 16.9 shows the same Web Form after a resource file for the de-DE encoding is added and German is selected from the drop-down list.

FIGURE 16.9
You can add resource files to automatically handle different culture encodings without having to write any additional code.

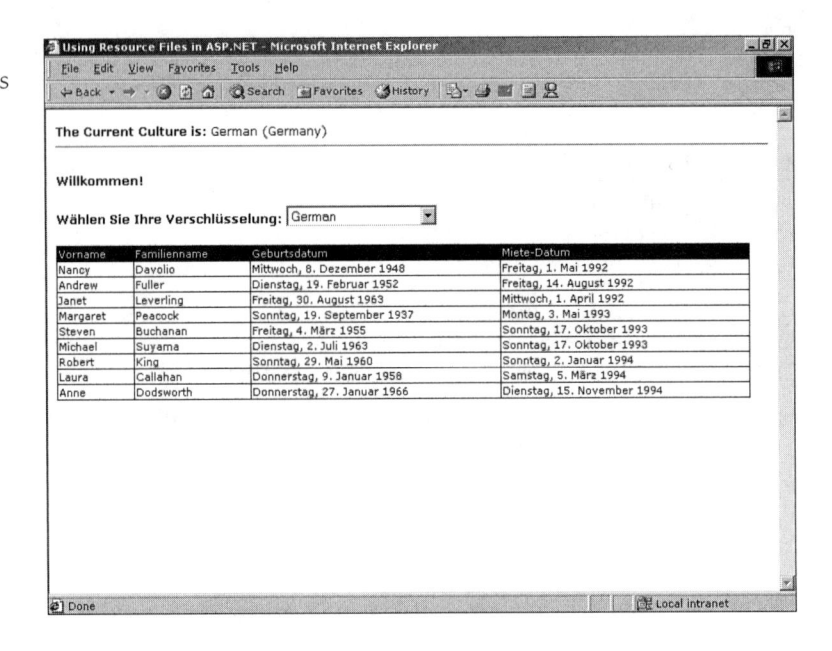

If there is not a resource file for a particular culture encoding, the base resource file will be used. If there is a resource file for the culture encoding but a key/value pair does not exist, the key/value pair from the base resource file will be used.

In Listing 16.3.5, we create a resource file for the en-NZ (English-New Zealand) culture encoding.

LISTING 16.3.5 A Resource File for a Similar-Language Culture Encoding

```
1: [strings]
2: Greeting = Good Day!
```

In Listing 16.3.5, we create a resource file that has only one key/value pair. All other key/value pairs will be used from the base resource file. Once we create the `.resources` file for Listing 16.3.5 (`resgen myResourceFile.en-NZ.txt`), we can browse the Web Form using the en-NZ encoding. Figure 16.10 shows the Web Form using the `Greeting` key/value pair from the en-NZ resource file and the other key/value pairs for the base resource file.

FIGURE 16.10
If no key/value pairs exist, the key/value pairs from the base resource file will be used.

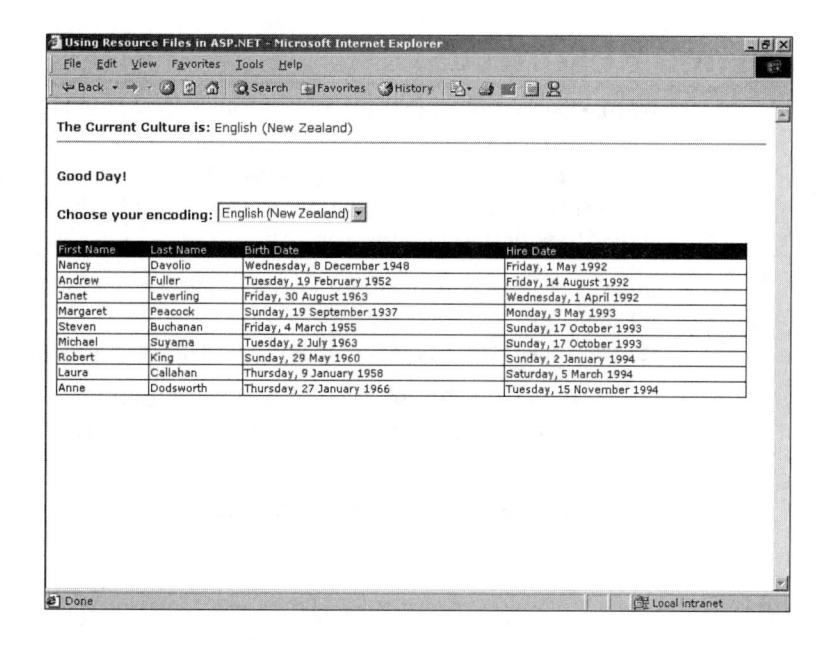

Summary

In this chapter you learned how to use Code-Behind techniques for ASP.NET Web Forms and user controls. By creating separate Code-Behind files and classes, you enable your Web Form or user control to inherit the programmatic functionality of the Code-Behind class. This enables you to maintain the presentation logic in one file and the programmatic code in another file. By declaring class instances of server controls in the Code-Behind class, you gain access to all the exposed properties and methods of the server controls.

Additionally, you learned how to localize a Web application using the `CultureInfo` class. With the `CultureInfo` class and the `CurrentThread` class, you are able to programmatically set the culture encoding to format culture-specific content, such as date formats. By incorporating resource files and the `ResourceManager` class, you are able to provide more culture-specific content. You can add new resource files for culture encodings at any time without having to write any new code.

Other Resources

- www.DotNetJunkies.com. This ASP.NET-focused site, authored and maintained by authors Doug Seven and Donny Mack, provides a plethora of information about ASP.NET for developers of any skill level. The site includes tutorials on getting started with ASP.NET and a repository for Web services and .NET components!
  http://www.DotNetJunkies.com

- Library of Congress standard for ISO639-2, "Codes for the Representation of the Names of Languages"
  http://lcweb.loc.gov/standards/iso639-2/langhome.html

- Language Codes: ISO 639, Microsoft and Macintosh
  http://www.unicode.org/unicode/onlinedat/languages.html

- Text of RFC 1766
  http://www.freesoft.org/CIE/RFC/Orig/rfc1766.txt

CHAPTER 17

MOBILE CONTROLS

by Steve Walther

In this chapter, you will learn
- How to configure Internet Information Server to work with WML files
- How to create multiple mobile forms in a single page
- How to display interactive lists of information
- How to accept and validate user input
- How to create device compatible mobile ASP.NET pages

*I*n this chapter, you'll learn how to write ASP.NET pages that work with mobile devices such as cellular phones, Pocket PC devices, and the Palm Pilot Web browser.

First, you'll be provided with an overview of the Wireless Application Protocol (WAP), a standard for communicating with wireless devices. You'll also learn the basics of the Wireless Markup Language (WML), the wireless version of HTML.

Next, you'll learn how to leverage your existing ASP.NET skills to create ASP.NET pages that generate content compatible with mobile devices. You'll be given an overview of the controls included with the Microsoft Mobile Internet Toolkit.

Finally, you'll learn how to create ASP.NET pages that are cross-device compatible. You'll learn how to detect features of specific devices and exploit their special capabilities.

1. Using Mobile Device Software Simulators

You can download software simulators for mobile devices so that you can test your ASP.NET pages from the comfort of your desktop computer. These simulators are a lot of fun to use. They display a mock telephone interface so that you can test your pages by clicking phone buttons.

One of the easiest simulators to set up is the one provided by Openwave. The Openwave simulator enables you to display a number of different phones by configuring different skins. For example, you can simulate phones from Samsung, Mitsubishi, and Ericsson by applying the proper skin (see Figure 7.1).

FIGURE 17.1
Openwave simulator with the Alcatel skin.

To download the Openwave phone simulator, go to `http://developer.Openwave.com` and download the UP.SDK. You'll need to register at the site before you can do this.

> **Note**
> Currently, there are two versions of the Openwave UP.SDK available for download: UP.SDK 3.2 and UP.SDK 4.0. The mobile controls have not been tested with every one of these phone simulators. See the .documentation for the Mobile Internet Toolkit for more information.

You also can download phone simulators from Nokia by going to `forum.nokia.com`. The Nokia Wap Toolkit 2.0 includes simulators for the Nokia 7110 phone and a "Blueprint" phone that has no counterpart in the actual world (it's a "concept" phone). Currently, the mobile controls will work only with the Nokia 7110 and not the Blueprint simulator (see Figure 17.2).

Finally, you can use the Microsoft Mobile Explorer version 2.01 software emulator (see Figure 17.3). This simulator is a free download from the Microsoft Web site (go to `www.microsoft.com/mobile/phones/mme/mmemulator.asp`). For installation instructions, see `http://www.microsoft.com/mobile/phones/mme/MME_2.01_Installation.doc`.

FIGURE 17.2
The Nokia 7110 phone simulator.

FIGURE 17.3
The Microsoft Mobile Explorer emulator.

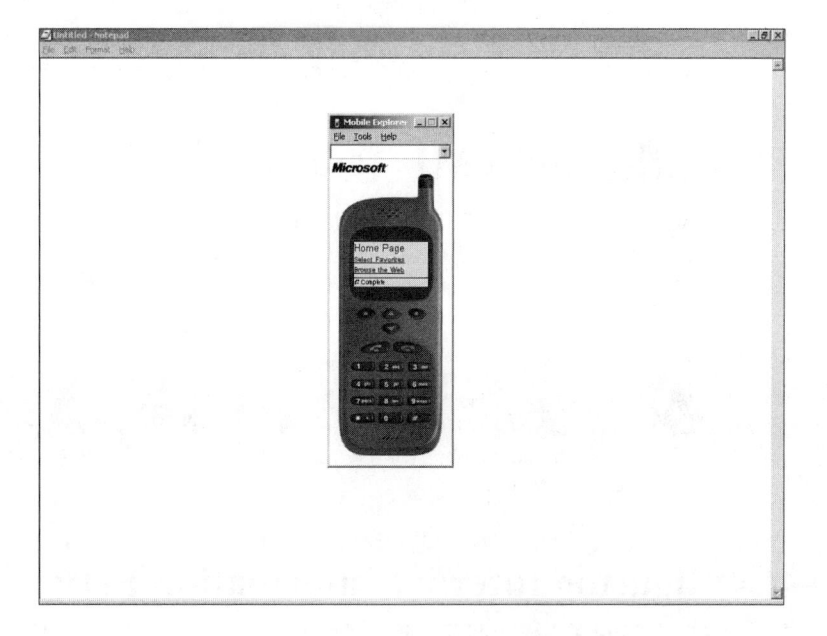

2. Introduction to the Wireless Application Protocol

Developing pages for mobile devices is a very different challenge than developing pages for standard Web browsers. One of the biggest differences is the available screen space. A typical mobile device, such as a cell phone, can display only 15 characters across and four characters down. A typical desktop Web browser, in contrast, can display 80 characters across and 40 characters down.

Another challenge concerns bandwidth. Most mobile devices do not have blazing fast connections to a network. When you use a mobile device, you typically get to enjoy watching each character slowly walk across the network and be displayed on your screen. Therefore, sending pages full of rich graphics and sound effects simply won't work.

In response to the unique characteristics of mobile devices, several alternative protocols to HTML were developed that are tailored specifically for mobile devices. In this chapter, we'll be discussing the Wireless Application Protocol (WAP). The WAP standard is an open standard developed and maintained by the WAP Forum (www.wapforum.org).

The WAP standard encompasses a number of different protocols. It includes a transport-level protocol named *WSP*, which performs the same function in the world of mobile devices that HTTP does on the Internet. It also includes an application level-protocol, the Wireless Markup Language (WML), which performs the same function in the wireless world that HTML does on the Internet.

Strictly speaking, you don't need to know anything about WML to use the mobile controls discussed in this chapter. The controls automatically render the correct WML content for you. However, it helps. The content in a WML file has a special organization, and it is useful to know what is happening under the hood when working with the mobile controls.

3. Building WML Pages

WML is similar to HTML. When building WML pages, you can continue to use familiar tags, such as the <b>, <i>, and <br> tags, with the same effect as in HTML pages. However, there are several significant differences between a WML page and an HTML page. In this section, you'll learn how to create and use simple WML pages.

> **Note**
> You can read the complete specification for WML at the WAP Forum Web site at www.wapforum.org.

Configuring Internet Information Server

You don't need to configure Internet Information Server to use the ASP.NET mobile controls. So, ignore this section if you plan to generate WML content only with the mobile controls. However, if you plan to serve static WML pages directly from your Web site, you'll need to configure Internet Information Server to use an additional MIME type for WML files.

To configure Internet Information Server 5.0 to serve static WML files, follow these steps:

1. Go to Start, Administrative Tools, Internet Services Manager.
2. Open the property sheet for your default Web site.
3. Choose the tab labeled HTTP Headers.
4. Click the button labeled File Types in the MIME Map section.
5. Enter a new file type with the extension `.wml` and content type `text/vnd.wap.wml`.

After you perform these steps, your server will send WML files with the correct MIME type.

WML and XML

Unlike HTML, WML is based on XML (the Extensible Markup Language). This fact has some inconvenient implications.

First, because WML is based on XML and XML is case sensitive, WML is case sensitive. Therefore, using the `<BR>` tag in a page will not have the same effect as using the `<br>` tag. In general, you must use all the tags in lowercase.

Second—and this requirement should be familiar to ASP.NET developers—you must be careful to close all the tags in a WML file. This requirement is very strict. For example, if you use the `<p>` tag, you must end it with a `</p>` tag. If you want to add a line break, you must use the `<br/>` tag. If you neglect to close a tag, an error will be generated.

Finally, all WML files must begin with the following document type declaration:

```
<?xml version="1.0"?>
<!DOCTYPE wml PUBLIC "-//WAPFORUM//DTD WML 1.1//EN"
➥"http:///www.wapforum.org/DTD/wml_1.1.xml">
```

Creating a Deck of Cards

WML uses a card metaphor for organizing content. When you request a WML file, you receive a deck of cards. Each card represents a screen of content.

Why this weird card metaphor? Remember that mobile devices are typically small and slow. You cannot display very much content at a time on a cell phone, and it takes a long time for the content to arrive. Under these circumstances, it makes a lot of sense to transmit multiple screens to a mobile device in a single file.

A WML card corresponds to an HTML page, and a WML deck corresponds to a group of HTML pages. Because a deck is transmitted as a single WML file, WML enables you to transmit multiple pages at a time.

The WML file in Listing 17.3.1 contains a simple WML deck for selecting a movie. (The page is named `selectmovie.wml` on the CD.)

LISTING 17.3.1   Selecting a Movie

```
 1: <?xml version="1.0"?>
 2: <!DOCTYPE wml PUBLIC "-//WAPFORUM//DTD WML 1.1//EN"
 3: "http:///www.wapforum.org/DTD/wml_1.1.xml">
 4:
 5: <wml>
 6:
 7:   <card id="card1" title="Movies">
 8:     <p>
 9:     <b>Select Movie:</b><br/>
10:     <a href="#card2">Star Wars</a><br/>
11:     <a href="#card3">Gone with the Wind</a><br/>
12:     <a href="#card4">Citizen Kane</a>
13:     </p>
14:   </card>
15:
16:   <card id="card2" title="Star Wars">
17:     <p>
18:     You selected:
19:     <b>Star Wars</b><br/>
20:     </p>
21:   </card>
22:
23:   <card id="card3" title="Gone with the Wind">
24:     <p>
25:     You selected:
26:     <b>Gone with the Wind</b><br/>
27:     </p>
28:   </card>
29:
30:   <card id="card4" title="Citizen Kane">
31:     <p>
32:     You selected:
33:     <b>Citizen Kane</b><br/>
34:     </p>
35:   </card>
36:
37: </wml>
```

The WML file in Listing 17.3.1 contains a deck with four cards. The first card has a menu of three movies. Each movie is a link to another card (see Figure 17.4). For example, if you click Star Wars, the contents of the second card are displayed.

When this WML file is transmitted to a cell phone or other mobile device, all the cards are available in the device's memory at the same time. This means that the user can navigate happily between the cards, displaying different screens of information, without performing any additional roundtrips to the server.

FIGURE 17.4
Output of a simple WML file.

Linking Files with WML

You can create a complete application with a single deck of cards. Typically, you'll want to do this for the sake of efficiency. However, you can also create links between decks of cards in separate WML files.

The WML file in Listing 17.3.2 illustrates how you would do this. It contains links to two WML files, named `selectmovie.wml` and `showcontacts.wml`. (This page is named `selectapp.wml` on the CD.)

LISTING 17.3.2 Selecting an Application

```
 1: <?xml version="1.0"?>
 2: <!DOCTYPE wml PUBLIC "-//WAPFORUM//DTD WML 1.1//EN"
 3: "http:///www.wapforum.org/DTD/wml_1.1.xml">
 4:
 5: <wml>
 6:
 7:   <card id="card1" title="app">
 8:     <p>
 9:     <b>Application:</b><br/>
10:     <a href="selectmovie.wml">Movies</a><br/>
11:     <a href="showcontacts.wml">Contacts</a><br/>
12:     </p>
13:   </card>
14:
15: </wml>
```

The card in Listing 17.3.2 functions as a menu. It enables you to pick other applications to execute. Notice that the link is created using standard HTML **HREF** syntax.

4. Using ASP.NET Mobile Controls

The ASP.NET mobile controls were designed to be compatible with a wide variety of mobile devices. The controls will render either WML or HTML content, depending on the device.

For example, if you request a page with a cell phone, the mobile controls will render WML 1.1–compliant content. If you request a page using a Palm Pilot or Pocket PC browser, HTML 3.2 content will be displayed.

You can also display ASP.NET pages that contain mobile controls in Internet Explorer 5.5 (or higher). This is useful for debugging pages because full error messages can be displayed.

To use the mobile controls, you must install the Microsoft Mobile Internet Toolkit. Currently, the .NET Mobile Web SDK is available as a free download from the Microsoft Web site (go to `http://msdn.microsoft.com/net`).

After you install the SDK, you can use the mobile controls in a page by including the following page directives:

```
<%@ Page Inherits="System.Web.UI.MobileControls.MobilePage" %>
<%@ Register TagPrefix="Mobile" Namespace="System.Web.UI.MobileControls"
Assembly="System.Web.Mobile" %>
```

All pages that use the mobile controls must inherit from a Code-Behind page called `System.Web.UI.MobileControls.MobilePage`. The second directive is used to associate the `Mobile` tag prefix with the mobile control namespace.

Creating Mobile Forms

A WML file typically contains multiple cards that represent different screens of content. When you create files with the ASP.NET controls, however, you create multiple screens with forms instead of cards.

> **Caution**
>
> An ASP.NET page that contains mobile controls is unlike a normal ASP.NET page. A normal ASP.NET page, unlike a mobile form page, cannot have more than one form control.

The page in Listing 17.4.1 illustrates how to create a simple page that displays movie choices using the mobile controls. (This page is named `selectmovie.aspx` on the CD.)

LISTING 17.4.1 Selecting a Movie

```
1: <%@ Page Inherits="System.Web.UI.MobileControls.MobilePage" %>
2: <%@ Register TagPrefix="Mobile" Namespace="System.Web.UI.MobileControls"
3: Assembly="System.Web.Mobile" %>
4:
5: <Mobile:Form runat="server" id="form1">
```

LISTING 17.4.1 Continued

```
 6: <b>Select Movie:</b><br/>
 7: <Mobile:Link runat="server" NavigateURL="#form2">Star Wars</Mobile:Link>
 8: <Mobile:Link runat="server" NavigateURL="#form3">Gone with the
➥Wind</Mobile:Link>
 9: <Mobile:Link runat="server" NavigateURL="#form4">Citizen Kane</Mobile:Link>
10: </Mobile:Form>
11:
12: <Mobile:Form runat="server" id="form2">
13: You selected:
14: <b>Star Wars</b>
15: </Mobile:Form>
16:
17: <Mobile:Form runat="server" id="form3">
18: You selected:
19: <b>Gone with the Wind</b>
20: </Mobile:Form>
21:
22: <Mobile:Form runat="server" id="form4">
23: You selected:
24: <b>Citizen Kane</b>
25: </Mobile:Form>
```

The page in Listing 17.4.1 contains four forms. The first form is a menu of three movie choices. Each choice is a link to one of the other three forms on the page. For example, if you click the Star Wars link, the mobile form labeled `form2` is activated and the text "You selected: Star Wars" is displayed (see Figure 17.5).

FIGURE 17.5
A simple mobile ASP.NET page displayed in a cell phone.

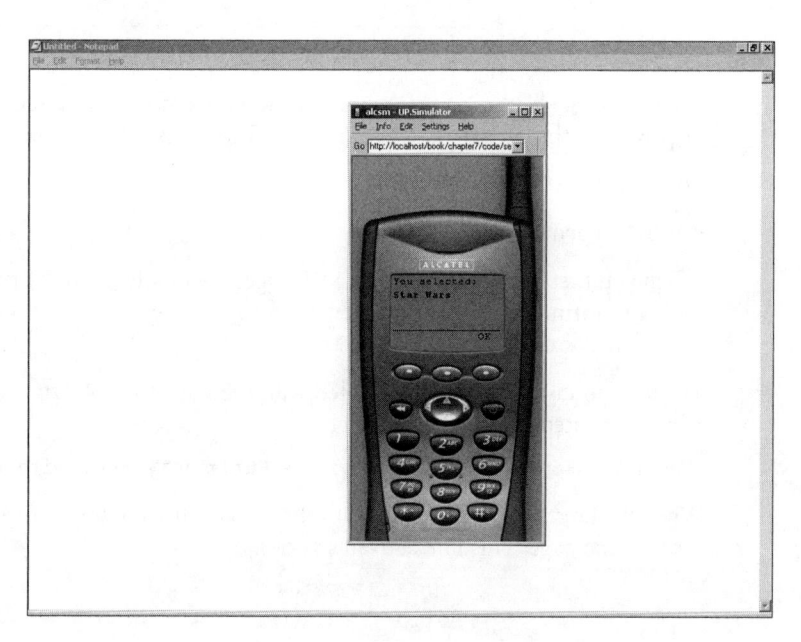

The mobile controls ASP.NET page in Listing 17.4.1 displays almost exactly the same content as the WML file in Listing 17.3.1. However, the page in Listing 17.4.1 will work with many more devices. In fact, Listing 17.4.1 will work with devices that support either WML or HTML 3.2. In addition to cell phones, the page in Listing 17.4.1 is compatible with Internet Explorer 5.5 and the Palm Pilot Web browser (see Figure 17.6).

FIGURE 17.6
A simple mobile ASP.NET page displayed in Internet Explorer 5.5.

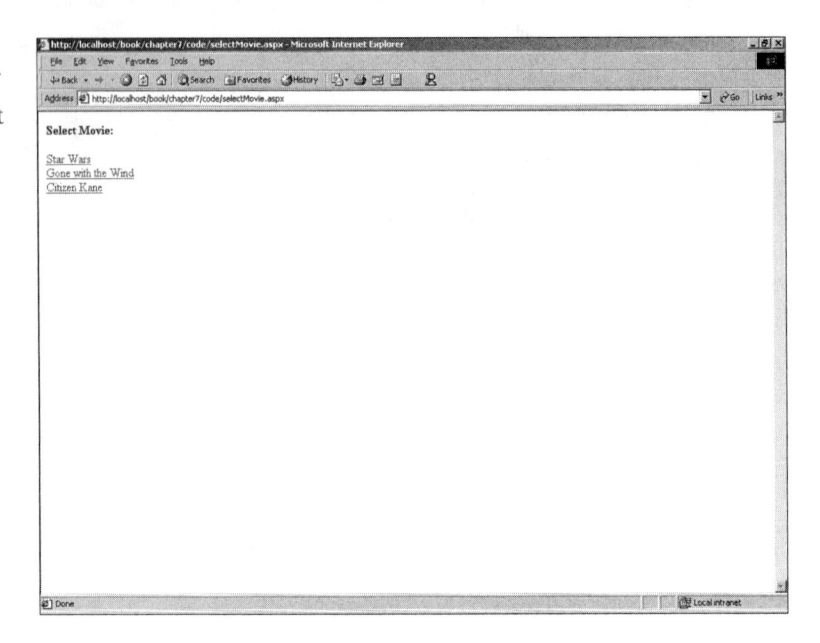

You should notice that each form is created with a mobile form tag. For example, the first form displayed by the page on lines 4-9 is created with the following tag:

```
<Mobile:Form runat="server" id="form1">
...
</Mobile:Form>
```

When you first open a mobile ASP.NET page, the first form in the page automatically becomes the active form. You can cause other forms to become active by linking to them or by modifying a page's `ActiveForm` property.

The links in Listing 17.4.1 are created with the Link control. For example, in line 7, a link to `form3` is created with the following tag:

```
<Mobile:Link runat="server" NavigateURL="#form3">Gone with the Wind</Mobile:Link>
```

When the target of a link begins with the `#` character, the link activates the corresponding form on the page. This link activates `form3`.

Dynamically Activating a Mobile Form

When you include multiple forms in a mobile control page, you can make any of the forms active by using the `ActiveForm` property. For example, the page in Listing 17.4.2 randomly displays one of three forms whenever the page is requested. (This page is included on the CD as `showquote.aspx`.)

LISTING 17.4.2 Showing a Random Quotation

```
 1: <%@ Page Inherits="System.Web.UI.MobileControls.MobilePage" %>
 2: <%@ Register TagPrefix="Mobile" Namespace="System.Web.UI.MobileControls"
 3: Assembly="System.Web.Mobile" %>
 4:
 5: <Script Runat="Server">
 6:
 7: Sub Page_Load( s As Object, e As EventArgs )
 8:   Dim myRand As New Random
 9:   Select Case myRand.Next( 3 )
10:     Case 0
11:       ActiveForm = form0
12:     Case 1
13:       ActiveForm = form1
14:     Case 2
15:       ActiveForm = form2
16:   End Select
17: End Sub
18:
19: </Script>
20:
21: <Mobile:Form runat="server" id="form0">
22: <i>Look before you leap!</i>
23: </Mobile:Form>
24:
25: <Mobile:Form runat="server" id="form1">
26: <i>He who hesitates is lost</i>
27: </Mobile:Form>
28:
29: <Mobile:Form runat="server" id="form2">
30: <i>The early bird gets the worm</i>
31: </Mobile:Form>
```

The page in Listing 17.4.2 randomly displays one of three quotations (see Figure 17.7). Whenever the page is requested, the `Page_Load` subroutine contained in lines 6-16 is executed and one of the three forms in the page is activated. A form is activated using the `ActiveForm` property. Notice that the `ActiveForm` property does not take a string as its value. Because the value is a mobile form control, it does not appear within quotation marks.

FIGURE 17.7
A Random Quotation displayed by a mobile form.

Displaying Text

You have three ways to display text in a mobile form control:

- You can display text directly within a form.
- You can display text in a Label control.
- You can display text within a TextView control.

For example, if you simply need to display some bold text within a form, you can display the text like this:

```
<%@ Page Inherits="System.Web.UI.MobileControls.MobilePage" %>
<%@ Register TagPrefix="Mobile" Namespace="System.Web.UI.MobileControls"
Assembly="System.Web.Mobile" %>

<Mobile:Form runat="server">
Here is some text:
<b>Hello World!</b>
</Mobile:Form>
```

If you want to display a small amount of text without any formatting, and you need to have programmatic access to the text, you can use a Label control. For example, the page in Listing 17.4.3 displays the phrase "Hello World!" in a Label control. (This page is named `label.aspx` on the CD.)

Chapter 17 • MOBILE CONTROLS

LISTING 17.4.3 Displaying Text with a `Label` Control

```
1: <%@ Page Inherits="System.Web.UI.MobileControls.MobilePage" %>
2: <%@ Register TagPrefix="Mobile" Namespace="System.Web.UI.MobileControls"
3: Assembly="System.Web.Mobile" %>
4:
5: <Mobile:Form runat="server">
6: <Mobile:Label Runat="Server" />
7: Hello World!
8: </Mobile:Label>
9: </Mobile:Form>
```

One disadvantage of the `Label` control is that it cannot contain any HTML tags. You cannot use such tags as the `<b>` or `<i>` tags within a `Label` control. You'll receive an error if you try.

The main advantage of a `Label` control is that you can modify the control's content within your code. For example, the page in Listing 17.4.4 displays the current date and time in a `Label` control. (This page is named label2.aspx on the CD.)

LISTING 17.4.4 Displaying Date and Time in a `Label` Control

```
 1: <%@ Page Inherits="System.Web.UI.MobileControls.MobilePage" %>
 2: <%@ Register TagPrefix="Mobile" Namespace="System.Web.UI.MobileControls"
 3: Assembly="System.Web.Mobile" %>
 4:
 5: <Script runat="Server">
 6: Sub Page_Load( s As Object, e As EventArgs )
 7:   myLabel.Text = DateTime.Now
 8: End Sub
 9: </Script>
10:
11: <Mobile:Form runat="server">
12: <Mobile:Label
13:   ID="myLabel"
14:   Runat="Server"/>
15: </Mobile:Form>
```

If you need to programmatically assign text that contains HTML formatting to a control, you can use the `TextView` control. The `TextView` control can contain the following HTML tags:

- `<p>`
- `<br>`
- `<b>`
- `<i>`
- `<a>`

For example, the following declaration of a `TextView` control is perfectly valid:

```
<Mobile:TextView runat="Server">
Here is some text:
<b>Hello World!</b>
</Mobile:TextView>
```

If you need to display a relatively large amount of text—such as a movie description or driving directions—you should enable pagination for a form. You enable pagination by setting the Paginate property of a Mobile Form to the value True.

For example, the text in Listing 17.4.5 will be displayed automatically on multiple pages on devices that have small screens (see Figure 17.8). This page is included on the CD with the name `paginate.aspx`.

LISTING 17.4.5 Paging Through Text

```
 1: <%@ Page Inherits="System.Web.UI.MobileControls.MobilePage" %>
 2: <%@ Register TagPrefix="Mobile" Namespace="System.Web.UI.MobileControls"
 3: Assembly="System.Web.Mobile" %>
 4:
 5: <Mobile:Form
 6:    Paginate="true"
 7:    Runat="Server">
 8:
 9: In this chapter, you'll learn how to write ASP.NET pages that work with
10: mobile devices such as cellular phones, Pocket PC devices, and the Palm
11: Pilot Web browser.
12:
13: First, you'll be provided with an overview of the Wireless Application
14: Protocol (WAP), a standard for communicating with wireless devices.
15: You'll also learn the basics of the Wireless Markup Language (WML),
16: the wireless version of HTML.
17:
18: Next, you'll learn how to leverage your existing ASP.NET skills to create
19: ASP.NET pages that generate content compatible with mobile devices. You'll
20: be given an overview of the controls included with the Microsoft
21: Mobile Internet Toolkit.
22:
23: Finally, you'll learn how to create ASP.NET pages that are cross-device
24: compatible. You'll learn how to detect features of specific devices and
25: exploit their special capabilities.
26:
27: </Mobile:Form>
```

You can control the alignment of the text in either a `Label` or `TextView` control by modifying the control's `Alignment` property. Possible values for `Alignment` are `NotSet`, `Left`, `Center`, and `Right`. The text displayed in the `Label` control in Listing 17.4.6 uses `Center` alignment. (This page is named `alignment.aspx` on the CD.)

FIGURE 17.8
The output of a Mobile Form with paging enabled.

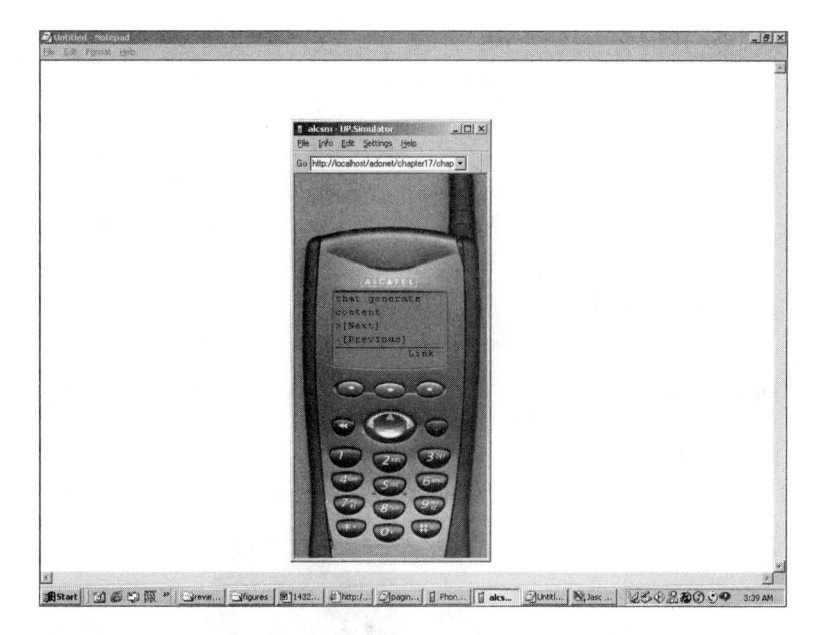

LISTING 17.4.6 *Aligning Text*

```
 1: <%@ Page Inherits="System.Web.UI.MobileControls.MobilePage" %>
 2: <%@ Register TagPrefix="Mobile" Namespace="System.Web.UI.MobileControls"
 3: Assembly="System.Web.Mobile" %>
 4:
 5: <Mobile:Form runat="server">
 6: <Mobile:Label
 7:   Alignment="Center"
 8:   Runat="Server">
 9:   Hello!
10: </Mobile:Label>
11:
12: </Mobile:Form>
```

You can control the way that text word-wraps in either a `Label` or `TextView` control by modifying the control's `Wrapping` property. Possible values for the `Wrapping` property are `NotSet`, `Wrap`, and `NoWrap`.

If you set the `Wrapping` property to `NoWrap`, then the lines of text contained in a form are not automatically wrapped to a new line. For example, the page in Listing 17.4.7 contains a long line of text in a form with wrapping disabled (see Figure 17.9 for the output of this page).

LISTING 17.4.7 *Controlling the Wrapping of Text*

```
 1: <%@ Page Inherits="System.Web.UI.MobileControls.MobilePage" %>
 2: <%@ Register TagPrefix="Mobile" Namespace="System.Web.UI.MobileControls"
 3: Assembly="System.Web.Mobile" %>
 4:
```

LISTING 17.4.7   Continued

```
 5: <Mobile:Form runat="server">
 6: <Mobile:TextView
 7:   Wrapping="NoWrap"
 8:   Runat="Server">
 9:
10: This is a line of text that goes off the side of the page because
➥it is very long
11:
12: </Mobile:TextView>
13: </Mobile:Form>
```

FIGURE 17.9
Setting Wrapping to NoWrap.

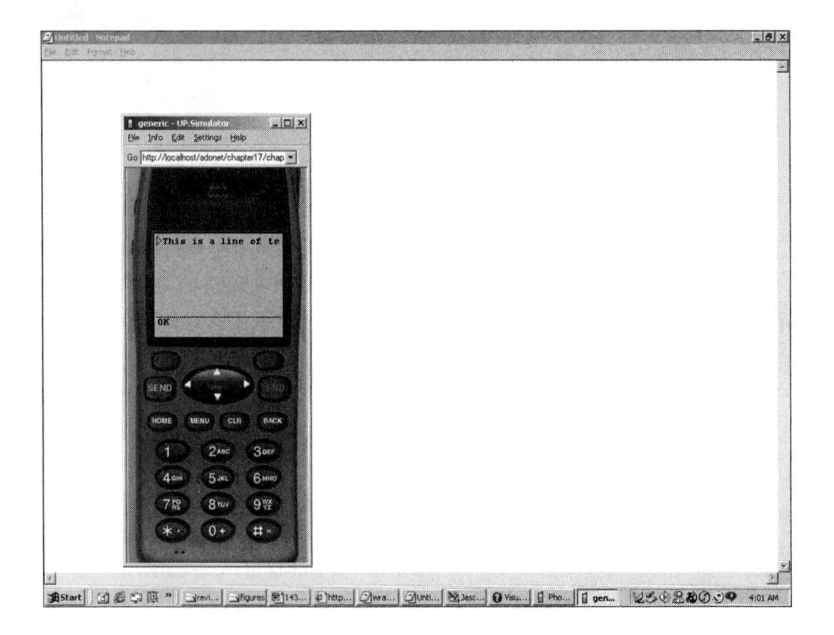

Displaying Lists

Included with the mobile controls is a `List` control that enables you to display lists of items. Imagine, for example, that you need to display a list of movies currently playing at a movie theater. Listing 17.4.8 demonstrates how you can display a list of information using the `List` mobile control. (This page is included on the CD with the name `currentmovies.aspx`.)

LISTING 17.4.8   Displaying a List of Current Movies

```
1: <%@ Page Inherits="System.Web.UI.MobileControls.MobilePage" %>
2: <%@ Register TagPrefix="Mobile" Namespace="System.Web.UI.MobileControls"
3: Assembly="System.Web.Mobile" %>
4:
5: <Mobile:Form runat="server">
```

LISTING 17.4.8 Continued

```
 6: <b>Now Playing:</b>
 7: <br/>
 8: <Mobile:List runat="Server">
 9: <Item Text="Star Wars" />
10: <Item Text="Gone with the Wind" />
11: <Item Text="Citizen Kane" />
12: </Mobile:List>
13: </Mobile:Form>
```

The `List` control is used in Listing 17.4.8 to display a list of three movies. When the page is opened in a device that supports HTML 3.2, the list is displayed within an HTML table. When displayed in a WML-compatible device, each list item is automatically separated by `<br/>` tags.

You can modify the manner in which each list item is displayed by changing the `List` control's `Decoration` property. This property can have the value `None`, `Bulleted`, or `Numbered`. For example, the page in Listing 17.4.9 displays the three movies in a numbered list. (This page is named `currentmovies2.aspx` on the CD.)

LISTING 17.4.9 Displaying a Numbered List

```
 1: <%@ Page Inherits="System.Web.UI.MobileControls.MobilePage" %>
 2: <%@ Register TagPrefix="Mobile" Namespace="System.Web.UI.MobileControls"
 3: Assembly="System.Web.Mobile" %>
 4:
 5: <Mobile:Form runat="server">
 6: <b>Now Playing:</b>
 7: <br/>
 8: <Mobile:List
 9:    Decoration="Numbered"
10:    Runat="Server">
11: <Item Text="Star Wars" />
12: <Item Text="Gone with the Wind" />
13: <Item Text="Citizen Kane" />
14: </Mobile:List>
15: </Mobile:Form>
```

Figure 17.10 illustrates how the `Decoration` property modifies the appearance of a `List` on Internet Explorer 5.5.

> **Note**
> Currently, the `Decoration` property only affects how a page is rendered in an HTML-compatible device. The `Decoration` property is ignored when rendering WML content.

Binding a `List` to a Data Source

You can bind a `List` control to a data source such as a database table or an `ArrayList` collection. For example, if you were really creating a page that displays a list of movies, you would most likely retrieve the list of movies from a database table rather than include a static list of movies.

FIGURE 17.10
Setting Decoration to Numbered on Internet Explorer 5.5.

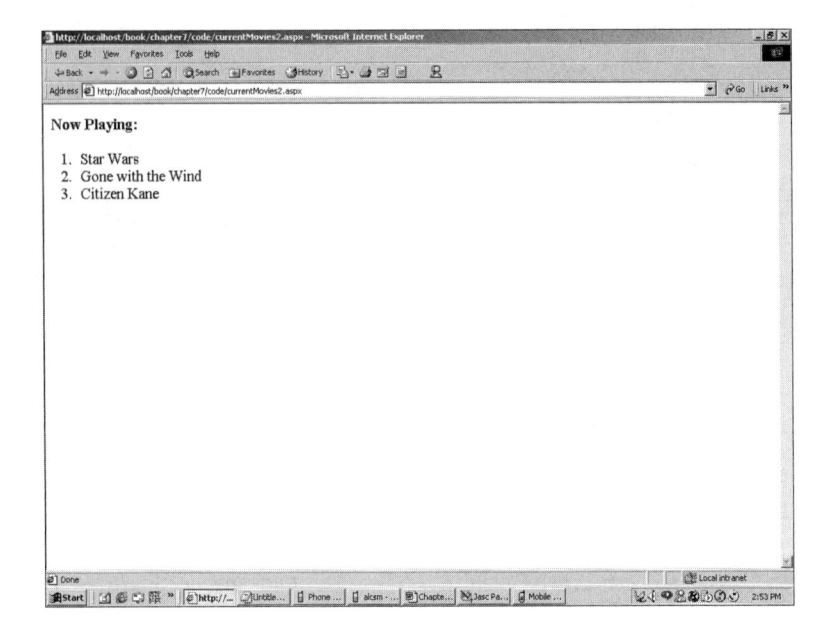

We covered data binding in detail in Chapter 7, "Data Presentation." However, I'll include a quick example using mobile controls here. The page in Listing 17.4.10 demonstrates how you can bind a List control named movies to an `ArrayList` collection named `myArrayList`. (Recall that we discussed using the `ArrayList` collection in Chapter 2, "Common ASP.NET Code Techniques.")

LISTING 17.4.10 Binding to an `ArrayList` Collection

```
 1: <%@ Page Inherits="System.Web.UI.MobileControls.MobilePage" %>
 2: <%@ Register TagPrefix="Mobile" Namespace="System.Web.UI.MobileControls"
 3: Assembly="System.Web.Mobile" %>
 4:
 5: <Script Runat="Server">
 6:
 7: Sub Page_Load( s As Object, e As EventArgs )
 8:   Dim myArrayList As New ArrayList
 9:   myArrayList.Add( "Star Wars" )
10:   myArrayList.Add( "Gone with the Wind" )
11:   myArrayList.Add( "Citizen Kane" )
12:   movies.DataSource = myArrayList
13:   movies.DataBind
14: End Sub
15:
```

LISTING 17.4.10 Continued

```
16: </Script>
17:
18: <Mobile:Form runat="server">
19: <b>Now Playing:</b>
20: <br/>
21: <Mobile:List ID="movies" Runat="Server"/>
22: </Mobile:Form>
```

In the `Page_Load` subroutine, an `ArrayList` collection is created and bound to the `List` control named movies. When `DataBind` is called, the items in the `List` control are populated from the items in `ArrayList`.

Paging Through a List

If you want to display a list that contains a lot of items, you can divide the list into multiple pages. When you enable paging for a form that contains a list, Next and Previous links are automatically created at set intervals in the list.

For example, the `List` control in Listing 17.4.11 displays 50 movies (named movie 1, movie 2, and so on). Because the Mobile Form's Paginate property has the value `True`, the list items are divided into multiple pages. (This page is named `currentmovies4.aspx` on the CD.)

LISTING 17.4.11 Paging Through a List

```
 1: <%@ Page Inherits="System.Web.UI.MobileControls.MobilePage" %>
 2: <%@ Register TagPrefix="Mobile" Namespace="System.Web.UI.MobileControls"
 3:   Assembly="System.Web.Mobile" %>
 4:
 5: <Script Runat="Server">
 6:
 7: Sub Page_Load( s As Object, e As EventArgs )
 8:   Dim myArrayList As New ArrayList
 9:   Dim i As Integer
10:   For i = 1 to 50
11:     myArrayList.Add( "movie " & i.toString )
12:   Next
13:   movies.DataSource = myArrayList
14:   movies.DataBind
15: End Sub
16:
17: </Script>
18:
19: <Mobile:Form
20:   Paginate="true"
21:   runat="server">
22: <b>Now Playing:</b>
23: <br/>
24: <Mobile:List
25:   ID="movies"
26:   Runat="Server" />
27: </Mobile:Form>
```

You can control the user interface displayed for paging through a form by setting properties of the `PagerStyle` element. For example, if you want to display a page number that indicates the current page, you can do this by displaying the value of the `PageLabel` property of the `PagerStyle` element. If you want to specify the text used for the next and previous page links, you can set the value of the `NextPageText` and `PreviousPageText` properties (see Figure 17.11). The page in Listing 17.4.12 illustrates how to set all three of these properties in a form. (This page is named `currentmovies5.aspx` on the CD.)

LISTING 17.4.12 Displaying a Page Number

```
 1: <%@ Page Inherits="System.Web.UI.MobileControls.MobilePage" %>
 2: <%@ Register TagPrefix="Mobile" Namespace="System.Web.UI.MobileControls"
 3:    Assembly="System.Web.Mobile" %>
 4:
 5: <Script Runat="Server">
 6:
 7: Sub Page_Load( s As Object, e As EventArgs )
 8:    Dim myArrayList As New ArrayList
 9:    Dim i As Integer
10:    For i = 1 to 50
11:       myArrayList.Add( "movie " & i.toString )
12:    Next
13:    movies.DataSource = myArrayList
14:    movies.DataBind
15: End Sub
16:
17: </Script>
18:
19: <Mobile:Form
20:    Paginate="True"
21:    PagerStyle-PageLabel="Page {0} of {1}"
22:    PagerStyle-NextPageText="Continue"
23:    PagerStyle-PreviousPageText="Back"
24:    Runat="server">
25: <b>Now Playing:</b>
26: <br/>
27: <Mobile:List
28:    ID="movies"
29:    Runat="Server" />
30: </Mobile:Form>
```

Creating Interactive Lists

You also can use the `List` control to display a list of choices. The choices appear as links when displayed in either WML or HTML devices.

FIGURE 17.11
Controlling pagination style.

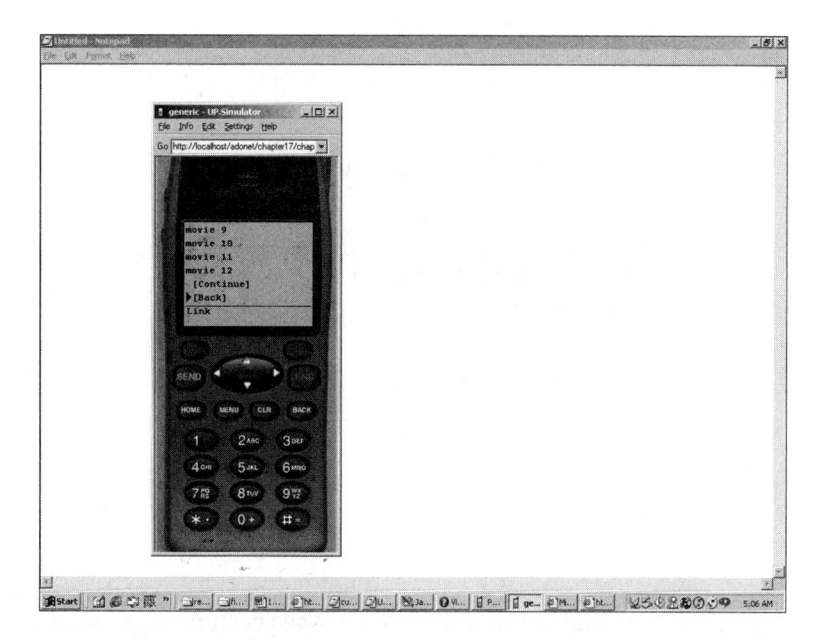

> **Note**
>
> As an alternative to the `List` control, you can use the `SelectionList` control to render an interactive list. The `SelectionList` control, unlike the `List` control, supports selecting multiple items at a time.

For example, the page in Listing 17.4.13 uses the `List` control to display a list of movie choices. (This page is named `selectmovie2.aspx` on the CD.)

LISTING 17.4.13 Displaying a List of Links

```
 1: <%@ Page Inherits="System.Web.UI.MobileControls.MobilePage" %>
 2: <%@ Register TagPrefix="Mobile" Namespace="System.Web.UI.MobileControls"
 3:    Assembly="System.Web.Mobile" %>
 4:
 5: <Script runat="Server">
 6:
 7: Sub doSomething( s As object, e As ListCommandEventArgs )
 8:    movieLabel.Text = e.ListItem.Text
 9:    ActiveForm = form2
10: End Sub
11:
12: </Script>
13:
14:
15: <Mobile:Form runat="server" id="form1">
```

LISTING 17.4.13 *Continued*

```
16: <b>Select Movie:</b><br/>
17: <Mobile:List
18:   ID="movies"
19:   OnItemCommand="doSomething"
20:   Runat="Server">
21: <Item text="Star Wars"/>
22: <Item text="Gone with the Wind"/>
23: <Item text="Citizen Kane"/>
24: </Mobile:List>
25: </Mobile:Form>
26:
27: <Mobile:Form runat="server" id="form2">
28: <b>You selected:</b>
29: <br/>
30: <Mobile:Label
31:   ID="movieLabel"
32:   Runat="Server"/>
33: </Mobile:Form>
```

When a `List` control has an event handler, each list item is displayed as a link (see Figure 17.12). In Listing 17.4.13, the `OnItemCommand` property associates the `doSomething` subroutine with the `ItemCommand` event. When you click any of the movie links, the `ItemCommand` event is raised and the `doSomething` subroutine is executed.

FIGURE 17.12
Displaying a list of links.

The `doSomething` subroutine retrieves the value of the `Text` property of the selected item and assigns the text to a `Label` control named `movieLabel`. Next, the `doSomething` subroutine activates `form2`, on `line 9`, so that the `Label` control is displayed.

Individual list items can have distinct **Text** and **Value** properties. The **Text** property is always displayed when an item is displayed and the **Value** property is hidden. You can use the **Value** property to pass additional information when an item is selected.

For example, in Listing 17.4.14, the **Value** property is used to pass the category of each movie. (This page is named **selectmovie3.aspx** on the CD.)

LISTING 17.4.14 Using the Value Property

```
 1: <%@ Page Inherits="System.Web.UI.MobileControls.MobilePage" %>
 2: <%@ Register TagPrefix="Mobile" Namespace="System.Web.UI.MobileControls"
 3:   Assembly="System.Web.Mobile" %>
 4:
 5: <Script runat="Server">
 6:
 7: Sub doSomething( s As object, e As ListCommandEventArgs )
 8:   movieLabel.Text = e.ListItem.Text
 9:   movieCatLabel.Text = e.ListItem.Value
10:   ActiveForm = form2
11: End Sub
12:
13: </Script>
14:
15:
16: <Mobile:Form runat="server" id="form1">
17: <b>Select Movie:</b><br/>
18: <Mobile:List
19:   ID="movies"
20:   OnItemCommand="doSomething"
21:   Runat="Server">
22: <Item text="Star Wars" value="scifi"/>
23: <Item text="Gone with the Wind" value="romance"/>
24: <Item text="Citizen Kane" value="drama"/>
25: </Mobile:List>
26: </Mobile:Form>
27:
28: <Mobile:Form runat="server" id="form2">
29: <b>You selected:</b>
30: <br/>
31: <Mobile:Label
32:   ID="movieLabel"
33:   Runat="Server"/>
34: <br/>
35: <b>Category:</b>
36: <br/>
37: <Mobile:Label
38:   ID="movieCatLabel"
39:   Runat="Server"/>
40: </Mobile:Form>
```

Each of the three items contained in the **List** control in Listing 17.4.14 have both a **Text** and a **Value** property. When an item is selected, the **ItemCommand** event is raised and the `doSomething` subroutine is executed. This subroutine assigns the value of the `Text` property to a `Label` control named `movieLabel` and the value of the `Value` property to a `Label` control named `movieCatLabel`.

Creating Object Lists

One significant limitation of the `List` control is that it enables you to select only one option for each item in the list. You click a list item and something happens. Imagine, however, that you need to display multiple options for each list item. For example, when displaying a list of movies, you may want the user to be able to view the description of the movie or buy a ticket for the movie. In other words, you may want two options associated with each list item.

To create more complicated lists, you need to use the `ObjectList` control instead of the `List` control. The `ObjectList` control is similar to the `List` control in that it enables you to display a list of links. However, unlike the `List` control, the `ObjectList` control enables you to associate multiple commands with each link. Also, unlike the `List` control, the `ObjectList` control requires you to bind the list to a data source.

> **Note**
> Data binding is discussed in Chapter 7, "Data Presentation."

The page in Listing 17.4.15 illustrates how you can use the `ObjectList` control to associate multiple commands with each list item. (This page is named `objectlist.aspx` on the CD.)

LISTING 17.4.15 Associating Multiple Commands with List Items

```
 1: <%@ Page Inherits="System.Web.UI.MobileControls.MobilePage" %>
 2: <%@ Register TagPrefix="Mobile" Namespace="System.Web.UI.MobileControls"
 3:    Assembly="System.Web.Mobile" %>
 4:
 5: <Script Runat="Server">
 6:
 7: Sub Page_Load( s As Object, e As EventArgs )
 8:    Dim myArrayList As New ArrayList
 9:
10:    myArrayList.Add( "Star Wars" )
11:    myArrayList.Add( "Citizen Kane" )
12:
13:    movieList.Datasource = myArrayList
14:    movieList.Databind
15:
16: End Sub
17:
18: Sub doSomething( s As Object, e As ObjectListCommandEventArgs )
19:    If e.CommandName = "Buy" Then
```

LISTING 17.4.15 Continued

```
20:      ActiveForm = BuyTicket
21:    Else
22:      ActiveForm = ShowDesc
23:    End If
24: End Sub
25:
26: </Script>
27:
28: <Mobile:Form id="displayMovies" runat="Server">
29:
30: <Mobile:ObjectList
31:   ID="movieList"
32:   OnItemCommand="doSomething"
33:   Runat="Server">
34: <Command Name="Buy" Text="Buy" />
35: <Command Name="Desc" Text="Desc" />
36: </Mobile:ObjectList>
37:
38: </Mobile:Form>
39:
40: <Mobile:Form id="ShowDesc" runat="Server">
41:   <b>Great Movie!</b>
42: </Mobile:Form>
43:
44: <Mobile:Form id="BuyTicket" runat="Server">
45:   <b>Buy Ticket!</b>
46: </Mobile:Form>
```

The `ObjectList` control in Listing 17.4.15 is bound to an `ArrayList` collection named `myArrayList`. This `ArrayList` collection consists of movie titles. Within the `ObjectList` control, two Command controls are declared on lines 34 and 35. The first command is labeled **Buy**, and the second command is labeled **Desc**. If you select a movie title or you select either of the two commands, the `doSomething` subroutine is executed.

Exactly how an `ObjectList` is displayed depends on the device. When the page in Listing 17.4.15 is displayed in Internet Explorer 5.5, each list item is rendered as a link (see Figure 17.13). When you click a link, the page in Figure 17.14 is displayed.

When displayed in a cell phone, such as the Alcatel cell phone, the Go command is displayed. When you press the Go button, a menu displaying Buy and Desc options is displayed (see Figure 17.15).

Unlike the `List` control, the `ObjectList` control can display multiple fields from a data source. For example, you can bind an `ObjectList` to a database table that contains `movieTitle`, `movieCat`, and `ticketPrice` columns and displays all these columns by using the `ObjectList`.

FIGURE 17.13
Displaying `ObjectList` links.

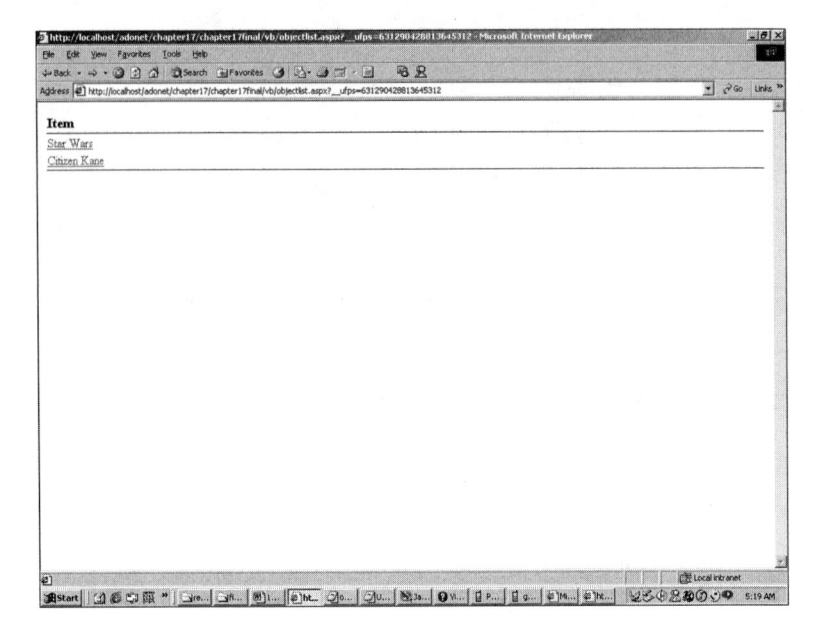

FIGURE 17.14
Output of `ObjectList` after clicking.

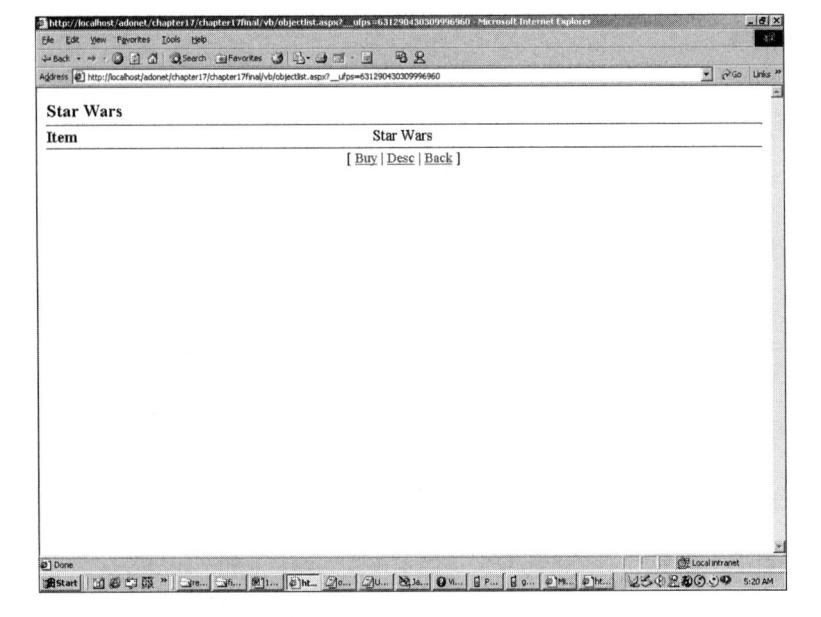

Chapter 17 • MOBILE CONTROLS   653

FIGURE 17.15
Output of `ObjectList` on Alcatel Phone Simulator.

The `ObjectList` in Listing 17.4.16 is bound to an `ArrayList` collection. Each item in the `ArrayList` collection is an instance of a class defined within the page named the `Movie` class (we need to create a class so that we can represent multiple fields for each item in the `ArrayList` collection). The `Movie` class has `movieTitle`, `movieCat`, and `ticketPrice` properties. When you select an item in the `ObjectList`, the values of all three of the properties are displayed. (This page is named `objectlist2.aspx` on the CD.)

LISTING 17.4.16   Displaying Multiple Database Fields

```
 1: <%@ Page Inherits="System.Web.UI.MobileControls.MobilePage" %>
 2: <%@ Register TagPrefix="Mobile" Namespace="System.Web.UI.MobileControls"
 3:    Assembly="System.Web.Mobile" %>
 4:
 5: <Script Runat="Server">
 6:
 7: Public class Movie
 8:
 9:    Private _movieTitle, _movieCat, _ticketPrice As String
10:
11:    ReadOnly Property movieTitle As String
12:    Get
13:      Return _movieTitle
14:    End Get
15:    End Property
16:
17:    ReadOnly Property movieCat As String
18:    Get
```

LISTING 17.4.16 *Continued*

```
19:    Return _movieCat
20:   End Get
21:  End Property
22:
23:  ReadOnly Property ticketPrice As String
24:   Get
25:    Return _ticketPrice
26:   End Get
27:  End Property
28:
29:  Sub New( movieTitle As String, _
30:      movieCat As String, _
31:      ticketPrice As String )
32:   _movieTitle = movieTitle
33:   _movieCat = movieCat
34:   _ticketPrice = ticketPrice
35:  End Sub
36:
37: End Class
38:
39:
40: Sub Page_Load( s As Object, e As EventArgs )
41:  Dim myArrayList As New ArrayList
42:
43:  myArrayList.Add( new Movie( "Star Wars", "SciFi", "$7.98" ) )
44:  myArrayList.Add( new Movie( "Citizen Kane", "Drama", "$4.00" ) )
45:
46:  movieList.Datasource = myArrayList
47:  movieList.Databind
48:
49: End Sub
50:
51: Sub doSomething( s As Object, e As ObjectListCommandEventArgs )
52:  ActiveForm = selectMovie
53: End Sub
54:
55: </Script>
56:
57: <Mobile:Form id="displayMovies" runat="Server">
58:
59:  <Mobile:ObjectList
60:   ID="movieList"
61:   AutoGenerateFields="False"
62:   LabelField="movieTitle"
63:   OnItemCommand="doSomething"
64:   Runat="Server">
65:  <Field DataField="movieTitle" Title="Movie" />
66:  <Field DataField="movieCat" Title="Category" />
67:  <Field DataField="ticketPrice" Title="Price" />
68:  </Mobile:ObjectList>
69:
```

LISTING 17.4.16 Continued

```
70: </Mobile:Form>
71:
72: <Mobile:Form id="selectMovie" runat="Server">
73:
74: <b>Movie Selected!</b>
75:
76: </Mobile:Form>
```

Creating Text Boxes

Entering text into most mobile devices is a cumbersome experience. For example, entering large amounts of text with a cell phone's numeric keypad is close to impossible. In most cases, you should enable users to make choices with the List controls discussed in the previous section.

However, there are certain circumstances in which you have no choice but to force the users of your application to enter text. For example, you might need the user to enter a password, a phone number, or some other type of data that cannot be selected from a list. In these situations, you will need to use the mobile `TextBox` control.

The mobile `TextBox` control is similar to the ASP.NET `TextBox` control. However, it does not support multiline input. All text must be entered into a single line (see Figure 17.16).

FIGURE 17.16
Entering text on a cell phone.

656 ASP.NET: TIPS, TUTORIALS, AND CODE

The page in Listing 17.4.17 illustrates how you can use the `TextBox` control. The first mobile form contains two mobile `TextBox` controls: one for a contact name and one for a contact phone. A `Command` control is used to enable the user to submit the form.

When the `Command` control is executed, the `doSomething` subroutine contained in lines 7-11 is executed and the second Mobile Form is displayed. This form simply redisplays the values entered into the `contactName` and `contactPhone` `TextBox` controls. (This page is named `textbox.aspx` on the CD.)

LISTING 17.4.17 Accepting User Input

```
 1: <%@ Page Inherits="System.Web.UI.MobileControls.MobilePage" %>
 2: <%@ Register TagPrefix="Mobile" Namespace="System.Web.UI.MobileControls"
 3:    Assembly="System.Web.Mobile" %>
 4:
 5: <Script Runat="Server">
 6:
 7: Sub doSomething( s As Object, e As EventArgs )
 8:    contactNameLabel.Text = contactName.Text
 9:    contactPhoneLabel.Text = contactPhone.Text
10:    ActiveForm = displayContact
11: End Sub
12:
13: </Script>
14:
15:
16: <Mobile:Form id="addContact" runat="Server">
17:
18: <b>Name:</b>
19: <Mobile:Textbox
20:    ID="contactName"
21:    Runat="Server"/>
22: <br/>
23: <b>Phone:</b>
24: <Mobile:Textbox
25:    ID="contactPhone"
26:    Runat="Server"/>
27: <br/>
28: <Mobile:Command
29:    ID="myCommand"
30:    Text="Submit!"
31:    OnClick="doSomething"
32:    Runat="Server" />
33: </Mobile:Form>
34:
35:
36: <Mobile:Form id="displayContact" runat="Server">
37: <b>You Entered:</b>
38: <br/>
39: <Mobile:Label
40:    ID="contactNameLabel"
41:    Runat="Server"/>
```

LISTING 17.4.17   Continued

```
42:   <br/>
43:   <Mobile:Label
44:     ID="contactPhoneLabel"
45:     Runat="Server"/>
46:
47:
48: </Mobile:Form>
```

The Mobile `TextBox` control has two properties, `Numeric` and `Password`, that indicate the type of information that can be entered into the text box. The `Password` value works with both HTML and WML clients. The `Numeric` value is unique to WML devices.

When the `Password` property is assigned the value `True`, any text entered into the text box is hidden (typically, the asterisk character is used to echo each character entered). When the `Numeric` property is assigned the value `True`, and the text box is rendered on a WML device, only numerals can be entered into the text box. The page in Listing 17.4.18 illustrates how to use both of these properties. The first `TextBox` control, labeled `Username`, has the default values for `Password` and `Numeric` (False). The `Username` `TextBox` control can accept any text input. The second `TextBox` control, labeled `Password`, will hide any text entered into it. The final `TextBox` control, labeled `PIN`, accepts only numeric values when rendered on a WML device. When rendered on an HTML device, a `Numeric` `TextBox` control behaves like a normal text box. (This page is named `textbox2.aspx` on the CD.)

LISTING 17.4.18   Displaying Different Input Types

```
 1: <%@ Page Inherits="System.Web.UI.MobileControls.MobilePage" %>
 2: <%@ Register TagPrefix="Mobile" Namespace="System.Web.UI.MobileControls"
 3:     Assembly="System.Web.Mobile" %>
 4:
 5: <Mobile:Form id="addContact" runat="Server">
 6:
 7: <b>User Name:</b>
 8: <Mobile:Textbox
 9:     ID="username"
10:     Runat="Server"/>
11: <br/>
12: <b>Password:</b>
13: <Mobile:Textbox
14:     ID="password"
15:     Password="True"
16:     Runat="Server"/>
17: <br/>
18: <b>PIN:</b>
19: <Mobile:Textbox
20:     ID="PIN"
21:     Numeric="True"
22:     Runat="Server"/>
23:
24: </Mobile:Form>
```

Validating User Input

All the ASP.NET `Validation` controls are shadowed in the mobile controls. For each of the ASP.NET `Validation` controls, there is a corresponding Mobile `Validation` control. The six Mobile `Validation` controls are detailed in the following list:

- *CompareValidator*—Compares the value entered into a control to a value or performs a data type check
- *CustomValidator*—Enables you to write a custom function to perform validation
- *RangeValidator*—Checks whether the value entered into a control falls between a certain range
- *RegularExpressionValidator*—Matches the value entered into a control against a regular expression
- *RequiredFieldValidator*—Checks whether a value has been entered into a control
- *ValidationSummary*—Displays a summary of validation errors

> **Note**
> To learn more about the standard ASP.NET Validation controls, see Chapter 3, "Form Field Input Validation."

These mobile Validation controls work almost, but not exactly, like the standard validation controls. First, unlike the standard `Validation` controls, the Mobile `Validation` controls do not use client-side JavaScript to display error messages. Error messages are not automatically displayed as you move from `TextBox` control to `TextBox` control.

Furthermore, the Mobile `ValidationSummary` control behaves differently than the standard ASP.NET `ValidationSummary` control. The Mobile `ValidationSummary` control is typically placed in a separate form and has a property named `formToValidate` that indicates the form to perform validation against.

The page in Listing 17.4.19 illustrates how to use the mobile `RequiredFieldValidator`, `RangeValidator`, and `ValidationSummary` validation controls. (This page is included on the CD with the name `validation.aspx`.)

LISTING 17.4.19 Validating User Input

```
1: <%@ Page Inherits="System.Web.UI.MobileControls.MobilePage" %>
2: <%@ Register TagPrefix="Mobile" Namespace="System.Web.UI.MobileControls"
3:     Assembly="System.Web.Mobile" %>
4:
5: <Script Runat="Server">
6:
7: Sub doSomething( s As Object, e As EventArgs )
```

LISTING 17.4.19 *Continued*

```
 8:    If Not isValid Then
 9:      ActiveForm = form2
10:    Else
11:      ActiveForm = form3
12:    End If
13: End Sub
14:
15: </Script>
16:
17: <Mobile:Form id="form1" runat="Server">
18:
19: <b>Enter a number between 3 and 12:</b>
20: <Mobile:Textbox
21:    ID="theNumber"
22:    Runat="Server"/>
23:
24: <Mobile:RequiredFieldValidator
25:    ErrorMessage="Input Required!"
26:    ControlToValidate="theNumber"
27:    Runat="Server" />
28:
29: <Mobile:RangeValidator
30:    ErrorMessage="Not in Range!"
31:    ControlToValidate="theNumber"
32:    Type="Integer"
33:    MinimumValue="3"
34:    MaximumValue="12"
35:    Runat="Server" />
36:
37: <Mobile:Command
38:    Text="Submit!"
39:    OnClick="doSomething"
40:    Runat="Server"/>
41:
42: </Mobile:Form>
43:
44: <Mobile:Form id="form2" runat="Server">
45:
46: <Mobile:ValidationSummary
47:    formToValidate="form1"
48:    Runat="Server" />
49:
50: </Mobile:Form>
51:
52: <Mobile:Form id="form3" runat="Server">
53:
54: <i>Good Job!</i>
55:
56: </Mobile:Form>
```

The first form in Listing 17.4.19 contains a mobile `TextBox` control. Both `RequiredFieldValidator` and `RangeValidator` mobile validation controls are associated with the `TextBox` control. The `RequiredFieldValidator` validation control is used to check whether a value has been entered into the control. The `RangeValidator` validation control is used to ensure that the entered value is between 3 and 12.

When you submit the form, the `doSomething` subroutine executes. If the `IsValid` property is not true, there is an error in the form. In that case, the second form is displayed. This form contains a `ValidationSummary` control that displays all the validation errors (see Figure 17.17).

FIGURE 17.17
Displaying a validation summary.

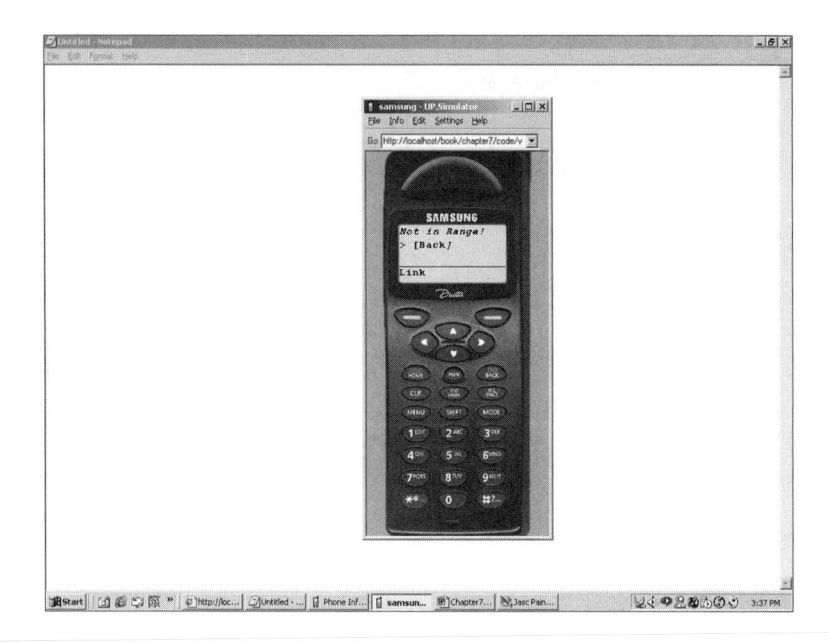

If there are no validation errors, the third form is displayed, which simply displays the message "Good Job!"

Displaying Images

Displaying images is a complicated proposition when it comes to mobile devices. The problem is that there are several different incompatible image formats that mobile devices support. Most Web browsers support GIF and JPEG image files. Many mobile devices, on the other hand, only support BMP or WBMP. The mobile controls need to support all these formats.

Microsoft's solution to this problem is elegant—a Mobile `Image` control. The `Image` control can detect different devices and display the proper image file format for the detected device. The page in Listing 17.4.20 illustrates how the `Image` control can be used with multiple devices. (This page is included on the CD with the name `image.aspx`.)

LISTING 17.4.20 Displaying Images with the Mobile `Image` Control

```
 1: <%@ Page Inherits="System.Web.UI.MobileControls.MobilePage" %>
 2: <%@ Register TagPrefix="Mobile" Namespace="System.Web.UI.MobileControls"
 3:    Assembly="System.Web.Mobile" %>
 4:
 5: <Mobile:Form id="form1" runat="Server">
 6:
 7: <Mobile:Image
 8:   ImageUrl="myImage.Gif"
 9:   AlternateText="myImage"
10:   Runat="Server">
11:   <DeviceSpecific>
12:     <Choice Filter="PrefersBmp" ImageURL="myImage.bmp" />
13:   </DeviceSpecific>
14: </mobile:Image>
15:
16: </Mobile:Form>
```

By default, the `Image` control in Listing 17.4.20 displays the `myImage.Gif` image. However, the `Image` control also contains a `<deviceSpecific>` tag on line 11. When a device that prefers a BMP image requests the page, a BMP image is displayed instead of the GIF image.

> **Note**
> The `<DeviceSpecific>` element makes use of a filter section in the `Web.config` file. (This `Web.config` file is included on the CD.) For more information on the `<deviceSelect>` element, see the last section of this chapter, "Creating Cross-Device-Compatible Mobile Pages."

When an Openwave (Phone.com) compatible cell phone is detected, a BMP image is displayed (see Figure 17.18). When an Internet Explorer 5 browser is detected, a GIF image is displayed.

> **Note**
> You have to create an image in each of the formats. The Image control isn't smart enough to generate the different image types for you.

If a device does not support any of the image formats, text is displayed instead. This alternative text is specified by the `AlternateText` property of the `Image` control.

Placing Phone Calls

One interesting thing that you can do with mobile controls that you cannot do in a normal ASP.NET page is place phone calls. When you use the `Call` control with a device such as a cell phone, the control enables you to place a call. When the `Call` control is used with a device that doesn't support placing phone calls, such as Internet Explorer 5.5, either a label or link is displayed.

FIGURE 17.18
Image displayed in a cell phone.

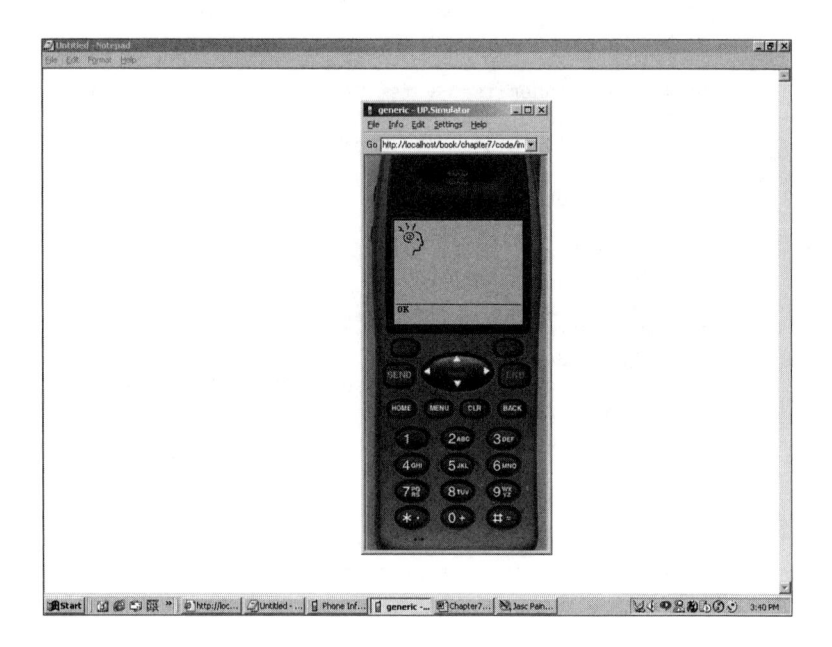

You can use the `Call` control to automatically call a phone number in a list of contacts. Or, you can imagine adding a customer service number to your mobile application.

The page in Listing 17.4.21 illustrates how to use the Call control (this page is included on the CD with the name `call.aspx`).

LISTING 17.4.21 Placing a Phone Call

```
 1: <%@ Page Inherits="System.Web.UI.MobileControls.MobilePage" %>
 2: <%@ Register TagPrefix="Mobile" Namespace="System.Web.UI.MobileControls"
 3: Assembly="System.Web.Mobile" %>
 4:
 5: <Mobile:Form id="form1" runat="Server">
 6:
 7: <Mobile:Call
 8:   Text="Call Information"
 9:   PhoneNumber="411"
10:   Runat="Server" />
11:
12: </Mobile:Form>
```

Displaying Advertisements with Mobile Controls

The Mobile controls include an `AdRotator` control that corresponds to the standard ASP.NET `AdRotator` control. The mobile `AdRotator` control displays links on WML devices and images on HTML devices.

Like the standard `AdRotator` control, the mobile `AdRotator` control uses an external XML file to list the banner advertisements that it displays. The XML file looks like this:

LISTING 17.4.22 The Ad Rotator File

```xml
<Advertisements>
   <Ad>
      <ImageUrl>ad1.gif</ImageUrl>
      <BmpImageUrl>ad1.bmp</BmpImageUrl>
      <NavigateUrl>http://www.AspWorkshops.com</NavigateUrl>
      <AlternateText>Click here for ASP.NET Training!</AlternateText>
      <Impressions>60</Impressions>
   </Ad>
   <Ad>
      <ImageUrl>ad2.gif</ImageUrl>
      <BmpImageUrl>ad2.bmp</BmpImageUrl>
      <NavigateUrl>http://www.superexpert.com</NavigateUrl>
      <AlternateText> Click here to visit superexpert.com! </AlternateText>
      <Impressions>60</Impressions>
   </Ad>
</Advertisements>
```

This advertisement file contains two banner advertisements. The `ImageURL`, `TargetURL`, and `AlternateText`, as well as the relative number of impressions to display, are declared for both banner advertisements.

Notice that two images are specified for each advertisement. A GIF image is contained in the `ImageUrl` tag and a BMP image is contained in the `BmpImageUrl` tag.

After you have created an advertisement file, you can use the file with the mobile AdRotator control by setting the `AdRotator` control's `AdvertisementFile` property. This is illustrated in Listing 17.4.23. (This page is included on the CD with the name `adrotator.aspx`.)

LISTING 17.4.23 Displaying Banner Advertisements

```
 1: <%@ Page Inherits="System.Web.UI.MobileControls.MobilePage" %>
 2: <%@ Register TagPrefix="Mobile" Namespace="System.Web.UI.MobileControls"
 3: Assembly="System.Web.Mobile" %>
 4:
 5: <Mobile:Form id="form1" runat="Server">
 6:
 7: <Mobile:AdRotator
 8:    AdvertisementFile="myAds.xml"
 9:    Runat="Server">
10:    <DeviceSpecific>
11:      <Choice Filter="PrefersBmp" ImageKey="BmpImageUrl"/>
12:      <Choice Filter="PrefersWBmp" ImageKey="WBmpImageUrl"/>
13:    </DeviceSpecific>
14: </Mobile:AdRotator>
15:
16: </Mobile:Form>
```

The output of Listing 17.23 is displayed in Figure 17.19. The `AdRotator` control in Listing 17.23 uses the `DeviceSpecific` tag to display the appropriate image for different devices. This page depends on the Filter section declared in the `Web.config` file. (This `Web.config` file is included on the CD that accompanies this book.)

FIGURE 17.19
Displaying a banner advertisement.

Displaying Calendars with Mobile Controls

The mobile controls include a `Calendar` control that corresponds to the standard ASP.NET `Calendar` control. You can use the `Calendar` control to select particular days, weeks, or months. It's useful for performing such activities as scheduling meetings and appointments.

When the Mobile `Calendar` control is displayed in an HTML-compatible device, a full calendar is rendered on the screen (see Figure 17.20). When the `Calendar` control is displayed in a WML device, you have a couple of options for selecting the date (see Figure 17.21). For example, you can select a date by typing the date or you can go through a series of menus and select a date without ever pressing a single number key.

The page in Listing 17.4.24 illustrates how to add a mobile `Calendar` control to a form. (This page is named `calendar.aspx` on the CD.)

Chapter 17 • MOBILE CONTROLS   665

FIGURE 17.20
`Calendar` Control displayed in Internet Explorer 5.5.

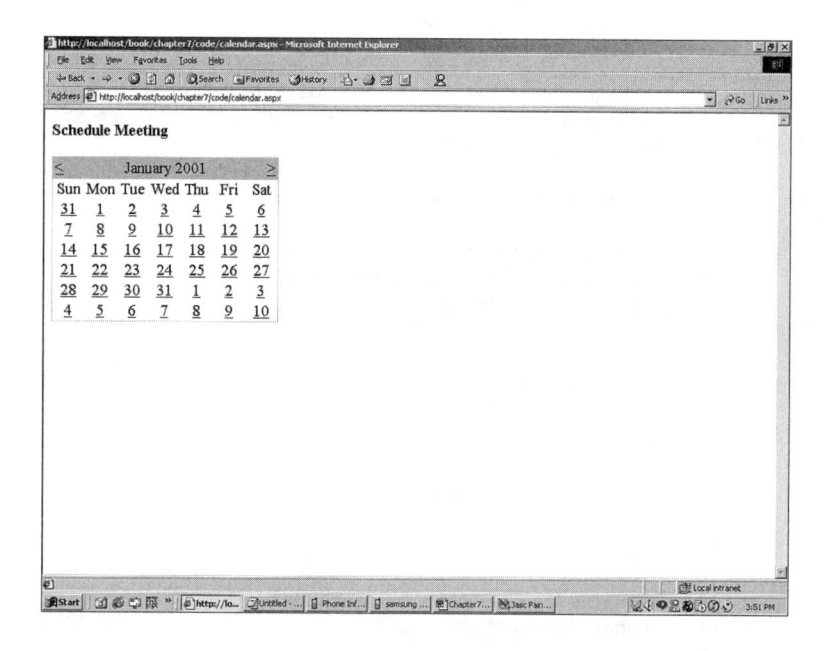

FIGURE 17.21
`Calendar` control displayed in cell phone.

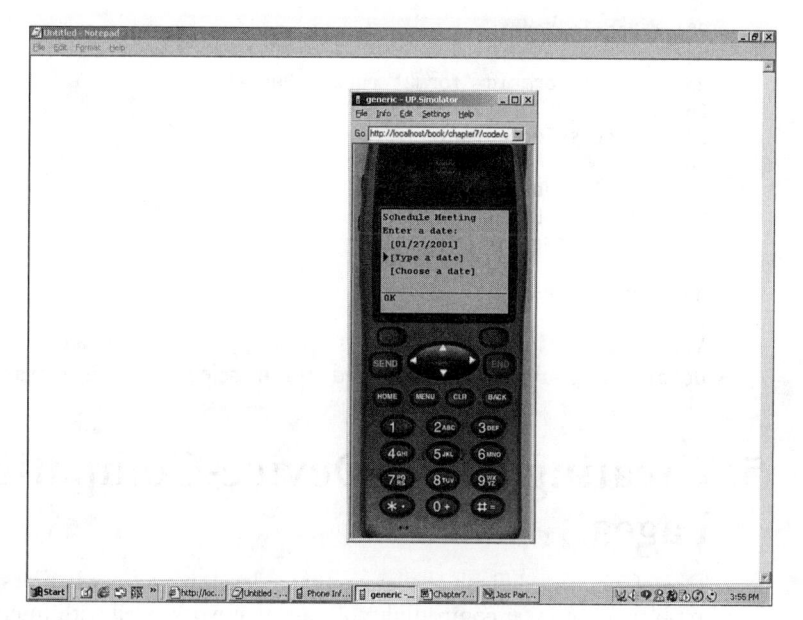

LISTING 17.4.24 *Displaying a Calendar*

```
 1: <%@ Page Inherits="System.Web.UI.MobileControls.MobilePage" %>
 2: <%@ Register TagPrefix="Mobile" Namespace="System.Web.UI.MobileControls"
 3: Assembly="System.Web.Mobile" %>
 4:
 5: <Script Runat="Server">
 6:
 7: Sub doSomething( s As Object, e As EventArgs )
 8:    DateLabel.Text = myCal.SelectedDate
 9:    ActiveForm = form2
10: End Sub
11:
12: </Script>
13:
14: <Mobile:Form id="form1" runat="Server">
15:
16: <b>Schedule Meeting</b>
17: <br/>
18: <Mobile:Calendar
19:    ID="myCal"
20:    OnSelectionChanged="doSomething"
21:    Runat="Server" />
22:
23: </Mobile:Form>
24:
25: <Mobile:Form id="form2" runat="Server">
26:
27: <i>You selected:</i>
28: <br/>
29: <Mobile:Label
30:    ID="DateLabel"
31:    Runat="Server" />
32:
33: </Mobile:Form>
```

When the page in Listing 17.4.24 is opened, you can select a date. Once a date is selected, the `doSomething` subroutine is executed and the selected date is displayed in the second form.

5. Creating Cross-Device-Compatible Mobile Pages

One of the most difficult challenges that a developer faces when designing HTML pages is the problem of browser compatibility. A page that works well with Internet Explorer 5.5 on a PC will not necessarily work well with Netscape Navigator 3.0 on the Macintosh.

Well, HTML designers have it easy. If you really want a tough challenge, try creating pages that are cross-device compatible rather than simply cross-browser and platform compatible. Making a page that looks good on a cell phone *and* on a full browser is a real challenge.

In this section, you'll learn about some of the features of mobile controls that you can exploit to detect the capabilities of different mobile devices. You can use these features to construct mobile pages that are cross-device compatible.

> **Note**
> For more information on creating pages that are compatible with different browser types see Chapter 4, "Enabling Better Browser Support."

Detecting Mobile Capabilities

When you install the mobile controls, your server's system `machine.config` file is also modified automatically. Additional entries are added to the `<browserCaps>` section, which describes the capabilities of various mobile devices. If you are curious, go ahead and open the `machine.config` file to look at these definitions. You can open the file with Notepad.

> **Note**
> The `machine.config` file is discussed in detail in Chapter 11, "ASP.NET Deployment and Configuration."

These entries in the `machine.config` file are used by the `MobileCapabilities` class. For example, the page in Listing 17.5.1 displays a number of features of the current device by displaying properties from the `MobileCapabilities` class. (This page is included on the CD with the name `mobilecapabilities.aspx`.)

LISTING 17.5.1 Displaying Mobile Capabilities

```
 1: <%@ Page Inherits="System.Web.UI.MobileControls.MobilePage" %>
 2: <%@ Register TagPrefix="Mobile" Namespace="System.Web.UI.MobileControls"
 3: Assembly="System.Web.Mobile" %>
 4:
 5: <Script Runat="Server">
 6:
 7: Sub Page_Load( s As Object, e As EventArgs )
 8:    Dim caps AS system.Web.Mobile.MobileCapabilities
 9:    caps = Request.Browser
10:    browserLabel.Text = caps.Browser
11:    typeLabel.Text = caps.Type
12:    preferredRenderingTypeLabel.Text = caps.PreferredRenderingType
13:    screenCharactersWidthLabel.Text = caps.ScreenCharactersWidth
14:    screenCharactersHeightLabel.Text = caps.ScreenCharactersHeight
15: End Sub
16:
17: </Script>
18:
```

LISTING 17.5.1 Continued

```
19: <Mobile:Form id="form1" runat="Server">
20:
21: <b>Browser:</b>
22: <Mobile:Label
23:     id="browserLabel"
24:     Runat="Server"/>
25: <br/>
26:
27: <b>Type:</b>
28: <Mobile:Label
29:     id="typeLabel"
30:     Runat="Server"/>
31: <br/>
32:
33: <b>PreferredRenderingType:</b>
34: <Mobile:Label
35:     id="preferredRenderingTypeLabel"
36:     Runat="Server"/>
37: <br/>
38:
39: <b>ScreenCharactersWidth:</b>
40: <Mobile:Label
41:     id="screenCharactersWidthLabel"
42:     Runat="Server"/>
43: <br/>
44:
45: <b>ScreenCharactersHeight:</b>
46: <Mobile:Label
47:     id="screenCharactersHeightLabel"
48:     Runat="Server"/>
49:
50: </Mobile:Form>
```

The page in Listing 17.5.1 displays five properties of the current device: `Browser`, `Type`, `PreferredRenderingType`, `ScreenCharactersWidth`, and `ScreenCharactersHeight`. The properties are retrieved by retrieving an instance of the `MobileCapabilities` class from the `Browser` class. Each property is displayed by assigning the value of each property to a Mobile Label control (see Figure 17.22).

The `Browser` property returns the type of browser used by the device—for example, `IE` or `Phone.com`. The `Type` property returns the general type of the device—`IE5` or `Pocket Internet Explorer`, for example. The `PreferredRenderingType` property returns the MIME type of the rendering language of the device. Examples are `html32` and `wml11`. Finally, the `ScreenCharactersWidth` and `ScreenCharactersHeight` properties return the number of characters that a device can display horizontally and vertically.

You can retrieve many more device properties than those returned in Listing 17.5.1. For example, you can use the `isColor` property to detect whether a device is capable of displaying color or the `CanInitiateVoiceCall` property to detect whether the device can place phone calls. For a complete list of properties supported by the `MobileCapabilities` class, consult the Mobile Internet Toolkit documentation.

FIGURE 17.22
Displaying device capabilities.

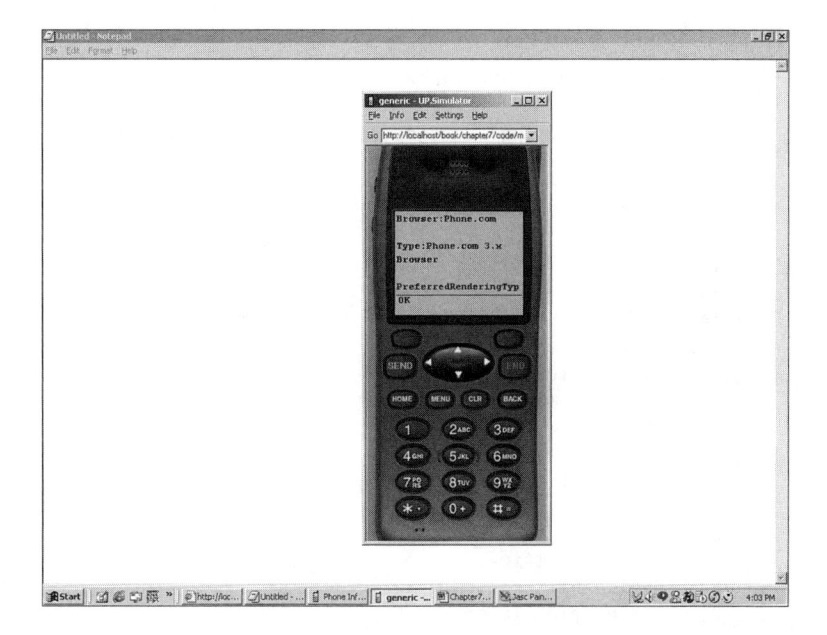

Choosing Devices with `DeviceSpecific`

The `MobileCapabilities` class can be used to display different content for different devices. You can use the properties from the `MobileCapabilities` class with a special element named the `<DeviceSpecific>` element.

The `<DeviceSpecific>` element works (very roughly) like a Visual Basic `Select Case` statement. The `<DeviceSpecific>` element can contain multiple `<Choice>` elements that match different device criteria. When a `<Choice>` element is matched, its content is returned.

Earlier in this chapter, in the section titled "Displaying Images," you saw how the `<DeviceSpecific>` element can be used with the Image control to display different image files, depending on the nature of the device that requests the page. You can also use `<DeviceSpecific>` with other controls, such as the `List` and `ObjectList` controls.

For example, the page in Listing 17.5.2 displays different content to HTML and WML devices. If the device is an HTML-compatible device, special formatting is applied to the `List` control's header and footer. Furthermore, each list item is formatted in the `List` control's `ItemTemplate`. (This page is included on the CD with the name `devicespecific.aspx`.)

LISTING 17.5.2 Selecting Different Devices

```
1: <%@ Page Inherits="System.Web.UI.MobileControls.MobilePage" %>
2: <%@ Register TagPrefix="Mobile" Namespace="System.Web.UI.MobileControls"
3: Assembly="System.Web.Mobile" %>
4:
```

LISTING 17.5.2 Continued

```
 5: <Script Runat="Server">
 6:
 7: Sub doSomething( s As object, e As ListCommandEventArgs )
 8:   movieLabel.Text = e.ListItem.Text
 9:   ActiveForm = form2
10: End Sub
11:
12: </Script>
13:
14: <Mobile:Form runat="server" id="form1">
15: <Mobile:List
16:    ID="movies"
17:    OnItemCommand="doSomething"
18:    Runat="Server">
19: <Item text="Star Wars"/>
20: <Item text="Gone with the Wind"/>
21: <Item text="Citizen Kane"/>
22:
23: <DeviceSpecific>
24: <Choice Filter="IsHTML32">
25:    <HeaderTemplate>
26:    <h2>Welcome to the Movie Reservation System!</h2>
27:    </HeaderTemplate>
28:
29:    <ItemTemplate>
30:    <p>
31:    <asp:Button
32:     Text='<%# Container.ToString() %>'
33:     Runat="Server" />
34:    </ItemTemplate>
35:
36:    <FooterTemplate>
37:    <p>
38:    <small>All Contents &copy; copyright 2002 by the Company</small>
39:    </FooterTemplate>
40: </Choice>
41: </DeviceSpecific>
42:
43: </Mobile:List>
44: </Mobile:Form>
45:
46: <Mobile:Form runat="server" id="form2">
47: <b>You selected:</b>
48: <br/>
49: <Mobile:Label
50:    ID="movieLabel"
51:    Runat="Server"/>
52: </Mobile:Form>
```

When the page in Listing 17.5.2 is displayed in an HTML 3.2–compatible browser, the special formatting in `HeaderTemplate` and `FooterTemplate` is displayed. For example, the

`ItemTemplate` shows a `Button` control for each list item. You also should notice that all the templates use HTML tags that are not WML compatible (see Figure 17.24).

FIGURE 17.24
Using templates with Internet Explorer 5.5.

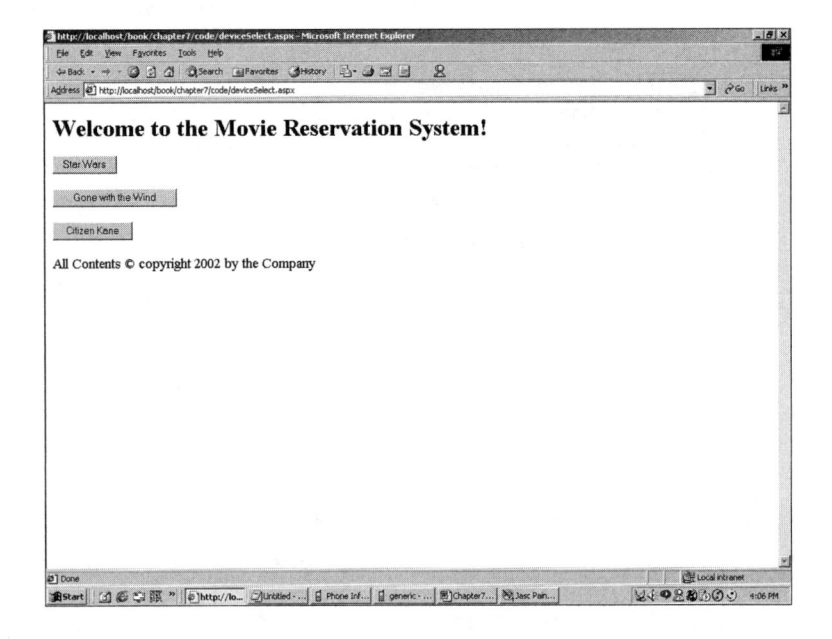

When the page in Listing 17.5.2 is displayed in a WML-compatible browser, all the templates are ignored. The `List` control is displayed with its default formatting.

Using Form Template Sets

As you saw in the previous section, the `<DeviceSpecific>` element can be used with `Image`, `List`, and `ObjectList` controls. You also can use the `<DeviceSpecific>` element with a Mobile `Form` control.

The Mobile `Form` control has both a `HeaderTemplate` and a `FooterTemplate`. You can create multiple `HeaderTemplates` and `FooterTemplates` and place them within different `<Choice>` elements. By creating multiple templates, you can display different content for different devices.

The page in Listing 17.5.3 demonstrates how to create three sets of templates. The first set of templates will render on WML-compatible devices, the second set on HTML 3.2–compatible devices, and the final set will render on other devices. (This page is included on the CD with the name `formTemplates.aspx`.)

LISTING 17.5.3 Displaying Different Content with Template Sets

```
 1: <%@ Page Inherits="System.Web.UI.MobileControls.MobilePage" %>
 2: <%@ Register TagPrefix="Mobile" Namespace="System.Web.UI.MobileControls"
 3: Assembly="System.Web.Mobile" %>
 4:
 5: <Mobile:Form runat="Server">
 6: <DeviceSpecific>
 7: <Choice Filter="IsWML">
 8:   <HeaderTemplate>
 9:     <b>Welcome to this Web site!</b>
10:     <br/>
11:   </HeaderTemplate>
12:   <FooterTemplate>
13:     <small>All Content Copyrighted 2001</small>
14:   </FooterTemplate>
15: </Choice>
16: <Choice Filter="IsHTML32">
17:   <HeaderTemplate>
18:     <table width="100%" bgcolor="yellow">
19:     <tr>
20:       <td>
21:       Welcome to this Web site!
22:       </td>
23:     </tr>
24:     </table>
25:   </HeaderTemplate>
26:   <FooterTemplate>
27:     <hr>
28:     <small>All Content Copyrighted &copy; 2001</small>
29:   </FooterTemplate>
30: </Choice>
31: <Choice>
32:   <HeaderTemplate>
33:     <b>Welcome to this Web site!</b>
34:     <br/>
35:   </HeaderTemplate>
36: </Choice>
37: </DeviceSpecific>
38:
39: <Mobile:Label
40:   Runat="Server">
41:   Here is the main body of the page.
42: </Mobile:Label>
43:
44: </Mobile:Form>
```

Summary

In this chapter, you learned how to use the Mobile controls to create ASP.NET pages that are compatible with cell phones, PDAs, and other mobile devices. First, you had an overview of WAP and WML—the standards for communicating with mobile devices.

In the next section, you looked at how to use the Microsoft Mobile controls. These mobile controls can be used to display text, lists, and other display elements, such as images and interactive calendars. Mobile controls also can be used to accept and validate text input with the `TextBox` control.

Finally, you examined how to make pages that are cross-device compatible and how to use the `MobileCapabilities` class to detect the features of a particular device. As you saw, the `<DeviceSpecific>` element can be used to display different content for devices with different features.

Other Resources

For more information on the material covered in this chapter:

- To view updated code samples and post questions about the topics covered in this chapter, visit the ASP.NET community at `www.superexpert.com`.

- For more information on WAP and WML, visit the WAP forum at `www.WapForum.org`. This Web site has developer forums, FAQs, and the latest news on the evolution of WAP.

- The Microsoft Mobile Devices Site contains announcements on the latest mobile device technologies offered by Microsoft in addition to information on the various Microsoft mobile devices. To visit the Microsoft Mobile Devices Site go to `www.microsoft.com/mobile`.

- To download the OpenWave phone simulators, visit `developer.openwave.com`. You'll want to download the UP.SDK.

- To download the Nokia phone simulators, visit `forum.nokia.com`. You'll want to download the Nokia Wap Toolkit 2.0.

CHAPTER 18

ASP.NET HTTP RUNTIME

by Billy Anders

In this chapter we will cover:
- The ASP.NET Http Runtime
- Intercepting Application Events using the Application File
- Intercepting Application Events using the IHttpModule interface
- Creating Http Handlers using .ASHX files
- Creating Http Handlers for files other than .ASHX
- ASP.NET Application File Directives

This chapter focuses on application-level programming using the ASP.NET Http Runtime. In this chapter, application-level programming refers to code and coding techniques that allow developers to access low-level request/response functionality of the Web server. This functionality is provided by the ASP.NET Http Runtime.

1. Http Runtime Overview

The ASP.NET Http Runtime is an extensible application runtime that allows changing the functionality of ASP.NET. The flexible design of the Http Runtime allows developers to extend its functionality beyond its out-of-box behavior. What this means for a .NET developer is that, if ASP.NET does not provide sufficient functionality in a particular area, the developer can change the underlying application infrastructure at a level that was once reserved for a different subset of developers.

In the past, to change the functionality of IIS (Internet Information Server) to include customized features such as custom logging, Internet-scale security, or data caching, you would need to use C/C++ and develop this functionality using the Internet Services Application Programming Interface (ISAPI). With the ASP.NET Http Runtime, advanced functionality can now easily be created using the .NET Frameworks and any .NET language.

The Http Runtime of ASP.NET exposes an object-oriented, event-driven infrastructure for developers to create advanced applications that participate during different stages of the request/response cycle. This infrastructure can be considered the logical .NET replacement for traditional ISAPI filters. Because of the event-driven model of the ASP.NET Http Runtime, developers are given the ability to participate at various stages of the application lifecycle using the .NET languages. Figure 18.1 shows the execution architecture for the Http Runtime.

FIGURE 18.1
ASP.NET Http Runtime execution architecture.

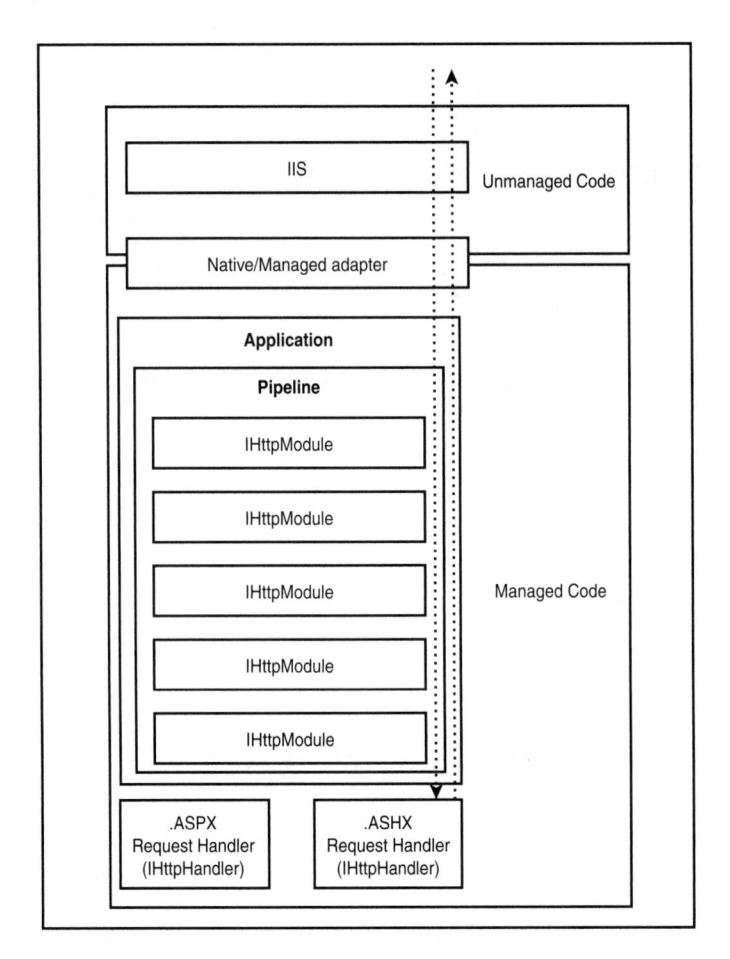

Another ISAPI-based advantage that has been available to C/C++ developers for years is the programming model that allows responding to particular URL and file extension requests. This model is referred to as an ISAPI *application* (or *extension*). In fact, the classic `ASP.DLL` itself is an ISAPI application mapped to files with the extension of `.asp`. With `ASP.DLL`, when IIS receives an HTTP request for a file with the `.asp` extension, the incoming request is dispatched to the `ASP.DLL` file. Using the ISAPI, `ASP.DLL` receives the request from IIS, loads the requested `.asp` file, interprets and executes the contents of the file, and sends the response back to the browser. The ASP.NET Http Runtime provides much of the same functionality through implementations of its `IHttpHandler` interface. An implementation of the `IHttpHandler` interface is typically called an `IHttpHandler` (also known as an HTTP Handler). An `IHttpHandler` can be developed using any .NET language in either a manually compiled and configured DLL (dynamic link library) or in a special `.ashx` file. Just as `.asmx` files are used for ASP.NET Web Services, `.ashx` files are used exclusively for creating HTTP Handlers. Both techniques offer the ASP.NET developer similar, powerful, yet easy to use, programming models.

With the ASP.NET Http Runtime the developer is no longer penalized for needing lower-level, customized application functionality. The Http Runtime continues to provide full access to the ASP.NET intrinsic objects. And since the functionality is provided by the .NET frameworks as opposed to a language-specific library such as MFC (Microsoft Foundation Classes) or ATL (Active Template Libraries), the programming model, features and functionality remain consistent across all of the languages. This means developers tasked with developing advanced, lower-level web application functionality can continue to use much of the higher-level services and functionality provided by the Http Runtime no matter what .NET language they choose to develop in.

Another important aspect to the Http Runtime is that it was designed to be host-agnostic; meaning it is not tied to any particular hosting environment. Currently the runtime is supported in versions 5 of IIS and greater and in command-line applications.

The `IHttpHandler` architecture of the runtime is used throughout ASP.NET. The installation of ASP.NET provides implementations of the `IHttpHandler` interface. These HTTP Handlers provide services for files with the extensions such as `.aspx`, `.ashx`, and `.asmx`. The `.aspx` files contain code for ASP.NET Pages; normally used for a graphical user-interface. The `.ashx` files contain HTTP Handlers. The files with an `.asmx` extension contain ASP.NET Web Services; programmable functionality most often exposed to other applications. For more information on Web Services in ASP.NET please see Chapter 13, "Web Services."

An `IHttpModule` is a class that implements the `System.Web.IHttpModule` interface. Some of the classes that implement `IHttpModule` interface (also known as *request interceptors* and *modules*) included with ASP.NET are for handling session state, authentication, authorization, logging, and output caching. The design of the Http Runtime allows for the removal of any unneeded `IHttpModule` from your application or from the machine entirely. This provides for occasions when you may simply not want a piece of default functionality in your application. The ASP.NET Http Runtime provides all of the facilities necessary to replace any of the *out-of-the-box* modules with ones of your own. For example, ASP.NET only provides authentication modules for a particular subset of possible authentication scenarios. However, just because your user account information is stored in a mainframe system, and not in a Microsoft Active Directory, does not mean that you have to forego using the rich authentication APIs provided by .NET. In this case, you would simply create your own custom `IHttpModule` to handle authenticating user credentials against your legacy system. The rest of the ASP.NET application can remain unchanged. For more information on Application Security in ASP.NET please see Chapter 12, "Security with ASP.NET."

Interception Events

The Http Runtime of ASP.NET exposes 12 events that enable a developer to register methods that get called at specific stages during the request/response lifecycle. As the events are raised, the registered methods are called and the developer is given the opportunity to act on the request. The developer can also terminate further processing of the request by the calling the `Response.End()` method.

Interception events can be developed using either the `global.asax` application file or precompiled components that implement the `IHttpModule` interface. Both the `global.asax` and precompiled methods expose the same events.

> **Tip**
>
> One of the advantages of the using the application file for interception events is that the compilation process is automatically handled by the ASP.NET Application compiler.
>
> However, parties interested in keeping their source code from prying eyes may be more interested in the precompiled technique. This will help conceal the source code and provide a distributable object that is un-editable by potential users of the component.

Listings 18.1.1 and 18.1.2 show all of the application-level events of the ASP.NET Http Runtime.

LISTING 18.1.1 Listing of All Deterministic Application-Level Events (in Order)

- BeginRequest
- AuthenticateRequest
- AuthorizeRequest
- ResolveRequestCache
- AquireRequestState
- PreRequestHandlerExecute
- PostRequestHandlerExecute
- ReleaseRequestState
- UpdateRequestCache
- EndRequest

These events are guaranteed to fire in the order listed. Listing 18.1.2 shows the non-deterministic application-level events.

LISTING 18.1.2 Listing of Non-Deterministic Application-Level Events

- Error
- PreSendRequestContent
- PreSendRequestHeaders

Listing 18.1.2 shows the non-deterministic application-level events. These events are not guaranteed to fire, and if and when any of them do, the order is not predetermined.

Using the Application-Level Events

Listing 18.1.3 shows the source of a `global.asax` application file.

LISTING 18.1.3 Provides a VB.Net Example of Handling the `BeginRequest` and `EndRequest` Events of the Application from Within the `global.asax` Application File

```
 1: <Script Language="VB" Runat="server">
 2:
 3: Sub Application_BeginRequest(ByVal Sender As Object, ByVal E As EventArgs)
 4:     Response.Write("Request Process Beginning!<br>")
 5: End Sub
 6:
 7:
 8: Sub Application_EndRequest(ByVal Sender As Object, ByVal E As EventArgs)
 9:     Response.Write("Request Process Ending!<br>")
10: End Sub
11:
12: </Script>
```

Inside of the `global.asax` application file two application events are being handled; `BeginRequest` and `EndRequest`. When raised by the ASP.NET Http Runtime, both of these events simply use the `Write` method of the `Response` object to output text to the response stream.

When this file is saved as the application file for an ASP.NET application, all requests for resources that ASP.NET is registered to service will have both "Request Process Beginning!" and "Request Process Ending!" in their content. For example, look at the contents of the following `default.aspx` file:

```
1: <html>
2: <head>
3:     <title>Test Page</title>
4: </head>
5:     <body>Hi, there!</body>
6: </html>
```

> **Note**
> Although the previous file listing contains no ASP.NET code, the file needed to end with `.aspx` in order to be processed by the ASP.NET Http Runtime.

Figure 18.2 shows the output when the file is requested by a Web browser.

FIGURE 18.2
Output from requesting the ASP.NET file.

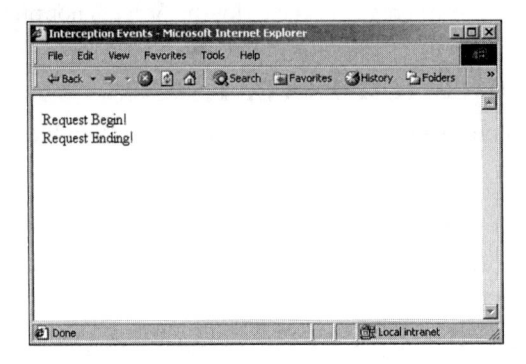

From the looks of Figure 18.2, it appears that we have injected our two lines of text and created a dynamic and well formed HTML page. Looking at the actual HTML output from the request shows when the events are actually fired.

When the file is requested by a Web browser, the resulting file is returned to the caller.

```
1: Request Processing Beginning!
2: <html>
3: <head>
4:     <title>Test Page</title>
5: </head>
6:     <body>Hi, there!</body>
7: </html>
8: Request Processing Ending!
```

Here you can see that our once well-formed HTML page is now less than well-formed. This example does a good job of demonstrating when the `BeginRequest` and `EndRequest` events of the `Application` object are raised.

These *interception events* are raised for all requests to ASP.NET-processed files. Only files that are registered in IIS with the ASP.NET ISAPI (`aspnet_isapi.dll`) will raise interception events. This means that requests to *non*-ASP.NET resources such as files with .GIF, .JPG, .TXT, and .HTM extensions, will not be processed by ASP.NET.

2. `Global.asax` Event Handlers

Earlier versions of Active Server Pages used an application file named `global.asa`. ASP.NET uses an application file with many of the same elements of the `global.asa`; however, the file is now named `global.asax`.

The `global.asax` application file is a text file that contains markup syntax for coding a server-side application object. The application file is parsed and compiled by the ASP.NET application compiler into a `System.Web.HttpApplication`-derived object during the first request to an ASP.NET resource within the application. The ASP.NET application compiler recompiles the application file automatically each time the file is modified.

> **Note**
> ASP.NET monitors the application file for changes, so the developer only needs to save the file for it to be recompiled during the next HTTP request.

Intercepting Events Using the `global.asax` Application File

The earlier example demonstrated both the `BeginRequest` and `EndRequest` events of the application. The next example demonstrates how one of the non-deterministic events, such as the `Error` event, can be handled.

There will undoubtedly be issues with any large-scaled, web application. The important thing is how you handle the issues. *Interception events* can be effectively used for wrapping your *entire* application with intelligent error handling code. In the case where something unexpected occurs in your application, you have the flexibility in deciding what you would like to do. When the application raises the `Error` event, you have a wealth of options available to you. Instead of showing the error to the end user, you can present the end-user with a custom message as simple as "Sorry, we are having technical difficulties." Another idea is that you can log the current state of all of the currently logged on users to an XML file. Of course, you will want to log the error and notify someone about the problem. To notify someone you can page the data center attendee about the situation. Once the problems with the application are fixed and the application begins executing normally, the application can be developed to do any number of things. Once started, the application can automatically check the contents of the XML file for users that were interrupted, look up their email addresses, and fire off emails saying, "Sorry we had problems early. But the system is back up now." These are just a few ideas, but the possibilities are endless.

Listing 18.2.1 shows how we can trap the `Error` event of the `Application` object and log the error to the Windows event log.

LISTING 18.2.1 Trapping the `Application_Error` Event and Logging the Error to the Windows Event Log

```
 1: <%@ Import Namespace="System.Diagnostics" %>
 2: <%@ Assembly Name="System.Diagnostics" %>
 3:
 4: <script language="VB" runat=server>
 5:
 6: Sub Application_Error(Sender as Object, E as EventArgs)
 7:
 8:    Dim LogName As String = "Web_Errors"
 9:    Dim Message As String = "Url " & Request.Path & " Error: " &
           Server.GetLastError.ToString
10:
11:    ' Create Event Log if It Doesn't Exist
12:    If (Not EventLog.SourceExists(LogName)) Then
13:      EventLog.CreateEventSource(LogName, LogName)
14:    End if
15:
16:    ' Log the Event
17:    Dim Log as New EventLog
18:    Log.Source = LogName
19:    Log.WriteEntry(Message, EventLogEntryType.Error)
20: End Sub
21: </script>
```

The example in Listing 18.2.1 intercepts the `Error` event of the `Application` object. The event is raised whenever there is an unhandled error within the application. When the `Error` event is raised, all HTTP handlers registered for this event will be called with two parameters: `Object` and `EventArgs`. Line 8 declares a String named `LogName` that contains the value "Web Errors." The `LogName` variable is used for creating a separate Event Log for the errors of our application. The `Message` variable that is created on line 9 contains the `Path` and text of the last error. Line 12 checks for the existence of the "Web Errors" event log. If the log does not exist, it is created on line 13. Line 17 creates a new `EventLog` object and gives it the name `Log`. Line 18 sets the `Source` property of the `Log` object to the `LogName` variable. The `WriteEntry` method of the `Log` object on line 19 simply writes the Message to the event log while setting the `EventLogEntryType` to `Error`.

For the `Application` object to actually raise the `Error` event, we need to write some faulty code. Listing 18.2.2 shows a simple ASP.NET page that forces an Application error to occur.

LISTING 18.2.2 Here Is an Intentionally Faulty Page to Force the `Application` Object to Raise the `Error` Event

```
1: <Script Language="VB" Runat="server">
2:
3: Sub Page_Load(O as Object, E As EventArgs)
4: Dim FakeObject as System.Object
5:
6: FakeObject.FakeMethod()
7: End Sub
```

LISTING 18.2.2 Continued

```
 8:
 9: </Script>
10:
11: <html>
12: <head>
13: <title>FakeObject Page</title>
14: </head>
15:
16: <body bgcolor="#FFFFFF">
17:
18: </body>
19: </html>
```

Line 4 of Listing 18.2.2 creates a `FakeObject` of type `System.Object`. Next on line 6, we call the `FakeMethod()` method of the `FakeObject`. This causes an error since the object does not contain a `FakeMethod()` method. Each time the page in Listing 18.2.2 is requested, it will cause the error to be logged to the Windows event log.

Figure 18.3 shows that the errors are indeed being logged to the Windows event log. All errors throughout the application will be logged here as well.

FIGURE 18.3
Windows event log showing the errors from our application.

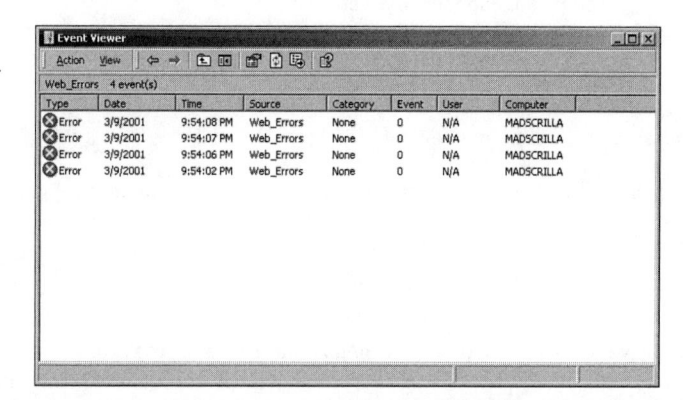

Figure 18.4 shows the details of one of the errors being logged to the Windows event log.

This error logging example could have been written to perform other tasks such as sending email to a pager, notifying a remote web service, etc. See Chapter 2, "Common ASP.NET Code Techniques," for more information on things like sending mail.

Interception events can also be used for creating a robust logging infrastructure in a *pay-per-use* billing system. Listing 18.2.3 shows how these events can be used in a *pay-per-use* scenario. The sample uses the `EndRequest` event of the `HttpApplication` object for logging all requests to web service files.

FIGURE 18.4
Details of one of the errors from our application.

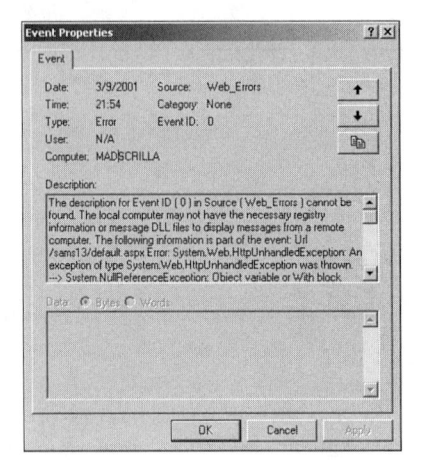

LISTING 18.2.3 Global.asax Application File for Logging Authenticated Requests to .asmx Files Within the ASP.NET Application

```
 1: <%@ Application Language="C#" Debug="True" %>
 2: <%@ Import Namespace="System.IO" %>
 3: <%@ Import Namespace="System.Data" %>
 4: <%@ Import Namespace="System.Data.SqlClient" %>
 5:
 6:
 7: <script runat="server">
 8:
 9: public void Application_EndRequest (object Sender, EventArgs E) {
10:
11: logInfo ((HttpApplication) Sender);
12: }
13:
14:
15: private void logInfo (HttpApplication application) {
16:
17: HttpRequest Request   = application.Request;
18: HttpResponse Response = application.Response;
19:
20: string UserName = Request.ServerVariables["REMOTE_USER"];
21: string IP= Request.ServerVariables["REMOTE_ADDR"];
22: string Method   = Request.ServerVariables["REQUEST_METHOD"];
23: string Path= Request.ServerVariables["PATH_INFO"];
24:
25: // Only log web service calls
26: if (Path.ToLower().IndexOf(".asmx")==-1)
27: return;
28:
29: String dsn = ConfigurationSettings.AppSettings["dsn"];
30:
```

LISTING 18.2.3 Continued

```
31:            SqlConnection conn = new SqlConnection(dsn);
32:            SqlCommand cmd = new SqlCommand("LogAccess", conn);
33:
34:            cmd.CommandType = CommandType.StoredProcedure;
35:
36:            SqlParameter prmUserName = new SqlParameter("@user_name",
➥SqlDbType.NVarChar, 30);
37:            prmUserName.Value = UserName;
38:            cmd.Parameters.Add(prmUserName);
39:
40:            SqlParameter prmPath = new SqlParameter("@path", SqlDbType.NVarChar,
➥255);
41:            prmPath.Value = Path;
42:            cmd.Parameters.Add(prmPath);
43:
44:            SqlParameter prmMethod = new SqlParameter("@method",
➥SqlDbType.NVarChar, 10);
45:            prmMethod.Value = Method;
46:            cmd.Parameters.Add(prmMethod);
47:
48:            SqlParameter prmIP = new SqlParameter("@remote_ip", SqlDbType.NVarChar,
15);
49:            prmIP.Value = IP;
50:            cmd.Parameters.Add(prmIP);
51:
52:            try {
53:                conn.Open();
54:                cmd.ExecuteNonQuery();
55:            }
56:            catch (Exception e) {
57:                // Eat the exception and return
58:            return;
59:            }
60:            finally {
61:                if (conn.State == ConnectionState.Open)
62:                    conn.Close();
63:            }
64:
65: return;
66: }
67:
68: </script>
```

Listing 18.2.4 creates the database, table, and stored procedure that are be used by the `global.asax` file for logging request to the `SimpleMath` web service. The database that is created is called `BillingSystem`. The `BillingSystem` database contains a single table called Log. For logging the web service request information we use the `LogAccess` stored procedure.

LISTING 18.2.4 SQL Script for Creating Database, Table, and Stored Procedure for Logging Web Service Usage

```sql
 1: CREATE DATABASE [BillingSystem]
 2: GO
 3:
 4: CREATE TABLE [Log] (
 5: [id] [int] IDENTITY (1, 1) NOT NULL ,
 6: [username] [nvarchar] (30) COLLATE SQL_Latin1_General_CP1_CI_AS NOT NULL ,
 7: [remote_ip] [nvarchar] (15) COLLATE SQL_Latin1_General_CP1_CI_AS NOT NULL ,
 8: [path] [nvarchar] (255) COLLATE SQL_Latin1_General_CP1_CI_AS NOT NULL ,
 9: [method] [nvarchar] (10) COLLATE SQL_Latin1_General_CP1_CI_AS NOT NULL ,
10: [timestamp] [datetime] NOT NULL ,
11: CONSTRAINT [PK_Log] PRIMARY KEY  CLUSTERED
12: (
13: [id]
14: )  ON [PRIMARY]
15: ) ON [PRIMARY]
16: GO
17:
18: CREATE Procedure LogAccess
19: @user_namenvarchar(30),
20: @pathnvarchar(255),
21: @methodnvarchar(10),
22: @remote_ipnvarchar(15)
23: As
24: INSERT INTO [Log]
25: (username, path, method, remote_ip, timestamp)
26: VALUES
27: (@user_name, @path, @method, @remote_ip, GETDATE())
28: RETURN
```

Now that we have our SQL database setup, we need to create a Web service to access. The `.asmx` file will allow users to do very simple arithmetic functions. Figure 18.5 shows the Web service client page.

FIGURE 18.5 `SimpleMath` Web service client page.

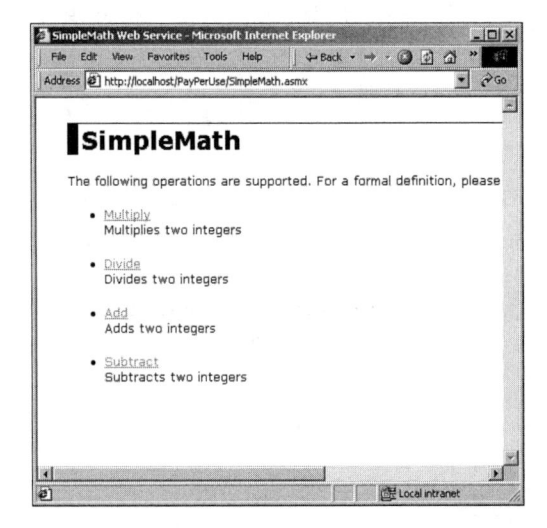

Listing 18.2.5 shows the code for our `SimpleMath` Web service.

LISTING 18.2.5 `SimpleMath` Web Service Source

```
 1: <%@ WebService Class="SimpleMath" Language="C#" Debug="True" %>
 2:
 3: using System.Web;
 4: using System.Web.Services;
 5:
 6:
 7: class SimpleMath {
 8:
 9: [WebMethod (Description="Adds two integers")]
10: public int Add (int first, int second) {
11:
12: return (first + second);
13: }
14:
15: [WebMethod (Description="Subtracts two integers")]
16: public int Subtract (int first, int second) {
17:
18: return (first - second);
19: }
20:
21: [WebMethod (Description="Multiplies two integers")]
22: public int Multiply (int first, int second) {
23:
24: return (first * second);
25: }
26:
27: [WebMethod (Description="Divides two integers")]
28: public int Divide (int first, int second) {
29:
30: return (first / second);
31: }
32: }
```

The service file contains four web service-exposed methods: `Add`, `Subtract`, `Multiple`, and `Divide`. Figure 18.7 shows the `Add` method of the `SimpleMath` service.

Listing 18.2.6 shows the `Web.config` file for the `SimpleMath` service. The service denies non-authenticated users from all pages. The `Web.config` file also establishes the `dsn` section that is used in both the `SimpleMath` service and in the `usage.aspx` page.

LISTING 18.2.6 `Web.config` Configuration File for the `SimpleMath` Service

```
1: <configuration>
2:
3: <system.web>
4: <authentication mode="Windows" />
5:
6: <authorization>
7: <allow users="*" />
```

LISTING 18.2.6 Continued

```
 8: <deny users="?" />
 9: </authorization>
10:
11: </system.web>
12:
13: <appSettings>
14: <add key="dsn" value="server=localhost;
➥                            uid=sa;
➥                            pwd=password;
➥                            database=BillingSystem;" />
15: </appSettings>
16:
17: </configuration>
```

Figure 18.6 shows the result of calling the Add method with 23 and 25 as the parameters.

FIGURE 18.6
Result of calling the Add method with 23 and 25 as the parameters.

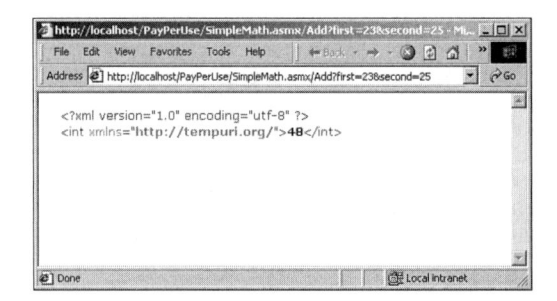

Next we need to show users how many times they have used the `SimpleMath` service. The page shows information such as the remote IP address, user name, time of request, and the path that was requested. Figure 18.7 shows a screenshot of the page.

FIGURE 18.7
Usage page that shows information about each request that was made with the current Windows account.

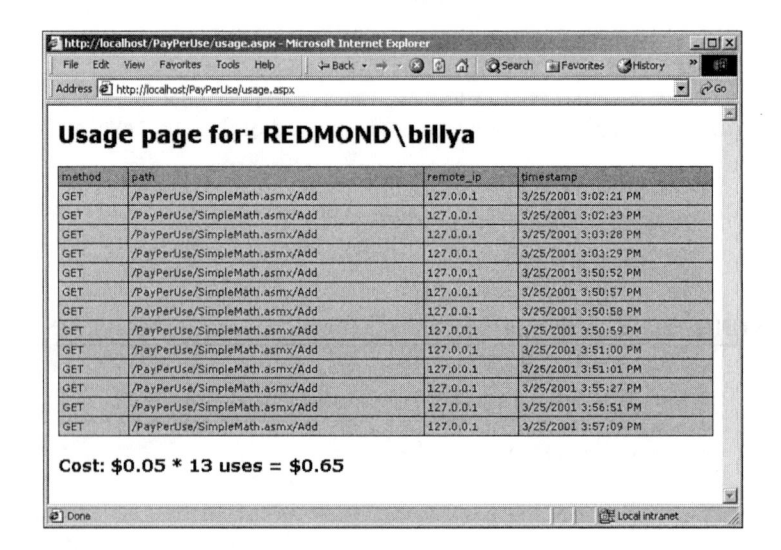

Listing 18.2.7 shows the source code for our `usage.aspx` page. This page gives the user information about each of their requests to a Web service file.

LISTING 18.2.7 Usage/Billing Page That Shows a User How Many Times They Have Used the Web Service and How Much Money They Owe

```
 1: <%@ Import Namespace="System.Data" %>
 2: <%@ Import Namespace="System.Data.SqlClient" %>
 3:
 4: <html>
 5: <script language="C#" runat="server">
 6:
 7:    protected void Page_Load(Object sender, EventArgs e) {
 8:
 9: // Each use costs 5¢
10: const double TRANSACTION_COST = 0.05;
11:
12: string username = User.Identity.Name;
13:
14: Message.Text = "Usage page for: " + username;
15:
16: String dsn = ConfigurationSettings.AppSettings["dsn"];
17:
18: SqlConnection conn = null;
19:
20: try {
21:
22: conn = new SqlConnection(dsn);
23: SqlDataAdapter myCommand = new
                   SqlDataAdapter("select method, path, remote_ip,
                   timestamp from Log where
                   username='" + username + "'", conn);
24:
25: DataSet ds = new DataSet();
26: myCommand.Fill(ds, "Usage");
27:
28: DataView dv = ds.Tables["Usage"].DefaultView;
29:
30: MyDataGrid.DataSource = dv;
31: MyDataGrid.DataBind();
32:
33: Fee.Text  = TRANSACTION_COST.ToString("c");
34: Uses.Text = dv.Count + " uses";
35:
36: Cost.Text = (dv.Count * TRANSACTION_COST).ToString("c");
37:
38: }
39: catch {
40: // Eat the exception
41: }
42:        finally {
43:            if (conn.State == ConnectionState.Open)
```

LISTING 18.2.7 Continued

```
44:                    conn.Close();
45:            }
46:    }
47:
48: </script>
49:
50: <body>
51:
52:    <h2>
53: <font face="Verdana">
54: <ASP:Label id="Message" runat="server" />
55: </font>
56:    </h2>
57:
58:    <ASP:DataGrid id="MyDataGrid" runat="server"
59:      Width="700"
60:      BackColor="#ccccff"
61:      BorderColor="black"
62:      ShowFooter="false"
63:      CellPadding=3
64:      CellSpacing="0"
65:      Font-Name="Verdana"
66:      Font-Size="8pt"
67:      HeaderStyle-BackColor="#aaaadd"
68:      EnableViewState="false"
69:    />
70:
71:    <h3>
72: <font face="Verdana">
73: Cost: <ASP:Label id="Fee" runat="server" /> *
74:        <ASP:Label id="Uses" runat="server" /> =
75:        <ASP:Label id="Cost" runat="server" />
76: </font>
77:    </h3>
78:
79: </body>
80: </html>
```

Intercepting Events Using HTTP Modules

As mentioned earlier in this chapter, HTTP Modules are the logical replacements for ISAPI filters. In essence, an `IHttpModule` is a class that implements the `System.Web.IHttpModule` interface.

The `IHttpModule` Interface

The `IHttpModule` interface contains the two members that must be implemented by all HTTP Modules.

```
Namespace System.Web {

    public interface IHttpModule {

        public void Init(HttpApplication application);
        public void Dispose();
        }
}
```

Init

The `Init()` method is invoked by the Http Runtime to enable a module to handle requests. The `Init()` method is almost always used to synchronize any `HttpApplication` events.

Here is an example of using the `Init()` method of `System.Web.IHttpModule` for adding the `Me.Application_Error()` method to the list of handlers for the `application.Error` event.

```
Public Sub Init(application As HttpApplication) Implements IHttpModule
    AddHandler application.Error , AddressOf Me.Application_Error
End Sub
```

This example uses the `Init()` method of the `IHttpModule` interface for registering the `Me.Application_Error()` method for handling all `Error` events raised by the `HttpApplication` object.

Dispose

The `Dispose()` method is called before the Http Runtime destroys your object. If there are any expensive resources still open, such as database connections, file handles, streams, and so on, they should be closed here.

Here is an example of the `Dispose` method of the `IHttpModule` interface.

```
Public Sub Dispose() Implements IHttpModule
    'Do some clean-up work here
    MyADOConn.Close()
End Sub
```

This example uses the `Dispose()` method for using ADO.NET for closing the database connection.

Listing 18.2.8 is an `IHttpModule` that traps the `Error` event of the `application` object and logs the information to the Windows event log.

LISTING 18.2.8 An Example of an `IHttpModule` for Logging Error Information

```
 1: 'vbc /target:library /r:System.Web.dll /r:System.dll error.vb
 2:
 3: Imports System
 4: Imports System.Web
 5: Imports System.Diagnostics
 6: Imports System.Collections
 7:
```

LISTING 18.2.8 *Continued*

```
 8: Public Class ErrorHandlerModule
 9:   Implements IHttpModule
10:
11:     Public Sub Init(application As HttpApplication)
12: ➥          Implements IHttpModule.Init
13:         AddHandler application.Error ,
14: ➥             AddressOf Me.Application_Error
15:     End Sub
16:
17:     Private Sub WriteEventLog(logName As [String], message As [String],
18: ➥         eventType As EventLogEntryType)
19:
20:         If EventLog.SourceExists(logName) = False Then
21:             EventLog.CreateEventSource(logName, logName)
22:         End If
23:
24:         Dim log As New EventLog()
25:
26:         log.Source = logName
27:         log.WriteEntry(message, eventType)
28:     End Sub
29:
30:     Private Sub Application_Error([source] As [Object],
31: ➥         e As EventArgs)
32:
33:         Dim application As HttpApplication = CType([source],
34: ➥             HttpApplication)
35:         Dim context As HttpContext = application.Context
36: Dim message As String = "Url: " + context.Request.Path +
37: ➥             "\n" + "Error: " + context.Error.ToString()
38:
39:         WriteEventLog(context.Request.ApplicationPath, message,
40: ➥             EventLogEntryType.Error)
41:     End Sub
42:
43:     Public Sub Dispose() Implements IHttpModule.Dispose
44:     End Sub
45:
46: End Class
```

As the number of lines of code between Listing 18.2.8 and 18.2.1 demonstrate, using the **global.asax** to code interception events can save some typing. However, if you are concerned with keeping your source code private, you undoubtedly need to endure the extra coding and configuration of using the **IHttpModule** interface.

IHttpModule *Registration*

Objects that implement the **IHttpModule** interface need to be registered with the ASP.NET Http Runtime before they can be used. In order to use your newly created **IHttpModule**, you must configure the hosting server. To do so, follow these steps:

1. Create an `HttpModule` implementing the `IHttpModule` interface.
2. Compile your `HttpModule` into a .NET library DLL.
3. Deploy your DLL into the `bin` directory under the application virtual root.
4. Register the `HttpModule` in the `<httpmodules>` section of the `web.config` file.

The `web.config` File

To add an `IHttpModule`, you will need to edit your `web.config` file. The syntax for adding a new `HttpModule` is listed below:

```
<configuration>
    <httpmodules>
        <add type="assemblyname#classname" />
    <httpmodules>
</configuration>
```

The `<add>` Directive

The `<add>` directive adds HttpModule classes to an application. The `<add>` directive has a single attribute: `type`. The `type` attribute is composed of an assembly and class combination (where the two values are separated by `#`). The assembly DLL is always resolved first against an application's private `bin` directory and then against the system assembly cache. The class part takes the name of a class within the assembly that implements the `System.Web.IHttpModule` interface.

Here is a sample of using the `<add>` tag:

```
<add type="MySample#My401k" />
```

The `<remove>` Directive

The `<remove>` directive removes an HttpModule class from an application. Deleting or commenting out the `<add>` directive of the `HttpModule` accomplishes the same thing. The `<remove>` directive is most useful when the system as a whole has one or more HttpModules that are added to all applications through the hierarchical configuration system but particular applications on the system do not want the HttpModules.

Here is an example of using the remove directive:

```
<remove type="MySample#My401k" />
```

The `<clear>` Directive

The `<clear>` directive removes all HttpModule mappings currently configured or inherited by a particular `web.config` file from the application. Here's an example:

```
<clear />
```

Listing 18.2.9 shows a simple `IHttpModule` that intercepts both the `BeginRequest` and `EndRequest` events of the application events.

LISTING 18.2.9 A Visual Basic Example of a Hello World `IhttpModule`

```
 1: Imports System
 2: Imports System.Web
 3: Imports System.Collections
 4:
 5: Public Class HelloWorldModule
 6: Implements IHttpModule
 7:
 8: Public Sub Init(application As HttpApplication)
➥Implements IHttpModule.Init
 9: AddHandler application.BeginRequest ,
➥AddressOf Me.Application_BeginRequest
10: AddHandler application.EndRequest ,
➥AddressOf Me.Application_EndRequest
11: End Sub
12:
13: Private Sub Application_BeginRequest([source] As [Object],
➥e As EventArgs)
14: Dim application As HttpApplication = CType([source],
➥HttpApplication)
15: Dim context As HttpContext = application.Context
16:
17: context.Response.Write("Beginning of Request")
18: End Sub
19:
20: Private Sub Application_EndRequest([source] As [Object],
    ➥e As EventArgs)
21: Dim application As HttpApplication = CType([source],
    ➥HttpApplication)
22: Dim context As HttpContext = application.Context
23:
24: context.Response.Write("End of Request")
25: End Sub
26:
27: Public Sub Dispose() Implements IHttpModule.Dispose
28: End Sub
29:
30: End Class
```

Listing 18.2.9 shows an `IHttpModule` in VB.Net. As mentioned earlier, the `Init()` method is used for registering for event notification. To dynamically add event handlers at runtime with VB, you use the `AddHandler` statement. The `AddHandler` statement takes two parameters. The first parameter is an event expression. The second parameter is an expression that must evaluate to a delegate instance of the appropriate type for the event hookup. Line 9 is effectively saying, "when the `BeginRequest` event of the application object occurs, please call my `Application_BeginRequest` method."

When called, the `Application_BeginRequest` method receives two parameters: a source parameter of type `Object` and an e parameter of type `EventArgs`. We use the `CType` function of VB to convert the source parameter to an `HttpApplication` object. Next, we call the `Context` property of the `HttpApplication` object in order to get an `HttpContext` object. Once we have an `HttpContext` (context) object, we can call the `Write` method of the `Response` object using the code on line 17.

IHttpHandlers

As mentioned earlier in this chapter, HTTP Handlers are the logical replacements for ISAPI applications. Tasks achieved using ISAPI applications can now be done using ASP.NET.

There are three ways in which to create an `IHttpHandler` with ASP.NET:

- ASHX file with inline code
- ASHX file with Code-Behind DLL
- Compiled DLL configured in `web.config`

Two of the three methods for creating `IHttpHandlers` involve using a file with the extension `.ashx`. An ASHX file is a declarative text file that contains markup syntax for either defining or referencing an ASP.NET `IHttpHandler`.

ASHX Files

All .ASHX files contain the `WebHandler` file directive:

```
<%@ WebHandler
➥    Language="Any installed .NET language"
➥    Class="IHttpHandler Class" %>
```

Use of the `WebHandler` directive requires the user specify a value for the `Class` attribute and optionally a value for the `Language` attribute. The value of the `Class` attribute should be the name of a class that implements the `System.Web.IHttpHandler` interface.

> **Note**
> Coding HTTP Handlers with `.ashx` files will be covered at length later in this chapter.
> The `.ashx` file technique is the recommended way for creating HTTP handlers for most developers.

Inline Code

An ASHX file gives you the flexibility of placing the code for the class either directly in the file or in a precompiled DLL within the `/bin` directory of the Web application.

When the code for the `IHttpHandler` is placed inline in the ASHX file, ASP.NET will dynamically compile and cache the code the first time the file is requested via a client. Listing 18.2.10 provides an example of using an ASHX file with inline code.

LISTING 18.2.10 A Very Simple HelloWorld `IHttpHandler`

```
 1: <%@ WebHandler Language="VB" Class="FirstHandler" %>
 2:
 3: Imports System.Web
 4:
 5: Public Class FirstHandler
 6: Implements IHttpHandler
 7:
 8: Public Sub ProcessRequest(Context As HttpContext) Implements
    ➥ IHttpHandler.ProcessRequest
 9:     Context.Response.Write("Hello, World!")
10: End Sub
11:
12: ReadOnly Property IsReusable() As Boolean Implements IHttpHandler.IsReusable
13:     Get
14:         Return true
15:     End Get
16:   End Property
17:
18: End Class
```

Listing 18.2.10 shows an HTTP Handler in VB that simply uses the `Write` method of the `HttpResponse` object for displaying the text "Hello, World!".

Listing 18.2.11 uses the `QueryString` property from the `Request` object to retrieve the `Name` parameter sent in the URL. Then a basic HTML page is produced, showing "Hello," and the value of the `Name` parameter.

LISTING 18.2.11 Simple `IHttpHandler` That Greets Users Using the `Name` Parameter from the Query String (`HelloHandler.ashx`)

```
 1: <%@ WebHandler Language="C#" Class="HelloHandler" %>
 2:
 3: using System;
 4: using System.Web;
 5:
 6: public class HelloHandler : IHttpHandler {
 7:
 8:     public void ProcessRequest(HttpContext context) {
 9:
10:         HttpResponse Response = context.Response;
11:         HttpRequest Request = context.Request;
12:
13:         Response.Write("<html><body>");
14:         Response.Write("<h1>");
15:         Response.Write("Hello ");
16:         Response.Write(Request.QueryString["Name"]);
17:         Response.Write("</h1>");
18:         Response.Write("</body></html>");
19: }
```

LISTING 18.2.11 *Continued*

```
20:     public bool IsReusable {
21:         get {return true;}
22:     }
23: }
```

The code in Listing 18.2.11 shows how to create an Http Handler in C# using a .ashx file. Lines 10 and 11 use the `Response` and `Request` properties of the `HttpContext` object for gaining access to the `Response` and `Request` intrinsic objects. Lines 13-18 simply use the `Write` method of the `Response` object for displaying an HTML page that displays the name value that was sent in the query string.

Code-Behind

Listing 18.2.12 affectively uses the same code as in Listing 18.2.11. One major difference between the Listing in 18.2.12 and that of 18.2.11 is that Listing 18.2.12 uses the more manual `IHttpHandler` technique.

LISTING 18.2.12 Simple `IHttpHandler` (`HelloHandler.vb`) That Displays the Contents of the Name Parameter

```
 1: Imports System
 2: Imports System.Web
 3:
 4: Public Class HelloHandler : Implements IHttpHandler
 5:
 6: Public Sub ProcessRequest (context As HttpContext) Implements
 7:          IHttpHandler.ProcessRequest
 8:
 9:     Dim Response As HttpResponse = context.Response
10:     Dim Request As HttpRequest = context.Request
11:
12:     Response.Write("<html><body>")
13:     Response.Write("<h1>")
14:     Response.Write("Hello ")
15:     Response.Write(Request.QueryString("Name"))
16:     Response.Write("</h1>")
17:     Response.Write("</body></html>")
18: End Sub
19:
20: Public Property IsReusable As Boolean Implements IHttpHandler.IsReusable
21:     Get
22:         Return True
23:     End Get
24: End Property
25:
26: End Class
```

The code in Listing 18.2.12 should be compiled with the following command:

```
vbc /t:library /r:System.Web.dll
➥       /out:HelloHandler.dll HelloHandler.vb
```

The resulting `HelloHandler.dll` file needs to be placed in the `/bin` directory of your application. You now have two ways available to you in which to configure ASP.NET to use your `IHttpHandler`. The simpler method involves creating a "stub" `.ashx` file that references your newly created `IHttpHandler` class.

In order to use the newly created `HelloHandler.dll` in the `/bin` directory from within a `.ashx` file we use the `@WebHandler` directive. The `WebHandler` directive below informs the ASP.NET compiler that it should check the assembly cache for a precompiled class called `HelloHandler`.

Here is an example of using the ASHX file with a Code-Behind DLL (`FirstHandler.ashx`):

```
<%@ WebHandler Class="HelloHandler" %>
```

One of the advantages to using a separately compiled DLL with either an ASHX file or `web.config` is that your source code can be hidden from prying eyes. All that someone can see is the `WebHandler` directive in the ASHX "stub" file. Your actual intellectual property is safely tucked away in the precompiled DLL.

Web.config

The downside to the `web.config` file approach is that there are additional configuration steps that need to be taken. You need to manually configure the file extension mappings in IIS to map a new file extension to the ASP.NET ISAPI (`aspnet_isapi.dll`). You must also add an `<httphandlers>` section to the `web.config` file of your application.

Listing 18.2.13 shows the `web.config` file for configuring ASP.NET to dispatch requests for `.hello` files to the `HelloHandler`

LISTING 18.2.13 Web.config File with `HelloHandler` Added to the `<httphandlers>` Section

```
1: <configuration>
2:     <httphandlers>
3:         <add verb="*" path="*.hello"
                 type="HelloHandler,HelloHandler"/>
4:     </httphandlers>
5: </configuration>
```

Although this approach requires more manual steps, it does offer at least one advantage. This approach allows you the flexibility of using any filename and/or extension for your `IHttpHandler`. For example, if your company creates sweaters for pot-bellied pigs, you might be interested in using a `.pig` extension for your Http Handler file.

Although simple in functionality, these examples demonstrate the basics for building an `IHttpHandler`. The `HelloHandler` class implements both members defined by the `IHttpHandler` interface: `ProcessRequest()` and `IsReusable`.

Here is the `IHttpHandler` interface.

```
namespace System.Web
{
    public interface IHttpHandler
    {
        public void     ProcessRequest(HttpContext Context);
        public boolean  IsReusable(get;)
    }
}
```

When called by the ASP.NET Http Runtime, the `ProcessRequest` method receives an `HttpContext` object. The `HttpContext` object encapsulates the entire HTTP-specific context used for processing the request. To gain access to the `HttpResponse` object we call the `Response` property of the `HttpContext` object. Using the `Response` object, we can write the contents of a simple HTML page that displays "Hello" and any information that is received in the query string variable `Name`.

The `IsReusable` property of the `IHttpHandler` interface informs the runtime whether the object can be pooled. If the object does not maintain state and can be reused, the property should return the Boolean value `True`. If the object should be re-created for each individual request, the method should return the Boolean value `False`.

The `HttpContext` Class

`HttpContext` is an object that encapsulates all information about an individual HTTP Request within ASP.NET.

Your code gains access to the ASP.NET request/response intrinsic objects via the `HttpContext` object. You can also add your own custom objects into the `HttpContext` object. All information, including newly added objects, are carried throughout the request.

Here is the definition for the `System.Web.HttpContext` object

```
namespace System.Web
{
    public class HttpContext
    {
        // Properties
        public IHttpHandler           Handler       { get; set; }
        public HttpPipeline           Pipeline      { get; }
        public HttpRequest            Request       { get; }
        public HttpResponse           Response      { get; }
        public HttpServerUtility      Server        { get; }
        public HttpApplicationState   Application   { get; }
        public SessionState           Session       { get; }
        public TraceContext           Trace         { get; }
        public DateTime               TimeStamp     { get; }
        public IPrincipal             User          { get; }
        public IDictionary            Items         { get; }
        public Exception              Error         { get; }
        public Exception []           AllErrors     { get; }
```

700 ASP.NET: TIPS, TUTORIALS, AND CODE

```
            // Methods
            public void        AddError(Exception error);
            public void        ClearErrors();
            public Object      GetConfig(String name);
            public Object      GetConfig(String name, String path);
        }
}
```

The `HttpContext` class contains all of the detail concerning the HTTP request that you would need.

Listing 18.2.14 shows how to iterate over all of the `ServerVariables` collection from within an Http Handler.

LISTING 18.2.14 Using the `ServerVariables` Collection from Within an `IhttpHandler`

```
 1: <%@ WebHandler Language="C#" Class="ServerVarsHandler" %>
 2:
 3: using System.Web;
 4: using System.Text;
 5: using System.Collections.Specialized;
 6:
 7:
 8: public class ServerVarsHandler : IHttpHandler {
 9:
10:     public void ProcessRequest(HttpContext context) {
11:
12: HttpRequest  Request  = context.Request;
13: HttpResponse Response = context.Response;
14:
15: NameValueCollection coll = Request.ServerVariables;
16:
17: string[] keys = coll.AllKeys;
18:
19: int iLength = keys.Length;
20:
21: for (int i=0; i < iLength; i++)
22: Response.Write (keys[i] + " = " + coll[i] + "<br>");
23:
24:     }
25:
26:     public bool IsReusable {
27:
28: get {return true;}
29:     }
30:
31: }
32:
```

Listing 18.2.14 shows an example of how to iterate over the `ServerVariables` collection. Lines 3-5 import the `System`, `System.Web`, `System.Text` and `System.Collections` namespaces into our `ServerVarsHandler`. Line 8 both declares the class with the name

ServerVarsHandler and instructs the C# compiler that this class implements the IHttpHandler interface. The ProcessRequest method is defined in the IHttpHandler interface and declared on line 10. On lines 12 and 13, the Request and Response properties of the Context object are called. These two properties return the current instances of the HttpRequest and HttpResponse objects and their returned values are set to the variables Request and Response, respectively. Once we have these objects, we have access to some the familiar methods such as the Write() method of the Response object. Line 15 uses the ServerVariables property of the request object and sets its returned value to a NameValueCollection named coll. The coll variable now contains the ServerVariables collection. Line 17 uses the AllKeys property of our new NameValueCollection. The AllKeys property returns an array strings that contain all of the names of the name/value pairs in the collection.

Line 20 creates an int and assigns the Length of the keys collection to it. Line 21 is the beginning of our for loop for iterating over the ServerVariables collection.

> **Note**
> The Length of the collection is 1-based, while collections are 0-based. On line 21 we must use count - 1 to compensate for this.

Line 24 uses the Write method of the Response object for displaying the values of the keys and values collection. The read-only IsReusable property on lines 26-39 is needed to satisfy our implementation of the IHttpHandler interface. The IsReusable method returns the bool true informing the ASP.NET Http Runtime that this particular IHttpHandler can be re-used and does not need to be destroyed first. Figure 18.8 shows a screen shot of the ServerVarsHandler.

FIGURE 18.8
The output of the ServerVars IhttpHandler.

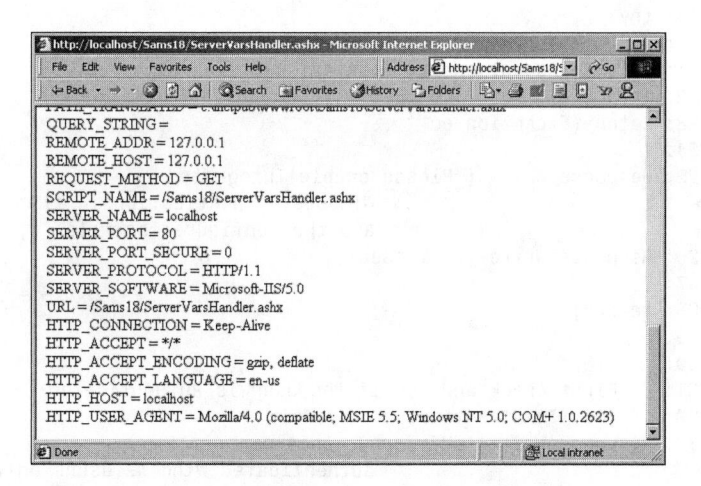

The `HttpRequest` Class

The `Request` and `Response` objects have been significantly enhanced in ASP.NET. The `Request` object has 25 new properties and three new methods. Some of the new additions include built-in stream, browser capabilities and file-uploading support.

Listing 18.2.15 demonstrates how to create an `IHttpHandler` that uses the `HttpPostedFile` and `HttpFileCollection` objects for allowing authenticated users to upload files to a predetermined directory on the server.

LISTING 18.2.15 Using the `HttpPostedFile` and `HttpFileCollection` Objects from Within an `IHttpHandler`

```
 1: <%@ WebHandler Class="FileUploadHandler" Language="C#" %>
 2:
 3: using System;
 4: using System.IO;
 5: using System.Web;
 6: using System.Web.Security;
 7: using System.Security.Principal;
 8:
 9:
10: class FileUploadHandler : IHttpHandler {
11:
12: public void ProcessRequest(HttpContext context) {
13:
14: HttpRequest Request   = context.Request;
15: HttpResponse Response = context.Response;
16:
17: WindowsIdentity id;
18:
19: try
20: {
21: id = (WindowsIdentity) context.User.Identity;
22: }
23: catch (Exception eo)
24: {
25: Response.Write ("Please enable Integrated
                     Windows Authentication in IIS
                     and the configuration file.");
26: Response.Write (eo.Message);
27:
28: return;
29: }
30:
31: // First check and see if the user is authenticated
32: if (!id.IsAuthenticated) {
33: Response.Write("<H2>Sorry, this page is for
                    authenticated Windows users only.</H2>");
34: Response.Write("Inform the administrator
                    that Anonymous access
                    must be disabled in IIS");
```

LISTING 18.2.15 Continued

```
35:
36: return;
37: }
38:
39: HttpFileCollection Files = Request.Files;
40:
41: // If there are no files, just return.
42: if (Files.Count == 0) {
43: Response.Write ("There were no files uploaded.<br>");
44:
45: return;
46: }
47:
48: // There is at least one file.
49: try
50: {
51: string[] FileNames;
52: string    FileName;
53: string SavePath;
54: string FileAndPath;
55: string UserName;
56:
57: HttpPostedFile File;
58:
59: int lastslash;
60: int iLoop;
61:
62: FileNames = Files.AllKeys;
63:
64: for (iLoop=0; iLoop < Files.Count; iLoop++) {
65:
66:
67: File = Files[FileNames[iLoop]];
68:
69: // Make sure that the HttpPostedFile object is not empty
70: if (File.FileName != "") {
71:
72: // Get the filename minus the path info
73: lastslash = File.FileName.LastIndexOf(@"\");
74: FileName = File.FileName.Substring(lastslash + 1);
75:
76: // Change the MachineName\UserName to MachineName-UserName
77: UserName = id.Name.Replace('\\','-');
78:
79: SavePath = @"c:\temp\" + UserName + @"\";
80: FileAndPath = SavePath + FileName;
81:
82: //  Create the directory
83: if(!Directory.Exists(SavePath))
84: Directory.CreateDirectory(SavePath);
85:
86: // Save the file
```

LISTING 18.2.15 Continued

```
 87: File.SaveAs(FileAndPath.ToLower());
 88:
 89: // Let the user know the file(s) were saved
 90: Response.Write("SAVED AS: " + FileAndPath.ToLower() + "<br>");
 91: }
 92: }
 93:
 94: }
 95: catch (Exception eo)
 96: {
 97: Response.Write("<H2>" + eo.Message +"</H2>");
 98: }
 99:
100:
101: }
102:
103: public bool IsReusable {
104: get {return true;}
105: }
106: }
107:
```

Listing 18.2.15 contains code for allowing users to upload files to the server. Lines 3-7 import the namespaces that will be needed during the rest of the code listing. After getting references to our `HttpRequest` and `HttpResponse` objects on lines 14 and 15, we declare a variable of type `WindowsIdentity` on line 17. The `id` variable declared on line 17 is set to the `WindowsIdentity` of the current user. This is done by calling the Identity property of the User object and casting the result to a `WindowsIdentity`. If the cast was not successful we inform the user and return.

> **Note**
> The cast can only work successfully if Integrated Windows Authenticated is enabled in both the configuration file and in IIS. Anonymous access must be disabled in IIS.

Even if the cast to a `WindowsIdentity` object is successful, we need to be sure that the user is authenticated. This is done on lines 32-37. If the user is not authenticated, we inform them and return. Figure 18.9 shows a screenshot of what an un-authenticated user will receive.

On line 39 we create `HttpFileCollection` object by calling the `Files` property of the `Request` object. The `HttpFileCollection` will contain the all of the files that were posted to the `IHttpHandler`. Just so that we do not waste further time and resources, line 42 checks to make sure that at least one file was sent to the handler using the `Count` property available to on the `HttpFileCollection` object. If there were no files sent, we inform the sender using the `Write` method of the `Response` object. Figure 18.10 shows what a user sees when they have not uploaded any files to the system.

FIGURE 18.9
A screenshot of what a user receives when they are not authenticated using Integrated Windows Authenticated.

FIGURE 18.10
Inform users that they have not uploaded any files.

Lines 51-55 declare strings and one array of strings. The `HttpFileCollection` is a collection of `HttpPostedFile` objects. Each `HttpPostedFile` object contains information about a single file that was potentially sent to the server. Line 57 declares our `HttpPostedFile` and assigns it the name `File`. Line 62 calls the `AllKeys` property of the `HttpFileCollection`. `AllKeys` returns an array of strings containing the names of all members in the file collection. Line 64 is the beginning of our `for` loop that iterates over all of the files that were potentially sent and saves them to the file system. Line 67 gets the current `HttpPostedFile` from the `HttpFileCollection`. Since the `HttpFileCollection` contains information on all files that were potentially sent, we need to check for the true existence of a file by calling the `FileName` property of each file. If the `FileName` property is not empty, then we can safely assume that there is indeed a file worth saving. The `FileName` property of each `HttpPostedFile` contains the fully-qualified path of the file (for example, `C:\Winnt\Notepad.exe`). We only want the actual filename (`Notepad.exe`), so the `LastIndex` method available on all strings is used for finding the `last` backslash (\) of the filename. The position of the last backslash is saved in the `lastslash` variable. Next, we use the `Substring` method of string for extracting only the filename from the fully-qualified filename. This is done using the `lastslash` position plus one.

Since we want user files saved in directories named after them, we need to extract the logon name of the user. Since the backslash (\) character designates directories the file system, we cannot use a standard Windows domain logon for the filename. Instead we need to do something with the backslash. In this case we simply convert the backslash to a dash (-). This is done using the `Replace` method of string. `Replace` either a `string` with another `string` or a `char` with another `char`. In this case, all that we need to replace is a single character, so a `char` works well. Line 77 replaces a single backslash with a dash and saves the result in the `UserName` string.

> **Note**
>
> The double-backslash (\\) on line 77 is really an escape sequence for a single backslash (\). Since line 77 is dealing with char types and not string types, we cannot use the @-quoted method of C#.
>
> The @-quoted method is reserved for string types only and allows C# strings to be treated literally. When a string uses the @-quoted method, escape sequences are not processed, which makes it easy to write things such as fully qualified file names. The following two string declarations result in identical strings. The first one uses @-quoting and is slightly easier to type and read.
>
> ```
> string filename = @"C:\Winnt\Notepad.exe ";
> string filename = "C:\\Winnt\\Notepad.exe ";
> ```
>
> Line 79 uses @-quoting for building the `SavePath` variable.

Line 79 builds a string that will be used as the path where the uploaded files will be saved. For this example we are using the `C:\temp` directory as the root directory for our user uploads. Each user will have a directory dynamically created within the `C:\temp` directory the first time they successfully upload a file to the system. Line 80 simply creates a string named `FileAndPath` that contains the `FileName` string appended to the end of the `SavePath` string. Lines 83 and 84 create the `FileAndPath` directory if it does not exist. Line 87 uses the `SaveAs` method of the `HttpPostedFile` for saving the uploaded file to the file system. The `ToLower()` method of string is used simply as a matter of style. Line 90 informs the user that their file upload was successful. If you look in the user directory within the `C:\temp` directory, you will see that the file was uploaded successfully.

In order to leverage the new `FileUploadHandler` we need to create a client that supports uploading files. Figure 18.11 shows the HTML page in Listing 18.3.13.

FIGURE 18.11
A simple HTML page for uploading multiple files to the `FileUploadHandler`.

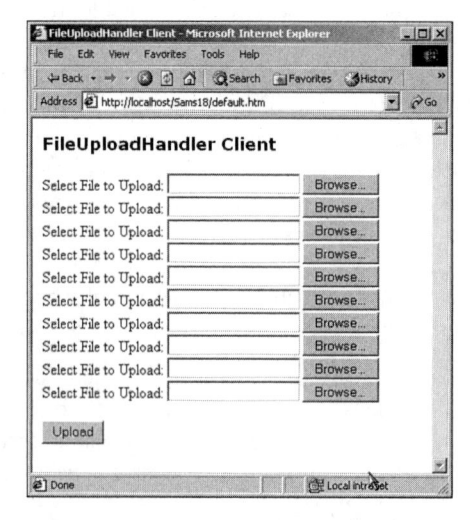

The client page allows for up to 10 files to be uploaded at a single time. Figure 18.12 shows our client page ready with 10 files ready to be uploaded.

FIGURE 18.12
The simple FileUploadHandler client page with 10 files ready for uploading to the `FileUploadHandler`.

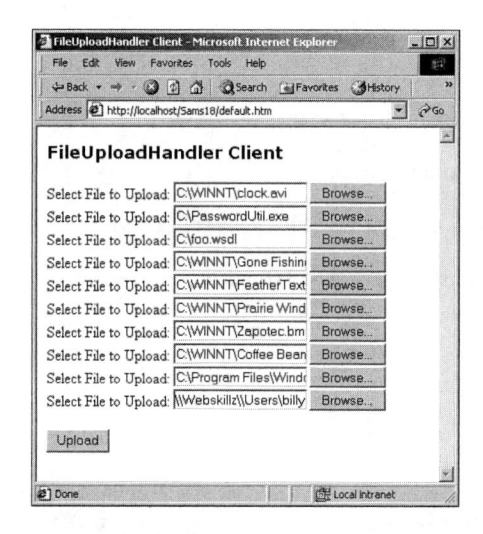

The HTML in Listing 18.2.16 can be used as a client page for uploading files to our new HTTP handler in Listing 18.3.15.

LISTING 18.2.16   HTML Client Page for Uploading Files to the File Upload `IhttpHandler`

```
 1: <html>
 2: <head>
 3: <title>FileUploadHandler Client</title>
 4: </head>
 5:
 6: <body>
 7:
 8:     <h3><font face="Verdana">FileUploadHandler Client</font></h3>
 9:
10:     <form name="form1" method="post"
11:         action="FileUploadHandler.ashx"
12:         enctype="multipart/form-data">
13:
14:         Select File to Upload:
15: <input id="File1" name="File1" type="file" size="20"> <br>
16:         Select File to Upload:
17: <input id="File2" name="File2" type="file" size="20"> <br>
18:         Select File to Upload:
19: <input id="File3" name="File3" type="file" size="20"> <br>
20:         Select File to Upload:
21: <input id="File4" name="File4" type="file" size="20"> <br>
22:         Select File to Upload:
23: <input id="File5" name="File5" type="file" size="20"> <br>
```

LISTING 18.2.16 Continued

```
24:          Select File to Upload:
25: <input id="File6" name="File6" type="file" size="20"> <br>
26:          Select File to Upload:
27: <input id="File7" name="File7" type="file" size="20"> <br>
28:          Select File to Upload:
29: <input id="File8" name="File8" type="file" size="20"> <br>
30:          Select File to Upload:
31: <input id="File9" name="File9" type="file" size="20"> <br>
32:          Select File to Upload:
33: <input id="File10" name="File10" type="file" size="20"> <br>
34:
35: <p><input type="submit" value="Upload"></p>
36:
37:     </form>
38:
39: </body>
40: </html>
```

Figure 18.13 shows that the files were received and saved by the `FileUploadHandler`.

FIGURE 18.13
Results from successfully uploading 10 files to the `FileUploadHandler`.

Figure 18.14 shows that the files were indeed saved to the directory on the file system.

Since and download files from our user directory on the server. we can upload files to the system it would be nice to be able to download files as well. The `WriteFile` method of the `Response` object allows information to be read from the file system and sent to the client. This can be done using instances of the .NET frameworks `Stream` class, but the `WriteFile` method makes it so much easier. Listing 18.2.17 demonstrates using the `WriteFile` method.

FIGURE 18.14
The user's directory now contains the 10 uploaded files.

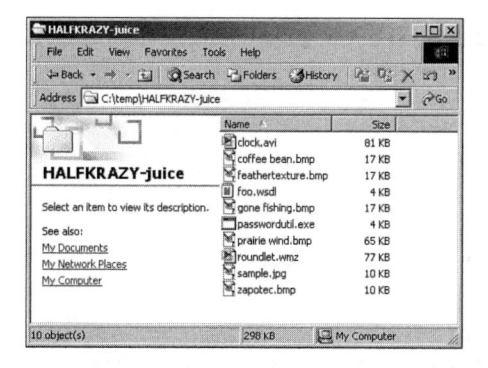

LISTING 18.2.17 Using the `WriteFile` Method for Reading Files on the Server and Sending Them Back to the Client

```
 1: <%@ WebHandler Class="FileDownloadHandler" Language="C#" %>
 2:
 3: using System;
 4: using System.IO;
 5: using System.Web;
 6: using System.Web.Security;
 7: using System.Security.Principal;
 8:
 9:
10: class FileDownloadHandler : IHttpHandler {
11:
12: public void ProcessRequest(HttpContext context) {
13:
14: HttpRequest Request   = context.Request;
15: HttpResponse Response = context.Response;
16:
17: WindowsIdentity id;
18:
19: try
20: {
21: id = (WindowsIdentity) context.User.Identity;
22: }
23: catch (Exception eo)
24: {
25: Response.Write ("Please enable Integrated
                    Windows Authentication in IIS
                    and the configuration file.");
26: Response.Write (eo.Message);
27:
28: return;
29: }
30:
31: // First check and see if the user is authenticated
32: if (!id.IsAuthenticated) {
33: Response.Write("<H2>Sorry, this page is for
                   authenticated Windows
                   users only.</H2>");
```

LISTING 18.2.17   Continued

```
34: Response.Write("Inform the administrator that
                               Anonymous access must
                               be disabled in IIS");
35:
36: return;
37: }
38:
39: string UserName = id.Name.Replace('\\','-');
40:
41:
42: // If there are no files, just return.
43: string FileToGet = Request.QueryString.Get("file");
44:
45: if (FileToGet==null) {
46: Response.Write ("File parameter was missing!");
47: return;
48: }
49:
50: FileToGet = @"c:\temp\" + UserName + @"\" + FileToGet;
51:
52: if (!File.Exists(FileToGet)) {
53: Response.Write("File Not Found!");
54: return;
55: }
56:
57: try
58: {
59: Response.Clear();
60: Response.WriteFile(FileToGet);
61: }
62: catch (Exception eo)
63: {
64: Response.Write(eo.Message);
65: }
66:
67:
68: }
69:
70: public bool IsReusable {
71: get {return true;}
72: }
73: }
74:
```

Listing 18.2.17 uses some of the code from the `FileUploadHandler` example earlier in this chapter. If the user is not authenticated with Integrated Windows Authenticated ,we will not allow them to download files. Line 43 uses the `Get` method from `NamedValueCollection` object to get the file attribute from the query string. The value, if found, is stored in the `FileToGet` variable. If the `FileToGet` variable is equal to `null` then we inform the user that the parameter was missing and then `return`. On line 50 we reuse the `FileToGet` variable for building the fully-qualified filename for retrieving from the file system. Line 52 checks that the file does indeed exist, and if it does not then the user is informed with a "File Not Found!" message. Lines 57-65 contain the *try-catch* block that first clears all content from the buffer stream and then uses the `WriteFile` method for reading a file from the local file system and sending the contents back to the client. Figure 18.15 shows the results when the `test.txt` file is requested.

FIGURE 18.15
User requesting a text file from their directory.

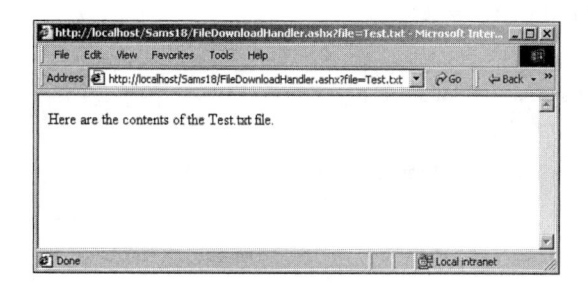

Using our two HTTP Handlers we can now upload and download files from our user directory on the server. To demonstrate that HTTP Handlers are not limited to only serving browser clients, we will now use a command-line test application for uploading and downloading files to the two HTTP Handlers. Listing 18.2.18 shows the code listing for the `FileUtil` console application.

LISTING 18.2.18 Command-Line Application That Allows Downloading and Uploading Files to the `FileUploadHandler` and `FileDownloadHandler`

```
 1: // Compile using
 2: //    csc FileUtil.cs
 3:
 4: using System;
 5: using System.Net;
 6: using System.IO;
 7: using System.Text;
 8:
 9:
10: class FileClient {
11:
12:
13: static void Main(string[] args)
14: {
15:
16: FileClientInfo fci;
17: FileClient fc;
18:
19: if ((args.Length > 2) && (args.Length < 6))
20: {
21: fci = new FileClientInfo();
22: fc = new FileClient();
23:
```

LISTING 18.2.18 *Continued*

```
24: fci.RemotePath = args[1];
25: fci.LocalPath  = args[2];
26:
27: // If credentials were given,
28: // we should try and use them
29: if (args.Length == 5)
30: {
31: fci.UserName = args[3];
32: fci.Password = args[4];
33: }
34:
35: // They want to upload a file
36: if (args[0].ToLower() == "-u")
37: {
38: fc.uploadFile(fci);
39: }
40: // The want to download a file
41: else if (args[0].ToLower() == "-d")
42: {
43: fc.downloadFile(fci);
44: }
45: else
46: {
47: ShowUsage();
48: }
49:
50: }
51: else
52: ShowUsage();
53:
54:
55: }
56:
57: private static void ShowUsage() {
58:
59: Console.WriteLine("\r\nExample Usage:");
60: Console.WriteLine("FileUtil -[u|d] [RemoteURL]
➥                    [LocalPath] [UserName] [Password]\r\n");
61: Console.WriteLine("** -u = Upload, -d = Download");
62: Console.WriteLine("** The UserName and
➥                    Password values are optional.\r\n");
63: }
64:
65: private void uploadFile (FileClientInfo info) {
66:
67: WebClient client = new WebClient();
68: ASCIIEncoding ascii = new ASCIIEncoding();
69:
70: byte[] retBytes = null;
71:
72: if ((info.UserName != null) || (info.Password != null))
```

LISTING 18.2.18   Continued

```
 73: client.Credentials = new NetworkCredential
➥                           (info.UserName, info.Password);
 74:
 75: try
 76: {
 77: // Are we uploading the contents of a directory?
 78: Console.WriteLine(info.LocalPath);
 79:
 80: DirectoryInfo di = new DirectoryInfo(info.LocalPath);
 81:
 82: if((di.Attributes & FileAttributes.Directory)
➥                           ==FileAttributes.Directory)
 83: {
 84: foreach (FileInfo file in di.GetFiles())
 85: {
 86: Console.WriteLine ("SENDING: {0}", file.FullName);
 87: retBytes = client.UploadFile
➥                                   (info.RemotePath,
➥                                           "POST",
➥                                           file.FullName);
 88: Console.WriteLine ("RESPONSE: {0}",
➥                                   ascii.GetString(retBytes));
 89: }
 90:
 91: }
 92: else
 93: {
 94: if (!File.Exists(info.LocalPath)) {
 95: Console.WriteLine(@"File\Path not found!");
 96: return;
 97: }
 98: else
 99: {
100: Console.WriteLine ("SENDING: {0}", info.LocalPath);
101: retBytes = client.UploadFile(info.RemotePath,
➥                                           "POST",
➥                                           info.LocalPath);
102: Console.WriteLine ("RESPONSE: {0}",
➥                                   ascii.GetString(retBytes));
103: }
104: }
105: }
106: catch (Exception eo)
107: {
108: Console.WriteLine(eo.Message);
109: }
110:
111:
112: }
113:
114: private void downloadFile (FileClientInfo info) {
115:
```

LISTING 18.2.18   Continued

```
116: WebClient client = new WebClient();
117:
118: if ((info.UserName != null) || (info.Password != null))
119:   client.Credentials = new NetworkCredential(info.UserName,
                                                 info.Password);
120:
121: Console.WriteLine ("REQUESTING: {0}", info.RemotePath);
122: try
123: {
124:   client.DownloadFile(info.RemotePath, info.LocalPath);
125:   Console.WriteLine ("RESPONSE SAVED TO: {0}", info.LocalPath);
126: }
127: catch (Exception eo)
128: {
129:   Console.WriteLine (eo.Message);
130: }
131: }
132:
133: internal struct FileClientInfo {
134:
135: FileClientInfo (string RemotePath,
                    string LocalPath,
                    string UserName,
                    string Password) {
136:
137:   _RemotePath = RemotePath;
138:   _LocalPath  = LocalPath;
139:   _UserName   = UserName;
140:   _Password   = Password;
141:
142:
143: FileClientInfo (string RemotePath, string LocalPath) {
144:
145:   _RemotePath = RemotePath;
146:   _LocalPath  = LocalPath;
147:   _UserName   = null;
148:   _Password   = null;
149: }
150:
151: private string _RemotePath;
152: private string _LocalPath;
153: private string _UserName;
154: private string _Password;
155:
156: internal string RemotePath {
157:   get {return _RemotePath;}
158:   set {_RemotePath = value;}
159: }
160:
161: internal string LocalPath {
162:   get {return _LocalPath;}
```

LISTING 18.2.18 Continued

```
163: set {_LocalPath = value;}
164: }
165:
166: internal string UserName {
167: get {return _UserName;}
168: set {_UserName = value;}
169: }
170:
171: internal string Password {
172: get {return _Password;}
173: set {_Password = value;}
174: }
175: }
176: }
177:
```

Listing 18.2.18 shows how we can leverage an HTTP Handler from clients other than web browsers. A brief walkthrough of the code shows that we allow both uploading and downloading of files. The `FileUtil` application also allows the user to send a username and password to the remote server. Without this, the handlers would not recognize the user and therefore would not know which directory files should be saved to and read from. As an added feature, the `FileUtil` client also allows sending the contents of an entire directory to handlers. This gives the `FileUtil` application functionality that could not have been implemented in the browser without some type of ActiveX control of Java applet.

Lines 13-55 contain the code for the static `Main()` method of the `FileUtil`. This method is called with an array of strings. This array of strings contain any arguments that were sent on the command line when the application was first executed. If three arguments were sent then we assume that the user did not want to set credential information. If five arguments were sent, we know that we will send the credentials. If the first argument was a "-u" then the `FileUtil` will do an upload. If the first argument was "-d", then we will download a file from the server. If any other value was found in first position, we call `ShowUsage()`. The `ShowUsage()` method, simply informs the user how to use the application.

Lines 65-112 contain the `uploadFile()` method. The `uploadFile()` method does just as its name implies. Lines 67 and 68 create instances of the `WebClient` and `ASCIIEncoding` classes.

> **Note**
>
> The .NET team noticed that everyone was writing the same code for doing very simple web requests, so they created an even higher-level API (Application Programming Interface) for sending and receiving data and files. This higher-level API is in the `System.Net.WebClient` class and makes everyday tasks such as getting a web page from a remote server a matter of just a few lines of code.

Line 72 checks to see if both the `Username` and `Password` properties of the `FileClientInfo` structure were set. If set, this means that we should create establish Credentials on our `WebClient` object.

Lines 114-131, contain the code for the `downloadFile()` method. Like the `downloadFile()` method, this method also uses the `WebClient` class for requesting a file from the remote HTTP handler. The `DownloadFile()` method of `WebClient` makes downloading and saving a file a matter of calling a single method.

Lines 133-175 define our `FileClientInfo` structure. When used by the `FileUtil` class, `FileClientInfo` will contain information such as the remote path, local path, user name, and password. The structure uses a series of `get`/`set` properties for allowing its user to access its various values. In addition the `FileClientInfo struct` has two constructors defined that allow the structure to be created and initialized by the caller at the same time.

> **Note**
>
> As stated in the Constructor Usage Guidelines of the .NET Frameworks SDK, it is a common pattern for constructors to have an increasing number of parameters for allowing the developer to specify a desired level of information. In our case, we could create our `FileClientInfo struct` with either 0, 2, or 4 parameters.

The remote path and local path both have dual duty depending if the application is uploading or downloading. When uploading to the `FileUploadHandler`, the remote path is the HTTP URL that should be used for uploading files to. When downloading from the `FileDownloadHandler`, the remote path contains the URL of the where files should be downloaded from. In our case, these will be two different HTTP handler paths. When uploading, the local path contains the local fully-qualified path and filename where the file that is to be sent is found. When downloading, the local path is used as the filename and path where the requested file will be saved to.

We have explored uploading and downloading files to and from the server with HTTP handlers. Next we will demonstrate creating images on-the-fly using the image creation resources available in the `System.Drawing` and `System.Drawing.Imaging` namespaces. Figure 18.16 shows some sample output from the `ImageHandler` HTTP handler.

FIGURE 18.16
`ImageHandler` creates images on the fly using a standardized format. Here we are requesting the `ImageHandler` to create a PNG file with "Hello, World!" as the image.

Listing 18.2.19 shows an example of how we can create images within an `IHttpHandler`.

LISTING 18.2.19 `IHttpHandler` That Uses Classes in the `System.Drawing` and `System.Drawing.Imaging` Namespaces for Generating Menu Images for a Web Site

```csharp
 1: <%@ WebHandler Language="C#" Class="ImageHandler" %>
 2:
 3: using System;
 4: using System.IO;
 5: using System.Web;
 6: using System.Drawing;
 7: using System.Drawing.Imaging;
 8:
 9:
10: class ImageHandler : IHttpHandler {
11:
12: public void ProcessRequest (HttpContext context) {
13:
14: CreateImage(ref context);
15: }
16:
17: public bool IsReusable {
18:
19: // Okay to reuse this object
20: get {return true;}
21: }
22:
23: public void CreateImage (ref HttpContext context) {
24:
25: HttpResponse Response = context.Response;
26: HttpRequest  Request  = context.Request;
27:
28: const string FONT_NAME= "Courier New";
29: const int FONT_SIZE= 12;
30:
31: Bitmap bmp = null;
32: Graphics g = null;
33:
34: // Set some default text to render
35: string RenderText = "[TEXT WAS UNDEFINED]";
36:
37: // Find out what the caller wants to render
38: if ((Request.QueryString.Get("Text") != null) &&
➥                    (Request.QueryString.Get("Text") != ""))
39: RenderText = Request.QueryString.Get("Text");
40:
41: // Find out what background color is desired
42: string BackgroundColorName = Request.QueryString.Get("BGColor");
43:
44: Color BackgroundColor = Color.CornflowerBlue;
45: try
46: {
47: if (BackgroundColorName != "")
48: BackgroundColor = ColorTranslator.FromHtml
➥                                 (BackgroundColorName);
49: }
```

LISTING 18.2.19 Continued

```
 50: catch {}
 51:
 52: try
 53: {
 54: Font font = new Font(FONT_NAME, FONT_SIZE);
 55:
 56: // calculate size of the string.
 57: bmp = new Bitmap(1,1,PixelFormat.Format32bppPArgb);
 58:
 59: g   = Graphics.FromImage(bmp);
 60: SizeF sSize = g.MeasureString(RenderText, font);
 61:
 62: // Get the Height and Width of our string
 63: int nHeight = (int)sSize.Height;
 64: int nWidth  = (int)sSize.Width;
 65:
 66:
 67: bmp = new Bitmap(nWidth, nHeight,
 68: PixelFormat.Format32bppPArgb);
 69:
 70: g = Graphics.FromImage(bmp);
 71: g.FillRectangle(new SolidBrush(BackgroundColor),
 72: new Rectangle(0, 0, nWidth, nHeight));
 73:
 74: g.DrawString(RenderText, font,
 75: new SolidBrush(Color.White), 0, 0);
 76:
 77: // Create a MemoryStream that will contain the image
 78: MemoryStream memStream = new MemoryStream();
 79:
 80: // Save the Image to the MemoryStream
 81: bmp.Save(memStream, ImageFormat.Png);
 82:
 83: // Clear the content from the buffer stream
 84: Response.Clear();
 85:
 86: // Inform the browser that this is a PNG file
 87: Response.ContentType= "IMAGE/PNG";
 88:
 89: // Take the image from the MemoryStream
 90: // and write it to the Response Stream
 91: Response.BinaryWrite(memStream.ToArray());
 92:
 93: // Send buffered output and fire the
 94: // EndRequest event of the Application
 95: Response.End();
 96:
 97: }
 98: catch {}
 99:
100: finally
101: {
```

LISTING 18.2.19   Continued

```
102: // Clean up the GDI+ surface
103: if (null != g)
104: g.Dispose();
105:
106: // Clean up the Bitmap
107: if (null != bmp)
108: bmp.Dispose();
109: }
110:
111: }
112:
113: }
114:
```

Listing 18.2.19 shows an example `IHttpHandler` for generating images on the fly. This handler generates standardized images using the `System.Drawing` and `System.Drawing.Imaging` namespaces. These namespaces contain all of the functionality we need in this example for creating PNG (Portable Network Graphics) files on the fly. You may notice in this example that the image is never persisted to disk. Beyond saving disk space, this also provides a significant performance gain. Lines 3-7 of our example import the namespaces that will be needed for the handler. Line 10 declares our `ImageHandler` class and informs the compiler that we are implementing the `IHttpHandler`. Lines 12-15 contain the code for the `ProcessRequest` method of the `IHttpHandler`. Line 14 of the `ProcessRequest()` method simply passes the `HttpContext` object to the `CreateImage()` method passing. Lines 17-20 contain the read-only `IsReusable` property. Line 20, simply informs the Http Runtime that this object can be re-used if need be.

> **Note**
>
> Properties are read-only when they only contain **get** methods. To make a property write-able as well, just add a corresponding set method as well.

Line 23 is the start of the `CreateImage()` method. The `CreateImage()` method receives a reference to the current `HttpContext` object. As was demonstrated earlier, the `HttpContext` object gives us access to objects such as the `Request` and `Response` objects. Lines 25 and 26 declare our `Response` and `Request` objects. Lines 28 and 29 declare to constant variable, `FONT_NAME` and `FONT_SIZE`, which will be used later in code listing. Lines 31 and 32 declare both our GDI+ `Bitmap` and `Graphics` objects. A `Graphics` object encapsulates GDI+ drawing surface. `Bitmap` objects encapsulate a GDI+ bitmap. Line 25 declares our `RenderText` string. `RenderText` is given a default value, but if the caller of the handler sent the proper Text parameter, it will be overwritten. Line 38 checks that the Text parameter was sent on the `QueryString`. If the parameter is present, it will be used; if not the default "[TEXT WAS UNDEFINED]" value will be used. Figure 18.17 shows what users will see if they do not send a text parameter.

FIGURE 18.17
When a user does not send the Text parameter in the query string, they will still receive an image, but the image will use default text instead.

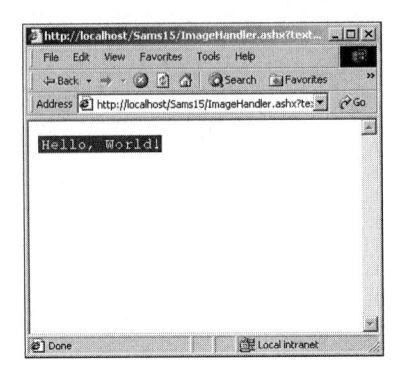

Line 42 requests the `BGColor` parameter from the `QueryString` collection and if present sets the value to the `BackgroundColorName` variable. Line 44 declares a Color object and sets its value equal to the `Color.CornflowerBlue` value. Lines 47-49 set the value of the `BackgroundColor` object to the value sent in the `BGColor` parameter of the querystring. Line 54 creates a new `Font` object using the `FONT_NAME` and `FONT_SIZE` constants declared on lines 28 and 29.

Line 57 creates a new 32-bit, RGB `Bitmap` object. Line 59 creates an instance of the `Graphics` object using the newly created `Bitmap` object. Line 60 creates a `SizeF` structure called `sSize`.

> **Note**
>
> A `SizeF` structure represents the size of a rectangular region.

We use the `MeasureString` method of the `Graphics` object in order to calculate the size of `RenderText` for use in the graphic. Lines 63 and 64 create our `Height` and `Width` variables. After a cast to `int`, the `Height` and `Width` variables contain the height and width of the `RenderText` string.

Lines 67 and 68 create a 32-bit RGB Bitmap named `bmp`. After we create a `Graphics` object from the `bmp Bitmap` object on line 70, we fill the rectangle with our `BackgroundColor`. Line 74 is where we draw the `RenderText` onto the `Graphics` surface. Even though there is no file to show it, the image has now been created. Line 78 declares and instantiates a `MemoryStream` object. Line 81 uses the `Save` method of the `Bitmap` object for saving a W3C PNG image to `memStream`. The type of image, in this case a PNG, is specified using one of the static properties of the `ImageFormat` class.

> **Note**
>
> Other image types that are exposed by `ImageFormat` are Bitmap (BMP), enhanced Windows Metafile (WMF), Exchangable Image Format (EXIF), Graphics Interchange Format (GIF), icon, Joint Photographers Expert Group (JPEG), memory bitmap, Tag Image File Format (TIFF), and Windows Metafile image formats.

Line 84 clears all content output from the `Response` stream. Line 87 sets the HTTP MIME (Multi-purpose Encoding) type of the output stream. This informs the browser that the content it is getting ready to receive is a PNG image. The default MIME type for ASP.NET is text/HTML. Line 92 uses the `BinaryWrite` method of the `HttpResponse` object for writing the contents of our `MemoryStream` object. The `BinaryWrite` method expects an array of bytes, so we use the `ToArray` method of the `MemoryStream`. Line 95 informs the ASP.NET Http Runtime that we are finished. The buffered output is sent and the `EndRequest` event of the `Application` is fired for all listeners of the event to intercept.

Lines 100-109 use the finally block for cleaning up the resources that were allocated earlier.

> **Note**
>
> In most cases `finally` blocks are used for cleaning up resources that were allocated during the try block. Control is always passed to the `finally` blocks regardless of how the try block exits. This means that an exception need not occur in order for the `finally` block to be called.

A sample use of the `ImageHandler` is an HTML page that uses standard HTML `IMG` tags that point to the `IHttpHandler`.

> **Note**
>
> This example is demonstrating returning a dynamically generated image to a browser. If this were going to be used in a real-world site, the image files would be saved to disk on the server and then called directly from the browser.

Instead of referring to an image file that resides on a server somewhere, the `IMG` tags of the page will point to our `ImageHandler` instead. Figure 18.18 shows a sample site menu that uses the `ImageHandler`.

FIGURE 18.18
Sample HTML page that demonstrates a site menu that leverages the `ImageHandler` for generating menu items on-the-fly.

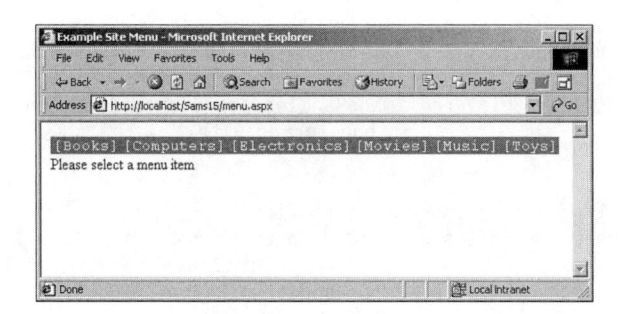

Listing 18.2.20 shows an HTML page that uses the `ImageHandler` for generating a menu for the site.

LISTING 18.2.20 HTML Page That Uses the `ImageHandler` for Generating a Site Navigation Bar Complete with Image Hovering

```
 1: <!doctype html public "-//W3C//DTD HTML 4.0 Transitional//EN">
 2: <html>
 3: <head>
 4: <title>Example Site Menu</title>
 5: </head>
 6:
 7: <body bgcolor="#FFFFFF">
 8: <p>
 9: <table cellspacing=0 cellpadding=0>
10: <tr>
11: <td>
12: <img
13: src="ImageHandler.ashx?text=[Appliances]"
14: onMouseOver="this.src='ImageHandler.ashx?text=[Appliances]&
➥                            bgcolor=cornflowerblue'"
15: onMouseOut="this.src='ImageHandler.ashx?text=[Appliances]&
➥                            bgcolor=gray'">
16: </td><td>
17: <img
18: src="ImageHandler.ashx?text=[Books]"
19: onMouseOver="this.src='ImageHandler.ashx?text=[Books]&
➥                            bgcolor=cornflowerblue'"
20: onMouseOut="this.src='ImageHandler.ashx?text=[Books]&
➥                            bgcolor=gray'">
21: </td><td>
22: <img
23: src="ImageHandler.ashx?text=[Computers]"
24: onMouseOver="this.src='ImageHandler.ashx?text=[Computers]&
➥                            bgcolor=cornflowerblue'"
25: onMouseOut="this.src='ImageHandler.ashx?text=[Computers]&
➥                            bgcolor=gray'">
26: </td><td>
27: <img
28: src="ImageHandler.ashx?text=[Electronics]"
29: onMouseOver="this.src='ImageHandler.ashx?text=[Electronics]&
➥                            bgcolor=cornflowerblue'"
30: onMouseOut="this.src='ImageHandler.ashx?text=[Electronics]&
➥                            bgcolor=gray'">
31: </td><td>
32: <img
33: src="ImageHandler.ashx?text=[Movies]"
34: onMouseOver="this.src='ImageHandler.ashx?text=[Movies]&
➥                            bgcolor=cornflowerblue'"
35: onMouseOut="this.src='ImageHandler.ashx?text=[Movies]&
➥                            bgcolor=gray'">
36: </td><td>
37: <img
38: src="ImageHandler.ashx?text=[Music]"
39: onMouseOver="this.src='ImageHandler.ashx?text=[Music]&
➥                            bgcolor=cornflowerblue'"
```

LISTING 18.2.20 *Continued*

```
40: onMouseOut="this.src='ImageHandler.ashx?text=[Music]&
➥                             bgcolor=gray'">
41: </td>
42: </p>
43: </body>
44: </html>
45:
```

The simple HTML page in Listing 18.2.20 even supports dynamically changing the images when the user hovers over an image. Figure 18.19 shows that when a user hovers over an image, the `ImageHandler` is re-called, this time the `bgccolor` parameter is set to `cornflowerblue`.

FIGURE 18.19
Hovering over an image causes the browser to request a another image with a background color of `cornflowerblue`.

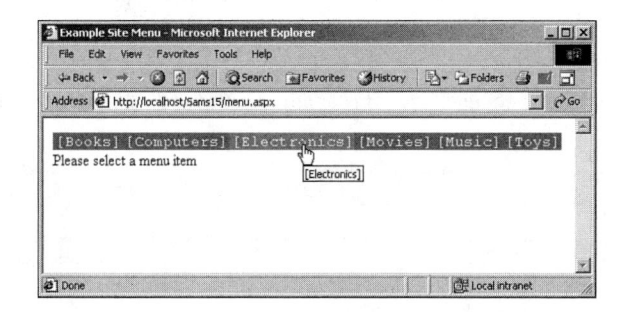

Each of the menu items in Listing 18.2.20 is a separate PNG image file. When the user hovers over a menu item, JavaScript is used for dynamically changing the `src` property of the current image tag. When a user clicks on an item, the page is refreshed and a message is displayed informing the user of which item was clicked.

This HTML page is just a sample use of the `ImageHandler`. It shows that images can be created for a site in a standardized way that would allow some of the tedium of generating new images for products, menus, and other items on a web site to be done using automated techniques.

3. Using Directives

Directives are used for specifying optional settings used by the ASP.NET page and application compilers. Although directives can be located anywhere in the `global.asax` file, the standard practice is to include them at the beginning of the file. Each directive can contain one or more attributes (paired with values) that are specific to that directive.

> **Note**
> ASP.NET treats any directive block (<%@ %>) that does not contain an explicit directive name as an @Page (<%@Page %>) directive.

Using the Application Directive

ASP.NET supports three different directives in the `global.asax` application file: `Application`, `Import`, and `Assembly`. Each of these directives will contain one or more name/value pairs specific to the directive. All directives need to be placed outside of the `<script>…</script>` tags of the application file. If you attempt to place a directive within the `<script>…</script>` tags, you will receive an error.

Here is the syntax for using a directive within the `global.asax` file:

```
 1: <%@ directive {attribute=value} %>
 2:
 3: <script language="VB" runat="server">
 4:
 5: Sub Application_BeginRequest(Sender As Object, EventArgs As E)
 6:     'Code goes here
 7: End Sub
 8:
 9: Sub Application_EndRequest(Sender As Object, EventArgs As E)
10:     'Code goes here
11: End Sub
12:
13: </script>
```

The following example causes an error because the directive is located within the `<script>` block:

```
 1: <script language="VB" runat="server">
 2:
 3: Sub Application_OnStart()
 4:     'Code goes here
 5: End Sub
 6:
 7: Sub Application_OnEnd()
 8:     'Code goes here
 9: End Sub
10:
11: 'Will result in a compiler error
12: <%@ directive {attribute=value} %>
13:
14: </script>
```

Figure 18.20 shows what happens when the attribute statements follow declarations within an application file.

The `Application` directive defines two application-specific attributes used by the application compiler: `Inherits` and `Description`.

The `Inherits` attribute is used for specifying a compiled .NET class that is derived from `System.Web.HttpApplication`.

Here is a simple example of the `Inherits` attribute:

```
<%@ Application Inherits="MyCompany.MyApplication" %>
```

FIGURE 18.20
Compilation error from attribute statement not preceding the declarations.

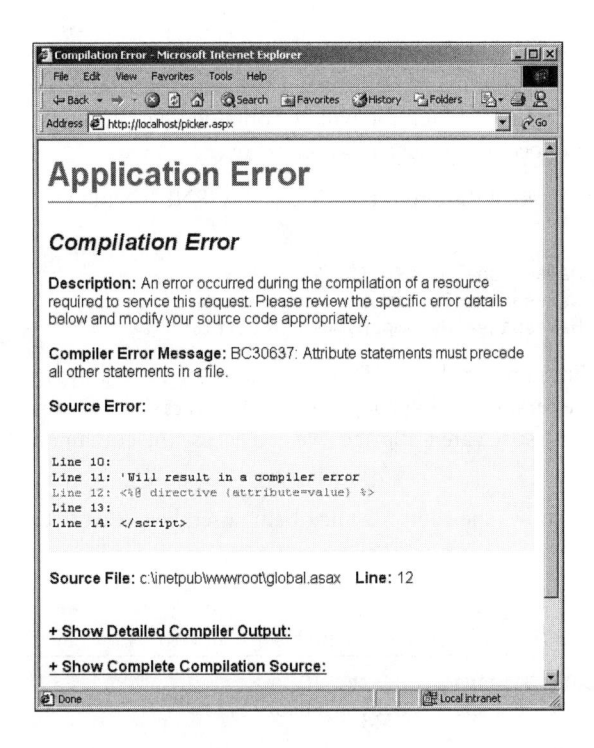

The preceding example instructs the ASP.NET application compiler to dynamically compile a new application class that extends the `MyCompany.MyApplication` class.

The `Description` attribute is used to provide a textual description of the application to anyone viewing the source of the `global.asax` file.

For example, you might decide to set the `Description` attribute to something like this:

```
<%@ Application Description="Employee Stock Purchase application" %>
```

> **Note**
>
> The `Description` attribute is ignored by both the application compiler and the Visual Studio designer.

Using the `Import` Directive

The `Import` directive is used for explicitly importing a namespace into an application class. Importing the namespace makes all classes and interfaces within the namespace available to the developer.

The `Import` directive only supports one attribute: `Namespace`. The `Namespace` attribute takes any valid .NET namespace as a valid value. The `Import` directive is synonymous with the

`Import` keyword in Visual Basic.NET and the `using` keyword of C#. Trying to use any of the language-specific namespace import keywords will result in an error because the code declaration section of the application file will be contained within a class structure, and namespace imports need to occur outside class declarations.

Here is an example of the `Import` directive of ASP.NET being used for importing three namespaces.

```
<%@ Import Namespace="System.IO" %>
<%@ Import Namespace="System.Collections" %>
<%@ Import Namespace="MyCompany.Web.Utilities" %>
```

These three lines import the .NET-supplied `System.IO` and `System.Collections` namespaces and the developer-supplied `MyCompany.Web.Utilities` namespace into the application class. Once these namespace are imported, we can access the contained classes and interfaces using a shorter syntax.

Listing 18.3.1 shows the shorter syntax being used because the `System.IO` namespace is being imported.

LISTING 18.3.1 An Example That Logs the User Name to a Log File

```
 1: <%@ Import Namespace="System.IO" %>
 2: <%@ Import Namespace="System.Security" %>
 3:
 4: <script language="VB" runat="server">
 5:
 6: Sub Application_EndRequest (Sender As Object, E as EventArgs)
 7:     Dim fs As FileStream = New FileStream("C:\log.txt", _
 8:         FileMode.OpenOrCreate, _
 9: FileAccess.Write)
10:
11:     Dim w As StreamWriter = New StreamWriter(fs)
12:
13:     w.BaseStream.Seek(0, SeekOrigin.End)
14:     w.WriteLine(User.Identity.Name)
15:
16:     w.Flush()
17:     w.Close()
18:
19: End Sub
20:
21: </script>
```

The example in Listing 18.3.2 uses the `FileStream` and `StreamWriter` object to log the user name to the `C:\log.txt` file.

Without using the `Import` directive, we would need to fully qualify the namespace and class for both the `FileStream` and `StreamWriter` objects.

Listing 18.3.3 shows the code listing without using the `Import` directive.

LISTING 18.3.3 An Example That Saves the User Name to a Log File—This Time There Are No `Import` Directives and Therefore Some of the Lines of Code Are Much Longer

```
 1: <script language="VB" runat="server">
 2:
 3: Sub Application_EndRequest (Sender As Object, E as EventArgs)
 4:     Dim fs As System.IO.FileStream = _
 5:         New System.IO.FileStream("C:\log.txt", _
 6:         System.IO.FileMode.OpenOrCreate, _
 7: System.IO.FileAccess.Write)
 8:
 9:     Dim w As System.IO.StreamWriter = New System.IO.StreamWriter(fs)
10:
11:     w.BaseStream.Seek(0, System.IO.SeekOrigin.End)
12:     w.WriteLine(User.Identity.Name)
13:
14:     w.Flush()
15:     w.Close()
16:
17: End Sub
18:
19: </script>
```

Listing 18.3.3 is effectively the same code as in Listing 18.3.2. As you can see from this example, the fully qualified name makes for longer lines of code, which sometimes appears messy.

Assemblies and Using the `Assembly` Directive

An assembly is the logical unit of functionality in .NET and also fundamentally the unit of deployment. In most cases you can think of an assembly as a file in the form of a DLL (Dynamically Linked Library) or EXE (Executable) although they can contain a wealth of information such as metadata and resources such as JPEG and GIF files. Assemblies can also be dynamically generated in memory as well. Technically, assemblies can span multiple files, but most often there will only be one file for a single assembly.

The `Assembly` directive of the application file allows a developer to use a declarative syntax for linking the application class to a .NET assembly. Assemblies can also be registered across either the entire application by using the `web.config` file, or registered across an entire machine using the `machine.config` file.

The `Assembly` directive supports only the `Name` attribute.

The `Name` attribute of the `Assembly` directive takes any valid assembly name. When used, the assembly will be linked to the current page during compilation. This will make all of the classes and interfaces within the assembly available for use on the page.

Here is an example of using the `Assembly` directive in an ASP.NET page to link to an assembly:

```
<%@ Assembly Name="MyCompany.MyApplication" %>

<script language="VB" runat="server">
```

```
Sub Page_Load(Sender As Object, E As EventArgs)
    Dim MyApp As New MyApplication
    Dim str As String

    str = MyApp.SomeMethod()
    Response.Write ("The method returned: " & str)
End Sub
```

</script>

This example links the current `Page` object to the `MyCompany.MyApplication` assembly located in the `\bin` directory of the application at compile time. This allows linking an assembly to a single page as opposed to an entire application.

> **Note**
> An assembly name does not include the file extension.

Assemblies that are located in the `\bin` directory of an application are automatically linked to pages within that application. As long as an application has automatic linking enabled, assemblies that reside in the `\bin` directory of an application do not require the `Assembly` directive.

To disable the automatic linking functionality, you can remove the following line from the `web.config` application file:

`<add assembly="*" />`

Removing the aforementioned line instructs the page compiler to not link against all (*) assemblies found in the `\bin` directory of the application. Adding the line back to the `web.config` file will re-enable the automatic linking feature.

If the desired effect is to have a particular assembly made available across an entire application, you alternatively can add the assembly to the `<assemblies>` section of the `web.config` file for the application using this syntax:

```
<assemblies>
    <add assembly="MyCompany.MyApplication" />
</assemblies>
```

This instructs the page compiler to automatically link the `MyCompany.MyApplication` assembly to all pages within the application.

> **Note**
> Notice that `<add assembly="*" />` is not present; therefore, all other assemblies in the `\bin` directory will not be linked to all pages within the application.

Using `Object` Tags

Like classic ASP, ASP.NET contains an `Object` tag that allows developers to use a declarative, tag-based syntax for instantiating server-side objects.

When the object tag is used, the object will not be instantiated until its first use. This way, if you were to declare 10 objects using the `object` tag directive but only access five of the objects, only five objects would be instantiated by ASP.NET. This saves resources and management overhead of the .NET Runtime.

The syntax for the object tag comes in one of three flavors:

```
<object id="id" runat="server"
➥    class=".NET Class Name" scope="appinstance" />
<object id="id" runat="server"
➥    progid="Classic COM ProgId" scope="session" />
<object id="id" runat="server"
➥    classid="Classic COM ClassID" scope="application" />
```

Server-side object tags can be used to create both .NET classes and COM classes. Here is an example of using the `object` tag to create a .NET class.

```
<object id="regex" runat="server"
➥    Class="System.Text.RegularExpressions.RegEx."
➥    scope="Application" />
```

For COM classes, you are given the choice of using either the `ProgID` attribute (programmatic identifier) or the `ClassID` (class identifier) attribute of the COM object to be instantiated.

Here are examples of both the `ProgID` and `ClassID` approaches.

```
<object id="id" runat="server"
➥    ProgId="Microsoft.FreeThreadedXMLDOM"
➥    scope="Application" />

<object id="id" runat="server"
➥    classid="{d63e0ce2-a0a2-11d0-9c02-00c04fc99c8e}"
➥    scope="Application" />
```

The Object tag supports three attributes: `ID`, `Runat`, `Scope`, `Class`, `ProgID` and `ClassID`. The `ID` attribute is used for identifying the object. The ID must be unique to other objects in the class. The `Runat` attribute only accepts the value `server`. Non-`server` values cause the application compiler to ignore the tag entirely. The `Scope` attribute is the scope that the object should be declared at.

In order to instantiate the object, you must use the `Class`, `ProgID`, or `ClassID` attribute. The `Class` attribute only accepts the fully-qualified name of the .NET class that is to be instantiated. `ProgID` is the programmatic identifier of a classic COM component to instantiate. The `ClassID` attribute accepts the class identifier (sometimes shown as CLSID) of a COM component to create.

The `ID` Attribute

The `ID` attribute of the object tag provides a unique identifier to use when declaring an object on the page. This unique identifier will be used when making subsequent requests in code.

Here is the syntax for the id attribute tag.

```
<object id="id" class="Class Name" runat=server />
```

The `Runat` Attribute

The `Runat` attribute must be set to `server` for ASP.NET to process the tag.

The `Scope` Attribute

The `Scope` attribute accepts one of four values: `AppInstance`, `Application`, `Session` and `Pipeline`. If no scope value is supplied, ASP.NET will default to `Pipeline` scope.

Pipeline

A scope value of `Pipeline` indicates that the object is only available to the `HttpPipeline` instance of the current application.

> **Note**
> Modules, such as for session state, are configured in the `HttpPipeline` section of the `machine.config` file.

AppInstance

`AppInstance` indicates that the object is only to be made available to the particular instance of the `HttpApplication`. By default, ASP.NET creates a pool of applications that are available to service requests. These pools of applications aid in both the scalability of ASP.NET as well as the stability. What this means for the developer is that if there are five applications within the pool, there will be five *independent* instances of a particular `AppInstance`-pooled object.

Here is an example of the scope attribute using the `AppInstance` value.

```
<object id="myWeb"
    class="System.Net.WebClient"
    scope="AppInstance"
    runat="server" />
```

In the previous example, the scope for the `Microsoft.XMLDOM` object is being set to `AppInstance`. In this example, an instance of the `Microsoft.XMLDOM` object will be created for each of the application-instances that are created by ASP.NET. Although each of the instances will be assigned the variable name of `myWeb`, each instance will be created independently of each other and will not share any state between them. What this means for a developer is that if the `Credentials` property of the `WebClient` object were set, and then later the `DownloadData()` method was called, the developer may not receive the results that were expected. This result is possible because the `Credentials` property may not have been set for the particular application instance.

Application

`Application` scope indicates that the object instance will be shared across all instances of the application. If five application instances are running within the ASP.NET application pool, there will still only be one instance of the object.

Here is an example of setting the scope of an object to `Application`.

LISTING 18.3.4 An Example That Counts the Page Requests and Reports Them at the End of Each Request

```
 1: <object id="MyCounter"
        class="System.Int32"
        scope="Application"
        runat="Server" />
 2:
 3: <script language="VB" runat="server">
 4:
 5: Sub Application_BeginRequest(O as Object, E as EventArgs)
 6:     Application("MyCounter") += 1
 7: End Sub
 8:
 9: Sub Application_EndRequest(O As Object, E As EventArgs)
10:     Response.Write ("There have been (" & Application("MyCounter") &
            ") requests to this site.")
11: End Sub
12: </script>
```

The code in Listing 18.3.4 shows a simple ASP.NET page request counter. This simple counter will count all ASP.NET requests for the entire application and append the count to the end of all requests. Line 1 shows the declaration for the `System.Int32` object that will be used for the counter. The `Int32` object is declared with the scope of `Application` and named `MyCounter`. Lines 5-7 show the `BeginRequest` event handler for the `Application` object. Line 6 uses the shortcut syntax for incrementing the value of the `MyCounter` variable by one. Lines 9-11 contain the `EndRequest` event handler for the `Application` object. This handler is the last deterministic event called before the current request terminates. Line 10 uses the `Write` method of the `Response` object for showing the request count.

> **Note**
> This example simply demonstrates the usage of the `Scope` attribute of the `Object` tag; it's not demonstrating an effective counter for a Web site. An effective counter should persist the counter information to durable storage, such as a database or a file.

Using multiple browsers and machines, you will notice that the scope of the `MyCounter` variable is indeed being shared across the entire scope of the application. Each request to an ASP.NET page, no matter where it comes from, will increment the `MyCounter` integer.

The `Scope` Attribute

The `Scope` attribute is used for establishing the scope for which an object is declared.

> **Note**
> If no scope is specified, the scope will default to `Pipeline`.

The `Session` Value

When the `Scope` attribute has its value set to `Session`, it indicates to ASP.NET that a new object instance should be instantiated and managed for each session created on the system. In the case where 500 sessions are active on the system, there will potentially be 500 instances of the object running. Each instance will have its own copy of data. When the session timeout is reached, the session state for the session is automatically cleaned up by ASP.NET.

Here is an example of using the `Scope` value for creating object instances within the scope of a session.

```
<object id="id"
    runat="server"
    class="MyCompany.Utilities.Class1"
    scope="Session" />
```

The `Class` Attribute

The `Class` attribute identifies the class name of the object to be created.

Here is an example of using the `Class` attribute of the object tag for creating a new instance of a .NET object.

```
<object id="myArray"
    class="System.Collections.ArrayList"
    runat="server" />
```

The example above uses the `class` attribute of the `object` tag in order to create an instance of the `System.Collections.ArrayList` object. Once created, the `ArrayList` object will be assigned the variable name `myArray`.

The `ProgID` Attribute

The `ProgID` attribute identifies the programmatic identifier of the COM object to be created.

Here is an example of using the `ProgID` attribute of the object tag for creating a new instance of a COM object.

```
<object id="myDOM"
    ProgID="Microsoft.XMLDOM"
    runat="server" />
```

The example above uses the `ProgID` attribute for creating an instance of the `Microsoft.XMLDOM` object. Once instantiated, the `Microsoft.XMLDOM` object will be assigned the name `myDOM`.

The ClassID Attribute

The `ClassID` attribute identifies the class identifier (CLASSID) of the COM object to be created. This is a 32-bit hexadecimal number.

Here is an example of using the `ClassID` attribute of the `object` tag.

```
<object id="myobj"
    ClassID="{2933BF90-7B36-11d2-B20E-00C04F983E60}"
    runat="server" />
```

The example above uses the `ClassID` attribute of the `object` tag for creating an instance of a COM object.

Code Declarations

The code declaration syntax of ASP.NET is enclosed within `<script>...</script>` tags.

Script

The `<script>` code declaration blocks are used for defining application, member variables, event handlers and methods.

Other than the `runat=server` attribute, the `<script>` code declaration block contains two other attributes; `language` and `src`.

The `language` attribute contains the name of any of the installed .NET language.

The `Src` attribute contains the path to any valid external source file on the local file system.

The Language Attribute

The optional `Language` attribute of the `Script` tag is used to explicitly inform ASP.NET which of the installed .NET language compilers should be used for compilation.

Here is an example of using the `Language` attribute of the `Script` tag.

```
<script language="VB" runat="server">

Sub Application_OnStart()
    'Startup code goes here
End Sub

</script>
```

The example above uses the `Language` attribute of the `Script` tag to establish the Visual Basic.NET compiler as the language compiler for this file.

To change the default language for the entire application, you edit the `<compilers>` section of the `Web.config` file for the application. The `<compilation>` section is nested in the `<system.web>` section of the `Web.config` file.

To change the default language for the application, the `defaultlanguage` attribute is used. This attribute indicates the default name of the language to be used during dynamic compilation of ASP.NET files. With the base install of ASP.NET, valid languages are Visual Basic.NET, C#, and JScript.NET.

An example `web.config` file for changing the default language for an application to C# is listed below.

```
<system.web>
    <compilation defaultlanguage="C#" />
</system.web>
```

Here the `defaultlanguage` attribute of the compilation section is being used for setting the default compilation language of ASP.NET to the C#. Once this setting is enabled, a developer using C# can forego placing the language attribute in the `<script>` declaration of their ASP.NET pages. Now, the C# developer for the application can use a `<script>` declaration like the one below.

```
<script runat=server/>
    void Application_EndRequest(Object sender, EventArgs E) {
        Response.Write("Here is the end of the request.");
    }
</script>
```

The example above shows a `global.asax` application file that appends "Here is the end of the request." to end of all ASP.NET resource requests. The important thing to note here is that our `<script>` declaration does not contain the language attribute because it is taken care of by the `Web.config` file for the application.

> **Note**
>
> The `defaultlanguage` attribute works across all ASP.NET compilation resources such as `.aspx`, `.asmx` and `.ashx` files.

If no default language is specified in the system-wide `machine.config` file or the application-specific `Web.config` file and the `<script>` tag does not specify a language to be used, the VB.NET language will be assumed by the ASP.NET compilers.

> **Note**
>
> If you know that most of the applications on a server will be using a particular programming language, you might want to edit the `machine.config` file for the machine.
>
> To make this change, edit the `<compilation>` section within the `<system.web>` section of the `machine.config` file. The `<compilers>` sub-section within `<compilation>` shows all of the valid values such as C#, VB, and JS.

The base install of ASP.NET includes the VB.NET, C#, and JScript.NET languages. After other .NET languages are installed, they can also become available to the ASP.NET dynamic compilation system.

The Runat Attribute

The Runat attribute of the <Script> tag only accepts Server as a valid value. Without the Runat="server" attribute/value pair, the code declaration will not be compiled.

Here is an example of using the Runat="server" attribute on the script declaration.

```
<script language="VB" runat="server">

Sub Application_OnStart()
    'Startup code goes here…
End Sub

</script>
```

The Src Attribute

Optionally, you can use the Src attribute to specify an external source code file. If the Src attribute is used, all code between the opening and closing <Script> tags will be ignored. If the Src attribute is used, a good practice is to use the shortcut syntax of XML for opening and closing tags:

```
<Script Language="VB" Src="MyGlobalasax.vb" Runat="Server" />
```

This syntax alleviates the possibility of code between the opening and closing tags being mistakenly ignored. Here's an example:

```
<script language="VB" Src="Application_Events.src" Runat="server" />
```

Server-Side Includes

The use of server-side includes allows you to insert the contents of another file directly into an ASP.NET application file. The contents of the file are inserted verbatim before any compilation or execution occurs. For C/C++ developers, it works very much like a preprocessor.

Path Type Meaning

The filename is a relative path from the directory containing the document with the #include directive. The included file can be in the same directory or in a subdirectory. It cannot be in a directory above the page with the #include directive.

Virtual

The filename is a full virtual path from a virtual directory in your Web site.

FileName

FileName specifies the name of the file to be included. The filename must be enclosed in double quotation marks (") and contain the extension of the file. Here is an example:

```
<script language="VB" runat="server">

Sub Application_OnStart() :
    'Code goes here
End Sub

Sub Application_OnEnd()
    'Code goes here
End Sub

</script>

<!-- #include virtual="/global/scriptlibrary.inc" -->
```

The preceding example has two event-handler methods for the `OnStart` and `OnEnd` events of the `Application` object. The server-side include directive after the closing `</script>` tag inserts the contents of a file named `scriptlibrary.inc`, which resides in the /global directory.

Summary

As was demonstrated in this chapter, ASP.NET provides a great deal of new and powerful functionality for .NET developers. During this chapter we learned that you can participate during the request/response cycle of an HTTP round-trip by writing code that intercepts the `HttpApplication` events. We demonstrated an `IHttpModule` that used the interception events triggered by the ASP.NET Http Runtime for simply logging all users that made requests into our ASP.NET application. Without the `IHttpModule` interface, we would have needed to either use the ISAPI to gain access to these types of low-level events or include classic ASP code into every page of our site. Creating your own `IHttpModule` allows a .NET developer to accomplish functionality that was once reserved only for C/C++ developers using the ISAPI. Not only do we now have access to these lower level functions, they are made easily accessible and programmable in either the `global.asax` application file or in separate `IHttpModule` classes. We also demonstrated how you could instrument a *pay-per-use* system that allows users to monitor not only how many times they have used your application, but how much money they owe for using it.

For developers that are interested in producing specialized content that may not be ideally produced using the page-focused `.aspx` or web service-focused `.asmx` files, you can now create and register your own file type and have those files deliver any content that you desire. We demonstrated this using our `HelloHandler`. Our `HelloHandler` was responsible for all requests to files with the `.hello` extension. Although there is a little more work involved in creating and registering a separate `IHttpHandler` class, they are ideal for ISV (Independent Software Vendors) and developers that would prefer that their work not be in source code format.

For users that need the flexibility of an `IHttpHandler`, but do not need special file extensions, paths, or source code obfuscation, the `.ashx` file type is the perfect solution. The file types were exercised using robust `IHttpHandler` examples that demonstrated the file upload classes offered by ASP.NET and the image generating classes of GDI+. Finally we walked through the application directives of ASP.NET and showed how these directives are used for specifying optional settings within your application.

The code examples in this chapter demonstrate that not only is the ASP.NET Http Runtime and .NET Frameworks an infinitely powerful combination, but together they provide the rich infrastructure necessary for creating additional functionality that seamlessly integrates with the rest of .NET.

Other Resources

Please see the following resource listing for more information on some of the topics covered in this chapter.

- `ftp://ftp.isi.edu/in-notes/rfc1867.txt`—When clients, such as web browsers, upload files to a server, they encode files the files and transmit them in the content body using multipart MIME format with an HTTP Content-Type header of multipart/form-data. This site contains the RFC that details how this works.

- `http://www.w3.org/Protocols/`—The W3C Hypertext Transfer Protocol (HTTP) page. This site contains all the information that you would ever need to know about the HTTP.

- `http://www.gotdotnet.com/quickstarts/`—These are the ASP.NET Quick Start guides that come with installations of ASP.NET.

- `http://www.w3c.org/Graphics/PNG/`—The Portable Network Graphics (PNG) file format is a lossless, portable, file format for raster images with support for up to 48-bit true color. Another benefit of PNG is that PNG is also patent-free.

- `ftp://ftp.isi.edu/in-notes/rfc1521.txt`—Multipurpose Internet Mail Extensions (MIME) RFC document.

CHAPTER 19

COM AND WIN32 IN ASP.NET WEB PAGES

by Adam Nathan

In this chapter we will examine

- Using COM components in an ASP.NET Web page
- Calling Win32 APIs in an ASP.NET Web page
- Using the `AspCompat` directive to gain compatibility with COM components designed to be used in ASP pages
- Performance concerns of using interoperability features

You've seen throughout this book that ASP.NET, as well as the entire .NET platform, is a hot technology that enables developers to write new kinds of Web-centric applications. The .NET platform also enables the same kind of applications to be written more productively than before. While this is great news for developers, .NET would take a long time to catch on if every project that wanted to take advantage of its great new features had to be written from scratch. After all, software developers and corporations have invested countless amounts of time and money into developing all the software applications and components that have been written prior to the arrival of .NET.

This is why one of the .NET platform's core features is its interoperability with non-.NET components. These non-.NET components fall into two broad categories:

- COM components. These are object-oriented components built on Microsoft's Component Object Model (COM), and are commonly used in ASP pages to provide a wide range of functionality. For example, ActiveX controls and pre-.NET Visual Basic components are based on COM technology.

- Dynamic-Link Libraries (DLLs) that expose static functions. Such components don't necessarily use COM, and expose functionality simply as a list of functions. The most widely used examples of this type of component are the Win32 APIs (application programming interfaces).

COM components and static DLL functions like the Win32 APIs are collectively called *native code* or *unmanaged code*. This is in contrast to VB.NET or C# code in an ASP.NET page, which is considered to be "managed" by the Common Language Runtime.

The goal of the .NET platform's native code interoperability is to enable the use of these existing components without modification and in a seamless manner. Therefore, interoperability is not about porting source code or rewriting any portions of it. It's about using the same functionality from the same components in a natural way when new .NET applications are written.

If you currently use COM components in an ASP application, and you want to convert the entire application to be COM-free (perhaps due to performance concerns described at the end of the chapter), interoperability can act as an intermediate step. First you can update your site to use ASP.NET instead of ASP, using the same COM components. Second, you could write or find .NET components that provide the same functionality as the COM components you were using. (You may even find the functionality provided inherently by ASP.NET!) The point is that the last step could be postponed indefinitely, because an ASP.NET Web site works with COM components just fine.

The examples in this chapter are relatively simple in order to focus specifically on the interaction with unmanaged code. Most of the concepts are presented in both VB.NET and C# because there are many noticeable differences when these interoperability features are used from both languages. Many subtleties are involved in interoperating with native code, so you'll see an abundance of cautions in this chapter to guide you in the right direction.

To get the most out of using COM and Win32 in the world of .NET, consult *.NET and COM for C#, Visual Basic, and C++ Programmers*, listed in the "Other Resources" section at the end of this chapter.

1. Using COM Components in an ASP.NET Web Page

COM components can be very useful in ASP.NET pages, just as they have been useful in ASP pages. A multitude of COM components already exist that can fill in missing functionality in the "pure" .NET world. For example, Chapter 8 ("Using XML") explained that the .NET Framework classes in `System.Xml` provide a pull model for parsing XML documents rather than the push model provided by the popular Simple API for XML (SAX). If you aren't concerned about the performance penalties of using a push model like SAX (or of using a COM object in an ASP.NET page), go ahead and use the same old MSXML3 COM object you're familiar with! There are COM objects for everything, from creating advanced 3D graphics, to performing low-level system tasks, to spell checking. If you're already an ASP developer, you probably have an arsenal of COM objects you'd still like to use in your ASP.NET Web pages.

The technology that enables COM objects to be used in the .NET Framework is called *COM Interoperability*. Although COM objects are very different from .NET objects, the Common Language Runtime and COM Interoperability make COM objects look just like .NET objects from the programmer's perspective.

In our examination of using COM components in an ASP.NET Web page, we'll start by looking at the variety of ways to create COM objects. Next, we'll look at how to take advantage of type information using a utility in the .NET Framework SDK. After that, we'll examine common interactions with COM objects and see how they can differ from the same interactions with .NET objects. Finally, we'll look at how the use of COM objects affects the deployment of your ASP.NET Web site.

Using COM Objects Created with the `<object>` Tag

As in ASP pages, COM objects can be created in ASP.NET Web pages with the `<object>` tag. Using the `<object>` tag with a `runat="server"` attribute enables us to use the COM object in server-side script blocks. The `<object>` tag can contain a class identifier (CLSID) or programmatic identifier (ProgID) to identify the COM component to instantiate. Every COM class has a CLSID that identifies it. The following code illustrates how to create an instance of a COM component using a CLSID:

```
<object id="MyObject" runat="server"
    classid="e2d9b696-86ce-45d3-8fc6-fb5b90230c11"
/>
```

A CLSID is guaranteed to uniquely identify the COM component. Because CLSIDs are not user friendly (imagine always having to refer to a class by "e2d9b696-86ce-45d3-8fc6-fb5b90230c11"), many COM components also have a ProgID—a human-readable string. Although ProgIDs are not guaranteed to be unique like CLSIDs, they are unlikely to conflict with other ProgIDs as long as component authors follow recommended conventions (usually *CompanyName.ProductName.ClassName*, or simply *ProductName.ClassName*). Instantiating a COM component using a ProgID can be accomplished with the following code:

```
<object id="MyObject" runat="server"
    progid="Excel.Chart"
/>
```

In ASP.NET pages, the `<object>` tag can also be used with a `class` attribute instead of the COM-specific `classid` or `progid` attribute. COM objects can be created using the `class` attribute, too, once you create .NET type information for such objects. This is covered in the upcoming section, "Taking Advantage of Type Information."

To demonstrate the use of COM components in an ASP.NET Web page, we're going to look at one of the most widely used COM components in ASP—ActiveX Data Objects, or *ADO*.

Note

The functionality provided by ADO is available via ADO.NET, a set of data-related classes in the .NET Framework. Using the classes in the `System.Data` namespace and the techniques described in Chapter 6, "Data Manipulation with ADO.NET," is the recommended way to perform data access in an ASP.NET Web page.

However, because a learning curve is involved in switching to a new data-access model, you may prefer to stick with the same ADO you've come to know and love. Thanks to COM Interoperability, you can continue to use these familiar COM objects when upgrading your Web site to use ASP.NET.

Listing 19.1.1 demonstrates using the ADO COM component in an ASP.NET page by declaring two ADO COM objects with the `<object>` tag.

LISTING 19.1.1 Traditional ADO Can Be Used in an ASP.NET Page Using the Familiar `<object>` Tag

```
 1: <%@ Page aspcompat=true %>
 2: <%@ Import namespace="System.Data" %>
 3: <script language="VB" runat="server">
 4: Sub Page_Load(sender As Object, e As EventArgs)
 5:   Dim strConnection As String
 6:   Dim i As Integer
 7:
 8:   ' Connection string for the sample "pubs" database
 9:   strConnection = _
10:     "DRIVER={SQL Server};SERVER=(local);UID=sa;PWD=;DATABASE=pubs;"
11:
12:   Try
13:     ' Call a method on the page's connection object
14:     connection.Open(strConnection)
15:   Catch ex as Exception
16:     Response.Write("Unable to open connection to database. " + ex.Message)
17:   End Try
18:
19:   Try
20:     ' Set properties and call a method on the page's recordset object
21:     recordset.CursorType = 1  ' 1 = ADODB.CursorTypeEnum.adOpenKeyset
22:     recordset.LockType = 3    ' 3 = ADODB.LockTypeEnum.adLockOptimistic
23:     ' 2 = ADODB.CommandTypeEnum.adCmdTable
24:     recordset.Open("titles", connection, , , 2)
25:   Catch ex as Exception
26:     Response.Write("Unable to open recordset. " + ex.Message)
27:   End Try
28:
29:   Dim table As DataTable
30:   Dim row As DataRow
31:
```

LISTING 19.1.1 Continued

```
32:     ' Create a DataTable
33:     table = New DataTable()
34:
35:     ' Add the appropriate columns
36:     For i = 0 to recordset.Fields.Count - 1
37:       table.Columns.Add(New DataColumn(recordset.Fields(i).Name, _
38:         GetType(String)))
39:     Next
40:
41:     ' Scan through the recordset and add a row for each record
42:     Do While Not recordset.EOF
43:       row = table.NewRow()
44:
45:       ' Look at each field and add an entry to the row
46:       For i = 0 to recordset.Fields.Count - 1
47:         row(i) = recordset.Fields(i).Value.ToString()
48:       Next
49:
50:       ' Add the row to the DataTable
51:       table.Rows.Add(row)
52:
53:       recordset.MoveNext()
54:     Loop
55:
56:     ' Update the DataGrid control
57:     dataGrid1.DataSource = New DataView(table)
58:     dataGrid1.DataBind()
59:
60:     ' Cleanup
61:     recordset.Close()
62:     connection.Close()
63: End Sub
64: </script>
65:
66: <html><title>Using ADO in ASP.NET</title>
67:   <body>
68:     <form runat=server>
69:       <asp:DataGrid id="dataGrid1" runat="server"
70:         BorderColor="black"
71:         GridLines="Both"
72:         BackColor="#ffdddd"
73:         />
74:     </form>.
75:     <object id="connection" runat="server"
76:       progid="ADODB.Connection"/>
77:     <object id="recordset" runat="server"
78:       classid="00000535-0000-0010-8000-00aa006d2ea4"/>
79:   </body>
80: </html>
```

You may be wondering about the `<%@ Page aspcompat=true %>` directive in line 1. Don't worry about this for now—it's covered in the "Using the `AspCompat` Directive" section of this chapter. The important parts of Listing 19.1.1 are lines 75–78, which declare the two COM objects used in the ASP.NET page. The `connection` object is identified by its ProgID, and the `recordset` object is identified by its CLSID, just to demonstrate the two uses in action. The HTML portion of the page contains one control—the DataGrid control. This data grid will hold the information that we obtain using ADO.

Now let's look at the `Page_Load` method, where all the work is done. Lines 9 and 10 initialize a connection string for the sample database (pubs) in the local machine's SQL Server. You may need to adjust this string appropriately to run the example on your computer. In line 14, we call a method on the `connection` COM object. As you can see, this doesn't look any different from calling a method on a .NET object. Lines 21 and 22 set some properties of the `recordset` COM object, again, just like setting the properties of a .NET object. Line 24 opens the "titles" table, so we're now ready to fill a `DataTable` object with information. Lines 21–24 use a few "magic numbers"—hard-coded values that represent various ADO enumeration values mentioned in the code's comments. A little later in the chapter we'll see how to use these values without having to know or type the numbers each represents.

After creating a new `DataTable` object in line 33, we add the appropriate number of columns by looping through the recordset's `Fields` collection. On line 37, each column added is given the name of the current field's `Name` property, and the type of the data held in each column is set to the type `String`. The `Do While` loop starting in line 42 processes each record in the `recordset` object. Once `recordset.EOF` is true, we've gone through all the records. With each record, we create a new row (line 43), add each of the record's fields to the row (lines 46–48), and add the row to the table (line 51). Each string added to a row is the current field's `Value` property. `ToString` is called on the `Value` property in line 47, in case the data isn't already a string. In lines 57 and 58, we associate the `DataTable` object with the page's DataGrid control and call `DataBind` to display the records. Finally, in lines 61 and 62, we call `Close` on the two ADO objects to indicate that we're finished with them. Calling `Close` should really be contained within a `Finally` block such that, even if an exception is thrown inside `Page_Load`, we're ensured that the ADO objects are closed. For simplicity, this is omitted from all the ADO listings. Figure 19.1 displays the output of Listing 19.1.1 as shown in a Web browser.

The important point to take away from this example is that although the `connection` and `recordset` objects are COM objects, interacting with them in the VB.NET code feels no different than interacting with the `table`, `row`, and `dataGrid1` objects. Additionally, the code that we used to work with the `Connection` and `Recordset` ADO objects is almost identical, in syntax, to the code we'd use in a classic ASP page.

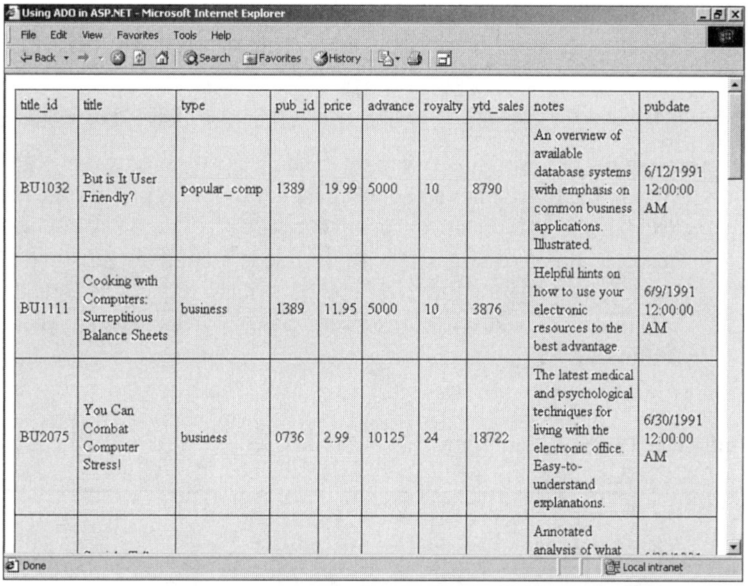

title_id	title	type	pub_id	price	advance	royalty	ytd_sales	notes	pubdate
BU1032	But is It User Friendly?	popular_comp	1389	19.99	5000	10	8790	An overview of available database systems with emphasis on common business applications. Illustrated.	6/12/1991 12:00:00 AM
BU1111	Cooking with Computers: Surreptitious Balance Sheets	business	1389	11.95	5000	10	3876	Helpful hints on how to use your electronic resources to the best advantage.	6/9/1991 12:00:00 AM
BU2075	You Can Combat Computer Stress!	business	0736	2.99	10125	24	18722	The latest medical and psychological techniques for living with the electronic office. Easy-to-understand explanations.	6/30/1991 12:00:00 AM
								Annotated analysis of what	

FIGURE 19.1
The output of Listing 19.1.1 when viewed through a browser.

Using COM Objects Created in the Source Code

In the last section, we looked at how to create COM objects within the HTML portion of an ASP.NET Web page using the `<object>` tag. There are, however, several ways to create COM objects inside the sever-side script block. In this section, we'll look at two ways to accomplish this:

- Using `Server.CreateObject`
- Using `Server.CreateObjectFromClsid`

The `Server.CreateObject` method should be familiar to ASP programmers. `Server.CreateObject` is a method with one string parameter that enables you to create an object from its ProgID. The following code illustrates how to create an instance of a COM component using `Server.CreateObject` in VB.NET:

```
Dim connection As Object
connection = Server.CreateObject("ADODB.Connection")
```

Caution

Although the same type of call to `Server.CreateObject` is done in many ASP pages, a small syntax change is required when updating VBScript code in an ASP page to VB.NET code in an ASP.NET page. VBScript requires the `Set` keyword when setting an `Object` variable in this fashion, for example:

```
Set connection = Server.CreateObject("ADODB.Connection")
```

However, the `Set` statement no longer exists in VB.NET, so it must be omitted. See Appendix A, "Upgrading to Visual Basic.NET," for more details.

746 ASP.NET: TIPS, TUTORIALS, AND CODE

`Server.CreateObjectFromClsid` works just like `Server.CreateObject`, but its string parameter must be set to a CLSID rather than a ProgID. For example

```
Dim recordset As Object
recordset = Server.CreateObjectFromClsid("00000535-0000-0010-8000-00aa006d2ea4")
```

Despite the multitude of ways to create a COM object we've seen so far, the result is the same. Regardless of whether an `ADODB.Connection` object is created with an `<object>` tag (via CLSID or ProgID), `Server.CreateObject` (via ProgID), or `Server.CreateObjectFromClsid`, the object that you interact with in code is no different. Listing 19.1.2 is an update to Listing 19.1.1, instantiating the COM components in server-side code instead of with `<object>` tags. Both the `Server.CreateObject` and `Server.CreateObjectFromClsid` methods are used in Listing 19.1.2.

LISTING 19.1.2 Traditional ADO Can Be Used in an ASP.NET Page by Declaring and Creating COM Objects Inside the `<script>` Block

```
 1: <%@ Page aspcompat=true %>
 2: <%@ Import namespace="System.Data" %>
 3: <script language="VB" runat="server">
 4: Sub Page_Load(sender As Object, e As EventArgs)
 5:   Dim connection As Object
 6:   Dim recordset As Object
 7:   Dim strConnection As String
 8:   Dim i As Integer
 9:
10:   ' Connection string for the sample "pubs" database
11:   strConnection = _
12:     "DRIVER={SQL Server};SERVER=(local);UID=sa;PWD=;DATABASE=pubs;"
13:
14:   Try
15:     ' Create instances of the two ADO objects
16:     connection = Server.CreateObject("ADODB.Connection")
17:     recordset = Server.CreateObjectFromClsid( _
18:       "00000535-0000-0010-8000-00aa006d2ea4")
19:   Catch ex as Exception
20:     Response.Write("Unable to instantiate ADO objects.  " + ex.Message)
21:   End Try
22:
23:   Try
24:     ' Call a method on the connection object
25:     connection.Open(strConnection)
26:   Catch ex as Exception
27:     Response.Write("Unable to open connection to database.  " + ex.Message)
28:   End Try
29:
30:   Try
31:     ' Set properties and call a method on the recordset object
32:     recordset.CursorType = 1  ' 1 = ADODB.CursorTypeEnum.adOpenKeyset
33:     recordset.LockType = 3    ' 3 = ADODB.LockTypeEnum.adLockOptimistic
34:     ' 2 = ADODB.CommandTypeEnum.adCmdTable
35:     recordset.Open("titles", connection, , , 2)
```

LISTING 19.1.2 *Continued*

```
36:     Catch ex as Exception
37:       Response.Write("Unable to open recordset.   " + ex.Message)
38:     End Try
39:
40:     Dim table As DataTable
41:     Dim row As DataRow
42:
43:     ' Create a DataTable
44:     table = New DataTable
45:
46:     ' Add the appropriate columns
47:     For i = 0 to recordset.Fields.Count - 1
48:       table.Columns.Add(New DataColumn(recordset.Fields(i).Name, _
49:         GetType(String)))
50:     Next
51:
52:     ' Scan through the recordset and add a row for each record
53:     Do While Not recordset.EOF
54:       row = table.NewRow()
55:
56:       ' Look at each field and add an entry to the row
57:       For i = 0 to recordset.Fields.Count - 1
58:         row(i) = recordset.Fields(i).Value.ToString()
59:       Next
60:
61:       ' Add the row to the DataTable
62:       table.Rows.Add(row)
63:
64:       recordset.MoveNext
65:     Loop
66:
67:     ' Update the DataGrid control
68:     dataGrid1.DataSource = New DataView(table)
69:     dataGrid1.DataBind
70:
71:     ' Cleanup
72:     recordset.Close()
73:     connection.Close()
74: End Sub
75: </script>
76:
77: <html><title>Using ADO in ASP.NET</title>
78:   <body>
79:     <form runat=server>
80:       <asp:DataGrid id="dataGrid1" runat="server"
81:         BorderColor="black"
82:         GridLines="Both"
83:         BackColor="#ffdddd"
84:       />
85:     </form>
86:   </body>
87: </html>
```

Listing 19.1.2 is identical to Listing 19.1.1, except for lines 5, 6, and 14–21 as well as the HTML portion. Notice that the HTML portion no longer has any `<object>` tags. Instead, the two COM objects are declared in lines 5 and 6, just like we'd declare any .NET objects. In line 16, we create the `connection` object using `Server.CreateObject`. In line 17, we create the `recordset` object using the `Server.CreateObjectFromClsid`. Again, two different methods are used just for demonstration purposes; using `Server.CreateObject` is preferred for both instantiations for its readability. The output of Listing 19.1.2 is the same as the output shown in Figure 19.1.

There's an important point to make about all the code we've seen so far in this chapter: The COM objects we're dealing with are treated as generic `Object` types in the code. This means that every method invocation and property access on the COM objects are resolved at run time rather than compile time. It's possible that a method called "`Open`" won't exist on the `connection` object at run time or have a different number of parameters (although we know otherwise), but all failures are reported at run time. This is commonly referred to as *dynamic invocation*, or *late binding*.

> **Note**
>
> Making a distinction between "compile time" and "run time" might seem odd in the context of an ASP.NET Web page because code in an ASP.NET Web page is compiled and run on-the-fly. However, compile-time errors tend to be much easier to diagnose than run-time errors. Also, invocations resolved at run time perform much more slowly than invocations resolved at compile time.

The fact that code like the following works is due to VB.NET hiding the plumbing of late binding:

```
Dim connection As Object
...
connection.Open(strConnection)
```

In a "strict" programming language like C# (or in VB.NET with `Option Strict` enabled), such code wouldn't compile successfully because the generic `Object` type defined by the .NET Framework doesn't have a method called `Open`. Instead, `Object` only has the methods `Equals`, `GetType`, `ToString`, and so on. Changing the declaration of the type from being an `Object` to being a more specific type like `ADODB.Connection` is not an option either (at this point in the chapter). This is because the compiler must locate a definition for the `ADODB.Connection` type, but no such definition exists in any of the .NET Framework libraries or in the page itself. The upcoming section, "Getting Type Information for COM Components," describes how to remedy this situation. In the mean time, life is not so easy if we want to write the same ASP.NET page from Listing 19.1.2 in C#. Listing 19.1.3 has all the gory details. ADO can be used in C# code the exact same way as in the previous listings, but the syntax isn't as nice when dealing with generic `Object` types.

LISTING 19.1.3 Late-Binding to Traditional ADO in C# Requires Much More Code Than VB.NET

```csharp
 1: <%@ Page aspcompat=true %>
 2: <%@ Import namespace="System.Data" %>
 3: <%@ Import namespace="System.Reflection" %>
 4: <script language="C#" runat="server">
 5: void Page_Load(object sender, EventArgs e)
 6: {
 7:   object connection = null;
 8:   object recordset = null;
 9:   object temp;
10:   string strConnection;
11:   int i;
12:
13:   // Connection string for the sample "pubs" database
14:   strConnection =
15:     "DRIVER={SQL Server};SERVER=(local);UID=sa;PWD=;DATABASE=pubs;";
16:   try
17:   {
18:     // Create instances of the two ADO objects
19:     connection = Server.CreateObject("ADODB.Connection");
20:     recordset = Server.CreateObjectFromClsid(
21:       "00000535-0000-0010-8000-00aa006d2ea4");
22:   }
23:   catch (Exception ex)
24:   {
25:     Response.Write("Unable to instantiate ADO objects.  " + ex.Message);
26:   }
27:
28:   try
29:   {
30:     // Call a method on the connection object
31:     connection.GetType().InvokeMember("Open", BindingFlags.InvokeMethod,
32:       null, connection, new object []
33:       {strConnection, Type.Missing, Type.Missing, Type.Missing});
34:   }
35:   catch (Exception ex)
36:   {
37:     Response.Write("Unable to open connection to database.  "
38:       + ex.Message);
39:   }
40:
41:   try
42:   {
43:     // Set properties and call a method on the recordset object
44:     recordset.GetType().InvokeMember("CursorType",
45:       BindingFlags.SetProperty, null, recordset, new object [] {1});
46:     recordset.GetType().InvokeMember("LockType", BindingFlags.SetProperty,
47:       null, recordset, new object [] {3});
48:     recordset.GetType().InvokeMember("Open", BindingFlags.InvokeMethod,
49:       null, recordset, new object []
50:       {"titles", connection, Type.Missing, Type.Missing, 2});
51:   }
52:   catch (Exception ex)
```

LISTING 19.1.3 Continued

```
53:     {
54:       Response.Write("Unable to open recordset.  " + ex.Message);
55:     }
56:
57:     DataTable table;
58:     DataRow row;
59:
60:     // Create a DataTable
61:     table = new DataTable();
62:
63:     // Get the value of recordset.Fields.Count ahead of time
64:     temp = recordset.GetType().InvokeMember("Fields",
65:       BindingFlags.GetProperty, null, recordset, null);
66:     int count = (int)temp.GetType().InvokeMember("Count",
67:       BindingFlags.GetProperty, null, temp, null);
68:
69:     // Add the appropriate columns
70:     for (i = 0; i < count; i++)
71:     {
72:       temp = recordset.GetType().InvokeMember("Fields",
73:         BindingFlags.GetProperty, null, recordset, new object [] {i});
74:       string name = (string) temp.GetType().InvokeMember("Name",
75:         BindingFlags.GetProperty, null, temp, null);
76:       table.Columns.Add(new DataColumn(name, typeof(String)));
77:     }
78:
79:     // Scan through the recordset and add a row for each record
80:     while (!(bool)recordset.GetType().InvokeMember("EOF",
81:       BindingFlags.GetProperty, null, recordset, null))
82:     {
83:       row = table.NewRow();
84:
85:       // Look at each field and add an entry to the row
86:       for (i = 0; i < count; i++)
87:       {
88:         temp = recordset.GetType().InvokeMember("",
89:           BindingFlags.GetProperty, null, recordset, new object [] {i});
90:         row[i] = temp.GetType().InvokeMember("", BindingFlags.GetProperty,
91:           null, temp, null).ToString();
92:       }
93:
94:       // Add the row to the DataTable
95:       table.Rows.Add(row);
96:
97:       recordset.GetType().InvokeMember("MoveNext",
98:         BindingFlags.InvokeMethod, null, recordset, null);
99:     }
100:
101:    // Update the DataGrid control
102:    dataGrid1.DataSource = new DataView(table);
103:    dataGrid1.DataBind();
104:
```

LISTING 19.1.3 Continued

```
105:    // Cleanup
106:    recordset.GetType().InvokeMember("Close", BindingFlags.InvokeMethod,
107:      null, recordset, null);
108:    connection.GetType().InvokeMember("Close", BindingFlags.InvokeMethod,
109:      null, connection, null);
110: }
111: </script>
112:
113: <html><title>Using ADO in ASP.NET</title>
114:   <body>
115:     <form runat=server>
116:       <asp:DataGrid id="dataGrid1" runat="server"
117:         BorderColor="black"
118:         GridLines="Both"
119:         BackColor="#ffdddd"
120:       />
121:     </form>
122:   </body>
123: </html>
```

Late binding is performed in the .NET Framework using a technology known as *reflection*. Therefore, in line 3, we import the `System.Reflection` namespace, which provides the definition of the `BindingFlags` enumeration used throughout the code. Besides the extra namespace imported, up until line 31, the C# code looks just like the equivalent VB.NET code, except for minor syntax differences. We create the `connection` object using `Server.CreateObject` and the `recordset` object using `Server.CreateObjectFromClsid`. As before, both of these variables are the generic `Object` type.

> **Note**
>
> Only a small subset of the reflection API (essentially just `Type.InvokeMember`) is useful on COM objects created in the ways you've seen so far. When following the procedure in the next section, "Getting Type Information for COM Components," we could use the full reflection API on COM objects if so desired. Reflection is briefly discussed in Chapter 16, "Separating Code from Content."

Line 31 is the first instance where we need to call a method on one of the generic objects. We dynamically invoke the `connection` object's `Open` method by calling `Type.InvokeMember`. The easiest way to get the connection's corresponding `Type` object is to call `GetType`. Note that we can directly call `connection.GetType` because the `GetType` method is defined on all objects in the .NET Framework. The simplest version of `Type.InvokeMember`, which is the only version used in Listing 19.1.3, has the following parameters:

- `name`—A string containing the name of the member to invoke. (If empty, the default member is invoked if one exists.)

- `invokeAttr`—A value of the `BindingFlags` enumeration that specifies what kind of member is being invoked—a public property, a private method, and so on.

- binder—A `Binder` object that can customize the invocation process. We always pass null (`Nothing` in VB.NET) to accept the default behavior.
- target—The object on which we're invoking the member.
- args—An array of objects that represent the parameters passed to the member. If the member has no parameters, we can pass null.

`Type.InvokeMember` returns an `Object` type that corresponds to whatever the member returns (or null if the member doesn't have a return value). Therefore, in line 31, we pass the string `"Open"`, the `InvokeMethod` binding flag, `connection` as the target object, and an array with objects that represent the parameters to `Open`. Why does the array have four elements (`strConnection` and three `Type.Missing` elements)? The reason is that `ADODB.Connection.Open` actually has four arguments, all of which are optional. The definition of `Open` (in VBScript syntax) is the following:

```
Sub Open( _
  Optional ConnectionString As String = "", _
  Optional UserID As String = "", _
  Optional Password As String = "", _
  Optional Options As Long = -1 _
)
```

We must pass an array with the number of elements matching the number of parameters (optional or not), so `Type.Missing` must be used as placeholders that represent optional parameters for which we aren't passing a value.

In lines 44–47, we set the `CursorType` and `LockType` properties of the `recordset` object, again using `Type.InvokeMember`. Setting a property is done just like invoking a method, but notice that the binding flag used is `SetProperty`. The one-element array represents the value that the property is being set to. Lines 48–50 call the `Open` method on the `recordset` object. Again, `Type.Missing` is used as placeholders in the argument array that represent omitted optional parameters.

In lines 64–67, we calculate the value of `recordset.Fields.Count` once rather than having to do it twice—once for each `for` loop. Due to the "clunkier" nature of reflection, it is a two-step process to invoke a property's property. In line 64, we first get the `Fields` property of `recordset` using the `GetProperty` binding flag and set the returned `Fields` object to a temporary variable. Then in line 66, we get the `Count` property of this temporary object and store it in the `count` variable used in lines 70 and 86. We must cast the returned object in line 66 to the type of `count` (an `int`) because the compiler can't know the type of the returned object.

Inside the first `for` loop, lines 72–75 use the same two-step process to get the value of `recordset.Fields[i].Value`. First, we get the `Fields[i]` property by using `GetProperty` and passing `i` as the parameter; then we get the `Name` property for this object and assign it to the local `name` variable. Once again, the cast to `string` is necessary because `Type.InvokeMember` returns a generic `Object` type.

Line 80 dynamically invokes the recordset's `EOF` property and casts it to a `bool` so we can use the ! operator. Lines 88–91 use the two-step process one last time to set the value of the current row to the string representation of `recordset.Fields[i].Value`. Notice that in lines 88 and 90 we're invoking the member specified with an empty string! This works because `Fields` is the default member of the `recordset` object, and `Value` is the default member of the `Fields` object. This is an interesting shortcut that reflection provides, but it's probably better to be more explicit rather than causing potential confusion for other programmers viewing the code. Those lines of code could be replaced with the following equivalent:

```
88:        temp = recordset.GetType().InvokeMember("Fields",
89:           BindingFlags.GetProperty, null, recordset, new object [] {i});
90:        row[i] = temp.GetType().InvokeMember("Value",
91:           BindingFlags.GetProperty, null, temp, null).ToString();
```

Notice that `ToString` is called directly on the object returned by `Type.InvokeMember` in lines 90 and 91. This is another way of expressing the cast to a string that we did in line 74. Finally, with the last `Type.InvokeMember` calls on lines 97, 106, and 108, the listing finishes the same way the VB.NET version finishes.

> **Tip**
>
> Although we continually called `GetType` each time we needed a `Type` to call `InvokeMember`, we could have optimized the code by saving a `Type` object for the `recordset` object and a `Type` object for the `connection` object. For instance, by simply adding
>
> `Type recordsetType = recordset.GetType();`
>
> we could replace each occurrence of `recordset.GetType()` in the listing with `recordsetType`. Listing 19.1.3 only scratches the surface of using reflection to dynamically invoke members. For more information about reflection, see the .NET Framework documentation.

The lesson of Listing 19.1.3 is that, unlike the previous listings, it became obvious when we were interacting with COM objects and when we were interacting with .NET objects. For example, every time we wanted to invoke a method of the `table` object (a .NET `DataTable`), we simply called it. In contrast, every time we wanted to invoke a method of the `recordset` object (a COM `Recordset`), we had to use convoluted syntax with `Type.InvokeMember`. The good news is that the difference has nothing to do with the COM objects themselves, only the way in which we used them. What we desire is to declare `recordset` as an `ADODB.Recordset` object and `connection` as an `ADODB.Connection` object so that the compiler can make use of these COM classes' type information, thereby saving us from making lengthy reflection calls. This would not only enable nicer syntax in C#, but it would result in substantial performance improvements in both C# and VB.NET because we're no longer late binding to the objects. The next section describes how to accomplish this.

> **Caution**
>
> The Common Language Runtime enables late binding to COM objects by communicating with a COM object through an interface called `IDispatch`. `IDispatch` has an `Invoke` method that functions much like `Type.InvokeMember` in the previous listing. Whether or not you use the simple late-binding syntax provided by VB.NET or the more explicit syntax in C#, `IDispatch.Invoke` is always called behind-the-scenes. This is no different than using a COM object in VBScript or JScript on an ASP page.
>
> However, unlike .NET objects, not all COM objects support dynamic invocation. Any COM object that does not implement the `IDispatch` interface does not support late binding. Therefore, if you try to use some COM objects via the mechanisms discussed so far, you might get an exception with the message "The COM target does not implement IDispatch."
>
> It's unlikely you'll run into this because most COM objects do support `IDispatch`, and any that don't support it cannot be used in ASP. The great news is that any such COM objects *can* be used in ASP.NET by following the procedures in the next section.

Getting Type Information for COM Components

Type information is metadata describing the definition of a type (such as a class or interface). In .NET, every type automatically has type information accompanying its definition. This type information is used by compilers, object browsers, IntelliSense in Visual Studio.NET, and so on, to discover what types exist in a given component and what members they contain. In COM, type information is often stored in a form known as a *type library*. Type libraries can be standalone files with a `.tlb` extension, or they can be embedded in a file as a resource. They are typically contained in files with the extension `.dll`, `.exe`, `.ocx`, or `.olb`. Plenty of utilities, such as `OLEVIEW.EXE`, are available for browsing the information inside a type library.

> **Tip**
>
> `OLEVIEW.EXE` is a part of the Windows Platform SDK and can be downloaded from Microsoft's MSDN Online Code Center (complete with source code) at `http://msdn.microsoft.com/code/`. It is also included with Visual Studio.NET. It's a good idea to familiarize yourself with this tool by opening and browsing several type libraries.

The key to making a COM component's type information readily available to ASP.NET is a mechanism that takes a type library and produces an equivalent .NET component (a.k.a. an *assembly*). This mechanism is called the *type library importer*. The assembly that it produces, known as an *Interop Assembly*, enables the VB.NET and C# compilers to find type definitions and resolve calls at compile time. An Interop Assembly contains type definitions; the actual implementation of the COM component remains in the original COM binary file(s). Therefore, the classes in an Interop Assembly are mostly "empty," delegating to the original COM component to do the real work at runtime.

Interop Assemblies are often called *wrappers* for the COM components they represent. To its users, an Interop Assembly looks no different from any other assembly. The mapping between type libraries and Interop Assemblies is one to one; the importer produces a single assembly for any type library, and any Interop Assembly corresponds to exactly one type library.

There are three ways of using the type library importer to generate an Interop Assembly:

- Referencing a type library in Visual Studio.NET
- Using `TlbImp.exe`, a command-line utility that is part of the .NET Framework SDK
- Using the `TypeLibConverter` class or `ITypeLibConverter` interface in the `System.Runtime.InteropServices` namespace

All three of these methods produce the exact same output, although each option gives more flexibility than the previous one. `TlbImp.exe` has several options to customize the import process, whereas using Visual Studio.NET mostly doesn't let you customize the process. Using the conversion APIs in `System.Runtime.InteropServices` gives you one additional capability compared to `TlbImp.exe`—the capability to import an in-memory type library. There's no compelling reason to use these APIs in an ASP.NET page, so the third option won't be covered here. Consult the resources listed at the end of this chapter if you're interested in using these APIs.

Referencing a Type Library in Visual Studio.NET

Visual Studio.NET makes the process of referencing COM components as seamless as referencing .NET components. In a VB.NET or C# Web Application project, you can choose the Project, Add Reference menu. You're then presented with a dialog box for referencing two kinds of components: .NET components and COM components. To add a reference to a COM component, click the COM tab. This dialog box is shown in Figure 19.2.

FIGURE 19.2
Adding a reference to a COM component using Visual Studio.NET is simply a matter of selecting the desired type library.

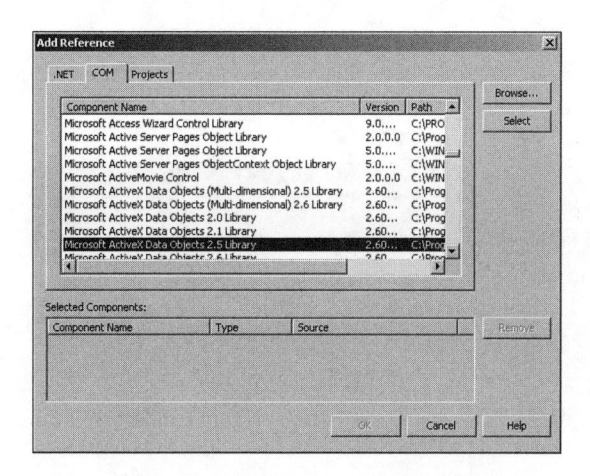

The list of COM components consists of type libraries that are registered in the Windows Registry. To add a reference to a type library that isn't listed, click Browse and select the file. This will also register the type library, so the next time it will be listed in the dialog box. Once you've selected the desired type libraries, click the OK button. Behind the scenes, Visual

Studio.NET invokes the type library importer, when appropriate, to generate an Interop Assembly for each type library selected.

Visual Studio.NET doesn't need to invoke the type library importer to generate an Interop Assembly if a *Primary Interop Assembly* can be located. A Primary Interop Assembly is an "official" assembly digitally signed by the author of the original COM component and made available specifically for .NET applications such as ASP.NET Web pages.

Not only might a Primary Interop Assembly have customizations that make its use in ASP.NET easier, but using Primary Interop Assemblies avoids subtle identity problems that can arise from the proliferation of Interop Assemblies generated for the same type library by different users. Therefore, Visual Studio.NET looks for a Primary Interop Assembly first and alerts you if it doesn't find one, so you can decide whether to generate your own Interop Assembly. This is shown in Figure 19.3.

FIGURE 19.3
Visual Studio.NET message when a Primary Interop Assembly cannot be located.

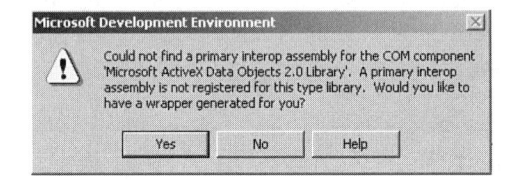

Microsoft has released Primary Interop Assemblies for several of its widely used COM components. For most ASP.NET applications, using a freshly-generated Interop Assembly is fine. See the .NET Framework documentation for more information about the need for Primary Interop Assemblies.

Once you've referenced an Interop Assembly, it's handy to use Visual Studio.NET's Object Browser (View, Other Windows, Object Browser) to view the contents of the Interop Assembly generated for the COM object, as shown in Figure 19.4.

FIGURE 19.4
Browsing the type information for a COM component can be done using Visual Studio.NET's object browser.

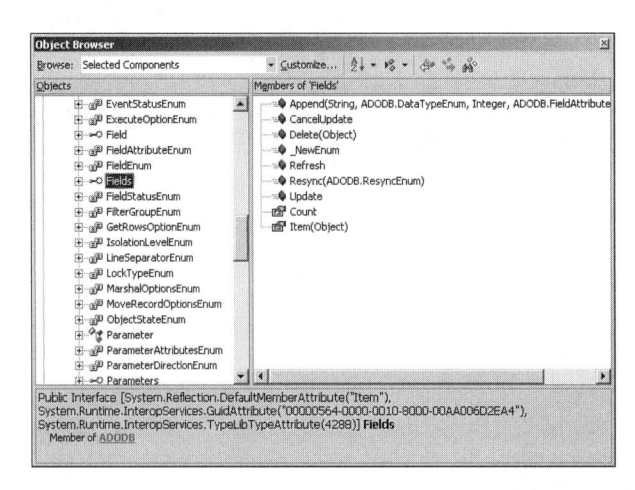

> **Caution**
>
> When browsing the type information in an Interop Assembly, you may be surprised by some of the members that show up. Many types and members and that are hidden from Visual Basic 6 and VBScript are visible and available to any .NET language. In particular, you may find yourself dealing with many interfaces beginning with an underscore. In ADO, the `Recordset` class implements a `_Recordset` interface, the `Connection` class implements a `_Connection` interface, and so on. This arises from the fact that Visual Basic used to provide the illusion that you didn't have to deal with interfaces, even though interfaces are the basis of communication in COM. In NET languages, you may find yourself having to use these interfaces in places where you used to use the classes directly.

Using `TlbImp.exe` to Generate an Interop Assembly

`TlbImp.exe`, the command-line utility mentioned earlier, stands for *Type Library Importer*. It is distributed as part of the .NET Framework SDK. To use it, you simply invoke it with the name of the input file containing the type library. Here's an example:

```
TlbImp "C:\Program Files\Common Files\System\ADO\msado21.tlb"
```

This produces an Interop Assembly called **ADODB.dll** in the current directory, because "ADODB" is the name of the library (which can be seen by opening the file using OLEVIEW). You can control the Interop Assembly's filename and namespace using the `/out` and `/namespace` options. Here's an example of using them:

```
TlbImp "C:\Program Files\Common Files\System\ADO\msado21.tlb"
➥ /out:Microsoft.Ado.dll /namespace:Microsoft.Ado
```

> **Caution**
>
> Sometimes COM components have a library name that is the same as the filename containing the type library. This is quite common for components authored in Visual Basic 6, because the default behavior of the IDE makes them the same (for example, `Project1`). An example of this can be seen by running `TlbImp.exe` on the Microsoft XML type library (`MSXML.dll`) from the same directory in which it resides on your computer:
>
> `C:\windows\system32> TlbImp msxml.dll`
>
> For this situation, `TlbImp.exe` gives the following message:
>
> > `TlbImp error: Output file would overwrite input file`
>
> The solution is to have `TlbImp.exe` place the output file in a different directory and/or choose a different name for the output file using the `/out` option:
>
> > `TlbImp msxml.dll /out:Microsoft.Xml.dll`
> > `TlbImp msxml.dll /out:C:\MyApplication\MSXML.dll`
>
> Be extremely careful with the `/out` option, however, because the name you choose for the filename will also become the namespace associated with all the type definitions contained within (minus the `.dll` extension, of course). The bad thing about this is whatever case you use—msxml, MsXmL, MSXML, and so on—will become the case of the namespace. To avoid this confusion, you should set the namespace independently of the output filename by using the `/namespace` option.

For more information on the rest of the `TlbImp.exe` command-line options, consult the .NET Framework documentation or, at the command line, enter `TlbImp /help`.

Once `TlbImp.exe` has generated the assembly, you can browse its contents using the IL Disassembler (`ILDASM.exe`), another utility that is included in the .NET Framework SDK. For an assembly with the filename `ADODB.dll`, you can type the following and get a graphical representation of the assembly's contents:

```
ildasm ADODB.dll
```

ILDASM is shown in Figure 19.5.

FIGURE 19.5
ILDASM can function as an object browser, showing the contents of any assembly.

Again, if you can find a Primary Interop Assembly for a COM component you wish to use in an ASP.NET page, you should use it instead of generating your own. `TlbImp.exe` warns you if it finds a Primary Interop Assembly for the type library you're importing.

Since the type library importer generates an Interop Assembly based on a type library, ASP.NET pages can take advantage of Interop Assemblies as long as COM components have type libraries. If you want to use a COM component that doesn't have a type library, you can use the late-binding techniques in the previous code listings. Or, you can attempt to generate an Interop Assembly manually by compiling C# or VB.NET code. This advanced technique is briefly discussed in the .NET Framework documentation. You can even manually define individual COM classes or interfaces directly on an ASP.NET page! This will be briefly seen toward the end of the section "Calling Win32 APIs in an ASP.NET Web Page," later in this chapter.

Taking Advantage of Type Information

When you have type information for a COM object, interacting with it is usually no different from interacting with a .NET object. This means that we can use the exact same techniques for creating COM objects that is used for creating .NET objects, rather than using COM-specific ProgIDs or CLSIDs. In this section, we'll look at

- Using the `<object>` Tag with its `class` Attribute
- Using `Server.CreateObject`
- Using the `New` Operator

Once obtaining an Interop Assembly containing the definitions of COM types such as `Recordset`, you can use the `<object>` tag and its `class` attribute as follows:

```
<object id="recset" runat="server"
    class="ADODB.Recordset, ADODB"
/>
```

The `class` string contains an "assembly-qualified" class name. This has the following format:

"*Namespace.ClassName, AssemblyName*"

For assemblies produced by the type library importer, the assembly name always equals the filename of the output file minus the ".dll" extension.

In ASP.NET, a new overload of the `Server.CreateObject` method has been added that has a `Type` object parameter instead of a string. To use this method, we can obtain a `Type` object from a method called `Type.GetType`. A `Type` object returned from `Type.GetType` corresponds to a definition in an assembly, so descriptive information about the class and its members is available to the compiler. `Type.GetType`, like the `class` attribute, takes a string parameter containing an assembly-qualified name. Therefore, the `Server.CreateObject` overload can be used as follows:

```
recset = Server.CreateObject(Type.GetType("ADODB.Recordset, ADODB"))
```

The `New` operator can also be used to create an early-bound COM object, just as we used it in previous listings for .NET classes such as `DataTable` and `DataColumn`.

> **Tip**
>
> Using `Server.CreateObject` with a `Type` object or using the `<object>` tag with the `class` attribute is the preferred method of creating a COM object. Besides giving you the massive performance benefits of early binding, it supports COM objects that rely on `OnStartPage` and `OnEndPage` notifications (whereas the `New` keyword does not). More about this is covered in Section 3 of this chapter.

Now let's go back to the ADO example and use type information as the cure to the unwieldy syntax of using reflection in C#. First, we need an Interop Assembly for the ADO type library. We could either use ADO's Primary Interop Assembly installed with Visual Studio.NET or use `TlbImp.exe`, like so:

```
TlbImp "C:\Program Files\Common Files\System\ADO\msado21.tlb"
```

Be sure to replace the preceding path with the location of the file on your computer. Alternatively, you could run `TlbImp.exe` on `msado15.dll`, which contains a type library embedded inside.

Whether you generated your own or used the Primary Interop Assembly, place a copy of the `ADODB` assembly in the `\bin` directory. Listing 19.1.4 uses the `ADODB` assembly in VB.NET code and demonstrates how to use "early binding" with a COM component using both the `New` operator and the `Server.CreateObject` overload that uses a `Type` parameter.

LISTING 19.1.4 Traditional ADO's Interop Assembly Can Be Used in VB.NET Code to Obtain Higher Performance

```
 1: <%@ Page aspcompat=true %>
 2: <%@ Import namespace="System.Data" %>
 3: <%@ Import namespace="ADODB" %>
 4: <%@ Assembly name="ADODB" %>
 5: <script language="VB" runat="server">
 6: Sub Page_Load(sender As Object, e As EventArgs)
 7:    Dim conn As Connection
 8:    Dim recset As Recordset
 9:    Dim strConnection As String
10:    Dim i As Integer
11:
12:    ' Connection string for the sample "pubs" database
13:    strConnection = _
14:      "DRIVER={SQL Server};SERVER=(local);UID=sa;PWD=;DATABASE=pubs;"
15:
16:    Try
17:      ' Create instances of the two ADO objects
18:      conn = New Connection()
19:      recset = Server.CreateObject(Type.GetType("ADODB.Recordset, ADODB"))
20:    Catch ex as Exception
21:      Response.Write("Unable to instantiate ADO objects. " + ex.Message)
22:    End Try
23:
24:    Try
25:      ' Call a method on the Connection object
26:      conn.Open(strConnection)
27:    Catch ex as Exception
28:      Response.Write("Unable to open connection to database. " + ex.Message)
29:    End Try
30:
31:    Try
32:      ' Set properties and call a method on the Recordset object
```

LISTING 19.1.4 Continued

```
33:      recset.CursorType = CursorTypeEnum.adOpenKeyset
34:      recset.LockType = LockTypeEnum.adLockOptimistic
35:      recset.Open("titles", conn, , , CommandTypeEnum.adCmdTable)
36:    Catch ex as Exception
37:      Response.Write("Unable to open recordset.  " + ex.Message)
38:    End Try
39:
40:    Dim table As DataTable
41:    Dim row As DataRow
42:
43:    ' Create a DataTable
44:    table = New DataTable
45:
46:    ' Add the appropriate columns
47:    For i = 0 to recset.Fields.Count - 1
48:      table.Columns.Add(New DataColumn(recset.Fields(i).Name, _
49:        GetType(String)))
50:    Next
51:
52:    ' Scan through the recordset and add a row for each record
53:    Do While Not recset.EOF
54:      row = table.NewRow()
55:
56:      ' Look at each field and add an entry to the row
57:      For i = 0 to recset.Fields.Count - 1
58:        row(i) = recset.Fields(i).Value.ToString()
59:      Next
60:
61:      ' Add the row to the DataTable
62:      table.Rows.Add(row)
63:
64:      recset.MoveNext()
65:    Loop
66:
67:    ' Update the DataGrid control
68:    dataGrid1.DataSource = New DataView(table)
69:    dataGrid1.DataBind()
70:
71:    ' Cleanup
72:    recset.Close()
73:    conn.Close()
74: End Sub
75: </script>
76:
77: <html><title>Using ADO in ASP.NET</title>
78:   <body>
79:     <form runat=server>
80:       <asp:DataGrid id="dataGrid1" runat="server"
81:         BorderColor="black"
82:         GridLines="Both"
```

LISTING 19.1.4 *Continued*

```
83:            BackColor="#ffdddd"
84:         />
85:      </form>
86:   </body>
87: </html>
```

Comparing Listing 19.1.4 to Listing 19.1.2, you'll see that the differences are subtle. In line 3, we're now importing the `ADODB` namespace, which contains the types in ADO's Interop Assembly. In line 4, we're referencing the assembly itself. Alternatively, this assembly could have been referenced by the site's configuration file, just like any other assembly. Remember, the assembly must be in your site's `\bin` directory or some other accessible location specified by your configuration file.

Besides these page directives, there are two differences in the code. One is the way the objects are created on lines 18 and 19. Because we have type information for the `Connection` and `Recordset` classes, we are able to use the `New` keyword and `Server.CreateObject` with `Type.GetType` to create new objects of these specific types. Rather than declaring the `Connection` and `Recordset` variables as the generic `Object` type, we were able to declare them as `Connection` and `Recordset` objects (lines 7 and 8). Also notice that we needed to change the variable names from `connection` and `recordset` to `conn` and `recset` because the names would conflict with the type names due to VB.NET's case insensitivity.

The only other changes are in lines 33–35. In these lines, we get to use the `enum` constants `CursorTypeEnum.adOpenKeyset`, `LockTypeEnum.adLockOptimistic`, and `CommandTypeEnum.adCmdTable` because these are defined in the `ADODB` assembly. Previously, we used the numeric values of these constants instead. Although the code doesn't look radically different, using the ADO Interop Assembly rather than late binding gives a substantial performance improvement.

Now it's time for the exciting part (that is, if you're planning on using C#). Listing 19.1.5 uses the ADODB assembly to take advantage of type information in C#. Such a measure saves us from relying on reflection to utilize the `Connection` and `Recordset` objects (thereby saving us the verbose and poorer-performing `Type.InvokeMember` calls).

LISTING 19.1.5 Traditional ADO Can Be Used in a C# ASP.NET Page Intuitively When ADO's Interop Assembly Is Referenced

```
 1: <%@ Page aspcompat=true %>
 2: <%@ Import namespace="System.Data" %>
 3: <%@ Import namespace="ADODB" %>
 4: <%@ Assembly name="ADODB" %>
 5: <script language="C#" runat="server">
 6: void Page_Load(object sender, EventArgs e)
 7: {
 8:    Connection connection = null;
 9:    Recordset recordset = null;
10:    string strConnection;
```

LISTING 19.1.5 *Continued*

```
11:    int i;
12:
13:    // Connection string for the sample "pubs" database
14:    strConnection =
15:      "DRIVER={SQL Server};SERVER=(local);UID=sa;PWD=;DATABASE=pubs;";
16:
17:    try
18:    {
16:      // Create instances of the two ADO objects
17:      connection = new Connection();
18:      recordset = (Recordset)Server.CreateObject(
19:        Type.GetType("ADODB.Recordset, ADODB"));
20:    }
21:    catch (Exception ex)
22:    {
23:      Response.Write("Unable to instantiate ADO objects.  " + ex.Message);
24:    }
25:
26:    try
27:    {
28:      connection.Open(strConnection, "", "", -1);
29:    }
30:    catch (Exception ex)
31:    {
32:      Response.Write("Unable to open connection to database.  "
33:        + ex.Message);
34:    }
35:
36:    try
37:    {
38:      // Set properties and call a method on the Recordset object
39:      recordset.CursorType = CursorTypeEnum.adOpenKeyset;
40:      recordset.LockType = LockTypeEnum.adLockOptimistic;
41:      recordset.Open("titles", connection, CursorTypeEnum.adOpenUnspecified,
42:        LockTypeEnum.adLockUnspecified, (int)CommandTypeEnum.adCmdTable);
43:    }
44:    catch (Exception ex)
45:    {
46:      Response.Write("Unable to open recordset.  " + ex.Message);
47:    }
48:
49:    DataTable table;
50:    DataRow row;
51:
52:    // Create a DataTable
53:    table = new DataTable();
54:
55:    // Add the appropriate columns
56:    for (i = 0; i < recordset.Fields.Count; i++)
57:      table.Columns.Add(new DataColumn(recordset.Fields[i].Name,
```

LISTING 19.1.5 Continued

```
58:                          typeof(String)));
59:
60:     // Scan through the recordset and add a row for each record
61:     while (!recordset.EOF)
62:     {
63:       row = table.NewRow();
64:
65:       // Look at each field and add an entry to the row
66:       for (i = 0; i < recordset.Fields.Count; i++)
67:         row[i] = recordset.Fields[i].Value.ToString();
68:
69:       // Add the row to the DataTable
70:       table.Rows.Add(row);
71:
72:       recordset.MoveNext();
73:     }
74:
75:     // Update the DataGrid control
76:     dataGrid1.DataSource = new DataView(table);
77:     dataGrid1.DataBind();
78:
79:     // Cleanup
80:     recordset.Close();
81:     connection.Close();
82: }
83: </script>
84:
85: <html><title>Using ADO in ASP.NET</title>
86:   <body>
87:     <form runat=server>
88:       <asp:DataGrid id="dataGrid1" runat="server"
89:         BorderColor="black"
90:         GridLines="Both"
91:         BackColor="#ffdddd"
92:       />
93:     </form>
94:   </body>
95: </html>
```

If you've forgotten how messy Listing 19.1.3 looks, go back and compare it with this listing. What a difference type information makes! Now the C# page looks much like the equivalent VB.NET page in Listing 19.1.4. Notice in line 17 that VB.NET's **New** keyword is equivalent to C#'s lowercase **new** keyword. Also notice in line 18 that the generic **Object** type returned from **Server.CreateObject** must be cast to the more-specific **Recordset** variable. The main difference in this listing is the lack of support for optional parameters, causing us to pass explicit values for both **connection.Open** in line 28 and **recordset.Open** in lines 41 and 42.

> **Tip**
>
> Although C# forces you to pass values for optional parameters, you often want to pass the default value. You can usually find the default value for each parameter in the component's documentation, its type library (when viewed with OLEVIEW), or the Interop Assembly (when viewed with ILDASM or the Visual Studio.NET Object Browser).
>
> However, if an optional parameter is the generic `Object` type, you can pass `Type.Missing` to indicate an omitted parameter. (This only works for `Object` types because the C# compiler won't let you pass such a type where a type like `String` is expected.) An example of using this would be to call `Connection.OpenSchema`, whose second and third parameters are optional `Object` types, as follows:
>
> ```
> recordset.OpenSchema(
>   SchemaEnum.adShemaViews, // Schema (a SchemaEnum type)
>   Type.Missing,            // Restrictions (an Object type)
>   Type.Missing             // SchemaID (an Object type)
> );
> ```
>
> This is similar to what was done when using reflection in Listing 19.1.3. Because `Type.InvokeMember` forces you to package parameters as arrays of `Object` types, you can always pass `Type.Missing` for any type of optional parameter when late-binding.

Now that you understand how an Interop Assembly is produced and used, you should see that interacting with it feels just as natural as interacting with any .NET component, regardless of programming language. There are some additional options and subtleties, however, and they're discussed in the next section.

Common Interactions with COM Objects

Let's take a look at some common interactions with COM objects and problems you might encounter when attempting to use your favorite COM components in an ASP.NET Web page. ADO, as used in the previous examples, didn't have too many "gotchas". With other COM components, you might not be so lucky. This section looks at some subtlies involved in using COM properties, handling errors, and more. COM concepts are presented that might be unfamiliar to programmers whose only exposure to COM is through VBScript or Visual Basic. Although they are briefly explained to the level required in these discussions, you may want to check out the "Other Resources" section at the end of the chapter for pointers to more in-depth COM coverage.

Calling Properties on a COM Object

To understand some of the subtleties that can arise when using COM properties, let's examine how COM properties are transformed into .NET properties.

In COM, properties are implemented as a set of methods, each associated with specific "property-like" semantics. Each property can contain up to 3 of these special methods known as *accessor methods*. For example, ADO's `Recordset.ActiveConnection` property, which contains all 3 possible accessor methods, would be implemented as follows in pre-.NET Visual Basic:

```
' The Get accessor method
Public Property Get ActiveConnection() As Variant
    ...
End Property

' The Let accessor method
Public Property Let ActiveConnection(ByVal x As Variant)
    ...
End Property

' The Set accessor method
Public Property Set ActiveConnection(ByRef x As Object)
End Property
```

In both COM and .NET, accessor methods can't usually be called directly. Instead, they are invoked through simple property notation.

The `Get` accessor method is called when the client gets the property's value. Here's an example in VBScript:

```
conn = recset.ActiveConnection
```

The `Let` accessor method is called when the client sets the property's value, shown here in VBScript:

```
recset.ActiveConnection = _
    "DRIVER={SQL Server};SERVER=(local);UID=sa;PWD=;DATABASE=pubs;"
```

or

```
Let recset.ActiveConnection = _
    "DRIVER={SQL Server};SERVER=(local);UID=sa;PWD=;DATABASE=pubs;"
```

Finally, the `Set` accessor method is called when the client sets the property to an object reference, shown here (again using VBScript syntax):

```
Set recset.ActiveConnection = conn
```

A COM property can implement any subset of these three methods and usually doesn't implement all three. .NET properties, on the other hand, typically only contain two accessors – a `Get` method and a `Set` method. For .NET components, the previously separate actions of setting a value and setting an object reference are handled by the same `Set` method. Therefore, C# and VB.NET only have "property-like" syntax for invoking two types of accessors: `Get` and `Set`.

The implementation of properties in existing COM components cannot be changed, so COM accessor methods must be presented to .NET applications in a way that makes them usuable as .NET properties. To make this happen, the type library importer performs the following actions when generating a .NET property that represents a COM property:

- A `Get` accessor method, if it exists, is left as a `Get` accessor for the .NET property.
- A `Set` accessor method, if it exists, is left as a `Set` accessor for the .NET property.

- A `Let` accessor method, if it exists, becomes the .NET property's `Set` accessor, as long as the COM property doesn't already have a `Set` method.

- If a property has both `Let` and `Set` accessor methods, the `Set` method remains the `Set` method and the `Let` method becomes an additional .NET accessor method with the name `let_PropertyName`.

The `Get` and `Set` accessors are used with the familiar property syntax in VB.NET and C#, but if you need to call the `Let` accessor method for a COM property that implements all three, you must call the `let_PropertyName` method explicitly.

> **Caution**
>
> A common mistake is made when pre-.NET Visual Basic code that calls a `Let` accessor method is ported to VB.NET. The source of the problem is that the VBScript/VB6 syntax for invoking a `Let` accessor is often identical to the VB.NET syntax for invoking a `Set` accessor. Fortunately, the problem can only arise for the rare cases when properties implement all three accessors (`Get`, `Set`, and `Let`). For example, the VBScript code
>
> ```
> ' Get
> someVariable = recset.ActiveConnection
> ' Let
> recset.ActiveConnection = someVariable
> ' Set
> Set recset.ActiveConnection = someVariable
> ```
>
> translates into the following VB.NET code:
>
> ```
> ' Get - the same familiar syntax.
> someVariable = recset.ActiveConnection
> ' Let - much different syntax than before!
> recset.let_ActiveConnection(someVariable)
> ' Set - the same as the old Let syntax!
> recset.ActiveConnection = someVariable
> ```
>
> Calling `Set` when you mean to call `Let` usually causes an exception to be thrown, but it depends on the property's implementation.

How do these property transformations fit in when we're using reflection and `BindingFlags` in C#? Listing 19.1.3 used `BindingFlags.SetProperty` to set properties. This flag causes either `Let` or `Set` accessor to be invoked, depending on which exists. If both exist, it's up to the object's implementation to interpret what this means and decide which one is called. If you're a "power user" and you'd like to specify exactly which accessor method gets invoked when both exist, there are two special flags for this purpose:

- `BindingFlags.PutDispProperty`—Always calls the `Let` accessor when both `Let` and `Set` exist

- `BindingFlags.PutRefDispProperty`—Always calls the `Set` accessor when both `Let` and `Set` exist

> **Note**
>
> The flags are named `PutDispProperty` and `PutRefDispProperty` because a COM property's `Let` and `Set` methods are often called `propput` and `propputref` methods, respectively. These names come from the representation of properties in COM's Interface Definition Language (IDL).

There's one additional subtlety to using COM properties, but it only affects C#, not VB.NET. C# has restrictions on properties defined and used in the language that other languages don't have. For instance, C# properties can't have parameters (excluding a default property known as an *indexer*, which may have one by-value parameter) or by-reference values. When encountering unsupported properties defined by COM objects in C# code, you can't use the convenient property notation, but you can call the accessor methods using regular method syntax and the method name `get_PropertyName` or `set_PropertyName`. C# only allows this when it isn't possible to use the property syntax.

An example of this can be seen when using the Microsoft SourceSafe 6.0 COM component. The SourceSafe type library defines a `VSSDatabase` type with a non-default `User` property containing a string `Name` parameter. Although this property can be called with regular property syntax in VB.NET:

```
user = database.User("Guest")
```

it must be called in C# as follows:

```
user = database.get_User("Guest");
```

Otherwise, C# compiler error CS1546 occurs with the message "Property or indexer 'User' is not supported by the language; try directly calling accessor method 'SourceSafeTypeLib.VSSDatabase.get_User(string)'".

Error Handling

Errors raised by COM objects are turned into .NET exceptions, so handling errors in COM objects is just like handling errors for .NET objects, which is described in Chapter 9 ("ASP.NET Error Handling Techniques"). Certain COM error codes (also known as `HRESULT`s) are transformed into well-known .NET exceptions, such as `OutOfMemoryException`, `NullReferenceException`, `InvalidCastException`, and more. If a COM object returns a custom error code, the type of exception thrown is `COMException`. Depending on the implementation of the COM object, the exception thrown might have a useful message, source, and "helplink". For a COM component written in Visual Basic 6, this would mean that the author had set the various properties of the `Err` object before raising the error. If the COM component doesn't give a message describing the error and if the operating system doesn't recognize the error code (in order to fill in a standard message), the exception could have a cryptic message, such as the following:

```
"Exception from HRESULT: 0x80090331"
```

To determine the meaning of the error code, consult the COM component's documentation.

> **Note**
>
> The rules governing the exception type seen for a COM-raised error are independent of the rules governing the exception contents. Therefore, it's possible to see a specific exception type thrown with the generic "Exception from HRESULT" message or a generic `COMException` exception type thrown with a user-friendly message.

The type of an exception is often the most important piece of information that enables us to choose an appropriate action. If we're stuck with a generic `COMException` exception type, we need a reliable way to programmatically determine what the problem was. Fortunately, `COMException` has a public `ErrorCode` property that contains the `HRESULT` value, so it's possible to check exactly which error code, returned by the COM object, caused this generic exception. Here's an example of doing this in VB.NET:

```
Try
  recset = New Recordset()
Catch ex as COMException
  If (ex.ErrorCode = &H80040154) Then
    Response.Write("Please check that ADO is properly installed on this machine.")
    Exit Sub
  Else
    ...
  End If
End Try
```

This code catches a `COMException` exception type when instantiating an ADO `Recordset` and checks for the `ErrorCode` value of `&H80040154`, which is VB.NET notation for the hexadecimal value 80040154. (This error code corresponds to the "Class not registered" COM error. Therefore, if the number matches, we print a special message explaining that ADO must not be installed correctly.)

In C#, the equivalent code looks as follows:

```
try
{
  recset = new Recordset();
}
catch (COMException ex)
{
  if ((uint)ex.ErrorCode == 0x80040154)
  {
    Response.Write("Please check that ADO is properly installed on this machine.");
    return;
  }
  else { ... }
}
```

Notice the cast in the `if` statement. This is needed since `COMException`'s `ErrorCode` property is defined as a signed integer yet we're comparing it to an unsigned integer. Doing the following in C#

```
if (ex.ErrorCode == 0x80040154) ...
```

would produce a compiler warning:

```
warning CS0652: Comparison to integral constant is useless;
  the constant is outside the range of type 'int'
```

and the expression inside the `if` statement would never evaluate to `true`! For more information about which `HRESULT` values are transformed into which .NET exceptions, consult the .NET Framework documentation.

Coercing COM Objects

In contrast to ASP, the ASP.NET programming environment is often *strongly-typed*. This means that to treat one type (such as a `String`) as another type (such as an `Integer`), an explicit conversion or *coercion* is sometimes necessary. Previous versions of Visual Basic have methods such as `CStr` (which converts an object to a `String`) or `CDbl` (which converts an object to a `Double`). VB.NET adds a new method—`CType`—that can coerce an object to any user-defined type.

Here is an example of using `CType` in VB.NET to coerce a `Recordset` COM object to the `_Recordset` COM interface type:

```
Dim i as _Recordset
Dim r as Recordset
...
i = CType(r, _Recordset)
```

From the programmer's perspective, coercing a COM object to a COM interface type works just like coercing a .NET object to a .NET interface type. Coercing objects to different types is done in C# using its casting operation. Here's the same example in C#:

```
_Recordset i;
Recordset r;
...
i = (_Recordset)r;
```

Behind the scenes, the coercion is performed by the CLR, which either inspects the object's type information or calls the COM object's `QueryInterface` method to ask if the coercion is legal. An explicit cast or `CType` call isn't always necessary when assigning a variable of one type to a variable of another type, depending on the type information.

> **Note**
>
> Just as every .NET object contains the methods of the `Object` class, every COM object contains the methods of an interface known as `IUnknown`. `IUnknown` contains three methods: `AddRef`, `Release`, and the previously mentioned `QueryInterface`. These methods cannot be called directly in Visual Basic or any .NET language, but are called by the CLR to handle low-level interactions with COM objects.

Many COM methods that appear to return classes in VBScript actually return interfaces, and in VB.NET and C#, it becomes obvious that you're dealing with interfaces. When calling such methods in VB.NET or C#, programmers often have the urge to cast a returned interface type to the class type that they know the object really is. You should avoid doing this in C# because it might not always work as you'd expect. This is explained in the following caution.

> **Caution**
>
> Although coercing a COM class type (such as `Recordset`) to a COM interface type (such as `_Recordset`) works as you'd expect, you can't always count on casting a COM interface type to a COM class type in C#, even if the object may really be the class type you're casting to. Due to fundamental differences in the way classes are used in COM compared to the .NET Framework, coercing to a COM class type is a separate action from a C# cast. This action is exposed by the `Marshal.CreateWrapperOfType` method in the `System.Runtime.InteropServices` namespace. The "wrapper" refers to any class defined in an Interop Assembly. Such classes are sometimes referred to as *CLR-Callable Wrappers*. VB.NET's `CType` calls `Marshal.CreateWrapperOfType` when appropriate (and VB.NET sometimes calls it implicitly), so this subtle detail is hidden from VB.NET users.
>
> If you have an Interop Assembly containing a definition of the COM class you wish to cast to in C#, there is a way to get the cast to work, as long as the following two conditions are met:
>
> - The class isn't marked [noncreatable] in the type library.
> - The object you're attempting to cast implements a COM interface known as `IProvideClassInfo`.
>
> If these two conditions are met, you can run an SDK utility called *RegAsm* (an assembly-registration utility) on the Interop Assembly. Here's an example:
>
> `RegAsm ADODB.dll`
>
> Although RegAsm is normally used for other purposes, it enables nicer casting behavior for languages such as C#. For more information, consult the .NET Framework documentation.

Passing the Right Type of Object

COM components may expose functionality that requires you to pass parameters of a type that no longer exists in the .NET Framework, such as `Currency`. If you're taking advantage of type information in an Interop Assembly, this usually isn't a problem—the CLR magically makes this work while exposing the type as a related one. For the case of `Currency`, it is exposed in the Interop Assembly as a `Decimal` type with a special custom attribute that automatically transforms it into the `Currency` type that the COM object expects. (This special custom attribute is `MarshalAsAttribute`, discussed in the "Calling Win32 APIs in an ASP.NET Web Page" section.) However, if you're late-binding to a COM object or if the method you're calling has a generic `Object` parameter, you need to do some extra work to make sure the COM object sees the right type of object.

> **Note**
>
> A COM method with a generic `Object` parameter means that the parameter is a `Variant` type from COM's perspective. VBScript's `Variant` is mapped to the .NET `Object` type. VBScript's `Object` type represents an interface known as `IDispatch` (introduced earlier), but this distinction between `Variant` and `Object` no longer exists in the .NET Framework.

This extra work entails using a "wrapper" object and passing it to the COM object. A few such objects are defined in the `System.Runtime.InteropServices` namespace—one for each basic COM type that doesn't exist in the .NET Framework:

- `CurrencyWrapper`—Used to make a `Decimal` type look like a `Currency` type
- `IDispatchWrapper`—Used to make an `Object` type look like an `IDispatch` interface pointer (`Object` in pre-.NET Visual Basic)
- `IUnknownWrapper`—Used to make an `Object` type look like an `IUnknown` interface pointer
- `ErrorWrapper`—Used to make either an integer or an `Exception` type look like an `HRESULT` (a COM error code)

All of these wrapper objects are used almost identically. For a method called `GiveMeAnything` with an `Object` parameter, `CurrencyWrapper` can be used as follows in VB.NET:

```
Dim d as Decimal = 123.456

' Make the COM object see a Variant containing a Decimal type
obj.GiveMeAnything(d)

' Make the COM object see a Variant containing a Currency type
obj.GiveMeAnything(New CurrencyWrapper(d))
```

> **Tip**
>
> Remember that using these wrapper classes is only necessary when late binding or when calling parameters of type `Object`.

Releasing a COM Object

The Common Language Runtime manages the lifetime of COM objects, so every COM object can be treated as a garbage-collected object, just like any .NET object. We usually don't need to worry about "releasing" a COM object when we're finished using it, but sometimes we might want to release it at a specific point in our code. In VBScript, this can be accomplished by setting the object equal to `Nothing`. This technique doesn't work in VB.NET, however. If you must release a COM object explicitly, you can use a method called `ReleaseComObject`, defined in the `System.Runtime.InteropServices` namespace. Here is an example in VB.NET:

```
Dim obj As MyCompany.ComObject
...
' We're finished with the object.
Marshal.ReleaseComObject(obj)
```

Attempting to use an object after passing it to `ReleaseComObject` raises a `NullReferenceException`. You should not call this method unless the semantics of the COM object require deterministic release. For example, a COM object holding onto scarce operating system resources should be released as soon as possible so calling `ReleaseComObject` when finished with it is a good idea.

Using COM+ Components

Just like COM components, COM+ components—formerly Microsoft Transaction Server (MTS) components—can be used in an ASP.NET application. However, due to differences between the ASP and ASP.NET security models, using COM+ components in an ASP.NET application might require changing their security settings.

If you get an error with a message such as "Permission denied" when attempting to use COM+ (MTS) components, you should be able to solve the problem as follows:

1. Open the "Component Services" explorer. On Windows 2000, this can be found by selecting Programs, Administrative Tools, Component Services from the Start menu.

2. Under the "Component Services" node, find the COM+ application you wish to use, right-click on it, and select "Properites".

3. Go to the "Identity" tab and change the account information to a brand new local machine account.

4. At a command prompt, run `DCOMCNFG.EXE`, a tool that lets you configure DCOM settings (such as security) for your COM+ application.

5. Go to the "Default Security" tab and click the "Edit Default..." button in the "Default Access Permissions" area.

6. Add the new user created in Step 3.

7. Restart Internet Information Services (IIS).

Deployment

Deploying an ASP.NET application that uses COM components is not quite as simple as deploying an ASP.NET application that doesn't. Besides satisfying the requirements of ASP.NET, you must satisfy the requirements of COM. This means registering COM components on the server, just as you would do with classic ASP. This is usually accomplished by running `regsvr32.exe`, a standard Windows utility, on each COM DLL. If you're relying on a component being installed, such as ADO, then no additional work is necessary besides the supplied installation.

Unless you late-bind to all COM components and only create COM types via ProgID or CLSID, you also must deploy any Interop Assemblies for the COM components you use. The deployment of these Interop Assemblies is no different from deploying any other assemblies used by your application. Again, if Primary Interop Assemblies are available for the COM components you use, you should deploy those.

2. Calling Win32 APIs in an ASP.NET Web Page

Thanks to the Common Language Runtime, we can call Win32 APIs directly from an ASP.NET page. The term *Win32 APIs* refers to static functions (*shared functions* in VB.NET terms) exposed by a collection of DLLs—`kernel32`, `gdi32`, `user32`, and more. Because the .NET Framework provides a rich set of APIs that provide much of the same functionality of the Win32 APIs, it's often not necessary to make use of this power. It's also not as easy, because you have to manually write Win32 function definitions that are callable from your code.

The Visual Basic language has had the capability to call Win32 APIs for years, but now every .NET language has this capability via a technology called Platform Invocation Services (or *PInvoke* for short). PInvoke enables you to call static entry points in *any* DLL, even ones you write yourself! Using function definitions you provide in your VB.NET or C# code, PInvoke transforms the arguments appropriately and calls the corresponding native function. This transformation is known as *marshaling*. Because the main application of PInvoke is to call functions exposed by the core Win32 DLLs, that is what we'll focus on. To begin, we'll look at using PInvoke in VB.NET and then in C#.

> **Tip**
>
> `DUMPBIN.EXE` is a useful utility for inspecting the contents of DLLs, such as the APIs they expose. To see a list of functions that any DLL exports, use the following command (shown here for `advapi32.dll`):
>
> ```
> dumpbin /exports advapi32.dll
> ```
>
> `DUMPBIN.EXE` is one of the many tools that comes with Visual Studio.

Calling Win32 APIs Using VB.NET

As just mentioned, we need to provide a suitable source code definition for any Win32 functions we'd like to call in an ASP.NET page. In VB.NET, this can be done using the `Declare` statement. The statement is structured as follows (in its simplest forms):

```
' For a subrountine (no return value)
Declare Sub FunctionName Lib "LibraryName" (Parameter list)

' For a function
Declare Function FunctionName Lib "LibraryName" (Parameter list) As ReturnType
```

Therefore, to call the `QueryPerformanceCounter` function in `kernel32.dll`, we need to declare the following in the script block:

```
Declare Function QueryPerformanceCounter Lib "kernel32.dll" _
  (ByRef lpPerformanceCount As Long) As Boolean
```

Then we call it just like we'd call any other method:

```
result = QueryPerformanceCounter(time)
```

> **Note**
> Functions exposed by DLLs have case-sensitive names, so even in VB.NET you must use the correct case when defining the function.

Listing 19.2.1 demonstrates a silly application for calling this `QueryPerformanceCounter` method in `kernel32.dll`—calculating the elapsed time between button clicks. A performance counter is a timer that gives time measurements with the highest resolution possible. This is a useful API for getting precise time measurements for games, scientific applications, performance testing, and more. The frequency of the counter depends on the capability of the computer and can be determined by calling `QueryPerformanceFrequency`, another function exposed by `kernel32.dll` and used in the listing.

LISTING 19.2.1 The `QueryPerformanceCounter` and `QueryPerformanceFrequency` Functions Enable High-Precision Measurement

```
 1: <script language="VB" runat="server">
 2: Declare Function QueryPerformanceCounter Lib "kernel32.dll" _
 3:        (ByRef lpPerformanceCount As Long) As Boolean
 4: Declare Function QueryPerformanceFrequency Lib "kernel32.dll" _
 5:        (ByRef lpFrequency As Long) As Boolean
 6:
 7: Sub Page_Load(sender as Object, e as EventArgs)
 8:    Dim CurrentTime as Long
 9:
10:    If Not Page.IsPostBack then
11:       lblTime.Text = ""
12:       CurrentTime = 0
13:       Session("LastTime") = New Long()
14:       Session("Frequency") = New Long()
15:
16:       If Not QueryPerformanceFrequency(Session("Frequency")) Then
17:          lblTime.Text = "Error: Server doesn't support performance counters"
18:          btnSubmit.Enabled = False
19:       End If
20:    Else
21:       ' a postback, so calculate the time elapsed
22:       If (QueryPerformanceCounter(CurrentTime) And Session("LastTime") <> 0)
23:          lblTime.Text = lblTime.Text & _
24:             ((CurrentTime - Session("LastTime"))_
```

LISTING 19.2.1 Continued

```
25:               / Session("Frequency")).ToString() _
26:               & " seconds since last click.<br>"
27:       Else
28:         lblTime.Text = lblTime.Text & "Please click again.<br>"
29:       End If
30:       Session("LastTime") = CurrentTime
31:     End If
32: End Sub
33: </script>
34: <html><title>Using Performance Counters in ASP.NET</title>
35: <body>
36:     <form method="post" runat="server">
37:        <b>Test Your Reflexes:</b><br>
38:        <asp:button id="btnSubmit" runat="server"
39:            type="Submit" text="Click Me!" />
40:        <p><hr><p>
41:        <asp:label runat="server" id="lblTime" />
42:     </form>
43: </body>
44: </html>
```

The page in Listing 19.2.1 contains a button and a label. The button is used to provoke the postback, and the label is used to display the time measurements. Lines 2–5 use the `Declare` statement to define the two Win32 functions used. The first time the page is loaded, we set the label text to an empty string and initialize `CurrentTime` to zero in lines 11 and 12. `CurrentTime` is a `Long` variable that will always hold the current value of the performance counter. In lines 13 and 14, we initialize two more `Long` variables, but this time they're session-level variables. `LastTime` will hold the value of `CurrentTime` from the previous page visit so we can calculate the elapsed time. `Frequency` will hold the value of the performance counter's frequency, obtained from the `QueryPerformanceFrequency` function, which we only call once when the page is first loaded. Alternatively, we could call the function every time rather than storing the value in a session-level variable, but this extra work isn't necessary.

The call to `QueryPerformanceFrequency` is done in line 16 to determine the capabilities of the system. Like many Win32 APIs, `QueryPerformanceFrequency` doesn't simply return the desired value. Instead, it requires you to declare a variable to contain the value and pass it by reference. Because a reference to the `Frequency` variable is passed to the method, it contains the value filled in by the method after the call. The "real" return value of the method is used to indicate success or failure. `True` means success and `False` means failure. If the call fails, we print an error message and disable the page's button. If it succeeds, there's nothing to do but wait for the postback. `Frequency` contains the necessary value because it was passed by reference, so when the postback occurs, we'll be ready to use that value in our calculations.

Line 20 begins the `Else` clause that handles the postback. We check for two conditions before performing the calculation. First, we call `QueryPerformanceCounter`. If the call fails, we fall into the `Else` clause where "Please click again" is appended to the text of the `lblTime` label in line 28. The `If` statement on line 22 also checks to see whether `LastTime` is equal to zero, which means that this is the first time the button has been clicked. We want to calculate the time elapsed between two button clicks, so we display the "Please click again" message to get our second data point if `LastTime` equals zero. At the end of the method, we set `LastTime` equal to `CurrentTime` so it will contain the correct value the next time around.

Once the button has been clicked at least twice, lines 24 and 25 perform the calculation every time the postback occurs. The calculation uses the following formula:

```
(CurrentTime - Session("LastTime")) / Session("Frequency")
```

The value we obtain from the difference between `CurrentTime` and `LastTime` isn't meaningful by itself. We must divide the difference by the frequency of the counter in order to determine how many seconds have passed. The resultant value is converted to a string and appended to the label. Figure 19.6 displays the output of Listing 19.2.1 in a browser once the button has been clicked a few times.

FIGURE 19.6
The output of Listing 19.2.1 when viewed through a browser.

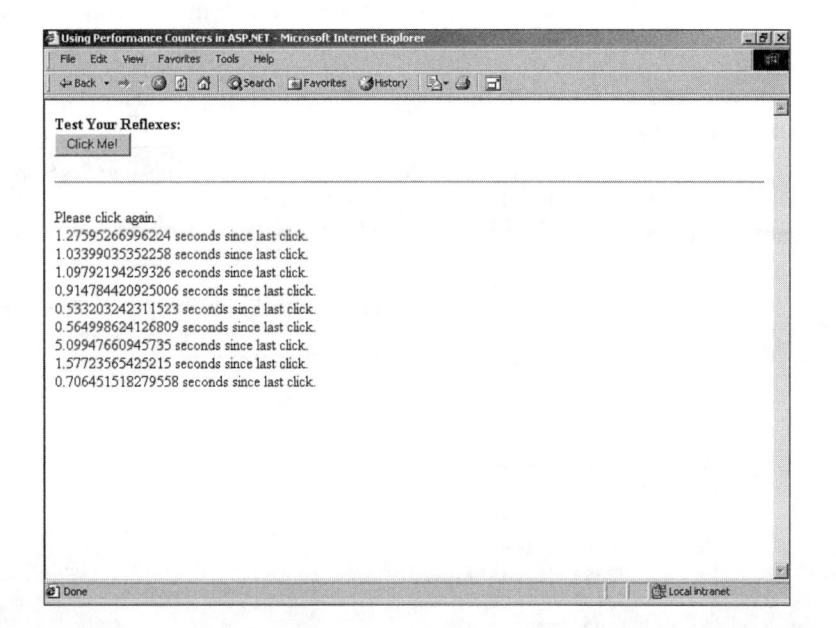

Calling Win32 APIs Using C#

C# doesn't have a built-in keyword equivalent to Visual Basic's `Declare`. Instead, a custom attribute is used to mark a method appropriately. This custom attribute is `DllImportAttribute`, defined in the `System.Runtime.InteropServices` namespace. Because C# allows you to drop the "`Attribute`" portion of a custom attribute's name, using this attribute is done as follows:

```
[DllImport("kernel32.dll")]
static extern bool QueryPerformanceCounter(out long lpPerformanceCount);
```

778 ASP.NET: TIPS, TUTORIALS, AND CODE

With this custom attribute, you specify the name of the DLL that exposes the method. Because you aren't providing an implementation for the method, C# requires that you use the **static** and **extern** keywords. The behavior caused by both of these keywords is implied by VB.NET's **Declare** statement.

Notice that the parameter to `QueryPerformanceCounter` uses C#'s **out** keyword. This could have been **ref** (C#'s equivalent to VB.NET's **ByRef** keyword), but C# enables us to be a little more specific regarding the method's intent. Because the purpose of the by-reference parameter is only for the method to send a value "out" to the caller, the method doesn't care what the value is coming "in." Whereas C#'s **ref** keyword indicates that the incoming value and outgoing value are both important, **out** makes it clear that we only care about the outgoing value. Besides resulting in clearer code, using **out** instead of **ref** when data doesn't need to be passed in can be a performance optimization. Listing 19.2.2 demonstrates the same code shown in Listing 19.2.1, but in C# using `DllImport` rather than in VB.NET using `Declare`.

LISTING 19.2.2 Using the `QueryPerformanceCounter` and `QueryPerformanceFrequency` Win32 APIs in C# Code

```
 1: <%@ Import namespace="System.Runtime.InteropServices" %>
 2: <script language="C#" runat="server">
 3: [DllImport("kernel32.dll")]
 4: static extern bool QueryPerformanceCounter(out long lpPerformanceCount);
 5: [DllImport("kernel32.dll")]
 6: static extern bool QueryPerformanceFrequency(out long lpFrequency);
 7:
 8: void Page_Load(object sender, EventArgs e)
 9: {
10:    long CurrentTime;
11:
12:    if (!Page.IsPostBack)
13:    {
14:      lblTime.Text = "";
15:      CurrentTime = 0;
16:      Session["LastTime"] = new long();
17:      Session["Frequency"] = new long();
18:      long temp;
19:      if (!QueryPerformanceFrequency(out temp))
20:      {
21:        lblTime.Text = "Error: Server doesn't support performance counters";
22:        btnSubmit.Enabled = false;
23:      }
24:      Session["Frequency"] = temp;
25:    }
26:    else
27:    {
28:      // a postback, so calculate the time elapsed
29:      if (QueryPerformanceCounter(out CurrentTime) &&
30:         (long)Session["LastTime"] != 0)
31:      {
32:        lblTime.Text = lblTime.Text + ((CurrentTime -
```

LISTING 19.2.2 *Continued*

```
33:            (long)Session["LastTime"]) / (long)Session["Frequency"]).ToString()
34:            + " seconds since last click.<br>";
35:      }
36:      else { lblTime.Text = lblTime.Text + "Please click again.<br>"; }
37:      Session["LastTime"] = CurrentTime;
38:    }
39: }
40: </script>
41: <html><title>Using Performance Counters in ASP.NET</title>
42: <body>
43:    <form method="post" runat="server">
44:      <b>Test Your Reflexes:</b><br>
45:      <asp:button id="btnSubmit" runat="server"
46:        type="Submit" text="Click Me!" />
47:      <p><hr><p>
48:      <asp:label runat="server" id="lblTime" />
49:    </form>
50: </body>
51: </html>
```

This listing serves the same purpose as Listing 19.2.1, with the function declarations in lines 3–6 and the function calls on lines 19 and 29. There are two additional things to point out. The first is on line 1: importing the `System.Runtime.InteropServices` namespace. This is necessary because `DllImportAttribute` is defined in this namespace. The second is the use of a temporary variable on lines 18, 19, and 24. This is a minor detail, but C# is picky when it comes to the type of by-reference parameters (whether `ref` or `out`). We must pass a reference to a `long`, yet using `Session["Frequency"]` directly would be a reference to a generic `object`, so it wouldn't work.

> **Note**
>
> C# enforces the rule that by-reference parameters must exactly match the by-reference parameter types in the method's signature because allowing more flexibility would violate the type-safety of the application. For more information, consult the C# reference documentation at http://msdn.microsoft.com.

Choosing the Right Parameter Types

The hardest part about PInvoke is defining each signature correctly. Unfortunately, there are no good diagnostics if you get the signature wrong—it just doesn't work. The first step is to know how to convert Win32 data types into .NET data types. Table 19.1 lists commonly used data types in Win32 functions and the .NET Framework's equivalent types. Keep in mind that many of the .NET types have aliases in VB.NET and C#. For instance, `Int16`, `Int32`, and `Int64` are identical to `Short`, `Integer`, and `Long`, respectively, in VB.NET.

> **Tip**
>
> Pasting `Declare` statements from pre-.NET versions of Visual Basic code into VB.NET code can be a handy way of getting function definitions. However, most `Declare` statements from earlier versions will need to be updated if used in VB.NET to account for the changes in data types. For example, `Short` is now `Integer`, and `Integer` is now `Long`. See Appendix A, "Upgrading to Visual Basic.NET," for more details.

TABLE 19.1 Common Win32 Data Types and Their Equivalent Data Types to Use in a `Declare` or `DllImport` Signature

Win32 Data Type	.NET Data Type
byte	System.Byte
char	System.Char
short	System.Int16
WORD	System.UInt16 or System.Int16
BOOL	System.Int32 or System.Boolean
int	System.Int32
long	System.Int32
DWORD	System.UInt32 or System.Int32
hyper	System.Int64
__int64	System.Int64
unsigned short	System.UInt16 or System.Int16
unsigned int	System.UInt32 or System.Int32
unsigned long	System.UInt32 or System.Int32
unsigned hyper	System.UInt64 or System.Int64
unsigned __int64	System.UInt64 or System.Int64
unsigned float	System.Single
unsigned double	System.Double
VARIANT	System.Object
LPSTR	System.String or System.Text.StringBuilder
LPCSTR	System.String

TABLE 19.1 Continued

Win32 Data Type	.NET Data Type
LPWSTR	`System.String` or `System.Text.StringBuilder`
LPCWSTR	`System.String`
BSTR	`System.String`
HANDLE	`System.IntPtr`
void*	`System.IntPtr`

> **Caution**
> To distinguish between the multiple unmanaged string types in Table 19.1, a custom attribute often must be added to a `System.String` parameter. This is covered in the upcoming section, "Customizing Parameters."

Notice in Table 19.1 that some of the Win32 types have two .NET types listed. We have a little bit of flexibility when defining the function signatures (even more than what the chart shows), but the options listed are the most commonly used. For example, although the Win32 `BOOL` type is really a 32-bit integer, it's handy to treat it as a `System.Boolean` type so you can check for `True` or `False` rather than a numeric value. However, treating a `BOOL` type as a `System.Boolean` type is slightly slower than treating it as an integer due to the transformation done by the Common Language Runtime. Similarly, because VB.NET doesn't support unsigned types, it's handy to just use a signed type such as `Int32` (or `Integer`) even when an `unsigned int` type more accurately represents the original type (assuming that the unsigned value always falls in the range of signed integers).

Strings are a different story; sometimes you must use `StringBuilder` instead of a simple `String` type. The `String` type in the .NET Framework is immutable. This means that once it's created, it can't be changed. This may not be obvious in C# or VB.NET code because you may "modify" strings all the time, such as in this example:

```
myString = myString + "."
```

However, code such as this doesn't actually modify the contents of `myString`; it creates a new `String` object with the contents of `myString` concatenated with "." and assigns the new object to `myString`. The old `myString` is discarded and cleaned up by the system.

`StringBuilder`, on the other hand, represents a string buffer whose contents can change. Therefore, this type should be used for any Win32 function that expects you to pass in an allocated buffer that the function fills with data.

Tip

As mentioned in Chapter 15, "ASP.NET Performance Tips," `StringBuilder` is useful in an ASP.NET page even if you're not using PInvoke. If you find yourself performing a lot of string concatenation and manipulation, you can boost performance by using `StringBuilder` types instead. This way, the Common Language Runtime doesn't have to create as many intermediate `String` objects.

Let's look at a canonical example of a Win32 API that expects a string buffer—`GetUserName` in `advapi32.dll`, which gives us the name of the user currently logged onto the computer. The Win32 documentation describes the method as follows:

```
BOOL GetUserName(
  LPTSTR lpBuffer,   // name buffer
  LPDWORD nSize      // size of name buffer
);
```

`lpBuffer` is an "out" parameter that points to a buffer that receives the string with the user's name. If the buffer isn't large enough to contain the whole string, the call fails. `nSize` is an "in/out" parameter. On the way in, it specifies the size of the `lpBuffer` string buffer. On the way out, it contains the number of characters copied to the buffer. If the call fails due to a buffer that isn't large enough, `nSize` will contain the size needed, so you can then increase the buffer's length to `nSize` and try calling the method again.

Tip

The previous information about parameters being "out" or "in/out" cannot be inferred from the function's signature alone. This information is described in the documentation for any Win32 function. Later, in the "Customizing Parameters" section, we'll see how such parameter designations can affect the corresponding signature definition in an ASP.NET page.

Listing 19.2.3 demonstrates how to define and call the `GetUserName` method in a C# ASP.NET page.

LISTING 19.2.3 Calling a Win32 API That Expects a String Buffer Must Be Called Using a `StringBuilder` Type in C# Code

```
 1: <%@ Import namespace="System.Runtime.InteropServices" %>
 2: <%@ Import namespace="System.Text" %>
 3: <script language="C#" runat="server">
 4: [DllImport("advapi32.dll")]
 5: static extern bool GetUserName(StringBuilder lpBuffer, ref int nSize);
 6:
 7: void Page_Load(object sender, EventArgs e)
 8: {
 9:   int size = 20; // Pick an arbitrary size
10:   StringBuilder sb = new StringBuilder(size);
11:   if (GetUserName(sb, ref size))
12:   {
```

LISTING 19.2.3 Continued

```
13:      Response.Write(sb.ToString());
14:    }
15:    else
16:    {
17:      sb.Capacity = size;
18:      if (GetUserName(sb, ref size))
19:      {
20:        Response.Write(sb.ToString());
21:      }
22:      else
23:      {
24:        Response.Write("Unable to get user name");
25:      }
26:    }
27: }
28: </script>
29: <html><title>StringBuilder Example</title>
30: </html>
```

To keep the example as simple as possible, we use an empty HTML section and use `Response.Write` to output our results. The first two lines import the necessary namespaces—`System.Runtime.InteropServices` for `DllImport` and `System.Text` for `StringBuilder`. Lines 4 and 5 define the `GetUserName` function, using `StringBuilder` to represent the buffer and a by-reference `int` to represent the size. Even though the contents of the buffer are modified by the function, we don't need to pass `StringBuilder` by reference; it is inherently a "reference type."

> **Note**
>
> Passing a reference type "by reference" means that the function can allocate and return a new object. In other words, it can change the reference. Passing a reference type "by value" means that the function cannot modify the reference itself but can change the contents of the type being referenced. This is in contrast to *value types* like `int`, `bool`, `double`, etc. The contents of a value type can only be changed by a function when it's passed by reference.

On line 9, we choose an arbitrary initial size that we hope is big enough. Line 10 creates a new `StringBuilder`, initializing it to the size we chose. In line 11, we call `GetUserName`, and if it succeeds, we simply print out the contents of the buffer. Notice that this is done in line 13 by simply calling the `StringBuilder`'s `ToString` method. If the method fails, it's likely that the buffer is too small. Because, according to the documentation, `nSize` contains the required buffer size in such a situation, we try to call `GetUserName` one more time after resizing the buffer. This is done in line 17 by setting the `Capacity` property. Finally, if that still fails, we give up and print an error message in line 24.

> **Tip**
>
> Many Win32 APIs that expect a buffer have documentation that specifies a maximum size that should always be sufficient. This way, you can avoid having to call the same method twice. For `GetUserName`, the documentation states that the maximum buffer size is UNLEN + 1. UNLEN is defined in `Lmcons.h` (a standard Windows header file) as 256.

For backward compatibility with Visual Basic 6, VB.NET enables you to pass a by-value `String` in a `Declare` statement to represent the same kind of "in/out" buffer. Listing 19.2.4 demonstrates the VB.NET way of achieving the functionality in Listing 19.2.3.

LISTING 19.2.4 Calling a Win32 API That Expects a String Buffer Can Be Called Using a Plain-Old String Type in VB.NET Code

```
 1: <script language="VB" runat="server">
 2: Declare Auto Function GetUserName Lib "advapi32.dll"_
 3: (ByVal lpBuffer as String, ByRef nSize As Integer) As Boolean
 4:
 5: Sub Page_Load(sender As Object, e As EventArgs)
 6:   Dim size As Integer = 20    ' Pick an arbitrary size
 7:   Dim s As String
 8:   s = New String(CChar(" "), size)
 9:   If (GetUserName(s, size)) Then
10:     Response.Write(Left(s, size))
11:   Else
12:     s = New String(CChar(" "), size)
13:     If (GetUserName(s, size)) Then
14:       Response.Write(Left(s, size))
15:     Else
16:       Response.Write("Unable to get user name")
17:     End If
18:   End If
19: End Sub
20: </script>
21: <html><title>String Example</title>
22: </html>
```

This example works just like the previous one, but the definition of the `GetUserName` function in lines 2 and 3 uses a by-value `String` instead of a `StringBuilder`. Notice that the `Declare` statement has something new—an `Auto` keyword. Ignore this for now; it is explained later in the chapter in the section "Customizing `Declare` and `DllImport`."

On line 8, we initialize the string to be a bunch of spaces with the length equal to our `size` variable. This is accomplished using a constructor on `String` that takes a character and a size. On line 9, we call `GetUserName`, and if it succeeds, we print out the contents of the buffer. We trim the printed string using VB.NET's `Left` function because we don't want the extra contents of the buffer printed (which doesn't really matter in this case because the rest of the buffer contains only spaces). We can trim the string to the number of characters specified with `size` because the by-reference value contains the number of characters filled in the buffer when the call is successful. If the method fails, we take the same approach we did in Listing 19.2.3. Notice that in line 12 we allocate a new `String` because we can't simply resize it like we could with `StringBuilder`.

> **Tip**
>
> If you prefer using `StringBuilder` in VB.NET, go ahead and use it just like you would in C#. Using `String` types for this case is simply a second option for backward compatibility.

Customizing Parameters

Because there are many different Win32 data types represented by the same .NET types, we sometimes need to place extra information on parameters used in a `Declare` or `DllImport` statement. This is done using the `MarshalAsAttribute` custom attribute (`MarshalAs` for short). This custom attribute is defined in the `System.Runtime.InteropServices` namespace and is used in conjunction with the `UnmanagedType` enumeration in the same namespace. `MarshalAs` tells the Common Language Runtime to marshal the given .NET ("managed") type as a particular native ("unmanaged") type. `UnmanagedType` has many values, but the most important ones for PInvoke are shown in Table 19.2.

TABLE 19.2 Commonly-Used Values of the `UnmanagedType` Enumeration Placed Inside the `MarshalAs` Custom Attribute

Attribute	Value
`UnmanagedType.BStr`	Can be placed on `String` to transform it into COM's string type, known as `BSTR` (which is also called `String` in VBScript)
`UnmanagedType.ByValArray`	Can be placed on an array, used in conjunction the `MarshalAs` property `SizeConst` to indicate the number of elements it contains
`UnmanagedType.ByValTStr`	Can be placed on `String` to transform it into a platform-dependent unmanaged string with a fixed length (either ANSI or Unicode depending on the operating system or other attributes)
`UnmanagedType.Currency`	Can be placed on `Decimal` to transform it into COM's `Currency` type
`UnmanagedType.IDispatch`	Can be placed on `Object` to transform it into the COM `IDispatch` interface
`UnmanagedType.IUnknown`	Can be placed on `Object` to transform it into the COM `IUnknown` interface

TABLE 19.2 Continued

Attribute	Value
UnmanagedType.LPTStr	Can be placed on String or StringBuilder to transform it into a pointer to a platform-dependent unmanaged string (either ANSI or Unicode, depending on the operating system or other attributes)
UnmanagedType.LPWStr	Can be placed on String or StringBuilder to transform it into a pointer to a Unicode string

Every parameter type has a default UnmanagedType value that is assumed if none is specified. For example, a String uses UnmanagedType.LPStr by default and a Short uses UnmanagedType.I2 (not shown in the table). Therefore, MarshalAs only needs to be used when the default behavior doesn't suffice.

> **Caution**
>
> Be aware that the default marshaling behavior when PInvoke is used sometimes differs from the default behavior when COM objects are used. For example, a .NET Framework String in a COM object's method is converted to a BSTR by default, whereas a String in a Declare or DllImport statement is converted to an LPSTR by default. Consult the .NET Framework documentation for the complete conversion rules.

Here's an example of using MarshalAs in C# to transform a StringBuilder into a Unicode string instead of an ANSI string:

```
[DllImport("advapi32.dll")]
static extern bool GetUserNameW(
  [MarshalAs(UnmanagedType.LPWStr)] StringBuilder lpBuffer,
  ref int nSize
);
```

Here's an example in VB.NET:

```
Declare Function GetUserNameW Lib "advapi32.dll" ( _
  <MarshalAs(UnmanagedType.LPWStr)> ByVal lpBuffer as StringBuilder, _
  ByRef nSize As Integer _
) As Boolean
```

Using MarshalAs isn't the only way to customize the behavior of a parameter. You can also use two more custom attributes in System.Runtime.InteropServices: InAttribute and OutAttribute (or simply In and Out). As stated earlier, documentation for Win32 APIs describes parameters as "in," "out," or "in/out." This means the following:

- For an "in" parameter, data flows from the caller to the function (or "callee").
- For an "out" parameter, data flows from the function to the caller.
- For an "in/out" parameter, data flows in both directions.

Here's what adding these attributes to the previous signatures looks like in C#:

```
[DllImport("advapi32.dll")]
static extern bool GetUserNameW(
  [MarshalAs(UnmanagedType.LPWStr),In,Out] StringBuilder lpBuffer,
  [In,Out] ref int nSize
);
```

Here's an example in VB.NET:

```
Declare Function GetUserNameW Lib "advapi32.dll" ( _
  <MarshalAs(UnmanagedType.LPWStr),InAttribute,Out> ByVal lpBuffer as StringBuilder, _
  <InAttribute,Out> ByRef nSize As Integer _
) As Boolean
```

> **Tip**
> VB.NET requires that you either use the full name of the `<InAttribute>` custom attribute or specify `<[In]>` rather than the usual `<In>` because `In` is a keyword. This doesn't apply to the `OutAttribute` custom attribute, however, because `Out` is not a keyword.

Notice that both the by-value `StringBuilder` and the by-reference `Integer` have in/out behavior by default. The `In` and `Out` attributes added to the previous signatures only make the default behavior explicit. Furthermore, just because you use the `In` and `Out` custom attributes doesn't mean that the system will respect them. For example, you can't mark a by-value integer with `[In,Out]` and expect the value to be modified after the call! You normally don't have to use these `In` or `Out` attributes because the default behavior is often sufficient.

> **Caution**
> One situation in which the default behavior is not sufficient involves reference types such as arrays. Although we're used to array parameters having in/out behavior (that is, the function may change the data contained in the array's elements), the default behavior in `Declare` and `DllImport` signatures is to treat reference types other than `StringBuilder` as "in only" unless its fields (or elements, in the case of arrays) are simple value types like `Short`, `Integer`, or `Long`. (Such simple value types are sometimes called *blittable*, meaning that the managed and unmanaged data representations are identical so complex marshaling is unnecessary.) Marshaling data only in the "in" direction performs better than marshaling data in both directions, and is acceptable when you don't care about the array contents after the call. If you do care about the contents afterward, however, be sure to mark a reference type parameter with `In` and `Out`!

> **Caution**
>
> Don't ever define a `Declare` or `DllImport` function with a by-reference array parameter. Such a function may pass back a completely new array with any number of elements (because the array itself was passed by reference), and PInvoke has no way to discover the size of the outgoing array. Therefore, only one element would be copied back to your array after the call; the array would always be resized to a length of 1.
>
> If you must call a function that uses a by-reference array parameter, you can define the parameter as a `System.IntPtr` type to expose a raw pointer and use methods of the `System.Runtime.InteropServices.Marshal` class to manipulate the pointer. If using C#, you can use *unsafe code* to accomplish the same task with more convenient syntax. Both of these are advanced options described in the .NET Framework documentation.

Calling APIs with Complex Types

Often Win32 functions use more complex types, such as structs (known as *User-Defined Types* or *UDTs* in Visual Basic), enums, and COM interfaces. When defining these functions in our ASP.NET page, we also need to define these parameter types. To demonstrate this, we'll create an ASP.NET page that uses some advanced Win32 APIs provided by Microsoft Video for Windows (VFW). These APIs reside in `avifil32.dll` and enable us (among other things) to open an AVI file and view its contents. We use these APIs on a file stored on the Web server. Such a technique could be useful for a multimedia repository site, ensuring that users are only uploading files with the appropriate format.

Listing 19.2.5 asks the user to upload an AVI movie file, using the same file upload technique from Chapter 2, "Common ASP.NET Code Techniques." Once we have the file on the server, we use the APIs to report some summary information regarding the file's contents.

LISTING 19.2.5 Using Microsoft Video for Windows in an ASP.NET Page to Report Information About an Uploaded AVI File

```
 1: <%@ Import Namespace="System.IO" %>
 2: <%@ Import Namespace="System.Runtime.InteropServices" %>
 3: <script language="VB" runat="server">
 4:   ' Initializes the AVIFile library.
 5:   Declare Function AVIFileInit Lib "avifil32.dll" () As Integer
 6:
 7:   ' Exits the AVIFile library.
 8:   Declare Function AVIFileExit Lib "avifil32.dll" () As Integer
 9:
10:   ' Opens the specified AVI file and returns a file interface (IAVIFile).
11:   Declare Function AVIFileOpen Lib "avifil32.dll" ( _
12:     ByRef ppfile As IAVIFile, szFile As String, mode As Integer, _
13:     pclsidHandler As Guid) As Integer
14:
15:   ' Returns a stream interface (IAVIStream) associated with an AVI file.
16:   Declare Function AVIFileGetStream Lib "avifil32.dll" ( _
17:     pfile As IAVIFile, ByRef ppavi As IAVIStream, fccType As Integer, _
```

LISTING 19.2.5 *Continued*

```
18:        lParam As Integer) As Integer
19:
20:    ' Returns the length of the input stream.
21:    Declare Function AVIStreamLength Lib "avifil32.dll" _
22:        (pavi As IAVIStream) As Integer
23:
24:    ' Converts a stream measurement in samples to milliseconds.
25:    Declare Function AVIStreamSampleToTime Lib "avifil32.dll" _
26:        (pavi As IAVIStream, lSample As Integer) As Integer
27:
28:    '
29:    ' The IAVIFile COM Interface used in the methods above
30:    '
31:    <ComImport(), InterfaceType(ComInterfaceType.InterfaceIsIUnknown), _
32:      Guid("00020020-0000-0000-c000-000000000046")> Interface IAVIFile
33:      Sub Info(ByRef pfi As AVIFILEINFO, lSize As Integer)
34:      Sub GetStream(ByRef ppStream As IAVIStream, fccType As Integer, _
35:        lParam As Integer)
36:      Sub CreateStream(ByRef ppStream As IAVIStream, psi As AVISTREAMINFO)
37:      Sub WriteData(ckid As Integer, lpData As IntPtr, cbData As Integer)
38:      Sub ReadData(ckid As Integer, lpData As IntPtr, _
39:        ByRef lpcbData As Integer)
40:      Sub EndRecord()
41:      Sub DeleteStream(fccType As Integer, lParam As Integer)
42:    End Interface
43:
44:    '
45:    ' The IAVIStream COM Interface used in the methods above
46:    '
47:    <ComImport(), InterfaceType(ComInterfaceType.InterfaceIsIUnknown), _
48:      Guid("00020021-0000-0000-c000-000000000046")> Interface IAVIStream
49:      Sub Create(lParam1 As Integer, lParam2 As Integer)
50:      Sub Info(ByRef psi As AVISTREAMINFO, lSize As Integer)
51:      <PreserveSig> Function FindSample(lPos As Integer, _
52:        lFlags As Integer) As Integer
53:      Sub ReadFormat(lPos As Integer, lpFormat As IntPtr, _
54:        ByRef lpcbFormat As Integer)
55:      Sub SetFormat(lPos As Integer, lpFormat As IntPtr, _
56:        cbFormat As Integer)
57:      Sub Read(lStart As Integer, lSamples As Integer, lpBuffer As IntPtr, _
58:        cbBuffer As Integer)
59:      Sub Write(lStart As Integer, lSamples As Integer, _
60:        lpBuffer As IntPtr, cbBuffer As Integer, dwFlags As Integer, _
61:        ByRef plSampWritten As Integer, ByRef plBytesWritten As Integer)
62:      Sub Delete(lStart As Integer, lSamples As Integer)
63:      Sub ReadData(fcc As Integer, lp As IntPtr, ByRef lpcb As Integer)
64:      Sub WriteData(fcc As Integer, lp As IntPtr, cb As Integer)
65:      Sub SetInfo(fcc As Integer, lp As IntPtr, cb As Integer)
66:    End Interface
67:
68:    '
```

LISTING 19.2.5 Continued

```
 69:    ' Structures used in the interfaces above.
 70:    '
 71:    <StructLayout(LayoutKind.Sequential, _
 72:      CharSet:=CharSet.Auto)> Public Structure AVISTREAMINFO
 73:      Public fccType As Integer
 74:      Public fccHandler As Integer
 75:      Public dwFlags As Integer
 76:      Public dwCaps As Integer
 77:      Public wPriority As Short
 78:      Public wLanguage As Short
 79:      Public dwScale As Integer
 80:      Public dwRate As Integer
 81:      Public dwStart As Integer
 82:      Public dwLength As Integer
 83:      Public dwInitialFrames As Integer
 84:      Public dwSuggestedBufferSize As Integer
 85:      Public dwQuality As Integer
 86:      Public dwSampleSize As Integer
 87:      Public rcFrame As RECT
 88:      Public dwEditCount As Integer
 89:      Public dwFormatChangeCount As Integer
 90:      <MarshalAs(UnmanagedType.ByValTStr, SizeConst:=64)> _
 91:      Public szName As String
 92:    End Structure
 93:
 94:    <StructLayout(LayoutKind.Sequential, _
 95:      CharSet:=CharSet.Auto)> Public Structure AVIFILEINFO
 96:      Public dwMaxBytesPerSec As Integer
 97:      Public dwFlags As Integer
 98:      Public dwCaps As Integer
 99:      Public dwStreams As Integer
100:      Public dwSuggestedBufferSize As Integer
101:      Public dwWidth As Integer
102:      Public dwHeight As Integer
103:      Public dwScale As Integer
104:      Public dwRate As Integer
105:      Public dwLength As Integer
106:      Public dwEditCount As Integer
107:      <MarshalAs(UnmanagedType.ByValTStr, SizeConst:=64)> _
108:      Public szFileType As String
109:    End Structure
110:
111:    Public Structure RECT
112:      Public left As Integer
113:      Public top As Integer
114:      Public right As Integer
115:      Public bottom As Integer
116:    End Structure
117:
118:    ' Constant used when opening the file
119:    Public OF_SHARE_DENY_WRITE As Integer = 32
120:
```

LISTING 19.2.5 *Continued*

```
121:    Sub Page_Load(sender As [Object], e As EventArgs)
122:      Dim result as Integer
123:
124:      If Page.IsPostBack AndAlso Not (fupUpload.PostedFile Is Nothing) Then
125:        ' Save the file if it has a filename and exists...
126:        If (fupUpload.PostedFile.FileName.Trim().Length > 0 And _
127:          fupUpload.PostedFile.ContentLength > 0) Then
128:          Const strBaseDir As String = "C:\My Projects\Uploaded Files\"
129:          Dim strFileName As String = _
130:            Path.GetFileName(fupUpload.PostedFile.FileName)
131:          fupUpload.PostedFile.SaveAs((strBaseDir & strFileName))
132:
133:          Dim pfile As IAVIFile = Nothing
134:
135:          ' Initialize the AVIFile library
136:          result = AVIFileInit()
137:          If (result < 0) Then
138:            lblResults.Text = _
139:              "<hr>Server Error: Cannot initialize the AVIFile library."
140:            Exit Sub
141:          End If
142:
143:          ' Open the AVI file
144:          result = AVIFileOpen(pfile, strBaseDir & strFileName, _
145:            OF_SHARE_DENY_WRITE, Guid.Empty)
146:          If (result < 0) Then
147:            lblResults.Text = _
148:              "<hr>The uploaded file is not a valid AVI or WAV file."
149:            Exit Sub
150:          End If
151:
152:          ' Display summary information
153:          Dim fileinfo As New AVIFILEINFO()
154:
155:          ' Call a method on the IAVIFile COM interface
156:          Try
157:            pfile.Info(fileinfo, Marshal.SizeOf(fileinfo))
158:          Catch ex As Exception
159:            lblResults.Text = "<hr>Unable to get file information."
160:            Exit Sub
161:          End Try
162:
163:          Dim samplesPerSecond As Double = _
164:            fileinfo.dwRate / fileinfo.dwScale
165:          lblResults.Text = "<hr>Information for file <b>" & _
166:            fupUpload.PostedFile.FileName & _
167:            "</b>:<hr>Type: <b>" & fileinfo.szFileType & _
168:            "</b><br>Width: <b>" & fileinfo.dwWidth & _
169:            "</b><br>Height: <b>" & fileinfo.dwHeight & _
170:            "</b><br>Samples/Sec: <b>" & samplesPerSecond & _
171:            "</b><br># of Streams: <b>" & fileinfo.dwStreams & "</b><br>"
172:
```

LISTING 19.2.5 Continued

```
173:        ' Look at each stream and print out summary information
174:        Dim i As Integer
175:        For i = 0 To fileinfo.dwStreams - 1
176:          Dim pstream As IAVIStream = Nothing
177:
178:          result = AVIFileGetStream(pfile, pstream, 0, i)
179:          If (result < 0) Then
180:            lblResults.Text = "<hr>Cannot get stream #" & (i+1).ToString()
181:            Exit Sub
182:          End If
183:
184:          Dim streaminfo As New AVISTREAMINFO()
185:
186:          ' Call a method on the IAVIStream COM interface
187:          Try
188:            pstream.Info(streaminfo, Marshal.SizeOf(streaminfo))
189:          Catch ex As Exception
190:            lblResults.Text = "<hr>Cannot get information for stream #" _
191:              & (i+1).ToString()
192:            Exit Sub
193:          End Try
194:
195:          Dim time As Integer = AVIStreamSampleToTime(pstream, _
196:            AVIStreamLength(pstream))
197:          Dim seconds As Integer = time / 1000
198:          Dim fraction As Integer = time Mod 1000
199:
200:          samplesPerSecond = streaminfo.dwRate / streaminfo.dwScale
201:
202:          lblResults.Text += "<hr><b>Stream #" & (i + 1).ToString() & _
203:            "</b><br>Name: <b>" & streaminfo.szName & _
204:            "</b><br>Frame Count: <b>" & _
205:            AVIStreamLength(pstream).ToString() & _
206:            "</b><br>Play Length: <b>" & seconds.ToString() & _
207:            "." & fraction.ToString() & " sec" & _
208:            "</b><br>Samples/Sec: <b>" & samplesPerSecond & "</b><br>"
209:        Next i
210:
211:        ' Called instead of AVIFileRelease,
212:        ' since it releases the COM interface.
213:        Marshal.ReleaseComObject(pfile)
214:
215:        ' Release the AVIFile library
216:        AVIFileExit()
217:      Else
218:        lblResults.Text = "<hr>You must enter a valid filename!"
219:      End If
220:    End If
221:  End Sub 'Page_Load
222: </script>
223: <html>
224: <body>
```

LISTING 19.2.5 *Continued*

```
225:    <form runat="server" EncType="multipart/form-data">
226:      <h1>Multimedia File Upload</h1>
227:      <b>Select the AVI or WAV file to upload:</b><br>
228:      <input runat="server" id="fupUpload" type="file" >
229:      <p>
230:      <asp:button id="btnSubmit" runat="server" Text="Upload File" />
231:      <p><asp:label runat="server" id="lblResults" />
232:    </form>
233: </body>
234: </html>
```

The uploading functionality of this listing is identical to the example in Chapter 2, so we won't discuss it here. The use of Win32 APIs begins in the postback after we have the uploaded file, in line 127. But before examining that, let's look at all the definitions we had to provide.

Lines 4–26 define all the APIs we're going to use. Besides simple types, the functions have parameters that are COM interfaces—`IAVIFile` and `IAVIStream`. If these interfaces were defined in a type library, we could use `TlbImp.exe` to generate an Interop Assembly containing these interface definitions and reference that assembly from our page. Because we don't have a type library with these definitions, we instead define them manually in lines 28–66. This is an advanced technique in which we mimic the work of the type library importer, creating interface definitions with the appropriate custom attributes. The process of doing this is much like the process of writing `Declare` statements, in which the signatures and attributes must faithfully represent the COM definitions. If any mistakes are made in the definitions, failure can occur in subtle and non-intuitive ways. For more information on manually defining COM interfaces, see the .NET Framework documentation.

Several of the methods on these COM interfaces have parameters that are structs. These structs—`AVIFILEINFO`, `AVISTREAMINFO`, and `RECT`—are defined in lines 68–116. These structs contain fields with types that are converted just like parameter types in function definitions. Notice the use of `<MarshalAs(UnmanagedType.ByValTStr, SizeConst:=64)>` in lines 90 and 107. This customizes the behavior of the `String` field to be a platform-dependent string with 64 characters. In Win32 documentation, this looks like `CHAR[64]` or `WCHAR[64]`. The `AVIFILEINFO` and `AVISTREAMINFO` structs also have additional customizations with the custom attribute `StructLayoutAttribute`. The use of this attribute is covered later in this section.

Finally, in line 133, we get to use these APIs. We call `AVIFileInit` in line 136 to initialize the library. (The Win32 documentation tells us that we need to do this before calling any of the other APIs). `AVIFileInit`, like a few of the other functions, returns an `HRESULT`—the same kind of error code used by COM. When `HRESULT`s are represented as signed integers, any value greater than or equal to zero indicates success, so we check if the returned value is *less than* 0 on line 137. If this call fails, there's nothing else we can do but print a message and exit.

In lines 144 and 145, we call `AVIFileOpen` to open the file that has been uploaded to the server in the `strBaseDir` directory. We check for failure the same way as with `AVIFileInit` and print an error message if we can't open the file. Although these APIs are meant to be used on AVI files, the functionality in this listing can also work on WAV sound files. Therefore, on failure, the message says that "the uploaded file is not a valid AVI or WAV file." The call to `AVIFileOpen` causes our `IAVIFile` interface variable declared in line 133 to point to a valid object. Therefore, after this call, we can call the interface's `Info` method to get the file information we want to display. The `Info` method has two parameters: a struct (`AVIFILEINFO`) that it will fill in with information and an `Integer` that needs to contain the size of the struct. This is the typical pattern when calling methods that expect structs. We create an instance of `AVIFILEINFO` in line 153 (called `fileinfo`) to pass as the first parameter to `Open`, and we pass the result of calling `Marshal.SizeOf` on the instance for the second size parameter. This is the way to calculate the size of structures in an ASP.NET page.

> **Tip**
>
> Use `Marshal.SizeOf` in `System.Runtime.InteropServices` to determine the size of a struct. A struct's size often needs to be passed as a parameter to Win32 APIs.

Because `Info` is a method on a COM interface rather than a static DLL entry point, we check for failure by catching an exception.

After the call, the fields of the `fileinfo` struct contain the information we want to display. In lines 163 and 164, we calculate the movie's "samples per second" by dividing `fileinfo.dwRate` by `fileinfo.dwScale`. In lines 165–171, we display some of the fields' values on the `lblResults` label. One of the fields of the `fileinfo` struct tells us how many streams are contained inside the file. There could be a video stream, audio stream, and more, and we want to print out summary information for each one just like we did for the file. Therefore, line 175 begins a `For` loop in which we examine each of the streams (numbered from 0 to `fileinfo.dwStreams − 1`).

Line 178 calls the API `AVIFileGetStream` to get each stream. We pass this method the `IAVIFile` instance (`pfile`), an `IAVIStream` variable that it should make point to a valid object, the type of the stream we want (we pass 0 to indicate that we'll accept any type), and the stream number. If this call succeeds, we call the `Info` method on the `IAVIStream` interface on line 188, just like we did with the `IAVIFile` interface, catching an exception in the case of failure. In lines 195 and 196, we call `AVIStreamSampleToTime` and `AVIStreamLength` to get a measurement of the stream's length in milliseconds. In lines 197 and 198, we split the value into two parts so we can format it nicely. Lines 202–208 print out the stream's information. Although the streams are counted from 0, we add one to the number we display so the user sees information for #1, #2, and so on, rather than #0, #1, and so on. Line 209 marks the end of the `For` loop used to check each stream.

The documentation for these Win32 APIs states that we should call `AVIFileRelease` when we're finished with a file to release the `IAVIFile` COM interface. This is contrary to the way COM objects are typically used, and because of this we shouldn't call it in an ASP.NET page. Doing so can cause unexpected run-time behavior, because the CLR would think it's still holding onto a valid COM object when it actually might get released without the runtime knowing about it. Instead, we call `Marshal.ReleaseComObject`, which is the only proper way to release a COM interface at a given point in time (as we read earlier in the chapter). The lesson here is that sometimes the way APIs are used needs to be altered slightly inside an ASP.NET page because they were designed for plain Win32 applications long before ASP.NET existed. Finally, in line 216, we call the `AVIFileExit` method to release the library. Figure 19.7 displays the output of Listing 19.2.5 on an AVI file that contains three streams.

FIGURE 19.7
The output of Listing 19.2.5 when viewed through a browser.

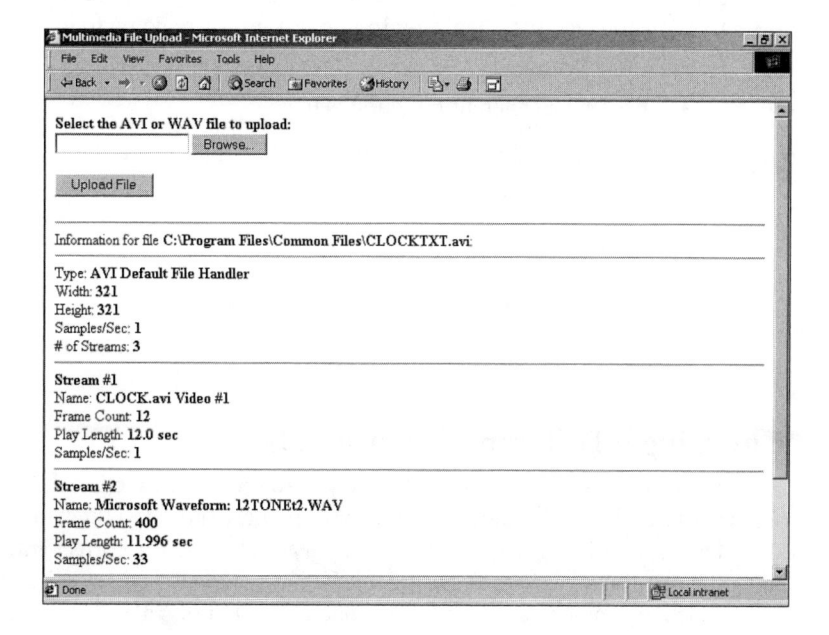

As you saw in the previous listing, the definitions of structs can be customized using `StructLayoutAttribute` in `System.Runtime.InteropServices`. `StructLayoutAttribute` requires that you specify a member of the `LayoutKind` enumeration. This can be one of three values:

- `Auto`—The CLR chooses how to arrange the fields in the structure. This should never be used when interacting with native code.
- `Sequential`—The fields are arranged sequentially, in the order they appear in source code. This is the default in C# and VB.NET.
- `Explicit`—The fields are arranged using byte offsets specified by the user on each field using a second custom attribute: `FieldOffsetAttribute`. This gives you complete control over the layout of a struct, and even makes it possible to define a union (by giving every field an offset of zero).

`StructLayoutAttribute` also enables you to optionally set some additional information, such as `CharSet`, used in the previous example. In fact, the only reason Listing 19.2.5 uses `StructLayoutAttribute` is to set `CharSet` to `CharSet.Auto`; the `LayoutKind.Sequential` value's associated behavior occurs by default. The details of `CharSet` are discussed in the "Customizing the Behavior of Strings" section.

Customizing `Declare` and `DllImport`

Sometimes it's necessary to alter an aspect of a PInvoke signature's behavior, depending on what the native entry point looks like and how it expects to receive its parameters. Other times, customizing a PInvoke signature's behavior is desirable to make its use more convenient. Fortunately, the `Declare` statement and `DllImport` custom attribute both have easy ways to achieve a variety of customizations. You'll see that `DllImport` has many more ways to be customized than `Declare`. In this section, we're going to look at all of the possible customizations:

- Choosing a Different Function Name
- Customizing the Behavior of Strings
- Changing the "Exact Spelling" Setting
- Choosing a Calling Convention
- Customizing Error Handling

The first two listed apply to both `Declare` and `DllImport`, but the last three are specific to `DllImport`.

Choosing a Different Function Name

Both `Declare` and `DllImport` enable you to give your function definition a name that's different from the "real" function (a.k.a. entry point) exposed in the DLL. When choosing a different name, you must specify the real name as an "alias" so the correct entry point can be found. For the first PInvoke examples using `QueryPerformanceCounter`, let's say we want to change the function's name to a more intuitive one like `GetTimerValue`. This is done as follows in VB.NET:

```
Declare Function GetTimerValue Lib "kernel32.dll" _
  Alias "QueryPerformanceCounter" (ByRef count As Long) As Boolean
```

And here's the same example in C#, which accomplishes the same behavior with an `EntryPoint` named parameter:

```
[DllImport("kernel32.dll", EntryPoint="QueryPerformanceCounter")]
static extern bool GetTimerValue(out long count);
```

For clarity, programmers typically keep the original name rather than using an alias. However, changing the function's name can come in handy for resolving name conflicts or if the function's name happens to be a keyword in your programming language.

The string given to `Alias` or `EntryPoint` can even be an *ordinal*—a number that identifies the entry point rather than a name. Using a tool such as `DUMPBIN.EXE`, we can see that the ordinal for `QueryPerformanceCounter` is 556, so a hard-core programmer could define the previous method as follows:

VB.NET:

```
Declare Function GetTimerValue Lib "kernel32.dll" Alias "#556" _
  (ByRef count As Long) As Boolean
```

C#:

```
[DllImport("kernel32.dll", EntryPoint="#556")]
static extern bool GetTimerValue(out long count);
```

Customizing the Behavior of Strings

Win32 functions with string parameters often come in two varieties—one to handle ANSI strings and one to handle Unicode strings (also known as *wide strings*). For example, the `GetUserName` function we used earlier doesn't really exist! Instead, `advapi32.dll` contains the following two entry points:

- `GetUserNameA`—An ANSI version of `GetUserName` (indicated by "A" at the end of the name)

- `GetUserNameW`—A Unicode version of `GetUserName` (indicated by "W" at the end of the name)

`Declare` and `DllImport` both have syntax that makes dealing with these multiple method definitions manageable. `Declare` enables you to specify `Ansi`, `Unicode`, or `Auto`, as follows:

```
Declare Ansi Function GetUserNameA Lib "advapi32.dll" (...) As Boolean
```

```
Declare Unicode Function GetUserNameW Lib "advapi32.dll" (...) As Boolean
```

```
Declare Auto Function GetUserName Lib "advapi32.dll" (...) As Boolean
```

Here are the ways in which these keywords change the `Declare` statement's behavior:

- `Ansi` is the default. This indicates that any string arguments are treated as ANSI strings unless otherwise specified with `MarshalAsAttribute`.

- `Unicode` means that any string arguments are treated as Unicode strings unless otherwise specified with `MarshalAsAttribute`.

- `Auto` means that any string arguments are treated as platform-dependent strings unless otherwise specified with `MarshalAsAttribute`. For platform-dependent strings, the Common Language Runtime chooses `Ansi` or `Unicode`, depending on the operating system of the server running the ASP.NET page. In addition, the system looks for the entry point name given plus an ending "A" or "W" depending on the platform.

`DllImport` exposes a similar-looking mechanism, but it does a little more by default. The attribute enables you to specify `Ansi`, `Unicode`, or `Auto`, as follows:

```
[DllImport("kernel32.dll", CharSet=CharSet.Ansi)]
static extern bool GetUserName(...);
```

```
[DllImport("kernel32.dll", CharSet=CharSet.Unicode)]
static extern bool GetUserName(...);

[DllImport("kernel32.dll", CharSet=CharSet.Auto)]
static extern bool GetUserName(...);
```

Here are the ways in which these settings change the `DllImport` attribute's behavior:

- `Ansi` is the default in C#. Besides affecting the string arguments just as `Declare`'s `Ansi` setting does, it looks for an entry point called `GetUserNameA` (for the previous example) and invokes that if an entry point called `GetUserName` doesn't exist. If the specified entry point exists, it will be invoked regardless of whether there is also one with an "A" suffix.

- `Unicode`, in addition to affecting the string arguments just as in `Declare`'s `Unicode` setting, causes the system to look for an entry point called `GetUserNameW`, *even if* there is an entry point called `GetUserName`. (If there is no `GetUserNameW` function, `GetUserName` would be invoked if it exists.) Notice the subtle ordering difference between the `Ansi` and `Unicode` options: the "W" version is chosen over the given name, but the "A" version is chosen only if the given name doesn't exist.

- `Auto` means that the choice of `Ansi` or `Unicode` will be made depending on the operating system of the server. Just as in `Declare`, the choice affects string arguments as well as the entry point name.

> **Note**
>
> The `CharSet` enumeration also has a `None` value, but this is obsolete and shouldn't be used. It has the same effect as specifying `Ansi`.

Therefore, setting `CharSet` using `DllImport` affects both how string arguments are marshaled and what entry point is called, whereas using the similar-looking setting in `Declare` (with the exception of `Auto`) only affects the string arguments. This is the reason `Auto` is used in Listing 19.2.4 when calling `GetUserName`. We needed to call either `GetUserNameA` or `GetUserNameW` without affecting the name of the `GetUserName` method called in the Web page and without worrying about marking the `String` parameter with the right custom attribute. If we cared which version is invoked, we could choose with the `Alias` keyword and make sure the `String` parameter is marked with `MarshalAs(UnmanagedType.LPWStr)` if choosing the "W" version.

As mentioned in the "Calling APIs with Complex Types" section, `StructLayoutAttribute` also enables you to set `CharSet` as a named parameter. You do this with the same values in the `CharSet` enumeration used with `DllImport`. When applied to a struct, the `Ansi`, `Unicode`, and `Auto` settings simply affect the behavior of any string fields. For example, Listing 19.2.5 defines the following struct:

```
<StructLayout(LayoutKind.Sequential, CharSet:=CharSet.Auto)> _
    Public Structure AVIFILEINFO
      Public dwMaxBytesPerSec As Integer
      Public dwFlags As Integer
      Public dwCaps As Integer
      Public dwStreams As Integer
```

```
        Public dwSuggestedBufferSize As Integer
        Public dwWidth As Integer
        Public dwHeight As Integer
        Public dwScale As Integer
        Public dwRate As Integer
        Public dwLength As Integer
        Public dwEditCount As Integer
        <MarshalAs(UnmanagedType.ByValTStr, SizeConst:=64)> _
        Public szFileType As String
    End Structure
```

`MarshalAsAttribute` is used with `UnmanagedType.ByValTStr` in order to indicate that `szFileType` is a fixed-length buffer of 64 characters. (`TStr` represents a platform-dependent string.) Using `UnmanagedType.ByValTStr` on a field means that the type of characters in the buffer depends on the character set marked on the containing struct. The characters are only plaftform-dependent if the struct is marked with `CharSet.Auto`. Because there's no choice of `ByValStr` or `ByValWStr`, the only way to specify that we want this to be a fixed-length *Unicode* buffer is to specify something other than the default `CharSet.Ansi` on the struct. This can be done with `CharSet.Unicode` on any platform or `CharSet.Auto` on a Unicode platform (such as Windows NT, 2000, and XP). As mentioned earlier, this is the only reason `StructLayoutAttribute` is used in our examples, because we always want `LayoutKind.Sequential`.

Changing the "Exact Spelling" Setting

With `DllImport` only, you can turn "exact spelling" on or off by setting a named parameter to `true` or `false`. Here's an example:

```
[DllImport("kernel32.dll", ExactSpelling=true)]
static extern bool GetUserName(...);
```

`ExactSpelling` refers to the name of the entry point and specifies whether the system searches for an alternative name ending in "A" or "W". Therefore, setting `ExactSpelling` to `True` along with setting `CharSet` causes `DllImport` to behave just like `Declare` when using `Ansi` or `Unicode`. This is demonstrated in the following signature:

```
' Behave just like Declare's Ansi option
[DllImport("kernel32.dll", CharSet=CharSet.Ansi, ExactSpelling=true)]
static extern bool GetUserNameA(...);
```

By default, `ExactSpelling` is set to `False` in C#. VB.NET's `Declare` statement only behaves with exact spelling off for the `Auto` character setting.

Choosing a Calling Convention

A function's *calling convention* refers to low-level details of how each call is handled. The calling convention of an entry point can be specified using another `DllImport` named parameter, called `CallingConvention`. The choices for this are as follows:

- `CallingConvention.Cdecl`
- `CallingConvention.FastCall`

- `CallingConvention.StdCall`
- `CallingConvention.ThisCall`
- `CallingConvention.Winapi`

`Declare` uses `Winapi`, and the default for `DllImport` is also `Winapi`. As you might guess, this is the calling convention used by Win32 APIs, so we never have to change this setting in our examples. See the .NET Framework documentation for descriptions of the differences in calling conventions.

Customizing Error Handling

In the previous listings, we saw a standard error handling technique for Win32 APIs - simply checking whether each method call returned `True` or `False`. This method of checking after each method is error-prone and cumbersome, and the `True/False` return value doesn't provide any detailed information about the cause or type of error that occurred. To enable improved error handling, `DllImport` has two options that can customize the way errors can be handled. One involves getting a Win32 error code, and the other involves transforming signatures to throw exceptions on failure.

Getting a Win32 Error Code

When Win32 functions fail, they often return `False`. If you'd like to get more information about why a failure occurred, you can often call the Win32 function `GetLastError` to obtain an error code (assuming that the function provides an error code by internally calling the `SetLastError` Win32 API). Due to the nature of the .NET Framework's interactions with the operating system, if you directly call `GetLastError` (defined in `kernel32.dll`) using PInvoke, the results would be unreliable. Instead, you must call `Marshal.GetLastWin32Error` in the `System.Runtime.InteropServices` namespace or use the `LastDllError` property in VB.NET's global `Err` object. The following code shows both ways to obtain the error code in VB.NET:

```
If (Not GetUserName(s, size)) Then
  Response.Write("Error Code " & Err.LastDllError)
  Response.Write("Error Code " & Marshal.GetLastWin32Error())
End If
```

Both `Err.LastDllError` and `Marshal.GetLastWin32Error` do the exact same thing, but `Err.LastDllError` is meant to be VB.NET-specific (and present for backward compatibility with earlier versions of Visual Basic) whereas `Marshal.GetLastWin32Error` is the language-neutral way of getting the same functionality.

Caution

Never define and use the `GetLastError` Win32 API directly via PInvoke. Instead, call `Marshal.GetLastWin32Error` in `System.Runtime.InteropServices` or the global `Err.LastDllError` in VB.NET code.

`DllImport` enables you to turn on or off the ability to successfully use `Marshal.GetLastWin32Error` by setting a named parameter to `true` or `false`. Here's an example:

```
[DllImport("kernel32.dll", SetLastError=true)]
static extern bool GetUserName(...);

[DllImport("kernel32.dll", SetLastError=false)]
static extern bool GetUserName(...);
```

Why would you ever want to set it to `false`? Turning this functionality off provides a slight performance improvement since the system doesn't need to worry about tracking the last error. In fact, `false` is the default in C#, so you must explicitly set it to `true` if you plan to use `Marshal.GetLastWin32Error`. With `Declare`, this functionality is always "on," so checking the `Err.LastDllError` property always works if the function you called returned additional information.

Causing Exceptions to be Thrown on Failure

Normally the signature of a DLL's function is "preserved" in the ASP.NET page. If the function returns a COM type known as an `HRESULT` (introduced earlier in the chapter), however, you can set the `DllImport` attribute's `PreserveSig` named parameter to `false`, meaning that a signature transformation occurs. As done with COM methods, the returned `HRESULT` is hidden from the signature and an exception is thrown instead if the `HRESULT` contains a value in a range corresponding to failure.

> **Note**
> `HRESULT` values can also be in a range that means "warning" or "informational note" instead of "error". If a returned `HRESULT` has a value outside the "error" range, no exception is thrown. Furthermore, the value of the HRESULT is lost in this case if `PreserveSig=false` is used.

This feature is not available using `Declare`. Most Win32 APIs do not return `HRESULT`s, but some of the ones we used in Listing 19.2.5 do. Therefore, we'll look at how to take advantage of setting `PreserveSig` equal to `false` by updating the listing using C# and `DllImport`. This is demonstrated in Listing 19.2.6.

LISTING 19.2.6 Using Microsoft Video for Windows in an ASP.NET Page with `PreserveSig=false` in Order to Catch Exceptions on Failure

```
1: <%@ Page aspcompat=true %>
2: <%@ Import Namespace="System.IO" %>
3: <%@ Import Namespace="System.Runtime.InteropServices" %>
4: <script language="C#" runat="server">
5:   // Initializes the AVIFile library.
6:   [DllImport("avifil32.dll", PreserveSig=false)]
7:   static extern void AVIFileInit();
8:
```

LISTING 19.2.6 Continued

```
 9:    // Exits the AVIFile library.
10:    [DllImport("avifil32.dll", PreserveSig=false)]
11:    static extern void AVIFileExit();
12:
13:    // Opens the specified AVI file and returns a file interface (IAVIFile).
14:
15:    [DllImport("avifil32.dll", PreserveSig=false)]
16:    static extern void AVIFileOpen(ref IAVIFile ppfile, string szFile,
17:      uint mode, Guid pclsidHandler);
18:
19:    // Returns a stream interface (IAVIStream) associated with an AVI file.
20:    [DllImport("avifil32.dll", PreserveSig=false)]
21:    static extern void AVIFileGetStream(IAVIFile pfile,
22:      ref IAVIStream ppavi, int fccType, int lParam);
23:
24:    // Returns the length of the input stream.
25:    [DllImport("avifil32.dll")]
26:    static extern int AVIStreamLength(IAVIStream pavi);
27:
28:    // Converts a stream measurement in samples to milliseconds.
29:    [DllImport("avifil32.dll")]
30:    static extern int AVIStreamSampleToTime(IAVIStream pavi, int lSample);
31:
32:    //
33:    // The IAVIFile COM Interface used in the methods above
34:    //
35:    [ComImport, InterfaceType(ComInterfaceType.InterfaceIsIUnknown),
36:      Guid("00020020-0000-0000-c000-000000000046")]
37:    interface IAVIFile
38:    {
39:      void Info(ref AVIFILEINFO pfi, int lSize);
40:      void GetStream(ref IAVIStream ppStream, int fccType, int lParam);
41:      void CreateStream(ref IAVIStream ppStream, AVISTREAMINFO psi);
42:      void WriteData(int ckid, IntPtr lpData, int cbData);
43:      void ReadData(int ckid, IntPtr lpData, ref int lpcbData);
44:      void EndRecord();
45:      void DeleteStream(int fccType, int lParam);
46:    };
47:
48:    //
49:    // The IAVIStream COM Interface used in the methods above
50:    //
51:    [ComImport, InterfaceType(ComInterfaceType.InterfaceIsIUnknown),
52:      Guid("00020021-0000-0000-c000-000000000046")]
53:    interface IAVIStream
54:    {
55:      void Create(int lParam1, int lParam2);
56:      void Info(ref AVISTREAMINFO psi, int lSize);
57:      [PreserveSig] int FindSample(int lPos, int lFlags);
58:      void ReadFormat(int lPos, IntPtr lpFormat, ref int lpcbFormat);
59:      void SetFormat(int lPos, IntPtr lpFormat, int cbFormat);
60:      void Read(int lStart, int lSamples, IntPtr lpBuffer, int cbBuffer);
```

LISTING 19.2.6 *Continued*

```
61:      void Write(int lStart, int lSamples, IntPtr lpBuffer, int cbBuffer,
62:        int dwFlags, ref int plSampWritten, ref int plBytesWritten);
63:      void Delete(int lStart, int lSamples);
64:      void ReadData(int fcc, IntPtr lp, ref int lpcb);
65:      void WriteData(int fcc, IntPtr lp, int cb);
66:      void SetInfo(int fcc, IntPtr lp, int cb);
67:    };
68:
69:    //
70:    // Structures used in the interfaces above.
71:    //
72:
73:    [StructLayout(LayoutKind.Sequential, CharSet=CharSet.Auto)]
74:    public struct AVISTREAMINFO
75:    {
76:      public int fccType;
77:      public int fccHandler;
78:      public int dwFlags;
79:      public int dwCaps;
80:      public short wPriority;
81:      public short wLanguage;
82:      public int dwScale;
83:      public int dwRate;
84:      public int dwStart;
85:      public int dwLength;
86:      public int dwInitialFrames;
87:      public int dwSuggestedBufferSize;
88:      public int dwQuality;
89:      public int dwSampleSize;
90:      public RECT rcFrame;
91:      public int dwEditCount;
92:      public int dwFormatChangeCount;
93:      [MarshalAs(UnmanagedType.ByValTStr, SizeConst=64)]
94:      public string szName;
95:    }
96:
97:    [StructLayout(LayoutKind.Sequential, CharSet=CharSet.Auto)]
98:    public struct AVIFILEINFO
99:    {
100:     public int dwMaxBytesPerSec;
101:     public int dwFlags;
102:     public int dwCaps;
103:     public int dwStreams;
104:     public int dwSuggestedBufferSize;
105:     public int dwWidth;
106:     public int dwHeight;
107:     public int dwScale;
108:     public int dwRate;
109:     public int dwLength;
110:     public int dwEditCount;
111:     [MarshalAs(UnmanagedType.ByValTStr, SizeConst=64)]
```

LISTING 19.2.6 Continued

```
112:       public string szFileType;
113:    }
114:
115:    public struct RECT
116:    {
117:      public int left;
118:      public int top;
119:      public int right;
120:      public int bottom;
121:    }
122:
123:    // Constant used when opening the file
124:    public const uint OF_SHARE_DENY_WRITE = 0x00000020;
125:
126:    void Page_Load(Object sender, EventArgs e)
127:    {
128:      if (Page.IsPostBack && fupUpload.PostedFile != null)
129:      {
130:        // Save the file if it has a filename and exists...
131:        if (fupUpload.PostedFile.FileName.Trim().Length > 0 &&
132:          fupUpload.PostedFile.ContentLength > 0)
133:        {
134:          const string strBaseDir = "C:\\My Projects\\Uploaded Files\\";
135:          string strFileName =
136:            Path.GetFileName(fupUpload.PostedFile.FileName);
137:          fupUpload.PostedFile.SaveAs(strBaseDir + strFileName);
138:
139:          IAVIFile pfile = null;
140:
141:          try
142:          {
143:            // Initialize the AVIFile library
144:            AVIFileInit();
145:          }
146:          catch (Exception ex)
147:          {
148:            lblResults.Text =
149:              "<hr>Server Error: Cannot initialize the AVIFile library." +
150:              "<br>Error Details:<br>" + ex.ToString();
151:            return;
152:          }
153:
154:          try
155:          {
156:            // Open the AVI file
157:            AVIFileOpen(ref pfile, strBaseDir + strFileName,
158:              OF_SHARE_DENY_WRITE, Guid.Empty);
159:          }
160:          catch (Exception ex)
161:          {
162:            lblResults.Text =
163:              "<hr>The uploaded file is not a valid AVI or WAV file." +
```

LISTING 19.2.6 Continued

```
164:              "<br>Error Details:<br>" + ex.ToString();
165:            return;
166:          }
167:
168:          // Display summary information
169:
170:          AVIFILEINFO fileinfo = new AVIFILEINFO();
171:
172:          try
173:          {
174:            // Call a method on the IAVIFile COM interface
175:            pfile.Info(ref fileinfo, Marshal.SizeOf(fileinfo));
176:          }
177:          catch (Exception ex)
178:          {
179:            lblResults.Text = "<hr>Unable to get file information." +
180:              "<br>Error Details:<br>" + ex.ToString();
181:            return;
182:          }
183:
184:          double samplesPerSecond = fileinfo.dwRate / fileinfo.dwScale;
185:          lblResults.Text = "<hr>Information for file <b>" +
186:            fupUpload.PostedFile.FileName + "</b>:<hr>" +
187:            "Type: <b>" + fileinfo.szFileType + "</b><br>" +
188:            "Width: <b>" + fileinfo.dwWidth + "</b><br>" +
189:            "Height: <b>" + fileinfo.dwHeight + "</b><br>" +
190:            "Samples/Sec: <b>" + samplesPerSecond + "</b><br>" +
191:            "# of Streams: <b>" + fileinfo.dwStreams + "</b><br>";
192:
193:          // Look at each stream and print out summary information
194:          for (int i = 0; i < fileinfo.dwStreams; i++)
195:          {
196:            IAVIStream pstream = null;
197:
198:            try
199:            {
200:              AVIFileGetStream(pfile, ref pstream, 0, i);
201:            }
202:            catch (Exception ex)
203:            {
204:              lblResults.Text = "<hr>Cannot get stream #" +
205:                (i+1).ToString() +
206:                ".<br>Error Details:<br>" + ex.ToString();
207:              return;
208:            }
209:
210:            AVISTREAMINFO streaminfo = new AVISTREAMINFO();
211:
212:            try
213:            {
214:              // Call a method on the IAVIStream COM interface
```

LISTING 19.2.6 Continued

```
215:                pstream.Info(ref streaminfo, Marshal.SizeOf(streaminfo));
216:              }
217:              catch (Exception ex)
218:              {
219:                lblResults.Text = "<hr>Cannot get information for stream #" +
220:                  (i+1).ToString() +
221:                  ".<br>Error Details:<br>" + ex.ToString();
222:                return;
223:              }
224:
225:              int time = AVIStreamSampleToTime(pstream,
226:                AVIStreamLength(pstream));
227:              int seconds = time / 1000;
228:              int fraction = time % 1000;
229:
230:              samplesPerSecond = streaminfo.dwRate / streaminfo.dwScale;
231:
232:              lblResults.Text += "<hr><b>Stream #" +
233:                (i+1).ToString() + "</b><br>" +
234:                "Name: <b>" + streaminfo.szName + "</b><br>" +
235:                "Frame Count: <b>" + AVIStreamLength(pstream).ToString() +
236:                "</b><br>Play Length: <b>" + seconds.ToString() + "." +
237:                fraction.ToString() + " sec" + "</b><br>" +
238:                "Samples/Sec: <b>" + samplesPerSecond + "</b><br>";
239:            }
240:
241:            // Called instead of AVIFileRelease,
242:            // since it releases the COM interface.
243:            Marshal.ReleaseComObject(pfile);
244:
245:            // Release the AVIFile library
246:            AVIFileExit();
247:          }
248:          else
249:          {
250:            lblResults.Text = "<hr>You must enter a valid filename!";
251:          }
252:        }
253:      }
254: </script>
255: <html><title>Multimedia File Upload</title>
256:   <body>
257:     <form runat="server" EncType="multipart/form-data">
258:       <b>Select the AVI or WAV file to upload:</b><br>
259:       <input runat="server" id="fupUpload" type="file" >
260:       <p>
261:       <asp:button id="btnSubmit" runat="server" Text="Upload File" />
262:       <p><asp:label runat="server" id="lblResults" />
263:     </form>
264:   </body>
265: </html>
```

The important parts of this listing are lines 5–22, which use `PreserveSig=false` on the functions that return an `HRESULT`, and lines 141–152, 154–166, and 198–208. These lines use these methods that now throw an exception on failure. The great addition inside each `catch` statement is that we can now easily print an error message that might have useful information as to why a method call failed.

> **Tip**
>
> We've covered many additional customizations available only to `DllImport`. Fortunately, all the additional customizations enabled by `DllImport` are also available in VB.NET because you can use `DllImport` in VB.NET! Simply put the attribute on an empty shared `Sub` or `Function`, like the following:
>
> ```
> <DllImport("avifil32.dll")> _
> Shared Function AVIFileInit() As Integer
> End Function
> ```
>
> Be aware that because the default behavior implied by the `Declare` statement is different from the default behavior chosen by the Common Language Runtime for `DllImport` (which also differs from C#'s default behavior), the statement
>
> ```
> <DllImport("avifil32.dll", _
>   CharSet:=CharSet.Ansi, _
>   ExactSpelling:=True, _
>   SetLastError:=True)> _
> Shared Function AVIFileInit() As Integer
> End Function
> ```
>
> is the exact equivalent of
>
> ```
> Declare Function AVIFileInit Lib "avifil32.dll" () As Integer
> ```

3. Using the `AspCompat` Directive

Some of the previous code examples in this chapter have used the following `@Page` directive:

```
<%@ Page aspcompat=true %>
```

This turns on what is known as *ASP Compatibility Mode*, which changes the behavior of the ASP.NET application in two ways:

- The page is executed inside a single-threaded apartment (STA) rather than inside a multi-threaded apartment (MTA), the default for ASP.NET pages. Such a page is said to execute on an *STA thread*. These COM concepts are explained in the upcoming "Executing on an STA Thread" section.

- The page exposes the ASP intrinsics through the mechanisms expected by COM and COM+ objects explained in the upcoming "ASP Intrinsics" section.

> **Caution**
>
> The `aspcompat=true` directive is only supported in ASP.NET Web pages (`.aspx` files), not in Web services (`.asmx` files).

> **Tip**
>
> Using ASP Compatibility Mode is not always necessary when interacting with COM components. It's only necessary if a COM component you're using requires one of the two behavior changes. COM components written in Visual Basic 6 do require `aspcompat=true` due to the STA thread requirement, described in the next section.

Executing on an STA Thread

Every COM object lives in an *apartment*, which is a logical container within a process. Apartments are used to group together objects that have the same threading requirements.

A COM object that lives in a single-threaded apartment (STA) can only be called by the thread that created the object. Any calls from different threads are synchronized with a queue used by the original thread. Most COM objects (and any authored in Visual Basic 6) must live in an STA. Such components are called *apartment-threaded components*. Writing apartment-threaded components is convenient because you don't have to worry about thread safety. A COM object that lives in a multi-threaded apartment (MTA) can be called by multiple threads concurrently. Such components are called *free-threaded components* and must handle synchronization themselves.

> **Note**
>
> Some COM objects are designed to only work inside an STA or only work inside an MTA, and some COM objects can work in both types of apartments. COM objects advertise their threading requirements in the Windows Registry with a `ThreadingModel` value set to a string such as `Apartment`, `Free`, or `Both`.

When calling into a COM object from an ASP.NET page, the current thread needs to create and initialize an apartment. A thread that creates an STA is known as an *STA thread*, and a thread that creates an MTA is known as an *MTA thread*. By default, ASP.NET uses MTA threads, but the use of `aspcompat=true` changes ASP.NET's behavior to use STA threads. This is helpful for two reasons:

- Some COM objects may simply be unusable if you attempt to create them from an MTA thread. Deadlocks are also possible.

- When the apartment needed by the object and the apartment created by the thread are incompatible, COM attempts to set up a proxy to make the calls work. Even if a proxy can be created (which can sometimes require extra registration of a proxy-stub DLL), performance suffers due to the extra work involved.

Therefore, setting `aspcompat=true` makes all apartment-threaded COM components useable and avoids a proxy, enabling you to call them directly without the extra performance penalty. The performance of free-threaded components can suffer, however, when using `aspcompat=true` since they aren't being used in a multi-threaded fashion.

Because using an apartment-threaded COM component is dangerous without `aspcompat=true`, and because it's not always obvious what a COM component's threading requirements are, ASP.NET sometimes checks for this scenario. Any page creating apartment-threaded objects via CLSID or ProgID with `Server.CreateObject`, `Server.CreateObjectFromClsid` or the `<object>` tag (with `runat="server"`) will cause an error if it's not marked with `aspcompat=true`. Note that ASP.NET does not check the threading model for objects created using type information generated by the type library importer (for example, using the `Server.CreateObject` overload that takes a `Type` parameter or using the `<object>` tag with the `class` attribute).

In addition, because `aspcompat=true` can only be marked on pages, ASP.NET doesn't allow you to create such objects anywhere except inside an ASPX file with `aspcompat=true`. This behavior can be seen with the ADO examples at the beginning of the chapter. If we remove `aspcompat=true` from Listing 19.1.1, we might get the output shown in Figure 19.8, depending on how ADO is registered.

> **Tip**
>
> If you are absolutely sure you want to create and use an apartment-threaded object from an MTA thread, but want to create the object using a CLSID or ProgID, check out `System.Activator.CreateInstance`, `System.Type.GetTypeFromCLSID`, and `System.Type.GetTypeFromProgID` in the .NET Framework documentation. These methods can provide the equivalent functionality as `Server.CreateObject` and `Server.CreateObjectFromClsid` but are more general methods meant to be used outside the context of an ASP.NET application. Therefore, they do not enforce any restrictions based on incompatible threading models.

This error occurs when the ADO components are marked with the **Apartment** threading model value in the Windows Registry.

FIGURE 19.8
The output of Listing 19.1.1 when viewed through a browser, if the `aspcompat=true` directive is removed and ADO is registered as apartment-threaded.

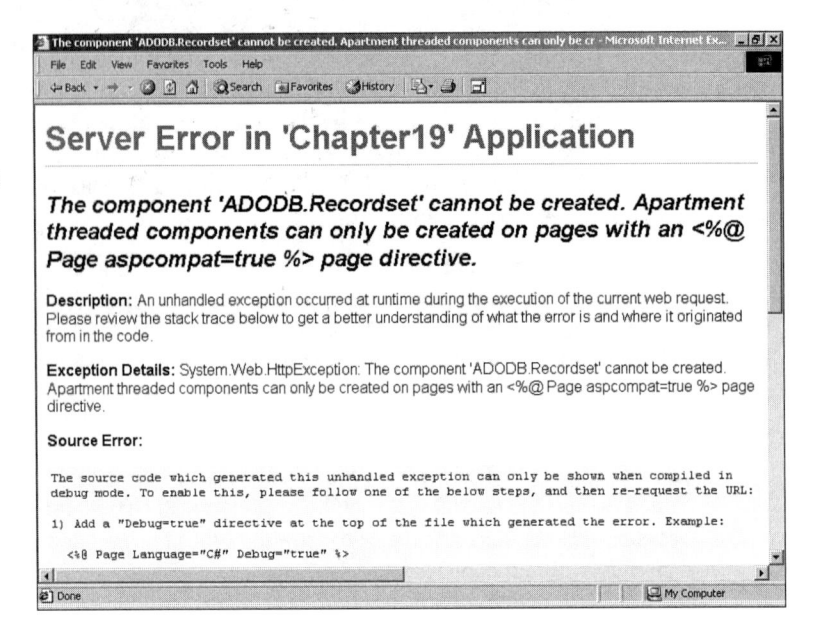

> **Tip**
>
> You can change the ADO Registry entries to be marked with either the `Both` threading model or the `Apartment` threading model. This should **never** be done for an arbitrary COM component, but this is supported by ADO. In fact, the directory containing the ADO DLLs contains two batch files for doing just this—`makfre15.bat` to make the ADO objects marked `Both` and `makapt15.bat` to make the ADO objects marked `Apartment`. The .NET Framework SDK and Visual Studio.NET installation programs change ADO's threading model to `Both`. Under this setting, you can use ADO on ASP.NET pages without restrictions.

ASP Intrinsics

ASP exposes a handful of *intrinsics*, or built-in objects. These objects are listed in Table 19.3.

TABLE 19.3 ASP Intrinsics That Expose Core Functionality to COM and COM+ Components

Intrinsics	Functionality
Application	Contains a collection of objects added to the application with the `<object>` tag or a script command
Response	Enables you to send output to the client
Request	Contains values that the client browser passed to the server during an HTTP request

TABLE 19.3 Continued

Intrinsics	Functionality
Server	Contains miscellaneous functions for object creation, error handling, string encoding, and more
Session	Stores objects and information for a single user's session

ASP.NET continues to support these intrinsics that can be accessed by .NET components and C# or VB.NET code in an ASP.NET page.

Many existing COM and COM+ components expect to be able to access these ASP intrinsics. This is achieved through two mechanisms:

- `OnStartPage` and `OnEndPage` *event handlers*. When defined appropriately, ASP calls the COM component's `OnStartPage` method when the client browser opens the page and the `OnEndPage` method when it closes the page.

- *The* `ObjectContext` *object.* `ObjectContext` provides COM+ components access to COM+ (previously MTS) features, such as transactional support, thread management, and object pooling, but it also provides access to the ASP intrinsics.

ASP.NET doesn't expose the intrinsic objects through these mechanisms unless the `AspCompat` directive is used. Therefore, by using `AspCompat`, existing components can continue to work as if an ASP page is invoking them because ASP.NET provides the intrinsics in a backward-compatible way *if* the COM object was created using `Server.CreateObject`, `Server.CreateObjectFromClsid`, or the `<object>` tag. For example, using the `New` keyword to instantiate a COM object won't enable ASP.NET to invoke an `OnStartPage` event handler even if `AspCompat` is used. If these backwards-compatible mechanisms are not exposed, existing components that depend on their behavior may fail in a variety of ways, depending on their implementation.

4. Performance Concerns

As you've seen, the .NET Framework provides many services that make it easy to leverage existing APIs and COM components in your ASP.NET page. However, it is important to understand that there is a cost associated with using Win32 APIs and COM objects. Calling methods on COM objects generally has a higher performance penalty than calling methods using PInvoke, due to more complex transformations performed by the CLR. Also, calling methods using PInvoke generally has a higher performance penalty than calling a method of a .NET object.

In many cases, any performance penalties for using the interoperability services is negligible, especially if the functions you're calling do a reasonable amount of work. That said, it's likely that rewriting your COM components to be .NET components will provide some degree of performance improvement. Here are ways in which you can boost the performance of your Web site and still use the same COM objects or Win32 APIs:

- Look for the places in which the transition is occurring from C# or VB.NET code into a COM object or Win32 API. Perhaps you can find ways to lessen the number of times these are called, by doing a little extra work in your own code.

- As in the cases where COM isn't involved, always try to take advantage of type information and early bind to COM objects rather than performing late binding. This means importing an Interop Assembly and creating instances using the `New` keyword (`new` in C#) `Server.CreateObject` with a `Type` object, or the `<object>` tag used with the `class` attribute.

- Be mindful of the threading requirements of the COM object. If it's an apartment-threaded component, you should see performance improvements by marking the page with `aspcompat=true`.

If you're in the position to redesign a COM object or the static entry points exposed by a DLL, there are three main things to consider:

- Expose a small number of methods, and each should perform a significant amount of work. This will cut down on the number of times an ASP.NET page needs to incur the cost of calling into your native code.

- Keep the data types exposed in your APIs as simple as possible. There is essentially no performance penalty for using simple parameters such as integers and doubles, but more complex types such as strings and User-Defined Types (UDTs) might incur more of a penalty because the CLR might need to transform them from one representation to another.

- If you're exposing static entry points in a DLL with string parameters, use Unicode strings because .NET strings are Unicode internally. If you're providing two versions of the function (ANSI and Unicode), be sure that your implementation of the Unicode version doesn't involve a conversion to ANSI.

If performance is still unacceptable, porting your COM components or other DLLs to .NET components might be in order.

Summary

In the final chapter of this book, we looked at the interoperability features provided by the .NET Framework. In "Using COM Components in an ASP.NET Web Page," we saw that creating and using COM objects can be just like creating and using any other objects. With the type library importer (`TlbImp.exe`), we can get type information so we don't always have to late bind to COM objects. We also encountered three issues specific to C# that often make VB.NET a more natural choice for using COM components:

- No optional parameters.
- Limitations in supported properties.
- Casting to a COM class type can't always be done.

Because C# is a brand-new language, its designers have made these decisions that promote certain design patterns moving forward. VB.NET, although having undergone many changes to fit well into the .NET Framework, is more sensitive to the needs of current COM components and their heavy use of optional parameters and parameterized properties.

In "Calling Win32 APIs in an ASP.NET Web Page," we looked at PInvoke (Platform Invocation Services) and what it means in VB.NET and C#. Although it's relatively easy to grasp the concept of PInvoke and use it for simple examples, a wide range of subtleties seems to arise with every new API you attempt to define a signature for! We've covered the basics for dealing with most Win32 APIs. Fortunately, using `Declare` in VB.NET is much like using it in Visual Basic 6.

In "Using the `AspCompat` Directive," we saw the ways in which ASP.NET is not backward compatible unless you flip the handy `aspcompat` switch on. Finally, in "Performance Concerns," we saw that all these great features don't come without a price. You must decide on a site-by-site basis whether the ease of using interoperability services is worth any performance penalties. Although the benefits of moving from ASP to ASP.NET are massive, the benefits of rewriting COM components to be .NET components may not always be significant.

Other Resources

For more information about COM, there are plenty of great books available. Here are some of them:

- *Inside COM*, by Dale Rogerson. Microsoft Press, 1997. This book is a classic introduction to COM.
- *Essential COM*, by Don Box, et al. Addison-Wesley, 1998. This book is written by a well-known COM guru who explains, as the book states, "the why, not just the how, of the Component Object Model."
- *Inside COM+ Base Services*, by Guy Eddon and Henry Eddon. Microsoft Press, 1999. This book is a comprehensive reference for COM programming, not just for C++ programmers but for Visual Basic and J++ programmers as well.

Here's where you can find more information about the .NET platform:

- `msdn.Microsoft.com/net`—This is Microsoft's official .NET Developer Center. Here you can find just about anything, including .NET Framework documentation, technical articles, code samples, and newsgroups.
- `www.gotdotnet.com`—This Microsoft-run web site contains extensive samples, tutorials, and even user-contributed .NET programs.

Finally, here's a great resource for more information about using COM and PInvoke with .NET:

- *.NET and COM for C#, Visual Basic, and C++ Programmers*, by Adam Nathan. SAMS Publishing, 2001. This book covers in depth the use COM components, ActiveX controls, and PInvoke in any .NET application - not just in an ASP.NET Web page. It also covers the use of .NET components by COM applications, enabling new .NET components to be "plugged into" existing client applications that use COM. As the title implies, the book caters to most programmers, regardless of language background.

APPENDIX A

UPGRADING TO VISUAL BASIC.NET

by Scott Mitchell

With classic ASP, you had a number of scripting languages to choose from to write your server-side scripts. The most popular choice was VBScript, a scripting language syntactically similar to Visual Basic. When creating ASP.NET Web pages, however, you must use a .NET-compliant language, such as Visual Basic.NET, C#, JScript.NET, and so on. Due to the popularity of VBScript, I suspect Visual Basic.NET will be the language of choice for creating ASP.NET Web pages.

Visual Basic.NET has many changes from the previous version of Visual Basic (version 6.0). Unfortunately, many of these changes are *breaking changes*, meaning that porting your ASP pages to ASP.NET Web pages will not likely be as easy as simply changing your old ASP pages' extensions to `.aspx`. Furthermore, if you're already familiar with VBScript or Visual Basic, there will likely be a bit of an additional learning curve associated with learning ASP.NET— not only do you have to learn about the new ASP.NET features, but you also have to learn about VB.NET's new features and breaking changes!

VB.NET is, in essence, the next version of Visual Basic. Although it does contain a number of new features, it is still Visual Basic and its syntax is strikingly similar. This appendix is intended to shorten the learning curve for VB/VBScript developers who are ready to get started with VB.NET.

> **Note**
>
> Although these new features and breaking changes may seem like an annoyance, they were needed to modernize Visual Basic. Also, because Microsoft's .NET approach aims at making component and application development "language independent," it is important that Visual Basic.NET mature into a language that can be compatible with more modern programming languages such as C#.

1. Variables

Visual Basic.NET has made some fundamental changes to certain variable data types and the way other variables are handled. This section delves into some of the more profound changes, such as Visual Basic.NET's extermination of the `Variant` and `Currency` data types and Visual Basic.NET's new array-indexing semantics.

The `Variant` Data Type

In VBScript, variables cannot be assigned a specific data type; they are all created as `Variant`s. In Visual Basic, variables can be created as `Variant`s as well, either implicitly or explicitly. A `Variant` could be created in Visual Basic with either of the two following statements:

```
Dim someVariable           'Implicit
Dim someVariable as Variant    'Explicit
```

With ASP.NET, however, the `Variant` data type is no longer supported. The new all-purpose data type is `Object`. For example, with VB.NET, if you want to create a variable that can be assigned values of any data type, you use this:

```
Dim somevariable as Object
```

> **Tip**
> You should always, if possible, create your variables with an appropriate data type. Your code's readability and performance drops when you create variables of type `Object` when you can specify a variable as a specific data type.

The `Currency` Data Type

Visual Basic.NET has stopped using the `Currency` data type due to insufficient accuracy of the `Currency` type, which, at times, resulted in rounding errors. Use the `Decimal` data type instead. The `Decimal` data type, stored as a 96-bit signed integer, can have up to 28 significant digits.

The `Integer` and `Long` Data Types

In previous versions of Visual Basic, variables declared as `Integer`s were represented as 16-bit numbers; variables declared as `Long`s were stored as signed 32-bit numbers. Visual Basic.NET increases the precision for each of these data types. In VB.NET, `Integer`s are represented as 32-bit numbers while `Long`s are represented as signed 64-bit numbers. If you need a 16-bit number use VB.NET's `Short` data type.

Code Blocks and Local Variables

With previous versions of Visual Basic and VBScript, you can create (using `Dim`) a variable inside a code block (such as an `If` statement), and that variable will be accessible in the script from its point of instantiation onward. For example, the following VBScript code produces the output "It's after noon…" when entered in an ASP page:

```
<%
  Option Explicit

  If Hour(Time()) > 12 then
    Dim strMessage
```

```
    strMessage = "It's after noon..."
  End If

  Response.Write strMessage
%>
```

Note that the creation of the `strMessage` variable (`Dim strMessage`) occurs within the `If` statement. With Visual Basic.NET, variables declared inside a code block are local *only* to that code block. This means that once outside of the code block, that variable can no longer be referenced. (This is similar in concept to creating a local variable in a function—that variable can only be accessed within the function it is created in.)

The following code, if entered into an ASP.NET Web page, would give a `"The name 'strMessage' is not declared"` error:

```
<%
  If Hour(Now()) > 12 then
    Dim strMessage as String
    strMessage = "It's after noon..."
  End If

  Response.Write (strMessage)
%>
```

This error occurs because `strMessage`'s scope is limited to the code block within which it was created.

Array Bounds

In previous versions of Visual Basic, developers can specify the lower bounds of their arrays by using the `Option Base` statement or specifying both a lower and upper bound when using `Dim` to create an array. With Visual Basic.NET (and all the .NET-compliant languages), *all* arrays have a lower bound of zero. There is no `Option Base` statement, and you cannot specify a lower bound when creating an array. The following statement will create an array with ten elements, having zero as its lower bound and nine as its upper bound:

```
Dim myArray (9) as integer
```

2. Short-Circuiting Operators

With the release of Visual Basic.NET, short circuiting is finally available in the Visual Basic syntax standard. Short circuiting is the bypassing of the second half of a logical operator when, after the first half is evaluated, it is known what the outcome will be for the logical comparison. This convoluted explanation can be better explained with an example. Imagine that we want to execute a block of code if both *variable1* and *variable2* are `True`. We could use a simple `If` statement, like so:

```
If variable1 AndAlso variable2 then ...
```

For the moment, assume that *variable1* is `False` when we run this code and this `If` statement is reached. Regardless of *variable2*'s value, we know that *variable1* And *variable2* will be `False`, so there's no need to waste time or resources checking *variable2*'s value. Similarly, if we want to check whether *variable1* or *variable2* is `True`, we don't need to bother checking *variable2*'s value if we find that *variable1* is `True`.

Although this might not seem like a big advantage, imagine that we have two long-running functions that both return Boolean values. We may have an `If` statement like the following:

`If LongRunningFunction1() And LongRunningFunction2() then ...`

With Visual Basic.NET's short circuiting, if we find that `LongRunningFunction1()` has returned a `False` value, there's no need to execute `LongRunningFunction2()`.

Note that to implement short-circuiting we used a new operator, `AndAlso`. Visual Basic 6 .NET provides two new operators to implement short-circuiting: `AndAlso` and `OrElse`. With `AndAlso`, the second expression is not evaluated if the first expression is False. With `OrElse`, the second expression is not evaluated if the first expression is True.

> **Note**
>
> Visual Basic .NET still supports the logical operators, `And` and `Or`. Like earlier versions of Visual Basic, these operators *do not* implement short-circuiting.

3. Functions and Subroutines

The changes VBScript and Visual Basic developers will have the most difficulty with, in my opinion, are the changes to the way Visual Basic.NET handles function and subroutine calls. These changes are not difficult to learn or understand, but if you've worked extensively with Visual Basic or VBScript in the past you may find yourself often forgetting about these needed changes as you develop your ASP.NET pages using VB.NET. For example, Visual Basic.NET now *requires* that developers use parentheses when calling a subroutine as opposed to Visual Basic and VBScript's requirement for *not* using parentheses when calling a subroutine.

Parentheses Required for Calling Subroutines and Functions

In previous versions of VB and VBScript, functions require parentheses around a parameter list, but subroutines require the absence of parentheses. For example, when calling a function, you need to use the following syntax:

`Result = MyFunction(param1, param2, ..., paramN)`

Note the required parentheses around the parameter list. When calling a subroutine in previous versions of Visual Basic or VBScript, you need to leave out the parentheses (or precede the subroutine name with the `Call` keyword):

```
MySub param1, param2, ..., paramN
--- or ---
Call MySub(param1, param2, ..., paramN)
```

> **Note**
>
> If you've created classic ASP pages in VBScript before, you may be thinking, "I can use parentheses when calling a subroutine. I do it all the time." For example, the following code snippet works just fine in VBScript:
>
> `Response.Write("Hello")`
>
> Parentheses are allowed here when the `Response.Write` method is called because VBScript is treating `("Hello")` as the first parameter. For more information, check out the article "Using Parentheses When Calling a Subroutine in VBScript" at http://www.4guysfromrolla.com/webtech/072800-1.shtml.

Visual Basic.NET has removed this confusing distinction, requiring that parentheses surround the parameter list for *both* subroutines and functions. Therefore, in an ASP.NET Web page, you will get an error if you try to use the following:

`Response.Write "Hello, World!"`

Rather, you must surround the parameter list with a set of parentheses, like so:

`Response.Write("Hello, World!")`

> **Note**
>
> Visual Basic.NET still supports the `Call` keyword for backward compatibility.

Function and Subroutine Parameters Now `ByVal` by Default

When parameters are passed into a subroutine or function, they can be passed in by value (`ByVal`) or by reference (`ByRef`). When a parameter is passed in using `ByVal`, a copy of the parameter is made and worked with throughout the subroutine or function. Therefore, any changes made to that parameter in the subroutine or function are not saved once the subroutine or function exits. If a parameter is passed in using `ByRef`, any changes made to the variable in the subroutine or function are seen once the subroutine or function exits.

By default, previous versions of Visual Basic and VBScript pass parameters as `ByRef`. In VB.NET, Visual Basic, and VBScript, you can explicitly specify whether a parameter should be passed using `ByRef` or `ByVal` with the following syntax:

`Function FunctionName(ByRef variable1, ByVal variable2, variable3, ...)`

However, if you do *not* specify either `ByRef` or `ByVal`, older versions of VB and VBScript will make the parameter `ByRef`. With VB.NET, however, this default is changed to `ByVal`.

> **Caution**
>
> This little change will surely be the cause of many hard-to-track-down errors. Many of the other changes can be checked at compile time. For example, if you attempt to create a variable of type `Currency`, you will receive an error at compile time.
>
> The compiler, however, cannot catch this change from `ByRef` to `ByVal` as the default. Therefore, if you have failed to explicitly declare your parameters as `ByRef` in your older VB and VBScript applications, be sure to take care to explicitly reference them as `ByRef` when porting them to ASP.NET.

4. The `While` Statement

In older versions of Visual Basic and VBScript, the `While` statement has the following syntax:

```
While booleanExpression
    ...
Wend
```

In Visual Basic.NET, however, this syntax has been modified to the following, more readable form:

```
While booleanExpression
    ...
End While
```

5. Default Properties

In previous versions of Visual Basic and VBScript, classes use the concept of *default properties*. With default properties, a developer can choose, when using a class, not to specify a property. In such an instance, the default property is assumed. ASP developers commonly used default properties when dealing with the ADO `Recordset` object. The following statement utilizes two default properties—the `Fields` property of the `Recordset` object and the `Value` property of the `Field` object:

```
SomeVariable = objRS("someColumnName")
```

This statement is semantically identical to the following statement, which explicitly specifies the default properties:

```
SomeVariable = objRS.Fields("someColumnName").Value
```

Due to the use of default properties, Visual Basic and VBScript require the `Set` keyword. The `Set` keyword is required with default properties because, without it, the compiler can't determine whether the developer is trying to access the object or its default property. For example, in the following code, does the developer want to assign *SomeVariable* to the recordset's `Field` object for *someColumnName* or to `objRS.Fields("`*someColumnName*`").Value`?

```
SomeVariable = objRS.Fields("someColumnName")
```

The previous line of code assigns `objRS.Fields("`*someColumnName*`").Value` to *SomeVariable*. If the developer wants to assign *SomeVariable* to the actual `Field` object representing *someColumnName*, she would have to use the following code:

```
Set SomeVariable = objRS.Fields("someColumnName")
```

With Visual Basic.NET, default properties are no longer supported. Therefore, when using .NET components or classic COM components, you *must* fully specify property names. For example, the following code will produce an error in an ASP.NET Web page:

```
SomeVariable = objRS("someColumnName")
```

Instead, you must fully specify the property names:

```
SomeVariable = objRS.Fields("someColumnName").Value
```

Also, Visual Basic.NET does not support the `Set` keyword. Because VB.NET did away with default properties, the `Set` keyword is no longer needed and has therefore been removed. Additionally, the `Let` keyword was removed from VB.NET's lexicon.

> **Caution**
> If you are porting code from a classic ASP page to an ASP.NET Web page, all of your object instantiations will need to have the `Set` keyword removed. For example, suppose you have an ASP page that contains the following line of code:
>
> ```
> Set ConnectionObject = Server.CreateObject("ADODB.Connection")
> ```
>
> In this case, you will need to remove the `Set` keyword, like so:
>
> ```
> ConnectionObject = Server.CreateObject("ADODB.Connection")
> ```

APPENDIX B

COMMONLY USED REGULAR EXPRESSION TEMPLATES

by Steve Walther

This appendix contains five common regular expressions that you can use in your ASP.NET applications. Most of these regular expressions work best for validating user input by ensuring that the input is in a valid format. As you saw in Chapter 3, "Form Field Input Validation," the `RegularExpressionValidator` validation control can be used to check a user's input against a regular expression.

Regular expressions can also be used in server-side code. Chapter 2, "Common ASP.NET Code Techniques," contains a section titled "Using Regular Expressions" that looks at using the regular expression classes in the `System.Text.RegularExpressions` namespace.

Although each regular expression template is followed by a brief explanation of how, exactly, the regular expression works, this appendix is not intended to serve as a resource for learning the ins and outs of regular expressions. For information on learning the basics of regular expressions, check out these great resources:

- *Regular Expressions Article Index*. This index contains a listing of must-read online regular expression articles. It's a great place to start for learning regular expressions. The index can be found at `http://www.4guysfromrolla.com/webtech/regularexpressions.shtml`.

- *Microsoft Beefs Up VBScript with Regular Expressions*. As its title implies, this Microsoft article is about using regular expressions in VBScript. Although this topic may seem out of date, the article provides a good introduction on pattern matching with regular expressions—definitely worth a read if you're new to regular expressions. The article can be found at `http://msdn.microsoft.com/workshop/languages/clinic/scripting051099.asp`.

- *Common Applications of Regular Expressions*. This article, by Richard Lowe, demonstrates several common uses of regular expressions, from form field input validation to reformatting text. The article can be found at `http://www.4guysfromrolla.com/webtech/120400-1.shtml`.

- *Mastering Regular Expressions*. This book, by Jeffrey E. Friedl (O'Reilly Press, 1997), is a must-have for anyone who wishes to become truly proficient at using regular expressions. Although the book presents most of its examples using Perl, it still does a fantastic job of explaining regular expressions.

1. Zip Code Validation

Zip codes are five or nine-digit codes used in the United States for postal mailing purposes. The five-digit zip code is simply five consecutive digits (such as 92109). The nine-digit zip code format differs slightly, containing a hyphen between the fifth and sixth digits (for example, 60126-8722).

A regular expression for zip code validation, then, should accept either five consecutive digits or five consecutive digits followed by a hyphen and four more consecutive digits. This can be expressed in a regular expression, like so:

`^\d{4}(\d|\d-\d{4})$`

If you are new to regular expressions, this, most likely, looks like complete gobbledygook. As we step through the regular expression and the meaning behind each character, it will (hopefully) begin to make more sense.

Regular expressions are designed to match patterns in strings. To assist with its pattern-matching capabilities, regular expressions have several "reserved" characters that have special meanings. For example, the caret (`^`) and dollar sign (`$`) characters both have special meanings. The caret indicates that the regular expression pattern must be found at the beginning of the string, whereas the dollar sign indicates that the regular expression pattern must be found at the end of the string. Therefore, if we had the regular expression pattern `Hello`, a match would be found in both "Hello, world!" and "John said Hello." If, however, we altered our regular expression pattern to use the caret (`^Hello`), only the first string ("Hello, world!") would provide a match, because the string starts with "Hello."

We can use the caret and dollar sign characters in conjunction to ensure that the string being searched for contains *just* the regular expression pattern specified. For example, if we want to determine whether a string equals "Hello" exactly (not just contain the substring "Hello"), we can use the pattern `^Hello$`. We'll use the caret and dollar sign in tandem for many of the regular expressions in this appendix.

The `\d` symbol also has a special meaning with regular expressions—it means "match any character." By following the `\d` symbol with `{n}`, we specify to match *n* instances. Therefore, if we want a regular expression to validate only on a five-digit zip code, we can use the following regular expression:

`^\d{5}$`

This expression only finds a match in a string that contains exactly five digits. However, because we want to validate five consecutive digits *or* five consecutive digits followed by a hyphen and four more consecutive digits, we need a slightly more complex regular expression.

We accomplish this by saying, essentially, "Match four consecutive digits, followed immediately by one other digit or one other digit, a hyphen, and four more consecutive digits. Here's what this looks like:

`^\d{4}(\d|\d\-\d{4})$`

The pipe (|) is another special character, serving as a Boolean OR. Therefore, inside the parentheses in the above regular expression, we are saying, "Match one digit *or* one digit followed by a hyphen (\-), followed by four more consecutive digits." The hyphen (-) is a special character like the caret, dollar sign, parenthesis, and curly brace ({ or }). If you want to use a special character in the regular expression as a literal character, you need to precede it with a backslash (\).

A number of regular expressions can be used to find a particular pattern. For example, here are some different regular expressions that all match a five- or nine-digit zip code:

```
^\d{4}(\d|\d\-\d{4})$
^\d\d\d\d(\d|\d\-\d\d\d\d)$
^((\d{5})|(\d{5}\-\d{4}))$
^(\d{5}(\-\d{4}){0,1})$
^(\d{5}(\-\d{4})?)$
```

2. Social Security Validation

In the United States, citizens are assigned social security numbers that uniquely identify them. A social security identification number is comprised of nine digits in total and is commonly represented in the following format:

XXX-XX-XXXX

Social security numbers are often needed in the United States for credit checks, proof of citizenship, and other identification purposes. A regular expression to match a social security number is fairly straightforward:

`^\d{3}\-\d{2}\-\d{4}$`

This regular expression matches against strings that contain exactly three digits followed by a hyphen, followed by two more digits, followed by a hyphen, followed by another four digits.

3. Telephone Number Validation

In the United States, telephone numbers are comprised of 10 digits—a three-digit area code followed by a seven-digit phone number. Phone numbers are commonly displayed or expected in one of a number of formats:

```
XXX XXX-XXXX
XXX-XXX-XXXX
(XXX) XXX-XXXX
(XXX)XXX-XXXX
```

Fortunately, we can write a single regular expression that will accept all these variations. You may, however, only want to accept one such format in order to keep your data as uniform as possible. Creating such a regular expression, though, shouldn't be hard, because it will look almost identical to the regular expression in the previous section, "Social Security Validation." That being said, here is a regular expression that will accept a phone number entered in *any* of the four formats:

`^(((\(\d{3}\)( )?)|(\d{3}( |\-)))\d{3}\-\d{4})$`

This regular expression starts by searching for either `(XXX)` followed by an optional space *or* `XXX` followed by a space or hyphen. Following either of these substrings, the regular expression pattern looks for three consecutive digits followed by a hyphen, followed by another four consecutive digits.

4. E-mail Address Validation

Because many Web sites like to be able to send newsletters, announcements, or advertisements to their visitors, collecting user e-mail addresses is a fairly common practice on the Web. As with any form of user-collected information, it is important that the e-mail addresses you collect from your users are valid. With regular expressions, we can ensure that the e-mail addresses are in a valid format, thereby reducing the number of invalid e-mail addresses in the database. The networking features of ASP.NET can be used to determine whether an e-mail address's domain (the part following the `@` sign) is valid. For more information on this topic, refer to Chapter 2.

In their most generic sense, e-mail addresses are comprised of one or more characters followed by an `@` sign, followed by a legal domain name. A domain name must contain one or more characters followed by a period and one or more characters. In the earlier days of the Web, validation routines could check to ensure that the domain ended in `.com`, `.edu`, `.mil`, `.gov`, `.org`, or `.net`. With the plethora of legal domain suffixes now, though, checking for *all* valid domains suffixes is a bit long-winded and impractical. Therefore, our regular expression will check for the most generic case:

`^\w+@\w+\.\w+$`

The `\w` symbol matches any word character, defined as the letters *a* through *z* (case insensitive), the underscore character, and the numbers 0 through 9, whereas the plus sign (+) matches one or more instances. The preceding regular expression, then, matches one or more word characters, followed by the `@` symbol, followed by one or more word characters, followed by a period, followed by one or more word characters.

The period is preceded by a backslash because it is a special symbol in regular expressions. Because we want to match a literal period, we must escape the special character with a backslash.

Note that this regular expression for e-mail address verification is far from perfect. For example, with the regular expression above, the following erroneous e-mail addresses would be considered valid:

```
hello@me.c
hiThere@test.whatTheHeckIsGoingOnHere
whoops@-.thisShouldNotBeValid
```

A more stringent e-mail validation regular expression could be concocted to be even more specific, but such a regular expression would be unwieldy due to its length and terseness. With ASP.NET the best way to validate e-mail address is to use a regular expression validation control with a rather simple regular expression (like the one above) *along with* using ASP.NET's `DNS.Resolve` method to validate that the domain name entered in the e-mail address is valid. Listing 2.6.2 in Chapter 2, "Common ASP.NET Code Techniques," examines how to accomplish this more stringent e-mail validation technique.

5. Censoring Offensive Language

One way to determine whether a string contains any offensive words is to simply use the `IndexOf` method of the `String` class to determine whether an offensive word exists within the string. Here is an example:

```
Dim strMessage as String
strMessage = "Go to hell."

'Does strMessage contain offensive words?
If strMessage.IndexOf("hell") = -1 then
   'hell was not found in strMessage
Else
   'Warning!  An offensive word!
End If
```

Although this may seem like a good strategy, imagine if `strMessage` contains the value "Hello, everyone." Unfortunately, in this instance, `strMessage` would be reported as containing profane language because the substring "hell" is found in "Hello". Obviously what we'd like to look for is not just the substring "hell" but the actual word *hell*.

Thankfully, this is quite simple with regular expressions. One of the special symbols in a regular expression is `\b`, which matches a word boundary. A *word boundary* is defined as the beginning or end of a word. Therefore, if we want a regular expression that will match any instances of "hell," we can use this:

`\bhell\b`

Of course, there are many more profane words than just *hell*. We can check for any number of profane words by separating each with a pipe (|). Here's an example:

`(\bCurseWord1\b)|(\bCurseWord2\b)|...|(\bCurseWordN\b)|`

APPENDIX C

COMMONLY USED STORED PROCEDURE TEMPLATES

by Scott Mitchell

This appendix contains 10 commonly used stored procedures you can cut and paste into your ASP.NET applications. This appendix does not contain any information on calling stored procedures or retrieving the return values from an ASP.NET Web page. To learn more about using stored procedures in an ASP.NET page, see Chapter 6, "Data Manipulation with ADO.NET."

Each of these sections contains both a stored procedure template and an example of implementing the template. Two different database tables are used for the various examples.

The first database table, `WebLinks`, serves as a repository of hyperlinks for a Web site. It contains an Identity column (`LinkID`), a name for the hyperlink (`Link_Name`), a URL for the hyperlink (`Link_URL`) and a count of how many times the hyperlink has been clicked (`ClickThroughs`).

The second database table, `UserList`, is a database table that might be found on Web sites that restrict certain parts of the site to registered users. This table contains an Identity column (`u_ID`), a column for the user's username (`u_username`), and a column for the user's password (`u_password`).

1. Selecting Rows

The following stored procedure template retrieves all the rows from a table that match a certain parameter value:

```
CREATE PROCEDURE selectRows
(
  @param1 DataType,
  @param2 DataType,
  ...
  @paramN DataType

)
As
SELECT * FROM TableName
  WHERE col1 = @param1,
```

```
    AND col2 = @param2,
    ...
    AND colN = @paramN
```

For example, the following stored procedure selects every row from a table named `WebLinks` where the value of the `Link_Name` column matches the value of the parameter:

```
CREATE PROCEDURE selectRows
(
  @LinkName Varchar( 100 )
)
As
SELECT * FROM WebLinks
  WHERE Link_Name = @LinkName
```

You also can pass in multiple parameters to the stored procedure through a comma-delimited list. For example, to return all of the rows from a table where the `Link_Name` column equals the value of one of the two parameters passed in, you could use the following code:

```
CREATE PROCEDURE selectRows
(
  @LinkName1 Varchar( 100 ),
  @LinkName2 Varchar( 50 )
)
As
SELECT * FROM WebLinks
  WHERE Link_Name = @LinkName1 OR Link_Name = @LinkName2
```

2. Inserting New Rows

The following stored procedure template inserts a new row into a table and returns the value of the identity column for the new row (if the table does not have an identity column, the stored procedure returns a value of 0):

```
CREATE PROCEDURE insertRow
(
  @param1 DataType,
  @param2 DataType,
  ...
  @paramN DataType
)
As
INSERT TableName
(
  col1,
  col2,
  ...
  colN
) VALUES (
  @param1,
  @param2,
  ...
```

```
  @paramN
)
RETURN @@IDENTITY
```

For example, to insert a new row into a table named `WebLinks` that contains `Link_Name` and `Link_URL` columns, you would use this:

```
CREATE PROCEDURE insertRow
(
  @LinkName Varchar( 100 ),
  @LinkURL Varchar( 255 ),
)
As
INSERT WebLinks
(
  Link_Name,
  Link_URL
) VALUES (
  @LinkName,
  @LinkURL
)
RETURN @@IDENTITY
```

3. Updating Existing Rows

The following stored procedure template updates existing database rows. The first parameter represents a new value and the second parameter is used to select the rows to be updated. Here's the template:

```
CREATE PROCEDURE updateRows
(
  @param1 DataType,
  @param2 DataType
)
As
UPDATE TableName SET
  Col1 = @param1
  WHERE Col2 = @param2
```

For example, the following stored procedure updates a table named `WebLinks` that contains `Link_Name` and `Link_URL` columns (the `Link_Name` column is updated with a new value):

```
CREATE PROCEDURE updateRows
(
  @oldValue Varchar( 100 ),
  @newValue Varchar( 100 )
)
As
UPDATE WebLinks SET
  Link_Name = @newValue
  WHERE Link_Name = @oldValue
```

4. Deleting Rows

The following stored procedure template deletes every row from a table where the row has a column with a certain value:

```
CREATE PROCEDURE deleteRows
(
  @param1 DataType
)
AS
DELETE TableName
  WHERE col1 = @param1
```

For example, the following stored procedure deletes every row from a table named `WebLinks` where the `Link_Name` column matches the value of the parameter:

```
CREATE PROCEDURE deleteRows
(
  @LinkName Varchar( 100 )
)
AS
DELETE WebLinks
  WHERE Link_Name = @LinkName
```

5. Selecting the Top 10 Rows

The following stored procedure template selects the top 10 rows from the database table `Tablename`:

```
CREATE PROCEDURE selectTop10
As
SELECT TOP 10 * FROM TableName
ORDER BY col1
```

For example, the following stored procedure retrieves the top 10 rows from a table named `WebLinks`. This `WebLinks` table contains a column named `ClickThroughs`, which tracks the total number of click throughs for a hyperlink. To view the most popular links we can implement the above stored procedure template like so:

```
CREATE PROCEDURE selectTop10
As
SELECT TOP 10 * FROM WebLinks
ORDER BY ClickThroughs Desc
```

6. Selecting Rows That Contain a Certain Substring

The following stored procedure template selects all the rows where a column with a character-based data type contains a user specified substring (`@target`). It uses SQL's wildcard characters (%) and the `LIKE` operator:

```
CREATE PROCEDURE selectLike
(
  @target VARCHAR( 100 )
)
AS

SELECT * FROM TableName
  WHERE col1 LIKE '%' + @target + '%'
```

For example, the following stored procedure retrieves all the rows from the `WebLinks` table where the `Link_Name` column contains the substring passed into the stored procedure (`@target`):

```
CREATE PROCEDURE selectLike
(
  @target VARCHAR( 100 )
)
AS

SELECT * FROM WebLinks
  WHERE Link_Name LIKE '%' + @target + '%'
```

7. Insert a Record if It Does Not Already Exist

The following stored procedure adds a new row only when the row doesn't already exist. If a new row is added, the value of the Identity column for the new row is returned. Otherwise, a negative number is returned. The absolute value of this returned number represents the Identity column of the existing row (`IdentityCol` is a special SQL Server keyword that serves as an alias for the value of an Identity column). Here's the code:

```
CREATE PROCEDURE insertNotAlready
(
  @param1 DataType,
  @param2 DataType,
  ...
  @paramN DataType
)
As
DECLARE @ID INT

SELECT @ID = IdentityCol FROM TableName
  WHERE col1 = @param1,
  AND col2 = @param2,
  ...
  AND colN = @paramN


IF @ID IS NOT NULL
  RETURN @ID * -1
ELSE
```

```
INSERT TableName (
  col1,
  col2,
  ...
  colN
  ) VALUES (
  @param1,
  @param2,
  ...
  @paramN

  )
  Return @@IDENTITY
```

For example, the following stored procedure inserts a new username and password into a table named `UserList` only when the username doesn't already exist:

```
CREATE PROCEDURE insertNotAlready
(
  @username Varchar( 100 ),
  @password Varchar( 100 )
)
As
DECLARE @ID INT

SELECT @ID = IdentityCol FROM UserList
  WHERE u_username = @username

IF @ID IS NOT NULL
  RETURN @ID * -1
ELSE
  INSERT UserList (
    u_username,
    u_password
    ) VALUES (
    @username,
    @password
    )
  Return @@IDENTITY
```

8. Update the Record if It Exists, or Else Insert the Record

The following stored procedure template updates a row, if it already exists; otherwise, it inserts the new row:

```
CREATE PROCEDURE insertUpdate
(
  @param1 DataType,
  @param2 DataType
)
```

```
As
Update TableName SET
  col2 = @param2
  WHERE col1 = @param1

IF @@ROWCOUNT = 0
  INSERT TableName (
    col1,
    col2
    ) VALUES (
    @param1,
    @param2
    )
```

For example, the following stored procedure either updates or adds a row to the `UserList` table. If there is already a row that contains the username, the row is updated with the new password. Otherwise, a new row is inserted with the username and password. Here's the stored procedure:

```
CREATE PROCEDURE insertUpdate
(
  @username Varchar( 100 ),
  @password Varchar( 255 )
)
As
Update UserList SET
  u_password = @password
  WHERE u_username = @username

IF @@ROWCOUNT = 0
  INSERT UserList (
    u_username,
    u_password
    ) VALUES (
    @username,
    @password
    )
```

9. Checking for a Valid Username/Password

The following stored procedure template could be used with a login page. The stored procedure expects two parameters, a username (`@username`) and password (`@password`). Assuming that the username and password are correct, the stored procedure returns the value of the identity column for the row that contains the username and password. If the username is found, but not the password, the stored procedure returns -1. If the username is not found, the stored procedure returns -2. Here's the stored procedure schema:

```
CREATE PROCEDURE checkPassword

(
  @username Varchar(100),
  @password Varchar(100)
)
As

DECLARE @ID INT

SELECT @ID = IdentityCol FROM TableName
  WHERE usernameCol = @username
  AND passwordCol = @password

IF @ID IS NOT NULL
  RETURN @ID
ELSE
  IF EXISTS( SELECT usernameCol
    FROM TableName
    WHERE usernameCol = @username )
    RETURN -1
  ELSE
    RETURN -2
```

For example, the following stored procedure checks a username and password against a table named UserList (the UserList table contains three columns—u_ID, u_username, and u_password):

```
CREATE PROCEDURE checkPassword

(
  @username Varchar( 100 ),
  @password Varchar( 100 )
)
As

DECLARE @ID INT

SELECT @ID = IdentityCol FROM UserList
  WHERE u_username = @username
  AND u_password = @password

IF @ID IS NOT NULL
  RETURN @ID
ELSE
  IF EXISTS( SELECT u_username
    FROM UserList
    WHERE u_username = @username )
    RETURN -1
  ELSE
    RETURN -2
```

10. Retrieving SQL Server System Objects

The following stored procedure returns information on database objects. By default, it will return a list of all user tables. You can view other bits of low-level SQL server information by passing in various values for the `@ObjectType` parameter. For example, passing the value `'system tables'` returns a list of system tables; passing the value `'stored procedures'` returns a list of stored procedures. Here's the code:

```
CREATE PROCEDURE systemInfo
(
  @ObjectType Varchar(30) = 'tables'
)
AS
SELECT @ObjectType =
  CASE @ObjectType
    WHEN 'tables' THEN 'U'
    WHEN 'system tables' THEN 'S'
    WHEN 'stored procedures' THEN 'P'
  END

SELECT name FROM sysobjects
  WHERE type = @ObjectType
```

For more information on the `sysobjects` table be sure to check out "Using the `sysobjects` Table." `http://www.4guysfromrolla.com/webtech/090899-1.shtml`

INDEX

Symbols

' (apostrophe)
    binding expressions, 257
    inserting data into databases, 202, 211
* (asterisk)
    database queries, 207
    Forms authentication, 439
    regular expressions, 72
    URL authorization, 481
\ (backslash)
    string escape sequence (C#), 60
    zip code validation (regular expressions), 825
{ } (braces), accessing system variables (C#), 46
^ (caret), zip code validation (regular expressions), 824-825
$ (dollar sign), zip code validation (regular expressions), 824-825
- (hyphen), zip code validation (regular expressions), 825
( ) parentheses
    calling Visual Basic.NET functions/subroutines, 818-819
    session variables, 46
. (period) special character (regular expressions), 72
    zip code validation, 826
| (pipe)
    offensive language censorship (regular expressions), 827
    zip code validation (regular expressions), 825
(pound sign), data-binding expressions, 244
+ (plus sign), zip code validation (regular expressions), 826
? (question mark) special character
    Forms authentication, 439
    URL authorization, 481
"" (quotation marks), server-side include filenames, 735
/l\: switch, creating proxy classes (Forms authentication), 461
@ Control directive, Code Behind for user controls, 603
@ Register directive, user controls, 174-175
@OutputCache directive
    Duration attribute, 558-562
    Location attribute, 564-565
    VaryByCustom attribute, 565-566
    VaryByHeader attribute, 566
    VaryByParam attribute, 562-564
@Page directive ErrorPage attribute, 365-368

A

Access databases. *See also* databases
    DataTables, 220
    deleting data, 205-206
    importing namespaces, 198
    inserting data, 201-202
    Northwind database
        caching based on named pair values, 560-561
        page caching with Data Access Pages, 558-560
    OleDb classes, 196-197
    opening database connections, 199
    storing data in tables (OleDb Save form), 237-238
        input form, 240-241
    updating data, 203-204
    using parameters, 213
access tokens, 485
accessing
    networks, 86-93
        DNS resolution/email address validation, 89-93
        listing 2.6.1, .NET Framework Internet access, 86
        listing 2.6.2, DNS resolving support, 90
    Queue elements, 41-44
    session variables, 46
    Stack elements, 44-49
    Windows event log, 105
        EventLog class, 106
        logging unhandled page exceptions, 122
        reading, 105-111
        writing, 111-113
accessor methods (COM objects), 765-767
Activator.CreateInstance method (COM Interoperability), 746-748, 759

ActiveForm property (mobile forms), 637-638
ActiveX Data Objects (ADO) COM Interoperability, 741-743
<add> tag (IHttpModule registration), 693
adding
    ArrayList elements (AddRange method), 31-34
    Hashtable elements (Add method), 35-37
    Queue elements (Enqueue method), 41-43
    SortedList elements (Add method), 38-40
    Stack elements (Push method), 44-49
admin.aspx page, list of registered users (Forms authentication), 456-458
Administrators group (file authorization), 480
ADO (ActiveX Data Objects) COM Interoperability, 741-743
ADO.NET, 196-197
    Access/Oracle classes, 196-197
    adding data to database, 200-202
        ' (apostrophe character), 202, 211
        variables, 210-211
    DataSets, 218-220
    DataTables, 218-219
        building programmatically, 223-224
        Columns/Rows properties, 221
        creating, 221
        DataAdapter, 228-230
        DataRelations, 226-227
        displaying automatically, 221-222
        filtering/sorting data, 225-226
        using with Access, 220
    deleting data, 204-206
    importing namespaces, 198
    Microsoft SQL Server classes, 196
    opening database connections, 198-200
    querying data, 207-209
        OleDbDataReaderclass, 210
        SqlDataReader class, 208-210
    SQL command parameters, 210-214
        output, 216-217
    SQL stored procedures, 214-217
    tables. *See* databases, DataTables
    updating data, 202-204
        DataAdapter Update method, 228-230
    versus ADO COM Interoperability, 726
    XML support, 339-345
        DataSet class, 339-342
        listing 8.9.1, Filling a DataSet Using SqlDataAdapter Class, 340
        listing 8.9.2, Using the DataSet's GetXmlSchema( ) and GetXml( ) Methods, 341
        listing 8.9.3, Using XmlDataDocument with DataSet Class, 342
        listing 8.9.4, Loading XML into a DataSet, 343
        listing 8.9.5, Mapping an XSD Schema to a DataSet, 343-344
        querying data within a DataSet using XPath, 341-342
        reading and writing XML using DataSet, 343
        viewing a DataSet's XML and schema, 341-342
adrotator.aspx code listing, 663
advertisements, displaying with mobile controls, 662-664
aligning text for mobile devices, 640
alignment.aspx code listing, 641
All (XmlNodeType enumeration member), 309
allow/disallow precendence (URL authorization), 483
AllowPaging property (DataGrid control), 292-295
AllowSorting property (DataGrid control), 289-291
anonymous access (Passport authentication), 471
apartment-threaded components (COM objects), 808-809
APIs (application programming interfaces). *See* Win32 APIs
apostrophes (')
    binding expressions, 257
    inserting data into databases, 202, 211
AppDomain class, 400
AppInstance value (Object tag Scope attribute), 730-731
Application directive (Http Runtime), 724-725
application localization. *See* localization
application programming interfaces. *See* Win32 APIs
Application property (HttpApplicationState object), 550
application settings section of Web.config, 419-420
application state management, 550-553
Application value (Object tag Scope attribute), 731-732
application-level code tracing, 383-385. *See also* debugging
    listing 10.1.2, Sample web.config File That Enables Tracing for an Application, 383
    viewing application trace information in trace.axd file, 384-385
application-level error handling, 368-376
    Application_Error event, 368-372
    page redirect, 372-376
        status codes, 373-376
ApplicationException class, 354. *See also* error handling
    creating exception objects, 360-363
appSettings section of Web.config, 416
    adding configuration settings, 419-420
    reading configuration settings, 420-421
ArrayList class, 31-35
    adding elements, 33
    binding collections to mobile controls, 644-645
    indexing/referencing elements, 33-35
    listing 2.1.1, 31-33
    listing 15.6.1, caching ArrayLists, 580
    removing elements, 33-34
arrays (Visual Basic.NET), bounds, 817
.ascx extension, 172
asmx files (Web services), 494-495
ASP intrinsics, 810-811
ASP Compatibility Mode. *See* AspCompat directive
ASP.NET Quick Start guides Web site, 737
ASP.NET SDK Documentation (state management), 554
ASP.NET Web site, 26, 169

AspCompat directive, 807-808
    ASP intrinsics, 810-811
    executing on STA threads, 808-810
aspnet_state.exe Session State Server process, 549
ASPNextGen.com Web site, 27
ASPNG.com Web site, 26
AspWorkshops.com Web site, 231
Asp:Xml Web control, 338-339
assemblies
    Assembly directive (Http Runtime), 727-728
    building versioned assemblies, 402-404
    compiling strong named assemblies, 404-405
    creating key files for strong named assemblies, 404
    global assembly cache, 401
        adding new assembly versions, 408-410
        registering assemblies, 405-406
    listings
        11.2.1, building the myData.myDataClass, 402
        11.2.2, sp_GetTenCustAndOutputParam stored procedure, 403
        11.2.3, building the assembly info, 403
        11.2.4, using a registered assembly on a Web Form, 407
        11.2.5, building the myDataClassV2.vb file, 408-409
        11.2.6, building the myDataAssemblyInfoV2.vb file, 409
        11.2.7, adding an assembly redirect to an application, 410-411
        11.2.8, updating Web Form to use myData v 2.0.0.0, 412
    running GacUtil.exe with list option, 410
    using multiple assembly versions, 410-412
    using registered assemblies, 406-408
asterisk (*) character
    database queries, 207
    Forms authentication, 439
    regular expressions, 72
    URL authorization, 481
asynchronous calls to Web services, 510-511
Attempted to divide by zero error message, 361
Attribute (XmlNodeType enumeration member), 309
attributes for URL authorization, 482-484
Attributes property (DirectoryInfo class), 58
authentication, 433-435
    authentication section of Web.config, 416, 419
    Forms (cookie-based) authentication. *See* Forms authentication
    integrated Windows authentication, 435-437
        displaying user's domain/username (Identity object), 435-436
        displaying user's name/authentication type, 437
        IIS Administration tool, 436
        Web.config file, 436
    Kerberos authentication scheme, 488

    Passport authentication, 467-469
        downloading Passport SDK, 469
        PassportAuthenticationModule, 469-474, 477-479
        registering as a Passport Partner site, 470
        test sites, 470
        typical Passport conversation, 468-469
    RFC 2617 authentication sections, 488
authorization, 434, 479
    authorization section of Web.config, 416, 419
    <authorization> tag, 481
    file authorization, 479-481
    impersonation, 485
        access tokens, 485
        enabling fixed NT account execution, 486-487
        impersonation disabled, 485
        impersonation enabled, 485-486
        UNC shares, 487
    URL authorization, 481
        role-based security, 484-485
        roles attribute, 482
        users attribute, 482
        verbs attribute, 482-484
Auto (XML ValidationType enumeration), 315-316
AVI movie files, uploading, 788-790, 793-795

B

Back.CSharp.aspx page listing, 48-49
backslash (\) character
    regular expressions, 825
    string escape sequence (C#), 60
backward compatability. *See also* compatibility
    AspCompat directive, 807
        ASP intrinsics, 810-811
        executing on STA threads, 808-810
    performance concerns, 811-812
    Visual Basic 6, 784-785, 800
banner ads, displaying with mobile controls, 662-664
bar charts, creating on-the-fly, 75-80
bin directory, deploying files to, 399-401
binary files, 66-68
BinaryWrite.aspx
    examining variables, 391-392
    stepping through applications, 389-391
binding lists to data sources (mobile controls), 643-645
binding data
    DataList control, 259
    DataSource property, 241-242
    DropDownList control, 251-255
    HyperLink control, 255-257
    Repeater control, 242-247
        binding to functions, 247-249
        displaying numbered lists, 248-250

842 ASP.NET: TIPS, TUTORIALS, AND CODE

binding flags (COM objects), 767-768
Bitmap class, generating images dynamically. *See* generating images dynamically
blocks (Visual Basic.NET local variables), 816-817
Boolean data types, converting to String, 162
BoundColumn property (DataGrid control), 277-279
braces { }, accessing system variables (C#), 46
breakpoints, debugging with CLR Debugger, 387-391
browsers
    navigation history stack, 44-49
        Back.CSharp.aspx page, 48-49
        ClearStackHistory.Csharp.aspx page, 47-48
    support, 155
        determining browser capabilities, 156-163
        dynamically redirecting users, 164
        uplevel versus downlevel browsers, 165-168
    viewing dynamically created images, 80-83
        listing 2.4.2, 80-81
        listing 2.4.3, IMG tag, 82
btnSubmit_OnClick event handler
    accessing networks remotely, 88
    creating graphics files, 74
    creating text files, 66
    email address validation, 91
    sending email, 84-85
    uploading files from Web browsers, 98-99
    viewing event logs, 111
building DataTables programmatically, 223-224
building versioned assemblies, 402-404
ByVal parameter default (Visual Basic.NET), 819-820

C

C#
    \ (backslash), string escape sequence, 60
    { } (braces), accessing system variables, 46
    c-sharpcorner Web site, 345
    calling Win32 APIs, 777-779
    casting, 47
    COM Interoperability, 749-751
    COM properties, 768
    DataAdapter Update method, 229-230
    file creation, 64-65
    foreach loop, 49-50
    foreach statement, 44
    out keyword, 778
    passing default values for optional parameters, 765
    String compatibility, 785
C++, cross-language debugging, 392-396
c-sharpcorner Web site, 345

Cache class, 578
    methods
        Get, 586
        GetEnumerator, 587
        Insert, 579, 581-582, 584
        Remove, 585-586
CacheDuration attribute (WebMethodAttribute class), 577
caching, 555-556
    entire Web forms (page output caching), 556-562
        @OutputCache Duration attribute, 558-562
        @OutputCache Location attribute, 564-565
        @OutputCache VaryByCustom attribute, 565-566
        @OutputCache VaryByHeader attribute, 566
        @OutputCache VaryByParam attribute, 562-564
    partial Web forms, 567-572
    programmatically (Cache class), 578
        Get method, 586
        GetEnumerator method, 587
        Insert method, 579-584
        Remove method, 585-586
    Response.Cache (HttpCachePolicy), 574-576
    Web services, 577-578
calendars, displaying with mobile controls, 664-666
Call control (mobile), 661-662
call.aspx code listing, 662
calling conventions (functions), 799-800
calling Visual Basic.NET functions/subroutines, 818-819
calling Win32 APIs, 774
    C#, 777-779
    choosing parameter types, 779-785
        data type equivalents, 780-781
        Declare statements, 780
        passing a by-value String, 784-785
        StringBuilder, 781-783
    complex type, 788, 791-795
        StructLayoutAttribute, 795
        uploadinging an AVI movie file, 788-790, 793-795
    customizing Declare and DllImport, 796
        calling conventions, 799-800
        different function names, 796-797
        error handling, 800-801, 804-807
        exact spelling setting, 799
        string behavior, 797-799
    customizing parameters, 785-787
    listing DLL functions with DUMPBIN.EXE utility, 774
    VB Net, 774-777
cancelling, DataList control (OnCancelCommand event), 262
cards, WML (Wireless Markup Language), 631-633. *See also* mobile controls, 616
caret (^), zip code validation (regular expressions), 824-825

case-sensitivity of DLL exposed functions, 775
casting, (C#) explicit, 47
catching exceptions
    general, 355-357
    specific, 358-359
        handling SQL Server Not Found error (listing 9.3.4), 357
standard predefined exception types, 358-359
    Try, Catch, Finally statement, 354-355
CategoryName property (PerformanceCounter class), 113-114
CDATA (XmlNodeType enumeration member), 310
CDONTS (Collaborative Data Object for NT Server), 83
cellular phone controls. See mobile devices and mobile controls
censoring offensive language, 827
character encodings, 613-618
charts, creating on-the-fly, 75-80
check box Web control, 23-25
classes
    ApplicationException, 354
        creating exception objects, 360-363
    ArrayList, 31-35
        adding elements, 33
        indexing/referencing elements, 33-35
        listing 2.1.1, 31-33
        removing elements, 33-34
    Bitmap, generating images dynamically. See generating images dynamically
    Cache, 578
        Get method, 586
        GetEnumerator method, 587
        Insert method, 579-584
        Remove method, 585-586
    Control (Web control events), 26
    CultureInfo class. See also resource files
        application localization by setting culture encoding programmatically, 615-618
        application localization with System.Globalization namespace, 612-613
    DataGridPagerStyle, 297
    DataSet, 339-342
        filling a DataSet using SqlDataAdapter, 340
        GetXml/GetXmlSchema( ) methods, 341
        mapping XSD schemas to DataSets, 343-345
        reading/writing XML documents, 343
        using with XmlDataDocument, 342
        viewing a DataSet's XML and schema, 341-342
    DataTable. See DataTables
default properties (Visual Basic.NET), 820-821
Directory, 57, 60
DirectoryInfo, 54, 56-60
    accessing methods/properties, 57
    Attributes property, 58
    CreateSubdirectory method, 59
    Delete method, 59-60

DisplayAttributes property, 58-59
FileAttributes property, 57-58
GetDirectories( ) method, 59
GetFiles( ) method, 59
listing 2.2.1, 54-56
EventLog, 105
    listing 2.9.1, 106
Exception, 352-354
FileInfo, 61-62
Graphics
    FillRectangle method, 78-79
    generating images dynamically. See generating images dynamically
Hashtable, 35
    adding elements, 35-37
    indexing/referencing elements, 35-38
    Keys/Values collections, 38
    listing 2.1.2, 36-37
    removing elements, 35-38
HtmlInputFile, 96
HttpBrowserCapabilities. See HttpBrowserCapabilities class
HttpCachePolicy, 574-576
HttpContext, 699-701
HttpPostedFile, 94-97
    InputStream property, 97-99
HttpRequest, 702
    client page for uploading files, 707-708
    command-line test application for uploading/downloading files, 711-716
    creating IhttpHandler to allow file uploads, 702-707
    creating images on-the-fly, 716-723
    downloading files, 708-711
    results from successful uploads, 708-709
IEnumerator, 50-53
IHttpHandler, 677, 695-699
    creating IhttpHandlers in .ashx files, 695-698
    creating IhttpHandlers in web.config files, 698-699
    creating images on the fly, 716-723
IHttpModule, 677
IHttpModule, intercepting events, 690-695
    <add> directive, 693
    <clear> directive, 693-695
    Dispose( ) method, 691-692
    IHttpModule registration, 692-695
    Init( ) method, 691
    <remove> directive, 693
ImageFormat, 79
Images, 79-81
MailMessage, 83-85
.NET Framework, 30
OleDb, 196-197
    OleDbDataReader, 210
    OleDbParameters, 213

Page
    Init event, 8
    listing 1.1.1, 8
    Load event, 8-10
    PreRender event, 8-9
    Tracing, 8-9
PerformanceCounter, 113-116
PerformanceCounterCategory, 116-121
    listing 2.10.2, 116-119
ProcessInfo, 100
    displaying currently executing aspnet_wp.exe process, 100-102
    displaying past instances of aspnet_wp.exe, 102-105
ProcessModelInfo, 100
    displaying past instances of aspnet_wp.exe, 102-105
    listing 2.8.2, 103-104
proxy classes, consuming Web services, 498-507
Queue, 41
    accessing elements, 41-44
    adding elements, 41-43
    listing 2.1.4, 42-43
    removing elements, 41-43
Regex, 69-70
    IsMatch method, 70-71
    listing 2.3.1, IsMatch method, 70
    listing 2.3.2, Matches method, 71
    Matches method, 71-73
    Replace method, 74
SmtpMail, 84-85
SortedList, 38-41
    adding elements, 38-40
    indexing/referencing elements, 38-40
    listing 2.1.3, 39-40
    removing elements, 38-40
SqlCommand, 196, 201
SqlConnection, 196-198
SqlDataAdapter, 197
    Fill( ) method, 340
SqlDataReader, 196, 201, 207-209
    listing 6.2.1, 208
    Read( ) method, 209
    using, 208
    using with C#, 209
Stack, 44
    accessing elements, 44-49
    adding elements, 44-49
    listing 2.1.5, 45-46
    listing 2.1.6, 48
    listing 2.1.7, 48-49
    removing elements, 44-49
System.Xml assembly. *See* System.Xml assembly

SystemException, 352-354
Type, JIT compiled user controls in Code Behind, 611
UserControl. *See also* user controls
    Code Behind for user controls, 603-605
WebAuth.cs proxy class, 461-462
WebMethodAttribute, 577
XML Document Object Model (DOM), 325-326
Clear method
    EventLog class, 111
    Queue class, 43
    SortedList class, 38
<clear> tag, IHttpModule registration, 693-695
ClearStackHistory.CSharp.aspx page listing, 48
client-side form validation, 124-125. *See also* form input validation
    CustomValidator control, 145, 147-148
ClientTarget property (Page class), 165-168
CLR Debugger
    attaching DbgCLR.exe to applications, 386-387
    breakpoints, 387-389
    cross-language debugging, 392-396
    Debug, Windows menu, 391
    debugging exceptions, 396-398
    detaching from currently attached processes, 387
    enabling debugging, 385-386
    examining variables, 391-392
    stepping through applications, 389-391
CLSIDs (class identifiers), COM objects, 741
code
    debugging. *See* debugging
    separating logic code from presentation markup. *See* Code Behind; localization; resource files
Code Behind, 596
    Code-Behind file extensions, 596
    dynamically loading user controls, 191-192
    user controls
        @ Control directive, 603
        declaring objects for controls that expose properties, 605-606
        inheriting UserControl, 603-605
        JIT compiled user controls (reflection), 609-611
        precompiled user controls, 606-608
    Web Forms, 596-603
        building the Code-Behind file, 597-598
        inheriting from Code Behind class, 596
        listing 16.1.1, 597
        listing 16.1.2, 598
        listing 16.1.3, 600
        listing 16.1.4, 601
        multiple events/controls, 600-603
        resource files, 621-622
        Src attribute, 598
code blocks, Visual Basic.NET local variables, 816-817

INDEX

code declarations (Http Runtime directives), 733-735
    <Script> blocks, 733
        Language attribute, 733-735
        Runat attribute, 735
        Src attribute, 735
    syntax, 733
code examples Web site, 122
code listings. *See* listings
coercing COM objects, 770-771
Collaborative Data Object for NT Server (CDONTS), 83
collections, 30-31
    ArrayList, 31-35
        adding elements, 33
        indexing/referencing elements, 33-35
        removing elements, 33-34
    Count property, 49
    enumerators, 50-53
    For Each... Next loops, 49-50
    Hashtable, 35
        adding elements, 35-37
        indexing/referencing elements, 35-38
        Keys/Values collections, 38
        removing elements, 35-38
    ICollection interface, 53
    Keys, 38
    Queue, 41-43
    SortedList, 38-41
    Stack, 44-49
    Values, 38
column layout (tables), controlling with DataList control, 260
columns (DataTables), 221
COM (Component Object Model) Interoperability, 739-741
    apartment-threaded components, 808-809
    deployment, 773-774
    free-threaded components, 808
    interacting with COM objects
        calling properties, 765-768
        coercing objects, 770-771
        error handling, 768
        passing right type of object, 771-772
        releasing objects, 772-773
        type libraries, 760-765
    IUnknown methods, 770
    objects created in source code
        Activator.CreateInstance method, 746-748, 759
        IDispatch.Invoke, 754
        late binding (dynamic invocation), 748-753
        Server.CreateObject method, 745-748, 759
        Type.InvokeMember, 751-753
    objects created with <object> tag, 741-744
        ADO (ActiveX Data Objects), 741-743
        CLSIDs/ProgIDs, 741
    performance concerns, 811-812
    type libraries, 754-755
        browsing assembly contents using IL Disassembler (ILDASM.exe), 758
        generating Interop Assembly with TlbImp.exe, 757
        Interop Assembly, 754-755
        referencing type libraries in Visual Studio.NET, 755-757
        taking advantage of type information, 759-765
CommandArgument property (LinkButton control), 266-268
commands (databases)
    DELETE, 205-206
    INSERT
        input, 200-202
        variables, 210-211
    UPDATE, 202-204
Comment (XmlNodeType enumeration member), 310
CompareValidator control, 131-135
    error message, 134
    listing 3.3.1, 131-132
    Operator property, 135
    Type property, 134-135
    valid input result, 134
compatability
    AspCompat directive, 807-808
        ASP intrinsics, 810-811
        executing on STA threads, 808-810
    performance concerns, 811-812
compilation section of Web.config, 416-418
compiling strong named assemblies, 404-405
Component Object Model. *See* COM
components
    configuring applications to use specific versions
        adding new assembly versions to global assembly cache, 408-410
        building versioned assemblies, 402-404
        compiling strong named assemblies, 404-405
        creating key files for strong named assemblies, 404
        global assembly cache, 401
        registering assemblies with global assembly cache, 405-406
        using a registered assembly, 406-408
        using multiple assembly versions, 410-412
    deploying to \bin directory, 399-401
configSections section of Web.config, 422-423
configuration of web.config file, 412-413
    adding
        application configuration settings, 419-420
        custom configuration settings, 421-422
    machine.config sections, 413-416
    reading
        application configuration settings, 420-421
        custom configuration settings, 422-423
    web.config sections, 416-419

console-based test application (Forms authentication), 463
consuming Web services, 498
    creating proxy classes, 498-507
        command line tools, 504
        disco files, 502-503
        disco.exe command line tool, 504
        listing 13.3.1, XML service contract, 499-500
        listing 13.3.2, disco document sample, 502
        listing 13.3.3, generated proxy class, Service1.vb, 505
        searching for Web services, 500-502
        Web Services Description Language (WSDLS), 498-500
        wsdl.exe command line tool, 505-507
    making asynchronous calls, 510-511
        listing 13.3.5, 511
    making synchronous calls, 507-510
        listing 13.3.4, 509
Contains method (Queue class), 43
ContainsKey method
    SortedList, 40
    HashTable, 37
ContainsValue method (HashTable), 37
Control class (Web control events), 26
Control Tree (trace output), 381
controls
    binding data. *See* data-binding, 242
        DataList control, 259
        DropDownList control, 251-255
        HyperLink control, 255-257
        Repeater control, 243-247
    Code Behind
        @ Control directive, 603
        declaring objects for controls that expose properties, 605-606
        inheriting UserControl, 603-605
        JIT compiled user controls (reflection), 609-611
        precompiled user controls, 606-608
        Web Forms with multiple events/controls, 600-603
    custom sever controls, 172
    DataGrid. *See* DataGrid control
    DataList. *See* DataList control
    DropDownList, binding data, 251-255
    HyperLink, binding data, 255-257
    LinkButton
        CommandArgument property, 266-268
        displaying menu items, 263-264
        editing items with DataGrid control, 284-285
    mobile controls. *See* mobile controls
    Passport Logo, 478-479
    Repeater. *See* Repeater control
    user controls. *See* user controls
    validation. *See* validation controls

Web controls
    event handlers, 23-26
    events, 26
cookies, 122
    cookie-based authentication. *See* Forms authentication; Passport authentication
    session state management, 543-546
        cookie munging (cookieless session management), 546-547
Cookies Collection (trace output), 381
copyright.ascx user control (DotNetJunkies.com Web site example), 173-174
Count property
    ArrayList class, 34
    collections, 49
CounterName property (PerformanceCounter class), 113-114
cpuMask attribute, processModel section of machine.config, 425, 428-430
CreateSubdirectory method (DirectoryInfo class), 59
CreateUser stored procedure (Forms authentication), 447-448
credit card validation
    CustomValidator control, 141-142
        client-side validation functions, 145-148
        server-side validation functions, 142-145
    Luhn formula, 142-145
cross-device compatibility (mobile controls), 666-671
    choosing devices with deviceSelect, 669-671
    detecting mobile capabilities, 667-668
    form template sets, 671
    listing 17.5.1, displaying mobile capabilities, 667
    listing 17.5.2, selecting different devices, 669
    listing 17.5.3, displaying different content with template sets, 672
cross-language debugging, 392-396
CultureInfo class, application localization. *See also* resource files
    setting culture encoding programmatically, 615-618
    System.Globalization namespace, 612-613
Currency data type (Visual Basic.NET), 816
currentmovies.aspx code listing, 642
currentmovies4.aspx code listing, 645
custom exceptions, 360-363
    changing Web.Config to allow custom errors, 366
    CustomErrors.aspx page, 371-374
    defaultredirect attribute (<customerrors>), 373
    implementing (<error>), 373
    redirecting to custom error pages, 367
    using HttpContext Error property to reference unhandled exception, 370
custom sever controls, 172
customer survey form listing, 234
CustomerList user control, 191
customErrors section of Web.config, 416-418
CustomErrors.aspx page, 371-374

customizing
    Declare and DllImport, 796
        calling conventions, 799-800
        different function names, 796-797
        error handling, 800-801, 804-807
        exact spelling setting, 799
        string behavior, 797-799
    parameters (Win32 APIs), 785-787
CustomValidator control, 141-142
    client-side validation functions, 145-148
        error message, 148
    listings
        3.6.1, server-side validation, 142-143
        3.6.2, client-side validation, 145-147
    Luhn formula, 142-144
    server-side validation functions, 142-145
        error message, 145
CustomValidator mobile validation control, 658

D

Data Access Pages, caching (listing 15.2.3), 558
data types
    Visual Basic.NET, 815-816
    widening conversion, 350-351
    Win32/Declare statment equivalents, 780-781
data-binding
    DataList control, 259
    DataSource property, 241-242
    DropDownList control, 251-255
    HyperLink control, 255-257
    Repeater control, 242-247
        binding to functions, 247-249
        displaying numbered lists, 248-251
DataAdapter (ADO.NET), 228-230
databases
    adding data, 200-202
        ' (apostrophe character), 202, 211
        variables, 210-211
    binding lists to data sources (mobile controls), 643-645
    DataTables, 218-219
        building programmatically, 223-224
        Columns/Rows properties, 221
        creating, 221
        DataAdapter, 228-230
        DataRelations, 226-227
        displaying automatically, 221-222
        filtering/sorting data, 225-226
        using with Access, 220
    deleting data, 204-206
    displaying multiple database fields, mobile controls, 653
    importing namespaces, 198
    in-memory databases, 197
    opening connections, 198-200
    performance checklist, 592
    querying data, 207-209
        OleDbDataReaderclass, 210
        SqlDataReader class, 208-210
    Response.Redirect method, 237
    retrieving database objects, stored procedure template, 837
    returning data from Web services, 512
        datasets, 514-519
        listing 13.4.1, data-access code for Web service, 513-514
        listing 13.4.2, returning an ADO.NET dataset, 515
        listing 13.4.3, returned XML data containing a DataSet, 516
        making decisions based on data, 513-514
    saving form data, 234-241
        Access/Oracle form (OleDb Survey form), 240-241
        IsValid property, 236
        SQL Server form, 238-240
        storing data in an Access or Oracle table (OleDb Save form), 237-238
        storing data in an SQL Server table, 235-237
    SQL command parameters, 210-214
        output, 216-217
    SQL stored procedures, 214-217
        output parameters, 216-217
    tables. *See also* databases, DataTables; rows (database tables)
        creating using Code Behind, 597-599
        stored procedure templates. *See* stored procedure templates
    updating data, 202-204
        DataAdapter Update method, 228-230
DataBinding event (Control class), 26
DataGrid control, 276-277
    creating tables using Code Behind, 597-599
    displaying specfic columns (BoundColumn property), 277-279
    editing data
        EditItemIndex property, 281-285
        EditItemTemplate property, 285, 288
    listing 7.4.1, using DataGrid, 277
    listing 7.4.2, BoundColumn property, 278
    listing 7.4.3, hiding columns, 279
    listing 7.4.4, editing items, 282
    listing 7.4.5, using template columns, 285
    listing 7.4.6, numeric paging through a DataGrid, 296
    listing 7.4.6, sorting data, 289
    listing 7.4.7, sorting certain columns of data, 291
    listing 7.4.8, paging through a DataGrid, 293-295
    listing 7.4.9, numeric paging through a DataGrid, 296-297

listing 7.4.10, paging through a DataGrid in chunks, 299-302
paging through table data (AllowPaging property), 292-295
    custom paging in chunks, 297-302
    displaying page numbers, 295-297
showing/hiding columns (Visible property), 279-281
sorting table data (AllowSorting property), 289-291
DataGridPagerStyle class, 297
DataList control, 258
    DataKeyField property, 269
    displaying data without a table, 261-262
    editing items (EditItemTemplate), 271, 274-276
    event bubbling, 262
        retrieving category Ids (DataKeyField property), 268-271
        retrieving category names, 266-268
        SelectedItemTemplate template, 265-267
        selecting menu items, 262-264
    events, 262
    listing 7.3.1, using DataList control, 258
    listing 7.3.2, displaying grid lines, 259
    listing 7.3.3, controlling column layout, 261
    listing 7.3.4, capturing OnItemCommand event, 263
    listing 7.3.5, using SelectedItemTemplate template, 265
    listing 7.3.6, using CommandArgument property, 267
    listing 7.3.7, DataKeyField property, 269
    listing 7.3.8, editing items, 271
    table properties, 258-259
        column layout, 260
DataRelations (ADO.NET), 226-227
DataSet class, 339-342
    filling a DataSet using SqlDataAdapter, 340
    GetXml/GetXmlSchema( ) methods, 341
    mapping XSD schemas to DataSets, 343-345
    reading/writing XML documents, 343
    using with XmlDataDocument, 342
    viewing a DataSet's XML and schema, 341-342
datasets
    ADO.NET, 218-220. *See also* DataTables
    returning from Web services, 514-516
        security, 517-519
DataSource property, binding data, 241-242
DataTables (ADO.NET), 218-220
    building programmatically, 223-224
    Columns/Rows properties, 221
    creating, 221
    DataAdapter, 228-230
    DataRelations, 226-227
    displaying automatically, 221-222
    filtering/sorting data, 225-226
DataValueField Property (DropDownList control), 254
date/time, displaying for mobile devices, 639
DbgCLR.exe. *See* CLR Debugger
de-DE (German) encoding resource file, 623-624

debugging
    CLR Debugger
        attaching DbgCLR.exe to applications, 386-387
        breakpoints, 387-389
        cross-language debugging, 392-396
        Debug, Windows menu, 391
        detaching from currently attached processes, 387
        enabling debugging, 385-386
        examining variables, 391-392
        exceptions, 396-398
        stepping through applications, 389-391
    tracing code execution
        adding messages to Trace Information section, 381-383
        application-level tracing, 383-385
        Control Tree section, 381
        Cookies Collection section, 381
        Headers Collection section, 381
        listing 10.1.1, Using Trace.Warn and Trace.Write, 382
        page-level, 380-381
        Request Details section, 381
        Server Variables section, 381
        Trace directive, 380-381
        Trace Information section, 381-383
Decimal data type (Visual Basic.NET), 816
decks of cards, WML (Wireless Markup Language), 631-633. *See also* mobile controls
Declare statement
    customizing, 796
        different function names, 796-797
        string behavior, 797-799
    defining with by-reference array parameters, 788
    in/out behavior, 787
    MarshalAsAttribute, 785-787
    passing a by-value String, 784-785
    Visual Basic.NET, calling Win32 APIs, 774-775
    Visual Basic, 780
        Win32 data type equivalents, 780-781
Decoration property (List control), 643-644
default properties (Visual Basic.NET), 820-821
default.aspx, welcome page for authenticated users (Forms authentication), 456
defaultlanguage attribute (<Script>), 734
defaultredirect attribute (<customerrors>), 373
Delete method
    Directory class, 60
    DirectoryInfo class, 59-60
DELETEcommand (databases), 205-206
deleting
    database data, 204-206
    directories, 59-60
    OnDeleteCommand event (DataList control), 262
    rows (stored procedure template), 832

deployment
    COM components, 773-774
    copying files to bin directory, 399-401
Dequeue method (Queue class), 41-43
Description attribute (Application directive), 725
<deviceSelect> element (mobile controls), 661, 669-671
<deviceSpecific> element (mobile controls), 661
Digest Authentication RFC 2617, 488
directives (Http Runtime), 723
    Application, 724-725
        Description attribute, 725
        Inherits attribute, 724-725
    Assembly, 727-728
    code declarations, 733-735
        Language attribute, 733-735
        Runat attribute, 735
        <Script> blocks, 733
        Src attribute, 735
        syntax, 733
    Import, 725-727
        logging user names to log file, 726
        logging user names to log file without Import, 727
        Namespace attribute, 725
    Object tag, 729
        Class attribute, 732
        ClassID attribute, 733
        ID attribute, 730
        ProgID attribute, 732-733
        Runat attribute, 730
        Scope attribute, 730-732
        syntax, 729
    server-side includes, 735-736
    syntax, 724-725
directories, 54-60
    available file attributes, 58
    creating, 54-57
    deleting, 59-60
    displaying file attributes, 58-59
    invalid directory error, 57
    listing 2.2.1, DirectoryInfo class, 54-56
    subdirectories, 59
Directory class, 57, 60
DirectoryInfo class, 54-60
    accessing methods/properties, 57
    Attributes property, 58
    CreateSubdirectory method, 59
    Delete method, 59-60
    DisplayAttributes property, 58-59
    FileAttributes property, 57-58
    GetDirectories( ) method, 59
    GetFiles( ) method, 59
    listing 2.2.1, 54-56
disco files (Web services), 502-503
    disco.exe tool, 504
Display property (validation controls), 128-129

DisplayAttributes property (DirectoryInfo class), 58-59
displaying database information
    binding data to DropDownList control, 251-255
    binding data to HyperLink control, 255-257
    binding data to Repeater control, 242-247
        binding to functions, 247-249
        displaying numbered lists, 248-251
    DataGrid control. *See* DataGrid control
    DataList control. *See* DataList control
    DataSource property, 241-242
    DataTables, 221-222
    encoding text with Server.HTMLEncode, 244
displaying file contents, 63-64
Dispose( ) method (IHttpModule class), 691-692
DllImport attribute, customizing, 796
    calling conventions, 799-800
    different function names, 796-797
    error handling, 800-801, 804-807
    exact spelling setting, 799
    string behavior, 797-799
DllImport statement
    defining with by-reference array parameters, 788
    in/out behavior, 787
    MarshalAsAttribute, 785-787
DLLs (Dynamic-Link Libraries). *See also* assemblies; Win32 APIs
    deploying files to bin directory, 399-401
    listing DLL functions with DUMPBIN.EXE utility, 774
DNS resolution, remote network access, 89-93
    DNS resolving support, .NET Framework Internet access, 90
Document (XmlNodeType enumeration member), 310
Document Object Model (DOM), XML, 322-324
    adding nodes to XML documents, 327
    DOM classes, 325-326
    DOM Level 2 specification, 323
    in-memory versus forward only cursor-based parsing, 324-325
    recursion, 327-330
    selecting nodes using XPath, 330-331
Document Type Definition (DTD) files (XML), 306
documentation, uploading files from Web browsers, 94
DocumentFragment (XmlNodeType enumeration member), 310
documents, XML. *See also* XML
    adding nodes using Document Object Model (DOM), 327
    creating (XmlTextWriter), 318-322
    listing 8.6.1, Generating XML with the XmlTextWriter Class, 319
    listing 8.6.2, Converting CSV Flat Files to XML with the XmlTextWriter Class, 320-322
    readingXML documents using DataSet class, 343
    selecting nodes in DOM using XPath, 330-331
    transforming with XSLT. *See* XSLT (Extensible Stylesheet Language Transformations)

validating (XmlValidatingReader), 314-318
walking the DOM using recursion, 327-330
writing XML documents using DataSet class, 343
XmlDataDocument class, 334, 342
XmlDocument class, 334
XmlPathDocument class, 334-336
DocumentType (XmlNodeType enumeration member), 310
dollar sign ($), zip code validation (regular expressions), 824-825
dotnet101 Web site, 345
DotNetJunkies.com Web site, 169, 593, 626
   copyright.ascx user control, 173-174
downlevel browsers, 165-168
downloading files (Http Runtime)
   command-line test application for uploading/downloading files, 711-716
   WriteFile method, 708-711
DrawBarChart function, 80
DrawBarGraph function, 75-79
DrinkBoyException custom exception, 362-363. *See also* custom exceptions
DropDownList control
   binding data, 251-255, 259
   listing 7.2.5, binding data, 251
   listing 7.2.6, DataValueField property, 254
DTD (XML ValidationType enumeration), 316
DUMPBIN.EXE utility, 774
Duration attribute (@OutputCache directive), 558-562
Duwamish Books Inc. Web site, 377
dynamic invocation (COM Interoperability), 748-753
   listing 19.1.3, 749-751
   reflection, 751-753
Dynamic-Link Libraries. *See* DLLs
dynamically loading user controls, 190-194
   code behind file, 191-192
   presentation file, 191

E

EDI (Electronic Data Interchange), 490
EditItemIndex property (DataGrid control), 281-285
EditItemTemplate property (DataGrid control), 285, 288
EditItemTemplate template (DataList control), 271, 274-276
Electronic Data Interchange (EDI), 490
Element (XmlNodeType enumeration member), 310
email
   address validation, 826
   email validation Web article, 122
   sending, 83-86
      address validation, 89-93
      listing 2.5.1, 83-84
en-NZ (English-New Zealand) encoding resource file, 624-625

enable attribute, processModel section of machine.config, 424
EnableViewState property (ViewState), 532-533
encoding database text with Server.HTMLEncode, 244
encryption, SHA1 algorithm, 444-446
EndElement (XmlNodeType enumeration member), 310
EndEntity (XmlNodeType enumeration member), 310
Enqueue method (Queue class), 41-43
Entity (XmlNodeType enumeration member), 310
EntityReference (XmlNodeType enumeration member), 311
enumerators, stepping through collections, 50-53
Error event (Page object), 363-365
error handling, 347-348. *See also* global.asax event handlers
   application level, 368-376
      Application_Error event, 368-372
      page redirect, 372-376
   catching errors at design time
      Option Explicit, 348-350
      Option Strict, 349-353
   COM object interaction, 768
   <customErrors> section of Web.config, 418
   Exception class, 352-354
   page level, 363-368
   structured, 354-355
      catching general exceptions, 355-357
      catching specific exceptions, 356-359
      creating custom exceptions, 360-363
      throwing exceptions, 360-361
      Try, Catch, Finally statement, 354-355
   Win32 APIs, customizing, 800-801, 804-807
      getting Win32 error codes, 800-801
      throwing exceptions on failure, 801-807
Error property (HttpContex), 370
ErrorPage attribute (@Page directive), 365-368
errors
   directives (Http Runtime), 724
   invalid directory, 57
      exceptions, 59
   System logs, 112-113. *See also* System event log
   validation controls
      CompareValidator, 134
      CustomValidator, client-side, 148
      CustomValidator, server-side, 145
      RangeValidator, 138
      RegularExpressionValidator, 141
      RequiredFieldValidator, 127
EuroConv.cs (cross-language debugging), 393-396
event bubbling in DataList control, 262
   retrieving category IDs (DataKeyField property), 268-271
   retrieving category names, 266-268
   SelectedItemTemplate template, 265-267
   selecting menu items, 262-264

INDEX 851

event handlers
    btnSubmit_OnClick
        accessing networks remotely, 88
        creating graphics files, 74
        creating text files, 66
        email address validation, 91
        sending email, 84-85
        uploading files from Web browsers, 98-99
        viewing event logs, 111
    CheckboxChanged, 23-25
    OnClick (postback forms), 22-23
    Page Init, 8
    Page Load, 8-10
    Page PreRender, 8-9
    Web control events, 23-26
event log (Windows), 105
    EventLog class, 106
    reading, 105-111
        display format, 107-110
    writing, 111-113
        logging unhandled page exceptions, 122
EventLog class, 105-106
events
    Application_Error, 368-372
    Control class, 26
    DataList control, 262
    Error (Page object), 363-365
    Http Runtime application-level events, 679-680
    Http Runtime global.asax event handlers. *See*
      global.asax event handlers
    Http Runtime interception events, 678-679
        intercepting using global.asax file. *See*
          global.asax event handlers, intercepting
          events
        intercepting using HTTP modules, 690-695
    OnClick, postback forms, 22-23
    Page class, 8-10
    SessionStart, 537-538
    Web controls, 26
        event handlers, 23-26
exact spelling setting (Win32 APIs), 799
Exception class, 352-354. *See also* error handling
exceptions. *See also* error handling
    catching
        general, 355-357
        specific, 356-359
          handling SQL Server Not Found error (listing 9.3.4), 357
          standard predefined exceptions, 358-359
    creating custom exceptions, 360-363
        changing Web.Config to allow custom errors, 366
        CustomErrors.aspx page, 371-374
        defaultredirect attribute (<customerrors>), 373
        implementing <error>, 373
        redirecting to custom error pages, 367
        using HttpContext Error property to reference unhandled exception, 370
    debugging, 396-398
    standard exception types, 358-359
    subdirectories, 59
    throwing, 360-361
explicit casting (C#), 47
expressions. *See* regular expressions
Extensible Markup Language. *See* XML

F

field input validation. *See* form input validation, 123
file authorization, 479-481
FileAttributes property (DirectoryInfo class), 57-58
FileInfo class
    FileMode enumeration, 67
    listing 2.2.2, 61-62
files, 53-54, 60-64. *See also* directories
    accessing (FileMode enumeration), 67
    binary, 66-68
    displaying contents, 63-64
    FileInfo class, 61-62
    formats (images), 79
    GetFiles( ) method (DirectoryInfo class), 59
    linking, WML (Wireless Markup Language), 633
    listing files, 62-63
    listings
        2.2.3, creating text files, 64-65
        2.2.4, binary files, 67
    Machine.config, 401
    saving files uploaded from Web browsers, 94-97
    text files, creating, 64-66
    uploading from Web browsers, 93-99
        HttpPostedFile class, 94-97
        RFC documentation, 94
        saving uploaded files, 94-97
        working with uploaded files, 97-99
    Web.config. *See* Web.config file
Fill( ) method (SqlDataAdapter class), 340
FillRectangle method (Graphics class), 78-79
filtering DataTable data, 225-226
First In, First Out (FIFO), 41
fixed NT account execution, 486-487
flat files
    converting to XML with XmlTextWriter, 320-322
    marking up with XML, 304-305
For...Next loop, drawing bar charts, 79
For Each...Next loop
    collections, 49-50
    Queue class iteration, 44
    stepping through collections, 34-35
foreach loop (C#), 49-50

foreach statement (C#), 44
foreign-language applications. *See* localization and resource files
form input validation, 123-125
    CompareValidator control, 131-135
        error message, 134
        listing 3.3.1, 131-132
        Operator property, 135
        Type property, 134-135
        valid input result, 134
    CustomValidator control, 141-142
        client-side validation functions, 145-148
        listing 3.6.1, server-side validation, 142-143
        listing 3.6.2, client-side validation, 145-147
        Luhn formula, 142-144
        server-side validation functions, 142-145
    Display property, 128-129
    RangeValidator control, 135-138
        error message, 138
        listing 3.4.1, 136-137
        valid input result, 138
    RegularExpressionValidator control, 139-141
        error message, 141
        listing 3.5.1, 139-140
        valid input message, 141
    RequiredFieldValidator control, 125-131
        error message, 127
        HTML form example, 127
        listing 3.2.1, RequireFieldValidator, 126
        listing 3.2.2, RequireFieldValidator Display property, 129
        listing 3.2.3, RequireFieldValidator list box, 129-130
    ValidationSummary control, 148-152
        listing 3.7.1, 149-150
        validation summary reports, 150-152
forms, 11. *See also* Web forms
    authentication. *See* Forms authentication
    input validation. *See* form input validation
    list boxes, RequiredFieldValidator control, 129-131
    mobile controls
        creating mobile forms, 634-636
        dynamically activiating forms, 637-638
        form template sets, 671
    processing input
        postback forms. *See* postback forms
        two-page form processing, 11-15
    processing scripts, 11
    Response.Redirect method, 237
    saving data, 234-241
        Access/Oracle form (OleDb Survey form), 240-241
        IsValid property, 236
        SQL Server form, 238-240
        storing data in an Access or Oracle table (OleDb Save form), 237-238
        storing data in an SQL Server table, 235-237
    uploading files from HTML forms, 93-99
        HttpPostedFile class, 94-97
        RFC documentation, 94
        saving uploaded files, 94-97
        working with uploaded files, 97-99
forms authentication, 437-439, 442-446
    advantages, 438
    authenticating against an XML file, 438, 442
    password encryption with SHA1 algorithm, 444-445
    redirection process, 437
    remote Web services, 458-465, 467
        advantages, 458
        console-based test application, 463
        creating a proxy using wsdl, 461-462
        creating Web service (WebAuth.asmx), 458-459
        incorporating authentication service into Web application, 464-465
        login.cs, 465-467
        SSL requirement, 459-460
        WebAuth.asmx test screen, 459-460
    SQL Server, 446-458
        admin.aspx, list of registered users, 456-458
        configuration file, 448-449
        CreateUser stored procedure, 447-448
        creating database and Logins table, 447
        default.aspx, welcome page for authenticated users, 456
        Login.aspx for authenticating users, 449-452
        register.aspx for creating new users, 452-455
        ValidateUser stored procedure, 447
    Web.config file, 439
        authenticating against credentials section, 443-444
        credentials section, 442-443
        SHA1 encrypted passwords, 445-446
free-threaded components (COM objects), 808
FTP site URLs
    Basic Authentication in HTTP (RFC 2617), 488
    Digest Authentication in HTTP (RFC 2617), 488
    MD5 hashing algorithm RFC, 488
    SHA1 hashing algorithm RFC, 488
functions
    binding to (Repeater control), 247-249
    calling conventions, 799-800
    choosing different function names (Win32 APIs), 796-797
    DrawBarChart, 80
    DrawBarGraph, 75-79
    Visual Basic.NET, 818-820
        ByVal parameter default, 819-820
        calling, 818-819
        QueryPerformanceCounter/QueryPerformance Frequency, 775-777

G

GacUtil.exe utility. *See* global assembly cache
generating images dynamically, 75
    saving images on Web servers, 75-80
        listing 2.4.1, 76-77
        listing 2.4.2, sending image to browser, 80-81
        listing 2.4.3, IMG tag, 82
    sending images to browsers, 80-83
German (de-DE) encoding resource file, 623-624
Get accessor method (COM object interaction), 766-767
Get method, 586
    exposing user control properties as Property objects, 181. *See also* Property objects, exposing user control properties
GetByIndex method (SortedList class), 39
GetConfig( ) method (Web.config file), 422-423
GetDirectories( ) method (DirectoryInfo class), 59
GetEnumerator method (Cache class), 587
GetFiles( ) method (DirectoryInfo class), 59
GetHistory method (ProcessModelInfo class), 102
GetKeyList method (SortedList class), 41
GetLastError method (HttpServerUtility), 369-370
GetSingleProduct user control, 181-186
GetValueList method (SortedList class), 39
GetXml( ) method (DataSet class), 341
GetXmlSchema( ) method (DataSet class), 341
GIF files. *See* binary files
global applications. *See* localization and resource files
global assembly cache, 401
    adding new assembly versions, 408-410
    registering assemblies, 405-406
        using a registered assembly, 406-408
global.asax event handlers, 681
    BeginRequest/EndRequest events, 679-680
    HttpContext class, 699-701
    HttpRequest class, 702
        client page for uploading files, 707-708
        command-line test application for uploading/downloading files, 711-712, 714-716
        creating IhttpHandler to allow file uploads, 702-707
        creating images on-the-fly, 716-723
        downloading files, 708-711
        results from successful uploads, 708-709
    IHttpHandlers, 695-699
        creating images on the fly, 716-723
        creating in .ashx files, 695-698
        creating in web.config files, 698-699
    intercepting events, 681
        logging for pay-per-use billing systems, 683-690
        trapping/logging Application_Error, 682-684

global.asax file
    Application_Error event, 368-372
    directives. *See* directives
    function, 368
    overriding GetVaryByCustomString method (caching), 566
    SessionStart/SessionEnd events, 537
globalization section of Web.config, 416, 419
GotDotNet.com Web site, 169
graphics
    binary files, 66-68
    creating images on-the-fly (Http Runtime), 716-723
    formats, 79
    generating images dynamically, 75
        listing 2.4.1, on-the-fly bar chart, 76-77
        listing 2.4.2, sending image to browser, 80-81
        listing 2.4.3, IMG tag, 82
        saving images on Web servers, 75-80
        sending images to browsers, 80-83
    mobile controls, 660-661
Graphics class
    FillRectangle method, 78-79
    generating images dynamically. *See* generating images dynamically
Guests group (file authorization), 480

H

handling errors, 347-348
    catching errors at design time
        Option Explicit, 348-350
        Option Strict, 349-353
    COM object interaction, 768
    Exception class, 352-354
    structured, 354-355
        catching general exceptions, 355-357
        catching specific exceptions, 356-359
        creating custom exceptions, 360-363
        throwing exceptions, 360-361
        Try, Catch, Finally statement, 354-355
    Win32 APIs, customizing, 800-801, 804-807
        getting Win32 error codes, 800-801
        throwing exceptions on failure, 801-807
handling Http Runtime interception events. *See* Http Runtime, interception events
hash tables, 30
Hashtable class, 35
    adding elements, 35-37
    indexing/referencing elements, 35-38
    Keys/Values collections, 38
    listing 2.1.2, 36-37
    removing elements, 35-38
headers, VaryByHeader attribute (@OutputCache directive), 566

Headers Collection (trace output), 381
HelloHandler.ashx code listing, 696-697
HelloHandler.vb code listing, 697
hiding table columns (DataGrid control), 279-281
history
    GetHistory method (ProcessModelInfo class), 102
    navigation history stack, 44-49
        Back.CSharp.aspx page, 48-49
        ClearStackHistory.Csharp.aspx page, 47-48
HRESULTs, 768, 801. *See also* handling errors
HTML (Hypertext Markup Language)
    postback forms, 18
        HTML received by the browser, 18
        HTML returned to browser, 20
        Page.IsPostBack property (Page_Load event), 21
        simple search form, 19-20
    tags
        IMG, 82-83
        INPUT, 96
        SPAN, 261
    uploading files from HTML forms, 93-99
        HttpPostedFile class, 96-97
        RFC documentation, 94
        saving uploaded files, 94-97
        working with uploaded files, 97-99
    user controls. *See* user controls
HtmlInputFile class, 96
Http Runtime, 675-677
    application-level events, 678-680
        deterministic, 678
        non-deterministic, 679
    directives. *See* directives
    execution architecture, 676
    global.asax event handlers. *See* global.asax event handlers
    HttpContext class, 699-701
    HttpRequest class, 702
        client page for uploading files, 707-708
        command-line test application for uploading/downloading files, 711-712, 714-716
        creating IhttpHandler to allow file uploads, 702-707
        creating images on-the-fly, 716-723
        downloading files, 708-711
        results from successful uploads, 708-709
    IHttpHandler class, 677, 695-699
        creating IhttpHandlers in .ashx files, 695-698
        creating IhttpHandlers in web.config files, 698-699
        creating images on the fly, 716-723
    IHttpModule class, 677, 690-695
        <add> directive, 693
        <clear> directive, 693-695
        Dispose( ) method, 691-692
        IHttpModule registration, 692-695
        Init( ) method, 691
        <remove> directive, 693
    interception events, 678-679. *See also* global.asax event handlers
        intercepting using global.asax file. *See* global.asax event handlers, intercepting events
        intercepting using HTTP modules, 690-695
HttpApplicationState object
    Application property, 550
    Lock method, 553
    UnLock method, 553
HttpBrowserCapabilities class, 155-156
    attributes, 156
    displaying browser capabilities, 158-163
    instantiating, 158
    JavaScript property, 164
    listing 4.1.1, 158-162
    properties, 157-158
    redirecting browsers, 164
HttpCachePolicy class, 574-576
HttpContext class, 699-701
    Error property, 370
<httpHandlers> section, web.config file, 416
<httpModules> section, web.config file, 417
HttpPostedFile class, 94-97
    InputStream property, 97-99
HttpRequest class, 702
    client page for uploading files, 707-708
    command-line test application for uploading/downloading files, 711-716
    creating IhttpHandler to allow file uploads, 702-707
    creating images on-the-fly, 716-723
    downloading files (WriteFile method), 708-711
    results from successful uploads, 708-709
<httpRuntime> section, web.config file, 417
HttpServerUtility GetLastError method, 369-370
HttpStatusCode, 373-376
hyperlinks
    HyperLink control
        binding data, 255-257
        listing 7.2.7, binding to Hyperlink control, 256
    interactive lists, mobile controls, 646
hyphen (-), zip code validation (regular expressions), 825

I

IbuySpy.com Web site, 27
ICollection interface, 53
ID attribute (Object tag), 730
Identity object (Integrated Windows aauthentication), 435-436
<identity> section, web.config file, 417

INDEX

IDispatch.Invoke (COM Interoperability), 754
idleTimeout attribute, processModel section of
   machine.config, 424-426
IEnumerator class, 50-53
   listing 2.1.8, 50-52
IHttpHandler class, 677, 695-699
   creating IhttpHandlers in .ashx files, 695-698
   creating IhttpHandlers in web.config files, 698-699
   creating images on-the-fly, 716-723
IHttpModule class, 677
IHttpModule class, intercepting events, 690-695
   Dispose( ) method, 691-692
   IHttpModule registration, 692-695
      <add> directive, 693
      <clear> directive, 693-695
      <remove> directive, 693
   Init( ) method, 691
IIS Administration tool, 436
IL Disassembler (ILDASM.exe), 742
Image control (mobile), 660-661
image.aspx code listing, 661
ImageFormat class, 79
images
   binary files, 66-68
   creating images on-the-fly (Http Runtime), 700-707
   formats, 79
   generating dynamically, 75
      listing 2.4.1, 76-77
      listing 2.4.2, sending image to browser, 80-81
      listing 2.4.3, IMG tag, 82
      saving images on Web servers, 75-80
      sending images to browsers, 80-83
Images class Save method, 79-81
IMG tag (HTML), 82-83
impersonation, 485. *See also* authorization
   access tokens, 485
   enabling fixed NT account execution, 486-487
   impersonation disabled, 485
   impersonation enabled, 485-486
   UNC shares, 487
Import directive (Http Runtime), 725-727
   logging user names to log file, 726
      without Import, 727
   Namespace attribute, 725
importing namespaces (databases), 198
in-memory databases, 197
include files, 171. *See also* user controls
indexing
   ArrayList elements, 31-35
   Hashtable elements, 35-38
   SortedList elements, 38-40
IndexOf method (ArrayList), 35
Inherits attribute (Application directive), 724-725
Init event
   Control class, 26
   Page class, 8

Init( ) method (IHttpModule class), 691
initialization of session state, 536-538
InProc (in process) running of Session State Server, 548
input
   mobile controls
      accepting, 656
      validating user input, 658-660
   processing
      postback forms. *See* postback forms
      two-page form processing, 11-15
   validating. *See* input validation
INPUT tag (HTML), 96
input validation, 123-125
   CompareValidator control, 131-135
      error message, 134
      listing 3.3.1, 131-132
      Operator property, 135
      Type property, 134-135
      valid input result, 134
   CustomValidator control, 141-142
      client-side validation functions, 145-148
      listing 3.6.1, server-side validation, 142-143
      listing 3.6.2, client-side validation, 145-147
      Luhn formula, 142-144
      server-side validation functions, 142-145
   Display property, 128-129
   mobile devices, 658-660
      listing 17.4.19, validating user input, 658
      Mobile Validation controls, 658
      Validation summaries, 660
   RangeValidator control, 135-138
      error message, 138
      listing 3.4.1, 136-137
      valid input result, 138
   RegularExpressionValidator control, 139-141
      error message, 141
      listing 3.5.1, 139-140
      valid input message, 141
   RequiredFieldValidator control, 125-131
      error message, 127
      HTML form example, 127
      listing 3.2.1, RequireFieldValidator, 126
      listing 3.2.2, RequireFieldValidator Display property, 129
      listing 3.2.3, RequireFieldValidator list box, 129-130
   ValidationSummary control, 148-152
      listing 3.7.1, 149-150
      validation summary reports, 150-152
InputStream property (HttpPostedFile class), 97-99
INSERT command (database input), 200-202
   variables, 210-211
Insert method (Cache class), 579-584
   caching ArrayList objects, 580-581
   caching DataSet objects, 581-583

caching XML data, 582-584
   parameters, 579
inserting rows (stored procedure template), 830-835
InstallSQLState.sql file, 539-540
InstanceName property (PerformanceCounter class), 113
Integer data type (Visual Basic.NET), 816
integrated Windows authentication, 435-437
   displaying user's domain/username (Identity object), 435-436
   displaying user's name/authentication type, 437
   IIS Administration tool, 436
   Web.config file, 436
interactive lists (mobile controls), 646-650
interception events (Http Runtime), 678-680. *See also* global.asax event handlers
   intercepting using global.asax file. *See* global.asax event handlers, intercepting events
   intercepting using HTTP modules, 690-695
      Dispose( ) method, 691-692
      IHttpModule registration, 692-695
      Init( ) method, 691
interface-based programming (Web services), 524-527
Internet remote network access, 86-93
   DNS resolution/email address validation, 89-93
   listing 2.6.1, .NET Framework Internet access, 86
   listing 2.6.2, DNS resolving support, 90
Internet Information Server, configuring for WML files, 630-631
Interop Assemblies (COM Interoperability), 754-755. *See also* COM Interoperability
   generating Interop Assembly with TlbImp.exe, 757
   referencing type libraries in Visual Studio.NET, 755-757
   RegAsm utiltiy, 771
   taking advantage of type information, 759-765
      listing 19.1.4, 760-762
      listing 19.1.5, 762-764
interoperability
   AspCompat directive, 807-808
      ASP intrinsics, 810-811
      executing on STA threads, 808-810
   performance concerns, 811-812
intrinsics (ASP), 810-811
invalid directory error, 57
   exceptions, 59
IPrincipal object (URL authorization), 482
IsMatch method (Regex class), 70-71
ISO 639, Microsoft and Macintosh Language Codes Web site, 626
ISO639-2 (Codes for the Representation of the Names of Languages) Web site, 626
IsValid property (forms), 236
IUnknown methods (COM objects), 770

J-K

Java, cross-language debugging, 392-396
JavaScript
   The JavaScript Source Web site, 153
   uplevel versus downlevel browsers, 165-168
   WebReference.com's JavaScript Tutorials and Article Index, 153
JavaScript property (HttpBrowserCapabilities class), 164
JIT compiled user controls (Code Behind), 609-611
JScript, cross-language debugging, 392-396

Kerberos authentication scheme Web site, 488
Keys collection, 38
keywords
   New, 762-764
   out (C#), 778
   Set (Visual Basic.NET), 820-821
   Throw, 360-361

L

Label control
   displaying text for mobile devices, 638-639
   time display, 562
label2.aspx code listing, 639
Language attribute (<Script> tag), 733-735
Language Codes: ISO 639, Microsoft and Macintosh Web site, 626
Last In, First Out (LIFO), 44
late binding (COM Interoperability), 748-753
   listing 19.1.3, 749-751
   passing right type of object, 771-772
   reflection, 751-753
Let accessor method (COM object interaction), 766-767
Library of Congress standard for ISO639-2 (Codes for the Representation of the Names of Languages) Web site, 626
LIFO (Last In, First Out), 44
LinkButton control
   displaying file contents, 63
   displaying menu items, 263-264
   editing items with DataGrid control, 284-285
   retrieving menu categories (CommandArgument property), 266-268
linking files, WML (Wireless Markup Language), 633
list boxes (RequiredFieldValidator control), 129-131
listing files, 62-63. *See also* lists
listings
   ArrayList class, 31-33
   assemblies
      adding an assembly redirect to an application, 410-411
      building the assembly info, 403
      building the myData.myDataClass, 402

INDEX

building the myDataAssemblyInfoV2.vb file, 409
building the myDataClassV2.vb file, 408-409
sp_GetTenCustAndOutputParam stored procedure, 403
updating Web Form to use myData v 2.0.0.0, 412
using a registered assembly on a Web Form, 407
authentication
  integrated Windows authentication, displaying user's domain/username (Identity object), 435-436
  integrated Windows authentication, displaying user's name/authentication type, 437
  integrated Windows authentication, Web.config file, 436
authorization
  enabling fixed NT account execution, 486
  enabling impersonation, 486
  login page (URL authorization), 483-484
  role-based security, 484
  web.config file (URL authorization), 481
  welcome page, 479
caching
  @OutputCache directive, 558
  ArrayList cache, 580
  Cache.GetEnumerator method, 587
  Cache.Remove method, 585
  CacheDuration attribute (WebMethodAttribute class), 577
  enabling page caching, 556-557
  named pair values, 560
  overriding GetVaryByCustomString method, 566
  page caching using HttpCachPolicy, 575
  page caching with Data Access Pages, 558
  user control for partial page caching, 568
  Web form for partial page caching, 568
  XML data, 583
CheckboxChanged event handler, 23
Code Behind
  ASP.NET Web form using Code Behind, 598
  building Code Behind for ASP.NET Web form, 597
  JIT compiled user controls—Part 1, 609
  JIT compiled user controls—Part 2, 609
  multiple events and controls, 600-601
  precompiled user controls—Part 1, 606
  precompiled user controls—Part 2, 606-607
  precompiled user controls—Part 3, 607
  precompiled user controls—Part 4, 608
  Using Code Behind with a User Control—Part 1, 604

Using Code Behind with a User Control—Part 2, 604
Using Code Behind with a User Control—Part 3, 604-605
COM Interoperability
  ADO <object> tag, 742-743
  creating COM objects in <script> block, 746-747
  Interop Assembly, 760-764
  late binding to ADO in C#, 749-751
databases
  adding data (INSERT command), 201
  adding data to Access, 201-202
  adding data to SQL Server, 200-201
  DataAdapter Update method, 228-230
  DataAdapter Update method in C#, 229-230
  DataTable, 219
  DataTable with Access, 220
  DataTables, building programmatically, 223-224
  DataTables, DataView filter, 226
  DataTables, displaying automatically, 221-222
  DataTables, master/detail relationship, 226-227
  DataTables, selecting DataRows, 225
  deleting data from Access, 205-206
  deleting data from SQL Server, 205
  inserting data with variables, 210-211
  OleDbDataReader, 210
  opening connections to Access, 199
  opening connections to SQL Server, 198
  output parameters, 216-217
  records affected by DELETE, 206
  records affected by UPDATE, 204
  records affected DELETE, 206
  SqlDataReader, 208
  stored procedures, 214-215
  updating Access data, 203-204
  updating SQL Server data, 203
  using SQL parameters, 212
  using SqlDataReader, 208
  using SqlDataReader with C#, 209
debugging
  sample web.config file that enables tracing for an application, 383
  using Trace.Warn and Trace.Write, 382
DirectoryInfo class, 54-56
displaying database data
  binding to a function, 247
  binding to DropDownlist control, 251
  binding to Hyperlink control, 256
  BoundColumn property of DataGrid control, 278
  capturing OnItemCommand event, 263
  column layout in a DataList, 261
  CommandArgument property, 267
  DataKeyField property, 269

DataList control, 258
displaying grid lines in a DataList, 259
DropDownlist DataValueField property, 254
editing DataList control items, 271
editing items in DataGrid control, 282
fancy repeater, 246
hiding column in DataGrid control, 279
numeric paging through a DataGrid, 296-297
paging through a DataGrid, 293-295
paging through a DataGrid in chunks, 299-302
Repeater control, 242
Repeater ItemIndex Property (displaying numbered lists), 249
sorting certain columns in DataGrid control, 291
sorting data in DataGrid control, 289
using DataGrid control, 277
using SelectedItemTemplate template, 265
using template column with DataGrid control, 285
dynamically generated images
IMG tag, 82
on-the-fly bar chart, 76-77
sending image to browser, 80-81
email output, 83-84
error handling
@Page directive ErrorPage attribute, 366
catching general exceptions, 356
changing Web.Config to allow custom errors, 366
combatting data type conversion errors, 352
combatting syntax errors with Option Explicit, 349
custom exceptions, 361-362
CustomErrors.aspx page, 371
defaultredirect attribute (<customerrors>), 373
handling SQL Server Not Found error, 357
HttpContext Error property, 370
implementing <error> sub-element, 373
Page object Error method, 364
throwing exceptions, 360
Try, Catch, Finally block, 354
Try, Catch, Finally example, 355
turning Option Explicit on/off, 349
turning Option Strict on/off, 352
using Application_Error within global.asax, 369
using HttpContext Error property to reference unhandled exception, 370
using HttpServerUtility GetLastError method, 369
event logs
adding entries, 112
displaying, 107-110
EventLog class, 106
FileInfo class, 61-62

files
binary files, 67
creating text files, 64-65
Forms authentication
authenticating against an XML file, 438
authenticating against Web.config file credentials section, 443-444
password encryption with SHA1 algorithm, 445
Web.config file credentials section, 442-443
Web.config file with SHA1 encrypted passwords, 445-446
Forms authentication with SQL Server
configuration file, 448-449
CreateUser stored procedure, 448
creating database and Logins table, 447
default.aspx, welcome page for authenticated users, 456
Login.aspx for authenticating users, 449-451
register.aspx for creating new users, 452-455
ValidateUser stored procedure, 447
Forms authentication with Web service
console-based test application, 463
incorporating authentication service into Web application, 464-465
login.aspx page, 465-467
WebAuth.asmx remote authentication service, 458-459
Hashtable class, 36-37
Http Runtime
application-level events, 678
application-level events (deterministic), 678
application-level events (non-deterministic), 679
command-line application for uploading/downloading files, 711-712, 715-716
command-line test application for uploading/downloading files, 711-715
creating images within an IHttpHandler, 717-719
faulty page that causes Application_Error, 682-683
handling BeginRequest and EndRequest events from within global.asax, 679
HTML client page for uploading files to File Upload IHttpHandler, 707-708
HTML page that uses ImageHandler for generating site navigation bar, 722-723
IHttpHandler, 696
IHttpHandler that displays contents of Name parameter (HelloHandler.vb), 697
IHttpHandler that greets users using Name parameter from Query String (HelloHandler.ashx), 696-697
IHttpModule, 694
logging user names to log files with Import directive, 726

INDEX

logging user names to log files without Import directive, 727
setting Application scope, 731
trapping/logging Application_Error, 682
using HttpPostedFile and HttpFileCollection objects from within IHttpHandler, 702-704
using ServerVariables collection from within IHttpHandler, 700
Web.config file with HelloHandler added to <httphandlers> section, 698
WriteFile method for downloading files, 709-710

HttpBrowserCapabilities class
    displaying browser capabilities, 158-162
    redirecting browsers, 164

IEnumerator class, 50-52

localization
    implementing CultureInfo class, part 1, 615-616
    implementing CultureInfo class, part 2, 616-617

machine.config file, 413-415
    enabling Web Gardening, 429
    modified section of processModel, 426
    processModel section, 425
    testing processModel settings, 427

mobile controls
    accepting user input, 656
    associating multiple commands with list items, 650
    displaying a random quotation, 637
    displaying banner ads, 663
    displaying different content with template sets, 672
    displaying input, 657
    displaying list of links, 647
    displaying multiple database fields, 653
    displaying text with a Label control, 639
    selecting a movie, 632
    selecting an application, 633
    validating user input, 658
    Value property, 649

network access
    DNS resolution/email address vaildation, 90
    DNS resolving support, 90
    .NET Framework Internet access, 86

Page events, 8
Page Load event handler, 9-10
Passport authentication
    information page, 472-478
    Passport Logo control, 478
    Web.config file for allowing anonymous access, 471
    Web.config file for enabling Passport authentication, 470
    welcome page, 472

performance counters
    gathering system information, 114-115
    PerformanceCounterCategory class, 116-119

postback forms
    ASP postback form, 15-16
    ASP.NET postback form, 17
    HTML received by the browser, 18
    HTML returned to browser, 20
    Page.IsPostBack property (Page_Load event), 21
    simple search form, 19-20
    Submit button OnClick event handler, 22

ProcessModelInfo class, 103-104
Queue class, 42-43
regular expressions
    complex search, 73
    IsMatch method (Regex class), 70
    Matches method (Regex class), 71

RequiredFieldValidator Server Control, 165
    Rendered HTML in an Downlevel Browser, 167
    Rendered HTML in an Uplevel Browser, 166-167

resource files
    base resource file (myResourceFile.txt), 619
    resource file for de-DE (German) encoding (myResourceFile.de-DE.txt), 623
    resource file for similar-language culture encoding, 624
    using a resource file from a Web Form, 619-620
    using resource files in Code Behind, 621-622

saving form data
    customer survey form, 234
    OleDb Save form, 237-238
    OleDb Survey form, 240-241
    SQL Save form, 235-236
    SQL Survey form, 238-240
    Thank-You page, 237

SimpleMath Web service pay-per-use logging example
    global.asax application file, 684-685
    source code, 687
    SQL script for creating database, table and stored procedure, 686
    usage/billing page, 689-690
    web.config file, 688

SortedList class, 39-40
Stack class, 45-46
    Back.CSharp.aspx, 48-49
    ClearStackHistory.CSharp.aspx, 48

state management
    adding information to session state, 541
    Application_Start event, 551
    cookie munging, 546
    handling SessionStart and SessionEnd with global.asax, 537
    InstallSQLState.sql file, 539

retrieving application state information, 551-552
Session State Server, running out-of-proc, 549
State Bag, 533-534
storing information with cookies, 544
using EnableViewState to disable automatic page-level management, 532
ViewState's SaveViewState method, 530

uploading files from Web browsers
accessing file contents (InputStream), 97-98
component-less file upload, 94-95

user controls
calling a public method, 189
copyright.ascx from DotNetJunkies.com, 173
CustomerList user control, 191
dynamically loading user controls, 192-193
exposing a public method, 188
exposing a public variable, 178
GetSingleProduct user control, 181-182
GetSingleProduct user control, including on a Web Form, 183
intrinsic user control properties, 176
programmatically accessing a public variable, 179
retrieving user control properties, 186-187
reusing a user control on a Web Form, 185

validation controls
CompareValidator, 131-132
CustomValidator, client-side, 145-147
CustomValidator, server-side, 142-143
RangeValidator, 136-137
RegularExpressionValidator, 139-140
RequiredFieldValidator, 126
RequiredFieldValidator Display property, 129
RequiredFieldValidator list box, 129-130
ValidationSummary, 149-150

Web services
asynchronous call to Web service, 511
autogenerated code for new Web service project, 494
data-access code for Web service, 513-514
disco document sample, 502
proxy class, Service1.vb, 505
returned XML data containing DataSet, 516
returning ADO.NET dataset, 515
returning an ADO.NET dataset, 515
securing the Dataset Web service, 517-518
SOAP headers, 517
synchronous call to Web service, 509
using Secure service from an ASP.NET page, 519-520
XML service contract, 499-500

web.config file, 417-418
adding application configuration settings, 420
adding custom configuration sections, 422
adding custom configuration settings, 420
reading application configuration settings, 421
reading custom configuration sections, 422-423

Win32 APIs
passing a by-value String, 784
QueryPerformanceCounter/QueryPerformance Frequency functions in C#, 778-779
QueryPerformanceCounter/QueryPerformance Frequency functions in VB Net, 775-776
StringBuilder, 782-783
throwing exceptions on failure, 801-806
uploading an AVI movie file, 788-793

XML
accessing DOM nodes using XPath, 331
adding nodes to an XML document, 327
BinaryWrite.aspx, sending an image to the client, 389-390
calling XmlTextReader's Read( ) method, 309
converting CSV flat files to XML with XmlTextWriter, 320-322
dynamically assigning source documents to asp:Xml Web control, 339
Euro Conversion Component (EuroConv.cs) source code, 393-395
filling a DataSet using SqlDataAdapter, 340
generating XML with XmlTextWriter class, 319
instantiating an XPathDocument class, 335
loading XML into a DataSet, 343
mapping an XSD schema to a DataSet, 343-344
marking up a comma-delimited file, 304-305
reading an XML document with XmlTextReader class, 312-313
result of XML transformation, 333
sample web.config file that enables debugging for an entire application, 386
simple example of setting a breakpoint (SetAbreakpoint.aspx), 387-388
Simple.aspx, using methods provided by Euro Conversion Component, 395-396
source code for the Euro Conversion Component (EuroConv.cs), 393
using DataSet's GetXmlSchema( ) and GetXml( ) methods, 341
using XmlDataDocument with DataSet, 342
using XsltArgumentList class, 337-338
using XslTransform class, 336
using xsl:param Element, 337
validate an XML document with XmlValidatingReader, 317-318
walking the DOM using recursive techniques, 328-329
XML document to transform to EDI, 332
XSLT style sheet, 332

lists
DataList control. *See* DataList control
DropDownList control. *See* DropDownList control

mobile controls, 642
    binding to data sources, 643, 645
    interactive lists, 646-650
    object lists, 650-653
    paging through lists, 645
Load event
    Control class, 26
    Page class, 8-10
loading user controls dynamically, 190-194
    code behind file, 191-192
    presentation file, 191
LoadViewState method, 531-532
local variables (Visual Basic.NET), 816-817
localization, 596
    specifying character encodings, 613-618
        <globalization> section of web.config file, 614
        listing 16.2.1, 615-616
        listing 16.2.2, 616-617
        setting culture encoding at page level, 614
        setting culture encoding programatically with CultureInfo class, 615-618
    System.Globalization namespace, 612-613
Location attribute (@OutputCache directive), 564-565
Lock method (HttpApplicationState object), 553
logging
    application errors, with global.asax event handlers, 681-684
    pay-per-use billing systems, 683-690
        client page, 686
        listing 18.2.3, global.asax application file, 684-685
        listing 18.2.4, SQL script for creating database, table and stored procedure, 686
        listing 18.2.5, source code, 687
        listing 18.2.6, web.config file, 688
        listing 18.2.7, usage/billing page, 688-690
    user names to log files
        Import directive, 726
        without Import directive, 727
logic code, separating from presentation markup. *See* Code Behind; localization; resource files
login page (URL authorization), 483-484
Login.aspx for authenticating users (Forms authentication), 449-452
login.cs page (Forms authentication), 465-467
logs, Windows events, 105
    EventLog class, 106
    logging unhandled page exceptions, 122
    reading, 105-111
      display format, 107-110
    writing, 111-113
Long data type (Visual Basic.NET), 816

loops
    For...Next, drawing bar charts, 79
    For Each...Next
        collections, 49-50
        Queue class iteration, 44
        stepping through collections, 34-35
    foreach(C#), 49-50
Luhn formula for credit card validation, 142-145

M

machine.config file, 413-416
    listing 11.3.1, 413-415
    location of machine.config, 406
    processModel section, 425
        enabling Web Gardening, 428-430
        enabling worker process restarts, 423-428
        settings, 424-426
        testing settings, 427-428
<machineKey> section, web.config file, 417
MailMessage class, 83-85
managing state. *See* state management
mapping XSD schemas to DataSets, 343-345
MarshalAsAttribute, 785-787
marshaling, 774
Matches method (Regex class), 71-73
MD5 hashing algorithm RFC URL, 488
memoryLimit attribute, processModel section of machine.config, 424-426
menus
    DataList control, 262-264
    retrieving category IDs (DataKeyField property), 268-271
    retrieving category names, 266-268
    SelectedItemTemplate template (DataList control), 265-267
methods
    accessor methods (COM objects), 765-767
    Add
        Hashtable class, 35-37
        SortedList class, 38-40
    AddRange (ArrayList class), 31-34
    Clear
        EventLog class, 111
        Hashtable, 35-38
        Queue class, 43
        SortedList class, 38
    Contains (Queue class), 43
    ContainsKey (SortedList class), 40
    ContainsKey (HashTable), 37
    ContainsValue (HashTable), 37
    CreateSubdirectory (DirectoryInfo class), 59

Delete
    Directory class, 60
    DirectoryInfo class, 59-60
Dequeue (Queue class), 41-43
DirectoryInfo class
    accessing, 57
    CreateSubdirectory method, 59
    Delete, 59-60
    GetDirectories( ) method, 59
    GetFiles( ) method, 59
Enqueue (Queue class), 41-43
FileInfo class, 68
FillRectangle (Graphics class), 78-79
GetByIndex (SortedList class), 39
GetDirectories( ), DirectoryInfo class, 59
GetFiles( ), DirectoryInfo class, 59
GetHistory (ProcessModelInfo class), 102
GetKeyList (SortedList class), 41
GetValueList (SortedList class), 39
Graphics class (FillRectangle), 78-79
IndexOf (ArrayList), 35
IsMatch (Regex class), 70-71
IUnknown (COM objects), 770
Matches (Regex class), 71-73
Open (FileInfo class), 68
Peek
    Queue class, 41-43
    Stack class, 47
Pop (Stack class), 44
Read (FileInfo class), 68
Redirect (Stack class), 49
Remove
    ArrayList, 31-34
    Hashtable, 35-38
    SortedList, 38
RemoveAt
    ArrayList, 31-34
    SortedList, 38
RemoveRange (ArrayList), 31-34
Replace (Regex class), 74
Save (Image class), 79-81
SaveAs (HttpPostedFile class), 96
SystemException class, 354
user controls
    custom methods, 187-190
    inherent methods, 175-178
Web services, adding during Web service creation, 495
Microsoft
    Component Object Model. *See* COM
    Developer Network Web site, 431
    Duwamish Books Inc. Web site, 377
    Kerberos authentication, 434
    MSDN Web site, user controls page, 194
    .NET Developer Center, 813
    .NET Mobile Web SDK, 634
    Passport authentication. *See* Passport authentication

Mobile Explorer, 628-629
SQL Server. *See* SQL Server
Web services resources, 528
MIME (Multipurpose Encoding), 721
    RFC, 737
mobile controls, 627, 634. *See also* mobile devices
    cross-device compatibility, 666-671
        choosing devices with deviceSelect, 669-671
        detecting mobile capabilities, 667-668
        form template sets, 671
        listing 17.5.1, displaying mobile capabilities, 667
        listing 17.5.2, selecting different devices, 669
        listing 17.5.3, displaying different content with template sets, 672
    displaying
        advertisements, 662-664
        calendars, 664-666
        images, 660-661
        random quotes, 637
    forms
        creating mobile forms, 634-636
        dynamically activiating forms, 637-638
        form template sets, 671
    input
        accepting, 656
        validating user input, 658-660
    lists, 642
        binding to data sources, 643-645
        interactive lists, 646-650
        object lists, 650-653
        paging through lists, 645
    .NET Mobile Web SDK, 634
    placing phone calls, 661-662
    software simulators for mobile devices, 629
    text
        alignment text, 640
        controlling wrapping, 641-642
        creating text boxes, 655-656
        displaying text, 638-642
        paging through text, 640-641
    validating user input, 658-660
        listing 17.4.19, 658
        Mobile Validation controls, 658
    Validation summaries, 660
mobile devices. *See also* mobile controls
    software simulators for mobile devices, 627-628
        Alcatel phone simulator, 651-653
        Microsoft Mobile Explorer, 628-629
        Nokia phone simulators, 628-629
        Openwave phone simulator, 628
    Wireless Application Protocol (WAP), 629-630
    Wireless Markup Language (WML), 630
        configuring Internet Information Server, 630-631
        decks of cards, 631-633

linking files, 633
listing 17.3.1, selecting a movie, 632
listing 17.3.2, selecting an application, 633
sample output, 633
WML specification Web site, 630
XML, 631
MTA (multithreaded apartment) threads (COM objects), 808-809
myDataAssemblyInfo.vb, 403. *See also* assemblies
myDataAssemblyInfoV2.vb, 409
myDataClass.vb, 402
myDataClassV2.vb, 408-409

N

Name attribute (Assembly directive), 727
named pair values, caching (listing 15.2.4), 560
namespaces
    importing (databases), 198
    System.Diagnostics, 113
    System.Drawing/System.Drawing.Imaging, creating images on-the-fly (Http Runtime), 716-723
    System.Globalization, localizing applications, 612-613
    System.Net, 86
    System.Reflection, JIT compiled user controls (Code Behind), 609-611
    Threading, character encoding, 618
native code interoperability. *See* interoperability
navigation history stack, 44-49
    Back.CSharp.aspx page, 48-49
    ClearStackHistory.Csharp.aspx page, 47-48
.NET Developer Center Web site, 813
.NET Framework, 30
.NET Mobile Web SDK, 634
.net101 Web site, 345
networks, remote access, 86-93
    DNS resolution/email address validation, 89-93
    listing 2.6.1, .NET Framework Internet access, 86
    listing 2.6.2, DNS resolving support, 90
New keyword, 762-764
nodes (XML documents)
    adding using Document Object Model (DOM), 327
    selecting nodes in DOM using XPath, 330-331
    walking the DOM using recursion, 327-330
NodeType property (XmlTextReader class), 309-311
Nokia phone simulators, 628-629
None
    XML ValidationType enumeration, 316
    XmlNodeType enumeration member, 311
Notation (XmlNodeType enumeration member), 311
Nothin' but ASP.NET article, 554
NTLM (Windows NT Challenge/Response), 435, 488
numbered lists, displaying, 248-251
    mobile controls, 643-644. *See also* lists, mobile controls

O

Object data type (Visual Basic.NET), 816
object lists (mobile controls), 650-653
Object tag, using COM objects, 741-744
    ADO (ActiveX Data Objects), 741-743
    CLSIDs, 741
    ProgIDs, 741
Object tag (Http Runtime directives), 729
    attributes, 729
        Class, 732
        ClassID, 733
        ID, 730
        ProgID, 732-733
        Runat, 730
        Scope, 730-732
    syntax, 729
objectlist.aspx code listing, 650
objectlist2.aspx code listing, 653
objects
    COM. *See* COM Interoperability
    retrieving database objects
    wrappers, 772
offensive language censor template, 827
OleDb classes, 196-197
    OleDbDataReader, 210
    OleDbParameters, 213
OleDb Save form, 237-238
OleDb Survey form, 240-241
OnCancelCommand event (DataList control), 262
OnClick event, postback forms, 22-23
OnDeleteCommand event (DataList control), 262
OnEditCommand event (DataList control), 262
OnItemCommand event (DataList control), 262-263
OnUpdateCommandevent (DataList control), 262
Open method (FileInfo class), 68
opening database connections, 198-200
Openwave phone simulator, 628
Operator property (CompareValidator control), 135
operators
    BitAnd, 58
    Visual Basic.NET, 818
        short circuiting, 817
Option Explicit statement, 348-350
    combatting syntax errors, 349
    turning on/off, 349
Option Strict statement, 349-353
    combatting data type conversion errors, 352
    turning on/off, 352
    widening conversions, 350-351
Oracle databases. *See also* databases
    Import statements, 198
    importing namespaces, 198
    OleDb classes, 196-197

storing data in tables
OleDb Survey form, 240-241
OleDb Save form, 237-238
out keyword (C#), 778
Out-of-Proc (out of process) running of Session State Server, 548-550
output
caching Web services, 577-578
email messages, 83-86
address validation, 89-93
listing 2.5.1, 83-84
page output caching. *See* page output caching
sending dynamically created images to browsers, 80-82
SQL stored procedures(databases), 216-217
trace output. *See* tracing code execution
overriding GetVaryByCustomString method (caching), 566

P

P/Invoke, 774
defining GetLastError Win32 API, 800
QueryPerformanceCounter, 796-797
UnmanagedType enumeration commonly used values, 785-786
Page class
ClientTarget property, 165-168
Init event, 8
listing 1.1.1, 8
Load event, 8-10
PreRender event, 8-9
Tracing, 8-9
Page Init event handler, 8
Page Load event handler, 8-10
listing 1.1.2, 9-10
Page.IsPostBack property, 21
Page object
@Page directive ErrorPage attribute, 365-368
Error event, 363-365
page output caching, 556-562
@OutputCache directive
Duration attribute, 558-562
Location attribute, 564-565
VaryByCustom attribute, 565-566
VaryByHeader attribute, 566
VaryByParam attribute, 562-564
Page PreRender event handler, 8-9
page-level code tracing, 380-381. *See also* debugging
listing 10.1.1, Using Trace.Warn and Trace.Write, 382
trace output, 380-381
adding messages to Trace Information section, 381-383
page-level error handling, 363-368

page-level state management (ViewState), 529-534
disabling state with EnableViewState property, 532-533
LoadViewState method, 531-532
SaveViewState method, 530-531
saving information with State Bag, 533-534
Page.IsPostBack property (Page Load event handler), 21
paging, mobile controls
lists, 645
text, 640-641
paging through table data with Data Grid control (AllowPaging property), 292-295
custom paging in chunks, 297-302
displaying page numbers, 295-297
Palm Pilot Web controls. *See* mobile devices and mobile controls
parameters
ByVal default (Visual Basic.NET), 819-820
calling Win32 APIs, 779-785
customizing parameters, 785-787
data type equivalents, 780-781
Declare statements, 780
passing a by-value String, 784-785
StringBuilder, 781-783
Insert method (Cache class), 579
SQL commands, 210-214
output, 216-217
xsl:param element, passing parameters into XSLT style sheets, 337-338
parentheses ( )
calling Visual Basic.NET functions/subroutines, 818-819
session variables, 46
parsing XML documents, 324-325
Passport authentication, 467-469
downloading Passport SDK, 469
PassportAuthenticationModule, 469-479
displaying information table, 472-478
Passport Logo control, 478-479
Web.config file for allowing anonymous access, 471
Web.config file for enabling Passport authentication, 470
welcome page, 471-472
registering as a Passport Partner site, 470
test sites, 470
typical Passport conversation, 468-469
passwords
encryption (SHA1 algorithm), 444-446
validating, 835-836
pay-per-use billing systems, 683-690
client page, 686
listing 18.2.3, global.asax application file, 684-685
listing 18.2.4, SQL script for creating database, table, and stored procedure, 686
listing 18.2.5, source code, 687

INDEX 865

listing 18.2.6, web.config file, 688
listing 18.2.7, usage/billing page, 688-690
Peek method
    Queue class, 41-43
    Stack class, 47
performance
    caching. *See* caching
    calling Win32 APIs/COM objects, 811-812
    counters, 113-121
        listing 2.10.1, gathering system information, 114-115
        listing 2.10.2, PerformanceCounterCategory class, 116-119
    database checklist, 592
    Web forms
        checklist, 588-590
        performance counters, 590-591
        Web Application Stress Tool, 591
    Web services checklist, 592
PerformanceCounter class, 113-116
    CategoryName property, 113-114
    CounterName property, 113-114
    InstanceName property, 113
PerformanceCounterCategory class, 116-121
    listing 2.10.2, 116-119
period (.) special character (regular expressions), 72
    zip code validation, 826
phone calls (mobile devices), 661-662
phone simulators, 627-629. *See also* mobile controls
    Alcatel, 651-653
PInvoke (Platform Invocation Services), 774
pipe character (|), regular expressions
    offensive language censorship, 827
    zip code validation, 825
Pipeline value (Object tag Scope attribute), 730
Platform Invocation Services (PInvoke), 774
plus sign (+), zip code validation, 826
PNG (Portable Network Graphics) files, 719
    creating images on-the-fly (Http Runtime), 720-723
    W3C PNG page, 737
Pocket PC controls. *See* mobile devices and mobile controls
Pop method (Stack class), 44
postback forms, 15-19
    DirectoryInfo class, 56
    listings
        1.2.5, ASP postback form, 15-16
        1.2.6, ASP.Net postback form, 17
        1.2.7, HTML received by the browser, 18
        1.3.1, simple search form, 19-20
        1.3.2, HTML returned to browser, 20
        1.3.3, Page.IsPostBack property, 21
        1.3.4, Submit button OnClick event handler, 22
    responding to postbacks, 19-23
        OnClick event handler, 22-23
        Page.IsPostBack property (Page_Load event), 21-22
PostedFile property (HttpPostedFile class), 96
pound sign character (#), data-binding expressions, 244
PreRender event
    Control class, 26
    Page class, 8-9
primary keys, DataKeyField property (DataList control), 269
procedures. *See* stored procedures
processes
    enabling process restarts, 423-428
        <processModel> settings (machine.config file), 424-428
    retrieving process information, 100
        currently executing aspnet_wp.exe process, 100-102
        past instances of aspnet_wp.exe, 102-105
ProcessInfo class, 100
    displaying currently executing aspnet_wp.exe process, 100-102
    displaying past instances of aspnet_wp.exe, 102-105
ProcessingInstruction (XmlNodeType enumeration member), 311
processModel section of machine.config, 423-428
    cpuMaskattribute, 425, 428-430
    settings, 424
        testing, 427-428
    webGarden attribute, 425, 428-430
ProcessModelInfo class, 100
    displaying past instances of aspnet_wp.exe, 102-105
    listing 2.8.2, 103-104
ProgIDs, COM objects, 741
properties
    CategoryName (PerformanceCounter class), 113-114
    COM objects, 765-768
        accessor methods, 765-767
        binding flags, 767-768
        C# restrictions, 768
    Count
        ArrayList class, 34
        collections, 49
    CounterName (PerformanceCounter class), 113-114
    DataGrid control
        AllowPaging, 292-295
        AllowSorting, 289-291
        BoundColumn, 277-279
        EditItemIndex, 281-285
        EditItemTemplate, 285, 288
        Visible, 279-281
    DataGridPagerStyle class, 297
    DataKeyField (DataList control), 269
    DataSource, binding data, 241-242

DirectoryInfo class
    accessing, 57
    Attributes, 58
    DisplayAttributes, 58-59
    FileAttributes, 57-58
HttpPostedFile class, 96
    InputStream, 97-99
InstanceName (PerformanceCounter class), 113
PostedFile (HttpPostedFile class), 96
SystemException class, 353
user controls
    custom properties. *See* user controls, custom properties/methods
    inherent properties, 175-178
validation controls
    Display, 128-129
    Operator, 135
    Type, 134-135
Visual Basic.NET defaults, 820-821
XmlTextReader class, NodeType, 309-311
Property objects, exposing user control properties, 181-187
    listings 5.3.4, 181-182
    listings 5.3.5, 183
    listings 5.3.6, 185
    listings 5.3.7, 186-187
    retrieving propeties, 185-187
    reusing controls, 183-186
proxy classes
    consuming Web services, 498-507
        command line tools, 504
        disco files, 502-503
        disco.exe command line tool, 504
        listing 13.3.1, XML service contract, 499-500
        listing 13.3.2, disco document sample, 502
        listing 13.3.3, generated proxy class, Service1.vb, 505
        searching for Web services, 500-502
        Web Services Description Language (WSDL), 498-500
        wsdl.exe command line tool, 505-507
    Web Authentication service, 461-462
public variables, exposing user control custom properties, 178-180

Q

querying
    data within a DataSet using XPath, 341-342
    database data, 207-209
        OleDbDataReader class, 210
        SqlDataReader class, 208-210
QueryPerformanceCounter/QueryPerformanceFrequency functions
    C#, 778-779
    VB Net, 775-777

question mark (?) special character
    Forms authentication, 439
    URL authorization, 481
Queue class, 41
    accessing elements, 41-44
    adding elements, 41-43
    listing 2.1.4, 42-43
    removing elements, 41-43
QuickStart documentation Web site, 153
quotation marks (""), server-side include filenames, 735

R

random quotes, displaying with mobile controls, 637
RangeValidator control, 135-138
    error message, 138
    listing 3.4.1, 136-137
    valid input result, 138
RangeValidator mobile validation control, 658
Read method (FileInfo class), 68
reading
    appSettings section of web.config, 420-421
    configSections section of web.config, 422-423
    directories. *See* directories
    Windows event log, 105-111
        display format, 107-110
        EventLog class, 106
reading XML documents (DataSet class), 343
reading XML documents (XmlTextReader), 307-314
    advantages of .NET pull model, 307-308
    associating XmlTextReader with XmlNameTable, 314
    calling XmlTextReader's Read( ) method, 309
    Simple API for XML (SAX) push model, 307
    XmlNodeType enumeration members (NodeType property), 309-311
records. *See* rows
recursion, XML Document Object Model (DOM), 327-330
Redirect method (Stack class), 49
redirecting
    browsers, 164. *See also* browser support
    redirecting error pages
        aplications-level error handling, 372-376
        page-level error handling, 365-368
reflection
    JIT compiled user controls (Code Behind), 609-611
    late binding, COM Interoperability, 751-753
RegAsm utility, 771
Regex class, 69-70
    IsMatch method, 70-71
    listing 2.3.1, IsMatch method, 70
    listing 2.3.2, Matches method, 71
    Matches method, 71-73
    Replace method, 74

register.aspx for creating new users (Forms authentication), 452-455
registering user controls, 174-175
regsvr32.exe utility, 773
regular expressions, 68-75
    articles online, 823-824
    listing 2.3.1, IsMatch method, 70
    listing 2.3.2, Matches method, 71
    listing 2.3.3, complex search, 73
    Regex class, 69-70
        IsMatch method, 70-71
        Matches method, 71-72
        Replace method, 74
    special characters/wildcards, 72
    System.Text.RegularExpressions namespace, 69
        Regex class, 69-70
    templates, 823-824
        e-mail address validation, 826
        offensive language censor, 827
        social security number validation, 825
        telephone number validation, 825-826
        zip code validation, 824-825
RegularExpressionValidator control, 139-141, 658
    error message, 141
    listing 3.5.1, 139-140
    valid input message, 141
relationships, DataRelations (ADO.NET), 226-227
releasing COM objects, 772-773
remote network access, 86-93
    DNS resolution/email address vaildation, 89-93
    listing 2.6.1, .NET Framework Internet access, 86
    listing 2.6.2, DNS resolution, 90
    listing 2.6.2, DNS resolving support, 90
remote Web authentication services, 458-467
    advantages, 458
    console-based test application, 463
    creating a proxy using wsdl, 461-462
    creating Web service (WebAuth.asmx), 458-459
    incorporating authentication service into Web application, 464-465
    login.cs, 465-467
    SSL requirement, 459-460
    WebAuth.asmx test screen, 459-460
Remove method
    Cache class, 585-586
    SortedList class, 38
<remove> tag, IHttpModule registration, 693
RemoveAt method (SortedList class), 38
removing
    ArrayList elements, 34
    Hashtable elements, 35-38
Repeater control
    binding data, 242-247
        binding to functions, 247-249
        displaying numbered lists, 248-251
    displaying hyperlinks, 256-257

    listing 7.2.1, 242
    listing 7.2.2, Fancy Repeater, 246
    listing 7.2.3, binding to a function, 247
    listing 7.2.4, ItemIndex Property (displaying numbered lists), 249
Replace method (Regex class), 74
Request Details (trace output), 381
Request object. *See* global.asax event handlers
requestLimit attribute, processModel section of machine.config, 424-426
requestQueueLimit attribute, processModel section of machine.config, 424
RequiredFieldValidator control, 125-130, 658
    Display property, 128-129
    error message, 127
    HTML form example, 127
    listings
        3.2.1, RequireFieldValidator, 126
        3.2.2, RequireFieldValidator Display property, 129
        3.2.3, RequireFieldValidator list box, 129-130
ResGen utility, creating resource files, 619, 623
resource files, 618-625
    building Web Forms to use .resources files, 619-620
    Code-Behind files associated with Web Forms, 620-622
    creating .resources files with ResGen utility, 619, 623
    creating basic text resource files, 618-619
    listing 16.3.1, 619
    listing 16.3.2, 619-620
    listing 16.3.3, 621-622
    listing 16.3.4, 623
    listing 16.3.5, 624
    requested Web Form results, 622-625
    resource file for de-DE (German) encoding, 623-624
    resource file for en-NZ (English-New Zealand) encoding, 624-625
responding to form postbacks, 19-23
    OnClick event handler, 22-23
    Page.IsPostBack property (Page_Load event), 21-22
Response object Cookies property, 543-545
Response.Cache (HttpCachePolicy), 574-576
Response.Redirect method (databases), 237
restarts, enabling worker process restarts, 423-428
    <processModel> settings (machine.config file), 424
        defaults, 425-426
        testing settings, 427-428
retrieving
    database objects, 837
    process information, 100
        currently executing aspnet_wp.exe process, 100-102
        past instances of aspnet_wp.exe, 102-105

RFC documentation
    RFC 1766 (Tags for the Identification of Languages) Web site, 626
    uploading files from Web browsers, 94
role-based security, 484-485. *See also* authorization
roles attribute, URL authorization, 482
rows (database tables), 829
    DataTables, 221
    deleting, 832
    inserting, 830-835
    selecting, 829-830
        rows that contain substrings, 832-833
        top 10 rows, 832
    updating, 831, 834-835
Runat attribute
    Object tag, 730
    Scrip tag, 735
runtime. *See* Http Runtime

S

Save method (Image class), 79-81
SaveAs method (HttpPostedFile class), 96
SaveViewState method, 530-531
saving
    files uploaded from Web browsers, 94-97
        working with uploaded files, 97-99
    form data, 234-241
        Access/Oracle form (OleDb Survey form), 240-241
        IsValid property, 236
        SQL Server form, 238-240
        storing data in an Access or Oracle table (OleDb Save form), 237-238
        storing data in an SQL Server table, 235-237
    state information with State Bag, 533-534
saving dynamically created images, 75-80
    listing 2.4.1, 76-77
SAX (Simple API for XML) push model, 307
Schema (XML ValidationType enumeration), 316
schemas (XML)
    mapping XSD schemas to DataSets, 343-345
    viewing a DataSet's XML and schema, 341-342
    validating documents, 314-318
        listing 8.5.1, Using XmlValidatingReader to Validate an XML Document, 317-318
        ValidationType enumerations, 315-316
Scope attribute (Object tag), 730-732
    AppInstance value, 730-731
    Application value, 731-732
    Pipeline value, 730
    Session value, 732

<Script> code declaration blocks, 733
    creating COM objects (listing 19.1.2), 746-747
    Language attribute, 733-735
    Runat attribute, 735
    Src attribute, 735
SDK RegAsm utility, 771
searches
    finding Web services on a Web site, 500-502
    regular expressions. *See* regular expressions
Secure Hash Algorithm version 1, 444-446
    RFC URL, 488
Secured Sockets Layer. *See* SSL
security
    authentication. *See* authentication
    authorization. *See* authorization
    source code, Http Runtime interception events, 678
    validation. *See* validating; validation controls
    Web services, 516-522
        listing 13.5.1, SOAP headers, 517
        listing 13.5.2, securing the Dataset Web service, 517-518
        listing 13.5.3, using Secure service from an ASP.NET page, 519-520
        SOAP headers, 517
        testing secure Web services, 519-520
SelectedItemTemplate template (DataList control), 265-267
selecting rows (stored procedure templates), 829-830
    rows that contain substrings, 832-833
    top 10 rows, 832
selectmovie2.aspx code listing, 647
sending email, 83-86
    address validation, 89-93
    listing 2.5.1, 83-84
separating logic code from presentation markup. *See* Code Behind; localization; resource files
Server Variables (trace output), 381
server-side form validation, 124-125. *See also* form input validation
    CustomValidator control, 142-145
server-side includes, 735-736
Server.CreateObject method (COM Interoperability), 745-748, 759
Server.HTMLEncode, encoding database text, 244
servers
    performance counters, 113-121
    saving dynamically created images, 75-80
        listing 2.4.1, 76-77
    uploading files from browsers, 93-99
        HttpPostedFile class, 94-97
        RFC documentation, 94
        saving uploaded files, 94-97
        working with uploaded files, 97-99
Session State Server, 547-548. *See also* session-level state management
    running InProc (in process), 548
    running Out-of-Proc (out of process), 548-550

INDEX

Session value (Object tag Scope attribute), 732
session variables, accessing, 46
session-level state management, 535-538
    controlling session expiration, 535-536
    controlling session initialization, 536-538
    cookieless, 546-547
    cookies, 543-546
    Session State Server, 547-548
        running InProc (in process), 548
        running Out-of-Proc (out of process), 548-550
    SQL server, 538-543
Set accessor method (COM object interaction), 766-767
Set keyword (Visual Basic.NET), 820-821
Set method, exposing user control properties as Property objects, 181. *See also* Property objects, exposing user control properties
SHA1 (Secure Hash Algorithm version 1), 444-446
    RFC URL, 488
short circuiting (Visual Basic.NET), 817
Short data type (Visual Basic.NET), 816
showing/hiding table columns (DataGrid control), 279-281
showquote.aspx listing, 637
shutdownTimeout attribute, processModel section of machine.config, 424-426
SignificantWhitespace (XmlNodeType enumeration member), 311
SignOut( ) method (FormsAuthentication object), 456
Simple API for XML (SAX) push model, 307
Simple Object Access Protocol. *See* SOAP
SimpleMath Web service pay-per-use logging example, 683-690
    client page, 686
    listing 18.2.3, global.asax application file, 684-685
    listing 18.2.4, SQL script for creating database, table and stored procedure, 686
    listing 18.2.5, source code, 687
    listing 18.2.6, web.config file, 688
    listing 18.2.7, usage/billing page, 688-690
single-threaded apartment (STA) threads, 808-810
SmtpMail class, 84-85
SOAP (Simple Object Access Protocol), 490
    Microsoft article URL, 528
    Web services, 490-491, 497, 507
        SOAP headers, 517
social security number validation template, 825
software simulators for mobile devices, 627-629
    Alcatel phone simulator, 651, 653
    Microsoft Mobile Explorer, 628-629
    Nokia phone simulators, 628-629
    Openwave phone simulator, 628
SortedList class, 38-41
    adding elements, 38-40
    indexing/referencing elements, 38-40
    listing 2.1.3, 39-40
    removing elements, 38-40

sorting
    DataTable data, 225-226
    table data with Data Grid control, 289-291
source code
    security, Http Runtime interception events, 678
    SimpleMath Web service, 687
special characters, regular expressions, 72
spelling, exact spelling setting (Win32 APIs), 799
SQL (Structured Query Language)
    command parameters, 210-214
        output, 216-217
    stored procedures, 214-217
SQL Save form listing, 235-236
SQL Server. *See also* databases
    classes, 196
    deleting data, 205
    Forms authentication, 446
        admin.aspx, list of registered users, 456-458
        configuration file, 448-449
        CreateUser stored procedure, 447-448
        creating database and Logins table, 447
        default.aspx, welcome page for authenticated users, 456
        Login.aspx for authenticating users, 449-452
        register.aspx for creating new users, 452-455
        ValidateUser stored procedure, 447
    handling SQL Server Not Found error (listing 9.3.4), 357
    importing namespaces, 198
    inserting data, 200-201
    opening database connections, 198
    session state management, 538-543
        UninstallSqlState.sql file, 543
    storing data in tables, 235-237
        input form, 238-240
    Tabular Data Stream (TDS) protocol, 197
    updating data, 203
SQL Survey form listing, 238-240
SqlCommand class, 196, 201
SqlConnection class, 196-198
SqlDataAdapter class, 197
    Fill( ) method, 340
SqlDataReader class, 196, 201, 207
    listing 6.2.1, 208
    Read( ) method, 209
    using
        listing 6.2.11, 208
        listing 6.2.12, 209
Src attribute
    declaring objects in Code Behind, 606
    using Code Behind with Web Forms, 598
SSL (Secured Sockets Layer), 459
    remote authentication services (Forms authentication), 459-460
STA (single-threaded apartment) threads, 808-810

Stack class, 44
    accessing elements, 44-49
    adding elements, 44-49
    listing 2.1.5, 45-46
    listing 2.1.6, ClearStackHistory.CSharp.aspx, 48
    listing 2.1.7, Back.CSharp.aspx, 48-49
    removing elements, 44-49
State Bag, 533-534
state management, 529
    application state, 550-553
    ASP.NET SDK Documentation Web page, 554
    listings
        14.1.1, ViewState's SaveViewState method, 530
        14.1.2, using EnableViewState to disable automatic page-level management, 532
        14.1.3, State Bag, 533-534
        14.2.1, handling SessionStart and SessionEnd with global.asax, 537
        14.3.1, InstallSQLState.sql file, 539
        14.3.2, adding information to session state, 541
        14.4.1, storing information with cookies, 544
        14.5.1, cookie munging, 546
        14.6.1, Session State Server, running out-of-proc, 549
        14.7.1, Application_Start event, 551
        14.7.2, retrieving application state information, 551-552
    Nothin' but ASP.NET article, 554
    page-level state (ViewState), 529-534
        disabling with EnableViewState property, 532-533
        LoadViewState method, 531-532
        SaveViewState method, 530-531
        saving information with State Bag, 533-534
    session-level state. See session-level state management
status codes (errors), 373-376
stepping
    through applications (debugging with CLR Debugger), 389-391
    through collections, 34-35
        enumerators, 50-53
stored procedures
    SQL commands, 214-217
        output parameters, 216-217
    templates
        deleting rows, 832
        inserting rows, 830-835
        retrieving database objects, 837
        selecting rows, 829-830
        selecting rows that contain substrings, 832-833
        selecting top 10 rows, 832
        updating rows, 831, 834-835
        validating usernames/passwords, 835-836
String data types, converting Boolean to String, 162
string escape sequence (C#), 60

StringBuilder, 781-783
    in/out behavior, 787
Strings
    C# compatibility, 785
    customizing string behavior (Win32 APIs), 797-799
    VB6 compatibility, 784
StructLayoutAttribute, 795
structured error handling, 354-355
    catching
        general exceptions, 355-357
        specific exceptions, 356-359
    creating custom exceptions, 360-363
        changing Web.Config to allow custom errors, 366
        CustomErrors.aspx page, 371-374
        defaultredirect attribute (<customerrors>), 373
        implementing <error>, 373
        redirecting to custom error pages, 367
        using HttpContext Error property to reference unhandled exception, 370
    throwing exceptions, 360-361
    Try, Catch, Finally statement, 354-355
subdirectories, 59
subroutines (Visual Basic.NET), 818-820
    ByVal parameter default, 819-820
    calling, 818-819
superexpert Web site, 231
switches, /l\:, creating proxy classes (Forms authentication), 461
synchronous calls to Web services, 507-510
    listing 13.3.4, 509
syntax
    code declaration, 733
    directives within global.asax file, 724-725
    Object tag (Http Runtime directives), 729
sysobjects table, 837
System event log
    reading, 105-111
        display forms, 107-110
    writing to, 111-113
        logging unhandled page exceptions, 122
System.Diagnostics namespace, 113
System.Drawing/System.Drawing.Imaging namespaces, creating images on-the-fly (Http Runtime), 716-723
System.Globalization namespace, localizing applications, 612-613
System.IO namespace, importing, 56
System.Net namespace, 86
System.Reflection namespace, JIT compiled user controls (Code Behind), 609-611
System.Text.RegularExpressions namespace, 69
    Regex class, 69-70
System.Xml assembly, 306-307
    .NET classes used in XSL transformations, 333-337
        XmlDataDocument, 334, 342
        XmlDocument, 334

INDEX 871

XPathDocument, 334-336
XsltArgumentList, 334
XslTransform, 334-337
XmlNameTable class, associating with XmlTextReader, 314
XmlTextReader class, 307-308
    advantages of .NET pull model, 307-308
    associating with XmlNameTable, 314
    calling Read( ) method, 309
    reading XML documents, 308-314
    Simple API for XML (SAX) push model, 307
    validating XML documents, 315-318
    XmlNodeType enumeration members (NodeType property), 309-311
XmlTextWriter class
    creating XML documents, 318-322
    listing 8.6.1, Generating XML with the XmlTextWriter Class, 319
    listing 8.6.2, Converting CSV Flat Files to XML with the XmlTextWriter Class, 320-322
XmlValidatingReader class
    listing 8.5.1, Using XmlValidatingReader to Validate and XML Document, 317-318
    validating XML documents, 315-318
    ValidationType enumerations, 315-316
SystemException class, 352-354. *See also* error handling

T

tables
    creating using Code Behind, 597-599
    databases. *See* DataTables (ADO.NET); rows (database tables); stored procedure templates
    displaying items with DataGrid control. *See* DataGrid control
    paging through data with DataGrid control (AllowPaging property), 292-295
        custom paging in chunks, 297-302
        displaying page numbers, 295-297
    setting table properties with DataList control, 258-259
        column layout, 260
    sorting data with DataGrid control, 289-291
    storing form data to a table
        Access or Oracle (OleDb Save form), 237-238
        Access/Oracle form (OleDb Survey form), 240-241
        SQL Server, 235-240
tags
    <add>, IHttpModule registration, 693
    <clear>, IHttpModule registration, 693-695
    <deviceSelect> element, mobile controls, 661, 669-671
    <deviceSPecific> element, mobile controls, 661
    <IMG>, 82-83

<INPUT>, 96
<Object>. *See* Object tag
<remove>, IHttpModule registration, 693
<Script>, 733
    Language attribute, 733-735
    Runat attribute, 735
    Src attribute, 735
TDS (Tabular Data Stream) protocol, 197
telephone number validation template, 825-826
templates
    DataList control
        EditItemTemplate, 271, 274-276, 285, 288
        SelectedItemTemplate, 265-267
    mobile control form template sets, 671-672
    regular expressions, 823-824
        e-mail address validation, 826
        offensive language censor, 827
        social security number validation, 825
        telephone number validation, 825-826
        zip code validation, 824-825
    Repeater control, 244-247
    stored procedures
        deleting rows, 832
        inserting rows, 830-835
        retrieving database objects, 837
        selecting rows, 829-830
        selecting rows that contain substrings, 832-833
        selecting top 10 rows, 832
        updating rows, 831, 834-835
        validating usernames/passwords, 835-836
text
    creating text files, 64-66
    mobile controls
        alignment, 640
        controlling wrapping, 641-642
        creating text boxes, 655-656
        displaying, 638-642
        lists. *See* lists, mobile controls
        paging through text, 640-641
Text (XmlNodeType enumeration member), 311
TextBox mobile control, 655-656
textbox.aspx code listing, 656
textview.aspx code listing, 640
Thank-You page listing, 237
The JavaScript Source Web site, 153
Threading namespace, characer encoding, 618
throwing exceptions, 360-361
    Win32 APIs, 801-807
time
    displaying for mobile devices, 639
    Label control time display, 562
timeout attribute, processModel section of machine.config, 424
Timeout property, controlling session expiration, 535
TlbImp.exe (Type Library Importer), generating Interop Assemblies, 757

872   ASP.NET: TIPS, TUTORIALS, AND CODE

TomorrowsLearning.com Web site, 345
ToString( ) method, 162
trace section of Web.config, 417-419
tracing
    Page events, 8-9
    user controls, 174
tracing code execution. *See also* debugging
    application-level tracing, 383-385
        listing 10.1.2, Sample web.config File That Enables Tracing for an Application, 383
        viewing application trace information in trace.axd file, 384-385
    listing 10.1.1, Using Trace.Warn and Trace.Write, 382
    page-level, 380-381
    Trace directive, 380-381
    trace output, 380-381
        Trace Information section, 381-383
Try, Catch, Finally statement, 354-355
two-page form processing, 11-15
Type class (JIT compiled user controls in Code Behind), 611
type libraries (COM Interoperability), 754-755
    browsing assembly contents using IL Disassembler (ILDASM.exe), 758
    generating Interop Assembly with TlbImp.exe, 757
    Interop Assembly, 754-755
    referencing type libraries in Visual Studio.NET, 755-757
    taking advantage of type information, 759-765
        listing 19.1.4, 760-762
        listing 19.1.5, 762-764
Type property (CompareValidator control), 134-135
Type.InvokeMember (COM Interoperability), 751-753

U

UDTs (User-Defined Types), Visual Basic, 788
UNC (Universal Naming Convention) shares, 487
Uniform Resource Identifiers (URIs), testing for with XmlNameTable, 314
UninstallSqlState.sql file (SQL Server session state management), 543
Unload event (Control class), 26
UnLock method (HttpApplicationState object), 553
unmanaged code interoperability. *See* interoperability
UnmanagedType enumeration commonly used values, 785-786
UPDATE command (databases), 202-204
Update method, DataAdapter class (ADO.NET), 228-230
updating
    database data, 202-204
        DataAdapter Update method, 228-230
        OnUpdateCommandevent (DataList control), 262
        rows, stored procedure template, 831, 834-835
uplevel browsers, 165-168

uploading
    AVI movie files, 788-795
    files from Web browsers, 93-99
        HttpPostedFile class, 94-97
        RFC documentation, 94
        saving uploaded files, 94-97
        working with uploaded files, 97-99
    files (Http Runtime)
        client page for uploading files, 707-708
        command-line test application for uploading/downloading files, 711-716
        creating IhttpHandler to allow file uploads, 702-707
        results from successful uploads, 708-709
URIs (Uniform Resource Identifiers), testing for with XmlNameTable, 314
URL authorization, 481
    role-based security, 484-485
    roles attribute, 482
    users attribute, 482
    verbs attribute, 482-484
UserControl class, Code Behind for user controls, 603-605
user controls, 172-174
    .ascx extension, 172
    creating, 172-174
    custom methods, 187-190
    custom properties
        exposing properties as Property objects, 181-187
        exposing properties as public variables, 178-180
    dynamically loading, 190-194
        code behind file, 191-192
        presentation file, 191
    example control from DotNetJunkies.com, 173-174
    hierarchy of UserControl inheritance, 178
    inherent properties/methods, 175-178
        hierarchy of inheritance, 176-178
        Visible property, 176-177
    registering, 174-175
    tracing information, 174
usernames, validating, 835-836
users attribute, URL authorization, 482

V

ValidateUser stored procedure (Forms authentication, 447
validating
    e-mail address, 89-93, 826
    mobile user input, 658-660
        listing 17.4.19, 658
        Mobile Validation controls, 658
        Validation summaries, 660
    social security numbers, 825

INDEX 873

telephone numbers, 825-826
usernames/passwords (stored procedure template), 835-836
XML documents, 314-318
    listing 8.5.1, Using XmlValidatingReader to Validate an XML Document, 317-318
    ValidationType enumerations, 315-316
zip codes, 824-825
validation controls, 123-125
    CompareValidator, 131-135
        error message, 134
        listing 3.3.1, 131-132
        Operator property, 135
        Type property, 134-135
        valid input result, 134
    CustomValidator, 141-142
        client-side validation functions, 145-148
        listing 3.6.1, server-side validation, 142-143
        listing 3.6.2, client-side validation, 145-147
        Luhn formula, 142-144
        server-side validation functions, 142-145
    Display property, 128-129
    RangeValidator, 135-138
        error message, 138
        listing 3.4.1, 136-137
        valid input result, 138
    RegularExpressionValidator, 139-141
        error message, 141
        listing 3.5.1, 139-140
        valid input message, 141
    RequiredFieldValidator, 125-131
        error message, 127
        HTML form example, 127
        listing 3.2.1, 126
        listing 3.2.2, Display property, 129
        listing 3.2.3, RequireFieldValidator list box, 129-130
    ValidationSummary, 148-152
        listing 3.7.1, 149-150
        mobile validation, 642
        validation summary reports, 150-152
validation.aspx code listing, 658
ValidationSummary control, 148-152
    listing 3.7.1, 149-150
    mobile validation, 642
    validation summary reports, 150-152
Value property (List control), 649
Values collection, 38
variables
    accessing session variables, 46
    examining (debugging with CLR Debugger), 391-392
    public, exposing user control custom properties, 178-180
    Server Variables (trace output), 381

SQL commands, 210-214
    output, 216-217
    Visual Basic.NET, 815-817
Variant data type (Visual Basic.NET), 816
Variant parameter (VBScript), 772
VaryByCustom attribute (@OutputCache directive), 565-566
VaryByHeader attribute (@OutputCache directive), 566
VaryByParam attribute (@OutputCache directive), 562-564
VB. *See* Visual Basic
VB.NET. *See* Visual Basic.NET
VBScript Variant parameter, 772
verbs attribute, URL authorization, 482-484
viewing
    DataSet XML and schema, 341-342
    dynamically created images, 80-83
        listing 2.4.2, 80-81
        listing 2.4.3, IMG tag, 82
    Windows event log, 105-111
        display format, 107-110
        EventLog class, 106
ViewState, 529-534
    disabling page-level state with EnableViewState property, 532-533
    LoadViewState method, 531-532
    SaveViewState method, 530-531
    saving information with State Bag, 533-534
Visible property
    DataGrid control, 279-281
    UserControl control, 176-177
Visual Basic
    backward compatibility, 785, 800
        passing by-value Strings, 784
    cross-language debugging, 392-396
    Declare statements, 780
        Win32 data type equivalents, 780-781
    User-Define Types (UDTs), 788
Visual Basic.NET, 815
    array bounds, 817
    calling Win32 APIs, 777-779
    data types, 815-816
    Declare statement. *See also* Declare statement
        defining with by-reference array parameters, 788
        in/out behavior, 787
        MarshalAsAttribute, 785-787
        passing a by-value String, 784-785
    default properties, 820-821
    DllImport attribute, customizing, 796
        calling conventions, 799-800
        different function names, 796-797
        error handling, 800-801, 804-807
        exact spelling setting, 799
        string behavior, 797-799

DllImport statement
            defining with by-reference array parameters, 788
            in/out behavior, 787
            MarshalAsAttribute, 785-787
    functions, 818-820
            ByVal parameter default, 819-820
            calling, 818-819
    operators, 818
            short circuiting, 817
    subroutines, 818-820
            ByVal parameter default, 819-820
            calling, 818-819
    variables, 815-817
    While statement, 820
Visual Studio
    creating Web services, 492-497
            Add Web Reference window, 500-502
            adding methods, 495
            default Web service files, 493-495
            listing 13.2.1, autogenerated code for new Web service project, 494
            Microsoft UDDI link, 500
            New Project dialog box, 492-493
            testing output, 495-497
            Web References folder, 503
    DUMPBIN.EXE utility, 774
    line-numbering feature, 495

W

W3C Hypertext Transfer Protocol (HTTP) Web page, 737
WAP (Wireless Application Protocol), 629-630
Web Application Stress Tool, 591
Web applications, deploying files to bin directory, 399-401
Web authentication services, 458-467
    advantages, 458
    console-based test application, 463
    creating a proxy using wsdl, 461-462
    creating Web service (WebAuth.asmx), 458-459
    incorporating authentication service into Web application, 464-465
    login.cs, 465-467
    SSL requirement, 459-460
    WebAuth.asmx test screen, 459-460
Web browsers
    navigation history stack, 44-49
            Back.CSharp.aspx page, 48-49
            ClearStackHistory.Csharp.aspx page, 47-48
    uploading files, 93-99
            HttpPostedFile class, 94-97
            RFC documentation, 94
            saving uploaded files, 94-97
            working with uploaded files, 97-99

viewing dynamically created images, 80-83
    listing 2.4.2, 80-81
    listing 2.4.3, IMG tag, 82
Web controls
    Asp:Xml, 338-339
    event handlers, 23-26
            listing 1.4.1, CheckboxChanged event handler, 23-24
    events, 26
Web forms
    caching entire forms (page output caching), 556-562
            @OutputCache Duration attribute, 558-562
            @OutputCache Location attribute, 564-565
            @OutputCache VaryByCustom attribute, 565-566
            @OutputCache VaryByHeader attribute, 566
            @OutputCache VaryByParam attribute, 562-564
    caching portions of forms, 567-572
    Code Behind, 596-603
            building the Code-Behind file, 597-598
            inheriting from Code Behind class, 596
            listing 16.1.1, 597
            listing 16.1.2, 598
            listing 16.1.3, 600
            listing 16.1.4, 601
            multiple events/controls, 600-603
            resource files, 621-622
            Src attribute, 598
            Web Form, 598-599
    customizing output for specific culture encoding. *See* localization; resource files
    listing browser capabilities, 158-162
    localization. *See* localization
    performance
            checklist, 588-590
            performance counters, 590-591
            Web Application Stress Tool, 591
    resource files. *See* resource files
    user controls. *See* user controls
Web Gardening, 428-430
Web servers
    saving dynamically created images, 75-80
            listing 2.4.1, 76-77
    uploading files from browsers, 93-99
            HttpPostedFile class, 94-97
            RFC documentation, 94
            saving uploaded files, 94-97
            working with uploaded files, 97-99
Web services, 489-492
    accessing (consuming) from client applications, 498
            creating proxy classes, 498-507
            listing 13.3.1, XML service contract, 499-500
            listing 13.3.2, disco document sample, 502
            listing 13.3.3, generated proxy class, Service1.vb, 505

listing 13.3.4, synchronous call to Web service, 509
listing 13.3.5, asynchronous call to Web service, 511
making asynchronous calls, 510-511
making synchronous calls, 507-510
asmx files, 494-495
caching, 577-578
creating, 492-497
    adding methods, 495
    default Web service files, 493-495
    listing 13.2.1, autogenerated code for new Web service project, 494
    New Project dialog box, 492-493
    testing output, 495-497
design considerations, 521
    failure response, 522-524
    interface-based programming, 524-527
    security, 521-522
disco files, 502-503
    disco.exe tool, 504
performance checklist, 592
returning database data, 512
    datasets, 514-519
    listing 13.4.1, data-access code for Web service, 513-514
    listing 13.4.2, returning ADO.NET dataset, 515
    listing 13.4.2, returning an ADO.NET dataset, 515
    listing 13.4.3, returned XML data containing a DataSet, 516
    making decisions based on data, 513-514
searching for services on a Web site, 500-502
security, 516-522
    listing 13.5.1, SOAP headers, 517
    listing 13.5.2, securing the Dataset Web service, 517-518
    listing 13.5.3, using Secure service from an ASP.NET page, 519-520
    SOAP headers, 517
    testing secure Web services, 519-520
SimpleMath pay-per-use logging example, 683-690
    client page, 686
    listing 18.2.3, global.asax application file, 684-685
    listing 18.2.4, SQL script for creating database, table and stored procedure, 686
    listing 18.2.5, source code, 687
    listing 18.2.6, web.config file, 688
    listing 18.2.7, usage/billing page, 688-690
SOAP (Simple Object Access Protocol), 490-491, 497, 507
    headers, 517
Web Services Description Language (WSDL), 461, 498-500

Web site URLs
    ASP.NET, 26, 169
    ASP.NET Quick Start guides, 737
    ASP.NET SDK Documentation (state management), 554
    ASPNextGen.com, 27
    ASPNG.com, 26
    AspWorkshops.com, 231
    c-sharpcorner, 345
    code examples, 122
    Cookies, 122
    DOM Level 2 specification, 323
    dotnet101, 345
    DotNetJunkies.com, 169, 593, 626
    Duwamish Books Inc. Web site, 377
    email validation article, 122
    GotDotNet.com, 169
    IbuySpy.com, 27
    Kerberos authentication scheme, 488
    Language Codes: ISO 639, Microsoft and Macintosh, 626
    Library of Congress standard for ISO639-2 (Codes for the Representation of the Names of Languages), 626
    Microsoft
        Mobile Devices, 673
        MSDN user controls page, 194
        .NET Mobile Web SDK, 634
        Web services, 528
    Microsoft Developer Network, 431
    .NET Developer Center, 813
    Nothin' but ASP.NET, 554
    NTLM, 488
    Openwave phone simulator, 628
    Portable Network Graphics (PNG) page, 737
    QuickStart documentation, 153
    regular expressions articles, 823-824
    RFC 1766 (Tags for the Identification of Languages), 626
    Simple API for XML (SAX), 307
    superexpert.com, 231, 673
    The JavaScript Source, 153
    TomorrowsLearning.com, 345
    W3C Hypertext Transfer Protocol (HTTP) page, 737
    WAP Forum, 630
    Web Application Stress Tool, 591
    WebReference.com's JavaScript Tutorials and Article Index, 153
    XPath, 330
web.config file, 412-413
    adding IHttpModules, 693
    changing to allow custom exceptions, 366
    configuration settings, 412-413
        adding application configuration settings, 419-420
        adding custom configuration settings, 421-422
        machine.config sections, 413-416

reading application configuration settings, 420-421
reading custom configuration settings, 422-423
web.config sections, 416-419
creating IhttpHandlers, 698-699
Forms authentication, 439
   authenticating against credentials section, 443-444
   credentials section, 442-443
   SHA1 encrypted passwords, 445-446
integrated Windows authentication, 436
listings
   11.3.1, 417
   11.3.2, 417-418
   11.4.1, adding application configuration settings, 420
   11.4.2, reading application configuration settings, 421
   11.4.3, adding custom configuration sections, 422
   11.4.4, reading custom configuration sections, 422-423
machine.config sections, 413-416
removing IHttpModules, 693-695
SimpleMath Web service, 688
<sessionState> section, 536
   cookieless mode, 546
   sqlserver mode, 540
   stateserver mode, 549-550
URL authorization, 481
WebAuth.asmx remote authentication service (Forms authentication), 458-459
WebAuth.cs proxy class (Forms authentication), 461-462
webGarden attribute, processModel section of machine.config, 425
WebMethodAttribute class, 577
WebReference.com's JavaScript Tutorials and Article Index Web site, 153
<webServices> section, web.config file, 417
While statement (Visual Basic.NET), 820
Whitespace (XmlNodeType enumeration member), 311
widening data types (Option Strict statement), 350-351
wildcards
   database queries, 207
   regular expressions, 72
Win32 APIs, 739-740, 774
   calling APIs with complex types, 788, 791-795
      StructLayoutAttribute, 795
      uploading an AVI movie file, 788-790, 793-795
   calling with C#, 777-779
   calling with VB Net, 774-777
   choosing parameter types, 779-785
      data type equivalents, 780-781
      Declare statements, 780
      passing a by-value String, 784-785
      StringBuilder, 781-783

customizing Declare and DllImport, 796
   calling conventions, 799-800
   different function names, 796-797
   error handling, 800-801, 804-807
   exact spelling setting, 799
   string behavior, 797-799
customizing parameters, 785-787
listing DLL functions with DUMPBIN.EXE utility, 774
performance concerns, 811-812
Windows authentication, 435-437
   displaying
      user's domain/username (Identity object), 435-436
      user's name/authentication type, 437
   IIS Administration tool, 436
   Web.config file, 436
Windows event log, 105
   EventLog class, 106
   reading, 105-111
      display format, 107-110
   writing, 111-113
      logging unhandled page exceptions, 122
Windows NT Challenge/Response (NTLM), 435
   Web site, 488
Wireless Application Protocol (WAP), 629-630
wireless devices. *See* mobile devices and mobile controls
Wireless Markup Language (WML), 630
   building WML pages
      configuring Internet Information Server, 630-631
      decks of cards, 631-633
      linking files, 633
      listing 17.3.1, selecting a movie, 632
      listing 17.3.2, selecting an application, 633
      sample output, 633
      XML, 631
   WML specification Web site, 630
worker process restarts, enabling, 423-428
   <processModel> settings (machine.config file), 424
      defaults, 425-426
      testing settings, 427-428
wrapper objects (COM Interoperability), 772
wrapping.aspx code listing, 641
WriteFile method, downloading files (Http Runtime), 708-711
writing
   Windows event log, 111-113
      logging unhandled page exceptions, 122
   XML documents (DataSet class), 343
   XML documents (XmlTextWriter), 318-322
      listing 8.6.1, Generating XML with the XmlTextWriter Class, 319
      listing 8.6.2, Converting CSV Flat Files to XML with the XmlTextWriter Class, 320-322
WSDL (Web Services Description Language), 498-500
wsdl.exe tool (Web services), 505-507

X-Y-Z

XDR (XML ValidationType enumeration), 316
XML (eXtensible Markup Language), 303
    ADO.NET support, 339-345
        DataSet class, 339-342
            listing 8.9.1, Filling a DataSet Using SqlDataAdapter Class, 340
            listing 8.9.2, Using the DataSet's GetXmlSchema( ) and GetXml( ) Methods, 341
            listing 8.9.3, Using XmlDataDocument with DataSet Class, 342
            listing 8.9.4, Loading XML into a DataSet, 343
            listing 8.9.5, Mapping an XSD Schema to a DataSet, 343-344
            mapping XSD schemas to DataSets, 343-345
            querying data within a DataSet using XPath, 341-342
            reading and writing XML using DataSet, 343
            viewing a DataSet's XML and schema, 341-342
    advantages, 304-306
    authenticating against an XML file (Forms authentication), 438-439, 442
    caching XML data (listing 16.6.3), 583
    creating XML documents, 318-322
        listing 8.6.1, Generating XML with the XmlTextWriter Class, 319
        listing 8.6.2, Converting CSV Flat Files to XML with the XmlTextWriter Class, 320-322
    Document Object Model (DOM), 322-324
        adding nodes to XML documents, 327
        DOM classes, 325-326
        DOM Level 2 specification, 323
        in-memory versus forward only cursor-based parsing, 324-325
        recursion, 327-330
        selecting nodes using XPath, 330-331
    Document Type Definition (DTD) files, 306
    marking up a comma-delimited file, 304-305
    .NET support, 303-304
    reading documents using DataSet class, 343
    reading XML documents (XmlTextReader), 307-314
        advantages of .NET pull model, 307-308
        associating XmlTextReader with XmlNameTable, 314
        calling XmlTextReader's Read( ) method, 309
        Simple API for XML (SAX) push model, 307
        XmlNodeType enumeration members (NodeType property), 309-311
    System.Xml assembly, 306-307
    transforming documents with eXtensible Stylesheet Language Transformations (XSLT), 331-333
        .NET XSLT classes, 333-337
        Asp:Xml Web control, 338-339
        listing 8.8.1, XSLT Style Sheet, 332
        listing 8.8.2, XML Document to Transform to EDI, 332
        listing 8.8.3, Result of XML Transformation, 333
        listing 8.8.4, Instantiating an XPathDocument Class, 335
        listing 8.8.5, Using XslTransform Class, 336
        listing 8.8.6, Using the xsl:param Element, 337
        listing 8.8.7, Using XsltArgumentList Class, 337-338
        listing 8.8.8, Dynamically Assigning Source Documents to the asp:Xml Web Control, 339
        passing parameters into style sheets, 337-338
        XmlDataDocument class, 334
        XmlDocument class, 334
        XPathDocument class, 334-336
        XsltArgumentList class, 334
        XslTransform class, 334-337
    validating XML documents, 314-318
        listing 8.5.1, Using XmlValidatingReader to Validate an XML Document, 317-318
        ValidationType enumerations, 315-316
    Web services contracts, 499-500
    WML (Wireless Markup Language), 631. *See also* Wireless Markup Language (WML)
    writing documents using DataSet class, 343
XmlDataDocument class, 334
    using with DataSet, 342
XmlDeclaration (XmlNodeType enumeration member), 311
XmlDocument class, 334
XmlNameTable class, associating with XmlTextReader, 314
XmlTextReader class, 307-308
    advantages of .NET pull model, 307-308
    associating with XmlNameTable, 314
    reading XML documents, 308-314
        calling Read( ) method, 309
        XmlNodeType enumeration members (NodeType property), 309-311
    Simple API for XML (SAX) push model, 307
    validating XML documents, 315-318
XmlTextWriter class, creating XML documents, 318-322
    listing 8.6.1, Generating XML with the XmlTextWriter Class, 319
    listing 8.6.2, Converting CSV Flat Files to XML with the XmlTextWriter Class, 320-322
XmlValidatingReader class
    listing 8.5.1, Using XmlValidatingReader to Validate an XML Document, 317-318
    validating XML documents, 315-318
        ValidationType enumerations, 315-316
XPath
    querying data within a DataSet, 341-342
    XML Document Object Model (DOM), selecting nodes, 330-331
XPathDocument class, 334-336
XSD schemas (XML). *See also* schemas (XML)

mapping to DataSets, 343-345
viewing a DataSet's XML and schema, 341-342
XSLT (eXtensible Stylesheet Language Transformations), 331
   transforming XML documents, 331-333
      Asp:Xml Web control, 338-339
      listing 8.8.1, XSLT Style Sheet, 332
      listing 8.8.2, XML Document to Transform to EDI, 332
      listing 8.8.3, Result of XML Transformation, 333
      listing 8.8.4, Instantiating an XPathDocument Class, 335
      listing 8.8.5, Using XslTransform Class, 336
      listing 8.8.6, Using the xsl:param Element, 337
      listing 8.8.7, Using XsltArgumentList Class, 337-338
      listing 8.8.8, Dynamically Assigning Source Documents to the asp:Xml Web Control, 339
      .NET XSLT classes, 333-337
      passing parameters into style sheets, 337-338
      XmlDataDocument class, 334
      XmlDocument class, 334
      XPathDocument class, 334-336
      XsltArgumentList class, 334
      XslTransform class, 334-337
XsltArgumentList class, 334
XslTransform class, 334-337

zip code validation template, 824-825

Hey, you've got enough worries.

Don't let IT training be one of them.

Get on the fast track to IT training at InformIT,
your total Information Technology training network.

InformIT | www.informit.com | SAMS

- Hundreds of timely articles on dozens of topics ■ Discounts on IT books from all our publishing partners, including Sams Publishing ■ Free, unabridged books from the InformIT Free Library ■ "Expert Q&A"—our live, online chat with IT experts ■ Faster, easier certification and training from our Web- or classroom-based training programs ■ Current IT news ■ Software downloads
- Career-enhancing resources

InformIT is a registered trademark of Pearson. Copyright ©2001 by Pearson.
Copyright ©2001 by Sams Publishing.

What's on the CD-ROM

The companion CD-ROM contains Microsoft's .NET Framework SDK Beta 2.

Windows 2000 Installation Instructions

1. Insert the disc into your CD-ROM drive.
2. From the Windows desktop, double-click the My Computer icon.
3. Double-click the icon representing your CD-ROM drive.
4. Double-click on `default.htm`. Microsoft's .NET Framework SDK Beta can be installed using the HTML interface.

> **Note**
> If you have the AutoPlay feature enabled, `default.htm` will be launched automatically whenever you insert the disc into your CD-ROM drive.